S P O R T
PSYCHOLOGY

Sport Psychology provides a synthesis of the major topics in sport psychology with an applied focus and an emphasis on achieving optimal performance.

After exploring the history of sport psychology, human motivation, and the role of exercise, there are three main sections to the text: Performance Enhancement, Performance Inhibition, and Individuals and Teams.

The first of these sections covers topics such as anxiety, routines, mental imagery, self-talk, enhancing concentration, relaxation, goals, and self-efficacy.

The section on Performance Inhibition includes chapters on choking under pressure, self-handicapping, procrastination, perfectionism, helplessness, disruptive personality factors, substance abuse, burnout, and injuries.

While much of the information presented is universally applicable, individual differences based on gender, ethnicity, age, and motivation are emphasized in the concluding section on Individuals and Teams. Leadership and team cohesion are also studied.

Throughout, there are case studies of well-known athletes from a variety of sports to illustrate topics that are being explored.

Nicholas T. Gallucci is a professor in the Department of Psychology at Western Connecticut State University. He received MA and PhD degrees in psychology at the University of Louisville, and a BA in psychology at Vanderbilt University. His research concerns personality and sport performance, and exercise and weight loss. He enjoys running, played intercollegiate soccer at Vanderbilt, and is a member of the St. Xavier High School Athletic Hall of Fame.

SPORT
PSYCHOLOGY

Performance Enhancement,
Performance Inhibition,
Individuals, and Teams

NICHOLAS T. GALLUCCI   Second Edition
Western Connecticut State University

Psychology Press
Taylor & Francis Group
NEW YORK AND LONDON

This edition published 2014
by Psychology Press
711 Third Avenue, New York, NY 10017

and by Psychology Press
27 Church Road, Hove, East Sussex BN3 2FA

Routledge is an imprint of the Taylor & Francis Group, an informa business

First edition published by Psychology Press 2008

Library of Congress Cataloging-in-Publication Data

Gallucci, Nicholas T.
Sport psychology : performance enhancement, performance inhibition,
    individuals, and teams / Nicholas T. Gallucci. — Second edition.
        pages cm
    1. Sports—Psychological aspects—Textbooks.   2. Athletes—Psychology.
    3. Teamwork (Sports)—Psychology.   I. Title.
    GV706.4.G34 2013
    796.01'9—dc23
    2013019062

ISBN: 978-1-84872-977-3 (hbk)
ISBN: 978-1-84872-978-0 (pbk)
ISBN: 978-1-315-88509-4 (ebk)

Typeset in Giovanni
by Apex CoVantage, LLC

Printed and bound in the United States of America by Sheridan Books, Inc. (a Sheridan Group Company).

CONTENTS

PREFACE

Sport Psychology: Performance Enhancement, Performance Inhibition, Individuals, and Teams is a textbook for university courses. It is intended for students and sportspersons interested in learning about psychology, sport, and exercise, and applying this learning to realize their full potential. It offers a synthesis of most of the major topics in sport psychology, and, true to its title, emphasizes topics related to optimal performance.

For this second edition, all of the chapters were revised to accommodate recent research. A chapter on exercise was added and the chapter on relaxation training was expanded to include mindfulness.

The book has four parts. Part I is the *Introduction* and provides the background and foundation for the other material in the book. The history of sport psychology is reviewed in Chapter 1. Human motivation is the subject of Chapter 2, and these theories are important for understanding motivation for sport, academic and vocational achievement, and the pursuit of personal interests. Exercise is considered in Chapter 3.

Performance Enhancement is the focus of Part II. Consistently realizing optimal performance involves the practice of strategies such as self-talk, enhancing concentration, mental imagery, relaxation training, goal setting, and promoting self-efficacy and sport self-confidence. Optimal performance is also more likely when the factors causing *Performance Inhibition* are limited. These topics are taken up in Part III: choking under pressure, self-handicapping, procrastination, perfectionism, helplessness, disruptive personality factors, substance abuse, burnout, and sport injuries.

Including factors that both enhance and inhibit performance, the chapters are organized on the basis of the degree to which the skills are to be practiced at times proximal or distal to the performance. Skills are proximal when their practice occurs immediately prior to and during performances, whereas those that are rehearsed at times farther removed from performances and competitions are distal. Therefore, strategies for enhancing performance that are practiced immediately prior to and during performances are presented in Chapters 4, 5, and 6, and psychological strengths and competencies that have a more distal influence on performance are related in Chapters 7 through 10. Similarly, psychological liabilities that inhibit performance as a result of their occurrence during performances are detailed in Chapter 11, and more distal, inhibiting factors are explained in Chapters 12 through 18. This organization of topics and chapters was influenced by practices that are common in areas of applied psychology. That is, the most expeditious way to solve problems and enhance performance is to first teach the skills necessary for success. If difficulties cannot be resolved after the acquisition of necessary skills, then inhibiting factors are analyzed. Additionally, since the distal causes of success and failure are often less apparent, and are altered more slowly and with greater effort, readers may find it unnecessary to alter the distal and more entrenched sources of success and failure if their performance improves adequately after making changes in the proximal factors.

To some degree this information is universally applicable. In addition, research with diverse populations is reviewed in Part IV: *Individuals and Teams*. The topics of gender and sport, ethnicity and sport, and youth and sport will be addressed in Chapters 19 through 21. The influence of leadership and coaching styles will be considered in Chapter 22 and team cohesiveness will be evaluated in Chapter 23.

The material in each chapter is introduced with a vignette, and photographs, figures, and illustrations are included in the chapters for the purpose of clarifying the material in the text. The illustrations are generally derived from the popular press, primarily concern well-known sport figures, and present dramatic and sometimes humorous examples of concepts in the text. Several illustrations are drawn from outside of the world of sport and these represent especially clear examples of concepts. For example, throughout 27 years in prison, Nelson Mandela never lost confidence that he would reach his goal of transforming South Africa.

Each chapter also includes suggestions for applying sport psychology in practice. These suggestions are organized in application sections. Boldface type is used to identify key terms and names for study.

Part I
INTRODUCTION

Chapter 1

INTRODUCTION TO SPORT PSYCHOLOGY

"I fell in love with football as I was later to fall in love with women: suddenly, inexplicably, uncritically, giving no thought to the pain or disruption it would bring with it" (Hornby, 1994, p. 1).

And so it goes with sport. This sentiment expressed by an Englishman about the sport Americans call soccer has undoubtedly been experienced by millions of men and women throughout the world. Regardless of the specific sport, gender, ethnicity, or nationality, interest and passion in sport endures. For example, recent estimates are that 23 million youth in the United States (U.S.) between the ages of 5 and 16

Getting started

participate in sports after school and another 6.5 million play sports that are sponsored by their schools (Participation Survey, 1999–2000).

Likewise, interest in psychology is widespread and enduring. In the year 2000, 74,060 Americans received bachelor's degrees with psychology majors (U.S. Department of Education, 2002). Sport psychology brings together these widespread interests.

WHAT IS SPORT PSYCHOLOGY?

Sport psychology is defined as the application of the knowledge and scientific methods of psychology to the study of people in sport and exercise settings. This knowledge is also applied to enhance sport performance and enjoyment, and the health and fitness of sportspersons. The scope of sport psychology includes understanding how psychological factors affect performance and how involvement in sport and exercise activities relates to psychological development, adjustment, and well-being (Williams & Straub, 2010). It is not surprising that college students have a keen interest in sport psychology, as college students have consistently demonstrated the greatest interest in topics in psychology that have direct applications in their daily lives (Ruch, 1937; Zanich & Grover, 1989).

HISTORY OF SPORT PSYCHOLOGY

By the start of the 20th century, theories about the benefits of sport were well-established. Theories to explain human motivation for involvement in sport and play were also developed. For example, play and sport were seen as inherently pleasurable, or as outlets for surplus energy (Hermann, 1921). Edward W. Scripture developed a widely recognized theory at the psychological laboratory of Yale University. According to Scripture (1900), involvement in sport built character, or fostered the development of favorable qualities of personality. He studied the effects of athletics, calisthenics, and manual training on the development of self-control among young felons in the Elmira Reformatory. Scripture argued that character strengths developed by motor activity could be transferred to areas of everyday living. Scripture was not alone in concluding that sport and play were methods by which people developed skills and qualities that would prepare them for life. Sport was said to develop alertness, judgment, and the capacity to react to changing environments. In scientific and popular literature, parallels were drawn between strong bodies and strong minds and sportspersonship and ethical conduct in other areas of life functioning (Bailey et al., 2009; Davis, Huss, & Becker, 1995).

RESEARCH AND TRAINING IN THE UNITED STATES

Norman Triplett (1898) is credited with conducting the initial research in sport psychology at the University of Indiana. Triplett discerned that bicycle racing performances were faster when cyclists competed in the presence of other cyclists who functioned as pacemakers or as competitors. Racing performances were slowest when cyclists rode alone. Triplett reasoned that the presence of pacemakers or competitors was "dynamogenic," or served as stimuli to release energy that was latent when cyclists rode alone. Visual and auditory cues from the other cyclists were also seen to inspire additional effort from cyclists. Triplett replicated these findings with children who were timed winding fishing reels, either alone or with another child. These results were later described as the **social facilitation effect** (Zajonc, 1965). This research was conducted while Triplett was in graduate school. He did not continue this research, as his professional career was spent in teaching and administration.

The first American psychologist to devote a significant portion of his career to research, teaching, and service in sport psychology was **Coleman Roberts Griffith** (Gould & Pick, 1995). Griffith and his students had a major impact on the field between the years of 1920 and 1940, as his was the first program for systematic research and training in sport psychology. He also championed sport for its capacity to develop virtues of character such as courage, honor, fair play, and team work (Green, 2006). He has been called the father of American sport psychology, and was the director of the Research in Athletics Laboratory at the University of Illinois. This lab was founded in 1925, five years after the first sport psychology laboratory in the world was established at the Institute of Physical Education by Robert Werner Schulte in Berlin, Germany. Griffith offered the first course in sport psychology, "Psychology and Athletics," in 1923 (Green, 2006).

Sport and character strengths—Diego Forlan

Diego Forlán Keeps His Promises

Diego Forlán's older sister, Alejandra, was left paralyzed at age 17 due to injuries suffered in a car accident. Although only 13 years of age, he promised that he would provide for her. "I told her while she was in her hospital bed that I would become a star so that I could ensure that she still has a good life," said Forlán.

Forlán pursued stardom in soccer. He left his native Uruguay at age 17 to play professional soccer with Argentina's Independiente. After scoring 40 goals in 91 games for Independiente, he was signed by Manchester United in the English Premier League at age 23. Subsequently he played for Villarreal and Atletico Madrid in Spain, and twice won scoring titles. He developed the Fundación Alejandra Forlán, and became an outspoken critic of dangerous driving.

Forlán led Uruguay, a country of approximately 3.3 million, to a fourth-place finish in the 2010 World Cup of soccer. He won the Golden Ball as the tournament's best player (Woitalla, 2010).

In addition to his research in his laboratory, Griffith functioned as an educator and consultant, and his career therefore presaged the roles of future generations of sport psychologists. In 1926 and 1928, his books *Psychology of Coaching* and *Psychology of Athletics* were published, and are considered classics. He also consulted with the Chicago Cubs professional baseball team and corresponded with the renowned Notre Dame Football coach Knute Rockne. Philip Knight Wrigley, the owner of the Chicago Cubs, advocated for Griffith's application of scientific rigor in the training and preparation of professional baseball players. However, the managerial and coaching staff of the Cubs undermined Griffith's efforts, perhaps fearing that their authority and influence would be diminished (Green, 2003).

Application

Griffith's experience with the Chicago Cubs illustrates the importance of working alliances between sport psychologists and coaching and managerial staffs. Griffith's efforts to impose scientific rigor on the homespun style and haphazard practices of manager Charlie Grimm resulted in division and conflict. Griffith's assistant John E. Sterrett summarized the atmosphere:

> I am convinced that Grimm is knocking our work as much as he can. Grimm said to one of the players that he was afraid we might say or do something worthwhile and that if the players or the head office knew about it, it would put him in a bad light (cited in Griffith, 1939, p. 48).

In turn, Griffith became increasingly critical of Grimm, and his successor at manager, Gabby Hartnett. Ultimately, Griffith had little influence with the Cubs, and Griffith's association with the Cubs came to an end in 1940 after only two years.

Griffith's sport psychology laboratory at the University of Illinois was also shut down in 1932. Ostensibly, budgetary restraint necessitated by the onset of the Great Depression was responsible for its closing. However, it was also rumored that Griffith lost the support of Illinois football coach Robert Zuppke (Green, 2003).

Griffith developed a view of the scope of sport psychology. First, he recommended that sport psychologists study the techniques and principles practiced by the best coaches of their day. Sport psychologists were then to abstract and summarize these principles and communicate them to young and inexperienced coaches. In this way, sport psychologists could help in the development of more effective coaches.

Second, Griffith studied psychomotor learning and the relationship between personality factors and physical performance and called for the integration of this information into sport psychology research. This practice has continued to the present day, and the extension of this practice is emphasized in this book. Third, Griffith recommended scientific, psychological research specific to sport psychology (Weiss & Gill, 2005). This research was to have practical applications in supporting improved athletic performance. Among the topics of research in his laboratory were the learning of athletic and motor skills and the influence of personality traits on athletic performance. Personality traits refer to ways of responding and behaving that are consistent over time and across situations.

Griffith introduced the concepts of automated responses and the development of optimal states of arousal for competitions. Automated responses occur without conscious or deliberate thought and are characteristic of sophisticated and elite motor responses and athletic performance (see Chapter 5). With the identification of optimal states of arousal, it was recognized that athletic performance could be inhibited if physiological activation was too low or too high. Arousal refers to the activation of the sympathetic branch of the autonomic nervous system. This activation is measured on the bases of heart rate, rate of breathing, systolic blood pressure, diastolic blood pressure, and galvanic skin response. Higher readings on these measures were considered indicative of players being ready for, or "up" for, games. Successful performance was seen to be associated with the majority of the team being prepared for competition. Current literature concerning the relationship between arousal and performance will be reviewed in Chapter 4. Griffith was also interested in the psychological growth that could be fostered by sport and physical training.

Rapid growth in sport psychology occurred between 1950 and 1980 (Landers, 1995; Wiggins, 1984). Topics in sport psychology that were identified during this period remain active areas of scientific inquiry. These areas include: optimal states of arousal and performance, mental imagery and performance, modeling of adaptive motor and psychological responses, performance anxiety, and achievement motivation. Between 1950 and 1965 there was an emphasis on personality factors associated with involvement in athletics. This literature was not especially conclusive, probably due in no small part to methodological limitations, such as reliably measuring the personality factors. More recent and promising research is reviewed in Chapter 15.

In the 1970s, the **interactionism paradigm,** or the interaction between individuals and their environments, was emphasized in sport psychology research (Williams & Straub, 2010). Research in sport venues rather than university laboratories was also emphasized in the 1970s. **Rainer Martens**'s 1979 article "About Smocks and Jocks" was credited with stimulating research in sport settings. Research in sport settings was considered more ecologically valid or directly applicable to real-life issues in sport.

Applied research occurred on a limited basis before the 1970s. For example, as early as 1952, psychologists studied the relationship between arousal and performance with professional American football teams (Freudenberger & Bergandi, 1994). Coleman Roberts Griffith lugged his "Sanborn reaction time outfit" to the practice facilities of the University of Illinois football team to test the quickness of players (Green, 2006, p. 155).

In the 1980s and thereafter, the breadth of research in sport psychology increased. Topics such as the cognitive factors associated with optimal performance, overtraining and burnout, the effects of athletic injuries, goal orientations, and exercise adherence were examined.

In the late 1960s and early 1970s, sport psychology regained the momentum on American campuses that it had experienced prior to 1932 in Coleman Griffith's laboratory. During this era, textbooks and scientific journals specific to sport psychology were published, and college courses and graduate training programs in sport psychology were founded. Sport psychology classes were also offered in university departments of Physical Education, Exercise, Sport Science, and Kinesiology, and to a lesser extent in departments of Psychology. The majority of graduate training in sport psychology has been provided in university departments of Physical Education, Exercise, Sport Science, and Kinesiology (Singer, 1989).

Recommendations for the enhancement of graduate training include implementing formal professional and peer mentoring programs (Watson, Clement, Blom, & Grindley, 2009), increasing the numbers of faculty in clearly defined Sport Psychology departments, and providing supervised practicum experiences for graduate students (Knowles, Gilbourne, Tomlinson, & Anderson, 2007; Silva, Conroy, & Zizzi, 1999). Practicum experiences involve the applied practice of sport psychology, such as consulting with teams and athletes, under the supervision of faculty. The development of comprehensive practicum training has lagged behind the establishment of strictly academic coursework, but is improving, as doctoral students in sport psychology averaged 446 hours of supervised experience between 1994 and 1999 (Williams & Scherzer, 2003).

RESEARCH AND TRAINING IN EUROPE AND CANADA

The development of sport psychology in Britain has been somewhat parallel to that in the U.S. The study of motor learning and the development of skill in sport were advanced at Cambridge University in the 1940s and 1950s (Biddle, 1989). The tradition of research concerning personality factors and athletics was pursued both in the U.S. and Britain. The eminent British psychologist Hans Eysenck was a pioneer in the scientific study of personality, and he extended his research to the evaluation of the personality of sportspersons (Eysenck, Nias, & Cox, 1982). A substantial portion of Chapter 15 will be devoted to reviewing Eysenck's theory of personality and its application in sporting contexts.

Professional organizations were developed and in 1985 the British Association of Sports Sciences was formed, which was an amalgamation of the Biomechanics Study Group, British Society for Sport Psychology, and Society of Sports Sciences. The British Psychological Society formed the Division of Sport and Exercise Psychology in 2004. Also consistent with practices in the U.S., academic programs in sport psychology have been developed and British sport psychologists have increasingly consulted with athletes. Since the 1980s, research in applied or sport settings has been more frequent, and the findings of this research will be presented in later chapters.

Similarly, sport and exercise psychology services have been available for many years in France, Germany, Australia, Canada, Italy, Sweden, Japan, the People's Republic of China, and the former Soviet Union (Kornspan, 2012; Pargman, 1998). For example, in 1925, Piotr Antonovich Roudik established the first sport psychology laboratory in the Psychology Department of the State Central Institute of Physical Culture in Moscow (Ryba, Stambulova, & Wrisberg, 2005), and soon thereafter, A. Z. Puni established a sport psychology laboratory at the Institute of Physical Culture in Leningrad (Roberts & Treasure, 1999). In 1946, Puni launched a Department of Sport Psychology at the Institute. Beginning in the 1950s, and continuing for approximately three decades, a rivalry ensued between Puni and Roudik for the acknowledged leadership of sport psychology in the Soviet Union. During this time period sport psychology was seen as an important ingredient in the success of Soviet Olympic athletes (Ryba et al., 2005).

The focus of Soviet/Russian sport psychology was on applied sport psychology and especially on interventions to optimize the performance of elite athletes (Stambulova, Wrisberg, & Ryba, 2006). Prior to 1963, applied sport psychology in the Soviet Union included consulting with athletes about preperformance preparation for competition, simulation training, mental rehearsals (see Chapters 5 and 6), goal setting (see Chapter 8), and the development of sport self-confidence (see Chapter 10; Ryba et al., 2005). Among Puni's contributions was a comprehensive model for optimal sport performance that included long- (e.g., goal setting) and short-term (e.g., practicing mental skills to realize optimal concentration) phases.

A great number of resources were devoted to performance enhancement with elite athletes in the former Soviet Union and East Germany. In these countries, elite athletes were exposed to as many as 30 hours of training in techniques to enhance performance, such as autogenic training, visualization, and self-hypnosis (Williams & Straub, 2010). Professional journals devoted to exercise and sport psychology are available in most of these countries.

Sport psychology also developed as a more applied discipline in Canada than in the U.S. in the 1960s and 1970s. Unlike their American counterparts, Canadian sport psychology consultants were supported by their national sport-governing organizations, such as the Coaching Association of Canada. As a result, the utilization of psychological services was more widespread among coaches and athletes in Canada. As was the case in the Soviet Union, there was also a greater emphasis on interventions to enhance and maximize athletic performance (Stambulova et al., 2006).

PROFESSIONAL ACTIVITIES OF SPORT PSYCHOLOGISTS

Sport psychologists based in universities are actively involved in scientific research, and therefore in the development of the basic facts and findings of the science of sport psychology. University-based sport psychologists also teach courses in sport and exercise psychology, and academia remains the primary area of employment for sport psychologists (Williams & Scherzer, 2003).

A group of sport psychologists consult with professional, university, and Olympic teams and athletes, and this **consultation** emphasizes the realization of optimal performance. Some of these consultants function as a "mental coach" in teaching athletes techniques to enhance performance and minimize inhibition. This consulting may involve techniques for decreasing anxiety during competition, as well as enhancing confidence and motivation (Singer, 1989). These consultants may be identified as **educational sport psychologists** and often have graduate training in sport and exercise science, physical education, and kinesiology as well as sport psychology (McCullagh & Noble, 2002). Other consultants are licensed clinical or counseling psychologists with specialized training in sport and exercise psychology. **Clinical psychologists** are licensed to diagnose and treat mental disorders and behavioral or adjustment problems. Examples of mental disorders that might be present among athletes are substance abuse, depression, and eating disorders. The practices of clinical and counseling psychologists have converged in recent years, as both have been increasingly involved in the delivery of psychotherapy. Psychotherapy is a verbal intervention by which the psychologist assists the client or patient in overcoming mental disorders or problems in living. Traditionally, counseling psychologists have been trained to identify impediments to psychological growth rather than discrete mental disorders.

Evolution of Consultation

From the 1960s to the present, the range of professional psychological services provided to athletes progressed. A sport psychologist was assigned to work with the U.S. Olympic team for the first time in 1976, and in 1978 the U.S. Olympic Committee (USOC) recruited advisors in four branches of sport science: biomechanics, exercise physiology, nutrition, and sport psychology. The USOC established a Sport Psychology Committee and a registry of qualified sport psychologists who specialized in research, education, or clinical sport psychology by 1983 (USOC, 1983). In 1984 and thereafter, sport psychology services were routinely provided to U.S. summer and winter Olympians. There were 11 psychological consultants for U.S. athletes at the 1984 summer and winter Olympics, with academic backgrounds in physical education and motor learning, clinical psychology, and counseling psychology (Suinn, 1985). The number of sport psychology consultants grew, and by 1988, 47 sport psychology consultants had consulted with U.S. Olympians and coaches (Gould, Tammen, Murphy, & May, 1989).

In the last 25 years, psychological preparation for peak performance has become increasingly important for the Olympic competition (Haberl & Zaichowsky, 2003). The psychological services most frequently provided by these consultants were training in concentration, relaxation, self-talk, the use of mental imagery and mental practice, and team cohesion.

In 2002, the Football Association of England initiated a "Psychology for Football" (soccer) educational program. The purpose of this initiative was to increase the awareness and application of sport psychology within professional clubs, youth academies, and national teams. Increasing numbers of professional clubs employ sport psychology consultants. In addition to teaching techniques for performance enhancement to professional footballers, these consultants focus on positive youth development within the youth academies of the professional teams (Harwood, 2008; Pain & Harwood, 2004). Russian and Swedish sport psychologists also emphasize a *whole person approach*, or guidance on how to balance athletic, academic, and social concerns (Stambulova, Stambulov, & Johnson, 2012).

It is not uncommon for innovations derived from psychological practice to precede the validation of these innovations via experimental study. For example, in 1971, Richard M. Suinn developed an intervention for athletes that combined mental imagery and relaxation. Suinn's **Visuo-Motor Behavioral Rehearsal** will be discussed in Chapter 7. It has been highly influential and has subsequently received solid empirical support (Seabourne, Weinberg, Jackson, & Suinn, 1985). In 1997, it was described as perhaps the most studied mental practice procedure in the literature of sport psychology (Onestak, 1997). Robert Nideffer's influential description and assessment of attentional styles was developed in 1976 and will also be discussed in Chapter 6 and in other chapters (Nideffer, 1985).

Bruce Ogilvie has been called the father of North American applied sport psychology because of his leadership in providing psychological services to elite and professional athletes. His book *Problem Athletes and How to Handle Them* (Ogilvie & Tutko, 1966) and questionnaire, the Athletic Motivational Inventory, were influential and controversial. Ogilvie and other pioneering consultants surveyed colleagues in 1979 regarding the training necessary for clinical psychologists to function effectively in consultation with athletes (Ogilvie et al., 1979). These clinicians placed the highest priority on knowledge about psychopathology, and they also made frequent use of relaxation training to reduce physiological anxiety. The clinicians stated that their experience as athletes competing at a high level was their most important experience or training to be an effective sport psychologist. Although not necessary for effective consulting, athletes are

Coleman Roberts Griffith
(Courtesy of the University of Illinois Archives, Photographic Subject File, RS 39/2/20)

not unimpressed by consultants' histories of athletic accomplishments, particularly if the athlete and consultant competed in the same sport (Lubker, Visek, Geer, & Watson, 2008). Participation notwithstanding, consultants who are deeply aware of the physical, technical, and tactical aspects of the client's sport are more capable of demonstrating empathy. An empathic understanding of the athlete's concerns is necessary for effective consultation (Sharp & Hodge, 2011).

These psychologists were probably self-trained or learned "on the job" to apply clinical services to athletes. Today, on-the-job training is not sufficient for certification as a sport psychologist. For example, the Division of Exercise and Sport Psychology of the **American Psychological Association (APA)** explicitly states that sport psychologists are not self-taught and also that experience as an athlete and training as a clinical psychologist does not provide the necessary education and training. Formal graduate coursework, supervised practice, and testing are necessary to insure that sport psychologists meet objective standards of competence and expertise. The **Association for Applied Sport Psychology (AASP)** developed criteria for certification for sport psychologists in 1991 that also requires supervised experience, graduate coursework in psychology and counseling, as well as knowledge of the biomechanical and/or physiological bases of sport (Zizzi, Zaichkowsky, & Perna, 2002). The USOC requires this certification for consultants to work with Olympic programs. Current sport consultants recognize the need for specialized training in sport performance enhancement (Lubker et al., 2008).

The clinicians in the 1979 survey (Ogilvie et al., 1979) recognized an ethical concern that has been codified as an ethical standard of sport psychologists, in that they considered confidentiality within the consulting relationship to be a highest priority. Sport psychologists and athletes continue to emphasize the importance of confidentiality (Petitpas, Brewer, Rivera, & Van Raalte, 1994), trustworthiness, and honesty (Lubker et al., 2008) in consulting relationships. It is especially important for sport psychology consultants to maintain appropriate professional boundaries and confidentiality, because consultations often occur in informal settings such as hotel lobbies and at training sessions (Sharp & Hodge, 2011).

Application

The ethical code of the AASP (1994) was modeled after that of the American Psychological Association (APA; 2002). The ethical code of the APA is an admixture of five general principles and specific rules that follow the general principles and relate to specific situations in the field of psychology. The general principles (Beneficence and Nonmaleficence, Fidelity and Responsibility, Integrity, Justice, Respect for People's Rights and Dignity) are considered universal or applicable to all human beings and to involve no contradictions (Whelan, Meyers, & Elkins, 2002). The specific rules are derived to some degree from the actual practice of psychology and are intended to enhance the well-being of the greatest majority of people. An example of a specific ethical obligation for professional psychologists is to maintain the confidentiality of information they obtain from clients (with certain exceptions) in professional counseling relationships.

Athletes' Views of Consulting Sport Psychologists

Given the aforementioned history of consultation with U.S. Olympic athletes since 1976, it is not surprising that in more recent times elite athletes routinely consult with psychologists (Gould, 1999; Gould & Maynard, 2009). However, perhaps due to less experience with sport psychologists (Maniar, Curry, Sommers-Flanagan, & Walsh, 2001), collegiate athletes in the U.S. and Britain are not entirely comfortable with the prospect of psychological consultations (Linder, Brewer, Van Raalte, & De Lange, 1991; Van Raalte, Brewer, Brewer, & Linder, 1992; Van Raalte, Brewer, Linder, & DeLange, 1990; Van Raalte, Brewer, Matheson, & Brewer, 1996). Sport psychologists are viewed as similar to mental health professionals such as clinical psychologists, counselors, and psychiatrists. However, they are often viewed to be less knowledgeable about mental health issues and more conversant with sport and physical topics than are mental health professionals. Coaches generally view the consultations of sport psychologists positively and recognize a need for their services (Pargman, 1998).

Athletes have underutilized mental health services and have been reluctant to take advantage of the services of sport psychologists. They are more likely to seek emotional help and support from family and professionals identified primarily as sport professionals, such as coaches (Maniar et al., 2001). It appears that athletes are uncomfortable with the title of psychologist due to its association with mental disorders and problems (Ravizza, 1988). African American and male Division I intercollegiate athletes were particularly uncomfortable with the prospect of accessing help from sport psychologists, as they feared being stigmatized by consulting sport psychologists (Maniar et al., 2001; Martin, Wrisberg, Beitel, & Lounsbury, 1997).

Metta World Peace Promotes Mental Health

At one time, Metta World Peace would have been an unlikely candidate for UCLA Medical Center's prestigious CICARE Award. This award honors someone for "healing humankind, one patient at a time, by improving health, alleviating suffering, and delivering acts of kindness" (Painter, 2010).

As an NBA player in 2004, and when named Ron Artest, World Peace was suspended for 86 games—the longest suspension in NBA history—for his part in a brawl involving the opposing team and fans. He served a seven-game suspension in 2007 for his no-contest plea to a domestic violence charge. In 2011, World Peace earned a one-game suspension for slamming his forearm into the face of an opposing player. He was slapped with a seven-game suspension in 2012 for an elbow to an opponent's head that resulted in a concussion. He was suspended for one game in 2013 for jabbing another player in the jaw.

World Peace has openly acknowledged mental health struggles. He thanked his psychologist, Dr. Santhi Periasamy, on national television after his Los Angeles Lakers won the NBA championship in 2010. World Peace has seen no less than eight therapists since adolescence. World Peace credits therapy for helping him to become a better person, husband, and father.

World Peace donated his NBA Championship ring to an auction to raise money for community mental health projects. He lends public support to the UCLA Resnick Neuropsychiatric Hospital and projects such as the Mental Health in Schools Act (Smith, 2010).

Female athletes appear to be more willing to accesses consultation from sport psychologists, and to acknowledge their need for help. Perhaps males are more likely to be socialized to be stoic, or to accept pain and the risk of injury without asking for help or complaining (Martin, Akers et al., 2001; Martin et al.,1997). Female athletes are less likely to believe that others will label them as having psychological problems due to their consultation with a sport psychologist. These women and girls are also less likely to express a preference for working with a consultant of their same culture, ethnicity, or race (Martin, 2005). High school athletes are also more likely than Division I collegiate athletes to associate consultation with a sport psychologist with the stigma of having psychological problems (Martin, 2005).

PROFESSIONAL ASSOCIATIONS AND JOURNALS

An important stimulus to the growth of sport psychology was the formation of academic societies and scholarly journals which fostered research and communication (Roberts & Treasure, 1999). The first journal to be devoted entirely to sport psychology was founded in 1970 as the *International Journal of Sport Psychology*. It is the official journal of the **International Society of Sport Psychology (ISSP)**, and the first president of ISSP and editor of the *International Journal of Sport Psychology* was the Italian psychiatrist Ferruccio Antonelli. The *Journal of Sport Psychology*, later called the *Journal of Sport & Exercise Psychology*, publishes basic and applied research and was established in 1979. Other important journals in this field are: *The Journal of Sport Sciences*, founded in 1983; *The Sport Psychologist*, established in 1986; the *Journal of Applied Sport Psychology*, founded in 1989 and the official journal of Association for Applied Sport Psychology (AASP); and the *Psychology of Sport and Exercise* founded in 2000. Division 47, Exercise and Sport Psychology, of the APA inaugurated its journal, *Sport, Exercise, and Performance Psychology*, in 2012. The relative youth and rapid development of sport psychology is reflected in this timeline for the development of journals.

Websites of Interest

With the development of the Internet, websites provide useful sources of information about sport psychology.

Sport and Exercise Psychology in North America

American Alliance for Health, Physical Education, Recreation and Dance
    http://www.aahperd.org
Association for the Advancement of Applied Sport Psychology
    http://www.appliedsportpsych.org
Canadian Society for Psychomotor Learning
    http://www.scapps.org

Division 47 of the American Psychological Association
    http://www.psyc.unt.edu/apadiv47
North American Society for the Psychology of Sport and Physical Activity
    http://www.naspspa.org

Information About Sport

American College of Sports Medicine
    http://www.acsm.org
Coaching Association of Canada
    http://www.coach.ca
National Collegiate Athletic Association
    http://www.ncaa.org
United States Olympic Committee
    http://www.olympic-usa.org

Sport and Exercise Internationally

Asian South Pacific Association of Sport Psychology
    http://www.humankinetics.com/associations/aspasp/index.cfm
British Association for Sport and Exercise Sciences
    http://www.bases.org.uk
Board of Sport Psychologists of the Australian Psychological Society
    http://psychsociety.com.au/units/colleges/sport
Canadian Society for Psychomotor Learning and Sport
    http://www.scapps.org
European Federation of Sport Psychology
    http://www.fepsac.org
International Olympic Committee
    http://www.olympic.org
International Society for Sport Psychology
    http://www.issponline.org

Associations for the study of sport psychology were established in the mid-1960s. In 1965, the International Society of Sport Psychology (ISSP) held the First International Congress of Sport Psychology in Rome, and in 1967 the first meeting of the North American Society for the Psychology of Sport and Physical Activity (NASPSPA) was held in Las Vegas (Landers, 1995; Wiggins, 1984). The Canadian Society for Psychomotor Learning and Sport Psychology (CSPLSP) was established in 1969. Initially, it was under the auspices of the Canadian Association for Health, Physical Education and Recreation, but became independent in 1977 (Williams & Straub, 2010). The Association for the Advancement of Applied Sport Psychology (renamed the Association for Applied Sport Psychology [AASP]) was launched in 1986. In 1987, the Division of Sport and Exercise Psychology was established as the 47th division of the APA.

Accreditation

Accreditation provides an objective index of the quality of training for educational programs and individuals. The AASP established standards for the accreditation of individual sport psychologists (Silva, 1989). Accreditation for graduate training programs in sport psychology has been recommended but is more controversial (Silva, 1989).

The precedent for accreditation was established by the APA for clinical psychology shortly after World War II (Report, 1947). This model is referred to as the scientist–practitioner model, reflecting its emphasis on training in academic and applied psychology, and as the Boulder model, in that it was established in a meeting in Boulder, Colorado (Raimy, 1950). Accreditation indicates that the academic courses, faculty, and facilities of academic institutions are sufficient to train competent professional psychologists.

Accreditation of graduate programs in sport psychology has been seen as slow to develop (Silva et al., 1999). Perhaps it has not been universally embraced due to concerns about the cost of the accreditation process, fears that programs that fail to meet accreditation standards will be eliminated, and beliefs that academic freedom will be imperiled if curriculums are imposed by outside organizations such as AASP. These issues appear to be less concerning to graduate students in sport psychology as they are largely in favor of accreditation (Students', 1997).

SPORT PSYCHOLOGY AND THE SCIENTIFIC METHOD

As mentioned earlier, a substantial body of scientific research is summarized in each chapter of this textbook. Although there is some explanation of how this information was obtained, the content rather than the methods of this scientific research will be emphasized in the ensuing chapters. Before continuing with the presentation of this content, a brief discussion of the methods by which this information was obtained is warranted. Due to space limitations, these topics are only introduced in this text, and readers are encouraged to explore these issues more thoroughly by referencing the suggested readings at the end of this chapter.

The majority of the research in this textbook was informed by the scientific method, which consists of developing hypotheses, often informed by prior research, and testing the correctness or accuracy of the hypotheses with sophisticated experimental and statistical methodology. The minimal elements necessary for scientific research in sport psychology are, therefore, testable hypotheses, valid experimental designs, and statistical procedures that mathematically evaluate hypotheses. The question "How many angels can stand on the head of a safety pin?" may be of metaphysical interest to some, but it does not represent a scientifically testable hypothesis. Tangible information cannot be obtained to test this question about angels. A question such as "Does pressure disrupt athletic performance?" is both testable and relevant to Sport Psychology.

Hypotheses are tested in **experiments** or **quasi-experiments.** True experiments have experimental and control groups, and participants or subjects are randomly assigned to both groups. Experimental groups are exposed to an intervention, whereas control groups are given no intervention or an intervention that would be expected to have no effect on the behavior of interest. With random assignment it is assumed that the experimental and control groups are equivalent before the intervention.

Returning to the question about the effects of pressure on performance, a sport psychologist might conduct a true experiment in which sport performance is measured by the accuracy of putting a golf ball. Specifically, accuracy could be measured by the distance between each putt and the target or pin. Pressure might be operationalized or represented in this experiment by filming students putting in the experimental condition, and informing them that golf coaches and other students would review the film. Undergraduate students without prior experience at golf might be randomly assigned to the experimental group that received instructions that their putting would be filmed and reviewed or to a control group that was given no instructions or instructions that were not intended to produce pressure, such as to try their best.

Differences in putting accuracy between the experimental and control groups would then be compared with statistical tests such as a *t-test*, a test of differences between the means of the two groups (Lindman, 1974). If between-groups differences are sufficiently large, then the *null hypothesis—* that the experimental and control groups are indistinguishable and that pressure has no effect on performance—would be rejected with some degree of statistical certainty. Experimental convention dictates that a 0.05 level of statistical significance or certainty is necessary to reject the null hypothesis, and at this level, the experimenter knows that differences as large as those recorded would occur by chance only five times in 100.

Returning to the potential study of pressure and putting performance, the experimenter might find that the average distances between putts and pins was 10 inches for the experimental or pressured group and 4 inches for the control group. The t-test would likely demonstrate that this difference is significant, perhaps at least at the 0.05 level. The experimenter may then reject the null hypothesis with the certainty that a difference between groups this large would occur only five times in 100 times. Following this procedure, the experimenter is also likely to conclude that the experiment has **internal validity** or that the intervention designed to induce pressure was responsible for the reduced putting accuracy of the pressured group.

The experimenter might pause before announcing that this study has external validity. **External validity** refers to the populations to which the results of a study can be generalized. This study was an analog study or a study in which realistic conditions were recreated in a laboratory environment. In that it was analogous but not identical to the study of pressure in actual sporting events, it is far from certain that the results of this hypothetical study can be generalized to all groups of golfers. For example, elite golfers may have developed skills for blunting the effects of pressure, or perhaps those susceptible to pressure quit, so that only golfers relatively unsusceptible to pressure advance to elite ranks.

Perhaps a study in a golf tournament with skilled golfers would provide more convincing evidence about the effects of pressure on performance. However, it is highly unlikely that participants in a golf tournament could be subjected to experimental conditions intended to increase pressure. Instead, performance in naturally occurring situations that produce pressure might be compared to performance where pressure is less obvious. For example, a gallery might be present on certain holes and not on others, and scores for holes with and without galleries might be compared. This study would probably have **ecological validity** in that it was conducted in naturalistic conditions and external validity in that it was conducted in the actual setting and with the population of interest. However, this study would lack the experimental control and random assignment necessary for true experiments, and therefore it would be a quasi-experiment (Shadish, Cook, & Campbell, 2002). Quasi-experiments are more open to challenges about causation or whether the experimental procedures resulted in the differences in measured variables (in this case, scores on holes). The benefits of external and ecological validity are balanced with potential challenges to internal validity when evaluating quasi-experiments.

Concerns about internal and external validity notwithstanding, true and quasi-experiments allow for inferences about causation. Some of the studies in this book utilized procedures, such as correlation and qualitative analyses, which were descriptive but did not allow for causal inferences. **Correlational studies** demonstrate associations between variables. **Qualitative analyses** (e.g., Gould, Tuffey, Udry, & Loehr, 1996; Lincoln & Guba, 1985; Patton, 1990) rely on semistructured interviews that are tape-recorded and transcribed verbatim. Independent investigators identify specific themes of the interviews, and the specific themes are subsequently organized into increasingly general themes. Qualitative analyses permit the discovery of information from the perspective of sportspersons. Another form of qualitative research, **ethnography,** has recently been advanced as a method of gaining insight into the behaviors and mental states of athletes. With ethnography, researchers become embedded in a particular sport and team, and collect data in the forms of participant observations, interviews, photography, and questionnaires (Krane & Baird, 2005).

Information from true experiments, quasi-experiments, correlational studies, and qualitative analyses is integrated throughout this textbook. With this research, the horizons of sport psychology are continually expanded.

SUMMARY AND APPLICATION

Sport psychology is a rapidly maturing area of research, teaching, and practice. The maturity of sport psychology is evidenced by the number of professional journals and organizations devoted to advancing and communicating the science and practice of sport psychology. The importance of applied sport psychology is perhaps best demonstrated by the observation that sport psychologists have consulted with U.S. Olympians since 1976.

As is true in other areas of applied psychology, such as clinical psychology, there have been periods of tension between practitioners and academics. Subsequent to the publication of Rainer Martens's 1979 article "About Smocks and Jocks," research in the actual venues of sport has been emphasized. Studies in such sport settings provide opportunities for research that is both ecologically and externally valid. This research diminishes the distance between academic and applied practice.

The effectiveness of psychologists in consulting, educational, and research settings is to some degree determined by the quality of their working alliances with students, supervisees, and clients. The effectiveness of working alliances merits monitoring on an ongoing basis. This monitoring may involve estimates of the degree of trust in the working alliance.

Key Terms

Norman Triplett 4

Social facilitation effect 5

Coleman Roberts Griffith 5

Rainer Martens 7

Consultation 10

Educational sport psychologist 10

Clinical psychologist 10

Visuo-Motor Behavioral Rehearsal 11

Bruce Ogilvie 11

American Psychological Association (APA) 12

Association for Applied Sport Psychology (AASP) 12

International Society of Sport Psychology (ISSP) 14

Accreditation 16

Experiments 17

Quasi-experiments 17

Internal validity 17

External validity 17

Ecological validity 18

Correlational studies 18

Qualitative analyses 18

Ethnography 18

Discussion Questions

Q1. What is the scope and focus of sport psychology?

Q2. Review the history of sport psychology, including the contributions of Edward W. Scripture, Norman Triplett, Coleman Roberts Griffith, and Rainer Martens.

Q3. Consider current recommendations for graduate training in sport psychology.

Q4. Describe training in sport psychology in the U.S., Europe, and Canada.

Q5. Differentiate educational sport psychologists and licensed psychologists.

Q6. Review the history of consultation in sport psychologists, including consultation with the USOC and the Football Association of England.

Q7. How do we remember Bruce Ogilvie?

Q8. What is the current status of "on the job" training in sport psychology?

Q9. How are competent consultants in sport psychology identified?

Q10. Review the general principles in the ethical code of the APA.

Q11. Which athletes might be initially favorably disposed to consultation with a sport psychologist?

Q12. What is the role of professional journals in the development of an academic discipline?

Q13. Define professional accreditation.

Q14. How is a testable hypothesis determined?

Q15. What differentiates experiments from quasi-experiments?

Q16. What is the role of the null hypothesis in research?

Q17. Define internal, external, and ecological validity.

Q18. Describe correlation studies, qualitative analysis, and ethnography.

Suggested Readings

Heiman, G. W. (2003). *Applied statistics for the behavioral sciences, 5th ed.* Boston, MA: Houghton-Mifflin.

Krane, V., & Baird, S M. (2005). Using ethnography in applied sport psychology. *Journal of Applied Sport Psychology, 17,* 87–107.

Ryba, T. V., Stambulova, N. B., Wrisberg, C. A. (2005). The Russian origins of sport psychology: A translation of an early work of A. Z. Puni. *Journal of Applied Sport Psychology, 17,* 157–169.

Shadish, W. R., Cook, T. D., & Campbell, D. T. (2002). *Experimental and quasi-experimental designs for generalized causal inference.* Boston, MA: Houghton-Mifflin.

Stambulova, N. B., Wrisberg, C. A., & Ryba, T. V. (2006). A tale of two traditions in applied sport psychology: The heyday of Soviet sport and wake-up calls for North America. *Journal of Applied Sport Psychology, 18,* 173–184.

Williams, J. M., & Straub, W. F. (2010). Sport psychology: Past, present, future. In J. M. Williams (Ed.), *Applied sport psychology: Personal growth to peak performance* (6th ed., pp. 1–17). New York, NY: McGraw-Hill.

Chapter 2

MOTIVATION FOR SPORT AND ACHIEVEMENT

Why do people strive to do their best?

Bouldering is practically all that interests 11-year-old Ashima Shiraishi. Bouldering is a form a climbing that was popularized in the 1990s, and consists of climbing without ropes or harnesses on rocks that are generally no higher than 20 feet. As a kindergartener, Ashima discovered bouldering when she joined other climbers and scurried up Rat Rock on the south end of Central Park in Manhattan. She found it so enjoyable that she begged her parents to stay through the dinner hour. She was convinced to go home only when it became too dark to see the rock.

Her parents, Tsuya and Hisatoshi Shiraishi, became aware that climbing was a sport, and now accommodate her insistence on climbing almost every day. She commutes daily with her father from Manhattan to the Brooklyn Boulders gym, where she trains from 4 to 7:30 PM. On Saturdays, she generally returns to the Brooklyn Boulders gym, and on Sundays, she travels by train to New Rochelle, NY, for a private climbing lesson. Wednesday afternoons are reserved for Japanese school.

On spring break, she flew to Hueco Tanks, a state park in Texas that is a center for bouldering enthusiasts. Arriving at the park entrance, she squirmed with excitement. "This is my favorite place to climb, the best place to climb," she said. "I just can't wait to get out there" (Bosman, 2012).

At age 10, she stunned the climbing world by climbing Crown of Aragorn at Hueco Tanks. The Crown of Aragorn is rated V13 (on a scale of V0 to V16). Only a few females climbers have "sent" (climbed) a V13, and none at age 10. At age 11, she weighs 63 pounds (28.58 kilograms) and stands 4 feet 5 inches (134.62 centimeters). She easily won the American Bouldering Series Youth National Championship in 2012.

Why do people strive to do their best? Why do people strive to reach their full potential? These questions have intrigued humankind since at least the time of the ancient Greeks. Aristotle divided human activity into two categories: labor and leisure. The former was the kind of work that created wealth and earned material goods. Leisure activities, on the other hand, were responsible for the creation of goods of the spirit and of civilization (Murphy, 1993). Labor and business were considered necessary but not ennobling for human life. Work did little for the self-esteem of ancient Greeks. By contrast, leisure allowed people to grow morally, intellectually, and spiritually, and made life worth living. In Greek society, slaves were the laborers, while aristocrats and most educated citizens spent their time engaged in leisure and recreation and activities related to the arts, sciences, business, and military enterprises.

Judaism and Christianity redefined the value of work. In these religions, men and women could emulate God, who worked six days to create the world. A full day's work came to have the highest ethical value, while play and leisure were seen to lead to sin. Work came to be seen as a virtue in itself. In 1904, the German sociologist **Max Weber** described the **Protestant work ethic** as a continual striving for perfection, or at least self-improvement, and to do one's best in every respect. Weber argued that the Protestant work ethic was catalyzed by John Calvin's theology of predestination (Weber, 1930). Predestination refers to the concept that heavenly salvation was predetermined by God and not to be won by the accumulation of good works and especially the purchase of indulgences. However, the concept that salvation was predestined did little to allay fears about damnation. By striving for perfection or to imitate a biblical figure, a believer could discover if he or she were one of the elect or predestined.

Approximately 100 years have passed since Weber's studies of work and achievement motivation. It may be disheartening to learn that after this interval, a unitary and perhaps straightforward explanation of achievement motivation does not exist. In the pages that follow, seven theories of human motivation are presented (Psychoanalytic, Humanistic, Achievement Motivation, Goals, Attribution, Motivational Orientation, and Flow). There are at least 32 distinguishable theories of motivation (Roberts, 2001), but these seven theories have influenced research and practice for decades. The underpinnings of these theories will be emphasized in this chapter and their application in sport settings will be described in detail in ensuing chapters.

PSYCHOANALYTIC VIEWPOINTS

Modern psychology has considered an absence of ambition as evidence of inhibition or psychopathology (American Psychiatric Association, 2000; Gelantzer-Levy & Cohler, 1993). However, **Sigmund Freud,** a Viennese physician and the developer of **psychoanalysis,** and considered one of the 100 most influential intellects in the twentieth century (Gay, 1999), argued that work was not a response to some innate internal drive but rather a response to external pressures and opportunities to make a living. Freud thought that society's proper role was to provide external pressure or coercion for work. Otherwise, he reasoned, the majority of humans would not put forth the effort necessary to create new wealth and care for themselves. He regarded the masses as "lazy and unintelligent" and not "spontaneously fond of work" (Freud, 1927, p. 7). Freud argued that each human being was innately endowed with an **Id,** or a psychological repository of libidinal or sexual and aggressive impulses. The **Pleasure Principle,** or the motive to seek immediate pleasures and to eschew delays of gratification in the pursuit of long-term goals, governs the Id. The Pleasure Principle is concordant with the **Hedonic Principle,** or the assumption that human motivation is determined by efforts to maximize pleasure and minimize pain. The Hedonic Principle has dominated the understanding of human motivation from the time of the ancient Greeks to the twentieth century. It is the basic motivational assumption in psychological theories as diverse as psychobiology, behavioral psychology, decision making, and social psychology (Higgins, 1997).

The psychological structure that allows for adaptive responses to societal pressure for work is the **Ego.** An important standard for psychological health is the Ego's uninhibited capacity to respond adaptively to external pressures and opportunities to make a living (normality was also related to the Ego's uninhibited capacity to respond freely to the Id's demands for enjoyment). Freud considered work to be a means by which people anchored themselves to reality as they established roles in the fabric of their societies. Perhaps due to the opportunities provided by their environments and their talents, some people were considered to find additional sources of gratification in their work. These people sublimated or redirected narcissistic, aggressive, or libidinal urges from their Ids into work productions.

Through processes of identification with parents and other important figures, children develop models for working, for persistence in solving difficult problems, and ultimately Ego strength. The **Superego,** or the psychological structure that contains the values and mores, also plays a role in directing ambition. The Super ego also contains the **Ego Ideal,** or the standards by which individuals judge their behavior. Together, the Super ego and the Ego Ideal determine the levels of goals and the methods for obtaining the goals to which people aspire. Freud's personal focus on work was notable. He had prodigious energy for work, and he feared the regressive pull of full contentment and hence thrived on irritation (Mahoney, 1997). For optimal achievement, Freud needed disgruntlement in the form of physical fatigue or psychic misery. In the last years of the nineteenth century, Freud was at his most creative and at the same time was suffering most from his neurosis. Freud wrote of these phenomena:

> I returned to a sense of too much well-being and have since then been very lazy because the modicum of misery essential for intensive work will not come back (Masson, 1985, letter of April 16, 1896, pp. 180–181). My style has unfortunately been bad because I feel too well physically; I have to feel somewhat miserable to write well (Masson, 1985, letter of September 6, 1899, p. 370).

The effects of work in diminishing discontentment notwithstanding, Freud also wrote that he found joy in work: "Creative imagination and work go together with me; I take no delight in anything else" (Mend & Federn, 1963, letter of March 6, 1910, p. 35).

Ultimately, Freud came to define mental health as the capacity to work and to love. Freud's emphasis on the importance of work, especially efficient work, achievement, and performance as a standard of mental health has been accepted as axiomatic or essentially unequivocal. Indeed the modern classification of mental disorders, the *Diagnostic and Statistical Manual of Mental Disorders-Fourth Edition, Text Revision* (DSM-IV-TR; American Psychiatric Association, 2000) identifies mental disorders as causing dysfunction vocationally, interpersonally, or intrapsychically.

Application

To Freud's definition of mental health—to work well and to love—modern psychology and psychiatry adds intrapsychic well-being. Students who work well have sufficient achievement motivation and discipline to persevere at studies, work, sports, and realize their potential. They are relatively comfortable in formal, informal, and intimate relationships. They have well-being and are not overly troubled with worries and unpleasant emotions.

NEO-ANALYTIC VIEWPOINTS

Psychoanalytic theorizing about the drive to reach one's full potential did not end with Freud. The neo-psychoanalytic perspective of Self Psychology considered the movement of children from activities that are merely playful to activities that are more purposeful to be motivated by wishes to obtain approval from important adults such as parents. Satisfaction in achieving self-set goals was considered to be integrated into the child's self-concept, and self-esteem was then partially determined by achievement (Wolf, 1997).

A member of Freud's inner circle, **Alfred Adler,** left to found the Society for Individual Psychology. One of the essential tenets of his theory of human motivation was that striving for success or superiority was the driving force behind human activity. Adler maintained that this drive was universal, as infants and children recognize their lack of stature and vulnerability, experience inferiority, and compensate with goals for superiority or success (Adler, 1964). Social recognition as a superior athlete was seen as an important motive for athletic participation among elite track and field athletes (Mallet & Hanrahan, 2004). Those with exaggerated feelings of inferiority strive for superiority regardless of the effects of their behavior on others. Psychologically secure people strive toward goals that are also consistent with the interests of their society.

Subsequent research inspired by Adler's work focused less on feelings of inferiority than on maintaining control over the factors that could influence the lives of others (Veroff, 1992). **The power motive** was understood to represent a fear of being in a weak position in relation to others and therefore unable to control one's fate. More recent, and perhaps complementary, empirical research concerning the power motive has not emphasized the fear of weakness but has conceptualized the power motive as the desire to influence others, to have authority, dominance, and leadership (Winter, 1992). The kind of power that was most important to people high in this latter power motive was direct and legitimate interpersonal power. These people are likely to make efforts to gain the attention of other people by making themselves more visible, and by building alliances with others. This power motivation is independent of motives for achievement, affiliation, and intimacy.

HUMANISTIC PSYCHOLOGY

The most widely recognized theory of motivation that is perhaps most at odds with Freud's notion that humans are inherently or instinctually lazy may be that of the American humanistic psychologist, **Abraham Maslow** (1973). Maslow argued that humans were instinctually motivated toward growth and **self-actualization,** or the realization of their full human potential. He maintained that growth was rewarding in itself and that the appetite for growth is whetted by growth rather than diminished by the realization of growth.

Self-actualization has at times been seen to be more compatible with community involvement, such as building better societies, nurturing the next generation, and helping others in need, than with individual preoccupations such as financial success and occupational status (Kasser & Ryan, 1993, 1996). Financial success and occupational status have been associated with external motivations or extrinsic goals as the individual strives to meet standards that are determined and perhaps imposed by others. Those working to make a better world have been seen as motivated by internal motives, as they sought to reach standards that were of their own making.

However, the question of whether one's ambitions are selfish versus altruistic matters less than the motives for pursuing those ambitions (Carver & Baird, 1998). People may pursue altruistic goals, such as building a better world, because they are freely pursuing their own interests and values or because of external pressure' such as the desire to please others, or by external pressure that is internalized' such as efforts to avoid or diminish guilt. Self-actualization is associated with goals that are self-selected or intrinsically rewarding regardless of whether one aspires to build a better world or simply better his or her position in the world.

Intrinsic motivation involves the pursuit of activities because they are inherently rewarding and people make their own decisions to pursue these goals. Conversely, if ambitions and goals are imposed externally, self-actualization is unlikely regardless of whether ambitions relate to financial success or community involvement.

With the mastery of skills and the development of competence come feelings of satisfaction and joy (Dweck, 1986). The development of competence and intrinsic motivation is somewhat domain-specific, and people experience varying degrees of cognitive, social, and physical competence. Competence in the cognitive, social, and physical spheres is more commonly experienced in academic performance, relationships, and in sport and exercise, respectively. The issue of intrinsic versus extrinsic motivation will be discussed in greater detail later in this chapter.

ACHIEVEMENT MOTIVATION

The American psychologist **John Atkinson**'s theories and research on achievement motivation (1957, 1964, 1978) were developed in the early 1950s, and continue to influence the direction of current research. He recognized and demonstrated scientifically that people differed in terms of levels of **achievement motivation** or need for accomplishments, and that achievement motivation was a trait or a stable characteristic (Thomassen & Hallgeir, 2007). However, even those with high levels of achievement motivation would not be expected to put forth maximum effort on all evaluations. Instead, tendencies to put forth optimal efforts and achieve success were determined by achievement motivation, the likelihood of being successful at a task, and the importance of the task.

Interestingly, those with high levels of achievement motivation were not drawn to tasks that were so difficult that the chances of success were slim. They preferred tasks of moderate difficulty, or perhaps fair tests of their ability (Capa, Audiffren, & Ragot, 2008). These fair tests provide clear evidence of effort and ability. People with lower achievement motivation prefer easy or unreasonably difficult evaluations.

Atkinson also recognized a **motive to avoid failure** or **fear of failure.** Just as was the case with achievement motivation, there are individual differences in the motive to avoid failure. Ultimately, when faced with a situation in which performance is evaluated, an achievement-oriented tendency is activated that is the result of the additive combination of the motive for achievement and the motive to avoid failure. If the motive to avoid failure exceeds achievement motivation, evaluations will be avoided (Capa, Audiffren, Andre, & Hansenne, 2011). The motive to avoid failure is most influential for tasks of moderate difficulty or fair tests of ability and effort, and those with high levels of this motive most vigorously avoid these tasks. People dominated by the tendency to avoid failure spend more of their time working on easier jobs and tasks. Of course, even those with extremely high levels of the motive to avoid failure cannot avoid all forms of evaluation.

With high levels of fear of failure, evaluations are seen as threats. For example, college students with high levels of fear of failure engaged in negative self-talk in which they blamed themselves for poor performances during recreational tennis (Conroy & Metzler, 2004). Ironically, this form of blame is what they most dreaded, and, therefore, this form of self-reproach appeared somewhat involuntary and automatic.

Even eminent performers experience fear of failure. Aspects of the fear of failure among elite female and male athletes and performance artists have been identified (Conroy, Poczwardowski, & Henschen, 2001, p. 318):

1. experiencing personal diminishment
2. demonstrating that I have low ability
3. demonstrating that I lack control
4. experiencing tangible losses
5. wasting my effort
6. making my future uncertain
7. losing a special opportunity
8. causing others to lose interest in me
9. disappointing or upsetting important others
10. experiencing an embarrassing self-presentational failure

Fears of experiencing shame and embarrassment were especially prominent among adolescents who feared failure in English soccer academies (Sagar, Busch, & Jowett, 2010). These fearful adolescents frequently engaged in emotion-focused coping strategies, perhaps because they considered failure to be beyond their control and, therefore, an experience to be endured.

Adolescent athletes with especially critical and punitive parents learn to fear failure. These parents may be threatening and withdraw their love in response to failure (e.g., "I don't want to see you the rest of the day because I'm disgusted with you"; Sagar & Lavallee, 2010, p. 182). Such parental practices create pressure as these adolescents associate failure with displeasing their parents. Further, these parental responses are internalized and children learn to become harsh in judging and blaming themselves for mistakes.

Some parents are overly involved in their children's training, practice, and preparation for competition. Perhaps these parents fear failure and believe that their involvement makes failure less likely. These ego-involved parents experience shame when their children fail, and their children have the additional burden of the necessity to succeed to provide emotional support to their parents (Grolnick, 2003).

When parents are highly controlling, they pressure their children to think and behave in accord with their wishes. This interferes with the autonomy and originality of the child and undermines intrinsic interest and creativity. Efforts to resist parental control may result in internal conflicts if these are seen to threaten relationships with parents (Ryan, 1982). Finally, excessively high parental expectations are associated with fear of failure, as adolescent athletes fear disappointing their parents (Conroy, 2008; Sagar & Lavallee, 2010).

Application

Highly involved parents who are preoccupied with their children's success and who are harshly critical of their imperfections develop ambivalent relationships with their children. Failure becomes overly important as it frustrates the child's wish for parental approval. The strength of the child's fear of failure may be directly proportional to his or her wish for parental love and approval. It may be difficult for anyone, especially a child, to gain insight into this internal conflict without professional guidance or self-study.

Achievement Motivation and Gender

Matina Horner (1973), another American psychologist, pioneered the examination of gender differences in achievement motivation in the context of Atkinson's expectancy value theory. She maintained that there was a psychological barrier that interfered with the achievement of women, and referred to this as the **motive to avoid success.** The motive to avoid success refers to the belief that negative consequences will accompany success. Horner reasoned that traditional conceptions of femininity involved the suppression of aggressive and competitive impulses. Therefore, success and competition would engender anxiety in women, as they would fear social disapproval and a "loss of femininity" (Horner, 1973, p. 223). The motive to avoid success was understood to be more influential when women competed with men and engaged in tasks considered masculine, such as mathematics.

Much of Horner's innovative research was conducted approximately 40 years ago. Despite refinements (Fleming & Horner, 1992), Horner's work came under a considerable amount of criticism due to her research methodology (Metzler & Conroy, 2004; Zuckerman & Wheeler, 1975) and because independent researchers did not replicate her findings. In groups of students in high school, college, and medical school, females did not show higher fear of success than did males (Costanzo, Woody, & Slater, 1992; Mednick & Thomas, 1993; Piedmont, 1988). Likewise, college women did not record higher levels of fear of success as they performed motor activities (Conroy & Metzler, 2004).

Elite male French athletes demonstrated higher levels of fear of success than did their female counterparts. They acknowledged more fear of facing higher expectations, experiencing jealousy and interpersonal rivalry, and competing time demands (Andre & Metzler, 2011).

However, women as a whole may be more uncomfortable demonstrating high levels of competence in the presence of men and women who have much less competence (Piedmont, 1988). Perhaps women are more sensitive than men to the emotional reactions of others and imagine that less-capable peers will be discomforted by their demonstration of prowess.

Both female and male elite athletes and performers acknowledged aspects of fear of success:

1. not learning and improving
2. facing an overly rigid future
3. accomplishing all my goals
4. facing higher expectations (own and others)
5. losing enjoyment of success
6. experiencing tangible costs (e.g., slumps, injuries, loneliness)
7. experiencing jealousy and interpersonal rivalry
8. experiencing increased recognition and appreciation
9. not receiving support from others
10. losing or not increasing motivation
11. becoming overconfident (Conroy et al., 2001, p. 318)

With high levels of fear of success, people may sabotage their opportunities for success by engaging in disparaging self-talk (Conroy & Metzler, 2004). This self-talk may direct attention from the instrumental behaviors that lead to success, and make success less likely.

SOCIAL-COGNITIVE APPROACH

Research in the **social-cognitive paradigm** of achievement motivation is consistent with the expectancy value models of Atkinson and his colleagues. From this perspective, the behavior of some people may be more determined by a **promotion focus** or a focus on approaching opportunities, advancement, and accomplishment and a relative lack of attention to potential risks and losses (Higgins, 1997, 2012). People with a promotion focus appear to be primarily motivated by the motive for achievement. They seek accomplishments and attempt to avoid the experience of nonfulfillment. They attempt to reduce the discrepancy between their current position in life and desired end-states or goals. People who are primarily concerned with avoiding negative outcomes, mistakes, and losses demonstrate a **prevention focus.** They are primarily motivated by the motive to avoid failure. These individuals seek safety and attempt to avoid danger. They seek to increase the distance between their current condition in life and undesired end-states or outcomes.

It is theorized that early socialization experiences with caretakers contribute to these differences in regulatory-focus (Higgins, 1997, 2012). Children with a promotion focus are more regularly rewarded and encouraged for accomplishments or positive outcomes, while the attention of children with a prevention focus is directed toward avoiding parental reproach.

Adults with a promotion focus demonstrate a risky bias in decision making or a tendency to insure against errors of omission. Those with a prevention focus demonstrate a conservative bias or an effort to avoid errors of commission or false alarms. When tasks become increasingly difficult, promotion-focused individuals are more persistent and successful because of their bias toward avoiding errors of omission or overlooking solutions to problems. Prevention-focused people quit more readily on difficult tasks, in an effort to avoid mistakes. The commitment of promotion-focused people to goals is determined by the interaction of their expectancy of achieving the goal and the degree to which they value the goal. The greater and more likely the payoff, the harder they work to achieve it. With a prevention focus, the likelihood of goal attainment is less important. Prevention-focused people focus on the value of a goal and pursue goals as if they were necessities, regardless of the likelihood of success or a payoff.

Research concerning promotion and prevention focuses has relevance in evaluating the hedonic principle (Higgins, 1997, 2012). The pleasure and pain sought and avoided is different depending on the regulatory focus. The stronger the promotion focus, the greater the feeling of cheerfulness upon achieving goals and dejection after failure. The more pronounced the prevention focus, the greater the sense of quiescence, calm, and relief upon goal attainment and the more the feeling of agitation and anxiety upon falling short of goals. Those with a promotion focus might experience pleasure upon the realization of a goal, and those with a prevention focus upon the successful avoidance of an outcome. Pain may be appreciated after an unsuccessful pursuit of a goal or after the failed avoidance of an outcome, depending on the presence of promotion or prevention regulatory focuses, respectively.

Members of national junior and senior (ages 16 through 21) hockey squads in Australia were shown to differ in terms of their tendencies to approach opportunities for success or avoid chances of failure (Watson, 1986). Those with approach orientations were motivated to capture the rewards of success, had high achievement motivation, had intrinsic motivation for involvement in hockey, and experienced low levels of anxiety. Athletes with avoidance orientations were prone to anxiety, were more concerned with social approval and disapproval, and were motivated more forcefully to avoid the sting of failure. Players with avoidance orientations demonstrated more anxiety, and more trait anxiety, or anxiety that was stable over time and across situations.

Hedonic principle?

Hedonic Principle?
"There are parts unknown with regard to human performance, and those are the parts when it's just about pain and forfeit. How do you make yourself do it? You remind yourself that you're fulfilling your obligation to get the best from yourself, and that all achievement is born out of sacrifice" (Armstrong & Jenkins, 2003, p 222).

GOALS

Simply put, a goal is what a person attempts to accomplish. Goals represent a person's current concerns, and can be as general and abstract as one's "life tasks" or as specific as getting a haircut (Ward, 2011). Goals regulate performance by directing activity toward objectives that have been prioritized in relation to less-important activities.

Achievement motivation influences the valence of goals (Elliot & Church, 1997). Goals may have an approach valence or a motive for accomplishment and achievement. With avoidance goals, the motive is to avoid failure and the demonstration of incompetence.

Four types of achievement goals have been identified: **mastery-approach, mastery-avoidance, performance-avoidance,** and **performance-approach** goals (Elliot & McGregor, 2001) (see Figure 2.1). The antecedents and consequences of these types of achievement goals are different (e.g., Conroy, Elliot, & Hofer, 2003; Elliot, 2005; Duda, 2005; Nien & Duda, 2008).

Both mastery-approach and performance-approach goals orient individuals toward the obtainment of positive outcomes (Elliot & Harackiewicz, 1996). The distal, underlying motivational disposition for mastery-approach goals is solely achievement motivation. With performance-approach goals, the motivational disposition consists of both achievement motivation and fear of failure (Nien & Duda, 2008; Stoeber & Crombie, 2010; Stoeber, Uphill, & Hotham, 2009). Sportspersons with mastery-approach goals are more likely to view competition with equally matched opponents as a challenge and an opportunity for accomplishment and personal growth. They rate competition as more enjoyable

FIGURE 2.1 A 2 × 2 Achievement Goal Framework (from Elliot & McGregor, 2001)

Definition of Competence

	Mastery (absolute or intrapersonal)	Performance (normative)
Valence of Striving		
Approach (striving for competence)	Mastery-Approach Goals	Performance-Approach Goals
Avoidance (striving to avoid incompetence)	Mastery-Avoidance Goals	Performance-Avoidance Goals

and fulfilling. Mastery orientations may even insulate people from developing fear of failure and self-consciousness during sport performance (Conroy & Elliot, 2004; Conroy, Elliot, & Hofer, 2003).

The motivational disposition for performance-avoidance and mastery-avoidance goals is fear of failure. Athletes with these avoidance goals expect failure and view competition as a threat. Athletes with mastery-avoidance goals are more likely to be concerned that they cannot meet their self-referenced standards and to view fair competition as threatening (Adie, Duda, & Ntoumanis, 2008; Adie, Duda, & Ntoumanis, 2010).

Sportspersons with mastery goals are more likely to pursue activities that they find intrinsically interesting (Wang, Sproule, McNeill, Martindale, & Lee, 2011). However, in both athletic and academic domains, skill development usually requires sustained practice at tasks that are not intrinsically interesting. For example, sportspersons may enjoy their game but not the training necessary to perform at the highest level. Those with performance-approach goals may have less intrinsic interest in topics than those with mastery goals, but have been shown to achieve higher grades in college classrooms (Elliot & Harackiewicz, 1996). Adolescent British soccer players were more likely to continue developing in an elite professional soccer academy when they endorsed performance-approach goals (Adie et al., 2010). Furthermore, athletes who recognize both mastery- and performance-approach goals may perform best on tasks that are interesting and uninteresting. Elite adolescent female soccer players with both self- and other-referenced goals demonstrated high levels of self-confidence and outperformed counterparts with task or mastery orientations (Burton, Gillham, & Glenn, 2011). These soccer players engaged in more positive self-talk and were less vulnerable to concentration disruption and worry.

Achievement tendencies that are dominated by performance-avoidance goals are not adaptive. Avoidance goals have global consequences on performance and phenomenological well-being. Avoidance goals result in less persistence in the face of failure, task involvement, intrinsic motivation, and poorer academic performance. Performance-avoidance goals influence the focus of attention during evaluation tasks, as people are more likely to focus on themselves and doubt their ability. For example, highly skilled French female soccer players with performance-avoidance goals questioned whether their play would confirm negative stereotypes of females' athletic ability (Chalabaev, Sarrazin, Stone, & Cury, 2008). This focus on oneself directs attention away from the specific activities necessary to achieve goals.

Avoidance goals motivate people to shy away from difficult challenges, and to attribute responsibility for success and failure to forces outside of themselves (Elliot & Harackiewicz, 1996; Elliot & Sheldon, 1997). Performance-avoidance goals also have an inimical effect on overall personal adjustment and well-being, and contribute to decreased self-esteem, personal control, and life satisfaction.

College students with performance-avoidance goals were shown to achieve the lowest grades on tests and to have the least interest in the subject matter. Performance-avoidance goals also correspond with anxiety, hopelessness, and shame about academic pursuits (Pekrun, Elliot, & Maier, 2006) and athletic performance (Adie et al., 2010). French professional golfers with performance-avoidance goals were less likely to make the cut at a tournament (Bois, Sarrazin, Southon, & Boiche, 2009). However, experience may moderate performance-avoidance goals. Among British soccer players who remained in elite academies, performance-avoidance goals decreased over time. Perhaps the experience of success made them less fearful of failure (Adie et al., 2010).

Finally, it is important to consider the influence of performance-avoidance goals with other achievement goals. British athletes who both endorsed performance-approach goals and disavowed performance-avoidance goals recorded better championship performances (Stoeber & Crombie, 2010; Stoeber et al., 2009). The endorsement of mastery-avoidance goals in isolation from approach goals may be relatively rare among intercollegiate athletes (Ciani & Sheldon, 2010).

Sportspersons with similar goal orientations are more likely to be compatible. Female athletes in dyadic sports (badminton, gymnastics, rowing, squash, tennis, and volleyball) marked higher satisfaction with and commitment for athletic partners who shared their mastery-approach or performance-approach goals. Again, performance-avoidance goals provided no benefit. Even if partners shared performance-avoidance goals, with these goals athletes were not only less committed to their sport but also less committed to and satisfied with their athletic partner. Athletes with mastery-avoidance goals were committed to and satisfied with sports partners regardless of whether partners shared this goal orientation. Perhaps their estimates of their abilities were so low that they depended on partners to compensate for perceived weaknesses (Jackson, Harwood, & Grove, 2010).

Achievement goals are also referred to as **goal orientations.** As will be described in Chapter 8, there are multiple systems for classifying goal orientations. Several of these systems have wider use in sport settings. However, comprehensive models of goal orientations, such as that provided by the mastery-approach, mastery-avoidance, performance-approach, and performance-avoidance models, have been seen as offering important new directions for the development of sport psychology (Duda & Hall, 2001).

Application

Those who approach games and matches as opportunities for accomplishment, personal growth, and the demonstration of competence are more comfortable at times distal and proximal to competition. Competition is experienced as engrossing, enjoyable, and fulfilling. Avoidance goals diminish achievement and well-being. Fearing failure, these sportspersons give up when tasks and skills are not easily mastered. With less practice, they develop less skill. With less intrinsic interest, sport and school is less fun and self-sustaining. During competition, attention is captured by concerns about the outcome and diverted from the tasks required in the "real time" of sport.

Without remediation, avoidance goals may diminish achievement, well-being, and even interpersonal adjustment. Teammates with avoidance goals may show less commitment and satisfaction.

ATTRIBUTION THEORY

Established in the 1950s, attribution theory understands people as active in construing the causes of their experiences (Heider, 1958; Jones & Davis, 1965; Kelley, 1967, 1972). **Attributions** are the explanations or reasons that people give for events such as successes and failures that occur in their lives and the lives of other people (Biddle & Hanrahan, 1998; Martin & Carron, 2012). Individuals are especially motivated to understand the causes of failures in achievement domains. They interpret failures to result from causal factors that are to varying degrees **internal** or **external** to themselves (locus), **global** or **specific, stable** or **unstable** over time, and **controllable** or **uncontrollable.** For example, if a person ascribes failure at a competition to an internal cause that is global, stable, and uncontrollable, such as a lack of talent, then that sportsperson will be more likely to experience shame and give up. A second person might also experience failure, but explain it as a result of a lack of effort. Effort is not stable over time and is controllable. The second sportsperson may therefore experience guilt, redouble his or her practice efforts, and continue to think of himself or herself as a capable athlete.

Global, internal, stable, and uncontrollable attributions for negative events are associated with a "depressive attributional style" (Seligman,

Abramson, Semmel, & von Baeyer, 1979). Tennis players who attributed losses to internal, stable, and global factors were also more likely to show helplessness, or attributions that they could not control the causes of success and failure (Prapavessis & Carron, 1988). College students who attributed failure at darts to stable, uncontrollable causes responded with lower self-efficacy (see Chapter 9) and poorer ensuing performance (Coffee, Rees, & Haslam, 2009). Fortunately, sportspersons more commonly demonstrate a self-serving bias in interpreting the causes of success and failure. That is, they attribute success to stable, internal, and controllable factors (Biddle, Hanrahan, & Sellars, 2001). If success is attributed to stable factors, such as talent, then success will be expected in the future (Allen, Jones, & Sheffield, 2010). Failure is less demoralizing when it is attributed to controllable factors that are unstable, such as a lack of effort. Attributions made by athletes for team outcomes are also self-serving. Athletes emphasize the influence of internal factors, especially team ability, in explaining wins, and downplay the role of internal factors for losses (Martin & Carron, 2012).

A lack of belief in one's abilities has a detrimental effect on a range of tasks in which performance is evaluated (Coffee & Rees, 2011; Thompson, Davidson, & Barber, 1995). Performance on tasks involving evaluative threat, such as intellectual or athletic aptitude, deteriorates after failures for those who lack confidence in their abilities; this is because they withdraw effort. Additional poor performances can then be attributed to the withdrawal of effort rather than to their lack of ability. The withdrawal of effort preserves the self-esteem of the person with low confidence at the cost of even poorer performance on the evaluative task. Self-esteem refers to self-worth, or how people value themselves, and is distinct from confidence in abilities in areas such as academics and athletics.

Even people who lack confidence in their ability can show improvements in performance on evaluative tasks following failures if the environment provides a ready explanation or excuse for failure. Students who attribute failure to unfair tests and runners who point to rainy weather as the cause of poor times in races, attribute poor performance to environmental conditions. In effect, the environmental explanation or external attribution for failure removes the evaluative threat from the task and, therefore, the threat to self-esteem or self-worth.

People who have high levels of confidence in their abilities appear to interpret successes and failures in a manner that is most beneficial to the preservation of their confidence (Thompson et al., 1995). That is, success is attributed to internal, stable factors, such as their talent, and failure is explained by external, unstable factors, such as bad luck. Regardless of whether they experience success or failure, those with high confidence retain the belief that they can control the factors that lead to success or failure. As stated above, people with little confidence in their abilities may also attribute failures to environmental or external factors. However, they differ from those with high self-confidence in that they also attribute the causes of success to external factors and have less belief in their control of the factors leading to successes and failures.

The coaching staff of the 1973 soccer team at the University of California at Los Angeles (UCLA) demonstrated attributional patterns that supported the confidence of their team (Lefebvre & Cunningham, 1977). This team came within one goal of winning a national championship. Coaches communicated to starting players that their successful performances were the results of internal factors such as ability and effort and that failures were due to external, unstable factors such as luck. These attribution patterns were more pronounced when evaluating the performances of the most talented starting players. The most talented soccer players attributed their successes to ability, a stable internal factor, and their failures to bad luck and a lack of effort. Less talented, but still starting soccer players were more likely to attribute success to an unstable, internal factor, effort, and failure to a lack of effort and ability.

Application

Why does not everyone practice the self-serving bias and attribute success to stable, global, internal characteristics and failure to external, unstable, and controllable factors? Why do people think pessimistically? People are probably unaware of maladaptive thought patterns; they occur automatically and often without conscious awareness. Keeping a record of maladaptive thought patterns is a good first step in their management. This may lead to an analysis of their origin and validity.

MOTIVATIONAL ORIENTATION: INTRINSIC AND EXTRINSIC MOTIVATION

Intrinsic motivation has been defined and discussed at various points in this chapter. Intrinsic motivation relates to the pursuit of activities and interests that are of an individual's own choosing and that are largely free of internal or external pressure and control. Three forms of intrinsic motivation have been identified: intrinsic motivation for *accomplishment, learning and knowledge,* and *experiencing stimulation or excitement* (Vallerand, 2007; Vallerand & Losier, 1994). Intrinsic motivation for accomplishment is not dependent on outcomes or results, as it is the experience of attempting to accomplish a goal or to surpass oneself that provides the rewards (Vallerand & Rousseau, 2001). All three forms of intrinsic motivation may come into play in the course of sport activities, as participants may find the mastery of difficult skills, the process of learning new skills, and the fun and excitement of sport to be rewarding. Most generally, freely chosen activities that produce feelings of competence, autonomy, and relatedness to others (e.g., Deci & Ryan, 1985, 2002; Gillet, Berjot, & Rosnet, 2009; Joesaar, Hein, & Hagger, 2011, 2012; Radel, Sarrazin, & Pelletier, 2009) are likely to be intrinsically rewarding.

The experience of external or internal regulation to engage in activities is referred to as **extrinsic** motivation. Behavior is externally regulated when it is controlled by external factors such as rewards and punishments. For example, athletes realize that prestige and honors accrue when they are successful and that coaches will penalize them for skipping practices. Athletic participation may also serve as extrinsic motivation for academic achievement. That is, students must attend school and maintain minimum grade point averages (GPA) to remain eligible for athletics (Jordan, 1999). Sometimes sportspersons engage in practices that they do not enjoy but believe that they "should" pursue. These sportspersons have *introjected* or internalized external regulations, and experience guilt when they violate these regulations. For example, soccer players who despise distance running and interval training may be faithful to these forms of training during off-seasons if they have internalized and honor the training regimen of their coach. With *identified regulation*, activities are pursued because they help people develop desired characteristics (e.g., weight training helps me to improve). Finally, *integrated regulation* results from the assimilation of activity into one's sense of self.

A third motivational orientation is **amotivation,** or the relative absence of motivation. Sportspersons who quit intensive training because they do not believe that it will result in improved athletic performance in competitions demonstrate this amotivation. Amotivated sportspersons may feel incompetent and directionless.

People are sometimes motivated by different forms of motivation in different situations. For example, athletes may be intrinsically motivated to play their sport, but attend class and complete schoolwork only when extrinsically controlled. Considering motivation at an even more specific level, sportspersons may relish and show intrinsic motivation for competition but loaf and require extrinsic control for practice (Vallerand & Rousseau, 2001).

Athletes who are intrinsically motivated enjoy sports to a greater degree. Intrinsically oriented athletes are more likely to experience flow or a state of well-being and efficiency that will be described at a later point in this chapter (Hodge, Lonsdale, & Jackson, 2009; Kowal & Fortier, 1999). With intrinsic motivation, sportspersons enjoy greater challenges and more difficult competition (Abuhamdeh & Csikszentmihalyi, 2009).

Extrinsically motivated athletes experience more anxiety and disruptions of concentration, perhaps because they are focused on the results of their performances. Extrinsically motivated athletes are more likely to "choke" under pressure or to perform poorly when optimal performance is most necessary (Baumeister, 1984; Baumeister, Hamilton, & Tice, 1985; Baumeister & Steinhilber, 1984). Intrinsically motivated athletes and people engaging in exercise programs are less likely to quit (Sarrazin, Vallerand, Guillet, Pelletier, & Cury, 2002), and this issue is especially important when considering athletic participation among children.

Athletes with intrinsic and self-determined motivation may perform better in competition. French adolescent and adult judokas or judo competitors with self-determined motivation were more successful in a national competition (Gillet, Vallerand, Amoura, & Baldes, 2010).

Intrinsically motivated athletes demonstrate more sportspersonship or respect and concern for other participants, rules, and fair play (Ntoumanis & Standage, 2009). For example, intrinsically motivated, elite male adolescent Canadian hockey players were more likely to demonstrate good sportspersonship throughout a hockey season (Vallerand & Losier, 1994). With intrinsic motivation, efforts are made to outdo oneself, and poor sportspersonship and cheating do not bring a sportsperson closer to this objective. Poor sportsmanship includes cheating to gain an advantage, and the use of performance-enhancing drugs is a form of cheating. It is therefore not surprising that extrinsically motivated athletes indicate a greater willingness to engage in doping (Donahue et al., 2006). Self-determined motivation also leads to instrumental (demonstrating energy for the game and not toward opponents) rather than reactive (intending to injure opponents) aggression (Chantal, Robin, Vernat, & Bernache-Assollant, 2005).

Intrinsic Motivation and Extrinsic Rewards

The experience of *external* or *internal regulation* may diminish intrinsic motivation at times, even if this regulation consists of rewards for achievement. This effect is paradoxical in that the activity becomes less rewarding in and of itself as a result of receiving rewards for engaging in the activity. For example, the interest of children between the ages of 9 and 11 in playing with the stabilometer, an interesting motor activity, decreased when they were given a reward to play with it (Orlick & Mosher, 1978). This paradoxical effect has also been reported for collegiate male and female athletes (Kingston, Horrocks, & Hanton, 2006) and football players (Vallerand, Deci, & Ryan, 1987). The athletes with scholarships reported less intrinsic interest in their sport than players who did not receive scholarships.

However, external rewards do not always diminish intrinsic motivation. External rewards only decrease intrinsic interest in activities when the reward is interpreted as an attempt to coerce and control behavior. Scholarship status did not diminish the intrinsic interest of female and male collegiate athletes in a range of sports (Amorose & Horn, 2000). Apparently, they considered the scholarship to be positive feedback that they had achieved a high level of competence, and evidence of competence may enhance intrinsic motivation. Rewards also did not diminish intrinsic motivation among elite athletes who finished in the top ten at major championships in track and field, as they likely also interpret awards and cash prizes as proof of competence (Mallet & Hanrahan, 2004).

Application

Athletic participation for elite and scholarship athletes is not all "fun and games." They may enjoy the game, but not the training necessary. They play through and cope with injuries and illnesses. Nevertheless, those who conscientiously apply themselves to structured practice for skill development and also devote the most time to playing their sport, develop most optimally (Ford, Ward, Hodges, & Williams, 2009).

Intrinsic Motivation and Feedback

Intrinsic interest increases when sportspersons achieve goals and receive positive feedback (Tauer & Harackiewicz, 2004; Vansteenkiste & Deci, 2003). Failure and feedback that performance is poor undermines intrinsic motivation (Vallerand & Rousseau, 2001). Negative feedback diminishes the belief of athletes in their competence or ability and subsequently their intrinsic interest in sport diminishes. However, the effects of failure, such as deselection from an elite team, are far more unpleasant for athletes who are not intrinsically motivated. For example, adolescent males who were deselected from the most elite Canadian hockey teams experienced more negative emotions when their participation was not self-determined and motivated by needs for autonomy, competence, and relatedness (Gaudreau, Amiot, & Vallerand, 2009).

Intrinsic Motivation and Competition

The effect of competition on intrinsic motivation is determined by whether the participant freely chose to compete. If athletes are obliged or coerced to compete, intrinsic motivation is likely to diminish (Reeve & Deci, 1996). However, when athletes chose to compete and perform well, intrinsic motivation is enhanced (Vallerand & Rousseau, 2001).

Team competition may be particularly enjoyable. Teammates experience the fun and enthusiasm of cooperating with one another, and the excitement of competing against opponents (Tauer & Harackiewicz, 2004).

If athletes engage in competition with a focus on beating others, then failure undermines intrinsic interest. However, the detrimental effects of failure on intrinsic motivation are mitigated if competitors recognize improvement and skill in their performance (e.g., Vansteenkiste & Deci, 2003). In addition, goals to beat competitors do not undermine intrinsic motivation and performance if athletes simultaneously endorse goals to improve and demonstrate technical mastery (Burton, Naylor, & Holliday, 2001).

Intrinsic and Extrinsic Motivation and Coaching

As mentioned earlier, coercion undermines intrinsic motivation. Athletes report less autonomy, competence, and relatedness to teammates when coaches are excessively coercive (Vallerand & Rousseau, 2001). Coaches tend to be more coercive when their jobs depend on the performance of their athletes, and with athletes who do not appear to be intrinsically motivated to reach their full potential. Paradoxically, the efforts of coaches to coerce greater effort from athletes often results in a slackening of effort, as people of all ages resist efforts to limit their autonomy (Vallerand, Deci, & Ryan, 1987). Intrinsically motivated athletes are more often "left alone" or supported in their development of competence.

Not surprisingly, coaches who are coercive encourage less intrinsic motivation in athletes than do coaches who are more supportive and encourage autonomy (Smith, Ntoumanis, & Duda, 2010). Coaches who support the autonomy and self-determined motivation in athletes may be more successful. Adolescent and adult French judokas or judo competitors with coaches who supported their autonomy for practice and competition were more successful in a national tournament (Gillet, Vallerand, Amoura, & Baldes, 2010).

The influence of coaching interventions on intrinsic motivation appears to be indirect, or mediated through the fundamental needs of perceived competence, autonomy, and relatedness (Deci & Ryan, 1985, 2002). For example, democratic coaching behaviors, such as allowing team members to participate in decision making, increased feelings of autonomy, which in turn enhanced intrinsic motivation among Division I collegiate athletes. Autocratic coaching behaviors had the opposite effects and led to decreased feelings of relatedness (Hollembeak & Amorose, 2005).

Coercion has a greater effect when athletes or students are younger. Interventions designed to promote autonomy and to decrease coercion from coaches have reduced dropout rates in athletic programs with children. Children tend to respond to interventions supporting autonomy by showing up for more team practices and performing better (Smith, 2010; Vallerand & Losier, 1999).

This does not mean that coaches should adopt a *laissez-faire* approach and keep a distance from athletes. The intrinsic motivation of athletes is enhanced by the skillful intervention of coaches. For example, novice golfers developed higher intrinsic interest when coaches taught them mental skills such as stress management, goal setting, and self-monitoring (Beauchamp, Halliwell, Fournier, & Koestner, 1996). Coaches of children who emphasize principles of positive control and avoid aversive control make sport fun and intrinsically rewarding. Positive control includes reinforcement for good performance, encouragement after mistakes, providing correction in a supportive manner, and technical instruction in the mechanics and strategies of sport (Smith & Smoll, 2005).

Before concluding this section, note that it is unlikely that sportspersons can find strong intrinsic motivation for all aspects of physical and mental training. As mentioned earlier, athletes may enjoy their sport but dislike aspects of training such as running distances or intervals. Introjected or internalized external regulations may be helpful to motivate adherence to these unpleasant or uninteresting aspects of training. The internalization of external demands does not make these aspects of training more interesting or rewarding but they motivate adherence with the threat of guilt.

PASSION IN SPORT

People who value sport and athletic participation may become dedicated and passionate about sport for years or even a lifetime. In doing so, athletic participation becomes part of their identity. When athletic participation is coerced due to external or introjected regulation, **passion** is more likely to be **obsessive.** Intrinsic motivation and identified regulation for sport activity more likely results in **harmonious passion** (Vallerand et al., 2006).

With obsessive passion, sportspersons may neglect other responsibilities in order to participate in sport, and experience shame and anxiety when prevented from engaging in athletic activities. With obsessive passion, sportspersons take risks, such as cycling on icy roads during winter (Vallerand et al., 2003) and training through injuries (Rip, Fortin, & Vallerand, 2006), rather than to miss workouts. Harmonious passion is inversely correlated with burnout (see Chapter 16; Curran, Appleton, Hill, & Hall, 2011).

ACHIEVEMENT, LIFE SATISFACTION, AND FLOW

Theory notwithstanding, achievement affects life satisfaction (Myers & Diener, 1995). This finding is certainly reasonable, given the portion of life devoted to activities related to achievement (Rain, Lane, & Steiner, 1991). Achievement contributes to a person's identity and to his or her network of supportive relationships. It provides a sense of meaning to life.

People who can become absorbed in their life's pursuits may experience a joyous state described as **flow** (Csikszentmihalyi, 1990). Flow occurs when people are engaged in optimal challenges, or when they work at tasks that are not so difficult that they exceed their capacities or so easy that they become bored. Confidence in one's skill level is especially important for entering the flow experience (Hodge, Lonsdale, & Jackson, 2009; Stavrou, Jackson, Zervas, & Karteroliotis, 2007). This is referred to as the **challenge-skills balance.** This flow experience has resulted in not only productive achievement, but also happiness. Absorption in meaningful activities, whether at work or play, is associated with greater happiness than is passive and mindless inactivity. Achievement, task absorption, and doing one's best are not the only factors associated with life satisfaction. Happy people also have high self-esteem, a sense of personal control over the factors that influence their lives, optimism, and extraversion. As will be described later in this book, these factors are also associated with optimal achievement and performance.

Flow is associated with optimal athletic performance (Chavez, 2008–2009; Jackson, 1995; Jackson & Roberts, 1992; Krane & Williams, 2010; Stavrou & Zervas, 2004), especially when athletic participation is autotelic or highly enjoyable (Stavrou et al., 2007). Sportspersons who experience flow want to continue athletic activity in the future (Schuler & Brunner, 2009). Flow and optimal performance are more likely with careful and exhaustive preparation. Elite international male and female athletes from Australia and New Zealand rated thorough *pre-competitive* and *competitive preparation* and *planning* as the factors most influential in leading to flow (Jackson, 1995). These preparations consisted of developing "game plans" and following pre-competitive routines. With thorough preparation, athletes were able to relax active monitoring of the impending performance and were more likely to engage in the *automatic* execution of actions during performances. With the automatic execution of actions there is less representation of actions in conscious thought, and automatic functioning is associated with elite performance and flow states (Hayslip, Petrie, MacIntire, & Jones, 2010). Athletes who experience flow during training may also prepare more thoroughly and perform better (Schuler & Brunner, 2009).

An equally important theme associated with flow is the maintenance of *self-efficacy* or confidence that one is at least equal to the challenge. High perceived ability and self-efficacy has been demonstrated to be critical to flow experiences, not only with elite athletes, but also with Division I collegiate athletes (Jackson & Roberts, 1992) and with older non-elite athletes (Jackson, Kimiecik, Ford, & Marsh, 1998). Faith in oneself, or self-efficacy, without action in the form of physical preparation is unlikely to lead to flow. These elite athletes recognized that optimal conditioning and pre-competitive *routines,* including proper rest, hydration, and nutrition, were necessary if flow was to be experienced during competitions. Deviations from this preparation disrupted flow, as did physical events such as *injuries.* Achieving optimal *arousal* or physiological preparation was often associated with flow, and for some athletes this consisted of relaxation and for others it involved becoming more energized. Interference due to excessive arousal or anxiety was more frequently disruptive than excessive relaxation. High motivation was important, especially the establishment of *goals. Mastery* goals or full attention to the instrumental behaviors necessary for good performances was a component of flow experiences. *Performance* goals or a focus on the outcome of performances is seldom a part of flow experiences (Jackson & Roberts, 1992). It was often necessary for athletes to feel that performances were going well for them to experience flow. *Concentration* was important to the elite athletes, and during flow task absorption is sometimes so complete that people are unaware of the passage of time (Csikszentmihalyi, 1990). Concentration and self-efficacy limit *cognitive interference* in the form of worries about the results or outcome of performances, about competitors, or about what others think of a performance. Cognitive anxiety or interference "is the antithesis of flow" (Jackson et al., 1998, p. 373), and cognitive interference disrupted performance to a greater degree than did *physiological anxiety* with the elite and older non-elite athletes. Flow requires letting go of worry about the self while maintaining control of one's thoughts (Jackson, Thomas, Marsh, Smethurst, 2001). When absorbed in activities and actions, there is a merging of action and awareness, and no room for self-reflection and self-consciousness. (Partington, Partington, & Olivier, 2009).

Optimal environmental and situation conditions relate to flow, and with *familiar* environments often seem less daunting or unfriendly. Prior experience in venues where competitions occur is especially helpful and serves to limit the influence of hostile crowds. Other environmental factors that disrupted flow states among the elite athletes were the behavior of competitors and bad calls from referees. When athletes' attention was given to the assertive play of competitors or other environmental disturbances, performances suffered and flow stopped (Jackson & Csikszentmihalyi, 1999).

If attention is not rapidly directed away from environmental disturbances and internal thoughts that disrupt concentration, performance can deteriorate to the degree that *choking under pressure* occurs. Choking under pressure refers to performance that is significantly below one's average level of performance at times when optimal performance is most important. Excessive self-consciousness is also associated with choking under pressure and flow is related to the loss of self-consciousness.

The factors that are italicized above and that contributed to flow are topics for examination in the chapters of this book. A review of the Table of Contents reveals that additional topics will be presented, especially about factors that disrupt performance. Perhaps the factors that disrupt performance are least understood, as elite athletes believed the factors that led to flow were controllable and that the factors that disrupted flow were uncontrollable (Jackson, 1995).

SUMMARY AND APPLICATION

Motivation for achievement has been established as an essential element of adaptive human behavior, and work satisfaction is an important contributor to life satisfaction. Indeed, vocational and academic inhibitions are criteria for the identification of mental disorders (American Psychiatric Association, 2000). Achievement motivation has been understood in context with the hedonic principle or the assumption that people strive to maximize rewards or pleasure and minimize losses and pain. The hedonic principle is an assumption contained in most of the theories reviewed in this chapter. However, people experience rewards and losses in different ways. With a promotion orientation there is an emphasis on the realization of rewards, and with a prevention orientation there is a focus on relief from tension when they avoid loss (Higgins, 1997). A focus on accomplishment or the realization of outcomes or goals rather than the avoidance of failures or mistakes is adaptive.

People also differ in terms of achievement motivation. Recent research has indicated the motives for achievement and to avoid failure also contribute to the development of achievement goals, and that achievement goals have a more direct effect on graded performance and intrinsic motivation than do the motives for achievement and to avoid failure (Elliot & Harackiewicz, 1996).

Self-confidence and good performance are sustained by the attribution of the causes of success to internal factors, such as talent and effort, and of failure to external, unstable factors, such as bad luck. Views that aptitudes are more innately determined and immutable foster withdrawal from problem-solving activities when solutions are not readily apparent (Dweck & Leggett, 1988). The optimal state of flow is more likely when self-efficacy and confidence are high and when people are optimally challenged. Optimal challenges are often associated with a balance between skills and challenges.

It should be noted that the causal pathways for constructs such as achievement goals, intrinsic and extrinsic motivation, causal attributions, and perceived competence have not been determined conclusively. In other words, there is disagreement among researchers in psychology about which of these constructs lead to or cause other constructs, which then contribute most directly to achievement behaviors. For example, Dweck (1986) maintained that people with intrinsic or mastery orientations are more likely to adopt learning or mastery goals, whereas Elliot and colleagues (Elliot & Harackiewicz, 1996) maintained that the causal pathway was in the opposite direction, or from mastery goals to intrinsic motivation.

In closing and considering the recent empirical literature, how do adaptive orientations toward achievement develop? The caretakers of children with a promotion focus encourage the value of proactively seeking accomplishments and realizing goals. The attention of children with a prevention focus is directed toward avoiding failures, mistakes, and the accompanying disapproval of caretakers. Intrinsic motivation is fostered by environments that allow for greater autonomy and choice and less coercion concerning the selection of activities. Perhaps these environments would provide clever ways of piquing the interest of children to master academic, interpersonal, and athletic skills necessary for adaptive functioning. Confidence and self-efficacy grow incrementally when youngsters are introduced to optimal challenges.

Key Terms

Discussion Questions

Q1. Explain the difficulties in arriving at a unifying theory of human motivation.

Q2. Review the development of the Protestant Work Ethic. Has this influenced current psychological theories?

Q3. Outline Freud's explanation of human emotion.

Q4. Consider the Hedonic Principle.

Q5. What is Freud's definition of mental health? Does it influence current definitions?

Q6. Explain how feelings of inferiority can be expressed as strivings for success of superiority.

Q7. How do Marlow's theories lead to a discussion of intrinsic and extrinsic motivation and mastery of goals?

Q8. Review the motive for achievement, motive to avoid failure, and motive to avoid success.

Q9. Outline the contributions of parents to fears of failure in their children.

Q10. Consider the evidence for the motive to avoid success among women.

Q11. Describe aspects of fear of success acknowledged by elite male and female athletes and performers.

Q12. Consider the dimensions of a promotion focus and a prevention focus.

Q13. Review mastery-approach, mastery-avoidance, performance-approach, and performance-avoidance goals.

Q14. Detail the four dimensions of attributions.

Q15. Review intrinsic and extrinsic motivation and amotivation.

Q16. Explain how external rewards influence intrinsic motivation.

Q17. Consider the influence of feedback on intrinsic motivation.

Q18. Describe the effect of competition on intrinsic motivation.

Q19. Are there suggestions for coaching intrinsically motivated athletes?

Q20. Detail the characteristics of passion in sport.

Q21. Explain flow.

Q22. How is flow beneficial?

Q23. When is flow likely to occur?

Suggested Readings

Atkinson, J. W. (1978). The mainsprings of achievement-oriented activity. In J. W. Atkinson & Joel O. Raynor (Eds.), *Personality, motivation, and achievement* (pp. 11–39). Washington, DC: Halsted Press.

Conroy, D E. (2008). Fear of failure in the context of competitive sport: A commentary. *Psychology of Sport and Exercise, 11*, 423–432. doi: 10.1016/j.psychsport.2010.04.013

Deci, E. L., & Ryan, R. M. (1985). *Intrinsic motivation and self-determination in human behavior.* New York, NY: Plenum Press.

Gaudreau, P., Amiot, C. E., & Vallerand, R. J. (2009). Trajectories of affective states in adolescent hockey players: Turning point and motivational antecedents. *Developmental Psychology, 45,* 307–319. doi: 10.1037/a0014134

Gillet, N., Vallerand, R. J., Amoura, S., & Baldes, B. (2010). Influence of coaches' autonomy support on athletes' motivation and sport performance: A test of the hierarchical model of intrinsic and extrinsic motivation. *Psychology of Sport and Exercise, 11,* 155–161. doi: 10.1016/j.psychsport.2009.10.004

Hodge, K., Lonsdale, C., & Jackson, S. A. (2009). Athlete engagement in elite sport: An exploratory investigation of antecedents and consequences. *The Sport Psychologist, 23,* 186–202.

Jackson, B., Harwood, C. G., & Grove, J. R. (2010). On the same page in sporting dyads: Does dissimilarity on 2 × 2 achievement goal constructs impair relationship functioning? *Journal of Sport & Exercise Psychology, 32,* 805–827.

Jackson, S. A., & Csikszentmihalyi, M. (1999). *Flow in sports.* Champaign, IL: Human Kinetics.

Joesaar, H., Hein, V., & Hagger, M. S. (2011). Peer influence on young athletes' need satisfaction, intrinsic motivation and persistence in sport: A 12-month prospective study. *Psychology of Sport and Exercise, 12,* 500–508. doi: 10.1016/j.psychsport.2011.04.005

Joesaar, H., Hein, V., & Hagger, M. S. (2012). Youth athletes' perception of autonomy support from the coach, peer motivational climate and intrinsic motivation in sport setting: One-year effects. *Psychology of Sport and Exercise, 13,* 257–262. doi: 10.1016/j.psychsport.2011.12.001

Maslow, A. (1973). Deficiency motivation and growth motivation. In D. C. McClelland, & R. S. Steele (Eds.), *Human motivation. A book of readings* (pp. 233–251). Morristown, NJ: General Learning Press.

Ntoumanis, N., & Standage, M. (2009). Morality in sport: A self-determination theory perspective. *Journal of Applied Sport Psychology, 21,* 365–380.

Radel, R., Sarrazin, P., & Pelletier, L. (2009). Evidence of subliminally primed motivational orientations: The focus of unconscious motivational processes on the performance of a new motor task. *Journal of Sport & Exercise Psychology, 31,* 657–674.

Sagar, S. S., Busch, B. K., & Jowett, S. (2010). Success and failure, fear of failure, and coping responses of adolescent academy football players. *Journal of Applied Sport Psychology, 22,* 213–230.

Sagar, S. S., & Lavallee, D. (2010). The developmental origins of fear of failure in adolescent athletes: Examining parental practices. *Psychology of Sport and Exercise, 11,* 177–187. doi: 10.1016.j.psychsport.2010.01.004

Vallerand, R. J. (2007). Intrinsic and extrinsic motivation in sport and physical activity. In G. Tenenbaum & R. C. Eklund (Eds.), *Handbook of sport psychology* (3rd ed., pp. 59–83). New York, NY: Wiley.

Weber, M. (1930). *The Protestant work ethic and the spirit of capitalism* (T. Parsons, Trans.). New York, NY: Scribner. (Original work published 1904).

Chapter 3

EXERCISE

Fitness as a way of life—Jack LaLanne

Jack LaLanne was called the Godfather of Fitness. Indeed, he credited exercise and a healthy diet with saving his life. Prior to age 15, he was so unhappy that he considered suicide. He described himself as a skinny, pimply, "sugarholic:" "[I] tried to kill my brother, had an uncontrollable temper, set the house on fire." "I can't believe it. I was a maniac. I was a psycho. Had these headaches all the day, couldn't stand the pain. All from sugar, sugar, sugar" (Goldman, 2011). LaLanne's transformation occurred after he attended a lecture by nutritionist Paul Bragg at the YMCA in Berkeley, CA. Exercise and nutrition became his life's work: "Exercise is King, nutrition is Queen, put them together and you've got a kingdom" (Jack.LaLanne.com).

He strictly controlled his diet: "If it tastes good, spit it out; if man made it, don't eat it; 10 seconds on the lips, lifetime on the hips" (Goldman, 2011; Murphy, 2007). His exercise routine of weight training, calisthenics, and aerobics was even stricter, and after 1930 he never missed a daily workout. He was a pioneer in the fabrication of weight training machines, and opened the first modern fitness club in Oakland, CA, in 1936 at the age of 21. In 1951, he began a television exercise program that continued for 34 years.

Prior to his death in 2011 at age 96, LaLanne was asked if working out was worth the effort. He reflected: "It's a pain in the gluties. But you gotta [sic] do it. Dying is easy, living is tough. I hate working out. Hate it. But I like the results" (Murphy, 2007).

In modern, industrialized countries, many people are not required to participate in physical labor and activity (Bauman et al., 2009). It may therefore be necessary to make deliberate efforts to incorporate physical activity into one's daily life. Physical activity consists of bodily movement that results in the expenditure of energy (Centers for Disease Control and Prevention, 2011). In the context of this chapter, the physical activity of primary interest is exercise. Exercise is a form of structured physical activity intended to improve physical fitness or health (Caspersen, Powell, & Christenson, 1985).

The physical and psychological benefits that result from regular exercise and physical activity are substantial. However, many people are sedentary, and it is, therefore, important to understand the motivation and barriers to exercise. There are several theoretical explanations for exercise adherence, and intervention strategies are established. While exercise adherence is the overriding public health goal, sometimes unhealthy behaviors, such as eating disorders, accompany preoccupations with exercise. These topics are addressed in this chapter.

EXERCISE AND PHYSICAL HEALTH

The consequences of physical inactivity are profound. In 2000, only tobacco use led to more deaths in the U.S. than did physical inactivity and poor diet. Indeed, 16.6 percent of the deaths in 2000 were due to physical inactivity and poor diet (Mokdad, Marks, Stroup, & Gerberding, 2004). Today, physical inactivity and poor diet may have overtaken tobacco as the leading cause of preventable death. Physical inactivity contributes to the deaths of approximately 200,000 Americans each year (Danaei et al., 2009). More specifically, physical inactivity contributes to cardiovascular disease, type 2 diabetes and metabolic syndrome (excessive fat around the waist, high blood pressure, low HDL cholesterol, high triglycerides, or high blood sugar, elevated BMI), colon and breast cancer, endometrial and lung cancer, and overweight and obesity (Centers for Disease Control and Prevention, 2011, 2012) (Figure 3.1).

Exercise slows the aging process. Competitive runners, cyclists, and swimmers in their 70s and 80s show little deterioration of musculature. Without exercise, people typically lose 8% of their muscle mass each decade after age 40. In addition to muscle loss, muscles become degraded as they become infiltrated with fat, among older, inactive people (Wroblewski, Amati, Smiley, Goodpaster, & Wright, 2011). Without exercise, the mitochondria within body cells—the microscopic organelles that combine oxygen and nutrients to create fuel for the cells—malfunction and die. With the loss of mitochondria, muscles shrink, brain volume decreases, and hair turns gray and falls out. Indeed, every bodily system studied in an animal sample benefited from exercise (Safdar et al., 2011). DNA loss is also mitigated by aerobic exercise. DNA strands are capped by telomeres. With age, telomeres shorten, a process that ultimately results in DNA loss and aging. The telomere length of older adults who participated in chronic aerobic exercise was similar to that of young adults (LaRocca, Seals, & Pierce, 2010).

FIGURE 3.1 BMI Formula

The formula for deriving the BMI is: weight (kg)/[height (m)]^2

Example: Weight = 70 kg, Height = 165 cm (1.65 m)

Calculation: $70 \div (1.65)^2 = 25.71$

Or   Weight (lb)/[height(in)]^2 x 703

Example: Weight = 155 lbs, Height = 5'5" (65")

Calculation: [155 ÷ (65)2] x 703 = 25.79

The standard weight status categories associated with BMI ranges for adults are as follows:

BMI	Weight Status
Below 18.5	Underweight
18.5 – 24.9	Normal
25.0 – 29.9	Overweight
30.0 and above	Obese

Exercise is also vitally important in limiting overweight and obesity. Worldwide, 502 million people are obese, with another 1 billion overweight (de Onis, Blossner, & Borghi, 2010). In the U.S., 33.1% of adults are overweight and another 35.7% are obese (Flegal, Carroll, Kit, & Ogden, 2012). Among U.S. children and adolescents, 20% and 18%, respectively, are obese (Ogden, Carroll, Curtin, Lamb, & Flegal, 2010).

The consequences of overweight are considerable. Overweight adults and young people are at risk for a myriad of health problems, such as cardiovascular disease, hypertension, type 2 diabetes, sleep apnea and asthma, and orthopedic and metabolic diseases (Centers for Disease Control and Prevention, 2011; Chief Medical Officers of England, Scotland, Wales, and Northern Ireland, 2011).

Exercise of moderate intensity is likely to confer health benefits. Moderate-intensity exercise consists of activity at sub-maximal workloads in which energy is supplied by the aerobic energy system. This energy supply is necessary when exercise passes the **anaerobic threshold,** or the point at which oxygen intake is required to continue an exercise. At this point energy is expended too rapidly to be supplied by the oxygen-requiring system. Exercise of this sort is **aerobic exercise,** and is typically a prolonged activity of moderate intensity. For example, running is an aerobic exercise that results in increased metabolic demand for oxygen. Exercise that does not pass the anaerobic threshold is **anaerobic exercise** (see Figure 3.2).

FIGURE 3.2   Exercise Definitions

Aerobic exercise is typically prolonged and of moderate intensity, and results in increased metabolic demand for oxygen. Examples are running, swimming, and cycling for long distances. Over time, this results in improved cardio-respiratory fitness.

VO_2 max is the maximum rate at which oxygen is absorbed and utilized

Maximum aerobic capacity is the maximal amount of exertion possible using oxidative metabolism. It is dependent on the capacity of the muscles to remove or tolerate lactic acid.

Moderate-intensity aerobic exercise is typically performed between 65% and 85% of VO_2 max.

Vigorous-intensity aerobic exercise is performed above 85% of VO_2 max.

Anaerobic exercise occurs in short, intense spurts with limited oxygen intake. Examples are weight training and sprinting.

Anaerobic threshold is the point at which oxygen intake is required to continue an exercise; energy is expended too rapidly to be supplied by the oxygen-requiring system.

Weight lifting is an example of this exercise that occurs in short, intense spurts, with limited oxygen intake.

Prolonged, moderate aerobic exercise results in improved cardio-respiratory fitness. Cardio-respiratory fitness is determined by the maximum rate at which oxygen is absorbed and utilized—known as the **VO$_2$ max**— and by **maximum aerobic capacity** (Astrand, Rodahl, Dahl, & Stromme, 2003). Maximum aerobic capacity is the maximal amount of exertion possible using oxidative metabolism.

EXERCISE AND COGNITIVE FUNCTIONING

Moderate- to high-intensity exercise for moderate durations is likely to have a positive, albeit small, *immediate* effect on cognitive functioning (Lambourne & Tomporowski, 2010). Following exercise, improvements are recognized for tasks such as decision making and problem solving. Exercise serves to increase levels of neurotransmitters, the brain chemicals that allow communication between cortical neurons. Among animals, and perhaps humans, improved cognitive functioning following exercise may be due to the greater availability of the neurotransmitters norepinephrine and serotonin (Ahmadiasl, Alaei, & Hanninen, 2003; Winter et al., 2007; Zouhal, Jacob, Delamarche, & Gratas-Delamarche, 2008).

Chronic exercise benefits cognitive functioning as well (Thomas, Dennis, Bandettini, & Johansen-Berg, 2012). Chronic aerobic exercise is particularly helpful for the development and preservation of frontal lobe or higher mental functioning among children and older adults, respectively (Colcombe & Kramer, 2003; Davis et al., 2007; Gow et al., 2012). Chronic exercise retards the atrophy of cortical neurons and prompts neurogenesis, or the development of new neurons (Pereira et al., 2007). Glia cells provide metabolic support for neurons, and these may also respond favorably to aerobic exercise. The brain's "white matter," or myelinated axons, serve a crucial function in connecting brain areas and allow the brain to function in concert as a "functional network." Some of these functional connections improve in concert with improvements with VO$_2$ max (Voss et al., 2010).

As suggested above, brain volume appears to be altered by aerobic exercise. Aerobic exercise leads to angiogenesis in the capillaries—the tiny blood vessels that distribute oxygenated blood from arteries to the brain and return deoxygenated blood into the veins. Angiogenesis consists of a sprouting process by which a new branch from one capillary merges with another capillary. Perhaps angiogenesis results from the sheer mechanical stress of blood flow on the walls of capillaries during aerobic exercise. In addition, angiogenesis may occur in response to hypoxia—decreased blood oxygenation—during aerobic exercise. Ultimately, cognitive performance is supported by greater availability of oxygen and less oxidative stress due to aerobic exercise.

Recommended and Actual Exercise Levels

The U.S. Department of Health and Human Services (2008) recommends at least 60 minutes of moderate-to-vigorous activity each day for youth and 150 minutes of moderate-intensity or 75 minutes of vigorous-intensity activity each week for adults. Only 42% of children of 6–11 years of age and 8% of adolescents meet this standard (Troiano et al., 2008). The amount of time devoted to physical activity decreases as people become older. Among adults, 39% are completely sedentary, 61% never engage in vigorous-intensity physical activity (Pleis & Lucas, 2009), and 23% engage in no leisure-time physical activity (Centers for Disease Control and Prevention, 2008).

Weightiest Countries

Americans tend to be well-rounded and have broad foundations—literally. The Body Mass Indices (BMIs) of Americans are the highest in the world. Mexico, Brazil, the United Kingdom, and Russia round out the top five. The average BMIs of the U.S., Mexico, and Brazil all exceed 25, the standard for overweight (Romei, 2012).

EXERCISE AND ANXIETY

People who exercise regularly report less trait anxiety and anxiety disorders (De Moor, Beem, Stubbe, Boomsma, & De Geus, 2006). As explained in Chapter 6, **trait anxiety** refers to anxiety levels that remain relatively stable across situations and over time (Spielberger, Gorsuch, & Lushene, 1970). **Anxiety disorders** are mental disorders. Examples of anxiety disorders are Generalized Anxiety Disorder (physiological and cognitive components of anxiety are almost always present), Specific Phobias (excessive fear of discrete things), and Panic Disorders With and Without Agoraphobia (fear of being trapped in a place where escape would be difficult). As mentioned in Chapter 2, the modern classification of mental disorders, the *Diagnostic and Statistical Manual of Mental Disorders-Fourth Edition, Text Revision* (DSM-IV-TR; American Psychiatric Association, 2000), identifies mental disorders as causing "clinically significant" dysfunction vocationally, interpersonally, or intrapsychically.

There is a **dose-response effect** for exercise and anxiety. Less anxiety is reported by those who engage in more exercise (Goodwin, 2003). Aerobic exercise is likely to be more effective in decreasing anxiety, and regular or chronic exercise is necessary to reduce trait or chronic anxiety. A single bout of aerobic exercise is likely to have an anxiolytic—anxiety reducing—effect, but without regular exercise, anxiety levels return to pre-exercise levels after two to four hours (Martinsen & Raglin, 2007; Motl,

O'Connor, & Dishman, 2004). Light- to moderate-intensity anaerobic exercise, such as weight training, may also be anxiolytic (Arent, Alderman, Short, & Landers, 2007; Physical Activity Guidelines Advisory Committee, 2008). High-intensity weight or resistance training has no anxiolytic effect.

Aerobic exercise of moderate-intensity effectively reduces anxiety symptoms among patients with anxiety disorders (Merom et al., 2008). Patients are also less hypervigilant about experiencing anxiety after bouts of aerobic exercise, especially high-intensity exercise (Broman-Fulks & Storey, 2008; Smits et al., 2008).

EXERCISE AND DEPRESSION

Regular exercise improves moods and alleviates depression (Annesi, 2005). Both aerobic and anaerobic exercise effectively reduces depression, and when the two forms are combined, exercise is even more beneficial (Rethorst, Wipfli, & Landers, 2009). Adolescents who are more physically active also have fewer (if frequency, less-depressed if a gauge of depression) depressed moods (Birkland, Torsheim, & Wold, 2009). As was the case for anxiety, there is a dose-response effect for cardiorespiratory fitness and depression and general well-being. Fitter people are less depressed and feel better (Legrand & Heuze, 2007; Rethorst et al., 2009). The same effect holds for weekly activity, such as walking and running, and physical activities, such as sports. The dose-response association between activity level and depression and well-being peaks at moderate levels. For example, running at a level of 11 to 19 miles per week would be considered moderate. Mileage above those levels has less effect on depression and well-being (Galper, Trivedi, Barlow, Dunn, & Kamert, 2006).

Exercise has an even larger effect in alleviating clinical depression (Rethorst et al., 2009). Early meta-analyses—statistical integration of extant research—indicated that exercise was an effective treatment for clinical depression such as Major Depressive Disorder (Craft & Landers, 1998; North, McCullagh, & Tran, 1990). More recent results have been more mixed (Eriksson & Gard, 2011). However, the preponderance of evidence supports the effectiveness of exercise—both aerobic and anaerobic—in reducing depression. Exercise also has a small but significant effect in reducing depression in children (Brown, Pearson, Braithwaite, Brown, & Biddle, 2013). An additional benefit of exercise is that it is fast-acting, compared to antidepressant medication (Knubben et al., 2007). Both aerobic (Dunn et al., 2005) and anaerobic exercise (Singh et al., 2005; Singh, Clements, & Fiatarone Singh, 2001) is much more effective if intensity levels are at least moderate. For example, Dunn et al. determined an effective dose of exercise to be 17.5-kcal/kg/week—the public health recommendation for physical activity mentioned above (U.S. Department of Health and Human Services, 2008).

Intense levels of exercise should not be prescribed, unless depressed patients self-select these levels. Depressed patients responded to intense exercise with immediate improvements in mood, but after 30 minutes they became even more depressed and listless (Weinstein, Deuster, Francis, Beadling, & Kop, 2010).

Depressed patients are likely to benefit from structured programming and psychoeducation with exercise. Without this support, they may be too pessimistic to believe that exercise will be beneficial and that they are capable of maintaining an exercise regimen. With diminished energy and efficacy they may withdraw from the experience of physical exertion (Pom, Fleig, Schwarzer, & Lippke, 2012).

Given the structure of a supervised program, exercise may reduce depression that is unresponsive to antidepressant medication (Trivedi et al., 2011). For those who have responded favorably to standard treatments for depressions, exercise serves to reduce sad moods that result from daily stressors (Mata, Hogan, Joormann, Waugh, & Gotlib, 2012).

Exercise also provides the benefit of increased total sleep, increased slow-wave sleep, and decreased REM sleep. REM sleep is rapid eye movement sleep, and is indicative of dreaming. Secretion of the neurotransmitter serotonin is inhibited during REM sleep, and depressed patients typically have lower levels of serotonin. Depressed people also have lower levels of norepinephrine, and exercise boosts the availability of this neurotransmitter. Finally, exercise often improves body image and self-esteem (Rethorst et al., 2009).

Fitness and Mental Toughness

One day after his right leg was amputated, Paul de Gelder was doing one-armed chin-ups from his hospital bed. One-armed chin-ups were necessary because he also lacked a right forearm. A diver for the Australian navy, de Gelder lost both limbs due to a shark attack in Sydney Harbor.

De Gelder continued training during a nine-week stay in the hospital. "Instead of getting back to where I was, I thought, 'Why don't I be better than what I was.'" Family and friends brought weights and tension bands, and he exercised from his hospital bed. Once equipped with prosthetic limbs, his training regimen expanded to 5-kilometer walks on the beach, cardiovascular workouts on an elliptical machine, and extensive weight training. He is equally conscientious about his diet.

De Gelder hopes to return to diving, swimming, and surfing. "Without fitness in my life, it really doesn't seem to be much of a life" (Tanaka, 2012).

EXERCISE AND BODY IMAGE

Body image refers to the manner in which one views, feels, and thinks about and acts toward her or his body. One's subjective view of her or his body is referred to as the *perceptual dimension* of body image. Body image also has an *affective dimension*. One may feel good about her or his body or their body image may invoke feelings of shame. Some people are more invested in their appearance. The degree to which people are concerned about their appearance is reflected in the *cognitive dimension*. The *behavioral dimension* provides clues to how the body is perceived and evaluated. This dimension is revealed by the style of dress and involvement in activities—such as swimming—that require a measure of bodily exposure. Finally, there is a *subjective satisfaction dimension* (Cash, 2004).

Unfortunately, the majority of women (56%), and a large minority of men (43%) are dissatisfied with their overall appearance (Garner, 1997). **Negative body images** contribute to low self-esteem, depression and anxiety (Stice & Whitenton, 2002), and eating disorders (Polivy & Herman, 2002). Those with negative body images are more prone to use alcohol and other drugs, smoke, and engage in unhealthy dieting (French, Story, Downes, Resnick, & Blum, 1995).

Exercise often, but not always (Lamarche & Gammage, 2012), improves body image. While improved fitness, muscularity, and weight loss may contribute to improved body image, the exerciser's satisfaction with his or her gains is particularly influential. When people perceive physical advancements due to exercise, their body image improves (Martin Ginis, Eng, Arbour, Hartman, & Phillip, 2005). Exercisers also gain self-efficacy for their capacity to manage their bodies. This efficacy contributes to improvements in body image (McAuley et al., 2000; McAuley et al., 2002).

Exercise that is at least of moderate intensity is more beneficial (Campbell & Hausenblas, 2009). There is also a dose-response effect such that body image improves as people log more time at exercise (Arbour & Martin Ginis, 2008).

NEGATIVE BEHAVIORS AND EXERCISE

Exercise Dependence

Given the list of benefits associated with exercise, it may be surprising to find dysfunctional behaviors associated with physical activity. A small number of people find it difficult or impossible to limit, alter, or stop exercise. They persist regardless of injury status, time limitations, and the degree to which exercise interferes with important obligations. These people may train despite serious injuries and the neglect of employment and family obligations. For these individuals, exercise is beyond their regulatory control (DiClemente, 2006). They may evidence **exercise dependence**. Exercise dependence is measured less by the sheer duration and intensity of exercise and more by the degree to which one "must" exercise and cannot stop.

The **Exercise Dependence Scale-Revised** (EDS; Symons Downs, Hausenblas, & Nigg, 2004) was developed to measure exercise dependence. Its seven factors were adopted from the criteria for dependence on substances in the DSM-IV-TR (American Psychiatric Association, 2000). Substance dependence is a category of mental disorders.

The seven factors of the EDS are tolerance, withdrawal, intentional effects, lack of control, time, reduction in other activities, and continuance (see Figure 3.3). With *tolerance,* increasing amounts of exercise are necessary to achieve the desired effect. There is less satisfaction with workouts that just maintain the status quo. *Withdrawal* consists of unpleasant physical or emotional experiences when workouts are missed. Withdrawal symptoms may prompt a feverish return to exercise to

---

FIGURE 3.3   Sample Items of the Exercise Dependence Scale-Revised (Symons Downs, Hausenblas, & Niggs, 2004)

Tolerance
I continually increase my exercise intensity to achieve the desired effect/benefits
I continually increase my exercise duration to achieve the desired effect/benefits

Withdrawal
I exercise to avoid feeling irritable
I exercise to avoid feeling anxious

Continuance
I exercise when injured
I exercise despite persistent physical problems

Lack of Control
I am unable to reduce how long I exercise
I am unable to reduce how often I exercise

Reduction in Other Activities
I would rather exercise than spend time with family/friends
I think about exercise when I should be concentrating on school/work

Time
I spend a lot of time exercising
I spend most of my free time exercising

Intentional Effects
I exercise longer than I intend
I exercise longer than I plan

alleviate the symptoms (Bratland-Sanda et al., 2011). *Intentional effects* reflect a loss of control over the duration of training so that exercise continues longer than expected. *Lack of control* is recognized when people are unable to reduce the length, duration, and intensity of exercise. The *time* factor registers the domination of exercise over one's schedule. This domination results in a *reduction of other* important *activities* in order to spend more time exercising. With *continuance*, people exercise to the point of injury and despite injuries.

Perhaps 9% of the population that is physically active is at risk for exercise dependence. Another 40% do not meet criteria for dependence, but show some symptoms of exercise dependence. Males register higher scores on the seven factors of the EDS (Weik, 2009), but females score higher on the factors of a competing exercise dependence questionnaire—the Exercise Dependence Questionnaire (Ogden, Veale, & Summers, 1997). Exercise dependence is more prevalent among elite and competitive athletes (McNamara & McCabe, 2012; Smith, Wright, & Winrow, 2010).

Among the risk factors for developing exercise dependence are perfectionism (see Chapter 13; Hall, Hill, Appleton, & Kozub, 2009; Hagan & Hausenblas, 2003; Hausenblas & Symons Downs, 2002) and the personality traits of extraversion, neuroticism, and agreeableness (see Chapter 15; Hausenblas & Giacobbi, 2004). Those who are hypervigilant about signs of illness are also more susceptible to exercise dependence (Pugh & Hadjistavropoulos, 2011).

Women who derive their self-worth from physical appearance are at greater risk for engaging in uncontrollable exercise patterns (Lamarche & Gammage, 2012). These women may go to extreme lengths to realize appearance goals. They are likely to diet to realize appearance goals, and are at greater risk for developing eating disorders (Cash, Melnyk, & Hrabosky, 2004).

Eating Disorders and Exercise

Obligatory and compulsive attitudes about exercise are associated with eating disorders (Meyer & Taranis, 2011). Exercise that is not compulsive enhances well-being and reduces the likelihood of developing eating disorders (Cook, Hausenblas, Tuccitto, & Giacobbi, 2011). Further, vigorous exercise for longer durations, as well as exercise to alleviate negative affect and enhance positive affect, is also associated with disordered eating among women with and without diagnosable eating disorders, such as Anorexia Nervosa and Bulimia Nervosa (Bratland-Sanda et al., 2011). With Anorexia Nervosa, restricted eating results in body weight that is less than 85% of normal for one's height. Bulimia Nervosa involves repeated episodes of binge eating followed by compensatory behaviors, such as purging, to prevent weight gain (American Psychiatric Association, 2000).

Exercise motivated solely or primarily to reduce weight is strongly associated with eating disorders and reduced well-being. Traditionally, obligatory and compulsive exercise was seen as a result of disordered eating. However, compulsive exercise may also lead to disordered eating.

For example, compulsive exercise may contribute to weight loss and to calorie restriction to further the weight-loss process. Compulsive exercise and disorder eating are probably reciprocally reinforcing (Meyer, Taranis, Goodwin, & Haycraft, 2011).

Exercise and Distorted Body Image

People with eating disorders often have distorted views of their body shape or weight. For example, patients with Anorexia Nervosa believe they are overweight despite undeniable evidence that they are emaciated. Compulsive exercise also accompanies another form of body image distortion, **muscle dysphoria.** This appears to be a type of Body Dysmorphic Disorder (American Psychiatric Association, 2000), whereby those affected become preoccupied with thoughts that they are not sufficiently muscular and lean. For example, a highly developed bodybuilder may imagine himself to be small and flabby. Weight trainers with muscle dysphoria are at risk for anabolic-androgenic steroid use (AAS; see Chapter 16) (Rohman, 2009). The use of AASs was 1.4 times higher for 16-year-old high school students in European countries who exercised on an almost daily basis (Kokkevi, Fotiou, Chileva, Nociar, Miller, 2008).

REASONS AND IMPEDIMENTS FOR EXERCISE

Given the benefits of exercise, how is it that so many people avoid it? The question may be answered by a bottom-up or a top-down approach. With the top-down approach, research is guided by theory. A bottom-up approach begins with data collection, and results drive interpretations of the data. Theoretical approaches will be reviewed in the next section.

Surveys indicate that people exercise to improve or sustain an attractive weight and appearance or to have fun and promote health. Those wanting to enhance health and have fun also realize better physical health—lower pulse rates and systolic blood pressure, and lower levels of cortisol—and well-being. Those who exercise for weight management and appearance are more likely to quit exercising, and to register symptoms of depression, eating disorders, and lower self-esteem (DiBartolo, Lin, Montoya, Neal, & Shaffer, 2007).

The importance of exercise as an outlet for competition and the demonstration of competence have been emphasized more by young males than by females and older males. The value of exercise for weight control and to enhance appearance is more important for women (Egli, Bland, Melton, & Czech, 2011). Younger adults are more likely to exercise to improve fitness, whereas older adults train for health benefits (Biddle & Nigg, 2000).

Some people experience barriers to exercise participation. Those who are obese, have lower socioeconomic status, less education, smoke cigarettes, and have medical problems are less likely to exercise. Some people also cite insufficient motivation and a lack of time as reasons for not exercising (Buckworth & Dishman, 2007).

THEORETICAL APPROACHES TO EXERCISE PROMOTION

Chapter 2 began with a question about why people strive to do their best and reach their full potential. While a simple answer was not available, the influential theories that have guided research were reviewed. Given that exercise involves voluntary, leisure-time activities designed to improve physical fitness (Bouchard, Blair, & Haskell, 2007), it may be understood as an aspect of striving for self-improvement. Again, the question of why people do and do not devote themselves to exercise cannot be answered simply. In the section that follows, the most influential theoretical explanations for exercise and health behavior are reviewed: **self-determination theory and organismic integration theory, social cognitive theory,** the **transtheoretical model,** the **theory of reasoned action/planned behavior,** and the **health belief model** (Painter, Borba, Hynes, Mays, & Glanz, 2008).

Self-Determination Theory, Organismic Integration Theory, and Exercise

People approach exercise with different motivational orientations. As first reviewed in Chapter 2, **intrinsic** motivation relates to the pursuit of activities and interests that are of an individual's own choosing and that are largely free of internal or external pressure and control. Three forms of intrinsic motivation have been identified: intrinsic motivation for *accomplishment, learning,* and experiencing *stimulation* (Vallerand, 2007; Vallerand & Losier, 1994). Intrinsic motivation for accomplishment is not dependent on outcomes or results; it is the experience of attempting to accomplish a goal or to surpass oneself that provides the rewards (Vallerand & Rousseau, 2001). All three forms of intrinsic motivation may come into play in the course of exercise as participants may find getting fitter, the process of learning new exercises and routines, and the fun and camaraderie of exercise to be rewarding.

The experience of external or internal regulation to engage in activities is referred to as **extrinsic** motivation. **Organismic integration theory** (Ryan & Deci, 2007) identifies four types of extrinsic motivation. Behavior is **externally regulated** when it is controlled by external factors, such as rewards and punishments. For example, a sedentary adolescent may be required to complete a mile jog in less than 12 minutes to earn a passing grade in physical education class. Sometimes sportspersons engage in exercise that they do not enjoy but believe that they "should" pursue. These sportspersons have **introjected,** or internalized, external regulations, and experience guilt when they violate these regulations. For example, obese adults may begin a walking program in order to lose weight and reduce hypertension if they have internalized and honor their doctors' warnings. With **identified regulation,** activities are pursued because they help people develop desired characteristics (e.g., "I want to be muscular and athletic"). Finally, **integrated regulation** results from the assimilation of activity into one's sense of self (see Figure 3.4).

The four types of extrinsic motivation are differentiated according to their relative level of self-determination (Ryan & Deci, 2007). Integrated regulation and identified regulation are considered to represent forms of self-determination. The three forms of intrinsic motivation are also forms of self-determination. Introjected and external regulations are considered controlling forms of motivation (see Figure 3.5).

FIGURE 3.4   Continuum of Motivation (adopted from Ryan & Deci, 2007; Li, 1999; Vallerand & Losier, 1999)

Continuum of Self-determination

Low--High

Amotivation	Extrinsic motivation				Intrinsic motivation		
	External regulation	Introjected regulation	Identified regulation	Integrated regulation	Learn	Accomplish task	Experience sensations

---

FIGURE 3.5   Basic Psychological Needs in Exercise Scale (sample items adopted from Vlachopoulos & Michailidou, 2006)

Autonomy   I feel very strongly that the way I exercise fits perfectly the way I prefer to exercise.

I feel very strongly that I have the opportunity to make choices with respect to the way I exercise.

Competence   I feel that exercise is an activity I do well.

I feel that I can execute very effectively the exercises of my training program.

Relatedness   I feel extremely comfortable when with the other exercise participants

I feel that I associate with the other exercise participants in a very friendly way.

A third motivational orientation is **amotivation,** or the relative absence of motivation. People who refuse to take the first step in an exercise program show this absence of motivation. With amotivation, exercisers may feel incompetent and directionless.

Self-determined motivation has a powerful effect on behavior. Among overweight and obese Portuguese women, self-determined motivation for exercise not only predicted actual exercise behavior, but also "spilled-over" and contributed to improved eating behavior (Mata et al., 2011). This spillover was also in evidence among Spanish adults with self-determined motivation to maintain healthy lifestyles. They enjoyed exercise (Gonzalez-Cutre, Sicilia, & Aguila, 2011).

With **self-determination theory** it was recognized that environments that permit a degree of autonomy are more likely to engender feelings of **competence, autonomy,** and **relatedness** to others (e.g., Deci & Ryan, 1985, 2002; Gillet, Berjot, & Rosnet, 2009; Joesaar, Hein, & Hagger, 2011, 2012; Radel, Sarrazin, & Pelletier, 2009; Wilson, Mack, & Grattan, 2008). Competence refers to belief in one's abilities and proficiencies, and autonomy to control over one's actions. Relatedness involves satisfying connections with others. With the experience of competence, autonomy, and relatedness, people are more likely to develop self-determined motivation, persist at difficult tasks, and develop proficiencies.

Competence was also associated with intrinsic and identified motivation for physical activity among first-year students in college. However, only intrinsic motivation predicted engagement in actual physical activity (Ullrich-French, Cox, & Bumpus, 2012). Competence predicted exercise behavior among overweight adults (Gay, Saunders, & Duda, 2011) and colorectal cancer survivors (Peddle, Plotnikoff, Wild, Au, & Courneya, 2008). Team-building interventions designed to increase group cohesiveness resulted in increased attendance in exercise classes among Canadian high school (Bruner & Spink, 2011) and university students (Spink, Wilson, & Priebe, 2010).

Adaptive Environments and Self-Determination Theory

Perhaps the basic needs of competence, autonomy, and relatedness are more likely to be fulfilled in **adaptive environments** (Edmunds, Ntoumanis, & Duda, 2006; Edmunds, Ntoumanis, & Duda, 2007; Edmunds, Ntoumanis, & Duda, 2008; Wilson & Rodgers, 2004). These environments provide *autonomy, structure,* and *involvement.* Autonomy support is provided when authority figures are empathic, do not pressure subordinates to comply with orders, provide rationales for decisions, offer choices, and acknowledge that behavioral changes are difficult and effortful (Edmunds et al., 2008). Structure and involvement are complimentary interventions. Structure consists of unambiguous and realistic feedback regarding progress and effort. Involvement refers to the quality of the relationships between those in charge and those taking direction.

Involvement concerns authentic relationships in which the well-being of others is supported.

Competence and relatedness increased in university exercise classes where autonomy, organization, and relatedness were emphasized. Attendance was also better in these classes (Edmunds et al., 2008). Cardiac patients who experienced autonomy and competence in exercise programs were more likely to develop self-determined motivation and to exercise independently in the future (Russell & Bray, 2009).

Autonomy support is particularly influential. In classes where instructors supported autonomy when teaching new exercises, young students registered more effort, self-determined regulation, and persistence across the four-month class. They were also more likely to enroll in future exercise classes (Vansteenkiste, Simons, Soenens, & Lens, 2004). Secondary school students were more likely to experience autonomy, competence, and relatedness in physical education classes when teachers supported their autonomy. Higher autonomy and competence contributed to autonomous motivation. Competence advanced the physical self-concepts of students, and relatedness directed the experience of higher health-related quality of life (Standage, Gillison, Ntoumanis, & Treasure, 2012). University students in physical education classes responded to autonomy support from instructors with increased perceived competence, autonomy, and self-determined motivation (Puente & Anshel, 2010).

Self-Efficacy and Exercise

As reviewed in Chapter 10, the belief that one has the capacity to organize and execute the actions necessary to realize attainments or goals in particular areas or domains of functioning is referred to as **self-efficacy.** The concept of self-efficacy was developed by Albert Bandura, and this concept has influenced research not only in sport psychology but also in social, clinical, industrial, and health psychology (Bandura, 1997; Feltz, Short, & Sullivan, 2008).

People with high **exercise efficacy** are more likely to begin and continue in programs of exercise. With weak efficacy beliefs, and inflated expectations about rapid gains from exercise, exercisers are more likely to quit. Of particular importance is **self-regulatory efficacy,** or the belief that one can stick with programs and resist temptations and excuses to quit. These temptations may include muscular fatigue and discomfort, as well as competing activities. Confidence that one can overcome obstacles to exercise, such as bad weather, is referred to as **barriers efficacy,** and **scheduling efficacy** concerns confidence that inconveniences associated with exercise are manageable (McAuley & Mihalko, 1998). Competing activities—such as eating snacks and watching sports on television—may offer more immediate reinforcement, whereas the benefits of exercise accrue in the future. Without this self-regulatory efficacy, people attend exercise sessions irregularly, do not exercise for sufficient intensities or durations to experience health benefits, and drop out. Efficacy that one can execute exercise skills is less influential since exercise often involves relatively simple skills, such as walking (Bandura, 1997; Luszczynska, Schwarzer, Lippke, & Mazurkiewicz, 2011).

Those with high efficacy are likely to enjoy exercise more and find it less stressful. Indeed, those with higher efficacy secreted less of the stress hormone cortisol during a bout of treadmill running (Rudolph & McAuley, 1995).

Effective strategies for maintaining exercise programs often integrate self-regulatory efficacy with proximal goals (see Chapter 8) and feedback about goal attainment. Exercisers are better motivated by proximal goals of moderate difficulty and feedback that they are realizing these goals. For example, the goal of walking 1 kilometer is likely to motivate more effectively than the goal of avoiding a heart attack in the distant future (McAuley et al., 2011).

It is also useful to incorporate the four primary sources of efficacy development into exercise plans for novice exercisers. As described in Chapter 10, efficacy develops with enactive attainments, social persuasion, feedback, by observing the success of similar people, and by observing physiological and emotional states. Access to observational learning and feedback is more readily available when exercising with others or in groups or classes. Knowledgeable staff may also help novice exercisers understand that transient physical and emotional discomfort is to be expected when getting fitter. Not surprisingly, exercise efficacy predicts exercise adherence and exercise efficacy increases as a result of successful experience with exercise (Park & Gaffey, 2007; Woodgate & Brawley, 2008).

Application

Suggestions for Enhancing Self-Efficacy (McAuley, 1994)

Mastery Experiences	Exercises: Gradually increase the (a) speed, grade, or duration of treadmills, (b) resistance or duration of stationary bicycles, and (c) load, repetitions, or sets in weight lifting. Daily activities: Walking to work, school, or errands instead of using motor transportation; using stairs instead of elevators or escalators; walking around golf courses instead of riding.
Vicarious Learning	Observe directly or watch videotapes of models successfully engaging in exercise; models should be similar in physical characteristics and exercise capacity. Provide leader or expert demonstrations. Encourage attendance at exercise orientation sessions at exercise facilities to observe others. Encourage group exercise and exercise partners.

Verbal Persuasion	Provide information about exercise in orientation meetings and forms of media.
	Develop networks of social support with "buddy systems" and group activities.
	Contact members of the exercise group when they are absent.
Psychological and Emotional States	Provide accurate information about proprioceptive feedback from exercise; for example, shortness of breath, fatigue, muscle soreness, and gradual fitness gains are to be anticipated.

Lapses and interruptions in exercise regimens are not uncommon and should be planned for. They are best understood as an unstable, specific, controllable, internal (e.g., "I got lazy"), or external (e.g., "My schedule made exercise impossible") event. Stable, global, uncontrollable attributions (e.g., "I'm hopeless") do not support efficacy.

Application

Getting Back to Exercise

Self-regulation strategies and efficacious beliefs require review and perhaps reinstatement when exercise regiments are stopped. The following may be considered:

1. Consider that relapses are a normal part of exercise regimens and that you may return to exercise without losing previous gains.
2. Identify impediments to regular exercise and plan for ways of surmounting them. For example, if you just cannot motivate yourself to exercise after 6:00 PM, it is necessary to find an earlier time—perhaps before work or school—to exercise.
3. Monitor declines in fitness when you stop exercising to serve as an incentive to return.
4. Review and reinstate exercise goals; identify self-incentives for exercise. An example of the latter might be to reward yourself with a fine pair of exercise shoes when you log 200 hours of exercise.
5. Try to enlist social support from others. Find compatible exercise buddies and groups.

The Transtheoretical Model and Exercise

The **transtheoretical model** of behavior change was developed to explain how people intentionally change addictive behaviors, with and without professional help. It is transtheoretical in that the common principles that drive behavior change are identified, regardless of the theoretical origin of the principles. Originated by James Prochaska (1979) and colleagues at the University of Rhode Island, it has influenced research in clinical, health, and exercise psychology for over 30 years.

Sometimes behavior changes suddenly. For example, someone may have an epiphany or a sudden insight that changes his or her life forever. However, behavior change is usually more gradual and effortful. Further, change seldom lasts forever, and people are often ambivalent about change. With ambivalence, people experience the positive and negative aspects of change. For example, a sedentary adult may wish to lose weight, sculpt his body, and lower his blood pressure with exercise. But, he may also find the experience of muscular exertion and oxygen debt to be unpleasant, and the necessity to change his schedule and budget time for exercise to be inconvenient.

Change is more likely a dynamic process that may involve movement through a series of stages. Five **stages of change** are identified in the transtheoretical model (see Figure 3.6). In **precontemplation,** change is not seriously considered. The possibility of change is entertained in **contemplation. Preparation** involves planning for and experimentation with behavioral and cognitive change. Active behavior change is embraced and enacted during the **action** stage. Change becomes a way of life—one's new homeostasis—during the **maintenance** stage (DiClemente, 2006). Maintenance begins after at least six months of sustained behavior change, and **termination** or an exit from the cycle of change is possible after five years of continuous exercise (Cardinal, 1999; Fallon & Hausenblas, 2001). Exercisers in the termination stage are more likely to engage in strenuous exercise.

This dynamic process of change is not necessarily in one direction. For example, an exerciser in the action stage may stop regular exercise and return to one of the preceding stage. Behavior change is considered resistant to relapse after five years of uninterrupted maintenance, but even after 10 years of continuous exercise, almost everyone experiences occasional **temptation** to avoid exercise (Fallon & Hausenblas, 2004). Temptation consists of affects, such as anger, and competing demands, including other time commitments (Hausenblas et al., 2001).

As mentioned above, people are often ambivalent about behavior change. With interventions informed by the stages of change model, ambivalence is clarified. Those considering change are encouraged to identify a **decisional balance** or a list of the *pros* and *cons* for behavior change. The pros of behavior change only begin to outweigh the cons during the preparation stage, whereas the balance shifts more definitely in favor of the benefits of change in the action stage. Similarly, self-efficacy increases during the contemplation stage and facilitates movement to the action stage of exercise (Gorely & Bruce, 2000; Prochaska, Wright, & Velicer, 2008). Temptation to avoid exercise is inversely related to self-efficacy (Hausenblas et al., 2001). Self-efficacy increases and temptation decreases with the maintenance of exercise (Dishman, Vandenberg, Motl, & Nigg, 2010).

Given the importance of moving people into the action, maintenance, and termination stages of exercise, there is an interest in matching

FIGURE 3.6	States of Change in the Transtheoretical Model (adopted from DiClemente, 2006)
Precontemplation	Changing or initiating behaviors is not seriously considered
	The environment is not supportive of behavior change
	There are few cues or environmental stimuli to prompt behavior change
Contemplation	Behavior change is considered
	Consciousness raising – gathering and considering important information
	Self-reevaluation and *environmental reevaluation*
	Decisional balance – weigh the pros and cons of exercise
Preparation	Experimentation with exercise
	Gradual and deliberate preparation for regular exercise
	Decisional balance – pros for exercise increase and cons decrease
	Self-efficacy for exercise increases
	Plan for how to include exercise in daily life

	FIGURE 3.6 (Continued)
Action	Decisional balance is skewed toward a positive view of exercise; supports engagement in exercise
	Stimulus generalization, more situations become cues for engagement in exercise
	*Reinforcement*s for exercise increase; e.g. one feels better and looks better, exercise is more enjoyable
	Fewer perceived barriers to exercise
	Self-efficacy for continued exercise increases
	Relationships, beliefs, attitudes, and environments are altered to support exercise
Maintenance	Exercise is a way of life
	Actively countering excuses to skip exercise
	Ensuring that the decision balance remains positive for exercise
	Establish a lifestyle, schedule, and environment that supports habitual exercise
	Further broaden the stimuli, cues, and relationships associated with exercise
Termination	An exit from the stages of change after five years of continuous exercise

interventions to the stages of change (Trost, Owen, Bauman, Sallis, & Brown, 2002). For example, consciousness raising—stimulating a consideration of the benefits of exercise and the hazards of inactivity—may be particularly beneficial for precontemplators. Interventions that are mismatched to stages of change may be ineffective or increase resistance to change. However, despite evidence that such mismatches result in ineffective or iatrogenic interventions in clinical populations (Miller & Rollnick, 2013), matching interventions to stages of change for exercise is determined less by empirical results (Fetherman, Hakim, & Sanko, 2011; Hutchinson, Breckon, & Johnston, 2008; Pfeffer & Alfermann, 2008) than by theory (Prochaska et al., 2008). Matching interventions to stages of change may not meaningfully increase exercise levels (Warner & Lippke, 2008). However, matched interventions are likely to move people to higher levels in the stages of change (Adams & White, 2003; Bridle et al., 2005).

The Theories of Reasoned Action and Planned Behavior

The theory of **reasoned action** is aimed at explaining intentional behavior (Fishbein & Ajzen, 2009). It emphasizes the importance of *intention*, or the degree of planning and effort someone is willing to invest in realizing a goal. Intention is a function of *attitudes* and *subjective norms*. Attitudes are defined in this model as one's evaluation of a behavior such as exercise. Subjective norms refer to the importance that significant others place on a behavior. For example, a sportsperson might realize that her coach highly values weight training because playing time is dependent on meeting weight training goals.

The realization that not all behavior is under volitional control led to an extension of the theory of reasoned action. With the theory of **planned behavior,** *perceived behavioral control* is placed alongside attitudes and subjective norms, and all three influence intentions (Ajzens, 1985). Perceived behavioral control refers to evaluations of barriers to goal attainment and judgments about whether one will realize goals. This construct overlaps somewhat with self-efficacy. Perceived behavioral control and attitudes are more influential in predicting exercise behavior, and the theory of planned behavior is more effective in explaining exercise behavior than the theory of reasoned action (Hagger & Charzisarantis, 2005; Hagar, Chatzisarantis, & Biddle, 2002).

Generally, intentions to exercise predict exercise behavior (Symons Downs, & Hausenblas, 2005). However, intentions to exercise are not always converted to actual behavior. Correspondingly, interventions designed to change intentions about exercise may not result in large changes in exercise behavior (Webb & Sheeran, 2006). People are more likely follow through on their intentions to exercise when they develop **implementation intentions** (see Figure 3.7). These are key cues that signal when and where intentions are to be implemented (Arbour & Martin

FIGURE 3.7 Theory of Planned Behavior (Ajzen, 1985)

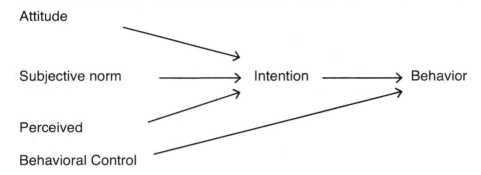

Ginis, 2009; Belanger-Gravel, Godin, & Amireault, 2011; Chatzisarantis, Hagger, & Thogersen-Ntoumani, 2008; Gollwitzer & Sheeran, 2006). For example, Dutch adults were far more likely to vigorously exercise when they endorsed intentions such as: "If I don't get my exercise on a day, I always try to catch up on another day that week," and, "When I notice that I have less than two days per week 30 minutes of intensive exercise, [sic] I examine how I can reorganize my week so that I can get this exercise" (de Bruin et al., 2012, p. 5).

Not all intentions have equal influence on behavior. When intentions are freely chosen and support autonomy, people are more likely to develop attitudes, perceived behavioral control, intentions, and effort necessary to engage in exercise behavior (Chatzisarantis, Hagger, Biddle, & Karageorghis, 2002; Hagger et al., 2002). As emphasized in self-determination theory, freely chosen activities that produce feelings of competence, autonomy, and relatedness to others (e.g., Deci & Ryan, 1985, 2002; Gillet, Berjot, & Rosnet, 2009; Joesaar, Hein, & Hagger, 2011, 2012; Radel, Sarrazin, & Pelletier, 2009) are likely to be intrinsically rewarding. Intrinsically rewarding activities are self-sustaining because they are their own reward.

The Health Belief Model

The **health belief model** has influenced thinking and research about health behavior since the early 1950s. It has informed research with a wide range of medical disorders including hypertension (e.g., Gatewood et al., 2008), cancers (e.g., Kiviniemi, Bennett, Zaiter, & Marshall, 2011), and immunizations (e.g., Smith et al., 2011). Its developers were social psychologists—Godfrey Hochbaum, Stephen Kegels, and Irwin Rosenstock—who worked for the U.S. Public Health Service. The focus of the U.S. Health Service at that time was on the prevention rather than the treatment of disease. The developers reasoned that people would make efforts to prevent diseases if they were informed about the benefits of preventive measures and sufficiently worried about contracting diseases. The developers recognized that people were more likely to comply with health care recommendations that were fast and easy to complete and that appeared effective. Finally, they understood that people needed internal and external cues or reminders to take action. For example, when individuals are convinced that flu shots are effective, worried about catching the flu, and when signs are posted at work or school that shots are given freely with no waiting, more people are expected to take the immunization.

Regular exercisers differ from non-exercisers in terms of the **perceived benefits** of exercise and the **perceived severity** of the disorders prevented by regular physical activity. Sedentary people more readily identify **perceived barriers** to exercise such as inconvenience, expense, lack of time, and discomfort. Those who exercise also have higher self-efficacy for adherence to regimens and more **cues to action** or reminders to engage (Bond, Aiken, & Somerville, 1992; Kiviniemi, Voss-Humke, & Seifert, 2007; Mahalik & Burns, 2011; Sullivan et al., 2008).

PHYSICAL ACTIVITY INTERVENTIONS

Enjoying exercise

It comes as no surprise that adults who enjoy physical activity and perceive it to be beneficial are more likely to exercise. Exercise is also more likely among those with clear intentions to exercise, self-motivation, and higher self-efficacy (Dishman et al., 2008).

Interventions designed to increase physical activity and exercise are likely to be equally effective for males and females and for individuals of different ethnic backgrounds. However, healthy individuals are more likely to continue participation in these exercise programs. People with physical disabilities, developmental disabilities, and obesity are more likely to discontinue exercise programs. Patients with coronary heart and other chronic disease are far less likely to persist with exercise (Dishman & Buckworth, 1996).

A first step in the rigorous development of interventions to increase participation in exercise is to identify the most promising theory of why people exercise. In the preceding section, five theoretical explanations for engaging in exercise behavior were reviewed. They all contribute to the understanding of why people adhere to exercise regimens. However, a rigorous method for selecting the most efficacious theory is not available.

The application of theory to practice does not have to wait until a "winning" theory is identified. Application may proceed with **intervention mapping** (Bartholomew, Parcel, Kok, & Gottleb, 2006). With this approach, intervention goals are identified, and theory-based methods that will most likely accomplish the intervention goals are selected across theories.

Meta-analyses indicate that adults are more likely to engage in exercise when interventions emphasize self-regulation strategies (Carver & Scheier, 1998). These strategies include goal setting, self-monitoring, self-rewards, providing cues and feedback for exercise, and actively monitoring physical activity behavior (e.g., keeping exercise logs). A common characteristic of these effective interventions is that they involve active behavior. Self-monitoring current behavior in relation to goals is particularly important. Adherence improves further when trainers model exercise behaviors. Booster interventions, such as reminding people to exercise by phone, mail, or Internet contact, also improves adherence. Strategies that are passive, such as efforts to influence knowledge, attitudes, and beliefs, are not as effective. Interventions are also more effective when they are delivered directly—face-to-face—to individuals rather than by mass media (Conn, Hafdahl, & Mehr, 2011; Michie, Abraham, Whittington, McAteer, & Gupta, 2009; Müller-Riemenschneider, Reinhold, Nocon, & Willich, 2008).

The identification of effective intervention strategies with children is more elusive. Again, considering meta-analyses, interventions only have a small effect (approximately four minutes more walking or running per day) on activity levels of children after the completion of physical activity programs. Programs were no more effective if administered at home or at school, if their duration was for less than or greater than six months, or if participants were obese or of normal weight (Metcalf, Henley, & Wilkin, 2012). Less elusive is the recognition that the involvement of parents is particularly important if children are to lose weight with physical activity and other interventions (Niemeier, Hektner, & Enger, 2012).

Application

Suggestions for Becoming More Physically Active (adopted from Hagger, 2012; Moran, 2012)

1. Make it fun! Engage with others! Exercise is easier to maintain if it is enjoyable and if it is a social activity.
2. Find a comfortable venue for exercise: where you feel comfortable, unselfconscious, and accepted (relatedness); where you can develop a sense of competence and efficacy as an active and healthy person (competence); and where you feel free to pursue your own regimens (autonomy).
3. Make the exercise your own. Can you find intrinsic rewards such as getting fitter, learning to handle training loads and oxygen debt, and enjoying the excitement of group participation? Can you develop motivation to improve your physique and health (identified regulation) and develop a view of yourself as healthy and athletic (integrated regulation)?

4. Make exercise purposeful. Incorporate exercise into other activities, such as yard work, walking the dog, walking to work, or shopping. Try to accumulate a minimum of 30 minutes of this activity per day.
5. Start with low- and moderate-intensity exercise for brief periods of time. Build intensity and duration levels at your own pace. This is especially important for exercisers who are older and sedentary.
6. Establish an exercise routine that fits realistically in your schedule.
7. Try an aerobic exercise that engages the major muscle groups in the legs.
8. Integrate exercise into an active lifestyle. Do not make exercise drudgery that is isolated to a gym or exercise setting.

SUMMARY AND APPLICATION

Due to the numerous health benefits of exercise, it was touted as "today's best buy in public health" in 1994 (Morris, 1994). After 19 years, this assessment is still valid, but motivating sedentary people to exercise remains a "tough sell" (Dishman, 2001).

Regular exercise of moderate intensity decreases the risk of cardiovascular disease, type 2 diabetes and metabolic syndrome, colon and breast cancer, endometrial and lung cancer, and overweight and obesity. Both aerobic and anaerobic exercise are beneficial. Aerobic exercise may confer additional benefits such enhancing cognitive development and functioning, and retarding cognitive decline due to aging.

Exercise also confers psychological benefits. Regular exercise improves mood and reduces anxiety. There is a dose-response effect for anxiety and depression. Those who exercise more have less anxiety and depression. Exercise is more fast-acting than antidepressant medications and effective with some patients who are unresponsive to antidepressant medication. Intense exercise may be iatrogenic for clinically depressed patients; perhaps feeling physically depleted contributes to listless and feelings of increased depression.

There is also a dose-response effect for exercise and body image. Body image improves as people log more hours at exercise. This is not surprising, since regular exercise is likely to result in objective fitness gains. Exercise also enhances self-efficacy for managing one's body.

While the overriding public health concern is to motivate sedentary people to become active, a sizable minority of the physically active exercise excessively. For these people, exercise is inordinately important and prioritized above interpersonal relationships, vocational and academic pursuits, and their own well-being. Those with exercise dependence train to the point of injury and may be perfectionistic, preoccupied with their appearance, and at risk for eating disorders. With these qualities people are also more likely to use ergogenic substances to enhance their appearance. Those with muscle dysphoria remain dissatisfied with their muscularity despite excessive exercise and perhaps doping.

Surveys indicate that people exercise to manage weight, improve appearance, promote health, and have fun. Those who exercise to promote health and have fun are more likely to stick with regimens. Unfortunately, people with health risks and lower socioeconomic status are less likely to exercise.

Five influential theories of exercise and health behavior were reviewed. *Self-determination theory* understands competence, autonomy, and relatedness to underpin self-determined motivation. With self-determined motivation, exercise is more likely to be self-sustaining and produce its own rewards. *Self-efficacy*, or confidence that goals in particular areas or domains will be accomplished, promotes and sustains exercise. People are more likely to be physically active with efficacy to self-regulate or persist despite fatigue, boredom, and competing activities, and efficacy to overcome barriers and scheduling difficulties.

Stages of change are emphasized in the *transtheoretical model*. For a sedentary person in the beginning stages of change—precontemplation and contemplation—the benefits of exercise are outweighed by the unpleasantness of the experience. The pros of exercise begin to outweigh the cons in the preparation stage, and the balance shifts in favor of change in the latter stages. Despite theoretical positions that people with five years of continuous exercise will not become inactive, exercisers experience occasional temptations to avoid exercise after 10 years of continuous physical activity.

The importance of one's intention to exercise was emphasized in the *theory of reasoned action*. The *theory of planned behavior* also recognized that exercise was more likely with perceived behavioral control, or judgments that barriers to goal attainments will be surmounted. With implementation intentions, or concrete plans for converting intentions to action, exercise is more likely.

With the *health belief model*, exercise is considered more likely when people clearly understand the benefits of exercise and the hazards of inactivity. Exercise is also more likely when scheduling inconveniences and costs are removed, and when people are given reminders.

The application of theories to practice is advanced with intervention mapping. With this approach, theory-based interventions are matched with specific goals for exercise. Self-regulation strategies that are proven to promote exercise adherence are goal setting, self-monitoring, self-rewards, and providing cues and feedback for exercise.

Key Terms

Discussion Questions

Q1. Identify the physical disorders resulting from physical inactivity.

Q2. What are the consequences of overweight for adults and young people?

Q3. How is the BMI calculated? Calculate your BMI .

Q4. Distinguish aerobic exercise, anaerobic exercise, the anaerobic threshold, maximum aerobic capacity, and VO_2 max.

Q5. Discuss the effects of chronic aerobic exercise on: neurotransmitters, cortical atrophy, neurogenesis, glia cells, myelinated axons, and capillaries.

Q6. How does trait anxiety differ from anxiety disorders?

Q7. What is the dose-response effect, and to what is it applied?

Q8. Discuss the effects of exercise on depressed moods and the depressive disorders. What benefits are conferred by exercise that are not as readily available with other interventions for depression?

Q9. Are there cautions when prescribing exercise for depressive disorders?

Q10. Describe the dimensions of body image.

Q11. How does exercise affect body image?

Q12. Describe the model for the definition of exercise dependence.
Q13. Review the seven factors of the Exercise Dependence Scale-Revised.
Q14. Consider the risk factors for exercise dependence.
Q15. How is it that exercise may both protect against and be a risk factor for eating disorders?
Q16. Distinguish Anorexia Nervosa and Bulimia Nervosa.
Q17. Discuss doping and its consequences.
Q18. Define muscle dysphoria and Body Dysmorphic Disorder.
Q19. Consider the reasons for exercise identified in surveys.
Q20. What are the contributions of self-determination theory and organismic integration theory?
Q21. Identify the forms of intrinsic motivation and extrinsic motivation. Which of these are self-determined versus controlling forms of regulation?
Q22. Define competence, autonomy, and relatedness.
Q23. What are the characteristics of adaptive environments?
Q24. Define self-efficacy, exercise efficacy, self-regulatory efficacy, barriers efficacy, and scheduling efficacy.
Q25. Review the derivation of the transtheoretical model.
Q26. Outline the characteristics of the five stages of change.
Q27. Explain the decisional balance.
Q28. Detail the feature of the theory of reasoned action. How did the theory of planned behavior add to this model?
Q29. What are implementation intentions?
Q30. Review the development of the health belief model.
Q31. What is intervention mapping?

Suggested Readings

Adams, J., & White, M. (2003). Are activity promotion interventions based on the transtheoretical model effective? A critical review. *British Journal of Sport Medicine, 37*, 106–114. doi: 10.1136/bjsm.37.2.106

Ajzens, I. (1985). From intentions to actions: A theory of planned behavior. In J. Huhl & J. Beckmann (Eds.), *Action-control: From cognition to behavior* (pp. 11–39). Heidelberg, Germany: Springer-Verlag.

Belanger-Gravel, A., Godin, G., & Amireault, S. (2011). A meta-analytic review of the effect of implementation intentions on physical activity. *Health Psychology Review, 5*, 1–32. doi: 101080/17437199.2011.560095

Birkland, M. S., Torsheim, T., & Wold, B. (2009). A longitudinal study of the relationship between leisure-time physical activity and depressed mood among adolescents. *Psychology of Sport & Exercise, 10*, 25–34. doi: 10.1016/j.psychsport.2008.01.005

Bruner, M. W., & Spink, K. S. (2011). Effects of team building on exercise adherence and group task satisfaction in a youth activity setting. *Group Dynamics: Theory, Research, and Practice, 15*, 161–172. doi: 10.1037/a0021257

Campbell, A., & Hausenblas, H. A. (2009). Effects of exercise interventions on body image: A meta-analysis. *Journal of Health Psychology, 14*, 780–793. doi: 10.1177/1359105309338977

Cook, B., Hausenblas, H., Tuccitto, D., & Giacobbi, P. R. Jr. (2011). Eating disorders and exercise: A structural equation modeling analysis of a conceptual model. Special issue article. *European Eating Disorders Review, 19*, 216–225. doi: 10.l002/erv.1111

De Bruin, M., Sheeran, P., Kok, G., Hiemstra, A., Prins, J. M., Hosers, H. J., & van Breukelen, G. J. P. (2012). Self-regulatory processes mediate the intention-behavior relation for adherence and exercise behaviors. *Health Psychology, 9*, 1–9. doi: 10.1037/a0027425

De Moor, M. H. M., Beem, A. L., Stubbe, J. H., Boomsma, D. I., & De Geus, E. J. C. (2006). Regular exercise, anxiety, depression and personality: a population-based study. *Preventive Medicine, 42*, 273-279. doi:10.1016/j.ypmed.2005.12.002

Fishbein, M., & Ajzen, I. (2009). *Predicting and changing behavior.* New York, NY: Psychology Press.

Hagger, M. S., & Chatzisarantis, N. L. D. (2005). First- and higher-order models of attitudes, normative influence, and perceived behavioural control in the theory of planned behaviour. *British Journal of Social Psychology 44*, 513–535. doi: 10.1348/014466604X16219

Lamarche, L., & Gammage, K. L. (2012). Predicting exercise and eating behaviors from appearance evaluation and two types of investment. *Sport, Exercise, and Performance Psychology, 1*, 145–157. doi: 10.1037/a0026892

Legrand, F., & Heuze, J. P. (2007). Antidepressant effects associated with different exercise conditions in participants with depression: A pilot study. *Journal of Sport & Exercise Psychology, 29*, 348–364.

Mata, J., Hogan, C. L., Joormann, J., Waugh, C. E., & Gotlib, I. H. (2012). Acute exercise attenuates negative affect following repeated sad mood inductions in persons who have recovered from depression. *Journal of Abnormal Psychology*, 1–6. doi: 10.1037/a0029881

Mata, J., Silva, M. N., Vieiera, P. N., Carraca, E. V., Andrade, A. M., Coutinho, S. R., . . . Teixeira, P. J. (2011). Motivational "spill-over" during weight control: Increased self-determination and exercise intrinsic motivation predict eating self-regulation. *Sport, Exercise, and Performance Psychology, 1*, 49–59. doi: 10.1037/2157-3905.1.S.49

McAuley, E., Mullen, S. P., Szabo, A. N., White, S. M., Wojcicki, T. R., Mailey, E. L., . . . Kramer, A. F. (2011). Self-regulatory processes and exercise adherence in older adults: Executive function and self-efficacy effects. *American Journal of Preventive Medicine, 41*, 284–290. doi: 10.1016/j.amere.2011.04.014

Meyer, C., & Taranis, L. (2011). Exercise in the eating disorders: Terms and definitions. *European Eating Disorders Review, 19,* 169–173. doi: 10.1002/erv.1121

Prochaska, J. O., Wright, J. A., & Velicer, W. F. (2008). Evaluating theories of health behavior change: A hierarchy of criteria applied to the transtheoretical model. *Applied Psychology: An International Review, 57,* 561–588. doi: 10.1111/j.1464-0597.2008.00345.x

Rethorst, C. D., Wipfli, B. M., & Landers, D. M. (2009). The antidepressive effects of exercise. A meta-analysis of randomized trials. *Sports Medicine, 39,* 491–511. doi: 0112-1642/09/0006-0491/$49.95/0

Ryan, R. M., & Deci, E. L. (2007). Active human nature: Self-determination theory and the promotion and maintenance of sport, exercise, and health. In M. S. Hagger, & N. L. D. Chatzisarantis (Eds.), *Intrinsic motivation and self-determination in exercise and sport* (pp. 1–19). Champaign, IL: Human Kinetics.

Standage, M., Gillison, F. B., Ntoumanis, N., & Treasure, D.C. (2012). A prospective cross-domain investigation of motivation across school physical education and exercise settings. *Journal of Sport & Exercise Psychology, 34,* 36–60.

Thomas, A. G., Dennis, A., Bandettini, P. A., & Johansen-Berg, H. (2012). The effects of aerobic activity on brain structure. *Frontiers in Psychology, 3,* 1–9. doi: 10.3389/fpsyg.2012.00086

Voss, M. W., Erickson, K. I., Prakash, R. S., Chaddock, L., Malkowski, E., Alves, H., . . . Kramer, A. F. (2010). Functional connectivity: A source of variance in the association between cardiorespiratory fitness and cognition? *Neuropsychologia, 48,* 1394–1406. doi: 10.1016/j.neuropsychologia.2010.01.005

Webb, T. L., & Sheeran, P. (2006). Does changing behavior intentions engender behavior change? A meta-analysis of the experimental evidence. *Psychological Bulletin, 132,* 249–268. doi: 10.1037/0033-2909.132.2.249

Wilson, P.M., Mack, D. E., & Grattan, K. P. (2008). Understanding motivation for exercise: A self-determination theory perspective. *Canadian Psychology, 49,* 250–256. doi: 10.1037/a0012762

Part II

PERFORMANCE ENHANCEMENT

Chapter 4

OPTIMAL LEVELS OF ANXIETY, INTENSITY, OR AROUSAL

Welsh golfer Ian Woosnam entered the final round of the 2001 British Open tied for the lead. He drove his first shot within six inches of the hole and scored a birdie 2 on the par-3 first hole of the final round. Prior to the start of the second hole, he was informed that he would be assessed a two-shot penalty for having 15 clubs in his bag, one over the limit. Earlier that day, he experimented with two drivers, and his caddy neglected to remove the extra club prior to the start of play. When informed of the penalty, Woosam said he "went ballistic," and later explained: "At the moment, it felt like I had been kicked in the teeth. It's hard enough to be level with the best players in the world. To give them a two-shot advantage wasn't something I was feeling too good about" (Sherman, 2001, p. C7).

Optimal levels of intensity (photo courtesy of Western Connecticut State University)

Woosnam pared the second hole but made bogeys on holes three and four. He said, "It took me a few holes to recover" (Sherman, 2001, p. C7). He did make an eagle on the sixth hole and birdies on holes 11 and 13. His final round score was 71, four strokes behind the tournament champion, David Duval. This unfortunate incident caused Woosnam to state: "I didn't really get it out of my head all the way around" (Shain, 2001, C1).

Mental skills and practices that promote and sustain optimal performance are the subjects of Chapters 4, 5, and 6. These techniques are intended for use during and immediately prior to competition, performances, and practice. However, just as physical skills must be practiced frequently and conscientiously, mental skills must be mastered during practice if they are to be useful during competition. The regular practice of mental skills also promotes better general well-being or psychological adjustment. Psychological skills that are practiced at times more distal to performances, such as goal-setting and the promotion of self-efficacy, also foster better psychological adjustment and are the subjects of Chapters 8, 9, and 10. Performance suffers if general well-being is poor, if thinking is dysfunctional, and if mental disorders are present.

STRESS AND PERFORMANCE

Performances, competitions, examinations, and evaluations are often stressful. Although there is not a universally accepted definition of stress, the **cognitive-relational theory** of Lazarus and Folkman (1984) has proven heuristic and influential:

> Psychological stress is a particular relationship between the person and the environment that is appraised by the person as taxing or exceeding his or her resources and endangering his or her well-being. (p. 19)

Stress is therefore understood to involve an environmental event and an individual's cognitive appraisal of the environmental challenge or threat (Folkman et al., 1991; Lazarus & Folkman, 1984). This appraisal process begins with an interpretation of whether the sources of stress or *stressors* impact important areas of functioning and whether one has resources adequate to cope with the magnitude of the stress (Ruiz & Hanin, 2011). There are four alternative appraisals. The event may be interpreted as a source of *harm/loss* if damage has already occurred or as a *threat* if there is potential for future damage. Alternatively, when stressors are considered to present a *challenge*, people feel joyous about ensuing struggles. Finally, environmental events are understood to be sources of *benefit* if they bring opportunities for advancement or success (Lazarus, 1999).

To illustrate, anticipated evaluations, performances, and competitions may be interpreted as threatening and sources of stress to the unprepared sportsperson. However, the same competitions might be welcomed as opportunities for advancement, recognition, and fun by the prepared sportsperson who feels equal to the challenge. When sportspersons interpret the stress of competition as a challenge, they are more likely to maintain confidence that they can control the action (Anshel, Kim, Kim, Chang, & Eom, 2001; Neil, Fletcher, Hanton, & Mellalieu, 2007). Very important competitions, such as championship games, may be sources of both high risk and opportunity, as the threat of loss and opportunities for advancement and recognition are heightened.

The cognitive appraisal of sources of stress is accompanied by emotional responses. Feelings of sadness, anger, guilt, and relief often occur with appraisals of loss. Anxiety, worry, and fear may be generated by appraisals of threat. Feelings of excitement, eagerness, and hopefulness may result from appraisals of challenge.

Application

During competition, appraisals and judgments—such as about the likely results of competition, the strength of the competition, and how one is doing—are likely to be distracting. These self-reactions and self-reflections (Bandura, 1997; Kitsantas & Zimmerman, 2002) should be saved until after competition. When attention is diverted from the moment-by-moment process of competition, performance suffers.

Stress and Coping

There are different ways of coping with situations that are seen as taxing or exceeding the resources of the person. **Coping** consists of what a person thinks or does in response to stressors. These thoughts and actions may change as situations unfold, and they may be relatively specific to stressors in specific environments (Nieuwenhuys, Vos, Pijpstra, & Bakker, 2011). There are three general categories of coping responses (Chesney, Neilands, Chambers, Taylor, and Folkman, 2006; Nicholls, Polman, & Levy, 2010). **Problem-focused coping** involves efforts to manage, change, or master the problem or challenge that is the source of stress. There are many examples of problem-focused coping, and those more relevant to the focus of this book include goal-setting, following regimens to prepare for evaluations and allowing adequate time for preparations, time management, visualization immediately prior to athletic performance, and self-talk to sustain concentration during competition. **Emotion-focused coping** concerns attempts to regulate emotional responses to the source of stress. Relevant examples of emotion-focused coping include the interpretation of stressors as challenges rather than as threats; engaging in relaxation, meditation, and physical exercises; and obtaining emotional support from others.

Social support is a form of **interpersonal coping** and consists of well-intentioned actions from other people. Examples of social support are: emotional support, esteem support, informational support, and tangible assistance (Bianco & Eklund, 2001; Chesney et al., 2006; Freeman,

Coffee, & Rees, 2011; Rees & Hardy, 2004). High-level British tennis players who received emotional and informational support maintained flow states (see Chapter 2) and avoided staleness despite the pressure of competition (Rees & Hardy, 2004). Tangible support helped to ameliorate technical problems and flatness and sustained flow despite competitive pressure.

With esteem support, athletes are more likely to feel in control of competitive situations and to interpret them as challenging rather than as threatening. With esteem support, athletes may come to believe that they have sufficient resources to manage the stress of competition. Esteem support was shown to be more influential than emotional, informational, or tangible support in determining the experience of control during competition among elite and skilled British golfers (Freeman & Rees, 2009). Esteem support improved not only their perception of control but also their scores. With more esteem support, a diverse group of British athletes recorded higher self-confidence and less "reduced sense of accomplishment" (Freeman, Coffee, & Rees, 2011, p. 68). In addition, with more informational support, athletes were less likely to devalue their sport and to register emotional and physical exhaustion.

Emotion-focused coping, such as interpreting the stress of competition as a challenge, may involve a cognitive reframing of experience. **Avoidance-focused** and **appraisal-focused coping** also focus on reformulating and reinterpreting experience (Cox & Ferguson, 1991; Giacobbi, Foore, & Weinberg, 2004; Kowalski & Crocker, 2001; Krohne, 1993). Avoidance-focused coping consists of efforts to ignore or discount the importance of stressors. It has been seen as desirable when the sources of stress are uncontrollable and transient, such as a "bad" call from a referee in sport. By ignoring the bad call, sportspersons avoid distractions and focus on aspects of performances that are under their control. Appraisal-focused coping refers to efforts to put current stressors in perspective by using logical analyses.

People differ in the degree to which they use problem- and emotion-focused coping. Problem-focused coping is also associated with the perception of control, whereas emotion-focused coping is correlated with the opposite (Anshel & Kaissidis, 1997; Daly, Brewer, Van-Raalte, Petitpas, & Sklar, 1995; Gaudreau & Blondin, 2002). In general, responses to problems or challenges that can be successfully resolved or mastered are more adaptive if they involve a greater proportion of problem-focused coping. More specifically, problem-focused coping is preferable when the sources of stress can be identified and controlled, and when it is necessary to stay "on task" for extended periods of time in order to master stressors (Roth & Cohen, 1986). Sources of stress for which there is no solution are responded to more successfully with greater proportions of emotion-focused coping. For example, major athletic injuries prompt worries about whether recovery will be complete, and athletes manage these worries by visualizing full recovery (Udry, 1997). It is clearly important to correctly size up a situation as changeable or uncontrollable and to also have effective problem- and emotion-focused coping skills.

Golfers were more satisfied with their performances and recorded better scores when they used task-oriented coping (similar to problem-focused coping; Gaudreau, Nicholls, & Levy, 2010). Mentally tough athletes are more likely to use problem-focused coping and are less likely to use emotion-focused coping strategies such as denial, humor, and behavioral disengagement (Kaiseler, Polman, & Nicholls, 2009). Mental toughness involves resistance to distractions, obstacles, adversity, and pressure, and a hearty work ethic. It also includes the capacity to "maintain concentration and motivation when things are going well to consistently achieve your goals" (Gucciardi, Gordon, & Dimmock, 2008, p. 278).

In many stressful situations, such as elite competition, all forms of coping are utilized as athletes attempt to both manage stress in the environment as well as their emotional reactions (Weston, Thelwell, Bond, & Hutchings, 2009). For example, U.S. Olympic wrestlers (Gould, Eklund, & Jackson, 1993), U.S. National Champion figure skaters (Gould, Finch, & Jackson, 1993), and U.S. professional soccer players (Kristiansen, Murphy, & Roberts, 2012) simultaneously used both problem-focused, such as conscientious practice, and emotion-focused strategies, such as relaxation techniques, for coping with the stress of competition and training. Other elite athletes and performance artists handled the stress of performances with not only avoidance-focused and appraisal-focused coping, but also with problem-focused and emotion-focused coping strategies (Poczwardowski & Conroy, 2002). The majority also remembered failing to cope sufficiently with stressors.

Coping and Mental Skills

Problem-focused, emotion-focused, and avoidance-coping strategies were all practiced by Irish adolescent international golfers. They interpreted situations and emotions positively, avoided stressful situations, and kept to pre-shot routines when coping well with the stress of competition (Nicholls, Holt, & Polman, 2005). Welsh international adolescent golfers primarily utilized problem- and avoidance-focused strategies—especially avoiding stress—to cope with the stress of practice and competition. They rated physical errors, mental errors, tough competition, and weather as the primary sources of stress (Nicholls, Holt, Polman, & James, 2005). Mental and physical errors and injuries were recognized most frequently as sources of stress in training and competition among professional rugby union players in the United Kingdom. They used problem-focused coping, such as increasing concentration and effort, emotion-focused coping, such as reinterpreting their experience in positive terms, and avoidance coping, such as withdrawing from the source of stress (Nicholls, Holt, Polman, & Bloomfield, 2006). U.S. professional soccer players engaged problem-, emotion-, and avoidance-focused coping strategies and interpersonal support to manage stress (Kristiansen et al., 2012).

Clearly, some people are more effective than others in coping with the stresses of examinations and performances. The mental skills and procedures discussed in this and ensuing chapters serve to improve coping strategies in close proximity to competitions. A key to understanding why these mental skills and techniques are helpful is that they increase awareness of phenomenology or psychological states during competition. Psychological states are more readily controlled when they are identified (Bortoli, Bertollo, Hanin, & Robazza, 2012; Ravizza, 2010). This process of identifying psychological states is referred to as **insight** or awareness, and a leitmotiv, or theme, in psychology, psychiatry, and philosophy is that awareness allows for greater control of thoughts and behavior. Corrective action can follow when problems with arousal level, preperformance preparation, attention, self-talk, concentration, and imagery are identified. The experience of control is fundamental to managing stress and anxiety.

ANXIETY, INTENSITY, OR AROUSAL LEVELS AND PERFORMANCE

The regulation of anxiety levels is related to optimal performance and doing one's best on tasks involving evaluation. The terms **anxiety, arousal,** and **intensity** have at times been used interchangeably. The practice of equating the terms has been criticized (Zaichkowsky & Baltzell, 2001; Uphill, 2008), but has continued. Some sport psychologists prefer the term intensity to anxiety or nervousness, because the latter refer to negative or dysfunctional conditions, or to **arousal,** as this latter term has been used to signify sexual responsiveness (Taylor, 1996). However, in terms of sports psychology, arousal has been defined as the activation of the body's resources for intense activity (Landers & Arent, 2010). Arousal refers to a general state of alertness, and arousal varies on a continuum from deep sleep to intense excitement (Gould & Udry, 1994). **Intensity** is defined as a condition within people that has an energizing function on the body and mind (Taylor & Wilson, 2002). It affects performance in the physiological, motor, and the cognitive domain. The physiological domain consists of the levels of heart rate, glandular and cortical activity, and blood flow. The motor area refers to behaviors such as changes in pace and coordination. The cognitive domain consists of the person's thoughts and emotions.

Descriptions of anxiety also often involve the identification of cognitive and physiological, or somatic, domains. The **cognitive** component consists of worries and apprehensions about the results of evaluations, potential failures, and personal inadequacies. The **physiological** component consists of reactions of the sympathetic nervous system, such as muscle tension, elevated heart rate, sweating, and feelings of being keyed up or on edge. Cognitive anxiety is particularly disruptive to athletic performance (Chamberlain & Hale, 2007; Jones, Swain, & Cale, 1991; Sanchez, Boschker, & Llewellyn, 2010; Smith, Bellamy, Collins, & Newell, 2001). These domains of anxiety are distinct, but intercorrelated. In other words, the experience of cognitive anxiety is more likely with the accompanying experience of physiological anxiety (Craft, Magyar, Becker, & Feltz, 2003).

Anxiety that is activated in response to specific situations, such as evaluations, has been referred to as **state anxiety,** whereas anxiety levels that remain relatively stable across situations and over time are considered **trait anxiety** (Spielberger, Gorsuch, & Lushene, 1970). It may also be important to distinguish between the cognitive and physiological activity that occurs when someone prepares for an evaluative event and the cognitive and physiological reactions to external input (Hardy, Jones, & Gould, 1996). In this context, reactions to external input are described as arousal and imply a lack of preparation for the external stimuli. Activation refers to the cognitive and physiological preparation for evaluative events. Not surprisingly, sportspersons with higher levels of trait anxiety are more likely to experience state anxiety prior to competition (Hanton, Mellalieu, & Hall, 2002; Mullen, Lane, & Hanton, 2009).

In the pages that follow, the terms arousal, intensity, and anxiety will be used in discussing the results of research. The use of these terms will follow the practices of the authors of this research, and generally reflects differences in the measurement of these constructs. For example, in some studies, questionnaires to measure anxiety were used, whereas in others questionnaires were used to assess arousal. Readers are advised to refer to the definitions of arousal, intensity, and anxiety as necessary to clarify these concepts.

Inverted-U Hypothesis

An early theory for conceptualizing the relationship between arousal and performance was the **inverted-U hypothesis** (Yerkes & Dodson, 1980). The tenet of this influential theory was that performance was poor when arousal was low. Performance improved as arousal rose to moderate levels, but then declined when arousal exceeded an optimal level (Arent & Landers, 2003; Levitt & Gutin, 1971). Therefore, a graph of this relationship between arousal and performance was curvilinear, or had the appearance of an inverted-U (Figure 4.1).

The effects of arousal on performance differ for tasks that require sustained concentration versus sustained information transfer (Humpreys & Revelle, 1984). Performance on tasks that required sustained concentration was shown to decrease as arousal increased. The human capacity for concentration is limited by the amount of information that can be sustained and processed in working or active memory at any given time. Working memory has an executive function, in that it allows for the prioritization of cognitions and behaviors and the inhibition of distracting information and stimuli (Engle, 2002; Kane, Conway, Hambrick, & Engle, 2007). Working memory is situated in the prefrontal cortex.

The average limit of working memory is seven units of information, and the active memory of most people falls within a range of five to nine units (seven plus or minus two; Kareev, 2000; Miller, 1956). As will

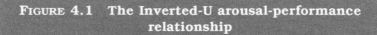

FIGURE 4.1   The Inverted-U arousal-performance
relationship

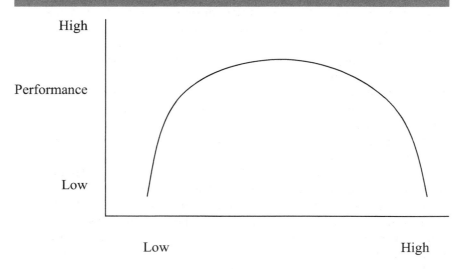

be explained later, arousal may compete with other information for the allocation of the approximate seven units of storage space in working memory and lead to poorer performances as arousal increases.

Performance on tasks that consist of sustained information transfer was shown to improve as arousal increased (Hardy et al., 1996). Sustained information transfer tasks do not require the maintenance of information in working memory or the transfer of information from working memory to long-term memory for permanent storage. Instead, they consist of simply remaining vigilant for signals and producing responses when the signals appear. Many tasks, however, do not simply involve working memory or sustained information transfer, but some combination of these mental processes. For example, a tenacious defender in basketball does not simply respond to the play of opponents. Instead, the defender draws on his or her knowledge of the tendencies of opponents and anticipates their play. The relationship between performance and arousal on these complex tasks does appear to correspond to the inverted-U, or curvilinear, graph. One possible explanation for this is that a moderate amount of arousal provokes optimal working memory capacity and sustained information transfer. Too little arousal results in performance

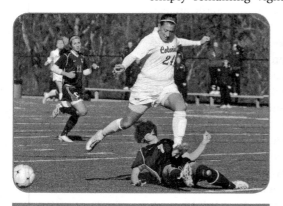

Physiological arousal and task requirements
(photo courtesy of Western Connecticut State University)

deficits on complex cognitive tasks because of deficient vigilance and preparation to respond (sustained information transfer) and too much arousal erodes performance due to competition for the allocation of working memory resources. Most generally, performance improves when arousal levels match task requirements (Landers & Arent, 2010).

Consistent with the history of science (Kuhn, 1970), there were anomalies that were not explained by the inverted-U hypothesis. Among these was the finding that the levels of intensity that were most facilitative for performance were different for different people (Landers & Arent, 2010; Whelan, Epkins, & Meyers, 1990).

Zone of Optimal Functioning

An understanding that people were different in terms of the level of arousal or anxiety associated with their best performance was integral to the current model of the **Individualized Zone of Optimal Functioning (IZOF;** Hanin, 2000a, 2000b). The IZOF was a refinement of the individual optimum zone model and the zone of optimal function model (Hanin, 1980; 1986). An individual might find his or her IZOF by regularly measuring the level of anxiety and his or her corresponding performances at various tasks. For example, athletes would assess their anxiety levels prior to or after a number of performances, and attempt to replicate the level of anxiety experienced prior to their best performances. This process enhances awareness of emotional states associated with optimal performance, as well as emotional conditions accompanying poor performances. Anxiety level could be assessed empirically by completing a questionnaire such as the State-Trait Anxiety Inventory (STAI; Spielberger, Gorsuch, & Lushene, 1970) or the sport-specific Competitive State Anxiety Inventory-2 (CSAI-2; Martens, Burton, Vealey, Bump, & Smith, 1990) or Sport Anxiety Scale (SAS; Smith, Smoll, & Schultz, 1990). Athletes may also receive counseling and guidance from sport consultants to become aware of the content and intensities of emotions associated with optimal performance (Robazza, Pellizzari, & Hanin, 2004; Woodcock, Cumming, Duda, & Sharp, 2012).

Successful sportspersons appear more capable of achieving and maintaining their desired level of physiological arousal and of experiencing this arousal as pleasant and not a source of stress (Hanin, 2000c; Kerr, 1997). Poorer performance is associated with deviations from optimal levels (Prapavessis & Grove, 1991). Optimal performance is not necessarily associated with low levels of arousal (Hanin, 2007). For example, squash players who competed in city and county teams in England, and members of the England National Under-19 squash team who won simulated tournaments experienced high but pleasant levels of arousal throughout the four matches of the tournament (Kerr & Cox, 1991).

Levels of precompetitive anxiety associated with optimal performances have been shown to vary considerably. Perhaps athletes with higher levels of trait anxiety, or who experience higher levels of anxiety not only prior to competition but also throughout their days, perform more optimally with higher levels of precompetitive anxiety (Raglin & Turner, 1996). Elite Belgian climbers were shown to climb optimally when experiencing high levels of physiological anxiety prior to competition. Their physiological anxiety was accompanied by positive affect, eagerness, and focused concentration (Sanchez, Boschker, & Llewellyn, 2010).

Elite athletes have been distinguished from non-elite athletes on the basis of performance-enhancing emotions prior to competition (Robazza & Bortoli, 2003). The IZOF model may also be less applicable to sub-elite performers than to elite athletes, as the former may be less capable of recognizing their anxiety levels associated with optimal performance (Thelwell & Maynard, 1998).

Research with collegiate female varsity softball players called into question the validity of the IZOF, and unlike previous studies concerning the IZOF, measured both cognitive and physiological anxiety (Randle & Weinberg, 1997). Subsequent research with measures of both cognitive and physiological anxiety (CSAI-2) have underlined the importance of identifying optimal preperformance states for individuals rather than groups because these states differ considerably among athletes (Annesi, 1998). Detailed discussions of how people differ in terms of their reactions to challenges and stress and of the influence of temperament and personality on performance will be presented in Chapter 15.

A further refinement of the IZOF has been to identify a range of emotions in addition to anxiety that is associated with optimal performance (Hanin, 2004, 2007; Hanin & Stambulova, 2002; Ruiz & Hanin, 2004; Woodman et al., 2010). To simplify, emotions are categorized on the bases of hedonic tone (pleasure or displeasure) and functional impact on performance (optimal or dysfunctional). The same emotion might be perceived quite differently by separate athletes. For example, anger, joy, and anxiety might be perceived as pleasant or unpleasant, depending on its functional impact on performance (Martinent & Ferrand, 2009). The athlete who performs well when angry would likely find it to be hedonically pleasing, because it serves the purpose of enhancing performance (Robazza, 2006; Ruiz & Hanin, 2011). These athletes may deliberately try to feel angry before competition (Lane, Beedie, Devonport, & Stanley, 2011). Athletes with a predominance of functional-pleasant and functional-unpleasant emotions are more capable of mobilizing and utilizing energy productively (Robazza, Bortoli, & Hanin, 2004; Robazza, Pellizzari, Bertollo, & Hanin, 2008). Conversely, with a predominance of dysfunctional-pleasant and dysfunctional-unpleasant emotions, sportspersons are more likely to be lethargic and distracted (Hanin & Stambulova, 2002).

Emotional states influence performance and performance influences emotional states. Emotional states are therefore subject to fluctuation in the course of competition. Not surprisingly, dysfunctional-unpleasant emotions follow poor athletic performances and successful performance results in optimal facilitative-pleasant emotions (Pellizzari, Bertollo, & Robazza, 2011).

Optimal performance is predicted more accurately when the IZOF is considered in conjunction with physiological measures of vigilance. Results with elite Italian air-pistol shooters indicated that more accurate shots were preceded by decelerating heart rates and levels of skin conductance—both measures of arousal (Bertollo et al., 2012).

Application

How does one arrive at optimal emotional states for competition? Emotional states are elicited with the conscientious practice of the preperformance routines reviewed in Chapter 5. Familiar routines promote efficacy and feelings of control. In the course of this practice, disruptive anxiety and arousal may be noticed and used as a cue to begin coping strategies. Methods for decreasing physiological anxiety are reviewed in Chapter 7.

Catastrophe Theory

Research with the inverted-U theory and early studies of the IZOF model have been criticized because it involved conceptualizations of anxiety or arousal as unidimensional. **Catastrophe theory** was postulated with the understanding that anxiety was a function of both physiological arousal and cognitive anxiety or worry (Gould & Udry, 1994; Hardy, 1990, 1996; Woodman & Hardy, 2001). The relationship between physiological arousal and performance was seen to be essentially the same as that outlined by the inverted-U hypothesis when cognitive anxiety was low. However, when cognitive anxiety was high, the deceleration of performance was extreme or catastrophic when physiological arousal (again, some authors refer to this construct as somatic or physiological anxiety) exceeded moderate levels (Cottyn, De Clercq, Pannier, Grombez, & Lenoir, 2006).

Catastrophe theory was later reformulated in light of processing efficiency theory (see Chapter 11; Eysenck & Calvo, 1992). Physiological arousal was understood to be a reflection of compensatory effort to concentrate and stay on task. As tasks become increasingly difficult, combined with cognitive anxiety, competitors may conclude that no amount of effort will be sufficient to produce success. If they withdraw effort, performance will plummet, and they will only reinvest effort if they are relatively assured that they can compete successfully (Hardy, Beattie, & Woodman, 2007).

The question of the ideal level of physiological arousal and cognitive anxiety associated with optimal performance has not been conclusively determined, and may also depend on the nature of the task under evaluation (Eccles et al., 2011). For example, high levels of physiological arousal have been shown to cause sharp performance decrements in closed skill sports involving fine motor control, such as bowling, golf, and pistol shooting (Gould, Petlichkoff, Simons, & Vevera, 1987; Woodman,

Albinson, & Hardy, 1997). These activities involve closed or fixed skills in that successful performance is a result of executing skills in a prescribed and relatively invariant way. Activities that involve open or generative skills require flexibility in responding to changing conditions and the behavior of competitors.

In general, performance on tasks which require complex motor responses or a great deal of thought or information processing is best under conditions of lower physiological arousal (Billing, 1980; Landers & Arent, 2010; Oxendine, 1970; 1984). These complex tasks require sustained concentration, decision making, multiple cue discrimination, fine motor control, movement fluidity, and manual dexterity. Activities performed best at high levels of physiological arousal involve power, strength, endurance, and speed. For example, high levels of physiological arousal probably facilitate Olympic weight lifting. However, attempts to categorize athletic tasks have been criticized because different activities in the same sport require different levels of complex thought and motor control, and because some athletic tasks require simple skills and complex information processing or complex skills and limited information processing (Hardy et al., 1996).

Identifying Prime Intensity

Finding **prime intensity** requires the assessment of physiological and cognitive intensity as well as the recognition that levels of intensity associated with optimal performance were different for different people. *A person* might find *their* ideal level of intensity by keeping records of their physiological responses, thoughts, and emotions, and the social conditions prior to and during competitive tasks (Taylor, 1996; Taylor & Wilson, 2002). People committed to this record-keeping become systematic in understanding themselves and their tendencies associated with optimal performance. As sportspersons become more aware of their levels of intensity, they become more capable of controlling intensity levels (Robazza & Bortoli, 1998).

The physical symptoms of overintensity are most apparent. Symptoms include muscle tension, shaking muscles, breathing difficulty, and excessive perspiration. More subtle physical symptoms consist of "butterflies" or feelings of anxiety in the stomach, fatigue, and decreased motor coordination. Overintensity may be revealed by changes in behavior' such as an increased pace or rushing during a performance, general agitation, and an increase in performance irrelevant, or "nervous," behaviors. Psychological signs of overintensity consist of negative self-talk, irrational thinking, problems with concentration, and the anticipation of poor results (Taylor, 1996; Taylor & Wilson, 2002). An example of negative self-talk is silent or audible criticism of one's performance or ability (e.g., "I'm the worst"). Irrational thinking might consist of all-or-nothing thinking (e.g., "If I can't hit a backhand, I might as well quit") or catastrophizing (e.g., "If I miss this penalty kick I'll go down in history as a choke artist").

Difficulties with overintensity are more common than problems with underintensity. The physical signs of underintensity are low levels of heart rate, respiration, adrenaline, and energy. The person may report feeling lethargic. Behavioral signs include reductions in pace and performance-relevant behaviors (e.g., routines), and increased distractibility. The psychological symptoms include apathy, loss of motivation to compete, and difficulty concentrating on tasks necessary for performance. The causes of underintensity have not been studied extensively. However, among the causes are overconfidence, or a belief that one's ability far exceeds the demands of the situation, and a lack of interest in competing (Taylor, 1996; Taylor & Wilson, 2002).

Optimal Pressure Model

The **optimal pressure model** (Costanzo, Woody, & Slater, 1992) incorporated concepts from the expectancy-value theory (Atkinson, 1978) described in Chapter 2 and the inverted-U theory (Yerkes & Dodson, 1908). However, this model emphasized situational sources of pressure rather than internal states of arousal or anxiety. Pressure was understood to derive from incentives for optimal performance. These incentives consisted of the intrinsic value of success compared to failure (the importance of the task), the situational consequences of success (social approval or disapproval), and the expectancy of success. High scores in all three of these areas were seen to contribute to pressure, and all three sources were understood to contribute essentially equal amounts of pressure. If attention is directed toward more than one source of pressure and if there are zero sources of pressure, performance suffers.

Doing one's best (at least by one's own estimate) when pressure is greatest may not be the norm. In a study of U.S. Olympic wrestlers at the 1988 Olympic Games, only 20% had their all-time best wrestling performance in Seoul (Gould, Eklund, & Jackson, 1992a). Thirty percent of the wrestlers indicated they had their worst Olympic performance in their most crucial Olympic match.

Anxiety Direction: Facilitative and Debilitative

Efficacy or confidence that one can achieve goals also has a significant influence on the **direction** of anxiety or how one interprets cognitive and physiological anxiety. People who believe that they exert control over the environment and themselves during evaluative tasks such as academic tests and athletic performances often interpret symptoms of anxiety as **facilitating** performance (Jones, 1995; Jones & Hanton, 2001; Hanton, Neil, & Mellalieu, 2008; Robazza et al., 2008; Williams, Cumming, & Balanos, 2010). For example, almost half of a sample of 91 competitive swimmers between the ages of 14 and 28 reported cognitive and physiological anxiety to be facilitative, and only 23% reported both kinds of anxiety as **debilitative** (Jones & Hanton, 1996). Sportspersons at elite, collegiate, and high school levels who believe they will achieve their goals use anxiety as a cue to become more engaged in the task, and show additional persistence and better performance when experiencing anxiety that is interpreted as facilitative (Chamberlain & Hale, 2007; Hanton & Connaughton, 2002; Ntoumanis & Jones, 1998; Wiggins, 1998).

Collegiate athletes who viewed anxiety as facilitative viewed their precompetitive emotional states more positively than did their counterparts who considered anxiety to be debilitative (Mellalieu, Hanton, & Jones, 2003). Athletes with facilitative anxiety were more likely to also be excited, focused, motivated, and eager. Heightened levels of physiological and cognitive anxiety are also more likely to be interpreted as facilitative with sports that call for explosive action, such as rugby (Mellalieu, Hanton, & O'Brien, 2004; Hanton, Jones, & Mullen, 2000).

Elite athletes with facilitative anxiety use imagery, self-talk, and goal-setting skills to counteract memories of mistakes and failure. Elite female hockey players remembered poor plays, but corrected mistakes in their mental imagery. They counteracted doubts and worries with positive self-talk and rationalizations, such as interpreting anxiety to be a sign of excitement (Thomas, Hanton, & Maynard, 2007). Jones and Hanton (1996) reasoned that swimmers might have interpreted anxiety as facilitative because they had previously experienced success while anxious. Perhaps this successful experience helps to explain why only 16% of a group of elite cricket players (Jones & Swain, 1995) and 21% of highly advanced tennis players (Perry & Williams, 1998) considered signs of cognitive and physiological trait anxiety to be debilitative.

Success enables sportspersons to interpret signs of anxiety as facilitative. Success does not eradicate the experience of anxiety. For example, the cognitive and physiological anxiety levels experienced by elite and non-elite swimmers (Jones, Hanton, & Swain, 1994); national and club rugby union, soccer, and field hockey players (Hanton, Thomas, & Maynard, 2004); and gymnasts (Jones, Swain, & Hardy, 1993) were of similar intensities. The elite (Jones et al., 1994; Jones et al., 1993) and national-level athletes (Hanton et al., 2004) were more likely to interpret this anxiety as facilitative. Professional golfers and rugby players with more experience were also more likely to interpret anxiety as facilitative (McKay, Selig, Carlson, & Morris, 1996; Mellalieu et al., 2004).

Sportspersons with lower levels of trait anxiety are also more likely to interpret competitive anxiety as facilitative than those with higher levels of trait anxiety (Mullen et al., 2009). For example, state anxiety prior to tournaments was experienced as more facilitative and less intense among competitive golfers with lower levels of trait anxiety (Jones, Smith, & Holmes, 2004). Collegiate footballers or soccer players who experienced trait anxiety that disrupted concentration were more likely to report state anxiety, or anxiety within one hour of matches, to be debilitative (Hanton et al., 2002).

As discussed in Chapter 2, some types of goals are more likely than others to facilitate performance. Competitive swimmers did not exclusively identify outcome goals for meets (Jones & Hanton, 1996). With outcome goals, performance is measured in relation to competitors. An example of an outcome goal would be to finish first in a race. Outcome goals were considered to engender debilitative anxiety because the swimmer had no control over the performance of competitors. Most of the swimmers chose a combination of goals that included performance (complete a race under a certain time) and process (attention to the technical elements of the swim) goals (24%) or outcome, performance, and process goals (49%).

Even the biochemical substrates of anxiety are influenced by the manner in which preperformance anxiety is interpreted. The catecholamine, cortisol, and testosterone levels of elite male marathon canoeists were measured prior to races for selection to the world championships (Eubank, Collins, Lovell, Dorling, & Talbot, 1997). Catecholamine, cortisol, and testosterone levels were measured 24, 2, and 1 hours prior to the start of the races. Elevations in testosterone and catecholamines have been associated with adaptive responses to challenges, and elevated cortisol has been associated with the disruptive effects of stress. Testosterone levels climbed for canoeists who believed that anxiety prior to races facilitated performance and fell for canoeists that interpreted their anxiety before races as debilitating. Cortisol levels increased for the debilitatory and facilitatory groups one hour prior to races, but the levels were much lower for the facilitatory group. The catecholamines consisted of epinephrine, norepinephrine, and dopamine, and they increased sharply for the facilitatory group, and remained steady or moved lower for the debilitatory group. The catecholamines were understood to activate the body to deal with the challenge of competition.

Hanton and Jones (1999a) went on to study how elite male swimmers developed their capacity to interpret cognitive and physiological anxiety as facilitative. Early in their competitive careers, these swimmers experienced cognitive and physiological symptoms of anxiety to be debilitative. For example, some were preoccupied with worry and even vomited before races. They came to take the perspective that anxiety could facilitate performance as a result of mentoring by parents, coaches, and more experienced swimmers. They were mentored to accept anxiety as a natural and necessary reaction to competition and evaluation, and to view anxiety as an aid to optimal performance. These swimmers came to welcome anxiety prior to competition and to try to use it to boost performance and preperformance preparation.

Perhaps successful athletes also learn to moderate the intensity of their anxiety. Elite and sub-elite Swedish adolescent athletes in cross country and swimming were more likely to rate cognitive anxiety as facilitative when its intensity was low (Lundqvist, Kentta, & Raglin, 2011).

> ### Novak Djokovic: "I want to be at one with nature."
>
> The Botanical Gardens in Melbourne, Australia, are situated across the Yarra River from the Ron Laver Arena where the Australian Open is contested. Visitors to this almost inexpressibly beautiful public garden were surprised to find Novak Djokovic stretching, jogging, or simply meditating on mornings during the Australian Open. Djokovic reasoned that he could arrive at optimal psychological states in the lush and serene garden.
>
> In ascending to the number one ranking in men's tennis, Djokovic learned to play "mentally lighter." In doing so, he plays with a calm serenity, knowing that he can impose his will on opponents and matches. He "adjusts the volume," or his level of arousal, during matches, and makes order out of the chaos of emotions, stress, and crowd reactions during matches.
>
> Djokovic won his third consecutive Australian Open title in 2013. He defeated Andy Murray, 6-7 (2), 7-6 (3), 6-3, 6-2 (Wertheim, 2013).

Coaches and mentors facilitate this process of learning from experience when they help athletes to reflect upon states of anxiety and results of competition. In this process, athletes not only learn to interpret anxiety as facilitative, but also focus on successful skill execution regardless of anxiety states. This knowledge is recalled in preparation for future competition (Hanton, Cropley, & Lee, 2009).

Not all elite athletes receive the benefits of nurturing relationships with coaches, mentors, and other athletes. These athletes may require focused consultations from sport psychologists to alleviate debilitative anxiety (Hanton, Thomas, & Mellalieu, 2009). This was in evidence in a group of female hockey players in the English Hockey League National Premier League. They responded favorably to training in self-talk, mental imagery, rationalization and restructuring, and goal setting. Their experience of facilitative anxiety and self-confidence increased, and their play in matches improved (Thomas, Maynard, & Hanton, 2007).

Facilitative and Debilitative Anxiety and Coping

Anxiety has been described as facilitative or debilitative, depending on its effects on behavior. Those with **facilitative anxiety** may also cope more effectively with stressors. For example, college students with facilitative anxiety about impending exams studied more effectively and scored better marks (Raffety, Smith, & Ptacek, 1997). They engaged in problem-focused coping, as they began studying well in advance, and sought help from others when help was needed. Collegiate students with debilitative test anxiety were more likely to show avoidant coping, or methods of distracting themselves from the stressor of the test and their anxiety. Students with **debilitative anxiety** were also beset with more cognitive anxiety and worries that distracted them from effective study. Students with debilitative and facilitative anxiety experienced physiological anxiety or "butterflies" in their stomachs prior to exams. However, those with facilitative anxiety "shook" these butterflies during exams, whereas students with debilitative anxiety did not. With facilitative anxiety, students were also not beset by cognitive anxiety or worry.

Anxiety, Intensity, or Arousal Levels and Performance

The question of the ideal level of physiological and cognitive anxiety associated with optimal performance has not been conclusively determined, and may be dependent not only on the differences between people, but on the nature of the task under evaluation. For example, high levels of somatic anxiety have been shown to cause performance decrements on complex tasks that require sustained concentration, decision making, multiple cue discrimination, fine motor control, movement fluidity, and manual dexterity. Clearly there are differences in the manner in which people interpret the signs of anxiety, and athletes may learn to interpret signs of anxiety as facilitative. However, not everyone interprets signs of anxiety as facilitative, especially when one doubts their efficacy to perform successfully (Lundqvist et al., 2011; Bandura, 1997). Even some children and adolescents base judgments about their competence in sports on pregame anxiety. Higher levels of anxiety in these children and adolescents were associated with lower estimates of their sports competence (Weiss, Ebbeck, & Horn, 1997). Finally, the question of when anxiety is experienced is important. The experience of anxiety before evaluations and competitions may facilitate performance if it motivates coping strategies that better prepare a person for the evaluation. However, better results have been associated with decreased anxiety prior to and during evaluations (Giacobbi & Weinberg, 2000) or with the ability to sustain concentration and task-absorption during competitions or evaluations despite some measure of anxiety.

SUMMARY AND APPLICATION

A considerable amount of research has been devoted to the relationship between arousal, intensity, or anxiety levels and performance. Attempts to find universal levels of arousal and anxiety that are most facilitative of performance have not been successful. This appears to be a result of the differences between people in terms of the levels of arousal or intensity that facilitate their best performances. Also, different levels of anxiety and arousal facilitate better performance on different tasks. High levels of physiological anxiety and arousal appear to be more disruptive to performance on tasks which require sustained concentration, complex motor responses, or a great deal of thought or information processing. Higher levels of anxiety may also be more facilitative during preparations for performances versus the actual performance. Preperformance anxiety is adaptive to the degree that it motivates the appropriate preparation for the performance or evaluation.

Recent research has emphasized the cognitive and physiological components of anxiety. Heightened physiological anxiety need not disrupt performance so long as a performer interprets it as a factor to facilitate performance. However, not all people are equally intrepid, and the self-efficacy of some people is diminished by the experience of their physiological anxiety. Techniques for gaining control over these physiological responses will be discussed in Chapter 7. These techniques are useful not only for controlling physiological responses proximate to evaluations and competitions, but also for enhancing well-being.

Key Terms

Cognitive-relational theory of stress   82

Coping   83

Problem-focused coping   83

Emotion-focused coping   83

Interpersonal coping   83

Avoidance-focused coping   84

Appraisal-focused coping   84

Insight   86

Arousal   86

Intensity   86

Cognitive and physiological anxiety   86

State anxiety   87

Inverted-U hypothesis   87

Individualized Zone of Optimal Functioning (IZOF)   89

Catastrophe theory   91

Prime intensity   92

Optimal pressure model   93

Anxiety Direction: Facilitative and debilitative anxiety   93

Discussion Questions

Q1. Explain the cognitive-relational theory of stress.

Q2. What are the four ways that stressors may be appraised or interpreted?

Q3. Review forms of coping: Problem-focused, emotion-focused, interpersonal, avoidance-focused, and appraisal-focused.

Q4. How is insight related to the deployment of mental skills and copying?

Q5. Differentiate anxiety, arousal, and intensity.

Q6. Describe cognitive and physiological anxiety.

Q7. Differentiate state and trait anxiety.

Q8. What is the relationship between arousal and performance according to the inverted-U hypothesis?

Q9. What tasks are performed better at moderate and lower levels of arousal?

Q10. What tasks benefit from increased arousal?

Q11. How does an individual determine the Individualized Zone of Optimal Functioning (IZOF) for optimal performance?

Q12. Explain the impact of hedonic tone and functional impact of emotions on performance.

Q13. Differentiate catastrophe theory from the inverted-U theory and IZOF.

Q14. How does one determine prime intensity for performance?

Q15. Review of optimal pressure model.

Q16. Differentiate facilitative and debilitative anxiety.

Q17. How is facilitative anxiety related to imagery, self-talk, and goal setting?

Q18. How is facilitative anxiety developed?

Q19. Is coping related to facilitative and debilitative anxiety?

Suggested Readings

Bortoli, L., Bertollo, M., Hanin, Y., & Robazza, C. (2012). Striving for excellence: A multi-action plan intervention model for shooters. *Psychology of Sport and Exercise, 13*, 693–701. doi: 10.1016/j.psychsport.2012.04.006

Freeman, P., Coffee, P., & Rees, T. (2011). The PASS-Q: The Perceived Available Support in Sport Questionnaire. *Journal of Sport & Exercise Psychology, 33*, 54–74.

Freeman, P., & Rees, T. (2009). How does perceived support lead to better performance? An examination of potential mechanisms. *Journal of Applied Sport Psychology, 21*, 429–441.

Gaudreau, Nicholls, A., & Levy A. R. (2010). The ups and downs of coping and sport achievement: An episodic process analysis of within-person associations. *Journal of Sport & Exercise Psychology, 32*, 298–311.

Gucciardi, D. F., Gordon, S., & Dimmock, J. A. (2008). Towards an understanding of mental toughness in Australian football. *Journal of Applied Sport Psychology, 20*, 261–281.

Hanin, Y. L. (2007). Emotions in sport: Current issues and perspectives. In G. Tenenbaum & R. C. Eklund (Eds.), *Handbook of sport psychology* (3rd ed., pp. 31–58), New York, NY: Wiley.

Hanton, S., Cropley, B., & Lee, S. (2009). Reflective practice, experience, and the interpretation of anxiety symptoms. *Journal of Sports Sciences, 27*, 517–533. doi: 10.1080/02640410802668668

Jones, G., & Hanton, S. (1996). Interpretation of competitive anxiety symptoms and goal attainment expectancies. *Journal of Sport and Exercise Psychology, 18*, 144–157.

Kaiseler, M., Polman, R., & Nicholls, A. (2009). Mental toughness, stress, stress appraisal, coping and coping effectiveness in sport. *Personality and Individual Differences, 47*, 728–733. doi: 10.1016/j.paid.2009.06.012

Kristiansen, E., Murphy, D., & Roberts, G. C. (2012). Organizational stress and coping in U.S. professional soccer. *Journal of Applied Sport Psychology, 23*, 207–233. doi: 10.1080/10413200.2011.614319

Landers, D. M., & Arent, S. M. (2010). Arousal-performance relationships. In J. M. Williams (Ed.), *Applied sport psychology: Personal growth to peak performance* (6th ed., pp. 221–246). New York, NY: McGraw-Hill.

Lazarus, R. S. (2000). Cognitive-motivational-relational theory of emotion. In Y. L. Hanin (Ed.), *Emotions in sport* (pp. 39–63). Champaign, IL: Human Kinetics.

Lundqvist, C., Kentta, G., & Raglin, J. S. (2011). Directional anxiety responses in elite and sub-elite young athletes: Intensity of anxiety symptoms matter. *Scandinavian Journal of Medicine & Science in Sports, 21*, 853–862. doi: 10.1111/j.1600-0838.2010.01102.x

Mullen, R., Lane, A., & Hanton, S. (2009). Anxiety symptom interpretation in high-anxious, defensive high-anxious, low-anxious and repressor sport performers. *Anxiety, Stress & Coping, 22*, 91–100. doi: 10.1080/10615800802203769

Nicholls, A. R., Polman, R., & Levy, A. R. (2010). Coping self-efficacy, precompetitive anxiety, and subjective performance among athletes. *European Journal of Sport Science, 10*, 97–102. doi: 10.1080/17461390903271592

Ravizza, K. (2010). Increasing awareness for sport performance. In J. M. Williams (Ed.), *Applied sport psychology: Personal growth to peak performance* (6th ed., pp. 189–200). New York, NY: McGraw-Hill.

Ruiz, M. C., & Hanin, Y. L. (2011). Perceived impact of anger on performance of skilled karate athletes. *Psychology of Sport and Exercise, 12*, 242–249. doi: 10.1016/j.psychsport.2011.01.005

Weston, N. J. V., Thelwell, R. C., Bond, D., & Hutchings, N. V. (2009). Stress and coping in single-handed round-the-world ocean sailing. *Journal of Applied Sport Psychology, 21*, 460–470.

Williams, S. E., Cumming, J., & Balanos, G. M. (2010). The use of imagery to manipulate challenge and threat appraisal states in athletes. *Journal of Sport & Exercise Psychology, 32*, 339–358.

Yerkes, R. M., & Dodson, J. D. (1908). The relation of strength of stimulus to rapidity of habit formation. *Journal of Comparative Neurology of Psychology, 18*, 459–482.

Chapter 5

PREPERFORMANCE ROUTINES

Kenya, an East African country of 41 million, "has produced more great runners (short- and long-distance) than just about any other nation on Earth" (Ghosh, 2012). For example, since 1988, 20 of the 25 male winners of the Boston Marathon have been Kenyans. Surprisingly, a Kenyan has not won an Olympic gold medal in the 10,000 meters since 1968.

Among the factors that contribute to Kenyan running eminence are training regimens at an altitude of 8,000 feet. Living and running at altitude results in the production of more red blood cells as the body adapts to less inspired oxygen pressure. With more red blood cells, more oxygen can be delivered to muscles to sustain exertion.

The three runners that represented Kenya in the 10,000 meter run at the 2012 Olympic Games in London were selected at a race in Eugene, Oregon. Atmospheric conditions in Eugene are similar to those in London, and Kenyan Olympic officials wanted to identify the runners most likely to perform well at sea level and in damp weather (Pilon, 2012a, 2012b).

Kenya realized 11 medals (two gold, four silver, and five bronze) in London; the most of any African country. Kenyan women won silver and bronze medals in the 10,000 meters.

Mental preparation

PSYCHOLOGICAL OR MENTAL SKILLS TRAINING

The development of sophisticated **preperformance routines** is an important aspect of psychological or mental skills training. As stated in Chapter 4, mental training also consists of instruction in goal setting, anxiety and arousal control, self-talk, concentration, and mental imagery and mental practice. The regular practice and use of these mental skills are directly related to the reduction of negative internal states such as anxiety and the enhancement of positive states such as confidence (Bois, Sarrazin, Southon, & Boiche, 2009; Jackson, 1995; Jackson & Csikszentmihalyi, 1999 ; Moore, 2009; Sheard & Golby, 2006; Thomas & Over, 1994). Elite athletes routinely practice these skills and use them to cope with adversity in the course of competitions (Dale, 2000; Hall, 2001). Less experienced athletes are not as conscientious in practicing mental skills (Hayslip, Petrie, MacIntire, & Jones, 2010; Neil, Mellalieu, & Hanton, 2006). Even experienced athletes utilize mental skills less frequently in away as opposed to home venues (Neil, Mellalieu, & Hanton, 2006).

Athletes who routinely focus more on their psychological processes and the emotional states of others are more likely to practice mental skills (Lane, Thelwell, Lowther, & Devonport, 2009). With practice, mental skills, like physical skills, can be automated so that their practice is less effortful (Brefczynski-Lewis, Lutz, Schaefer, Levinson, & Davidson, 2007).

Like physical practice, mental practice is effective if practiced on a regular and perhaps daily basis (Weinberg & Williams, 2010). Simply becoming casually aware of these techniques does not result in appreciable gains in performance (Munroe-Chandler, Hall, Fishburne, Murphy, & Hall, 2012; Wakefield & Smith, 2009). Sportspersons may be much more patient in devoting the time and attention necessary for physical skills than these mental skills (Hardy, Roberts, Thomas, & Murphy, 2010), and in employing mental skills in competition rather than practice (Frey, Laguna, & Ravizza, 2003; Hall et al., 2009). However, the neglect of mental skills training may inhibit the development of athletic potential. For example, Canadian Olympians and world champions recognized that their ascendancy as elite athletes was delayed by as much as four years because the development of their mental skills lagged behind physical skill development (Orlick & Partington, 1988).

Despite the understanding that the neglect of mental skill practice retards the development of athleticism, it may be difficult to encourage people who are not self-motivated to regularly practice mental skills. Attrition rates from psychological skills training programs are approximately 20% to 25% (Shambrook & Bull, 1999).

Intercollegiate athletes were also shown to infrequently practice mental skills after a four-week training program (Bull, 1991). In the eight weeks that followed the training, the average amount of time devoted to practicing mental skills was only 17 minutes per week. Some athletes practiced the mental skills far more than others, and the key factor in determining the frequency and duration of practice was self-motivation or commitment to persevere.

Athletes neglect practicing mental skills because they are not convinced of their efficacy. They also cite a lack of time, disruptions in their home environments, and laziness as reasons for not practicing mental skills (Thelwell, 2008). Sportspersons without high levels of self-motivation may benefit from individualized training to boost their motivation and mental skills techniques.

Athletes may also be more motivated to learn and practice different mental skills. For example, Bull (1991) found that 38.2% of the collegiate athletes rated relaxation training, 29.4% rated visualization, 11.8% rated concentration, and 11.8% rated positive thinking to be the most valuable elements of their mental skills training. Female intercollegiate swimmers frequently utilized goal setting, positive self-talk, and visualization, whereas most "never" used autogenic training, meditation, or Transcendental Meditation (Thiese & Huddleston, 1999).

Athletes may be less compliant with mental as compared to physical training because their primary concern is to advance their physical skills. Some athletes may shy away from mental skills training provided by psychologists because they associate psychological services with psychopathology. Traditionally, young athletes have been seen as less willing to independently practice mental skills. However, recent evidence contradicts this view, as adolescents training in U.S. Luge Development Camps independently practiced mental skills eight times weekly (Copeland, Bonnell, Reider, & Burton, 2009). Young athletes benefit substantially from the practice of mental skills (Copeland et al., 2009; Fournier, Calmels, Durand-Bush, & Salmela, 2005; Mamassis & Doganis, 2004; Sheard & Golby, 2006).

The idea of devoting large blocks of time to mental training may be unappealing, but brief periods devoted to mentally organizing actions necessary for successful performance, and periods of mental practice interspersed with physical practice, can be beneficial (Callow, Roberts, & Fawkes, 2006; Shambrook & Bull, 1999). Regular mental practice may also enhance motivation for physical practice.

Mental practice is facilitated by the maintenance of daily logs, and some people have to practice this journaling for some time before they experience benefits. The most successful Canadian Olympian athletes refined their mental skills by keeping logs of the mental factors associated with successful and disappointing competitions (Orlick & Partington, 1988).

Innovative instruction also promotes the practice of mental skills (Horn, Gilbert, Gilbert, & Lewis, 2011). For example, the Psychological UNIFORM program provides mental skills instruction in a Game Plan Format (Gilbert, Gilbert, Loney, Wahl, & Michel, 2006). Student-athletes are divided into teams and given *conditioning* (applied activities and discussion about mental skills), *practice* (homework), *games* (quizzes), *statistics* (individual and team quiz scores), *films, and playbooks* (journal entries about the skills).

The practice of mental skills need not be distasteful. Highly motivated athletes devise strategies for improving performance even without formal mental skills training. Female and male members of the Italian national pentathlete teams developed mental skills strategies on the basis of their own intuition. They simulated competition during training and used visualization with both internal and external perspectives. These sportspersons kept records of arousal states associated with optimal performance and attempted to replicate these states prior to competition. They appeared to appreciate the benefit of facilitative anxiety: "I try to relax myself as much as possible and at the same time to remain concentrated and not lose the tension, because tension when controlled is productive, stimulating" (Bertollo, Saltarelli, & Robazza, 2009, pp. 248–249). All the athletes had well-developed precompetitive routines.

Coaches acknowledge the importance of mental skills but do not teach them to athletes in a systematic way (Hardy, Roberts, Thomas, & Murphy, 2010). Elite coaches showed limited interest in learning to teach mental skills such as imagery to their athletes. Coaches may respond more favorably to a needs-based approach to training, in which sport psychologists provide training in the topics of greatest interest to coaches (Callow, Roberts, Bringer, & Langan, 2010).

In summary, athletes who have the strongest desire to succeed in their sport and who believe that the psychological skill training will enable them to reach their goals are most likely to practice these skills. Individual consultations with sport psychologists sometimes help less-motivated athletes discern the benefits of, and become more compliant with, the practice of mental skills. For athletes who are not self-motivated, regular supervised practice of mental skills may be as necessary as the supervision of their physical training and nutritional regimen. With regular practice, mental skills techniques often result in improved performance, and when athletes see these benefits, they are more likely to practice the mental skills.

PREPERFORMANCE ROUTINES

Preperformance routines consist of the preparations taken for competition. They facilitate experiences of familiarity, order, consistency, and control (Boutcher & Crews, 1987; Vealey, 2009). Preperformance routines probably should include all aspects that may influence performance, such as sleep, diet, physical and mental practice and preparation, the inspection and preparation of equipment, travel to the venue, mental imagery, and the establishment of prime intensity (Robson-Ansley, Gleeson, & Ansley, 2009; Scott, McNaughton, & Polman, 2006; Stambulova, Stambulov, & Johnson, 2012). Elite athletes practice elaborate preperformance routines that may involve the use of mental imagery, self-talk, goal setting, managing media relations, and the experience of consistent and familiar levels of cognitive and physiological anxiety (Gould, 1999; Gould, Flett, & Bean, 2009; Hanton & Jones, 1999b; Kristiansen, Halvari, & Roberts, 2011; Kristiansen, Hanstad, & Roberts, 2011; Orlick & Partington, 1988; Thelwell & Maynard, 2002). Mental imagery and self-talk will be discussed in Chapter 6, and goal setting will be reviewed in Chapter 8. Pre-evaluation routines may extend up to the time of a performance (Taylor, 1996). Some authors limit the definition of preperformance routines to just the sequence of behaviors that precede a discrete closed skill such as shooting a free-throw shot in basketball (Lidor, 2007).

Application

The concept of facilitative anxiety was introduced in Chapter 3. Facilitative anxiety motivates preperformance preparation well in advance of actual performances. Well-prepared athletes are less likely to experience anxiety immediately prior to competition. Last minute preparations are more likely to be fraught with anxiety and to be incomplete and inconsistent. Important steps in preperformance preparation and even equipment are less likely to be forgotten if written outlines are followed.

Athletes may even prepare for anticipated pain associated with competition or oxygen debt. Athletes who sustain self-efficacy during the experience of pain (such as "I can do it") have greater pain tolerance (Birrer & Morgan, 2010). Efficacy beliefs are also associated with the release of endogenous opioids that inhibit the experience of pain (Motl, Gliottoni, & Scott, 2007).

Many athletes listen to their favorite music and watch motivational videos prior to practice and competition (Karageorghis, 2008; Tracey, 2011). For example, elite British tennis players frequently listened to music and reported that that regulated preperformance moods. The young tennis athletes often experienced negative emotional states, and music was used to psych up, relax, or dissociate from stressors (Bishop, Karageorghis, & Loizou, 2007).

Even body language prior to competition is important. Sportspersons are likely to believe that their chances of success are greater when opponents represent a lack of confidence by hanging their heads and chins downward and hunching their shoulders. When opponents emanate confidence, sportspersons are less confident of success (Greenlees, Buscombe, Thelwell, Holder, & Rimmer, 2005; Jones & Harwood, 2008). Sportspersons who fix their gaze upon opponents or targets for longer durations are also estimated to be more assertive, confident, and efficacious (Greenlees, Leyland, Thelwell, & Filby, 2008).

Weakens Your Legs?

In preparing for the Olympic Games in approximately 444 B.C., Ikkos of Tarentum ate large quantities of wild boar, goat meat, and cheese, coated his body with olive oil, and abstained from sex. He won the Olympic Pentathlon, and the tradition of abstaining from sex prior to athletic competition began (Spencer, 2006). U. S. Olympic triathlete Victor Plata abstained from sex for 233 days prior to the 2004 Olympic Games in

Athens. Lightweight boxing champion Diego Corrales goes without sex for 11 weeks prior to fights. He reasoned, "If you have sex, you're in a very good mood. That's a problem when you get in a ring" (Spencer, 2006, A1). Professional football teams often lodge teams in hotels even before home games to sequester players from wives or partners. Shaun Smith, defensive tackle for the Cincinnati Bengals, noted, "You don't want to feel relaxed, weak and laid back before a football game. You want to be jumpy and excited" (Spencer, A1). Smith's pregame routine includes drinking virgin daiquiris and praying with his mother and wife on the phone from his hotel room.

Athletes abstain from sex prior to competition because they believe that sexual satisfaction will decrease their aggressiveness and cause distraction and fatigue. However, the fatiguing effects of heterosexual coitus among married couples is minimal and results in the expenditure of only 25 to 50 calories, or "the energy equivalent of walking up two flights of stairs" (McGlone & Shrier, 2000). Theories that sexual satisfaction and ejaculation drains testosterone, the hormone associated not only with sex drive but also muscle development and aggression, are also likely to be false. Indeed, testosterone levels may increase for both men and women who regularly experience sex.

Ultimately, whether performance is disrupted by sexual activity is likely to depend on whether it has been a part of the sportsperson's routine throughout their training and preparation. Disruptions to routines generally impair performance.

An early arrival at athletic venues not only allows for mental and physical preparation (Blumenstein & Lidor, 2008), but also facilitates the emergence of pre-evaluative, debilitative anxiety. This anxiety can be recognized and alleviated prior to the actual performance. For example, university athletes in England and Wales rated physical and psychological preparation as more important than other factors such as the strength of competition and expectations for winning in determining cognitive anxiety 30 minutes prior to competitions (Jones, Swain, & Cale, 1991). Female university athletes who believed they were well-prepared were more self-confident prior to competition.

Preperformance routines sometimes involve written algorithms or specific steps or procedures that are to be accomplished in a certain order. With written preperformance routines, it is less likely that key aspects will be overlooked. However, routines should allow for some degree of flexibility, otherwise a sportsperson may become anxious if their routine is interrupted (Gould et al., 2009). For example, it may be difficult to adhere to a routine of going to sleep at 10 P.M. on nights before competitions. Sleep may be interrupted by anxiety or by external events, such as travel to a venue.

Flexibility is also necessary when the time of competition is not precisely controlled. For example, the start of match may be delayed because of weather or the duration of preceding matches. In these circumstances, it may be necessary to manage frustration, boredom, and anxiety during the delay, and to reinvigorate preperformance routines after the delay (Mellalieu, Neil, Hanton, & Fletcher, 2009).

Preperformance routines occur prior to the execution of self-paced skills within athletic competitions. When the sequence of these behaviors is consistent, better performance is likely (Boutcher & Crews, 1987; Lidor & Mayan, 2005). For example, prior to kicking "conversions" and penalty kicks, the most prolific kicker in professional rugby, Neil Jenkins, consistently took four steps back from the ball and two steps to the left of the ball. However, there was variability in the amount of time spent concentrating prior to kicks, as he concentrated for longer durations prior to more difficult kicks (Jackson & Baker, 2001). Players in the 1999 World Rugby Cup also took longer to prepare for the most difficult kicks (Jackson, 2003). More complex and sustained visualization may be necessary prior to difficult kicks or shots, and performers may also need more time to regain focus if they are distracted by internal stimuli, such as negative self-talk or excessive physiological anxiety, or by external stimuli, such as crowd noise.

Application

In the seconds between the completion of preperformance preparation and the initiation of a self-paced skill, it is essential that distractions are screened out of working memory. The information from the preperformance routine (whether visual or verbal) is the basis for forming the optimal sport skill. If this schema is displaced by distractions, the cognitive guide for the sport skill will be missing. Information in visual working memory is particularly transient and vulnerable to displacement by cognitive interference.

For example, golfers extract information about the direction and placement of shots from their visual fixation on targets. Ideally, this is a quiet eye period that consists of a fixation on the target for a sufficient period of time to extract the necessary information about direction and distance. If distractions enter the working memory in the seconds between the last fixation and the swing, the information about direction and distance will be compromised or lost.

When preperformance routines are enacted prior to initiating self-paced sport skills, athletes visualize a plan of action, engage in self-talk, use key words, and practice relaxation strategies. Golfers especially rely on visualization (Cotterill, Sanders, & Collins, 2010). Concentration is focused to screen out internal and external distractions, such as ruminations about poor play and worries about the outcome of competition. With consistent routines, sportspersons are more capable of staying in the present moment, and feelings of efficacy and control are increased (Boutcher, 1992; Lidor, 2007). Preperformance motor routines also serve to select the appropriate motor skill—for example, the proper kick for penalty kicks in rugby—and inhibit excessive attention to the mechanics of automatic motor skills (see the discussion below). Visualization also contributes to the representation of closed skills in long-term memory (Velentzas, Heinen, & Schack, 2011).

Novak Djokovic

Novak Djokovic's CVAC Pod

Since the 2010 U.S. Tennis Open, Novak Djokovic has attempted to improve his fitness and recovery by utilizing the CVAC Systems pressure chamber. The CVAC pod is an egg-shaped, bobsled-sized (7 feet long—3 feet wide), enclosed pressure chamber. With computerized-assisted technology, it boosts the production of oxygen-rich red blood cells and compresses muscles to speed the removal of lactic acid. With greater availability of oxygen, muscular fatigue is decreased. Lactic acid is a byproduct of muscular fatigue and decreases muscular productivity. While blood doping is banned by most governing sports agencies, as well as the U.S. Tennis Association, the CVAC pod is not.

During that year, he also stopped eating food with gluten, after his nutritionist discovered he was allergic to the protein found in common flours. He lost several pounds and improved his stamina (Karp, 2011). Djokovic also improved his serve, forehand, and fitness. Since 2011, he has won five Grand Slam tournaments: the Australian Open three times, Wimbledon, and the U.S. Open. He also won the Australian Open in 2008.

Preperformance Preparation at the Site of Competition

Gaining as much experience as possible with the actual competition venues serves to decrease anxiety and increase self-efficacy. The more similar the experience is to the conditions under which the performance will occur, or to actual "game conditions," the more useful it is in diminishing unfamiliarity. Therefore, actual performances, competitions, or evaluations in the same setting are most effective in diminishing unfamiliarity (Gould et al., 2009; Menzel & Carrell, 1994). For example, elite divers cited a lack of experience in managing high levels of pressure, such as the pressure to qualify for national teams, as responsible for their less-successful performances (Highlen & Bennett, 1983).

Preparing for the Weather

From a weather station overlooking the Olympic ski slopes, a team of meteorologists and snow experts provided weather reports at 10-minute intervals during the 2006 Olympic Games in Turin, Italy (Kahn, 2006). The cost for this weather service was an estimated minimum $4.2 million dollars, and yet most Olympics teams used weather information from their own meteorologists because they did not trust the accuracy of the local weather station. In sports such as alpine skiing, the air and snow temperatures and humidity levels determine the composition of the waxes that are applied to skis. The optimal wax allows for reduced friction and faster times. In cross-country skiing, wax technicians often apply a wax that provides traction when skiers kick or propel themselves forward, and a second wax to help skiers glide. Weather conditions influence the delicate mix of the two waxes. Prior to the 2002 Winter Games in Salt Lake City, UT, the Norwegian team requested samples of snow from different months in the year. The snow was then analyzed in labs in Oslo.

Practice under conditions that approximate game conditions results in the reduction of novelty and provides experience in ignoring distractions. These "dress rehearsals" may include simulations of loud and distracting behaviors by spectators and opponents, and practice under the most adverse conditions (Schmid & Peper, 1993). This is referred to as **simulation training**, and has been shown to be a high priority for Olympic athletes (Orlick & Partington, 1988). Simulation training may begin with scheduling practice at the time of the actual competition. Simulation training may involve recreating aspects of competitions which have disrupted an athlete's concentration, such as a bad line call in tennis (Hardy et al., 1996).

Preparing for the Worst

The Giro d'Italia bicycle race consists of 21 stages or individual races over a 23-day period. Most of the stages are contested in Italy, and the winner is often determined by who has the most skill and courage in descending mountains at speeds of 60 miles (96.56 kilometers) per hour. Among the skills required are exceptional hand-eye coordination and riding technique, and a "soft focus" on the whole road and potential hazards. Mistakes can result in more than just a nasty fall. Belgian cyclist Wouter Weylandt died of injuries from a crash on the descent from the Passo del Bocco in 2011 (Fotheringham, 2011).

Simulation training is necessary in preperformance preparation because race conditions cannot be fabricated in practice. During race stages, the entire road is used by cyclists so as to "flatten" turns at top speeds. In practice, riders have only one lane available. It is also impossible to memorize the course, as the total distance of the 2013 Giro d'Italia will be 2,116 miles (3,405 kilometers).

Andy Hampsten, the only American to win the Giro d'Italia, learned descending skills from three-time Tour de France champion Greg LeMond and Polish coach Eddie Borysewicz. Borysewicz also taught Hampsten how to crash. The latter training consisted of learning tumbling skills so that he would roll, rather than slide over surfaces, with his hands wrapped around his head to protect from injuries.

Hampsten credited this training with helping him to take risks and not fear crashes. He secured his win in 1988 by widening his lead on the 25-kilometer descent from the Gavia Pass during a snowstorm, on roads covered with snow and ice (Albergotti, 2009).

The sport psychology consultants for the Taiwanese Olympic archery teams recommended preparing athletes for potential insomnia during the Olympic Games. This was accomplished by exposing athletes to bouts of sleep deprivation during preparation (Hung, Lin, Lee, & Chen, 2008).

Very Exhaustive Preperformance Preparation or Superstition?

Wade Boggs was inducted into the National Baseball Hall of Fame in 2005 (Doyle, 2005). His insistence on eating chicken before every game is well-documented, and he even developed his own chicken cookbook, *Fowl Tips*. His pregame routine extended well beyond his diet, and has been described as **superstitious** (inclined to irrationally believe that actions are related to outcomes). His pregame routine consisted of the following steps (Heyman, 1993, March 23):

1. Eats chicken every day.
2. Grows his beard when hitting well with it, shaves when he hits a slump.
3. Draws the Hebrew letter *Chai* in the batter's box.
4. Does everything at the same time each day. He eats at 2:00, leaves his house at 3:00, changes into his uniform at 3:30, goes to the dugout at 4:00, takes grounders at 4:15.
5. After taking grounders, he ends the drill at 4:40 by stepping on third base, second base, and first base, then steps on the foul line and takes two steps in the first base coach's box before heading for the dugout.
6. When he takes his position each inning, he steps over the foul line.
7. Runs wind sprints at 7:17 to signify a 7-for-7 game.
8. Has lucky bats, gloves, and T-shirts. Slumps can make them unlucky bats, gloves, and T-shirts.
9. Throws the ball against the dugout wall for five minutes before each game.
10. Leaves his glove and ball in the same spot in the dugout every game.
11. Arranges pine tar, weighted doughnut, and resin in a precise way in the on-deck circle and applies them in that order.

Although the insistence on this ritual may be seen as superstitious behavior (Heyman, 1993), this routine may have contributed to his sense of personal control. Boggs maintained that this routine relieved worry: "All superstition is a positive framework for your mind" (Heyman, 1993). This routine was elaborate but not overly rigid, because circumstances probably rarely prevented following this algorithm. Bogg's preparation and consistency are reflected by career statistics. In 1999, he became the 23rd major leaguer to have 3,000 hits. He had the highest batting average in the American League four times in a five-year period, had seven consecutive seasons in which he had 200 hits, was an All-Star for 11 consecutive years, and is in the Baseball Hall of Fame. Perhaps Bogg's extensive preparation shielded him from distractions. In 1986, a year he won a batting title, his mother died in a June auto accident. He also won a batting title in 1988 despite being at the center of a considerable scandal. The scandal concerned a lawsuit by his traveling companion, Margo Adams. Ms. Adams claimed breach of contract after Boggs apparently tried to end their four-year affair. She pleaded for compensation for wages lost while she accompanied him on road trips (Gammons, 1988; Swift, 1989).

Even if game conditions cannot be simulated, preperformance simulations are helpful. For example, walking through a performance, such as figure skating, has positive effects on performance and improves confidence and self-efficacy that the performance will be successful (Garza & Feltz, 1998).

The use of mental practice, or just imagining performance in the setting or learning about the setting from others with first-hand experience, is also helpful, especially when actual practice is not possible. An additional level of familiarity is added to mental practice if it occurs in the venue where the competition is to take place, and this mental practice may involve the use of external as well as internal imagery (Nideffer, 1985). Internal imagery is directed toward one's thoughts and emotions, and external imagery is focused on outside details. When mental practice at actual competition venues is impossible, familiarity is added to mental practice when athletes are provided with photographs of sites for competition, warm-up areas, and training rooms (Vealey & Greenleaf, 2010).

Deviation from Preperformance Routines

In general, performance is compromised by **deviations from routines** and by the introduction of novelty and unpredictability prior to and during a performance (Lidor, 2007). Indeed, junior soccer players who represented England in international tournaments and their coaches cited disruptions to preperformance routines as the most disruptive factor influencing performance (Pain & Haywood, 2008). Disruptive effects occur even when aspects of preperformance routines consist of superstitious behaviors. Superstitious behaviors do not have technical functions in preparing sportspersons to execute skills, but are associated with better performance (Moran, 1996). For example, free-throw accuracy decreased when collegiate and club basketball players in England where inhibited from engaging in pre-shot superstitious rituals (Foster, Weigand, & Baines, 2006). Perhaps rituals such as "taps own head 3 times prior to shooting" (Foster et al., 2006, p. 171), promoted feelings of emotional stability and control.

One aspect that introduces unfamiliarity and deviation from routines is travel for competition. Individuals and teams perform better and prefer to compete at home (Courneya & Carron, 1992; Nevill & Holder, 1999). For example, of the 175 no-hitters thrown by U.S. major league pitchers between 1900 and 1989, 63% occurred at home ballparks; also, 78% of the perfect games in this era were thrown at home ballparks (Irving & Goldstein, 1990). Further, the performance of professional or college basketball teams is disrupted by travel to other cities for games. In the eight seasons between 1987–1988 and 1994–1995, home teams won 64% of the games by an average margin of 4.6 points in the National Basketball Association (NBA) (Steenland & Deddens, 1997). Home teams have also performed better in deciding games of NBA playoff series, especially in Game 7 (Tauer, Guenther, & Rozek, 2009). Home teams won 65% of the games in the Atlantic Coast Conference (ACC) during a 10-year period from 1971–1981 (Silva & Andrew, 1987). Visiting teams were less accurate at shooting from the field, turned the ball over more often, and committed more fouls.

Elite adolescent male hockey players in Canada won 58.8% of games on home ice (Agnew & Carron, 1994). Countries were more likely to win Olympic metals when they hosted the Olympics (Leonard, 1989). World Cup soccer teams won 63% of their games at home, 37% away, and 40% at neutral sites in 1987 and 1998 (Brown et al., 2002). Soccer clubs in the European Champions League were twice as likely to score goals at home, and away teams were twice as likely to receive yellow cards (for committing serious fouls). Home teams won 67% of the matches in the Champions league (Poulter, 2009).

Until recently, most research demonstrated that performance was worse for visiting teams that traveled longer distances. This result was observed with World Cup or continental championship games and European soccer matches (Pollard, 2006). Travel between time zones may disrupt the sleep-wake cycle of athletes, especially if there is a change of three hours or more and if travel is eastbound, so that the timing of the sleep-wake cycle is advanced (Savis, 1994). Sleep loss disrupts concentration, mood, fine motor and perhaps gross motor skills. Sleep-deprived athletes show less willingness to train hard, and their immune functions are perhaps compromised (Robson-Ansley et al., 2009).

However, examining the results of soccer matches in the German Football Premier League (Bundesliga) over 21 seasons, team performance decreased with travel up to a distance of about 450 kilometers (280 miles). For travel longer than 450 kilometers, teams adapted by taking more comfortable means of travel, such as flying, and by arriving one or two days prior to matches to practice and gain familiarity with the pitch (Oberhofer, Philippovich, & Winner, 2010).

Performance is influenced by unfamiliar living accommodations, court composition and lighting, physical confinement while traveling, and by opposing crowds (Courneya & Carron, 1992; Nevill & Holder, 1999). Crowd noise influences not only the participants in athletic matches but also the referees, as, for example, referees called fewer fouls against the home team in the English Premier League (Nevill, Balmer, & Williams, 2002). Athletes are also less likely to practice mental skills such as self-talk, imagery, and goal setting in preparation for away matches (Thelwell, Greenlees, & Weston, 2009).

Opposing Crowds

The U.S. has struggled to win World Cup Soccer qualifying games in Central America. Local fans do what they can to disrupt the preperformance routines and sleep of the U.S. team. In Honduras in 2001, a San Pedro Sula newspaper published a diagram of the U.S. team's hotel and their room numbers. In Mexico, late-night fire alarms and calls to player's rooms are routine. In Costa Rica in 2001, two massive speakers were hauled outside of the U.S. team's hotel. Local fans then serenaded the U.S. team with loud music at two in the morning (Wahl, 2009).

Soccer teams are more likely to be offensively oriented at home (Poulter, 2009). Home teams control the ball for longer periods of time, take more shots on goal, and make more penetrative passes. With penetrative passes, possession is maintained, and the ball is moved in the direction of the opponent's goal and passes at least one opponent player. Visiting teams more often adopt defensive and cautious playing tactics (Tenga, Holme, Ronglan, & Bahr, 2010).

Preperformance Routines and Performance

The establishment of preperformance routines facilitates preparation for and performance in a variety of sports, including golf, tennis service, basketball free throws, soccer, volleyball service, bowling, gymnastics, wrestling, skiing, skating, and diving (Taylor, 1996; Velentzas, Heinen, & Schack, 2011). U.S. Olympic wrestlers who won Olympic medals were systematic and highly conscientiousness in adhering to pre-match routines throughout the Olympic tournament, whereas non-medalists and wrestlers who had their worst Olympic performance deviated from routines prior to matches with lightly regarded opponents and when it was inconvenient (Gould, Eklund, & Jackson, 1992a). U.S. Olympic wrestlers were more likely to follow their strategic plans during their best matches (Gould, Eklund, & Jackson, 1992b). They refocused as necessary, and some used breathing techniques as cues to refocus. During best matches, wrestlers maintained concentration throughout and were highly motivated to put forth their best efforts. By contrast, during their worst matches, Olympic wrestlers were distracted, experienced negative emotions, deviated from strategic plans, and reported cognitive interference. The most successful Canadian Olympic athletes also emphasized the importance of remaining focused on the specific components of their strategic plans (Orlick & Partington, 1988). Canadian Olympians who made major changes to preperformance routines and strategic plans for competition immediately before the Olympics were less successful. The topic of cognitive interference will be discussed in Chapter 11, and it represents a form of cognitive anxiety that displaces attention to the actions necessary for successful performance. Basketball players with more consistent preperformance routines were more accurate in shooting free throws (Wrisberg & Pein, 1992).

Wearing Red in Competition

It is widely recognized that Tiger Woods wears red on Sundays or on the final day of golf tournaments. Red is a unique color in the animal kingdom in that intense red hues are associated with male dominance and testosterone levels (Hill & Barton, 2005). At the 2004 Olympic Games, contestants in four combat sports (boxing, tae kwon do, Greco-Roman wrestling, and freestyle wrestling) were randomly assigned red uniforms or body protectors. Athletes wearing red won more frequently in all weight classes when they were evenly matched with opponents. The same held true at the Euro 2004 international soccer tournament, as teams wearing red had better results, largely due to scoring more goals.

Success or failure in sports such as wrestling is determined in a matter of minutes. Given the difficulty of devising a new strategy in such a brief time and with the stress of competition, it is not surprising that deviations from strategic plans were associated with worst performances. Competition plans probably represented the best thinking of athletes and coaches for exploiting weaknesses and tendencies of opponents and capitalizing on the strengths of sportspersons (Rumbold, Fletcher, & Daniels, 2012). Carefully developed plans are therefore more likely to be successful than strategies developed in a matter of seconds during the pressure of competition. When carefully developed strategies may prove to be ineffective during competition, sportspersons may consider their "Plan B."

Andre Agassi, a Loose Toupee, and Disappointment

The night before playing in his first Grand Slam championship tennis match, the 1990 French Open, Andre Agassi's toupee disintegrated. Esteemed for both tennis brilliance and his appearance, his hairpiece was a secret. In a panic, he reconfigured the hairpiece and attached it with at least 20 bobby pins. Taking the court he was "catatonic," or preoccupied with worry that his hairpiece would slip:

> The whole world would be laughing. With every lunge, every leap, I picture it landing on the clay, like a hawk my father shot from the sky. I can hear a gasp going up from the crowd. I can picture millions of people suddenly leaning closer to their TVs, turning to each other and in dozens of languages and dialects saying some version of: "Did Andre Agassi's *hair* just fall off?" (Agassi, 2009, p. 152).

Agassi lost the match to Andres Gomez 6-3, 2-6, 6-4, 6-4.

"PLAN B"

Unexpected events that occur in the course of competition or evaluative tasks contribute to beliefs that one has little control over the causes of success and failure. Unexpected events are less likely to happen if thorough preparation has been completed prior to the evaluative task. This thorough preparation will likely include predictions about the nature of the evaluation (e.g., what can I expect at tryouts, what questions will be on the test), the competition, the competition's tendencies, and the competition's probable plan of attack (e.g., a scouting report). Unexpected events may still occur, but developing a **"Plan B"** can minimize their impact (Birrer & Morgan, 2010; Taylor, 1996). A "Plan B" refers to alternative strategies for problem solving, performances, and competitions that are adopted when the "Plan A," or primary strategy or game plan, is not successful. The presence of alternative or "B" plans facilitates the preservation of self-efficacy in the face of initial failures and unexpected obstacles. For example, U.S. winter Olympians considered the ability to make tactical adjustments during the course of competition to be an important determinant of performance (Gould, 1999).

The experience of problems and distractions during the course of a performance is not uncommon. For example, elite male decathlon participants who represented the United States in international competition uniformly identified competitions in which they struggled to overcome problems. All of the decathletes had struggled with poor weather, pain, fatigue, a poor performance in at least one event, and worries due to comparing themselves to other competitors (Dale, 2000). Performance is disrupted less by unfavorable conditions, such as bad weather, if preperformance preparation has included practice in inclement weather, (Gould, 1999). With this preparation, athletes can develop tactics suited to particular weather conditions.

Preparation for pain and discomfort is also likely to be beneficial. Responding to the experience of pain with thoughts such as "I can handle this" enhances pain tolerance and minimizes pain sensation.

It is sometimes difficult to prepare a "Plan B" for all the things that can go wrong in the course of a competition. As illustrated in the vignette about Welsh golfer Ian Woosnam at the 2001 British Open at the start of Chapter 4, surprises do occur. Perhaps at these points mental skills and relaxation exercises are especially crucial.

WHY PREPERFORMANCE ROUTINES ARE HELPFUL

There are several theoretical explanations for the benefits of preperformance routines involving movement (Cohn, 1990b):

1. *Schema* theory holds that groups of skills (such as a serve in volleyball; Velentzas et al., 2011) are stored in permanent or long-term memory in the form of schemas or mental representations. Preperformance routines have the effect of selecting the most appropriate motor schemas and tailoring those schemas for the particular situation. For example, just prior to serving, a tennis player may visualize a flat, wide serve to an opponent's backhand in the deuce court.

2. The *Stage* theory of motor learning emphasizes the amount of thinking and attention required to execute newly acquired skills. With practice, the execution of skills require less thought, and attention can be devoted to making minor adjustments in the sequence of movements. As skills are mastered, they can be executed with little conscious attention to how the skills should be performed and sequenced; this is described as **the autonomous phase**. Skills become autonomous as a result of extensive practice. Practice enhances the organization of skills into an organized schema or mental representation of the skills. This schema can be quickly and directly retrieved from memory and skills are executed automatically.

With this automatic execution of skills, minimal demands are placed on attentional resources, thus allowing the performer to focus on other information such as tactics or strategy. Preperformance routines may promote the automatic execution of autonomous skills (Singer, 2002). The Stage theory has direct implications for routines that occur immediately prior to the execution of skills. If skills cannot be executed automatically, preperformance mental and physical rehearsals should include thought about how to execute the skills and cue words or self-talk to direct attention to the sequence of skills in the performance.

3. The *Set* hypothesis recognizes that preperformance routines facilitate attention to skills, strategies, tactics, and physiological arousal levels associated with good performance. Preperformance routines serve to direct attention to behaviors instrumental to good performance, and away from cognitive anxiety and regret about prior errors in a competition. Preperformance routines also promote feelings of control (Lidor, 2007).

4. Finally, the benefits of preperformance routines may be understood to be the results of *mental rehearsal* or practice. This topic will be taken up in Chapter 6, and one theory of the benefits of mental rehearsal is psychoneuromuscular priming, or the preparation of muscular groups to react as a result of imagining the execution of skills (Fourkas, Bonavolonta, Avenanti, & Aglioti, 2008; Vealey & Greenleaf, 2010; Velentzas et al., 2011). Perhaps these routines facilitate a shift in brain hemisphere activation prior to actual performance. For example, among highly skilled marksmen there was a reduction in activation in the left hemisphere (verbal processes) and an increase in activation in the right hemisphere (spatial, nonverbal processes) prior to competition (Hatfield, Landers, & Ray, 1984, Salazar et al., 1990).

Feel

Golf instructor, analyst, and writer Dave Pelz's description of "feel" for golf strokes is consistent with the previous explanation of autonomous skills execution (Pelz & Frank, 1999). For example, Pelz maintained that "feel" is based on a great deal of practice that results in memories of actual golf swings and strokes, and the results of these swings. With this practice and these memories, golfers have a basis for predictions and expectations about the likely results of individual swings or strokes. The golfer with "feel" develops expectations about how a golf ball will fly, and where it will land. The putter with "feel" makes predictions about the speed, slopes, and breaks of greens before balls are struck. In effect, Pelz's definition of "feel" melds visualization and automatic execution of skills, and recognizes no clear demarcation between the two.

"Feel" becomes available to golfers after they have mastered the mechanical aspects of various golf strokes, and mechanical shortcomings keep even professional golfers from developing "feel" in some aspects of their game. Once mechanics have been mastered, Pelz encourages golfers to try to remember the results of each swing or stroke. This builds the "memory bank of knowledge and expertise called 'feel'" (p. 115). He recommends visual and kinesthetic mental practice (see the discussion of mental practice and imagery in the next chapter) prior to every shot in practice and competition as a way of pulling "the right 'feel' out of your memory for the shot at hand" (p. 115). This cueing for the development of "feel" involves visualizing the desired shot and taking practice swings to retrieve the kinesthetic memory of the proper swing.

Given this discussion, it appears that "feel" and autonomous skill execution does not occur "automatically," but with strict preperformance routines, visualization, and preparation. When the golfer "feels" the perfect swing, she or he is encouraged to visualize the desired result for the ensuing shot. With visual and kinesthetic "feel" for the shot, the golfer is encouraged to take one look at the landing spot and then to swing.

Elite golfers focus primarily on the mechanical aspects of shot making while their "feel" for shots has a subconscious influence. Others focus more directly and primarily on "feel." Even among golfers who routinely approach the game with "feel," their attention may periodically be directed toward mechanical aspects of their strokes. This focus on mechanics typically occurs when there are flaws in the technical aspects of their strokes.

SUMMARY AND APPLICATION

The establishment of preperformance routines facilitates experiences of familiarity, order, consistency, and control. Practice should occur under conditions that most closely approximate "game conditions." Generally, they should be carefully scripted and followed throughout periods of preparation and up to the time of the actual performance.

It is more difficult to stick to preparation schedules during periods of travel and in unfamiliar locals. To the degree possible, athletes are advised to keep to sleep routines and to deviate only minimally from their normal diets.

However, flexibility should be included in preperformance routines, because environmental conditions may necessitate changes in routines. Efficacy that is dependent on the rigid adherence to preperformance routines and "game plans" may be brittle and easily shattered by environmental conditions that force changes in routines, by unexpected questions on examinations, and by surprising tactics by opponents. By adding flexibility to preperformance routines and to game plans, the experience of control can more readily be maintained. Sportspersons may be advised to develop "Plan Bs" for both preparation and performances.

Preperformance techniques have to be practiced on a regular basis to be effective, as the introduction of novel interventions prior to and during performances is typically disruptive. The benefits of preperformance routines are due in no small degree to the order and control that they bring to the schedules and psychological states of athletes.

Key Terms

Preperformance routines   102

Superstitious behavior   109

Simulation training   109

Deviation from preperformance
routines   111

"Plan B"   114

Autonomous phase   115

Discussion Questions

Q1. Review the UNIFORM program.

Q2. Consider the components of preperformance routines.

Q3. What benefits are conferred by preperformance routines?

Q4. An early arrival at performance venues invites to emergence of debilitative anxiety. How is this beneficial?

Q5. How are written algorithms beneficial with preperformance routines?

Q6. Why is it necessary to have some flexibility with preperformance routines?

Q7. Review the benefits of preperformance routines at the site of the competition.

Q8. What is simulation training?

Q9. What evidence is there for the argument that deviations from preperformance routines are harmful or disruptive?

Q10. Why are athletes generally more successful when they follow "game plans"?

Q11. What is a "Plan B"?

Q12. Review the theoretical explanations for the benefits of preperformance routines involving movement.

Suggested Readings

Carver, C. S., & Scheier, M. F. (1998). *On the self-regulation of behavior.* Cambridge, UK: Cambridge University Press.

Carver, C. S., & Scheier, M. F. (2011). Self-regulation of action and affect. In K. K. Vohs & R. F. Baumeister (Eds.), *Handbook of self-regulation research, theory, and applications,* (2nd ed., pp 3–21). New York, NY: Guilford.

Hardy, L, Jones, J. G., & Gould, D. (1996). *Understanding psychological preparation for sport: Theory and practice of elite performers.* Chichester, UK: John Wiley.

Lidor, R. (2007). Preparatory routines in self-paced events. In G. Tenenbaum & R. C. Eklund (Eds.), *Handbook of sport psychology* (3rd ed., pp. 445–465), New York, NY: Wiley.

Orlick, T., & Partington, J. (1988). Mental links to excellence. *The Sport Psychologist, 2*, 105–130.

Shambrook, C. J., & Bull, S. J. (1999). Adherence to psychological preparation in sport. In S. J. Bull (Ed.), *Adherence issues in sport and exercise* (pp. 169–196). Chichester, UK: Wiley.

Singer, R. N. (2002). Preperformance state, routines, and automaticity: What does it take to realize expertise in self-paced events? *Journal of Sport & Exercise Psychology, 24*, 359–375.

Spielberger, C. D., & Vagg, P. R. (1995). Test anxiety: A transactional process model. In C. D. Spielberger & P. R. Vagg (Eds.), *Test anxiety. Theory, assessment, and treatment* (pp. 3–13). Washington, DC: Taylor & Francis.

Chapter 6

MENTAL IMAGERY, SELF-TALK, AND CONCENTRATION

The American golfer Jack Nicklaus won 18 "major" golf tournaments (six Masters, four U.S. Opens, three British Opens, five PGAs), and placed second 19 times at majors. He won his first major, a U.S. Open in 1962, and his last, a Masters, in 1986 at age 46. To place this record in context, the players with the next highest numbers of victories of comparable majors are Tiger Woods with 14, and Gary Player and Ben Hogan, each of whom have 10. Bobby Jones won 13 of the 21 majors he entered. During his era, however, the majors were considered the U.S. and British Opens and Amateurs.

Nicklaus has been meticulous in his practice of mental skills and adherence to mental simulation regimens during golf tournaments:

> *Before every shot I go to the movies inside my head. Here is what I see. First, I see the ball where I want it to finish, nice and white and sitting up high on the bright green grass. Then, I see the ball going there; its path and trajectory and even its behavior on landing. The next scene shows me making the kind of swing that will turn the previous image into reality. These home movies are a key to my concentration and to my positive approach to every shot (Nicklaus, 1976, p. 45).*

Mental imagery—Jyoti Randhawa

Elite athletes such as Jack Nicklaus routinely use mental imagery to facilitate the execution and development of sport skills and strategies (e.g., Calmels, d'Arripe-Longueville, Fournier, & Soulard, 2003; Cumming & Hall, 2002; Hellstrom, 2009; Murphy, 1994). The terms "mental imagery," "mental practice," "mental rehearsal," and "mental simulation" are at times used interchangeably. Imagery appears to be the major component of mental practice (Hall, 1985), and the term "mental imagery" will be used in this discussion. **Mental imagery** consists of intentionally bringing images to mind or rehearsing performances without actually physically enacting the performance. Mental imagery is not limited to visualization, and it has been recommended that it involve all the senses (Vealey & Greenleaf, 2010). This means that imagery should involve mental representations of sights, sounds, smells, and touch. In addition, imagery should involve representations of kinesthetic or bodily movement (Callow & Roberts, 2010). Imagery should also include the recall or anticipation of emotional responses during competitions, especially if athletes intend to gain control of these emotional responses (Williams, Cumming, & Balanos, 2010).

Mental imagery is no substitute for the acquisition of skills through physical practice (Taktek, 2004). Physical skills are best acquired through physical practice, and physical practice generally has a greater effect than mental practice on performance. However, mental imagery may be substituted for some of the physical practice without decreasing the acquisition of skills. After skills have been developed, the use of imagery supplements regular physical practice (Hall, 2001). The substitution of mental imagery is sometimes welcomed, such as during times of injury, fatigue, and travel.

The mental imagery of highly skilled athletes is more vivid than that of athletes with less expertise (Roberts, Callow, Hardy, Markland, & Bringer, 2008). Their imagery is likely to engage multiple sensory modalities and internal and external perspectives. They have control over the content of their mental imagery—removing images of failure, using images of prior poor performances to motivate practice, and identifying and avoiding hazards (MacIntyre & Moran, 2007a, 2007b).

Athletes who are not elite (Arvinen-Barrow, Weigand, Thomas, Hemmings, & Walley, 2007; Hall et al., 2009; Mahoney & Avener, 1977) and younger (Gregg & Hall, 2006) are less likely to practice visualization. Perhaps less-elite athletes have less awareness of and instruction in the practice of mental skill. Although some people appear to have more aptitude for visualizing movement than others, visualization abilities improve with practice (Hall, 2001).

MENTAL IMAGERY: WHEN AND WHERE

Sportspersons engage in imagery during training, competition, and rehabilitation. Mental imagery is often used prior to a motor action or performance, but is also engaged during and after the execution of skills (Bernier & Fournier, 2010). The more that activities depend on mental operations and the less on physical strength, endurance, and coordination, the greater the benefit of mental imagery (Driskell, Copper, & Moran, 1994).

Traditionally, effective mental imagery was seen to begin with feelings of relaxation. For example, with Richard Suinn's (1986) **Visuo-Motor Behavior Rehearsal (VMBR),** athletes are taught to relax with a form of progressive muscle relaxation (PMR; discussed in Chapter 7) and then to practice visualizing successful performance. The pairing of relaxation and imagery should, of course, occur during practice and stages of skill acquisition (Murphy & Martin, 2002). Perhaps by pairing relaxed states with images of stressful performances, the two become associated so that a person may perform with less anxiety. Athletes also reduce performance anxiety when they visualize themselves successfully handling stressful athletic situations (Martin et al., 1999).

More recently, the importance of visualizing sport skills in environments that most closely resemble "game conditions" has been emphasized (Holmes & Collins, 2001; Ramsey, Cumming, Edwards, Williams, & Brunning, 2010; Smith, Wright, Allsopp, & Westhead, 2007). Athletes have been instructed to engage in imagery during arousal states that correspond to arousal states during competition or practice (Guillot & Collet, 2008). Accurate mental images of movement are equally likely in relaxed and aroused states (Louis, Collet, & Guillot, 2011).

The Duration of Mental Imagery

Imagery often unfolds in real-time or at the same pace as the actual motor actions. For example, the times required to image and execute complex vaults were similar among elite gymnasts (Calmels, Holmes, Lopez, and Naman, 2006). Slow-motion imagery is more likely to occur when learning skills and strategies, as athletes form and refine mental representations of skills (Fournier, Deremaux, & Bernier, 2008; O & Hall, 2009). The imagery of novice sportspersons may also unfold more slowly as motor actions are analyzed, deconstructed, and integrated (Reed, 2002). Fast-motion imagery is more probable after skills have been mastered. Mental imagery also unfolds more slowly when practiced in relaxed states (Louis, Collet, & Guillot, 2011).

Application

Visualization is often a component of preperformance routines in closed skill sports. Closed skills—such as free throws in basketball—are often executed in a self-paced and somewhat invariant manner. Visualization not only prepares the athlete for optimal skill execution, but also occupies working memory with what he or she intends to do, and therefore screens out distractions, such as anxiety.

Novice golfers putted more accurately with longer periods of mental imagery. The opposite was true for expert golfers. Apparently, the experts imaged an automated or proceduralized putting stroke. Proceduralized skills are developed with extensive practice and are executed without consciously bringing to mind the component parts that make up the omnibus skill. Novice putters do not have procedural skills, and their performance is best when the component motor skills are brought to mind. Neural substrates for motor imagery and execution overlap. Therefore, imaging proceduralized skills recruits the neurons required for optimal execution of proceduralized motor skills and imaging component skills engages the appropriate neurons for best performances among novices (Beilock & Gonso, 2008).

Experts need not image in real-time. Elite golfers slowed or speeded the pace of imagery depending on the function of their imagery (Bernier & Fournier, 2010). The **function** of imagery refers to the purpose for engaging in imagery (Murphy, Nordin, & Cumming, 2008). The golfers also adapted the content and the characteristics to the function of their imagery. The **content** consists of what is seen in the image and whether the perspective is internal or external. Imagery **characteristics** consist of the sensory modalities, vividness, duration, and control.

Mental Imagery in the NBA

B.J. Armstrong prepared for NBA games by engaging in mental imagery:

> I believe that if I can take twenty or thirty minutes before each game and visualize what's going to happen, I'll be able to react to it without thinking, because I'll already have seen it in my mind. When I'm lying down before the game, I can see myself making a shot or boxing out or getting a loose ball. And then when I see that come up during the game, I don't think about it, I do it. There are no second thoughts, no hesitation. Sometimes, after the game, I'll go, 'Wow! I saw that! I anticipated it before it happened' (Jackson & Delehanty, 1995, p. 121).

Cognitive and Motivational Imagery

Mental imagery may involve the execution of specific sport skills, groups of skills in larger routines, or entire game plans. For example, in soccer, a player might visualize the specifics of a corner kick to deliver a ball to a teammate positioned in front of the goal. Footballers or soccer players might also imagine interactive plays with teammates. Game plans might include strategies to exploit the weaknesses of opposing teams, anticipation of the tendencies and strategies of opponents, and a "Plan B" should game plans prove ineffective. Sportspersons use the type of imagery they believe to be most effective (Weinberg, Butt, Knight, Burke, & Jackson, 2003).

Imagery that promotes the acquisition of sport skills is considered to serve a cognitive function: either imaging specific skills (Cognitive Specific or CS) or general strategies in sport (Cognitive General or CG; Paivio, 1985). CS imagery is especially related to skill development among child athletes (Munroe-Chandler, Hall, Fishburne, Murphy, & Hall, 2012).

Imagery focused on the steps necessary for goal attainment serves more of a motivational function. Motivational General (MG-A) imagery augments affect and arousal, and Motivational Specific (MS) imagery focuses on the specific steps for goal attainment. Motivational General imagery that is focused on mastery (MG-M; e.g., "I imagine giving 100%") is especially endorsed by intercollegiate athletes (Arvinen-Barrow et al., 2007; Ross-Stewart & Short, 2009), elite adult and adolescent (Callow & Hardy, 2001; Mills, Munroe, & Hall, 2001; Vadocz, Hall, & Moritz, 1997), and younger athletes (Munroe-Chandler, Hall, & Fishburne, 2008). It is effective in building, maintaining, and regaining confidence and self-efficacy. When sportspersons identify goals, they are often motivated to develop plans for reaching their goals and managing emotions, such as anxiety, that emerge in the process of pursuing these goals.

MG-A imagery has also been used to decrease debilitative anxiety. By imagining the successful execution of skills under pressure, arousal was interpreted as increasingly facilitative and self-efficacy increased among male collegiate rugby union players (Mellalieu, Hanton, & Thomas, 2009). Athletes more frequently engage MG-M imagery in competition and CS imagery in practice (Hall et al., 2009). MG-A and MS imagery are used least in both competition and practice.

At the risk of introducing excessive detail, it is noted that the content of imagery does not always determine its function. For example, a particular image may have a cognitive function for one athlete and a motivational function for another (Short, Monsma, & Short, 2004).

Finally, these forms of mental imagery are measured with the Sport Imagery Questionnaire (SIQ; Hall, Stevens, & Paivio, 2005) with adults, and among children and young adolescents with the Sport Imagery Questionnaire for Children (SIQ-C; Hall, Munroe-Chandler, Fishburne, & Hall, 2009).

Productive Mental Imagery

The **direction** of imagery may be toward images of success or failure. The visualization of images of failure, especially immediately prior to performance, is detrimental, and successful images should precede performance. Coping images may be entertained at a time somewhat distant from the actual performance. Coping imagery refers to the consideration of difficulties and setbacks during performance, and how to overcome obstacles.

Generally, more **vivid** mental imagery is more beneficial (Hall, 2001), and therefore, ideally, and as mentioned earlier, imagery should involve the five senses and not consist of just visualization. It is also important to be able to **control** the imagery, or to reliably bring the elements of a successful performance to mind in their proper sequence. Without this control, mental imagery might consist of a series of somnambular "bad dreams," as it might bring to mind images of failed or faulty performances (Murphy et al., 2008). With practice, imagery generally becomes more controllable and vivid (Evans, Jones, & Mullen, 2004). Productive imagery skill generally predicts its use (Gregg, Hall, McGowan, & Hall, 2011).

The use of both **internal** and **external perspectives** may be helpful (Gould & Damarjian, 1996). An internal perspective involves how one might experience the elements of a successful performance, and an external perspective refers to how the performance would appear to other people. External perspectives have been recommended for closed skill sports. Internal perspectives have been recommended for open skill sports, such as soccer, that require flexibility in responding to changing conditions and the behavior of competitors (Hardy, 1997; Hardy & Callow, 1999; White & Hardy, 1995). However, athletes in open and closed skill sports make regular use of vivid imagery with internal and external perspectives (Cumming & Ste-Marie, 2001; Highlen & Bennett, 1983; Orlick & Partington, 1988; Robazza & Bertoli, 1998).

Mental imagery is often selected and tailored to fit the requirements of specific sports (Martin et al., 1999). For example, divers have been encouraged to focus on the most critical elements of dives in preperformance preparations. They are advised to visualize these elements performed perfectly and to attempt to imagine the kinesthetic experiences of the dive during this visualization. Divers are also directed to use a verbal cue to sustain attention on these performance keys throughout the execution of the dive (Cohn, 1990).

Viewing **videotapes** of oneself during a successful performance or of a successful person to be emulated may facilitate effective visualization. While viewing these "success" tapes, one might listen to favorite music. Replaying that music may then bring associations of the success and facilitate productive mental imagery. Productive mental imagery may also be associated with key words that may be repeated during actual performances. Repeating the key words might facilitate associations to the mental imagery and direct attention to the correct organization and sequencing of behavior during performance (Moran, 2009).

Athletes have been encouraged to use imagery during **transition points** in practice and athletic contests, such as prior to the start of routines in figure skating or springboard dives (Nideffer, 1985). Mental imagery can be integrated with centering at these transition points. Centering is a relaxation technique and is described in greater detail at a later point in this chapter. By centering, mental imagery can become more vivid. For example, a diver might achieve a calm focus by centering and using imagery prior to initiating dives in practice and competition.

Mental Imagery Controversies

Mental imagery that consists simply of imagining the fruits of success has been criticized as little more than wishful thinking. There is even evidence that devoting time to imagining successful results is detrimental. Levels of aspiration and performance decreased for college students who devoted their attention to the joy they would experience after achieving high grades. Their wishful thinking was pleasant but did not motivate more study (Taylor, Pham, Rivkin, & Armor, 1998). The time that could have been given to preparing for exams may have been squandered on the pleasant experience of imagining success.

These criticisms of the visualization of successful outcomes notwithstanding, highly skilled athletes devote time to visualizing successful performances. Elite female netball players were likely to visualize sporting success and to report high levels of sport confidence (Callow & Hardy, 2001). The association of images of success and sport confidence was not as strong for less-skilled female netball players. The less-skilled players were more likely to report sport confidence when their visualization focused on technical aspects and persistent effort in the practice of netball. This pattern of visualization may support skill acquisition among the athletes that are in need of additional instruction and practice in order to achieve their goals.

However, visualization of specific successful performance has been shown to be helpful, even for novices. Beginning golfers who visualized successful putts set higher goals and practiced more than beginners who just visualized perfect putting strokes (Martin & Hall, 1995).

Clearly Iatrogenic Mental Imagery

As discussed above, negative imagery such as unsuccessful putting, is detrimental to performance (Short et al., 2002). Attempts to suppress negative images are also detrimental. For example, when instructed to be careful to not undershoot the target, putting accuracy at golf decreased; even when putters tried to suppress the images (Beilock, Afremow, Rabe, & Carr, 2001). Persistent attempts to suppress negative thoughts and images can have the ironic effect of increasing the likelihood that these thoughts and images will impact performance (Wegner, 1994, 1997a, 1997b, 2011).

Why Mental Imagery Is Beneficial

There are at least 11 explanations for the psychological benefits of mental imagery (Driskell et al., 1994; Gould & Damarjain, 1996):

- *First*, skills become symbolized or mentally represented and organized in the process of mental imagery. These mental representations or schemas become the standard by which physical practice and performance are evaluated. Skills are refined as athletes shape their performance to match schemas. Conversely, athletes recognize that their internal representations are not adequate when they execute a skill in a manner that comports with their schema and still the performance is not sufficient. This informs the person that they have more to learn and to practice. If novice sportspersons do not have accurate schemas of skills, then their mental imagery may consist of the rehearsal of "bad habits" or the wrong set of skills (Hall, 2001; Noel, 1980). Once a high level of expertise and skill has been established, visualization may serve as a conduit for the transfer of skills from practice to competition.

- Explanations two, three, four, and five are related. The *second* explanation is that sportspersons are more likely to believe that skills will be successfully executed if skills were successfully performed in mental imagery. The *third* is that mental simulation may promote self-efficacy and sport confidence (e.g., Callow, Hardy, & Hall, 2001; Evans et al., 2004; Mamassis & Doganis, 2004; Short et al., 2002), and self-efficacy competes with feelings of helplessness and anxiety. Of course, if imagery is to enhance efficacy beliefs, it must include images of success, competence, and confidence (Moritz, Martin, Hall, & Vadocz, 1996). *Fourth*, mental imagery may divert attention from questions about the likelihood of successful performance and direct attention to the behavioral elements that will result in successful performance (Bandura, 1997; Calmels, Berthoumieux, & d'Arripe-Longueville, 2004). *Fifth*, mental simulations may lead people to place greater value on their goals, and to believe that their goals are more proximal or close to being realized.

- *Sixth*, the automation of complex skills occurs during the process of mental and physical practice. Automation occurs as discrete skills become organized into integrated routines, as specific courses of action are developed for particular situations, and as sportspersons become more efficient in using feedback to correct actions during the process of a performance.

- *Seventh*, in the course of forming mental simulations, people can anticipate problems and "think through" their solutions.

- *Eighth*, mental simulations may evoke anxiety, but by mentally representing realistic and successful mastery in these situations, anxiety can be diminished (Page, Sime, & Nordell, 1999; Taylor, Pham, Rivkin, & Armor, 1998). Anxiety is reduced as people reinterpret their anxiety and understand it as controllable and manageable, as they are more effective in obtaining support and emotional solace from other people, and as plans for coping with stressors are developed.

- *Ninth,* the benefits of mental imagery that occurs immediately prior to performances may also be due to psychoneuromuscular "priming," or activation of the muscular groups that are responsible for the actual performance (Beilock & Gonzo, 2008; Fourkas, Bonavolonta, Avenanti, & Aglioti, 2008; Vealey & Greenleaf, 2010).
- *Tenth,* motor imagery is functionally equivalent to movement, because they share common neurological mechanisms and substrates. There is a transfer of training at the cortical level (MacIntyre & Moran, 2010).
- *Finally,* mental rehearsal appears to be an efficient way of invoking a state of intensity or arousal that corresponds to the state of intensity that occurs during actual physical practice (Hardy et al., 1996). Mental rehearsal is, therefore, an efficient way of maintaining intensity levels and attentional focus during delays in the action of athletic contests (Moran, 1996).

SELF-TALK

Self-talk refers to what people say to themselves. It may be silent or audible to others. Audible self-talk is more likely among children, and with maturation self-talk becomes more covert. Sport psychologists have studied self-statements that direct attention (e.g., what to expect next from an opponent), provide motivation (e.g., "I can"), label oneself or others (e.g., "I don't perform well under pressure"), judge performance (e.g., "I'm the worst"), and enhance or undermine performance (Hardy, 2006; Hatzigeorgiadis, Zourbanos, & Theodorakis, 2009; Theodorakis, Hatzigeorgiadis, & Chroni, 2008; Williams & Leffingwell, 1996). Self-talk is used for skill acquisition ("point the toe down and strike the soccer ball with the instep"), self-instruction ("chop steps as necessary to plant your take-off foot"), and breaking bad habits ("follow the ball all the way to the racket"; Cutton & Landin, 2007; Landin & Hebert, 1999).

Self-talk—Andy Murray

Self-talk that supports a positive self-concept and self-confidence directs attention to the tasks necessary for successful performance, and diminishes self-doubt and anxiety (Hardy et al., 1996; Hatzigeorgiadis, Zourbanos, Galanis, & Theodorakis, 2012; Schuler & Langens, 2007) is adaptive. Adaptive self-talk is parsimonious and focused on the keys necessary for optimal performance (Latinjak, Torregrosa, & Renom, 2011). Self-talk that diverts attention away from task-absorption and to questions about whether performance will be successful or the reaction of others is referred to as **negative self-talk** (Hayslip, Petrie, MacIntire, & Jones, 2010). Negative self-talk may also focus on past mistakes or direct attention to the future, such as whether one will win or lose a competition. Surprisingly, the effects of negative self-talk on performance has not been studied extensively (Tod, Hardy, & Oliver, 2011).

Unfortunately, the self-talk of junior tennis players during competition was sometimes balanced toward self-critical and judgmental statements (Van Raalte, Brewer, Rivera, & Petitpas, 1994). The self-talk of skilled adult tennis players was also negative in tone. Negative self-talk as frequent as six times in a match was demonstrated by 94% of the competitors, whereas comparable frequencies of positive self-talk were recorded by only 11% (Van Raalte, Cornelius, Hatten, & Brewer, 2000). Additionally, self-talk was often in response to prior action in the match and did not appear to systematically direct attention to actual match play or to the anticipation of opponents' play. All the competitors complimented their opponents at least twice. Although compliments may demonstrate sportspersonship, they may also be distracting during the course of play and may best be reserved until the end of matches.

This negative self-talk was recorded in actual tennis matches. When asked on questionnaires about their self-talk, collegiate athletes reported that their self-talk was more positive than negative (Hardy, Gammage, & Hall, 2001). Perhaps athletes understand the benefit of positive self-talk, but have difficulty maintaining a positive focus during the stress of competition.

Motivational self-talk enhances confidence, inspires a greater expenditure of effort, and develops a positive mood (Hatzigeorgiadis, Zourbanos, Mpoumpaki, & Theodorakis, 2009). For example, football players might augment intensity levels and prepare for especially aggressive play with exhortations of "this is my kind of party." It enhances self-efficacy and performance (Hatzigeorgiadis, Zourbanos, Goltsios, & Theodorakis, 2008).

Instructional or **cognitive self-talk** facilitates concentration as well as the development and deployment of sport skills and strategies (Zervas, Stavrou, & Psychountaki, 2007). An example of instructional self-talk is the self-instructions that are rehearsed by more successful elite divers prior to and during competition (Highlen & Bennett, 1983).

Traditionally, motivational self-talk has been seen as more beneficial in facilitating performance at tasks that predominantly require muscular strength and endurance, but instructional self-talk also enhances this performance. For example, instructional and motivational self-talk were equally effective in enhancing movement kinematics and increasing power, strength, and coordination during vertical jumps (Tod, Thatcher, McGuigan, Thatcher, 2009).

Instructional self-talk enhances performance to a greater degree on tasks that require fine motor movements, sustained concentration, anticipation, planning, and the flexible selection and application of strategies. Motivational self-talk also enhances performance at these tasks (Hatzigeorgiadis et al., 2011; Tod et al., 2011).

Some authors encourage the use of instructional self-talk during the acquisition of skills. For example, while learning to strike soccer balls, young footballers might recite instructions for placement of their plant foot, striking the ball with their instep, and for keeping their eyes on the ball to the point of contact. As skills become automated, self-talk may refer to more global aspects of sports skills such as how to "set-up" or trick defenders (Zinsser, Bunker, & Williams, 1998). The development of automated skills will be discussed at a later point in this chapter. However, even skilled athletes benefit from instructional self-talk that directs attention to specific techniques (Hatzigeorgiadis et al., 2011). For example, elite, under-14 female soccer players fired shots on goal more accurately when they used the cue word "downlock" to direct their attention to proper technique involving pointing their toe down and locking their ankle (Johnson, Hrycaiko, Johnson, & Halas, 2004). Collegiate, Division I female tennis players demonstrated improved volleying with the use of the cue words "split" and "turn" to direct their attention to optimal techniques (Landin & Herbert, 1999).

Both instructional and motivational self-talk have the additional benefit of inhibiting negative self-talk or cognitive interference (Hatzigeorgiadis, Theodorakis, & Zourbanos, 2004; Hatzigeorgiadis et al., 2008; Tod et al., 2011). Positive self-statements can be a part of an adaptive preperformance routine, and may be helpful in focusing attention in the course of performance. The practice of keeping a log of thought patterns prior to and during performances can help to identify self-talk that has accompanied satisfactory and unsatisfactory performances. Efforts can then be made to initiate patterns of self-talk that have been historically associated with good performances during and prior to competitions and practice.

In actual competition, all of these forms of self-talk are likely to occur. For example, skilled and elite Greek athletes engaged in positive and negative self-talk and motivational and instructional self-talk during competition (Zourbanos, Hatzigeorgiadis, Chroni, Theodorakis, & Papaloannou, 2009). Their self-talk formed eight distinct categories:

1. Psych up: e.g., "Let's go; give 100%."
2. Confidence: e.g., "I believe in me; I can make it."
3. Instruction: e.g., "Focus; bend your knees."
4. Anxiety control: e.g., "Relax; no stress."
5. Worry: e.g., "I'm going to lose; I am not as good as the others; what will others think of my poor performance."
6. Disengagement: e.g., "I want to get out of here; I can't keep going; I think I'll stop trying."
7. Somatic fatigue: e.g., "I am tired; my body doesn't help me today."
8. Irrelevant thoughts: "I am hungry; I want to take a shower."

Psych up, confidence, instruction, and anxiety control are examples of positive self-talk, and worry, disengagement, somatic fatigue, and irrelevant thoughts are forms of negative self-talk. With the exception of the instruction factor, positive self-talk was primarily motivational.

NEGATIVE SELF-TALK OR COGNITIVE INTERFERENCE

As mentioned above, negative self-talk disrupts concentration and performance. Negative self-talk may involve doubts and questions about the likelihood of success and the reactions of spectators. Negative self-talk diverts attention from the skills and strategies necessary for optimal performance and is detrimental to performance. A general term for thoughts such as this negative self-talk is **cognitive interference** (Yee & Vaughan, 1996), and cognitive interference will also be discussed at a later point in this chapter.

Sportspersons may be unaware of negative self-talk, as it may occur automatically or unintentionally. The effects of these automatic thoughts are insidious, as they direct attention away from the task at hand and toward concerns about the adequacy of performances. Sportspersons may become more aware of negative self-talk by keeping a log of its occurrence and content (Hardy, Roberts, & Hardy, 2009).

Concentration may be disrupted and cognitive interference may increase during the course of performance. This occurs because of expected events or obstacles (e.g., a particularly tough opponent or surprising tactics by an opponent) or because of anxiety that occurs prior to or during a performance (Hatzigeorgiadis & Biddle, 2008). Recall that anxiety has physiological and cognitive dimensions, and cognitive anxiety in competition often includes worries about success and expectations of failure (Baumeister & Showers, 1986; Humphreys & Revelle, 1984; Sarason, Pierce, & Sarason, 1996).

Cognitive interference may motivate audible negative comments directed toward oneself (e.g., "loser") and opponents (e.g., "cheat"), as well as unsporting behaviors (e.g., hitting one's legs with a tennis racquet). These unsporting behaviors not only undermine performance but also increase the confidence of competitors as they recognize when opponents are "losing it" (Hanegby & Tennenbaum, 2001).

Phil Jackson on Negative Self-Talk

When I was a player, not surprisingly, my biggest obstacle was my hyperactive critical mind. I'd been trained by my Pentecostal parents to stand guard over my thoughts, meticulously sorting out the "pure" from the "impure." That kind of intense judgmental thinking—*this* is good, *that's* bad—is not unlike the mental process most professional athletes go through every day. Everything they've done since junior high school has been dissected, analyzed, measured, and thrown back in their faces by their coaches, and, in many cases, the media. By the time they reach the pros, the inner critic rules. With the precision of a cuckoo clock, he crops up whenever they make a mistake. *How did that guy beat me? Where did that shot come from? What a stupid pass!* The incessant accusations of the judging mind block vital energy and sabotage concentration (Jackson & Delehanty, 1995, p. 117).

The degree to which people can become absorbed in tasks is relative, and athletes may question whether they will be successful during the course of a performance. However, intrusive and repetitive thoughts about the adequacy of one's performance are likely to adversely affect performance. Furthermore, the more often the person queries themselves about whether they will be successful, the more likely that they will answer "no" (Carver, 1996).

Self-Talk, Cognitive Interference, and Self-Efficacy

People with high **self-efficacy** and confidence are more capable of maintaining positive self-talk and focused attention in the course of evaluations and in the face of adversity. With traits of confidence and self-efficacy, athletes can remain task-focused, and, to relative degrees, ignore setbacks and their own fears and uncertainties in the pursuit of goals. If the attention of confident people is directed to questions of whether they will accomplish goals, they show even greater task absorption and persistence because they believe they have the capacity to reach the goals. In addition, the process of sustaining attention on the elements of one's performance is likely to enhance efficacy because the sportsperson is focused on events in their control (Bandura, 1997; Cheng, Hardy, & Markland, 2009; Craft, Magyar, Becker, & Feltz, 2003; Mellalieu, Hanton, & Fletcher, 2006; Vealey, 2009). The behavior of observers and competitors is less under a person's control.

With high self-efficacy, sportspersons also more quickly rid themselves of ruminations about mistakes and failures that inevitably occur during the pursuit of difficult goals. They are more likely to attribute mistakes to external and unstable factors such as bad luck, and are less apt to exacerbate the effects of setbacks by getting "down on themselves," or by judging themselves harshly and by having punitive self-reactions. They learn, perhaps with the help of mentors, to identify and modify the specific elements in their performance that led to unsuccessful performances, and do not make global judgments about their competency.

When self-efficacy is shaky, people more frequently brood about mistakes and feel lousy about them. As attention is drawn to self-judgments and self-reactions and away from the elements in a performance, performance suffers further and people with low self-efficacy may judge that they are having a "bad day" or that momentum has shifted in the favor of an opponent (Jones & Harwood, 2008). The attention of doubtful people is captured by concerns that they will not be equal to tasks, and their fears will be realized.

The effects of efficacy and performance interact, so that lowered efficacy disrupts performance and problems with performance lower efficacy. If this cycle of declining performance and efficacy is not interrupted, the quality of performance will diminish rapidly (Lindsley, Brass, & Thomas, 1995). When this focus on past mistakes extends past a single performance, the person may believe they are in a "slump." A slump consists of a period of substandard athletic performance for which there is no ready explanation (Taylor, 1988).

The performance of sportspersons that lack confidence suffers as they disengage mentally or physically from challenges. As they engage in off-task behaviors such as procrastination, daydreaming, and negative and perhaps self-deprecatory ruminations, time that could be devoted to mental and physical practice is lost.

Training in positive, motivational self-talk increases self-efficacy and performance (Hatzigeorgiadis et al., 2008). For example, skilled and elite adolescent Greek tennis players improved the depth and accuracy of forehand shots when they overtly or covertly recited either "I can," "strong," "let's go," or "got it" during the strokes.

Disengaging Cognitive Interference

It may be difficult to disengage from this cycle of cognitive interference in the course of a performance. To do so requires an interruption in the process of critically evaluating oneself and a return of attention to the present moment of the contest (Zinsser, Bunker, & Williams, 2006). Sophisticated preparations for performances should probably include cue words or techniques for interrupting performances that deteriorate in this manner. For example, sportspersons may slow themselves down between parts of their performance, become aware of their critical self-focus, and redirect attention to the current moment. Self-talk or cue words can be rehearsed during physical practice, mental practice, and preperformance preparation, and repeated during performances to sustain concentration and to redirect concentration when cognitive interference occurs ("Developing your mental pacemaker," 1989). For example, the word, "anticipate" might be a cue word in tennis to sustain attention. This may cue a player to predict likely shots from opponents and to attend to their own game plan. Generally, cue words direct attention to the process of performance and away from attention to outcomes. Cue words should be brief and easy to pronounce and the number of cue words should be kept to a minimum (Landin & Hebert, 1999). Self-talk or written notes can serve as reminders of the key components for successful performances.

top-down focus need not be inflexible, as alternative tactics may supplant game plans that are not working. A top-down focus also facilitates optimal allocation of attentional resources to the most salient external cues. For example, competitors may be scrutinized for clues that give away strategies and game plans.

Athletes also counter negative self-talk by reminding themselves that difficult conditions are even more detrimental to the performance of competitors (Hays, Thomas, Maynard, & Bawden, 2009; Suinn, 1986). For example, in her semifinal tennis match in the 1999 U.S. Open, Martina Hingis was exhausted and trailing 3 games to 2 in the third set, after losing her serve. She recalled matches with Steffi Graf, who presented an image of impeccable conditioning and composure. She initiated the self-talk: "She must get cramps, too. She can't be so fresh. It paid off. It was a mental game" (Jacobs, 1999, September 11). Hingis prevailed over Venus Williams 6–1, 4–6, 6–3.

Athletes who are losing in competition may counter negative self-talk by reminding themselves that opponents are unlikely to perform flawlessly throughout matches, and that they may have opportunities to capitalize on the errors of opponents (Williams & Underwood, 1970). As mentioned in Chapter 5, careful preparation sometimes includes the development of a "Plan B," or alternative, if a primary game plan fails to produce the desired results. With a "Plan B," sportspersons are more likely to sustain belief that they have control over the outcome of competitions and are less likely to experience cognitive interference and debilitating anxiety.

The effects of symptoms of physiological and cognitive anxiety can be mitigated if they are interpreted as likely to facilitate performance (Hardy et al., 1996; Williams et al., 2010), or at least as expectable reactions to stressors and not signs that one is "choking" or that performance is about to rapidly deteriorate. As has been emphasized throughout this text, careful and exhaustive preparation is associated with optimal performance. For example, elite swimmers were more likely to interpret signs of anxiety as facilitative if they followed precompetitive routines that included goal setting, imagery, and self-talk (Hanton & Jones, 1999a, 1999b).

As previously mentioned, people may interpret symptoms of anxiety more benignly if they have received direct and empathic instruction that anxiety commonly accompanies performances. An instructor, coach, or a more experienced performer who has already "been there" or experienced similar anxiety reactions prior to and during performances might provide this mentoring.

People who have not had the benefit of mentoring or coaching to interpret signs of anxiety as facilitative can benefit from psychological interventions. For example, Hanton and Jones (1999b) intervened with elite swimmers who interpreted cognitive and somatic anxiety as debilitating. The swimmers were provided with instruction in goal setting, mental imagery, preperformance regimens, positive thinking and self-talk, and self-talk and reminder cue cards. The cognitive and somatic anxiety of the swimmers did not decrease, but they learned to interpret their anxiety as facilitative and demonstrated improved swimming performances. Swimmers reported improved confidence, probably because they felt more comfortable with their thoughts and bodily reactions prior to competitions. Alternatively, the confidence of swimmers may have improved because they actually were swimming faster due to the psychological interventions. Sportspersons may not be able to rid themselves of "butterflies" in their stomach, but by interpreting them as facilitative, they can make them "fly in formation" (Hanton & Jones, 1999a, p. 19).

Application

It comes as no surprise that we often avoid the sources of anxiety. However, when anxiety is precipitated by impending competition, this strategy is of little benefit. Unless one drops out, competition cannot be avoided. When athletes avoid concerns about upcoming performances, they miss opportunities to confront and resolve debilitative anxiety, such as worries about failure. They also neglect visualization, self-talk, and thorough reviews of game plans.

Sportspersons are better advised to directly confront the sources of their anxiety. For example, an early arrival at the site of competition allows cognitive interference and anxiety to come to mind. This anxiety may then be more directly managed or resolved; perhaps in consultation with coaches. For example, persistent fears of failure may be recognized, and used as a cue to focus on the moment during competition. Distractions from opponents and hostile crowds may be anticipated and used as reminders to focus on game plans. Sportspersons may experience increased arousal or physiological anxiety when they arrive at the venue, and begin to manage arousal and perform optimally with heightened arousal levels.

Anxiety also tends to dissipate over time. It is far better to begin this process well in advance of competition than to avoid the unpleasant experience of anxiety until game time.

Taking time off and regaining focus on the process of performances may interrupt slumps. Strategies for coping with slumps that are problem-focused, or that identify and correct flaws in performance, are also helpful in resolving slumps and increasing self-efficacy (Hardy et al., 1996; Taylor, 1988). Guidance and information from knowledgeable and supportive people such as mentors are also helpful in resolving slumps. Strategies that involve avoiding thoughts about slumps, engaging in less corrective practice, and wishful thinking are not adaptive.

CONCENTRATION AND ATTENTION

Motor sports place extreme demands on attention

Concentration has been described as a learned skill of becoming absorbed in tasks and not reacting to or being disturbed by irrelevant stimuli (Schmid & Peper, 1993). This process has also been described as **attentional control,** and consists of a process by which individuals selectively attend to stimuli in the environment or to their own thoughts (Kane & Engle, 2003; Moran, 2009). External stimuli, such as the efforts of other people to interfere with concentration, novel environments and situations, and pressure in the form of daunting challenges, can disrupt concentration. Elite athletes are often adept at blocking both internal and external distractions and at directing attention to the specific skills necessary for successful performances (Robazza & Bortoli, 1998). High levels of self-confidence and concentration have been described as two factors that differentiate successful from unsuccessful elite athletes (Highlen & Bennett, 1983; Moran, 1996). Intense concentration is a cardinal feature of flow experiences (Jackson & Csikszentmihalyi, 1999), and flow is associated with optimal performance and well-being. Preparing Olympians to avoid distractions was seen as the single most important intervention by sport consultants and coaches (Gould, Guinan, Greenleaf, & Chung, 2002).

The capacity for concentration is limited to the amount of information that can be sustained and processed in working or active memory at any given time. The limit of working memory is approximately seven, plus or minus two units of information (Kareev, 2000; Miller, 1956). That is, at any given time, people attend to approximately seven bits or units of information from the environment or their own minds and bodies and screen out any number of other stimuli.

Concentration and Automated Skills

With practice, skills may become more **automated** or autonomous in that they can be performed without attention to the specific procedures necessary for their execution (Beilock, Carr, MacMahon, & Starkes, 2002; Logan, 1988). Automatic processing takes place unconsciously, whereas controlled processing occurs with conscious effort. Controlled processing proceeds more slowly, as thoughts progress sequentially in working memory (Abernethy, Maxwell, Masters, Van Der Kamp, & Jackson, 2007). Highly skilled and elite performance is associated with autonomous skills execution.

The process by which autonomous skills develop is complex and may involve dedicated neural architectures (e.g., Masters & Maxwell, 2004, Milner & Goodale, 1995; Wulf & Prinz, 2001). However, a reasonable model of its development involves three processes. The first, *mergerization*, consists of merging progressively larger segments of a skill into a single integrated routine. The entire routine is thereafter represented as a single cognitive unit or schema (Keele, 1968; Schmidt, 1975, 1982), rather than the individual segments and the linkages of the segments. The second process consists of *automation*, or the immediate execution of certain skills in certain situations. For example, hockey players may always shoot when positioned in the goalmouth. The third process consists of a *shift in attention* from the execution of skills to strategies concerning when to use the skills (Bandura, 1997). For example, a tennis player may decide to serve to an opponent's backhand on crucial points.

Less of the limited capacity of working memory is occupied during the execution of skills that have this over-learned or automatic quality (Hardy et al., 1996). Additional active memory resources are, therefore, available during the execution of autonomous skills. These resources can be put to good use in monitoring environmental conditions, such as the behavior of competitors or teammates.

Expert athletes attend to and extract more information from advance behavior cues that are unwittingly provided by opponents (Abernethy, 2001; Moran, 1996; Williams & Ward, 2007). Experts are more efficient in recognizing the relevant behavioral cues that "give away" their opponents' next move. In this way, experts are more generally prepared for ensuing action in competitions. They are less frequently "fooled" and more frequently "get the jump" on opponents. For example, skilled tennis players are more adept at detecting subtle cues about the direction of forehand and backhand shots by identifying shifts in the head, shoulders, and hips of opponents (Williams, Ward, Knowles, & Smeeton, 2002). Elite soccer players as young as age 9 are capable of recognizing patterns of play on the basis of the position of players on the field and on the postures of opposing players (Ward & Williams, 2003). Elite footballers or soccer players are also more selective in focusing on the players who are most likely to initiate or respond to action.

Expert athletes use these cues to anticipate actions and prepare responses. The action in sport is often so rapid that decisions about how to respond must be made prior to as opposed to after the action. While prepared for the most likely action, elite athletes still remain vigilant for the unexpected (Hung, Spalding, Santa Maria, & Hatfield, 2004).

With experience, athletes gain understanding about where to direct their focus to pick up cues about ensuing action. For example, expert karate performers focus more on the torso area of opponents and detect information about movements of opponents' hands and feet with peripheral vision (Williams & Elliott, 1999; Williams, Janelle, & Davids, 2004). Skilled tennis players are particularly adept at anticipating the direction of serves and ground strokes by observing the trajectory of the ball toss, and they also attend to the positioning of the racket, wrist, and right arm (Jackson & Mogan, 2007; Singer, Cauraugh, Chen, Steinberg, & Frehlich, 1996). Less-skilled tennis players are more likely to focus on the whole body or the head.

In addition, expert sportspersons also use their knowledge of opponents' tendencies, strengths, weaknesses, and position on the court or pitch to anticipate play (Buckolz, Prapavesis, & Fairs, 1988; Williams & Ward, 2007). Tennis experts recognize when opponents have limited shot options, such as when they control play with firm approach shots, and move to the net (Crognier & Fery, 2005).

Concentration and Batting

Ted Williams was rated as the third best baseball player of all time and was the last Major League Baseball player to hit over .400 ("Baseball's best," 1999). He opined that hitting a baseball was the most difficult skill in sport. A Major League Baseball pitcher delivers a baseball to the strike zone in 0.40 seconds. Batters must recognize whether the pitch is a fastball, slider, curve, or changeup within 0.10 seconds. Williams concluded that even superior baseball players must anticipate or guess what pitch will be thrown next if they are to be able to respond in this amount of time. He maintained that "proper thinking" was 50% of effective hitting, and that guessing or anticipating what pitch a pitcher would throw was essential for every plate appearance (Williams & Underwood, 1970).

Expert athletes appear to have a **quiet eye period** prior to the initiation of closed motor skills (Janelle et al., 2000; Vickers & Williams, 2007; Vine & Wilson, 2010). Prior to executing these skills, expert sportspersons focus their vision on targets for longer periods of time than do less-skilled players. During this time, experts fine-tune motor responses. More difficult shots require longer quiet eye periods (Williams et al., 2002).

Concentration and Distraction

The additional attentional resources that are available with automization of skills can also be captured by distractions. Distractions divert attention from the instrumental tasks necessary for skilled performance. Distractions include internal thoughts or worries and stimuli from the environment, and compete for attentional resources in working memory. Distractions can also disrupt the flow of automated actions and cause sportspersons to become more self-conscious. With "deautomation," performances become clumsy.

Cognitive interference is a form of **internal distraction** and was described as a form of negative self-talk. With increasing worry, less attention is given to tasks necessary for successful performance and more attention is focused inward toward feelings and thoughts such as self-conscious focus on oneself (Baumeister & Showers, 1986; Eysenck, Derakshan, Santos, & Calvo, 2007; Nideffer & Sagal, 2006). The topic of cognitive interference will be reviewed in Chapter 11, and it will be shown to be a primary determinant of "choking under pressure." Optimal performance occurs when athletes are "in the moment" or when their attentional resources are fully focused on each moment of play. Choking under pressure is more likely when distractions about the results of competitions occupy the attention of sportspersons. Distracting thoughts about the results of a match are apparently not uncommon, because teams in sports such as hockey and soccer may concede a goal soon after having scored one due to this lapse of concentration.

Another form of internal distraction is regret about poor performances or missed opportunities earlier in a match or competition. In addition, some athletes find it difficult to concentrate when they are pitted against an opponent they clearly outmatch. Negative emotions such as dejection, anger, and anxiety also compete for storage space in working memory (Vast, Young, & Thomas, 2010).

Examples of **external distractions** are noise or unwanted sound, weather and playing conditions, and visual distractions. Given the discussion of the importance of preperformance routines in Chapter 5, it comes as no surprise that unfamiliar venues and atmospheric conditions disrupt concentration and performance. Unexpected changes in ambient noise are often distracting. Changes in ambient levels of noise may increase athletes' arousal levels and result in a narrow attentional focus. There are many opportunities for visual distractions. Athletes lose concentration when they attend to visual cues, such as members of the audience or scoreboards listing their performance in relation to competitors.

Where have you gone, Jackie Stewart?

Almost one million automobile crashes occur each year in Britain because drivers cannot keep their eyes on the road. They are too busy ogling attractive pedestrians of the opposite sex. Men are troubled most with these lapses of attention, especially in the summer when women are wearing less clothing. Indeed, 60% of male drivers confessed to being distracted by attractive women. Women were better at focusing, as only 12% snuck peeks while driving.

Driver Martyn Beard's trouble is representative:

> I was on my way into Birmingham when I saw this lovely looking blond girl standing on the side of the road. She was outside a pub and wearing pretty much next to nothing. I couldn't take my eyes off her; she had the classic long legs and lovely figure. My concentration drifted and suddenly I realized I was about to crash into the car in front. I slammed on my brakes and this bloke went into the back of me. . . . I was gutted the girl didn't come and check if I was OK, she just walked off and I was stuck swapping insurance details with this big hairy bloke instead (Edwards, 2012).

On his way to three World Drivers' Championships in Formula One auto racing, Scotland's Jackie Stewart was likely untroubled by similar lapses in concentration. He was ranked as the fifth greatest Formula One driver of all time and awarded the rank of Knight Bachelor in the British honors system.

The behavior of opponents may also disrupt performance. For example, in World Cup and European Championship soccer matches, penalty kicks in "shootouts" were converted less frequently when opponents scored the preceding penalty kick and pridefully celebrated. Shootouts decide matches that end in ties after regulation and overtime periods. Prideful celebrations involve extending both hands—perhaps signaling a goal, expanding the chest, and making both hands into fists (Moll, Jordet, & Pepping, 2010). Prideful celebrations may be "contagious," so that teammates also experience pride and a boost in their confidence. Teams were more likely to win shootouts when they pridefully celebrated. The emotional contagion may extend to the opposing teams such that prideful celebrations signal dominance and evoke feelings of inferiority in opposing teams.

Michael Jordan on Trash-talking

Trash-talking is a means of (1) giving you confidence, and (2) taking your opponent's mind off what he's trying to do and putting a little more pressure on him. I don't talk trash to demean people. I don't talk about their parents or any of that. But I do love talking trash, no matter who I'm playing. President Clinton is the only U.S. president I've played golf with, and I talked trash with him, too. . . .I enjoy moments like that. I love competitiveness. So why would I do anything less? (Jordan & Bestrom, 2009, p. 87).

Deliberate efforts to disrupt the attention of opponents are known as "gamesmanship" (Potter, 1947). Gamesmanship does not violate the rules of competition but is inconsistent with sportspersonship because it is an attempt to psychologically unsettle opponents. Gamesmanship may take on many forms. For example, by rendering a pseudo-compliment to an opponent, the opponent may become overly self-conscious and automatic execution of skills may be disrupted. Comments masquerading as altruistic may also represent subtle forms of gamesmanship. For example, a diver may caution an opponent to be careful when taking off from a springboard because of its slippery surface (Nideffer, 1985). Another form of gamesmanship is to call a time-out prior to an opponent's free throw in basketball in an effort to cause cognitive interference and worries about missing the free shot. It is unlikely that this practice will abate despite empirical evidence that it does not decrease the accuracy of free throws (Kozar, Whitfield, Lord, & Mechikoff, 1993). Gamesmanship may also be far less subtle and may consist of deliberate intimidation through verbal or physical means.

Materazzi to Zidane: "The mother is sacred"

Zinedine Zidane was the captain of the French soccer team. At age 34, he played his final match before retiring in the 2006 World Cup championship with Italy. He was International Footballer of the Year in 1998, 2000, and 2003, and scored two goals in France's only World Cup championship in 1998. He scored France's only goal in the 2006 championship match and won the Golden Ball as the outstanding player in the 2006 World Cup. He was also given a red card or expelled in the 110 minute of the 120-minute overtime championship match for head butting Italy's Marco Materazzi. With the match tied 1-1 after 90 minutes and two 15-minute overtime periods, the game was decided with penalty kicks. Italy won, five kicks to three. France's coach Raymond Domenech commented: "He was missed in the last 20 minutes tonight. It weighed heavily in the outcome" ("Top of the World, Italy wins shootout with France for fourth Cup title," 2006).

A "Paris-based advocacy group" cited "several very well informed sources from the world of football" in alleging that the provocation for the head butt was that Materazzi called Zidane a "dirty terrorist" ("Butt Why?," 2006, C2). Zidane's parents immigrated to France from Algeria. Materazzi denied calling him a terrorist: "I'm not cultured and I don't even know what an Islamic terrorist is" ("Italian Admits to Insult," 2006, C3). Materazzi acknowledged insulting Zidane, "It was one of those insults you've told tens of times that always fly around the pitch," but denied saying anything about racism, religion, or politics. Ultimately, Zidane said that the insult concerned his mother and sister ("Zidane: 'I don't regret anything that happened,'" 2006); a charge that Materazzi also denied: "The mother is sacred" ("Italian Admits to Insult," 2006, C3).

Two months after the World Cup, the mystery was revealed. After Materazzi held his opponent's shirt, Zidane said: "If you want, I'll give you the jersey later." "I responded that I preferred his sister, it's true," Materazzi said ("Italian Player Ends Mystery," 2006, C7).

Attentional Width and Direction

The influential **Nideffer** (1981a) model of attention in athletic activities maintained that attentional style varies along the dimensions of width and direction. Attention can be given to a **broad** or **narrow** range of cues or information. The direction of attention can range from an internal focus on one's thoughts and emotions to an external focus on outside details. Therefore, the direction of attention could be **internal-broad, internal-narrow, external-broad, or external-narrow.** A narrow focus of concentration is appropriate when strength and intensity are key elements of a successful performance. Tasks such as auto racing are performed best by maintaining a broad and external focus of attention, as drivers have to attend to their own driving, the positions of other drivers, information from their crew, and the condition of their car and the track. Successful diving might demand a narrow and internal focus, as performers would optimally attend to their self-talk or visualization related to the elements of their dive. Some distance runners maintain a broad and internal focus as they ration energy and monitor fatigue throughout their bodies. Hitting a baseball requires a narrow and external focus on the behavior of the pitcher and the flight of the ball.

Efficient control of attention often requires the capacity to adjust both the width and the direction of focus to adapt to the requirements of given situations (Williams, Nideffer, Wilson, Sagal, & Peper, 2010). For example, when planning a golf shot, golfers must attend to the characteristics of a particular hole, such as distance, the placement of hazards like sand traps, and atmospheric conditions, such as the direction of the wind. This requires an external-broad focus. Efficient golfers then shift to an internal-broad focus, as they recall prior shots in similar situations and select the proper club. When golfers engage in visualization and mental imagery prior to striking the ball, attention is directed efficiently if it has an internal-narrow focus. Finally, when swinging, attention is on the ball itself, and attention is focused externally and narrowly.

Attentional Width and Direction and Anxiety

People may differ in their capacities to sustain the various widths and directions of attentional focus (Nideffer, Sagal, Lowry, & Bond, 2001). As anxiety and pressure increase, people may rely more strongly on their preferred widths and directions of attention. High levels of physiological arousal can result in a perceptual focus that is overly narrow and internal and cause deficits for performances that require a broad and external attentional focus (Moran, 1996; Murray & Janelle, 2003; Nieuwenhuys, Pijpers, Oudejans, & Bakker, 2008; Nideffer, 1993). Anxiety and pressure also interfere with the flexibility with which attentional focus may be adjusted. If the width and direction of attention do not fit well with the task at hand, performance suffers (Smith, 1996).

In addition to physiological arousal, cognitive anxiety results in **attentional narrowing** (Pijpers, Oudejans, Bakker, & Beek, 2006). With cognitive or physiological anxiety, drivers respond more slowly to signals in the periphery of their visual field, and more frequently misidentify signals (Janelle, Singer, & Williams, 1999). Paradoxically, with high anxiety and attentional narrowing drivers spend more time gazing in the periphery of their visual fields, as it takes them longer to identify and respond to signals in the periphery. Of course, time given to hunting and responding to peripheral information is taken from attention to the central peripheral field where most of the information relevant for fast and skilled driving was to be found, and the anxious drivers were slower in races. The attention of the anxious drivers is therefore deployed inefficiently in the periphery and center of their visual fields. English karate performers also directed a greater proportion of their attention to the periphery when experiencing anxiety (Williams & Elliott, 1999). Anxiety was also shown to disrupt the performance and attentional processes of tennis players (Williams, Vickers, & Rodrigues, 2002). However, their attentional deficits appeared to be due to excessive tracking of the ball flight with the fovea or central area of their visual field. Anxiety appears to disrupt the functional connection between perception and action by reducing the sportsperson's capacity to identify relevant visual information.

Michael Schumacher's Working Memory

With seven Formula One driving championships, Michael Schumacher is the most successful driver in the sport's history. By comparison, Juan Manuel Fangio has the second most championships with five. Rory Byrne, the chief designer for Schumacher's Ferrari racing team, considered Schumacher's abilities:

"Does Schumacher have an analytic ability? The difference between the great ones and the merely good is, as John Barnard has already underlined, the great ones do it so naturally they still have brain space available."

"Yes, that's true, that's absolutely true."

"So he can come in and say X, Y or Z when he's done a really hot lap?"

"Not only that but during a race. He can be turning in really quick laps and be on the radio asking questions or telling us various things. Most drivers don't really like to be bothered on the radio when they're really going for it, whereas he's got the mental capacity to drive quickly and still consider the other aspects of the race or whatever it is to be considered" (Hilton, 2006, p. 226).

Potential Techniques for Improving Concentration

With optimum concentration, there is no separation between what athletes are thinking and what they are doing. They make deliberate decisions to "switch on" and direct their focus to factors under their control. When anxious, they focus their attention outward and toward what they intend to do, rather than inward and on worries (Moran, 2009).

Sport psychologists and coaches have identified techniques for focusing attention during athletic performances. It is necessary to practice and refine these techniques prior to actual performances, and they will be more effective if they become a part of practice and preperformance routines (Greenlees, Thelwell, & Holder, 2006; Harris & Harris, 1984; Moran, 1996). As sportspersons come to recognize when attention is compromised, they can develop strategies for refocusing on the factors that support good performance.

First, fatigue compromises concentration, and therefore maintaining **optimal physical fitness** enhances concentration. This includes the maintenance of **sleep hygiene,** as sleep deprivation results in impaired concentration. Athletes can use fatigue as a cue that they are vulnerable to distractions and make conscious efforts to redouble efforts to concentrate (Moran, 1996; Scott, McNaughton, & Polman, 2006).

As mentioned in Chapter 5, practice under conditions that approximate game conditions results in the reduction of novelty and provides experience in ignoring distractions. These "dress rehearsals" may include simulations of loud and distracting behaviors by spectators and opponents and practice under the most adverse conditions (Wilson, Peper, & Schmid, 2006; Schmid & Peper, 1993). This is referred to as **simulation training,** and has been shown to be a high priority for Olympic athletes

(Orlick & Partington, 1988). Simulation training may involve recreating aspects of competitions, which have disrupted an athlete's concentration, such as a bad line call in tennis (Hardy et al., 1996).

Mental rehearsals of performances also provide opportunities for recognizing cognitive interference and redirecting attention to the elements responsible for good performances. Mental imagery may include visualizations of the novel aspects of venues, and athletes may post photographs of athletic venues at home and at practice so that the venues appear less foreign.

Careful preparation before performances and game plans that focus on the details that are under the control of the performer facilitates concentration. Detailed competitive plans may direct or lead attention in that they create states of preparedness to implement responses or strategies at specific times during a competition, in certain situations, or when opponents give certain responses. For example, runners may plan to run splits or segments of the race in certain times, and may also have strategies for responding to surges or bursts of speed by competitors. Preperformance routines also direct attention to the productive action and inhibit cognitive interference. Athletes may also prepare for responding to their mistakes in the course of competition, and mentally rehearse executing skills perfectly after errors (Wilson, Peper, & Schmid, 2006).

Less-experienced athletes and test-anxious students may profit from observing how experienced and skilled athletes and students screen out distractions. **Social support** has been empirically demonstrated to diminish self-preoccupation and enhance performance. For example, performance improved when greater cohesiveness was developed among youthful athletes and between athletes and coaches, and when students experienced empathic understanding of and solutions to evaluation anxiety (Moran, 1996).

Athletes have been trained in adjusting the width and focus of their attention during the course of a competition (Moran, 2009). This training is informed by the understanding that an intense and narrowed focus of attention cannot be maintained indefinitely. Athletes are therefore trained to **"soften"** or maintain a relaxed external focus during times when performances are interrupted, but then to "zoom in" on critical stimuli at critical moments (Williams et al., 2010). It may be speculated that this process of hardening and softening attentional focus serves to maintain self-efficacy as athletes may come to understand that they can control their attention. Behavioral routines that occur during the time that attention is softened may not be trivial because they may suppress cognitive interference and cue sportspersons to harden their focus. The elaborate routines of Wade Boggs, which were described in Chapter 5, may facilitate this hard focus. Boggs maintained that when batting, his attention was so focused on the point at which the ball was released from the pitcher's hand that he could see the spin on the ball as it left the pitcher's fingers.

More generally, training to improve perceptual focus and attention in actual game conditions appears to hold promise for improving the attentional efficiency of beginning, intermediate, and even elite athletes during competition. Midfield soccer players from the Norwegian World Cup team were trained to develop and rehearse personalized imagery scripts whereby they imagined game sequences, such as receiving the ball and moving their bodies and heads to scan for opportunities (Jordet, 2005). Two of the three midfielders improved their visual exploration of the soccer pitch by improving their scanning of play to their rear. This pair also demonstrated improvement by continuing to focus on their surroundings until literally the last second prior to receiving the ball.

English recreational tennis players were trained to anticipate the direction of serves in tennis with on-court instruction and practice (Williams, Ward, Smeeton, & Allen, 2004). This training allowed the tennis players to pick up cues about the flight of serves by "reading" postural cues of the server, and to more quickly initiate moves to the right or left to return serves.

English intermediate junior tennis players responded with greater speed and accuracy when they received instruction about how to anticipate the direction of ground strokes (Smeeton, Williams, Hodges, & Ward, 2005). Some juniors were taught to focus on the shoulders, hips, and racket swings of opponents for clues about shot direction. Others were guided to discover these cues on their own. All forms of anticipation training produced improvements in speed and accuracy of movement, but those that received on-court training improved most. Performance under pressure was better for those that discovered the cues, probably because they did not consciously bring the verbal cues to mind, a process that is cumbersome under pressure (see Chapter 11).

Comprehensive cognitive training strategies result in additional gains in response speed and accuracy, especially if this training is in actual game conditions. For example, with *situational awareness* training, tennis players were taught to: identify the most relevant perceptual cues during a point, interpret these cues to anticipate shots and identify leverage points or opportunities to take control of on-court points, and anticipate the opponent's intended shot in the future. This training resulted in quicker responses to shots among young adults in tennis classes (Caserta & Singer, 2007). Senior tennis players who were trained in situational awareness were quicker to respond to the shots of opponents and were more accurate in predicting the direction of and moving to these shots (Caserta, Young, & Janelle, 2007).

Anticipation skills may also be honed with video-based instruction. English recreational tennis players positioned themselves to return forehand and backhand shots with greater speed and accuracy after viewing videotapes and receiving instruction about how to read the postural cues of opponents (Williams et al., 2002). These recreational players benefited from implicit instruction concerning body cues and from instruction consisting of a guided discovery technique about where to look for these cues.

Focusing Concentration with Centering

A technique that has been empirically related to improved performance is centering (Nideffer, 1993). It has been described by some martial arts experts as a way of controlling anxiety and concentration under pressure. **Centering** involves directing the focus of attention to a point immediately below the navel, or the body's center of gravity. This focus is paired with recommendations to let one's mind rest on the experience of strength and balance. With centering, attention is briefly directed inward to check one's pattern of breathing and muscular tension. In preparation for performances, this centering focus should be associated with deep, abdominal breathing, so that under pressure an athlete can very quickly control either his or her focus and breathing. Shallow, thoracic breathing has been associated with anxiety and muscle tension. The process of checking the pattern of breathing has the secondary benefit of interrupting cognitive interference.

It is beneficial to learn to center from the standing position because athletes are often standing in competition, and because it is most difficult to control breathing and muscular tension from the standing position. From the standing position, athletes are directed to spread their legs to shoulder width and to flex slightly at the knees. Then inhaling deeply, athletes should scan for tension in arms, shoulders, and neck muscles, and consciously let these muscle groups relax. When exhaling, athletes allow the muscles in their thighs and calves to relax, permit their knees to bend slightly, and their hips to lower. Thoughts of relaxation, heaviness and the purging of anxiety are associated with exhalation (Nideffer, 1985). With practice, the purpose of centering is to shed excessive physiological anxiety and muscle tension in a single breath. It is a technique for gaining momentary control over physiological anxiety or arousal and concentration. It is recommended for use just prior to crucial points in a match or competition when anxiety is likely to be highest. Its practice is also recommended during natural pauses in competitions, prior to the start of a performance, and after its completion.

After centering, it is necessary to quickly pull oneself away from the centering exercise and back to the action of the competition. Athletes may pull concentration back to internal or external and narrow or broad stimuli, or they may take stock of their performance, strategies, and tactics. As is true with all the strategies discussed in this chapter, centering will be more helpful to athletes if they incorporate it into their daily practice as a method for controlling physiological anxiety. A more detailed discussion of techniques for controlling cognitive and physiological anxiety and reducing cognitive interference will be provided in Chapter 7.

Centering, along with other mental skills, such as self-talk, are often used by professional hockey players (Botterill, 1990; Halliwell, 1990). They are seen as effective ways of refocusing and remaining confident after bad shifts. The play of hockey goaltenders in the elite Canadian

Junior-A league improved after they were taught a mental skills "package" consisting of centering and self-talk (Rogerson & Hrycaiko, 2002). These goaltenders, who were between the ages of 16 and 18, improved their save percentages, or the number of shots stopped, when they engaged in centering with self-talk during league games. A mental skills package consisting of relaxation, imagery, self-talk, and goal-setting improved the times of an elite male runner and three male triathletes in 1600-meter runs (Patrick & Hrycaiko, 1998). Collegiate midfield soccer players (Thelwell, Greenlees, & Weston, 2006) and skilled amateur midfield players (Thelwell, Greenlees, & Weston, 2010) benefited from a mental skills package consisting of relaxation, imagery, and self-talk.

COMPARING FORMS OF MENTAL SKILLS TRAINING

There has been some inquiry regarding whether some psychological skills are more effective and appropriate for different types of performance. For example, Lohasz and Leith (1997) evaluated the effects of self-talk, self-determined mental preparation strategies, and efforts to enhance and sustain attentional focus on the reaction times of college athletes. The athletes were required to attend to the center of a computer monitor and to press a series of buttons when a signal was flashed in the periphery of the monitor. All of the mental preparation strategies were equally effective in this and other studies (Kornspan, Overby, & Lerner, 2004; Malouff, McGee, Halford, & Rooke, 2008) in decreasing the reaction times of athletes. In addition, efforts to systematically identify people more comfortable with visualization or self-talk and then tailor training to enhance their preferred mode of mental preparation have not yet been successful. This has led to suggestions to offer training in both self-talk and visualization so that sportspersons can use either or both techniques (Thomas & Fogarty, 1997). It is also not surprising that research has not proven one form of mental preparation to be superior, because the same person commonly uses more than one form of mental preparation prior to and during performances. For example, professional tennis players consistently use a variety of mental preparation techniques, such as self-talk and visualization prior to serving and returning a serve (DeFrancesco & Burke, 1997). The effects of visualization and self-talk may also interact, as for example facilitative self-talk may counteract the effects of facilitative visualization (Cumming, Nordin, Horton, & Reynolds, 2006). Self-talk may serve an "imagery stopping" function to inhibit negative imagery (Hanton, Mellalieu, & Hall, 2004). Given that sportspersons exchange one skill for another during competition, future research may evaluate the efficacy of mental skills "packages" as opposed to individual mental skills (Rogerson & Hrycaiko, 2004; Thelwell & Greenlees, 2003).

SUMMARY AND APPLICATION

Five components of proximal preparation for optimal performance were discussed in Chapters 4, 5, and 6. These were the control of arousal, anxiety, or intensity; preperformance preparation; self-talk; concentration; and mental imagery. All have been shown to enhance athletic performance, and there is every reason to incorporate them in preparation for competition and training. There are no empirical or scientific bases for emphasizing certain techniques or of determining which techniques work best for different people, and readers may be comfortable with some techniques and not with others (McKenzie & Howe, 1997). Successful athletes often use these techniques in combination (Patrick & Hryciako, 1998), and different athletes select different combinations. Clearly, all the techniques have to be practiced on a regular basis to be effective, as the introduction of novel interventions prior to and during performances is typically disruptive.

Mental imagery is most productive when it is vivid or involves all of the senses, takes an internal and external perspective, and is under the control or direction of the sportsperson. The benefits of visualizing successful results are controversial. The visualization of success has been criticized as a waste of time that could be devoted to productive mental or physical practice. However, successful athletes imagine victory, and novice golfers who visualized success set more demanding goals for putting accuracy.

Self-talk or self-statements that direct attention to the tasks necessary for successful performance are adaptive. Self-talk that promotes a focus on the results of a performance, the reactions and judgments of others, and to doubts about whether goals will be accomplished inhibit performance and are consistent with cognitive interference.

Concentration can be maintained during performances by remaining focused on one's game plan or strategies and tactics, anticipating obstacles, challenges, and initiatives of opponents, and quickly recognizing cognitive interference and physiological anxiety. The execution of automatic or over-learned skills and responses demand less of peoples' limited attentional resources. The unused attentional resources can be utilized to focus on strategies and tactics that will augment performance. For example, if tennis skills are automated, less attention is required to execute specific shots, and additional attentional resources may be devoted to how an individual shot sets up future shots, how to best attack an opponent, and to anticipating the tactics of opponents.

With the systematic application of these techniques discussed in Chapters 4, 5, and 6, order, predictability, and control is imposed on training schedules and performances, and performance is enhanced. The techniques advance greater awareness and control over one's psychological states or phenomenology.

Key Terms

Discussion Questions

Q1. Define mental imagery and discuss its dimensions.

Q2. Review Visual-Motor Behavior Rehearsal (VMBR). How is this integrated with mental imagery?

Q3. Is imagery always paired with relaxation?

Q4. Review the various speeds at which mental imagery unfolds.

Q5. Discuss the tempos for visualizing proceduralized and nonproceduralized skills.

Q6. Review the function, content, and characteristics of mental imagery.

Q7. Examine cognitive and motivational imagery.

Q8. Consider all the aspects of productive mental imagery.

Q9. Review centering.

Q10. What are the arguments for and against visualizing successful outcomes?

Q11. What is iatrogenic mental imagery?

Q12. Consider the 11 explanations for the psychological benefits of mental imagery.

Q13. Describe the characteristic of positive and negative self-talk.

Q14. Consider motivational and instructional or cognitive self-talk.
Q15. In actual practice, are the forms of self-talk segregated?
Q16. Define cognitive interference.
Q17. Explain how self-efficacy affects self-talk.
Q18. Discuss concentration.
Q19. Review working memory in detail.
Q20. How do autonomous skills develop?
Q21. What demands do automated skills place on working memory?
Q22. Review the forms of distraction.
Q23. Describe attentional width and direction.
Q24. What is attentional narrowing?
Q25. Consider forms of improving concentration.
Q26. How is centering integrated with mental skills?
Q27. Compare the forms of mental skills.

Suggested Readings

Beilock, S. L., & Gonzo, S. (2008). Putting in mind versus putting on the green: Expertise, performance time, and the linking of imagery and action. *The Quarterly Journal of Experimental Psychology, 61,* 920–932. doi: 10.1080/17470210701625626

Bernier, M., & Fournier, J. F. (2010). Functions of mental imagery in expert golfers. *Psychology of Sport and Exercise, 11,* 444–452. doi: 10.1016/j.psychsport.2010.05.006

Caserta, R. J., Young, J., & Janelle, C. M. (2007). Old dogs, new tricks: Training the perceptual skills of senior tennis players. *Journal of Sport & Exercise Psychology, 29,* 479–497.

Eysenck, M. W., Derakshan, N., Santos, R., & Calvo, M. G. (2007). Anxiety and cognitive performance: Attentional control theory. *Emotion, 7,* 336–353.

Fournier, J. F., Deremaux, S., & Bernier, M. (2008). Content, characteristics and function of mental images. *Psychology of Sport and Exercise, 9,* 734–748. doi: 10.1016/j.psychsport.2007.12.003

Hardy, J., Roberts, R., & Hardy, L. (2009). Awareness and motivation to change negative self-talk. *The Sport Psychologist, 23,* 435–450.

Janelle, C. M., Hillman, C. H., Apparies, R., Murray, N. P., Meili, L., & Hatfield, B. D. (2000). Expertise differences in cortical activity and gaze behavior during rifle shooting. *Journal Sport & Exercise Psychology, 22,* 167–182.

Moran, A. P. (2009). Attention, concentration and thought management. In B. W. Brewer (Ed.), *Handbook of sports medicine and science, sport psychology* (pp. 18–29). Chichester, England: Wiley-Blackwell.

Munroe-Chandler, K., Hall, C., & Fishburne, G. (2008). Playing with confidence: The relationship between imagery use and self-confidence and self-efficacy in youth soccer players. *Journal of Sports Sciences, 26,* 1539–1546. doi: 10.1080/026404108002315419

Munroe-Chandler, K., Hall, C., & Fishburne, G., & Strachan, L. (2007). Where, when and why young athletes use imagery: An examination of developmental differences. *Research Quarterly for Exercise and Sport, 78,* 103–116.

Murphy, S. M., Nordin, S. M., & Cumming, J. (2008). Imagery in sport, exercise and dance. In T. S. Horn (Ed.), *Advances in sport and exercise psychology* (3rd ed., pp. 297–324). Champaign, IL: Human Kinetics.

Nicklaus, J. (1976). *Play better golf.* New York, NY: King Features.

Nieuwenhuys, A., Pijpers, J. R., Oudejans, R. R. D., & Bakker, F. C. (2008). The influence of anxiety on visual attention in climbing. *Journal of Sport & Exercise Psychology, 30,* 171–185.

Roberts, R., Callow, N., Hardy, L., Markland, D., & Bringer, J. (2008). Movement imagery ability: Development and assessment of a revised version of the Vividness of Movement Imagery Questionnaire. *Journal of Sport & Exercise Psychology, 30,* 200–221.

Smith, D., Wright, C., Allsopp, A., & Westhead, H. (2007). It's all in the mind: PETTLEP-Based imagery and sports performance. *Journal of Applied Sport Psychology, 19,* 80–92.

Vast, R. L., Young, R. L., & Thomas, P. R. (2010). Emotions in sport: Perceived effects on attention, concentration, and performance. *Australian Psychologist, 45,* 132–140. doi: 10.1080/000500060903261538

Vine, S. J., & Wilson, M. R. (2010). Quiet eye training: Effects on learning and performance under pressure. *Journal of Applied Sport Psychology, 22,* 361–376. doi: 10.1080/10413200.2010.495106

Williams, J. M., Nideffer, R. M., Wilson, V. E., Sagal, M-S., & Peper, E. (2010). Concentration and strategies for controlling it. In J. M. Williams (Ed.), *Applied sport psychology: Personal growth to peak performance* (6th ed., pp. 336–358), New York, NY: McGraw-Hill.

Williams, S. E., Cumming, J., & Balanos, G. M. (2010). The use of imagery to manipulate challenge and threat appraisal states in athletes. *Journal of Sport & Exercise Psychology, 32,* 339–358.

Zourbanos, N., Hatzigeorgiadis, A., Chroni, S., Theodorakis, Y., & Papaioannou, A. (2009). The Automatic Self-Talk Questionnaire for Sports (ASTQS): Development and preliminary validation. *The Sport Psychologist, 23,* 233–251.

Chapter 7

RELAXATION TRAINING

Calming the Physiology

Relaxation training

Standing on the platform, Karen prepared for the most difficult dive in her program. She was too nervous to visualize the elements of the dive and she noticed that she was shaking. She thought of how disappointed spectators and teammates would be with a poor dive. Fortunately, she recognized this anxiety and had a routine for disengaging it. She stalled for time by adjusting the springboard, not once, but twice. Breathing deeply, she noticed muscle tension and a nervous stomach. She focused on a point immediately below the navel or at the body's center of gravity. Flexing at the knees, she took a deep breath and while exhaling she experienced a release of tension and anxiety. She thought, "Now I'm in control."

In Chapter 4, the inverted-U hypothesis, Individualized Zone of Optimal Functioning (IZOF) model, catastrophe theory, and prime intensity were discussed. Each hypothesis or theory evaluated the effects of the physiological or somatic aspects of anxiety, and presented data indicating that either singularly or in some combination with cognitive anxiety, heightened levels of the physiological aspects of anxiety disrupted performance. Some researchers have minimized the importance of physiological anxiety on sport performance. These studies indicated the effects of physiological anxiety had less influence on performance than did the interpretation of that anxiety (Jones & Hanton, 1996, 2001; Robazza et al., 2008; Williams, Cumming, & Balanos, 2010). However, even if anxiety is interpreted as facilitative, physiological anxiety is only associated with better performance when accompanied by positive emotions, such as eagerness and pleasurable engagement (Sanchez, Boschker, & Llewellyn, 2010), as well as relaxation, which is a characteristic of peak performance in athletics (Hardy, Jones, & Gould, 1996; Roberts, Spink, & Pemberton, 1999). Further, there are significant differences between individuals in their capacity to interpret signs of physiological anxiety as facilitative. Prior experience in performing well while experiencing heightened arousal and perhaps empathic mentoring may be necessary to interpret heightened physiological anxiety as facilitative (Hanton & Jones, 1999a).

The experience of the physiological aspects of anxiety may be distracting, as attention is diverted from the performance to bodily signs of anxiety. As performers focus on their physiological responses, they miss critical environmental cues that determine optimal performance (Nideffer & Sagal, 2006).

Physiological anxiety also leads to fatigue. People with high anxiety have more unnecessary muscle activity and wasted energy before, during, and after athletic activities. They simultaneously contract agonist and antagonist muscle groups, and this **bracing** contributes to wasted muscular activity and inhibited coordination (Weinberg, 1977; Williams, 2010).

Physiological anxiety has less impact on performance that requires strength, speed, and power, but has a greater and detrimental influence on tasks that call for decision-making and fine motor control (Jones & Hanton, 1996). Athletes may attempt to increase somatic anxiety or arousal prior to sport requiring explosive power through "psyching-up" procedures. However, these procedures may easily become detrimental and result in "psyching-out" performers (Hardy, 1997). Superior performance often requires sustained practice across the course of years, and factors that contribute to overall adaptive functioning, such as the control of physiological anxiety, eventually influence performance on specific tasks.

BENEFITS OF CONTROLLING ANXIETY

Gaining control of physiological anxiety contributes to self-efficacy (Bandura, 1997), enhanced sport performance (Bois, Sarrazin, Southon, & Boiche, 2009; Greenspan & Feltz, 1989; Meyers, Whelan, & Murphy,

1996), and improved control of cognitive anxiety. For example, the practice of progressive muscle relaxation (PMR; Jacobson, 1938) produced significant reductions in cognitive anxiety among semiprofessional soccer players (Maynard, Hemmings, & Warwick-Evans, 1995). PMR will be discussed in this chapter and is a technique for reducing physiological anxiety. True to its design, PMR had a greater impact on the physiological than the cognitive anxiety of the semiprofessional soccer players. However, the footballers with PMR training came to interpret signs of physiological anxiety as facilitative, perhaps because they developed a greater belief in their ability to control arousal levels.

The control and management of cognitive anxiety appears to be an additional benefit of the reduction of physiological anxiety. Techniques that target cognitive anxiety have the greatest impact on reducing and managing cognitive anxiety (Lehrer, 1987; Norton & Johnson, 1983). For example, among the semiprofessional footballers (Maynard, Warwick-Evans, & Smith, 1995), the practice of a cognitive treatment for anxiety (Positive Thought Control; Suinn, 1987) reduced both the cognitive and physiological anxiety of footballers, but the reduction in cognitive anxiety was more marked. With Positive Thought Control, the footballers were more likely to interpret symptoms of cognitive and physiological anxiety as facilitative.

All findings considered, learning to control or contain physiological anxiety is adaptive. The focus of this chapter will be the psychological interventions for reducing physiological anxiety or arousal that have been the most reliably validated. Although these interventions are useful at a time proximal to evaluations, they require daily practice to be effective prior to and perhaps during evaluations. The regular practice of these techniques contributes to general well-being, as they serve to diminish the physiological and psychological reactions to chronic stress. Pharmacological interventions have also been used to reduce forms of anxiety. Of course, the use of medications requires the supervision of physicians, and the potential for side effects may outweigh their benefits (Lehrer, 1987). Beta blockers, as well as other drugs for controlling anxiety, are banned substances in many athletic venues, such as the Olympic Games (World Anti-Doping Agency, 2009). At some point after strenuous exercise, anxiety is reduced (Landers & Petruzzello, 1994). But this, of course, would be impractical before and during athletic competition, as it would deplete physical resources.

Furthermore, the practice of the relaxation and mindfulness techniques reviewed in this chapter confer additional benefits. With regular practice, these techniques support more positive moods, heightened immune functioning, and enhanced concentration. These benefits are realized not only during the practice of sport, but also throughout one's daily life (Conrad & Roth, 2007; Jha, Krompinger, & Baime, 2007).

The relaxation methods in this chapter may appear to be in conflict with many of the other recommendations discussed in this book. Most of these other recommendations involve active and goal-directed strivings and require analytic thought, awareness, and insight. Relaxation occurs when goal-directed activity ceases. Paradoxically, the harder one works to be relaxed, the less it occurs. Relaxation is more likely the result of "trying without trying" (Smith, 1990, p. 43). However, consistent with the techniques for mental proximal preparation discussed in Chapters 4, 5, and 6, the methods for realizing relaxation require systematic and regular practice.

PROGRESSIVE MUSCLE RELAXATION

Progressive muscle relaxation (PMR) is perhaps the most widely utilized technique for relaxation training in sport settings (Hanton, Thomas, & Mellalieu, 2009). **Edmund Jacobson,** an American physician and psychologist, developed PMR in the 1930s (Jacobson, 1938). The purpose of training in progressive relaxation is to recognize and eliminate tension in skeletal muscles (Lehrer & Carr, 1997). Jacobson conceptualized relaxation as a method of preserving adenosine triphosphate (ATP), one of the body's principle energy sources, avoiding deterioration of the skeletal muscles, and limiting fatigue. The theoretical rationale for PMR was that one of the routes by which brain structures, or specifically the ascending reticular activation system and the hypothalamus, received information about environmental stress is through the skeletal muscular system. By relaxing the skeletal muscles, the ascending reticular activation system and hypothalamus receive less information that the sympathetic branch of the autonomic nervous system should be activated to prepare the body for emergencies (Carlson & Bernstein, 1995; Field, 2009). It has also been proposed that the effects of PMR are due to the activation of the parasympathetic branch of the autonomic nervous system, which then inhibits the sympathetic branch. Nerve fibers also run from the ascending reticular activation system to the cortex, or the center for higher thinking. Therefore, skeletal muscle tension results in activation of the reticular action system, which then contributes to increased alertness and nervousness.

To review (Carlson & Bernstein, 1995), the autonomic and somatic nervous systems comprise the peripheral nervous system. The central nervous system consists of the brain and the spinal cord. The somatic nervous system allows for voluntary muscle control and regulates the functioning of the internal organs. Historically, the somatic nervous system has been labeled the voluntary peripheral nervous system and the term involuntary nervous system has been applied to the autonomic nervous system. The latter terms reflected the assumption that the functioning of the autonomic nervous system could not be consciously controlled, and that its function did not require conscious, volitional regulation. This belief in the uncontrollability of the autonomic nervous system waned after research with biofeedback demonstrated that voluntary regulation of autonomic processes was possible.

The **autonomic nervous system** consists of two branches, which to some degree are mutually inhibitory, such that the activation of one branch inhibits the activation of the other. Given optimal functioning of the autonomic system, the **sympathetic** and **parasympathetic** branches would be mutually self-regulatory. Under these conditions, optimal states of arousal would be maintained; the sympathetic branch would increase arousal in preparation for stressors ("fight-or-flight"), and the parasympathetic branch would decrease arousal levels when external threats or challenges were no longer present. Examples of sympathetic activation include increased heart rate, respiration, sweating, blood pressure, and other physiological components of arousal.

Application

The capacity to manage arousal and physiological anxiety under pressure is a welcome addition to a sportsperson's armamentarium. This skill comes with regular practice—something many athletes find unappealing. Practice may be more palatable if it is introduced in predictable quiet times, such as prior to going to sleep.

Instruction in PMR is available to the public without professional consultation. For example, Roberts et al. (1999) provided a script for the induction of PMR and recommended that individuals make a tape-recording of the script and then play the tape to induce relaxation. PMR training provided by audiotape has been shown to result in significant reductions in somatic or physiological arousal (Lehrer, 1982). However, the originator of PMR and other psychologists have subsequently cautioned that PMR should be taught by clinicians (Borkovec & Sides, 1979; Carlson & Bernstein, 1995; Jacobson, 1938; Lehrer, 1982; Lehrer & Carr, 1997), and medical clearance has been considered a prerequisite for relaxation-based therapy (Carlson & Bernstein, 1995). There are several reasons for this caution. First, people may differ in their capacity for observing and reporting on muscle tension. It is necessary for the person undertaking PMR training to be capable of observing and reporting on muscle tension. Second, PMR training by clinicians is probably more effective, as the training can be tailored on the basis of the trainee's responses and progress (Borkovec & Sides, 1979; Lehrer, 1982). For example, a trainee may have difficulty relaxing certain muscle groups and may require additional time and instruction before he experiences tension reduction in that muscle group. Third, sympathetic nervous system overactivation will probably remit more slowly in response to PMR if it is a chronic condition. Self-diagnosing sympathetic nervous system overactivation without medical consultation may also be risky, as forms of medical pathology may be overlooked or misdiagnosed. The symptoms of medical disorder, such as hyperthyroidism, nerve root compression, and cardiovascular disorders, may mimic symptoms of sympathetic overactivation. Finally, relaxation-induced anxiety may result from the practice of PMR and other forms of relaxation.

Relaxation-induced anxiety is rare and occurs most frequently in people who have preexisting anxiety disorders or significant anxiety problems (Carlson & Bernstein, 1995). Relaxation-induced anxiety has occurred with relaxation techniques that have cognitive (e.g., Transcendental Meditation, TM) or somatic (PMR) focuses, but appears more common for techniques with cognitive focuses (Heide & Borkovec, 1984; Norton, Rhodes, & Hauch, 1985). Indeed, a suggestion for counteracting this ironic process of becoming more anxious when attempting to relax is to downplay the importance of mental control and provide highly motivational instructions about how to achieve relaxation (Wegner, 1994, 2011; Wegner, Broome, & Blumberg, 1997).

There are several explanations for the mechanisms underlying relaxation-induced anxiety. Relaxation may increase anxiety in people who try to insure their well-being by continuously monitoring factors related to their safety. If they decrease these efforts at monitoring and vigilance, anxiety may increase due to their fear of losing control of themselves and their environment. Relaxation-induced anxiety may also result from increased attention and awareness of existent physiological anxiety, or to sources of cognitive anxiety or worry. Sequelae of parasympathetic nervous system dominance during relaxation can be frightening for chronically tense people, as they might experience heaviness, tingling, heat or cold, numbness, and even sensations of floating. Relaxation-induced panic and perhaps relaxation-induced anxiety have also been associated with hyperventilation, especially in persons prone to hyperventilation.

With these cautions in place, the procedures for PMR, Visuo-Motor Behavior Rehearsal, autogenic training, TM, the relaxation response, and centering will be outlined for the purpose of academic instruction. Readers interested in practicing these techniques may seek appropriate consultation.

The PMR Technique

PMR is a skill that improves with practice. People learning PMR begin by tensing and rapidly releasing tension in muscle groups. In this way muscles become deeply relaxed, and awareness about the sensations associated with tense versus relaxed muscles increases. There are 16 basic muscle groups, and a sequence of tensing each of them is as follows (Carlson & Bernstein, 1995, p. 25):

1. Dominant hand and forearm—make a tight fist
2. Dominant upper arm—push elbow down against chair
3. Nondominant hand and forearm—same as dominant
4. Nondominant upper arm—same as dominant
5. Forehead—raise eyebrows as high as possible
6. Upper cheeks and nose—squint and wrinkle nose

7. Lower face and jaw—clench teeth and pull back corners of mouth
8. Neck—pull chin toward chest and try to raise it simultaneously
9. Chest, shoulders, upper back—pull shoulder blades together
10. Abdomen—make stomach hard
11. Dominant upper leg—tense muscles on upper side and lower side
12. Dominant calf—pull toes toward head
13. Dominant foot—point toes downward, turn foot in, and curl toes gently
14. Nondominant upper leg—same as dominant
15. Nondominant calf—same as dominant
16. Nondominant foot—same as dominant

Each muscle group is tensed for five to seven seconds and relaxed for 30 to 40 seconds. Muscle groups should not be flexed to the point of pain, and the presence of injuries may necessitate the omission of muscle groups from this sequence or a reduction in the time it is flexed. Muscle spasm may occur, and are interpreted to trainees as signs of deep muscle relaxation. PMR is typically practiced in a seated position with eyes closed, and with support for the head and spine, and a reclining chair often provides optimal seating. Even with a reclining chair, trainees may be more comfortable if they are able to support body parts with pillows. Trainees adjust clothing and make visits to the restroom prior to initiating PMR so as to become as comfortable as possible. A minimum of muscle contractions, movements, and vocalizations should occur prior to initiating PMR. People with bronchial problems may have difficulty breathing or may cough frequently. Adjustments in seating positions may alleviate bronchial problems, but severe difficulties may necessitate postponement of PMR training.

Clinicians instruct trainees to tense and relax each muscle group twice. After the second time, trainees signal by raising the index finger on the dominant hand only to indicate that the muscle group is completely relaxed. Trainees try not to move muscle groups after they have been relaxed with this procedure, and try to remain silent except for the aforementioned finger signals. This emphasis on stillness is intended to encourage relaxation and attentional focus on the muscle groups that are sequentially relaxed. Breathing should be slow and rhythmic. As muscles are tensed and relaxed, the trainee focuses on the difference in sensations. After the sequence of 16 exercises, trainees are asked to indicate with their index finger if their entire body is relaxed. If muscle groups are still tense, the appropriate exercise should be used to induce relaxation.

This entire sequence of 16 exercises comprises an abbreviated version of PMR, and can be completed in a training session of approximately 45 minutes. If trainees faithfully practice this PMR on a twice-daily basis for 15 to 20 minutes, they will probably be capable of realizing deep relaxation with the 16-muscle-group procedure after approximately three training sessions. From this point, the PMR procedure can be abbreviated in a number of steps. The goal of abbreviating the induction of PMR is to induce relaxation rapidly, without the necessity of muscle contractions, and in a range of venues.

First, the 16 exercises can be condensed to a group of seven exercises. The seven exercises are conducted in the same manner as the original 16, and are as follows (Carlson & Bernstein, 1995, p. 28):

1. Dominant hand, forearm, and upper arm
2. Nondominant hand, forearm, and upper arm
3. All muscles in the face
4. Neck
5. Chest, shoulders, upper back, and abdomen
6. Dominant upper leg, calf, and foot
7. Nondominant upper leg, calf, and foot

With approximately two weeks of practice, most trainees are able to experience deep relaxation with this seven-step procedure. Some may have difficulty combining certain steps, and it may be necessary to separate and individually practice the components of the steps that cause difficulty. When the seven-step process has been mastered, the process can be condensed to the following four steps (Carlson & Bernstein, 1995, p. 28):

1. Both arms and both hands
2. Face and neck
3. Chest, shoulders, back, and abdomen
4. Both legs and feet

With mastery of these four steps, relaxation can be induced in approximately 10 minutes. Throughout this process, PMR is practiced twice daily.

The next step in the process of condensing the PMR process is to achieve relaxation by simply recalling the sensations in the each of the four muscle groups included in the four steps above. Trainees are first asked to recall the sensations in the both arms and hands after they were first tensed and then relaxed. Trainees direct their attention to these sensations with the cue words "O.K., relax." If this "relaxation by recall" has been successful, attention is directed to the face and neck, and the same cue words are used to initiate relaxation in those regions. If muscle groups are not relaxed with this recall procedure, attention is redirected to the sensations of releasing tension from the muscle groups with the same cue words. If the muscle groups remain tense, the process of tensing and relaxing that muscle group is repeated. This process continues for Steps 3 and 4, and this relaxation by recall is practiced at home on a twice-daily basis.

Once the recall procedure has been developed to reliably induce relaxation, adding a counting procedure deepens relaxation. At the end of a relaxation by recall procedure, the trainee is encouraged to relax more deeply as the therapist or trainer counts from 1 to 10. A number is recited at each exhalation, and the trainee may imagine descending to deeper relaxation as the numbers increase.

The last step in the process of streamlining PMR, to make it as rapid and portable as possible, consists of inducing relaxation with only the counting-from-1-to-10 procedure. Alternately, trainees may scan their bodies for signs of tension, and release the tension ("O.K., relax") in tight muscles (Williams, 2010). If the trainee is unsuccessful in realizing relaxation with just this counting or scanning process, he or she is instructed to recall muscle relaxation in the four muscle groups. If the trainee remains tense, then one or more tense-release-relax cycles with the four muscle groups are initiated. After relaxation is reliably achieved by counting alone, the relaxation by counting-alone procedure should be practiced at least once daily.

PMR has been used successfully with athletes. For example, after PMR training, the accuracy of serves increased and anxiety decreased among female high-school varsity volleyball players (Lanning & Hisanaga, 1983).

VISUO-MOTOR BEHAVIOR REHEARSAL

A procedure similar to the final step in the streamlined PMR procedure described above has been used in athletic venues (Suinn, 1986). This onsite relaxation does not appear to be as streamlined as the PMR described above. In addition to focusing on breathing and using cue words such as "O.K., relax," the visualization of relaxation in muscles is encouraged. Trainees are encouraged to visualize each muscle group loosening up "like light bulbs being turned off one by one" (Suinn, 1986, p. 9).

Whether mastery of PMR would strengthen the capacity to relax on cue and accomplish relaxation during competitions remains an open question. Despite the similarities between the two approaches, this question has not been answered with empirical research.

This discussion has focused on streamlining PMR so that relaxation can be realized more rapidly and during performances. Relaxation has also been coupled with mental rehearsal, mental practice, and visualization in **Visuo-Motor Behavior Rehearsal (VMBR;** Suinn, 1986). VMBR calls for the induction of relaxation and then mental practice. The objective of these exercises is to transfer the relaxation experienced during mental practice to conditions of actual practice and competition (Suinn, 1986), and it has been shown to enhance athletic performance in golf, cross-country running, gymnastics (Lohr & Scogin, 1998), karate (Weinberg, Seabourne, & Jackson, 1981), tennis serving (Lohr & Scogin, 1998; Noel, 1980), basketball free-throw accuracy (Hall & Erffmeyer, 1983; Gray & Fernandez, 1989; Lohr & Scogin, 1998), pistol marksmanship (Hall & Hardy, 1991), racquetball (Gray, 1990), and Frisbee tossing (Andre & Means, 1986).

Relaxation has also been combined with the recall of successful performances to encourage the emergence of the IZOF, or Individualized Zone of Optimal Functioning. Of course, the mental practice during relaxed states should emphasize competence, mastery of challenging situations, and self-efficacy in competitions. Mental practice of this sort may lead not only to the emergence of optimal states of intensity, but also makes it more likely that intensity is interpreted as facilitative of good performance (Hale & Whitehouse, 1998).

VMBR has been used to decrease daily stress among NCAA Division II swimmers and NCAA Division I football players. A correlate of stress is susceptibility to injuries, and injuries among swimmers and football players were reduced by 58% and 33%, respectively, during the years VMBR was instituted (Davis, 1991). The competitive records of both teams improved dramatically during the same years. This was not an experimental study, and the degree to which VMBR contributed to these results is not entirely clear. As explained in Chapter 6, visualization and mental practice is not a substitute for physical practice. Further, mental practice is unlikely to bring improvements in performance if the skills that are visualized have not already been mastered physically (Noel, 1980).

AUTOGENIC TRAINING

Although the title of this chapter is "Calming the Physiology," the techniques to accomplish this calming or reduction in anxiety or arousal are generally described as having more wide-ranging benefits. For example, **autogenic training (AT)** has been described as a physiological self-control therapy and a psychophysiologic form of psychotherapy (Linden, 1990; Luthe, 1970). The benefits of AT have been shown to extend beyond the acute reduction of arousal. People trained in autogenic techniques demonstrated less cortisol production in response to stress. Cortisol has routinely been identified as a hormonal correlate of stress reactions. Patterns of brain waves are routinely altered during the practice of AT. Typical changes include increased synchronicity of brain waves and predominance of alpha waves during AT practice. Alpha waves have been reliably associated with deep relaxation. Respiration decreases during AT practice, and skin temperature increases during the warmth formula, which will be described below. AT practice results in reduced heart rates, and contractions of the muscles in the forehead (Blumenstein, Breslav, Bar-Eli, Tenenbaum, & Weinstein, 1995).

The term "autogenic" is derived from the Greek, and is defined as a type of self-induced therapy. AT is a method by which people can gain greater control of their autonomic nervous system. AT has been proposed as a method to maintain optimal homeostasis or balance of the autonomic system, and this may often involve decreasing the activation of the sympathetic branch. AT involves a passive focus on bodily sensations and involves elements of a self-hypnotic trance. Johann H. Schultz, a German neurologist, developed AT, and his first book on the topic was published in 1932 (Schultz, 1932). AT is probably the most widely practiced self-regulation therapy in the world, but it is infrequently applied and studied in English-speaking countries. AT may occur individually or in groups. AT instruction should be provided by experienced therapists (Linden, 1990; Pikoff, 1985).

AT has been shown to be efficacious in the treatment of disorders such as insomnia, migraine headaches, and Raynaud's disease (Linden, 1994; Pikoff, 1985). Raynaud's disease is a functional disorder of the cardio-vascular system involving intermittent vasospasms, or constriction of the blood vessels, causing restricted blood flow to the hands, feet, or face on exposure to low temperatures or stress.

When combined with mental imagery training, AT enhanced performance among biathletes. The biathlon is a winter sport that combines cross-country skiing with rifle marksmanship. Biathletes held their rifles more stably while standing and aiming, and shot more accurately, after AT and mental imagery training (Gieremek, Osialdlo, Rudzinska, & Nowotny, 1994; Groslambert, Candau, Grappe, Dogue, and Rouillon, 2003).

AT is also rightly described as a method of calming the physiology, as, unlike most psychological interventions, it has a direct effect on physiological functioning (Linden, 1994). AT is not considered appropriate for young children or people with mental retardation or acute central nervous system disorders. The minimum age necessary for trainees to benefit from AT has been estimated to be between 6 and 10 years. The cautions described in the section in PMR about relaxation-induced anxiety pertain. The trainee's concerns about loss of control may be mitigated if trainees understand relaxation training as another method for controlling themselves.

The degree to which these techniques can be self-taught has not been determined. There may be a risk in attempting AT without the supervision of a therapist, in that "autogenic discharges" or anxiety may be precipitated by AT. Clearly, AT will be more effective if practiced regularly (Linden, 1994).

Due to space limitations, the following is an abbreviated description of AT. AT consists of instruction in six standard formulas or exercises. In the first formula, trainees are taught to focus on muscular relaxation, which is experienced as heaviness. Unlike PMR, there is no instruction to flex muscle groups, and attention is focused on just the experience of heaviness in the dominant arm. The specific procedures for the first formula are as follows:

1. The trainee assumes a comfortable sitting or lying position. With eyes closed, attention is given to bodily reactions for a period of two minutes.
2. The first formula consists of silently repeating, "My right (left) arm is very heavy" (Linden, 1990, p. 27) six times and for a duration of approximately one minute.
3. The trainee is then instructed to direct attention from the arm, to silently repeat, "I am very quiet" (Linden, 1990, p. 28), and to enjoy the experience of relaxation for a duration of approximately two minutes.

4. Procedure 2 is repeated.
5. Procedure 3 is repeated.
6. A "take back" procedure is initiated. This allows for a gradual emergence from the autogenic state of relaxation. It consists of four steps, and a waiting period of 15 seconds precedes each step.
7. The trainee is instructed to make several fists with their hands in rapid succession to "get the blood pumping."
8. The arms are bent inward several times.
9. A few deep breaths are taken and the lungs are filled with air.
10. The trainee opens his or her eyes and is instructed to feel relaxed and alert.

The focus of the second formula is the entire peripheral cardiovascular system. It involves the same six procedures as the first formula, with the exception that the formula "My arm is very warm" (Linden, 1990, p. 30) replaces "My right (left) arm is very heavy" on procedures 2 and 4. All of the formulas are silently repeated six times. This formula results in an increase of at least one-degree Celsius in body warmth after it has been mastered. This formula relies on vascular dilation and should be attempted only by individuals without cardiovascular impairment.

Perhaps in the third of eight training sessions, the first and second formulas are combined. The formula "My right (left) arm is very heavy" is used on procedure 2 and "My arm is very warm" is repeated on procedure 4. The remaining four procedures are identical to those described in exercise one.

The focus of the third formula is the regulation of the heart. This begins with an awareness of the heart beating. Some may be able to feel their heart beating, and others may become aware of their heart beating by monitoring their pulse. Still others may be instructed to lie flat on their back with their right hand placed over their heart so that they can monitor their heartbeat. When trainees can recognize and monitor their heartbeat, formula three "My heartbeat is calm and strong" (Linden, 1990, p. 33) is introduced and repeated on procedure 4. The formula, "My arms are very heavy and warm" (Linden, 1990, p. 27) is repeated on procedure 2. The purpose of this formula is not to reduce the heart rate because this could lead to damage.

Formula four concerns the regulation of breathing. This does not result from intentional changes in the rate of breathing, as breathing in AT is to function autonomously and in a self-regulatory manner. The fourth formula "It breathes me" (Linden, 1990, p 34) reflects this passive focus on breathing. Trainees are encouraged to find their own breathing rhythm. The fourth formula is introduced as procedure 6 and procedures 1 through 5 are the same as described above.

The focus of formula five is the regulation of the visceral organs and especially the area of the solar plexus. The solar plexus is located halfway between the navel and the lower end of the sternum. The sternum is also referred to as the breastbone and is located by tracing a line from the navel northward to the bone from which the ribs arch. The fifth formula is "Warmth is radiating over my stomach" (Linden, 1990, p. 36), and the trainee is encouraged to think of solar plexus as a sun that sends warm rays to other areas of the body. The fourth formula is introduced as procedure 8 and procedures 1 through 7 are the same as described above.

The goal of formula six, "The forehead is cool" (Linden, 1990, p. 38), is the regulation of the head. The trainee might imagine that a cool cloth has been placed on the forehead or that they experience a cool breeze. This formula involves vasoconstriction and occasionally has resulted in migraine headaches or fainting. The fourth formula is introduced as procedure 10 and procedures 1 through 9 are the same as described above.

TRANSCENDENTAL MEDITATION

PMR and AT target peripheral manifestations of arousal or anxiety, such as muscle tension, breathing, and heartbeat. Forms of meditation emphasize the importance of achieving states of mental stillness, and decreased arousal or anxiety occurs in the process of quieting thought. Decreased arousal is considered a necessary but not sufficient condition for meditation, as the latter requires an alertness associated with coordinated or organized neuronal functioning in the brain (Jevning, Wallace, & Beidebach, 1992). **Transcendental Meditation (TM)** is a widely practiced relaxation method. Consistent with other techniques reviewed in this chapter, the regular practice of TM produces additional health benefits, such as the treatment and prevention of hypertension (elevated systolic and diastolic blood pressure; Schneider, Alexander, & Wallace, 1992).

TM History

TM has probably existed for thousands of years, but its current form was widely disseminated by Maharishi Mahesh Yogi (Russell, 1976). According to TM teachings, Maharishi acquired the TM technique from the Indian sage Brahmananda Saraswati. Brahmananda Saraswati spent the majority of his life living in solitude in the Himalayas and was referred to as the "Divine Teacher." Maharishi brought the TM technique to Western nations from India, and the first permanent Western teaching center was established in California in 1959. To facilitate the rapid growth of TM, Maharishi trained instructors, and by 1975, approximately 10,000 people were qualified to teach TM. The Beatles focused international attention on TM as a result of their TM training at the Maharishi's training center, or ashram, in Rishekesh in northern India in 1968 (Brown & Gaines, 1983). The Maharishi International University was established in Iowa to integrate the study of TM with conventional academic disciplines, and the Foundation for the Science of Creative Intelligence was built to offer TM services to business and industry. By 1975, TM was estimated to be the fastest-growing organization in the world, as approximately 35,000 people per month were trained in TM. By 1975, there were an estimated 550,000 trainees in the United States and one million worldwide. Today, it is practiced by as many as five million people worldwide (Transcendental

Medication, n.d.). In excess of 500 studies concerning the effects of TM have been conducted in 33 countries around the world and in over 100 peer-reviewed journals (Orme-Johnson, Zimmerman, & Hawkins, 1997).

TM training has been standardized and is provided only by certified instructors. The standard fee for adults for TM training is $1,500, but scholarships are available based on need. The Maharishi has been adamant that there be no alteration in the TM technique. It is provided in four lessons on four consecutive days. Three additional sessions are then provided to determine that the meditation is progressing properly. The novice at TM checks with the instructor after approximately two weeks to evaluate progress, and this process of checking on the progress of trainees becomes less frequent with the passage of time.

The TM Technique

Essentially, the goal of TM is to achieve a state of mental stillness. TM trainees are assigned **mantras,** or words that carry no meaning but that are phonetically soothing or pleasant sounding. Mantras serve as vehicles for directing attention inward and ferry thought to deeper levels that are quiet or relatively devoid of conscious meaning. Indeed, TM has been labeled transcendental because it was considered to allow for transcending the usual forms of conscious thought and foster the experience of the source of human thought or pure consciousness.

This diminution of mental activity is considered to be imminently satisfying, rewarding, and charming (Orme-Johnson et al., 1997). Therefore, meditators did not have to make efforts to rid their minds of distracting thoughts, as they would seek this self-reinforcing state of pure consciousness once they were provided with TM instruction.

Realizing this state of mental stillness is a result of a paradoxical technique of not trying to rid the mind of distractions, but rather of passively allowing attention to move toward the satisfying state of stillness. This technique may be counterintuitive for many people concerned with achievement, as it operates on the basis of "the less effort, the better" (Russell, 1976, p. 43). The Maharishi taught that this technique was so surefire that it would inevitably carry meditators to states of mental silence regardless of whether the meditators believed that TM was worthwhile.

Effects of TM

Physiological changes in the activity of the brain occur during the practice of TM. Brain activity during TM is similar to that during the transition from waking to sleeping, and brain waves consisting of theta-alpha and delta waves are often recorded. Alpha waves are associated with an alert mind that is not focused on solving problems and delta waves have been associated with deep sleep. The presence of theta-alpha and delta waves has been interpreted by advocates of TM as an indication of transcendental consciousness (Travis, 1994). Brain waves appear to synchronize across sections of the cortex during TM, and advocates of TM interpret this synchrony as an indication of intellectual flexibility and efficiency (Orme-Johnson et al., 1997).

The effects of TM that are most central to the focus of this chapter are the degree to which TM reduces somatic arousal during meditation and whether the regular practice of TM allows one to respond more adaptively to stressors. It is unlikely that TM practice reduces physiological arousal more than simply resting with eyes closed (Holmes, 1984) At most, in comparison to resting with eyes closed, TM practice may result in greater reductions in somatic arousal as measured by skin resistance, respiration rate, and plasma lactate, but not heart rate or spontaneous skin resistance (Dillbeck & Orme-Johnson, 1987). Simple rest may lower these physiological measures sufficiently so that additional decreases in arousal are unlikely regardless of the technique utilized to reduce arousal (Morrell, 1986). There is no evidence that the practice of TM is associated with less somatic arousal or release of stress hormones in response to threatening situations (Dillbeck & Orme-Johnson, 1987; Holmes, 1984; MacLean et al., 1997).

In the interest of fairness, it should also be noted that TM has been evaluated more thoroughly than other relaxation techniques, and there is no proof that the regular practice of other techniques prepares athletes to respond more adaptively to stressors. Furthermore, the physiological and psychological effects of TM and PMR are similar (Lehrer, Woolfolk, Rooney, McCann, & Carrington, 1983; Throll, 1982; Zuroff & Schwarz, 1978).

TM and Golf

The members of the golf team at Maharishi High in Fairfield, Iowa, practiced an advanced form of meditation known as TM-Sidhi. This form of TM is also known as yogic flying. The distinguishing feature of yogic flying is levitation during the practice of TM (TM-Sidhi Program, n.d.). A member of the Maharishi High golf team levitated by bouncing "on his bum like a human Super Ball," and experienced "a zap of bliss" (Lidz, 1996, p. 123) when in the air.

Fairfield, Iowa, is also the home of the Marharishi University of Management, and the golf coach at Maharishi High, Ed Hipp, was also a TM instructor. For these golfers and Coach Hipp, TM presented a unifying principle for practice, competition, and the conduct of their daily lives: "Our whole lives are a preshot routine" (Lidz, 1996, p. 123). In just his third year as coach, Hipp's Maharishi Pioneers won the Iowa State 1A Golf Championship by 19 strokes.

THE RELAXATION RESPONSE

The concepts of minimizing conscious thought and movement, utilizing mantras, and descending to transcendental states of consciousness are not unique to Eastern cultures. Christians in the fourteenth century utilized meditative practices to achieve unity with God, and suggestions for mantras included the words "love" or "God" (Benson, 1983). Examples of Jewish mysticism date to the second century BC. Early Islamic mysticism also involved the repetition of the name of God, as well as rhythmic breathing. These examples notwithstanding, mysticism has not been as integral to Western religious practices and to everyday life in the West, as has been the case in the East. Benson noted that in the sixth century BC, Indian scriptures outlined the basic principles of meditation, and that meditative practices are outlined in Zen Buddhism, Shintoism, Taoism, and Shamanism.

The American cardiologist Herbert Benson studied forms of meditation and relaxation (e.g., Wallace & Benson, 1972) and argued that a common variable accounted for the physiological benefits and altered states of consciousness associated with these meditation techniques and with TM, AT, and hypnosis. Benson (Benson, Greenwood, & Klemchuk, 1975) and independent researchers (Lehrer, Carr, Sargunaraj, & Woolfolk, 1994) described this variable as the **relaxation response.** The relaxation response was seen to be responsible for parasympathetic nervous system activation and inhibition of the sympathetic nervous system, and decreased oxygen consumption and carbon dioxide elimination. Altered states of consciousness associated with the relaxation response were a result of cortical activity or brain waves associated with relaxation and well-being. This activity consists of increased slow alpha waves, occasional theta waves, and decreased beta waves (Jacobs, Benson, & Friedman, 1996).

Consistent with other methods of calming physiological arousal, practice of the relaxation response is helpful for decreasing blood pressure, hypertension, cardiac arrhythmias (Everly & Benson, 1989), and the number of premature ventricular contractions (a risk factor for mortality in patients with ischemic heart disease). It is recommended as an intervention to facilitate recovery from athletic injuries (Walsh, 2011).

Benson (1983) described the relaxation response as a simple nonreligious technique, and it is the simplest method described in this chapter. The aforementioned changes in alpha, theta, and beta waves were observed with volunteer subjects during their first exposure to the relaxation response technique, which consisted of listening to tape-recorded instructions (Benson, 1983). There are four steps for realizing the relaxation response:

1. Sit quietly in a comfortable position with eyes closed.
2. Deeply relax all of the muscle systems, beginning with the feet, and progressing to the face. Maintain this relaxation in the muscle systems.
3. Breathe through the nose. During exhalation, silently repeat the word *one*. Continue this process

Pathways to the relaxation response

or silently repeating the word *one* during exhalation for approximately 20 minutes. After 20 minutes, sit quietly for a few minutes, first with eyes closed and then with eyes open.

4. Maintain a passive attitude about whether a state of deep relaxation is realized. That is, do not worry about or become concerned about whether one is "getting it right" or achieving a state of deep relaxation. Allow relaxation to occur at its own pace. Also, do not attempt to fight off intrusive thoughts so as to focus solely on the word *one*. Ignore distracting thoughts by thinking "Oh well" (Benson et al, 1975), and continue to repeat the word *one*. Practice the relaxation response once or twice daily, but not within two hours of eating, because digestive processes may interfere the subjective experience.

CENTERING

In Chapter 6, centering was discussed as a relaxation technique for use not only before but also during athletic performances (Nideffer, 1993). To review, **centering** involves directing the focus of attention to a point immediately below the navel, or the body's center of gravity. This focus is paired with recommendations to let one's mind rest on the experience of strength and balance. With centering, attention is briefly directed inward to check one's pattern of breathing and muscular tension. In preparation for performances, this centering focus should be associated with deep, abdominal breathing, so that under pressure an athlete can very quickly control both his or her focus and breathing. Shallow, thoracic breathing is associated with anxiety and muscle tension.

Centering has the secondary benefit of interrupting cognitive interference. It is beneficial to learn to center from the standing position, both because athletes are often standing in competition and because it is most difficult to control breathing and muscular tension from the standing position. From the standing position, athletes are directed to spread their legs to shoulder width and to flex slightly at the knees. Then inhaling deeply, athletes should scan for tension in arms, shoulders, and neck muscles, and consciously let these muscle groups relax. When exhaling, athletes allow the muscles in their thighs and calves to relax, permit their knees to bend slightly and their hips to lower. Thoughts of relaxation, heaviness, and the purging of anxiety are associated with exhalation (Nideffer, 1985). With practice, the purpose of centering is to shed excessive physiological anxiety and muscle tension in a single breath. It is a technique for gaining momentary control over physiological anxiety or arousal and concentration. It is recommended for use just prior to crucial points in a match or competition when anxiety is likely to be highest. Its practice is also recommended during natural pauses in competitions, as well as prior to and after performances.

Characteristics of centering are similar to those of the relaxation response. Both emphasize attention to breathing and techniques are straightforward.

Centering offers the considerable promise of being maximally "portable," in that it can be practiced before, after, and during competitions.

MINDFULNESS AND ACCEPTANCE-BASED BEHAVIOR THERAPIES

As was the case with TM and centering, **mindfulness** is based on Eastern spiritual traditions, primarily Buddhism (Kabat-Zinn, 2003). Mindfulness meditational practices were reinterpreted as a set of skills that were independent of religious beliefs by Western mental health and medical professionals, such as John Kabat-Zinn, an American biologist. Among the interventions based on mindfulness are: mindfulness-based stress reduction (Kabat-Zinn, 1982, 1990), mindfulness-based cognitive therapy (Segal, Williams, & Teasdale, 2002), acceptance and commitment therapy (Hayes, Strosahl, & Wilson, 1999), and the Mindfulness-Acceptance-Commitment approach (Gardner & Moore, 2004, 2006, 2007).

Two components underlie mindfulness: directing attention to the present moment, and observing immediate experience with curiosity, openness, and acceptance (Bishop et al., 2004). Attention is redirected to the present moment if it wanders. Rumination or elaborative processing is inhibited. That is, one suspends efforts to enhance the present moment with thoughts of getting more of what one wants, such as pleasure or advancement, or to rid oneself of undesirable experiences or qualities, such as anxiety or feelings of failure (Shapiro & Carlson, 2009). Focusing on desired outcomes or on avoiding failure not only detracts from well-being, but is also inimical to optimal performance in sport (see Chapter 11).

Mindfulness practice promotes more efficient use of attentional resources (Salmon, Hanneman, & Harwood, 2010). As explained in Chapter 6, attentional resources are limited to the amount of information that can be sustained and processed in working or active memory at any given time. The limit of working memory is approximately seven, plus or minus two units of information (Kareev, 2000; Miller, 1956). Experienced meditators have heightened capacities for sustaining attention on target while suppressing distractions. This process of mindful attention becomes automated or less effortful with practice (Marks, 2008). Storage space in their working memories is captured less by verbal and emotional distractions. Additional working memory resources are therefore available for sustained attention on targets in the environment (Brefczynski-Lewis et al., 2007).

With mindfulness practice, efforts to directly control the contents of one's thoughts are discouraged (Schwanhausser, 2009). Efforts to suppress thoughts and emotions may create ironic processes (Wegner, 2011) that exacerbate internal conflicts when expectations of how life "should be" fail to match how life actually is (Siegel, 2007). With mindful awareness, people are more capable of stepping outside their immediate experience, and observing their thoughts with detachment and objectivity. For example, under pressure, a sportsperson may perceive anxiety without becoming embedded in it: "The anxiety is not me; I notice myself having worries; just distractions, nothing really."

Phil Jackson on Zen

As coach of the Chicago Bulls and Los Angeles Lakers, Phil Jackson won a record 10 NBA (National Basketball Association) Championships. His coaching philosophy was influenced by instruction in Christianity from his parents, studying the teachings of the Lakota Sioux (a Native American tribe), and by his practice of Zen:

> In basketball—as in life—true joy comes from being fully present in each and every moment, not just when things are going your way. Of course, it's no accident that things are more likely to go your way when you stop worrying about whether you're going to win or lose and focus your full attention on what's happening *right this moment* (Jackson & Delehanty, 1995, p. 4).
>
> In Zen it is said that the gap between accepting things the way they are and wishing them to be otherwise is "the tenth of an inch of difference between heaven and hell." If we can accept whatever hand we've been dealt—no matter how unwelcome—the way to proceed eventually becomes clear. This is what is meant by right action: the capacity to observe what's happening and act appropriately, without being distracted by self-centered thoughts. If we rage and resist, our angry, fearful minds have trouble quieting down sufficiently to allow us to act in the most beneficial way for ourselves and others (Jackson & Delehanty, 1995, p. 69).

This capacity to dispassionately observe the contents of one's consciousness—*reperceiving*—has been understood as the underlying mechanism for the benefits of mindfulness practice (Shapiro & Carlson, 2009). As practitioners of mindfulness become more aware of, and less frightened of, their thoughts, they are more capable of coping effectively with problems and worries. The mere willingness to keep uncomfortable thoughts and images in mind leads to a decrease in their emotional intensity and negative valence (Marks, 2008). If the scope of mindfulness extends to a consideration of values, practitioners may clarify whether priorities have been objectively chosen or simply internalized from family and cultural experience.

Application

Emotionally valenced, anxiety-arousing thoughts are fully capable of hijacking working memory resources and diverting attention from the present moment. Ironically, one's imagination may be more influential than the physical reality of the external world. The persistence of these thoughts may be frustrating, annoying, and even distressing, but ultimately, these are mere thoughts. Just as sportspersons may compete when sick or injured, they can also take the field when beset by emotionally valenced thoughts. The influence of cognitive interference is likely to lessen as athletes immerse themselves in the very tangible reality of play and competition.

The benefits of mindfulness are wide-ranging. Mindfulness is associated with heightened abilities to regulate emotion and limit symptoms of anxiety, depression, addictive behaviors, and Borderline Personality Disorder (Shapiro & Carlson, 2009). Its practice is inversely correlated to neurotic perfectionism (Argus & Thompson, 2008; Teasdale et al., 2000). It is related to optimistic mindsets and physical health. MBSR practice serves to reduce pain symptoms among chronic pain patients (Kabat-Zinn, 1982; Randolph, Caldera, Tacone, & Greak, 1999). Healthier immune, hormone, and blood pressure profiles resulted from MBSR practice among cancer patients (Carlson, Speca, Patel, & Faris, 2007; Carlson, Speca, Patel, & Goodey, 2004). ACT practice reduced the likelihood of seizures among epilepsy patients (Lundgren, Dahl, Melin, & Kies, 2006; Lundgren, Dahl, Yardi, & Melin, 2008).

Mindfulness Practice

A general model of mindfulness practice consists of three core elements: intention, attention, and attitude (Shapiro, Carlson, Astin, & Freedman, 2006). **Intention** refers to the motivation for practicing mindfulness. Outcomes are correlated with intensions. For example, the intention to manage stress and anxiety is more likely to lead to this result. **Attention** refers to focusing on internal and external experiences in the present moment. This attention is sufficiently sustained to allow for a thorough examination of experience. When attention is disrupted by judgments and wishes for things to be different, it tends to be less focused. **Attitude** relates to qualities that one brings to this focused attention. The attitudes of acceptance, openness, caring, and curiosity are productive for focusing attention. The attitudes of patience, compassion, and nonstriving contribute to capacities to relinquish habitual striving for pleasant experiences and avoiding unpleasant experiences.

The formal practice of mindfulness involves activities such as sitting meditation, body scan meditation, and walking meditation. Mindfulness is practiced informally when people engage in daily activities with mindful awareness (Baer & Krietemeyer, 2006).

As mentioned above, there are several forms of mindfulness acceptance-based behavior therapies. The **mindfulness-based stress reduction (MBSR;** Kabat-Zinn, 1982, 1990) intervention consists of eight weekly sessions of 150 to 180 minutes. In week six, an all-day intensive session is conducted. Participants commit to mindfulness practices for 45 minutes per day, six days per week.

Among the practices of MBSR are the raisin exercise, body scan, sitting meditation, hatha yoga, and walking meditation. The raisin exercise involves directing one's attention entirely to the sight, smell, feel, and taste of a single raisin. For the body scan, reclining participants notice sensation in body parts. They systematically scan the body, and notice tension with curiosity and a nonjudgmental attitude. The body is scanned from toe to head in a manner similar to that described above for PMR.

Unlike PMR, no effort is made to relax muscles. Sitting meditation involves a focus on breathing and observation of the thoughts that enter conscious awareness. Hatha yoga cultivates awareness of the body while stretching, moving, or holding a position. Attention is focused on bodily experiences during walking meditation. All of these principles are incorporated in the all-day session. Participants are also encouraged to remain silent and avoid eye contact during the all-day session.

Mindfulness-based cognitive therapy (MBCT; Segal, Williams, & Teasdale, 2002) incorporates many of the components of MBSR. It is taught in eight weekly sessions of 120 minutes. MBCT also offers the three-minute breathing space exercise. Participants are taught to focus on their current experience—thoughts, emotional states, bodily sensations—for one minute. Full attention is directed to one's breathing for the second minute of the exercise. In the third minute, awareness is expanded to bodily sensations and posture, again with acceptance and without judgment. Participants are also invited to deliberately bring difficulties to mind during periods of sitting meditation. This counteracts usual tendencies to avoid difficult or painful feelings. Facing difficulties with curiosity and openness allows for their mastery and results in desensitization or a reduction in attendant anxiety.

The goal of **acceptance and commitment therapy** (ACT; Hayes, Strosahl, & Wilson, 1999) is to increase awareness and understanding of emotional states, and to help people accept and tolerate forms of distress, such as anxiety (Moore, 2009). Indeed, forms of distress such as worry and perfectionism are considered inefficient attempts to regulate emotional states. Participants are taught to embrace thoughts and emotions that were previously feared and avoided. They develop a capacity for cognitive defusion, or the ability to objectively observe their thoughts and emotions without becoming consumed by them. With cognitive defusion, people realize that thoughts are not necessarily true or productive, and that they do not have to act in accordance with their content. There is less pressure to ward off thoughts if they are understood to be relatively harmless and temporary. Thoughts and emotions are also less threatening if they are understood as separate from oneself, transient, and relatively inconsequential. The self is the context in which thoughts and experiences occur and is not synonymous with these experiences. ACT understands the statement "I am a choke artist" as evidence that the self is considered synonymous with experience. A statement such as "I am having the thought that I am a choke artist" facilitates recognition that the self is separate from unproductive thoughts and experiences.

The **Mindfulness-Acceptance-Commitment** approach (MAC; Gardner & Moore, 2004, 2006, 2007) is an integration of MBCT and ACT. With the MAC practice, athletes focus attention in the present moment and accept internal experiences in a nonjudgmental manner. They are also trained to direct their attention to performance-related cues in the environment during competition and to valued athletic goals (commitment) during training and practice. This focus on values and goals counteracts tendencies to avoid discomfort in pursuit of goals. For example, tendencies to avoid painful experiences in training, such as oxygen debt, may be counteracted by reminding oneself that the experience of suffering is the price one pays to reach goals.

There are five components to MAC training. With *psychoeducation*, athletes are taught to identify internal cues to performance difficulties. Mindfulness practice is modified for athletic participation and includes: *mindful drill/practice skills, mindful pre-game stretching and warm-ups, full body-scan mindfulness*, and *mindfulness of the breath* (Gardner & Moore, 2004). The objective of this practice is to increases nonjudgmental awareness of internal experience.

Mindfulness and Sport

Mindfulness techniques have been seen essentially as an opposite perspective to traditional methods of mental skills training. Traditional methods are seen as "control"-based interventions, whereas mindfulness eschews efforts to control in lieu of a moment-to-moment awareness and acceptance of mental states (Moore, 2009). This theoretical discrepancy notwithstanding, more mindful athletes were also more likely to endorse the practice of mental skills, such as attentional control, emotional control, goal-setting, and self-talk (Kee & Wang, 2008).

The regular practice of mindfulness results in efficient use of attentional resources among sportspersons (Davidson et al., 2003). This occurs when attention is allocated to the internal or external cues most essential to optimal performance. Concurrently, attention is not captured by external or internal distractions, such as gamesmanship or worries, respectively (Marks, 2008).

Elite adolescent French golfers who were trained in mindfulness and acceptance-based behavioral therapy became more aware of their thoughts and more capable of directing their attention to task-relevant cues. They made better decisions, such as selecting the right clubs for shots, and improved their national rankings (Bernier, Thienot, Codron, & Fournier, 2009). With higher levels of mindfulness, division I male basketball players shot free throws with greater accuracy in games (Gooding & Gardner, 2009).

Mindful athletes are also more likely to become optimally absorbed in sport or to experience flow (see Chapter 2; Csikszentmihalyi, 1990; Jackson & Csikszentmihalyi, 1999). For example, Taiwanese intercollegiate athletes who were characteristically mindful were more likely to experience an optimal challenge-skills balance. Sport was sufficiently challenging to be interesting but not overwhelming and anxiety inducing. They were also more likely to concentrate deeply, experience efficacy, recognize clear goals, and to experience less self-consciousness (Kee & Wang, 2008). Flow and mindfulness were also associated during optimal performances among elite French female and male swimmers (Bernier, Thienot, Codron, & Fournier, 2009).

Efforts to train athletes in forms of mindfulness and AABT show promise (De Petrillo, Kaufman, Glass, & Arnkoff, 2009; Schwanhausser, 2009), and this is especially apparent with closed skill sports (Kaufman, Glass, & Arnkoff, 2009). Elite athletes who participated in mindfulness training were more likely to experience aspects of flow: clearer goals and a heightened experience of control (Aherne, Moran, & Lonsdale, 2011).

SUMMARY AND APPLICATION

Has one form of relaxation been proven to be superior in decreasing somatic anxiety or arousal? In a word, no. However, there are at least eight factors to consider in evaluating the practicality of relaxation techniques for sportspersons.

First is a consideration of whether professional instruction is necessary for a form of relaxation training. Forms of relaxation training such as AT, TM, and the mindfulness and acceptance-based behavioral therapies require formal instruction that must be acquired from qualified instructors. The relaxation response can be acquired through self-instruction, but medical clearance is suggested. Professional instruction is generally recommended for PMR, but there are many examples of PMR training through self-instruction.

Second, some forms of anxiety or arousal reduction may require less skill and practice than do others. Proponents of TM maintained that the process of maintaining attention on mantras was surefire and effortless (Russell, 1976). However, meditation may effectively reduce arousal only for those with the capacity to focus or maintain attention on simple stimuli for extended periods of time (Smith, 1990). This skill in focusing may be refined with practice (Davidson, Golemen, & Schwartz, 1976), but PMR appears to be more effective in reducing anxiety for people who have difficulty focusing and becoming absorbed in mental stimuli (Weinstein & Smith, 1992). Under conditions of situational stress, PMR may be preferable, as stress might interfere with absorption with mantras (Tellegen, 1981). The mindfulness and acceptance-based therapies are effective treatments for anxiety; the use of these techniques to manage anxiety and enhance performance under pressure has not been evaluated.

The third consideration may be which intervention seems most creditable or likely to produce positive results (Kirsch & Henry, 1979). A creditable intervention is likely to be practiced more regularly and to lead to self-efficacy or confidence that arousal can be brought under conscious control. In the future, it may be possible to recommend relaxation techniques on the basis of demographic or personality characteristics (Friedman & Berger, 1991). However, at present, that time appears far in the future, and such tailoring of relaxation techniques would also require additional consultation with professionals.

Fourth, consistent and even daily practice appears to be the critical variable in determining the effectiveness of relaxation techniques (Kirsch &

Henry, 1979; Throll, 1982). Techniques that can be practiced in the least amount of time in the greatest variety of settings may be more attractive for the greatest number of people.

Fifth, if relaxation-induced anxiety occurs during the practice of one technique, it is recommended that it be replaced by another relaxation method. Relaxation-induced anxiety has been shown to be somewhat specific to the particular form of relaxation (Heide & Borkovec, 1983).

Sixth, if the primary purpose for practicing a relaxation technique is to gain control over arousal during challenging performances, then a technique that is portable or capable of being practiced prior to and during the course of performances should be selected (Schwartz, Davidson, & Goleman, 1978). For example, jogging reduces anxiety (Long & Haney, 1988), but it would be impractical during competitions such as archery. Jogging and other forms of exercise would also deplete physical resources prior to performances that are physically demanding, such as athletic events.

A related and seventh concern is whether the cognitive skills and structures associated with particular relaxation techniques compete with the attentional focus necessary for optimal performance during the evaluation or competition. Relaxation techniques differ in the degree to which they place demands on the cognitive skills of focusing, passivity, and receptivity (Smith, 1990). As previously stated, focusing refers to the maintenance of attention on simple stimuli, such as mantras, for extended periods of time. The ability to stop unnecessary goal-directed activity and analytic thinking is the definition of passivity, and receptivity concerns openness to uncertain, unfamiliar, and paradoxical experiences. Forms of meditation such as TM are most dependent on these cognitive skills, whereas PMR places minimal demands on these mental resources (Smith, Amutio, Anderson, & Aria, 1996). It appears obvious that the practice of TM during the course of a challenging evaluation would be impractical, as concentration on a mantra would compete with the task absorption necessary for optimal performance.

As mentioned above, one relaxation technique has not been shown to be more effective than others. It is still important to demonstrate that relaxation techniques are efficacious in sport settings, and this is consideration eight. PMR and AT are the relaxation techniques that are most widely practiced in athletic, academic, and musical settings (Kirkcaldy, 1984). AT is frequently practiced in Europe, whereas PMR is utilized most frequently among English speakers in athletic (Greenspan & Feltz, 1989; Onestak, 1991), academic, and musical settings. In sporting contexts, PMR may be more effective in reducing physiological anxiety, and cognitive interventions may more effectively relieve cognitive anxiety (Maynard, Hemmings, & Warwick-Evans, 1995). Perhaps both interventions reduce both cognitive and physiological anxiety because they enhance self-efficacy (Hamann, 1985; Kirsch & Henry, 1979) and prompt athletes to interpret signs of anxiety as facilitative to performance.

Given these eight considerations, PMR appears to be the most relevant relaxation technique for the largest number of people. PMR has been identified as the treatment of choice for reducing physiological anxiety among athletes (Onestak, 1991), and it is the most widely utilized technique among professional psychologists who consult with elite athletes (Ogilvie, Haase, Kranidiotis, Mahoney, & Nideffer, 1979).

Centering has been developed specifically for use in athletic contests and also serves to focus attention and inhibit cognitive interference. With practice, centering is seen to reduce arousal and inhibit cognitive interference with just a single deep breath. Centering (Nideffer, 1993) was developed more recently and has less empirical background than PMR (Jacobson, 1938), but it is perhaps the most portable and its cognitive demands are perhaps the least.

Given this portability and simplicity, centering may be the technique of choice if it is proven to be as effective as PMR. Even if PMR is proven to be superior, it may be reasonable to explore integrating centering with PMR. This process might involve moving the practice of counting from 10 to one to the penultimate step in the PMR streamlining process and making the centering exercise the final step. This integration process might be facilitated if athletes are taught to take a deep and relaxed inhalation and exhalation when relaxing muscle groups (Suinn, 1980). Whether the integration of centering with PMR is superior to retaining the aforementioned procedure with the practice of counting from 10 to one as the final step remains an empirical question.

It is probably unrealistic to expect that PMR or other relaxation techniques will relieve all somatic anxiety, and as discussed in Chapter 2, the objective is to induce an optimal level of arousal for the task at hand. As discussed earlier in this chapter, PMR can assist in both inducing an optimal level of activation or arousal, and in helping performers to interpret somatic and cognitive anxiety to be facilitative to performance. PMR and other relaxation techniques are best utilized in combination with the other strategies for proximal and distal preparation for evaluations and performances. To some degree, somatic and cognitive anxieties are related reciprocally. The management of somatic anxiety contributes to the preservation of confidence or self-efficacy during performances, and self-efficacy leads to the management and control of somatic anxiety (Hamann, 1985; Kirsch & Henry, 1979).

Mindfulness and acceptance-based therapies have only recently been studied in sport settings. In lieu of directly targeting physiological and cognitive anxiety, these therapies train people to objectively process internal and external stimuli. They are intended as comprehensive systems for performance enhancement and well-being. Indeed, the developers of the MAC approach (Gardner & Moore, 2004, 2006, 2007) note disappointing efficacy for traditional mental skills training programs, and encourage the MAC approach for enhancing skills and well-being. Mindfulness-based interventions also offer promise for the development of mental skills such as the management of attentional resources and autonomic arousal (Marks, 2008).

Key Terms

Bracing   153

Progressive muscle relaxation (PMR)   155

Edmund Jacobson   155

Autonomic nervous system   156

Sympathetic & parasympathetic nervous system   156

Visuo-Motor Behavior Rehearsal (VMBR)   160

Autogenic Training (AT)   161

Transcendental Meditation (TM)   164

Mantras   165

Relaxation response   167

Centering   168

Mindfulness   169

Intention   171

Attention   171

Mindfulness-Based Stress Reduction (MBSR)   171

Mindfulness-Based Cognitive Therapy (MBCT)   172

Acceptance and Commitment Therapy (ACT)   172

Mindfulness-Acceptance-Commitment approach (MAC)   172

Discussion Questions

Q1. Why is it beneficial to control physiological anxiety?

Q2. In addition to managing physiological anxiety, relaxation training confers additional benefits. Review these benefits.

Q3. Describe the development of progressive muscle relaxation (PMR).

Q4. Review the PMR technique.

Q5. Describe Visuo-Motor Behavior Rehearsal.

Q6. Explain autogenic training (AT).

Q7. Review the AT technique.

Q8. Consider and explain Transcendental Meditation (TM).

Q9. Outline the TM technique.

Q10. What are the effects of TM?

Q11. Describe the relaxation response.

Q12. How is centering accomplished?

Q13. What are the basic components of mindfulness?

Q14. Review mindfulness-based cognitive therapy, acceptance and commitment therapy, and the Mindfulness-Acceptance-Commitment approach.

Q15. What is reperceiving?

Q16. How does mindfulness promote the more efficient use of attentional resources?

Q17. Review the wide-ranging benefits of mindfulness.

Q18. Consider the three core elements of mindfulness practice.

Q19. Review the application of mindfulness techniques in sport.

Suggested Readings

Aherne, C., Moran, A.M., & Lonsdale, C. (2011). The effect of mindfulness training on athletes' flow: An initial investigation. *The Sport Psychologist, 25,* 177–189.

Benson, H. (1983). The relaxation response: Its subjective and objective historical precedents and physiology. *Trends in Neurosciences, 6,* 281–284.

Bernier, M., Codron, R., Thienot, E., & Fournier, J. F. (2011). The attentional focus of expert golfers in training and competition: A naturalistic investigation. *Journal of Applied Sport Psychology, 23,* 1153–1571. doi: 10.1080/10413200.2011.561518

Carlson, C. R., & Bernstein, D. A. (1995). Relaxation skills training: Abbreviated Progressive Relaxation. In W. O'Donohue, & L. Krasner (Eds.), *Handbook of psychological skills training: Clinical applications and techniques* (pp. 20–35). Boston, MA: Allyn & Bacon.

De Petrillo, L. A., Kaufman, K. A., Glass, C. R., & Arnkoff, D. B. (2009). Mindfulness for long-distance runners: An open trial using Mindful Sport Performance Enhancement (MSPE). *Journal of Clinical Sport Psychology, 4,* 357–376.

Gardner, F. L., & Moore, Z. E. (2007). *The psychology of enhancing human performance: The Mindfulness-Acceptance-Commitment (MAC) approach.* New York, NY: Springer Publishing.

Hayes, S. C., Strosahl, K., & Wilson, K. G. (1999). *Acceptance and commitment therapy.* New York, NY: Guilford Press.

Kabat-Zinn, J. (2003). Mindfulness-based interventions in context: Past, present, and future. *Clinical Psychology: Science and Practice, 10,* 144–156.

Kaufman, K. A., Glass, C. R., & Arnkoff, D. B. (2009). Evaluation of Mindful Sport Performance Enhancement (MSPE): A new approach to promote flow in athletes. *Journal of Clinical Sport Psychology, 4,* 334–356.

Linden, W. (1990). *Autogenic training. A clinical guide.* New York, NY: Guilford Press.

Marks, D. R. (2008). The Buddha's extra scoop: Neural correlates of mindfulness practice and their relevance for clinical sport psychology. *Journal of Clinical Sports Psychology, 2,* 216–241.

Moore, Z. E. (2009). Theoretical and empirical developments of the mindfulness-acceptance-commitment (MAC) approach to performance enhancement. *Journal of Clinical Sports Psychology, 4,* 291–302.

Schwanhausser, L. (2009). Application of the Mindfulness-Acceptance-Commitment (MAC) protocol with an adolescent springboard diver. *Journal of Clinical Sports Psychology, 4,* 377–395.

Segal, Z. V., Williams, J. M., & Teasdale, J. D. (2002). *Mindfulness-based cognitive therapy for depression: A new approach to preventing relapse.* New York, NY: Guilford Press.

Shapiro, S. L., & Carlson, L. E. (2009). *The art and science of mindfulness. Integrating mindfulness into psychology and the helping professions.* Washington, DC: American Psychological Association.

Suinn, R. M. (1980). *Psychology in sport. Methods and applications.* Minneapolis, MN: Burgess.

Suinn, R. M. (1986). *Seven steps to peak performance: The mental training manual for athletes.* Toronto, Canada: H. Huber.

TM-Sidhi Program. (n.d.) Retrieved from http://www.maharishi.org/sidhi

Williams, J. M. (2010). Relaxation and energizing techniques for regulation of arousal. In J. M. Williams (Ed.), *Applied sport psychology: Personal growth to peak performance* (6th ed., pp. 247–266). New York, NY: McGraw-Hill.

World Anti-Doping Agency. (2009). *World anti-doping code.* Retrieved from http://www.wada-ama.org

Chapter 8

GOALS AND SELF-REGULATION

Jurgen Klinsmann

Jurgen Klinsmann was a member of three German National soccer teams, including the 1990 team that won the World Cup. He was twice Footballer of the Year in Germany and once in England. He was the coach of the German National team and is the current coach of the U.S. National team. In his view, optimal development in sport requires continuous—24/7—efforts to reach goals:

When you talk about 24/7, it's that you're accountable for what you eat, accountable for how you sleep, how you live your life, how serious you take your job. You're accountable for what you do with your money, choosing your agent, choosing your girlfriend or your wife. All that stuff. Ultimately, it will all affect your performance. That's why, big teams around the world, they try to kind of overcontrol, maybe. With La Masia at Barcelona, they think about everything. They hire an amazing chef to make sure they eat all gluten-free [laughs]. Or whatever. I don't know.

The stage where we are with soccer in this country, and also the stage with a lot of American players that are actually in Europe, is a stage where there's a lot of education still necessary. A lot of them were not introduced—and it's not their fault—they were not introduced yet to what it means to perform consistently on their own personal highest level. They think: "What I do off the field is no big deal. I know how to perform on the field." But they can't read themselves yet, and say: "You know what? That was only an 80-percent performance." The player thinks it was a good performance. I come as a coach and say, "No that was not good enough."

They were not benchmarked, really, in the past, and that's why I came in and said: "Your benchmark should be higher. Clint Dempsey, your benchmark should be a Champions League team. That's your benchmark, not Fulham." All due respect to Fulham, obviously. Wherever you are right now, that's not really your benchmark. If you really want to become a so-called exceptional player, your goal should be a Champions League team. Your goal should be, within a Champions League team, to become a leader. Your goal should be winning a competition like that. At the end of the day, you want to get to the World Cup and get a couple of rounds further than you ever did before. That's the level of the Champions League. If you want to go to the World Cup quarter or semifinal one day, you've got to perform with the best out there. And the best out there play the Champions League in Europe (Keh, 2013).

Goals motivate preparation for competitions at times distal to actual performances, and also direct attention and guide behavior prior to and during performances. Simply put, a goal is what a person attempts to accomplish. Goals represent a person's current concerns, and can be as general and abstract as one's "life tasks" or as specific as getting a haircut (Ward, 2011). Goals regulate performance by directing activity toward objectives that have been prioritized in relation to less important activities. Goals identify benchmarks or standards for evaluating performances and judging accomplishments. They have been described as the minimal level of performance with which a person will be satisfied with himself or herself. Given that goals reflect a standard to be obtained in the future, movement from one's current situation is necessary to reach the goals.

Theories of the definition and function of goals have evolved over the past century, and there are approximately 31 theories that posit goal-like constructs. In the mid-1960s, goal-setting theory developed with the premise that human behavior is purposeful and directed by conscious goals (Locke & Latham, 2002; Latham & Locke, 2007). This theory has influenced much of the information in this chapter. The focus of this chapter will be on goals that people set for themselves, as opposed to goals that are assigned by outside parties, and on the ways in which goals relate to performance.

Goals regulate behavior throughout the lifespan, and even young children demonstrate the ability to plan and organize their behaviors to achieve goals. For example, Bauer, Schwade, Wewerka, and Delaney (1999) found that children as young as 21 months of age were capable of completing three steps to build objects when they were shown an example of the completed object. The example of the completed object represented the goal that the children were to achieve by sequencing the three steps. These very young children were apparently able to think for themselves in determining what steps to take to reach these goals.

Application

As reviewed in Chapters 2 and 3, motivation for autonomy and control of one's life is counted as essentially universal (Ryan & Deci, 2007). Yet, ironically, many people never get around to setting their own course and establishing their own direction (Murray, 2010). They do not systematically establish goals. Without goals, there is less prioritization, impetus to move forward, and fewer opportunities to anticipate roadblocks. Not seeing the road ahead and establishing their own course, sportspersons and students find themselves reacting to pressures and demands that seem externally imposed.

GOAL DIMENSIONS

Goals are a source of motivation and an incentive for action. The establishment of goals often stimulates planning to reach that goal. People consistently work faster, harder, longer, and more successfully when their behavior is guided by goals (Burton & Weiss, 2008). Relevant dimensions of goals are content, intensity, and difficulty. The **content** of a goal is the object of an action. **Intensity** refers to the degree of effort exerted to reach a goal, the importance of a goal, and the **commitment** to achieving a goal (Latham & Locke, 2007; Locke, Latham & Erez, 1988). As demonstrated in industrial and sporting venues, goal commitment increases when goals are determined more by individuals and less by outside coercion. When people are committed to **difficult goals,** they are more tenacious in pursuing those goals. Goals are often adopted in the absence of instructions or training to set goals. Some argue that when people are motivated to action, they always pursue goals, even when they are not explicitly aware of these goals (Sheldon & Elliot, 1999).

Goal Difficulty

Over 400 research studies have demonstrated that higher achievement results from setting more difficult goals, so long as people possess the requisite ability and knowledge to reach the difficult goals (Bueno, Weinberg, Fernandez-Castro, & Capdevile, 2008; Locke & Latham, 2002; Ward, 2011). People with difficult goals exert greater effort at physical tasks, such as lifting weight and peddling a bicycle. They also exert more effort at cognitive tasks, such as mental arithmetic and solving puzzles; they work longer and rest less. Effort is roughly proportional to the difficulty of goals, and greater persistence is demanded to reach difficult goals. However, when someone reaches the limit of his or her skill and ability, there is little room for improvement, regardless of the level of goal difficulty.

People come to realize how to regulate the expenditure of effort to reach difficult versus easy goals. People realize that to reach a goal, they have to direct their attention to that goal, to the exclusion of activities that would compete with the realization of that goal.

Goals serve as standards for satisfaction with oneself. People who set higher goals demand more of themselves (Locke & Latham, 2002). More intense feelings of satisfaction and failure result from attaining or failing to reach more important goals.

When goals are assigned by outside sources, it is important to determine whether individuals actually accept the assigned goals. For example, Weinberg, Bruya, Jackson, and Garland (1987) demonstrated that the level of difficulty of assigned goals was not related to the performance of college students on sit-up tasks in physical education classes. The number of sit-ups was closely related to the internal goals of the students. However, an independent study of male college students in physical education classes demonstrated that personal goals are influenced by assigned goals. When these students were assigned difficult goals, such as the number of sit-ups to achieve in one minute, their personal goals for sit-ups also increased (Lerner & Locke, 1995).

The performance of novice athletes, who may not be intrinsically motivated to perform at a high level, may be best motivated by goals that are assigned by experts. For example, college students enrolled in beginning tennis classes showed more rapid progress in serving accurately when assigned goals by instructors (Boyce, Wayda, Johnston, Bunker, & Eliot, 2001).

Goal Specificity

In addition to goal difficulty, higher performance has consistently been related to the specificity of goals. However, specific goals are likely to lead to higher performance only when the goals are not only specific, but also difficult. **Goal specificity** is obtained primarily by quantifying goals (e.g., improve by 10%) or by enumeration (e.g., a list of tasks to be completed on a given day). Specific goals are also more likely to lead to greater consistency across performances. Greater variability occurs with vague goals because the standards for good performances are never clear. Specific goals designate the amount and type of effort necessary for their attainment, and allow for self-satisfaction upon reaching goals (Bandura & Simon, 1977). Vague goals, such as just doing one's best, have little effect on performance. Vague goals can be redefined after the fact to accommodate low performance. If specific standards are not set for goals, people are more likely to be satisfied with modest performances.

Better performance is associated with difficult and specific goals. For example, following the completion of a summer wrestling camp, male high school wrestlers described goals for the upcoming preseason, wrestling season, and long-term goals (Kane, Baltes, & Moss, 2001). The wrestlers with difficult and specific goals for their preseason (such as bench press double my weight) tended to have more difficult and specific goals for their wrestling seasons (such as win over 25 matches and better on my feet [takedowns]). Wrestlers with more specific and difficult goals for the preseason and season showed more improvement, as rated by their coaches.

Goal Commitment

Specific and difficult goals lead to higher performance if people are committed or have strong, stable intentions to reach these goals (Li & Chan, 2008). Specific and difficult goals do not lead to high performance when goal commitment is low, and commitment to easy goals does not lead to higher performance (Klein, Wesson, Hollenbeck, & Alge, 1999). Goal commitment refers to one's determination to reach a goal. Goal commitment is a function of one's conviction or belief that the goal is important, attractive, or attainable, and that progress toward its attainment is possible. With histories of attaining similar goals and challenges, and with the requisite ability, experience, and training, people are more likely to believe that their goals are attainable.

Goal commitment is a dynamic process in that it involves more than making an initial decision to reach a goal. Consciously recalling goals and reminding oneself of commitments to goals enhances goal commitment. This involves consciously reviewing the importance of specific goals and how specific goals are integrated with long-range goals, objectives, and values. Goal commitment is also enhanced by analyzing or taking stock of the training and knowledge that must be obtained to make goal attainment possible. Bringing goals to mind is an effective way to blunt the demoralizing effects of setbacks. Noting progress toward goal realization or toward reaching **subgoals** also enhances maintaining commitments to goals.

Goal Commitment
Michael Phelps, winner of 22 Olympic medals set goals: Every year since I have been swimming competitively, I have set goals for myself. In writing.

The goal sheet was mandatory. I got used to it and it became a habit. When I was younger, I used to scribble my goals out by hand and show the sheet to Bob [his coach]. Every year, he would take a look at what I'd given him, or sent him, and that would be that. He wouldn't challenge me, say this one's too fast or that one's not.

I usually kept my original paper version by the side of my bed.

The two of us are the only ones who have it, who ever got to see it.

The goal sheet was famously secret for a long time . . . Until now (Phelps & Abrahamson, 2008, p. 14).

GOALS AND FEEDBACK

Feedback about progress toward goals contributes to effective goal setting. It provides information about whether performance standards have been met. If feedback indicates that performance standards have been met, then the behavior and effort exerted in pursuit of a particular goal is often sustained. Information that performance falls beneath standards motivates improved performance. The effects of explicit feedback are enhanced if clear goals have been established and if self-efficacy for realizing goals is high (Cervone & Wood, 1995). This process sustains self-confidence and goal commitment (O'Brien, Mellalieu, & Hanton, 2009).

GOALS AND SELF-EFFICACY

Self-efficacy, or confidence that one can accomplish a range of related goals, has a direct and stable effect on self-set goals. Those that have high self-efficacy set higher goals and expect more of themselves (Latham & Locke 2007). Conversely, self-efficacy and self-confidence increases as a result of setting and achieving goals (Burton & Weiss, 2008; Phillips & Gully, 1997). Prospective Olympic athletes who set multifaceted goals— short- and long-term goals, psychological goals, process and outcome goals (see Chapter 9)—experienced both higher self-efficacy and athletic success (Burton et al., 2010). High **self-esteem**—a global sense of self-worth—has also been associated with setting higher goals and better performance (Martin & Murberger, 1994; Tang & Reynolds, 1993).

By systematically setting and achieving goals, athletes are likely to become more committed to the goal-setting process. Conversely, those who do not believe that goals are beneficial are less likely to commit to them in the future, and their performance and self-confidence is also more likely to suffer (Burton et al., 2010).

Setting the level of goal difficulty beyond the limits of one's abilities is not recommended, as people tend to reduce effort or give up when goal attainment appears impossible. Repeated failures to reach goals that exceed one's abilities are demoralizing and decrease self-efficacy (Bandura, 1989a, 1989b; Bueno et al., 2008).

PROXIMAL AND DISTAL GOALS

Feedback is more abundant if difficult end goals or omnibus goals are divided into subgoals. Goals that are structured with difficult end goals and progressively more difficult subgoals provide the most specific information about what is necessary to reach both the end goal and subgoals (Bandura & Simon, 1977). If subgoals are also **proximal** or to be accomplished in the near future, then an almost constant stream of feedback is available about whether current behavior is leading to goal accomplishment. Explicit, proximal goals lead to better performance in sport and other settings (Gould, 2010; Kyllo & Landers, 1995), and when people are simply provided with end goals, they often develop their own proximal goals. For example, people spontaneously developed subgoals when assigned distal goals for weight loss (Bandura & Simon, 1977) and training (Burton & Weiss, 2008).

Perhaps more successful athletes set more specific proximal goals. For example, the most successful Canadian Olympic athletes set specific, daily goals (Orlick & Partington, 1988). These Olympians established what they wanted to accomplish each day and in each workout.

Long-term goals provide direction and sustain motivation in practice and competition (Jones, Hanton, & Connaughton, 2007). However, a focus on **distal goals** may contribute to procrastination, because distal goals provide less information about what immediate action is necessary. Distal goals do not provide adequate markers against which a person may gauge his or her progress, and demoralization and negative emotions often occur when progress seems minimal (Kanfer & Ackerman, 1989).

Proximal goals are especially important in the early stages of work on complex tasks because progress can be gauged against the marker of the subgoal. If timely progress does not occur in relation to subgoals, alternative strategies can be tried while there is still time to reach the distal goal. Self-efficacy is also enhanced with the attainment of proximal goals, as people become more convinced that the attainment of the distal goal will result from the orderly process of reaching the proximal goals (Latham & Seijts, 1999).

Proximal goals not only guide the behavior necessary for the accomplishment of distal goals, but they also provide **incentives.** Self-satisfaction or dissatisfaction in relation to the proximal goals provides a chain of incentives in the process of working toward the accomplishment of the ultimate goal. This discussion of proximal and distal goals assumes that goals are self-selected and serve one's self-interest.

Goals are most motivating when they are proximal or just beyond a person's reach. In fact, people may be expected to work approximately twice as hard when they are approaching their goal as when they have exceeded it. This finding is consistent with the frequently reported result that difficult and challenging goals evoke better performance. If a goal is difficult and challenging, it is less likely to have been met and greatly exceeded. Goals are less influential when they are distal, when they have already been met, and especially when they have been greatly exceeded (Heath, Larrick, & Wu, 1999).

Application

It is not unusual to have a "starting problem" when attempting to start work on a very difficult long-term goal. This is due to the difficulty in measuring progress toward distal goals. For example, when starting a book, an initial day's work might result in the production of only a few paragraphs or notes. Training for a first marathon (26.2 miles or 42 kilometers) may begin with efforts to jog 1,600 meters. Even the most elite scholars and athletes experience difficulty initiating highly demanding projects. When asked how to write a book, the Nobel Prize-winning novelist Ernest Hemingway replied that you first clean the refrigerator.

GOALS IN SPORT: CONTROVERSIES

Approximately 90% of the studies conducted in industrial and business settings were consistent with the findings reported above about the benefits of specific and difficult goals. The effects of goals on sport and exercise performance have been more equivocal. It has been reasoned that goals may be less necessary in sport environments because athletes are typically already highly motivated, and because their performances are judged against objective standards such as time or scores.

An important limitation of some of the studies in sporting contexts is that they did not evaluate the goals that athletes set for themselves. In some studies, goals were assigned by experimenters, and in others, participants set their own quantitative goals, but only within parameters defined by experimenters (e.g., Lerner & Locke, 1995; Weinberg et al., 1987). As described above, goal commitment is an important determinant of the influence of goals in motivating behavior. People are more committed to goals that are important to them and that are self-selected. It is reasonable to question the motivating effects of assigned goals, such as to perform a given number of sit-ups (Weinberg, Bruya, & Jackson, 1985) or to complete coordination tasks (Smith & Lee, 1992).

This controversy about the influence of goals in sporting contexts has been at least partially resolved in a study that statistically aggregated the body of research concerning goals and sport performance (Kyllo & Landers, 1995). Moderately difficult, but not extremely difficult goals, led to better sport and exercise performance. More precisely, if participants in the sport and exercise studies were assigned goals that were achieved by no more than 10% of the participants, there was no improvement in performance. The assignment of goals that were accomplished by no more than 25% of participants contributed to improved performance. The motivating qualities of goals diminish if participants do not have the ability to reach goals, and the participants in these sporting studies may have realized that the extremely difficult goals were unrealistic. Moderately difficult goals are more motivating in sport and exercise settings if they are specific and if short- and long-term goals are used in combination.

The effects of goals are as great for endurance tasks as for skill-related tasks such as archery. Skilled and experienced athletes perform better when they set their own goals or cooperate with mentors in setting goals, as opposed to receiving assigned goals. Sportspersons may be in the best position to evaluate their abilities and to set a standard for an optimal performance.

Athletes' Goals

Goals of improving overall performance, winning, and having fun with others were most important to Division I college athletes (Weinberg, Burton, Yukelson, & Weigand, 1993). The goals of improving overall performance, winning, and having fun were also rated as most important by 187 male and 151 female U.S. Olympic athletes representing 12 different individual and team sports (Weinberg, Burton, Yukelson, & Weigand, 2000). Given the emphasis on winning medals in Olympic competition, it was notable that 42% of the athletes rated improving overall performance as their most important goal, whereas 25% rated winning and 15% rated having fun as their most important goals. Perhaps the Olympians perceived these goals to be interrelated, such that improvement accompanied winning and enjoyment.

Highly skilled young athletes also rated improving performance, having fun, and winning as their most important goals (Weinberg, Burke, & Jackson, 1997). The goals of younger athletes are more likely to focus on skill acquisition, and the goals of more advanced athletes are more focused on skilled performance. For example, the most effective goals for younger athletes such as tennis players appear to focus on physical conditioning, practice, and the refinement of skills and techniques.

The Olympic athletes and college athletes set realistic goals. Notwithstanding the level of Olympic competition, 52% of the Olympians reported that they set moderately difficult goals, with 25% reporting very difficult goals. College athletes (Weinberg et al., 1993) and young athletes (Weinberg et al., 1997) are also more likely to set moderately difficult goals.

Only One Gold

The sporting press hyped Michael Phelps as a likely candidate for eight Olympic gold medals in men's swimming at the 2004 Olympic Games in Athens, Greece; one more than Mark Spitz's record seven goal medals at the 1972 Olympics in Munich, Germany. Phelps' goal was to win one gold medal: "That's the only goal I have. Bringing back one Olympic medal to the U.S. would be an honor for me" (Hine, 2004a, E10). Still, Phelps did not want to rule out winning more medals: "I'll wait and see what happens.

I want the best chance to succeed. I can't stress enough how important it is to prepare properly" (Hine, 2004a, E10).

Phelps did not win eight gold medals. Still, his haul of six gold and two bronze medals matched the most won by any Olympian (Dillman, 2004).

Phelps did win eight gold medals at the 2008 Olympic Games in Beijing, China, and an additional four gold and two silver medals at the 2012 Olympic Games in London, England. His total of 22 medals (18 gold, two silver, and two bronze) is easily the largest in Olympic history. The runner-up, Larissa Latynina, a gymnast from the former Soviet Union, has nine gold, five silver, and four bronze, for a total of 18.

Coaches' Goals

Comparable surveys of the percentages of coaches who make use of goals are not available. However, information about the goal-setting techniques of eight male and six female high school coaches is available (Weinberg, Butt, & Knight, 2001). These coaches had reputations for integrating goal setting in their coaching practices. These coaches were shown to set goals for individual athletes, teams, and for themselves. There was wide variability in the degree to which goal-setting techniques were systematically applied. More specifically, there was variability with regard to writing down goals, measuring progress toward goals, and having practice time available for the review of goals.

There was greater agreement between coaches regarding the importance of short-term goals, as most coaches set individual and team short-term goals. The coaches appreciated the value of measuring progress and motivating athletes with proximate goals, and understood the position of short-term goals in goal hierarchies with long-term goals. The coaches set goals to provide direction to athletes, teams, and coaches, and valued goals as sources of feedback. The high school coaches estimated that a lack of cohesion or agreement among teammates was the primary barrier to achieving team goals. They recognized the hazards of setting unrealistically high goals, as they believed that this would lead to demoralization. However, the coaches tended to set very difficult goals, and this is at variance with the information presented earlier indicating that moderately difficult goals were most motivating (Kyllo & Landers, 1995).

GOAL HIERARCHIES

Goals are often organized not only on the basis of standards that are distal and proximal, but also in **hierarchies.** Goals for the most discrete and concrete actions are at the bottom of these hierarchies and omnibus, abstract goals are at the top. Goals at higher levels in the hierarchy relate to "why or for what effect" (Brett and VandeWalle, 1999, p. 864) one engages in activities. Goals at lower levels in hierarchies relate to how particular actions are accomplished. The pursuit and accomplishment of lower-order goals is instrumental in attaining higher-order goals.

For example, readers of this book may have the abstract, omnibus goal of doing their best in situations where performance is evaluated. Beneath that goal might be less abstract but still broad goals, such as to achieve the highest grades possible in college. Beneath that level of abstraction might be goals for grades in a particular class in which this textbook is used. Next down in the hierarchy would be goals for daily and weekly strategies for budgeting time for study. Additional goals at this level of abstraction might include using the adoption of principles for managing one's own behavior described in this chapter. The most concrete and discrete goals in this hierarchy would concern behaviors immediately prior to and during examinations. For example, students might attempt to practice the principles detailed in Chapters 4, 5, and 6 to control the anxiety in evaluations. Goals that have a higher-order in the hierarchy set the standards for the goals at the next lower level in the hierarchy. An example of a goal hierarchy is represented in Figure 8.1.

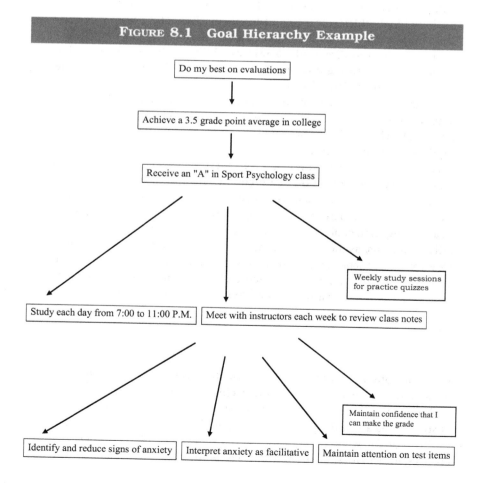

FIGURE 8.1   Goal Hierarchy Example

Do my best on evaluations

Achieve a 3.5 grade point average in college

Receive an "A" in Sport Psychology class

Study each day from 7:00 to 11:00 P.M.

Meet with instructors each week to review class notes

Weekly study sessions for practice quizzes

Identify and reduce signs of anxiety

Interpret anxiety as facilitative

Maintain attention on test items

Maintain confidence that I can make the grade

ABSTRACT GOALS

With clear linkages between lower- and higher-order goals, progress toward **abstract goals** is more discernable. However, when this linkage is apparent, there is more negative affect when progress toward lower-order and concrete goals is poor, because of the realization that the attainment of omnibus goals is also threatened (McIntosh, 1996).

Not all people strive for equally abstract goals. Goals that are more abstract are less manageable and more difficult to accomplish than more concrete goals. The pursuit of higher-level goals typically results in more negative affect, because progress toward their realization is often slower. Conversely, people directed by lower-level goals may not pursue aspirations that provide as much fulfillment and meaning in their lives. They experience less negative affect, at the cost of avoiding very difficult and challenging projects (Emmons & Kaiser, 1996).

Abstract goals that are of intrinsic interest are more likely to lead to life satisfaction, and these activities often provide the experiences of competence, autonomy, and interpersonal relatedness (Deci & Ryan, 1987). People limit their potential life satisfaction when they pursue abstract goals that are not concordant with their intrinsic interests (Sheldon & Elliot, 1999). In place of the selection of goals that will lead to the most life satisfaction, they may adopt the goals assigned by others. Goals that are concordant with intrinsic interests are likely to be enduring and to sustain effort over time. By contrast, goals that are pursued due to external pressure or to introjected guilt or shame have less capacity to sustain effort over time. For example, children may halfheartedly cooperate with parents by attending sport practices and camps, and later drop the sport because the sport did not capture their interest.

Goals sustain effort

When abstract goals are in conflict, people spend more time ruminating about goals and less time in the productive pursuit of these goals (Li & Chan, 2008). Goals are in conflict when the attainment of one goal interferes with the attainment of another goal. For example, a student may be conflicted about playing a collegiate club sport, such as rugby, because time spent at practice, competition, and travel is taken from study time, and potentially interferes with her pursuit of a superior GPA (grade point average). When there is a great deal of goal conflict, people seldom experience psychological well-being, because they almost always feel they are not making adequate progress toward at least one of their goals. People with a high degree of goal conflict do not have a coherent structure for directing their activities and for rendering meaning to their lives.

WHY GOALS ARE MOTIVATING

When goals are set at a level above one's current level of performance, people deliberately establish a state of internal **disequilibrium**. This disequilibrium creates self-dissatisfaction, because one's current status falls beneath goals, and this disequilibrium is only ameliorated when goals are reached. Positive and negative emotions are not only experienced at the time of goal attainment or nonattainment, but also during the pursuit of goals. If progress toward goals is rapid, positive emotions are experienced. Positive emotions can, therefore, be experienced even when the discrepancy between one's current status and goals is large, so long as the rate of movement or velocity toward the reduction of this discrepancy is rapid. Indeed, sport is likely to be more enjoyable when goals are systematically established and progress is measured in relation to goals (McCarthy, Jones, Harwood, & Davenport, 2010). Conversely, if the rate of movement toward goals is slower than one's expectations or is nonexistent, negative emotions are experienced. Negative emotions could, therefore, be experienced even when goals are close at hand if progress toward these proximal goals is slow or nonexistent. Extremely rapid progress produces a rush of excitement, and rapid deceleration produces a "sinking feeling" (Carver, Lawrence, & Scheier, 1996).

Application

The process of improving fitness and athletic skill is often not linear. Not uncommonly, intensive training results in periods of staleness or relative fatigue and lethargy. Athletes may misinterpret these periods as evidence that they are not making progress toward goals and experience disappointment and discouragement. Extreme responses consist of using ergogenic substances to enhance performance and dropping out of sport. If athletes are prepared for periods of relative fatigue or staleness followed by recovery and further advancement, they may avoid the disappointment associated with experiencing plateaus in fitness and skill development.

Is movement toward goals motivated more by efforts to capture positive emotion or to avoid negative emotion? Perhaps ironically, it appears to be the latter. The amount of dissatisfaction and negative emotion experienced when goals are not realized is significantly greater than the amount of positive emotion and self-satisfaction experienced when exceeding a goal (Heath, Larrick, & Wu, 1999). Therefore, negative emotions and dissatisfaction, and to a lesser extent the anticipation of self-satisfaction, drive people toward goals (Wiese & Freund, 2005).

Negative emotion may provide information that goal attainment is threatened, whereas positive emotion may signal that one can "coast" or take it easy and still reach goals on schedule. When satisfied with goal attainment, people may divert attention and energy to collateral goals and pursuits and lose momentum toward goal attainment. This satisfaction with goal attainments may be temporary, as people with high self-efficacy set new goals for themselves after goals are realized.

Coasting After Goal Attainment

After winning the state open tennis championship as a sophomore, Brian seemed to lose direction. He avoided tennis camp in the summer, and joined his high school swim team. Although rusty at the start of the tennis season in his junior year, he was certain that he would round into form by the time of the state open tournament. With an early round loss, he was almost inconsolable. He realized that he had been coasting, and that a single-minded commitment to tennis would be necessary to return to championship form.

When performance falls short of goals, sportspersons experience negative emotions (Graham, Kowalski, & Crocker, 2002), and self-dissatisfaction motivates corrective action (Bandura & Simon, 1977). People with higher self-efficacy are more dissatisfied when they do not reach goals, and they also demonstrate a greater intensification of effort to reach goals after learning that they have fallen short of standards (Bandura & Cervone, 1986). Negative emotions not only motivate efforts to reach goals, but also reconsiderations of strategies for goal attainment and goal reprioritization.

Intercollegiate athletes were shown to set goals for performances in track and field events at levels higher than their best previous performances. They almost always "raised the bar" in this fashion, as athletes set goals that were above their best previous performances during the season prior to 98% of individual events in track and field competitions. Athletes adjusted goal difficulty and set proximate goals that were reasonably above their current levels of performance. Goals that were too difficult were adjusted downward, and when goal realization was at hand, goal difficulty was increased. If athletes concluded that they could not control the factors related to the realization of their goals, goal difficulty was adjusted downward. If they believed that they controlled the factors that determined the realization of goals, they set goals at higher levels and were more persistent in attempting to reach these goals (Williams, Donovan, & Dodge, 2000).

IATROGENIC EFFECTS OF GOALS

There are **iatrogenic** or negative effects of working to achieve goals. People that are unable to relinquish goals that are unattainable are likely to experience depression. An additional iatrogenic effect occurs when goals are conceptualized in an all-or-none fashion such that if goals or subgoals are not met, the goal is renounced. Goals are more likely to be conceptualized in an all-or-none manner when they refer to behaviors that people are trying to avoid instead of behaviors to be increased. Often, "slips" in these **inhibitional goals** of abstaining from certain behaviors are seen as losses because the goal requires perfection or total abstinence.

An example of an inhibitional goal is to keep the daily consumption of calories beneath a certain limit. Exceeding the calorie limit may be perceived as a failure and a loss of the daily subgoal, and the person may subsequently greatly exceed their daily calorie limit and demonstrate the "what the hell effect" (Cochran & Tesser, 1996, p. 101). The "what the hell effect," or the renunciation of goals, appears to be the result of monitoring inhibitional behavior with proximal subgoals. Applying these findings to the problem of weight loss, the maintenance of optimal health and weight is more likely if inhibitional goals such as calorie limits are combined with positive goals, such as frequent or daily exercise.

Goals that call for positive action or increased behavior to reach a standard allow for the perception of incremental advancement toward the standard. Goals that simply refer to avoiding behavior are more likely to promote all-or-none thinking, because lapses are readily equated as a loss of the goal or the subgoal. Failure to make progress toward a goal that one wishes to achieve is less likely to be perceived as such a loss, because the person has not yet achieved the goal and so cannot lose it.

Acquisitional or positive goals direct attention toward the correct actions for goal realization. Inhibitional goals direct focus to behaviors to be decreased and to one's errors. Focusing on the negative aspects of one's behavior increases anxiety and leads to avoidance of feedback or of monitoring progress toward goals. As feedback is avoided, behavior becomes less regulated by goals, and self-confidence and self-efficacy is eroded. Focusing on behaviors to be avoided can also foster negative emotions or cognitive interference, and these reactions compete with attention to the tasks necessary to accomplish goals (Cervone & Wood, 1995).

An excessive focus on inhibiting behavior can also produce a rebound effect and actually result in a greater production of the behavior that was to be inhibited. For example, golfers consistently putted balls long of the target when cautioned to not leave putts short, and short of the target when instructed to not push it long (De La Pena, Murray, & Janelle, 2008).

In short, frequent monitoring of progress toward inhibitional subgoals has the opposite effect of frequent monitoring of progress toward acquisitional goals. It erodes confidence and performance because the feedback often reflects failure. Goals should be framed in terms of what to do, not what not to do.

RECOMMENDATIONS FOR A GOAL-SETTING PROCESS IN SPORT

A comprehensive goal-setting process involving seven steps has been recommended for sportspersons (Burton, Naylor, & Holliday, 2001):

1. Establish a hierarchy of long-term and short-term goals. There should be goals for practice and competition.
2. Enhance commitment to reaching goals. Commitment is enhanced when athletes collaborate with others such as coaches in setting goals, when goals are self-set, when there are external rewards such as championships, and when reaching goals is supported by others. Writing down and publicly posting goals also enhance commitment.
3. Evaluate barriers to goal attainment. Barriers may involve conditions that are internal to athletes, such as inadequate knowledge, skill, and conditioning, and external factors, such as family commitments.
4. Construct a plan of action to reach goals.
5. Monitor feedback about progress toward goals.
6. Evaluate goal attainment. Step six is considered crucial in sustaining motivation and confidence to reach goals (O'Brien, Mellalieu, & Hanton, 2009), and the topic of why goals are motivating was discussed earlier in this chapter.
7. Reinforce goal attainments. As mentioned earlier, with short-term and proximate goals, there are abundant opportunities for feedback and rewards en route to the attainment of long-term and distal goals.

Athletes are also more likely to set effective goals when they establish **SMARTS goals** (Smith, 1994):

- Specific, precise performance standards
- Measurable or quantifiable standards
- Action-oriented goals that indicate what is to be done as opposed to inhibitional goals
- Realistic or reachable goals as opposed to impossibly difficult goals
- Timely goals, achievable in a reasonable period of time
- Self-determined or established by the participant or with input from the participant

SELF-REGULATION

Goals have been understood to compose an element of a larger process of **self-regulation** (Zimmerman, 2000). Self-regulation refers to processes by which people manage their own behavior in the absence of external controls or constraints. This self-management involves not only the identification and pursuit of goals, but also resisting temptation to engage in activities that compete with the pursuit of these goals (Kirschenbaum,

1984). Competing activities may offer rewards and gratification that are more immediate, and the pursuit of difficult and long-term goals often requires delaying gratification (Anshel, 1995). Elite athletic achievement is associated with highly developed self-regulation skills (Jonker, Elferink-Gemser, Toering, Lyons, & Visscher, 2010).

Goals are established during a **forethought** phase of self-regulation. These goals include process and performance goals. With the development of athletic expertise, more specific performance and process goals are set. For example, expert male high school basketball players and female collegiate volleyball players (Kitsantas & Zimmerman, 2002) set more specific technique or process goals than did less-skilled teammates. Expert athletes also demonstrate higher levels of intrinsic motivation and expectations for reaching higher performance standards.

In a **performance control** phase, strategies such as self-instruction, imagery, and attentional focusing are used to optimize performance. Not unexpectedly, expert athletes use these strategies more frequently and effectively. Experts self-monitor and observe their athletic responses in "real time" or in the process of athletic performances. For example, during practice, expert collegiate female volleyball players more frequently monitored process goals, or the technical aspects of serves, as well as performance goals, or where the serves landed (Kitsantas & Zimmerman, 2002).

The last phase of this self-regulation process is **self-reflection.** In this phase, performance is compared to goals and adjustments necessary to direct performances nearer to goals are identified. Expert athletes are more accurate and objective in scrutinizing aspects of performances that are in need of improvement and refinement. They more readily identify techniques in need of modification, whereas less-skilled sportspersons are less likely to know what to do to improve. Experts are also more adept at recognizing when they need help and coaching and in soliciting this assistance. Even elite child and adolescent athletes make frequent use of reflection. This reflection may allow them to learn more from previous experience and develop expertise more rapidly. They try harder and are more persistent in advancing their expertise (Toering, Elferink-Gemser, Jordet, & Visscher, 2009).

In addition to this model with the phases of forethought, performance-control, and self-reflection, a five-stage model has been identified. These five stages consist of problem identification, commitment, execution, environmental management, and generalization (Kirschenbaum, 1984). Consistent with the three-stage model (Zimmerman, 2000), this model emphasizes the importance of self-monitoring. Continuous and even unremitting or "obsessive-compulsive" (Kirschenbaum, 1984, p. 163) monitoring of sport performance has been associated with elite performance. Without this commitment to continuous self-monitoring, the benefits of self-monitoring may be transient and unimpressive (Young, Medic, & Starkes, 2009).

When learning new skills, improvement is most rapid when sportspersons focus on their successes and maintain positive expectations.

For example, unskilled bowlers and golfers marked better scores when focusing on the positive rather than negative aspects of their form (Kirschenbaum, Ordman, Tomarken, & Holtzbauer, 1982; Johnston-O'Connor & Kirschenbaum, 1884). After skills have been mastered, negative self-monitoring, or attention to areas in need of improvement, has been associated with skill enhancement.

Self-regulation processes, such as self-monitoring, evaluating progress, and planning to overcome setbacks, are more likely in task-involving climates. Task-involving environments also promote self-control processes such as directing attention and effort and avoiding negative self-talk. Self-regulation may be less relevant in ego-involving climates if sportspersons understand that success is determined less by their efforts and more by innate ability (Gano-Overway, 2008).

SUMMARY AND APPLICATION

People become more productive when they establish goals. The most effective goals establish not only what is to be accomplished but also when the task should be completed. In athletic and other venues, goals serve to direct attention toward standards. Goals sustain the behavior and effort necessary to reach standards, and provide feedback about progress. With this feedback, athletes can more readily recognize when techniques and strategies must be altered or improved if goals are to be accomplished.

Goals identify what current behaviors are necessary to reach standards that are either proximal or distal. Difficult and specific goals direct and require effort for their realization, but they have this effect only when people accept assigned goals or establish them themselves and when they have the requisite skill to reach the difficult goals.

Goals that are self-selected or to which there is a high degree of commitment and that represent highly important accomplishments are more likely to motivate higher performance in sporting venues. If coaches or other mentors assign goals, commitment can be enhanced if athletes cooperate in the goal-setting process.

Not surprisingly, people with high self-efficacy or belief in their capacity to reach goals, establish more challenging goals for themselves. However, even those with unshakable self-efficacy are ill-advised to underestimate the effort and resources necessary to reach difficult goals.

Goals are often organized in hierarchies of long- and short-term goals. Long-term goals provide coherent structures for activities and in the most general sense, can provide a sense of purpose in life. However, distal or long-term goals provide little information about whether current efforts are likely to be sufficient to reach future, distal goals. It is difficult to gauge progress toward distal goals, whereas proximal goals allow for a steady stream of feedback about whether current behaviors are successful in reaching short-term standards.

By setting proximal and distal goals, people create a state of internal disequilibrium, because one's current state is beneath the proximal or distant standard for satisfactory attainment. Dissatisfaction drives people to reach their goals, and goals that are just beyond one's reach are most motivating. The pursuit of goals is not accompanied by unremitting negative emotion, as positive emotions are experienced if progress toward goal attainment is satisfactory. However, as trajectory of movement toward goal attainment flattens and reverses, the emotional experience becomes increasingly unpleasant.

The body of information about goals has practical applications in sport settings. A process of seven stages has been recommended. It is important for sportspersons to not only establish goals, but to nest short-term goals in hierarchies, identify action necessary to realize goals, remove barriers to goal attainment, and continually monitor progress toward goals.

Goals have been understood to be a part of a larger process of self-regulation. Self-regulation involves at least three phases: The forethought phase; the performance control phase; and the self-reflection phase. In the forethought phase, goals are established. In the performance control phase, skills are deployed of to optimize performance and athletes monitor progress toward goals. Sportspersons evaluate progress during the self-reflection phase, and identify areas in need of improvement.

Key Terms

Discussion Questions

Q1. Define goals.
Q2. Review goal dimensions.
Q3. How is it that difficult goals drive productivity?
Q4. How does goal commitment influence performance?

Q5. Does feedback influence progress toward goals?
Q6. Consider the influence of self-efficacy on self-selected goals.
Q7. Review the benefits of proximal and distal goals.
Q8. Evaluate the goals set by athletes.
Q9. Evaluate the goals set by coaches.
Q10. Explain goal hierarchies.
Q11. Differentiate abstract and concrete goals.
Q12. Why are goals motivating?
Q13. Review the goals that are iatrogenic.
Q14. Describe the seven steps for goal setting in sport.
Q15. Review SMARTS goals.
Q16. Detail the components of self-regulation.

Suggested Readings

Bueno, J., Weinberg, R. S., Fernandez-Castro, J., & Capdevila, L. (2008). Emotional and motivational mechanisms mediating the influence of goal setting on endurance athletes' performance. *Psychology of Sport and Exercise, 9*, 786–799. doi: 10.1016/j.psychsport.2007.11.003

Burton, D., & Weiss, C. L. (2008). The fundamental goal concept: The path to process and performance success. In T. Horn (Ed.), *Advances in sport psychology* (3rd ed., pp. 339–375). Champaign, IL: Human Kinetics.

Carver, C. S., & Scheier, M. F. (2011). Self-regulation of action and affect. In K. K. Vohs & R. F. Baumeister (Eds.), *Handbook of self-regulation research, theory, and applications*, (2nd ed., pp 3–21). New York, NY: Guilford.

De La Pena, D., Murray, N. P., & Janelle, C. M. (2008). Implicit overcompensation: The influence of negative self-instructions on performance of a self-paced motor task. *Journal of Sport Sciences, 26*, 1323–1331. doi: 10.1080/02640410802155138

Gano-Overway, L. A. (2008). The effect of goal involvement on self-regulatory processes. *International Journal of Sport and Exercise Psychology, 6*, 132–156.

Gould, D. (2010). Goal setting for peak performance. In J. M. Williams (Ed.), *Applied sport psychology: Personal growth to peak performance* (6th ed., pp. 201–220). New York, NY: McGraw-Hill.

Jonker, L., Elferink-Gemser, M. T., Toering, T. T., Lyons, J., & Visscher, C. (2010). Academic performance and self-regulatory skills in elite youth soccer players. *Journal of Sports Sciences, 28*, 1605–1614. doi: 10.1080/02640414.2010.516270

Li, K.-K., & Chan, D. K.-S. (2008). Goal conflict and the moderating effects of intention stability in intention-behavior relations: Physical activity among Hong Kong Chinese. *Journal of Sport & Exercise Psychology, 30*, 39–55.

Locke, E. A., & Latham, G. P. (2002). Building a practically useful theory of goal setting and task motivation: A 35-year odyssey. *American Psychologist, 57,* 705–717.

McCarthy, P. J., Jones, M. V., Harwood, C. G., & Davenport, L. (2010). Using goal setting to enhance positive affect among junior multievent athletes. *Journal of Clinical Sport Psychology, 4,* 53–68. doi: 10.1016/j.psychsport.2007.01.005

Toering, T. T., Elferink-Gemser, M. T., Jordet, G., & Visscher, C. (2009). Self-regulation and performance level of elite and non-elite youth soccer players. *Journal of Sports Sciences, 27,* 1509–1517. doi: 10.1080/02640410903369919

Ward, P. (2011). Goal setting and performance feedback. In J. K. Luiselli & D. D. Reed (Eds.), *Behavioral sport psychology* (pp. 99–112). New York, NY: Springer. doi: 10.1007/978-1-4614-0070-7_6

Young, B. W., Medic, N., & Starkes, J. L. (2009). Effects of self-monitoring training logs on behaviors and beliefs of swimmers. *Journal of Applied Sport Psychology, 21,* 313–428.

Zimmerman, B. J. (2000). Attaining self-regulation: A social cognitive perspective. In M. Boekaerts. P. Pintich, & M. Seidner (Eds.), *Self-regulation: Theory, research and application* (pp. 13–39). Orlando, FL: Academic Press.

Chapter 9

GOAL ORIENTATION

John Wooden won a record 10 national championships in basketball as the head coach for UCLA. He was the first to be inducted into the NCAA Basketball Hall of Fame as a coach and a player. He described his view of success:

First and foremost is my belief that success is within the grasp of each and every one of us. Success, as I define it, is not determined by fame, fortune, or being number 1. Of course, this is heresy for many leaders—to suggest that something could be more important than being number 1.

Motivational climates (photo courtesy of Western Connecticut State University)

Over and over, I have taught those under my supervision that we are all given a certain potential unique to each one of us. Our first responsibility is to make the utmost effort to bring forth that potential in service to our team. For me, that is success.

Then, perhaps when circumstances come together, we may find ourselves number 1. If that happens, it is merely a by-product of the effort we make to realize our own competency—our full potential. Success may result in winning, but winning does not necessarily mean you are a success. I also believe it is harmful to compare yourself to others—to judge your own success based on how you stack up against someone else. Others will do that for you. My approach is to judge myself—and those under my supervision—on the effort we make to become our best as a team (Wooden & Jamison, 2007, pp. xv–xvi).

In the mid- to late 1970s, it became increasingly clear to psychologists at the University of Illinois that people differed in terms of goal orientations, or the types of goals they pursued (Roberts, 2001). The conceptualizations of Carol Dweck and John Nicholls have been particularly influential in explaining why people strive for achievement in areas such as athletics and academics (Elliot, 2005). Nicholls's formulation has been most influential in athletic settings. A basic distinction in both conceptualizations is whether competence is *defined* in relation to self-referenced versus external standards. Learning goals (Dweck) and task orientations (Nicholls) orient individuals to self-referenced progress, intrinsic interest in tasks, and a range of positive outcomes. Performance goals (Dweck) and ego orientations (Nicholls) measure performance normatively or in relation to others. Normatively referenced goals lead to a range of negative outcomes, especially when people judge their ability to be inferior to competitors.

The models of goal orientations from these and other research traditions will be examined and compared in this chapter. Comparisons of models of goal orientations are controversial, and the foremost experts disagree about their similarities and differences (Duda, 1997; Duda & Hall, 2001; Hardy, 1997; Treasure, Duda, Hall, Roberts, Ames, & Maehr, 2001). Although readers are advised to regard these comparisons with caution, the comparisons help to organize information from the different models.

TASK AND EGO ORIENTATIONS

Task orientations focus on self-referenced mastery or improvement in relation to one's personal standards. With task orientations, success is perceived when learning, improvement, and mastery are achieved (Williams, 1994). Athletes with **ego orientations** are concerned with gaining favorable judgments from others and compare their performance to that of competitors (Nicholls, 1989). With ego orientations, ability is perceived when performance exceeds that of others, especially when less effort is exerted. Task and ego orientations do not simply influence how progress and success is measured in discrete settings or situations. For example, adolescents who endorsed task or ego orientations in athletic venues were more likely to measure their school progress with the same orientation (Duda & Nicholls, 1992).

Athletes with ego orientations are vulnerable to cognitive and somatic anxiety before and during performances if they rate their ability as inferior to competitors. With ego orientations and low estimates of abilities, people are more likely to drop out of competitions or performances, rate evaluations or competitions as unimportant, and set standards for their performance that are unrealistically high or very low. By setting extremely high or low standards, performers essentially avoid or escape comparing their performance to others, as neither provides a fair comparison of performance.

Ego orientations are also associated with pressure from parents and coaches to reach exacting goals, and with concern over making mistakes. With task orientations, sportspersons may set exacting goals, but these goals conform to the athlete's own standards (Dunn, Causgrove, Dunn, & Syrotuik, 2002).

People with ego orientations are also more likely to view ability as a fixed, innate quality, so that a failure at any point in time signals a future of failures (Donovan & Williams, 2003). However, if sportspersons withhold effort and do not try to do their best during competitions and evaluations, failure is less diagnostic of inadequate ability and can be attributed to a lack of effort. Failure is most threatening to those with ego orientations when they put forth maximum effort, because it can then be attributed only to insufficient ability (Duda & Hall, 2001). With ego orientations, failure is more threatening because it threatens self-esteem (Dweck & Leggett, 1988). As described in the Chapter 8, self-esteem and competence are abstract goals and likely to occupy higher-order positions in goal hierarchies. Threats to higher-order goals evoke powerful, negative emotional reactions.

Not surprisingly, athletes who approach competition with ego orientations are more likely to experience cognitive anxiety prior to and during competition (White & Zellner, 1996). Athletes who adopt task orientations have less vulnerability to cognitive and somatic anxiety (Hall & Kerr, 1997). They have more control over the factors that lead to success and failure, whereas with performance orientations sportspersons have little control over the performance of others. Control over the standards of success and failure also contributes to heightened intrinsic interest (Duda & Hall, 2001; Roberts, Treasure, & Conroy, 2007) and enjoyment (McCarthy, Jones, & Clark-Carter, 2008) in sport.

Ego orientations are particularly problematic for athletes when they perceive their talent to be inadequate to win. In these competitions, they are more likely to experience cognitive interference, to be less flexible in selecting strategies during the course of a performance, and to wish to escape or withdraw from competition. For example, British club snooker and tennis players with ego orientations wanted to escape competition when they thought they were unskilled in comparison to opponents. Adult club athletes with task orientations recorded little cognitive interference during competition and few wishes to avoid competition (Hatzigeorgiadis & Biddle, 1999).

Task and Ego Orientations and Prosocial Behavior

Young sport participants of approximately 11.5 years of age were more likely to perceive sports as a means of enhancing self-esteem, developing good citizenship, developing increased skill and cooperation, and being physically active when they endorsed task goals (Cetinkalp & Turksoy, 2011; White, Duda, & Keller, 1998). Adolescent female soccer players in Norway were more likely to emphasize companionship, loyalty, and constructive relationships with friends on their team when they also endorsed task orientations (Ommundsen, Roberts, Lemyre, & Miller, 2005). With high task orientations and low ego orientations, Norwegian adolescent soccer players were more likely to endorse aspects of sportspersonship such as respect for social conventions, rules and officials, and opponents, and to make a full commitment to their sport. Soccer players with high ego orientations and high perceived soccer ability endorsed one aspect of sportspersonship, respect for rules and officials (Lemyre, Roberts, & Ommundsen, 2002).

Task orientations have also been associated with good sportspersonship, prosocial choices (Sage & Kavusannu, 2007) and behavior (Kavussanu & Boardley, 2009), greater respect for social conventions in hockey, and for the rules and officials (Dunn & Causgrove Dunn, 1999; Sage & Kavussanu, 2007) among elite male hockey players of approximately 13 years of age in Canada. Young hockey players with ego orientations were more comfortable with aggressive play. Similarly, high school basketball players (Duda, Olson, & Templin, 1991) and adolescent soccer players (Sage & Kavussanu, 2007) with ego orientations were more likely to endorse the use of aggression and unsporting behaviors in games (Duda, Olson, & Templin, 1991). Male high school basketball players were more likely than females to demonstrate ego orientations.

Joe Torre's (Manager of Four New York Yankee World Series Championship Teams) Take on Success

But in my book, success and winning are not always one and the same....To me, success is playing—or working—to the best of your ability. And *winning* is a by-product of living up to your highest standards for yourself, getting the most out of your natural talents, reaching down and rooting out your own drive, courage, and commitment. In other words, if you succeed in realizing your own abilities, the chances that you'll be a winner in objective terms—with all the rewards—are maximized (Torre & Dreher, 1999, p. 7).

MEASUREMENT OF GOAL ORIENTATIONS

The most extensively employed questionnaires for assessing goal orientations are the **Task and Ego Orientation in Sport Questionnaire (TEOSQ;** Chi & Duda, 1995; Duda, 1989; Duda & Nicholls, 1992) and Perceptions of Success Questionnaire (POSQ; Roberts, Treasure, & Belague, 1998). Both assess task and ego orientations, as does the Goal Orientation in Exercise Scale, a questionnaire developed for measuring goal orientation in exercise venues (Kilpatrick, Bartholomew, & Riemer, 2003). Clearly defined cutting points or scores for identifying individual task and ego orientations have not been established with the TEOSQ and POSQ (Harwood, 2002; Lemyre, Roberts, & Ommundsen, 2002). Further, although goal orientations have been shown to be stable (Treasure & Roberts, 1998), they are still influenced by situational pressure, such that in actual competition, elite sportspersons are likely to focus more on ego and less on task orientations (Harwood, 2002). A measure of clinical judgment is therefore necessary in assessing goal orientations among individual athletes (Harwood, 2002).

The Achievement Goal Scale for Youth Sports (AGSYS) was recently validated for use with children and adolescents (Cumming, Smith, Smoll, Standage, & Grossbard, 2008). It measures ego and mastery goals, and the latter are similar to task orientations. The ego and mastery scales of the AGSYS correlated highly with their corresponding scales on the POSQ, and with mastery and performance-approach and performance-avoidance goals (see the definitions below) in school classrooms. Youth who registered high scores on the mastery goal scale demonstrated intrinsic, identified, and introjected motivation for sport (see Chapter 2), whereas those with high ego scale scores experienced external control. Those with mastery goals were more likely to show higher self-esteem and lower anxiety, whereas youth with ego goals recorded more anxiety and lower self-esteem.

TASK AND EGO ORIENTATIONS AND MOTIVATIONAL CLIMATES

The goal orientations of young athletes correspond with their perceptions of the goal orientations of their parents (Escarti, Roberts, Cervello, & Guzman, 1999). Peers also influence goal orientations, especially during adolescence (Carr & Weigand, 2002; Vazou, Ntoumanis, & Duda, 2006). Parents and coaches create **motivational climates** that encourage the development of task and ego orientations (Boyce, Gano-Overway, & Campbell, 2009; Cumming et al., 2008; Smith, Smoll, & Cumming, 2009; Vazou, 2010). Indeed, a single episode of feedback by parents that emphasized measuring performance relative to others (performance orientation) or relative to oneself (task orientation) influenced 12-year-old soccer players to identify motivational climates as performance- or task-oriented, respectively (Gershgoren, Tenenbaum, Gershgoren, & Eklund, 2011).

Application

How are children to learn that there is more to sport than how they compare to others if both their parents and coaches emphasize ego orientations? One solution is to introduce the principles of task orientations in coach effectiveness training programs. Representative programs are reviewed in Chapter 20. After training, coaches are encouraged to further these principles in meetings with parents.

Child athletes with task orientations are more likely to play for coaches who emphasize mastery of skills and enjoyment of sport. In task-involving climates, success and improvement is understood to result from effort. Cooperative learning and important roles for all participants are also emphasized in task-oriented environments. In motivational climates that encourage ego orientations, young athletes rate normative ability and deception as the most important causes of success. Ego-involving climates prompt intra-team rivalry, unequal recognition of participants, and punishment for mistakes (Newton, Duda, & Yin, 2000).

Positive emotional experiences are more likely in task-oriented environments. Young Italian athletes were happier and experienced more positive emotions in mastery climates and with task orientations. Ego orientations and climates provoked unpleasant emotional states (Bortoli, Bertollo, & Robazza, 2009; Bortoli, Bertollo, Comani, & Robazza, 2011). Elite adolescent athletes who trained in climates encouraging task orientations experienced less performance anxiety and greater satisfaction about being members of their teams (Treasure & Roberts, 1998). Indeed, overall anxiety related to sport performance, as well as somatic anxiety and worry, was shown to decrease over the course of a basketball season for boys and girls on teams with mastery-oriented motivational climates (similar to task-involving motivational climates; Smith, Smoll, & Cumming, 2007).

Ego-involving climates are associated with negative personal development (MacDonald, Cote, Eys, & Deakin, 2011). These climates prompt sportspersons to consider unproductive strategies for enhancing skills, such as the avoidance of practice. Athletes also claim handicaps (see Chapter 12), such as fatigue and a lack of preparation in ego-involving atmospheres (Coudevylle, Ginis, Famose, & Gernigon, 2009). In these climates, adolescents worry more about success and failure, and are less content with team membership (Vazou et al., 2006; Ommundsen, Roberts, Lemyre, & Miller, 2006; Walling, Duda, & Chi, 1993). Adolescents are more likely to drop out of sports when the motivational climates are not mastery-oriented (Ntoumanis et al., 2012; Smith, Smoll, & Cumming, 2007) or highly ego-involving and when they judge their athletic ability to be low (Duda & Hall, 2001).

Motivational Climates and Team Cohesion

Team cohesion is more likely in task-involving climates. Elite French female basketball and handball squads were more cohesive when team environments were task-involving (Heuze, Sarrazin, Masiero, Raimbault, & Thomas, 2006). Constructive relationships were forged among adolescent Norwegian female soccer players when team climates were task-oriented (Ommundsen et al., 2005). Estonian adolescents in task-involving peer motivational climates recognized not only greater relatedness, but also higher levels of autonomy and competence (Joesaar, Hein, & Hagger, 2011). When their coaches provided autonomy support—considered their perspectives when making decisions—these adolescents were more likely to treat teammates respectfully and establish task-involving team climates (Joessar, Hein, & Hagger, 2012).

Elite Spanish handball players between the ages of 17 and 34 were more satisfied with their individual and team improvement and with their coaches when these coaches created motivational climates that encouraged task orientations (Balaguer, Duda, Atienza, & Mayo, 2002). In motivational climates that are more task-involving and less ego-involving, elite Spanish handball and tennis players were more likely to view coaches as closer to their "ideal" coach, or someone who was helping them to improve and do their best (Balaguer, Duda, & Crespo, 1999). Task-involving team environments also promoted greater satisfaction with coaches among young adolescent Catalan (Spain) soccer players (Boixados, Cruz, Torregrosa, & Valiente, 2004).

Coaches with winning records are judged by young athletes as knowledgeable and skillful, but young athletes do not necessarily enjoy playing or want to continue playing for them. They do enjoy playing and want to continue with coaches who promote mastery-oriented motivational climates. They judge these coaches to be capable, and expect that their parents also like them (Cumming, Smoll, Smith, & Grossbard, 2007). They are more likely to return to play for additional seasons with coaches who create task climates, and are less likely to experience burnout (Ntoumanis, Taylor, & Thogersen-Ntoumani, 2012).

Application

Children are more likely to enjoy and persist at sport in task-oriented milieus. The public health goal of youth sport is served when as many children as possible enjoy the benefits of exercise. Children who engage in sport also have opportunities to socialize and make friends. Through participation, children also learn to value sport traditions and sportspersonship.

Motivational Climates and Sportspersonship

Sportspersonship and moral behaviors, such as considering the impact of one's behavior on others, are influenced by motivational climates. Norwegian collegiate athletes who perceived the environment of their teams to be highly ego-involving were less likely to view athletic participation as a means for the development of social responsibility and skills for use throughout their lifetimes (Ommundsen & Roberts, 1999). Underserved adolescent baseball and softball players who played in ego-oriented climates were less likely to develop life skills (Gould, Flett, & Lauer, 2012). Experienced Norwegian male soccer players between the ages of 12 and 14 with coaches who emphasized performance-oriented goals were likely to use whatever means necessary to pursue victory, including aggressive and cheating behaviors (Ommundsen et al., 2003). Similarly, experienced Catalan male soccer players between the ages of 10 and 14 who played on teams that emphasized ego-involving and de-emphasized task-involving motivational climates were more likely to endorse rough play and cheating (Boixados et al., 2005). English adolescent male soccer players who identified ego-involving motivational climates were more likely to engage in antisocial behaviors in matches (e.g., late tackles, shirt pulling, elbowing, pretending to be injured) and less likely to show prosocial behavior (Kavussanu, Seal, & Phillips, 2006). The converse is also true. Among English male and female adolescent soccer players, antisocial behavior early in soccer seasons predicted the perception of ego-involving climates later in seasons (Sage & Kavussanu, 2008).

The longer adolescent athletes engage with coaches who foster ego climates, the greater the likelihood that they endorse cheating and gamesmanship. For example, although the attitudes of British adolescent athletes concerning gamespersonship and cheating did not correspond with the motivational environments of teams at midseason, they were more likely to acknowledge gamespersonship and cheating at the end of seasons and at the start of new competitive seasons (Ntoumanis et al., 2012).

Dirtiest Teams at the 2006 World Cup

The British Office of Information Builders created the Foul Play Index (FPI) as a measure of the dirtiest teams in the 2006 World Cup soccer tournament. Teams are assigned points for dirty play for yellow (major foul) and red (expulsion) cards, dives (exaggerating contact from another player in an effort to draw a foul), faked injuries, tantrums, and bullying referees. Prior to the championship game, Paraguay lead the tournament with a FPI of 45, followed by Italy (40), the Netherlands, Ivory Coast, and Portugal (37; Ranking the Dirtiest Teams, 2006).

Good sportspersonship develops more readily in task-involving climates. Youthful Norwegian soccer players who played for coaches who nurtured mastery climates demonstrated respect for game rules, and opponents, as did urban American tennis players from lower socioeconomic backgrounds (Fry & Newton, 2003; Ommundsen, Roberts, Lemyre, & Treasure, 2003). The commitment of adolescent British athletes to their athletic clubs and to the conventions of their sports grew over the course of seasons when coaches created task climates (Ntoumanis et al., 2012).

Motivational Climates, Intrinsic Interest, and Meta-Cognitive Strategies

Motivational climates, along with goal orientations, contribute to intrinsic interest in sport (Joesaar et al., 2011, 2012). Mastery-oriented climates promote intrinsic interest in sport, self-esteem, and decrease performance anxiety. Ego-involving climates elicit performance anxiety, amotivation, and decrease self-esteem and intrinsic interest (Smith, Cumming, & Smoll, 2008).

Perhaps motivational climates provide opportunities for experiencing competence, self-determination, and relatedness to others, characteristics that are considered primary motives for investment in sport (Duda & Hall, 2001). For example, in ego-involving climates, elite English dancers experienced less competence and relatedness to fellow competitors, whereas in task-involving climates, dancers experienced higher levels of competence, relatedness, and autonomy (Quested & Duda, 2010).

Climates that emphasize mastery and task-involvement also teach meta-cognitive strategies. Meta-cognitive strategies provide individuals with cognitive frameworks or models for evaluating current skills and for future self-regulated learning (Ommundsen, 2006). People with meta-cognitive learning strategies have "learned how to learn." Examples of meta-cognitive strategies in evidence among adolescent physical education students include procedural knowledge, or knowing how to sequence motor skills, self-monitoring, or determining if a skill was performed precisely, and debugging, or identifying and correcting mistakes. Students with internalized task orientations also demonstrate these meta-cognitive cognitive processes (Theodosiou & Papaioannou, 2006), and both task orientations and task-involving climates predispose physical education students to engage in sport and exercise in out-of-school settings (Papaioannou, March, & Theodorakis, 2004).

Task-involving climate

GOAL ORIENTATIONS AND CHANGE

Goal orientations become more internalized with experience, and therefore the influence of internal goal orientations is less for children than for adults (Boyce et al., 2009). However, by adolescence, goal orientations are stable internal characteristics, and both goal orientations and motivational climates influence the beliefs of adolescents about what leads to athletic success and failure. For example, the perceptions of female, adolescent basketball players about the motivational climates of summer basketball camps as well as their goal orientations influenced their beliefs about the causes of success and failure (Treasure & Roberts, 1998). Task orientation was the most important factor in determining efforts for mastery in comparison to one's own baseline, and its influence was augmented when the basketball players thought that coaches created mastery environments. The striving for social approval of adolescents with ego orientations was decreased by motivational climates that encouraged mastery.

Motivational climates are subject to change. The motivational climates of adolescent, elite tennis players in England were influenced by interventions with the players and their coaches and parents (Harwood & Swain, 2002). These interventions encouraged self-directed goals involving measuring in relation to the adolescents' baselines of prior tennis skills, as well as goals to prevail in individual matches. Intervention also de-emphasized attention to gaining social approval and encouraged self-efficacy.

Motivational climates may also change to emphasize winning. Competition is generally experienced as more ego-involving and less task-involving than training (van de Pol & Kavussanu, 2011; van de Pol, Kavussanu, & Ring, 2012). Intense media scrutiny of elite athletes increases the experience of stress, especially for athletes with ego orientations and when there is a performance climate on teams. For example, Norwegian athletes at the 2010 Winter Olympics in Vancouver experienced extra pressure to perform due to media coverage: "For the media it is all about gold medals, everything else is a failure. The joy and fun of doing my sport, which is my biggest motivation, is missing" (Kristiansen, Hanstad, & Roberts, 2011, p. 449). The stress of media scrutiny was mitigated by avoiding Olympic reports by the Norwegian press, and by fostering mastery or task-oriented climates on teams.

SIMULTANEOUS TASK AND EGO ORIENTATIONS

Sportspersons may approach competitions and practice with multiple goal orientations. That is, sportspersons with high, moderate, or low task orientations may have either high, moderate, or low ego orientations; those with high, moderate, or low ego orientations may endorse high, moderate, or low task orientations.

Optimal performance may result from the endorsement of moderate to high levels of task and ego orientations (Barron & Harackiewicz, 2001; Burton, Gillham, & Glenn, 2011; Horn, Duda, & Miller, 1993). With high ego and low task orientations, sportspersons are more likely to endorse unsportspersonlike conduct, such as doping or the use of illicit ergogenic substances (Sas-Nowosielski & Swiatkowska, 2008).

Athletes who finished in the top 10 in major track and field championships were driven by both task (e.g., producing a perfect performance) and ego (e.g., beating opponents) goals (Mallett & Hanrahan, 2004), as ~e the most mentally tough English cricketers during the 1980s and (Bull, Shambrook, James, & Brooks, 2005). The negative effects ,ı ego orientations may be buffered by concurrent high task orientions (Hodge & Petlichkoff, 2000). Elite adolescent female soccer .yers with both task and ego involvement demonstrated high levels of self-confidence, and outperformed counterparts with task or mastery orientations (Burton et al., 2011). With both task and ego involvement, soccer players engaged in more positive self-talk and were less vulnerable to concentration disruption and worry.

Situational pressure or demands for competent performance may also determine how influential a goal orientation is during a particular competition or at specific times in a competition (Harwood, Hardy, & Swain, 2000; Harwood & Swain, 2002). With both task and ego goals, athletes may also default to task goals when they perform poorly in relation to competitors (Duda, 2001).

Goal orientations also influence the mental imagery of athletes. The imagery of competitive, adolescent Canadian swimmers corresponded somewhat to their goal orientations, as swimmers with moderate-task/higher-ego orientations focused more of their mental resources on imagining themselves besting others (Cumming, Hall, Harwood, & Gammage, 2002). Elite, adolescent British athletes in a broad range of sports who maintained higher task/higher ego goal orientations were more likely to use imagery than were counterparts with combinations of moderate and low task and ego goal profiles (Harwood, Cumming, & Hall, 2003). Elite, British adolescent athletes with higher-task/moderate-ego goal orientations also use more imagery and self-talk than counterparts with lower task/higher ego and moderate task/lower ego goal orientations. With higher task/moderate ego goal orientations the adolescent athletes engaged in more goal setting in practice and competition than counterparts with lower task/higher ego profiles and more goal setting in competition than counterparts with moderate task/lower ego profiles (Harwood, Cumming, & Fletcher, 2004).

MASTERY-APPROACH, MASTERY-AVOIDANCE, PERFORMANCE-APPROACH, PERFORMANCE-AVOIDANCE GOALS

To this point, goal orientations have been distinguished on the basis of how competence is defined: self- or other-referenced. Goals may also have different underlying motives or *valences*. This is, not all goals have an **approach** valence or a motive for accomplishment and achievement. With **avoidance** goals, the motive is to avoid failure and the demonstration of incompetence.

Like task-oriented and learning goals, **mastery** goals are self-referenced. **Performance** goals are similar to ego-oriented goals and are other-referenced (e.g., Conroy, Elliot, & Hofer, 2003; Elliot, 2005; Duda, 2005). Both **mastery** and **performance** goals may have an **approach** or **avoidance** valence (see Figure 9.1).

In the previous section, motivational climates were shown to influence how competence is defined—self- or other-referenced goals. Motivational climates also influenced goal valences. Children who swam for coaches who emphasized avoidance goals came to also focus on avoiding the demonstration of incompetence, in comparison to others or to their own baselines. English collegiate athletes who trained in mastery team climates also were more likely to endorse mastery-approach goals (Morris & Kavussanu, 2008).

As discussed in Chapter 2, the underlying motive for **performance-avoidance** goals is the fear of failure (Nien & Duda, 2008). With performance-avoidance goals, people are likely to become anxious and self-conscious, and question their competence in the face of difficult tasks (Cury, Da Fonseca, Rufo, Peres, & Sarrazin, 2003; Cury, Elliot, Sarrazin, Da Fonseca, & Rufo, 2002; Elliot & Harackiewicz, 1996; Elliot & Sheldon, 1997). Not surprisingly, performance-avoidance goals have an inimical effect on well-being and performance in the classroom and in sport contexts (Conroy & Elliot, 2004; Conroy, Elliot, & Hofer, 2003; Duda & Hall, 2001; Elliot, Cury, Fryer, & Huguet, 2006; Pekrun, Elliot, & Maier, 2006). Elite adolescent British soccer players with performance-avoidance goals were more likely to interpret competition as threatening (Adie, Duda, & Ntoumanis, 2010). French professional golfers with

FIGURE 9.1 A 2 × 2 Achievement Goal Framework (from Elliot & McGregor, 2001)

Definition of Competence

Valence of Striving	Mastery (absolute or intrapersonal)	Performance (normative)
Approach (striving for competence)	Mastery-Approach Goals	Performance-Approach Goals
Avoidance (striving to avoid incompetence)	Mastery-Avoidance Goals	Performance-Avoidance Goals

performance-avoidance goals were less likely to make the cut at a tournament (Bois, Sarrazin, Southon, & Boiche, 2009).

Norwegian Olympic-level athletes who acknowledged fear of failure were also more likely to endorse performance-avoidance goals (Halvari & Kjormo, 1999). When performance-avoidance goals were fostered, adolescent French physical education students experienced heightened anxiety prior to an evaluation of their competence at dribbling a basketball, and indicated that their performance was of less importance (Cury, Elliot, Sarrazin, Da Fonseca, & Rufo, 2002; Cury, Da Fonseca, Rufo, & Sarrazin, 2003). This anxiety and discounting of the importance of the dribbling evaluation probably interfered with their preparation, as they spent less time practicing. With mastery and performance-approach goals, the physical education students did not experience this anxiety, discounting of task importance, and avoidance of practice.

As discussed in Chapter 12, people who expect to perform poorly sometimes engage in self-handicapping, such as the avoidance of practice. Handicaps provide explanations for failure and poor performances other than a lack of ability.

On a more positive note, experience may moderate performance-avoidance goals. Among British soccer players who remained in elite academies, performance-avoidance goals decreased over time. Perhaps the experience of success made them less fearful of failure (Adie et al., 2010).

The underlying motives for **performance-approach** goals are the fear of failure and achievement motivation, or the concurrent motives to demonstrate performance superior to others and to avoid failure. Performance-approach goals are associated with high achievement (Elliot & Harackiewicz, 1996). Indeed, students with performance-approach goals are more likely to achieve higher grades than those motivated solely by achievement motivation and mastery goals. With performance-approach goals, study may focus on the material likely to appear on tests, whereas those with mastery goals may focus on topics of intrinsic interest. British athletes who both endorsed performance-approach goals and disavowed performance-avoidance goals recorded better championship performances (Stoeber & Crombie, 2010; Stoeber et al., 2009).

Those with **mastery-approach** goals focus on self-referenced achievement. With mastery-approach goals, people try to improve on what they have done previously. Mastery-approach goals may insulate people from developing fear of failure and self-consciousness during sport performance (Conroy, 2008; Conroy & Elliot, 2004; Conroy et al., 2003). Sportspersons with mastery-approach goals are more likely to view competition with equally matched opponents as a challenge and an opportunity for accomplishment and personal growth. They rate competition as more enjoyable and fulfilling (Adie et al., 2008; Adie et al., 2010).

Individuals with **mastery-avoidance** goals strive to avoid failure, as measured by their own standards or baseline (Chen, Wu, Kee, Lin, & Shui, 2009). They try to avoid doing worse than they have done previously. Athletes with mastery-avoidance goals are more likely to be concerned that they cannot meet their self-referenced standards and to view fair competition as threatening (Adie et al., 2008; Adie et al., 2010). Further, when highly skilled French female soccer players questioned whether their play would confirm negative stereotypes of females' athletic ability, they were more likely to adopt performance-avoidance goals (Chalabaev, Sarrazin, Stone, & Cury, 2008). The endorsement of mastery-avoidance goals in isolation from approach goals may be relatively rare among intercollegiate athletes (Ciani & Sheldon, 2010).

Intrinsic Interest

As reviewed in Chapter 2, sportspersons with mastery goals are more likely to pursue activities that they find intrinsically interesting (Wang, Sproule, McNeill, Martindale, & Lee, 2011). In support of this point, swimming league participation was considered less intrinsically rewarding and self-determined by children who endorsed mastery-avoidance, performance-avoidance, and performance-approach goals. Children with mastery-approach goals consistently rated their swimming experience as intrinsically rewarding (Conroy, Kaye, & Coatsworth, 2006).

However, in both athletic and academic domains, skill development usually requires sustained practice at tasks that are not intrinsically interesting. Performance-approach goals are influential in motivating diligent practice at tasks that are of less intrinsic interest. For example, sportspersons may enjoy their game but not the training necessary to perform at the highest level. Adolescent British soccer players were more likely to continue developing in an elite professional soccer academy when they endorsed performance-approach goals (Adie et al., 2010).

Furthermore, athletes who recognize both mastery and performance-approach goals may perform best on tasks that are interesting and uninteresting. Elite adolescent female soccer players with both self- and other-referenced goals demonstrated high levels of self-confidence and outperformed counterparts with task or mastery orientations (Burton et al., 2011). These soccer players engaged in more positive self-talk and were less vulnerable to concentration disruption and worry.

Application

Perhaps deliberate practice is not as intrinsically rewarding as deliberate play. Deliberate practice requires repetition, error identification and correction, and maximum effort and concentration. Deliberate play is not structured by authorities and is pursued just because it is fun and enjoyable. The development of elite physical and mental skills may require both deliberate practice and play. Those who love their sport are more likely to add deliberate play to practice and accumulate the number of hours or practice necessary for the emergence of expertise. For example, the accumulated practice necessary to become a professional soccer player was estimated to be 9,332 hours (Helsen, Starkes, & Hodges, 1998).

Achievement-Goal Similarity

Sportspersons with similar goal orientations are more likely to be compatible. Female athletes in badminton, gymnastics, rowing, squash, tennis, and volleyball marked higher satisfaction and commitment for athletic partners who shared their mastery-approach or performance-approach goals. Again, performance-avoidance goals provided no benefit. Even if partners shared performance-avoidance goals, with these goals athletes were not only less committed to their sport but also less committed to and satisfied with their athletic partner. Athletes with mastery-avoidance goals were committed to and satisfied with sports partners regardless of whether partners shared this goal orientation. Perhaps their estimates of their abilities were so low that they depended on partners to compensate for perceived weaknesses (Jackson, Harwood, & Grove, 2010).

OUTCOME, PERFORMANCE, AND PROCESS GOALS

Another convention in athletic settings is to categorize goals into **outcome, performance, and process** types (Burton, Naylor, & Holliday, 2001). The focuses of outcome goals are the results of a performance and are usually based on social comparisons, such as to beat others in a competition. Performance goals refer to an end-product of a performance, but the end-product is a self-referenced standard. For example, a swimmer might try to swim seconds faster than her personal best time. Process goals refer to the actions necessary to reach an outcome.

British competitive swimmers between the ages of 14 and 28 have been shown to rarely endorse outcome goals (Jones and Hanton, 1996), such as winning a race or beating opponents. Goals of this sort are more likely to engender debilitative cognitive anxiety because one is not able to control the performance of competitors. Most of the swimmers choose a combination of goals that include performance (e.g., complete a race under a certain time) and process (e.g., attention to the technical elements of the swim) goals (24%) or outcome, performance, and process goals (49%). Perhaps the goal orientations of these competitive swimmers were shaped by experience and mentoring from coaches. For example, high school coaches have been shown to use all three types of goals, and to focus on performance and process goals, especially when setting individual goals for athletes (Weinberg et al., 2001). In addition, swimmers with less-adaptive goal orientations, such as outcome goals, may not have reached the competitive level of the swimmers in this sample. Elite athletes are also likely to endorse multiple goal orientations, and to have process goals or systematic plans for reaching their goals (Wilson, Hardy, & Harwood, 2006).

Outcome, Performance, and Process Goals and Proximity to Competition

Various combinations of performance goals have been recommended at times distal and proximal to performances. Athletes have been encouraged to make explicit outcome goals several weeks prior to competitions. Public commitments, such as to win a competition, have been seen to motivate greater efforts to prepare for competitions and for the development of sophisticated strategies for competition. Athletic performance and process goals are recommended to support practice and training for competitions. Athletic performance goals have been shown to support self-confidence and self-efficacy, as athletes record progress in relation to their baseline of prior performance. Process goals are effective in directing attention to instrumental behaviors necessary for good performances. Athletes have been advised to focus on outcome and performance goals immediately prior to competition, and to attend to process goals during competitions. These process goals should include holistic aspects of techniques, such that the automatic execution of skills is not disrupted (Hardy, Jones, & Gould, 1996). Motor skills achieve automaticity when they are capable of being executed without conscious attention to the motor elements that compose the overall motor skill.

The influence of performance and process goals was studied with British male amateur golfers across a duration of 54 weeks. Golfers who set either performance or process goals showed more improvement across the 54 weeks (as measured by handicap) and less anxiety than golfers who did not set goals (Kingston & Hardy, 1997). Golfers who were guided by process goals had the additional advantages of gaining in self-efficacy and concentration during golf rounds. Complex tasks such as golf involve the development of many different skills and strategies, and process goals guide attention to the developments of these facets. As mentioned above, process goals do not necessarily disrupt the automaticity of over-learned actions, such as a golf swing, because attention may be given to key global components rather than the swing's minor elements.

Kitsantas and Zimmerman (1998) reported that process goals were particularly influential in the successful acquisition of novel motor skills, such as throwing darts. They reported that process goals directed the attention of female high school students to the elements of the skill that were to be mastered, and skill acquisition is enhanced further if athletes self-monitor or record their progress in skill acquisition.

SUMMARY AND APPLICATION

There are differences between people in terms of the types of goals they pursue. An extensive research tradition has examined the effects of goals that compare behavior to self-referenced standards versus external standards or norms. Self-referenced goals have been identified as task orientations, athletic performance, or process goals. Goals that determine success in relation to the performance of others have been defined in the same research traditions as ego orientations, and outcome goals. Initially, goals that defined success in relation to others or to norms were seen to impede achievement, persistence at difficult tasks, and intrinsic interest in activities, and to result in higher levels of anxiety during performances. This finding was, of course, ironic, as the focus on winning in relation to others resulted in impaired performance.

Goal orientations that emphasized mastery in relation to one's own baseline were also seen to encourage the development of self-esteem and good sportspersonship. This finding had direct applications, especially with young students and athletes. For example, with the understanding that parents, coaches, and adolescent peers contribute to motivation climates for athletic performance, efforts might be made to develop climates that encourage task orientations.

Subsequent studies demonstrated that goals that measured performance in relation to others did not always impede achievement. In athletic venues, high ego orientations are not iatrogenic if athletes also maintain high task orientations. Almost half (49%) of a sample of competitive adolescent and adult British swimmers endorsed goals of winning in relation to other swimmers, as well as goals of improving performance in relation to their baselines of prior performances, and of focusing on the process of skilled swimming. Successful athletes may learn by experience to develop combinations of goals and to avoid goals that simply focus on performance in relation to others.

Exclusive attention to winning in relation to others competes with concentration on technical skills necessary for skilled performance. This is especially true in the face of superior competition. If competitors are seen to be more formidable than oneself, anxiety increases, and attention is directed away from the technical aspects of skilled performances. However, it should be emphasized that although anxiety about the formidability of competitors may serve as an impediment during performances, it may motivate thorough preparation for performances. "Healthy respect" for opponents may motivate exhaustive practice and preparation for performances. "Healthy respect" or outcome goals facilitate preparation at times distal to competition, and performance during competition is better directed by a combination of goals that are to some degree self-referenced.

Key Terms

Task orientation   202

Ego orientation   202

Task and Ego Orientation in Sport Questionnaire (TEOSQ)   205

The Achievement Goal Scale for Youth Sports (AGSYS)   205

Motivational climates   205

Approach goals   211

Discussion Questions

Q1. Review the models of goal orientations were developed by Carol Dweck and John Nicholls.

Q2. Define task and ego orientations.

Q3. Review the benefits and liabilities of task and ego orientations.

Q4. How is it that ego orientations provoke anxiety prior to and during competition?

Q5. Consider the relationship between task and ego orientations and prosocial behavior.

Q6. How are goal orientations measured?

Q7. Describe the influence of motivational climates on goal orientations.

Q8. Review the influence of motivational climates on team cohesion.

Q9. Describe the development of sportspersonship in motivational climates.

Q10. What is the relationship between simultaneous task and ego orientations and performance?

Q11. Review goal valences.

Q12. Differentiate mastery-approach, mastery-avoidance, performance-approach, and performance-avoidance goals.

Q13. Review the valence of striving and the point of reference for mastery-approach, mastery-avoidance, performance-approach, and performance-avoidance goals.

Q14. Review the underlying motives for mastery-approach, mastery-avoidance, performance-approach, and performance-avoidance goals.

Q15. Are mastery-approach, mastery-avoidance, performance-approach, performance-avoidance goals associated with intrinsic interest?

Q16. Describe outcome, performance, and process goals.

Q17. How is proximity to competition related to the endorsement of outcome, performance, and process goals?

Suggested Readings

Adie, J. W., Duda, J. L., & Ntoumanis, K. (2010). Achievement goals, competition appraisals, and well- and ill-being of elite youth soccer players over two competitive seasons. *Journal of Sport & Exercise Psychology, 32,* 555–579.

Boyce, B. A., Gano-Overway, L. A., & Campbell, A. L. (2009). Perceived motivational climate's influence on goal orientations, perceived competence, and practice strategies across the athletic season. *Journal of Applied Sport Psychology, 21,* 381–394.

Conroy, D E. (2008). Fear of failure in the context of competitive sport: A commentary. *Psychology of Sport and Exercise, 11,* 423–432. doi: 10.1016/j.psychsport.2010.04.013

Duda, J. L. (2005). Motivation in sport: The relevance of competence and achievement goals. In A. J. Elliot & C. S. Dweck (Eds.), *Handbook of competence and motivation* (pp. 318–335). New York, NY: Guilford Press.

Kristiansen, E., Hanstad, D. V., & Roberts, G. C. (2011). Coping with the media at the Vancouver Winter Olympics: "We all make a living out of this." *Journal of Applied Sport Psychology, 23,* 443–458. doi: 10.1080/10413200.2011.598139

MacDonald, D. J., Cote, J., Eys, M., & Deakin, J. (2011). The role of enjoyment and motivational climate in relation to the personal development of team sport athletes. *The Sport Psychologist, 25,* 32–46.

Roberts, G. C., Treasure, D.C., & Conroy, D. E. (2007). Understanding the dynamics of motivation in sport and physical activity. Anticipation and decision making. In G. Tenenbaum & R. C. Eklund (Eds.), *Handbook of sport psychology* (3rd ed., pp. 3–30). New York, NY: Wiley.

Stoeber, J., & Crombie, R. (2010). Achievement goals and championship performance: Predicting absolute performance and qualification success. *Psychology of Sport and Exercise, 11,* 513–521. doi: 10.1016/j.psychsport.2010.07.007

van de Pol, P. K. C., & Kavussanu, M. (2011). Achievement goals and motivational responses in tennis: Does the context matter? *Psychology of Sport and Exercise, 12,* 176–183. doi: 10.1016/j.psychsport.2010.09.005

van de Pol, P. K. C., Kavussanu, M., & Ring, C. (2012). Goal orientations, perceived motivational climate, and motivational outcomes in football: A comparison between training and competition contexts. *Psychology of Sport and Exercise, 13,* 491–499. doi: 10.1016/j.psychsport.2011.12.002

Chapter 10

SELF-EFFICACY, SPORT SELF-CONFIDENCE, AND MENTAL TOUGHNESS

Self-efficacy and striving for difficult goals

Michael Phelps won 22 Olympic medals (18 gold, two silver, and two bronze); easily the most in Olympic history. He evidenced self-efficacy: "When I'm focused, there is not one single thing, person, anything that can stand in my way of doing something. There is not. If I want something bad enough, I feel I'm gonna [sic] get there. That's just how I've always been" (Phelps & Abrahamson, 2008, p. 38).

SELF-EFFICACY

Self-efficacy has been referenced in five of the seven preceding chapters. Its influence on performance begins at points distal to competition and evaluations, and continues throughout competition and practice. It is a concept that is highly relevant to the topic of performance enhancement, because it relates to efforts to control the circumstances and events in one's life.

In a larger sense, people influence the course of their lives by exerting control over their pursuits. With high self-efficacy, people are more likely to take action to control their environment and less likely to disengage from challenges and the stress of competition (Chesney, Neilands, Chambers, Taylor, & Folkman, 2006; Haney & Long, 1995; Nicholls, Polman, & Levy, 2010). With stronger and sturdier efficacy beliefs, people tackle more difficult projects, and overwhelming evidence is necessary before they admit defeat (Beattie, Hardy, Savage, Woodman, & Callow, 2011). This belief that one has the capacity to organize and execute the actions necessary to realize attainments or goals in particular areas or domains of functioning is referred to as **self-efficacy.** The concept of self-efficacy was developed by Albert Bandura, and this concept has influenced research not only in sport psychology, but also in social, clinical, industrial, and health psychology (Feltz, Short, & Sullivan, 2008; Bandura, 1997). The concept of sport self-confidence was developed specifically to measure confidence for successful athletic performance (Vealey, 2001, 2007, 2009).

Sportspersons with sturdy self-efficacy are also described as mentally tough. Mentally tough performers approach competition with confidence and believe they are in control of the factors that will determine success. They cope well with pressure and adversity in competition, practice, and their personal lives, and recover quickly from setbacks (Galli & Vealey, 2008; Jones, Hanton, & Connaugton, 2002; Nicholls, Levy, Polman, & Crust, 2011; Nicholls, Polman, Levy, & Backhouse, 2008; Thelwell, Weston, & Greenlees, 2005).

Self-Efficacy and Expectations about Future Success

Self-efficacy reflects expectations about future success. It is an especially important determinant of performance when people compete in unfamiliar venues and against unfamiliar opponents. In these situations, performers are uncertain about their chances of success. Competitors are also likely to be uncertain of their chances of success when they are evenly matched. Relative physical equality is not uncommon at elite levels of athletic competition. Among elite, collegiate, and high school athletes, self-confidence distinguishes more and less successful counterparts (Covassin & Pero, 2004; Feltz & Magyar, 2006; Moritz, Feltz, Fahrbach, & Mack, 2000; Vealey, 2009).

For example, the physical skills of wrestlers in overtime matches are roughly equivalent. Perceived efficacy was the sole determinant of success in wrestling matches with high school boys that extended into overtimes

(Kane, Marks, Zaccaro, & Blair, 1996). As will be discussed later, an important source of self-efficacy is one's history of prior success at similar tasks. However, self-efficacy reflects more than just memories of prior win-loss records, because it represents expectations about success with new and evenly matched opponents. High and sturdy efficacy sustains belief in successful outcomes when clear information about one's likelihood of success is unavailable.

Application

Efficacious athletes believe in their ultimate success when uncertain about the strength of opponents or when evenly matched. How is efficacy possible when one is clearly overmatched?

    Efficacious athletes may remember that competition would be unnecessary if the outcome was certain. The strongest competitor and team do not always win. Opponents have off days, and play with injuries and illnesses. Favored teams and individuals also experience the greatest pressure to win.

Until recently, the influence of efficacy on estimates of success was shown to be greatest during the early stages of skill development. As sportspersons gained experience in practicing skills and in competition, past performance was seen to be more important than efficacy beliefs in determining additional progress (Feltz, 1982; Feltz & Mugno, 1983; Haney & Long, 1995). For example, as female athletes practiced back dives, their actual diving proficiency was a more important determinant of diving performance than efficacy beliefs (Feltz, 1982; Feltz & Mugno, 1983).

Efficacy beliefs and actual performance are temporally recursive; efficacious beliefs result in better performance, which then reinforce the efficacious beliefs (Bandura, 1977). A truer picture of the influence of self-efficacy and past performance on future performance is obtained when the recursive influence of one on the other is statistically removed. This statistical procedure was applied in a recent reanalysis of the results of the aforementioned study with female divers. The results indicated that self-efficacy was a better predictor of diving proficiency that were past diving performance, even after diving practice (Feltz, Chow, & Hepler, 2008).

Optimistic Self-Efficacy Beliefs

Both in athletic venues and more generally, people do not always make accurate determinations of their capabilities. This occurs when new tasks are undertaken and feedback about progress is not forthcoming. Self-efficacy judgments are often derived from assessments of performances on similar tasks, and, of course, these assessments may be faulty because of differences in the tasks, misinterpretations of the similarities of the tasks, and faulty judgment of one's success at the similar task. Underestimating efficacy results in the avoidance of activities that could lead to advancement and greater life satisfaction, whereas overestimating efficacy on tasks that involve considerable risk can easily result in loss or injury. Significant personal, scientific, and athletic advancements often involve the acceptance of risk, because they require prolonged effort for an uncertain reward. With optimistic self-efficacy beliefs, people are more willing to take these risks because they have a sturdy belief in their ability to prevail in advance of proof that they will be successful. For example, French rock climbers who took the greatest risks while climbing rated themselves as most competent at safe climbing. They had reserves of efficacy due to actual experience at executing dangerous climbs (Martha, Sanchez, & Goma-i-Freixanet, 2009).

Optimistic assessments of efficacy can be detrimental not only when dangers are ignored, but also when the difficulty of acquiring new skills and knowledge is underestimated. As described in Chapter 5, it is adaptive to be realistic about the necessity of thorough and even exhaustive preparation for optimal performances. It is unlikely that even elite athletes can ignore the challenge of highly difficult athletic accomplishments. For example, male and female divers from the U.S. national team were acutely aware of the difficulty of the dives in their programs. They were more cautious in their efficacy assessments prior to the execution of the more difficult dives (Slobounov, Yukelson, & O'Brien, 1997). Similarly, the French climbers referenced above were realistic in assessing the potential for injury in the course of dangerous climbs (Martha et al., 2009). Still, efficacy increased over the course of a program with the successful execution of difficult dives. Of course, it is important to maximize efficacy from the first moment of competitions, and the strategies for optimal proximal preparation make this more likely.

During performances, self-doubt undermines the execution of the skills acquired during preparation. In extreme sports, such as rock climbing without ropes, white water kayaking, and skiing on terrain so dangerous that, "if you fall you die" (Slanger & Rudestam, 1997, p. 359), both efficacy and preparation must be very high, because there is no room for error. So long as dangers and thorough preparation are not ignored, optimistic efficacy beliefs allow people to do their best with the talent and skills they possess.

Self-Efficacy and Persistence

Disappointments and setbacks often occur in the pursuit of significant accomplishments, and, therefore, efficacy beliefs must be sturdy, so that optimism is quickly restored after discouragement (Beattie et al., 2011). Innovative and creative artistic and scientific work is routinely received, at least initially, with disinterest or rejection, perhaps because it provides a paradigm or worldview that is unlike what exists at its time. Truly creative work is "outside the box" of conventional thinking, and, therefore, the self-efficacy of innovators must be especially sturdy, as they must believe they cannot only reach a standard necessary for success, but that they can establish a new standard.

Efficacy beliefs can shape the course and direction of the lives of people. With higher efficacy beliefs, people are more likely to consider a wider range of career options. These career options are more likely to be available to them because efficacy for academic achievement resulted in greater academic competency, and because they are more likely to persist throughout difficult education programs to realize career goals.

Higher self-efficacy leads to higher levels of motivation and effort, persistence at difficult tasks, and higher achievement at sports, such as cricket, tennis, gymnastics, diving, and endurance exercises with adults and children (Bandura & Cervone, 1983; Bull, Shambrook, James, & Brooks, 2005; Weinberg, 1985; Weinberg, Gould, & Jackson, 1979; Weinberg, Gould, Yukelson, & Jackson, 1981; Wurtele, 1986). It sustains performance under pressure, in the face of stiff competition, adversity, and setbacks, and is particularly influential in face-to-face competition. In the vernacular of sport, participants with very high self-efficacy are said to not "have an ounce of quit" in them. Efficacy beliefs are vital not only during performances or the demonstration of acquired skills, but also during the acquisition or learning of skill. Sustained effort is often necessary to master the skills and subskills necessary for successful performances.

Heightened self-efficacy is associated with improved problem solving, heightened physical stamina, and increased pain tolerance. In the face of difficulties or obstacles, people with lower efficacy reduce their efforts and settle for mediocre results, whereas those with high efficacy intensify their efforts to reach goals. The persistence of people with high efficacy may be due to their commitment to reach goals. With higher goal commitment and higher self-efficacy, people set loftier goals for performance (Theodorakis, 1995, 1996). People with high self-efficacy do not become satisfied and quiescent upon reaching a goal, but instead set additional and higher goals.

Nelson Mandela
(photo by Dave Hogan/
Getty Images)

Self-Efficacy and Persistence

As a black South African lawyer and political activist in the African National Congress (ANC), Nelson Mandela devoted his adult life to ending apartheid and gaining legal and political equality for black South Africans. He was convicted of conspiracy, which was similar to treason, and for which he could have received the death penalty. He served 27 years in prison. After his release, he was awarded the Nobel Peace Prize in 1993.

After helping to develop a new constitution and obtain the voting franchise for South Africans of all races, he was elected president in 1994.

Reflecting on his odyssey from a childhood in a traditional African tribe, to imprisonment, and to the presidency of South Africa, at age 76, Nelson Mandela wrote:

I have walked that long road to freedom. I have tried not to falter; I have made missteps along the way. But I have discovered the secret that after climbing a great hill, one only finds that there are many more hills to climb. I have taken a moment here to rest, to steal a view of the glorious vista that surrounds me, to look back on the distance I have come. But I can rest only for a moment, for with freedom comes responsibilities, and I dare not linger, for my long walk is not yet ended (Mandela, 1994, p. 544).

Self-Efficacy and the Use of Skills

As mentioned in Chapter 2, efficacy beliefs are not a substitute for skill, as without the skills and training necessary for successful performance, unshakable efficacy may be little more than wishful thinking. But efficacy beliefs allow people to make optimal use of their acquired skills. Skills often have to be selected, organized, and integrated in novel ways during performances, and efficacious beliefs allow for this flexibility. With heightened self-efficacy, people make optimal use of the skills they have mastered, and more quickly acquire new skills and knowledge.

With high self-efficacy, skills can be applied flexibly and in various combinations, and performance is more consistently excellent. For example, female and male divers from the U.S. national team with higher self-efficacy were more consistent in performing key elements of dives, such as the placement of feet on the board and the angle of takeoff (Slobounov, Yukelson, & O'Brien, 1997). These elements occurred near the point of takeoff from the board. There was more flexibility and variability in the movements of the most efficacious divers prior to the point of takeoff. Variability in preparatory movements apparently offers divers ways of self-regulating performance and finding the combination of movements that lead to optimal dives.

Self-Efficacy and Anxiety

People with high self-efficacy are not easily daunted by difficult tasks and initial failures in problem solving. Perhaps this is due to their tendency to attribute initial difficulties to insufficient effort rather than to inadequate talent. Without high efficacy beliefs, the same initial difficulties prompt doubts about whether one has the skills to perform successfully. Self-doubts and concerns about the consequences of failure compete with the planning and execution of skills necessary for success at the task. When self-efficacy is low, difficult tasks are more readily seen to be threats rather than challenges, and unsuccessful performances cause demoralization that is enduring.

As will be discussed in Chapter 11, a firm belief that one has the capacity to reach standards necessary for successful performances serves as a powerful source of psychological insulation against cognitive interference and cognitive anxiety during performances (Chamberlain & Hale, 2007; Craft, Magyar, Becker, & Feltz, 2003; Mellalieu, Hanton, & Fletcher, 2006; Mullen, Lane, & Hanton, 2009). For example, male high school wrestlers with higher self-efficacy had less anxiety prior to matches and more positive emotions (Treasure, Monson, & Lox, 1996). The wrestlers with higher self-efficacy also had better win-loss records and scored more points during matches. Among male university athletes in England and Wales, expectations for winning were the most important determinants of cognitive anxiety measured two hours and thirty minutes before competitions (Jones, Swain, & Cale, 1991). Those who expected to win experienced less cognitive anxiety.

There is a place for self-doubt in the course of evaluations, performances, and competitions, and it is in the preparatory stage (Feltz, Short, & Sullivan, 2008). Realistic evaluations of areas in need of improvement and strategies to counter strengths of opponents promote better preparation for performances (Bandura, 1997; Bandura & Locke, 2003; Woodman, Akehurst, Hardy, & Beattie, 2010). Motivation might best be maintained by combining a resilient sense of efficacy with realistic appraisals of the likelihood of accomplishing difficult tasks.

Application

With sturdy efficacy, sportspersons have less need to query themselves about the likelihood of success during competition. With low efficacy, athletes more frequently ask themselves if they will be successful. With each query, they increase the likelihood that they will answer, "No."

Generalizability of Efficacy Beliefs

Efficacy beliefs pertain to domains of functioning such as academic or athletic aptitude. For example, efficacy for math performance predicts higher achievement in mathematics across ability levels for college students. With high efficacy for math performance, children complete more math problems correctly, and rework problems they missed. Children with higher academic self-efficacy are more conscientious and effective in completing homework assignments, in working at their classroom desks, and achieve higher grades (Pajares, 1996).

However, some people have efficacy beliefs that are quite general, so that they believe they can function successfully in a wide range of domains. Sometimes these domains are only superficially dissimilar and rely on similar subskills. For example, a coach and university professor might have efficacy for her facility to provide lectures to college students and effective coaching to her soccer team. Both tasks may rely on similar subskills, such as skill in public speaking and sensitivity to the reactions of others. Self-efficacy about public speaking and responding empathetically to others may further generalize to beliefs about her capacity to conduct workshops for high school coaches.

Efficacy beliefs also generalize when facilities in different domains are developed contemporaneously. Continuing with the previous example, efficacy beliefs in functioning as a professor and coach could be the result of gaining competency as a graduate assistant coach and scholar during graduate school training.

The development of metastrategies also leads to the generalization of efficacy beliefs. Metastrategies refer to skills that can be used in a variety of situations. For example, techniques to control somatic or physiological anxiety were discussed in Chapter 7. These techniques could be practiced in a range of settings, such as prior to athletic competitions and prior to tests in school. The successful deployment of techniques to control somatic anxiety would foster a generalized belief in the controllability of anxiety (Smith, 1999). Efficacy beliefs are also generalized from experiences in which fears are mastered. For example, upon the mastery of snake phobias, people were emboldened to tackle other fears, such as fear of public speaking (Bandura, Jeffery, & Gajdos, 1975).

Highly salient or meaningful mastery experiences are more likely to result in heightened general or widespread self-efficacy. For example, women who obtain training in self-defense are likely to view personal safety as an important issue. The amelioration of this vulnerability was shown to have more general effects among college women who were taught methods of physical self-defense (Weitlauf, Cervone, Smith, & Wright, 2001; Weitlauf, Smith, & Cervone, 2000). This training included the use of verbal resistance and persuasion, and physical resistance. The physical resistance techniques were based on the Japanese martial arts of Shotokan karate and aikido. With these techniques, women were trained to free themselves from assailants and to disable opponents with punches and kicks to vulnerable areas of the body. These women gained self-efficacy not only in the domain of self-defense, but also for their capacity to master other physical skills and demands, and most generally for their ability to master challenges in areas of life not related to physical functioning. These women appeared to have gained confidence in their capacities to channel anger and aggression in adaptive ways.

SELF-EFFICACY VERSUS SELF-ESTEEM

Self-efficacy is not synonymous with **self-esteem.** Self-esteem refers to self-worth, or how people value themselves. Self-efficacy relates to convictions that one can initiate and sustain sufficiently skilled actions to realize a range of goals in domains of functioning. High self-esteem may be unrelated to high achievement because this self-esteem may be dependent on sources other than high achievement, and people may be satisfied with low levels of achievement. For example, the high self-esteem of college students was unrelated to setting goals for high grades in college courses and to the realization of high grades in college courses (Mone, Baker, & Jeffries, 1995).

Conversely, high achievement does not inevitably lead to high self-esteem. This is because self-worth may be dependent on realizing standards that are impossibly high and that have been internalized in the context of important relationships, such as the relationship between a child and his or her parents. The internalization of impossibly high standards has been associated with relationships with parents who almost chronically reflect a degree of disappointment in their children and who do not set clear and attainable standards for their children. With lofty and "fuzzy" internal standards, dissatisfaction with oneself may persist because external accomplishments are unlikely to match internal standards for self-satisfaction. These children strive to escape feelings of disappointment but do not experience increased self-worth after reaching goals, because the standards for self-satisfaction are not clear. The topic of striving for impossibly high standards and perfectionism will be explored further in Chapter 13.

Application

Recent research indicates that those with higher self-esteem not only feel better about themselves, but also about their work and relationships. However, self-esteem does not result in achievement in areas such as occupational status (Orth, Robins, & Widaman, 2012).

Conversely, individuals may accomplish a great deal and still feel disappointed in themselves because their accomplishments do not rise to the level of their internal standards. These standards may be difficult to objectively evaluate, as they may originate in childhood and in the context of essential relationships. A child may internalize the viewpoint of a parent and unwittingly take a similar view when evaluating him- or herself.

Self-esteem and self-confidence are correlated. Basketball players with higher self-esteem also demonstrated higher self-confidence (Coudevylle, Gernigon, & Ginis, 2011). Failure appears to decrease self-efficacy to a greater extent among sportspersons with lower self-esteem. Following a loss in a tiebreak, adolescent and young adult national standard tennis players with lower self-esteem reported larger decreases in self-efficacy compared to their counterparts with higher self-esteem (Lane, Jones, & Stevens, 2002).

SOURCES OF SELF-EFFICACY

Self-efficacy develops from successful experience at related tasks or enactive attainments, watching a person similar to oneself accomplish a task, and from encouragement and persuasion from others (Chase, Feltz, & Lirgg, 2003; Freeman & Rees, 2010; Jackson, Knapp, & Beauchamp, 2008). Self-efficacy is also judged on the bases of one's thoughts and emotional reactions, especially the reactions that occur in the process of performances and competitions. Finally, childhood experiences form the bases of judgments about self-efficacy.

Enactive Attainments

The actual experience of success is the most persuasive source of self-efficacy (Chase et al., 2003). For example, the United States Tennis Association (USTA) ratings of adult league tennis players strongly predicted the perceived tennis abilities of these tennis players (Sheldon & Eccles, 2005). The USTA ratings were assigned by certified teaching professionals. High self-efficacy then makes future success more likely, and the ensuing experiences of success further augment self-efficacy (Bond, Biddle, & Ntoumanis, 2001; Bueno, Weinberg, Fernandez-Castro, & Capdevila, 2008). Resilient self-efficacy requires experience in overcoming obstacles and learning to persist in the face of difficulties. Self-efficacy built on experiences of easy successes is vulnerable under conditions in which success depends on sustained effort and initial failures are experienced. Experience in overcoming adversity is beneficial in that it teaches that success at difficult tasks requires sustained and sometimes extraordinary effort, and provides information about how to hone and organize skills to reach difficult goals (Galli & Vealey, 2008; Bandura, 1997).

It is not the experience of success that influences self-efficacy, but how the person understands his or her contribution to the success. Success that is attributed to internal and stable characteristics, such as talent and ability, augments efficacy beliefs (Bond et al., 2001; Coffee, Rees, & Haslam, 2009). For example, confidence in tennis abilities is built on more than just USTA ratings but also on confidence in one's psychological skills and knowledge of strategy (Sheldon & Eccles, 2005).

Resilient efficacy beliefs are somewhat difficult to dislodge. When self-efficacy is low, success experiences can be readily discounted, attributed to luck, or to inordinate effort rather than talent. These success experiences may also be ignored, because people selectively attend to information that is consistent with their self-efficacy beliefs and ignore disconfirming information. If experience is to alter low efficacy beliefs, the discordance between the experience and the beliefs must be confronted and reconciled. The resiliency of efficacy beliefs is advantageous when self-efficacy is high. In these instances, failures do not easily deflate efficacy and are attributed to inadequate effort, preparation, and external factors, such as bad luck. Efficacy beliefs are reinforced and strengthened by selectively recalling successful performances.

Application

The objectives of cognitive behavioral psychotherapies include the identification and modification of dysfunctional attributional biases. Those with low self-efficacy evidence such biases, as they attribute success to external, uncontrollable, and unstable factors, such as luck. They are unlikely to attribute success to internal, global, stable, and controllable traits, such as talent.

Success that is largely due to the help or efforts of others does little to enhance self-efficacy. Failure is less likely to diminish efficacy if little effort is exerted and if it is attributed to environmental conditions rather than to talent. However, the withdrawal of effort when confronted with challenges is hardly an adaptive strategy, and if adopted routinely leads to a pattern of **self-handicapping** that will be discussed in Chapter 12. By self-handicapping, people are spared failure experiences at the cost of avoiding opportunities in which success is not assured. To try hard and fail under optimal conditions undermines efficacy beliefs, especially if failure occurs prior to a pattern of successes in a realm of functioning and prior to the establishment of a sturdy sense of efficacy.

Observational Learning

People engage in observational learning by watching others demonstrate a desired behavior (Bandura, 1986). It is an efficient and effective way of teaching sport skills (Rink, 1988), and it influences efficacy. For example, observational learning increased both self-efficacy and performance among French boxers (Legrain, d'Arrippe-Longueville, & Gernigon, 2003a, 2003b). The skills of novice climbers advanced more quickly with observational learning (Boschker & Bakker, 2002).

People estimate their efficacy by evaluating the competence of people to whom they are similar, and the successes and failures of others they resemble increases and decreases efficacy, respectively (George, Feltz, & Chase, 1992; Hall et al., 2009; McCullagh & Weiss, 2001). The influence of this vicarious experience is greatest when people have little prior experience in the realm of functioning and when the models are highly similar to the observer (Bandura, 1997). In effect, with little prior experience, the results obtained by the model present the best information about the probable results of one's own performance. If one model of similar status is convincing, then observing several similar models is even more convincing to the observer that they can also execute that function.

Vicarious experience affects not only efficacy beliefs, but also provides instruction about the skills, strategies, and optimal arousal levels and mental states necessary for successful performance (Cumming, Clark, Ste-Marie, McCullagh, & Hall, 2005; Law & Hall, 2009; Wesch, Law, & Hall, 2007). The observer forms a mental representation of action that serves to both initiate imitation and as a reference for judging the correctness of motor actions (Black & Wright, 2000; Blandin & Proteau, 2000; Hodges, Chua, & Franks, 2003; McCullagh & Weiss, 2001). Some models also provide information about the influence of efficacious beliefs, as they voice their determination to surmount obstacles. Models can also verbalize problem-solving strategies to the benefit of observers. Instructive models help observers predict threats that may occur in the course of a performance, and also to respond to and control these sources of threat.

People who have serious doubts about their ability to function in various domains may find a **coping model** most similar. Coping models do not demonstrate initial proficiency in domains, such as academic problem solving, but demonstrate a process by which they build competence. This process may involve learning general rules for solving problems and techniques for managing anxiety. The observer learns that he or she will also have to learn new skills and techniques for managing anxiety. The coping model demonstrates that successful performance is due to effort and persistence rather than to initial talent.

Coping models have been seen to be preferable to mastery models for the acquisition of novel motor skills (Feltz & Magyar, 2006). Girls in the ninth grade who learned to throw darts by observing an adult coping model achieved higher dart scores, self-efficacy, and gained greater intrinsic interest in darts than did girls who observed an adult mastery model (Kitsantas, Zimmerman, & Cleary, 2000). In the coping condition, girls learned to identify subskills necessary for good throws and how to correct errors in their throws. Feedback improved the girls' identification of proper skills and subskills, self-efficacy, and intrinsic interest in throwing darts. Exposure to the coping model appeared to teach the ninth graders that missed shots were due to strategy limitations and limited experience and effort. These limitations are subject to remediation and do not result in demoralization and decreased intrinsic interest in darts. Training with the mastery model was more likely to lead to attributions that misses were due to inadequate ability.

Similar models also help children overcome anxiety and develop self-efficacy. For example, children who were fearful of swimming became less fearful, made more progress with swimming lessons, and developed greater self-efficacy when observing peer models (Weiss, McCullagh, Smith, & Berlant, 1998).

Coping and **mastery models,** or models that demonstrate skills proficiently and with limited anxiety, are both most effective to the degree that they explicitly demonstrate and verbalize the step-by-step actions that the observer must follow to perform competently (Clark & Ste-Marie, 2002). It may also be unnecessary to demonstrate initial ineptitude, such as would be the case in true coping modeling, to foster feelings of similarity between the observer and model. In place of enacted ineptitude, the model can simply detail their historical difficulties and demonstrate the skills that allow them to master problems. By verbalizing their conviction that solutions to problems are found after the expenditure of sufficient effort, models encourage observers to be persistent and to not attribute difficulties to insufficient talent.

Regardless of whether models demonstrate coping or mastery, they are most influential if they demonstrate **competence.** The benefits of observing competent models are especially apparent when observers have much to learn and believe they are similar to the competent model.

Observing a videotape of oneself or **self-modeling** is also informative. For example, by viewing a tape on one's golf swing (McCullagh & Weiss, 2001) or gymnastic routines (Hars & Calmels, 2007), flaws can be detected and modified. Divers used self-modeling to identify the component parts of complex dives that were correctly executed (Rymal, Martini, & Ste-Marie, 2010). Commentary and direction from an expert can facilitate this process. Progress can be recorded on tape, and this data enhances self-efficacy. Self-efficacy is also enhanced when self-modeling contributes to visualization prior to the execution of closed skills (Rymal et al., 2010).

Feedback

The comments of others can augment or erode self-efficacy and performance (Hutchinson, Sherman, Martinovic, & Tenenbaum, 2008). For example, the self-efficacy and performance of experienced weightlifters was influenced not simply by the actual amount of weight they lifted, but how much they believed they lifted. When feedback exaggerated the amount they actually lifted, their efficacy and performance increased (Fitzsimmons, Landers, Thomas, & Van der Mars, 1991). Similar findings were reported with adults between the ages of 45 and 65. The middle-aged participants pedaled at submaximum intensity on a bicycle ergometer and were given feedback that exaggerated their performance. This feedback lifted their efficacy for walking, cycling, and doing push-ups (McAuley, Duncan, Wraith, & Lettunich, 1991). Further, in a study involving Spanish college students and performance in the track and field event of hurdling, feedback not only influenced self-efficacy and performance, but also decisions to participate in more difficult hurdling events in the future (Escarti & Guzman, 1999). Feedback was altered to reflect slower or faster times for the completion of a 70-meter hurdle event with seven hurdles. Self-efficacy, subsequent hurdling times, and decisions to tackle difficult hurdle events in the future were all influenced by feedback.

Adults are sensitive to encouraging feedback that does not sound **authentic.** Faint praise may or may not be damning, but it does erode efficacy, as people interpret it as indicating that little is expected of them. Feedback that focuses on progress toward goals enhances efficacy and performance, whereas feedback about shortfalls has the opposite effect. Criticism about shortfalls offers little information about how to correct or improve performance.

Feedback is more persuasive if it comes from **experts.** Experts may have mastery of the skill they are evaluating, and may also be qualified on the basis of their training, credentials, and experience. Persuasive feedback is also **believable.** For example, feedback that performance can improve moderately is more believable than is advice that rapid, huge improvements can be easily realized. Feedback that raises expectations to unrealistic levels is likely to be discounted soon after sportspersons follow instructions and do not realize rapid gains.

With feedback and verbal persuasion, people can recognize when they have the requisite skills for success and when these skills must be developed. In the former case, the skills may be misapplied. In the latter, the missing skills are identified, performers are persuaded to believe that they have the ability to acquire the skills, and a competent model demonstrates the execution of the skills. New skills are best acquired if they are deconstructed and taught as a series of subskills. Attempts to master subskills are more likely to result in success, and with this success and confirmatory feedback, performers develop efficacy that all of the skills and the ultimate goal will be mastered (Bandura, 1997; Smith, 2010).

Feedback and Coaches

In many instances, the influence of verbal persuasion, vicarious experience, and enactive attainments interact. For example, effective coaches diagnose skills that require refinement or development, develop practice that makes it likely that skills and subskills are mastered, model the execution of skills, recognize when skills as misused, and provide feedback that focuses on attainments rather than deficits. Effective coaches recognize that that this is a daily process and that passing comments and random critiques are of little benefit. Effective coaches understand that the self-efficacy of their athletes is strengthened when they model confidence and make liberal use of praise, when athletes engage in positive self-talk, and when skills are refined with drilling and instruction (Vargas-Tonsing, Myers, & Feltz, 2004).

Efficacy is enhanced when athletes sense that their coaches and teammates believe in their ability. Efficacy is also enhanced when athletes have confidence in the skills of their partners in sports such as tennis (Jackson, Beauchamp, & Knapp, 2007). Athletes and coaches also appear to be more committed to and satisfied with each other when they are confident in the other's ability (Jackson & Beauchamp, 2010). These findings support a *tripartite efficacy* model for close, dyadic relationships, such as that between a coach and an athlete. In these dyadic relationships, complementary efficacy beliefs are developed: the athlete's self-efficacy, the athlete's confidence in the ability of the coach, and the athlete's estimation of the coach's confidence in his or her ability (Jackson, Gucciardi, & Dimmock, 2011; Lent & Lopez, 2002).

Coaching for Efficacy

The efficacy of Michael Phelps—winner of 22 Olympic gold medals—was honed by his only coach, Bob Bowman: "Bob has, without question, helped refine my intense drive and dedication. He has also, without question, helped me believe that anything is possible. Two seconds faster than the world record? Doesn't matter. Three seconds faster? Doesn't matter. You can swim as fast as you want. You can do anything you want. You just have to dream it, believe it, work at it, go for it" (Phelps & Abrahamson, 2008, p. 18).

Physical and Emotional States

Physical and emotional states also provide information about efficacy. Physiological anxiety, physical dysfunction and fatigue, and emotional dysphoria provoke doubts about competence. However, as discussed in Chapter 4, physiological anxiety or arousal can be interpreted as facilitative or debilitative to performance. Conviction that one can achieve goals and standards for performance, regardless of arousal and environmental disruptions, is a critical element for minimizing the disruptive effects of physiological arousal and concomitant cognitive interference (Sanchez, Boschker, & Llewellyn, 2010). Confidence in the capacity to control one's emotions is also associated with less physiological anxiety during athletic performance (Haney & Long, 1995).

Childhood Experiences

Youth who develop in caring environments are more likely to develop efficacy that they can express and moderate emotions. Children feel safe, supported, valued, and respected in caring environments (Gano-Overway et al., 2009; Newton et al., 2007). When treated with kindness, children express positive and negative emotion with less fear of ridicule. Adolescents free to express positive emotions are more likely to engage in prosocial behavior, such as concern for the well-being of others. Adolescent females who lack confidence for managing negative emotions are more likely to experience depression. With insight and efficacy, less time is spent brooding over anger, frustration, and disappointment (Bandura, Caprara, Barbaranelli, Gerbino, & Pastoreli, 2003).

Children and adolescents who experienced caring environments in five-week summer sport camps were more capable of expressing positive emotions and negative emotions. The expression of positive emotion contributed to greater happiness and hope and to less sadness and depression. The expression of negative emotion contributed to the experience of hope. Perhaps those youngsters who do not overreact and dwell on the negative more readily consider that better times are ahead (Fry et al., 2012). The influence of coaches is instrumental in nurturing caring environments (Gould, Flett, & Lauer, 2012).

Adults contribute to the efficacy of children by providing challenges that are just beyond a child's current level of competency, so that with effort and guidance, successful performance is likely. These adults recognize when children need more and less help, and withdraw assistance as children become more capable of completing tasks on their own. They avoid offering challenges that are too difficult or too easy, as the former are likely to result in failure, the latter in no new learning, and both in the diminishment of self-efficacy. When adults respond contingently to the skill levels of children, they demonstrate an intense interest in the well-being of children, and this interest is expressed in an ongoing process of hypothesis testing about the nature of optimal challenges that children might enjoy and master. With stable, supportive attachment to competent adults, children develop psychological resiliency that contributes to efficacy and recovery after setbacks (Bandura, 1997).

When adults offer feedback that links the successes of children to abilities, they provide greater support for efficacious beliefs than when they extol the virtues of work for the attainment of future success (Schunk, 1989). In effect, efficacious beliefs develop more reliably if children are taught that achievement is due to their abilities. As is true with adults, children who consider their success to result only from extraordinary effort may harbor doubts about their talents. Virtuosity is likely to be the result of talent and hard work. The parents of U.S. Olympic champions communicated confidence in their athletic children's capacities, while also emphasizing the importance of hard work and persistence (Gould, Dieffenbach, & Moffett, 2002).

Efficacy is promoted in school when progress is measured in relation to students' own prior performance rather than to the performance of other children. Frequent social comparisons encourage students to think of ability as fixed or stable rather than malleable and emerging. By focusing on improvement relative to one's baseline, learners are more likely to emphasize personal improvement and skill mastery, and to focus on the intrinsic rewards of learning (Duda & Hall, 2001; Kavussanu & Roberts, 1996; Wood & Bandura, 1989).

Intrinsic interest in learning and achievement accompanies increased efficacy (Gano-Overway et al., 2009; Newton et al., 2007). Bandura (1986) maintained that practically any task could become intrinsically interesting. Intrinsic interest develops when people assign performance standards or goals to tasks. When reaching these standards, people experience satisfying self-reactions. Meeting goals and achieving a level of competency at tasks contributes to feelings of self-efficacy, and a threshold of competency is necessary prior to the experience of intrinsic interest. For example, competition in a five-day wrestling camp in which high school wrestlers competed in the equivalent of one-third to one-half of a season's matches may appear more like work than fun. However, wrestlers who were pleased with their performances and who had high efficacy for their wrestling competence discovered intrinsic interest and satisfaction with the camp experience (Kane et al., 1996).

HANDLING FAILURE

Despite the best preparation and sturdy self-efficacy, failures occur. Efficacious beliefs also serve to restore positive moods after losses (Brown, Malouff, & Schutte, 2005). As mentioned earlier, the effects of failure on self-efficacy are substantially determined by how the failure is interpreted. When failure is ascribed to stable, internal factors, such as a lack of "natural ability," self-efficacy and ensuing performance worsens (Coffee, Rees, & Haslam, 2009). People are also more likely to avoid future opportunities for failure. When interpretations of failures focus on inadequate preparation, execution of skills, and premature efforts to execute complex skills without first mastering subskills, failures are not interpreted as the "final word" about whether skills and anxiety will be mastered (Kitsantas & Zimmerman, 1998; Zimmerman & Kitsantas, 1997).

Therapists, coaches, teachers, and mentors help people resolve anxiety about performances by modeling subskills and skills, by identifying the subskills in complex skills, and by correcting trainees' dysfunctional attributions of failure to stable, internal characteristics. This guidance is particularly helpful when provided in the setting where the actual performance will occur. Once complex skills have been performed successfully, it is important to practice variations of the skills in a variety of situations. Skill should be practiced under diverse conditions, and resilient skills can still be properly executed after setbacks and with adversity (Bandura, 1997).

SPORT SELF-CONFIDENCE

Recall that self-efficacy pertains to confidence for reaching goals in domains of functioning. The domain of greatest interest in this book is sport. The concept of sport self-confidence was developed specifically to measure confidence for successful athletic performance (Vealey, 2001, 2007, 2009). With high sport self-confidence, athletes are more capable of successfully deploying their skills to reach goals (Hayes et al., 2009). U.S. Olympic athletes at the Winter Games in Nagano, Japan, in 1998 rated self-confidence and confidence in teammates as the most influential factors in determining performance (Gould, 1999).

Theory and research about sport self-confidence has accounted for unique social and cultural factors that affect confidence in sport venues. Aspects of sport venues that affect confidence include the level of competition, coaching behavior, and motivational climates. Athletes are sometimes acculturated to participate in certain sports on the bases of gender and ethnicity, and dissuaded from participation in other sports. For example, ethnic minorities and women are infrequent drivers in certain motor sports.

The sources of sport self-confidence have been reliably measured with the Sources of Sport Confidence Questionnaire (SSCQ; Vealey, Hayashi, Garner-Holman, & Giacobbi, 1998). The SSCQ identifies nine specific sources of sport self-confidence: *mastery, demonstration of ability, physical/ mental preparation, physical self-presentation, social support, vicarious experience, coach's leadership, environmental comfort, situational favorableness.*

The nine categories form three larger domains of sport self-confidence. The first domain involves sport self-confidence from actual *achievement. Mastery* and *demonstration of ability* are sources of confidence in this domain. Sport self-confidence is increased when skills are mastered or improved. Sportspersons also obtain confidence from the demonstration of ability and when they show off or demonstrate more skill than opponents. Mastery and demonstration of ability are the two most important sources of self-confidence for high school, college, and world-class athletes (Kingston, Lane, & Thomas, 2010). As was demonstrated with self-efficacy, nothing builds confidence like success. Sport self-confidence is unlikely in the absence of quality training, practice, and skill development. Coaches rate physical conditioning and practice as the most important sources of self-confidence, and athletes also recognize the importance of physical preparation.

The second domain is *self-regulation*. *Physical/mental preparation*, and *physical self-presentation* are sources of confidence in this domain. With proper physical and mental preparation for performances, confidence increases. The physical self-presentation of athletes, or how the athlete believes that he or she looks to others, is a source of confidence for some. Physical self-presentation is a more important source of confidence in individual sports and for female athletes, perhaps due to the societal focus on the appearance of women.

The third domain is the *social climate*. The sources of confidence in this domain are *social support, vicarious experience, coach's leadership, environmental comfort*, and *situational favorableness*. Coaches, family, and teammates are potential sources of social support. Teammates are important sources of social support. Support from teammates boosted the confidence of collegiate athletes and insulated them from the detrimental effects of performance-related stress (Freeman & Rees, 2010). Vicarious experience can enhance confidence when others such as teammates perform successfully, as can confidence in the leadership of coaches. Environmental comfort often is the result of familiarity with venues, such as with home fields. Situational favorableness occurs when athletes believe that the "breaks" or luck is in their favor.

Even at the highest levels, confidence is a multidimensional construct. World class athletes (Olympic Games, World Championship, and/or World Cup) identified nine sources of confidence that were consistent with the sources in the SSCQ: Preparation, both physical and mental; performance accomplishments; coaching; innate physical and mental talent; social support; experience in sport; belief in their competitive advantage; trust; and self-awareness. Female athletes focused to a greater degree on perceived competitive advantages, such as viewing opponents perform badly under pressure. Vicarious experience was not identified as a source of confidence, perhaps because the performance of others is of less importance to athletes at the highest levels (Hays, Maynard, Thomas, & Bawden, 2007). Elite senior athletes derived sport confidence from thorough physical and mental preparation and by demonstrating athletic ability (Wilson, Sullivan, Myers, & Feltz, 2004).

As was the case with high self-efficacy, with high sport self-confidence, athletes are less vulnerable to cognitive interference during competition and are more likely to interpret physiological anxiety to be facilitative (Cresswell & Hodge, 2004). For example, a world-class athlete described confidence as his "shield" that protected him from worries, such as the strength of opponents and the audience (Hayes et al., 2007, p. 1189). Confident world-class athletes experience flow states and automaticity. They are relaxed, calm, and happy. They present themselves as confident to both boost their internal confidence and to shake the confidence of opponents.

Confident athletes establish more difficult goals and show greater persistence in pursuit of these goals. Confident athletes more frequently establish mastery goals. With mastery goals, athletes compare progress to their baseline of prior performance, and have greater control over factors contributing to success. Sport self-confidence is more likely to be stable over time and across venues when it is derived from controllable factors, such as the demonstration of ability and mental and physical preparation (Kingston, Lane, & Thomas, 2010).

A measure of stable self-confidence was developed recently: the Trait Robustness Self-Confidence Inventory (TROSCI; Beattie et al., 2011). Robust trait self-confidence is stable over time. With robust trait self-confidence, sportspersons expect success even in the face of mistakes, defeats, and negative feedback.

MENTAL TOUGHNESS

Athletes who remain cool under pressure are also identified as **mentally tough**. Mentally tough athletes experience intense emotions in pressurized and adverse situations, but are more effective in concentrating on the task at hand and limiting cognitive interference (Crust, 2009). By remaining focused on game plans for competition, they avoid emotional overreactions (Bull, Shambrook, James, & Brooks, 2005) and the attendant attentional narrowing (Janelle, Singer, & Williams, 1999) and impulsive behavior (Leith & Baumeister, 1996) that results in impaired performance. They make use of visualization, self-talk, and relaxation strategies to manage their emotions (Crust & Azadi, 2009; Holland, Woodcock, Cumming, & Duda, 2010; Nicholls, Polman, Levy, & Backhouse, 2008).

Mentally tough performers approach competition with high self-efficacy and confidence and believe they are in control of the factors that will determine success. They cope well with pressure and adversity in competition, practice, and their personal lives, and recover quickly from setbacks (Galli & Vealey, 2008; Jones, Hanton, & Connaugton, 2002; Nicholls, Polman, Levy, & Backhouse, 2008; Thelwell, Weston, & Greenlees, 2005). They are more likely to use problem-focused and less likely to use emotion-focused coping strategies, such as denial, humor, and behavioral disengagement (Kaiseler, Polman, & Nicholls, 2009). An example of problem-focused coping is to increase effort levels in response to adversity, obstacles, pressure, and when they are having an "off" day (Gucciardi, Gordon, & Dimmock, 2008). They use motivational imagery to augment their belief that they can maintain control in difficult situations (Mattie & Munroe-Chandler, 2012).

Mental toughness represents more than an aptitude for optimal performance at sport. It likely indicates life skills that predict optimal development in youth (Gucciardi & Jones, 2012). For example, mentally tough young cricketeers endorsed greater commitment to learning, positive values, positive identity, and social competencies—internal assets. These children and adolescents also experienced more support, empowerment, boundaries, and expectations—external assets (Benson, 2002). The young cricketeers experienced less negative emotion such as depression.

SUMMARY AND APPLICATION

Self-efficacy consists of beliefs that one can exert sufficient control over the environment and oneself to realize goals. Self-efficacy refers to convictions that one will obtain future goals, and it motivates behaviors that make actual goal attainment more likely. With higher self-efficacy, effort is sustained despite difficulties and obstacles. Effort is also deployed in purposeful ways, as people with higher self-efficacy are flexible in their selection, organization, and integration of skills. Difficult and even unyielding problems do not daunt people with high self-efficacy, as they persist in the application of sophisticated strategies to solve difficult problems. With beliefs that one can reach goals, failures provide information that one must both try harder and think better to discover an answer or solution that is already in one's repertoire, or to learn new skills to solve problems. Efforts to master difficult tasks have the effect of "keeping you humble," because such tasks require sustained effort. A realistic appreciation of the difficulty in reaching certain goals is not inconsistent with high self-efficacy, and it motivates the preparation necessary to acquire skills.

The cliché "nothing builds confidence like success" has been shown to be accurate. That is, the most convincing source of self-efficacy is actual success in similar domains of functioning. The development of resilient self-efficacy does not occur with singular success experiences, but is the result of mastering increasingly difficult tasks and of sustaining effort to accomplish complex tasks and reach long-term goals. Mentors such as parents, coaches, teachers, therapists, and senior colleagues can facilitate the development of efficacy by providing encouragement and support, and modeling behaviors that will likely lead to success. Sensitive mentors patiently build self-efficacy in others by issuing challenges that are neither too difficult, so as to result in consistent failure and weakened self-efficacy, nor too easy, so that trainees do not learn how to sustain effort. Efficacy also grows and develops when success is attributed to skill and talent and failure to inadequate preparation and execution of skills. Little is accomplished by noticing unfavorable comparisons between oneself and others with greater endowment, and efficacy is fostered when progress is noted in relation to a baseline of one's own behavior. Progress or enactive attainments enhance efficacy, which then leads to additional progress and a cycle of continuing achievement and confidence that additional achievement is within one's grasp.

Sport self-confidence is similar to self-efficacy for achieving goals in sport. The study of sport self-confidence has emphasized the sources of sport self-confidence that are unique to athletic settings. For example, sport self-confidence is influenced by the leadership of coaches, by comfort and familiarity with athletic venues, and by belief that the breaks will fall in one's favor. Sport self-confidence is not a substitute for the training and practice that is necessary to become highly skilled at sport. Indeed, the development and demonstration of ability are the most influential source of sport self-confidence. With sport self-confidence, athletes can more successfully deploy existing skills and abilities to reach goals.

Mentally tough athletes have high self-efficacy. They are in control of their thoughts and emotions. They keep their "head in the game" and ignore distractions. They cope well with pressure and bounce back quickly from setbacks.

Key Terms

Self-efficacy   221

Self-esteem   227

Self-handicapping   230

Optimistic self-efficacy beliefs   222

Self-efficacy and persistence   223

Self-efficacy and the use of skills   225

Self-efficacy and anxiety   225

Generalizability of efficacy beliefs   226

Self-efficacy versus self-esteem   227

Sources of self-efficacy: enactive attainments, observational learning,

feedback, physical and emotional states, childhood experiences   229

Coping models   231

Mastery models   231

Competence   232

Self-modeling   232

Feedback: authentic, experts, believable   232

Sport self-confidence: mastery, demonstration of ability, physical/mental preparation, physical self-presentation, social support, vicarious experience, coach's leadership, environmental comfort, situational favorableness   236

Mentally tough   238

Discussion Questions

Q1. Define self-efficacy and sport self-confidence.

Q2. Explain the relationship between self-efficacy and success.

Q3. How are efficacy beliefs and actual performance temporally recursive?

Q4. What are the advantages and hazards of optimistic efficacy beliefs?

Q5. How is it that efficacious sportspersons do not "have an ounce of quit in them."

Q6. Consider how efficacious people respond to difficulties and setbacks in the pursuit of goals.

Q7. How is self-efficacy positioned in relation to physical and cognitive skills and abilities?

Q8. Explain how efficacy caps anxiety.

Q9. Review the processes by which efficacy beliefs become generalized.

Q10. Differentiate self-efficacy and self-esteem.

Q11. Consider the sources of self-efficacy: enactive attainments, observational learning, feedback, physical and emotional states, and childhood experiences.

Q12. Consider how efficacious people interpret the causes of failure.

Q13. Describe the similarities of self-efficacy and sport self-confidence.

Q14. Identify the nine sources of sport self-confidence.

Q15. Review the components of mental toughness.

Q16. How is mental toughness related to self-efficacy?

Suggested Readings

Bandura, A. (1997). *Self-efficacy. The exercise of control.* New York, NY: Freeman.

Coffee, P., Rees, T., & Haslam, A. (2009). Bouncing back from failure: The interactive impact of perceived controllability and stability on self-efficacy beliefs and future task performance. *Journal of Sports Sciences, 27,* 1117–1124. doi: 10.1080/02640410903030297

Feltz, D. L., Short, S. E., & Sullivan, P. J. (2008). *Self-efficacy in sport. Research and strategies for working with athletes, teams, and coaches.* Champaign, IL: Human Kinetics.

Fry, M. D., Guivernau, M., Kim, M-s, Newton, M., Gano-Overway, L. A., & Magyar, T. M. (2012). Youth perceptions of a caring climate, emotional regulation, and psychological well-being. *Sport, Exercise, and Performance Psychology, 1,* 44–57. doi: 10.1037/a0025454

Galli, N., & Vealey, R. S. (2008). "Bouncing back" from adversity: Athletes' experiences of resilience. *The Sport Psychologist, 22,* 316–335.

Gano-Overway, L. A., Newton, M., Magyar, T. M., Fry, M. D., Kim, M., & Guivernau, M. R. (2009). Influence of caring youth sport contexts on efficacy-related beliefs and social behaviors. *Developmental Psychology, 45,* 329–340. doi: 10.1037/a0014067

Gucciardi, D. F., & Jones, M. I. (2012). Beyond optimal performance: Mental toughness profiles and developmental success in adolescent cricketers. *Journal of Sport & Exercise Psychology, 34,* 16–36.

Jackson, B., Gucciardi, D. F., & Dimmock, J. A. (2011). Tripartite efficacy profiles: A cluster analytic investigation of athletes' perceptions of their relationship with their coach. *Journal of Sport & Exercise Psychology, 33*, 394–415.

Kingston, K., Lane, A., & Thomas, O. (2010). A temporal examination of elite performers sources of sport confidence. *The Sport Psychologist, 18*, 313–332.

Martha, C., Sanchez, X., & Goma-i-Freixanet, M. (2009). Risk perception as a function of risk exposure amongst rock climbers. *Psychology of Sport and Exercise, 10*, 193–200. doi: 10.1016/j.psychsport.2009.07.004

Nicholls, A. R., Levy, A. R., Polman, R. C. J., & Crust, L. (2011). Mental toughness, coping self-efficacy, and coping effectiveness among athletes. *International Journal of Sport Psychology, 42*, 513–524.

Nicholls, A. R., Polman, R., & Levy, A. R. (2010). Coping self-efficacy, pre-competitive anxiety, and subjective performance among athletes. *European Journal of Sport Science, 10*, 97–102. doi: 10.1080/17461390903271592

Sanchez, X., Boschker, M.S.J., & Llewellyn, D. J. (2010). Pre-performance psychological states and performance in an elite climbing competition. *Scandinavian Journal of Medicine & Science in Sports, 20*, 356–363. doi: 10.1111/j.1600-0838.2009.00403.x

Vealey, R. S. (2009). Confidence in sport. (2009). Management of competitive stress in elite sport. In B. W. Brewer (Ed.), *Handbook of sports medicine and science, sport psychology* (pp. 43–52). Chichester, England: Wiley-Blackwell.

Woodman, T., Akehurst, S., Hardy, L., & Beattie, S. (2010). Self-confidence and performance: A little self-doubt helps. *Psychology of Sport and Exercise, 11*, 467–470. doi: 10.1016/j.psychsport.2010.05.009

Part III

PERFORMANCE INHIBITION

Chapter 11

CHOKING UNDER PRESSURE AND PERFORMANCE ANXIETY

Performance and pressure

As soon as Dominick saw the seedings for the state championship soccer tournament, he realized that a high school championship game between Xavier and Trinity was very likely. The traditional powers had the best records in the regular season, and were placed in opposite brackets. The rivalry between the schools was beyond bitter. As teammates realized the implications of the seedings, a spontaneous cheer swept across their group. The cheer betrayed exhilaration and anxiety. Xavier had lost 3–1 to Trinity during the regular season.

True to expectations, Xavier and Trinity met in the championship match. Almost as soon as the game began, all of the physical and psychological preparation of Dominick, and perhaps most of Xavier's team, seemed moot. They seemed to be more spectators than players, as they watched Trinity's front line and central midfielder move effortlessly toward their goal. In the first twelve minutes, Trinity's all-state forward, Kevin Strauss, initiated four breakaway scoring opportunities, or chances to score when the number of offensive players exceeded the number of defenders. He scored, assisted halfback Kenny Chung's score, sent a shot off the goal post, and had a shot blocked by Xavier's goalie, Henry Strohbler. Dominick didn't have a Plan B for winning as the presence of Xavier's all-state sweeper, Paul Geiss, usually made concerns about the offense of opposing teams a non-issue.

As the final twelve minutes of the game began, Dominick looked to the stands. He imagined the disappointment in the faces of classmates, the "soccer groupies," and his parents. He knew they would be thinking, "X chokes again." He didn't know how he could face them. Xavier's sophomore phenomenon, Wayne Bleighley, had other things on his mind. He simply picked up a free ball and scored. It was almost as if he said, "I'm not waiting for you guys." The game mind had changed. The attention of Trinity's players was turned to attempts to counter Xavier's initiatives. Within minutes, Dominick found himself in front of Trinity's goal with a ball presenting itself for a volley. In an instant, it was in the back of the goal, the equalizer.

Readers who have practiced the techniques in Chapters 4, 5, 6, and 7 prior to and during evaluations and performances and have found themselves to be entirely focused and free of debilitative anxiety may be uninterested in this chapter. For the rest of us, Chapter 11 is the first of eight chapters devoted to the exploration of the psychological factors that impede performance. In some ways, Chapter 11 is a companion chapter to Chapters 4, 5, 6, and 7, because the proximal factors that impede performance are often countered by the techniques described in Chapters 4, 5, 6, and 7. As will be explained in ensuing chapters, people differ in their psychological and physiological reactions to the stress of evaluations and performances. However, most people find evaluations and performances to be stressful. Readers interested in additional information about how anxiety impairs performance are referred to the discussion in the Appendix on test anxiety. Like choking, test anxiety is paradoxical because it impairs performance when people are highly motivated to perform optimally. The literature about test anxiety is largely consistent with that of choking, and, in addition, there is information about how to ameliorate test anxiety that may have applications in sport settings.

As explained in Chapter 4, stress can be conceptualized as a relationship between the person and the environment in which the person evaluates the stressor or the source of stress as exceeding his or her coping resources and endangering his or her well-being (Lazarus & Folkman, 1984). The process of comparing the source of threat to one's capacity to handle and master that source is accompanied by emotional responses. If one's coping resources are appraised to be inadequate to handle the stressor, the experience of anxiety, worry, and fear is likely. If the stress overwhelms coping resources, choking may occur (Hill, Hanton, Fleming, Matthews, 2009). Conversely, if coping resources are seen to be adequate, the stressor may be seen as a stimulus for excitement, eagerness, and hopefulness. These positive emotions are also more likely if the stressor is interpreted as an opportunity for advancement (Burton & Naylor, 1997).

ANXIETY DIRECTION: FACILITATIVE AND DEBILITATIVE

As described in Chapter 4, anxiety does not always result in performance deficits and may be interpreted as facilitative or debilitative. In everyday life, anxiety is adaptive or useful to the degree that it serves as an internal signal of future danger. Anxiety that is **facilitative** motivates forward planning and preparation for activities such as performances and evaluations. In this context, anxiety facilitates problem-focused coping strategies that confront the source of the stress (Zeidner, 1994). Students and athletes who experience facilitative anxiety are not free from physiological anxiety, but their anxiety serves as a signal to prepare for the stress of an evaluation or performance, and they interpret the physiological anxiety as an indication that they are ready to do their best. Students with low debilitating test anxiety are more likely to reduce their levels of physiological anxiety or "shake their butterflies" when it matters most, during exams (Raffety, Smith, & Ptacek, 1997). Athletes with facilitative anxiety have confidence that they can control themselves and the environment, and that they will realize their goals (Jones & Hanton, 1996, 2001). Anxiety is **debilitative** if it disrupts preparation and planning to resolve or master the sources of stress and threat.

Anxiety that is debilitative often orients people to the protection of their well-being at the expense of goal-directed behavior. This may involve the protection of their personal safety or of their reputation or image in the eyes of others (Carver & Scheier, 1992; Tallis & Eysenck, 1994). Preoccupation with one's personal well-being interferes with attention to the tasks necessary for optimal performance.

TRAIT AND STATE ANXIETY

The focus of this chapter will be the debilitative effects of anxiety on performance. To review, anxiety has **cognitive** and **physiological** manifestations. The physiological component consists of reactions of the sympathetic nervous system, such as muscle tension, elevated heart rate, sweating, and feelings of being keyed-up or on edge. The cognitive aspect of anxiety has been referred to as cognitive interference, and will be discussed at length in this chapter. Anxiety that is activated in response to specific situations, such as competitions and evaluations, is **state anxiety**, whereas anxiety levels that remain relatively stable across situations and over time is considered **trait anxiety** (Spielberger, Gorsuch, & Lushene, 1970).

Specific questionnaires have been developed to measure competitive trait anxiety and competitive state anxiety in sport settings. These include the Sport Competition Anxiety Test (SCAT; Martens, 1977), Competitive State Anxiety Inventory-2 (CSAI-2; Martens, Burton, Vealey, Bump, & Smith, 1990), and the Sport Anxiety Scale-2 (SAS-2; Smith, Smoll, Cumming, & Grossbard, 2006). The SAS-2 has been validated with adults and children (Grossbard, Smith, Smoll, & Cumming, 2009), and measures cognitive and somatic anxiety, concentration disruption, and overall anxiety related to sport performance.

COGNITIVE INTERFERENCE AND DISTRACTION THEORIES

High levels of anxiety and pressure reduce the processing and storage capacity of working memory, decrease the efficiency of mental processing, and lead to performance deficits on a wide range of cognitive (MacLeod, 1996; Markman, Maddox, & Worthy, 2006; Wine, 1971) and motor (Gray, 2004; Memmert & Furley, 2007) tasks. These deficits are more marked for tasks that require complex motor control, higher-level mental processes, and decision making (MacLeod, 1996; Taylor, 1996). Tasks that require only sustained vigilance, such as to respond whenever a particular sign or signal is detected, are not as adversely affected by anxiety (Humphreys & Revelle, 1984). In general, higher levels of cognitive and physiological anxiety lead to greater distractibility (Yee & Vaughan, 1996).

As discussed in Chapter 6, the human capacity for concentration is limited by the amount of information that can be sustained and processed in working or active memory at any given time. The average limit of working memory is seven units of information, and the working memory of most people falls between a range of five and nine (Kareev, 2000; Miller, 1956). Information in working memory is temporary in that it is kept in mind only so long as other information does not crowd it out and capture the seven units of space. Working memory is taxed when people attempt to solve difficult problems, and people with higher working memory capacities have an advantage on such tasks (Kane & Engle, 2000). This advantage evaporates under pressure, perhaps because their superior attention capacities are captured by anxiety about their performance (Beilock & Carr, 2005; Gimmig, Huguet, Caverni, & Cury, 2006).

This information in working memory may be in a verbal or visual and spatial form. Working memory has separate components for holding and sustaining this information: the articulatory loop for verbal information and the visuospatial sketchpad for visual and spatial information. A third component, the central executive, has three functions. The central executive is responsible for inhibiting distractions and directing attention, shifting attention back and forth between multiple tasks, and updating and monitoring the contents of working memory. An episodic buffer integrates information from these systems and from long-term memory (Baddeley, 2001: Friedman & Miyake, 2004; Miyake et al., 2000). Working memory is situated in the prefrontal cortex and has an executive function in that it allows for the prioritization of cognitions and behaviors and the inhibition of distracting information and cognitive interference (Engle, 2002; Kane, Conway, Hambrick, & Engle, 2007).

Application

The demands on working memory, and specifically on the central executive, are considerable during athletic competition. Input from the outside world and from long-term memory must be processed rapidly and under the load of pressure and anxiety. Functioning optimally, the central executive allocates all working memory resources to the keys in the present moment. For example, a defender in football integrates play on the pitch with scouting reports and knowledge of the tendencies of opposing players in diagnosing and responding to play. When concentrating most optimally, play may seem to "slow down" and sportspersons are capable of anticipating play.

Cognitive anxiety affects both the central executive and the articulatory loop when the central executive cannot exclude worries (nonvocalized verbal information) from the limited space in the articulatory loop. More generally, anxiety decreases the degree to which attention is goal directed and controlled centrally and increases the likelihood that it is captured and directed by stimuli that are peripheral to goals, such as worries and environmental distractions (Eysenck, Derakshan, Santos, & Calvo, 2007).

Cognitive interference refers to intrusive thoughts that compete for the attentional resources that would ideally be devoted to other tasks, such as decision making, anticipating the responses of opponents, and integrating automated skills during evaluations and performances (Macquet, 2009; Pierce, Henderson, Yost, & Lofreddo, 1996). These cognitive activities are not only complex but also dynamic, as the process of imposing a game plan and anticipating and thwarting the initiatives of opponents unfolds in real time (Seve, Saury, Leblanc, & Durand, 2005).

Although the execution of over-learned, automated, or proceduralized skills (Beilock, et al., 2002; Fitts & Posner, 1967; Proctor & Dutta, 1995) requires little attentional storage space, cognitive interference is still disruptive to their execution. This is because forms of cognitive interference can occupy the space in working memory that is not required to execute the automatic skills (Mullen, Hardy, & Tattersall, 2005). Working memory space that is available during the execution of automated skills is usually needed for metacognitive processes, such as sequencing and organizing automated skills, monitoring the effectiveness of game strategies, and anticipating the next moves of opponents (Bandura, 1997). Cognitive interference may also affect the flexibility of performers in adjusting the breadth and direction of attentional focus and in adjusting from soft to hard attentional focuses (Nideffer, 1993; Wilson, Smith, Chattington, Ford, & Marple-Horvat, 2006).

Forms of Cognitive Interference

Cognitive interference can be seen as a loss of control over one's thoughts, as **emotionally-valenced thoughts** take precedence over attention to tasks and skills necessary for optimal performance (Sarason, Pierce, & Sarason, 1996). Thoughts are emotionally valenced when associated with the experience of emotion. Two forms of emotionally valenced thoughts include worry about the consequences of **unsuccessful performance** and the **reactions of spectators**. A third form of cognitive interference is **preemptory thoughts**, or thoughts related to general themes that color the manner in which people view themselves and their potential for achievement and happiness. An example of a preemptory thought is "I don't perform well under pressure," and this theme might influence performance across venues. A fourth form of cognitive interference is **self-doubt** (Schwarzer, 1996).

The forms of cognitive interference are influenced by the age and sport of participants. For example, the cognitive anxiety of collegiate Canadian hockey players was shown to form four categories (Dunn, 1999). The hockey players were fearful of: (1) injury and physical danger; (2) performance failure; (3) negative evaluation by others such as teammates, coaches, and spectators; and (4) the unknown, such as the strengths and weaknesses of opponents. Not surprisingly, younger athletes are more concerned about the reactions of parents. For example, male wrestlers and soccer players between the ages of 9 and 14 worried about: failure, evaluations by parents and coaches, and pleasing oneself and others (Scanlan, T. K., & Lewthwaite, 1984; Scanlan, Lewthwaite, & Jackson, 1984). The worries of other young wrestlers prior to a tournament consisted of: concern about pleasing oneself and others, negative evaluations from the father of the wrestler, and failure and negative evaluations from other adults (Gould, Eklund, Petlichkoff, Peterson, & Bump, 1991).

As mentioned in Chapter 6, cognitive interference may motivate audible negative comments directed toward oneself (e.g., "loser") and opponents (e.g., "cheat"), as well as unsporting behaviors (e.g., hitting one's legs with a tennis racquet). These unsporting behaviors not only undermine performance but also increases the confidence of competitors, as they recognize when opponents are "losing it" (Hanegby & Tennenbaum, 2001).

Fear of Failure and Cognitive Interference

The **fear of failure** in sport has five dimensions: "(a) fears of experiencing shame and embarrassment, (b) fears of devaluing one's self-estimate, (c) fears of having an uncertain future, (d) fears of important others losing interest, and (e) fears of upsetting important others" (Conroy, 2004, p. 484). Four of the five dimensions of fear of failure have been associated with hostile forms of self-talk and cognitive interference among students and athletes (Conroy, 2003; Conroy & Coatsworth, 2007). Examples of hostile self-talk include self-blame and self-attack. Fears of upsetting important others were not associated with hostile self-talk, but still were related to diminished self-esteem.

Application

Note that the five forms of fear of failure as well as the four types of emotionally valenced thoughts all involve judgments about performance. These forms of cognitive interference divert scarce working memory resources from input from the environment and long-term memory that is directed to the present moment. The time for self-evaluations and self-reactions is after play is completed.

Those who fear failure view athletic competition as a threat and perhaps dread "the agony of defeat" (Smith, 2010, p. 45). Those who fear failure focus their attention inward and become vigilant to signs of mistakes, errors, and flaws in their performance (Schmader, Johns, & Forbes, 2008). Attention that is captured by fears of failure is taken from concentration on the instrumental behaviors necessary for skilled performance, and choking under pressure is more likely. Such fearful athletes are also more vulnerable to injury (Smith, Smoll, & Passer, 2002).

Trait Anxiety and Cognitive Interference

Environmental stressors such as evaluations, competitions, and performances cause a measure of situational or state anxiety in most people. State anxiety is more likely to escalate and lead to cognitive interference among people who are generally anxious, or who have high levels of trait anxiety (Smith, Bellamy, Collins, & Newell, 2001). People with trait anxiety and with anxiety disorders have a particular sensitivity to processing information that relates to the primary domain of their worry (Wilson et al., 2006; Weierich, Treat, & Hollingworth, 2008). For example, students with test anxiety have high levels of intrusive and threatening thoughts concerning poor performance when working on demanding intellectual tasks. College students who experienced cognitive interference during one examination were likely to report cognitive interference on other examinations (Pierce, Henderson, Yost, & Lofredo, 1996). College football players who reported cognitive interference during examinations were also likely to report cognitive interference during football games. Thoughts concerning imminent danger and threat are also characteristic of people with anxiety disorders, such as Generalized Anxiety Disorder (physiological and cognitive components of anxiety almost always present), agoraphobia (fear of being trapped in a place where escape would be difficult), simple phobias (excessive fear of discrete things), and panic disorders.

It is difficult for people with anxiety disorders and trait anxiety to ignore signs of threat in their environment and to devote their attention to thoughts related to problem solving on intellective tasks (Weierich et al., 2008). They encode or bring information related to threat into their working memory. People with high levels of trait anxiety and people with anxiety disorders are also likely to selectively impose threatening interpretations on ambiguous information from the environment. This interpretation results in cognitive interference, because the outcomes of performances are often ambiguous. For example, opponents in competition may be relatively evenly matched, and success or failure may only result from prolonged effort and concentration on the tasks necessary for successful performance. Athletes with high trait anxiety might prematurely conclude that they are beaten by an opponent, and use unproductive coping strategies, such as self-blame, if they do not experience easy success (Giacobbi & Weinberg, 2000).

The interpretive bias of anxious people to selectively encode information related to threat occurs **automatically** or at a level outside of their conscious awareness. This automatically encoded information becomes, in effect, the raw material for their thoughts. They may engage in self-talk that consists of blaming themselves for poor performances, and, ironically, this blaming may be what they fear most (Conroy & Metzler, 2004). State anxiety caused by evaluations is often not disruptive to the performance of people with low levels of trait anxiety, as they demonstrate a bias toward automatic attentional avoidance of the sources of stress and threat in the environment. Clearly, the latter attentional bias is adaptive, as environmental stress is largely inevitable.

People high in trait anxiety have an overly pessimistic assessment of future outcomes. They expect the worst, expect to be less successful than others (Eysenck & Derakshan, 1997), and perform more poorly under pressure. For example, basketball players who were high in trait anxiety were less accurate in shooting free throws than were less-anxious counterparts (Wang, Marchant, Morris, & Gibbs, 2004). Those high in trait anxiety were also shown to be shown to be slower in scanning and responding to signals in their visual field in competition (Murray & Janelle, 2003).

Why Cognitive Interference Exists

Why does cognitive interference exist? Perhaps it represents deviations of normal, adaptive patterns of thought (Moran, 2009). The average amount of time that college students kept any single thought in mind was shown to be five seconds. In a 16-hour day, these undergraduates shifted the content of their thought 4,000 times (Klinger, 1996). Attention shifts whenever a person encounters an environmental cue or has a thought that arouses emotion because of its relation to one's current concerns or what is considered important. The more closely an environmental cue or thought relates to one's current concerns, the more likely that thought will shift to that current concern. For example, if a golfer is concerned about the strength of an opponent, seeing that opponent's name at the top of the leader board is likely to augment cognitive interference about the strength of the opponent. Cognitive interference occurs when a cue initiates emotional responses and patterns of thought that compete and interfere with the behaviors necessary for successful performances.

This cognitive interference may be unwanted and puzzling, because it occurs automatically when cues are encountered. That is, cues may initiate a shift in thought content even though a person does not intend to think about the subject of that cue. Indeed, if people receive spoken cues related to their concerns while they are sleeping, the content of their dreams will correspond to the spoken cues. It is, therefore, more difficult to keep one's mind on the tasks necessary for successful performances in environments rich with cues related to important concerns or while experiencing strong emotion that prompt internal thoughts.

Cognitive interference in the form of fear of failure occurs when athletes have been punished excessively for mistakes. For example, some coaches infrequently reinforce success, growth, and effort, and are relentless in chastising sportspersons when they make errors. Under these circumstances, athletes become afraid of taking risks of any sort in competition, and, ironically, are more likely to make the same errors for which they were chastised (Conroy, 2008; Petri & Govern, 2004).

The Physiology of Distraction

Stress and pressure, especially coupled with the belief that one will not perform well in important competitions, affects the cortex (Baumeister, Twenge, & Nuss, 2002). These effects include elevated responsiveness of the sympathetic nervous system (specifically the sympathetic-adrenal-medullary system and the hypothalamic-pituitary-adrenal axis) and increased release of corticosteroids and catecholamines hormones (Schommer, Hellhammer, & Kirschbaum, 2003). Working memory is mediated by the prefrontal cortex, an area with a high concentration of neurons that are sensitive to corticosteroids. With excessive activation of the prefrontal cortex, working memory is impaired, and concentration and focus may, therefore, be impaired under pressure due to these physiological processes. This overactivation is particularly detrimental to performance on tasks that are complex or require sustained attention.

EXPLICIT MONITORING AND CONSCIOUS PROCESSING HYPOTHESES

An alternative explanation for the disruptive effects of pressure and anxiety on performance is the **explicit monitoring** (Beilock & Gray, 2007) or **conscious processing hypothesis** (CPH; Masters, 1992). According to the CPH, pressure increases anxiety and self-focus (Liao & Masters, 2002). With this self-focus, expert sportspersons monitor or form conscious mental images of the step-by-step components and processes that make up automated or proceduralized skills. Automated skills become "dechunked" (Masters, 1992), or executed as individual units of motor behavior, as opposed to omnibus and proceduralized composites of the individual units (Beilock, Bertenthal, McCoy, & Carr, 2004; Beilock & Carr, 2001; Beilock, Carr, MacMahon, & Starkes, 2002; Beilock & Gray, 2007; Hardy, Mullen, & Martin, 2001; Jackson, Ashford, & Norsworthy, 2006; Masters, 1992; Mullen & Hardy, 2000; Singer, 2002; Smith, 1996). This process of bringing the individual components of automated skills into conscious awareness slows their execution and creates opportunities for errors to occur in the sequencing, timing, and transitions between individual units. This monitoring process is characteristic of the cognitive activity of beginners rather than experts, and often involves explicit knowledge that is conscious and capable of being verbalized (Beilock & Carr, 2001). Recall that proceduralized skills are so well practiced that they "run" with minimal demands on working memory, as they involve implicit knowledge that is abstract, unconscious, and difficult to articulate (Berry & Dienes, 1993).

Audience distraction—the vuvuzela

In the parlance of sport, some performers become "tight," stiffen-up, or freeze under pressure. Biomechanical analyses suggest that pressure does indeed compromise the fluid and skilled movement of sportspersons, due to the "freezing" or reduced mobility of joints (Bernstein, 1967; Collins, Jones, Fairweather, Doolan, & Priestley, 2001; Higuchi, Imanaka, & Hatayama, 2002; Pijpers, Oudejans, & Bakker, 2005; Vereijken, van Emmerik, Whiting, & Newell, 1992). Stiff, awkward, clumsy, and dechunked motor behavior is associated with inferior performance.

For example, the batting of Division I intercollegiate baseball players became clumsier when they were asked to determine whether their swings were directed upward or downward at the precise times that tones were sounded (Gray, 2004). This direction caused the batters to explicitly monitor the motor components of their swings, and pressure exacerbated the degradation of batting performance. Their batting coordination did not suffer when they merely indicated whether a tone had a high or low pitch, as this requirement directed their attention outward and not to components in the automated skill of batting a baseball. The batting skill of novices was not disrupted by attention to the components motor skills of swinging a bat because the skill was not automated and they were, therefore, already monitoring these component skills (Gray, 2004).

Explicit monitoring is also a likely contributor to the "yips." The yips consist of involuntary movements that disrupt the execution of automated motor skills. With the yips, sportspersons feel as if they have little control over their actions. The yips disrupt putting strokes in golf with twitching, freezing, or flinching movements (McDaniel, Cummings, & Shane, 1989; Smith et al., 2003; Stinear et al., 2006). Cricket bowlers experienced the yips as tension in the hand and a sensation of not being able to release the ball (Bawden & Maynard, 2001).

Explicit instructions to focus attention on external cues may enhance performance under pressure once skills are automated. An external focus is more likely to sustain automaticity and conserve working memory resources. Skilled baseball players batted more effectively when they concentrated on the direction of the ball after it left the bat (Castaneda & Gray, 2007). Skilled golfers chipped more accurately when they focused on the direction in which they intended to set the ball and engaged in self-talk by repeating "straight flight" immediately prior to shot execution (Bell & Hardy, 2009; Perkins-Ceccato et al., 2003). When focusing on the intended effects of movement, performers may be advised to focus on an effect that is "intermediately distant" (ball landing near the flag in golf or the direction of the ball leaving the bat or club) from the actual movement (Wulf, 2007; Wulf & Prinz, 2001; Wulf & Su, 2007). A focus that is too close (e.g., club striking the ball) to the movement (motor components of the golf swing) may promote a focus on the actual movement, whereas a focus on a result that is too distant (e.g., saving par) results in confusion about what motor action leads to the desired effect. This focus on the effects of motor actions is consistent with the **common-coding theory:** that sensory (intended outcome) and motor (bat or club swing) information for distal, environmental events are coded in the same cortical areas. Attention directed to the relatively distal results of a motor action is, therefore, likely to elicit the sequence of motor skills necessary to produce those results.

Michael Jordan: In Golf Keep It Simple

My instructor, Ed Ibarguen, has me focus on a specific target before every swing. One of my biggest problems is, sometimes when I see water to the right, I try extra hard to stay away from it. And what happens? You end up going right in the water. That's because you're focusing on the wrong thing.

Eddie tells me to pick a blade of grass on my line or a building in the distance and to blindfold myself to everything else. That's keeping it simple, and that works especially well in pressure situations (Jordan & Bestrom, 2009, p. 86).

In addition to focusing on the intended effects of movements, skilled sportspersons may be advised to engage in self-talk or the repetition of key words to facilitate the "running" of automated skills under pressure. For example, experienced golfers putted more accurately with and without performance anxiety when they focused on a global cue word or "swing thought" (e.g., "easy" or "smooth"; Jackson & Wilson, 1999) while putting. This global cue may have brought to their working memory the correct global motor program or schema for their automated putting stroke. This global representation likely involved implicit and automatic thought and placed minimal demands on working memory. Consistent with previous research, putting accuracy was least accurate with performance anxiety when the golfers brought to mind the step-by-step components of their putting strokes (Gucciardi & Dimmock, 2008).

The most productive focus of attention for unskilled sportspersons has not been conclusively determined. There is evidence that skills are acquired most efficiently with an internal focus on the component skills (Castaneda & Gray, 2007; Perkins-Ceccato, Passmore, & Lee, 2003) or a focus on the wielded implement in sports, such as table tennis (Caliari, 2008). However, other studies indicate that motor learning is enhanced (Abernethy et al., 2007; Wulf & Prinz, 2001) or equivalent (Lam, Maxwell, & Masters, 2009) when sportspersons are taught to focus on the effects of their movements, or when skills are learned by analogy. An analogy used in teaching a top-spin forehand in table tennis was "strike the ball while bringing the bat up the hypotenuse of the triangle" (Liao & Masters, 2001, p. 310). Perhaps an additional benefit to learning motor skills without explicit, conscious representations of their components is that under pressure, reinvestment is less likely (Abernethy et al., 2007; Lam et al., 2009; Poolton, Masters, & Maxwell, 2007). That is, if skills have been acquired implicitly, explicit representations of these skills under pressure—and more clumsy performance—is less likely, because the explicit representations were never acquired.

However, to complicate matters even more, after extensive practice, skills may be executed automatically and without explicit representations, regardless of whether they were acquired with or without explicit instructions. For example, after practicing 1,400 forehand shots in table tennis, the skill was automated, and reinvestment did not occur under pressure for a group that learned with explicit instruction (Koedijker, Oudejans, & Beek, 2008). Explicit rules may be remembered, but not brought to mind during the execution of skills once automatization is intact.

COMPARING DISTRACTION AND EXPLICIT MONITORING THEORIES

Whether pressure-induced performance deficits are due primarily to distraction or explicit monitoring depends on the nature of the task (Beilock & Gray, 2007). Skills that primarily tax higher-order mental processes, such as strategizing, problem solving, decision making, and perceptual classification tasks (Markman et al., 2006), are more likely to fail because working memory space has been captured by cognitive interference. Many of these tasks, such as solving modular mathematical problems, where it is necessary to retain the solutions to sequences of problems in working memory, are primarily cognitive (Beilock, Kulp, Holt, & Carr, 2004). However, some athletic pursuits also place considerable demands on working memory. For example, as a midfielder in soccer, it is necessary to sustain a broad, external focus of attention in order to monitor the positions of other players, anticipate action, direct teammates, and coordinate play. Tasks that place greater demands on the motor control system, such as trampolining, golf, and baseball, may be more disrupted by consciously monitoring the component motor skills (Hardy, Mullen, & Martin, 2001). The executions of sensorimotor skills that are not proceduralized also require representation in working memory. However, these tasks tax working memory to a lesser degree because it is often not necessary to sustain representations of sequential motor skills.

Most, if not all, sport skills are performed with a combination of controlled and automated processing (Abernethy et al., 2007). Therefore, the best explanation of why skills fail under pressure may be a combination of the processing efficiency theory and conscious processing hypothesis (Edwards, Kingston, Hardy, & Gould, 2002).

PROCESSING EFFICIENCY/ATTENTIONAL CONTROL THEORY

As stated above, cognitive interference reduces the processing and storage capacity of working memory and decreases the efficiency of mental processing. However, despite the distraction of intrusive thoughts, performance may not suffer if individuals compensate for cognitive interference with redoubled effort to stay on task and with additional caution to minimize errors (Eysenck & Calvo, 1992; Eysenck et al., 2007; Murray & Janelle, 2003). In effect, worries about suboptimal performance may motivate sportspersons to suppress distractions and cognitive interference, and allocate more of their attentional and physical resources to improve their performance (Wilson, Chattington, Marple-Horvat, & Smith, 2007).

Elite athletes with high levels of trait anxiety perform well despite the presence of high levels of state anxiety and cognitive interference. For example, female field hockey players with high trait anxiety experienced more frequent worries about their performance during international female field hockey games when pressure was greatest. Their performance did not suffer, however, because they countered cognitive interference with increased effort to efforts concentrate and try harder (Wilson & Smith, 2007).

Continuing, the shooting accuracy of three of the ten members of the junior and senior Canadian national biathlon teams was not diminished under very considerable pressure. Prior to taking standing rifle shots, these athletes exercised on a bike ergometer at prescribed power output levels of 55%, 70%, 85%, and 100% of their maximum oxygen uptake. The pressure consisted of understanding that members of the Canadian national team would be selected on the basis of their shooting performance (Vickers & Williams, 2007). The three who performed well under pressure increased the duration of the final visual fixation on the target prior to shooting (the **quiet eye period**). This prolonged quiet eye period was especially important in preserving accuracy in the 100% power output condition. Longer quiet eye periods allow for more efficient processing of visual information in pistol and rifle shooting (Janelle et al., 2000), golf putting (Vickers, 1992), dart throwing (Vickers, Rodrigues, & Edworthy, 2000), billiards (Williams, Singer, & Frehlich, 2002), and basketball shooting (Vickers, 1996). The efficient processing of the quiet eye period also suppresses distractions and supports performance under pressure (Vine & Wilson, 2010).

If the quiet eye period is disrupted, performance will likely suffer. This was the case among intercollegiate basketball players. Under pressure, durations of quiet eye periods declined by 34% and free-throw accuracy dropped 26% (Wilson, Vine, & Wood, 2009). Elite clay target shooters were also less accurate when quiet eye periods for aiming at targets were briefer and initiated later (Causer, Holmes, Smith, & Williams, 2011). When the quiet eye period is disrupted, gaze is directed to the sources of threat or anxiety, and away from the goals for motor action. For example, anxious male university soccer players fixed their visual gaze on goalkeepers for longer periods when attempting penalty kicks (Wilson, Wood, & Vine, 2009). Penalty shots are more likely to be accurate when players focus on their target rather than when they focus on goalies. If kickers do glance at the goalkeeper and the side of the goal opposite from where they intend to strike, shots will more likely be successful if their last visual fixation is on their intended target (Wood & Wilson, 2008). Ironically, by focusing on the source of threat or challenge—the goalie—penalty shots are placed closer to the goalkeeper's reach (e.g., Van der Kamp & Masters, 2008).

Performance will also suffer if the compensatory behavior for managing anxiety slows performance due to excessive caution. Anxious Dutch climbers visually examined more handholds and fixated on handholds for longer durations. Due to cognitive interference, they need more time to select handholds and climbing paths. They spent more time standing still before initiating movement. They selected handholds that were closer to their body, and therefore needed more holds and movements to scale a climbing wall (Nieuwenhuys, Pijpers, Oudejans, & Bakker, 2008).

In some instances, extra effort is not always sufficient to counteract the detrimental effects of cognitive anxiety on performance (Hardy & Hutchinson, 2007; Smith et al., 2001; Williams, Vickers, & Rodrigues, 2002). This occurs when there are no working memory resources available for compensatory activities because the resources are occupied by either the demands of the task or cognitive interference (Eysenck et al., 2007). For example, with trait anxiety, working capacity is routinely occupied, and therefore reduced, by cognitive interference. Medium-handicap golfers with high trait and state anxiety exerted greater mental effort, were somewhat slower to make putts in a pressure condition, and fixated on the hole more frequently before initiating their putts. Nevertheless, the highly anxious golfers putted less accurately under pressure (Wilson, Smith, & Holmes, 2007). In addition, students with high trait anxiety were both more anxious and slower at a driving task under pressure (Wilson et al., 2006).

In other instances, extra effort may not be compensatory because processing resources in the central executive are not available. In these instances, the central executive cannot efficiently allocate working memory resources to either the articulatory loop or the visual sketchpad. For example, quiet eye periods among elite clay target shooters were disrupted under pressure, indicating that they did not allocate sufficient resources to the visual sketchpad (Causer et al., 2011).

In general, anxiety disrupts performance to a greater degree when task demands on the central executive increase. This is most evident with intense anxiety and panic. For example, skydivers experience extreme pressure and face death when their primary parachutes fail to deploy. Under these conditions, even experienced skydivers fail to deploy reserve parachutes and fall to their deaths (Leach & Griffith, 2008).

Application

Readers are advised to prepare for the potential of compromised performance under the most intense pressure. One strategy is to simplify the task and lessen demands on working memory. Sportspersons may rely on aspects of their game in which they have the most confidence. With successful skill execution and the progression of play, anxiety is likely to lessen and play selection may become more expansive.

Furthermore, when the contents of attention or working memory are stimulus driven, performance suffers. The contents of attention are stimulus driven or bottom-up when external threats (such as the behavior of goalies) or cognitive interference co-opt working memory. A top-down or goal-directed process by which performers control the contents of working memory is generally associated with optimal performance (Eysenck et al., 2007; Navarro et al., 2012; Wilson, 2008).

Tiger Woods Plays It Safe

Until 2010, Tiger Woods never lost a major (Masters, U.S. Open, British Open, PGA) golf tournament when he began the final round with a share of the lead, and is 41-2 overall on the PGA Tour when leading after three rounds. He plays cautiously when pressure is highest:

> Every successful player has a go-to shot that holds up under the most intense pressure. Mine is a stinger or knockdown shot off the tee with a fairway wood. I've used

it many times and in all kinds of conditions. It's my ultimate control shot. Although it's conservative in nature, it's also a scoring shot because it helps me avoid trouble while putting me in position to play aggressively onto the green when necessary.

The No. 1 key to hitting this shot is making an on-plane swing. I also focus on turning the back of my left hand down so it faces the ground more at impact. I start my release when the shaft is parallel to the ground, turning my left hand downward, which delofts the club. I knock the ball down not by leaning on it or moving forward but with the release.

I also want to keep my arms relaxed through impact. Trying to muscle the ball results in a poor release and a higher shot with more backspin—the opposite of what I want (Woods, 2008, p.55).

STEREOTYPE THREAT

Sportspersons and others who are simultaneously concerned about demonstrating competence and worried that their performance will confirm stereotypes or expectations of inferiority, are more likely to choke under pressure (Beilock et al., 2006; Beilock & McConnell, 2004; Beilock, Rydell, & McConnell, 2007; Chalabaev, Sarrazin, Stone, & Cury, 2008; Schmader et al., 2008). During the course of competitions, they actively monitor their progress and attempt to avoid failure and the confirmation of negative stereotypes (such as that one is a gagger, choker, or choke artist). They simultaneously monitor their performance for indications that they are disconfirming negative stereotypes. These self-conscious processes increase stress, anxiety, self-doubts, feelings of dejection, and tax the same attentional resources that are needed to perform optimally. Such sportspersons may consciously attempt to suppress thoughts about the negative stereotypes, and these efforts further compromise working memory space and have the ironic effect of making the anxiety-related stereotypes more prominent (Muraven & Baumeister, 2000; Wenzlaff & Wegner, 2000).

The performance deficits of those stereotyped are not simply due to working memory interference. The process of explicitly monitoring behavior to determine if it confirms stereotypes may cause people to respond more slowly and deliberately (Vorauer & Turpie, 2004). Others may rush and respond less accurately, as they are more susceptible to the "pull" of environmental stimuli and distractions. Performers that rush appear less capable of inhibiting responses and executing deliberate, planned strategies that will result in more sophisticated and accurate visual tracking and motor responses (Jamieson & Harkins, 2007).

CHOKING UNDER PRESSURE

"**Choking**" is a term that is widely recognized in the vernacular of sport and refers to inferior performances under pressure. Performances that do not measure up to a person's acquired skill level are considered inferior. **Pressure** refers to the conditions or factors that increase the importance of performing well. Pressure is increased when the rewards for superior performance are high, when an evaluating audience is present, when competition is stiff, when the outcome of a performance is especially important, and when there is only one chance to be successful (Baumeister & Showers, 1986; Hill, Hanton, Matthews, & Fleming, 2010). For example, championships are often contested on a yearly basis, and championship opportunities may occur only once in a lifetime. Pressure may also increase when the costs of failure are high.

The cost of failure is higher for those favored in competition (Gibson, Sachau, Doll, & Shumate, 2002), and for recognized superstars, as failure threatens their status as superior talents. This increased pressure may undermine performance. For example, footballers who were recipients of international soccer awards scored fewer penalty kicks in shootouts in World Cup, European Championship, and European Football Associations Champions League play than did their counterparts who were future recipients of the same awards (Jordet, 2009a). More generally, teams representing countries with the most European Championships and with the most players who were recipients of international soccer awards also scored fewer penalty kicks in shootouts in World Cup and European Championship matches (Jordet, 2009b). England was the country with the highest number of Championship League titles and the second most recipients of international awards. Together with the Netherlands, they were the least accurate in shootouts.

In general, those who are concerned with protecting their self-worth and public impressions of their ability are prone to anxiety, disrupted concentration (Cheryan & Bodenhausen, 2000), and choking under pressure (Thompson & Dinnel, 2007). They may also engage in sandbagging or underestimates of their ability, so as to reduce audience expectations and pressure (Gibson, Sachau, Doll, & Shumate, 2002).

Choking is paradoxical because performers are often most highly motivated to do their best when the stakes or consequences of performances are highest. However, choking does not occur as a result of insufficient effort, but rather because pressure impairs skilled performance by altering the contents of working memory (Wallace, Baumeister, & Vohs, 2005).

Choking occurs when physiological anxiety or arousal increases and attention is involuntarily directed inward and to a narrow range of topics (Liao & Masters, 2002; Williams et al., 2010). These topics include concerns that one cannot meet a standard of performance, cannot measure up to a competitor (Edwards et al., 2002; McGrath, 1970), and thoughts about the result of a performance rather than the process. These self-conscious concerns constitute cognitive interference, because they compete with attention to the details necessary for successful performances. These thoughts are emotionally valenced in that they prompt cognitive and physiological anxiety. Attention is captured by these thoughts and taken from the cues in the environment that require recognition, such as game plans and how to counter the strategies and exploit the vulnerabilities of opponents. With attention captured by emotionally valenced thoughts and the experience of physiological anxiety, the execution of automated skills is inhibited. As stated above, efforts to consciously monitor and control the proceduralized elements of a performance disrupt their automatic and skilled execution (Beilock & Carr, 2001; Beilock, Carr, MacMahon, & Starkes, 2002; Beilock & Gray, 2007; Jackson, Ashford, & Norsworthy, 2006; Singer, 2002; Smith, 1996).

Under pressure, athletes may become impulsive and abandon game plans or strategies for performances. Game plans typically represent strategies that present the greatest opportunities for optimal performance. In lieu of these carefully crafted game plans, pressured athletes may become hurried and impulsive and adopt high-risk, high-reward strategies (Leith & Baumeister, 1996).

The most elite soccer players or footballers in the world appeared to alter their preparation for penalty kicks in World Cup and European Championship matches that were determined by penalty kick "shootouts" (Jordet, 2009b; Jordet & Hartman, 2008). Shootouts decide matches that end in ties after regulation and overtime periods, and pressure is greatest when matches will be lost if a penalty kick is not converted. The most crucial shots—those that would result in their team losing if missed—were rushed. The elite footballers spent less time studying the goalkeeper prior to these penalty kicks; after setting the ball on the penalty mark, they turned their back to the goalkeeper and walked back to prepare for their run-up. They were more deliberate in preparation for penalty kicks that would only result in a win if converted, and those that would not result in either a win or a loss. Prior to these shots, they were more likely to keep their eyes on the goalkeeper and walk backward to prepare for their run-up. Perhaps most importantly, penalty kicks were successful on 92% of the efforts that would result in wins if converted, 61.8% that would result in losses if missed, and 73.7% when the kicks would not result in either a win or a loss.

When penalty takers turn their backs prior to the run-up and rush kicks, goalkeepers judge them as weak and insecure. Goalkeepers expect them to produce less precise kicks, and delay in initiating their first movements to deflect shots. Goalkeepers may more successfully defend penalty kicks if they delay in this manner because the majority of penalty takers use a keeper-dependent strategy. With a keeper-dependent strategy, penalty takers determine where to place shots by watching and anticipating the movement of the goalkeeper (Furley, Dicks, Stendtke, & Memmert, 2012).

Application

It is especially important to adhere to game plans and preperformance routines under pressure. In doing so, athletes not only sustain efficacy but also reduce the cognitive load.

Not all people become impulsive under pressure. In fact, some become overly deliberative or slow in making decisions (Butler & Baumeister, 1998; Heaton & Sigall, 1991; Janelle, 2002; Seibt & Förster, 2004). These sportspersons may be overly cautious and focus on avoiding failure rather than initiating action to gain success. For example, in basketball, an anxious player may pass up an open shot under pressure because he or she does not want to be the one who misses the critical basket. In effect, these sportspersons play to avoid losing rather than to win (Wallace et al., 2005). Perhaps both hurried and overly deliberative disruptions to tempo impair the automatic execution of skills.

John Wooden: Play to Win

John Wooden won a record 10 national championships in basketball as the head coach of the UCLA men's basketball team. He was the first to be inducted into the NCAA Basketball Hall of Fame as a coach and a player. He considered it essential to play to win:

I was taught not to fear making a mistake. My college coach at Purdue, Ward 'Piggy' Lambert, often told us that the team that makes the most mistakes usually wins. His point? If you're not making some mistakes, you're not doing anything—not trying to make things happen. And to win basketball games, you have to make something happen. Just like anywhere else (Wooden & Jamison, 2007, pp. 18-19).

The Effects of Pressure

Pressure often disrupts the performance of not only average adults (Wilson, Wood, & Vine, 2009) but also elite athletes (e.g., Jordet, Hartman, Visscher, & Lemmick, 2007; Wang, Marchant, & Morris, 2004). For example, Lewis and Linder (1997) described the effects of pressure on the putting accuracy of college students. A condition of moderate pressure was created by informing students that they would receive twice the usual class credit if they could place 10 putts within an average of 5 cm from the putting target. Putting accuracy decreased under pressure as the average distances from the target for the low-pressure and high-pressure groups were 55.5 and 81.5 cm, respectively. Of interest, some of the students spontaneously verbalized: "'Don't choke!' 'The pressure's on now!' and 'The pressure's getting to me!'" (Lewis & Linder, 1997, p. 941).

Among elite athletes ranked in the top four for their sport in the U.S., 13.7% acknowledged being panic-stricken prior to performances, 18.4% acknowledged intense panic while performing, and 49.6% indicated that they became very anxious during performances if they make mistakes (Mahoney, Gabriel, & Perkins, 1987). As mentioned in Chapter 4, 30% of the U.S. wrestlers at the 1988 Olympic Games in Seoul said that their worst Olympic performance was in their most crucial match (Gould, Eklund, & Jackson, 1992a). Elite soccer players were highly distressed when taking penalty kicks in "shootouts" that determined the outcomes of matches, and they performed worse when the importance of the kick was highest (Jordet, Elferink-Gemser, Lemmink, & Visscher, 2006; Jordet, Hartman, Visscher, & Lemmink, 2007).

Even the most elite performers acknowledge choking. For example, after his record-tying seventh singles title at Wimbledon and, at that time, record-breaking 13 Grand Slam singles titles in the open era (seven Wimbledon, four U.S. Open, and two Australian Open), Pete Sampras acknowledged choking at a critical juncture in the first set of the match. Despite Sampras's dominating serve, his opponent Patrick Rafter won five of his twelve points in a first set tiebreaker on Sampras's serve. Regarding his erratic play in the tiebreaker, Sampras reflected, "We all choke. . . . The title could be won or lost in a matter of a couple shots" (Hersh, 2000, p. C2). Sampras went on to win a 14th Grand Slam singles title at the 2002 U.S. Open.

As will be emphasized in Chapter 15, people are different, and not everyone is adversely affected by pressure. Approximately 19% of a sample of undergraduate students did not evidence physiological signs of stress (elevated cortisol and heart rate) and their performance did not erode under pressure in a simulated soccer penalty kick task (Navarro et al., 2012).

Elite athletes learn to perform well under pressure. Members of the Professional Golfers' Association (PGA) Tour, Ladies' Professional Golfers' Association (LPGA) Tour, and Senior Professional Golfers' Association (Senior PGA) Tour, generally won top-tier tournaments (such as the four Majors) and second-tier tournaments when leading and within one stroke of the lead after three of four rounds (Clark, 2002). The performance of male professional golfers in Australia was also not compromised by elevated levels of cognitive and physical anxiety (McKay et al., 1997).

CHOKING ON THE THRESHOLD OF VICTORY

Is victory more difficult to grasp when it is close at hand? Baumeister and Steinhilber (1984) maintained that professional baseball players more often "choked" or began to perform poorly when victory was close at hand and when they began to imagine themselves as champions. This choking process was seen to be more likely in front of supportive home crowds and in final or deciding games of championship series. The support of the home crowd was understood to intensify the ball players' focus on themselves as impending champions, and to distract attention from the hitting and fielding necessary to win. This self-attention or daydreaming about oneself was maintained because it was pleasant. However, this self-attention also disrupts the automatic and unselfconscious execution of skills that characterize elite performance. Perhaps similar processes occurred among British golfers in the final round of the British Open Golf Championship, as their performance was inferior to that of foreign golfers on final rounds (Wright & Jackson, 1991). Home field was not a disadvantage for major league baseball players in championship games only when the victorious team was a decided underdog, perhaps because the players were less likely to be drawn to fantasies about their status as champions.

These finding of Baumeister and Steinhilber (1984) were derived from the archival statistics of the World Series of Major League Baseball in the U.S., and were counterintuitive and inconsistent with a larger body of research conducted in controlled, laboratory settings. This laboratory research demonstrated that self-attention disrupted performance when stakes were high and when performers expected failure. Self-attention facilitated performance when the level of pressure was high and when success was expected. The findings of Baumeister and Steinhilber were also inconsistent with evidence summarized in Chapter 5 that home teams are advantaged in terms of won-loss records. For example, World Cup soccer teams won 63% of their games at home, 37% away, and 40% at neutral sites in 1987 and 1998 (Brown et al., 2002). A home advantage was particularly evident for World Cup championship games, and performance was worse for visiting teams that traveled longer distances. Home teams have also performed better in deciding games in NBA playoff series, especially in Game 7 (Tauer, Guenther, & Rozek, 2009).

In addition, independent analyses of archival data from the World Series of Major League Baseball revealed that home teams won 60% of the decisive sixth or seventh games in the World Series between 1924 and 1993 (Schlenker, Phillips Boniecki, & Schlenker, 1995). Further, during the seventh games of World Series, fielding errors were made three times as often when the home team was behind rather than ahead in the score. Therefore, Schlenker et al. attributed choking to self-attention concerning failure rather than to self-attention regarding the anticipation of success. The combination of wanting to impress the hometown fans and having self-doubts about the likelihood of success apparently impaired the performance of the professional baseball players. Expectations of success and self-efficacy facilitate performance, even when the expectations of others are high and when a public performance is important. Schlenker et al. considered the essential ingredients of choking in athletic and other venues to be self-doubts and high motivation to impress others.

The Kinder and Darker Forms of Choking on the Threshold of Victory

Whether choking on the threshold of victory is due to a "**dark form,**" or belief that standards for success and expectations of others will not be met, or a "**kinder form**" of pleasant fantasies about an impending change in status to that of champions has not been conclusively determined (Baumeister, 1995). Both the dark and kind forms of choking divert the limited attentional resources of performers to conditions in the future rather than to the skilled and sometimes automatic execution of tasks in the here-and-now. (Sanders, Baron, & Moore, 1978). However, both forms of choking appear to be more than just forms of distraction, and both represent cognitive interference in that they are emotionally valenced.

On the Threshold of Victory

John McEnroe was ranked number one in professional men's tennis from 1981 to 1985. He won 77 career singles titles and 77 doubles titles, more than any other tennis professional. In 1984, he won 13 of the 15 tournaments he entered, including the Masters and the Grand Slams of Wimbledon and the U.S. Open. Yet his loss in the finals of the 1984 French Open, a Grand Slam event, still causes him sleepless nights and days of nausea when he returns to the site of the French Open to do commentary for television (McEnroe & Kaplan, 2002). McEnroe considered this loss to be the worst in his life and to have cost him a legitimate claim to being the best player ever.

McEnroe won the first two sets of the French open from Ivan Lendl, and was leading 4-2 in the third set. McEnroe thought he could read the facial expressions of friends in the audience. He imagined that they were thinking that he had essentially won the tournament and that it would be a *fait accompli* in a half hour. He found himself wondering: "*I've been playing so amazingly. How can I keep it up*" (McEnroe & Kaplan, 2002, p. 177). A squawking headset from a television cameraman also distracted him. He lost his composure and complained throughout the remainder of the match. A largely supportive crown turned hostile. McEnroe lost in five sets.

Self-Efficacy and Choking on the Threshold of Victory

In the sixth and seventh games of World Series, it is reasonable to assume that opponents are somewhat evenly matched. Competition with individuals or teams that are equal or superior in skill can cause performers to question whether they have the capacity to prevail over these competitors (Baumeister, 1984; Gould et al., 1992a). These questions erode confidence that one can reach a standard necessary for success and allow for involuntary surrender of storage capacity in working memory to cognitive interference. Self-efficacy or confidence that an individual or team will prevail when evenly matched is a vital determinant of performance under conditions of high pressure and intense competition (Bandura, 1997; Cheng, Hardy, & Markland, 2009; Craft, Magyar, Becker, & Feltz, 2003; Mellalieu, Hanton, & Fletcher, 2006; Vealey, 2009).

Efficacy beliefs are especially important in determining the results of face-to-face competition. For example, elite soccer players who believed that they were in control when taking penalty kicks in shoot-outs were more likely to score than were their counterparts who considered the results of penalty kicks to be determined by luck (e.g., the goalie might guess the direction of their shot and deflect it; Jordet et al., 2006). Undergraduates who believed that they were in control and knew what they were doing shot free throws more accurately under pressure (Otten, 2009).

Efficacy beliefs may also be influenced by the behavior of teammates. Team efficacy may erode when skilled teammates perform poorly. Concurrently, estimates of the abilities of opponents may be inflated.

Teams with high collective efficacy are resilient in the face of pressure and are not easily daunted by defeat (Jones & Harwood, 2008).

Audience Effects

Supportive audiences communicate their interest in seeing a performer do well. They may identify with performers and experience gains and losses in self-esteem and moods as a result of the successes or failures the performers. The supportive audience may experience the glory reflected from their favorite successful performers. Supportive audiences have a strong interest in how performers do, whereas neutral audiences have little or no stake in the results of performances. Hostile audiences root for poor performances. Supportive audiences may provide an emotional buffer for performers so that their attention is not captured by negative emotions and so that efficacy is preserved under adverse conditions. Perhaps performers believe that they will not lose the esteem of supportive audiences because the members of supportive audiences are aware of their past histories of competent performances.

Performers generally prefer a supportive audience (Gould, Greenleaf, Guinan, & Chung, 2002; Pain & Harwood, 2008), but its presence is not necessarily associated with better performance. This is especially true when the standards for a successful performance are high, and success is far from assured. Sportspersons do not want to disappoint supportive audiences, especially when the audience has a personal investment in the outcome (Wallace, Baumeister, & Vohs, 2005).

Supportive audiences have detrimental effects on performance when students and athletes lack confidence that will be successful (Butler & Baumeister, 1998). When performers lack confidence, the presence of a supportive audience may increase the pressure to obtain a goal that they considered to be beyond their reach (Baumeister, Hamilton, & Tice, 1985), and contribute to choking. Supportive audiences tend to closely scrutinize performers, and this may increase the self-consciousness of performers. Performers sometimes demonstrate higher levels of physiological anxiety before supportive audiences.

Self-esteem may provide a psychological buffer to moderate the effects of audience support on performance. Those with high and stable self-esteem may be less worried about winning the approval of or disappointing audiences (Baumeister, Tice, & Hutton, 1989).

Audience Effects and Self-Consciousness

A leitmotiv or theme for understanding choking under pressure is the direction of attention inward to self-conscious concerns, such as whether a performance will be successful or how one appears to an audience. It would, therefore, appear obvious that those with high levels of trait self-consciousness would perform more poorly under pressure and with an audience. Indeed, accuracy at shooting basketball free throws (Wang,

Marchant, Morris, & Gibbs, 2004) with an audience and under pressure was shown to deteriorate for sportspersons with high self-consciousness. There are, however, conflicting reports that demonstrate that those with high self-consciousness perform better under pressure and with an audience (Baumeister, 1984; Heaton & Sigall, 1993). In these reports, it is emphasized that people who are more self-conscious are less concerned with the responses of audiences, and are more likely to concentrate on their own standards of success. Individuals low in trait self-consciousness are described as typically focusing their attention on factors external to themselves, and, therefore, are more sensitive to external sources of pressure, such as the responses of an audience.

These conflicting results are not readily reconciled on the basis of evidence, although it has been suggested for the highly self-consciousness, pressure disrupts performance only on complex motor skills, such as golf putting (Wang et al., 2004). Perhaps those who are able to maintain their routine attentional focus, whether this is inward or outward, are less likely to perform more poorly and choke under pressure (Ford, Hodges, & Williams, 2005; Reeves, Tenenbaum, & Lidor, 2007). This latter suggestion is also consistent with the leitmotif that consistency and routine in preparation and performance is associated with optimal performance.

Worst Choke in Golfing History?

In 1996, the world's top ranked golfer, Greg Norman, said, "One of my great motivations in life is a fear of failure" (Garber & Berlet, 1996, p. K1). In that year, Norman "suffered the worst collapse in major tournament history" (Reilly, 1996, p. 24) at the Masters golf tournament. He entered the final day of this tournament leading the field by six strokes and ended the day five strokes behind the eventual winner, Nick Faldo. News reports did not provide information about whether Norman may have adopted performance-avoidance goals (such as not to lose; Elliot & McGregor, 1999), but there was evidence of state anxiety: " 'His routine is so different,' said Faldo's coach David Leadbetter. 'He's standing over the ball an *incredible* amount of time. I'd say he's spending six, seven seconds longer per shot, fidgeting, moving around in ways I've never seen him do' " (Reilly, 1996, p. 26). In a list of the "Top 10 Chokes in Majors" in *Golf Magazine*, this performance was rated as the worst choke in golfing history (Top 10 Chokes in Majors, 2002).

Norman entered the final round with the lead in seven of golf's major tournaments. He lost the 1986 Masters to Jack Nicklaus on the final hole. He entered the final round of the 1986 U.S. Open with a one stroke lead and finished six shots behind winner Ray Floyd. He led starting the final round of the 1986 British Open and won by five shots. He started the final round of the 1986 PGA Championship with a lead of four shots, but lost by two strokes. In the 1987 Masters, he started the final round with a one stroke lead and lost on a second playoff hole. Norman was tied with Faldo as they entered the final round of the 1990 British Open, but lost to Faldo by nine shots. By 1996, Norman was well aware that he had been identified in the press as a choke artist. The degree to which Norman internalized choking as a stable, internal characteristic is open to speculation. However, in 1996, he defended himself to the press: "I know I'm not a loser. There's a lot of golf left in me. They'll call you a choker, and a gagger. But it's only a game. I'm a better person for it. I will achieve my goals in life" (Garber & Berlet, 1996, p. K1).

Perhaps more than any golfer prior to Tiger Woods, Greg Norman had been considered the heir apparent to golf greatest champion, Jack Nicklaus (McDermott, 1986). He was a crowd favorite due to his skill and finesse, power, and good looks. Galleries and audiences were supportive, but their expectations were high. The high expectations of galleries may have placed additional pressure on Norman, especially if he had doubts about whether he was a winner. His career has been far from unsuccessful, as he has been named as the 22nd best golfer of all time (Yocom et al., 2000).

THE CHOKING EXPERIENCE CYCLE

The personal experiences of female and male collegiate golfers who choked during competition largely confirm the findings described above (Guicciardi, Longbottom, Jackson, & Dimmock, 2010). Worries about the results of competition distracted them from focusing on play in real time. Fear of failure was another prominent source of cognitive interference. Automaticity was also disrupted as they focused on the step-by-step execution of shots.

Importantly, golfers lost control of not only their concentration but also their emotions, and extended periods of subpar performance were more likely when emotions "got the better" of them. Golfers were also more likely to consistently choke when they set standards for their performance that were excessively high and exceeded their abilities. These golfers also deviated from preperformance routines and often rushed preparations for shots. These findings, as well as the consequences and the learning event from choking, are summarized in Figure 11.1.

CHOKING IS NOT INEVITABLE

To this point, choking has been described as somewhat normative. It is not inevitable, and clearly some sportspersons choke or respond less favorably to pressure than do others. Sportspersons who characteristically respond to pressure with an inward focus that involves cognitive interference and explicit monitoring and control of proceduralized skills are more likely to choke (Masters, Polman, & Hammond, 1993; Wang et al., 2004). An external focus on game situations and the desired outcome of action is generally preferable (Abernethy et al., 2007; Bell & Hardy, 2009; Hill et al., 2010; Moran, 2009; Vast, Young, & Thomas, 2010). As mentioned above, skilled baseball players performed better under pressure

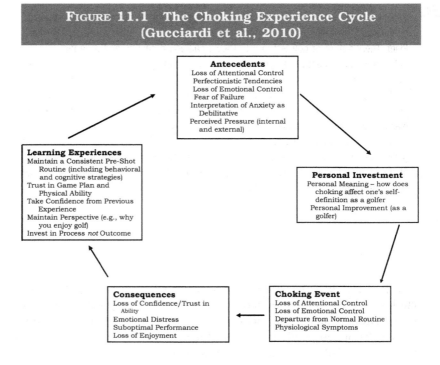

FIGURE 11.1   The Choking Experience Cycle
(Gucciardi et al., 2010)

when they focused on the direction the ball followed after it had left the bat (Castaneda & Gray, 2007), and skilled golfers made more accurate chip shots when they focused on where they intended to place the ball after it left the clubface and engaged in self talk ("straight flight") prior to shot execution (Bell & Hardy, 2009).

These findings notwithstanding, expert French golfers estimated that they focused on technical aspects, procedural rules, club motion, and body positions during approximately 43% of golf swings. They focused on the outcome during approximately 40% of swings (Bernier, Codron, Thienot, & Fournier, 2011).

Sportspersons may also redouble efforts to maintain performance levels while managing high levels of pressure, cognitive and physiological anxiety, and fatigue (Vickers & Williams, 2007). For example, by selecting a "safe" shot under the most extreme pressure, a golfer might sustain attention on where he intends to place the ball on the fairway as well as his efficacy for executing this shot (Woods, 2008). Perhaps choking under pressure is also less likely in sports that generally require a broad and external attentional focus and almost constant action and movement. For example, evidence of home-ice disadvantage in championship matches in the National Hockey League is at most equivocal (Gayton, Matthews, & Nickless, 1987; Wright & Voyer, 1995).

With experience in actual competition and with simulation training, sportspersons and performers learn to perform well and optimally under pressure (Hill, Hanton, Matthews, & Fleming, 2011). For example, in the Lewis and Linder (1997) and Beilock and Carr (2001) studies cited earlier, some college students practiced putting while being videotaped. These students expected that sport psychologists, coaches, instructors, and members of the golf team would examine the films of their putting. These students were in effect "inoculated" to putt accurately under conditions of heightened self-awareness, and the high-pressure condition did not interfere with their accuracy. Skilled basketball players shoot free throws more accurately under pressure when they practiced free throws under simulated competitive pressure. Dart players threw darts more accurately when experiencing anxiety after practicing while experiencing anxiety (Oudejans & Pijpers, 2009).

Sportspersons also learn to manage the disruptive effects of supportive and unsupportive audiences with experience (Wallace et al., 2005). A measure of inoculation against reinvestment, or attention to the step-by-step components of motor skills, may be obtained by practicing the motor skills without self-focused attention or without explicit instructions about how to perform the skill (Abernethy et al., 2007; Liao & Masters, 2002). For example, visualization of sport skills rather than verbal instructions might be emphasized (Masters, 2000).

As mentioned in Chapter 5, ideal preperformance planning involves developing game plans and anticipating problems, impediments, and the tactics of opponents. Thorough preperformance preparation may also involve strategies for interrupting cognitive interference and choking. Cue words and breathing exercises are examples of strategies for interrupting cognitive interference. If cognitive interference and emotionally valenced thoughts are interrupted, performance is likely to improve, even if the disruption is distracting. For example, in the Lewis and Linder (1997) study, collegiate putters who were required to count aloud backward from 100 by twos were relatively unaffected by the high-pressure condition. Their putting was roughly as accurate as students in low-pressure conditions without distractions, and far more accurate than the putting of students in high-pressure conditions that were not counting backward. The explanation for this curious finding was that students in the high-pressure condition were less able to focus on themselves because their attention was occupied by the task of counting backward. Do the results of this study suggest that people should look for distractions such as counting backward when attempting expert performance? No. This form of distraction disrupted performance under low-pressure conditions and attenuated the inoculating effects of practice under conditions of heightened self-awareness.

Preperformance routines that are practiced immediately prior to the execution of closed skills, such as shooting free throws in basketball and penalty kicks in soccer, also inhibit choking. As discussed in Chapter 5, preperformance routines include behavioral rehearsal of sport skills, visualization, self-talk, and strategies to reduce physiological anxiety (such as centering) or reinterpret anxiety as facilitative (Williams, Cumming, &

Balanos, 2010). Preperformance routines reduce choking by enhancing the experience of efficacy and control and by reducing physiological anxiety and negative self-talk. Preperformance routines also direct attention outward and toward the intended result of actions rather than inward and toward oneself (Mesagno, Marchant, & Morris, 2008). In a closed skill sport such as golf, preshot routines that included practice swings (focusing on the feel of the swing rather than explicitly monitoring and deconstructing the automated skill) and visualization served to increase confidence and decrease distraction and self-focus (Hill et al., 2011).

It is also not recommended that sportspersons attempt to suppress cognitive interference by simply making efforts to block these thoughts from conscious awareness. Intentional efforts to suppress thoughts may activate two cognitive processes: an "intentional operating process" and an "ironic monitoring process" (Wegner, 1994, 1997a, 1997b, 2011). The intentional process consists of a conscious, effortful search for a desired mental state, such as a focus on a game plan. The ironic monitoring is an unconscious and automatic search for mental contents that indicate that one has mentally strayed from the desired mental state, such as thoughts about getting nervous and choking under pressure. Under stress and pressure, the ironic monitoring process may supersede the intentional operating process, causing the unwanted thoughts about choking to come to mind with even greater frequency.

It is also not beneficial to attempt to block sensory information from entering conscious awareness, as this results in ironic perceptual-motor processes. For example, instructions to "make sure the goalkeeper could not reach the ball" influenced soccer players to direct their gaze at the goalkeeper prior to taking penalty kicks (Bakker, Oudejans, Binsch, & Van der Kamp, 2006, p. 273). The placement of penalty kicks followed the direction of their gaze, and therefore within proximity to the keeper. Footballers who focused on where they intended to place the ball kicked more accurately. Eye movements are coordinated with movements of the arms and legs. A visual focus on the intended target is more likely to elicit the motor schema to produce the desired action (Land, 2009). The direction and duration of the final visual fixation—the quiet eye period—prior to initiating motor action is especially important (Wilson, Vine, & Wood, 2009; Wilson, Wood, & Vine, 2009; Wood & Wilson, 2008). If this final visual fixation is abbreviated and directed away from the target of impending motor action, performance suffers (Vine & Wilson, 2010). Motor action is also continuously coupled with perceptual input, and therefore it is necessary to sustain visual focus on intended targets to elicit motor sequences with the proper force and direction. Sportspersons generally need not be concerned that their gaze will "give away" the direction of shots, as in sports such as soccer, defenders do not anticipate shot direction on the basis of gaze direction.

Instead of focusing on thoughts and input to suppress, sportspersons are better served by preparing to focus, and refocus as necessary, their attention on task-relevant cues throughout competitions and practices (Conroy, 2008; Dugdale & Eklund, 2002; Martens, 1987; Hill et al., 2010).

For example, cue words may be used to disrupt choking and refocus attention (Moran, 2009). Cue words and other strategies are most useful when they promote concentration on the instrumental behaviors responsible for optimal performance. Attention will, therefore, be directed toward the sportsperson's intentions, plans, strategies, and tactics at specific points in contests and in response to the play of opponents (Seve, Saury, Theureau, & Durand, 2002). Cue words may also represent global motor skills that require minimal explicit thought and working memory space, and that may also inhibit regressions to explicit monitoring of proceduralized skills (Jackson & Wilson, 1999; Masters, 2000; Todd & Gigerenzer, 2000). For example, a tennis player may cue a proceduralized serve at a strategic point in match (e.g., "my kicker") without consciously monitoring the specific motor skills (ball toss, knee bend, brush up the back of the ball, uncoil) required to hit a high bouncing, twisting serve.

The downward performance spiral of choking may also be disrupted by decreasing the attendant physiological anxiety or arousal. For example, athletes may use the centering technique (described in Chapter 6) to reduce tension during practice and competition (Williams et al., 2010). Sportspersons may be advised to simply assume that the centering technique reduces arousal rather than to engage in emotion-focused coping and monitor whether they are effectively reducing anxiety. The process of monitoring anxiety levels is likely to hijack the same attentional resources required for optimal performance. Sportspersons may also benefit from understanding that anxiety "comes with the territory" of performance under pressure and need not disrupt performance (Ben-Zeev, Fein, & Inzlicht, 2005; Schmader et al., 2008).

Most generally, the detrimental effects of anxiety and pressure on performance are not all-or-none phenomena. Anxiety and pressure may engender cognitive interference and distraction and interfere with performance during one point in a performance, but not in others. For example, collegiate wrestlers experienced some doubts before peak performances, but transformed doubts into states of confidence during their matches (Eklund, 1994). In the 2001 U.S. Open in golf, the three leaders three-putted the final hole of the tournament. It can easily be argued that the eventual winner Ratief Goosen choked when he three-putted from ten feet, and missed his second putt from three feet, a putt that would have won the championship. The somewhat universal recognition of the effects of anxiety on performance and choking under pressure was reflected in the title of newspaper article about this match, "Gag Order" (Berlet, 2001, p. C1). Goosen may have gagged when victory was within three feet, but this gagging was short-lived. He won the U.S. Open in a playoff on the next day.

Performers regain their concentration and composure by redirecting attention to their game plans or strategies for performances (Eklund, 1994, 1996), by reestablishing efficacy or conviction that their performance will exceed standards necessary for success (Hill et al., 2009; Otten, 2009), and by controlling their physiology. Efficacy may also be restored if opponents are recognized to be vulnerable.

Nagging doubts about being a "choker," "gagger," or "choke artist" are likely to be highly detrimental to performance. To see oneself as a choke artist implies that choking is a stable, internal characteristic, and that performance is likely to be impaired across venues or situations and over time (Elliot & McGregor, 1999). With the conviction that one is a choker, a state of imbalance is created when individuals attempt to perform optimally. This imbalance and threat is amplified if one has acquired a reputation or stereotype as a choker, as these individuals experience even greater pressure to not conform to their reputation. In effect, the conviction that one is a choke artist means that there is no end to one's choking. The recognition that choking during performances is not uncommon is helpful if it contributes to convictions that choking is relatively universal and situational.

Lastly, focused professional intervention may be beneficial. For example, a structured visualization procedure resulted in a significant reduction in putting "yips" among accomplished golfers (Bell, Skinner, & Fisher, 2009).

SUMMARY AND APPLICATION

Choking occurs when external pressure for skilled performance has the paradoxical effect of producing inferior performances. Choking happens when attention is captured by concerns that one cannot measure up to a criterion necessary for success or to competitors. In the course of a competition, the likelihood for victory or defeat becomes more apparent. Choking is more likely if the attention of performers is captured by these potential outcomes and diverted from the skilled execution of tasks in the here-and-now. Performers may be distracted by pleasant fantasies of an impending change in status to that of a champion, or by aversive thoughts of lacking what it takes to win. Supportive audiences comfort performers, but if they lack confidence that they can reach standards necessary for success, this standard is raised by the presence of an audience. If negative emotions such as fear or embarrassment are experienced during a performance, and perhaps if the opportunity for success is believed to be slipping away, performers may engage in novel and untested strategies that have little chances for success. For example, performers may attempt high-risk strategies that have little chance for success, and may also become overly impulsive or deliberate.

The recognition of cognitive interference is an important step in its amelioration. Recognition serves to interrupt the automatic occurrence of interfering thoughts and provide a greater sense of control of these thoughts. With, guidance, social support, and coaching, cognitive interference and physiological anxiety can be recognized and interpreted as facilitative anxiety. Attention can be directed to the elements of a performance that will lead to an optimal or at least satisfactory performance. An effective method of providing guidance and coaching is to model or demonstrate effective problem solving in response to obstacles and to enunciate the strategies used in surmounting obstacles.

The importance of confidence that one can realize standards necessary for success has been emphasized throughout this chapter. In keeping with this theme, choking is less likely if goals are not set beyond one's capabilities. Efficacy and confidence are more likely to be maintained if goals are attainable with some margin for error. Focusing on aspects of a performance over which one has control also support efficacy beliefs. Repeated queries to oneself about whether goals will be realized during the course of a performance are not helpful. These queries compete with attention to the planning, ordering, and execution of elements of a performance. These queries can take the form of cognitive interference, as a performer may conclude that they will not reach standards necessary for success.

Effective control of debilitative anxiety and cognitive interference during evaluations and performances begins with the conscientious practice of the techniques described in Chapters 4, 5, and 6. This preparation provides performers with direction and solutions to obstacles that occur during the course of a performance. Well-prepared performers are more likely to believe that they are the equal to challenges and opponents and to maintain self-efficacy when success is not readily achieved.

Careful preparation should probably include measures to "inoculate" performers against the disruptive effects of audiences. Without this inoculation, the presence of an audience may cause greater self-consciousness and prompt overly expeditious or deliberate performance in place of the execution of automatic skills. The importance of preparing to perform under conditions that are similar to "game conditions" was discussed in Chapter 5. This discussion can now be expanded to physical and mental practice with friendly, hostile, and neutral crowds.

Key Terms

Debilitative and facilitative anxiety   247

Cognitive and physiological anxiety   247

Trait and state anxiety   248

Working memory   248

Cognitive interference   249

Emotionally-valenced thoughts: unsuccessful performance, reactions of spectators   250

Preemptory thoughts   250

Self-doubt   250

Fear of failure   251

Automatically   252

Explicit monitoring or conscious processing hypothesis   254

Common-coding theory   255

Processing efficiency/attentional control theory   257

Quiet eye period   258

Choking under pressure   260

Stereotype threat   260

Kinder and darker forms of choking on the threshold of victory   265

Supportive audiences   267

The choking experience cycle   269

Discussion Questions

Q1. Review facilitative and debilitative anxiety.

Q2. Review trait and state anxiety.

Q3. Summarize cognitive interference and distraction theories.

Q4. Describe working memory.

Q5. Consider forms of cognitive interference: emotionally valenced thoughts, preemptive thoughts, and self-doubt.

Q6. What are the five dimensions of fear of failure in sport?

Q7. Explain why those with trait anxiety are more likely to experience state anxiety during competition.

Q8. Consider the interpretive bias of people with trait anxiety.

Q9. Why does cognitive interference exist?

Q10. Detail the explicit monitoring or conscious processing hypothesis.

Q11. Do sportspersons actually become tight or stiffen-up under pressure?

Q12. Describe the yips.

Q13. Once automated, skills are more likely to sustain automaticity when athletes maintain an external focus. Explain why.

Q14. Describe the common-coding theory.

Q15. Review the arguments for teaching sport skills with and without explicit instructions.

Q16. Consider the conditions under which pressure-induced performance deficits result primarily from distraction or explicit monitoring.

Q17. Distinguish processing efficiency/attentional control theory from distraction theories.

Q18. Review the quiet eye period.

Q19. Considering visual gaze, what contributes to more accurate penalty kicks in soccer?

Q20. Review the conditions under which additional effort is unlikely to compensate for the distracting effects of anxiety.

Q21. Explain bottom-up and top-down attentional processes.

Q22. How does the threat of confirming stereotypes disrupt performance?

Q23. Review the influence of pressure on performance.

Q24. Consider the disruptive effects of being favored in competition.

Q25. How does pressure disrupt the behavior of athletes in sports such as soccer?

Q26. Discuss the "darker" and "kinder" explanations for choking on the threshold of victory.

Q27. Review the influences of supportive, neutral, and hostile audiences on performance.

Q28. Reconcile the conflicting evidence for the influence of self-consciousness and audience effects.

Q29. Describe the choking experience cycle.

Q30. Consider suggestions for counteracting choking under pressure.

Suggested Readings

Baumeister, R. F. (1995). Disputing the effects of championship pressures and home audiences. *Journal of Personality and Social Psychology, 68*, 644–648.

Baumeister, R. F., & Steinhilber, A. (1984). Paradoxical effects of supportive audiences on performance under pressure: The home field disadvantage in sports championships. *Journal of Personality and Social Psychology, 47*, 85–93.

Dugdale, J. R., & Eklund, R. C. (2002). Do *not* pay attention to the empires: Thought suppression and task-relevant focusing strategies. *Journal of Sport & Exercise Psychology, 24*, 306–319.

Lewis, B. P., & Linder, D. E. (1997). Thinking about choking? Attentional processes and paradoxical performance. *Personality and Social Psychology Bulletin, 23*, 937–944.

Petri, H. L., & Govern, J. (2004). *Motivation: Theory, research, and applications* (5th ed.). Belmont, CA: Wadsworth/Thomson Learning.

Schlenker, B. R., Phillips, S. T., Boniecki, K. A., & Schlenker, D. R. (1995). Championship pressures: Choking or triumphing in one's own territory. *Journal of Personality and Social Psychology, 68*, 632–643.

Williams, J. M., Nideffer, R. M., Wilson, V. E., Sagal, M-S., Peper, E. (2006). Concentration and strategies for controlling it. In J. M. Williams (Ed.), *Applied sport psychology. Personal growth to peak performance* (6th ed., pp. 336–358). New York, NY: McGraw-Hill.

Chapter 12

SELF-HANDICAPPING

Self-handicapping and sport

As a six-time U.S. champion and four-time world champion, 21-year-old Michelle Kwan was the favorite for the gold medal in women's figure skating at the 2002 Winter Olympics in Salt Lake City, Utah. A scant five months prior to these Olympic Games, Kwan fired her highly regarded longtime skating coach, Frank Carroll. In a move widely interpreted as desperation, if not outright insanity (Starr, 2002a), Kwan trained and competed without a coach, an endeavor unprecedented in Olympic competition. Elite coaches are instrumental in supervising the training of skaters, organizing their skating programs, and in advancing the interests of their skaters with judges and other officials in backroom wheeling-dealing. After firing Carroll, she was accompanied only by her father, described as a cheerleader but without technical knowledge of elite figure skating.

With reasoning that was described as "dreamy" and "New Age," Kwan maintained that this solo act was motivated by a desire to "listen to the voice inside of me" and "take control of my life" (Howard, 2002a). This reasoning was questioned in the sporting press, with suggestions that fears of failure were behind this move that appeared to make success less likely or at least more difficult. More specifically, it was described as "a move by a worried woman locked in a quixotic chase that's ended with her falling short of gold once before" (Howard, 2002a).

In 2002, Kwan led the Olympic women's figure skating competition after the short program or the first day of competition, and it appeared as if she would fulfill expectations as the Olympic favorite. Despite skating a conservative program without the technical difficulty of her closest competitors, Kwan could not muster a critical triple-triple jump, and "doubled" the second jump by landing on two rather than one blade (Starr, 2002b). She later put a hand to the ice to avoid falling on a triple flip. She finished third and won the bronze medal.

If competing without a coach represented a form of self-handicapping, it did not "work" or was not successful in excusing her below-par Olympic performance in the eyes of others. In the sporting press, her performance was seen as an example of "her self-inflicted history of Olympic mishaps—nearly all of them brought on by a lack of guts" (Howard, 2002b).

Kwan hired Scott Williams as her coach in September 2002 (Hine, 2003a). She won her seventh U.S. Figure Skating Championship in January 2003 (Hine, 2003b), and her fifth world championship in March 2003 (Hine, 2003c). By 2005, she won a record-tying nine U.S. Figure Skating Championships (Associated Press, 2005, January 16).

The gold medal winner, 16-year-old Sarah Hughes, went to the 2002 Olympics with her coach Robin Wagner. The two became particularly close in 1999 when Hughes's mother was receiving treatment for breast cancer, and Wagner was described as a best friend and second mother (Starr, 2002b). Six times weekly, the two would drive 90 minutes to practice from Hughes's home on Long Island, New York to an ice rink in Hackensack, New Jersey.

Hughes was in fourth place after the first day and short program of Olympic competition. Working with Wagner, Hughes boldly changed the final 90 seconds, or last third, of her long program to ratchet up its technical difficulty and artistic merit. A second triple-triple jump combination was added and a triple jump was fit in at the end to provide a bigger finish. On the day of the long program, Wagner kept her skater to her normal routine of morning practice, lunch, light walking, afternoon nap, and a snack prior to competition. Hughes slept in her good-luck Peggy Fleming (former Olympic champion figure skater) pajamas. In preparing for the Olympics, Wagner oversaw every detail of preparation, including custom skates, skating outfits, coiffure, and even the sharpening of Hughes's skates. "Team Hughes" won out.

SELF-HANDICAPPING

Choking under pressure and performance anxiety were examined in the previous chapter and shown to inhibit performance during evaluations and competitions. Sources of performance inhibition that have a negative effect on performance and well-being at times distal and proximal to competitions are described in Chapters 11 through 17.

To this point in this book, the literature presented has rested on the assumption that people are motivated to do their best by the hedonic principle. The basis of the hedonic principle is that human motivation is determined by efforts to maximize pleasure and minimize pain. As described in Chapter 2, the hedonic principle has dominated the understanding of human motivation from the time of the ancient Greeks to the 20th century. It is the basic motivation assumption in psychological theories as diverse as emotion in psychobiology, behavioral psychology, decision making, and social psychology (Higgins, 1997, 2012). The focus of this chapter is self-handicapping, and self-handicapping has the paradoxical effect of making success less likely. A key to understanding this paradoxical behavior is that under some circumstances, people avoid diagnostic information about their own capabilities and talents. They avoid knowing precisely what they are capable of accomplishing at their best, perhaps because they doubt their abilities (Chen, Wu, Kee, Lin, & Shui, 2009; Coudevylle, Ginis, & Famose, 2008; Jones & Berglas, 1978). Indeed, those prone to self-handicapping experience anxiety and cognitive interference after noncontingent success or success that is not due to their efforts and abilities (Thompson, 2004). They are more likely to attribute their success to luck and to doubt the likelihood of future success.

The first of these paradoxical dispositions or tendencies was described in 1978 by Edward Jones and Steven Berglas. They identified people who created or claimed impediments prior to performance that made their success less likely. Since these people performed with handicaps, their failures could be excused and attributed to the handicaps and their successes could be seen as truly extraordinary. This strategy was described as self-handicapping. It had the effect of attributing failure in athletic and academic settings to external, unstable, and specific factors, such as drunkenness, illness, injury, or inadequate practice. Self-handicappers also avoid internal, stable, global, and uncontrollable attributions for failure, such as a lack of talent (Arkin & Oleson, 1998; Greenlees, Jones, Holder, & Thelwell, 2006). Self-handicaps are anticipatory excuses that are presented to obscure the link between performance and ability. Self-handicaps protect people's images of self-competence in the event of poor performances.

Other forms of self-handicapping include reduced effort and academic underachievement, choosing to perform under adverse conditions, and laziness. Symptoms of anxiety, physical illness, and depression (Baumgardner, 1991; Ferrand, Tetard, & Fontayne, 2006) have also been cited as self-handicaps (Riggs, 1992). As explained in Chapter 10, failure provides information about one's competence to the degree that one prepared optimally and attributes failure to internal, stable, and uncontrollable factors. If success occurs despite the presence of handicaps, the self-handicapper can claim and receive additional credit for overcoming obstacles. By imposing handicaps such as a lack of preparation, tasks become more difficult, and failing at a highly difficult task is less damaging to self-esteem than failure on tasks of moderate difficulty.

By avoiding "fair" tests of their competence, self-handicappers defend beliefs in their abilities and bolster their self-esteem at the cost of optimal performance and achievement. Indeed, if success occurs despite the presence of a handicap, performers may not only claim exceptional talent, but others may also concede that the handicapped person possesses exceptional talent. **Acquired handicaps,** such as drunkenness and an actual lack of preparation, serve as an excuse for poor performance and decrease the chances for a successful performance. **Claimed handicaps,** such as anxiety, depression, illness, fatigue, and stress, serve to excuse poor performances but do not necessarily lessen the chances for success. Perhaps a fundamental self-handicap is the claim of being unconcerned about doing one's best in an event or competition that is of critical importance (Kuczka & Treasure, 2005; Tice & Baumeister, 1990).

Application

Self-handicaps make subpar performances more likely. The behavior of self-handicappers suggests that this fact is less motivating than discovering that they are not as talented as they hope to be. Self-handicappers regard talent as fixed and somewhat immutable. This view, and their sensitivity to disappointment, results in the avoidance of practice and study that would increase abilities and talent.

SELF-HANDICAPPING AND SPORT

Jones and Berglas (1978) estimated that self-handicapping was common in sport and athletic venues. Claimed handicaps have been seen as most influential in explaining a lack of adherence to exercise regimens of adults. Handicaps that are routinely claimed to interfere with exercise are difficulties incorporating exercise into daily routines, accessing adequate exercise facilities, and poor health/physical ailments (Shields, Paskevich, & Brawley, 2003).

Competitive athletes both cite and acquire handicaps. Sportspersons cite handicaps, such as a lack of preparation, competing school, work, and family obligations, injuries and illness, and conflicts with teammates and coaches (Maddison & Prapavessis, 2007; Prapavessis, Grove, & Eklund, 2004). Such cited handicaps served to obscure the relationship between an unsuccessful competition and perceived judo ability among nationally ranked male judo players. Further, these athletes perceived greater increments in judo talent after successful matches (Greenlees et al., 2006).

Athletes withdraw effort and acquire handicaps when they avoid optimal practice and training. For example, male college swimmers who were high in trait self-handicapping practiced less than did low self-handicappers, and were rated by their coach as putting less effort into practice before important swim meets (Rhodewalt, Saltzman, & Wittmer, 1984). Professional golfers who competed at the state level and who were high in trait self-handicapping also spent less time practicing than did low self-handicappers before important golf tournaments. High self-handicappers also practiced less on average than did low self-handicappers. With both the swimmers and golfers, the high self-handicappers did not decrease their preparation time prior to important performances, but they did not increase the amount of practice before these performances as much as the low self-handicappers. Sportspersons may acquire handicaps, such as the avoidance of practice, because they lack self-efficacy that they will perform successfully (Coudevylle et al., 2008).

Perhaps the handicaps identified by female and male athletes differ. For example, the disruptions in training and practice identified by late adolescent and young adult, elite male and female athletes who competed in basketball, volleyball, swimming, rowing, wrestling, and track and field were different (Hausenblas & Carron, 1996). Female athletes more frequently cited handicaps related to the sport itself, such as cancelled practices, illness and fatigue, and problems with family and friends. Both females and males frequently cited school commitments as handicaps.

Acquired Handicap?

Pedro Martinez finished second to Barry Zito in the 2002 voting for the Cy Young award as the best pitcher in the American League of American Professional Baseball. As a two-time Cy Young winner, Martinez believed that he deserved the honor in 2002. Martinez claimed that baseball writers made excuses for not giving him the most votes, such as not facing as many tough teams as Zito had. He stated that bias was the real reason for his second-place finish, in that baseball writers did not want to give all of baseball's awards to Dominican players. Martinez also claimed that this bias victimized him in 1999 when he should have received the league's Most Valuable Player award in addition to the Cy Young.

Given Martinez's expectation that writers would search for excuses to support their bias, it is difficult to explain why he delivered a convincing reason for judging his record to be second to that of Zito. After getting his 20th victory on September 22, 2002, and with his team, the Boston Red Sox, having no chance for the playoffs, Martinez declared himself through for the season even before his manager made a decision about his last start. Baseball writers went on record to attribute Martinez's second-place finish to his decision to skip his last start of the season, as well as to Zito's superior season (Heuschkel, 2002). Zito also made all of his 35 starts and compiled a record of 23 wins versus five losses, and an Earned Run Average (ERA) of 2.75. Zito helped his team, the Oakland Athletics, win the American League West, the strongest division. His peers voted Zito as the winner of the Players Choice Award, and *The Sporting News* named him the top pitcher.

AUDIENCE FOR SELF-HANDICAPPING

The audience for self-handicapping is apparently both the self and other people (Prapavessis et al., 2004). That is, self-handicappers do not want to discover and reveal a lack of ability to themselves and to others. Handicapping is probably augmented in the presence of other people, but the public value of handicapping has been considered secondary to its importance in protecting the self-handicapper's own private conception of self-competence.

Self-handicapping "works" or has the desired effects, in so far as self-esteem is preserved following failure and enhanced after success. As explained in previous chapters, self-esteem refers to how well or poorly people regard themselves. Without handicaps, failure is more detrimental to, and success less bolstering of, self-esteem (Feick & Rhodewalt, 1997). This self-esteem protection comes at the cost of achievement in areas such as college grades and physical fitness. Self-handicapping also provides a buffer to negative affect or mood following poor performances (Drexler, Ahrens, & Haaga, 1995). Handicappers even claim altruism when they lessen their chances of success by providing opponents an advantage in competition. Perhaps the self-handicapper limits the sting of underachievement with thoughts of the future successes that will result from the application of their innate talent.

Application

As mentioned throughout this text, a focus on success or failure during competition or practice is a form of cognitive interference. This focus directs attention to the future and away from the moment-to-moment process of sport.

Self-handicapping "works" not only to protect self-esteem, but also to preserve enjoyment (Bailis, 2001; Coudevylle, Ginis, Famose, & Gernigon, 2008) and intrinsic interest in tasks. Intrinsic interest in activities is typically lessened after failure, but not if failure is attributable to handicaps. For example, male college students who handicapped themselves by not availing themselves of practice prior to competitive pinball games performed worse than did those who practiced (Deppe & Harackiewicz, 1996). However, the handicappers responded with a measure of indifference to feedback that they had failed in competition. Failure sapped the enjoyment of those who practiced for the pinball competition and they practiced less for future games. The college students who self-handicapped in many situations involving evaluation or with high dispositional or **trait self-handicappers** stated that they enjoyed and were more absorbed in the pinball games than did the men who seldom self-handicapped. They apparently believed they had little to lose, since failure could be blamed on the handicaps rather than on their ability at pinball. High self-handicappers did indeed blame failure on their lack of practice and were still able to see themselves as "good" pinball players after not practicing and failing. Men who were high in the self-handicapping trait and who practiced prior to the competition did not enjoy the competition. Men with low self-handicapping traits enjoyed the competition more and were more absorbed in the game when they thoroughly prepared and less when they did not practice.

Despite the performer's claim of exceptional talent, success that occurs with the presence of a handicap does not resolve the handicapper's uncertainty about their ability and efficacy. This is because self-handicapping blocks not only the attribution of failure but also of success to internal factors. High self-handicappers experience less happiness, satisfaction, relief from anxiety, and feelings of control as a result of their successes (Thompson & Richardson, 2001). Self-handicappers may want to believe that at some point they can remove the handicap and demonstrate their potential. Perhaps that is why withholding effort and not trying to do one's best is a frequently observed handicap. It can be readily removed and it is not a permanent impediment. Of course, until the impediment is removed and the self-handicapper succeeds in fair competitions, uncertainty persists.

RECOGNITION OF SELF-HANDICAPPING

People who cite handicaps to excuse poor performance may be quite unaware that they engage in a consistent pattern of behavior that both spares them attributions about inadequate abilities and also results in underachievement. At other times, people may be quite aware of their self-handicapping and consciously adopt strategies that will provide viable excuses for poor performances. For example, female college students claimed the handicap of test anxiety to avoid responsibility for poor performances on intelligence tests. However, when test anxiety was discounted as a viable excuse for poor performances, these students simply identified another handicap, a lack of effort (Smith, Snyder, & Handelsman, 1982). Similar results have been demonstrated with high school students (Riggs, 1992).

Self-handicapping is not routinely recognized by others. Others do not hold people as responsible for irresponsible behaviors when they have handicaps such as drunkenness. Just as the handicapper does not attribute failure to a lack of ability, the presence of a handicap convinces outside observers that failures do not reflect inadequate ability. For example, if a runner performs badly at a road race but does not train properly, outside observers are less likely to judge the failure as a reflection of ability. Outside observers generally do not recognize that the self-handicapper is doubtful about his or her abilities and is using a strategy to protect self-esteem. Some observers are impressed that handicapping techniques such as not studying for tests is a reflection of confidence or cockiness. Men are more likely to confuse handicapping with confidence, but self-handicappers spot handicapping in others and do not associate it with confidence or cockiness.

Observers do, however, have less favorable impressions of self-handicappers. If outside observers believe that handicaps are self-imposed, such as inadequate preparation or drunkenness, then the handicapper may be seen as lazy and weak. People who cite self-handicaps that appear to be under their volitional control, such as putting forth little effort in training, are viewed less favorably than are people who present handicaps over which they have less control, such as anxiety (Rhodewalt, Sanbonmatsu, Tschanz, Feick, & Waller, 1995). Another handicap that appears to be outside of the handicapper's control is the pursuit of an extraordinarily difficult goal. Observers do not ascribe negative attributes to handicappers who strive to reach extraordinarily difficult goals.

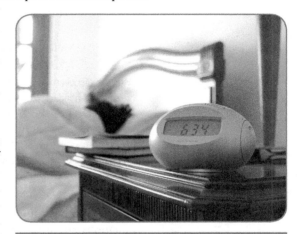

Self-handicapping and inadequate preparation

Observers may be relatively sympathetic to self-handicapping, because it is a way of offering excuses before rather than after performances take place. Excuses for failures that are given after performances receive a less favorable reception if a handicap has not been claimed or imposed prior to the performance (Crant, 1996).

ETIOLOGY OF SELF-HANDICAPPING

Why do people undermine their chances for success? Berglas and Jones (1978) stated that handicapping begins with a hunch that success is uncertain in situations and on tasks. For example, people who suspect that prior successes and accomplishments were not due to their talent and abilities avoid future evaluations, for fear that their suspicions will be confirmed. Male college students who believed that their high scores on intelligence tests were due to luck were more likely to self-handicap prior to taking a second test of intelligence. These students handicapped by taking apparent performance-inhibiting drugs as opposed to performance-enhancing drugs prior to the second test. Self-handicapping is also more likely after success that was not contingent on or the result of a person's effort. Since the person does not understand what they did to achieve this success and doubt that the success can be repeated, they fear another evaluation.

Jones and Berglas (1978) reasoned that self-handicappers somehow believe that love is conditional on performance and ability. They concluded that some children are placed in emotional binds in which their parents expect the demonstration of high ability, yet still do not provide a high degree of warmth and acceptance after ability has been demonstrated. Under these circumstances, the child learns that success does not ensure unconditional love. By withholding effort, they both protect themselves from the demonstration of average or below-average ability, as well as from the realization that unconditional acceptance will not be provided by their parents if they actually demonstrate good ability. Therefore, self-handicapping keeps alive hope that parents will deliver the longed for unconditional love in the future. Under these conditions, it is understandable that fair tests of ability would threaten those prone to self-handicapping.

Application

With the discovery of self-handicapping, what is one to do about it? The unwinding of trait self-handicapping may be complex, as it may originate in relationships with parents during childhood. Self-awareness, insight, and commitment to change are important first steps in changing the handicapping dynamic. Consultation with a psychologist or professional who is knowledgeable about these dynamics may facilitate the resolution of self-handicapping.

It may appear ironic that self-imposed handicaps are more likely when evaluations are most important. However, it is on these tasks that ability is revealed and imagined unconditional love is at risk. Although the self-handicapper has doubts about his or her abilities, by avoiding fair tests they sustain uncertainty about their talent and their likelihood for success.

No Need for Self-Handicaps

The Australian tennis professional Patrick Rafter provided a lesson about how to face the possibility of defeat without being daunted. He was two points from defeat in a match with American Andre Agassi in the semifinals of the 2001 men's championship tennis match at Wimbledon. He recalled his thoughts at that juncture:

> Just give it a go and see what happens. When you walk off, you hold your head up high. Bad luck, gave it my best shot, lost 6-4 in the fifth. Instead, here I am with a big smile on my face (Bricker, 2001, p. C2).

Rafter won the match 2-6, 6-3, 3-6, 6-2, and 8-6.

SELF-ESTEEM AND SELF-HANDICAPPING

Given that a primary motivation for self-handicapping is to protect self-esteem, it is understandable that it occurs when people are faced with evaluations that that are important to their self-image (Martin & Brawley,

2002). For example, college students were more likely to self-handicap when taking tests of verbal intelligence compared to tests of hand-eye coordination and fine motor control (Tice, 1991).

Generally, sportspersons with higher self-esteem make fewer self-handicapping claims, because they have higher self-confidence (Coudevylle, Gernigon, & Ginis, 2011). However, even those with high self-esteem may engage in self-handicapping as a way of **enhancing** their public image and self-image. That is, they engage in self-handicapping as a means of making their successes appear truly outstanding. People with low self-esteem self-handicap to **protect** against the esteem-threatening implications of failure. For example, college students with high self-esteem were more likely to self-handicap by not practicing for tests of verbal intelligence when successful performances were seen to reflect superior ability (Tice, 1991). College students with low self-esteem were more likely to avoid practice for tests of verbal ability when failure was shown to indicate poor aptitude.

Paradoxically, the collegians prepared more optimally when tasks were less important and relevant to their self-esteem. College students with high self-esteem practiced more in preparation for tests of hand-eye coordination and fine motor control when they understood practice to enhance their chances of performing outstandingly. Student with low self-esteem practiced more on the same tasks when they understood practice to lessen their chances of failure.

Over time, self-handicapping contributes to lower self-esteem and to poorer moods and to decreased well-being. Of course, lower self-esteem and performance uncertainty makes self-handicapping more likely and thus a cycle is created in which self-handicapping, poor performance, and decreased self-esteem all become more likely (Zuckerman, Kieffer, & Knee, 1998).

STABILITY OF SELF-ESTEEM AND SELF-HANDICAPPING

Self-esteem is more **stable** in some people than others, and daily successes and failures have a greater influence when self-esteem is unstable. Those with unstable and high self-esteem are more dependent on activities that enhance their image than are those with stable, high self-esteem. People with unstable and low self-esteem are more active in avoiding activities that will confirm their low self-regard than are those with stable, low self-esteem. People with unstable self-esteem are somewhat more likely to self-handicap than are college students with stable self-esteem. When taking nonverbal intelligence tests, college students with unstable, high self-esteem were more likely to self-handicap to enhance the impressiveness of their performance, and students with unstable, low self-esteem were more prone handicap to avoid the embarrassment of failure (Newman & Wadas, 1997).

TRAIT SELF-HANDICAPPING AND SELF-ESTEEM

Self-handicapping is also more stable in some people than in others, and trait self-handicapping refers to a disposition to handicap in different situations and over time (Rhodewalt, Morf, Hazlett, & Fairfield, 1991). For example, French athletes with trait self-handicapping claimed handicaps before tests of athletic ability in both high and low ego-threatening conditions. In the high ego-threatening condition, the test was described as a measure of physical abilities. Their counterparts with low trait self-handicapping claimed handicaps only in the high ego-threatening condition. Athletes with low self-esteem were also more likely to claim handicaps in both the high and low ego-threatening conditions (Finez, Berjot, Rosnet, & Cleveland, 2011). With both high self-esteem and high trait self-handicapping, people are more likely to invent handicaps to enhance attributions about ability. Low self-esteem and high trait self-handicapping increase the likelihood of creating handicaps to avoid attributing failure to ability (Rhodewalt, More, Hazlett, & Fairfield, 1991).

Highly skilled male golfers who frequently engage in self-handicapping were shown to have lower self-esteem (Prapavessis & Grove, 1998). Perhaps the self-handicappers were more uncertain about the outcome of tournaments. Of course, the question of whether athletes and performers with high self-esteem claim or acquire handicaps to enhance the impressiveness of performances would be of interest, especially among elite athletes.

People with low self-esteem who seldom handicap may attribute failure to inadequate ability, and thus further decrease their self-esteem. This attributional style resembles the style of people with depression, in that negative outcomes are ascribed to stable, internal factors, and positive outcomes to external, unstable factors.

GENDER AND SELF-HANDICAPPING

There has been a debate about whether men and women are equally likely to **acquire** handicaps. For example, preliminary research demonstrated that both women and men who characteristically self-handicapped claimed stress as a handicap for poor performance, but only men avoided extra practice when they were informed that practice would improve their chances for success (Hirt, Deppe, & Gordon, 1991). It was reasoned that these gender differences were due to socialization practices. That is, failure in boys tends to be attributed to a lack of effort, whereas failure in girls is attributed to a lack of ability. Therefore, effort withdrawal may not "work" as an effective excuse for poor performance in females, since their failure is already more likely to be attributed to a lack of ability. If effort withdrawal is not considered a reasonable excuse for failure, women would be better off practicing as much as possible to improve their chances for success.

Another explanation for the gender difference in acquired versus claimed handicaps is that certain handicaps simply involve behaviors that are more common in males. For example, in the initial studies of self-handicapping, men were shown to more frequently acquire the handicap of debilitating drug use (Berglas & Jones, 1978). Substance use and abuse is far more common in males than in females (Kessler et al., 1994).

Gender does not generally influence the **number** of claimed handicaps or the attributional benefits of the claimed excuses. For example, both college women and men claimed handicaps such as having a heavy course load, sickness, lack of sleep, having other exams for which to study, and having studied the wrong material prior to taking college tests. With handicaps, both males and females discounted failure as reflective of their ability, and claimed extra talent when they performed well with handicaps (Feick & Rhodewalt, 1997).

The differences between genders with regard to claimed versus acquired handicaps may be **historical**. Recent research demonstrated that when men and women who were high in trait self-handicapping were given the opportunity to both claim stress and to acquire a handicap by avoiding practice, both the women and men selected the claimed handicap (Thompson & Richardson, 2001). These high self-handicappers availed themselves of an excuse for poor performance but did little to sabotage their chances for success, as they practiced as much as the low self-handicappers for the evaluations. The claimed handicap appeared to have all of the "benefits" of the acquired handicap, in that it excused failure. In addition, the claimed handicap did not disrupt performance and, therefore, offered the additional benefit of enhancing attributions about talent when they performed well. Perhaps women and men would more readily acquire handicaps if they sensed that claimed handicaps would not "play well" or be believable to skeptical audiences. Other recent research demonstrated that male basketball players even claimed more handicaps than did their female counterparts in ego-involving motivational climates (Coudevylle et al., 2009).

Perhaps most generally, there are likely no gender differences in claimed, situational self-handicaps when competitions are equally important or ego relevant to female and male athletes. For example, prior to a prestigious national intercollegiate NCAA Division I golf tournament, the number of claimed situational handicaps was essentially equivalent for male and female golfers (Kuczka & Treasure, 2005).

SELF-HANDICAPPING AND GOALS

Self-handicappers tend to regard characteristics such as athletic and academic ability as **fixed** and **immutable entities** (Ommundsen, Haugen & Lund, 2005). Failure is seen to be highly threatening, because it is seen to reveal permanent deficiencies in academic (Covington, 1992; Midgley, Arunkumar, & Urdan, 1996) or athletic talent (Ommundsen, 2001).

Despite histories of exceptional achievement, self-handicappers are inclined to doubt their ability on the basis on one unambiguous failure or one failure that cannot be attributed to handicaps. On the other hand, this understanding occurs quite early, as ninth-grade physical education students in Norway (Ommundsen, 2001) and American eighth-graders (Midgley, Arunkumar, & Urdan, 1996) who viewed abilities as fixed were prone to self-handicapping, especially when they doubted their abilities.

Self-handicappers are also more likely to pursue other-referenced goals (see Chapter 9), such as **performance, ego**, or **performance-avoidance** goals, which focus on the demonstration of competence in comparison to others (Midgley, Arunkumar, & Urdan, 1996; Rhodewalt, 1994). They are also more likely to endorse **mastery-avoidance goals** (Chen et al., 2009). By contrast, people with **mastery-approach, learning**, or **task** goal orientations (the three refer to similar goal orientations) to achievement regard ability as a mutable characteristic that is built by their efforts to develop and refine their skills (Dweck & Leggett, 1988). With mastery or learning goals, people are more prone to strive for incremental development of their skills in relation to their own baseline of prior performance. Failure is less threatening with these orientations, because deficits are understood to be subject to remediation. For example, failure might indicate that additional training and practice are necessary to master aspects of a particular element in sport performance. Given that failure denotes inadequate effort rather than inadequate ability, people with mastery goal orientations are not particularly vulnerable to threats to their self-worth, and are, therefore, less likely to self-handicap (Martin, Marsh, & Debus, 2001; Thill & Cury, 2000). With mastery or task orientation, people are less likely to have negative expectations about performance, and to spend more time and effort reflecting on or thinking about what needed to be done to prepare optimally for performances.

Self-handicapping was more prevalent among boys and girls between the ages of 10 and 17 who played recreational and competitive soccer when the children had performance goals and played on teams in which children were commonly compared to each other (Ryska & Yin, 1999). The children with performance goals were prone to using self-handicapping strategies, such as making excuses and effort reduction, as protection from threatening attributions about their abilities. Children are particularly likely to engage in self-handicapping in classrooms and gymnasiums (Standage, Treasure, Hooper, & Kuczka, 2007; Urdan, Midgley, & Anderman, 1998) in which there is an emphasis on performance relative to others. Intercollegiate athletes are also more likely to self-handicap when their performance is frequently compared to teammates (Kuczka & Treasure, 2005).

Examining performance goals more closely, physical education students with **performance-avoidance goals** were likely to endorse self-handicapping, whereas **performance-approach goals** and task orientations were not associated with self-handicapping (Ommundsen, 2004). Seventh-graders with performance-avoidance goals were also prone to self-handicapping (Midgley & Urdan, 2001). Physical education students between the ages of 11 and 13 with performance-avoidance orientations were more likely to acquire and claim handicaps prior to assessments of their basketball dribbling competence (Elliot, Cury, Fryer, & Huguet, 2006). They acquired handicaps by avoiding practice, and claimed handicaps by minimizing the importance of the basketball evaluation, and both handicaps eroded actual performance.

Performance-approach goals refer to the attainment of competence in relation to norms or to other people, and performance-avoidance goals refer to orientations to avoid demonstrating incompetence in relation to norms or in the eyes of others (Elliot, 1999). With mastery or task and performance-approach orientations, people strive to grasp possibilities. With both performance-approach and performance-avoidance orientations, success is measured in relation to others. However, with performance-avoidance goals success involves avoiding mistakes and failures and dodging blunders. The distal, underlying motive disposition of those with mastery goals is solely the motive for achievement and that for people with performance-avoidance goals is the motive for avoiding failure (Atkinson, 1957; 1964). The underlying motives for people with performance-approach goals are both the motive for achievement and for avoiding failure (Elliot & Harackiewicz, 1996).

Norwegian male and female tenth-grade physical education students who endorsed performance-approach and task orientations also considered themselves to be competent at athletics (Ommundsen, 2004). With expectations of competence, there was less endorsement of self-handicapping or strategies to excuse athletic inadequacies. Additionally, when the tenth-graders held task orientations in combination with either performance-approach or performance-avoidance goals, they were less likely to acknowledge self-handicapping. Apparently, the emotional valence of efforts to avoid failure (as with performance-avoidance goals) is countered by the positive emotional valence associated with striving for success and with intrinsic interest in athletic tasks.

SELF-HANDICAPPING AND COPING

People who engage in self-handicapping have been seen to engage in **emotion-focused coping** (Lazarus & Folkman, 1994). As discussed in Chapter 4, emotion-focused coping consists of managing emotional responses to stressors such as competitions and evaluations, and **problem-focused coping** involves taking action to master or resolve the source of stress. College students with high dispositional or trait self-handicapping demonstrated emotion-focused coping prior to tests and evaluations (Zuckerman et al., 1998). Their emotion-based coping strategies consisted of withdrawing from the challenge of preparing optimally for examinations. They studied less and were less efficient in studying for tests.

Emotion-focused coping may temporarily ease the stress of evaluations and soothe the sting of poor performances. This soothing comes at the cost of lower achievement (Martin et al., 2001; Zuckerman et al., 1998). Further, emotion-focused coping does not spare people from ruminations or intrusive and repetitive thoughts about poor performances. Perhaps difficulties in accepting the consequences of performances motivated their involvement in self-handicapping. That is, if people with high dispositional self-handicapping cannot accept and move on after performances, having excuses for poor performances may make their ruminations about poor performances less painful.

Australian athletes who were prone to self-handicapping were also more likely to use emotion-focused coping when experiencing slumps or prolonged periods of poor performance (Prapavessis, Grove, Maddison, & Zillmann, 2003). As was the case for college students, emotion-focused coping may promote disengagement from active problem solving and prolong slumps. Self-handicapping tendencies did not spare recreational and elite athletes from the experience of cognitive and somatic anxiety prior to competitions, and self-handicapping tendencies were also associated with lower self-esteem.

TEAM COHESIVENESS AND SELF-HANDICAPPING

Athletes who are high in trait self-handicapping are more likely to claim handicaps when they are members of cohesive teams. Female and male athletes high in the trait of excuse making rated disruptions in training and practice schedules disruptions as unimportant when team cohesion was low, but as highly disruptive when the team cohesion was high (Carron, Prapavessis, & Grove, 1994). Athletes who were low on the self-handicapping trait of excuse making rated disruptions to practice and training as trivial regardless of whether team cohesion was low or high. Perhaps cohesiveness provides reassurance that claimed self-handicaps will be received sympathetically. Alternatively, athletes may experience more responsibility to the group and cite handicaps to excuse disappointing the cohesive team.

SUMMARY AND APPLICATION

The literature about self-handicapping demonstrates that some people will go to considerable lengths to avoid diagnostic information about their own capabilities and talents and a precise understanding of what they are capable of accomplishing at their best. Self-handicappers have an accurate, naïve understanding that failure under ideal conditions is highly diagnostic about their abilities. With self-handicaps, they forward anticipatory excuses that obscure the link between performance and internal and stable attributions about their ability. The benefits of claimed or acquired handicaps are the protection of self-esteem, mood, and intrinsic interest in tasks. These benefits are realized at the price of lower achievement. Self-handicappers preserve faith in their potential ability but are unlikely to be entirely free of self-doubts, because they have not actually demonstrated this ability. As discussed in Chapter 10, the most convincing source of self-efficacy is enactive attainments or actual successful performance. Other people generally do not recognize the defensive qualities of self-handicapping, and may even consider it to reflect cockiness. Other people do not attribute poor performance to insufficient ability in the self-handicapper, but are likely to attribute unfavorable qualities to the handicapper, such as laziness, if the handicaps are self-imposed.

At times, the motivation for self-handicapping is not to breach the connection between performance and ability, but rather to enhance the impressiveness of accomplishments. People with high self-esteem are more likely to self-handicap to embellish their achievements and attributions about their abilities.

Failure is more threatening if ability is considered to be innately determined and immutable, and people with performance or ego goals often hold this view of talent. People with this goal orientation are at risk for self-handicapping because task difficulty signals inadequate ability. By withdrawing effort, or engaging in some other form of self-handicapping, those with performance goals attempt to break the link between performance and ability and avoid attributions that their innate or genetic talent is puny. With performance-avoidance goals, self-handicapping is especially likely because these goals focus attention on avoiding failure. With learning, mastery, or task goals, ability is considered to be acquired and success to be a result of effort. Stubborn problems are expected to yield to persistent effort. Since failure is considered to be subject to remediation, it is far less threatening. Success is marked in relation to one's baseline of prior performance, and therefore improvement and effort are more likely to be counted as successes, and these successes can enhance confidence in one's abilities.

Self-handicapping allows for the avoidance of unfavorable attributions about one's ability. Of course, competitions, performances, evaluations, and occasional failure cannot be avoided. Guilt occurs when poor performance results from minimal effort, whereas humiliation is experienced when failure occurs despite putting forth one's best efforts (Covington, 1992; Thompson & Dinnel, 2007). Despite the prospects for guilt and underachievement, self-handicappers accept these outcomes rather than diagnostic information about their ability. Self-handicappers may be counseled about the possibility of an alternative interpretation of failure: inappropriate strategy. This offers an attribution for failure that is internal, unstable, and controllable, and is more likely to enhance self-efficacy and intrinsic interest. Ultimately, it is necessary to remove self-handicaps to realize one's full potential. The systematic application of the principles described in Chapters 4 through 10 serve to inhibit self-handicapping. As discussed in this chapter, self-handicapping is less likely with the adoption of mastery or performance-achievement goals and the relinquishing of performance-avoidance goals.

If Jones and Berglas's (1978) explanation for the etiology of self-handicapping is accurate, then the renunciation of archaic wishes for unconditional parental love and prizing with extraordinary success may be necessary. This process of relinquishing the unfinished business of childhood may be difficult because it implies going on with life without capturing coveted parental supplies of unconditional love, and it may be necessary to consult sophisticated counselors and therapists to resolve resistance to this process. However, with both self-handicapping and procrastination, which will be discussed in the next chapter, action is not taken and opportunities are lost. Squandered and lost opportunities are regretted most with the passage of time (Gilovich & Medvec, 1995).

Key Terms

Acquired handicaps   281

Claimed handicaps   281

Trait self-handicapping   283

Stability of self-esteem   287

Stability of self-handicapping   287

Acquire hardships

Number   289

Historical   289

Fixed and immutable entities   289

Performance, ego, and performance avoidance goals   290

Mastery-avoidance goals   290

Mastery-approach, learning, task   290

Performance-avoidance goals   290

Performance-approach goals   290

Emotion-focused coping   291

Problem-focused coping   291

Discussion Questions

Q1.   Review acquired and claimed self-handicaps.
Q2.   Consider handicaps that are claimed and acquired in sport.
Q3.   What is the audience for self-handicapping?
Q4.   Does self-handicapping "work"?
Q5.   Is self-handicapping recognized?
Q6.   Review the etiology of self-handicapping.
Q7.   Consider the motivation for self-handicapping for sportspersons with high versus low self-esteem.
Q8.   Evaluate self-handicapping among athletes with trait self-handicapping.
Q9.   Does self-handicapping differ by gender?
Q10. Explain why failure is so threatening to self-handicappers.
Q11. Review the goal orientations of self-handicappers.
Q12. Consider the coping strategies of self-handicappers.
Q13. Does team cohesiveness influence self-handicapping?

Suggested Readings

Berglas, S., & Jones, E. E. (1978). Drug choice as a self-handicapping strategy in response to noncontingent success. *Journal of Personality and Social Psychology, 36,* 405–417.

Ommundsen, Y. (2004). Self-handicapping related to task and performance-approach and avoidance goals in physical education. *Journal of Applied Sport Psychology, 16,* 183–197.

Prapavessis, H., Grove, J. R., Maddison, R., & Zillmann, N. (2003). Self-handicapping tendencies, coping, and anxiety responses among athletes. *Psychology of Sport and Exercise, 4,* 357–375.

Ryska, R. A., & Yin, Z. (1999). The role of dispositional goal orientation and team climate on situational self-handicapping among young athletes. *Journal of Sport Behavior, 22,* 410–425.

Thompson, T., & Richardson, A. (2001) Self-handicapping status, claimed self-handicaps and reduced practice effort following success and failure feedback. *British Journal of Educational Psychology, 71,* 151–170.

Chapter 13

PROCRASTINATION AND PERFECTIONISM

Herb decided that he would reach his goal of bench pressing 225 pounds for 12 repetitions during the summer before his senior year in high school. He was also determined to start the wrestling season at 147 pounds and to be first in his weight class. Since he could only press 155 pounds for 12 repetitions, he knew he had to get busy. He took advantage of a Memorial Day sale and purchased four new 45 pound plates, which he neatly arranged in his basement with the other weights. He decided that he did not want to do a "half-way" job of weight training, so planned to delay weight training until school ended on June 22. After all, the body builders in "Muscle and Fitness" trained for at least six hours per day. Just when he was ready to start, he remembered that his family was going to the beach for the 4th of July week. "Oh well," he reasoned, he still would have a good seven weeks of summer after that week.

Procrastination and inadequate preparation

In July, Herb was offered a landscaping job at which he would earn $10 per hour. He could work 10-hour days and save quite a bit of money. He remembered his goals for weight training, but figured the manual labor would also be a good form of training. Besides, he read an article in "Popular Psychology Journal" that said that athletes should not be too perfectionistic or else they will burn out. He convinced himself that he would know the right time to start training if he adopted an "Eastern philosophy" of "letting the weights come to him."

As August approached, the weights had still "not come" to Herb, and he began avoiding the basement and a visual sighting of his weight bench. At the preseason meeting for the wrestling team, Herb weighed in at 162 pounds. He wondered if the extra weight would contribute to his bench press.

As described in Chapter 12, procrastination with regard to studying was identified as the most prevalent form of self-handicapping among students. It is a form of withholding effort, and is also prevalent among sportspersons. As an acquired handicap, it not only obscures the link between performance and ability but also erodes actual performance and achievement. Procrastinators are also at risk for acquiring and claiming other handicaps. Procrastination and other forms of self-handicapping are more likely to occur when facing tasks that threaten self-esteem, such as such as competitions and tests (Ferrari & Tice, 2000). Procrastination involves a unique form of self-handicapping, in that it extends over a period of time, and compromises optimal preparation at times both distal and proximal to performances and competitions. Given that optimal athletic performance typically requires discrete periods of overtraining and tapering, procrastination may be especially disruptive to sportspersons (Raglin & Wilson, 2000). It may, therefore, be surprising that it has been studied less extensively than have other forms of self-handicapping in sport venues. The review of procrastination in this chapter will be brief and focus on its etiology and theoretical similarities with perfectionism.

The term **procrastination** is derived from the Latin verb *procrastinare*, which is defined as putting off, or postponing until another day (DeSimone, 1993). It has been described as an irrational tendency to delay tasks that require completion. Procrastination may occur when tasks are considered important but unattractive. The unattractive tasks are avoided in favor of more enjoyable activities. Interest in overcoming procrastination is due to the long-term rewards that will follow the execution of aversive or unattractive actions or work.

Procrastination has been a concern in modern times and in technologically advanced countries where timeliness and punctuality is emphasized. Approximately 20% to 30% of college students identified themselves as "problem procrastinators," in that postponing tasks decreased both their academic achievement and enjoyment of life. Among adults in the general population, 25% acknowledged that procrastination was a significant problem and 40% allowed that procrastination caused them financial loss during the past year. Procrastination is most prevalent at approximately ages 20 to 25 for women and men, respectively, in the general population (Ferrari, Johnson, & McCown, 1995). Forms of frequent or chronic procrastination are referred to as **trait procrastination**.

COSTS OF PROCRASTINATION

It is not uncommon for procrastinators to discount the costs of their dawdling. For example, some procrastinators say that they do their best work under the pressure of deadlines, and that when squeezed by deadlines they experience excitement. They might also argue that by delaying the start of work projects, they preserve leisure time and increase their quality of life. This view that dawdling is adaptive or at least not harmful does not withstand scientific scrutiny (Steel, Brother, & Wambach, 2001). College student procrastinators receive lower grades on term papers and on exams (Tice & Baumeister, 1997) and experience higher levels of worry about tests (Flett, Blankstein, & Martin, 1995). During the early portions of college semesters, procrastinators experience lower levels of stress and have fewer physical illnesses and problems, perhaps because they avoid the stress of preparing for classes. However, at the end of the semester and in total, procrastinators reported more physical symptoms, experienced more stress, and made more visits to health-care professionals than non-procrastinators (Tice & Baumeister, 1997).

Collegiate sport administrators reported experiencing guilt when procrastinating, perhaps because they also associated procrastination with laziness, lack of confidence, and poor time management skills (Parsons & Soucie, 1988). These administrators also attributed procrastination to institutional problems, such as having too much work and too little direction.

It is even more difficult to rationalize procrastination as beneficial to athletic training. Athletic and mental skills are often developed incrementally and maintained through regular practice. As described in Chapter 5, extensive and regular practice is necessary for athletic skills to become autonomous or capable of execution with little conscious attention and regulation. Skills and fitness also develop over time with the systematic management of overtraining, staleness, and tapering (Kentta, Hassmen, & Raglin, 2006; Raglin & Wilson, 2000). Delays in the initiation or maintenance of athletic training cannot be remediated with feverish last-minute preparations.

PROCRASTINATION AND COPING

Procrastination is associated with more stress in the form of daily hassles or problems and annoyances, depression, negative self-concepts, and lower self-esteem and self-efficacy (Lay, 1995). Because of their tendency to avoid the sources of stress in their lives, procrastinators use coping strategies that are far less effective in mastering the sources of stress. Procrastination involves an **emotion-focused coping** response to the stress of accomplishing a difficult or unpleasant assignment (Lazarus & Folkman, 1984). As mentioned above, these avoidance behaviors serve the short-term purpose of reducing anxiety but incur considerable long-term costs. When procrastinating, it is sometimes difficult for people to completely rid their mind of thoughts about what they are avoiding or what they should be doing. They live with the knowledge that adverse consequences loom and they do not control aversive stimuli, such as deadlines. Like the self-handicapper, procrastinators live with pervasive and consistent doubts about their ability.

Martina Navratilova Was a Procrastinator

Or maybe you're a born procrastinator. Okay, I'll admit it, so am I—or I was. Procrastination is an old habit that many times in my life kept winning out. I'd let problems slide and slide, mostly because I needed shelter from them when I was playing tennis. Conflict, for example—I tried to avoid it at all costs. I would just let things build, and they'd get worse. But just imagine what might happen if you let your health slide. Who wants to hear a doctor say, "If you don't stop smoking, you'll be dead in 6 months," or, "If you don't stop drinking, your liver will give out in 2 years"? Don't let things deteriorate into a life-or-death situation. Please! I learned to deal with problems head on, and sooner rather than later. You can as well (Navratilova, 2006, p. 13).

Procrastinators also live with disappointment about lost opportunities and regret how they waste time. This regret does not typically teach people to stop procrastinating. Instead, people try to avoid future experiences of regret, and therefore demonstrate even greater avoidance of the challenges in the future (Van Eerde, 2000).

As has been mentioned at several points in this book, **task-focused coping** strategies are, effective in reducing the effects of stressors that must be faced and mastered. Task-focused coping refers to rational preparation and responses to stressors, such as the use of the strategies for optimizing performance that were discussed in Chapters 4 through 10.

THEORETICAL AND SCIENTIFIC EXPLANATIONS FOR PROCRASTINATION

Psychoanalytic

Procrastination has been explained in the contexts of some of the most influential paradigms in psychology. The **psychoanalytic** paradigm began with Sigmund Freud and was introduced in Chapter 2. In Freud's model of the psyche, the Ego conducted executive functions, such as the detection of anxiety. The Ego employs a variety of methods for reducing anxiety, and these include intrapsychic defenses, which push the causes of anxiety out of conscious awareness. For example, thoughts that cause anxiety are repressed and tasks that cause anxiety are avoided by procrastination. Although difficult to validate empirically, the psychoanalytic perspective has fostered research. For example, procrastination has been seen to reflect an unconscious preoccupation with death, in that tardiness reflects an attempt to put off death until a later date (Blatt & Quinlan, 1967).

Psychodynamic

From a **psychodynamic** perspective, procrastination is understood to be a result of childrearing practices. For example, parents of procrastinators have been shown to make love and approval contingent on achievement, to set unrealistically high goals for their children, and to be overly coercive in emphasizing achievement. As described earlier in context with self-handicapping, these experiences place the child, and later the adult, in a bind that encourages procrastination. Task avoidance allows for avoidance of anxiety related to fear of failing to achieve the lofty goals and also keeps alive hope of obtaining parental love in the future. Excessive parental coercion also fosters **reactance**, or efforts to reestablish autonomy and independence, and dawdling demonstrates that the child will not be pushed at the parents' schedule.

Children who are involved in struggles about achievement with parents may also procrastinate as a passive aggressive way of expressing anger at the parents. Passive aggressive behaviors typically frustrate and anger the other person without a direct display of aggression. There is a certain naïve genius to procrastination in response to an authoritarian parent who pushes for the accomplishment of unrealistic goals. There are probably few other responses available to the child that would cause equal frustration to the parent and also sustain the parents' belief in the child's abilities. College students with trait procrastination report conflict with not only their parents but also with best friends of the same sex (Ferrari, Harriott, & Zimmerman, 1999).

Developmental Psychology

A related explanation from **developmental psychology** regards procrastination as originating in a context of high levels of parental criticism and expectations. These parents may respond with harsh criticism when their children fail to meet their expectations. Given all the learning that occurs throughout development, there are practically unlimited opportunities for authoritarian parents to see their children as falling short. Children form primary attachments to these critical parents, and must accommodate their behavior and manners of viewing themselves and others to fit these relations or attachments to their parents. These children may, therefore, come to judge themselves in overly harsh and critical ways, and expect the same judgments from people outside of their family of origin. Expecting harsh judgments, these children are less likely to turn to others when they need help, and more likely to compare their performance to that of others in achievement contexts (Flett, Blankstein, & Martin, 1995). These children often compare their academic or athletic ability to their most capable peers, and feel dumb or clumsy in comparison. Children escape from these negative social comparisons by avoiding competitions and evaluations, and one form of this avoidance is procrastination.

An assumption of the psychoanalytic and psychodynamic perspectives is that procrastination is a trait or characteristic that appears consistently over time and across situations. This assumption is almost certainly correct. Empirical research has demonstrated that trait procrastination can be reliably and validly measured (Lay, 1986; McCown & Johnson, 1989), and that these measures of procrastination predict tardiness in completing assignments across settings (Tice & Baumeister, 1997).

Behaviorism

The psychological perspective that is perhaps the most theoretically opposed to psychoanalytic and psychodynamic paradigms is **behaviorism**. Behavioral psychologists have also reported that people procrastinate prior to initiating and completing tasks that are unpleasant, difficult, or boring. Such tasks are often put aside in favor of activities that appear to have more immediate rewards and fewer aversive characteristics. People procrastinate when faced with such tasks because it is often difficult for them to sustain effort until these tasks are completed. If difficult and boring tasks are to be completed, people must inhibit interference from competing thoughts and activities. Similarly, when frustrated, it is necessary to inhibit behaviors that are more rewarding and less frustrating. Sometimes people are frustrated and resentful when others impose tasks and jobs on them. With resentment, people may procrastinate as a means of reacting against the imposition of duties by others (Blunt & Psychl, 2000).

From a behavioral paradigm, a key to overcoming the tendency to avoid the difficult and seek the easy tasks is to follow **Grandma's Law** or, "First clean up your plate, then you may have your dessert" (Homme, 1970, p. 17). Applying Grandma's Law to academic venues, students would be advised to study first and play later. Athletes will be far more successful if they practice or train first and relax afterwards. Continuing with the analogy, procrastinating athletes and students may be as likely to do their work after "goofing off" as the grandchildren are to eat broccoli after ice cream.

Fear of Failure

Another explanation for procrastination that is consistent with behavioral paradigms is that procrastination is a result of **fears of failure**. For example, students who fear failing on tests avoid the stimulus for their fear, the test, by procrastinating. By avoiding the stimulus for their fear, anxiety is reduced. Despite the intuitive appeal of this explanation, empirical studies demonstrate that only a minority of procrastination is due to fears of failure (Schouwenburg, 1995).

Cognitive Psychology

Cognitive psychology examines the beliefs that lead to procrastination. From this perspective, procrastinators often hold unreasonably high standards for their performance (Ferrari et al., 1995). This perspective is consistent with the discussion of self-handicapping in Chapter 12, in that by withdrawing effort and delaying the initiation of tasks, individuals provide themselves with excuses for not reaching their extreme standards for performance. This perspective is also consistent with a discussion of perfectionism that will follow, as perfection is the highest goal for a performance.

Personality Traits and Procrastination

There are a number of personality traits associated with procrastination. Procrastinators often show low levels of conscientiousness, and **conscientiousness** and procrastination are negatively correlated for children as young as 8 years old (Lay, Kovacs, & Danto, 1998). With low levels of conscientiousness, people lack self-discipline, dutifulness, achievement striving, orderliness, and strong commitments to reach their goals. Procrastinators underestimate that amount of time necessary to complete assignments. Trait **neuroticism** also appears to be higher among procrastinators.

Neuroticism refers to as depression, self-consciousness, impulsiveness, anxiety, somatic concerns, and social discomfort. The influence of neuroticism has been more equivocal than that of conscientiousness (Steel et al., 2001).

PROCRASTINATION AND SELF-ESTEEM

The self-esteem of procrastinators is lower than average, and, therefore, more easily threatened. Like self-handicappers, procrastinators avoid fair tests of their ability and prefer to work on easy, unchallenging tasks. Because of their difficulty in starting and finishing tasks, they live with any number of unfulfilled ambitions, intentions, and dreams. For procrastinators, it is sometimes preferable to do nothing than to risk failure and look foolish (Ferrari & Tice, 2000). As was true for self-handicappers, procrastinators protect their self-esteem at the cost of underachievement, unrealized goals, and wasted potential. Perhaps ruminations about "what might have been" sustain hope in abilities, but again this comes at the considerable cost of regret regarding lost and squandered opportunities.

Application

Theoretical explanations and insight notwithstanding, readers may not be able to resist procrastination. For example, a student may find the prospect of studying for a test so unpleasant or anxiety-arousing that they cannot practice "Grandma's Rule." That is, no reinforcer is sufficiently potent to elicit the operant of productive study.

In these circumstances, students may need additional help—perhaps a study partner. The procrastinator might commit to outline chapters from textbooks and share the outlined material with the study partner on a regular basis and well before deadlines. This process might redirect attention away from internal dynamics and anxieties and to the interpersonal obligation.

SUMMARY AND APPLICATION

Procrastinators avoid the stress, anxiety, and work of challenges during times that are distal to evaluations and performances. Since they do not prepare optimally during times that are distal and moderately distal to evaluations, they perform more poorly and underachieve. After evaluations, they are left with disappointment and ruminations about lost opportunities. The cumulative effects of procrastination are lower self-esteem and self-efficacy and higher risks for depression. At times proximal to evaluations, stress, anxiety, and somatic or physical symptoms accelerate and become intrusive, as procrastinators can no longer avoid and deny the impeding evaluation and their lack of preparation.

In reviewing the factors that inhibit optimal performance, two themes will persist. First, the conscientious practice of the techniques for optimal proximal and distal preparation competes with and counteracts the inhibiting factors. The preparation of procrastinators for performances is faulty at times distal and proximal to evaluations. It is likely necessary to identify optimal but realistic challenges, and to be systematic in establishing timetables for accomplishing goals and subgoals. Competing goals may be prioritized so that procrastination is recognized when time is given to or wasted on tasks that are not of a high priority. It is often important to schedule adequate chunks of time to muster the concentration necessary to accomplish difficult subgoals. Intrinsic interest in tasks can be strengthened and boredom decreased when efficacy for the accomplishment of the task is increased. Almost any task can be interesting or rewarding if one is good at it. Efficacy builds with the experience of successfully realizing goals.

The second theme that will be present in many reviews of the factors that inhibit performance is that in some instances, it will be necessary to consult mentors who are knowledgeable about these issues for advice, coaching, guidance, counseling, or therapy. This process of gaining help from others may be accomplished with formal or informal mentoring relationships. Formal mentoring relationships often occur with recognized professionals, such as coaches, teachers, and psychologists.

PERFECTIONISM

Urban Meyer III won his first national championship as the head coach of the University of Florida football team in 2006. It was particularly poignant because his team defeated Ohio State University, the team he had "worshipped" throughout his childhood in Ashtabula, Ohio. Meyer accomplished this at age 42, in just his sixth year as a head coach.

Meyer's father, Urban "Bud" Meyer Jr., was waiting for him on the sidelines after the game. His father commented: "Well, it's about time you did that" (Price, 2009, p. 137).

Meyer described his father's expectations as "almost unachievable." The Meyer children were expected to be impeccable, to achieve straight A's, and to skip grades. On Saturdays, Meyer Jr. lectured the children on Latin, German, ethics, and advanced mathematics. Success earned the faintest of praise and failure was treated harshly. For example, as a senior in high school, Meyer took a curveball for a called strike three. In response, Meyer Jr. made him run the eight miles home. Meyer struggled as a minor league professional baseball player with the Cleveland Indians. After going hitless at bat and being hit in the eye with a ground ball, he called his father and tearfully announced his intention to quit.

> *"You're never welcome in this house again," Bud said. "There's no such thing as a quitter in the Meyer household. Do you understand me?" Meyer was speechless. "Your mother will want to talk to you," Bud added. "Make sure you give her a call at Christmas" (Price, 2009, p. 137).*

Meyer won his second national championship at Florida in 2008. In 2009, he was hospitalized for chest pains and dehydration. He was treated for esophageal spasms and severe headaches that were later identified as related to stress, perfectionism, and burnout (Thamel, 2009; Mandel, 2011). He retired in 2010.

Meyer returned to coaching in 2012 as the head football coach at Ohio State. With a record of 12–0, his 2012 team was undefeated.

Definitions of perfectionism are influenced by the theories and empirical research of teams of psychologists, and, therefore, are not identical. As is often the case with complex psychological phenomena, alternative viewpoints or explanations for these phenomena are not necessarily in competition, and at this point can be understood to be heuristic. Moreover, different teams emphasize several common dimensions. Most theoretical and empirical discussions of perfectionism emphasize the setting of **extreme standards** for performance. As discussed in Chapter 8, setting difficult and even extreme goals is not dysfunctional and leads to higher achievement. Perfectionism associated with very high standards for performance is normal, to the degree that one does not feel compelled to perform flawlessly on unimportant tasks, and that efforts to excel are saved for situations when excellence is warranted and rewarded (Rehm, 1982). **Normal perfectionism** is distinguished by lofty but achievable goals, intrinsic pleasure in tasks, and satisfaction upon reaching goals (Rehm, 1982). Exacting and adaptive goals allow for some margin of error during performances and competitions. Normal perfectionists sometimes experience facilitative anxiety or excitement prior to evaluations and performances, as well as hope for success (Stoeber & Rambow, 2007).

NEUROTIC PERFECTIONISM

Neurotic perfectionists differ from normal perfectionists in a number of important ways. First, their perfectionism does not motivate higher performance and achievement. Ironically, with goals of perfection, people try harder but do worse (Frost & Marten, 1990), because their attention is given to detecting flaws in their performances and avoiding mistakes. This focus on avoiding mistakes results in accurate but slow performance (Slade, Coppel, & Townes, 2009). In effect, neurotic perfectionists "worry about their deficiencies and concentrate on how to avoid doing things wrong" (Hamachek, 1978, p. 28). Attention to flawlessness is excessively self-focused, and self-focused attention frequently gives way to cognitive interference and performance inhibition and deterioration (Anshel & Mansouri, 2005). Examples of this cognitive interference are self-derogatory or self-critical internal monologues (Cervone, 2000), and perhaps this cognitive interference slows performance on tasks requiring speed and precision (Rheaume et al., 2000). These monologues are also distracting and neurotic perfectionists sometimes miss important feedback about progress toward their goals. This feedback provides information about whether efforts are producing desired results and is essential for understanding when efforts, such as training regimens, should be altered. Neurotic perfectionists are prone to "end-state" daydreaming about the consequences of reaching goals. As discussed previously in context with mental practice, this kind of daydreaming interferes with the instrumental behaviors that make goal attainment more likely.

Neurotic perfectionism directs attention to the negative aspects of performance and allows for little satisfaction with the results of performances. It is generally not sufficient for neurotic perfectionists to be perfect in one domain of life (McArdle, 2010), as they often strive toward perfection in other domains (Flett, Sawatzky, & Hewitt, 1995). Given that this perfection is largely unattainable, neurotic perfectionists remonstrate themselves that their performances should have been better. Neurotic perfectionists are harsh in their self-criticism when they make mistakes, and especially when they fail. The thinking of perfectionists is often dichotomized such that they regard themselves as perfect or as failures. Since perfection is all but unattainable, this all-or-nothing thinking often leaves the neurotic perfectionist feeling like a failure.

NEUROTIC PERFECTIONISM AND DEPRESSION

Feeling that they are lacking, being angry with themselves for their lack of perfection, and seeing themselves as failures, neurotic perfectionists are vulnerable to depression (Flett, Hewitt, Blankstein, & Gray, 1998). This type of depression tends to be characterological or long-standing (Hewitt, Flett, Ediger, Norton, & Flynn, 1998), and its amelioration requires an extended course of psychotherapy (Blatt, 1995). In cases of extreme perfectionism, failure and humiliation can foster suicidal thoughts and behavior.

Paradoxically, depression may contribute to the further elevation of self-set standards, because depressed people may achieve high goals and still feel depressed rather than a measure of self-satisfaction upon realizing goals. In effect, the depressed person makes a tacit assumption the relief from depression will result from the realization of even more difficult goals. Of course, the realization of extreme goals is unlikely, and as the depressed person experiences fewer successes in relation to their self-set goals, negative moods are likely to deepen (Cervone, Kopp, Schaumann, & Scott, 1994).

The impossibility of reaching standards of perfection serves only to increase the likelihood of rumination about the perfectionistic goal. Ruminative thinking and depression commonly result when unattainable goals are not renounced (McIntosh, 1996). Perfectionists have a difficult time disengaging from unattainable goals and brood about "what might have been" if they were perfect. This thinking brings to mind depressing thoughts about the gulf between the standards of perfection and the neurotic perfectionist's current status and level of functioning.

THEORETICAL AND SCIENTIFIC EXPLANATIONS FOR PERFECTIONISM

Psychoanalytic Theory

Psychoanalytic theory identified a harsh and punitive Superego as the source of perfectionism. As indicated in several previous chapters, Sigmund Freud determined that the dynamic structures of the psyche were the Superego, Ego, and Id. The Superego was seen to be the moral seat of the psyche and to contain the equivalent of the conscience and the standards for performance, also known as the **Ego Ideal** (Freud, 1917/1957; 1923/1961). Metaphorically speaking, the Superego and Ego Ideal sits in judgment of the individual and her or his accomplishments. If the standards of the Superego and Ego Ideal are too extreme, people may incessantly push themselves toward perfection, but never experience satisfaction with their accomplishments. People with these extreme Superegos may experience a need to maintain a personal and public image of strength and perfection, and feel as if they are always on trial and in need of proving themselves. This need for perfection may also inhibit them from turning to others when help is needed (Blatt, 1995).

Multidimensional Perfectionism: Flett and Hewitt

Contemporary psychologists have determined that perfectionism is a **multidimensional** construct or psychological trait, and that there are adaptive features to perfectionism. Perfectionism may simply consist of high personal standards, and it is associated with ambitiousness and conscientiousness. With this **self-oriented** perfectionism, people tend to focus on the rewards associated with realizing goals, rather than the punishments and losses that may result from failed performances (Hill, Hall, Appleton, & Murray, 2010). Learning or mastery goals and intrinsic motivation are more likely associated with self-oriented perfectionism. Perhaps intrinsic motivation and efficacy for reaching extreme goals shield those with self-oriented perfectionism from procrastination. In fact, greater procrastination occurs when self-oriented perfectionism and standards are low, and when expectations for success are low (Flett, Hewitt, & Martin, 1995).

Athletes with self-oriented perfectionism are also more likely to engage in problem-focused coping and to spurn avoidant coping. As explained in Chapter 4, examples of problem-focused coping include active problem-solving, planning, prioritization of activities, and seeking help and advice from others. Examples of avoidant coping include denial, wishful thinking, and self-blame (Hill, Hall, & Appleton, 2010).

It appears that self-oriented perfectionism is adaptive under conditions of low stress. With the experiences of high levels of stress and negative life events, the belief of self-oriented perfectionists in their personal control is shaken, and they are at risk for depression (Flett & Hewitt, 1995) and cognitive and physiological anxiety (Flett & Hewitt, 1994, Martinent &

Ferrand, 2007). Self-oriented perfectionists are especially prone to experiencing anxiety prior to and during important evaluations and performances. For example, dancers with high self-oriented perfectionism and low personal control experienced debilitating anxiety during performances (Mor, Day, Flett, & Hewitt, 1995). Self-oriented perfectionists are also prone to self-handicapping (Hobden & Pliner, 1995). Self-oriented perfectionists also bombard themselves with criticism following imperfect performances, and, over time, these negative, global, and stable attributions take their toll in the form of depression (Hewitt, Flett, & Ediger, 1996). Self-oriented perfectionists are also at greater risk for exercise dependence (Hall, Hill, Appleton, & Kozub, 2009). Exercise dependence refers to an unreasonable prioritization of exercise and adherence to rigid exercise schedules.

Perfectionism is **other-directed** when individuals expect and demand that others perform and behave perfectly. Other-directed perfectionism often sparks hostility because other people do not meet standards of perfectionism, and this promotes efforts to dominate and control the people who are not performing perfectly.

A third kind of perfectionism occurs when people believe that others expect them to reach standards that are difficult or impossible to achieve, and that acceptance and approval is dependent upon achieving these standards. This **socially prescribed** perfectionism probably originates with expectations of perfectionism imposed by significant others. This socially prescribed perfectionism promotes excessive attention to the reactions of others and fears of their negative evaluations (Hill, Hall, Appleton, & Murray, 2010). With socially prescribed perfectionism, there is a pervasive fear of failure and negative evaluations, and feelings of failure, anxiety, anger, and helplessness are common. Given that these perfectionists anticipate negative reactions from others, it is not surprising that they keep their emotional reactions under control and are careful to not upset others (Flett, Hewitt, & De Rosa, 1996).

Socially prescribed perfectionism is associated with performance goals and less intrinsic interest in tasks. Socially prescribed perfectionists lack efficacy and confidence that externally imposed goals will be realized, and are prone to attributing the causes of their successes and failures to external factors (Flett & Hewitt, 1998). It promotes efforts to avoid challenges and potential failures rather than to approach opportunities and potential gains. It is also associated with procrastination (Flett, Blankstein, Hewitt, & Koledin, 1992; Hill, Hall, & Appleton, 2010) and burnout (Hill, Hall, Appleton, & Murray, 2010).

As was the case with self-oriented perfectionism, socially prescribed perfectionism is associated with cognitive and physiological anxiety (Flett & Hewitt, 1994). It inhibits performance and promotes self-handicapping. It is related to unhappiness and lower life-satisfaction and vitality (Gaudreau & Verner-Filion, 2012). Finally, perfectionism has been associated with eating disorders in women, and this association appears stronger with socially prescribed perfectionism (Hewitt, Flett, & Ediger, 1995).

Multidimensional Perfectionism: Frost et al.

An independent research team (Frost, Marten, Lahart, & Rosenblate, 1990) also determined that perfectionism is multidimensional. The dimensions, however, are not determined by whether perfectionism is directed at the self or at others, but by the manner in which the self is evaluated and judged. These dimensions of perfectionism consist of: **Personal Standards, Organization, Parental Expectations, Parental Criticism, Concern Over Mistakes, and Doubts About Actions** (Frost et al., 1990).

The dimensions of Personal Standards and Organization are associated with high levels of achievement, effective work habits, a lack of procrastination, and normal perfectionism (Brown et al., 1999). Organization is also related to neatness, efficiency, and order. High Personal Standards are especially adaptive when athletes voluntarily engage in sport. These athletes are more likely to find sports interesting, enjoyable, and important. They are more likely to cope with the stresses of competition and to train independently (Mouratidis & Michou, 2011). High Personal Standards are less adaptive when athletes feel obliged to engage in sport and when they perceive that approval is contingent on perfection (DiBartolo, Frost, Chang, LaSota, & Grills, 2004; Gaudreau & Thompson, 2010).

Concern Over Mistakes, excessive Parental Expectations, and Doubts About Actions are associated with procrastination, fear of failure, and depression and anxiety. Doubts About Actions relates to a vague sense of doubt about the quality of one's performance. With high levels of Doubts About Actions, people have a pervasive sense that something is wrong, but they cannot identify specific mistakes or correct what is considered to be wrong. Concern Over Mistakes disposes people to lack confidence during evaluations when mistakes are likely and to experience negative moods during these tasks. With high Concern Over Mistakes, people are more concerned that other people will think they lack intelligence during these evaluations and they are grudging about sharing the results of their performances with others (Frost et al., 1995). Obligatory exercise was associated with high levels of Concern Over Mistakes and Personal Standards among English middle distance runners (Hall, Kerr, Kozub, & Finnie, 2007). Obligatory exercisers run through injuries, experience anxiety if they miss a workout, and increase training loads following missed workouts. Athletes and students who express high levels of Concern Over Mistakes and Doubts About Actions are more likely to have experienced harsh parental criticism during childhood (Kawamura, Frost, & Harmatz, 2002; McArdle & Duda, 2008).

Correlations Between the Two Multidimensional Perfectionisms

Both of the aforementioned characterizations of multidimensional perfectionism identified adaptive and maladaptive aspects, and these aspects are statistically related. Socially prescribed perfectionism is maladaptive, and correlates highly with Concern Over Mistakes, excessive Parental Expectations, and Parental Criticism (Frost et al., 1993). High Parental Expectations and socially prescribed perfectionism are also related to wishes for perfect interpersonal relationships (Flett, Sawatzky, & Hewitt, 1995).

Concern Over Mistakes, Doubts About Actions, Parental Criticism, Parental Expectations, and socially prescribed perfectionism have been seen to form a broad dimension of perfectionism referred to as **perfectionistic concerns** (Kaye, Conroy, & Fifer, 2008; Stoeber & Otto, 2006) or **evaluative concerns perfectionism** (Dunkley, Blankstein, Halsall, Williams, & Winkworth, 2000). The dimensions of self-oriented, other-directed, Organization, and Personal Standards perfectionism have been seen to form a second broad dimension referred to as **perfectionistic strivings** or **personal standards perfectionism.**

The perfectionistic strivings dimension is associated with mastery-approach and performance-approach goals and the perfectionistic concerns dimension is associated with mastery-avoidance and performance-avoidance goals (Fletcher, Shim, & Wang, 2012; Kaye et al., 2008; Stoeber, Stoll, Pescheck, & Otto, 2008). The dimensions of perfectionistic concerns are also correlated with the dimensions of fear of failure: experiencing shame and embarrassment, devaluing one's self-estimate, having an uncertain future, important others losing interest, and upsetting important others (Conroy, Willow, & Metzler, 2002). Perfectionistic concerns has been characterized as a form of unhealthy perfectionism (Stoeber & Otto, 2006), and is associated with unhealthy concerns about body image among female figure skaters (Dunn, Craft, Dunn, & Gotwals, 2011).

Application

As reviewed in Chapter 8, when students and sportspersons set difficult goals, they usually accomplish more. Difficult goals are likely beyond one's current reach, and goals lose their motivating qualities after their realization. Goals of perfection are clearly difficult and not realized. However, the goals of those with perfectionistic concerns are also iatrogenic or harmful and have inhibitional qualities. Inhibition goals—avoiding imperfection—direct attention to what is to be avoided rather than pursued. With goals of perfection and motivated by fears of failure, there is much to avoid and to fear. Inhibitional goals also mark progress in an all-or-nothing manner—failure is avoided or one failed. The goal of perfection is unattainable, and depression results when unattainable goals cannot be renounced.

The dimension of perfectionistic strivings has aspects for normal or positive perfectionism. However, while people with perfectionistic strivings may take on challenges, they are simultaneously motivated to avoid incompetence. They "approach to avoid failure" (Kaye et al., 2008, p. 128). It is associated with less cognitive anxiety and physiological anxiety and with higher self-confidence (Stoeber, Otto, Pescheck, Becker, & Stoll, 2007). Positive perfectionism is associated with putting forth maximum mental and physical effort (Slade et al., 2009).

Multidimensional Perfectionism in Sport

Perfectionism that is specific to athletic domains (Dunn, Gotwals, & Causegrove Dunn, 2005) has been measured with the **Sport Multidimensional Perfectionism Scale** (Sport-MPS), and consists of the dimensions of Personal Standards, Concern Over Mistakes, Perceived Parental Pressure, and Perceived Coach Pressure (Dunn et al., 2006). The Sport-MPS was modeled after the multidimensional model of perfectionism of Frost et al. (1990). A revised version of the Sport-MPS scale (the Sport-MPS-2; Gotwals & Dunn, 2009) was developed with two additional scales: Doubt About Action and Organization. Consistent with the work of Frost et al. (1995), the Doubt About Action scale was associated with uncertainty and dissatisfaction with training and practice prior to competition. Concern Over Mistakes is associated with mastery-avoidance and performance-avoidance goals, and the latter is particularly inimical to well-being and performance in the classroom and in sport contexts (Conroy & Elliot, 2004; Conroy, Elliot, & Hofer, 2003; Duda & Hall, 2001; Elliot, Cury, Fryer, & Huguet, 2006). The Organization scale reflects readiness for competition and thorough preperformance preparation (Gotwals & Dunn, 2009).

The Personal Standards dimension is also associated with adaptive striving and mastery-approach and performance-approach goals (Gotwals, Dunn, Dunn, & Gamache, 2010; Stoeber, Stoll, Salmi, & Tiikkaja, 2008). Athletes with high Personal Standards booked faster times in triathlons in the United Kingdom (Stoeber, Uphill, & Hotham, 2009). However, it does not appear that merely having this adaptive form of perfectionism is sufficient to produce higher achievement in specific contests. Rather, triathletes with high Personal Standards, who also endorsed performance-approach (Elliot & McGregor, 2001) goals as well as specific goals for their times and rank in the race, performed better. Perceived Coach Pressure and Perceived Parental Pressure are important dimensions of perfectionism in sport settings that predispose athletes to fear of failure (Sagar & Stoeber, 2009).

In the previous section, perfectionistic strivings and perfectionistic concerns were characterized as forms of healthy and unhealthy perfectionism, respectively. The dimensions of the MPS also form dimensions of adaptive and maladaptive perfectionism. In a sample of elite athletes from a variety of sports, maladaptive perfectionism was characterized by high levels of Concerns Over Mistakes, Perceived Parental Pressure, and Perceived Coach Pressure (Gucciardi, Mahoney, Jelleh, Donovan, & Parkes, 2012). Adaptive perfectionism was characterized by low to moderate levels on these dimensions. The Personal Standards dimension was elevated for both forms of perfectionism. Of course, not all athletes are perfectionistic, and in this sample of elite athletes, the nonperfectionists were more clearly identified by lower scores on the Personal Standards and Concern Over Mistakes dimensions.

Adaptive perfectionists appear to strive for internally derived standards of excellence. Maladaptive perfectionists make efforts to realize externally derived standards of competence and to avoid internally and externally identified standards of incompetence. Adaptive perfectionists and nonperfectionists have less fear of failure than maladaptive perfectionists. In short, adaptive perfection that consists of striving for exacting standards is not problematic unless accompanied by overly-critical self-evaluations.

ETIOLOGY OF PERFECTIONISM

Neurotic perfectionism is more likely to result when people have histories of high levels of Parental Criticism and Parental Expectations. As explained above, these parental characteristics are also associated with procrastination (as well as Fear of Failure in sport [Conroy, 2003]). Children who receive little parental love and approval and who lose these short supplies when they do not perform successfully consequently fear initiating tasks and chancing failure. These parents may be overly controlling and authoritarian, and appear to value performance above closeness and affection (Fletcher et al., 2012). These parents may readily provide criticism when the child behaves in ways that are considered unacceptable, and fail to provide clear standards for behavior and direction about how to reach acceptable standards. In these environments, children can only escape criticism if their performance is flawless, but they experience performance inhibition because they are never sure what constitutes a flawless performance. When parents chronically withhold approval and urge their children to do better, they provide a model that, when internalized, results in the child's chronic dissatisfaction with his or her performance. With this implicit model, children "see themselves through their parent's eyes." In adulthood, these models exist in abstract or metabolized forms, not necessarily as expectations of parental responses, but as perfectionistic standards for judging oneself and others (Pacht, 1984; Neumeister, 2004).

The parents of normal perfectionists may also communicate high expectations. However, their love and support is not withheld when their children fall short. These parents are more likely to be available, responsive, and nurturing, and to allow their children greater latitude to make decisions. Elite, adolescent male soccer players with high scores on the Sport-MPS-2 Organization scale were also more likely to view their parents as providing support for their athletic development, as well as for their autonomy (Sapieja, Dunn, & Holt, 2011).

It has also been hypothesized that neurotic perfectionists have histories of **insecure attachments** to parents and caregivers. Consistent with the previous theorizing, these parents are understood to make approval conditional on the child's performance and to impose harsh criticism when performance has flaws. In response to the harsh and punitive responses of these parents and caregivers, their children learn to avoid others when they experience distress (Flett, Blankstein, & Martin, 1995). Children with insecure and ambivalent/anxious attachments are quite dependent on caretakers, but are also vigilant to avoid this criticism. These children are more likely to compare their performance to that of others in achievement contexts. These children often compare themselves with people who set the standard for performance in their sphere. For example, a child who is uncertain about his or her athletic ability may compare herself or himself to the swiftest runner in her or his class, and as a result experience demoralization and inadequacy.

The parents of perfectionists may also be **perfectionistic** in their own right, and model or demonstrate perfectionism in their own behavior. For example, High Personal Standards and Organization in parents were correlated with the same dimensions of normal perfectionism in college women (Frost, Lahart, & Rosenblate, 1991). Elite English junior athletes also modeled the perfectionism of their parents. When juniors viewed their parents as self-oriented and other-oriented perfectionists, they were more likely to identify these characteristics in themselves. Juniors were also prone to manifest socially prescribed perfectionism when their parents demonstrated other-oriented perfectionism (Appleton, Hall, & Hill, 2010).

Annika Sorenstam

PERFECTIONISM AND SPORT

Neurotic Perfectionism

Research about the impact of perfectionism on sport performance has emphasized the effects of neurotic or maladaptive perfectionism (Flett & Hewitt, 2005). For example, neurotic perfectionism was shown to be higher among runners who felt "obliged" to run, or who were excessively uncomfortable with the idea of skipping a day's run (Coen & Ogles, 1993). The obliged runners experienced more fear of making mistakes and performance anxiety. They had high levels of trait anxiety, and experienced intense state anxiety when their self-esteem was threatened. More generally, perfectionism is associated with exercise dependence (Hagan & Hausenblas, 2003; Hausenblas & Symons Downs, 2002). Aspects of exercise dependence include the experience of anxiety if one cannot exercise and the organization of one's life around exercise.

Neurotic perfectionism is also associated with anxiety about the appearance of one's physique. This finding was reported with elite male and female Australian athletes (Haase, Prapavessis, & Owens, 2002). Among the elite female Australian athletes, neurotic perfectionism and anxiety about the appearance of one's physique was associated with negative eating attitudes. Neurotic perfectionism has also been described as negative perfectionism, and positive and negative perfectionism have been measured with the Positive and Negative Perfectionism Scale. The Positive and Negative Perfectionism Scale (Terry-Short, Owens, Slade, & Dewey, 1995) has been validated with elite athletes from Australia and New Zealand (Haase & Prapavessis, 2004).

Perfectionism and Anxiety

Perfectionism has consistently been associated with cognitive anxiety in groups of athletes. This finding was reported with female softball players and male baseball players in high school (Castro & Rice, 2003), and female and male high school runners (Hall, Kerr, & Matthews, 1998). With the high school runners, higher levels of perfectionism were associated with higher levels of cognitive anxiety when both were measured one week, two days, one day, and thirty minutes prior to cross-country meets. Higher levels of perfectionism were related to higher somatic anxiety when they were measured one week prior to competition. Perfectionism was more closely related to anxiety than perceived ability and goal orientation. However, maladaptive perfectionism is related to ego orientations, and perhaps both direct the attention of athletes to external standards for measuring performance (Dunn, Causgrove Dunn, & Syrotuik, 2002).

Considering the dimensions of perfectionism identified by Frost and colleagues (Frost et al., 1990), high levels of Concern Over Mistakes and Doubts About Actions were associated with higher levels of cognitive and somatic anxiety among current or potential Olympic athletes in Sweden (Koivula, Hassmen, & Fallby, 2002). Concern Over Mistakes was associated with anxiety and Concern Over Mistakes and Doubts About Actions were associated with less self-confidence during athletic competition among intercollegiate Division II female athletes (Frost & Henderson, 1991). Concern Over Mistakes, Doubts About Actions, and Parental Criticism were associated with lower general self-esteem and self-esteem in sport among female and male intercollegiate athletes (Gotwals, Dunn, & Wayment, 2003).

As mentioned above, Concern Over Mistakes and Parental Criticism are correlated with socially prescribed perfectionism, and both relate to expectations that others expect perfection and will not brook blunders (Frost et al., 1993). Athletes with high levels of perfectionism on the dimensions of Concern Over Mistakes and Doubts About Actions apparently view competition as an opportunity for failure.

Perfectionism and Cognitive Interference

With high levels of Concern Over Mistakes, Doubts About Actions, and Parental Criticism, athletes experienced cognitive interference when they made mistakes (Frost & Henderson, 1991; Koivula et al., 2002). This cognitive interference consisted of worries about disappointing coaches and teammates, focusing attention on the mistake, self-talk about the mistake, experiencing pressure to make up for the mistake, having difficulty forgetting about the mistake, and having intrusive images about the mistake. Even the coaches of these athletes were aware of their difficulties recovering from mistakes during the course of performances.

High levels of Concern Over Mistakes, Doubts About Action, and Parental Criticism are likely to foster attention that is self-focused rather than task focused. As explained in the discussion of choking under pressure, with self-focused attention there is a greater risk for cognitive interference and questioning whether one has the capacity to reach standards necessary for success. If the standard for success is perfection, then the answer will usually be "no" (Carver, 1996). With this answer, anxiety and cognitive interference are likely to rise and self-efficacy is likely to shrink.

Perfectionism and Anger

Given that perfectionists judge themselves by excessively high standards, it is not surprising that they become especially angry when they make mistakes. This anger is internally directed in the form of self-blame and also expressed at others. The most perfectionistic elite male adolescent Canadian football (Dunn, Gotwals, Causegrove Dunn, & Syrotuik, 2006) and hockey players (Vallance, Dunn, & Dunn, 2006) reported the highest levels of anger following mistakes in games and the highest levels of trait anger. These elite athletes were especially vulnerable toward anger when mistakes occurred in critical game situations.

Perfectionism and Relationships with Teammates

Maladaptive perfectionism has also been associated with a reduced quality of relationships with teammates among experienced adolescent female and male Norwegian soccer players (Ommundsen et al., 2005). The maladaptive perfectionism of the adolescent males appeared to stem from excessively high Parental Criticism and expectations and criticism and Concern Over Mistakes. Perhaps the perfectionistic footballers become impatient and critical with teammates who do not perform to their excessively high standards. Alternatively, the perfectionistic adolescents may withdraw from more interactions with teammates as they expect that the judgments of peers will be as harsh as their own self-criticism.

Normal Perfectionism

Athletes who endorsed the high Personal Standards factor of perfectionism are more likely to enjoy thoughts concerning the opportunities for success in competitions. They are also less likely to fear experiencing shame and embarrassment due to athletic failure (Sagar & Stoeber, 2009). Canadian high school footballers who recorded high Personal Standards also endorsed task orientations (Dunn et al., 2002). It has been speculated that task orientations provide a buffer against maladaptive perfectionism (Dunn et al., 2002); however, athletes with high Personal Standards were still concerned with avoiding failure (Frost et al., 1993). U.S. Olympic champions recorded high levels of Personal Standards and Organization, and low levels of Concern Over Mistakes, Doubts About Actions, Parental Expectations, and Parental Criticism (Gould, Dieffenbach, & Moffett, 2002).

Athletes who acknowledged high Personal Standards and self-oriented perfectionism were more likely to engage in task-oriented coping—to directly address the sources of stress and the accompanying thoughts and emotions—during competition. These athletes more often engaged in sport because of intrinsic motivation and because sport is seen to be an integral part of the identity. These athletes were more likely to realize competitive goals and experience life satisfaction. Conversely, athletes who marked high scores on Concern Over Mistakes, Doubts About Actions, and Parental Criticism were more frequently engaged in sport because of extrinsic and introjected motivation and disengaged from actively coping with the stress of competition. There were less likely to be satisfied with the results of their competitive efforts and to realize goals (Gaudreau & Antl, 2008).

Perfectionism and Burnout

Perfectionism is recognized as one reason why junior tennis players lost interest in and became apathetic about playing tennis or "burned out" (Gould, Udry, Tuffey, & Loehr, 1996a). Burned-out juniors recorded significantly higher scores for Parental Criticism, Parental Expectations, and Concern Over Mistakes, as well as Personal Standards and Organization, than juniors who were enthusiastic about tennis. Some burned-out juniors became immobilized and withdrew from competition (Gould, Udry, Tuffey, & Loehr, 1996a).

Socially prescribed perfectionism was also associated with burnout among elite junior athletes in the United Kingdom (Appleton, Hall, & Hill, 2009; Hill, Hall, & Appleton, 2010; Hill, Hall, Appleton, & Kozub, 2008), but self-oriented perfectionism was not associated with burnout (Hill, Hall, Appleton, & Murray, 2010). With standards of perfection and a focus on gaining approval from others, burnout is more likely.

Intercollegiate tennis coaches who experienced maladaptive or neurotic forms of perfectionism were more likely to regard the demands of coaching as stressful and threatening, and to experience burnout (Tashman, Tenenbaum, & Eklund, 2010). However, coaches with forms of normal perfectionism, such as high standards for themselves and others, were not as likely to experience the pressures of coaching to be as stressful and to experience burnout. As explained in Chapter 4, situations are considered stressful if one's resources are deemed insufficient to meet the demands of the stressor (Lazarus, 1999). Perfection is likely an impossible standard, especially for extended periods of time, and neurotic perfectionists may be increasingly likely to experience stress and burnout over time.

WHAT TO DO ABOUT PERFECTIONISM

Neurotic perfectionists have been encouraged to accept imperfection as a goal (Lundh, 2004; Pacht, 1984), and to essentially work toward becoming normal perfectionists. As normal perfectionists, they can strive for excellence, but also relax their standards when situations warrant. Neurotic perfectionists have also been advised to limit their perfectionism to one or two important areas of life functioning. They were advised to give themselves permission to be less than perfect in areas outside of the aforementioned one or two important areas. They were encouraged to set reasonable goals and to develop at least one area in which they can function without any self-evaluation (Hamachek, 1978). Perfectionists are also advised to avoid harsh criticisms when they fall short of perfection and to avoid making self-worth dependent on achieving perfection (DiBartolo, Frost, Chang, LaSota, & Grills, 2004; Dunkley, Zuroff, & Blankstein, 2006).

The adaptive aspects of normal perfectionism notwithstanding, performance may improve if all perfectionism is removed and replaced with exacting proximal and distal goals, mastery and performance-approach goals, and high and sturdy self-efficacy. This conclusion is based on the observation that aspects of perfectionism, with the exceptions of high Personal Standards and Organization, interact with situational pressure to erode performance (Frost & Henderson, 1991). For example, high levels of stress and negative life events disrupt the self-efficacy and sense of personal control of normal perfectionists and place them at risk for depression (e.g., Blatt, 1995). The stress of very important evaluations provokes self-handicapping and vulnerably to anxiety among normal perfectionists. The tendency to compare performances to standards of perfection represents a specific vulnerability to cognitive interference (Frost & Henderson, 1991; Koivula et al., 2002). Furthermore, even normal perfectionism is likely to have aspects of fear of failure and incompetence.

Optimal athletic performances often have dynamic and creative qualities, whereas perfectionism implies that performance will be compared to an abstract, static, and pre-established standard. This suggests that, rather than attempting to replicate perfect performances that have somehow been identified by others, athletic performers should attempt to stamp performances with their unique signature while still staying within the boundaries of the competition. This advice might hold even for a closed skill sport that appears to allow for little creativity, such as archery. It might be quite different for an athlete to enter a competition with the goal of having every one of *their* arrows hit *their* bull's-eyes, and believing that they have the efficacy and the competence to control the flight of each of *their* arrows. Conversely, greater anxiety may result if archers believe that their performance must not deviate from a standard of perfection that has been established or imposed by others.

Replacing perfectionism with self-efficacy and optimally adaptive goals is not necessarily accomplished with minimum effort. Altering perfectionism is especially difficult if it developed in the context of relationships with parents and important attachment figures throughout childhood. These important relationships form the bases for implicit models by which the self and others are judged and evaluated. Their entrenched nature makes them both difficult to recognize and to change. In addition to self-exploration and introspection, guidance from highly skilled mentors such as coaches and psychologists (Blatt, 1995) may be necessary to alleviate the dysfunctional aspects of perfectionism.

SUMMARY AND APPLICATION

Perfectionism is "normal" so long as it facilitates setting realistic and achievable goals, even if the goals are lofty and perhaps extreme. It is also normal if it does not involve a somewhat compulsive drive to behave perfectly in all situations and at all times. High Personal Standards and Organization direct people to higher levels of achievement.

With neurotic adherence to perfectionism, performance and well-being suffers. The neurotic perfectionist demonstrates a slavish adherence to perfectionism such that they appear subject to the extreme goals rather than the goals under their direction and control. The neurotic perfectionist asks a lot of her or himself, and does not excuse imperfect performances. They count themselves as total failures when they are unsuccessful, and do not credit themselves for improvements that occur within the context of unsuccessful performances. They are unlikely to hold mastery, learning, or task goals. They develop performance-avoidance goals as they focus on avoiding mistakes and unfavorable comparisons to others. Goals of flawlessness provoke all-or-nothing thinking, and neurotic perfectionists frequently see themselves as having "nothing" of the perfection they desire. With the recognition of imperfections, they can be harshly critical and remonstrate themselves as failures. To regard oneself as a failure and devoid of good qualities is to make stable, internal, and global attributions that are starkly negative, and that lead to depression.

The self-efficacy of the neurotic perfectionist is flimsy under the pressure of important performances, and they are vulnerable to cognitive interference and anxiety during performances. The attention of the neurotic perfectionist is excessively self-focused during performances, as they direct attention away from the instrumental behaviors necessary for optimal performance and toward comparisons of their performance to an ideal standard.

Some psychologists have suggested guiding neurotic perfectionists to a form of normal perfectionism. Another suggestion is to replace perfectionism with a focus on exacting proximal and distal goals, mastery and performance-approach goals, and resilient self-efficacy. This refocusing may require guidance from highly skilled mentors.

Key Terms

Discussion Questions

Q1. Define and consider the prevalence of procrastination.

Q2. What are the consequences of procrastination?

Q3. Consider procrastination as a form of coping.

Q4. Outline the theoretical explanations for procrastination: psychoanalytic, psychodynamic, developmental psychology, behaviorism, fear of failure, cognitive psychology, and personality traits.

Q5. Consider the self-esteem of procrastinators.

Q6. What are common dimensions in most definitions of perfectionism?

Q7. Is it possible to differentiate neurotic and normal perfectionism?

Q8. Consider the relationship between neurotic perfectionism and depression.

Q9. Review the theoretical explanations for perfectionism: psychoanalytic, multidimensional perfectionism: Flett and Hewitt; multidimensional perfectionism: Frost et al.

Q10. Compare the multidimensional models of Flett and Hewitt, Frost et al., and multidimensional perfectionism in sport.

Q11. Evaluate the etiology of perfectionism.

Q12. How is neurotic perfectionism recognized among sportspersons?

Q13. Describe the influence of perfectionism on anxiety among sportspersons.

Q14. Are perfectionistic sportspersons vulnerable to anxiety; to anger?

Q15. Consider the effects of perfectionism on relationships with teammates.

Q16. Identify normal perfectionism in athletes.

Q17. Identify the influence of perfectionism on burnout.

Q18. How is perfectionism managed?

Suggested Readings

Blatt, S. J. (1995). The destructiveness of perfectionism. *American Psychologist, 50*, 1003–1020.

Ferrari, J. R., Johnson, J. L., & McCown, W. G. (1995). *Procrastination and task avoidance. Theory, research and treatment.* New York, NY: Plenum.

Flett, G. L., Hewitt, P. L., & Martin, T. R. (1995). Dimensions of perfectionism and procrastination. In J. R. Ferrari, J. L. Johnson, & W. G. McCown (Eds.), *Procrastination and task avoidance. Theory, research and treatment* (pp. 113–136). New York, NY: Plenum.

Flett, G. L., Hewitt, P. L., & De Rosa, T. (1996). Dimensions of perfectionism, psychosocial adjustment, and social skills. *Personality and Individual Differences, 20,* 143–150.

Frost, R. O., Marten, P., Lahart, C., & Rosenblate, R. (1990). The dimensions of perfectionism. *Cognitive Therapy and Research, 14,* 449–468.

Gotwals, J. K., & Dunn, J. G. H. (2009). A multi-method multi-analytic approach to establishing construct validity evidence: The Sport Multidimensional Perfectionism Scale 2. *Measurement in Physical Education and Exercise Science, 13,* 71–92.

Haase, A.M., & Prapavessis, H. (2004). Assessing the factor structure and composition of the Positive and Negative Perfectionism Scale in sport. *Personality and Individual Differences, 36,* 1725–1740.

Hamachek, D. E. (1978). Psychodynamics of normal and neurotic perfectionism. *Psychology, 15,* 27–33.

Sagar, S. S., & Stoeber, J. (2009). Perfectionism, fear of failure, and affective responses to success and failure: The central role of fear of experiencing shame and embarrassment. *Journal of Sport & Exercise Psychology, 31,* 602–627.

Sapieja, K. M., Dunn, J.G.H., & Holt, N. L. (2011). Perfectionism and perceptions of parenting styles in male youth soccer. *Journal of Sport & Exercise Psychology, 33,* 20–39.

Stoeber, J., & Otto, K. (2006). Positive conceptions of perfectionism: Approaches, evidence, challenges. *Personality and Social Psychology Review, 10,* 295–319.

Chapter 14

LEARNED HELPLESSNESS

Lacking control over the environment

The Futility Index was developed to provide an answer to questions about which sport teams were the biggest all-time failures. It is a mathematical measure of the likelihood of a team not winning a championship over consecutive years. "In math terms, the probability of a team not winning a championship in a given season is $(n-1)/n$, where n equals the number of teams in the league. Multiplying that fraction over and over for every year a team doesn't win and then taking the reciprocal yields the Futility Index" (Fatsis, 1998, p. B1).

Among American professional sport teams, the Chicago Cubs took the Futility Index prize, as they did not win a World Series in more than 100 years. "'It's nice to know you're No. 1 in something,' says Ed Cohen, founder of Cubs Anonymous, a group of long-suffering fans. 'And yet it's very sad'" (Fatsis, 1998, p. B1).

The essence of **learned helplessness** is the conviction that one has little or no control over events in one's life. It is the converse of self-efficacy, in that it refers to beliefs that one cannot accomplish tasks and goals (Pryce et al., 2011; Seligman, 1975). First identified in the 1960s by Martin Seligman and colleagues (Seligman & Maier, 1967; Seligman, Maier, & Geer, 1968), it is a widely recognized paradigm for understanding disruptions to adaptive striving, performance, and mood. It refers to the debilitating consequences of uncontrollable events, and it has been studied extensively with humans and infrahuman species, such as dogs, cats, and rats (Abramson, Seligman, & Teasdale, 1978). An outcome is uncontrollable when its occurrence is not related to the responses of the person or animal. For example, college students exposed to uncontrollable loud noise in a first condition tended to do nothing to turn off loud noise in subsequent situations where the termination of the noise was under their control. These students did not flip a switch that was in plain view and that would have terminated the noise. Conversely, students who were exposed to loud noise that could be terminated by pressing a button in the first condition were quick to flip the switch to turn off the noise in the second condition. Students who received no noise in the first condition were also quick to switch off the noise in the second condition. Humans, but not animals, can also acquire helplessness by observing the helplessness of others (Peterson, Maier, & Seligman, 1993).

The experience of uncontrollability produces expectations that future outcomes will be uncontrollable, and voluntary responses to exercise control on the environment are inhibited. With helplessness, little effort is exerted to control events and situations that are truly controllable. Helplessness is associated with a belief that current and future success is not contingent on effort. For example, French adolescents of approximately 14 years of age practiced less by taking fewer shots at a target in a pistol shooting task after first taking a test of pistol shooting accuracy in which their performance was unrelated to outcomes. In the first test of pistol shooting accuracy, signals to indicate hits on targets were unrelated to actual shooting accuracy (Gernigon, Thill, & Fleurance, 1999).

HELPLESSNESS AND COGNITIVE BIAS

More than just exposure to uncontrollable events and insolvable problems is necessary for the development of learned helplessness. People must attribute their lack of control to their inadequacies, and in this way develop a **helpless cognitive bias** (Peterson, Maier, & Seligman, 1993). For example, a sportsperson may attribute failure to his or her lack of athletic aptitude. This interpretation or attribution is **internal,** in that it refers to a stable characteristic that is likely to be expressed in future situations. Athletic aptitude also refers to a **global** ability that would be expressed in diverse sports and exercises. Athletic aptitude is also likely to be seen as **chronic** (similar to the stable dimension discussed in Chapter 2), and perhaps **uncontrollable,** or not subject to change with practice and training.

Application

Thinking is biased when the true relationships between causes and effects—between one's efforts and results—are distorted. A bias in favor of efficacy is adaptive, except when danger and the necessity for exhaustive preparation are ignored.

A second sportsperson might consider failure at a competition to be an unfair and biased reflection of his or her ability. This attribution is **external,** and this sportsperson would be less likely to believe that they are helpless to influence their future athletic achievements. The attribution is also **specific,** in that it refers to a particular competition, **transient,** or subject to change in the future, and **controllable.** Failure is also attributed to external sources when people fail at impossibly difficult goals that others also fail to achieve. For example, not running 100 meters in less than nine seconds is unlikely to be demoralizing, because no one has run that fast.

The attribution of failures to internal, stable, and global causes, such as a lack of athletic talent, results in the greatest amount of helplessness (Au, Watkins, & Hattie, 2010; Mikulincer, 1986). The view that one's entire self is deficient contributes to hopelessness (Abramson, Metalsky, & Alloy, 1989). To the degree that uncontrollability is attributed to external, specific, and transient factors, helplessness beliefs will be brief or time limited and relegated to specific domains of functioning.

For example, elite male and female tennis players between the ages of 11 and 25 who demonstrated a helpless pattern during performances and matches attributed failure to internal, stable, and global factors (Prapavessis & Carron, 1988). They doubted their ability and capacity to control the factors leading to success or failure. Helplessness was equally distributed among male and female tennis athletes. As is true for self-efficacy, attributions of helplessness are independent of actual skill level. Some players with the highest level of skills thought and behaved as if they could not control the outcome of matches, and some with lesser skills stubbornly believed that they held the keys to success and failure. The athletes who attributed success and failure to external, unstable, and specific factors showed little helplessness.

The attribution of failure to stable, uncontrollable factors lowers not only efficacy but also future performance. For example, after failing at darts, college students who attributed failure to uncontrollable factors were less than half as accurate in ensuing dart tests as counterparts who attributed failure to controllable factors (Coffee, Rees, & Haslam, 2009).

LEARNED HELPLESSNESS AND OPTIMISM AND PESSIMISM

The helpless cognitive bias has also been described as **pessimism.** As was the case with depression, pessimism is associated with the attribution of difficulties and failures to internal characteristics that are stable over time, and with the attribution of successes to external, unstable, and specific factors. The opposite pattern of attributions holds for **optimists** (Helton, Dember, Warm, & Matthews, 1999).

Pessimism and optimism predicted the number of poor swimming performances among nationally ranked collegiate swimmers at the University of California at Berkeley (Seligman, Nolen-Hoeksema, Thornton, & Thornton, 1990). The pessimists had more poor or disappointing swims during their collegiate swim seasons. Also meriting notice was the finding that the women swimmers were far more pessimistic than the males. These elite women swimmers were no more optimistic than typical college women. The men were as optimistic as any group tested by the authors, and their scores were comparable to the scores of insurance salesmen.

After the season, a subset of the most elite swimmers participated in a second experiment. They were timed at their best event and then given a false and disappointingly slow time. After a 30-minute rest, they swam the event again. The swimmers with the optimistic style were unfazed by their apparent poor performance and swam times that were at least as fast as their first efforts. The performance of the pessimists deteriorated after the apparent defeat. It should be noted that the participants in the second experiment had remained on campus to prepare for the 1988 Olympic trials, and were, therefore, seasoned performers who had experienced a high level of success. Pessimism is not determined solely by one's history of successes and failures, but also reflects one's attributions about the causes of success and failure.

Pessimism also predicted performance in samples of male soccer players and French high school students. Pessimistic soccer players lowered their effort levels when losing a match, whereas their optimistic counterparts sustained performance levels during losing matches (Gordon, 2008). Pessimistic French high school students dribbled basketballs with less dexterity after failure feedback. They also expected to do more poorly on their next evaluation of this basketball skill, and their elevated heart rate suggested heightened anxiety. Their optimistic counterparts dribbled with greater dexterity, expected better results, and did not evidence state anxiety at such high levels (Martin-Krumm, Sarrazin, Peterson, & Famose, 2003).

Pessimistic teams perform more poorly after losses. For example, press reports of the statements of members of the five teams of the Atlantic Division of the National Basketball Association (NBA) were rated for optimism and pessimism. Teams that explained bad events such as losses and slumps in an optimistic manner during the 1982–1983 season were more likely to perform better during the 1983–1984 season. The optimistic teams were significantly more likely to beat the Las Vegas point spread for the games following losses (Rettew & Reivich, 1995). Press reports of player statements were also rated for optimism and pessimism for the 12 teams in the National Baseball League during the 1985 and 1986 seasons. Team optimism in 1985 and 1986 after bad events were powerful predictors of team-winning percentages during the 1986 and 1987 seasons, respectively. Team optimism predicted performance for these professional basketball and baseball teams even after controlling statistically for the abilities of team members.

Failure may not demoralize optimistic teams and people, because they attribute it to external, unstable, and situational factors. Pessimists do not have this form of attributional protection, as they take the blame for their failures. Optimists are more likely to believe that challenges will be mastered, and are more likely to use what Lazarus and Folkman (1984) have described as **problem-focused coping** strategies. As previously explained in this book, problem-focused coping consists of initiatives for confronting and finding solutions to stressors such as evaluations. Examples of problem-focused coping strategies include planning, seeking social support, interpretation of failures as a result of situational and environmental events, acceptance of occasional poor performances, and suppression of competing activities when training. Pessimists are more likely to practice **emotion-focused coping** or to be sensitive to their emotional reactions when confronted by stressors. Emotion-focused coping is more likely to involve passive strategies or ways of tolerating conditions that are considered to be beyond one's control.

The trait of optimism (Norlander & Archer, 2002) appears similar to that of sport confidence among athletes (Grove & Heard, 1997). Both are positively related to problem-focused coping and negatively related to emotion-related coping. They are both also negatively related to avoidance-oriented coping, or the tendency to deny and avoid stressors. Optimism is also related to mental toughness. The components of mental toughness are "challenge, commitment, interpersonal confidence, confidence in own abilities, emotional control and life control" (Nicholls, Polman, Levy, & Backhouse, 2008, p. 1185).

ALTERNATIVE THEORIES OF LEARNED HELPLESSNESS

There are alternative views of the processes responsible for learned helplessness. One view is that repeated failures—rather than merely the disconnection between responses and outcomes—are necessary for helplessness. For example, in groups of French adolescents who practiced a pistol shooting task, failure, along with a disconnection between shooting accuracy and signals that targets were hit, appeared to be more influential in lowering self-efficacy expectations and influencing future shooting accuracy (Gernigon, Fleurance, Reine, 2000). Conversely, adolescents who received success feedback that was contingent on actual shooting performance were subsequently more accurate in pistol shooting.

Another view is that helplessness emerges in uncontrollable situations, because people cannot find solutions to problems. According to this view, when faced with problems, people generate hypotheses about potential solutions. Solvable problems provide clues about which hypotheses are likely to be successful. These clues may emerge quickly, as with easy problems. Difficult problems yield clues only after extended study and hypothesis generation. Unsolvable problems provide no information about potential solutions, and people spin theories about their solutions but come no closer to reaching those solutions. This condition of hypothesis generation without reductions in uncertainty about problem solutions is uncomfortable, and after a period of time most people give up trying. They experience cognitive exhaustion and stop thinking of potential solutions. With cognitive exhaustion, people do not generate hypotheses about solutions to new and solvable problems and performance deteriorates. With cognitive exhaustion, the sophistication of hypotheses suffers; people have difficulty concentrating on problems, and intrinsic interest in problems decrease. People may then not have the energy to carefully think about problems and challenges and to develop novel and creative hypotheses and solutions to problems. Instead, they may adopt strategies that they have used in the past, because pulling up "ready-to-use" (Sedek & Kofta, 1990, p. 741) strategies requires less energy. This "tired" thinking may be implicated in depression, because the attribution of misfortunes to internal, global, and stable factors requires little exertion of mental energy.

With helplessness, adaptive responses to failures are derailed. Failure signals that one's knowledge and behavioral repertoires are insufficient to meet the demands of the environment. Adaptive responses to failures are to learn more, try harder to solve problems, and even to ruminate about problems and the causes of failures (Mikulincer, 1996). This rumination involves the active search for solutions to problems, and interrupts perseveration or the repetition of failed solutions.

If failure continues despite continued efforts to solve problems, people often begin off-task rumination. People who are depressed may engage in off-task rumination after a single failure, and those with high self-efficacy are resistant to off-task rumination. Off-task rumination often includes automatic, intrusive thoughts concerning failure, such as the cognitive interference discussed in Chapter 11. Off-task ruminations also consist of thoughts that are simply irrelevant to the problem at hand.

Some people cope with the threat of failure by attempting to avoid or suppress the source of threat or failure. This strategy is unlikely to be successful when failure threatens important goals, as thoughts related to failure are readily cued by associated thoughts or environmental stimuli. In effect, the person fighting off these thoughts of failure has lost a measure of control over his or her thoughts as ruminations of failure spring to mind automatically when cued in the aforementioned manner. When preoccupied with off-task ruminations or automatic thoughts about failure, attention is diverted from problem solving.

Ruminations may be disrupted by interventions, such as aerobic exercise, guided imagery, and ingesting sugar (Weisenberg, Gerby, & Mikulincer, 1993). Aerobic exercise and ingesting sugar in the form of chocolate reduce anxiety and task-irrelevant cognitions, and guided imagery decreases anxiety related to the experience of helplessness. With the reduction of anxiety and cognitive interference, performance improves.

LEARNED HELPLESSNESS AND ACHIEVEMENT

The effects of helplessness on academic achievement are in some ways the converse of self-efficacy. Students with helplessness beliefs are not persistent in working to solve difficult problems and to remove barriers to their success. College students with helplessness beliefs had lower grade point averages (GPA) than did college students of equivalent ability with optimistic attributional styles. College students with helplessness beliefs were more passive than were peers with efficacious beliefs, in that they sought out less help from academic advisors (Peterson & Barrett, 1987). College freshmen with helplessness attributional styles made internal, stable, and global attributions for poor academic performances, such as a lack of ability, and external, stable, and specific attributions for their academic successes, such as "the course was easy" (Kamen & Seligman, 1986).

The effects of helplessness beliefs were evident in elementary and middle school students, and their helplessness beliefs were reflected in physical education and other classes (Martinek, 1996; Walling & Martinek, 1995). Children with helplessness beliefs attributed failures to internal and stable factors such as a lack of ability or to internal and unstable factors such as a loss of ability (Diener & Dweck, 1978; Fincham, Hokoda, & Sanders, 1989). As is also the case with their older counterparts (Mikulincer, 1996), young students with helplessness beliefs avoid grappling with difficult problems, engage in daydreaming when they are faced with failure and difficult problems, and are prone to depression (Nolen-Hoeksema, Girgus, & Seligman, 1986).

Athletes with helpless beliefs and pessimism are also less persistent in learning new athletic skills and improving performance. This lack of persistent effort has been demonstrated with young elite Canadian tennis players (Prapavessis & Carron, 1988), British college students with majors in sport studies (Johnson & Biddle, 1989), and American collegiate swimmers (Seligman et al., 1990). The presence of helpless orientations among elite athletes is perhaps surprising, given their histories of high achievement (Hale, 1993; Prapavessis & Carron, 1988).

Athletes with helplessness beliefs also attribute failure to internal, stable characteristics (Prapavessis & Carron, 1988). They express less confidence in their ability to control and change the factors that led to disappointing performances.

MASTERY ORIENTATIONS AND HELPLESSNESS

By the age of 10, children differ in their response to failure. Some show a helpless pattern with negative affect, negative thoughts about themselves, and a tendency to give up easily. These children tend to avoid challenging tasks in which failure is possible (Dweck & Leggett, 1988). By the same age, children may also show a mastery-oriented pattern, which consists of persistence in attempting to solve difficult problems, the maintenance of positive affect, and high expectations for success (Heyman, Dweck, & Cain, 1992).

Children with **mastery orientations** simply count failures as "mistakes" (Dweck, 1980). Children and adults with mastery orientations are optimistic, intrinsically motivated, and measure performance against their own baseline of prior performances. They experience less pressure and anxiety when performing because of their stable, internal attributions about their competence. With this stable, internal foundation of confidence, individual successes and failures are less threatening, as their efficacy is not dependent on singular performances. With mastery orientations, children are able to look past singular failures and expect stubborn problems to yield to their problem-solving efforts. With helplessness orientations, children are able to look past successes and expect future failures.

Even at this early age, children hold theories about the nature of their abilities. The young children who do not view ability as a malleable quality demonstrate the helpless pattern, because failures demonstrate that problems exceed their capacities. These children view abilities as stable and uncontrollable. They are concerned with the adequacy of their abilities and seek to avoid public recognition of their shortcomings. Young children who view abilities as mutable qualities are persistent in study and practice, because they view intelligence and achievement to be a reflection of effort (Sarrazin et al., 1996). They seek to master challenges because they have faith that their efforts will both be sufficient to solve problems and that they will improve their abilities and aptitudes as a result of their efforts to solve problems.

When engaged in a challenging task, the attention of children with mastery orientations is devoted primarily to the task rather than to questions of whether they have the ability to meet the challenge. They are more capable of thinking of ways of meeting the challenge or of resolving the problem, and their optimism leads to enhanced performance.

ETIOLOGY OF HELPLESSNESS AND EFFICACY

The seeds of self-efficacy and helpless are first sown in infancy. Infants develop beliefs in their personal efficacy by recognizing that their behaviors influence the things and people in their world (Bandura, 1997). They learn this most readily if the environmental influences occur soon after their actions. If the effects or actions are separated by some period of time, infants will not recognize that their action caused the effect, because they cannot sustain mental representations of their actions and

Helplessness, a lack of control

the effects of those actions, due to their limited working memory capacity. For younger infants to recognize the connection between their behavior and its effects, the effect must be produced in the vicinity of their action. For example, it would be difficult for an infant to learn the association between moving a rattle and the noise it produced if the rattling sound emerged from an area distant to the rattle.

An especially important source for the development of personal agency in infants is the contingent responses of adults. Attentive adults who take interest and delight in studying the behaviors of infants, attempting to discern the meaning of the infants' actions, and then responding contingently, provide clear evidence to the child that his or her behaviors are efficacious.

Very young children do not have conceptualizations of specific traits, such as ability and effort. Instead, they think of human characteristics in global terms. The dichotomy of "good" and "bad" is perhaps the most basic and global distinction by which very young children categorize other people and themselves. These very young children may judge their goodness and badness on the basis of the reactions of important others, such as parents, and also on the basis of their performances in venues, such as school. Children just starting school may interpret their successes or failures on achievement tasks as reflections of their goodness or badness. Children who have routinely experienced **punitive responses** to their failures are more likely to lack persistence in attempting to solve problems and to show passivity and helplessness (Boggiano, Barrett, & Kellam, 1993; Heyman et al., 1992). These children are sensitive to criticism from adults. In response to adult criticism, they are more likely to rate themselves as not good at a task, not smart, not a good person, or not nice, and to view their imagined deficiencies as unchangeable.

The development of helpless versus mastery achievement patterns is influenced more by the consistent responses of parents than of teachers (Hokoda & Fincham, 1995). For example, children who demonstrate helplessness in the classroom more commonly have parents who attribute their children's failures to a lack of ability. Children's explanations of their failures correspond with their parent's explanations, and parents who ascribe failure to their children's inability commonly have children who attribute their failures to internal and stable traits. Mothers of helpless children are sometimes not subtle in discouraging self-efficacy, as they have been shown to make derogatory comments about their children's ability and to encourage them to quit when working at difficult problems. These mothers were also more likely foster the development of performance goals, or achievement measured in relation to the performance of others.

These mothers responded to the negative moods of their children with their own negative moods, and this may have validated feelings of demoralization in their children. Mothers of helpless children may have modeled passivity and a lack of productivity in response to difficulties, because they often did nothing in response to their children's requests for help. This lack of parental responsiveness may augment helplessness, as the child's effort to elicit help is unrelated to receiving help. In this context of help seeking, the child is exposed to another uncontrollable situation.

ETIOLOGY OF HELPLESSNESS AND MASTERY ORIENTATIONS

Children that are bathed in parental attentiveness are more likely to develop mastery motivation, perhaps because they form global images of themselves and the world as good (Boyce, Gano-Overway, & Campbell, 2009). These parents reflect warmth and a positive mood toward their children. Responsive parents are attentive and provide help to children when it is needed. The help they provide directs children's attention toward the technical aspects of problems and does not impart beliefs that the child is incapable at sport or in school.

Mothers of children with mastery orientations frequently compliment their children for having high ability. They maintain a positive affect or mood, even as they children struggle with difficult problems. These mothers encourage their children to find solutions to difficult problems, and they do not lose confidence in their children if they struggle with difficult puzzles (Hokoda & Fincham, 1995). These mothers discourage helplessness and conclusions that failures reflect inadequate ability, and redirect their children toward strategies for mastering difficult tasks. They even contradict statements from their children that reflect discouragement with reminders of their children's high ability.

Application

Mastery and helpless orientations in children reflect their home and school environments. Children with helpless orientations internalize viewpoints such as: "It is too hard, you are not good at it, you need help, there is nothing you can do, others are better, and I cannot help you." Children with mastery orientations have internalized parental responses that suggest: "I know you can do it, you are good at it, stay positive, you might have to work harder and learn more to get this, do not give up, and I am here if you need me."

ETIOLOGY OF HELPLESSNESS AND TRAUMATIC EVENTS

It should be noted that the reactions of parents is but one, albeit a very important, potential cause for helplessness and depression in children. **Traumatic, uncontrollable events** that affect the lives of children for long periods of time, such as the death of a parent, are also associated with depression in children. These traumatic events may provoke pessimistic explanatory styles, which then lead to entrenched negative moods (Nolen-Hoeksema et al., 1986). Indeed, traumatic events have been shown to be most influential in predicting future depression for third-graders in a five-year longitudinal study (Nolen-Hoeksema, Girgus, & Seligman, 1992). Depressive symptoms also lead to pessimistic attributional styles, and these pessimistic attributions persist even after depressions have subsided.

The association between helplessness and depression is also not surprising, because people with depression tend to attribute their failures to internal, stable, and global factors, and their successes to external, specific, and unstable factors (Forgeard et al., 2011). If failures result from actions that were controllable, a greater amount of self-criticism, self-blame, and guilt often ensues. Depression and decreased self-esteem are more likely when people experience helplessness in areas of functioning that are particularly important to their well-being.

ETIOLOGY OF HELPLESSNESS AND CLASSROOM, PHYSICAL EDUCATION, AND RECREATION ENVIRONMENTS

The responses of teachers are also important in the development of helplessness in children. In physical education classrooms and recreational settings (Firmin, Hwang, Copella, & Clark, 2004; Yeh, 2010) where the greatest efforts are made to exert external control of students' learning through the use of rewards, punishments, and pressure from instructors, children are oriented toward extrinsic or external learning orientations. In these environments, children tend to focus on pleasing, and avoiding the displeasure of others. This motivational orientation results in decreased intrinsic interest in learning, and places children at greater risk for helplessness, because desired outcomes, such as praise from instructors, is to some degree outside of their control. Indeed, children with strong **extrinsic motivation** may credit powerful others, such as teachers, with successes that are entirely due to their own efforts and abilities.

Children who pursue activities because the activities are inherently satisfying have **intrinsic motivation,** and are less vulnerable to experiencing helplessness. These children attend more to internal standards for determining their successes and failures, and to some degree these factors remain under their control, even if others do not recognize their accomplishments. Intrinsic motivation is more likely in environments that promote mastery orientations.

Children and adults with intrinsic orientations are more likely to attribute the results of evaluations to their self-initiated and self-regulated efforts. People with extrinsic orientations are more likely to attribute their successes and failures to the reactions of others (Boggiano et al., 1992). For example, children with intrinsic orientations might consider attempts to solve problems to be successful if they credited themselves for the amount of effort expended and with the acquisition of knowledge, even if efforts to solve specific problems were unsuccessful. Extrinsically motivated children are more interested in the demonstration of ability to others, and, therefore, are more likely to experience helplessness when their efforts do not result in notices of approval from the others.

Children with intrinsic orientations are not only undaunted by failures to solve problems, but also develop even more sophisticated strategies to solve problems after experiencing failure (Boggiano, 1998). The opposite trend has been demonstrated for children with extrinsic orientations, as their sophisticated problem solving deteriorated after their first experience of failure.

GENDER DIFFERENCES AND HELPLESSNESS

The question of whether girls or boys are more susceptible to helplessness remains equivocal. Some researchers have argued forcefully that girls more often demonstrate helplessness than do boys, and that girls also more frequently blame failure on their lack of ability and show negative affect after failure information (Boggiano & Barrett, 1991). An influential hypothesis for these gender differences is that "socializing agents," such as teachers and parents, have different expectancies for boys and girls in academic and competitive arenas. They expect helpless behaviors from girls, because they are consistent with stereotypes of females as dependent. The socializing agents expect mastery-oriented responses from boys, as these responses are deemed consistent with stereotypes of males as independent. The different expectancies of parents and teachers motivate differential treatments of boys and girls. Girls receive more support when they behave in dependent and helpless ways, and when boys are supported more when they act in independent and mastery-oriented fashions. Adults respond more stridently to control and limit mastery-oriented and independent behaviors in girls and helpless and dependent responses from boys.

Gender differences have also been demonstrated among athletes. Female Japanese intercollegiate swimmers endorsed higher levels of helplessness related to daily life and competitive life (Yasunaga & Inomata, 2004).

Research with adults has identified differences in the attributional styles of men and women. Women have been seen to be more pessimistic in their explanatory styles, in that they more often attribute failures to internal and stable factors. As discussed earlier in this chapter, nationally ranked collegiate female swimmers at the University of California at Berkeley were far more pessimistic than their male counterparts (Seligman et al., 1990). Men more commonly consider failure to result from external factors. With tendencies to make internal attributions and to ruminate or have repetitive thoughts about failures, women have been seen to be prone to depression (Nolen-Hoeksema, 1990; Nolen-Hoeksema, Parker, & Larson, 1994; Seligman, 1990).

Perhaps the gender of the person providing failure feedback is important. Fifth-grade girls have shown more helplessness, when females as compared to males provided failure feedback (Dweck & Bush, 1976). When the girls received failure feedback from the adult males, they more frequently attributed failure to effort rather than ability, and performance subsequently improved. These findings were considered to reflect tendencies of female teachers to provide less-explicit feedback to students about the causes of incorrect responses on evaluations or to ask additional questions so that students can respond correctly. The pursuit of correct solutions following failure may discourage internal attributions for failure, such as ascribing failures to inadequate ability. College students have also demonstrated less helplessness when males delivered failure information (Rozell, Gundersen, & Terpstra, 1997).

Several studies have identified limited gender differences regarding helplessness. For example, Farmer and Vispoel (1990) asked high school students to recall failure experiences and their responses to the failures. They identified attributional patterns that were characteristic of helplessness after failures, and determined that high school boys and girls are highly similar with regard to attribution patterns characteristic of helpless. Confidence in the results of this study is limited by its design, as the recollections of high school students may be susceptible to a variety of distortions and biases. Both boys and girls most frequently recalled school failures, and boys more frequently recalled athletic failures and girls more often remembered failures in their families.

In other studies, attributional patterns were evaluated immediately after actual failures (Eccles, Adler, & Meece, 1984). Boys and girls were shown to respond similarly after the failures, both in terms of the time spent trying to solve problems and actual successful performance. There were differences in attributions immediately after failure, as the girls' expectancy of success dropped lower than the boys'. However, after completing all of the problems in the experiment, the expectancies of success of both genders were equivalent.

SUMMARY AND APPLICATION

Learned helplessness was described as the converse of self-efficacy, because it refers to stable beliefs that one has little or no control over events in one's life. With helplessness, people believe that stable, global, and internal qualities, such as a lack of talent, make control over events in the future unlikely, and people do not put forth the efforts that lead to successful performances and achievements. Helplessness is associated with pessimism, whereas efficacy corresponds with optimism or beliefs that challenges will be mastered and difficulties will yield given sufficient effort. With optimism, efficacy is shielded from the effects of failure, as failures are blamed on external, unstable, and situational factors. Helpless people not only "give up trying" to perform successfully, but they give up the difficult work of thinking of complex and novel ways of solving problems and reaching goals. Instead of selecting strategies and skills to meet the demands of a specific situation, they show a form of prolonged mental exhaustion by attempting solutions to problems that have already been shown to fail.

There is evidence that helplessness and pessimism develop early in life. If young children are consistently exposed to harsh criticism of their work products by parents and teachers, they internalize helplessness and passivity. Children who attribute their failures to their lack of ability often have parents who attribute the failures of their children to the same stable and internal traits. Mastery motivation, which consists partially of resistance to helplessness, is associated with parental confidence in children's abilities and with their empathic support of children's efforts to achieve. Empathic support implies that parents make accurate judgments about when to provide help and when to let children work independently when no help is needed. The parents of helpless children are more likely to be passive as their children struggle with problems, and, thus, their children learn that they are helpless to solve problems and helpless in gaining assistance from their most important attachment figures.

Children who are consistently exposed to classroom environments that emphasize external control of students' learning place children at greater risk for helplessness and extrinsic motivation for achievement. These children focus to a greater extent on eliciting favorable responses from others, something that they can control only partially. Conversely, when children are aware of the intrinsic benefits of achievement pursuits, they are more likely to compare progress and success against their own internal standards or baseline. Efficacy is more likely to be preserved when progress is measured in relation to one's baseline.

The question of whether girls or boys are more susceptible to helplessness remains equivocal. The evidence that girls blamed failure on a lack of ability and showed negative affect after failure is stronger than the evidence that girls spent less time trying to solve problems and actually solved fewer problems after failures on problems. The effects of socialization practices may accumulate or have differential effects at different stages in life, as adult women demonstrate more pessimism than men.

Key Terms

Learned helplessness   323

Helpless cognitive bias   323

Internal attribution   323

Global ability   323

Chronic and uncontrollable athletic aptitude   323

External attribution   324

Specific attribution   324

Discussion Questions

Q1. Review the development of the learned helplessness construct.

Q2. Examine the cognitive bias associated with learned helplessness.

Q3. Consider the pessimism of those with learned helplessness.

Q4. How does pessimism influence sport performance?

Q5. How do optimistic teams rationalize failure?

Q6. Consider the coping strategies of optimists and pessimists.

Q7. Outline the theoretical explanations for learned helplessness.

Q8. Review the influence of learned helplessness on achievement.

Q9. Compare mastery and helplessness orientations.

Q10. Review the development of learned helplessness.

Q11. Consider the behavior of parents that lead to the development of mastery orientations.

Q12. Explain the contribution of traumatic events to helplessness and depression in children.

Q13. Examine the influence of teachers on the development of helplessness in children.

Q14. Is there evidence for gender differences in helplessness?

Suggested Readings

Abramson, L. Y., Seligman, M.E.P., & Teasdale, J. D. (1978). Learned helplessness in humans: Critique and reformulation. *Journal of Abnormal Psychology, 87*, 49–74.

Boyce, B. A., Gano-Overway, L. A., & Campbell, A. L. (2009). Perceived motivational climate's influence on goal orientations, perceived competence, and practice strategies across the athletic season. *Journal of Applied Sport Psychology, 21*, 381–394.

Coffee, P., Rees, T., & Haslam, A. (2009). Bouncing back from failure: The interactive impact of perceived controllability and stability on self-efficacy beliefs and future task performance. *Journal of Sports Sciences, 27*, 1117–1124. doi: 10.1080/02640410903030297

Gernigon, C., Fleurance, P., & Reine, B. (2000). Effects of uncontrollability and failure on the development of learned helplessness in perceptual-motor tasks. *Research Quarterly for Exercise and Sport, 71,* 44–54.

Gernigon, C., Thill, E., & Fleurance, P. (1999). Learned helplessness: A survey of cognitive, motivational and perceptual-motor consequences in motor tasks. *Journal of Sports Sciences, 17,* 403–412.

Gordon, R. A. (2008). Attributional style and athletic performance: Strategic optimism and defensive pessimism. *Psychology of Sport and Exercise, 9,* 336–350. doi: 10.1016/j.psychsport.2007.04.007

Helton, W. S., Dember, W. N., Warm, J. S., & Matthews, G. (1999). Optimism, pessimism, and false failure feedback: Effects on vigilance performance. *Current Psychology: Developmental, Learning, Personality, Social, 18,* 311–325.

Peterson, C., Maier, S. F., & Seligman, M. E. P. (1993). *Learned helplessness. A theory for the age of personal control.* New York, NY: Oxford.

Seligman, M. (1975). *Helplessness: On depression, development, and death.* San Francisco, CA: Freeman.

Seligman, M.E.P. (1990). *Learned optimism.* New York, NY: Pocket Books.

Seligman, M.E.P., Nolen-Hoeksema, S., Thornton, N., & Thornton, K. M. (1990). Explanatory style as a mechanism of disappointing athletic performance. *Psychological Science, 1,* 143–146.

Yasunaga, M., & Inomata, K. (2004). Factors associated with helplessness among Japanese collegiate swimmers. *Perceptual and Motor Skills, 99,* 581–590.

Chapter 15

PERFORMANCE INHIBITION DUE TO PERSONALITY FACTORS

Personality traits influence sport participation

John Terry was twice named as the captain of the England national football (soccer) team. Twice, he has been stripped of one of his nation's highest honors.

In 2001, on the day after the 9/11 attacks at the World Trade Centers, Terry and three teammates stripped naked and vomited at a London Heathrow

Airport hotel bar as American tourists watched television coverage of the attacks. A year later, he was filmed urinating into a beer glass, which he then dropped on the floor. He was fined for parking his Bentley in a spot reserved for handicapped drivers in 2008. In December 2009, he was secretly filmed by undercover journalists as he gave unauthorized tours of Chelsea's training grounds, the club for which he was captain, in exchange for £10,000 ($15,900).

Yet, published reports of his violating a taboo in soccer cost him the captaincy of the national team in 2010. These reports concerned an extramarital affair with the girlfriend of a teammate on the Chelsea and national football teams. The woman and teammate were the parents of a child, and the woman was a close friend of Terry's wife. At this time, Terry was the married father of three-year-old twins. He was voted Dad of the Year in 2009.

Terry's captaincy was restored but soon removed again. In 2012, he was accused of racially abusing an opponent in a football match. He was tried for a "racially aggravated public order offense," but cleared by Westminster magistrates' court. The FA (Football Association, the governing body of English football) later found Terry guilty of a similar offense. The FA imposed penalties of a four-game ban from Premier League play and a fine of £22,000. Terry resigned from the England national team (Clegg & Orwall, 2010; Davies & Davies, 2012; Hughes, 2012; Lawton, 2012; McIntosh, 2010; "Terry to fight," 2012).

The focus of this chapter will be the personality characteristics that inhibit performance. In addition, personality traits associated with optimal sport performance will be described. As is true for most topics in psychology, a definition of personality that is universally accepted does not exist. Rival theories of personality were reviewed in Chapter 2. These include the psychoanalytic and neo-analytic viewpoints, humanistic theories, and social-learning approaches, such as self-efficacy theory. The influence of self-efficacy on sport performance was considered in Chapter 10, and the inhibiting influence of the related construct of helplessness was addressed in Chapter 14.

Another paradigm or theoretical model that has generated a body of research in sport psychology is trait theory. With this model, personality is conceptualized as a composite of a number of discrete traits or enduring characteristics. Hans Eysenck's model of personality (Eysenck & Eysenck, 1985) has influenced the greatest number of empirical studies. The five-factor model is another trait approach to personality that has influenced research in sport psychology.

The Profile of Mood States (POMS; McNair, Lorr, & Droppleman, 1971) and the Athletic Coping Skills Inventory (ACSI; Smith, Schutz, Smoll, & Ptacek, 1995) will also be reviewed in this chapter. Neither measure dimensions of behavior that are as broad and stable over time as are traditional personality traits (Lane & Terry, 2000). Nevertheless, tradition dictates that the POMS and ACSI are examined in treatments of personality and sport psychology (Cox, 2011; Gill & Williams, 2008;

Weinberg & Gould, 2010), as the ASCI was developed specifically for differentiating more and less successful athletes, and the POMS has been utilized extensively in sport settings. The topic of temperament will also be examined in this chapter. Temperament, especially biological vulnerability to experience anxiety is related to Eysenck's theory of personality and provides useful information for understanding performance under pressure.

TRAIT THEORIES OF PERSONALITY

Regardless of theory, trait approaches identify major dimensions of behavior that are consistent over time and in different situations. These traits or enduring characteristics are distributed normally in human populations (see Figure 15.1). Normal distributions form a bell curve, such that the mean (average score), median (point that divides evenly the population), and the modal (most frequent) score are the same. Normal distributions and bell curves are symmetrical so that 68% of the scores of the entire population fall within a unit of plus or minus one standard deviation from the mean. Fully 95% of the normal distribution falls within plus or minus two standard deviations from the mean.

Theory and data indicate that personality traits in the five-factor and Eysenck models are not only normally distributed, but also orthogonal (Costa & McCrae, 1992; Eysenck, 1992). Traits are orthogonal when they are statistically independent. In other words, knowledge of whether someone is high or low on a trait such as neuroticism provides absolutely no information about whether that person will be high or low on any of the other two traits in Eysenck's model or the other four traits in the five-factor model.

Even extreme scores on these dimensions of personality do not guarantee that behavior consistent with the particular dimension will be expressed in a given situation and at a given time. Instead, high scores on personality traits produce a statistical likelihood or greater probability that the behavior in question will occur. Behavior is often understood in terms of diathesis and stress. These dimensions of personality create a **diathesis** or likelihood that characteristics are expressed in response to certain environmental **stressors.** Common stressors in sport psychology are the demands of competition, especially pressure for optimal performance during critical times in crucial competitions. To complicate matters further, the behavior of some people is more consistent than that of others (Mischel & Shoda, 1995; Smith, 2006). In general, the behavior of adults is more consistent than that of children and adolescents.

Finally, although the focus of this chapter will be the effects of personality on performance, sport and exercise have an influence on personality (Dishman & Chambliss, 2010). Sport and exercise may influence personality as a result of their influence in diminishing anxiety and depression and improving mood. Anxiety and depression are important components of personality traits such as neuroticism, which will be described later. Exercise and sport may also improve fitness and appearance, and physique improvements may lead to improved self-esteem. As described in Chapter 10, mastery in the areas of sport and exercise may also foster improved self-efficacy. Sport and exercise regimens may result in patterns of socialization, and the influence of other people may alter personality.

HANS EYSENCK'S THEORY OF PERSONALITY

Hans Eysenck at the University of London developed the most influential of the trait theories in terms of generating scientific research in sport psychology. Eysenck was a student of Sir Cyril Burt, and Eysenck's theorizing about personality reflects Burt's emphasis on the genetic influences on behavior. Eysenck identified three major dimensions or traits in personality, **neuroticism, psychoticism,** and **extraversion** (Eysenck, 1994). People who demonstrate high levels of the psychoticism, neuroticism, and extraversion dimensions do not necessarily evince these characteristics at all times. As mentioned earlier, high levels of traits represent dispositions to demonstrate certain behaviors when these behaviors are elicited by environmental conditions.

These traits are bipolar such that the opposite pole of extraversion is introversion, the opposite pole of neuroticism is stability, and the opposite pole of psychoticism is superego or a strong conscience. Extraversion is characterized by: sociable, lively, active, assertive, sensation-seeking, carefree, dominant, surgent, and venturesome. Primary characteristics defining neuroticism are: anxious, depressed, guilt feelings, low self-esteem, tense, irrational, shy, moody, and emotional. Psychoticism is defined by the characteristics of: aggressive, cold, egocentric, impersonal, impulsive, antisocial, unempathic, creative, and tough-minded. True to the name of this trait, Eysenck (1992) also argued that the psychoticism dimension represented a continuum of mental disorders. At the extreme of this continuum were people prone to severe mental illness, such as bipolar, schizoaffective, and schizophrenic disorders. Eysenck considered bipolar, schizophrenic, and schizoaffective disorders to represent dimensions on the continuum of psychoticism, with schizophrenic disorders occupying the most extreme position and representing the most severe disturbance.

People with extreme scores on Eysenck's personality dimensions are more likely to demonstrate a wider range of the behaviors characteristic to that dimension and to demonstrate the behaviors more forcefully. People with moderate levels of these traits may show fewer and less extreme characteristic behaviors. But moderate levels of these traits still contribute to important differences in behavior. Given that these traits are normally distributed, the majority of people have moderate levels of introversion or extraversion, stability or neuroticism, and superego or psychoticism.

EXTRAVERSION AND CORTICAL AROUSAL

Eysenck maintained that these traits were largely determined by genetic factors. For example, introverts were seen to have higher levels of **cortical arousal** than extraverts and to have stronger and more labile autonomic nervous system responses. Cortical arousal level was seen to be a function of the activity level of the **ascending reticular-activating system** (ARAS). Extraverted behavior patterns are produced by a relatively underreactive ARAS and therefore higher levels of environmental stimulation are necessary for extraverts to realize an optimal hedonic level. The tension and excitement of sport afford means for augmenting cortical activation. Exercise and movement may also augment cortical activation, as the ARAS receives propioceptive feedback from the muscles and somatic or peripheral nervous system. Conversely, introverts have an overactive ARAS, and realize optimal hedonic tone with limited environmental input.

The cortical activation of extraverts is lowest in the morning and increases during the day, perhaps due to the effects of environmental stimulation (Kirkcaldy, 1980). State anxiety is experienced as increasingly facilitative of performance with the nearing of competition (Cerin, 2004). Extraversion also diminishes with increasing age, so that extraversion is generally lower in older than younger people.

This conceptualization of cortical arousal is overly simplified by modern neurophysiological standards (Rammsayer, 2004). The activation of the brain involves a number of cortical structures and neurotransmitters. Neurotransmitters are chemicals responsible for communication between neurons, or the tiny structures that provide for information processing in the brain. The neurotransmitter dopamine has been identified as important in cortical activation, and it appears that introverts have dopamine in greater abundance than extraverts, or that introverts are more responsive to dopamine.

Extraverts tend to habituate to environmental stimuli more quickly than do introverts. Habituation is measured by both the amplitude of cortical arousal and by the degree to which people continue to pay attention to input from the environment. Extraverts lose interest quickly in redundant stimuli and seek out novel experiences. Extraverts are, therefore, more easily distracted by environmental stimuli. Introverts demonstrate a more narrow focus of attention and are more likely to sustain their attentional focus and inhibit responses to environmental stimuli. Extraverts are not only more likely to be distracted by environmental stimuli, but are also more likely to respond physically to the stimuli. Because of the relative hunger of marked extraverts for external stimulation, they are less precise at some tasks that call for sustained vigilance and responding to feedback in the environment. For example, extraverts have more accidents while driving automobiles, as their attention wanders from vigilance for danger.

People tend to seek out environments that provide for an optimal level of stimulation. Environments that introverts find optimal are counted as boring to extraverts, while extraverts are most comfortable in situations that cause anxiety to introverts. Introverts are less "hungry" for environmental stimulation than extraverts because of their higher level of cortical stimulation. Extraverts are far more comfortable than introverts in situations involving risk and danger. For example, extraverts were more likely to take risks when engaged in high-risk sports (downhill skiing, mountaineering, rock climbing, and skydiving; Castanier, Le Scanff, & Woodman, 2010).

Both introverts and extraverts will make efforts to place themselves in environments that provide for the optimal hedonic tone or the optimal amount of cortical arousal. Therefore, introverts may seek to avoid too much stimulation from the environment, whereas extraverts are more willing to take physical and social risks for varied, novel, and complex sensations and experiences that are stimulating, exciting, and even thrilling.

Research indicates that extraverts are more motivated by the possibilities of realizing gains and rewards and introverts are more sensitive to avoiding loss and punishment. Eysenck's theorizing (1952) anticipated this research, and Eysenck's theorizing also anticipated, by perhaps 40 years, sophisticated recent research concerning people who were motivated primarily by the opportunities for gains versus the avoidance of loss. For example, and as discussed in Chapter 2, people with a *promotion* focus attend to opportunities for accomplishments and are relatively unconcerned with potential risks and losses (Higgins, 1997, 2012). They seek to avoid the experience of nonfulfillment. Those with a *prevention* focus seek safety and attempt to avoid danger.

EYSENCK'S THEORY AND SPORT

Perhaps the most widely reported finding concerning Eysenck's theory of personality and sport is that athletes are likely to be extraverted. Competitive sports often produce a high level of stimulation and excitement, and extraverts may be especially drawn to sports that involve risk, excitement, and aggression (Daino, 1985; Eysenck, Nias, & Cox, 1982; Newcomb & Boyle, 1995). Athletes have also traditionally been shown to have relatively low levels of neuroticism and high levels of psychoticism, although the latter finding is less well-established.

Comparing female athletes and nonathletes, female athletes typically show higher extraversion and psychoticism scores, perhaps reflecting traits that have been identified as masculine or androgynous (e.g. Bem Sex Role Inventory; Bem, 1974, 1978) in groups of female athletes (Francis, Kelly, & Jones, 1998).

More successful and elite sportspersons demonstrate higher levels of extraversion and psychoticism and lower levels of neuroticism than do average sport performers. These results have been reported among Olympic athletes, college football players, elite swimmers, and international table tennis and badminton players (Davis & Mogk, 1994). Extraversion appears to be particularly sensitive in differentiating elite from sub-elite athletes. For example, among candidates for the male 1974 U.S. Heavyweight Rowing Team, extraversion was more accurate than measures of state and trait anxiety, a measure of bodily perception during stressful situations, and the tension, depression, anger, vigor, fatigue, and confusion scales of the Profile of Mood States (POMS; McNair, Lorr, & Droppleman, 1971) in identifying oarsmen who made the team (Morgan & Johnson, 1978). Among candidates for the 1974 U.S. Lightweight Rowing Team, higher levels of extraversion and vigor differentiated the oarsmen who made the team.

It should be noted that these findings hold true for groups of elite performers, and that individual elite athletes sometime have higher levels of neuroticism and lower levels of extraversion. For example, tennis players of Wimbledon standard have been identified with levels of neuroticism that exceed the mean of psychiatric patients with depressive disorders (Eysenck et al., 1982).

MORE ON EXTRAVERSION AND SPORT

The acceptance of risk among the highly extraverted is rewarded in sports where explosive actions and very rapid decisions are necessary. For example, when heading a soccer ball—especially on plays such as corner kicks—soccer players accept the possibilities of intense ball-to-head contact, and contact with the head or boot of another player. Extraverted collegiate soccer players were more likely to pursue head balls (Webbe & Ochs, 2007).

Extraverts appear more likely to participate in team sports (Eagleton, McKelvie, & deMan, 2007; Newcombe & Boyle, 1995). Extraversion and a lack of neuroticism may contribute to team cohesion, at least in the workplace (van Vianen & De Dreu, 2001).

Participants in "extreme" sports such as hang-gliding, powerboat racing, white-water canoeing, parachuting, and mountaineering have been shown to be particularly extraverted and to show low levels of neuroticism (Watson & Pulford, 2004). Consistently high scores on the psychoticism dimension have not been reported for athletes who engage in extreme sports (Egan & Stelmack, 2003). Mountaineering involves extreme risks and consists of mountain climbing, mountain skiing, and alpinism, or climbing at altitudes greater than 8,000 meters. The death rate for athletes in the Spanish Federation of Mountaineering was 15% in 1988 (Freixanet, 1991). Alpinists have been considered to take the greatest risks of any of the extreme athletes, and they have been shown to achieve the most extreme elevation on the extraversion dimension. The marked extraversion of extreme athletes reflects their seeking of risk, but not impulsiveness or failure to plan and to act without forethought. Consistent with the earlier discussion of extraversion, extreme athletes are motivated more by the opportunities for rewards, such as thrill and adventure-seeking, than by the threat of punishment. Alpinists were least influenced by the potential for punishment (Freixanet, 1991).

Participants in high-risk sports have been shown to not only be willing to assume risks, but also to be drawn to activities that provide intense, complex, and novel sensations (Cazenave, Le Scanff, & Woodman, 2007). This tendency to seek intense experiences that may present risk has been identified as the trait of **Impulsiveness-Sensation Seeking** by the American psychologist Marvin Zuckerman (1994). People high on the trait of Impulsiveness-Sensation Seeking are willing to take not only physical risks, but also social, financial, and legal risks in order to capture intense, novel, and complex sensations. Participants in high-risk sports have consistently demonstrated higher levels of this Impulsiveness-Sensation Seeking trait than have athletes in low-risk sports (Rhea & Martin, 2010). For example, female and male athletes in New Zealand between the ages of 13 and 76 who engaged in the high-risk sports of hang-gliding, mountaineering, skydiving, and automobile racing demonstrated higher levels of the Impulsiveness-Sensation Seeking quality than did athletes involved in the low-risk sports of swimming, marathon running, aerobics, and golfing (Jack & Ronan, 1998). However, consistent with the results of Freixanet with Spanish alpinists, athletes in high-risk sports did not demonstrate higher levels of impulsiveness or a lack of planning than did the low-risk athletes.

Long-distance runners are more likely to be introverted and to demonstrate less sensation-seeking than athletes who engage in high-risk sports and athletes who engaged in the low-risk sports or swimming, aerobics, and golf (Jack & Ronan, 1998). They are not, however, more introverted than general populations of people who do not exercise regularly or engage in sports (Egloff & Gruhn, 1996). It is not surprising that distance runners are not markedly introverted, given that their training requires a high level of activity, some socialization, and a willingness to tolerate pain, all characteristics associated with extraversion (Eysenck et al., 1982). Participants in sports involving explosive action are more likely to be mesomorphic or muscular, and mesomorphy is associated with extraversion. Distance runners are more likely to have ectomorphic or thin physiques, and ectomorphy is associated with introversion.

Extraverts are less deterred by potential adverse consequences in sport, such as failure, and are less fazed by the disapproval of others. Extraverts worry less about the prospect of aversive encounters with others and maintenance of harmonious relationships is not particularly appealing to extraverts. Extraverts find competition with others to be less aversive than introverts (Graziano, Feldesman, & Rahe, 1985). Indeed, extraverts find competitive situations to be more arousing, rewarding, interesting, and likable (Wolfe & Kasmer, 1988).

As explained in Chapter 11, the presence of an audience creates additional pressure for performance, and this is often accompanied by increased levels of cortical arousal. Given the higher levels of resting cortical arousal among introverts, it is not surprising that their performance erodes markedly with the presence of an audience (see Figure 15.1). Conversely, the performance of extraverts is enhanced by the presence of an audience, as the additional pressure may bring their cortical arousal to optimal levels. For example, the accuracy of serves in table tennis was evaluated in a group of English male college students with majors in sports studies and physical education. The students who were clear extraverts served far more accurately in the presence of 12 male peers as well as a table tennis coach. The accuracy of the serves of the introverts decreased dramatically in the presence of this audience (Graydon & Murphy, 1995). The debilitative effects of the audience on the performance of introverts may have been due to excessive levels of cortical arousal, or the introverts may have been more distracted by the audience. If the active memory resources of the introverts were captured by attention to the behavior of the audience, then fewer resources would be devoted to the instrumental behaviors necessary for skilled performance.

FIGURE 15.1 Mean Scores and Standard Deviations (SD) on Points Scored for Introverted and Extraverted Groups in Audience and No Audience Conditions (from Graydon & Murphy, 1995)

	Audience		No Audience	
	Mean	SD	Mean	SD
Extravert	23.9	7.5	18.1	7.6
Introvert	18.1	4.5	26.3	4.2

The tendency of introverts to sustain attention may provide them with an advantage at sports such as rifle shooting and archery, which call for deliberate preparation and execution of skills. Extraverts tend to trade vigilance and accuracy for speed, and their records for automobile accidents reflect this orientation. However, many sports reward participants for initiating action and anticipating the responses of others, especially in open skill sports such as tennis. The attention of the extravert is given more to anticipating and predicting changes in sporting and other environments, whereas introverts are less proactive and focused more on reacting to changing environmental conditions and the reactions of others.

MORE ON NEUROTICISM AND SPORT

A primary aspect of the neuroticism trait is the experience of **anxiety.** The relationship between anxiety and arousal or intensity and performance was discussed in Chapter 4. Distinctions between cognitive and physiological, trait and state, and facilitative and debilitative anxiety were identified. Neuroticism has aspects of trait anxiety, and performance on tasks that require complex motor actions, thought, and decision making are likely to be negatively affected by high levels of neuroticism and high state and cognitive anxiety. For example, male British squash players who were winners in a tournament were much lower in the trait of neuroticism than were counterparts who were losers (Cox & Kerr, 1990; Kerr & Cox, 1991).

With high levels of neuroticism, people may also avoid competition and athletic activity (Davis, Elliott, Dionne, & Mitchell, 1991). With high levels of neuroticism, runners may overestimate their susceptibility to running-related injury and avoid intense but safe training (Stephan, Deroche, Brewer, Caudroit, & Le Scanff, 2009).

Higher levels of neuroticism have also been related to the experience of state anxiety and negative mood states among female and male adults who competed in a National Championship for rifle shooting in Australia (Prapavessis & Grove, 1994). The rifle shooters with higher neuroticism experienced higher levels of tension, depression, anger, fatigue, confusion, and vigor prior to competition.

Anxiety is experienced as increasingly debilitative with the nearing of competition among athletes with high levels of neuroticism. For example, cognitive anxiety was experienced as increasingly debilitative in the week prior to competition among Tae Kwon Do practitioners high in the trait of neuroticism (Cerin, 2004). Levels of somatic anxiety were comparable one week prior to competition among practitioners high and low in neuroticism. However, practitioners who were low in the neuroticism trait experienced this anxiety as increasingly facilitative as they approached competition.

People with high levels of neuroticism often display cognitive anxiety or cognitive interference during complex motor tasks such as sport and automobile driving. Cognitive interference occupies attentional resources that can be put to best use focusing on motor tasks and changing environmental conditions. People who are both highly neurotic and extraverted have been shown to have particularly poor driving records (Shaw & Sichel, 1971).

MORE ON PSYCHOTICISM AND SPORT

Aggression and sport

With high trait psychoticism, people are more likely to be **aggressive** and comfortable with behavior that violates social norms or that is even antisocial. Eysenck et al. (1982) maintained that this trait was adaptive in sport. Psychoticism and extraversion are associated with Machiavellianism or with taking every advantage to advance personal interests (Allsopp, Eysenck, & Eysenck, 1991). More specifically, psychoticism is associated with the Machiavellianism attitudes of deceitfulness, cunning, manipulation, ruthlessness, and power seeking. Extraversion is more closely related to a Machiavellianism focus on social influence and power.

> ### Aggression and Sport
>
> Aggressive behavior is integrated into the flow of some sports, such as hockey, where aggressive acts in various levels of European male hockey have been shown to occur every third minute (Isberg, 2000). Very few of these aggressive acts in hockey games resulted in penalties, and coaches and other players encouraged players to commit aggressive acts during the game. Youth hockey players have discriminated good from bad penalties on the basis of whether the penalized player's team gained an advantage or avoided a disadvantage as a result of the illegal action.
>
> Aggression in hockey that resulted in penalty minutes has not consistently proven to be adaptive in terms of producing victories in the National Hockey League (McGuire, Courneya, Widmeyer, & Carron, 1992). This is reasonable, since the penalized team plays for a period of time with a disadvantage in terms of the number of skaters, while the penalized player sits in the penalty box. There was also no significant correlation between penalty minutes and team victories among male participants in the Ontario University Athletic Association (Widmeyer & Birch, 1979). All-stars in this University Athletic Association were penalized less than were non-all-stars.
>
> When attentional resources are occupied with concerns about opponents, fewer attentional resources are free for a focus on instrumental behaviors that contribute to optimal performance. Anger and hostility directed toward opponents or to oneself serve as a source of this distraction (Silva & Conroy, 1995).

FIVE-FACTOR MODEL OF PERSONALITY

Eysenck's model of personality was discussed in detail because it has generated the greatest amount of research concerning personality and sport. Other influential theories of personality propose a greater number of traits or dimensions of personality. Raymond Cattell identified 16 personality factors, and some research with this model has been conducted in sport settings (e.g., Schurr, Ashley, & Joy, 1977). The five-factor model identifies five traits (Costa & McCrae, 1992). In addition to the aforementioned traits of **neuroticism** and **extraversion,** the traits include **agreeableness, conscientiousness,** and **openness to experience.** The authors of the most influential five-factor model maintained that it provided a broader description of personality than did that of Eysenck (Costa & McCrae, 1995). Eysenck and others (Draycott & Kline, 1995) demonstrated that agreeableness and conscientiousness were not independent traits, but rather were negatively correlated with psychoticism. Costa and McCrae (1995) countered that psychoticism was an arbitrary conflation of two independent dimensions, agreeableness and conscientiousness. Openness to experience has also shown to share characteristics of extraversion.

The Eysenck Personality Questionnaire (EPQ; Eysenck & Eysenck, 1994) was developed to measure the traits of extraversion, neuroticism, and psychoticism. Perhaps it is useful to consider that the EPQ contains 100 questions and the questionnaire used by Costa and McCrae to measure the five factors, the NEO-PI-R, contains 240 questions. The questions are not identical, and the NEO-PI-R measures aspects of personality that are not included in the EPQ. A 60-item version of the NEO-Five Factor Inventory (NEO-FFI; Costa & McCrae, 1992) is also available.

Consistent with the results for the EPQ, sportspersons with high scores on extraversion are more likely to engage in risky sports, such as paragliding, rafting, and rock climbing. These risk takers also registered higher scores on openness, and lower scores on conscientiousness and neuroticism (Tok, 2011). As was the case with the EPQ, extraversion was shown to be adaptive for sport. Participants in a 100-mile ultra-marathon conducted in Alaska during February recorded higher scores on the extraversion scale (Hughes, Case, Stuemple, & Evans, 2003). They also endorsed higher levels of openness to experience.

Extraverted athletes use more problem-focused coping, such as increasing effort and analyzing problems. Extraverted athletes who had low scores on neuroticism and high scores on openness to experience were especially prone to opt for problem-focused coping. Athletes with high scores on extraversion, openness, and agreeableness endorsed emotion-focused coping strategies such as attempting to regulate their emotions. Highly conscientious athletes also focused on emotion-focused coping. Athletes who tend to ignore or avoid problems—those that engage in avoidance-focused coping—are more likely high in neuroticism and low in openness (Allen, Greenlees, & Jones, 2011).

Conscientious sportspersons more regularly put in their best efforts during practice and competition, and act on intentions to engage in strenuous training (de Bruijn, de Groot, van den Putte, & Rhodes, 2009). Conscientious Division I female soccer players fulfilled their responsibilities at practice and performed better during games. Better game performance was marked by the number of assists, shots on goal, scored goals, and the number of games played (Piedmont, Hill, & Blanco, 1999).

Application

Consistency, growth and development, and maintaining standards of excellence are esteemed traits in many athletic settings. Coaches value players who respond well to direction, instruction, and criticism. "Team players" are important to teammates and coaches. These qualities are reflected in the trait of conscientiousness.

Coaches rate conscientious players favorably and neurotic players unfavorably. Athletes with high levels of neuroticism were viewed as performing worse in games and as having less coachability, athletic ability, and "team playerness." Conscientious players were considered to have higher coachability, game performance, and work ethic. Coachability refers to the athlete's response to the instructions and directions of coaches. Highly conscientious athletes are more committed to their partnership with coaches; the same holds for conscientious coaches in relation to their athletes. Neurotic athletes show less commitment to coaches (Jackson, Dimmock, Gucciardi, & Grove, 2011).

Conscientiousness
In 2011, Ron Simpson became the sixth person in the United States to jog every day for 40 years. Mark Covert, a 60-year-old track coach, has the longest streak of daily running—43 years. To sustain this streak, he "hobbled" through his run the day after minor knee surgery. On another occasion, he was spooked by a rattlesnake and sprained his ankle. He stabilized the ankle in a lace-up boot to continued jogging. Jon Sutherland, who has the second-longest streak, ran with a broken hip that took nine months to heal. After taking a hard fall, Ken Young defied doctor's orders and jogged 1.1 miles with new steel plates in his broken wrists. Jim Pearson had a "scary" episode of jogging with blood clots in his lungs. Steve DeBoer preserved his membership in this 40-year club by scheduling a layover of sufficient duration to accommodate a jog during a flight to Australia. After tearing his meniscus in 2011, Mark Covert briefly considered stopping. However, he reasoned: "What we are doing is not a mark of intelligence" (Cacciola, 2011).

The combination of low neuroticism and high conscientiousness has been associated with high achievement in a variety of settings. This combination is associated with setting high standards and sufficient emotional stability and self-confidence to withstand setbacks and frustration in the pursuit of long-term goals.

The importance of setting high standards and goals was recognized among competitive male and female English gymnasts (Woodman et al., 2010). Gymnasts who regulated their behavior by setting goals were more likely to realize quality training, irrespective of personality traits. Further, conscientiousness was also associated with quality training, and those with lower levels of neuroticism coped better with adversity.

Higher-level athletes show higher levels of conscientiousness. Consistent with research with the EPQ, they are also more likely to be stable and to record low levels of neuroticism (Allen et al., 2011)

People generally recognize that competition is not all "fun and games." For example, college students understood competitive situations to involve fewer friendly interactions and few harmonious relationships than did situations requiring cooperation with others (Graziano, Hair, & Finch, 1997). Competitive situations were seen as more challenging, difficult, and enjoyable, and to cause more anxiety. However, competitive situations are seen to be even more problematic by people who are high in the trait of agreeableness. Those high in agreeableness are more highly motivated to maintain harmonious relationships with others and to avoid competitive interactions. Competition may present a greater conflict for highly agreeable people, because their victories often involve defeating others and disrupting interpersonal harmony. It may be difficult to reconcile defeating an opponent with wishes for interpersonal harmony, because the agreeable person recognizes that opponents also want to win.

Athletes who are agreeable, conscientious, and open to experience show greater commitment to partners in sports such as doubles tennis, badminton, rowing, and beach volleyball (Jackson, Dimmock, Gucciardi, & Grove, 2010). Further, athletes who are perceived as agreeable, conscientious, and open to experience inspire greater commitment from their partners in these sports. Agreeableness also provoked trust, emotional closeness, and commitment in athlete-coach dyads (Jackson et al., 2011). The commitment and trust of coaches and athletes may result from the cooperation, empathy, and emotional warmth displayed by the agreeable sportspersons.

Boris Becker and Personality Traits?

Boris Becker was the youngest-ever men's champion at Wimbledon in 1985. He won the tournament at 17 years of age, and was also the first unseeded winner and the first from Germany. He won an additional two titles at Wimbledon, two at the Australian Open, and one at the U.S. Open, for a total of six major tennis titles. Yet, he expressed conflicting reactions to competition. He compared tennis matches to gladiatorial contests in which one wins and the other "dies" (Atkins, 1990). He explained:

> My opponents are human beings, not enemies. In order to survive a tournament, you have to be some kind of beast. You have to beat your opponent psychologically. After tough tournaments I frequently go through phases of deep depression and see no reason to go on. I can't bear to go out and be among people who touch me and ask how I am, especially after a big success like Wimbledon (Atkins, 1990, p. 5).

He also likened competitive tennis to art and sex:

> That Sunday afternoon: You're in the Wimbledon final, it's the third set, and you're about to win. . .This is something I miss. Because even with a great business deal, it's not the same sensation. Tennis is an art form. I feel as if I'm performing on a stage in front of millions of people, and I was sometimes able to fascinate them for two weeks. This culminates with a Sunday final, match point, and then all the celebrations. It's like a long foreplay that ends with a huge orgasm. That's what it is (Price, 2001, p. 90).

Becker was also acutely uncomfortable with the understandable adulation of German fans, and appeared to associate expressions of national pride with Nazi fanaticism. He commented, "When I looked into the eyes of my fans I thought I was looking at monsters. When I saw this kind of blind, emotional devotion I could understand what happened to us a long time ago in Nuremberg" (Atkins, 1990, p. 5). Of course, the emotional devotion of fans "comes with the territory" of sporting virtuosity, perhaps especially with tall, powerfully built prodigies who are "strikingly handsome" (Atkins, 1990, p. 3). This adulation is independent of ethnicity or country of origin.

NARCISSISM

Narcissism is a trait that refers to an excessive focus on oneself, and a relative lack of concern for others, except as sources of admiration. Narcissists may believe that they are special human beings who are capable of accomplishing special things. With this trait, people tend to focus on gaining glory and, therefore, put forth greater effort and achieve better results in the presence of an audience and under pressure. They perform equally well in the presence of supportive and unsupportive audiences, as they focus on demonstrating their superiority rather than on the responses of the audience. Their objective is to gain the admiration, not the affection, of the audience. They perform beneath their capabilities when an audience is not present, as they put forth less effort when there are no opportunities for self-enhancement (Roberts, Callow, Hardy, Woodman, & Thomas, 2010; Wallace & Baumeister, 2002; Williams & Cumming, 2011; Woodman, Roberts, Hardy, Callow, & Rogers, 2011).

Narcissists are less cooperative with exhortations of coaches to adopt team goals and to put forth extra effort. Narcissistic athletes may view such efforts as diminishing opportunities for their individual aggrandizement (Arthur, Woodman, Ong, Hardy, & Ntoumanis, 2011).

Readers will recall that that the performance of extraverts is enhanced in the presence of an audience (Graydon & Murphy, 1995). However, this is likely due to the augmented cortical arousal perpetuated by environmental pressure. The traits of psychoticism (high) and agreeableness (low) are also associated with a lack of empathy or concern with the welfare of others and narcissism is associated with low levels of agreeableness (Bagby et al., 2005) and high levels of psychoticism and extraversion (Raskin & Hall, 1981).

TEMPERAMENT

Theories of personality, such as Eysenck's, that hypothesize, and to some degree, document associations between traits and brain functions are consistent with theory and research on temperament. **Temperament** refers to inherited or genetically determined physiological and psychological processes that are apparent in very young children. Temperament creates biases or tendencies to behave in certain ways, but does not guarantee that this behavior will occur. Conversely, without a temperamental bias, behaviors, such as excessive fearfulness, are far less likely, even in environments that provoke this fearfulness. An analogy for the illustration of the relationship between a temperamental bias for fearfulness and the actual expression of fearful behavior is the relationship between temperatures under 32 degrees Fahrenheit, or zero degrees Celsius or centigrade, and the likelihood of a blizzard. Blizzards often do not occur when the temperature is below 32 degrees, but if they are to occur, chances are that the temperature will be below 32. Blizzards never occur when the temperature is above 50 degrees Fahrenheit (Kagan, 1994).

Jerome Kagan (1994) asserted that temperamental differences were due to inherited differences in the levels of norepinephrine, a primary neurotransmitter in the brain and sympathetic nervous system, and corticotrophin-releasing hormone (CRH). Higher levels of norepinephrine result in greater activation of the parts of the **amygdala,** an area of the brain associated with fear and anxiety. The amygdala is a part of the limbic system—the brain structures most responsible for the experience of emotion. CRH contributes to the bodily or physiological experience of anxiety. CRH production leads to the production of cortisol. Cortisol has been described at several points in this text as a sign of stress. With this constellation of norepinephrine and CRH, children have a more reactive circuit from the limbic system to the sympathetic nervous system. Perhaps because the amygdala has neuronal projections to the frontal lobes of the cerebral cortex, higher levels of activation of the amygdala are associated with higher levels of beta wave activity and lower levels of alpha wave activity, especially in the right frontal cortex. This pattern of beta and alpha wave activity is associated with unpleasant and anxious feelings (Kagan, Snidman, McManis, & Woodward, 2001).

Children with this biochemical diathesis are more likely to be inhibited, withdrawn, and shy, especially when faced with unfamiliar situations. They resemble Eysenck's introverts. They are prone to experience heightened states of anxiety when faced with unfamiliarity and challenges, and in response they have difficulty processing information and remembering new information. They also show less willingness to take risks.

The diathesis for inhibition is particularly evident in novel situations and in social settings, and is therefore relevant to the issue of performance anxiety and choking under pressure. For example, children classified as inhibited in the second year of life are more likely to develop social anxiety or to become anxious and inhibited in the presence of others, especially strangers, at age 13. Indeed, 61% of a group of 13-year-olds who demonstrated withdrawal during their second year of life demonstrated social anxiety, whereas 27% who were uninhibited in their second year demonstrated this later social anxiety (Kagan et al., 2001).

Ectomorphy and Inhibition

Kagan reported that the biochemical predisposition to inhibited and fearful behavior was not democratically distributed. He found that about 60% of inhibited children had blue eyes and 60% of uninhibited children had brown eyes. He also discovered that 60% of ectomorphic boys with thin faces were inhibited. The combination of ectomorphy and blue eyes resulted in the greatest chance for behavioral inhibition. Placed in a larger context, approximately 20% of Caucasian children begin life with this inhibited disposition, and 40% begin with the uninhibited characteristic. These dispositions are to a large degree determined by genetic factors, but are influenced by experience. For example, parents who understand when inhibited children profit from a bit of a nudge to master tendencies to withdraw, help their children become less fearful. Parents who place demands on uninhibited children to follow rules, assist these children to reign in their fearlessness.

Women and girls are also more likely to demonstrate inhibition and anxiety. This may be due to differences in the norepinephrine, CRH, cortical, and peripheral structures. Alternatively, these differences may be due to greater environmental demands on women, especially well-educated women, in the U.S. and Europe. These women commonly experience pressure to meet high standards of beauty, success in sustaining relationships and attachments, and vocational competence. Believing that they fall beneath standards in one or more of these areas, women may respond with social anxiety and withdrawal.

THE PROFILE OF MOOD STATES (POMS)

There are alternative models of psychological factors associated with enhanced versus impaired athletic performance. These models are commonly referred to as personality theories, even though they do not refer to stable dimensions of behavior that are consistent over time and across situations. For example, the American psychologist William Morgan developed the Mental Health Model for differentiating more and less successful athletes. Athletic performance was seen to rise and fall in relation to the mental health of athletes. Successful athletes were seen to experience fewer psychological problems than did less successful athletes. For example, elite senior male weightlifters, junior male weightlifters, and female weightlifters that were ranked in the top three of their weight categories by the U.S. Weightlifting Federation had fewer psychological problems than their counterparts who were ranked lower than eleventh or were unranked (Mahoney, 1989). The elite weightlifters had less depression, psychoticism, and fewer overall problems.

Working within this model, mental health was commonly measured with the **Profile of Mood States (POMS).** The POMS is a self-report questionnaire designed to measure the mood states of tension, depression, anger, fatigue, confusion, and vigor. The POMS was created in 1971 as a measure of reactions to current life situations. The POMS was especially designed to measure progress in psychotherapy or counseling in outpatient settings (McNair, Lorr, & Droppleman, 1971; Bourgeois, LeUnes, & Meyers, 2010). It was also developed for use in measuring mood states among normal subjects of at least 18 years of age, and has been used extensively in exercise and sport settings. The POMS had been used in at least 258 published studies by 1998 (LeUnes & Burger, 2000), and in over 1,400 studies that were listed on PsycInfo by 2006.

THE POMS ICEBERG PROFILE

The POMS has been shown to be sensitive to fluctuation in the moods that influence athletic performance. This quality has been demonstrated most convincingly among groups of athletes that were homogenous with regard to skill level and physical conditioning (Terry, 1995). More successful athletes have traditionally been identified by the **"iceberg profile"** on the POMS, which consists of high levels of vigor, or an abundance of energy, and low levels of tension, depression, anger, fatigue, and confusion (Figure 15.2). The term "iceberg" refers to the graphic picture that is created when this configuration of scores is plotted on a POMS profile sheet rather than to predictions that these successful athletes would be cool under pressure. In the vernacular of sport, athletes who are cool under pressure and unlikely to choke are referred to as having "ice water" in their veins. With the iceberg profile, the tension, depression, anger, fatigue, and confusion scales are suppressed beneath the "water line" or the average scores for these scales, and there is a sharp spike for the vigor scale.

The POMS was seen as a technique for predicting successful performances among elite athletes. For example, wrestlers who qualified for the 1976 U.S. Olympic team demonstrated this iceberg profile, whereas wrestlers who were not selected for the team demonstrated less vigor and more depression, anger, fatigue, and confusion (Morgan, 1980). Similarly, wrestlers and speed skaters from the 1972 U.S. Olympic team,

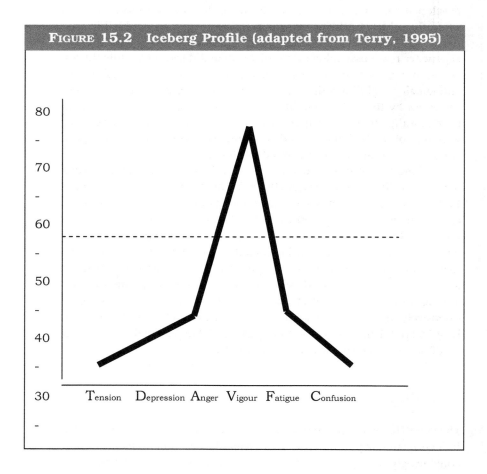

FIGURE 15.2   Iceberg Profile (adapted from Terry, 1995)

international rowers, and international runners also gave iceberg profiles on the POMS. Collegiate tennis players who won matches at an NCAA regional (VII) tournament were more likely to evidence the iceberg profile than were counterparts who lost (Covassin & Pero, 2004).

The success of the POMS in differentiating elite and non-elite athletes has not been consistent. For example, the POMS did not differentiate between elite and non-elite athletes in a sizeable number of studies involving marathoners, field hockey players, basketball, and football players, and ultramarathoners (Prapavessis, 2000).

It is somewhat unreasonable to expect that the POMS, or any measure of mood or personality, will always distinguish between winners and losers at extremely elite levels of competition. For example, the POMS did not identify World Netball Championship titlists (Miller & Miller, 1985). Among elite competitors, physical and psychological differences are often quite small. Further, the POMS profile associated with elite performance may be somewhat variable depending on the demands of particular sports (Hadala, Cebolla, Banos, & Barrios, 2010).

HOW THE MOODS MEASURED BY THE POMS AFFECT PERFORMANCE

Most generally, better athletic performance is associated with vigor, whereas confusion, fatigue, and depression are related to poorer performance (Beedie, Terry, & Lane, 2000). Sportspersons are very unlikely to report depression on the POMS, and approximately 50% of athletes endorse none of the depression items (Lane, 2008). However, depression moderates the effects of anger and tension on performance. For sportspersons without depression, anger and tension facilitated performance, whereas the opposite was observed for athletes who reported depression (Lane, 2007).

THE POMS AND SATISFACTORY PERFORMANCES

Precompetitive moods as measured by the POMS differentiate between athletes who are satisfied or dissatisfied with performances. Athletes with POMS profiles that approximated the iceberg profile are far more likely to report that their performance in competition met their expectations. For example, the iceberg profile consistently identified athletes in rowing and bobsledding Olympic and World competitions who were satisfied with performances. Similarly, satisfied oarsmen at the 1993 World Rowing Championships and participants in the 1993–1994 Bobsled World Cup event were distinguished by the iceberg profile (Terry, 1995). The greatest differences for these athletes who were satisfied with performances versus those whom believed they had underperformed were on the vigor scale of the POMS.

As mentioned above, the POMS measures moods, and these are more transient than traits. It is, therefore, unreasonable to expect that POMS scores taken prior to competitions will predict performance if moods change in the course of the competition. Further, the POMS appears more predictive of performance in sports that involved closed skills and that are self-paced. In open skill sports, there are more external influences that influence performance (Durtschi & Weiss, 1986).

INDIVIDUAL DIFFERENCES IN POMS AND OPTIMAL PERFORMANCE

The association between the iceberg profile and successful performance notwithstanding, elevated anger scores on the POMS promotes better performance in violent sports. For example, the anger scores were almost twice as high for collegiate rodeo athletes in steer wrestling compared to roughstock, roping, and barrel racing. Steer wrestling, involves the most violent interaction between man and animal (Meyers & Sterling, 1990; Meyers & LeUnes, 1996).

Further, as has been emphasized throughout this book, people are different. As many as 26% of successful performances in Olympic and World Championship competitions occurred with athletes who did not show the iceberg pattern prior to competition. Conversely, 54% of these elite athletes produced these iceberg profiles and subsequently had unsuccessful performances (Terry, 1993). The understanding that the POMS profile associated with optimal performance may be different for different athletes has led to suggestions that athletes learn from experience what POMS "works best" for them, and then attempt to reproduce that POMS profile prior to competitions (Hanton, Cropley, & Lee, 2009).

Deviations from this pattern of moods and POMS may serve as warnings to athletes that they are not emotionally prepared to perform, and they may then take action to alleviate negative moods. For example, athletes in the closed skill sport of clay-target shooting recorded POMS profiles prior to competition for a period of 12 months (Prapavessis & Grove, 1991). Comparing the POMS scores prior to acceptable and worst performances, the POMS scores for acceptable performances were far closer to each athlete's optimal POMS profile. POMS profiles that are stable for days prior to competition suggest a better impending performance than do POMS reflecting fluctuating moods.

THE INVERSE ICEBERG PROFILE

An **"inverse iceberg"** POMS profile has been considered to reflect staleness, especially low scores on the vigor factor. Staleness is a state of psychological and physical fatigue that results in impaired sport performance and an inability to train at customary levels (Morgan, Brown, Raglin,

O'Connor, & Ellickson, 1987). Staleness is often the result of overtraining, but overtraining or progressively increasing training loads is necessary to improving performance with endurance sports. Staleness is most likely during cycles of intense training, and is represented on the POMS by increased fatigue and global mood disturbance, and decreased vigor. The inverse iceberg profile may also present after an athlete is injured. A return to an iceberg profile may coincide with the physical recovery of injured athletes and tapering or reducing the training load of fatigued athletes (Zehsaz, Azarbaijani, Farhangimaleki, & Tiidus, 2011).

The POMS in Practice

It appears that the POMS should be used as a suggestion of readiness to do one's best rather than as an absolute sign of impending difficulties. It is not sufficiently accurate for use in selecting members to teams. The influence of preperformance mood as measured by the POMS on athletic performance is small in comparison to the importance of other psychological factors, physiological characteristics of athletes, training schedules, and histories of prior athletic success. Sophisticated statistical analyses have demonstrated that less than 1% of athletic performance was predicted by preperformance POMS (Rowley, Landers, Kyllo, & Etnier, 1995). Of course, if outcomes of athletic events were 100% predictable on the basis of prior information, it would be unnecessary to hold actual competitions. This being said, the remaining 99% of the factors that determine outcomes of athletic events remain to be determined if only preperformance POMS scores are available. Information about the many other psychological factors, physiological characteristics of athletes, training schedules, and histories of prior athletic success would be referenced to make more accurate predictions about athletic performances.

As has been emphasized throughout this book, it is unrealistic to expect that one will feel full of vigor and self-efficacy if proper physical training has been neglected. Athletes with the iceberg profile are prepared to do their best in competition, and a history of success in competition and excellent preparation, training, and the development of superior skills are likely to lead to the development of the iceberg profile. For example, successful athletes who produced iceberg profiles prior to competitions had better records throughout the athletic season, more experience, and superior training facilities and programs (Heyman, 1982).

ATHLETIC COPING SKILLS INVENTORY

The **Athletic Coping Skills Inventory (ACSI)** was developed to measure resiliency and coping effectiveness. With scales designed to measure social support, psychological coping skills, and life stress, it has proven effective in evaluating psychological resiliency and vulnerability to athletic injury. Originally developed in the 1980s, the most recent and scientifically sound version consists of 28 questions that compose seven scales: **Coping with Adversity, Peaking Under Pressure, Goal Setting/Mental Preparation, Concentration, Freedom From Worry, Confidence and Achievement Motivation,** and **Coachability** (Smith, Schutz, Smoll, & Ptacek, 1995).

The scales of the ACSI-28 have validity in that they measure what they purport to measure. Further, as athletes progress in elite sport, athletic coping skills also develop (Meyers, Stewart, Laurent, LeUnes, & Bourgeois, 2008). The Freedom From Worry scale correlates negatively with measures of anxiety in sporting contexts. The Concentration, Confidence and Achievement Motivation, Coping With Adversity, Goal Setting/Mental Preparation, and Peaking Under Pressure were all highly correlated with general self-efficacy. Successful performance at the Australian Age National Swimming Championships was associated with higher scores on the Coping with Adversity and Peaking Under Pressure scales (Mummery, Schofield, & Perry, 2004). The Coping with Adversity scale also differentiated recruits that cracked starting lineups in American Division I AA football programs (Spieler et al, 2007). A composite score of the ACSI items was shown to correlate .58 with a measure of general self-efficacy. Similar, albeit slightly less robust, correlations were seen between these ACSI-28 scales and a measure of self-esteem (Smith et al., 1995).

The ACSI-28 was also used to predict the performance of professional minor league baseball players (Smith & Christensen, 1995). The Confidence, Coping with Adversity, and Total, or composite, score for the ACSI-28 predicted the batting averages of position players. The Confidence and Peaking Under Pressure scales were significant correlates of low earned run averages (ERA) among pitchers. As mentioned above, the Confidence scale resembles self-efficacy, and this factor predicted both hitting and pitching skill. Information from the ACSI-28 allowed for significantly more accurate predictions of batting averages for position players and ERAs for pitchers than was possible solely on the basis of the ballplayers' physical talent. In fact, coaches' estimates of pitchers' physical talent (e.g., velocity, control, movement of fast ball, adequacy of breaking ball, and changeup) were practically unrelated to ERAs. The ACSI-28 was seen to be at least as accurate in predicting baseball performance as tests of intelligence (IQ tests) were in predicting academic performance for college students.

Composite ACSI-28 scores also allowed for more accurate predictions of which minor league players would still be in baseball after two and three years. Estimates of physical talent were also accurate predictors of the players who would avoid being cut after two and three years. Competition in professional baseball is so keen that only 74% survive after two years and only 26% have managed to stick with their team after three years.

SUMMARY AND APPLICATION

Hans Eysenck's proposed that personality consists of three large dimensions or traits that were at least somewhat determined by genetic inheritance. Traditionally, athletes have been seen as high in the traits of extraversion and psychoticism and low in neuroticism. Of course, athletes are not the only people with these profiles or traits, as, for example, sports fans show similar profiles. Because of higher levels of cortical and sympathetic nervous system arousal, introverts are more reactive to environmental stress than are extroverts. Given that introverts might chose to shun environments that include tension and excitement, their comfort in many sports may be problematic. This was forcefully illustrated in the study of English college students with majors in sports studies and physical education (Graydon & Murphy, 1995). The presence of an audience eroded the performance of introverts when the accuracy of table tennis serves was measured. Extraverts "came alive" in the presence of an audience, and the accuracy of their table tennis serves improved relative to their accuracy when serving in solitude. Extraverts habituate or stop attending to environmental stimuli quickly, and their poorer performance without an audience may be because table tennis serving in solitude is not sufficiently exciting to sustain their attention. Competition may also be more aversive to introverts because of their concerns about maintaining harmonious relationships with others. Extraverts count competition as arousing, interesting, and rewarding.

Jerome Kagan's descriptions of withdrawn children were similar to Eysenck's characterizations of introverts. These children became behaviorally inhibited when stressed or anxious. This temperamental bias for inhibition and withdrawal was seen to be the result of highly reactive amygdalae and, more generally, limbic systems and sympathetic nervous systems.

With high levels of neuroticism, people may also avoid competition and athletic activity. Neuroticism has characteristics of trait anxiety, and those high in neuroticism are prone to state anxiety during performances of complex motor tasks.

The five-factor model was discussed and compared to the three factors of Eysenck. The trait of agreeableness partially reflects low scores on the psychoticism dimension. Those high in the agreeableness trait are more uncomfortable with interpersonal conflict. Competition often presents a form of conflict in that achieving victory and protecting opponents from the sting of defeat are mutually exclusive goals.

Should introverts be consigned to sports that do not involve explosive action and which are better suited to ectomorphic physiques, such as distance running? Given their capacity to sustain attention, are they better candidates for closed skill sports such as target shooting? These questions cannot currently be answered on the basis of empirical evidence. However, given that marked extraversion is a statistical rarity, to reserve competition, especially with audiences and pressure for optimal performance, to these extraverts with "ice water in their veins" would be to deny the majority the benefit of competition and sport. Further, many factors such as physical talent determine performance, and elite athletes such as tennis players of Wimbledon standard have been identified with levels of neuroticism that exceed the mean of psychiatric patients with depressive disorders (Eysenck et al., 1982).

Research with the POMS has traditionally indicated that athletes with the iceberg profile were prepared to do their best in competition. The iceberg profile reflects a high level of vigor or an abundance of energy, and low levels of tension, depression, anger, fatigue, and confusion. It appeared that the vigor scale was most sensitive in predicting satisfactory performances. However, the finding that POMS profiles associated with optimal performance may be different for different athletes led to suggestions that athletes learn from experience what POMS is associated with best performances, and then attempt to reproduce that POMS prior to competitions. When moods are clearly different from these optimal profiles, athletes may be warned that they are not prepared to do their best. Other deviations from profiles that are optimal for performers, such as the inverse iceberg, may indicate staleness or injury.

The POMS measures psychological states, whereas the Eysenck and five-factor models described traits or stable characteristics. The Athletic Coping Skills Coping Inventory (ACSI-28) was developed specifically for use in sporting contexts and offers the promise of measuring skills that are closely related to performance. For example, a composite score from the ACSI-28 was shown to correlate with a measure of general self-efficacy.

Ancient Greek philosophers encouraged people to "Know yourself," as armed with self-knowledge people were better able to predict their own responses and tendencies. With self-knowledge, people can build on their strengths and work around their weaknesses (Eysenck & Wilson, 1976). These themes have been consistently presented throughout the chapters of this book. A greater understanding of one's psychology serves to take the mystery out of the factors that relate to performance.

It may also be difficult to determine one's personality based on the descriptions provided in this book, and personality can certainly be evaluated more precisely by a professional psychologist. However, the descriptions provided in this chapter may at least stir the curiosity and provide insight to those troubled by performance inhibition.

Whether traits are as genetically determined and relatively immutable as argued by Eysenck is a matter of controversy. However, the traits of extraversion and neuroticism have been shown to influence performance in sporting contexts, and knowledge of one's tendencies to respond with anxiety or enthusiasm to situational pressure during performances appears useful. Scientific research is necessary before clear directions can be provided about how to use information about personality to enhance performance.

An appreciation of the influence of personality traits on performance is probably best considered at times distal to performances and competitions. Information about traits may provide performers with information about their tendencies. This information may be integrated into training regimens and preperformance routines. For example, knowledge that one is likely to respond with cognitive and physiological anxiety, perhaps due to introversion or neuroticism, may signal that techniques described in previous chapters to control anxiety and choking under pressure are especially relevant. Athletes who are excessively agreeable may consider whether their overly empathic responses to the psychological well-being of competitors is unreasonable under rules of fair play.

Key Terms

Discussion Questions

Q1. Review the assumptions of trait theories of personality.
Q2. Consider the personality theory of Hans Eysenck.
Q3. Review the dimensions of extraversion-introversion, neuroticism-stability, and psychoticism-superego.
Q4. Consider Eysenck's explanation of the genetic determinants of extraversion.
Q5. Consider environments in which introverts and extraverts would be most comfortable.
Q6. Identify the traits Eysenck associated with athletes.
Q7. Review the traits associated with extraversion that are adaptive in sport.
Q8. Consider sports most associated with extraversion and introversion.
Q9. Explain how neuroticism is not adaptive in sport?
Q10. Eysenck considered psychoticism to be adaptive in sport. Does the evidence support this?
Q11. Compare and contrast Eysenck model with the five-factor model of personality.
Q12. What traits are associated with high achievement?
Q13. Is narcissism adaptive in sport?

Q14. How does the topic of temperament fit in a chapter on personality?
Q15. Review the dimensions of the Profile of Mood States (POMS).
Q16. Does the POMS measure personality traits?
Q17. How is the POMS used in practice?
Q18. Review the scales of the Athletic Coping Skills Inventory.
Q19. Consider the usefulness of the Athletic Coping Skills Inventory in consulting with athletes.

Suggested Readings

Allen, M. S., Greenlees, I., & Jones, M. (2011). An investigation of the five-factor model of personality and coping behaviour in sport. *Journal of Sports Sciences, 29*, 841–850. doi : 10.1080/02640414.2011.565064

Castanier, C., Le Scanff, C., & Woodman, T. (2010). Who takes risks in high-risk sports? A typological personality approach. *Research Quarterly for Exercise & Sport, 81*, 478–484.

Cazenvae, N., Le Scanff, C., & Woodman, T. (2007). Psychological profiles and emotional regulation characteristics of women engaged in risk-taking sports. *Anxiety, Stress, & Coping, 20*, 421–435. doi: 10.1080/10615800701330176

Costa, P. T., Jr., & McCrae, R. R. (1995). Primary traits of Eysenck's P-E-N system: three- and five-factor solutions. *Journal of Personality and Social Psychology, 69*, 308–317.

De Bruijn, G-J., de Groot, R., van den Putte, B., & Rhodes, R. (2009). Conscientiousness, extroversion, and action control: Comparing moderate and vigorous physical activity. *Journal of Sport & Exercise Psychology, 31*, 724–742.

Dishman, R. K., & Chambliss, H. O. (2010). Exercise psychology. In J. M. Williams (Ed.), *Applied sport psychology: Personal growth to peak performance* (6th ed., pp. 563–595). New York, NY: McGraw-Hill.

Eysenck, H. J., & Eysenck, M. W. (1985). *Personality and individual differences.* New York, NY: Plenum.

Jackson, B., Dimmock, J. A., Gucciardi, D. F., & Grove, J. R. (2010). Relationship commitment in athletic dyads: Actor and partner effects for Big Five self- and other-ratings. *Journal of Research in Personality, 44*, 641–648. doi: 10.1016/j.jrp.2010.08.004

Jackson, B., Dimmock, J. A., Gucciardi, D. F., & Grove, J. R. (2011). Personality traits and relationship perceptions in coach-athlete dyads: Do opposites really attract? *Psychology of Sport and Exercise, 12*, 222–230. doi: 10.1016/j.psychsport.2010.11.005

Kagan, J. (1994). *Galen's prophecy. Temperament in human nature.* New York, NY: Basic Books.

Prapavessis, H. (2000). The POMS and sports performance: A review. *Journal of Applied Sport Psychology, 12,* 34–48.

Roberts, R., Callow, N., Hardy, L., Woodman, T., & Thomas, L. (2010). Interactive effects of different visual imagery perspectives and narcissism on motor performance. *Journal of Sport & Exercise Psychology, 32,* 499–517.

Smith, R. E., Schutz, R. W., Smoll, F. L., & Ptacek, J. T. (1995). Development and validation of a multidimensional measure of sport-specific psychological skills: The Athletic Coping Skills Inventory-28. *Journal of Sport & Exercise Psychology, 17,* 379–398.

Tok, S. (2011). The big five personality traits and risky sport participation. *Social Behavior and Personality, 39,* 1105–1112. doi: 10.2224/sbp. 2011.39.8.1105

Van Vianen, A.E.M., & De Dreu, C.K.W. (2001). Personality in teams: Its relationship to social cohesion, task cohesion, and term performance. *European Journal of Work and Organizational Psychology, 10,* 97–120.

Webbe, R. M., & Ochs, S. R. (2007). Personality traits relate to heading frequency in male soccer players. *Journal of Clinical Sport Psychology, 1,* 379–389.

Chapter 16

SUBSTANCE ABUSE

Alcohol consumption is associated with sport

"Despite their roles in promoting healthy pursuits, sports clubs in Australia are notorious for the rates of unregulated, high-risk drinking common among many club members. High-risk drinking is normative at all levels in much Australian sport and particularly among male team sports. At the community

level, this culture is manifest in ritual binge drinking, the use of alcohol as rewards for sporting performances, and end-of-season trips that resemble a drinking 'safari' " (Duff and Munro, 2007, p. 1992). Offensive behavior, physical and relational violence, assaults, and drunk driving have been accepted as collateral damage. In the most graphic example, a player died at a suburban club in Melbourne in 1992 following a drinking bout that lasted 12 hours. "The victim collapsed in the club toilet and asphyxiated after vomiting. Sporting clubs reproduce problematic drinking cultures by introducing young people into the practice. Many underage people report being able to purchase alcohol in community sporting clubs more easily than in other licensed venues" (Duff and Munro, 2007, p. 1992). The Good Sports program was introduced in Victoria in 2001 as a means of establishing safer norms for alcohol use. Approximately one-quarter of the sporting clubs in Victoria participate in this program.

The use of alcohol and other substances is widespread. Substance use disorders are among the three most frequently diagnosed mental disorders in the U.S. (American Psychiatric Association, 2000). The prevalence or frequency of substance use and abuse among sportspersons is comparable to that of the general population. Among athletes and the general population, substance abuse results in interpersonal and vocational dysfunction and decreases well-being. Substance use and abuse may directly impair motor and cognitive performance. Performance suffers from substance abuse at times proximal and distal to performance. Due to this focus on performance impairment, the topic of performance-enhancing or ergogenic substances will be addressed more briefly, and with a focus on the health hazards associated with their use.

The most widely abused drugs are alcohol, nicotine, cannabis, cocaine/crack, and prescription-type drugs (pain relievers, tranquilizers, stimulants, and sedatives) used nonmedically. Due to space limitation, the treatment of substance use in this chapter will be primarily limited to a review of the effects of alcohol and cannabis. Cannabis is most often consumed in the form of smoked marijuana. Alcohol use has been studied in greatest detail, perhaps because it is a legal substance and the most widely used. Far more people use tobacco than cannabis, but the effects of tobacco on performance are less immediate. However, tobacco use has profoundly negative effects on health, such as increased risks for bronchitis, obstructive lung disease, cardiovascular disease, and forms of cancer. Tobacco users become profoundly dependent on nicotine, and experience painful withdrawal symptoms when its use is stopped. Cocaine/crack is a powerfully addictive drug that also promotes dependence and painful withdrawal. Its use is far less frequent than alcohol and cannabis. Both nicotine and cocaine/crack are stimulant drugs. College athletes are less likely to engage in nonmedical prescription drug use (Ford, 2008).

PROBLEMS CAUSED BY SUBSTANCE ABUSE

The abuse of alcohol and other drugs leads to untoward events. The World Health Organization (WHO, 2011) reports that the harmful use of alcohol is the world's third largest risk factor for disability and disease. Alcohol consumption results in almost 4% of deaths worldwide, more deaths than are caused by HIV/AIDS, violence, or tuberculosis. It is the leading risk factor for male deaths between the ages of 15 and 59. In the Americas and Europe, approximately 31% to 41% of male deaths between the ages of 15 and 29 are attributable to the harmful use of alcohol. These deaths are largely attributable to accidents, violence and conflict, and higher levels of heart disease.

Substance abuse and other mental disorders lead to absences from work and decreased work productivity (Cartwright, 2008; Kessler & Frank, 1997; U.S. Department of Health and Human Services, 2010). The annual medical costs for people in the U.S. with substance abuse or depressive disorders are $1,766 higher than that for people without these mental disorders (Druss & Rosenheck, 1999). The total U.S. health care costs for treating substance abuse disorders were $32.1 billion in 1998.

Drug abuse cost the U.S. economy an additional $98.5 billion in lost earnings due to absenteeism and lost productivity. Crime-related expenses caused by drug use totaled $88.9 billion, and these costs included property damage and police and criminal justice expenses ("Report finds," 2002). Alcohol alone results in total economic costs of $837 per individual in the U.S., $358 in Scotland, $384 in France, and $420 in Canada (WHO, 2011).

These costs would be considerably higher if everyone in need of treatment obtained it. National surveys demonstrated that 50% of Canadians, 60% of Mexicans, and 72% of Americans with substance abuse or dependence disorders seek help for their addictions (Kessler et al., 2001). However, there is an average lag of 10 years between the occurrence of their substance disorder and this help seeking. Unfortunately, people who begin substance abuse at a younger age are less likely to seek treatment.

The likelihood of suicide attempts increases with drug use and abuse. The odds of suicide for current heroin users was six times as great as for people who do not abuse drugs, and at least twofold for cocaine users. The risk of first suicide attempts increased as the number of substances currently used increased (Borges, Walters, & Kessler, 2000). Among people with a genetic predisposition for schizophrenia, those who used cannabis during adolescence had a much higher likelihood of developing schizophrenic-type disorders (U.S. Department of Health and Human Services, 2010).

People with substance abuse and other mental disorders are more likely to drop out of high school and college (Kessler, Foster, Saunders, & Stang, 1995; U.S. Department of Health and Human Services, 2010). Among college students, increasing alcohol use is related to lower average grades and a contributing factor in 28% of all college dropouts. Alcohol use is involved in about 80% of campus vandalism, 95% of campus violence, and two-thirds of campus suicides (Bower & Martin, 1999).

Teenage females with substance abuse and other mental disorders are more likely to give birth and to give birth prior to marriage (Kessler et al. 1997). Alcohol use and abuse also contributes to sexual aggression, unintended sexual liaisons and pregnancies, and infections from sexually transmitted diseases including HIV (Centers for Disease Control and Prevention [CDC], 1998). The use of alcohol and cannabis during pregnancy can compromise brain development in the fetus (Hart, Ksir, & Ray, 2012; Trezza et al., 2008).

Nate Newton up to 388 Pounds—of Pot

Six-time All-Pro lineman Nate Newton was a bedrock of the Dallas Cowboys professional football team that won three Super Bowls in the 1990s. In December 2001, he was arrested for the second time in five weeks for marijuana possession. Police found 213 pounds of pot in Newton's van in the first bust and 175 pounds of weed in the second arrest. Together, the 388 pounds of pot approached Newton's playing weight of 350 pound ("Newton up to 388 Lbs.—of Pot," 2001).

SCOPE OF SUBSTANCE USE IN THE U.S.

The best estimates of substance use in the U.S. are provided by national surveys conducted by the Substance Abuse and Mental Health Services Administration. The most recent survey was conducted with approximately 67,500 people (SAMHSA, 2011). Among the results were that 21.5% of the population who were 18 to 25 years were current illicit drug users; 25.8% of the males and 17.0% of the females. Current use was defined as use in the month prior to the interview. The most commonly used illicit drug was marijuana, as 18.5 % of this sample used it during the month prior to the survey. Prescription-type drugs that were consumed nonmedically were the next most frequently used, with 5.9% of young adults acknowledging this use. Sizable percentages of young adults also used hallucinogens, 2.0%, and crack/cocaine, 1.5%. Tobacco products were used by 40.8% in the prior month; 48.9% for males and 32.5% for females. Ethnic differences in illicit drug use are summarized in Figure 16.1.

Among Americans between 18 and 25 years of age, 61.5% were current alcohol users; 65.9% for males and 57.0% for females. Binge drinking consists of drinking five or more drinks on the same occasion on at least one day in the past month, and 40.6% (48.4% males, 32.6% females) met this criterion. Heavy drinking consists of drinking five or more drinks on the same occasion on at least five days in the past month, and 13.7%

FIGURE 16.1 Current Illicit Drug use Among Americans 18 to 25 years of Age (SAMHSA, 2011)	
	Use in past month
Caucasian	24.4%
Black or African American	20.0%
American Indian or Alaska Native	32.1%
Asian	8.4%
Hispanic or Latino	16.2%

FIGURE 16.2 Alcohol Use for Americans 18 to 25 years of Age (SAMHSA, 2011)			
	Use in past month	Binge use	Heavy use
Caucasian	67.7%	46.1%	17.3%
Black or African American	49.6%	27.9%	5.7%
American Indian or Alaska Native	52.0%	41.8%	no estimate reported
Asian	52.9%	25.8%	5.8%
Hispanic or Latino	53.5%	36.8%	10.2%
More than one race	63.3%	34.1%	9.4%

(19.0% males, 8.4% females) were heavy drinkers in 2010. Ethnic differences in alcohol consumption are summarized in Figure 16.2.

Alcohol consumption reaches its peak among Americans between the ages of 21 and 25, and many of the studies in sport psychology involve college-age participants who are in this age group. Binge drinking occurred among 41.9% of those in this age group, and heavy drinking was reported by 15.3% of these young adults; both percentages are approximately double that of the entire population. Males, especially Caucasian males, are the largest consumers of alcohol.

DIAGNOSES OF SUBSTANCE ABUSE

Substance Abuse and Dependence Disorders are classified as mental disorders in the *Diagnostic and Statistical Manual of Mental Disorders, Fourth Edition* (DSM-IV-TR; American Psychiatric Association, 2000). The DSM-IV-TR is the essential nosology or classification of mental disorders in the U.S. The terms of the DSM-IV-TR are compatible with the terms and codes in Chapter V, "Mental and Behavioural Disorders," of the *International Classification of Diseases and Related Health Problems*, Tenth Revision (ICD-10). The ICD-10 was developed by the World Health Organization and is the classification system for diseases throughout much of the world. All mental disorders identified in the DSM-IV-TR result in "clinically significant" dysfunction in **interpersonal, vocational**, or **intrapsychic** spheres.

In the DSM-IV-TR there are 11 classes of substance-related disorders: alcohol, amphetamine (e.g., methamphetamine, Dexedrine), caffeine, cannabis (e.g., marijuana), cocaine, hallucinogen (e.g., LSD), inhalant (e.g., paint, glue), nicotine, opioid (e.g., heroin), phencyclidine (e.g., PCP), and sedative, hypnotic, or anxiolytic (e.g., barbiturates such as secobarbital and benzodiazepines such as Valium). Obviously people use legal drugs such as alcohol and caffeine in ways that do not impair their functioning. However, the use of alcohol and any of the other classes of substances warrants a DSM-IV-TR diagnosis if this use significantly impairs interpersonal or vocational functioning or intrapsychic well-being. There are two general categories of diagnoses for significantly problematic use of the 11 classes of substances, **Substance Abuse Disorders** and **Substance Dependence Disorders**.

In brief summary, diagnoses of Substance Abuse Disorders refer to recurrent patterns of substance use that result in significant problems in a person's life. Diagnoses of Substance Dependence Disorders imply even more serious impairment. With substance dependence disorders, individuals have for practical purposes lost control of their use of substances or of their ability to use substances in moderation. This loss of control is reflected in their use of larger amounts of substances over a longer period of time than intended. There may also be repeated, unsuccessful efforts to limit or stop substance use. A great deal of time may be devoted to finding, obtaining, or scoring the substance, and recovering from the intoxicating effects of the substance. The substance may also be used despite clear knowledge that this use results in physical or psychological damage. For example, an athlete might drive while drunk, despite knowledge that he or she will lose a scholarship if caught.

With Substance Dependence Disorders, there is often more chronic or habitual use of substances over an extended period of time. With habitual use, **tolerance** develops for most of the aforementioned 11 classes of substances. Tolerance consists of the need for increasing amounts of the substance to achieve the desired level of intoxication. This, of course, promotes the use of the substance in increasing amounts, as intoxication does not occur if the substance-dependent person continues to use the same amount of the substance.

With Substance Dependence Disorders, **withdrawal** may also be experienced when the use of the substance is terminated. In general, withdrawal consists of physical and psychological reactions that are the opposite from that produced by the consumption of the abused substance (American Psychiatric Association, 2000). For example, amphetamines are stimulant drugs and their use results in the speeding up of thought, action, and the sympathetic nervous system, a decreased need for sleep, and possibly euphoria. Amphetamine withdrawal includes fatigue, dysphoric mood, and often slowing of movement. Alcohol is a depressant drug and results in disinhibition and sedation. Alcohol withdrawal includes motor agitation and sympathetic nervous system overactivity.

George Best: "I Spent a Lot of Money on Booze, Birds, and Fast Cars—the Rest I just Squandered."

George Best has a place in the pantheon of the all-time greatest soccer players. He was signed to a professional soccer contract with Manchester United of the English Premier League at age 15. Two years later, in 1965, he helped United win its first championship in eight years; United won again in 1967. In 1968, United became the first English team to win the European cup and he was voted the English and European footballer of the year. With flowing black hair, good looks, and a playboy lifestyle, Best was dubbed the "fifth Beatle" (Davies, 2009). In 1972, at age 26, he retired from Premier League football (Best: Decline, 2005).

Best struggled with alcoholism during and after his playing career. He tried unsuccessfully to control his drinking with psychological therapies, confinement, and Antabuse—a medication that causes violent illness when combined with alcohol. By 2000, his liver was destroyed by alcohol. A liver transplant saved his life in 2002 (Milmo, 2003).

Despite a vow of abstinence, Best returned to drinking in 2003. Prior to his death in 2005 at age 59, he issued a warning to young people "not to live and die as I had done" (George Best, 2005).

PREVALENCE OF SUBSTANCE ABUSE IN THE AMERICAS, EUROPE, AND NEW ZEALAND

Prevalence rates for alcohol and drug disorders are also high in the U.S. in comparison to other countries, as illustrated in the Figure 16.3. There is also evidence of substantial substance use that is not reflected in this table. Approximately 52% of New Zealanders who were 21 years of age used cannabis in 1992, and 9.7% met DSM-III-R criteria for cannabis dependence (Poulton, Brooke, Moffitt, Stanton, & Silva, 1997). High school students in Spain also consume considerable amounts of alcohol (Lopez-Frias et al., 2001). Spanish males between the ages of 14 and 19 consume an average of 15 drinks per week, and more than half of the drinks are consumed on Saturday. Spanish high school girls drink about eight drinks per week, and more than four of these on Saturday. Spanish adolescents who consumed more alcohol were more likely to drop out of school. These Spanish teenagers drank more beer than wine or distilled spirits, and this preference for beer has also been reported among French teenagers. Spanish adolescents who do not attend school consume even more alcohol.

PREVALENCE OF ALCOHOL USE AMONG ATHLETES

Among the initiatives to prevent underage drinking have been efforts to engage young people in sport. Ironically, adolescents who engage in team sports are more likely to use alcohol and cannabis (Fauth, Roth, &

FIGURE 16.3   Lifetime Prevalence Rates by Country (from Merikangas et al., 1998)

	% Lifetime Alcohol Dependence	% Lifetime All Other Drug Dependence
Germany	6.2	2.1
Mexico	6.7	0.7
Netherlands	5.5	1.8
Ontario, Canada	9.1	3.2
USA	14.3	7.5

Brooks-Gunn, 2007; Linver, Roth, & Brooks-Gunn, 2009; Moore & Werch, 2005) and to be heavy drinkers as adolescents and young adults (Taliaferro, Rienzo, & Donovan, 2010). This observation holds true for American, French, Norwegian (who participated in team and technical sports, but not endurance sports), and male Swedish adolescents (Peretti-Watel, Beck, & Legleye, 2002; Stafstrom, Ostergren, & Larsson, 2005; Wichstrøm & Wichstrøm, 2009). This pattern was not repeated among high school athletes in Italy, who drank less than did peers who were not sportspersons (Gutgesell & Canterbury, 1999).

Among the team sports associated with substance use for both genders are school-sponsored football, swimming, wrestling, and out-of-school dance/cheerleading/gymnastics, skateboarding, surfing, and tennis (Moore & Werch, 2005). Sports may provide a supportive context for drinking in high school (Eccles & Barber, 1999; Darling, Caldwell, & Smith, 2005).

Indeed, there is evidence that alcohol abuse increases with increasing involvement in athletics, in that team leaders were more likely to engage in binge drinking than were other teammates (Leichliter, Meilman, Presley, & Cashin, 1998). Athletic leaders were also more likely to experience negative consequences as a result of drinking, such as hangovers and arguments.

College students are more likely to be current binge and heavy drinkers than their nonmatriculated peers (SAMSHA, 2011; Wechsler, Davenport, Dowdall, Grossman, & Zanakos, 1997). College athletes drink more than collegians who are not athletes (Hildebrand, Johnson, & Bogle, 2001; Yusko, Buckman, White, & Pandina, 2008b), get drunk more often, and consume more drinks during peak drinking episodes (Turrisi, Mastroleo, Mallett, Larimer, & Kilmer, 2007). Division I male athletes drank an average 5.64 times per month and female athletes averaged 4.51 episodes of monthly drinking (Grossbard, Hummer, LaBrie, Pederson, & Neighbors, 2009). Male and female athletes averaged 6.06 and 4.16 drinks, respectively, in average drinking episodes, and 10.5 and 6.65 drinks, respectively, in their peak drinking episode. Division I athletes are especially likely to engage in binge drinking on Saturday, perhaps because they did not practice or play games on Sunday (Yusko, Buckman, White, & Pandina, 2008a).

Division I male and female athletes who consumed alcohol in combination with energy drinks (drinks with high levels of stimulants, such as caffeine) consumed an average of 18.35 alcoholics drinks during their peak binging episodes (Woolsey, Waigandt, & Beck, 2010). Australian Rules football players averaged 14 drinks per week, 12 of which were consumed after matches (Burke & Read, 1988). Recall that the standard for binge drinking is five drinks in an episode (SAMHSA, 2011).

The influence of teammates and coaches contributes to the increased alcohol use among athletes. Intercollegiate athletes recognize that teammates drink often and heavily, and believe teammates approve of them drinking in a similar manner (Lewis, 2008; Turrisi et al., 2007).

Intercollegiate athletes who engage in binge drinking also perceive that coaches have lenient attitudes about drinking. Some teams also have traditions of socializing and drinking together (Zamboanga, Rodriguez, & Horton, 2008).

Application

Teammates and coaches make important contributions to atmospheres that foster heavy drinking. Perhaps their commitment to responsible drinking or even abstinence would be equally influential. Teams that establish norms about substance use might even become more cohesive.

The high levels of heavy drinking among intercollegiate swimmers and divers may be due to traditions of male and female swimmers and divers socializing and "partying together" (Martens, Watson, & Beck, 2006). Alcohol may also be more readily available for athletes. Perhaps members of teams have larger social networks of drinking buddies, and teammates may also purchase alcohol for underage teammates (Eitle, Turner, & Eitle, 2003; Wichstrøm & Wichstrøm, 2009). It is not surprising that college students who were both athletes and members of fraternities or sororities drank more than any other identifiable college group. In fraternities, sororities, and sports, there are opportunities for social activities at which alcohol is typically consumed (Meilman, Leichliter, & Presley, 1999).

Among African American intercollegiate athletes, 14% reported drinking at least four drinks per sitting during athletic seasons, and 46% reported drinking at this level out of season (Bower & Martin, 1999). Consistent with the larger literature about alcohol use, binge drinking was most common among Caucasian male athletes, or among those who smoked marijuana or cigarettes.

Heavy Drinking among Athletes Is Nothing New

The association between drinking and athletics is not a recent phenomenon. The sportswriter Dick Schaap spent a week in the 1961 NFL (National Football League) season chronicling the activities of Paul Hornung. Hornung was a Heisman Trophy winner and an NFL All-Pro halfback for the Green Bay Packers. Hornung began drinking martinis at about three in the afternoon. Martini time was over at about six, when it was time for scotch before dinner and wine with dinner. After-dinner drinks were brandy, and then it was back on scotch. Schaap was not able to determine the exact number of drinks consumed by Hornung during the week, but estimated it to be in excess of 60, a number nowhere near the club record (Maraniss, 1999).

PREVALENCE OF CANNABIS USE AMONG ATHLETES

Intercollegiate athletes are less likely to use marijuana than are nonathletes (Yusko et al., 2008b; Wechsler et al., 1997). Twelve percent and 10% of male and female intercollegiate athletes, respectively, used cannabis regularly, whereas 16% and 11% of male and female college students, respectively, who did not participate in athletics used marijuana. The finding that collegiate athletes use less cannabis has been consistently reported, and athletes have also been shown to use less powder and crack cocaine (Anderson, Albrecht, McKeag, Hough, & McGrew, 1991).

However, substantial numbers of intercollegiate athletes use cannabis at least once yearly. Approximately 23.8% (Grossbard, Hummer, LaBrie, Pederson, & Neighbors, 2009) of Division I athletes and 22.6% of the intercollegiate athletes in Divisions I, II, and III use marijuana yearly (Bracken, 2012). Intercollegiate athletes who use marijuana are likely to consider it normative, as female athletes estimated that 83.9% of typical female athletes used marijuana and male athletes estimated that 88.8% of their counterparts smoked marijuana (LaBrie, Grossbard, & Hummer, 2009).

German adolescent athletes were less likely to use cannabis than did their peers who did not engage in sports (Wanjek, Rosendahl, Strauss, & Gabriel, 2007). Norwegian adolescents who participated in team sports were less likely to use cannabis as they matured. Norwegian sportspersons also smoked less tobacco, which could serve as a gateway to smoking cannabis (Wichstrøm & Wichstrøm, 2009).

Adolescents who use substantial quantities of cannabis are less likely to engage in conventional tasks, such as athletics and extracurricular sport activities, and are more frequently involved with delinquent or substance-using peers (Brook, Kessler, & Cohen, 1999; Lynskey & Hall, 2000). Cannabis has a direct effect on decreasing motivation and attention to study and training, a condition referred to as **amotivational syndrome**.

Marijuana and the NBA

Major new sources have consistently reported that American professional basketball players in the National Basketball Association (NBA) routinely smoke marijuana. For example, Jay Williams recently acknowledged that teammates on the Chicago Bulls smoked marijuana before games during the 2002-03 season ("Jay Williams," 2013). The extent of marijuana use in the NBA has not been established by scientific surveys, but *The New York Times* cited sources such as two dozen active players, former players, basketball agents, and basketball executives in estimating that 60% to 70% of NBA players smoked marijuana (Roberts, 1997). The NBA's drug policy does not list marijuana as a prohibited substance, and therefore differentiates between cannabis and other illegal substances, such as cocaine, heroin, amphetamines, and LSD. The current NBA policy states that teams *may* drug screen rookies once during training camp and no more than three times during the Regular Season. Veterans face random testing no more than one time during the Regular Season or during the first 15 days in which he reports to his team, typically training camp (Wise, 2000). League policy calls for a ban of players guilty of a crime involving cocaine or heroin, and this policy was developed in response to arrests of NBA players involving these drugs in the 1970s and early 1980s.

The NBA initiated a screening program for cannabis during training camps in 2000. They boasted that only 2.8% of the players tested positive for cannabis (Wise, 2000). The players were aware when they would be tested. Therefore, the "hit rate" of 2.8% reflects less a true survey of cannabis use in the NBA and more the percent that were "extremely stupid or really dependent on the drug" (Keteyian, 1999) so that they were unable to stop prior to the drug test. Players cannot be dismissed from the league for testing positive for cannabis, but can be banished for a single positive test of the other illegal drugs.

NBA players and their union president Billy Hunter have defended their resistance to more frequent and unannounced screening with the argument that the cannabis use in the NBA mirrors its use in society. Of course, this argument is spurious, as 18.5% of the U.S. population between the ages of 18 and 25 smoke marijuana as frequently as monthly (SAMHSA, 2011).

How is it that there is such a potential disparity between the levels of cannabis use among college and the potential use among professional athletes? One explanation is that the wealth and influence of professional athletes provides them access to almost unlimited party scenes. With average salaries in excess of $2 million in the NBA, plenty of free time, and little mentoring by senior adults, players accept this access.

MOTIVATION FOR SUBSTANCE USE

It should come as no surprise that the primary motivation for using cannabis and alcohol is to experience their effect. Cannabis users report a "high" that includes feelings of intoxication and pleasure. However, some experience anxiety and even paranoia when trying cannabis. Drinkers find the sedating effects of alcohol to be rewarding. Some experience disinhibition and report they are better able to enjoy themselves after using alcohol (Hart, Ksir, & Ray, 2012).

The motivation for alcohol use has been studied more extensively than the use of other substances. Perhaps this is due to the greater prevalence of alcohol use and the fact that it is a legal substance. Three factors have been shown to motivate the drinking of adults and adolescents (Cooper, 1994; Cooper, Russell, Skinner, & Windle, 1992; Segal, 1986). First, the drinking of some adolescents and adults is determined primarily by peer-related or **social** motives. These people consider drinking to be the thing to do when socializing, when at parties, or when celebrating. A second group is primarily motivated by sensation-seeking or efforts for **enhancement** of phenomenological states. This group is more likely to be extraverted and interested in exciting and even risky activities. Tension-reduction or **palliation** motives are primary when alcohol is used for self-medication of depression and anxiety or to palliate or reduce anhedonia, or an absence of pleasure.

Drinking that is primarily determined by social motives has been shown to be least related to excessive drinking and difficulties controlling drinking. The social use of illicit drugs by adolescents may be a different matter. Approximately 90% of adolescent substance abusers have friends that use the same drugs (Dinges & Oetting, 1993). Alcohol use that is motivated by enhancement and palliation motives is more likely to be problematic (Cloninger, 1987; Gallucci, 1997; Kessler, Crum et al., 1997; MacAndrew, 1980, 1981; Merikangas et al. 1998; Mezzich et al., 1993; Schuckit, 1994).

ATHLETES' MOTIVATION FOR SUBSTANCE USE

Collegiate athletes also use alcohol and other drugs during social interactions and celebrations, to enhance phenomenology or feeling states, and to palliate or self-medicate unpleasant feelings (Evans, Weinberg, & Jackson, 1992). Alcohol may palliate stress that is attendant to athletic competition. Athletes also experience peer pressure and positive reinforcement for drinking from teammates (Martens, Watson, Royland, Beck, 2005). For example, athletes may compete in drinking games with the objective of drinking more than teammates (Grossbard, Geisner, Neighbors, Kilmer, & Larimer, 2007; Serrao, Martens, Martin, & Rocha, 2008).

ACUTE EFFECTS OF ALCOHOL ON PSYCHOMOTOR PERFORMANCE

A universally recognized psychomotor task that is influenced by substance use is automobile driving. In the U.S., blood alcohol concentrations (BAC; grams of alcohol per 100 milliliters of blood) of 0.08 or 0.1 are commonly recognized as the standard for determining illegal driving under the influence of alcohol. The National Highway Traffic Safety Administration determined that BACs as low as 0.02 impaired driving performance ("Tests show," 2000). Compared to drivers who did not drink alcohol, the risk of fatal accidents for drivers with BACs from 0.05 to 0.09 is approximately 11 times greater, 48 times greater for drivers with BACs between 0.1 to 0.14, and 385 times greater for drivers with BAC levels of at least 0.15 (Zador, 1991). BAC levels as low as .05 are more generally associated with lowered alertness, impaired judgment, and disinhibition. At higher levels, motor coordination and reaction times become increasingly impaired.

Given the increased likelihood of automobile accidents after drinking

Police officer giving sobriety test

alcohol, it is no surprise that alcohol consumption impairs concentration, reaction time, complex motor skills, and complex decision-making. Skills that are automatic are also more likely to be negatively affected (Stainback, 1997).

The consumption of the equivalent of one alcoholic drink significantly decreases aerobic power output. Alcohol increases cardiovascular strain and results in disturbances in lactate production and oxidation and its conversion into glucose, and these process may explain the reduced aerobic power output. Alcohol consumption also inhibits the synthesis of glycogen—and its conversion into glucose—in both the liver and muscles (Maughan, 2006). Psychological processes may also be partially responsible for reduced output after taking one standard drink of alcohol. Specifically, athletic challenges, such as cycling as far as possible in 60 minutes, may seem more difficult and effortful after consuming one drink (Lecoultre & Schutz, 2009).

Aerobic power output is also less the day after a bout of drinking. During this "hangover" phase, heart rate and blood pressure are elevated, there is relative dehydration, and there are alterations in glucose metabolism (Wiese, Shilpak, & Browner, 2000).

GENDER DIFFERENCES AND ALCOHOL

Alcohol causes more cognitive impairment in women than in men. This impairment is apparent on tasks that require working memory, reaction time, and hand–eye coordination. This impairment has a negative effect on driving, and piloting a commercial aircraft with even trace amounts of alcohol in one's bloodstream is forbidden. With driving and flying, the ability to attend to two or more sources of information is especially important and easily disrupted by alcohol consumption. Women have proportionally more body fat and less water in the body than do men of equivalent body weights. Alcohol is dispersed in the water in the body, and women reach higher levels of blood alcohol concentration (BAC) with equivalent amounts of alcohol and adjusting for body weight. These gender differences in response to alcohol do not appear to result from changes in levels of sex steroid hormones throughout the menstrual cycle of women (Mumenthaler & Taylor, 1999).

ACUTE EFFECTS OF CANNABIS ON PSYCHOMOTOR PERFORMANCE

Cannabis intoxication impairs judgment, decreases sustained attention and concentration, and slows reaction time. It is, therefore, not surprising that drivers who are intoxicated with cannabis are more likely to be involved in and cause accidents (O'Malley & Johnston, 2007; Richer & Bergeron, 2009).

In addition to disrupting attention and concentration, cannabis intoxication is traditionally correlated with difficulties in working memory or with learning new information, and with distorted estimates of time (Montgomery & Fisk, 2007). While intoxicated, the cannabis user overestimates the passage of time.

Traditional correlates of cannabis use notwithstanding, the influence of cannabis on performance has been controversial, with some scientists maintaining that the effects are relatively benign (Hart, van Gorp, Haney, Foltin, & Fischman, 2001). In addition, tolerance to the cognitive and psychomotor effects of cannabis almost surely occurs. Even with tolerance, performance on some tests of visual-motor coordination, such as matching geometric patterns with numbers during a span of 90 minutes, is impaired (Haney et al., 1999).

Furthermore, it is not only the acute effects of cannabis intoxication on performance that are of concern, but also the effects of withdrawal from cannabis. In a sample of adult males who smoked about six marijuana cigarettes per day, performance was actually impaired on a task requiring sustained concentration following abstinence from cannabis, and these effects were seen even on the fourth day of abstinence (Haney et al., 1999).

Abstinence from cannabis affects not only performance, but also mood, food intake, sleep, and social behavior (U.S. Department of Health and Human Services, 2010). Heavy cannabis users report heightened anxiety, stomach pain, and irritability after abstinence. They also eat less often and socialize less. The withdrawal symptoms are most severe on about the fourth day of abstinence, but persist after the fourth day. For example, aggressive behavior and irritability persist for at least seven days.

CANNABIS USE AND LONG-TERM IMPAIRMENT

Does heavy and frequent use of cannabis lead to impairment in cognitive functioning that persists beyond the time of acute intoxication? Historically, studies have yielded minimum evidence of cognitive impairment among chronic cannabis users. As the sophistication of scientific inquiries has increased, the effects of cannabis on the brain have been shown to be far from harmless.

The finding that long-term cannabis use results in subtle impairments in verbal memory has been consistently reported. For example, comparing males who used cannabis almost every day of the month, memory functions were impaired for a group using an average of 23 years but not for a group with 10 years of use (Solowij et al., 2002). The group with 23 years of cannabis abuse demonstrated impaired attention and was more easily distracted (Croft, Mackay, Mills, & Gruzelier, 2001). More recent research demonstrated that college students who consumed an average of two marijuana cigarettes daily for a duration of three years also demonstrated **memory impairment** (Bartholomew, Holroyd, & Heffernan, 2010).

Smoking cannabis causes pathological changes to the lungs that are similar to those caused by smoking tobacco. However, the pathological changes occur more rapidly with cannabis due to the respiratory burden of inhaling large puffs of cannabis and holding the smoke in the lungs. Young adult marijuana smokers in New Zealand had significantly more wheezing apart from colds, shortness of breath caused by exercise such as climbing hills, production of sputum in the morning, and nocturnal wakening with chest tightness (Taylor, Poulton, Moffitt, Ramankutty, & Sears, 2000). Many of the marijuana smokers also smoked tobacco. Smoking both tobacco and cannabis produced more respiratory symptoms than does smoking either alone. The magnitude of these respiratory symptoms caused by cannabis dependence was similar to smoking up to ten cigarettes per day.

ALCOHOL USE AND LONG-TERM IMPAIRMENT

The long-term effects of alcohol are less controversial than those for cannabis. Most dramatically, alcohol has been shown to be the third leading external or nongenetic contributor to death, trailing only tobacco use and diet and activity patterns (Grant, DeBakey, & Zobeck, 1991; McGinnis & Foege, 1993). Cirrhosis of the liver due to alcohol abuse usually occurs after approximately ten years of drinking about a pint of whiskey per day. With such heavy and prolonged alcohol consumption, Wernicke-Korsakoff syndrome may also occur. This syndrome includes loss of many important brain functions, including memory (Hart et al., 2012).

Chronic exposure to alcohol produces diffuse brain dysfunction. The severity of this function varies from mild to severe, with perhaps 50% demonstrating significant impairment. Chronic alcoholics lose mental efficiency or the facility to identify important and accurate information and ignore irrelevant and inaccurate. Deficits with cognitive efficiency are especially apparent on timed tasks, or when jobs and performances must be completed by deadlines or during discrete periods of time (Nixon, 1999).

Chronic alcoholism does not appear to cause muscle atrophy or diminished muscle size, but does result in decreased speed and force of muscle movements. Deficits in the speed and force of muscle contractions due to alcoholism have been considered small because they were less than 10% (York, Hirsch, Pendergast, Glavy, 1999). However, in competitive athletics, differences of this magnitude are enormous. Muscle energy is partially recovered within two weeks of abstinence from alcohol among chronic alcoholics.

ALCOHOL AND SPORT

The American College of Sport Medicine took a position in 1982 that the use of alcohol was of no benefit for sport, and that its use may be detrimental for athletes. It should be obvious that the acute effects of alcohol on sport performance are detrimental. As discussed earlier, with recent alcohol consumption, reaction time, eye-hand coordination, accuracy, and balance are compromised. Alcohol use among young leisure sport participants contributes to serious injuries in activities such as cycling, boating, swimming, snow skiing, and ice-skating. These injuries result from impaired psychomotor functioning and judgment. Approximately half of the victims of fatal leisure boat accidents were intoxicated. About half of the spinal cord injuries that occurring when diving into pools and more than half of the young adult drowning victims were using alcohol at the time of their accidents.

Alcohol provides no benefit in terms of increasing stored energy sources, such as glycogen, that can be converted to glucose and used to fuel muscle performance. The typical increase in glucose levels in the blood that occurs with exercise is inhibited after the consumption of alcohol. Alcohol consumption, even on the night before competition, contributes to dehydration due to the suppression of antidiuretic hormones, and this results in increased volume of sweat and urine. This loss of fluid has an especially deleterious effect on endurance performance. Alcohol also disrupts performance in cold weather. With alcohol use, peripheral veins and arteries become dilated or increase in diameter. This results in excessive heat loss and interferes with the normal vasoconstriction of blood vessels in cold weather. The use of alcohol during competition is also banned by the International Olympic Committee.

ALCOHOL AND SLEEP

Alcohol has been used since ancient times as a folk remedy to facilitate sleep. About 15% of the U.S. population use alcohol to induce sleep at least 30 times in one year, and 6% drank to go to sleep 180 times or more in the course of a year (Johnson, Roehrs, Roth, Breslau, 1998).

In actuality, alcohol consumption worsens sleep quality. People who use alcohol to induce sleep are more tired and less alert during the day. Perhaps the appeal of alcohol as a sleep tonic is due to its sedating effects. Drinking even a small amount of alcohol, such as one to three drinks prior to bedtime, provides sedation and an immediate enhancement of slow-wave sleep and a concurrent suppression of REM or rapid eye movement sleep (Casteneda, Sussman, Levy, O'Malley, & Westreich, 1998). Slow-wave sleep is associated with deep sleep, and dreaming occurs during REM sleep. With the metabolization of alcohol, blood alcohol levels reach zero after approximately two to three hours. At that point, a rebound effect occurs that consists of elevated heart rate and a greater likelihood of awakening. With this rebound, the drinker is not only no longer sedated, but also more alert than would be the case without alcohol.

With nightly use of alcohol and alcohol tolerance, these disruptions of the sleep cycle may diminish, but rebound effects and sleep disruptions will reoccur with the discontinuation of alcohol use. Indeed, insomnia is a symptom of alcohol withdrawal (American Psychiatric Association, 2000).

Alcohol consumption serves to obstruct airflow during sleep. Normal sleepers who consume a single large alcoholic drink can develop sleep apnea or obstructions of airflow when trying to breathe. Chronic snorers are likely to develop frank apneas during the first hours of sleep when alcohol levels are highest, and airflow is decreased further for those with preexisting sleep apnea. With sleep apnea, air flow to the brain is decreased.

People who have at least two drinks per day have more restless sleep than do those who do not drink. They are especially likely to move their legs about during sleep. About the same amount of alcohol also suppresses melatonin. Melatonin is a pineal hormone, and its secretion prompts drowsiness and sleep. Regular schedules of bedtime capitalize on the secretion of melatonin and allow for easy transitions to sleep and more restful sleep. With the regulation of sleep, circadian rhythms, or patterns of wakefulness and drowsiness, are predictable and more under the control of athletes. Inadequate sleep impairs performance and may result in lethargy, fatigue, difficulties with concentration, and depressed mood.

Growth hormone or somatomedin is released during the first hours of sleep, and is also suppressed by a few drinks prior to bed. Of course, growth hormone stimulates growth during childhood and adolescence, the latter being a time when drinking is not uncommon. In adults, growth hormone plays a role in sustaining the health of aging body tissues.

CANNABIS AND SLEEP

Regular cannabis users fall asleep more quickly after smoking marijuana (Chait, 1990). Abstinence from marijuana following prolonged, heavy use is associated with sleep disturbances. Sleep disturbance occurs even with abstinence after smoking five marijuana cigarettes per day for three days. With abstinence, it takes longer for marijuana users to fall asleep and to begin the REM or dream cycle of their sleep.

Application

Athletes who rely on cannabis as a soporific or a means of inducing sleep may be particularly resistant to quitting. Even faced with a urine screen, they may try to use cannabis until the last possible day prior to the screening. This is a risky strategy. Cannabis has a half-life of 19 hours, and heavy users may test positive for cannabis for up to four weeks.

DOPING

The use of drugs to enhance sport performance and muscularity is referred to as doping or ergogenic substance use, and both licit and illicit drugs are used in doping (World Anti-Doping Agency, 2009; Zelli, Lucidi, & Mallia,

2010). This topic may appear disconnected to the previous examination of substances that inhibit or impair performance. However, athletic careers and the physical well-being of athletes are imperiled by ergogenic substance use. For example, Tim Montgomery was banned from track competition by the Court of Arbitration for Sport for two years when it was determined that he used an anabolic-androgenic steroid (AAS; Litsky, 2005). He was also stripped of honors and prize money acquired after March 31, 2001, as well as his former world record of 9.78 seconds in the 100 meters.

The former president, Manfred Ewald, and chief sport physician, Dr. Manfred Hoppner, of the former East German Sports Federation were convicted of causing bodily harm to minors as a result of secretly mixing anabolic-androgenic steroids such as Turinabol in the sports drinks of adolescent and preadolescent athletes (Ungerleider, 2001). This illegal doping produced dramatic results such as in the 1976 Olympics when the East German female swimmers swept 11 of 13 gold medals. It also resulted in bodily harm that included clitoral enlargement, excessive body hair, deepened voice, and damage to the liver and heart.

Anabolic-androgenic steroids (AAS), prohormones such as Androstenedione, growth hormone (GH) derived from human, animal, or synthetic sources, insulin, amphetamines, blood doping, and Erythropoietin (EPO) are illicit forms of doping. Androstenedione, AAS, and GH are used to build muscular strength, power, and endurance. Caffeine, ephedrine, and amphetamines are central nervous system stimulants and used in doping to decrease fatigue, increase aggressiveness, and enhance confidence. Blood doping consists of adding red blood cells to the blood stream of athletes so as to augment the amount of oxygen that can be carried to muscles. With greater availability of oxygen, muscular fatigue is decreased. Erythropoietin (EPO) is the body's hormone that stimulates the production of red blood cells.

Creatine and caffeine are legal, readily available, and increasingly sanctioned for performance enhancement. The use of increasing amounts of caffeine as a stimulant has been recently publicized in the popular press. Caffeine is currently delivered from not only traditional sources such as coffee, but also in bottled water and drinks, and even soap. "Shower Shock" is a soap that is advertised to deliver 250 milligrams of caffeine per soaping. Soft drinks such as "Whoop Ass" have been "enriched" with large doses of caffeine (Shea, 2002).

There are serious health hazards associated with the use of these substances. AASs are the most widely used class of illicit ergogenic drugs. The medical and psychiatric complications of AAS use include hepatic or liver abnormalities such as peliosis hepatis, cholestasis, and benign and malignant tumors. AASs also result in changes in cardiovascular risk factors, such as increased low-density lipoprotein and decreased high-density lipoprotein cholesterol levels and hypertension. Endocrinologic effects resulting from AAS use include decreased plasma testosterone and gonadotropin levels, testicular atrophy and gynecomastia in men, and inhibition of ovulation, hirsutism, deepened voice, and acne in women (Bahrke, Yesalis, & Brower, 1998; Hallagan, Hallagan, Snyder, 1989; Holt & Sonksen, 2008; Kanayama, Hudson, & Pope, 2010; Maior et al., 2010). Aggressive behavior (Bahrke, Yesalis, & Wright, 1996) and mood disorders with depressive and manic features are also associated with the use of and withdrawal from AASs (Copeland, Peters, & Dillon, 2000; Malone, Dimeff, Lombardo, & Sample, 1995; Pope & Katz, 1994).

College students who are AAS users are also much more likely to use marijuana, ecstasy, and tranquilizers/sedatives, and to be alcohol dependent (Kokkevi, Fotiou, Chileva, Nociar, & Miller, 2008; McCabe, Brower, West, Nelson, & Wechsler, 2007). Male AAS-using weightlifters were more likely to abuse opioids than did weightlifters who did not use AASs (Kanayama, Hudson, & Pope, 2009).

In the U.S., Europe, and Brazil, at least 3% of young men have used AASs at some time in their lives (Centers for Disease Control, 2009; Kanayama et al., 2010). A recent survey of 2,793 diverse adolescents from 20 urban middle and high schools in the U.S. indicated that 34.7% used protein powders or shakes and 5.9% took AASs (Eisenberg, Wall, & Neumark, Sztainer, 2012). AAS use is considerably lower in Asian countries and among females (Kanayama et al., 2010). Prevalence rates for AAS use among 16-year-olds in other countries are listed in Figure 16.4. In most samples, AAS use is nearly twice as high for males as for females.

Regulatory agencies such as the World Anti-Doping Agency (WADA) and the International Olympic Committee (IOC) oppose and attempt to eliminate doping for several reasons. In addition to imperiling the health

FIGURE 16.4 Life Use of AAS (Kokkevi et al., 2008)

	Total	Boys	Girls
Bulgaria	2.2	4.0	0.7
Croatia	3.5	4.4	2.4
Cyprus	2.3	4.5	0.5
Greece	2.0	3.2	1.2

of athletes, doping provides an unfair competitive advantage. The use of ergogenic substances by elite athletes may also encourage use by competitors and aspiring athletes. Finally, the integrity of sport is more nearly maintained when competition is seen to be fair (International Olympic Committee, 2011; Smith & Stewart, 2008; World Anti-Doping Agency, 2009). Those engaging in doping engage in an ongoing "cat and mouse" game with agencies such as the WADA. This involves the development of doping substances that elude current methods of detection (Catlin, Fitch, & Ljungqvist, 2008).

SUMMARY AND APPLICATION

Alcohol and cannabis use is not infrequent in the general population and among athletes. For example, 12% and 10% of male and female intercollegiate athletes, respectively, used cannabis, whereas 16% and 11% of male and female college students who did not participate in athletics used marijuana on a monthly basis, respectively. Collegiate athletes have been shown to be almost twice as likely to drink on a twice-weekly basis as do college students who do not play sports at the high school or college level. Americans of European descent and who are not Hispanic have been shown to consume more alcohol than do Native, African, Asian, and Hispanic Americans. Women of all ethnic groups drink less than men.

The prevalence of alcohol and other drug-dependence disorders is high in the U.S. in comparison to other countries. However, 9.7% of New Zealanders who were 21 years of age were determined to have Cannabis Dependence Disorders. Considering that Spanish males and females between the ages of 14 and 19 average 7.5 and four drinks on Saturday, respectivly, many of these teenagers would meet the Substance Abuse and Mental Health Services Administration (SAMHSA) standards for heavy or binge drinking.

Drinking motivated by efforts to palliate anxiety and depression or to enliven oneself is more problematic than is drinking in the context of socialization. Moderate drinking in the context of social rituals is less likely to lead to substance abuse or dependence disorders.

The importance of preperformance routines was discussed in Chapter 5. Readers were encouraged to simulate "game conditions" during all phases of preperformance preparation and training. Unnecessary deviations and disruptions in preperformance routines are to be avoided, as they counter the benefits of systematic preparation to do one's best. With this in mind, the use of any psychoactive drugs other than small amounts of alcohol and prescription medications cannot be defended, and even small amounts of alcohol can disrupt sleep. Alcohol consumption prior to practice or competition, even in low doses, worsens performance (American College of Sports Medicine, 1982).

The use of substances may impair performance in at least three ways. First, if alcohol and cannabis are routinely used during training and preperformance preparation, psychomotor skill acquisition may be delayed, concentration disrupted, and sleep impaired. Hormonal disruptions secondary to sleep changes and muscular impairments are potential consequences of chronic alcohol abuse. Chronic marijuana smoking compromises the respiratory system. Moreover, the time wasted while high or drunk is taken from purposeful activities, such as physical and mental practice, and an amotivational syndrome that contributes to inadequate effort and poor school performance may also erode motivation for optimal training and sport performance. Second, athletes are likely to experience disequilibrium if psychoactive drugs are routinely used during training and discontinued prior to competition and performances. In effect, these athletes would train with some measure of alcohol or cannabis in their bodies or in some state of withdrawal, and then compete with less alcohol or cannabis in their systems and in perhaps heightened states of withdrawal. These differences in physiology and phenomenology could range from subtle to very noticeable, and would be contrary to the best preperformance preparation strategies. The most extreme form of disequilibrium would be diagnosable alcohol or cannabis withdrawal, which would involve insomnia, irritability, lethargy, anxiety, sympathetic nervous system overactivity, and changes in appetite and food intake. Third, athletes may routinely use alcohol and cannabis during training and competition. These steady substance users avoid the aforementioned disruptions in equilibriums at the cost of the acute effects of alcohol and cannabis on psychomotor performance. These acute effects include decreased visual-motor speed and accuracy, impaired concentration and memory, and reduced aerobic power output.

The benefits of preperformance routines are due in no small degree to the order and control that they bring to the schedules and psychological states of athletes. Perceived control and self-efficacy are vital ingredients for sustaining effort in the face of obstacles and across years of practice and preparation. Self-efficacy or beliefs that one is equal to challenges is also crucial in limiting choking under pressure. The most convincing source of efficacious beliefs is enactive attainments or actual successful experience. The self-efficacy and confidence of teams is influenced by the skillful performance of its members. With substance abuse, there are fewer opportunities for successful training experiences and less potential for the establishment of sturdy self-efficacy.

Among the recognized costs and consequences of substance abuse are family dysfunction, injuries, stunted academic achievement, and even suicide. Doping or ergogenic substance use imperils the physical well-being of athletes as well as the integrity of sport.

However substantial the recognized costs, the loss of human potential due to substance abuse is probably underestimated. Teenage substance abusers miss important social experiences with peers and family, and academic training during the brief time of their adolescence. Once past, opportunities for these experiences cannot be retrieved, though social and academic skills can perhaps be remediated at a later point in life.

Squandered opportunities for achievement are even more damaging in athletic venues because the time available for athletic careers is limited and often discrete, as in collegiate athletics. With poignancy and scientific accuracy it can be said that lost opportunities are a primary source of life's disappointments.

Key Terms

Diagnostic and Statistical Manual of Mental Disorders, Fourth Edition: interpersonal, vocational, or intrapsychic impairment   371

Substance abuse disorders   371

Substance dependence disorders   371

Tolerance   372

Withdrawal   372

Amotivational Syndrome   376

Motivation for substance use: Social, enhancement, and palliation motives   377

Memory impairment   380

Discussion Questions

Q1. Consider the psychological, physical, social, and economic costs of alcohol abuse.

Q2. Review the patterns of substance use in the U.S.

Q3. Examine ethnic differences in alcohol consumption.

Q4. Do those who meet criterion for binge and heavy drinking also meet DSM-IV-TR standards for abuse and dependence?

Q5. Mental disorders identified in the DSM-IV-TR involve significant disruption in what areas of functioning?

Q6. Consider the suggestion that adolescents should engage in sports to avoid substance abuse.

Q7. How do team norms contribute to alcohol consumption?

Q8. Compare cannabis use among athletes and nonathletes.

Q9. Review the motivations for substance use.

Q10. Why do athletes use substances?

Q11. Explain the impact of alcohol on cognitive and physical performance.

Q12. Describe gender differences in response to alcohol.

Q13. Review the acute effects of cannabis on performance.

Q14. Review the long-term effects of cannabis use.

Q15. Consider the impairment resulting from long-term alcohol use.

Q16. How does drinking alcohol benefit a sportsperson?

Q17. Evaluate alcohol as a sleep aid.

Q18. Describe the effects of cannabis on sleep.

Q19. How is doping differentiated from other substance use?

Q20. How is doping problematic?

Suggested Readings

Appleton, P. R., Hall, H. K., & Hill, A. P. (2009). Relations between multidimensional perfectionism and burnout in junior-elite male athletes. *Psychology of Sport and Exercise, 10*, 457–465. doi: 10.1016/j.psychsport.2008.12.006

Bartholomew, J., Holroyd, S., & Heffernan, T. M. (2010). Does cannabis use affect prospective memory in young adults? *Journal of Psychopharmacology, 24*, 241–246. doi: 10.1177/0269881109106909

Bracken, N. M. (2012). *Substance use: National study of substance use trends among NCAA college student-athletes*. Indianapolis, IN: NCAA.

Cartwright, W. S. (2008). Economic costs of drug abuse: Financial cost of illness and services. *Journal of Substance Abuse Treatment, 34*, 224–233. doi: 10.1016/jsat.2007.04.003

Catlin, D. H., Fitch, K. D., & Ljungqvist, A. (2008). Medicine and science in the fight against doping in sport. *Journal of Internal Medicine, 264*, 99–114. doi: 10.1111/j.1365-2796.2008.01993.x

Fauth, R. C., Roth, J. L., & Brooks-Gunn, J. (2007). Does the neighborhood context alter the link between youth's after-school time activities and developmental outcomes? A multilevel analysis. *Developmental Psychology, 43*, 760–777. doi: 10.1037/0012-1649.43.3.760

Grossbard, J., Hummer, J., LaBrie, J., Pederson, E., & Neighbors, C. (2009). Is substance use a team sport? Attraction to team, perceived norms, and alcohol and marijuana use among male and female intercollegiate athletes. *Journal of Applied Sport Psychology, 21*, 247–261.

Hill, A. P., Hall, H. K., & Appleton, P. R. (2010). Perfectionism and athlete burnout in junior elite athletes: The mediating role of coping tendencies. *Anxiety, Stress, & Coping, 23*, 415–430. doi: 10.1080/10615800903330966

Hill, A. P., Hall, H. K., Appleton, P. R., & Kozub, S. A. (2008). Perfectionism and burnout in junior elite soccer players: The mediating influence of unconditional self-acceptance. *Psychology of Sport and Exercise, 9*, 630–644. doi: 10.1016/j.psychsport.2007.09.004

Hill, A. P., Hall, H. K., Appleton, P. R., & Murray, J. J. (2010). Perfectionism and burnout in canoe, polo and kayak slalom athletes: The mediating influence of validation and growth-seeking. *The Sport Psychologist, 24*, 16–34.

LaBrie, J. W., Grossbard, J. R., & Hummer, J. F. (2009). Normative misperceptions and marijuana use among male and female college athletes. *Journal of Applied Sport Psychology, 21 (Supp. 1)*, S77-S85.

Lecoultre, V., & Schutz, Y. (2009). Effects of a small dose of alcohol on the endurance performance of trained cyclists. *Alcohol & Alcoholism, 44*, 278–283.

Substance Abuse and Mental Health Services Administration (2011). *Results from the 2010 national survey on drug use and health: Summary of national findings*. NSDUH Series H-41, HHS Publication No. (SMA)

11–4658. Rockville, MD: Substance Abuse and Mental Health Services Administration.

Taliaferro, L. A., Rienzo, B. A., & Donovan, K. A. (2010). Relationships between youth sport participation and selected health risk behaviors from 1999 to 2007. *Journal of School Health, 80,* 399–410.

Turrisi, R., Mastroleo, N. R., Mallett, K. A., & Larimer, M. E. (2007). Examination of the meditational influences of peer norms, environmental influences, and parent communications on heavy drinking in athletes and nonathletes. *Psychology of Addictive Behaviors, 21,* 453–461. doi: 10.1037/0893–164X.21.4.453

Ungerleider, S. (2001). *Faust's gold. Inside the East German doping machine.* New York, NY: Thomas Dunne.

Woolsey, C., Waigandt, A., & Beck, N. C. (2010). Athletes and energy drinks: Reported risk-taking and consequences from the combined use of alcohol and energy drinks. *Journal of Applied Sport Psychology, 22,* 65–71.

World Health Organization. (2011). *Global status report on alcohol and health.* Retrieved from http://www.who.int/substance_abuse/publications/global_alcohol_report/msbgsruprofiles.pdf

Chapter 17

BURNOUT

Dick Vermeil became the head coach of the Philadelphia Eagles National Football League (NFL) team in 1976 at age 39. His philosophy was emblazoned on a sign in the Eagles's locker room: "The best way to kill time is to work it to death" (Coates, 1997, p. 3C). He became known as the "poster boy of coaching burnout" (Coates, 1997, p. 3C), as he worked from early morning to past midnight and often slept on a cot in his office. He considered an average workweek for NFL coaches to be 96 hours, and he tried to squeeze as much work as possible in each 24 hours. He kept a notebook by his bed to record the thoughts that woke him during the night, and interviewed his first assistant coaches during his spare hours between midnight and 3:00 A.M. Vermeil took the Eagles to the Super Bowl in 1981, losing to the Oakland Raiders 27 to 10.

Coach Dick Vermeil (photo by Jed Jacobsohn/Getty Images)

After the 1982 season and at age 46, Vermeil resigned and admitted that he was burned out. He recognized that he continued to add hours to his workweek in order to be the best in his profession until he finally ran out of hours. He pushed himself and his team to be the best until, "I finally ran out of things to push with. I couldn't relax. I couldn't turn it off" (Coates, 1997. p. 3C).

Vermeil sought psychotherapy for burnout, and spent several years dealing with issues such as anger and perfectionism. The influence of his relationship with his father remained with him in his adult life. His father was a perfectionist, and although Vermeil acknowledged his love for his father, he stated that this relationship left him with emotional scars. Vermeil said that his father invented the phrase "verbal abuse," and, "I was 16 before I realized my real first name wasn't Dumb Bastard " (King, 2000). This therapy was successful and he reasoned, "There's such a stigma in this country about seeking help like that, but I can tell you it's one of the best things I've ever done. It really helped me in this job" (King, 2000).

After 14 years and at age 60, Vermeil returned to the NFL as the head coach of the St. Louis Rams in 1997. The Rams won the Super Bowl in 2000.

Burnout is a syndrome that consists of mental, physical, and emotional fatigue and even exhaustion. It is characterized by psychological, emotional, and sometimes physical withdrawal from activities that were previously enjoyable. Burnout may also involve chronic fatigue, sleep disturbances, susceptibility to illness, and even depression. The term was originally applied to the emotional depletion of volunteers in an alternative health agency in the U.S. in the mid-1970s (Freudenberger, 1974, 1975). More generally, it has referred to the emotional depletion that occurs in the practice of human service and helping professions. These volunteers gradually lost their motivation and commitment and became more cynical and less idealistic and productive (Farber, 1983). Burnout has been seen as a response of prolonged work stress that overwhelms the coping resources of employees (Maslach & Schaufeli, 1993), or from too much work for too long a time with too little rest. The concept of burnout has achieved wide recognition in the world of sport (Goodger, Lavallee, Gorely, & Harwood, 2010). While highly motivated athletes may be "burning" with competitive desire, with burnout these flames are extinguished. It is a malady of those with high levels of achievement motivation, conscientiousness, and idealism, especially if their hard work is devoted to pursuits that are unrewarding.

With burnout, sportspersons lose their energy and purpose, perceive that they are accomplishing little, and devalue participation in sport (Eklund & Cresswell, 2007). It becomes more difficult to sustain lofty goals and single-minded devotion to these goals. Athletes may develop a reduced sense of accomplishment and lowered athletic efficacy as a result of burnout (Cresswell & Eklund, 2006a, 2006c; Henschen, 1998). Burnout may persist even after an athlete withdraws from sport (Goodger, Wolfenden, & Lavallee, 2007).

With burnout, athletes often develop negative attitudes toward their sport and question whether it is "worth it" to engage in sport (Dubuc et al., 2010; Smith, 1986). There is often a reduced sense of accomplishment, as, for example, athletes report that they are making little progress and that their efforts are a waste of time (Raedeke & Smith, 2001). The rewards or benefits of sport seem to be outweighed by the costs or unpleasant aspects. There are intrinsic rewards, such as the sheer enjoyment of sport and competition, the experience of gaining mastery or improving, and self-approval or feeling good about one's progress. Extrinsic rewards include trophies, money, privileges, and the admiration of others. Intrinsic costs include the time, effort, and pain necessary to reach high levels of fitness and skill, and self-derogation and disappointment after poor performances. Extrinsic costs include the disapproval of others after failure, and sometimes enduring unpleasant coaches, parents, teammates, and spectators. In general, burnout is less associated with intrinsic and identified motivation and more associated with extrinsic and introjected motivation and amotivation (Cresswell & Eklund, 2005a, 2005b; Lemyre, Treasure, & Roberts, 2006; Lonsdale, Hodge, & Rose, 2009). Indeed intrinsic motivation for sport participation is negatively correlated with burnout (Curran, Appleton, Hill, & Hall, 2011).

Application

People will work very hard and endure hardship and suffering when pursuing their own goals. For example, recreational marathon competitors freely engage in hundreds of hours of grueling training for nothing other than to better their personal record in the 26.2 mile (42.17 k) race. As explained in Chapter 3, the experience of external coercion—of being forced into participation—readily undermines interest and contributes to burnout.

A sportsperson might pursue athletics even if the costs outweigh the benefits if they decide that they have nothing better to do. However, if they identify competing activities that were more rewarding, such as goofing off, they may drop the athletics in pursuit of the activities that seem to return more at less cost. It is also possible that it will be difficult to decide what to do at a particular time because two activities are relatively equal in terms of costs and benefits. Using the same example, a sportsperson might realize that the eventual benefits of proper training are far greater than the benefits of goofing off, but the immediate costs of goofing off are minimal and it is fun.

MEASURING BURNOUT

Burnout has been reliably measured in workplace and sport settings. The Maslach Burnout Inventory (MBI; Maslach & Jackson, 1981, 1986) became the most widely utilized measure of burnout in workplaces. It has also been used to measure burnout among athletic personnel (e.g., Hendrix, Acevedo, & Hebert, 2000; Kelley, Eklund, & Ritter-Taylor, 1999; Martin, Kelley, & Eklund, 1999). A modified version has been validated with athletes (Cresswell & Eklund, 2006b). The **Athlete Burnout Questionnaire (ABQ**; Raedeke, 1997; Raedeke & Smith, 2001) was developed specifically for use in sport settings. It measures three dimensions of burnout among sportspersons: 1) emotional and physical exhaustion, 2) reduced sense of accomplishment, 3) sport devaluation.

STRESS AND BURNOUT

How is it that the flames of competitive desire burn brightly for years in some sportspersons, whereas others burnout? Clearly, burnout is not simply the result of a great deal of intense practice and competition. For example, elite junior tennis players may believe that 35 hours per week of practice is not enough (Gould, Tuffey, Udry, & Loehr, 1996b). One important part of this answer is the individual's response to the stress of competition and training. In discussing stress, the reader is reminded of the definition provided by Lazarus and Folkman (1984) and first mentioned in Chapter 4:

> Psychological stress is a particular relationship between the person and the environment that is appraised by the person as taxing or exceeding his or her resources and endangering his or her well-being. (p. 19)

Psychological stress is, therefore, determined by not only the demands and challenges of particular situations and conditions, but also by the athlete's determination of whether their skill and will are equal to the challenge.

Forms of external challenges or stressors in athletic settings include severe practice conditions, inadequate social support, poor coaching, strength of opponents, and, as discussed in Chapter 11, pressure in competition. Athletes' estimates of their internal resources are influenced by factors such as self-efficacy and helplessness, expectations about choking under pressure and anxiety, perfectionism, procrastination, and self-handicapping (Smith, 1986). When perceived internal resources are equal to environmental challenge, athletes do not feel stressed and drained by pressure, and are unlikely to experience burnout.

Burnout does not occur overnight. If the imbalance between environmental challenge and internal resources persists, burnout is likely to ensue. With burnout, there is a downward cycle of demoralization, diminished performance, withdrawal from practice and preparation, and, at worst, helplessness. This cycle is perpetuated by increased anxiety, depression, and sleeplessness, and withdrawal from and alienation of sources of social support.

STRESS, SELF-EFFICACY, AND GOALS

The importance of **self-efficacy** in influencing performance has been emphasized throughout this book, and it is a vital determinant of burnout (Nicholls, Polman, Levy, & Borkoles, 2010). Athletes with burnout often lack self-efficacy or conviction that they will work their way through external challenges and reach their goals. A devotion to unrealized or unrealistic goals is also associated with burnout. **Unrealistic goals** are often overly **narrow, intense**, and established at a very early age.

With a narrow focus, athletes judge themselves exclusively or largely on the basis of their success in competition. When this focus is overly intense, athletes devalue themselves when performance is flawed. As explained in Chapter 13, extreme standards for performance are a cardinal feature of perfectionism, and it is, therefore, not surprising that athletes with perfectionistic qualities are more likely to report burnout (Appleton, Hall, & Hill, 2009; Hill, Hall, & Appleton, 2010; Hill, Hall, Appleton, & Kozub, 2008; Hill, Hall, Appleton, & Murray, 2010). For example, burnout was more common among Norwegian Olympians and junior elite athletes with goals that were **perfectionistic** as well as **ego-oriented** and who trained in ego-oriented motivational climates (Lemyre, Hall, & Roberts, 2008).

Goals of perfection in all areas of functioning are unachievable, and unattained goals lead to burnout. Athletes who are especially sensitive to the reactions of others, who find criticism especially painful, and are overly concerned with pleasing others, are also more vulnerable to burnout.

Application

Exacting and even extreme goals are not necessarily maladaptive. As explained in Chapter 13, there are forms of normal perfectionism. Perfectionistic strivings are associated with high levels of achievement motivation and intrinsic interest. The expectation that others expect and require perfection—perfectionistic concerns—is a more likely cause of burnout.

COPING WITH STRESSORS

There are different ways of coping with situations that are seen as taxing or exceeding one's resources. Coping consists of what a person thinks or does in response to stressors. These thoughts and actions may change as situations unfold, and they may be relatively specific to stressors in specific environments. As explained in Chapter 4, there are two general categories of coping responses. Problem-focused coping involves efforts to manage, change, or master the source of the stress. There are many examples of problem-focused coping, and those more relevant to the focus of this book include goal setting, following regiments to prepare for competition, time management, problem solving and decision making, information gathering, and advice seeking. Emotion-focused coping concerns attempts to regulate emotional responses to the sources of stress. Relevant examples of emotion-focused coping include interpreting the stressor as a challenge rather than a threat, engaging in relaxation, meditation, and physical exercises, and obtaining emotional support from others. In many stressful situations, both problem- and emotion-focused coping are utilized. People differ in the degree to which they use problem- and emotion-focused coping. In general, problem-focused coping is more adaptive when there are tangible solutions to problems and resolutions to challenges. With problem-focused coping, the sources of stress are confronted (Zeidner, 1994). Emotion-focused coping is more successful when stressors cannot be eliminated or removed and must be endured or managed. It is important to correctly size up a situation as changeable or uncontrollable and to also have effective problem- and emotion-focused coping skills (Kowalski, Crocker, Hoar, & Niefer, 2005; Poliseo & McDonough, 2012).

MEASUREMENT OF SPORT STRESS

The **Recovery-Stress Questionnaire for Athletes** (RESTQ-Sport; Kellmann & Kallus, 2001) was developed to measure current sources of stress in the lives of individual athletes (King, Clark, & Kellmann, 2010). It is also a measure of current activities that promote the reestablishment of psychological and physical resources. With the RESTQ-Sport, athletes rate sources of general life stress, sport specific stress, and recovery activities that have occurred during the past three days. The recovery process occurs over time and concerns the alleviation of stress. Recovery consists of psychophysical regeneration, or a systematic, planned, and intentional process for creating the best possible conditions for recovery. Preparations for upcoming stressors, such as competitions, are also taken during the recovery process (Kellmann & Kallus, 2001).

Recovery is not a passive process, as athletes take action—such as attending to needs for sleep, hydration, nutrition, and reinforcing relationships with others—to speed it along. In the time between two competitions, three phases have been proposed to facilitate optimal recovery. During the *evaluation* phase, sportspersons evaluate results from the first competition or match. In the *transition* phase, athletes tailor restful activities to regenerate physical and psychological energy. The *final* phase is the preparation phase for the next competition, and this involves mental and physical preparation.

Application

Not infrequently, athletes find themselves with free time between matches. This is especially likely during tournaments and when traveling. Sportspersons may fill this time by sightseeing, shopping, and searching for good restaurants. Although enjoyable, these pursuits may result in standing and walking for hours. These pursuits also expose sportspersons to potential stressors, such as getting lost, conflicts with pedestrians, problems with transportation, and running late. Recovery is more likely when athletes deliberately rest by reclining and remaining inactive.

The scales of the RESTQ-Sport are listed in Figure 17.1. Sources of stress that are specific to sport settings are described in seven scales and more general sources of stress are detailed in the remaining 12. This empirically derived instrument provides sportspersons with an estimate of stress and burnout, recovery and well-being, and preparation for performance and competition.

Predictably, there is a dose-response relationship between stress and recovery. Acute increases in training volume and/or intensity are associated with decreased recovery and increased mood disturbance (Armstrong & VanHeest, 2002; Coutts, Wallace, & Slattery, 2007). However, elite and highly motivated athletes are capable of managing higher training volumes without correspondingly increased levels of stress and under-recovery states (Hartwig, Naughton, & Searl, 2011).

BURNOUT AND DROPOUT

The terms "burnout" and "dropout" are not synonymous. Burnout athletes may continue with a sport if they cannot find preferable alternative activities. Those experiencing burnout may also persist if they have invested a great deal of time and effort in attaining proficiency in their sport (Butcher, Lindner, & Johns, 2002; Schmidt & Stein, 1991). Other athletes may feel "entrapped" in that they do not believe quitting is an option (Gustafsson, Hassmen, Kentta, & Johansson, 2008). They may feel obligated to participate, perhaps due to pressure from parents and coaches. These athletes may not *want* to continue in sport but believe they *have* to. For example, female and male adolescent competitive swimmers who felt entrapped or obligated to train and compete were relatively burned out but swam on (Raedeke, 1997). Some of these teenagers were very negative on competitive swimming, as they experienced minimal rewards and high costs. Other burnt out teenagers did not find swimming to be equally aversive, but they also did not rate swimming as particularly rewarding. They were emotionally and physically exhausted, but continued out of a sense of obligation. Both groups of burnt out swimmers "went through the motions"

FIGURE 17.1 Scales of the Recovery-Stress Questionnaire for Athletes (Kellmann & Kallus, 2001)

1. General Stress: Mental stress, imbalance, depression, listlessness

2. Emotional Stress: Frequent irritation, anxiety, inhibition

3. Social Stress: Interpersonal conflicts and annoyances

4. Conflicts/Pressure: Unresolved conflicts, goals not achieved

5. Fatigue: Time pressure at work, training, school, overfatigue, lack of sleep

6. Lack of Energy: Ineffective work due to inability to concentrate, lack of energy, inefficient decision making

7. Physical Complaints: Bodily complaints

8. Success: Success, pleasure, and creativity at pursuits

9. Social Recovery: Pleasurable social contacts

10. Physical Recovery: Restoration of physical vigor

11. General Well-Being: Good moods and contentment

12. Sleep Quality: Absence of sleep disorders and sleeping through the night

13. Disturbed Breaks: Interruptions during recovery periods

14. Burnout/Emotional Exhaustion: Athletic burnout

15. Fitness/Injury: Vulnerability to injuries

16. Fitness/Being in Shape: Fitness, efficiency, vigor

17. Burnout/Personal Accomplishment: Function in team context and enjoyment of sport

18. Self-Efficacy: Optimal preparation and resources sufficient for challenges

19. Self-Regulation: Mental resources to meet goals

of training and competing and endured burnout because their sense of obligation prohibited quitting. Swimmers who did not rate themselves as obligated to swim were free to either participate for the rewards of training and competition, or to quit if they did not find swimming sufficiently enjoyable or if alternative activities were preferred.

With a large investment of time and effort, athletes are more likely to stick with sports that have temporally become unrewarding, because they expect some return on their large investment. People often expect some return on their investments, and sportspersons who have invested a great deal of time and energy in training may expect to reap intrinsic and extrinsic rewards in the future.

SOCIAL TIES

Social support is often seen as a way of blunting the effects of stress and preventing burnout. This view assumes that the comments and reactions of others are uniformly positive. Of course, this is not the case, as the reactions of others can do more harm than good and serve to increase one's sense of isolation. Elite male and female junior or late-adolescent tennis players who identified themselves as burnt out recognized that the influence of their parents and coaches was sometimes negative (Udry, Gould, Bridges, & Tuffey, 1997). These tennis players said that parents and coaches actually created a high-stress environment by emphasizing ego or performance goals, such as winning, and comparing their performance to other junior players. The tennis juniors responded negatively to excessive coercion by their parents to practice and compete in tournaments. Parental criticism that ascribed internal, global, and stable negative attributes, such as being a weakling, was demoralizing. Some players complained that coaches were not sensitive to their lack of self-efficacy and performance anxiety. They complained that their coaches expected them to be uniformly confident in matches.

It is probably helpful for parents to recognize when to push their children and when to back off, as the juniors found "pushing in a good way" (Udry et al., 1997, p. 376) to be helpful and supportive. This supportive pushing involved providing the resources necessary for elite participation and avoiding excessive pressure for winning performance. When parental approval is contingent on defeating others, young athletes experience performance anxiety, fear of failure, and lose intrinsic interest in sport. Indeed, the more intensely parents emphasize ego-oriented goals (see Chapter 9), the greater the child's anxiety. Conversely, even intense parental pressure for self-improvement, giving maximum effort, and for learning from mistakes does not result in evaluative pressure and anxiety in young sportspersons. When parents create mastery climates by emphasizing self-referenced goals, young athletes experience greater control over the factors that determine success (O'Rourke, Smith, Smoll, & Cumming, 2011).

Parents may be highly involved in the athletic careers of their children, provide appropriate structure, and also support the autonomy of their children. This form of support is likely to encourage intrinsic interest in sport and does not discourage elite achievement (Holt, Tamminen, Black, Mandigo, & Fox, 2009). For example, the parents of Olympic champions exerted little pressure to win (Gould, Dieffenbach, & Moffett, 2002). The parents did emphasize discipline and hard work and probably "pushed in a good way," in that they would at times challenge their children while remaining supportive and empathic. These parents also provided the resources necessary for athletic participation.

It is reasonable to assume that the parents and coaches of the juniors with burnout were well-intentioned in encouraging, and even pushing, them to perform at a high level. These efforts did not, however, have their desired effect, as the juniors described the influence of coaches and parents as more negative than positive. Coaches and parents may not have understood that interventions such as comparing players to others were harmful. However, insensitivity to the causes of burnout may not be the rule among coaches. Male coaches of late-adolescent swimmers with an average of 19 years of coaching experience demonstrated an accurate understanding of the causes and potential ways of avoiding burnout (Raedeke, Lunney, & Venables, 2002).

Application

"Pushing in the right way" is probably not experienced as coercive. People generally resist coercion and push back. Indeed, the experience of coercion results in even greater resistance and unwillingness to cooperate (Miller & Rollnick, 2013). Pushing in the right way may be promoted by an empathic understanding of an athlete's current motivational states. For example, there are days when young sportspersons are ambivalent about giving the time and effort necessary for quality practice. Parents and coaches may acknowledge the young athlete's disinterest. In addition, mentors may help athletes to recall their goals and the reasons they choose to participate. Hopefully, the athlete can recognize that the pros for sport outweigh the cons, and that quality practice and fitness gains can result even on "off" days.

The Influence of Coaches

As mentioned above, the behavior of coaches influences burnout in athletes. Burnout was more likely among female intercollegiate basketball and softball players when their coaches lacked empathy and were autocratic, critical, and preoccupied with winning (Vealey, Armstrong, Comar, & Greenleaf, 1998). Coaching was also a contributing factor in determining burnout among elite female and male French adolescent handball players. Handball players experienced less autonomy when their coaches were highly controlling. Handball players experienced more relatedness to their teams and autonomy when their coaches supported their autonomy (Isoard-Gautheur, Guillet-Descas, & Lemyre, 2012). As outlined in Chapter 2, sport is more likely to be intrinsically rewarding when participants experience competence, autonomy, and relatedness to others (e.g., Deci & Ryan, 1985, 2002; Gillet, Berjot, & Rosnet, 2009; Joesaar, Hein, & Hagger, 2011, 2012; Radel, Sarrazin, & Pelletier, 2009).

Male and female coaches of female high school soccer players who demonstrated the emotional exhaustion feature of burnout were less active in coaching (Price & Weiss, 2000). Their players said that they provided less instruction and training and less social support. These emotionally exhausted coaches may have relinquished tight and effective control of their teams. Consistent with the findings with college basketball and softball players (Vealey et al., 1998), athletes reported more burnout and anxiety about competition and less enjoyment and belief in their abilities when their coaches were burnt out and made decisions autocratically or with little input from players, and when coaches gave minimal training, positive feedback, and social support.

Coaches who are less autocratic and who focus on the personal growth of their athletes are less likely to burn out. These coaches are more likely to have collaborative leadership styles and encourage input from their team. They develop deep personal connections with team members, and are gratified when their players improve and succeed (Ryska, 2009).

Nevertheless, burnout is not uncommon among coaches. Estimates of burnout include 43% to 63% of high school and college coaches admitting to burnout (Vealey, Udry, Zimmerman, & Soliday, 1992). Over half of a group of college tennis coaches also acknowledged aspects of burnout, including emotional exhaustion, depersonalization, and a reduced sense of personal accomplishment (Kelley, Eklund, & Ritter-Taylor, 1999). Among coaches in the Premier soccer league for women in Sweden, 71% reported Emotional Exhaustion on the MBI; 23% of the coaches in the Premier league for men acknowledged Emotional Exhaustion. Stressors for coaches in the league for women were greater, as these coaches had fewer support staff and only 10% of these coaches had full-time appointments (Hjalm, Kentta, Hassmenan & Gustafsson, 2007). The coping resources of coaches with burnout are not equal to the external demands of coaching, such as the pressure to win, and to interact successfully with administrators, parents, the media, and the members of the team. Coaches with burnout reported less autonomy and control in their coaching roles and fewer meaningful accomplishments as coaches. Coaches without social support were more vulnerable to burnout.

There are varying types of commitment to coaching. For example, among swim coaches, there are those who coached primarily because of their attraction to the actual tasks of coaching, such as teaching sport skills, developing programs, and developing the sportspersonship and character of athletes. Others were less attracted to these aspects of coaching but felt relatively entrapped or obliged to continue in their roles as coaches (Raedeke, Granzyk, & Warren, 2000). These coaches reported decreasing satisfaction with coaching and increasing exhaustion over the course of one year. These coaches may have been overly stressed, as the time and energy demands of coaching may have exceeded perceived resources. A third group was comparatively less interested in coaching. The relative disinterest of the third group increased over the course of one year, and perhaps they became less committed to coaching and more drawn to competing activities (Raedeke, 2004).

SOCIOLOGY AND BURNOUT

In this discussion of stress and burnout, the balance between environmental stressors and pressure and internal coping resources was considered. So long as internal coping resources were seen as sufficient to handle the environmental stressors, burnout was not likely. The socio-logical approach of Jay Coakley to burnout takes issue with the emphasis on individual coping resources. From this vantage point, burnout is not due to individual coping limitations, but instead to the organization of athletic institutions. These institutions were seen as "disempowering" athletes from meaningful control over areas of their lives (Coakley, 1992). Sport institutions were criticized as emphasizing competition at the expense of providing opportunities for the overall social development of young sportspersons. This emphasis on competition encouraged athletes to develop identities that were relatively dependent on successful athletic performance rather than on competence in a wider range of roles.

Coakley also hypothesized that families tightly and excessively con-trolled the lives of burnt out young athletes. He conjectured that families that were capable of providing more time and money to support the ath-letic careers of their children were more likely to encourage a unilateral focus on athletic performance and that children in these families were prone to participate in sport out of a sense of obligation.

Jennifer Capriati and Burnout

Jennifer Capriati was described as "tennis' new legend in the making" (Scheiber, 1990), the "The Can't Miss Kid," and "eighth-grade wonder of the world" (Leershen & Barrett, 1990). At age 12, she won the U.S. Tennis Association 18-and-under competitions on clay and hard courts, and was named Junior Player of the Year by *Tennis* magazine. At age 16, she won an Olympic gold medal as the woman's singles champion.

Capriati turned pro as a tennis player on her 14th birthday in 1990, the first day she was eligible for professional status. At age 14, she became the youngest woman to be ranked in the top 10 of women's professional tennis, and the youngest to reach the semifinals of a Grand Slam tournament at the French Open. As a 14-year-old, she earned in excess of $4 million, primarily from endorsement contracts, such as racket maker Prince and Italian apparel maker Diadora. The figure was estimated to be $6 million when she was 15. Renowned sport psychologists described her as having an almost insatiable hunger for practice and training, and as earning highest marks for psychological fitness. At age 14, the press gushed that she "represents an evolutionary advance, a superior approach to the game" (Leershen & Barrett, 1990, p. 63).

The expectations and pressure foisted on her by the media, sponsors, and tourna-ment promoters were excessive. The pressure of being the "most hyped tennis player of all time" (Starr & Reiss, 1994) probably contributed to her sense of failure when her career stalled. She did not make the predicted meteoric ascent to the top of profes-sional women's tennis, and discovered that becoming "number one" was more difficult than anticipated. Perhaps this was due to the fact that young Grand Slam winners such as Steffi Graff and Monica Seles were not easily pushed aside by 16-year-old prodigies. At age 15, Ms. Capriati reached the semifinals of two Grand Slam events, but she won only one title as a 16-year-old, and described 1992 as a waste. She was plagued by tendonitis and bone chips in her elbow and suffered a first round loss as a 17-year-old in the 1993 U.S. Open. Prior to the Australian open in January 1992, Ms. Capriati complained openly and often about "a lot of pressure from everyone" (Harwitt, 1992).

At age 18, Ms. Capriati confirmed that this pressure led to burnout (Finn, 1994). Signs of mental and physical exhaustion were evident prior to her 16th birthday in 1992. She was pushed to compete in so many tournaments that tennis was no longer fun (Jenkins, 1992). She had so little fun playing tennis in 1992, she simply went through the motions, perhaps because her career was so important to others, such as her sponsors, tennis fans, and parents. She was also the primary breadwinner in her family.

Ms. Capriati returned to tennis eminence and in 2001 won two major tennis tournaments in the Australian and French Opens. In 2002, she won the Australian Open for the second time. This return was possible when she rediscovered intrinsic motivation for playing, training, and competing.

STALENESS

As mentioned above burnout does not occur overnight. It is the result of the cumulative effects of emotional and physical exhaustion. Staleness is a related concept, but it refers to the acute rather than long-term effects of physical and emotional fatigue and exhaustion. The psychological aspects of staleness are the same for both genders. Staleness results in impaired sport performance and an inability to train at customary levels. It is not uncommon with about 10% of college athletes experiencing it every year and more than 50% of elite distance runners reporting it at some point in their careers (Raglin & Wilson, 2000; Tobar, 2005). Staleness is often accompanied by body aches and physical complaints, such as headaches and stomach aches. Staleness has been seen as an early warning sign of burnout. If the signs of staleness are not heeded, burnout will likely follow.

Readers may also recall that the topic of staleness was introduced in Chapter 15 in the discussion of the "inverse iceberg" POMS (Profile of Mood States; McNair, Lorr, & Droppleman, 1971) profile. The inverse iceberg profile consists of low levels of vigor or energy, and high levels of tension, depression, anger, fatigue, and confusion (Morgan, Brown, Raglin, O'Connor, & Ellickson, 1987), and this profile identifies staleness. The inverse iceberg profile may also present after an athlete is injured. A return to an iceberg profile may coincide with the physical recovery of injured athletes and tapering or reducing the training load of fatigued athletes. More complete rest is necessary if tapering does not alleviate staleness (Raglin & Wilson, 2000). Ironically, some athletes respond to staleness by training harder.

Staleness is often the result of overtraining, but overtraining is necessary to improve physical performance (Kentta, Hassmen, & Raglin, 2006; Raglin & Wilson, 2000; Robson-Ansley, Gleeson, & Ansley, 2009). Overtraining is a prescribed period of the most intense training during a training cycle. The goal of overtraining is to provide maximal training stress without injury. Overtraining is a positive training stress when it leads to improved performance over time. Physiological adaptations to increasing training loads are necessary to improve performance with endurance and other sports. With the development of more scientific training regimens, training loads are increasing markedly. For example, Mark Spitz reportedly swam 9,000 meters per day in preparation for his seven Olympic gold medals in the 1972 Olympics. The training load of some current Olympic swimmers exceeds 18,000 meters per day.

Overtraining is typically followed by brief tapering periods during which training volume, but perhaps not intensity, is decreased. As training intensity increases, additional recovery time is necessary, and overtraining and tapering periods can be balanced to optimize performance and improvements (Kellmann & Kallus, 2001; O'Connor, 2007).

Overtraining has not been balanced with tapering when there is excessive difficulty in recovering from fatigue and regaining vigor between workouts, and inability to return to former levels of performance (Hollander & Meyers, 1995; Zehsaz, Azarbaijani, Farhangimaleki, & Tiidus, 2011). At times, it may be difficult to distinguish appropriate levels of fatigue that accompany overtraining from staleness. However, careful record-keeping provides unambiguous evidence of an inability to reach prior performance levels and the necessity of adjustments in training schedules. There is no single biological marker that reliably identifies staleness, but increases in heart rate during rest, exercise and recovery, and decreases in testosterone and increases in cortisol, a marker of stress, suggest that overtraining has not been balanced with rest (Maso, Lac, Filaire, Michaux, & Robert, 2004; McKenzie, 1999). Overtraining for endurance sports results in an increased susceptibility to upper respiratory tract infections. Overtraining for endurance sports results in less production of a hormone, IgA, that provides resistance to upper respiratory tract infections.

Long and continuous athletic seasons are a contributor to staleness. This source of staleness is difficult to reverse, as in many U.S. universities athletes are expected to practice and train formally and "informally" for about twelve months of the year (Henschen, 1998).

Boring practices and training regimens also lead to staleness. Practice that consists of simply "going through the motions" is more likely to lead to staleness, and the antidote to meaningless practice may be to develop specific long- and short-term goals for practice. As explained in Chapter 8, goals that are just beyond one's reach are most motivating, and a sense of purpose is established by organizing proximate goals within a hierarchy. Proximal goals allow for a steady stream of feedback about whether current behaviors are successful in reaching short-term standards. The adequacy of current training and technique mastery can estimated by determining if short-term goals are accomplished, and strategies can be altered in time to achieve distal goals.

Sources of Burnout
1. Imbalances between internal coping resources and environmental challenges
2. Fatigue, staleness, sleeplessness, anxiety, and depression
3. Alienation from sources of social support
4. Participation in sport because of perceived social pressure rather than because you *want to*
5. Parents and coaches emphasize performance goals, such as winning
6. Coercive and authoritarian coaching and parenting styles
7. Training for twelve months of the year
8. Boring practices
9. See the Recovery-Stress Questionnaire for Athletes

Recommendations for Avoiding Burnout

1. Systematically manage overtraining and tapering, reducing training load, rest
2. Set realistic goals for training, practice, and competition; not perfectionistic goals
3. Set short- and long-term goals for training, practice, and competition
4. Develop intrinsic interest in sport
5. Make training, practice, and competition fun
6. Do not isolate athletes from friends and sources of social support
7. Avoid parental overinvolvement
8. More democratic and less dictatorial coaching and parenting styles
9. See the Recovery-Stress Questionnaire for Athletes

(Gould et al., 1996b; Henschen, 1998; Kellmann & Kallus, 2001; Raedeke & Smith, 2001; Raglin & Wilson, 2000; Smith, 1986; Udry et al., 1997)

OVERTRAINING

Definitions of staleness and overtraining are not consistent. As mentioned above, overtraining is recognized as a contributor and forbearer to staleness. Alternatively, staleness has been defined as the psychological component of physical overtraining (Hollander & Meyers, 1995). A third alternative considers staleness, overtraining, and burnout to all represent forms of negative responses to training stress (Silva, 1990). In this formulation, overtraining is distinguished from training overload, and the term "overtraining" is reserved for maladaptive responses to prescribed training overload (Lee, 2010). The definition of training overload in this formulation is similar to that given earlier for overtraining. It is a period of progressively increased training loads, during which the volume and intensity of training are maximized in an effort to produce physical improvements (Kellmann, 2010). Staleness is then defined as the initial failure to respond adaptively to progressive training loads (Silva, 1990). In this context, staleness is considered an expectable response as mental and physical adjustments are made to increasing training stress. During this "lag period," sportspersons experience training plateaus and show no improvements or perhaps some slippage in performance.

With this definition, approximately 73% of male and female collegiate athletes experience staleness during athletic seasons, and many notice it at the midpoint and end of their seasons (Silva, 1990). Athletes either "train through" this plateau and prepare for new and additional cycles of training, or make adjustments to training schedules, such as tapering, to provide for rejuvenation and a return to physiological homeostasis. The athlete that accomplishes neither in response to staleness is at risk for the overtraining response. This overtraining response consists of physical and mental exhaustion, but this fatigue is entrenched and longstanding. It also is not uncommon among female and male collegiate athletes, with about 66% experiencing the overtraining response during athletic seasons. The athlete unable to train through or taper and recover from overtraining is more likely to progress to burnout. Intercollegiate athletes identified burnout as the most unfavorable response to training stress. The most common response to burnout was the wish to quit playing their sport. Recovery from burnout was seen as less likely and to predispose athletes to drop out of their sport or to fail to realize prior levels of performance.

SUMMARY AND APPLICATION

The concept of burnout is well-established in sport. It describes the mental, physical, and emotional fatigue that results from the experience of excessive stress and pressure. The experience of psychological stress is only partially determined by situational or environmental demands for training and practice and pressure for skilled performance. These situational stressors are balanced by the coping strategies and resources of individual athletes. Athletes who confront situational pressure with well-established and highly functional coping strategies are likely to be undaunted, and may interpret pressure as a source of excitement and heavy training loads as means of advancement. Emotion- and problem-focused coping strategies are useful for mastering stressors, and problem- focused strategies are especially useful if it is necessary to take action to master environmental demands and pressure. Coping strategies do not simply concern what individuals do to address sources of stress, but also include the solicitation of information and help from others.

Burnout does not occur overnight, but is the result of a persistent imbalance between internal coping resources and the stressors of training and competition. Athletes with certain characteristics are more or less likely to successfully cope with the pressure of competition and training loads of practice. With high self-efficacy for athletic competence, sportspersons persist in training and competition and remain confident that goals will be obtained. Lacking this confidence, athletes may question whether the time, effort, discomfort, and inconvenience of training, practice, and competition is "worth it." Athletic participation is more likely to be worth it if intrinsic rewards, such as having fun and self-improvement, and extrinsic rewards, such as approval and occasional "pats on the back" from important others, are realized (Scanlan, Russell, Magyar, & Scanlan, 2009). Coercion for athletic participation from parents and coaches, the establishment of ego or performance and perfectionistic goals diminish intrinsic rewards and increase the likelihood of burnout.

Levels of self-efficacy and goals notwithstanding, burnt out athletes often question whether the sacrifices and costs of athletic participation are worth the intrinsic and extrinsic rewards. When the costs predominate, athletes may wish to dropout. However, burnout does not always result in dropping out of athletic participation, especially when athletes feel an obligation to others, such as parents and coaches, to continue. Athletes may also continue in their sport when burnt out if there are no preferable alternative activities and if they have already invested a great deal in gaining proficiency.

Sociological theories of burnout de-emphasize individual coping strategies and focus on the stress placed on athletes by athletic institutions. These institutions were seen as fostering the development of identities that are overly narrow and determined primarily by continuing athletic participation. Institutions were criticized as disempowering burned out athletes and limiting the overall social development of sportspersons.

In responding to these criticisms of athletic institutions, the question arises of whether the correction of these problems will require a radical reworking of athletic institutions, hardly a likelihood, or whether parents and coaches should be encouraged to limit or stop interventions that are not helpful. For example, burnt out junior tennis players complained when coaches and parents pressured them to win and compared their performance to that of other juniors. Derogatory comments about mental toughness and talent of juniors had a detrimental effect. Juniors complained if tennis dominated their lives to the degree that socialization with peers was prevented, and multifaceted identities may be developed if competent peer and academic functioning is emphasized.

The topics of staleness, overtraining, and training overload were also addressed in this chapter. There is a lack of agreement on the precise definition of these terms, but definitions that are best integrated with the larger topic of burnout were emphasized. In this context, staleness refers to the acute effects of physical and emotional fatigue and exhaustion. Staleness is often the result of overtraining, or cycles of intense training intended to advance the physical status of athletes. Staleness is distinguished, however, from normal levels of fatigue that result from overtraining. One reliable measure of staleness is diminished performance, and accurate record keeping provides unambiguous evidence of impaired performance.

Staleness is a harbinger of burnout, and efforts to identify and reverse staleness are, therefore, useful. The most direct way of reducing staleness is to determine if overtraining is balanced with periods in which training is tapered. Tapering may involve reducing the either or both the volume and intensity of training exercise. Establishing proximal goals for practice, and integrating proximal goals in hierarchies also help to make training meaningful, interesting, and challenging and counteract staleness. Practice is also less likely to be meaningless if athletes adhere to the techniques presented in Chapters 4, 5, 6, and 7, and understand practice as not only a time for physical training but also for mental preparation for competition.

Key Terms

Stress and Burnout   394

Athlete Burnout Questionnaire (ABQ)   394

Self-efficacy   395

Unrealistic goals: narrow, intense, perfectionistic, ego-oriented   395

Recovery-Stress Questionnaire for Athletes   396

Social support   399

Discussion Questions

Q1. Review the development of the burnout concept.
Q2. Describe the measures of burnout.
Q3. Explain the relationship between stress and burnout.
Q4. Consider how self-efficacy and goal-setting are related to burnout.
Q5. Review the forms of coping.
Q6. Review the process of recovery as measured by the Recovery-Stress Questionnaire for Athletes.
Q7. How is it that some athletes pursue sports despite being burnt out?
Q8. Explain the relationship between social support and burnout.
Q9. Review the coaching behaviors that predict burnout.
Q10. Describe the characteristics of coaches who are burnt out.
Q11. Explain burnout from a sociological perspective.
Q12. Differentiate staleness and burnout.
Q13. Review overtraining.

Suggested Readings

Cresswell, S. L., & Eklund, R. C. (2006a). Athlete burnout: Conceptual confusion, current research and future research directions. In S. Hanton & S. D. Mellalieu (Eds.), *Literature reviews in sport psychology* (pp. 91–126). New York, NY: Nova Science Publishers.

Curran, T., Appleton, P. R., Hill, A. P., & Hall, H. K. (2011). Passion and burnout in elite junior soccer players: The mediating role of self-determined motivation. *Psychology of Sport and Exercise, 12,* 655–661. doi: 10.1016/j.psychsport.2011.06.004

Freudenberger, H. J. (1974). Staff burnout. *Journal of Social Issues, 30,* 159–165.

Goodger, K., Lavallee, D., Gorely, T., & Harwood, C. (2010). Burnout in sport: Understanding the process. In J. M. Williams (Ed.), *Applied sport psychology: Personal growth to peak performance* (6th ed., pp. 492–511). New York, NY: McGraw-Hill.

Goodger, K., Wolfenden, L., & Lavallee, D. (2007). Symptoms and consequences associated with three dimensions of burnout in junior tennis players. *International Journal of Sport Psychology, 38,* 342–364.

Gustafsson, H., Hassmen, P., Kentta, G., & Johansson, M. (2008). A qualitative analysis of burnout in elite Swedish athletes. *Psychology of Sport & Exercise, 9,* 800–816. doi: 10.1016/j.psychsport.2007.11.004

Holt, N. L., Tamminen, K. A., Black, D. E., Mandigo, J. L., & Fox, K. R. (2009). Youth sport parenting styles and practices. *Journal of Sport & Exercise Psychology, 31,* 37–59.

Kellmann, M., & Kallus, K. W. (2001). *Recovery-stress questionnaire for athletes: User manual.* Champaign, IL: Human Kinetics.

O'Rourke, D. J., Smith, R. E., Smoll, F. L., & Cumming, S. P. (2011). Trait anxiety in young athletes as a function of parental pressure and motivational climate: Is parental pressure always harmful? *Journal of Applied Sport Psychology, 23,* 398–412. doi: 10-1080/10413200.2001.552089

Poliseo, J. M., & McDonough, M. H. (2012). Coping effectiveness in competitive sport: Linking goodness of fit and coping outcomes, *Sport, Exercise, and Performance Psychology, 1,* 106–119. doi: 10.1037/a0026382

Raedeke, T. D., & Smith, A. L. (2001). Development and preliminary validation of an athlete burnout measure. *Journal of Sport & Exercise Psychology, 23,* 281–306.

Smith, R. E. (1986). Toward a cognitive-affective model of athletic burnout. *Journal of Sport Psychology, 8,* 36–50.

Chapter 18

SPORT INJURIES

Prior to becoming the first Irish gymnast to qualify for the Olympic Games in 2012, Kieran Behan overcame a spate of serious injuries. After tearing a second anterior cruciate knee ligament in 2010, one of his coaches, Simon Gale, feared for his safety. "He couldn't handle it. I wouldn't say he was suicidal, but I'm just glad that his girlfriend was there to watch him at night" (Macur, 2012).

As a child, he broke his arm and wrist. As a teenager, he visited the hospital so often that authorities suspected he was being abused. At age 10, a benign tumor was surgically removed from his left leg. A tourniquet was left on for too long after surgery and he suffered nerve damage that resulted in limited feeling in his left foot. Although despondent, he refused to believe doctors who advised him to prepare for life in a wheelchair. After fifteen months, he regained function and returned to gymnastics. However, within eight months, he banged his head against a metal apparatus during a gymnastics routine and suffered an injury to his brain and semicircular canal in his vestibular system. With the latter injury, he lost consciousness if he made the slightest of movements.

Why has he been so resilient? "I think it's probably just in my blood. I was born to do this."

Athletic injuries

Athletic injuries are not uncommon. There are about 17 million sport injuries per year in the U.S. Athletic participation accounts for 44% of the injuries that occur to students 14 years of age and older (Boyce & Sobolewski, 1989). Among intercollegiate athletes in the U.S., 13.8 significant sport injuries occurred for every 1,000 athletic contests, and 4.0 injuries happened in every 1,000 practices (Hootman, Dick, & Agel, 2007). Among the 7 million students in the U.S. who participate in high school sports, there are 1.4 million annual sports injuries (Centers for Disease Control and Prevention, 2006). Approximately 14.9% of injuries incurred in high school athletics are severe or result in a loss of at least 21 days of athletic participation (Darrow, Collins, Yard, & Comstock, 2009). Recurrent injuries are not uncommon, and account for 10.5% of the injuries in high school athletics. Comparing recurrent and new injuries, high school athletes are three times more likely to discontinue athletic participation after a recurrent injury (Swenson, Yard, Fields, Comstock, 2009). Among the most elite male soccer players in the Netherlands, 26.65 significant injuries occurred for every 1,000 hours of match competition, and 6.74 injuries happened for every 1,000 training hours (Brink et al., 2010). Approximately 7.7% of German children and adolescents experience sports injuries yearly (Bruhmann & Schneider, 2011). Hundreds of millions of dollars are allocated for the treatment of these injuries.

PREDICTING SPORT INJURIES

Injuries do not occur randomly. The likelihood of injuries increases when training and practice, biomechanics, coaching, equipment, playing and practice venues, and luck are less than optimal. Injuries are also more

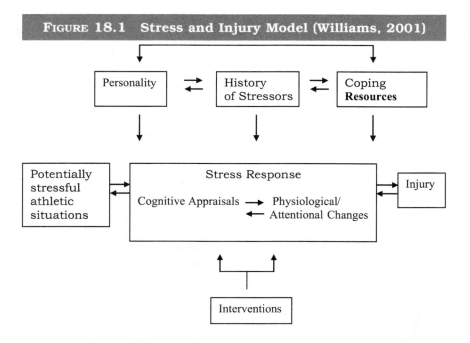

FIGURE **18.1** **Stress and Injury Model (Williams, 2001)**

likely during periods of overtraining (Brink et al., 2010). Psychological and social factors also increase the chances of athletic injuries, and the relationship between these variables is probably best explained in the following model.

The **stress and injury model** (Figure 18.1) is consistent with the cognitive-relational theory (Lazarus & Folkman, 1984) of stress that has been described throughout the chapters of this book. Athletic competitions and practice that are demanding and that involve pressure are environmental stressors that affect sportspersons differently, depending on their history of stressors and coping resources. Athletic stressors will produce more intense stress responses in the forms of threatening cognitive appraisals, physiological anxiety, and attentional disruptions if **personality** factors augment the effects of the stressors, if there is **a history of** exposure to **stressors**, and if there are few **coping resources**. Without intervention, the highly stressed athlete is at greater risk for injury (Williams, 2001) and illness (Brink, 2010). In general, when internal and external resources are seen to be insufficient to meet challenges presented by environmental pressure, stress responses increase and vulnerability to injury increases.

Depending on a sportsperson's **cognitive appraisal**, environmental stressors may be seen as a source of excitement and attraction or as a source of danger to be avoided. When stressors are seen to be sources of danger, cognitive appraisals can serve as cognitive interference and disrupt **attention** and also to increase **physiological anxiety** (Kerr & Goss, 1996). These responses can accompany unwanted simultaneous contraction of agonist and antagonist muscle groups, a response referred to as bracing. This

bracing leads to fatigue, reduced flexibility, and decreased motor coordination and fluidity of motion and, consequently, to increased risk of injury.

When athletes take the field with cognitive interference and physiological anxiety, they have fewer attentional resources available to focus on sources of danger from opponents, and to anticipate action and avoid sources of injury (Johnson & Ivarsson, 2011). Not concentrating fully, athletes are less able to make split-second decisions and physical maneuvers to avoid musculoskeletal trauma. Peripheral narrowing may also occur so that athletes focus less attention on action in the periphery of their visual fields (Rogers & Landers, 2005; Williams, Tonymon, & Andersen, 1991). Prior physical injuries also create risk factors for future injuries, because they potentially represent physical vulnerability as well as a psychological vulnerability if the athlete fears reinjury (Petrie & Falkstein, 1998).

How is it that some athletes appraise environmental challenges to be dangerous whereas others find them to be exciting? In the model under discussion, the answer is found by considering the athlete's personality characteristics, history of stressors, and coping resources. As mentioned throughout this book, personality characteristics refer to stable internal traits. One's history of stressors is determined by identifying major life events, daily hassles or problems, and previous injuries. Coping resources include skill in handling stress and interpersonal resources or help from others.

History of Stressors

Negative **major life events** are a category of **stressors** or stress that has a fairly dramatic effect on athletic injuries in sports such as football, wrestling, gymnastics, and alpine skiing, with most studies showing that highly stressed athletes were two to five times as likely to incur injuries (Williams, 2001). Examples of negative major life events include poor performances in major competitions, problems maintaining academic eligibility, and conflicts with coaching staff, and pressure from parents (Johnson & Ivarsson, 2011). In fewer studies, it was found that injuries were more likely among athletes with higher levels of total life stress, or both positive and negative major life events, and in fewer still injuries were associated with positive life stress (Steffen, Pensgaard, & Bahr, 2008).

Application

Some athletes have the enviable experience of being able to concentrate deeply during competition, regardless of external distractions and major stressors. Indeed, some report taking refuge from external stress during match play.

More are distracted by external stress, especially when stressors are emotionally valent or provoke emotional responses. It is difficult to disengage emotional responses. Emotionally valent stressors are especially distracting, as they compete for space in working memory.

This relationship between stress and injuries holds across competitive levels and from youth to elite levels. There has been less research about the relationship of daily hassles and prior injuries and future injuries. An example of a daily hassle is an inconvenience, such as having to drive one hour for swim practice at 5 A.M. However, there is evidence that athletes who have more current hassles in their life (Fawkner, McMurray, & Summers, 1999) as well as prior injuries (Williams, Hogan & Anderson, 1993) were more susceptible to injury. Prior injuries are also potential stressors, especially for athletes who lack social support and who are not fully rehabilitated (Williams & Andersen, 2007). Previously injured athletes feel more susceptible to injury reoccurrence (Stephan, Deroche, Brewer, Caudroit, & Le Scanff, 2009).

Gymnastics and Injuries

Female gymnasts at the 2012 Olympic Games in London competed while recovering from injuries. Russia's Viktoria Komova twice had surgery on her right ankle. American McKayla Maroney suffered a broken nose and mild concussion during the Olympic trials, and reinjured a broken toe in the weeks before the Olympic Games. Romania's Larisa Andreea Lordache competed with an injured left foot, and China's Yao Jinnan struggled with a bruised knee ligament. American Chellsie Memmel and China's Cheng Fei missed the Games due to injuries.

Memmel and others blame increasingly difficult routines for the injuries. Prior to 2006, the highest potential score in gymnastics was 10. With this limit, there was less incentive to pack a routine with risky and extremely difficult elements. Today, gymnastics scoring is open-ended, and routines must have high degrees of difficulty if a gymnast is to have a chance to medal. For example, a decade ago, an uneven-bars routine might have two release moves. Today, it has five.

Bruno Grandi, the president of the International Gymnastics Federation, recognized the difficulties caused by the Code of Points—the system for scoring gymnastics routines. He characterized it as "a time bomb that we are wholly unable to contain."

Maroney views injuries as simply part of the sport. "Sometimes you just have to go through the pain and do what you've done in the gym every day," she says. "I'm positive that every single girl here has something that bugs them" (Fowler, 2012).

Personality

Personality factors serve to augment or blunt the effects of stressors (Ivarsson & Johnson, 2010). For example, competitive trait anxiety or anxiety that occurs during most competitions is associated with higher injury rates. Among starting collegiate football players, the combination of competitive trait anxiety and high life stress made athletes particularly susceptible to injury (Petrie, 1993). Trait anxiety is a major component of the personality trait of neuroticism. Rugby players who endorsed high levels of neuroticism and low levels of global self-esteem considered themselves vulnerable to injury (Deroche, Stepahn, Brewer, & Scanff,

2007). The trait of sensation-seeking was discussed in Chapter 15 and is seen as similar to extreme extraversion. Professional hockey players who were high in sensation-seeking suffered more injuries in the course of seasons (Osborn, Blanton, & Schwebel, 2009). Intercollegiate athletes in football, volleyball, and cross-country who maintained positive states of mind were less likely to sustain injuries. These positive states served to keep athletes focused, concentrating, an relaxed, and fostered social support (Williams et al., 1993). Positive mood states appear to buffer the stress of competition and training. Negative mood states, such as anxiety and depression, increase risks for injury (Galambos, Terry, Moyle, & Locke, 2005). With negative mood states, athletes appear to have fewer resources available to cope with the stress of competition.

Self-handicapping and defensive pessimism have also been cited as personality factors related to injuries. Intercollegiate female field hockey players with low self-concepts were shown to self-handicap by being more likely to sustain injuries on the day before competitions. These injuries offered excuses for the avoidance of competition or at least for poor play (Lamb, 1986). Defensive pessimism consists of expectations for poor performance, which then provide motivation to work hard to avoid failure (Norem & Illingworth, 1993). With defensive pessimism and high life stress, athletes have been shown to be injury prone. Defensive pessimists also took few days' rest, especially under high stress conditions, and even when injured (Williams, 2001).

Coping

Coping resources serve to blunt environmental stress (Maddison & Prapavessis, 2005). There are three forms of coping resources. Not surprisingly, higher levels of these coping resources are associated with fewer injuries. **General coping behaviors** relate to sleep patterns, nutritional habits, and reserving time for recreation. **Psychological coping skills** include the techniques for controlling physiological anxiety and preparing for competitions that were presented in Chapters 4 through 7. Social support is a form of **interpersonal coping** and consists of well-intentioned actions from other people. Social support has been seen as a buffer to stress, and athletic injuries are less frequent when stress is reduced (Johnson, 2007). For example, collegiate football players in the starting lineup who experienced high stress and negative life events were more likely to sustain an athletic injury only when they had little social support (Petrie, 1993). Similar results were found with adult male and female ballet dancers affiliated with a major ballet company in the western U.S. Dancers with little social support were vulnerable to the effects of negative life events and especially negative daily hassles (Patterson & Smith, 1998). They were more frequently injured.

Moderate or high levels of either psychological coping skills or social support insulate athletes against the effects of athletic stressors. Professional, collegiate, and high school Korean ballet dancers with higher levels of psychological coping skills were less likely to experience injuries (Noh, Morris, & Andersen, 2005). Varsity male and female high school athletes who were low in both psychological coping skills and social support were shown to be at greatest risk for injury when hit with negative life events (Smith et al., 1990). Athletes who were unable to call on internal coping resources or help from other people apparently had no strategies to reduce arousal and physiological anxiety and to sustain attention and avoid harm during practice and competition. Despite the young age of these high school athletes, it appears that if they felt equal to athletic challenges, negative life events did not distract them or produce unremitting physiological anxiety sufficient to lead to injury.

Intervention to Reduce the Risk of Injury

Intervention prior to injury is recommended to lessen the risk of injury (Johnson, 2007; Maddisson & Prapavessis, 2005; Williams, 2001). This intervention is directed at faulty cognitive appraisals as well as at excessive physiological anxiety. The techniques and interventions discussed in Chapters 4 through 7 are useful in helping athletes form realistic evaluations of athletic stressors and of their capacities to masters the stressors. Perceived stress and pressure may also diminish if there is team cohesion and helpful communication between athletes and coaches. Physiological anxiety is reduced by the regular practice of the techniques described in Chapter 6.

Stress inoculation training produced good results in preventing injuries with gymnasts who competed at national and international levels (Kerr & Goss, 1996). In a course of stress inoculation training that consisted of 16 one-hour training sessions, gymnasts learned techniques for mental practice, interrupting negative thoughts, and rational evaluation of the sources of stress and their capacities to master these sources. The benefits of stress inoculation training began to accrue at midseason, or about four months after the start of practice, and persisted through the second four months of the gymnastic season. The gymnasts reported less total and less negative stress in their lives. The gymnasts who practiced stress inoculation training spent about half as many days injured, five versus ten, as the gymnasts who did not practice. Less injury time during the second half of the season was important for these gymnasts, because National Championships were held at the season's end. A form of stress inoculation training was also shown to be effective in reducing the prevalence of injuries and illnesses among male and female collegiate rowers (Perna, Antoni, Baum, Gordon, & Schneiderman, 2003).

Intercollegiate swimmers and football players had significantly fewer injuries during seasons in which they practiced **progressive muscle relaxation** (PMR) and mental practice and rehearsal (Davis, 1991). Similar results were reported for U.S. alpine skiers who were trained in mental practice, attention control, communication skills, team building, and crisis intervention (May & Brown, 1989).

Highly competitive to elite female and male Swedish soccer players who received training to manage stress were less likely to be injured than were their untreated counterparts. Those who received the stress management intervention recorded 0.22 injuries per person during the intervention period that lasted through the first half of their spring competitive season, whereas the untreated players had 1.31 injuries per person (Johnson, Ekengren, & Andersen, 2005). The reduction in injuries may have been the direct result of instruction in somatic and cognitive relaxation, stress management, goal setting, and attribution and self-confidence training. The athletes also kept a critical incident diary, and this may have heightened their awareness of stress and allowed them to better prepare for practice and competition and to avoid unnecessary stress at work or school.

An intervention that included stress inoculation training and biofeedback showed promise with elite adolescent Swedish soccer players. Footballers receiving the intervention were less frequently injured (Evardsson, Ivarsson, & Johnson, 2011).

Application

Interventions designed to reduce injuries focus on external stress and relaxation techniques. Athletes are not taught to play cautiously to prevent injuries. Perhaps instructions for avoiding injury during practice and competition may result in an ironic process (see Chapter 11) and more injuries. However, coaches may protect athletes from unnecessary injuries by pulling them from competition when teams are comfortably ahead or games are out of reach. Coaches may also limit an athlete's playing time when they are visibly stale and in need of rest.

AFTER THE OCCURRENCE OF INJURIES

Stress is not only a predictor of the occurrence of injuries, but injuries are also an ongoing source of stress. Stress has been seen as deriving from three potential sources: **major life events, chronic stress**, and **daily hassles**. Sport injuries are serious sources of stress because they meet all three criteria. Injuries threaten or postpone advancement in the athlete's area of primary interest and threaten potential careers and livelihoods. They linger for a period of time and are sources of ongoing pain. They are bothersome on a daily basis as athletes adjust their routine to cope with disabilities and limitations.

Serious, season-ending injuries are common among elite skiers. Male and female members of the U.S. Ski team identified stress caused by season-ending injuries (Udry, Gould, Bridges, & Beck, 1997a). The majority of the injuries were to the anterior cruciate ligaments of knees. Psychological worries and concerns were a source of stress for all of the injured skiers. They worried that they would never be the same, that they would lose their spot on the team, that teammates would surpass

After the injury
(photo courtesy of Western Connecticut State University)

them, and that they would be reinjured. About two-thirds felt socially isolated and found the lack of attention by coaches and teammates to be a source of stress. Many found the physical limitations caused by the injury to be stressful, and some also worried about the adequacy of medical and rehabilitation care. Rehabilitation consists of the retraining or reconditioning of the musculoskeletal system to return to pre-injury levels of physical fitness. The suspension of financial support and career opportunities during injury was an additional source of stress. Prior physical injuries appear to create risk factors for future injuries because they represent potential physical vulnerability as well as a psychological vulnerability if the athlete fears reinjury (Petrie & Falkstein, 1998).

Sport Injury and Grieving

Grief can be defined as an emotional response to a loss. It is often understood to occur in response to the loss of a loved one or someone to whom someone has formed an emotional attachment. Injuries result in losses and sometimes grief. As athletes invest more effort, time, and aspects of their identity in their sport, the greater is the loss due to injury.

The losses from injuries include restricted athletic participation, career opportunities, status, playing time, and attention from coaches, teammates, and the media. Athletic injuries portend a loss of independence, mobility, vitality, and control. Additional losses occur with physical separation from teammates, coaches, and training routines and opportunities for athletic achievement during physical primes. If injuries are career ending, athletes may experience losses to vital aspects of their identity and to their purpose in life (Evans & Hardy, 1995). Grief responses are more likely when injuries are serious and irreversible (Johnston & Carroll, 1998).

Over the past fifty years, there has been a considerable amount of theorizing about the process of resolving grief. Although not proven scientifically (Brewer, 2007, 2009), it has been almost axiomatic that there are several stages of grieving process. Kubler-Ross (1969) advanced the most widely recognized **stage theory** of grief. She recognized five stages in the grief process of dying patients: **denial, bargaining, anger, depression,** and **acceptance**. That is, when confronted with the likelihood of death, patients first respond with disbelief or an unwillingness to accept the news. As denial erodes, patients try to bargain or make deals about what they will offer in exchange for their life being spared. For example, dying patients might promise God to make amends if they survive. The bargaining phase is followed by anger about one's fate, and depression when the loss of life appears inevitable. With acceptance, patients acknowledge and accept the inevitability of death.

Stage models have been developed to describe responses to athletic injuries. McDonald and Hardy (1990) advanced a two-stage process. The first stage involves an intense emotional experience of shock, panic, disorganization, and helplessness. In this stage, the athlete is faced with accepting the reality of the injury. In the second stage, athletes mobilize their energy for the rehabilitation process. Heil (2000) described three components in a cyclical process of recovering from injury. In the first, athletes experience distress in the form of anger, depression, anxiety, guilt, bargaining, complaining, and self-doubt. Second, athletes are seen to engage in denial or unwillingness to accept the severity of injuries. Third, athletes begin determined coping responses and get on with the effort of rehabilitation. In the determined coping stage, athletes seek out and evaluate resources, clarify goals, learn new skills, and commit to rehabilitation plans. Athletes may cycle through the three components several times before completing rehabilitation, but successful rehabilitation implies progress toward the determined coping component.

There are other stage theories that are less widely recognized (Rose & Jevne, 1993). These stage models focus on the psychological reactions to injuries. Medical and psychological stages in the injury process have also been described: Preinjury, immediate post injury, treatment decision and implementation, early postoperative/rehabilitation, late postoperative/ rehabilitation, specificity, and return to play (Heil, 2000).

The responses of athletes to severe injuries have been evaluated to determine if they conform to stage theories of grief (Newmark & Bogacki, 2005). For example, male and female members of the U.S. Ski team were interviewed to evaluate their reactions to season-ending injuries (Udry, Gould, Bridges, & Beck, 1997). The majority of the injuries were to the anterior cruciate ligaments of knees. The elite skiers recalled the acute and persistent pain of their injuries. They often engaged in a process of attempting to rapidly determine the severity of their injuries. Soon thereafter, they came to appreciate the costs of their injuries, both in terms of lost potential and the inconvenience of rehabilitation. The injured skiers experienced emotional upheaval. They were frustrated and angry, and often had no clear direction for this anger. Some were anxious and scared to the point of panic. Dejection, depression, and disappointment were expectable. Some felt disconnected from teams and alone in hospitals. Despite initially responding with denial and disbelief, many came to accept their injuries and to focus on rehabilitation.

Upon reflection and over time, most of the skiers came to appreciate opportunities for growth that resulted from their injuries. For example, some gained perspective on the importance of skiing and clarified their priorities. Some also thought they matured as a result of their injuries and came to be more empathic to others with injuries. Others attempted to improve other aspects of their life, such as academics (Udry, 1999). Other benefits included increased mental toughness and self-efficacy due to successful rehabilitation. Finally, the work ethic, physical fitness, and skiing techniques of some athletes improved as a result of their experience with rehabilitation. In general, athletes are better able to cope with career-ending injuries when they focus on the social and personal growth obtained in sport and when they have the opportunity to remain involved with their sport in some way postinjury.

Consistent with the Kubler-Ross stage theory of response to loss, the injured skiers experienced anger, depression, and acceptance (Udry, 1999; Udry et al., 1997). They did not, however, engage in denial and bargaining. The responses of the skiers appeared consistent with the stages of distress and determined coping in the Heil stage theory, but not with the denial stage of this theory. Initial emotional upheaval followed by adaptive responses such as getting on with the job of rehabilitation, were common reactions of the skiers. This two-step process was consistent with a two-stage model described by McDonald and Hardy, but skiers also emphasized their intense interest in finding out all that they could about their injuries.

Moreover, the grief reactions of athletes often involve a complex pattern of emotional responses that do not fit neatly into a stage model (Brewer, 2007, 2009). For example, injured athletes may experience anger, depression, and anxiety simultaneously, and they may not pass through sequential stages in recovering emotional homeostasis (Gould, Udry, Bridges, & Beck, 1997). Just as people in general are different, injured athletes are different in their emotional responses to injuries. When injuries are severe and status as an athlete is very important, sportspersons experience strong and negative emotional reactions. A cognitive-appraisal model for understanding the response of athletes to athletic injuries appears to be a better fit for these findings.

Application

It is difficult to identify stages of grief that are invariable and adaptive for most people. People grieve losses differently.

Differences notwithstanding, mindful awareness may be helpful (Kumar, 2010). Athletes approach grief with mindful awareness when they suspend efforts to rid themselves of the emotional pain of grief and explore their worries and uncertainties. This process of embracing rather than avoiding grief may facilitate, rather than delay, problem-focused coping and physical rehabilitation.

COGNITIVE-APPRAISAL MODELS AND INJURIES

The responses of athletes to athletic injuries appear to fit reasonable well with the cognitive-appraisal model (Figure 18.2). This model is also consistent with the cognitive-relational theory of stress and the stress and injury model that were discussed previously in this chapter. This model

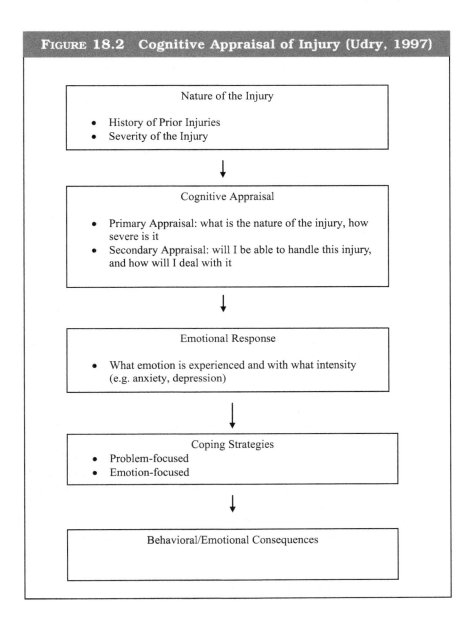

FIGURE 18.2   Cognitive Appraisal of Injury (Udry, 1997)

Nature of the Injury

- History of Prior Injuries
- Severity of the Injury

Cognitive Appraisal

- Primary Appraisal: what is the nature of the injury, how severe is it
- Secondary Appraisal: will I be able to handle this injury, and how will I deal with it

Emotional Response

- What emotion is experienced and with what intensity (e.g. anxiety, depression)

Coping Strategies
- Problem-focused
- Emotion-focused

Behavioral/Emotional Consequences

understands reactions to injuries to be due to preinjury characteristics, such as personality, coping resources, history of stressors, and interventions such as stress inoculation training. Postinjury responses involve the personal attributes of the injured athlete as well as the resources in the rehabilitation setting and social support.

Following injuries, athletes evaluate the nature and severity of the injury. They evaluate their capacity to handle the injury and the rehabilitation process, and the amount of social support available for rehabilitation. To the degree that athletes believe that they have suffered irreversible losses and that their self-esteem and well-being is dependent on their athletic status, negative emotional responses are likely to be greater. Injuries present a much greater threat to self-esteem and well-being when an individual's identity is woven to their role as an athlete (Brewer, 1993; Green & Weinberg, 2001) and when sportspersons have aspirations of becoming professional athletes (Kleiber & Brock, 1992). These negative emotional reactions may include diminished self-esteem and confidence about athletic abilities, and in some cases, depression. Athletes are most likely to experience depression after severe injuries, when they fail to return to preinjury levels despite working hard in rehabilitation, and when their futures as elite athletes are threatened by injury. With these considerations in mind, it is not surprising that estimates of clinical depression and emotional disturbance among injured athletes range from five percent to 27% (Appaneal, Levine, Perna, & Roh, 2009; Brewer, 2007).

Nature of the Injury

Efficacy and confidence are more likely to be shaken if injuries are severe. For example, beliefs in full recovery are more likely following ankle sprains than tears to the anterior cruciate ligament (ACL; Wiese-Bjornstal, Smith, Shaffer, & Morrey, 1998).

In general, negative emotional responses decrease across the course of rehabilitation (Brewer, 2001), and self-efficacy improves with the recovery of function (Thome et al., 2007). However, the negative emotional responses after injuries may not be transient. Negative emotional responses are likely to decrease when confidence in recovery is higher and to increase when athletes are presented with evidence that they may be left with limitations. For example, after ACL reconstructive surgery, mood was initially negative, improved for several months, and then again turned more negative (Wiese-Bjornstal et al., 1998). Perhaps the optimism and self-efficacy (Quinn & Fallon, 1999) of athletes postsurgery was difficult to sustain when they tested their injured knees in their sports and experienced frustration with their initial performance post injury. The most productive channel for frustration and anger postinjury may be especially conscientious adherence to the rehabilitation process.

Coping Strategies

Athletes recovering from injuries use a range of coping strategies to handle the loss caused by major injuries and the stress of rehabilitation (Van Wilgen, Kaptein, & Brink, 2010). For example, the male and female members of the U.S. Ski team who experienced season-ending injuries used a number of coping **strategies** to handle the stress of rehabilitation (Gould et al., 1997). As described in Chapter 4, coping strategies can be categorized as problem-focused or emotion-focused. The former involves taking action to handle the sources of stress and the latter consists of managing one's emotional reactions to the sources of stress. Approximately 90% of the injured skiathletes used some form of problem-focused coping during rehabilitation. These strategies included attempting to keep to daily schedules and doing things for themselves. They also refocused their determination to compete again, set new goals, and devoted themselves to rehabilitation exercises and training. Some athletes also did new and useful activities, such as going to college to occupy free time during the rehabilitation process. About half of the skiers sought support from others, and the female skiers were twice as likely as the males to utilize this resource.

Injured male rugby, soccer, and basketball players also realized growth as a result of injury. They became more capable of empathizing with other injured athletes, more caring, and unselfish (Wadey, Evans, Evans, & Mitchell, 2011). They developed greater resilience and mental toughness.

It may be that diverse and varied coping strategies are required to meet a major stressor such as a season-ending injury (Carson & Polman, 2010). Emotion-focused coping has previously been seen to be less important in the rehabilitation process, but skiers whose performance postinjury equaled or exceeded preinjury performance were more likely to actively manage their emotions and use visualization techniques (Van Wilgen et al., 2010). However, coping that consists primarily of emotion-focused or palliative coping is associated with poorer adherence to rehabilitation schedules (Udry, 1997).

INTEGRATED MODEL OF PSYCHOLOGICAL RESPONSE TO INJURY

At the risk of overwhelming and confusing the reader, one final model for understanding psychological responses to injuries is presented (Figure 18.3). This integrated model (Wiese-Bjornstal et al., 1998) is similar to the cognitive appraisal model presented above, in that appraisals or interpretations of injuries influence behavioral responses, emotional responses, and recovery outcomes. It includes aspects of the stress and injury model that was also previously discussed in this chapter. The stress and injury model organized the factors that represented vulnerabilities for injuries. The integrated model takes in more of the variables that influence an athlete's response to injuries. Of particular interest for the ensuing discussion in this chapter are the situational and behavioral responses and cognitive appraisal factors in the integrated model. In the original model (Wiese-Bjornstal et al., 1998), there are longer lists of examples of personal and situational factors. For the sake of clarity, these lists have been abbreviated to include the items discussed in this chapter.

Goals and Rehabilitation (Cognitive Appraisal)

Athletes have been encouraged to establish goals for physical rehabilitation postinjury (Gilbourne & Taylor, 1998). As explained in Chapters 8 and 9, behavior that is goal oriented is likely to be more productive and

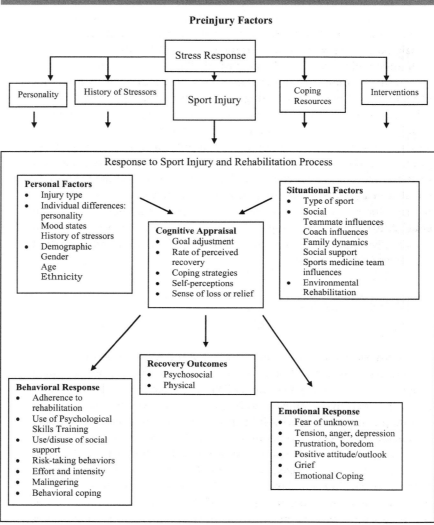

FIGURE 18.3 Integrated Model of Psychological Response to Sport Injury and Rehabilitation (Wiese-Bjornstal et al., 1998) (Abbreviated to account for variables discussed in this chapter)

successful, and athletes who set goals for rehabilitation are more likely to adhere to rehabilitation regimens both at home and in clinics (Scherzer et al., 2001), and also develop greater efficacy so that they can realize rehabilitation goals (Evans & Hardy, 2002a; Evans & Hardy, 2002b). With social support, athletes are more likely to establish task goals for their rehabilitation (Magyar & Duda, 2000). Task goal orientations are likely to be most adaptive, with athletes measuring progress in relation to their own baseline and persisting throughout the difficult process of rehabilitation

(Levy, Polman, & Clough, 2008). With ego goals, competence is measured in relation to others, and the injured athlete will certainly function at a level beneath healthy peers. Injured athletes with ego orientations may also compare rehabilitation progress to other injured athletes. Injuries are not identical and further injury can result from trying to outdistance other injured athletes rather than simply attempting to improve one's health status. Ego goals during the rehabilitation process are also problematic, because they sustain effort and confidence when athletes believe that their competence is high. When competence is thought to be suspect, as during rehabilitation, maladaptive behaviors, such as becoming discouraged, not putting forth maximum effort, missing rehabilitation appointments, and dropping out of rehabilitation, are likely. Athletes with ego orientations may also try to return to action prior to full recovery so as to reestablish their position on teams. Task goals concern standards that are under the control of the athlete. By keeping written records, athletes more accurately measure progress toward task goals.

Some athletes with ego orientations adopt task orientations during the process of rehabilitation. For example, some injured collegiate athletes with ego orientations adopted task orientations by the midpoint of treatment (Magyar & Duda, 2000). Perhaps the atmospheres in training rooms clearly encouraged athletes to measure progress in relation to their own baselines.

Athletes with task orientations are more likely to enhance the rehabilitation process by engaging in mental imagery and positive self-talk. The use of imagery during rehabilitation may further augment motivation and confidence (Sordoni, Hall, & Forwell, 2000).

Recall that there are several nosologies for categorizing athletic goals. Athletic performance goals refer to an end product of a performance, but the end product is a self-referenced standard. Process goals refer to the actions necessary to reach an outcome. Both process and athletic performance goals are seen to be helpful during rehabilitation from season-ending injuries (Evans, Hardy, & Fleming, 2000), and process goals were emphasized by the coaches of elite Australian athletes (Podlog & Dionigi, 2010). With athletic performance goals, sportspersons are able to structure the rehabilitation process, and process goals direct attention to the specific behaviors necessary to reach these goals.

Athletes who reflect on their experiences and gain self-awareness may learn more from the rehabilitation process. They may put their injuries in perspective, and improve their capacities to cope with adversity (Ghaye & Ghaye, 1998).

Injury Rehabilitation (Behavioral Response and Situational Factors)

The behavior most frequently associated with recovery from sport injury is adherence to prescribed rehabilitation programs (Brewer, 2009). Adherence to sport injury rehabilitation is more likely when athletes believe that their health status is subject to their personal control and when they have higher tolerance for pain (Brewer, 2001). Adherents to rehabilitation processes have confidence that following treatment regimens will lead to recovery (Brewer et al., 2000; Brewer et al., 2003).

Psychological Skills Training (Behavioral Response and Situational Factors)

Regardless of goal orientation and self-efficacy, training in psychological skills helps injured athletes in rehabilitation (Clement, Shannon, & Cannole, 2011). Athletes make more productive use of the rehabilitation process when they understand the purpose of rehabilitation exercises and procedures and the likely duration of the rehabilitation process (Williams & Scherzer, 2010).

Examples of specific psychological intervention techniques are the use of mental imagery and mental practice. In addition, the use of techniques to control physiological arousal or anxiety, such as progressive muscle relaxation (PMR) and guided imagery designed to parallel the rehabilitation process, has been encouraged. The use of PMR and guided imagery with athletes recovering from ACL reconstruction produced more rapid rehabilitation, less reinjury, and less anxiety (Cupal, 1998; Cupal & Brewer, 2001). With less anxiety and higher motivation, athletes may participate more fully in physical therapies.

An example of an integrated psychological intervention for injured athletes was the stress inoculation training provided to adult male athletes who received arthroscopic surgery to repair a torn meniscus in one knee (Ross & Berger, 1996). The stress inoculation training consisted of information about emotional responses, such as anxiety and pain. This was given to forewarn the injured athletes that these responses were likely and to prepare them for their management. They were advised to monitor themselves for pain and anxiety responses, and were taught deep-breathing exercises and progressive muscle relaxation, positive self-talk, and visualization strategies to decrease pain and anxiety responses. The athletes who practiced this stress inoculation reported less pain and anxiety during rehabilitation, and returned to preinjury levels of fitness more rapidly. An understanding of how the stress inoculation training helped is subject to speculation. For example, by inducing relaxation, vasodilation may have occurred and allowed greater quantities of blood to flow to injured knees. Alternatively, with a better grasp of the rehabilitation process, athletes are more likely efficacious and compliant with the rehabilitation process.

Social Support (Behavioral Response and Situational Factors)

Social support consists of well-intentioned interactions between people. For example, when a coach calls an injured player to inquire about progress, the coach implicitly communicates that she or he cares about and values the athlete (Bianco & Eklund, 2001). In providing social support, people intend or try to do something, such as providing practical help or emotional support, which will benefit the recipient. Three categories of social support have been identified. **Emotional support** consists of nonjudgmental listening, expressions of concern about the well-being of others, and sometimes challenging others. **Informational support** consists of clarifying similarities and differences in how people understand problems, acknowledging the effort of others, and challenging others to work harder and be more creative. Social support may also involve **tangible assistance** such as money and other help.

Social support facilitates emotion- and problem-focused coping in the injured and stressed athlete. Social support serves to buffer the detrimental effects of stress on the well-being of injured athletes (Malinauskas, 2010; Rees, Mitchell, Evans, & Hardy, 2010). With social support, people may become more resourceful in responding to stressors and less likely to simply brood about negative life events. Brooding and self-preoccupation retard rehabilitation and are risk factors for injuries. These preoccupations can disrupt attention and increase bracing during competition and performances, both of which were discussed above as representing risk factors for injury.

When people grow up in environments rich with social support, they develop expectations that stress is manageable and that they will be equal to many of the stressors they face. With this background, people have a degree of inoculation against the effects of stress. Regardless of inoculations, when social support is accessed in times of stress, the effects of stress are mitigated. People with low self-esteem are in greater need of social support and less likely to ask for it. Those with low self-esteem do not risk losing face and appearing weak and incompetent. For example, injured skiers who had not proven themselves to coaches were less likely to seek the support of coaches (Bianco & Eklund, 2001).

The presence of a support network or a group of people capable of providing support is a necessary but not sufficient condition for the receipt of social support. Those in the network must deliver it. Injured athletes receive more help with feelings of anxiety and frustration when supported by family or friends with whom they have a degree of emotional intimacy. In general, intimate relationships, such as those with spouses, have the largest impact on mental health.

Support in the form of information is most helpful when provided by those who know what they are talking about. For example, physicians best provide medical reassurance, and injured athletes often are in need of information about the severity of injuries and the duration of rehabilitation. People knowledgeable about sport are also more likely to be on target in recognizing what type of support is needed, and injured athletes are likely to seek support from knowledgeable people (Bianco, 2001; Podlog & Eklund, 2007; Yang, Peek-Asa, Lowe, Heiden, & Foster, 2010). Athletic trainers are important sources of social support (Arvinen-Barrow, Penny, Hemmings, & Corr, 2010), and injured intercollegiate athletes were somewhat more satisfied with the social support received from athletic trainers than from coaches or teammates (Clement & Shannon, 2011).

The coaches of elite Australian athletes secured the professional help needed by their injured athletes. They coordinated the interventions of "teams" of professionals, such as exercise physiologists, physiotherapists, and sport psychologists. Coaches directly supported the emotional needs of their athletes by involving them in team meetings and training sessions, and by monitoring the frustration of athletes about the loss of fitness and skill. They intervened when overzealous athletes attempted to return to sport prematurely (Podlog & Dionigi, 2010).

Confidence in Medical and Coaching Staffs

Brittany Hunter was perhaps the most highly recruited female high school basketball player in the U.S. when she accepted an athletic scholarship to Duke University in 2003. Playing as a freshman, she had a tear in her lateral meniscus. She resumed play four weeks after arthroscopic surgery, but the knee kept swelling and did not feel stable. The knee was drained of fluid repeatedly and she received three cortisone shot in the joint. There was a second operation after the basketball season.

Hunter lost confidence in the medical, training, and coaching staff, commenting, "There were no lines of communication." Her mother stated: "I had a problem with her being brought back after she was injured. I said I thought she should have sat down. I'm pretty bitter. I think that bringing her back exacerbated the injury and prolonged her healing" (Riley, 2005, p. C3).

Hunter transferred to the University of Connecticut (UCONN), and still the knee continued to swell from basketball practice. She underwent a third operation in which the meniscus was replaced with the meniscus of a cadaver.

At peace at UCONN, she commented:

> I've got more drive than I've ever had. Even when I first got hurt, I was like, I'm going to come back, I'm all right. And when I didn't, I was kind of sulking about it. There's a drive to me now. Like there's no doubt in my mind that I'm going to come back the same way. I think that helps you a lot (Riley, 2005, p. C3).

Sometimes, the social support is well matched to the needs of the recipient (Chan, Hagger, & Spray, 2011). For example, an injured athlete in a grieving process may benefit more from emotional support, whereas an athlete who is focused on physical rehabilitation may find information about the restoration of physical function to be most supportive. Even if the social support offered is not a good match to the needs of the recipient, it is still likely to be helpful if it communicates concern about the well-being of the recipient (Podlog, Lochbaum, & Stevens, 2010; Rees & Hardy, 2000). The needs of sportspersons for social support wanes somewhat as they move closer to recovery (Johnston & Carroll, 1998).

Social Support and Adherence to Rehabilitation

Social support facilitates rehabilitation. With social support from others, such as sports medicine providers and teammates, injured athletes are more likely to adhere to rehabilitation programs and realize more complete recoveries (Ruddock-Hudson, O'Halloran, & Murphy, 2012; Udry, 1996). Injured intercollegiate athletes who felt they had the support of parents, teammates, and trainers continued to look to others for guidance and comfort throughout the rehabilitation process (Magyar & Duda, 2000).

Athletes make more productive use of the rehabilitation process when they understand the purpose of rehabilitation exercises and procedures and the likely duration of the rehabilitation process (Williams & Scherzer, 2010). Consultation with rehabilitation professionals is helpful in understanding whether pain is a necessary aspect of rehabilitation exercises or whether it is a sign of further injury. Without this form of social coping, athletes may skip painful exercises that will return a full range of function to an injury site. Alternatively, they may persist at procedures that will cause further damage. Athletes are encouraged to express negative emotions to rehabilitation personnel. Professional counseling or therapy has been recommended for athletes who remain despondent and hopeless after injury.

In addition to feedback from trainers, athletes are sensitive to feedback from other rehabilitating athletes, and they learn by watching others in rehabilitation. Athletes also size up their prospects for good recoveries on the basis of their experience during the first days of rehabilitation. If they are assigned exercises and tasks at which they are likely to be successful, they will more likely to be successful at later points in the rehabilitation process.

Lacking Social Support

To this point, this discussion of social support has assumed that the comments and reactions of others are uniformly positive. Of course, this is not the case, as the reactions of others can do more harm than good, and serve to increase one's sense of isolation. For example, members of the U.S. Ski team who sustained season-ending injuries, the majority of which involved anterior cruciate ligament damage, did not find the social support from family, teammates, and coaches to be uniformly positive (Udry, Gould, Bridges, & Tuffey, 1997). Family and teammates most often provided emotional support in the form of understanding, reassurance, and supporting the decisions of athletes such as to return to skiing. Family and teammates were also supportive in encouraging the injured skiers throughout rehabilitation, and by providing transportation and help with daily living. Coaches who remained in contact with injured skiers, supported and encouraged the skiers, and consulted about rehabilitation provided injured skiers with positive emotional support.

All of the injured skiers experienced some form of this positive support, but a minority reported negative experiences with family and teammates. These negative influences included losing contact with teammates and friends, and not receiving support from family with decisions to return to skiing or to retire from skiing. Injured skiers also identified a lack of contact with coaches as a negative influence. Some complained that coaches did not call until they were back on the snow. Some injured skiers also wanted coaching advice and guidance throughout the rehabilitation process. In general, the injured skiers in this study and athletes from other sports (Brewer, 2001) viewed the social influence of coaches as more negative than positive and the influence of family and teammates as more positive than negative. Injured female intercollegiate athletes from other sports also were more critical of the quality and quantity of social support they received from coaches (Granito, 2002).

Parents of injured elite athletes recognized that their children missed bonding opportunities with teammates during injury rehabilitation. With social support, these adolescents were also more likely to trust that they would meet and exceed their prior performance standards and less worried that they would be outdistanced by teammates during rehabilitation (Podlog, Kleinert, Dimmock, Miller, & Shipherd, 2012).

CAREER TERMINATION

Athletes forced into retirement by serious career-ending athletic injuries often report low life satisfaction. This is particularly true if their identities are closely and exclusively tied to their sport; they see themselves only as athletes and without other purposes in life (Douglas & Carless, 2009: Park, Tod, & Lavallee, 2012). Some have chronic pain and physical restrictions. Moreover, the most important sources of their unhappiness appears to be unresolved feelings of loss and inadequate career planning (Alfermann & Stambolova, 2007; Petitpas, 2009; Wylleman, Alfermann, & Lavallee, 2004).

Deselection

Approximately 85% of the elite junior footballers (soccer players) who receive scholarships to the football academies of the teams of the Premier League in the United Kingdom are not offered professional contracts. Four deselected 19-year-old players reflected:

> I felt as though I didn't know who I was anymore because football was my life and I didn't have that anymore. It was a difficult time in my life and there was a lot of uncertainty regarding my future . . . It was as though they had taken away my identity and stripped me of everything I knew.
>
> When you're first told you're like what am I going to do? You're just so confused and you worry about what you're going to do . . . didn't know what to think and I

guess I was in shock . . . Everything I had worked for in my life had come crashing down in front of me . . . Being released makes you think that you are a failure. It makes you upset and angry.

I think it definitely killed me emotionally and I lost all confidence. I felt lost and confused. I didn't know what to do next. I got very depressed and didn't know where my life was going. I really didn't know how to handle it.

I guess I felt a failure and rejected . . . You've sort of failed in a way haven't you. All your life you've been put on this pedestal and then all of a sudden you're brought down to earth again and it's humiliating. It's not a nice feeling telling everyone that you've failed. It's the end of an era you know of being at a professional club and being put on a pedestal and everyone talking about you and suddenly you're no longer that (Brown & Potrac, 2009, p. 151).

There is little reason to believe that adjustment problems are the norm after retirement from high school and college athletic careers. Indeed, high school athletes are more likely to attend college, graduate from college, and have greater occupational success than are classmates who did not play sports. Life satisfaction is generally not less for collegiate athletes and nonathletes at the time of graduation from college (Perna, Ahlgren, Zaichkowsky, 1999). Collegiate athletes and elite junior athletes may miss the excitement, camaraderie, and fun of their playing days, but they have been shown to be no less satisfied with or successful in careers. Transitioning from involvement in sport at this level is similar to the transitions and adjustment to new roles in young adulthood, such as to work after college and to marriage after being single.

There are several issues to be considered in predicting adjustment to retirement among elite and professional athletes (Taylor & Ogilvie, 2001). The first concerns the causes of career termination among athletes. Retirement is often the result of aging and the erosion of speed, strength, and coordination, and sometimes the desire to intensely train and compete. Retirement may also be due to being deselected or cut from teams, or to injury. Sometimes athletes decide to retire because they have had enough of the training and lifestyle demands of their sport and they have reached their goals. Retirement is far more aversive if it is not "on time" or of their choosing (Petitpas, 2009).

There are varying estimates of the percentage of elite athletes that experience significant adjustment problems after retirement, with perhaps the best estimate at 19% experiencing serious adjustment problems (Grove, Lavallee, Gordon, & Harvey, 1998). The highest estimate of adjustment difficulties among elite athletes was 70% of elite female gymnasts (Kerr & Dacyshyn, 2000). Ironically, athletes who are vulnerable to deselection may redouble their efforts to train and practice sport skills, and spend less time planning for career transitions (Petitpas, 2009).

A second important issue in evaluating adjustment after athletic careers is the degree to which athletes define their self-worth and social identity on the basis of accomplishment and participation in sport (Brewer, Van

Raalte, & Petitpas, 2000; Grove et al., 1998; Pearson & Petitpas, 1990). Elite athletes with the most serious adjustment problems after retirement based their identities exclusively on sport and had few other competencies and sources of life satisfaction (Brown & Potrac, 2009). Retiring athletes with few other social and vocational competencies experience marked drops in status and show awkwardness functioning outside the role of an athlete (Park, Tod, & Lavallee, 2012; Wylleman & Lavallee, 2004).

Lacking these competencies, retired elite gymnasts had difficulties with self-identity and body image, and felt a general void in their lives (Warriner & Lavallee, 2008). The parents of elite female gymnasts are also strongly affected by their child's retirement. Relationships between parents and children were altered, as family life was no longer organized around gymnastics practice and competition. Parents also questioned whether the benefits of elite gymnastics were worth the experience of pain and injuries and the potential loss of a wider range of social experiences during adolescence. The parents also sometimes regretted allowing elite coaches to usurp their authority and make decisions for their children (Lally & Kerr, 2008).

Elite female rhythmic gymnasts may struggle to maintain leanness and muscle mass after retirement. Weight gain is not unlikely, because these gymnasts chronically restrict calorie consumption during their athletic careers. Food cravings and binge eating are not unlikely after periods of restrained eating. During binges, restraint and control are lost, and individuals consume large amounts of food in brief periods of time. Laxatives, diet pills, and obsessive exercise may be used to control weight (Stirling, Cruz, & Kerr, 2012).

Of course, distress is not universal. For example, 50% of recently retired female tennis professionals were relieved to be free of the pressure and grind of competition and available for more traditional lifestyles (Allison & Meyer, 1988). Elite Korean tennis players also reported relief and positive emotions after deciding to retire. At that point, they also became more actively engaged in planning for their lives after sport (Park et al., 2012).

Mike Richter: Life Goes On

Mike Richter made this comment after retiring from a professional hockey career that spanned fifteen years in the National Hockey League (NHL) and included four All-Star selections and a Stanley Cup championship (Hine, 2005, p. C2). Richter continued, "In the locker room, there are 20 guys. There's a support group. It's your life, and all of a sudden, it's just gone. You're very much alone for the first time. You've lost your support group" (Hine, 2005, p. C2).

Richter was more fortunate than many athletes in that he had two important support groups outside of hockey; one at home with his wife and three children, and the other at Yale University where he was enrolled as a student at age 39. Richter described the support from Yale faculty and advisors as "unbelievable," and accepted the challenge of disciplining himself to a schedule of study and family responsibilities. He reflected: "But playing hockey doesn't mean you retire and do nothing the rest of your life. You can, but I'd like to develop the different aspects of my personality" (Hine, 2005, p. C2).

Career Transitions

European nations took the lead in the development of programs to assist elite athletes in career transitions. The Canadian Olympic Athlete Career Centre was launched in 1985 to prepare athletes for life after elite competition. The Career Assistance Program for Athletes was initiated by the U.S. Olympic Committee in 1988 and the Lifeskills for Elite Athletes Program was established in Australia in 1989, both for the purpose of assisting elite athletes with career transitions (Taylor & Lavallee, 2010). These organizations help athletes to identify skills that were valuable in their athletic careers and which may be transferred to the workplace (Petitpas, 2009). Emotional support and referrals for necessary services are also provided.

Professional Athletes and Financial Planning

NFL football players are more successful after retirement if they have prepared for post-NFL careers. Despite average salaries of $1.25 million in 2003 (Heath, 2004), many NFL athletes need to generate income after retirement and, in addition, need to "downsize" or reduce their levels of spending (Wethe, 2004). Organizations such as the Sports Professionals Foundation and the NFL Players Association have been established to promote this career development among NFL players. Nevertheless, it is difficult for some NFL players to plan for a future that portends fewer rewards and adulation. For example, the NFL Players Association has established off-season internships in corporations to provide job training and assistance in making transitions to jobs post-NFL. Perhaps 30 of the 1,600 NFL players participated in these internships in 2001 (Greenberg, 2001).

Individual NFL athletes have embraced the world of work after retirement. Former Dallas Cowboys wide receiver Raghib "Rocket" Ismail is the owner of a hip-hop record company in Dallas and a performer in the *3 Dot* and *3 Pieces* ensembles. Former Dallas Cowboys defensive back George Teague developed new skills running Touch of Lace, a lingerie shop in North Richland Hills, TX (Wethe, 2004).

Careful financial planning during peak earning years as an athlete also makes retirement more comfortable. Rod Smith, wide receiver for the Denver Broncos, banks about $1 million of his $2.5 million pretax annual salary. He saved almost half of his $11 million signing bonus. Brad Daugherty lived in an apartment that rented for $625 per month during his playing days with the Cleveland Cavaliers of the NBA. He saved $5 million in his first four years and began investing in car dealerships. He is estimated to be worth tens of millions of dollars (Heath, 2004).

The well-being of athletes after retirement is better when they redirect time and energy to new concerns and develop new routines or rhythms to their days. This is more difficult for retired athletes who are largely dependent on their former athletic organizations for social support. Their adjustment is to a greater degree determined by support from these organizations. Some athletes resist occupational planning because they do not want to look to a future after sport that will have less financial remuneration and status. As mentioned earlier, career preparation is a vital determinant of life satisfaction after athletic careers (Alfermann & Stambulova, 2007).

SUMMARY AND APPLICATION

Injuries often occur in the course of athletic participation. There are about 17 million athletic injuries annually in the U.S. There are many factors associated with athletic injuries, such as inadequate training and practice, poor athletic techniques and equipment, and bad luck. The psychological factors associated with the prediction of sport injuries and with optimal rehabilitation were emphasized in this chapter.

Athletic competition and practice are environmental stressors, especially when they are demanding and involve pressure. However, the degree to which they produce stress responses in sportspersons is explained by their personalities, history of stressors, and coping resources. Athletes coping with a greater number of stressors, with fewer resources for coping with stress, and with personality characteristics such as trait anxiety experience more intense stress responses from athletic stressors. These stress responses result in cognitive interference as athletes are more likely to interpret pressure as a source of threat. Cognitive interference and physiological anxiety disrupt attention and produce bracing or the simultaneous contraction of agonist and antagonist muscle groups. Athletes are then less able to anticipate and respond fluidly and automatically to the flow of competitions and more likely to become exposed to musculoskeletal trauma.

Coping resources provide an important function in moderating cognitive interference, physiological anxiety, and attentional impairment. Psychological coping skills such as techniques for controlling physiological anxiety and preparing for competitions and interpersonal coping skills such as accessing social support provide a buffer to stress responses. Athletes who can access at least one form of coping resource have strategies for reducing stress responses and the chance of injuries. Coping resources can be developed. Athletes who were taught stress inoculation training and PMR had fewer resources injuries.

After the occurrence of injuries, the injuries are a source of stress. Injuries are potential major negative life events, sources of chronic stress, and negative daily hassles. Negative emotional reactions commonly occur with injuries. Psychologists have given considerable thought and energy to the question of whether these negative emotional reactions follow a sequential pattern consistent with stage theories of grief. As emphasized throughout this book, people are different. There are some common reactions to injuries, but not enough consistency between athletes to maintain that athletes invariably move through stages of grief such as the five-stage theory of Kubler-Ross.

The responses of athletes to injuries are determined not only by the stressor of the injury itself, but also by their cognitive appraisal. This appraisal includes consideration of their ability to cope with the rehabilitation process, the amount of social support available, and the likelihood of recovery. Severe injuries are major negative stressors, and negative emotional responses are more likely if athletes believe their internal and external resources are not sufficient for rehabilitation. If injuries are seen to present irreversible losses, and if an athlete's well-being is dependent on their status as an active athlete, negative emotional responses are likely to be greater. Negative emotional responses are understandable following severe injuries. Mood is seen to brighten as rehabilitation progresses, but mood and self-efficacy are sensitive to the full return of function. The recognition of limitations or incomplete recovery of function is associated with persistent negative emotional responses diminished efficacy. Athletes handle the stress of injuries by engaging problem-focused coping strategies, such as adhering to rehabilitation programs, and also handle negative emotional responses with emotion-focused coping.

Sportspersons call on not only their own coping resources during rehabilitation, but also support and help from family, friends, and professionals. The support of others not only makes injured athletes feel better, but also more likely to make productive use of problem- and emotion-focused coping strategies and to adhere to rehabilitation programs. Athletes who received social support or help from others throughout their development develop confidence in their own capacities to handle difficult situations and in the likelihood that others will deliver help when it is needed. Absent development in supportive environments, sportspersons are less likely to ask for help and more likely to need it.

Professional intervention is helpful in the rehabilitation process. This involves not only medical and physical therapy intervention, but also guidance in using techniques for positive self-talk, visualization, and the control of physiological anxiety. Task orientation or athletic performance and process goals are encouraged during rehabilitation from injuries. These goal orientations measure progress against the athlete's baseline of prior functioning. The severity of injuries and rehabilitation schedules are somewhat idiosyncratic and, therefore, little is to be gained by comparing progress in rehabilitation to that of other injured athletes. Further injury can result from efforts to compete with and return to play quicker than other rehabilitating athletes. Ego orientations also sustain effort and confidence when confidence is high, and confidence typically drops after injury. Injured sportspersons are sensitive to guidance and interventions from professionals in rehabilitation settings, and some adopt more adaptive task orientations as a result of their experience in rehabilitation.

Injuries may result in the end of athletic careers. Career termination or retirement is especially difficult if the goals of the athlete have not been met, and if the athlete does not have alternative vocational opportunities and sources of social support. Career termination is also particularly unhappy if the self-worth of athletes is tied exclusively to their playing status. Professional and elite athletes gain more rewards from sport than high school and college athletes, and, therefore, are likely to experience a greater loss upon career termination. Career termination may bring feelings of loss, but may also provide freedom to pursue other interests and opportunities.

Key Terms

Stress and Injury Model   412

Personality factors   412

History of stressors   412

Coping resources   412

Cognitive appraisal   412

Attention   412

Physiological anxiety   412

Bracing   413

Major life events   413

Stressors   413

Personality   414

Coping resources: general coping behaviors, psychological coping skills, interpersonal coping   415

Psychological Skills Training: Stress inoculation training, progressive muscle relaxation   416

Stage theory of grieving: denial, bargaining, anger, depression, and acceptance   418

Strategies   422

Social Support: emotional support, informational support, tangible assistance   427

Discussion Questions

Q1. How does stress contribute to the vulnerability to injury?

Q2. Consider the personality factors that lead to injury.

Q3. Explain how effective coping reduces the vulnerability to injury.

Q4. Examine interventions that may lessen the risk of athletic injuries.

Q5. Consider the influence of stress in the rehabilitation process.

Q6. Critically examine stage models of grieving.

Q7. Review the theoretical foundation for cognitive-appraisal models of injuries.

Q8. Some injuries are more difficult to manage than others. Consider the impact of the nature of the injury on the rehabilitation process.

Q9. Are there suggestions for types of coping after the occurrence of injuries?

Q10. Consider suggestions for goal setting in the rehabilitation process.

Q11. Examine psychological skills that are helpful in the rehabilitation process.

Q12. Describe the forms of social support that help injured athletes.

Q13. How does social support contribute to rehabilitation?

Q14. Review the reasons for retirement that lead to higher and lower life satisfaction after athletic careers.

Q15. Consider productive career transition programs.

Suggested Readings

Alfermann, D., & Stambulova, N. (2007). Career transitions and career termination. In G. Tenenbaum & R. C. Eklund (Eds.), *Handbook of sport psychology* (3rd ed., pp. 712–733). New York, NY: Wiley.

Brink, M. S. (2010). Monitoring stress and recovery: New insights for the prevention of injuries and illnesses in elite youth soccer players. *British Journal of Sports Medicine, 44,* 809–815.

Brink, M. S., Visscher, C., Arends, S., Zwerver, J., Post, W. J., Limmink, K. A. (2010). Monitoring stress and recovery: New insights for the prevention of injuries and illnesses in elite youth soccer players. *British Journal of Sports Medicine, 44,* 809–815. doi: 10.1136/bjsm. 2009.069476

Brown, G., & Potrac, P. (2009). "You've not made the grade son": De-selection and identity disruption in elite level youth football. *Soccer & Society, 10,* 143–159.

Chan, D. K-C., Hagger, M. S., & Spray, C. M. (2011). Treatment motivation for rehabilitation after a sport injury: Application of the trans-contextual model. *Psychology of Sport and Exercise, 12,* 83–92. doi: 10.1016/ j.psychsport.2010.08.005

Darrow, C. J., Collins, C. L., Yard, E. E., Comstock, R. D. (2009). Epidemiology of severe injuries among United States high school athletes. *The American Journal of Sports Medicine, 37,* 1798–1805. doi: 10.1177/0363546509333015

Douglas, K., & Carless, D. (2009). Abandoning the performance narrative: Two women's stories of transition from professional sport. *Journal of Applied Sport Psychology, 21,* 213–230.

Evardsson, A., Ivarsson, A., & Johnson, U. (2011). Is a cognitive-behavioural biofeedback intervention useful to reduce injury risk in junior football players? *Journal of Sports Science and Medicine, 11,* 331–338.

Hootman, J. M., Dick, R., Agel, J. (2007). Epidemiology of collegiate injuries for 15 sports: Summary and recommendations for injury prevention. *Journal of Athletic Training, 42,* 311–319.

Ivarsson, A., & Johnson, U. (2010). Psychological factors as predictors of injuries among senior soccer players. A prospective study. *Journal of Sports Science and Medicine, 9,* 347–352.

Johnson, U. (2007). Psychosocial antecedents of sport injury, prevention, and intervention: An overview of theoretical approaches and empirical findings. *International Journal of Sport and Exercise Psychology, 5,* 352–369. doi: 10.1080/1612197X.2007.9671841

Johnson, U., & Ivarsson, A. (2011). Psychological predictors of sport injuries among junior soccer players. *Scandinavian Journal of Medicine & Science in Sports, 21,* 129–136. doi: 10.1111/j.1600.0838.2009.01057.x

Maddison, R., & Prapavessis, H. (2005). A psychological approach to the prediction and prevention of athletic injury. *Journal of Sport & Exercise Psychology, 27,* 289–300.

Newmark, T. S., & Bogacki, D. F. (2005). The impact of injury on the adolescent athlete and the family. *Directions in Psychiatry, 25,* 91–99.

Park, S., Tod, D., & Lavallee, D. (2012). Exploring the retirement from sport decision-making process based on the transtheoretical model. *Psychology of Sport and Exercise, 13,* 444–453. doi: 10.1016/j.psychsport.2012.02.003

Petitpas, A. J. (2009). Sport career termination. In B. W. Brewer (Ed.), *Handbook of sports medicine and science, sport psychology* (pp. 113–120). Chichester, England: Wiley-Blackwell.

Podlog, L., Kleinert, J., Dimmock, J., Miller, J., & Shipherd, A.M. (2012). A parental perspective on adolescent injury rehabilitation and return to sport experiences. *Journal of Applied Sport Psychology, 24,* 175–190. doi: 10.1080/10413200.2011.608102

Rees, T., Mitchell, I., Evans, L., & Hardy, L. (2010). Stressors, social support and psychological responses to sport injury in high- and low-performance standard participants. *Psychology of Sport and Exercise, 11,* 505–512. doi: 10.1016/j.psychsport.2010.07.002

Rogers, T. J., & Landers, D. M. (2005). Mediating effects of peripheral vision in the life event stress/athletic injury relationship. *Journal of Sport & Exercise Psychology, 27,* 271–288.

Smith, R. E., Ptacek, J. T., & Smoll, E. L. (1992). Sensation seeking, stress, and adolescent injuries: A test of stress-buffering, risk-taking, and coping skills hypotheses. *Journal of Personality and Social Psychology, 62,* 1016–1024.

Thome, P., Wahrborg, P., Borjesson, M., Thome, R., Eriksson, B. I., & Karlsson, J. (2007). Self-efficacy, symptoms and physical activity in patients with an anterior cruciate ligament injury: A prospective study. *Scandinavian Journal of Medicine & Science in Sports, 17,* 238–245.

Udry, E. (1997). Coping and social support among injured athletes following surgery. *Journal of Sport & Exercise Psychology, 19,* 71–90.

Udry, E., Gould, D., Bridges, D., & Beck, L. (1997). Down but not out: Athlete responses to season-ending injuries. *Journal of Sport & Exercise Psychology, 19,* 229–248.

Wadey, R., Evans, L., Evans, K., & Mitchell, I. (2011). Perceived benefits following sport injury: A qualitative examination of their antecedents and underlying mechanisms. *Journal of Applied Sport Psychology, 23,* 142–158. doi: 10.1080/10413200.2010.543119

Wiese-Bjornstal, D. M., Smith, A. S., Shaffer, S. M., & Morrey, M. A. (1998). An integrated model of response to sport injury: Psychological and sociological dynamics. *Journal of Applied Sport Psychology, 10,* 46–69.

Part IV

INDIVIDUALS AND TEAMS

Chapter 19

GENDER AND SPORT

Women and sport (photo courtesy of Western Connecticut State University)

As a fourth-grader, Rebecca Lobo was unable to play basketball on a girls' team because only two girls signed up to play. Her mother, a teacher and the Title IX compliance officer at her school, insisted that she play on the boys' team. "On the first day of practice, my mother told the coach, 'I realize Rebecca is the only girl on the team but I want you to treat her exactly the same as the boys. When they run sprints, she runs sprints. When you yell at them, you yell at her. Everything needs to be the same. Except when you scrimmage shirts and skins. Then I want her on the shirts team.' "

When Rebecca was in the fifth grade, her mother intervened when a teacher counseled Rebecca to "act more like a girl" and "dress more like a girl." "My mother flipped her lid. After hearing what my teacher had said, my mom immediately drove me to the school. I was terrified—for the teacher."

As a collegiate all-American, Lobo led the University of Connecticut in 1995 to its first national championship in women's basketball. In 2009, the oldest of her four children happened to view a UCONN men's basketball game on television and asked her father, "Are those boys playing basketball?" When he answered "yes," she replied, "I didn't know boys played basketball, too" (Lobo, 2012).

The view that women and men are so different that they derive from separate planets was fostered in popular literature with the publication of *Men Are from Mars, Women Are from Venus* (Gray, 1992). Not surprisingly, this view is described as the "difference hypothesis." Feminist scholars disagree with this view and instead note that practically all physical and psychological human characteristics are distributed among both sexes (Oglesby & Hill, 1993). This view, the similarities hypothesis, recognizes that psychological differences are mostly small or nonexistent. For example, a recent review of research concerning gender differences on cognitive, social and personality, communication, well-being, and motor variables demonstrated that there were close-to-zero or small differences on 78% of the indices (Hyde, 2005). Furthermore, even when gender differences are identified, these differences may be less the result of innate differences between males and females, and more the result of the conformity of the males and females to social expectations or gender roles.

This is not to say that the brain structures of males and females are identical. Androgens, such as testosterone, that circulate during prenatal and adolescent development contribute to between-sex differences in cortical anatomy. To some degree, between-sex differences are related to the rate of development for brain structures. For example, frontal lobe development lags in males versus females. The behavioral consequences of this delayed development of frontal lobes is impulsive and risk-taking behaviors—behaviors more common in adolescent males. However, despite differences in the rate of development, by adulthood the brain structures of females and males are more similar (Raznahan et al., 2010).

Gender and biological sex are not interchangeable terms. Sex refers to biological characteristics, such as chromosomes, internal and external genitalia, gonads, hormones, and secondary sexual characteristics. Secondary sexual characteristics appear with the onset of puberty. **Gender** is a psychosocial phenomenon based not only on biological sex, but also on cultural customs, social identities, roles, and expectations associated with being female or male (American Psychological Association, 2007).

Biological sex differences for physical characteristics, such as muscle strength and maximal oxygen consumption, are not categorical such that all men have greater strength and maximum oxygen consumption. Maximum oxygen consumption is a measure of endurance. Instead, there is considerable overlap between the sexes, so that groups of women and men have comparable strength and maximum oxygen consumption. On average, adult American males are 50% stronger in most muscle groups and their maximal oxygen consumption exceeds that of women by 20% (Brooks & Fahey, 1984). Women show greater flexibility and balance (Hudson, 1978). In Olympic track and field and swimming events, the gender gap was 11% in favor of males (Thibault et al., 2010).

While these differences might be cited as evidence of biological differences between the sexes, even these differences are influenced by culture and experience, as muscles are typically trained differently in male and female sport and exercise. For example, traditional sports for women, such as figure skating, place a greater emphasis on beauty, grace, and flexibility, whereas traditionally male sports, such as Olympic weightlifting, emphasize explosive power. Prior to the different recreational and sport experiences of the genders, there are greater similarities in physical performance. For example, among elementary school children, girls scored only 2% lower than boys on a number of motor skills tests. However, by the end of the first grade, girls rated their skills as 14% lower than boys (Eccles & Harold, 1991; Fredericks & Eccles, 2005). This is in part because parents encourage boys to engage in sport and physical activity, which in turn leads to higher levels of athletic confidence (Brustad, 1993; Fredericks & Eccles, 2004). Children are rather accurate in perceiving their parents' appraisals of their athletic ability, and these appraisals influence the corresponding self-appraisals of children (Bois et al., 2005). Women and men enjoy similar physiological benefits from exercise and physical training, including increased muscle metabolism and strength, decreased body fat, and increased maximum oxygen consumption.

Girls are less likely to participate in sports than are boys (Roper, 2012). Adolescent females are more likely than males to withdraw from sports. Among the reason for this difference is the perception that athletic participation is not "cool." Girls may view forms of athletic participation as incompatible with femininity, whereas involvement in sport is viewed as enhancing masculinity in boys. Girls may also be concerned with how they appear in certain athletic uniforms, such as those that are more revealing (Slater & Tiggemann, 2010).

Application

The importance of encouraging girls to participate in sport should not be underestimated. The health of girls is enhanced when they participate in sport and vigorous exercise. Girls develop sport skills and learn the rules, history, and tradition of sport as a result of participation. Sport provides opportunities to expand friendship networks. Psychological competencies are developed when youngsters accept direction and team roles, cooperate with teammates, and manage discomfort, fatigue, and frustration in pursuit of goals. Most importantly, sport provides opportunities to have fun.

Female adolescent and adult athletes are also at greater risk for sport injuries, especially to knees, ankles, and feet. Female high school basketball players are especially vulnerable to severe knee injuries (Darrow, Collins, Yard, & Comstock, 2009). The risk is greatest with team sports that involve contact, jumping, pivoting, or sprinting. Adolescent female athletes may also be more vulnerable to injury when experiencing fatigue or emotional stress (Frisch et al., 2009).

HISTORICAL CONTEXT OF GENDER AND SPORT

Historically, gender differences have been emphasized to a greater extent in departments of physical education rather than psychology, because of the belief that curriculum for women's physical education was separate from the counterpart for men. Separate curricula were considered necessary because women were thought to be too frail to engage in outdoor play and physical activity. Mary Bissell questioned this assumption about the frailty of women in the late 1800s (Gill, 1998). Another canard of this era was that women should refrain from physical activity during menstruation, but Mary Putnam Jacobi (1877; cited in Denmark & Fernandez, 1993) argued that there was no scientific basis for this cultural norm.

There were commonalties in the emphases of physical education programs for women and men in the late 1800s. Physical education programs of both women and men emphasized physical training as a component in the development of healthy and well-rounded individuals. However, by 1923, the emphases of physical education programs diverged further along gender lines. Men's programs encouraged competitive athletics, whereas an **anticompetitive movement** gained support in women's physical education. This movement was led by the leading women scholars of this era and by organizations such as the Committee on Women's Athletics of the American Physical Education Association (Pfister, 2000). Sportspersonship, enjoyment of physical activity for all women rather than just elite athletes, and the well-being of athletes were emphasized. Women scholars in physical education did not condemn competition; rather, they opposed an emphasis on winning at the expense of participation in athletics by greater numbers of women.

Opposition to the participation of women in rigorous athletics and competition persisted. Beginning in the 1920s in the U.S. and Europe, theories about the physiological incompatibility of women for athletics were supported by mainstream medicine (Pfister, 2000; Roper, 2012). A central assumption of these theories was that women were obliged to bear children and that vigorous athletics would compromise their **reproductive fitness.** It was argued that women had only a limited ration of energy, and that this energy would be dissipated in sport and, therefore, unavailable for childbearing and childrearing. Physicians maintained that the uterus was the most fragile organ in the female anatomy and that it could be displaced and even tilted backward by strenuous activity such as running or the long jump. Medical men pronounced it unwise to firm the muscles of the abdomen and pelvis through training, reasoning that tautening of the muscle fibers would make childbirth difficult or impossible. Sport was feared to masculinize women, disrupt the polarity of the sexes and the social order, and even lead to homosexuality. These myths endured for some time despite abundant scientific evidence as early as the 1930s that sport did not produce these feared consequences.

Competition in women's athletics received a far greater emphasis in the U.S. with **Title IX.** Title IX was an aspect of the Higher Education Act of 1972 (U.S. Dept. of Education, 1972), and was probably fostered by the civil rights and women's movements (Gill, 2002). With its three-part **Compliance Test,** Title IX required universities that received federal assistance to demonstrate that they did not discriminate on the basis of sex in all education programs. This ban extended to intercollegiate and intramural sports. The first part of the Title IX Compliance Test requires that the number of males and females who participate in athletics must be substantially proportionate to the full-time undergraduate enrollment at a university. Therefore, if approximately 50% of the undergraduates are women at a university, the number of female athletes should be 50%. Second, Title IX requires universities to demonstrate expansion of women's athletic programs, and third, that the interests and abilities of the underrepresented sex have been fully accommodated.

As a result of Title IX, the number of women in intercollegiate sports has increased six- to ten-fold and women constitute approximately one-third of the Olympic, college, and high school athletes in the U.S. (Gill, 2002). The 2001–2002 Gender-Equity Report of the National Collegiate Athletic Association (NCAA) indicated that 44% of Division I athletes were female and 39% of the athletes in Divisions II and III were female (Gender-Equity Report, 2002). The increase in spending for women's programs has not been concomitant with the increase in female participation. This disparity is primarily due to the costs associated with football programs for men. Female head coaches at Division I universities received 36% of the average salaries of their male counterparts, and the greatest equity in coaches' salaries occurred at Division II schools, where women received 47% of the salaries of their male colleagues. At Division I and II universities, the recruiting budgets for women's sports were no more than 40% of the budgets for male sports.

An unexpected result of Title IX was the exclusion of women from almost all positions of leadership in amateur sports in the U.S. This occurred when women's and men's athletic departments and athletic governing organizations merged. For example, the Association for the Intercollegiate Athletics for Women (AIAW) was absorbed into the NCAA, which was controlled by men (Fasting, 2000). Prior to Title IX, women coached more than 90% of women's athletic teams, whereas women today coach 42.8% of the same (Carpenter & Acosta, 2008). The number of female athletic directors is increasing, as for example in 2006, 18.6% were female and in 2008, 21.3% where female. The most common administrative structure consists of three administrators: a male athletic director and male and female assistant/associate athletic directors.

Some sport governing bodies, such as the International Olympic Committee (IOC), excluded women from its inception. This was not surprising, considering the exclusion of women from Olympic events as described below. Women first joined the IOC in 1981, and in 2007 12.6% (14 of 111) of the members of the IOC were women. The first IOC conference on women and sport was conducted in 1996, and recommendations included providing equal opportunities for women in the athletic, coaching, and administrative ranks.

It has been difficult to increase the number of women in athletic organizations because entrance to these organizations is often determined by relationships with those currently in power (Fasting, 2000; Whisenant, Pedersen, & Clavio, 2010). Positions in these athletic organizations are typically filled informally rather than through formal announcements and competitive application processes. A process by which those in power restrict entry into their organizations to people like themselves is referred to as an **"old boys' network."**

Women may have fewer opportunities to cultivate relationships with those in power in athletic organizations because they carry a disproportionate share of domestic duties and responsibilities for the care of children and elderly parents in their households. They are, therefore, less available for travel and committee meetings. With greater flexibility in terms of the scheduling of meetings and requirements for travel, more women may have more opportunities to cultivate relationships in "old boys' networks" and gain greater access to positions in the hierarchies of athletic organizations.

Requirements for positions in athletic administration may also be written so as to effectively exclude women. For example, a review of all advertisements for high school athletic directors in Texas in a one-year period revealed that for 75% of the positions, the head coach was also required to serve as head football coach (Whisenant, Miller, & Pedersen, 2005).

WOMEN AND THE OLYMPIC GAMES

The first modern Olympic Games were held in Athens, Greece, in 1896. Women first competed in the Olympic Games in 1900, but this participation was limited to seven women in tennis competitions and ten in golf competitions. Women were also allowed to participate in sailing as members of crews with males. At the 1908 Games in England, women competed in tennis, ice-skating, and archery, and in mixed crews in sailing and motor boating. In the 1912 Games in Sweden, women began competing in swimming events. Resistance to parity between the genders in Olympic participation mirrored resistance recognizing equal rights to women in vocational, academic, and political arenas (Pfister, 2000).

Women first competed in track and field at the Olympic Games in 1928. After female competitors in the 800-meter race dropped to the ground in exhaustion, the IOC responded by excluding women from this event in 1932, reasoning that endurance events were not made for them. Even in recent history, women were excluded from events considered too traumatic for the feminine physique. For example, women did not run the marathon (26.2 miles) until 1984. Surprisingly, women did not compete in the 10,000-meter race (6.2 miles) until 1988. Women began participating in Olympic volleyball in 1964, basketball and handball in 1976, hockey in 1980, and soccer in 1996. Women's boxing debuted at the 2012 Olympic Games (Bruni, 2012).

In 2012, for the first time in Olympic history, all participating countries included female athletes. This occurred only after the International Olympic Committee allowed a female judo athlete from Saudi Arabia to wear headwear (although not a hijab or head scarf) during competition (Longman, 2012). To put this in perspective, 26 nations did not send female athletes to the 1996 Olympic Games in Atlanta. As recently as 10 or 15 years ago, "it would have been unheard of" for a member of the U.S. soccer team to publicly announce that she was lesbian. Megan Rapinoe did so prior to the 2012 games, and the response was widely supportive.

Also in 2012, a shooter from Malaysia became one of the first Olympians to compete while pregnant. "I feel her kicking. But I said to her, 'O.K., be calm; Mummy is going to shoot now' " (Longman, 2012).

GENDER ROLES AND PARTICIPATION IN SPORT

Cultural institutions such as family, school, church, and state shape **gender roles** (Gill, 2002). These institutions convey information about behaviors, tasks, and attitudes associated with gender in a particular culture (Oglesby & Hill, 1993). Traditional conceptions of femininity include characteristics such as beauty, grace, submissiveness, and passivity. The attributes of strength and aggressiveness are more often associated with **traditional ideas of masculinity** and these characteristics are also often productive in sport (Martin & Martin, 1995). Socialization practices that encourage nurturing, cooperative, and passive behaviors are seen as somewhat inconsistent with sport and are more frequent among girls. Perhaps athletic participation has been more consistent with gender roles and femininity in African-American communities (Howard-Hamilton, 1993).

Joan Benoit Samuelson and Gender Roles

In 1984, and prior to assuming the name Samuelson with her marriage, Joan Benoit won the first Olympic marathon. She grew up in a loving and supportive family in Maine, but experienced conflict between gender roles and sport:

It seemed to me that almost everything I had dreamed of doing with my life had overtones of boyishness. The climate of the times encouraged revolution, but my friends and I were slow to shoulder the barricades. As far as we could see, girls were supposed to be finished with boys' games when they were eleven. They weren't supposed to dream of careers in athletics. I can still remember watching a friend playing catch with her male teacher and being envious of her, but at the same time being glad I wasn't blatantly advertising my interest in sports. None of the girls I knew would have been flattered if described as "athletic" or (God forbid) "strong." I used to look at my brother's high school yearbooks and hope to make the "senior superlatives" section: not as Most Athletic, but as Friendliest or Most Optimistic.

My love of sports went underground. If I had known that the boys were missing any insights into their future sexuality, I would have thought they were lucky. The insights I was having made me sad and uneasy. A girl who wanted to be an athlete was suspect; maybe we could aspire to be doctors and lawyers now, but we shouldn't want muscles (Benoit & Baker, 1987, p. 43).

Certain sports, such as gymnastics and swimming, have been seen to be more appropriate for women. These sports often emphasize aesthetic qualities and do not emphasize matches against other competitors. These sports remain faithful to traditional notions of femininity, such as gracefulness, beauty, and a lack of aggression. In a masculinist culture, the female body is an object for the aesthetic enjoyment of others, and sports that provide for aesthetic pleasure are consistent with stereotypic ideas of femininity (Koivula, 2001). The first men's singles Lawn Tennis Championship at Wimbledon was contested in 1877, and a women's singles Championship began in 1884. Interest in the women's game and media coverage has increased but does not equal that in the men's game. In 2004, 59% of the articles and 58.3% of the photographs in *The Times* (London), *The New York Times*, and *The Globe & Mail* (Canada) concerning the Championship were about male players (Crossman, Vincent, & Speed, 2007).

Sports that call for the use of physical force to overcome an opponent, such as boxing, or to overcome the resistance of a heavy object, such as weightlifting, were considered less appropriate for women (Metheny, 1965; Sage & Loudermilk, 1979). As mentioned earlier, aggressiveness has been considered especially characteristic of masculinity and male sport. However, these traditions have yielded as women have engaged in a wide range of athletic activities in venues such as the Olympics. For example, ice hockey requires a high degree of aggressiveness, and it became an Olympic sport for women in 1980.

Socialization that builds **confidence in athletic aptitude** is important. Children and adults are more likely to enjoy and participate in sport and exercise if they believe they are competent and reasonably skilled athletically. Guidance to facilitate belief in athletic competence is often necessary, because children cannot accurately make assessments of their own athletic ability. Children as old as 13 years of age are inaccurate in judging their athletic ability (Raudsepp & Liblik, 2002). If girls and women perceive themselves to be competent, they are more likely to find sport and exercise to be intrinsically rewarding. For example, female collegiate athletes demonstrated only slightly less intrinsic interest in sport than did their male counterparts (Amorose & Horn, 2000). Both genders may have interpreted their status as scholarship athletes to be evidence of their competence. However, female children and adolescents who participated in organized athletics in Central England were less likely to enjoy sport than their male counterparts. Perhaps the young males enjoyed greater social recognition for their sporting prowess (McCarthy, Jones, & Clark-Carter, 2008).

Women and girls have received increased social support for athletic participation. Comparing the responses of female, collegiate volleyball players in Division I programs in the years 1979 and 1989, the latter cohort were encouraged to participate in athletics to a greater degree by family members and male and female best friends (Weiss & Barber, 1995). Mothers of athletes were seen to be increasingly influential in fostering interest in athletics.

However, even female collegian athletes may experience conflicts with regard to body types (Krane, Choi, Baird, Aimar, & Kauer, 2004). Western European cultures have increasingly characterized the ideal female body type as quite thin, and the ideal male body type as more **mesomorphic** or muscular (Sheldon, 1940, 1942). Regardless of gender, the mesomorphic body type is likely to be more adaptive in the greater number of sports. Female collegiate athletes have been shown to have a higher incidence of eating disorders and concerns about weight than do their male counterparts. Female athletes more commonly engage in unhealthy eating practices in order to control their weight. Coaches are more likely to believe that female athletes need to lose weight and that males need to gain weight, and more male than female coaches attribute being overweight to laziness (Griffin & Harris, 1996).

Femininity and Strength

With a number-one ranking in women's professional tennis, and grand slam victories in the French Open, Wimbledon, and the U.S. Open, Serena Williams was the Sportswoman of the Year in *Sports Illustrated*'s annual report of 2002. The bodacious "all-black, one-piece short-shorts catsuit" ("The Queen," 2002, p. 63) that she wore at the U.S. Open made it difficult to ignore the symmetry and muscularity of her physique. Standing close to 5 ft. 10 in. with wide shoulders and hips, her beauty did not conform to traditional feminine stereotypes and required the incorporation of strength and muscularity into traditional images of beauty.

In 2001 and 2002, Annika Sorenstam was the most dominant golfer in the world. During that time, she reconfigured her physique with a grueling regimen of weightlifting, running, and stretching. This regimen included as many as 1,000 sit-ups a day. As she prepared to be the first woman in the modern era to compete in the men's Professional Golf Association (PGA) tour in the U.S., she was pronounced "built for battle, with industrial-strength arms, the thighs of a sprinter" (Bamberger, 2003). Perhaps photographs that accompanied this *Sports Illustrated* article were intended to document the results of Ms. Sorenstam's training regimen. These photographs captured Ms. Sorenstam's golf swing, but she was clothed only in a leotard that resembled a two-piece bathing suit. Perhaps they were also intended to draw attention to Ms. Sorenstam's physical attractiveness.

Gender Role Orientation and Athletes

The study of gender roles progressed rapidly in the 1970s with the development of questionnaires for assessing gender role orientation. Prominent among these questionnaires was the **Bem Sex Role Inventory** (BSRI; Bem, 1974, 1978). With the BSRI, people are rated for characteristics that are traditionally feminine (sensitive to the needs of others, affectionate) or masculine (willing to take risks, independent). People are then identified as feminine if ratings are high on feminine and low on masculine traits, masculine if scored as high on masculine and low on feminine traits, **androgynous** if rated as high on both feminine and masculine traits, and undifferentiated if they score low on both. The Children's Sex Role Inventory (CSRI) was developed to assess gender roles in children (Boldizar, 1991). It is comparable to the BSRI and appropriate for the assessment of sex typing and androgyny from middle school through adulthood.

Items From the BSRI (Bem, 1974)	
Masculine Items	**Feminine Items**
Acts as a leader	Affectionate
Aggressive	Cheerful
Ambitious	Childlike
Analytical	Compassionate
Assertive	Does not use harsh language
Athletic	Eager to soothe hurt feelings
Competitive	Feminine

Another influential model and measure of gender roles was the **Personality Attributes Questionnaire** (PAQ; Helmreich & Spence, 1977). Research with this questionnaire and the BSRI consistently demonstrated that female athletes were either androgynous or masculine, whereas the average college woman rated as feminine. These findings have been reported for collegiate athletes (Edwards, Gordin, & Henschen, 1984; Gill, 1995; Koca, Asci, & Kirazci, 2005), high school athletes (Andre & Holland, 1995), and younger children (Salminen, 1990). These findings are not surprising, given that athletics are likely to call for assertive and competitive behaviors, and these characteristics are classified as masculine on the PAQ and BSRI.

Gender differences have also been evaluated with the **Sport Orientation Questionnaire** (SOQ; Gill & Deeter, 1988). Men were shown to score higher on scales measuring competitiveness and a focus on winning. Women scored slightly higher on a scale measuring an emphasis on achieving personal goals. Access to and experience with competitive athletics probably influenced the gender differences in competitiveness.

These differences all but disappeared when international and collegiate athletes were evaluated (Gill, 1993).

How is it that athletes of both genders endorse masculine or androgynous gender roles? It has been theorized that the experience of sport, with its emphasis on instrumental behavior, or initiating action to reach goals, aggressiveness, and competitiveness is responsible for fostering masculine (traditionally or stereotypically) characteristics in both genders. In support of this theory, male athletes have been shown to have more traditional views of the roles of women than do male nonathletes. However, if this theory were precise, it would also be reasonable to expect that females, who participated in sports that were traditionally defined as more aggressive and, therefore, more masculine, such as basketball, would have less traditional views of gender roles than their counterparts in traditionally feminine sports, such as figure skating. That is, by engaging in activities traditionally identified as masculine, female athletes would adopt androgynous or masculine gender role perspectives. Instead, female and male college (Burke, 1986) and high school athletes (Andre & Holland, 1995) who participate in more aggressive sports, such as males in American football and females in basketball, do not endorse more masculine gender roles than do their counterparts in less-aggressive sports. An alternative hypothesis is that males with traditional views of gender roles and females who do not carry traditional gender role views choose to engage in sport.

Males have more rigid ideas about sports that are appropriate for each gender. These ideas are likely reified or solidified during childhood and adolescence. For example, children in third grade viewed a range of sporting activities, including weightlifting and cheerleading, as appropriate for both genders. By the eighth grade, 80% of a group of boys viewed weightlifting as an activity for boys, whereas 53% of the girls saw it as appropriate for both genders (Meaney, Dornier, & Owens, 2002). It is unlikely that these boys in the eighth grade made conscious decisions to adopt stereotypical views of gender roles, and more likely that their perceptions reflected societal expectations of gender-appropriate behavior for males. Participation in athletics may also shape views about masculine norms. For example, collegiate male football players with higher levels of athletic identity identified more strongly with traditional masculine norms (Steinfeldt & Steinfeldt, 2012).

Aggression, Sport, and Gender

There are gender differences in the expression of aggression in sport. Female athletes are more likely to express aggression in socially acceptable ways and in ways that do not violate the rules of their sport. Girls are also more likely to manifest prosocial behaviors, such as supporting peers (Baar & Wubbels, 2011). Socialization practices appear to legitimize aggressive behavior to a greater degree in males than females. For example, prior to the start of the basketball season, first-year varsity female basketball players in high school considered aggression to be more acceptable than did experienced female high school basketball players (Ryan, Williams, & Wimer, 1990). Among the aggressive acts that the inexperienced players were more likely to endorse were: verbal intimidation, shoving, knocking the wind out of an opponent so that she would have to leave the game for a few minutes, throwing elbows at opponents with the intention of causing a nosebleed and causing an opponent to leave the game, causing a knee injury and eliminating an opponent from play for an entire season, and inflicting permanent disability. Basketball players who considered these forms of aggression to be more legitimate prior to the start of the basketball season were actually more aggressive during the season.

As a result of actual experience in organized high school athletics, the beliefs of the first-year basketball players about the legitimacy of aggression changed. After the season, the first-year players rated aggression as no more acceptable than did their experienced teammates. It has been theorized that without actual sport experience, females may assume that aggression and violence are a part of the experience of sport, because of the prevalence of information and media coverage of men's athletics.

The International Society of Sport Psychology has deemed that behavior that is violent and inflicts physical harm as well as acts that are aggressive and cause psychological injury are unacceptable (Tenenbaum, Stewart, Singer, & Duda, 1996). These forms of aggression bear no direct relationship to the competitive goals of sport, and they are committed with the intention of harming opponents. Athletes may legitimately attempt to dominate opponents and use aggression to realize competitive goals. Aggression that is legitimately channeled within the boundaries of fair play is described as assertive.

Unacceptable Aggression

On March 8, 2004, Todd Bertuzzi of the National Hockey League's (NHL) Vancouver Canucks punched the Colorado Avalanche's Steve Moore in the head from behind and slammed his head in the ice. With two broken vertebrae and a concussion, Moore ended up face-first in a pool of his own blood. The president-elect of the American College of Sports Medicine commented, "It's time to stop these muggings masquerading as sport" (Farber, 2004, p. 56). The NHL suspended Bertuzzi for the remainder of the season and the playoffs, and he forfeited at least $501,926.39 in salary. These penalties to Bertuzzi notwithstanding, the NHL may have a culture of fighting, such that "the ultimate game for most players is a Gordie Howe hat trick: a goal, an assist and a fight" (Farber, 2004, p. 56).

Gender and Exercise

There are gender differences in the reasons for participation in exercise. The importance of exercise as an outlet for competition and the demonstration of competence have been emphasized more by young males than by females and older males. The value of exercise for weight control and to enhance appearance is more important for women (Egli, Bland, Melton, & Czech, 2011). There is a question about whether women value exercise as a means to facilitate social interaction to a greater degree than do men, as independent research has produced conflicting results.

These gender differences are more pronounced among males that identify more strongly with traditional masculine roles and females that identify with traditional feminine roles. For example, Swedish college students who exercised for the experience of competition were more likely to be males who identified with traditional masculine motives. To a lesser extent, androgynous men and women exercised for the experience of competition (Koivula, 1999). Women and men who strongly endorsed traditional feminine motives said they exercised to enhance appearance.

Similar results have been reported for exercise and sport participation for boys and girls. For example, in the U.S., girls emphasized friendship and fitness and considered achievement and status as important reasons for participation in sport and exercise (Gill, Gross, & Huddleston, 1983; Gould, Feltz, & Weiss, 1985). Australian boys also rated opportunities for competition and status as important reasons for engagement in sport and exercise, and girls were more interested in learning skills, improving health, and engaging in cooperative activities (Weinberg et al., 2000).

Application

Are coaches and athletic department personnel sufficiently aware of and responsive to the weight concerns of female athletes? Perhaps they are not. About half of a sample of Division I female athletes were dissatisfied with their current weight. Most wanted to lose weight—an average of 13.58 pounds. Sizable numbers reported binge eating at least weekly (16.63%), restricted food intake following a binge (22.55%), and exercised at least two hours per day to burn calories (25.5%; Greenleaf, Petrie, Carter, & Reel, 2009).

Girls were also more likely to consider the benefits of physical fitness and playing on a team as reasons for sport participation. Gender differences for sport participation by adolescents between the ages of 13 and 18 appear consistent regardless of whether the adolescents reside in the U.S., Australia, or New Zealand (Weinberg et al., 2000). Adolescent boys were more likely than adolescent girls to say they played sports for the competition and status benefits and because it provided independence, social outlets, and means of releasing tension and energy. The female and male adolescents in all three countries played sports and exercised because they found the activities to be intrinsically rewarding or to provide its own benefits and rewards, and because of extrinsic or external rewards. Examples of the intrinsic rewards for sport and exercise participation were "to have fun" and "improve my skills" (Weinberg et al., 2000, p. 337). The most commonly identified extrinsic benefits were to stay in shape and gain status and recognition.

His daughter, Amantle Montsho, seemed to be different from other children, and especially other girls, in rural Botswana, Africa. She engaged less in free play and gentle running over long distances. She ran sprint after sprint, and with great strength and intensity. She ran without the benefit of a track program or even a track. Maun, her village, had only one gymnasium. Her mother recalled, "It was a struggle that the kids would have things to eat."

Montsho had no role models for sport, as Botswana had never produced an acclaimed female athlete. Intensive training and muscular development was considered incompatible with Botswanian conceptions of femininity. Furthermore, a slender and athletic physique was considered problematic because of the association between weight loss and AIDS—approximately one-quarter of those between the ages of 15 and 49 are living with HIV in Botswana.

At age 16, Montsho was selected for a newly developed training program in Gaborone, the capital. For three years, she shuttled between her home in Maun and Gaborone. Her development continued at a more advanced training facility in Dakar, Senegal. Montsho finished eighth in the 400 meters in the 2008 Olympics in Beijing, and received sponsorship from Nike.

Montsho entered the 2012 Olympic Games in London as the favorite in the 400 meters. Win or lose, she had already become an icon in Botswana. Gaborone's track at the University of Botswana Stadium attracts young athletes from throughout the country, and a new generation of female runners is being cultivated (Pilon, 2012).

Intrinsic rewards are proximate or contiguous to the exercise activity and have been associated with the maintenance of exercise programs. The intrinsic reward of exercise enjoyment or fun is an important factor associated with the continuation or maintenance of exercise in African American and Caucasian adolescent girls (Motl, Dishman, Saunders, Dowda, Felton, & Pate, 2001). Extrinsic rewards have been more closely related to the initiation of exercise programs. Extrinsic rewards, such as the improvement of appearance, accrue more distally or in the future. (Bartlewski, Van Raalte, & Brewer, 1996; Diehl & Petrie, 1995).

Achievement motivation (photo courtesy of Western Connecticut State University)

ACHIEVEMENT MOTIVATION AND GENDER

As explained in Chapter 2, Matina Horner (1973) pioneered the examination of gender differences in achievement motivation in the context of Atkinson's expectancy value formula. She maintained that there was a psychological barrier that interfered with the achievement of women, and referred to this as the **motive to avoid success** (MAS). The MAS refers to the belief that negative consequences will accompany success. Horner reasoned that traditional conceptions of femininity involved the suppression of aggressive and competitive impulses. Therefore, success and competition would engender anxiety in women, as they would fear social disapproval and a "loss of femininity" (Horner, 1973, p. 223). She (1978) recognized that the tendency to avoid success in a given situation (T-S) was a function of a stable, internal characteristic (MAS), subjective estimates of the probability of success in the situation (Ps), and the negative incentive value for success (Ias):

$$T\text{–}S = MAS \times Ps \times Ias$$

Ias was greater for women in competitive situations, when their competitors were men, and when engaged in tasks considered masculine, such as mathematics.

The tendency to avoid success inhibits competitive and adaptive strivings and adversely affects performance; this tendency was far more frequent in college females than in college males. Horner demonstrated that the performance on achievement tests of two-thirds of male college students improved in competitive versus noncompetitive conditions, whereas improvements in performance occurred for only one-third of female college students. For female students high in the motive to avoid success, 75% achieved at a significantly higher level in the noncompetitive condition, compared with 7% of the women low in the motive to avoid success. Women high in the motive to avoid success indicated that doing well was significantly more important to them in noncompetitive conditions, and doing well was rated as least important in competitive conditions with men. Statistical trends indicated that the motive to avoid success was more influential for college women high in ability and achievement motivation and who had a history of academic success.

Criticism of Horner's Fear of Success Construct

Much of Horner's innovative research was conducted approximately 40 years ago. Despite refinements (Fleming & Horner, 1992), Horner's work came under a considerable amount of criticism due to her research methodology (Metzler & Conroy, 2004; Zuckerman & Wheeler, 1975) and because independent researchers did not replicate her findings. In groups of students in high school, college, and medical school, females did not show higher fear of success than males (Costanzo, Woody, & Slater, 1992; Mednick & Thomas, 1993; Piedmont, 1988). Likewise, college women did not record higher levels of fear of success as they performed motor activities (Conroy & Metzler, 2004). Elite male French athletes demonstrated higher levels of fear of success than did their female counterparts (Andre & Metzler, 2011).

Other studies have demonstrated that while women had higher scores than men on measures of fear of success, these measures did not predict grade point averages or ACT scores. Further, performance during competition for those high in T-S may be impaired for both sexes, and some adolescent boys are more affected by competition with a girl than with a boy (Graham & Weiner, 1996).

Regardless of whether women are uncomfortable demonstrating prowess in competition with men, women as a whole may be more uncomfortable demonstrating high levels of competence in the presence of men and women who have much less competence (Piedmont, 1988). This finding was demonstrated in a study in which female and male college students with high nonverbal ability completed half of a test of nonverbal ability alone, and half with a male or female student of much lower ability. The performance of the women versus the men with high ability was suppressed when they were paired with a student of lower ability, regardless of the gender of the latter. Those that suppressed their performance when paired with the less-capable student also had lower college grades, Scholastic Aptitude Test (SAT) scores, need for achievement, and aspirations for higher education. Social needs may be more influential in females, such that they suppress their performance if they believe that success will cause discomfort in their less capable peers or result in their being disliked (Costanzo et al. 1992).

Female athletes have been shown to be more agreeable and compassionate than their male counterparts (Allen, Greenlees, & Jones, 2011). They also register higher levels of conscientiousness and trait anxiety (Newcombe & Boyle, 1995). As a broad generalization, it may be more difficult for them to dispassionately ignore the struggles of others.

Both female and male elite athletes and performers acknowledged aspects of fear of success (Conroy, Poczwardowski, & Henschen, 2001, p. 318):

1. Not learning and improving
2. Facing an overly rigid future
3. Accomplishing all my goals
4. Facing higher expectations (own and others)
5. Losing enjoyment of success
6. Experiencing tangible costs (e.g., slumps, injuries, loneliness)
7. Experiencing jealousy and interpersonal rivalry
8. Experiencing increased recognition and appreciation
9. Not receiving support from others
10. Losing or not increasing motivation
11. Becoming overconfident.

Elite French male athletes acknowledged greater fear of facing higher expectations, experiencing jealousy and interpersonal rivalry, and competing time demands (Andre & Metzler, 2011). With high levels of fear of success, people may sabotage their opportunities for success by engaging in disparaging self-talk (Conroy & Metzler, 2004). This self-talk may direct attention from the instrumental behaviors that lead to success, and make success less likely.

Achievement Motivation and Sport

Expectancy value theories have been shown to be valid for evaluating motivation in sporting contexts, and gender differences have been considered. Males in high school and college were more likely than females to acknowledge an achievement orientation that consisted of a willingness to participate in and strive for success in competitive sports (Gill, 1998). These males said they had more interest in winning and avoiding losing than did their female classmates, but the females were as interested as the males in achieving their own goals and in achievement across areas of life functioning. These males also reported more activity and experience with competitive sports.

Differences in achievement motivation between younger girls and boys in athletic contexts have also been demonstrated. Girls have been shown to be more receptive than boys to games with cooperative rules. Boys have been shown to focus more on winning at games. These results hold for Caucasian and Native American children. Native American children were more receptive to cooperative games, perhaps due to cultural influences (Duda, 1986; McNally & Orlick, 1975).

Female club athletes recorded higher levels of concern about their appearance while engaged in sport. They marked concerns about performance/composure inadequacy, appearing fatigued/lacking energy, physical appearance, and appearing athletically untalented. These concerns about appearance correlate with anxiety in competition (Lorimer, 2006).

Gender differences in achievement motives are minimal among more accomplished athletes (McElroy & Willis, 1979). Accomplished female athletes have demonstrated no particular vulnerability to being uncomfortable with success, although male collegiate athletes have been shown to rate themselves as having less fear of success than do female collegiate athletes and female and male nonathletes (Silva, 1982). Gender differences in achievement orientation were shown to be minimal for college athletes in Iowa and for international athletes and university athletes in Taiwan (Gill, 1998). Involvement in athletics may foster this achievement orientation, as female college and international athletes scored higher on this achievement orientation factor than male nonathletes (Gill, 1993). Alternatively, women with higher achievement orientation may be drawn to athletics.

Are audiences uncomfortable with the success of female athletes? This question is reasonable if sport is considered to represent masculine activities and, therefore, be inconsistent with the roles of women. If audiences were uncomfortable in this way, then the success of female athletes might be attributed to luck, cheating, and the lack of serious competition. Regardless of whether sports were seen to be more stereotypically masculine (e.g., handball) or feminine (e.g., figure skating), the success of female and male athletes was considered to be due to talent (Duda & Roberts, 1980).

STRESS AND COPING

Both female and male athletes use a range of **problem- and emotion-focused coping** strategies to handle stress. The similarities in coping responses of women and men are far greater than the differences, especially when considering elite athletes. However, some gender differences in the coping strategies of sportspersons have been noted (Nicholls & Polman, 2007). Female athletes who competed at highly skilled to elite levels (Anshel, Porter, & Quek, 1998; Crocker & Graham, 1995), as well as adolescents (Hoar, Crocker, Holt, & Tamminen, 2010; Kowalski & Crocker, 2001), were more likely than males to utilize emotion-focused coping by seeking out emotional support from others when their goals were thwarted. Among elite skiers with season-ending injuries, about half sought support from others, and the female skiers were twice as likely as the males to utilize this resource (Gould, Udry, Bridges, & Beck, 1997b). In response to slumps or periods of below average performance, female elite runners more frequently utilized emotion-focused coping and males preferred problem-focused coping (Madden, Kikby, & McDonald, 1989). The elite women responded with stronger emotion, such as anger, and accepted sympathy from others, whereas the men attempted more direct solutions to emerge from slumps, such as altering their training regimen.

MENTAL SKILLS

Gender differences in the amount of cognitive anxiety or worry have been noticed. Female collegiate athletes acknowledged more cognitive anxiety or worry prior to competition, and especially thirty minutes prior to matches (Jones & Cale, 1989). Gender differences in the nature of cognitive anxiety have also been reported. Female collegiate athletes were shown to worry about reaching their personal goals and about whether they were sufficiently prepared for competition (Jones, Swain, & Cale, 1991). Males were more concerned with the strength of competition and the outcome of the competition. Findings that the self-confidence of female as compared to male athletes drops and the somatic anxiety (muscular tension and elevated heart rate) increases prior to competition (Jones & Cale, 1989) have been less consistent (Jones et al., 1991).

Female and males do not differ in their capacity to interpret signs of cognitive and physiological anxiety as facilitative of their efforts to reach goals. For example, almost half of a sample of 91 competitive swimmers between the ages of 14 and 28 reported cognitive and physiological anxiety to be facilitative, and only 23% reported both kinds of anxiety as debilitative (Jones & Hanton, 1996). The swimmers who believed they would achieve their goals used anxiety as a cue to become more engaged and persistent in training and competition.

Negative self-talk interferes with optimal performance. The self-talk of female junior tennis players during competition was weighted toward self-critical and judgmental statements, especially during losing matches (Van Raalte, Brewer, Rivera, & Petitpas, 1994).

The sport self-confidence of female athletes may be less stable than that of males. Stable sport self-confidence is based on controllable factors, such as the demonstration of ability. Sport self-confidence derived from sources over which athletes have less control, such as perceptions of body image, the leadership of coaches, and comfort in competitive venues, is less stable (Kingston, Lane, & Thomas, 2010). Confidence in athletic ability is a component of mental toughness, and female athletes also scored lower on this and other dimensions of mental toughness, such as emotional control (Nicholls, Polman, Levy, & Backhouse, 2009).

GOAL ORIENTATIONS

As discussed in Chapter 9, goal orientations refer to the manner by which progress is measured. With task orientations, progress is measured in relation to one's baseline of prior performance. Both female and male athletes benefit from task orientations (Petherick & Weigand, 2002). For example, junior elite female gymnasts who trained with coaches who were seen to encourage task orientations demonstrated more enjoyment for their sport, more positive body images, and higher self-esteem (Duda, 2001). The 11-year-old gymnasts in this sample who trained with coaches that encouraged ego orientations were more likely to experience competitive stress. Ego orientations involve measuring performance in relation to external standards, and present an additional threat to female athletes, in that they may encourage body dysphoria or dissatisfaction, perfectionism, and eating disorders. Perfectionism among young, elite female gymnasts is an insidious consequence of coaching that emphasizes ego orientations, and this perfectionism contributes to disordered eating and preoccupation with food (Duda & Kim, 1997).

Female basketball players between 10 and 14 years of age evidenced higher levels of task orientations and lower ego orientations than did their male counterparts (Grossbard et al., 2007). However, the young females with task and ego orientations recorded more competitive anxiety than did males with corresponding goal orientations. Similar results were reported among elite British adolescent athletes, as the females were more likely to have higher levels of task orientation and anxiety, and lower ego orientation levels (Harwood, Cumming & Fletcher, 2004). Elite male and female Norwegian athletes endorsed relatively high levels of both task and ego orientations (Abrahamsen, Roberts, & Pensgaard, 2008). They also had similar impressions of the motivational climates of their teams and training venues. However, the elite females recorded more performance anxiety than did the males. They also experienced more concentration disruption in motivational climates that encouraged ego orientations.

SEXUAL HARASSMENT AND ABUSE

Female athletes are more likely to be coached by males and to experience sexual harassment and abuse from coaches and other sporting officials (Brackenridge, 2000). **Sexual harassment** consists of unwanted attention that is motivated by sexual interest. **Sexual abuse** consists of coerced sexual contact. Coerced sexual contact occurs not only with actual physical force, but also when someone, such as a coach, uses a position of authority to obtain sexual contact. Athletes are coerced when they believe that they risk alienating coaches and jeopardize their careers by resisting unwanted sexual contact. A **hostile atmosphere** exists when references to gender and sex create an uncomfortable and debilitating environment. Sexual exploitation may occur at elite levels of competition (Weiss, Amorose, & Allen, 2000) or at beginning levels where coaches are volunteers and have minimal preparation and screening.

Estimates of the prevalence of sexual harassment vary across settings. For example, prevalence rates were 79% and 54% among Czech and Norwegian female sport students, respectively. Norwegian female athletes experienced disgust, fear, irritation, and anger in response to sexual harassment. A number of the women passively accepted the harassment. They rationalized that the harassment was not serious and wished that it would end. Others coped by avoiding the harasser. Still others confronted harassers directly or with humor (Fasting, Brackenridge, & Walseth, 2007).

Sexual Harassment

The ethical code of the Association for Applied Sport Psychology (Association for the Advancement of Applied Sport Psychology, 1994) is based in large part on the Ethical Principles of the American Psychological Association (2002). Both ethical codes forbid multiple relationships with clients, students, and supervisees. For example, a psychologist would not supervise a student and have that student as a client. A psychologist would also avoid business or financial relationships with clients or students. Both ethical codes forbid sexual relations with students, supervisees, and clients over which the psychologist has authority. These multiple or dual relationships are likely to impair the judgment of psychologists, and most importantly are exploitative.

The subject of sexual relations between coaches and athletes has recently received attention in the popular press (Wahl, Wertheim, Dohrmann, 2001). Public statements from governing bodies for coaches are inconsistent in their treatment of this topic, but such affairs are clearly in violation of ethical standards for psychologists. The WNBA (Woman's National Basketball Association), WUSA, NCAA (National Collegiate Athletic Association) and U.S. Track and Field, and U.S. Soccer organizations have no policies about this issue. The U.S. Soccer organization does not prohibit coaches and players from dating and considers dating a personal activity. The U.S. Basketball organization has no written policy, but the Federation stated that coaches and athletes are discouraged from dating.

A survey of Canadian elite athletes revealed that 21.8% of the 266 surveyed stated that they engaged in sexual intercourse with a coach or sports authority figure. The majority of the authority figures and coaches were male and 80% of the athletes who engaged in sexual intercourse were female. Coaches and tennis athletes spend large blocks of time together, and former player Pam Shriver opined, "For every one [that becomes a romance], I'll bet there are sexual feelings in 99% of the other player-coach relationships that never surface" (Wahl et al., 2001, p. 68).

Regardless of whether the authority figure is male or female, the effects of such sexual contact on athletes and teams appear similar and detrimental. Coaches or other officials are in a position of authority and make myriad decisions that affect the careers of athletes, such as playing time and roles on teams and in individual sports. Because of the power differential in these relationships, there is a question about whether a sexual relationship between an athlete and a coach or other authority figure in sport can be consensual. Team members may wonder if team selections, roles, and playing times were influenced by intimacies between coaches and players.

For example, the U.S. Olympic woman's volleyball team was described as on the edge of disintegration prior to the 1996 Olympics. Five months prior to the Olympics, team captain Tammy Liley broke off an affair with assistant coach Kent Miller. Team sources said that Miller became so distraught that he could not function effectively as a coach. The head coach suspended Miller and stripped Liley of her captaincy. These events altered team chemistry to a degree that a player on this team said, "After this happened, we were toast before we ever set foot on the floor" (Wahl et al., 2001, p. 70).

WOMEN AND COACHING

As mentioned earlier, prior to the passage of Title IX in 1972, approximately 90% of the coaches of women and girls were women. By 2008, this number was 43% (Carpenter & Acosta, 2008). With Title IX, the number of collegiate athletic teams for women increased markedly and there was a concordant need for more college coaches. Men filled many of the new coaching positions.

Male athletic directors reasoned that more men were hired as coaches because of a dearth of qualified female applicants, whereas female athletic administrators cited discriminatory hiring practices to be the cause of the declining number of female coaches. The number of women in the upper echelons of athletic administrations is limited, and women may not benefit from the "old boys' network" or assistance from acquaintances to secure coaching jobs (Acosta & Carpenter, 1985). That is, given that the majority of athletic directors are male, they may be more favorably acquainted with coaches of their gender.

Some athletes also believe that female coaches are less qualified than their male counterparts. Female high school athletes demonstrated **gender biases** when estimating the skill of female coaches, the likelihood that a coach will be successful, and when making hypothetical choices about playing for a female or male coach (Parkhouse & Williams, 1986; Williams & Parkhouse, 1988). These biases have diminished more recently, as female swimmers between the ages of 10 and 19 (Medwechuk & Crossman, 1994) and elite Swedish soccer players (Fasting & Pfister, 2000) preferred female coaches. The young swimmers also demonstrated preferences for coaches of the same sex, perhaps because of experience with competent female coaches. British collegiate athletes considered coaches of the other sex as having less efficacy in building character and motivation (Kavussanu, Boardley, Jutkiewicz, Vincent, & Ring, 2008).

Biases about the qualifications of collegiate female head coaches are unfounded. They are as likely as their male counterparts to have collegiate athletic playing experience, while male coaches were more likely to have experience as a high school athlete. Collegiate female head coaches are more likely to have a professional background in physical education. This professional background may provide a greater amount of training for coaching positions (Hasbrook, Hart, Mathes, & True, 1990). Female high school soccer coaches were shown to have more experience as soccer players than did their male counterparts (Millard, 1996).

The decrease in the number of female coaches is due to not only this influx of men, but also to women dropping out of the profession. Specific **training** and mentoring in coaching facilitates the entry and retention of women in the coaching profession (Sisley, Weiss, Barber, & Ebbeck, 1990). Even programs that provide limited training in the specifics of how to coach and manage practice, and that did not screen coaching mentors to insure their wholehearted cooperation (Weiss et al., 1991), markedly improved retention rates for women in coaching. With highly competent coaches as mentors, intercollegiate female athletes show greater coaching self-efficacy and interest (Moran-Miller & Flores, 2011). Perhaps, novice coaches can profit from instruction about the technical aspects of their sport, training in the management of overly involved and intrusive parents (see Chapter 21), and in the management of schedules and practices (Sisley et al., 1990).

The ongoing development of **coaching competence** is an important motivator for female and male coaches. There are similarities in the ways by which female and male head coaches of high school girls' volleyball, basketball, softball, and soccer teams evaluate their competence (Barber, 1998). Both genders attend to improvements in their athletes, the emotional tone of their athletes, and their own coaching skills in evaluating their competence and performance. Female coaches may well judge their competence in teaching sport skills to be superior to the male coaches (Barber, 1998), but inferior in developing game strategies (Kavussanu et al., 2008). Female coaches with extensive educational backgrounds in physical education are more likely to have more training in teaching sport skills. Both female and male coaches rate time demands as the most important reason for withdrawing from coaching.

If women are to remain in coaching, the **costs** as well as the **benefits of coaching** will be important considerations. For both current and former female high school coaches, the costs of coaching include: time demands, inadequate professional compensation, lack of support, stress, and low perceived competence. Administrators who provided flexible schedules and adequate staff were more likely to retain coaching mothers at Division I universities (Breuning & Dixon, 2008). The benefits of coaching include the success of their programs and the opportunity to experience and participate in athletics (Weiss & Stevens, 1993).

Application

Felice Schwartz initiated a firestorm of controversy as a result of her 1989 Harvard Business Review article "Management Women and the New Facts of Life." In this work she maintained that while some women prioritize work above all else, most want children. Women with children were seen as willing to trade some career growth and compensation for freedom from incessant pressure to work long hours and weekends. Schwartz argued that these women were more valuable to companies than men at similar job levels. These men might remain in their positions only until they claw their way up the management ladder. Other men at similar levels might compensate for less talent by working an excessive number of hours.

Schwartz was criticized as promoting a "mommy track" of dead-end jobs for women. In coaching, even mommy tracks may not be available for women. Much of the work of coaches extends into evenings and weekends, and elite coaches must travel for games and recruiting. Family and administrative support—especially for the care of young children—is especially important if women are to advance in coaching. This support is possible. In the world of business, between 21% and 27% of women have both careers and children by age 40 (Postrel, 2011).

COACHING INTERVENTIONS AND GENDER

The topic of effective coaching and leadership will be addressed in greater depth in Chapter 22. In brief summary, positive reinforcement, encouragement following mistakes, technical advice, and avoidance of negative feedback and criticism, have been identified as positive characteristics of coaches (Smith & Smoll, 1990; Smoll & Smith, 1989).

Some differences in the coaching interventions of female and male high school soccer coaches during games were noted. Males were more given to providing technical instruction and females provided more encouragement (Millard, 1996).

Does Gender Influence Reactions to Coaches?

Adult female and male Australian athletes showed similar preferences for coaching interventions (Sherman, Fuller, & Speed, 2000). These athletes consisted of female and male basketball players, female netball players, and male Australian Rules football players. The coaching responses preferred by both females and males in descending order were positive feedback, training and instruction, democratic behavior, social support, and autocratic behavior. Autocratic behavior often consists of decision making without input from team members (Chelladurai & Doherty, 1998).

Although not unequivocal (Black & Weiss, 1992), perhaps female adolescents and children respond somewhat differently to coaching interventions. For example, Allen and Howe (1998) reported that confidence was higher among female field hockey athletes between the ages of 14 to 18 who played for coaches who emphasized praise and technical information following skilled performance and who made fewer comments in the form of encouragement and corrective information after mistakes. However, these players on regional teams in Canada were more satisfied with their field hockey experience if they perceived coaches as providing praise and information following good performances as well as encouragement and corrective information following mistakes. Both feelings of confidence and satisfaction with hockey experiences were influenced by the actual athletic skill of the athletes, and the more skilled players were more confident in and satisfied with their sport.

Collegiate female athletes in a variety of sports appear to respond more unfavorably to **autocratic coaching styles** than do their male counterparts (Amorose & Horn, 2000). These women were negatively affected by autocratic behaviors, such as punishing feedback, and comments from coaches and when coaches ignored their successes and failures. Male athletes were also negatively affected by autocratic coaching styles, but less so than were the women. Coaches who manifested aspects of democratic leadership, such as praise and recognition after good performance and encouragement and informational feedback after failures, enhanced the intrinsic motivation of their athletes. These democratic interventions supported athletes' beliefs in their efficacy and competence at their sport. Democratic coaching interventions also encouraged athletes to think of their athletic experience to be under their personal control. Beliefs in personal control, efficacy, and competence contribute to intrinsic interest in sport.

Women as Sport Psychologists

By the year 2000, 46% of the members of the Association for Applied Sport Psychology (AASP) were women, and 43% of AASP Certified Consultants were women.

Nevertheless, elite, senior female sport psychologists experienced gender bias in the early years of their academic careers (Whaley & Krane, 2012). Female sport psychologists have not been seen to have equal opportunities for consultation with athletes, perhaps because male coaches or athletic administrators are likely to select male consultants (Roper, 2002).

SUMMARY AND APPLICATION

The benefits of sport and exercise include increased muscle metabolism and strength, decreased body fat, increased maximum oxygen consumption, and improved well-being. It is, therefore, reasonable to encourage children, adolescents, and adults to participate in exercise and sport if they are medically capable. Historically, the participation of women in some forms of sport and exercise has been limited, discouraged, or prohibited. Efforts to exclude women from athletic participation have decreased more recently, as it has been recognized that impediments to their involvement have been due to social constructions rather than to physiological limitations. The participation of women in collegiate athletics was enhanced dramatically in the U.S. with Title IX federal legislation in 1972. However, the representation of women in collegiate and other coaching and athletic administrative positions remains limited. It also appears that social factors continue to influence girls to underestimate their motor skills and to lose confidence and expectations for success in future activities that require these motor skills.

Gender roles that were construed to exclude the involvement of women in sport have also receded and support for the participation of girls and women in sport has increased with the passage of time. However, girls continue to judge their athletic ability more negatively than do boys, and their doubts about athletic competence are likely to limit intrinsic interest and involvement in sport. Those women who play sports through their collegiate years show levels of intrinsic interest in sport that are comparable to their male counterparts. They also demonstrate gender-role orientations that are less traditionally feminine. Female athletes continue to have greater conflicts between body images that are conceptualized as ideal for women in general and for women in sport. This conflict is negligible for men, as mesomorphic or muscular physiques are prized for men aesthetically and athletically.

There are also gender differences in the motivation for exercise, and these differences are more pronounced for males and females that identify with traditional roles. For example, with masculine gender roles, men more commonly pursued exercise for the experience of competition. With traditional feminine gender roles, women exercise to enhance appearance.

The Motive to Avoid Success (MAS) has been evaluated for over thirty years, and reliable evidence that women inhibit achievement in the presence of men is lacking. In athletic contexts, males acknowledged more interest in winning and avoiding losing than do females, but these differences are minimal among accomplished athletes. Further, evidence that women suppress their athletic performance in the presence of males or less-capable competitors is lacking. However, there was evidence that women were uncomfortable demonstrating superior intellectual ability in the presence of less-capable peers, irrespective of the peers' gender. Perhaps the women were more sensitive to the potential reactions of the peers and suppressed their performance if they suspected that their success would cause discomfort to others.

This interpersonal sensitivity has also been evidenced in the coping strategies of female athletes. They more frequently seek out emotional support from others.

Athletes of both genders are capable of interpreting signs of anxiety as facilitative, and when sportspersons are confident that they will reach their goals, anxiety is more likely to facilitate performance. Female sportspersons may be more vulnerable to disruptive cognitive anxiety prior to performances and to self-critical thoughts during competition. Sportspersons are more likely to adopt task orientations in environments or motivation climates that encourage and support these task orientations.

Parents and coaches make important contributions to the motivational climates of athletes. The conduct of coaches and other sporting officials with female athletes is especially important because of the greater likelihood that males will coach them. The ethical codes of the AASP and APA forbid sexual harassment and relationships between psychologists and clients, students, and supervisees. The governing bodies of other organizations are less decisive.

Training, mentoring, administrative, and interpersonal support are important factors for introducing and retaining women in coaching professions. Athletes respond more negatively to autocratic than to democratic coaching styles. Collegiate women athletes responded more negatively to autocratic coaching interventions than did their male counterparts.

Key Terms

Discussion Questions

Q1. Consider the historical understanding of the fitness of women for rigorous athletics.

Q2. Review Title IX.

Q3. Describe the obstacles that women experience in pursuing careers in athletic administration.

Q4. Outline the history of participation in the Olympic Games by women.

Q5. Explain gender roles.

Q6. Consider the sports associated with traditional notions of femininity.

Q7. Do some sports result in the development of body types that are inconsistent with traditional female body types?

Q8. Describe the Bem Sex Role Inventory.

Q9. Review the results for female athletes on the Bem Sex Role Inventory, the Personality Attributes Questionnaire, and the Sport Orientation Questionnaire.

Q10. Describe gender differences in the expression of aggression in sport.

Q11. Review gender differences in the reasons for exercise.

Q12. How convincing is the evidence for gender differences in the motive to avoid success?

Q13. Consider aspects of fear of success endorsed by females and male athletes and performers.

Q14. Gender differences in achievement motives are likely to differ most at what levels of participation?

Q15. Review the coping strategies of female and male athletes.

Q16. Consider the mental skills of female and male athletes.

Q17. Examine gender differences in task and ego orientations.

Q18. Discuss the impact of sexual harassment and abuse.

Q19. Review the challenges faced by women in coaching.

Q20. Do female athletes respond more favorably and unfavorably to specific coaching styles?

Q21. Do female sport psychologists realize equal opportunities with their male counterparts?

Suggested Readings

Carpenter, L. J., & Acosta, R. V. (2008). Women in intercollegiate sport: A longitudinal, national study thirty-one year update 1977–2008. Retrieved from http://www.acostacarpenter.org.

Conroy, D. E., & Metzler, J. N. (2004). Patterns of self-talk associated with different forms of competitive anxiety. *Journal of Sport & Exercise Psychology, 26,* 69–89.

Gill, D. L., & Kamphoff, C. S. (2010). Gender and cultural considerations. In J. M. Williams (Ed.), *Applied sport psychology: Personal growth to peak performance* (6th ed., pp. 417–439). New York, NY: McGraw-Hill.

Oglesby, C. A., & Hill, K. L. (1993). Gender and sport. In R. N. Singer, M. Murphey, & L. K. Tennant (Eds.), *Handbook of research on sport psychology* (pp. 718–728). New York, NY: MacMillan.

Pfister, G. (2001). Women and the Olympic Games: 1900–97. In B. L. Drinkwater (Ed.), *Women in sport* (pp. 3–19). Oxford, England: Blackwell Science.

Raznahan, A., Lee, Y., Stidd, R., Long, R., Greenstein, D., Clasen, L., Addington, A., Gogtay, N., Rapoport, J. L., & Giedd, J. N. (2010). Longitudinally mapping the influence of sex and androgen signaling on the dynamics of human cortical maturation in adolescence. *Proceedings of the National Academy of Sciences, 107*, 16988–16993.

Slater, A., & Tiggemann, M. (2010). "Uncool to do sport": A focus group study of adolescent girls' reasons for withdrawing from physical activity. *Psychology of Sport and Exercise, 11*, 619–626.

Weiss, M. R., Barber, H., Ebbeck, V., & Sisley, B. L. (1991). Developing competence and confidence in novice female coaches: II. Perceptions of ability and affective experiences following a season-long coaching internship. *Journal of Sport & Exercise Psychology, 13*, 336–363.

Chapter 20

ETHNIC AND CULTURAL DIFFERENCES AND SPORT

"In effect, 1970 (World Cup; championship of soccer) was the first major confrontation between Europe and South America that the world had had the opportunity to witness. When Czechoslovakia went one up in Brazil's opening game, David Coleman observed that 'all we ever knew about them has come true,' he was referring to Brazil's sloppy defense, but the words are those of a man whose job it was to introduce one culture to another.

In the next eight minutes, everything else we knew about them came true, too. They equalized with a direct

Men's 100 meters final, Beijing Olympics 2008

free kick from Rivelino that dipped and spun and swerved in the thin Mexican air (had I ever seen a goal scored direct from a free kick before? I don't remember one), and they went 2–1 up when Pele took a long pass on his chest and volleyed it into the corner. They won 4–1 and we in 2W (in England), the small but significant center of the global village, were duly awed.

It wasn't just the quality of the football, though; it was the way they regarded ingenious and outrageous embellishment as though it were as functional and necessary as a corner kick or a throw-in. The only comparison I had at my disposal then was with toy cars: although I had no interest in Dinky or Corgi or Matchbox, I loved Lady Penelope's pink Rolls-Royce and James Bond's Aston Martin, both equipped with elaborate devices such as ejector seats and hidden guns which lifted them out of the boring ordinary. Pele's attempt to score from inside his own half with a lob, the dummy he sold to the Peruvian goalkeeper when he went one way round and ball went the other. . . these were football's equivalent of the ejector seat, and made everything else look like so many Vauxhall Vivas. Even the Brazilian way of celebrating a goal—run four strides, jump, punch, run four strides, jump, punch—was alien and funny and enviable, all at the same time" (Hornby, 1992, p. 37).

A s mentioned in Chapter 1, most of the information in this book is presented without reference to gender, ethnicity, culture, or socio-economic status. This emphasis on universal human responses to competition and training notwithstanding, individual differences that are determined by ethnicity and culture have also been identified. The study of these ethnic and cultural differences is its rudimentary stages (Duda & Allison, 1990). A recent analysis of influential sport psychology journals demonstrated that the cultural background of study participants was identified in only 11.5% of the articles published between 1987 and 2000. Furthermore, cultural background was a substantial focus of study in only 1.5% of these research articles (Ram, Starek, & Johnson, 2004). Considering articles published in these journals between 2001 and 2006, cultural background was a primary component of theoretical frameworks in 4.8% of the articles (Peters & Williams, 2009). Similarly, cultural diversity was a focus in only 10.5% of the presentations in the annual conferences of the Association for Applied Sport Psychology (AASP) between 1986 and 2007 (Kamphoff, Gill, Araki, & Hammond, 2010). It is likely that the study of culture and ethnicity will progress, as psychologists attempt to refine their interventions with increasingly diverse and international athletes.

Ethnic and cultural differences may also exist between sport psychologists and clients. There is less cultural and ethnic diversity among sport psychologists than among the sportspersons with whom they are likely to consult. For example, in the U.S. sport psychologists are predominantly Caucasians (Gill, 2002; Roper, 2002; Williams & Scherzer, 2003). Psychologists and sport psychologists are also ethically obliged to become educated and sensitive to cultural and ethnic concerns (as well as gender issues), and to recognize and avoid bias in their professional functioning (American Psychological Association, 2002; Association for the Advancement of Applied Sport Psychology, 1994; Gill & Kamphoff, 2010). **Culture** and ethnicity are not synonymous. Cultures share attitudes, beliefs, values, norms for judging behavior, and often geographic regions and languages. Ethnic or racial backgrounds include African, Asian/Pacific Island, and European. However, the division of people into distinct racial groups is controversial (Cavalli-Sforza & Cavalli-Sforza, 1995; Helms, Jernigan, & Maschler, 2005). These racial groups have been seen to differ phenotypically (in appearance), but geneticists emphasize the similarities between races, as racial groups are genetically 99.9% alike (Smedley & Smedley, 2005).

African and European and Asian
Immigration and intermarriage has resulted in a demographic shift in the U.S. One in seven marriages is between spouses of different ethnic groups. Multiracial and biracial college students are increasingly identifying themselves as such, and may find it inauthentic to identify with dominant phenotypes (Saulny, 2011).

Ethnicity, culture, and gender are often studied in a multicultural framework. Within this framework, individuals are understood to have multiple, intersecting identities based on intersecting cultural identities. Multicultural psychologists evaluate power relations based on gender and cultural identities and intertwined and advocate for fairness (Gill, 2007).

ATHLETIC PARTICIPATION AND ACADEMIC ENGAGEMENT AND ACHIEVEMENT

Given the representation of African American athletes in American sports, such as the National Basketball Association (NBA) and National Football League (NFL), it might be assumed that higher percentages of African Americans are involved with sport at all levels. This assumption has greater validity in evaluating participation in certain sports at elite levels. For example, among National Collegiate Athletic Association (NCAA) athletes, 68.4% of men's basketball players, 51.7% of football players, and 53.2% of women's basketball players were ethnic minorities (NCAA Research Staff, 2004). These percentages were higher than the corresponding percentage, 29%, of U.S. citizens who were not of European descent. This assumption would however be inconsistent with estimates that only 18% of African American students participated in team sports by the tenth grade. Nearly 10% of these African American students participated in individual sports by the tenth grade (Jordan, 1999). More Caucasian students participated in team (23%) and individual (16%) sports by the tenth grade.

Non-Latino Blacks and Hispanics are also less likely to engage in leisure time activities, such as exercise and sports, which require physical exertion than were non-Latino Whites. These differences are not entirely due to socioeconomic factors, such as educational and income levels, or the greater likelihood that non-Latino Blacks and especially Hispanics are more likely to be employed at jobs that require physical activity (Marquez, Neighbors, Bustamante, 2010).

Athletic participation among Native Americans has been limited by factors such as poverty, insufficient athletic equipment and facilities, and inadequate coaching and instruction (Coakley, 2001). Native Americans may also have concerns that athletic participation will result in their cultural alienation.

For African, European, and Hispanic American high school students, athletic participation led to **higher academic achievement** and grades, higher academic self-confidence, and better self-concepts. Participation in sports and other extracurricular activities increases students' interest in school, facilitates positive relationships with coaches, teachers, and administrators, and motivates athletes to achieve adequate grade point averages (GPA) so as to maintain athletic eligibility (Jordan, 1999).

Hank Aaron and Vocational Advancement for African Americans

Hank Aaron held the Major League Baseball record for home runs (755) until it was broken by Barry Bonds in 2007. As an owner of a BMW dealership in Atlanta, Aaron encouraged BMW to start the MetroSTEP program in 2004. The MetroSTEP program provides seven-month paid internships in automobile technician training for minority-group members. Graduates of this program are guaranteed jobs at BMW dealerships with starting salaries of almost $40,000 a year (Bluestein, 2004).

Life Satisfaction

Male African Americans on the verge of graduation from college demonstrate slightly less life satisfaction or well-being than do their male Caucasian counterparts. This relationship holds regardless of whether the students were Division I athletes or whether the athletes sustained significant injuries during their college careers (Perna, Ahlgren, & Zaichkowsky, 1999). Further, regardless of athletic participation, students without post-collegiate career plans have less well-being.

African American collegiate athletes are more likely to participate in "revenue-generating" sports, such as football and basketball (Upthegrove, Roscigno, & Charles, 1999). Graduation rates for African American Division I National Collegiate Athletic Association (NCAA) male football and basketball players are increasing, but still lag behind the rates for Caucasians. As of 2006, 55% of African American football players graduated six years after enrolling as freshmen in 2000. By comparison,

77% of Caucasian, 54% of Asian/Pacific Island, and 64% of Hispanic football players graduated in the same period (NCAA Research Staff, 2006). Considering men's basketball, 51% of African American males graduated and 76% of Caucasians graduated in this time interval. The graduation rates for women are considerably higher. For example, 72% of African American women and 89% of Caucasian women graduated from Division I basketball programs during this time period.

Application

Comparing the academic performance of African American males and females, males significantly underperform. Their academic self-concepts differ. Males are less likely to identify as good students, to develop academic proficiencies, or intrinsic interest in school. Mentors and school personnel who are approachable and caring are in the best position to help African American males integrate academic achievement into their identities (Cokley, McClain, Jones, & Johnson, 2011).

Athletics may be overemphasized at the expense of academic achievement by the families and communities of African American males. Athletic role models may be especially esteemed, and sports may be seen as routes to college scholarships and professional careers (Beamon, 2010; Howard-Hamilton, 1993).

Application

The majority of African Americans are involuntary immigrants due to slavery in the U.S. prior to 1865. Voluntary immigrants realize higher academic achievement than do involuntary immigrants. For example, Black male college students from Africa and the Caribbean interacted more effectively in classrooms than did African American students. Perhaps the foreign-born students are more accepting of the White middle-class norms of classrooms (Ogbu & Simons, 1998). Their families also provide more support for academic progress (Williamson, 2010).

MOTIVATIONAL ORIENTATION AND ETHNICITY

The **motivational orientation** of sportspersons of several ethnic groups and cultures differ. Mexican American and Navajo adolescents are more likely to focus on the amount of effort exerted and improvement in comparison to one's baseline of prior performance when evaluating successful performance. This focus is consistent with a task orientation to motivation. Task orientations were discussed in Chapter 9, and to review briefly, they refer to evaluating performance in terms of improvement relative to prior performance, the amount of effort exerted, and the fulfillment of individual potential. Navajo and Mexican American adolescents also focus on their contribution to group or team success to a greater degree than American adolescents of European descent. European American adolescents more commonly focus on ego goals or judge success in relation to outperforming others. Evidence of task orientations among Mexican American adolescents contradicts theory (Ryska, 2001) that a cultural ideal of *machismo* disposes Hispanic males to adopt particularly strong ego orientations in an effort to prove themselves superior to male counterparts. Machismo refers to an exaggerated sense of masculinity, stressing attributes such as courage and aggressiveness.

Individual members of ethnic groups within the U.S. are not monolithic or identical in terms of acculturation, or the adaptation of values, attitudes, and behaviors consistent with mainstream culture in the U.S. Acculturation among Mexican Americans is typically measured on the basis of language use (English versus Spanish), use of media in English versus Spanish, and the ethnic identities of friends and associates (Kontos, 2012; Marin, 1993).

Although it may be expected that Mexican American adolescents who are more acculturated would more strongly endorse ego goals, evidence of this is available only for females. However, the motivation for athletic participation among female and male American-born adolescents of Chinese descent was more similar to non-Chinese American counterparts than to adolescents in China (Yan & McCullagh, 2004). The American-born adolescents participated for the experience of competition and skills improvement, while the adolescents in China worked at getting fit and socializing.

The influence of motivational climates extends beyond shaping goal orientations (Duda, 1985). In Greece, physical education students with ego orientations, and who functioned in motivational climates that encouraged comparisons between students, were less interested in interacting with members of other ethnic groups. Minority students also felt marginalized or not comfortable with their ethnic group or the larger Greek society. Task-oriented environments, as well as individual task orientations, promoted mutual understanding and respect for individuals of different ethnic groups, and promoted cross-cultural education (Kouli & Papaioannou, 2009).

Korean middle school athletes were shown to score higher in ego orientations and lower on task orientations and intrinsic interest in sport than did their American counterparts (Kim, Williams, & Gill, 2003). These differences were significant but small, and the motivational climates for sport in the U.S. and Korea may be different. Admission to high schools is limited in Korea, and athletic excellence provides a route for winning admission. Korean middle school athletes, therefore, compete for limited seats in high school. Chinese college students also registered higher scores on scales of ego orientations and lower scores for task orientations than did their American counterparts (Gao, Ziang, Harrison, Guan, & Rao, 2008).

Perhaps distinct task and ego orientations are not evident in Eastern cultures. Among Chinese college students, there was evidence of a somewhat undifferentiated and vehement drive for achievement, and high scores for task orientations were correlated with high scores for ego orientations and self-efficacy (Gao et al., 2008). The correlates of ego and task orientations may also differ across cultures. Persistence in learning sport skills was correlated with ego orientations among Chinese collegians and with task orientations for Americans. Self-efficacy was correlated with this persistence among both groups.

ETHNICITY AND COPING STRATEGIES

The strategies used by national level athletes in Korea to cope with the stress of competition overlapped with those of U.S. Olympic wrestlers (Gould, Eklund, & Jackson, 1993) and U.S. National Champion figure skaters (Gould, Finch, & Jackson, 1993). The most frequently cited coping strategy by the Korean athletes (97.2%) was mental training, including visualization, meditation, and a category defined as psyching-up that included positive self-talk (Park, 2000). The Korean athletes also cited somatic relaxation, including stretching and sleeping, focusing on training and strategies during competition, hobbies, and prayer, as coping strategies. Meditation techniques such as Zen, breath control, and contemplation are practiced more frequently in Eastern countries, such as Korea, Japan, India, and China.

Also consistent with the coping responses of Americans, Korean athletes engaged in forms of problem-focused, emotion-focused, and avoidance-focused coping. Additionally, Korean athletes may engage in a form of transcendent coping or give up their own efforts to control events in the face of adversity and turn their destiny over to the course of nature (Yoo, 2000). Both avoidance-focused and transcendent coping are described as indirect and passive ways of managing stress in a detached manner (Yoo & Park, 1998a, 1998b). Elite, as opposed to state and local level, Korean athletes were more likely to engage in transcendent coping, perhaps because the elite athletes practiced Zen meditation or Confucian philosophy (Yoo, 2001).

Continuing, highly skilled adolescent tennis players from Mexico and the U.S. rated the disapproval of coaches and spectators as important sources of stress in matches. Mexican adolescents were more likely to identify potential injury as a source of stress and U.S. adolescents focused on opponent's cheating. While Mexican adolescents were more likely to use both problem- and emotion-focused coping strategies, cultural differences were relatively small (Puente-Diaz & Anshel, 2005).

ATTRIBUTIONS AND ETHNICITY

Navajo and Mexican American adolescents have been seen to be more likely to attribute athletic success to effort and failure to inadequate ability (Duda, 1986; Duda & Allison, 1982). European American adolescents have been seen to be more likely to attribute success to ability and failure to a lack of effort. Native Americans adolescent athletes may understand the causes of success and failure to be less internal and controllable because of cultural values that define success in terms of group and team performance (Morgan, Griffin, & Heyward, 1996).

SELF-TALK AND CULTURE

East Asian and European American students have been shown to differ in the proportion of negative to positive self-talk during a dart-throwing task (Peters & Williams, 2006). East Asian college students engaged in a higher proportion of negative self-talk. However, unlike their European American counterparts, poorer performances were not associated with higher proportions of negative self-talk among the East Asians. Perhaps negative self-talk reflects a fear of future failure that is detrimental to the performance of European Americans and those who emanate from individualistic cultures, and beneficial to performance of East Asians and those from a collectivist cultural background. As mentioned in the above section on motivational orientation, the culture of European Americans has been said to emphasize individual accomplishments. East Asian culture has been seen to focus on the relationships of individuals within a group.

STEREOTYPES AND SPORT

Racial **stereotypes** in sport represent overgeneralized beliefs about the sources of athletic ability or aptitude. Among the problems associated with stereotypes is the fact that they potentially interfere with performance on evaluations (Steele, 1997). This interference occurs when individuals becomes concerned that their performance will confirm a negative stereotype. That is, individuals develop expectations that their performance is likely to be poor and, therefore, confirm the negative stereotype that their racial or ethnic group has less ability than others. Negative stereotypes are not confined to explanations of ethnic differences, as concern about confirming negative stereotypes have also been shown to have debilitating effects on the performance of women in areas of mathematical reasoning (Spencer, Steele, & Quinn, 1999).

Hostile Native American Images

The NCAA banned schools with mascots or nicknames deemed hostile or abusive to Native Americans from NCAA championship competitions effective February 1, 2006. Upon appeal, three schools were permitted to continue using nicknames of specific tribes, because the affiliated tribes supported the use of these names: Central

Michigan (Chippewas), Florida State (Seminoles), University of Utah (Utes; Davis, 2005, Lederman, 2005). The University of North Dakota was denied an appeal to continuing using Fighting Sioux as a nickname after it was concluded that the majority of the Sioux tribes opposed its use. The NCAA also denied appeals to use nicknames that referred to Native Americans as a group, such as the Indians (seven colleges), Braves (two colleges), Redmen (Carthage College), and Savages (Southeastern Oklahoma State University). Specific names of tribes were seen to be owned by the tribe, whereas names that made general reference to Native Americans were not considered the property of tribes and to present the potential for hostile and abusive imagery.

Theories about ethnic differences in athletic aptitude have been published since the 1880s. Social scientists, medical doctors, biologists, and most notably, coaches have advanced these theories (Wiggins, 1997). Over the years, theory and lore have focused on differences between Black and White athletes, and have forwarded notions that the dominance of Black athletes in some sports was due to genetic advantage. For example, in 1971, Martin Kane, a senior editor of *Sports Illustrated*, wrote "An assessment of 'Black is best' " in which he gave voice to lay or unscientific theories of Social Darwinism. According to these theories, the Africans that survived the oppression of slavery in the U.S. possessed superior physical traits, and the less physically capable were casualties of slavery. Since only the more physically capable and superior survived to produce offspring, it was argued that superior athletic aptitude was genetically transmitted to ensuing generations.

Of course, an alternative explanation for the survival of slavery would be that superior intelligence and character were necessary (Edwards, 1973). Continuing within the context of Social Darwinism, Africans with superior intellect and character would survive slavery, produce offspring, and superior intellect would be genetically transmitted to subsequent generations.

The ascendancy of Black athletes in sport is perhaps best considered in historical context. Black athletes were denied access to sport venues in the U.S. in the 20th century, and the color barrier was only broken in Major League Baseball in 1947 when Jackie Robinson assumed the field for the Brooklyn Dodgers. Even after the introduction of athletes of African descent, an implicit quota called the "50% color line" existed (Kahn, 1971). This quota limited the number of Blacks to four of the starting nine members of a baseball team. This color line was breached with the Brooklyn Dodgers in 1954. Jim Brown, a member of the National Football League (NFL) Hall of Fame, maintained that when he entered the NFL in 1957 there was a quota of no more than eight Blacks on a team roster (Brown & Delsohn, 1989). A mere twenty-four years after Black men began playing professional baseball, sportswriters pondered whether "Black is Best" (Kane, 1971). In the 1984 Summer Olympic Games in Los Angeles, Blacks won 40 of the 49 medals awarded in track and field, and 10 of 11 medals awarded in boxing to Americans. Women and men of African descent hold world records in track and field events that require speed and explosive power, and have held these records for at least 40 years (Ashe, 1993). Africans have more recently dominated distance running events.

Consumer Discrimination against Black College Basketball Players

Economists have determined that attendance at Division I college basketball games increases with the addition of Caucasian players. In the 1988-89 season, Division I schools had an average of seven African American and six Caucasian players. The addition of one Caucasian player to this average ethnic distribution resulted in the realization of more than $100,000 in additional annual gate revenues (Brown & Jewell, 1994). This consumer discrimination among largely Caucasian audiences may motivate college basketball programs to discriminate against African Americans in awarding scholarships. Denying minority and low-income students college scholarships is particularly harmful, as they already have more limited employment opportunities.

More recently, consumer discrimination was seen to be minimal among NBA fans. However, there is price discrimination among the management of NBA teams, as African American players are paid significantly less than are Caucasian players of equivalent ability (McCormick & Tollison, 2001).

In Major League Baseball (MLB), attendance has increased with the addition of players born outside of the United States. At its peak in 2000, the addition of an additional foreign-born player to team rosters resulted in $595,632 in additional stadium revenue. In 2000, the average MLB teams fielded 10.78 foreign-born players on rosters, and their presence resulted in an additional $6,000,000 in revenue (Tainsky & Winfree, 2010).

Implicit in theories of athletic superiority of Africans is the understanding that other races such as Caucasians possess less athletic ability (Powell, 2008). Continuing with these genetic theories or stereotypes, skilled or superior athletic performance among Whites is understood to be more the result of effort, training, and mental preparation and practice rather than natural ability. These concepts have been popularized in films such as "White Men Can't Jump" and "Hoop Dreams."

Disrespecting Larry Bird by Guarding Him with White Players

"I really got irritated when they put a White guy on me." "Come on, you got a White guy coming out here to guard me, you got no chance." "As far as playing, I don't care who guarded me, red, yellow, black, I just didn't want a White guy guarding me. Because it's disrespect to my game" (Caesar, 2004, p. C7).

These comments by NBA Hall of Fame player and president of the Indiana Pacers, Larry Bird, reflect his belief that "the greatest athletes in the world are African American." Bird, who is White, opined that basketball "is a Black man's game, and will be forever" (Caesar, 2004, p. C7).

These stereotypes are widespread. College football coaches rated African American athletes as having better speed, quickness, and achievement motivation, and Caucasians as more reliable and mentally facile (Williams & Youssef, 1975). African and European American college students endorsed similar beliefs (Sailes, 1993). The effects of expectations about athletic ability and race were also illustrated in a recent study in which White adults listened to the broadcast of a basketball game. Half of the listeners were informed that a very successful player was Black and the other half were led to believe that the player was White. Despite the fact that all the listeners heard the same broadcast, those that thought the player was White attributed success to "court smarts" and "hustle" rather than to natural athletic ability. When the player was thought to be Black, success was attributed to natural ability and less to court smarts and hustle (Stone, Perry, & Darley, 1997). Moreover, the player was considered better when thought to be Black.

Negative Stereotypes and Performance

Negative stereotypes have been shown to affect the athletic performance of African Americans. The accuracy of African American college students at putting golf balls decreased significantly when they were prompted to think that putting measured their sports intelligence or even when they were required to indicate their race prior to putting (Stone, Lynch, Sjomeling, & Darley, 1999). Instructions that putting was a measure of natural athletic ability had no effect on putting accuracy. Just the opposite effects were found for White college students when given instructions that putting measured sports intelligence, natural athletic ability, or when required to indicate race. White college students were shown to hold negative stereotypes about their athletic ability, and this belief diminished their putting accuracy.

Stereotypes about athletic and other abilities only present a threat when ability represents an area that is important to one's self-worth or self-esteem. In the case of the White college students, instructions that putting accuracy was a measure of natural athletic ability impaired the performance of only those whose self-worth was determined partially from their athletic achievement.

Negative stereotypes provoke self-doubts or worries that one's performance will confirm a negative stereotype. This worry represents a form of cognitive interference. As discussed in Chapters 6 and 11, cognitive interference disrupts attention to the tasks necessary for optimal performance.

Stereotypes?

Despite being drafted in the third round, Bill Romanowski has experienced considerable success in the National Football League (NFL). In his 16 years as a linebacker, he has played for two Super Bowl Championship teams in San Francisco and two with the

Denver Broncos. His effort for a fifth Super Bowl win fell short in 2003 as his Oakland Raiders team lost in the Super Bowl. His commitment to physical training has been equaled perhaps only by Jerry Rice, a future Hall of Fame receiver and arguably the best ever at his position. Off-season training was shown to include three hours on a track refining sprint mechanics, thirty minutes of swimming, and three hours of weight training (Murphy, 1998).

Efforts to boost performance includes more than physical training. His regimen of nutritional supplements prompted teammates to nickname him Rx (shorthand for prescription; Yaeger, 2000). On August 9, 2000, a Colorado grand jury handed down a felony indictment charging Romanowski with using family and friends to acquire phentermine, a diet drug. Used in sufficient doses, the effects of phentermine mimic amphetamines. Family and friends acquired upward of 500 phentermine pills, and ephedrine was also delivered to Romanowski's Colorado home. No one denied that the drugs were for Romanowski. Romanowski was acquitted of these charges. In November 2003, the NFL notified Romanowski that he tested positive for the steroid THG, or tetrahydrogestrinone, and in 2005, he acknowledged that he stayed one step ahead of the NFL drug policy by taking supplements that were not yet banned (Associated Press, 2005, May 18).

Stimulants of this sort mask the experience of fatigue and pain and increase alertness and aggressiveness. Whether stimulant use was related to his fierce demeanor in games is a matter for speculation. Extracurricular aggression in games has included spitting in the face of wide receiver J. J. Stokes, repeatedly kicking running back Larry Centers in the helmet, breaking the jaw of quarterback Kerry Collins with a helmet-to-helmet hit in a preseason game, and tearing the helmet off teammate Marcus Williams and punching him in the face so as to break the left eye socket (Associated Press, 2005, March 23). Romanowski was ordered to pay $340,000 for damages that ended the career of Williams.

A White teammate maintained that Romanowski reasoned that stimulant use was necessary for him to compete on a level playing field with African American players: "They're faster and stronger, and we have to take advantage of this. It is the only way we can compete with the Black guys" (Yaeger, p. 28). Romanowski's lawyer denied that his client said anything about Black players. The results of a recent NCAA survey (2001) demonstrated similar levels of use of ergogenic substances such as anabolic-androgenic steroids among Caucasian (1.3%) and African American (1.6%) athletes. Ergogenic substances are (see Chapter 16) are taken to enhance performance, and many of these substances, such as amphetamines, violate rules for athletic competition

COACHES' RESPONSES AND ETHNIC DIFFERENCES

Do coaches demonstrate biases in responding to athletes of different ethnic groups? This question has been addressed, but not answered convincingly. For example, the coaching interventions of college coaches of female and male basketball players were studied (Solomon et al., 1996).

The gender of the coaches was not specified, and the responses of female and male basketball players were pooled. Coaches provided less praise and more instruction to players of African versus European descent. Technical instruction consists of advice about how to improve action and encouragement involves comments that the athlete can be successful. Whether this difference is due to a stereotype about ethnicity is a matter for speculation. The finding that coaches provided African American players with more technical instruction would appear inconsistent with the stereotype that the skilled performance of athletes of African descent is due to natural ability.

An alternative explanation is that the differences in coaching interventions were stimulated by actual differences in basketball abilities. Coaches provided more instruction to the basketball players who they rated as having the highest ability. Of the eight players rated with the highest ability, seven were African American (Solomon et al., 1996). Less instruction and praise were given to the less-talented players, as coaches rationed disproportionate amounts of time to more talented athletes.

AFRICAN AMERICAN FOOTBALL PLAYERS AND REACTIONS TO COACHES

The responses of African American football players to coaches are not always apparent, as demonstrated with African American football players at a Division I program in the southwestern U.S. The head coach and nine assistant coaches were White, and one assistant coach was African American. The coaches were perceived as insensitive to the individual and sociocultural interests of the African American athletes, and also as not objectively assessing their skill. The athletes reported a lack of communication and trust. They did not think that their coaches understood their background, family, and culture. There was a suspicion of unfair treatment on the basis of race. The African American coach was seen as an extension of the White coaching staff. African American collegiate athletes are also sensitive to the underrepresentation of African Americans in athletic administrations (Agyemang, Singer, & DeLorme, 2010).

The African American football players did not respond well to harsh criticism, and wanted coaches to earn their respect. These football players said that a greater portion of their self-esteem was drawn from their athletic performance, and harsh criticism and limited playing time was therefore more threatening to their self-esteem and confidence. These athletes were embarrassed and decreased rather than increased subsequent efforts in response to harsh criticism. As explained by one player, "When the coach yells at me, that's it. I feel no motivation; I don't want to have anything to do with it" (Anshel, 1990, p. 241).

Some believed that personal accomplishments were more important than team accomplishments. They preferred pregame preparation strategies that were subdued and individualized, as opposed to their coach's pregame talks and coaching instructions (Anshel, 1990). Compared to White players, African American footballers considered coaches to be too authoritarian and untrustworthy, and were unhappier if their team won but they played poorly (Anshel & Sailes, 1990).

The mental skills employed by the African American and Caucasian players differed. The African American footballers reported that they ignored or minimized the importance of scouting reports, coaching instructions, and pregame talks. They did not want to get caught up in these "head games," and prepared by focusing on their own internal responses rather than on the coach's instructions. They believed that coaches underestimated their achievement motivation because they responded to the demands of competition in a less intense and emotionally demonstrative way.

An independent group of African American football players rated mental preparation as less significant in determining the outcome of competition. They emphasized the importance of physical preparation, and showed fewer tendencies to engage in introspection (Nation & LeUnes, 1983). They felt more confident of performing well even when depressed, were less likely to brood over past poor performances, and attributed athletic outcomes to physical rather than psychological factors.

It is unlikely that all or perhaps the majority of athletes who are members of ethnic minorities are equally uncomfortable and suspicious of White coaches. However, sport psychologists and professional psychologists are ethically obliged to be knowledgeable and sensitive to differences on the bases of ethnicity, culture, gender, physical disabilities, sexual orientation, and socioeconomic differences, and to avoid bias on the basis of any of these factors (American Psychological Association, 2002; Association for the Advancement of Applied Sport Psychology, 1994). Being knowledgeable about and open to the discussion of racial and cultural differences has been seen as important in developing effective working alliances between sport psychologists and clients (Cogan & Petrie, 1996; Petrie, 1998).

Ethics and Differences

The ethical code of the Association for Applied Sport Psychology (Association for the Advancement of Applied Sport Psychology, 1994) is based in large part on the Ethical Principles of the American Psychological Association (2002). Both codes of ethics emphasize competence or the limitation of practice to areas in which the psychologist has received training, education, or experience.

The ethical codes mandate that psychologists are aware of cultural, individual, and role differences, including those due to gender, ethnicity, race, religion, sexual orientation, language, disability, and socioeconomic status.

African American Athletes and Responses to Sport Psychologists

As mentioned in Chapter 1, African American and male Division I intercollegiate athletes were particularly uncomfortable with the prospect of accessing help from sport psychologists, as they feared being stigmatized by consulting sport psychologists (Martin, Wrisberg, Beitel, & Lounsbury, 1997). The stigma consists of being cast or viewed as someone with mental disorders or problems. These athletes estimated that coaches and teammates would think less of them and perhaps harass them if they received the services of a sport psychologist. The African American athletes indicated that they would be more comfortable consulting a sport psychologist of their own race, and African Americans are also more mistrustful of Caucasian counselors (Watkins, Terrell, Miller, & Terrell, 1989). Hispanics, Asian Americans, and Native Americans also tend to access professional counseling to a lesser degree than do Caucasian Americans (Kontos & Breland-Noble, 2002).

BECOMING KNOWLEDGEABLE ABOUT ETHNIC DIFFERENCES

This issue of becoming knowledgeable about ethnic differences is not straightforward, because the scientific bases for this literature are often limited, and, therefore, students from different cultures are often not certain if the information is accurate, is accurate for subsets of cultural communities, or if it reinforces stereotypes. For example, in contrast to Anshel's (1990) findings that African American athletes approached competition with less demonstration of emotion, Lee and Rotella (1991) argued that "Black expressiveness," "soul," and "core Black experience" is characterized by a high degree of emotion expression and a merging of thought, emotion, and movement. Adding to this distinction of emotional expressiveness is the contention that African American athletes have not only the goal of winning, but also the goal of stamping performances with elements of their own individual stylistic flair (Kochman, 1981). Coaches also rated African American athletes higher than Caucasians on exhibitionism (as well as impulsivity, and lower on orderliness, understanding, and abasement; Chu, 1982).

No Espresso, Ever

Jurgen Klinsmann, the coach of the U.S. national soccer team and former coach of the German national team, played professionally in Germany, England, and Italy. In his view, the style of play of the national team should reflect the mentality and culture of the U.S. (Futterman, 2011):

[In Germany before the 2006 World Cup] everybody was in the same boat. We said the only way was we got to attack we got to go forward, maybe it's in our DNA, maybe it was wrongfully in our DNA in two world wars. Who knows that? I don't know; I was not even born yet. But I just said we Germans, we can't take just defending, just sitting back, and waiting and countering. We're not good at that. We need to take things into our own hands. We are a hard-working nation, we are doers. We can't react to whatever happens. The Italians, they react, they sit back, they relax, they have a nice espresso, and they say, "O.K., now, once you make your wrong move, [we] are going to counter-break and kill you."

I can't come with my German approach and say this is how I want to do it in the U.S., because in the U.S., it would fail. I have certain experiences in different countries, I can understand many connections there, but I have to do it the way it is best for the players here, not how I would like to have it if I were somewhere else (Futterman, 2013).

Perhaps both stoicism and emotional expressiveness are integrated among African American male athletes in a "cool pose" (Majors, 1998). The cool pose was seen as a response by African American males to their experience of less socioeconomic status than that of Caucasians. With the demonstration of both unflappability and expressive styles of demeanor, gestures, and speech, the cool pose was seen to imply strength, uniqueness, and masculinity.

Some African American athletes of previous generations were especially aware that their behavior might be scrutinized by Caucasians, and were, therefore, especially careful to present a restrained and dignified image. Their current counterparts may experience a pull to manifest "street cred" (credibility) or rebelliousness, exhibitionism, and unwillingness to conform to the norms of mainstream American culture (Powell, 2008).

Jalen Rose: Duke "Uncle Toms"

In a television documentary about Michigan's "fab five" basketball team, the film's African American executive producer, and one of the fab five, Jalen Rose, stated that Duke recruited only African American players he considered "Uncle Toms." To be labeled an Uncle Tom is inflammatory, as it refers to Black subservience to Caucasians.

Grant Hill, a member of the Duke Basketball team that defeated the fab five in the 1992 Final Four, responded that Rose's hint that African Americans who grow up two-parent households and who excel academically are "less Black" [sic] is "beyond ridiculous." "I caution my fabulous five friends to avoid stereotyping me and others they do not know in much the same way so many people stereotyped them back then for their appearance and swagger" (Hill, 2011).

There is also some empirical support for an interest in expression of individual flair in performances among African American high school track athletes, and it does not appear to be in conflict with adaptive motives for achievement (Gano-Overway & Duda, 1999). However, this interest in expressing individual flair is only slightly higher for African American than for European American track athletes, and this interest in stylistic expression was likewise not in conflict with adaptive goals among the European Americans.

The culture of European Americans has also been seen to be consonant with independence, efforts to be unique and distinct from others, and the demonstration of success in comparison to others. Cultural differences between European American and Native Pacific Islanders in Hawaii and European Americans from the mainland of the U.S. have also been considered. Hawaiians, regardless of ethnic heritage, have been considered to share aspects of culture. The Hawaiian culture was considered to emphasize interdependence, affiliation with others, and harmony within one's reference group (Hayashi, 1996). However, the reasons for recreational weightlifting were much the same among Hawaiian and mainland European American males. They all demonstrated interest in maintaining interpersonal bonds with other weightlifters. They lifted for a variety of goals, such as demonstrating improvement in relation to their own baseline of fitness and to look better than others. The Hawaiians were more humble and shunned showing off or "acting."

Shared culture of sport

Perhaps this study also illustrates how shared activities bring together people with similar interests, experiences, and goals, regardless of their ethnic and cultural backgrounds. Alternatively, the common psychological characteristics of these weightlifters may have been shaped by the shared experience of weightlifting. These weightlifters were approximately 27 years of age, and the average number of years of weightlifting was in excess of fifteen years.

MULTICULTURAL TRAINING IN SPORT PSYCHOLOGY

Multicultural training consists of formal learning experiences for graduate students or professionals in sport psychology or counseling. The goal of this training is to prepare students for more effective counseling and consulting services to clients of different ethnic and cultural groups. Multicultural training may also involve instruction and experience in providing counseling services to lesbian/gay/bisexual/transgendered and disabled clients (American Psychological Association, 2003; American

Psychological Association, 2012; Mio, Barker-Hackett, & Tumambing, 2006). One way of accomplishing this is with a formal curriculum in graduate school with textbooks, classroom discussion, and supervised applied experience (Gill & Kamphoff, 2009; Martens, Mobley, & Zizzi, 2000).

In addition to learning about different cultures, a multiculturally competent counselor strives to understand how culture influences client expectations for the counseling relationship. These competent counselors and consultants should be open to considering how their own beliefs, values, and biases influence their perceptions of clients and clients' problems. Given this understanding of themselves and clients, multiculturally competent sport consultants should intervene in ways that are culturally relevant and sensitive (Sue, 2006).

Bad Multicultural Training

As the public relations director for the NFL's San Francisco 49ers, Kirk Reynolds produced a video to coach players about how to handle media questions in diverse San Francisco. In the video, Reynolds impersonated San Francisco Mayor Gavin Newsom and officiated at a topless lesbian wedding and a 49ers trainer traveled to Chinatown to make ethnic slurs about Chinese. Team owners John York fired Reynolds, calling the video offensive and inexcusable. York stated: "Ostensibly, the video was created to raise player awareness about how to deal with the media and to demonstrate by example how poor conduct can unintentionally make news. Unfortunately, this video is an example in itself" (Associated Press, 2005, June 2, C7).

PRACTICAL ADVICE

Are the methods of sport psychologists dominated by "white middle-class approaches to thinking" (Lee & Rotella, 1991, p. 365), which depend on logical analysis and the isolation of thought and emotion? Are these methods viewed by different cultural and racial groups with suspicion and concern that it will "tie them up in knots" (Lee & Rotella, 1991, p. 365)? Perhaps the best way of answering these questions is to ask the athletes and determine whether the athletes utilize the suggestions of consultants.

To avoid stereotyping, it is important to remember that any of the differences described above pertain only for ethnic or cultural groups as a whole, and not necessarily for the individual members of that group (Andersen, 1993; Murphy, 2005; Parham, 2005). For example, while it may be true that some evidence exists that European American football players rated mental skills as more important than did their African American counterparts, it would be misleading to consider athletes of European descent to be generally interested and conscientious in the practice of mental skills (Shambrook & Bull, 1999).

> ### Application
>
> Helpers, such as sport consultants, are not infrequently reluctant to address sources of discomfort in relationships. However, unless and until these concerns are identified and ameliorated, counseling and consultation is not likely to be effective. Without this resolution, the helper and perhaps the client is likely to be incongruent or somewhat inauthentic in the helping relationship (Hill, 2009).
>
> Effective consultants examine their biases and also help clients to talk about discomfort due to the ethnic and cultural status of the helper. These skills are best developed with supervision from senior mentors.

Regardless of racial, cultural, and gender differences, successful consultations depend on the development of effective working alliances. Effective working alliances are more likely when athletes trust and believe that the consultant's interest is in helping the athlete reach her or his potential. Trust is fostered by efforts to learn about and understand the whole person who is also an athlete, and this includes differences due to culture and gender. There may be more impediments to trust in relationships between Caucasian consultants and African American athletes, as the latter may be socialized to expect racism and bias (Agyemang et al., 2010; Butryn, 2002; Peters, 1981).

Caucasian consultants are advised to be sensitive to their own biases, such as beliefs that athletes of African descent achieve eminence through natural ability in place of mental skills and effort, and that their "whiteness" has no effect on athletes of other ethnic groups (Butryn, 2002; Cogan & Petrie, 2002). Sport psychologists have been encouraged to consider whether they share the values and worldviews of the ethnically diverse athletes with whom they consult (Kontos & Breland-Noble, 2002: Parham, 2005; Sue & Sue, 1999). It is generally not sufficient to ignore potential cultural differences by claiming "color blindness." Regardless of whether the consultant is entirely comfortable with athletes of all ethnic and cultural groups, clients or athletes may be uneasy with consultants with different cultural backgrounds. If the discomfort of clients and athletes is ignored, they are more likely to discontinue the consulting relationship (Peters & Williams, 2009).

Ethnic and cultural considerations should not obscure the presenting problem or the reason the athlete consulted the sport psychologist (Kontos & Breland-Noble, 2002). Ethnic and cultural concerns should be considered in context with the presenting problem.

Finally, sport psychologists may advocate within institutions when racism is identified (Cogan & Petrie, 2002). Examples of this advocacy include providing diversity training with coaches and management and working to end discrimination in recruitment and hiring. African American athletes are sensitive to the relative dearth of African Americans in leadership positions within athletic departments and as academic counselors. They often do not have sufficient financial resources for incidental expenses during the academic year (Singer, 2009).

SUMMARY AND APPLICATION

In proclaiming 2005 as the International Year for Sport and Physical Education, United Nations Secretary-General Kofi Annan described sport as a "universal language" and a force for unifying people irrespective of their origin, background, or religious beliefs ("Universal language," 2005). The study of ethnic differences in sport psychology is in its nascent or beginning stages. As this study progresses, the responses of sportspersons may be shown to be increasingly similar or dissimilar across ethnic and cultural groups.

The beneficial effects of sport are similar for African, European, and Hispanic American high school students. High school athletes realized higher academic achievement and academic self-confidence, and better self-concepts. African and European collegiate athletes also demonstrated comparable life satisfaction as they prepared for graduation, and well-being was lower for those without plans for careers after college.

Differences in motivational orientations have been noted for Navajo, Mexican, and European American adolescent sportspersons. The Navajo and Mexican adolescents were more likely to acknowledge task orientations. However, they also attributed failure to a lack of ability and success to effort more frequently than did their European counterparts. Task orientations are adaptive in sustaining effort, as progress is measured in relation to the individual's baseline of prior performance. The attribution of failure to internal, global, and uncontrollable factors, such as a lack of talent, do not promote persistent effort in response to failure. It was also noted that more recent research indicated that Mexican American males were more likely to endorse ego goals or orientations.

There is little disagreement about the detrimental effects of negative stereotypes on performance both in athletic and academic venues. African and European Americans, as well as women, have been negatively affected by stereotypes. Stereotypes appear to interfere with performance when individuals who are aware of the negative stereotypes think that they will perform ineptly and confirm the negative stereotypes. These thought processes resemble cognitive interference, a topic for Chapter 11.

The population of athletes is far more diverse than the population of sport psychologists, at least in the U.S. Athletes may be more comfortable consulting with a psychologist of their own race, and sensitivity to these concerns and historical and cultural differences by Caucasian psychologists is warranted. Trust is an essential element of the working alliances between psychologists and clients regardless of ethnicity, culture, gender, and socioeconomic status. The development of multicultural scholarship and competencies should be a component of graduate study in sport psychology.

Key Terms

Culture   471

Higher academic achievement   472

Motivational orientation   473

Stereotypes   476

Discussion Questions

Q1. How is culture differentiated from ethnicity?

Q2. Consider participation rates of African Americans in sports at all levels.

Q3. Consider the benefits of athletic participation across ethnic and cultural groups.

Q4. Is it possible to overemphasize sports, especially with African American males?

Q5. Review the motivational orientations of the ethnic groups identified in this chapter.

Q6. Consider ethnic differences in coping strategies.

Q7. Do the attributions about the causes of success and failure differ across ethnic and cultural groups?

Q8. Review ethnic differences in self-talk.

Q9. Describe stereotypes and their impact on performance.

Q10. Consider the responses of coaches to ethnic and cultural differences.

Q11. Review and evaluate the reactions of African American football players to coaching interventions.

Q12. What are the ethical obligations of sports psychologists when working with clients of different ethnic groups?

Q13. Consider the practical advice for working with people of different ethnic and cultural backgrounds.

Suggested Readings

Agyemang, K., Singer, J. N., DeLorme, J. (2010). An exploratory study of Black male college athletes' perceptions on race and athlete activism. *International Review for the Sociology of Sport, 45*, 419–435. doi: 10.1177/1012690210374691

Gao, Z., Xiang, P., Harrison, L., Jr., Guan, J., & Rao, Y. (2008). A cross-cultural analysis of achievement goals and self-efficacy between American and Chinese college students in physical education. *International Journal of Sport Psychology, 39*, 312–328.

Martens, M. P., Mobley, M., Zizzi, S. J. (2000). Multicultural training in applied sport psychology. *The Sport Psychologist, 14*, 81–97.

Powell, S. (2008). *Souled out?* Champaign, IL: Human Kinetics.

Smedley, A., & Smedley, B. D. (2005). Race as biology is fiction, racism as a social problem is real: Anthropological and historical perspectives on the social construction of race. *American Psychologist, 60,* 16–26.

Solomon, G. B., Wiegardt, P. A., Wayda, V. K., Yusuf, F. R., Kosmitzki, C., Williams, J., & Stevens, C. E. (1996). Expectancies and ethnicity: The self-fulfilling prophecy in college basketball. *Journal of Sport & Exercise Psychology, 18,* 83–88.

Stone, J., Lynch, C. I., Sjomeling, M., & Darley, J. M. (1999). Stereotype threat effects on Black and White athletic performance. *Journal of Personality and Social Psychology, 77,* 1213–1227.

Chapter 21

YOUTH AND SPORT

Youth and sport

"We believe in the power of play to unite and heal and provide development for children," said John McFarland of General Motors after the corporation agreed to buy 1.5 million One World Futbols and donate them to needy children. One World Futbols were developed by Tim Jahnigen, and financed by Rock and Roll Hall of Fame musician Sting. Jahnigen was moved to develop a practically

indestructible ball after viewing a documentary about children in Darfur who pursued their love of soccer with balls fashioned from garbage and string. One World Futbols are made of PopFoam, a type of hard foam made of ethylene-vinyl acetate. These fabricated balls were necessary because proper balls made of leather or rubber are easily punctured in the hardscrabble settings that double as soccer pitches.

One World Futbols withstood the stresses of these pitches in Rwanda, Haiti, and Iraq. A lion at the Johannesburg Zoo and a German shepherd were also unable to deflate these balls. Currently, 45,000 balls per month are shipped throughout the world.

Jahnigen hopes to distribute millions of these balls: "A child can play to their heart's content where there are no content [sic] hearts." McFarland, of General Motors, reflected: "We don't want to focus on the beautiful game, but what is beautiful about the game" (Belson, 2012).

Sport often serves important functions in the lives of children, families, and coaches. Many of the topics reviewed in this book have applications with children and adolescents. Furthermore, the etiologies of the factors that facilitate and inhibit performance were shown to often date to childhood. In this chapter, topics specific to sport participation by youth, or children and adolescents, will be examined. These topics include: the goals of youth sport, factors that promote and inhibit sport participation, stress associated with youth athletics, and coaching and leadership with youth.

Athletic participation is beneficial because it affords children and adolescents with opportunities for physical, psychological, social, and educational growth (Bailey et al., 2009; Smoll, 1998; Smoll & Cumming, 2006). Athletics promote weight control, academic achievement, school attendance, self-esteem, and self-efficacy (Faude et al., 2010; Taliaferro, Rienzo, & Donovan, 2010). Participation in sports may offer even more benefit than involvement in other structured activities, and appears responsible for less depression among sportspersons. Athletic participation is also more accessible than other out-of-school activities to youth who come from homes, schools, and neighborhoods that have fewer resources. These children and adolescents may not have opportunities to participate in activities such as Boy and Girl Scouts, performing arts, and school clubs. Sports may offer the most important form of structured activity to promote positive youth development among youth born to less privilege (Zarrett et al., 2009).

The social and emotional benefits conferred by athletic participation are especially impressive when adolescents engage in sports in combination with other structured extracurricular activities. This combination enhances confidence and the experience of connectedness to one's school (Linver, Roth, & Brooks-Gunn, 2009). Further, adolescent athletes are shielded somewhat from emotional upheaval resulting from athletic failures when their self-concept is not determined exclusively by their identity as an athlete. With self-concepts determined both by success on the ice and in the classroom, the most elite junior Canadian hockey players were less vulnerable to emotional ups and downs in their athletic careers (Gaudreau, Amiot, & Vallerand, 2009).

It may be surprising to realize that athletic participation prior to age 12 was not always considered to be beneficial in the U.S. Little League baseball was inaugurated in Williamsport, PA, in 1939, and with its success, it was recognized that sport was not overly strenuous for boys who were 12 years of age and younger. Little League is now an international organization with at least 2.5 million participants (Franklin, 1989), and softball programs for girls enroll approximately 400,000 players.

By the 1950s, it was recognized that physical activity programs in the U.S. were not sufficiently strenuous. American children were shown to be physically unfit in comparison to their European counterparts. In 1955, during the Eisenhower administration, the President's Council on Youth Fitness was established to promote youth fitness (Kraus & Hirschland, 1954).

Today, physical activity is a priority for counteracting childhood obesity (Faude et al., 2010; Morrow, Zhu, Franks, Meredith, & Spain, 2009). Obesity is a health epidemic in the U.S. that is "out of control" (Wadden, Brownell, & Foster, 2002, p. 520). For example, the National Health and Nutrition Examination Survey (NHANES) results for 2007 demonstrated that 48% of the children and adolescents in the U.S. were overweight or obese, as defined by a body mass index (BMI; kg/m^2) at or above the 85th percentile (Singh, Kogan, & van Dyck, 2010).

Sport represents the most popular form of structured activity for youth (Mahoney, Larson, Eccles, & Lord, 2005). Estimates are that 23 million youth in the U.S. between the ages of 5 and 16 participate in sports after school and another 6.5 million play sports that are sponsored by their schools (Participation Survey, 1999–2000). Approximately 76% of Canadians between the ages of 6 and 17 participate in at least one structured sport activity yearly (Guevremont, Findlay, & Kohen, 2008). The participation of females has increased markedly in the past thirty years, as in 1972–1973, 17.8% of young sportspersons were females and in 1999–2000, this figure had increased to 40%. These youth engage in traditional sports such as baseball, basketball, and swimming, as well as more regional sports such as rodeo and cross-country skiing (Ewing, Seefeldt, & Brown, 1996).

GOALS OF YOUTH SPORTS: THE FUNDAMENTAL GOAL

A fundamental goal of youth sport is to provide an **education experience** for the development of desirable psychological and physical qualities (Smoll, 1998; Smoll & Cumming, 2006). These life skills are useful not only in childhood or while engaged in sport. Some of these attributes are physical, such as improved fitness and athletic competence. Others are psychological, and these include leadership skills, discipline, respect for authority, and achievement motivation (Jones & Lavallee, 2009). Sport participation promotes the development of positive identities, or feelings of control and empowerment among young sportspersons. Feeling empowered, valued, and useful, youngsters are more likely to enjoy sport and be less susceptible to burnout (Strachan, Cote, & Deakin, 2009).

Sport provides venues for learning social skills, making friends, and spending time with family members (McCarthy & Jones, 2007). Young people sometimes seek to experience the excitement of sport, the challenge of competition, and the experience of success and winning (Keegan, Spray, Harwood, & Lavallee, 2010; Gould & Petlichkoff, 1988). Perhaps the most important reason that children engage in sport is to have fun (Smith & Smoll, 2002b).

The Fun of Golf in Sweden

In Sweden, it is impossible to play golf outdoors during the long, snowy winters. Yet, this country of 8.8 million produces a disproportionate number of elite professional female and male golfers.

This success is partially due to the efforts of the Swedish Golf Federation to promote golf as an inexpensive family sport. Golf club memberships are minimal, averaging $500 a year for adults and $200 for children. Players who cannot afford these fees can pay daily green fees. Entry fees for tournaments are $50, and the Swedish Golf Federation sponsors promising young golfers.

Swedish golf officials also make a conscious effort to avoid putting too much pressure on young golfers. Elite young golfers are not sequestered in golf academies, and practice sporadically and mostly indoors in winters. Lennart Larsson, the former administrator of junior golf at the Swedish Golf Federation commented, "We try to always remember to make it fun" (Echikson, 2008, p. R8).

The psychological benefits of sport are more readily realized in a caring environment. Children feel safe, supported, valued, and respected in caring environments (Gano-Overway et al., 2009; Newton et al., 2007). When treated with kindness, children express positive and negative emotion with less fear of ridicule. Adolescents free to express positive emotions are more likely to engage in prosocial behavior, such as concern for the well-being of others. Adolescent females who lack confidence for managing negative emotions are more likely to experience depression. With insight and efficacy, less time is spent brooding over anger, frustration, and disappointment (Bandura, Caprara, Barbaranelli, Gerbino, & Pastoreli, 2003).

Children and adolescents who experienced caring environments in five-week summer sport camps were more capable of expressing positive and negative emotions. The expression of positive emotions contributed to greater happiness and hope and to less sadness and depression. The expression of negative emotions contributed to the experience of hope. Perhaps those youngsters who do not overreact and dwell on the negative more readily consider that better times are ahead (Fry et al., 2012). The influence of coaches is instrumental in nurturing caring environments (Gould, Flett, & Lauer, 2012; Nicolas, Gaudreau, & Franche, 2011).

Application

Even in caring environments, some children become easily frustrated when skills are not readily mastered. Some also try the patience of instructors as they sulk and give in to exaggerated bouts of anger.

Instructors and parents who wish to keep children engaged in sport are advised to respond soon after a pattern of this sort is noticed. Children benefit when they understand that frustration is normal and universal when learning new skills. It is helpful to learn that almost everyone has similar frustrations when learning sport skills, and that everyone has to learn to deal with it. When young sportspersons "get a handle" on their frustration, they are in better shape to respond to technical advice regarding skill development. Instructors may then remain vigilant to praise success and to point out that successes and growth experiences make sport worth the work and frustration. Responses that tease and shame children are effective in getting children to stop displays of anger—as well as sport participation.

The psychological benefits of sport are also more likely to be realized in environments that create opportunities for positive interactions with teammates. In addition to encouraging affiliation with peers, these environments are more likely to promote the exertion of effort, self-referenced goals, and task orientations (see Chapter 9). In these environments, youthful athletes are more likely to demonstrate initiative, set goals, and develop personal and social skills (MacDonald, Cote, Eys, & Deakin, 2011).

Goals of Youth Sports: Public Health, Elite-Development, Sport Practices

In addition to this fundamental goal of youth sport, three additional goals have been recognized (Siedentop, 2002). These are the **public health goal,** the **elite-development goal,** and the goal of preserving and protecting the **sport practices.** Public health is enhanced when youth and adults exercise and play sports, and the practice of vigorous activities serves to prevent health problems. When the most talented and interested young athletes are encouraged to reach their athletic potential, elite-development goals are served. Varsity sport programs in U.S. high schools and colleges pursue elite-development goals, in that a select few make prestigious teams such as basketball.

Youth sport provides educational and recreational experiences and is differentiated from **professional sport.** The goal of the latter is to entertain and to produce income. Winning is fundamental to professional sport because it delivers an audience and this income. Winning is not the primary goal of youth sport, although success may be conceptualized as striving to win and putting forth maximum effort. The most important product of youth sport is the quality of the experience provided for the participants (Hanlon, 1994). Effective coaching and parental involvement begins with an understanding of the purpose of youth sport and its differentiation from professional sport.

Sport and Peer Relationships

A fundamental goal of youth sport is to encourage the development of social skills and friendships, and children who are competent at sport are more popular with peers. For example, boys in grades four through six rated being good at sports as most important in determining popularity among peers. The boys rated achieving good grades as the next most determinant of **popularity.** Girls in these grades rated having good grades followed by good sport achievement as most influential in determining popularity (Buchanan, Blankenbaker, & Cotton, 1976). The finding that boys identified sport competence as most important in determining popularity was replicated with boys between the ages of 8 and 13 (Chase & Dummer, 1992). Physical attractiveness or good looks and good grades followed skill in sport as the next most important factors. Girls in the same age group rated being pretty as most important, and sport and academic achievement followed good looks in their estimates of the sources of popularity with peers.

Relationships are often forged in the course of athletic participation. Female and male children and adolescents between the ages of 8 and 16, who were current or former participants in a university summer sports program, identified twelve dimensions of the relationship with their best friend in sports (Weiss, Smith, & Theeboom, 1996). Almost all of these young sportspersons rated companionship or spending time together as an important quality of this friendship. The friendship boosted the self-esteem of most of the youngsters. Friends helped each other with sport skills, schoolwork, and offered advice. The friends were often prosocial, in that they tried to be nice and to avoid being unkind to one another. Friendships had aspects of intimacy in that friends trusted each other with their thoughts and feelings. Best friends were loyal to one another, and like intimacy, loyalty indicates a deep emotional bond. Common interests, such as sports, were aspects of many of the friendships of these sportspersons. Finally, friends were esteemed for attractive psychological and physical qualities, because they provided emotional support, and because disagreements could be resolved with the best friend.

Children and adolescents who experience acceptance and friendship from teammates are more likely to continue athletic participation

(Ullrich, French, & Smith, 2009) and to emerge as team leaders. Team leaders also manifest strong work ethics and advanced levels of skills and tactical sport knowledge (Glen & Horn, 1993; Moran & Weiss, 2006; Wright & Cote, 2003).

The development of social skills begins in the relationship between the child and the parental figures. Children form internal representations of their consistent experiences with attachment figures, and these serve as models or cognitive maps for future relationships. Children that are securely attached—those who consistently experience parental figures as sources of comfort, support, and security—are more likely to expect other people to be responsive and helpful, and to see themselves as deserving to be treated well (Ainsworth, 1989). Children develop a generalized view of a "non-supportive world" (Ainsworth, Blehar, Waters, & Wall, 1978, p. 666) when their needs for safety, nurturance, and empathy are not met in parental relationships. Insecurely attached children often suffer from low self-esteem, as they reason that they do not merit these emotional resources.

Securely attached adolescent males on cricket or soccer teams in the United Kingdom were more popular with teammates. They were more likely to be socially skilled and to find relationships with teammates to be rewarding. They experienced intimacy, loyalty, self-esteem enhancement, and support in the relationship with their best friend on the team. They also viewed themselves as sharing interests and capable of resolving conflicts with best friends. Friendships were viewed most positively when both friends were securely attached to parental figures (Carr, 2009).

ENCOURAGING CHILDREN TO PARTICIPATE IN SPORT

Children come to value athletic participation and to develop confidence in their capacity to function well or adequately as sportspersons as a result of a number of influences (Dorsch, Smith, McDonough, 2009; Keegan et al., 2010). Parents are an important source of encouragement when they communicate their beliefs in the value of athletic participation and their expectations that their children will be competent sportspersons (Wiese-Bjornstal, LaVoi, & Omli, 2009). This encouragement is especially important, as children younger than 10 years of age are poor judges of their physical abilities (Toftegaard-Stoeckel, Groenfeldt, & Andersen, 2010). Parents who enjoy physical activity are more likely to encourage their children to participate in sport, and to provide opportunities for this participation. These encouraged children are more likely to develop confidence in their athletic aptitude. Boys are more likely to receive this encouragement from parents and to develop greater confidence in their athletic aptitude (Brustad, 1993). Closeness and affection is communicated when parents attend the sporting activities of their children (Turman, Zimmerman, Dobesh, 2009). Parental support buffers stress related to athletic performance (Van Yperen, 1995). Parents may also enjoy being involved in their children's athletic careers, and develop emotional ties to the parents of other athletes (Dorsch et al., 2009).

The majority of the parents of junior tennis players at tennis academies were rated by elite junior coaches as "supportive and very, very helpful" (Gould, Lauer, Rolo, Jannes, & Pennisi, 2008, p. 23). They emphasized a task focus in their children or improvement in relation to their own baseline of performance rather than in comparison to other children. They encouraged the total development of their child. This included character development, the advancement of social skills, and the emotional well-being of their children. They provided financial, logistical, and emotional support, and families were required to flex schedules to accommodate practices and tournaments. They often modeled sportspersonship and provided unconditional love and caring.

A minority of parents were overinvolved, overbearing, and pushy. They readily compared their children to others and emphasized winning. They behaved poorly in matches and interfered with the coaching process. Indeed, elite junior tennis coaches estimated that 35.9% of parents hurt their child's development in tennis (Gould, Lauer, Jannes, & Pennisi, 2006). Junior athletes who are poor sports are more likely to have parents who show poor sportspersonship (Authur-Banning, Wells, Baker, & Hegreness, 2009).

As mentioned in Chapter 17, it is possible for parents to push children "in a good way" (Udry et al., 1997, p. 376). This typically involves encouragement for self-improvement and giving maximum effort. When parental approval is contingent on defeating others, young athletes experience performance anxiety and fear of failure, and lose intrinsic interest in sport. Indeed, the more intensely parents emphasize ego-oriented goals (see Chapter 9), the greater the child's anxiety. However, even intense parental pressure for self-improvement, giving maximum effort, and for learning from mistakes, does not result in evaluative pressure and anxiety in young sportspersons. When parents create mastery climates by emphasizing self-referenced goals, young athletes experience greater control over the factors that determine success (O'Rourke, Smith, Smoll, & Cumming, 2011).

Application

Words like, "I can't wait to get to the pitch, court, or pool," are "music to the ears" of supportive parents and coaches. These words signal intrinsic motivation and interest in sport. When this interest is not apparent, promoting sport requires more thought and effort.

Children with close and affectionate attachments to parents are more likely to identify with their parents' interests. These parents have an easier job of promoting sport participation with direct encouragement and modeling. It is, nevertheless, important to help children find activities that best suit their interests and aptitudes. For example, a child may find golf impossibly difficult but volleyball relatively effortless.

In families where children are less closely and affectionately attached, children may respond to direct encouragement with indifference and even resistance. Under these circumstances, parents may be advised to help children discover that they like sport, and to think that it is "their idea." Children are more likely to make this discovery when they associate with other youngsters who participate in sport. This process is also kindled when children are exposed to media that conveys the opportunities for fun and development that sport offers. Interest is continued by coaches who nurture caring team environments.

The roles of parents in supporting athletic participation may differ at various stages in the athletic development of their children. For example, among elite junior Canadian female and male athletes in rowing and tennis, parents were responsible for getting their children involved with and encouraging the enjoyment of sport during the *sampling* years or prior to adolescence (Cote, 1999). Participation in a number of extracurricular activities and sports has been encouraged during the sampling years (Carlson, 1988, 1997). In the course of this sampling process, children are more likely to spend time with family members and other adults in the community such as coaches, and this promotes positive development in youth (Strachan et al., 2009; Wilkes, MacDonald, Horton, & Cote, 2009). Parents of future elite athletes may notice special gifts or natural talents in their children and especially encourage the development of these talents.

Generally, early specialization and "professional-like training" does not promote the development of elite athletes (Johnson, Tenenbaum, Edmonds, & Castillo, 2008). This generalization does not hold in sports such as diving, women's rhythmic gymnastics, and women's figure skating, where long hours of deliberate practice prior to age 16 is associated with elite performance (Deakin & Cobley, 2003; Law, Cote, & Ericsson, 2007; Stambulova, Stambulov, & Johnson, 2012; Wiese-Bjornstal et al., 2009). Deliberate practice consists of structured activities for the purpose of improving performance. It includes repetition, feedback to correct errors, and requires maximal effort and concentration (Ericsson, 2003; Ericsson, Krampe, & Tesch-Romer, 1993). Early specialization also results in overtraining injuries and decreased enjoyment of sport (Baker, Cobley, & Fraser-Thomas, 2009), and has been discouraged by the National Athletic Trainers' Association (McLeod et al., 2011).

Fun and excitement remain important reasons for athletic participation among elite athletes during the *specialization* years, or between the ages of 13 and 15 (younger for some sports such as gymnastics; Cote, 1999). However, elite athletes often increasingly focus on one or two sports and make increasing commitments to practice during these years. Parents devote more of their time and financial resources to support the increasing commitment of their children to sport, and mothers sacrifice engaging in competing social activities (Harwood & Knight, 2009; Wolfenden & Holt, 2005). Fathers of elite adolescent male soccer players were also important sources of informational support (Holt & Dunn,

2004). Many of these fathers were experienced soccer players and, therefore, capable of providing their sons with technical advice about soccer.

Athletes who achieve elite status may enter the *investment* years at approximately age 15 (perhaps younger in sports such as tennis; Wolfenden & Holt, 2005). This period is characterized by intense commitments to practice and the development of expertise in one sport. For example, the amount of accumulated practice necessary to become a professional soccer player was estimated to be 9,332 hours (Helsen, Starkes, & Hodges, 1998). This may also be a time of investment for parents and other family members, as the adolescent athlete's training and competition requirements may dominate the schedule of the entire family. Parents may need to ration their attention to avoid creating jealousy among siblings.

Sensitive parents help their elite adolescent athletes to balance intense athletic commitments with other priorities such as family life, academics, and friendships. This balance serves to reduce the pressure and increase the enjoyment experienced in competition. This balance is disrupted when parents adopt an all-encompassing emphasis on winning and make their love conditional on success. Sensitive parents may challenge their elite children to reach their full potential while recognizing that their child has ultimate "ownership" of their athletic careers (Harwood & Knight, 2009; Lauer, Gould, Roman, & Pierce, 2010; Scanlan et al., 2009). Maintaining this balance may require "emotional intelligence," as parents recognize when their children welcome challenge and structure because they do not possess the skills to regulate their own behavior.

Deliberate Play

In addition to formal practice, instruction and training under the tutelage of adults, it is important for children to engage in **deliberate play.** Deliberate play is a form of physical activity that is not supervised by adults and pursued because it is fun and enjoyable (Cote, Baker, & Abernethy, 2007). Children develop fitness and expertise in the course of playing, and learn to think for themselves. Elite Australian Rules football players who were expert decision makers spent more time in deliberate play as children than did their counterparts who were not as skilled in making decisions on the pitch (Berry & Abernethy, 2003). Children who engage in deliberate play are also more likely to develop intrinsic interest in sport and to obtain formal instruction in their teens. The importance of fun, creative play was also shown to be critical to the development of intrinsic interest and expertise among elite and sub-elite cricketers (Weissensteiner, Abernethy, & Farrow, 2009).

Perhaps extensive engagement in both deliberate practice and play at the same sport during the sampling or preadolescent years results in a sufficient balance of skill development, intrinsic interest, and fun (Ford, Ward, Hodges, & Williams, 2009). For example, members of elite English preadolescent soccer academies spent approximately 200 hours at deliberate practice and 50 hours in competition per year between the ages of 6 and 12. At age 16, those given professional scholarships to the soccer academies of the English Premier League logged approximately 300 hours of deliberate soccer play between the ages of 6 and 12; those not selected "played" at soccer for about 150 hours per year during this time period.

English soccer coaches for under-9, under-13, and under-16 of elite, sub-elite, and non-elite teams engaged in playing form activities for only a third of total practice times. Playing form activities resembles actual match play. The majority of practice time was given to training form activities, such as improving fitness and developing isolated technical skills. Coaches were also highly prescriptive in teaching technical skills and managing practice sessions (Ford, Yates, & Williams, 2010).

MENTAL SKILLS TRAINING WITH CHILDREN

The development of mental skills promotes the personal development of children and enhances motivation to engage in sport and physical activity across the life span (Weiss, 1991; Wiese-Bjornstal et al., 2009). The range of mental skills was discussed in Chapters 4, 5, and 6, and sport psychologists in Canada, Sweden, and the U.S. have taught many of these skills to children to help them function more effectively and with less stress and anxiety (Copeland, Bonnell, Reider, & Burton, 2009; Devonport, Biscomb, Lane, Mahoney, & Cassidy, 2005; Orlick & McCaffrey, 1991). The forms and functions of mental imagery are similar for children, young adolescents, and adults (Munroe-Chandler, Hall, Fishburne, & Strachan, 2007).

Mental skills are adapted to appeal to children, and are simplified and described in terms that children are likely to understand (McCarthy, Jones, Harwood, & Olivier, 2010; Visek, Harris, & Bloom, 2009). As is the case with adults, mental skills must be practiced regularly if they are to be reliable, and their practice is more likely if they are incorporated into practice schedules. The ongoing integration of mental skill and physical skill development is more certain if adults, such as assistant coaches, assume the responsibility of continuously reminding youthful athletes to engage in the practice of mental skills. This training is likely to be more successful if the parents of youthful sportspersons understand and support the procedures, and if they are in positions to prevent or reduce sources of stress in the lives of their children.

An example of a mental skill that was adapted for children is the **Spaghetti Toes** procedure (Orlick, 1992). This technique is a derivative of Progressive Muscle Relaxation (PMR), a technique described in Chapter 7. To illustrate the concept of tension, children are shown pieces uncooked and stiff spaghetti. The concept of relaxation is next illustrated with cooked and soft spaghetti. The children are then instructed to wiggle the toes on either foot and to then make the toes soft and sleepy and similar to cooked spaghetti lying on a plate. The wiggling is comparable to instructions in PRM to flex muscles and instructions to imagine cooked spaghetti corresponds to directions to relax muscles and experience tension flowing from muscles.

After wiggling and relaxing toes, this procedure is repeated with both legs, and the buttocks. Next, the procedure is applied to either set of fingers, and to either arm. Finally, children are asked to let their entire body become sleepy and warm like soft spaghetti. While relaxed, children are instructed that this relaxation technique may be utilized to respond to cognitive or physiological anxiety. Children are encouraged to think that they can become "the boss of your body by talking to it" (Orlick & McCaffrey, 1991, p. 325). Lastly, children are asked to repeat the flexing and relaxation procedure with their mouth, tongue, and eyebrows.

Adolescent athletes may spontaneously practice mental skills without professional intervention. For example, elite adolescent rugby union players in the United Kingdom engaged in goal setting, self-talk, and visualization (Holland, Woodcock, Cumming, & Duda, 2010). Adolescent athletes gain additional benefits from traditional programs in mental skills training as well as mental toughness training (Gucciardi, Gordon, & Dimmock, 2009a, 2009b). Mental toughness involves resistance to distractions, obstacles, adversity and pressure, and a hearty work ethic. It also includes the capacity to sustain concentration and motivation under pressure and in the face of adversity (Gucciardi, Gordon, & Dimmock, 2008, p. 278). Adolescent Australian footballers who participated in these programs improved their mental toughness, resilience, and flow. The improvement was probably due to the common components of these programs: self-regulation, arousal regulation, mental rehearsal, attentional control, and self-efficacy. Perhaps these components allow adolescents to gain awareness of their strengths and weaknesses, monitor their cognitions and emotional states, and gain needed mental skills. Similarly, adolescent, male ice hockey players learned to control aggression when they learned to recognize the sources of their anger, control arousal, and refocus on the game (Lauer & Paiement, 2004).

WHY YOUTH DISCONTINUE SPORT PARTICIPATION

Given that youth participate in sport to have fun, to improve and learn skills, to enhance their fitness, to affiliate with teammates, to experience the excitement of sport, and for the challenge of competition, it is not surprising that they drop out when these interests are not realized (Gould & Petlichkoff, 1988). Further, youth who drop out believe that they have less sport competency, and are not given "playing time" during games (Figueiredo, Goncalves, Coelho E Silva, & Malina, 2009; Ullrich-French, & Smith, 2009; Weiss & Chaumeton, 2002). As discussed in Chapter 10, a threshold of competency is necessary prior to the experience of intrinsic interest. Tasks that are intrinsically interesting are fun, and it is difficult to enjoy sport if youngsters believe they have little competency and demonstrate the same.

Efficacy and perceived competency are also supported in atmospheres that identify skill development to be the result of effort and learning (Butcher, Lindner, & Johns, 2002; Kavussanu & Roberts, 1996). Coaches and other adults can promote efficacy and perceived sport competence by encouraging young sportspersons to evaluate their performance in relation their own baselines of performance rather than to the performance of other children. By focusing on improvement relative to one's baseline, youngsters are more likely to emphasize personal improvement and skill mastery and to focus on the intrinsic rewards of learning. Frequent social comparisons encourage young athletes to think of ability as reified or innate rather than malleable and emerging.

As mentioned in Chapter 19, adolescent females are more likely than males to withdraw from sports. Among the reason for this difference is the perception that athletic participation is not "cool." Girls may view forms of athletic participation as incompatible with femininity, whereas involvement in sport is viewed as enhancing masculinity in boys. Girls may also be concerned with how they appear in certain athletic uniforms, such as those that are more revealing (Slater & Tiggemann, 2010).

Application

Parents and coaches are often surprised when their promising daughters and players unexpectedly dropout of athletics during adolescence. They are surprised only because they are not privy to the implicit and explicit influences of peers that discourage athletic participation. It is difficult to change the minds of adolescents after they decide to drop out of sport.

Parents and coaches are more likely to be influential if they anticipate and counteract these influences. They can reflect their admiration for female athletes with successful careers and personal lives. They may challenge stereotypes about the incompatibility of sport and femininity, and identify the many examples of accomplished women with happy families. Indeed, through sport and higher education, women have more opportunities to meet desirable partners. Misconceptions about the masculinizing effect of sport on the female physique are also readily discredited. Rather than avoiding strenuous exercise, it may be embraced as a means of improving body tone, weight, and overall appearance.

Burnout

Some youth discontinue sport participation because of burnout. As described in Chapter 17, **burnout** occurs when youthful participants lose interest and no longer find sport to be enjoyable. With burnout, athletes develop negative attitudes toward their sport and question whether it is "worth it" to engage in sport (Smith, 1986). There is often a reduced sense of accomplishment, and these youth may believe that they are making little progress and that their efforts are a waste of time (Raedeke & Smith, 2001). The rewards or benefits of sport and other activities seem to be outweighed by the costs or unpleasant aspects of the sport or activity.

Youthful sportspersons might pursue athletics even if the costs outweighed the benefits if they decided that they had nothing better to do. However, if they identified competing activities that were more rewarding, such as spending free time with friends, they might drop out of athletics in pursuit of the activities that seem to return more at less cost. Early specialization and intensive training regimens are associated with dropping out of athletics (Baker et al., 2009).

Perfectionism has been identified as a precursor of burnout and dropout among youthful athletes (Hill, Hall, & Appleton, 2010). As discussed in Chapter 13, perfectionism, or efforts to be flawless, inhibits not only performance but also interest and enjoyment in sport. Perfectionism was recognized as an important reason why elite junior female and male tennis players lost interest in and became apathetic about playing tennis (Gould, Tuffey, Edry, & Loehr, 1997; Gould, Uldry, Tuffey, & Loehr, 1996a). Elite juniors who dropped out of tennis lost motivation to exert the energy necessary for elite play (Gould, Tuffey, Udry, & Loehr, 1996b). The burnt out tennis players found it difficult to concentrate. Negative emotions, such as anxiety, irritability, and depression, accompanied burnout, and athletes often reported low self-esteem. Many became isolated and kept their problems to themselves.

The burnt out juniors often complained that too much of their time was dominated by tennis. With the demands of training and travel, they felt they had too little time for socializing with peers. If young athletes become isolated from peers, they have fewer opportunities for social support to blunt the stress of competition. If they do not have friends with whom to share their tennis experiences, it may become less fun. Competing activities that involve peers may also become more attractive if playing tennis requires being cloistered from peers. The importance of balancing sport with social activities during adolescence and keeping sport enjoyable was confirmed with a group of male high school golfers (Cohn, 1990a).

Early Pro

Hall of Fame LPGA (Ladies Professional Golf Association) golfer Nancy Lopez criticized Michelle Wie and her inner circle for the decision to play professional golf at age 14 and for her interest in skipping over the LPGA to play on the professional men's tour.

"I feel bad for her," said Lopez, the mother of three girls. "If I had a daughter that played the type of golf that she's playing, I would have the patience to let her be a little girl for a little while and enjoy that time of her life, because she may choose not to play this game. We don't know what kind of pressure she's under, but I saw so many players who were really good amateur players not make it on the LPGA Tour. There was too much pressure behind closed doors, and they ended up really hating the game instead of loving it the way I did" (Berlet, 2005, C3).

Six days prior to her 16th birthday, Ms. Wie announced that she was turning pro. With the announcement came notice that Nike and Sony would be corporate sponsors and pay her $5 million each for her endorsements (Bonk, 2005).

Some junior tennis players appeared to lack intrinsic motivation for the rigors of training at an elite level, and appeared to endure these demands in order to please their parents (Gould et al., 1996b). Lacking intrinsic motivation, tennis was not fun. Indeed, these juniors said they would advise other juniors to find intrinsic motivation and enjoyment for their game.

The tennis juniors said that they would encourage parents of other juniors to avoid overinvolvement in the tennis careers of their children and suggested that parents not coach their children. They encouraged other parents to try to understand and empathize with the emotions of their children, and to not push their children beyond their limits. These young women and men wished that parents would place less emphasis on winning and the outcome of matches. As discussed in Chapter 2, external pressure and coercion, a focus on outcomes, results, or evaluations, and an emphasis on comparing children to others serve to undermine intrinsic motivation. Intrinsic motivation sustains deep interests and enjoyment in activities, as well as the persistence necessary to develop elite skills.

The juniors advised coaches to be less dictatorial and more democratic. This would involve listening and utilizing input from players and trying to empathize with the feelings of players. Some of the burnt out juniors would also like coaches to intervene with parents who place too much pressure on their children.

STRESS AND YOUTH SPORT

As explained in Chapter 4, stress originates in the environment or external world, and discrete sources of stress are described as stressors. As is the case for adults, competition is often stressful for youthful sportspersons. For example, among elite American male adolescent wrestlers, common sources of stress associated with competition were not wrestling well, losing, not performing up to their ability, and not improving on prior performances (Gould, Horn, & Spreemann, 1983). The most frequently reported source of acute stress for Australian field hockey players between the ages of 10 and 12 was "bad" calls from umpires (Anshel & Delany, 2001). Making physical errors in games was also a common source of stress for these youngsters. The pain of injury, the sudden success of opponents, and unpleasant comments and cheating from the opposition were also stressors. Female hockey players were more discomforted by hearing unpleasant comments from the sidelines, whereas males found getting bad scores in games to be more frequent sources of stress.

The most frequent coping responses to these game stressors were examples of **avoidance coping** (Anshel & Delany, 2001). These included trying to ignore stressors, forgeting incidents, and accepting that there was nothing that they could do in response to stressors. This avoidance coping has been seen as desirable when the sources of stress are uncontrollable and transient. With avoidance coping, attentional resources are directed to aspects of performances that are under the control of youthful athletes.

Sportspersons cope with stress with intrapersonal or individual strategies, such as avoidance coping, and with interpersonal strategies, such as gaining social support from others. Parental support is an example of **interpersonal support.** Parental support provides an interpersonal buffer to interpersonal stress from teammates and coaches when young athletes are performing poorly.

The importance of interpersonal support was illustrated with Dutch male soccer players between the ages of 15 and 22 years who were pupils at an elite soccer school from which the majority of the Dutch national team was selected. The soccer players who were rated by coaches as less skilled than teammates experienced less conflict with teammates and disgruntlement about their roles on the team when they had close emotional bonds with parents (VanYperen, 1995). The players with similarly lower levels of skill but also with lower levels of parental support reported less interpersonal support from teammates. Perhaps the latter players were more sensitive to and in need of interpersonal support from teammates because they received less support from their parents.

Players with higher skill levels and higher parental support reported more interpersonal stress with teammates than did their counterparts with higher skill and less parental support (VanYperen, 1995). With high skill and high parental support, players were more attentive to their discontent with the performances of teammates. Perhaps with high skill and low parental support, players were more in need of interpersonal support from teammates and less likely to be critical of teammates.

With maturation, adolescent athletes expand their repertoire of coping strategies (Reeves, Nicholls, & McKenna, 2011). Older adolescents are more likely to vent emotions and less likely to use mental imagery. They more frequently engaged in emotion-focused coping, and viewed mental distraction as a more effective coping technique than their younger counterparts. Females found mental distraction to be more useful than males (Nicholls, Poleman, Morley, & Taylor, 2009).

COACHING, LEADERSHIP, AND YOUTH SPORT

Coaches are influential leaders. Indeed, there is evidence that child athletes rate positive evaluations from coaches as more important than similar parental evaluations (Smith, Smoll, & Smith, 1989). Several interventions by coaches have been shown to have a considerable impact on youthful athletes. These interventions consist of **positive feedback** or recognition and verbal reinforcement for skilled action, **encouragement** or comments that the athlete can be successful, **technical information** or advice about how to improve action, and **negative feedback** or criticism following mistakes (Smoll & Smith, 2002).

Male Little League baseball coaches who provided more positive feedback and encouragement following mistakes supported the development of higher general self-esteem among their male players, and coaches who provided more technical instruction or instrumental support encouraged higher levels of athletic self-esteem (Smoll & Smith, 1989). Little Leaguers (ages 12 and younger) also liked coaches better who were supportive and provided technical assistance (Smith & Smoll, 1990). These players responded favorably to coaches who emphasized encouragement and technical assistance, but not to coaches who were punitive or frequently made negative comments or gave correction in a hostile manner. Young baseball and basketball players not only liked their coaches better and had more fun when coaches emphasized positive reinforcement for desirable performance and effort, but also liked their teammates better (Cumming, Smoll, Smith, & Grossbard, 2007; Smoll & Smith, 2010).

Young basketball players responded similarly to positive feedback, encouragement, technical instruction, and criticism (Smith, Zane, Smoll, & Coppel, 1983). Athletes on high school female and male basketball teams were more satisfied with the atmospheres of their teams when coaches were more supportive and gave more frequent positive reinforcement and less frequent negative feedback (Fisher, Mancini, Hirsch, Proulx, & Starowsky, 1982). High school football coaches who were active in providing instruction and training, positive feedback, and social support, and who allowed athletes to participate in decision making also fostered team cohesion and satisfaction among teammates (Westre & Weiss, 1991). Positive feedback from parents as well as coaches promoted motivation and engagement among sportspersons younger than 12 in the United Kingdom (Keegan, Harwood, Spray, & Lavallee, 2009).

Elite, young adolescent Canadian hockey players preferred more positive and technical feedback, less negative feedback, and less nonreinforcement for good performances than they actually received. The elite male hockey players who wanted more positive and technical feedback were more likely to perceive the motivational climate of their team as ego-involved (see Chapter 9). Those who were dissatisfied with their coach's nonreinforcement of good performances viewed team climates as less task-involved (Stein, Bloom, & Sabiston, 2012).

When coaches are perceived as pressuring, athletes are at risk for maladaptive forms of coping. French adolescent and adult athletes with unsupportive coaches disengaged, vented negative emotions, and resigned themselves to failure in competition. Their counterparts with supportive coaches were more likely to engage task-oriented coping (thought control, mental imagery, exerting additional effort) during competition. The athletes who practiced task-oriented coping more nearly realized their personal goals (Nicolas et al., 2011).

Coaches and Fear of Failure

Children identify with and internalize the responses of important adults, such as coaches and parents. Critical and controlling coaching behaviors, even if subtle, contribute to fear of failure among young sportspersons. For example, the self-talk of children in a summer swim league became increasingly self-controlling and self-blaming, when they were assigned to coaches who were controlling and blaming (Conroy & Coatsworth, 2007). The youthful swimmers who were more self-blaming came to increasingly fear failure throughout the summer. Fear of failure decreased for the swimmers lucky enough to be assigned to coaches who were least critical and who established good relationships with their teams. In short, when the swimmers were confident that their coaches truly understood and appreciated them and what they offered, they had less fear of failure.

Andre Agassi's Self-talk

Tennis Magazine rated Andre Agassi as the seventh greatest male tennis player of all time. He won an Olympic Gold Medal, all four of tennis' Grand Slam tournaments, and eight "majors" in total. He is a member of the International Tennis Hall of Fame. In his autobiography, he recalled his thinking after losing a tennis tournament at age 7:

> After years of hearing my father rant at my flaws, one loss caused me to take up his rant. I've internalized my father—his impatience, his perfectionism, his rage—until his voice doesn't just feel like my own, it is my own. I no longer need my father to torture me. From this day on, I can do it all by myself (Agassi, 2009, p. 38).

Self-Esteem and Response to Coaches

Children with low **self-esteem** are especially sensitive to the reactions of coaches. With low self-esteem, children are also more likely to interpret the responses of coaches to be punitive. For example, Little Leaguers with low self-esteem judged coaches to be less supportive and more punitive than did teammates with high self-esteem (Smith & Smoll, 1990).

Little Leaguers with low self-esteem responded most negatively to coaches who did not provide encouragement and technical support, and most positively to coaches who provided either form of support (Smith & Smoll, 1990). Little Leaguers who had high self-esteem were less influenced by the leadership behavior of coaches.

Athletes and students with low self-esteem are more dependent on support from coaches. They have a shallow reservoir of positive self-regard or positive feelings about themselves (Rogers, 1954; Tice, 1991), and this reserve is apt to be exhausted if they do not receive a regular supply of encouragement and technical advice. When self-esteem is high, youth are affected less by supportive and punitive responses from others, because they have internal reserves available for the preservation of positive self-regard. With high self-esteem, people may also be more capable of eliciting support from a greater number of people, and, therefore, less dependent on the reactions of just one person, such as a coach (Smith & Smoll, 1990).

Coach Effectiveness Training (CET)

Leadership styles are not immutable or unchangeable. Coaches can be trained to provide more encouragement, technical support, and less-punitive responses with interventions such as **Coach Effectiveness Training** (CET; Smith, Smoll, & Curtis, 1979). CET is a systematic program of instruction that trains coaches to emphasize principles of positive control and to avoid aversive control. Positive control includes reinforcement for good performance, encouragement after mistakes, providing correction in a supportive manner, and technical instruction in the mechanics and strategies of sport. Aversive control includes nonreinforcement or failure to respond to good performance or effort, verbal or nonverbal punishment, and providing instruction in a sarcastic and punitive manner. The motivating factor for aversive control is fear.

Coaching and positive control

There are five core principles of CET (Smith & Smoll, 2005). First, winning is defined in terms of the self-referenced goals of giving maximum effort and demonstrating improvement in relation to individual baselines of prior performance (Smith & Smoll, 2002a). Coaches are directed to emphasize the values of having fun, taking satisfaction from being a member of a team, learning sport skills, and increasing the self-esteem of team members. Coaches are encouraged to de-emphasize the goal of winning, and certainly not a "win at all costs" orientation (Smith & Smoll, 1997). This approach is likely to decrease competitive anxiety (Smoll & Smith, 1988). Fear of failure is reduced when sportspersons are encouraged to separate feelings of self-worth from the results of their sport performance and game outcomes. The importance of winning is not ignored with CET, but it is regarded as subsidiary to the objectives of having fun, increasing self-esteem, and developing skills. CET also emphasizes that success consists of giving maximum effort, demonstrating improvement, and having fun.

The second principle of CET is for coaches to emphasize positive reinforcement, encouragement, and technical instruction and to avoid punitive behaviors and excessive criticism. Reinforcement should not be reserved for just the learning and mastery of sport skills. Coaches should also reinforce teamwork, leadership, sportspersonship, and, especially, effort (Smith & Smoll, 2002b). Athletes have control over the amount of effort they exert but only partially control the outcome of competitions. Encouragement is recommended especially after mistakes, and again effort rather that results should be the focus of encouragement. Teammates should be reinforced for encouraging other teammates, and this form of peer support enhances cohesion.

The provision of corrective instruction is seen as consistent with this emphasis on a positive approach. Sportspersons are described as receptive to corrective instruction after mistakes, and coaches are encouraged to include ample supplies of encouragement with this instruction. Coaches are encouraged to wrap instruction following errors in a "**positive sandwich**" (Smith & Smoll, 1997). The "bread" or the first and third statements by the coach are reinforcements. For example, a coach might first reinforce a player for effort, and lastly reassure the sportsperson that they will improve with practice. Between the two reinforcing comments, coaches with this positive approach provide the technical correction and emphasize that he or she expects the player to master the skill in the future.

The use of harsh criticism, punishment, and even sarcasm is strongly discouraged in CET. Such responses are seen to contribute to the decisions of youngsters to drop out of sports. It is also regarded as destructive to team cohesion.

Third, coaches are taught to establish norms for their teams that require members to help and support teammates. The purpose of these norms is to build team cohesiveness and commitment. By focusing on the game and supporting teammates, even benchwarmers contribute to the team effort and cohesion. Coaches support "we're in this together" (Smith & Smoll, 1997) team norms when they acknowledge the verbal support of players on the bench and when they give the reserves attention, encouragement, and instruction in practice. Some coaches encourage team cohesion by "buddying" more-skilled with less-skilled teammates. High school athletes are more likely to endorse the use of aggression in competition when they perceive that teammates are also aggressive (Chow, Murray, & Feltz, 2009).

The fourth principle of CET is to engage team members in making decisions about team rules and in monitoring compliance with rules. Rules should be established at the start of seasons and should be fair and consistent. If coaches can create an atmosphere in which teammates monitor each other, they remove themselves from the position of exclusively policing their team and responding punitively. If team members have a say in the determination of team rules, then individuals violate team norms when they break rules rather than merely the order of a coach.

Fifth, coaches monitor themselves and perhaps seek feedback from others on an ongoing basis to determine if they remain consistent in emphasizing positive reinforcement, encouragement, and technical instruction and de-emphasizing punitive responses.

Empirical Support for CET

There are at least four training programs currently available in the U.S. for training coaches of youthful athletes, but CET is the only program that has been systematically evaluated (Smith & Smoll, 2002b). Little Leaguers who played for coaches who completed CET played with less anxiety and had more fun playing (Smith, Smoll, & Barnett, 1995). They liked their coaches and teammates better and thought their coaches liked them better. They also rated coaches as better teachers of baseball skills. Their anxiety about making mistakes and not playing well decreased significantly across the course of the Little League season. Players with low self-esteem were especially responsive to the CET coaches, and their self-worth increased across the course of the season.

The leadership provided by the CET coaches also influenced dropout from Little League, as 95% of the players on teams with CET coaches returned to play the next year, whereas only 74% of the players on the teams without CET coaches returned (Barnett, Smoll, & Smith, 1992). The won-loss records of teams did not influence dropout as the teams with and without CET coaches had approximately equal records. Children on teams without CET coaches were more likely to drop out because playing was a bad experience.

More generally, quality leadership from adult coaches is an important determinant of the experience of children and adolescents in sport. Problems and difficulties with coaches are important reasons why children and adolescents drop out of athletics. Dropout is an important concern, in that as many as half of the children who begin a sport stop playing.

The 5Cs Coaching Efficacy Program

Another empirically derived intervention for increasing the effectiveness of coaches, teaching psychological skills, and promoting positive youth development is the **5Cs Coaching Efficacy program** (Harwood, 2008). The 5Cs are *commitment, communication, concentration, control,* and *confidence*. Commitment is represented by characteristics such as intrinsic motivation and task/mastery goals. Examples of communication are peer praise and encouragement. Concentration training involves focusing attention to internal or external, broad or narrow cues (see Chapter 6). Control includes the management of arousal and use of positive self-talk and body language. Confidence is enhanced with coaching to not fear mistakes, engage fully in practice and competition, and accept challenging goals. The foundation for training is the development of team climates that are task- or mastery-oriented, cooperative, and supportive.

Coaches and Parents

It is sometimes necessary for coaches of children and adolescents to practice effective leadership with not only their youthful athletes but also their parents (Smoll, 1998, Smoll & Cumming, 2006). At one end of a spectrum of problematic parental involvement are parents who are **disinterested** in the participation of their children in athletics. At the other end of this spectrum are parents who are overly involved. These parents may experience achievement by proxy (Tofler, Knapp, & Drell, 1998). They may see their child as an extension of himself or herself, and in some ways define their self-worth in terms of the child's success. Overly involved parents experience losses to their self-image if their children do not perform well and may require that their children excel before they grant their approval. The children of overly involved parents experience pressure to excel and the parents may demonstrate the **reversed-dependency trap** (Smith & Smoll, 2002b) in that their well-being is dependent on their children's success (Coakley, 2006). At its most extreme, parents who are overly identified with the success of their children push for success even at the risk of overtraining and injury.

Andre Agassi at Age Seven

I'm seven years old, talking to myself, because I'm scared, and because I'm the only person who listens to me. Under my breath I whisper: "Just quit, Andre, just give up. Put down your racket and walk off this court, right now. Go into the house and get something good to eat . . . Wouldn't that feel like heaven, Andre? To just quit? To never play tennis again?"

But I can't. Not only would my father chase me around the house with my racket, but something in my gut, some deep unseen muscle, won't let me. I hate tennis, hate it with all my heart, and still I keep playing, keep hitting all morning and all afternoon, because I have no choice. No matter how much I want to stop, I don't. I keep begging myself to stop, and I keep playing, and this gap, this contradiction between what I want to do and what I actually do, feels like the core of my being (Agassi, 2009, p. 27).

My father says that if I hit 2,500 balls each day, I'll hit 17,500 balls each week, and at the end of one year I'll have hit nearly one million balls. Numbers, he says don't lie. A child who hits one million balls each year will be unbeatable (Agassi, 2010, p. 29).

Effective leadership with overly involved parents involves diplomatic efforts to clarify that youth athletics are for the growth and development of the children. As was described in Chapter 11, simultaneous goals of winning in relation to competitors and winning parental approval are likely to provoke performance anxiety and choking under pressure.

Coaches may also have to intervene with parents in the viewing area that scream to such a degree that they disrupt play, embarrass their children, and represent a nuisance. Parents model self-control and discipline during the athletic contests of their children. Coaches face a more difficult task in teaching good sportspersonship when parents are poor sports and prone to emotional outbursts. Parents who coach from the sidelines or who are overprotective also may require tactful intervention from coaches. Some coaches attempt to limit parental coaching from the sidelines by asking them to not sit directly behind the bench for their child's team (Strean, 1995).

Parents Out of Control

Upset that his daughter, Melanie, received a three-game suspension for missing a softball game to attend a senior prom at North Haven (CT) High School, Mark Picard appealed to coach John Corvo to resend the suspension and allow Melanie, a senior, to play on senior's day. Corvo, the softball coach of the all-girls Sacred Heart Academy in Hamden, CT, refused and stated that he did not want Melanie at practice and to take her home. As Corvo walked away, Picard struck him several times about the head and shoulders with an aluminum softball bat (Eagan & Gonzalez, 2005). Corvo sustained injuries to his neck and chest, his ear canal collapsed, and he had severe swelling in his right knee (Gonzalez & Courchesne, 2005). Dave Cypher, the former coach at Sacred Heart Academy, said that part of the reason he resigned was a run-in with Picard. In 2004, Cypher allowed all the seniors to play as a group on Senior Night. After Sacred Heart was beaten badly, Picard, "was screaming, 'You are the worst coach I've ever seen. You were just sitting on the bench saying nothing'" (Gonzalez, 2005, p. C8). Cypher speculated that the Picards might have been upset with him because he did not choose Melanie to be a team captain. Picard was instrumental in building equipment sheds for the track and softball teams and raised money for athletic programs at Sacred Heart. Picard had taught art and photography at Notre Dame High School in nearby West Haven, CT, since 1980.

Coaches show leadership with disinterested parents by inviting them to participate and by explaining that their support is of value to their children. Busy parents are often unable to balance other commitments with time to watch their children's matches. Coaches are advised to have parents make reasonable commitments to attend games and practices and to not promise more time than they can actually deliver. Coaches may also explain to their teams that not all parents can attend games and practices due to work and other commitments.

Regardless of their availability and time constraints, some demands are placed on the parents of youthful athletes. These parents must entrust their child to the guidance of coaches, and accept the coaches' authority in matters relating to sport (Smoll & Cumming, 2006). Disappointment occurs in the course of athletic striving, and children benefit when they can share disappointments with parents (Dorsch et al., 2009; Fredericks & Eccles, 2004). Parents should avoid shaming children about their disappointment and even about crying following poor performances. Parents support their children when they help them to learn from disappointments and losses.

Parents also have a responsibility to protect their children from aversive control by coaches. This may be difficult when coaches have prestige and power; such as coaches who make decisions about selection to Olympic teams. Parents may also become "socialized" to ignore bullying behavior by coaches because other parents do not find the behavior objectionable. Indeed, even young athletes may implore parents to not question coaches because they fear retaliation. However, parents who remain silent bystanders as coaches berate, threaten, and denigrate their children may experience guilt and regret that they allowed coaches to usurp their authority to protect the emotional well-being of their children (Kerr & Stirling, 2012).

A final demand placed on the parents of youthful athletes is the need to understand when to allow children to make their own decisions about sports. Parents play an important role in motivating children to participate in sports, but some children choose not to participate despite the best efforts of parents.

Preseason Meetings with Parents

Coaches are more likely to be effective leaders with parents when they clarify the roles of parents and coaches in meetings with parents. The roles and responsibilities of coaches, parents, and athletes, and the objectives of the sport program are explained in such meetings. These meetings are considered vital to avoiding misunderstandings and to avoiding problems with parents such as overinvolvement, sideline coaching, abusive verbal behavior from parents in the stands, and disagreements about the playing time of children.

These goals may best be accomplished in **preseason meetings** with parents. Follow-up meetings may be held at other times in the season. A guide for coaches in planning meetings with parents and for providing effective leadership with parents and athletes is provided in the book *Way to Go, Coach!* (Smith & Smoll, 2002a).

On the Need for Leadership with Parents

In July 2000, Thomas Junta watched his son practice ice hockey at the Burbank Ice Arena in Reading, Massachusetts. Junta complained to the coach, Michael Costin, that play was too rough. Costin disagreed and after practice, the two scuffled (Campo-Flores & Kirsch, 2002). The two were separated by bystanders, but Junta returned within minutes. At 275 pounds, Junta wrestled the 156-pound Costin to the floor. With Costin lying on his back and Junta kneeling over him, Junta pummeled him with from three to ten punches, and according to several witnesses, slammed Costin's head to the floor. The blows ruptured a vital artery in Costin's neck, and he died after spending two days in a coma. At the ensuing trial, a medical examiner testified that Costin's brain was so severely damaged that during the autopsy it "came squeezing out like toothpaste" (Campo-Flores & Kirsch, 2002, p. 38). The men's sons and the other children on the hockey team witnessed this fatal dispute about rough play.

Organizers of youth hockey in Massachusetts considered ways of reining in parents and preventing violence in the future, such as holding educational sessions with parents and requiring parents to sign codes of conduct.

SUMMARY AND APPLICATION

The benefits of youth sport include the enhancement of physical fitness and athletic competence and the development of leadership skills, discipline, respect for authority, and achievement motivation. In the course of athletic participation, children and adolescents learn social skills, make friends, spend time with family members, and have fun. Youth sport also serves a public health interest, preserves the tradition of organized sport, and develops elite athletes. Unlike professional sport, the fundamental goal of youth sport is not winning, but young sportspersons are encouraged to put forth maximum effort and to strive to win.

There are also social benefits for youth sport. Young sportspersons are more likely to be popular with peers. These youth also have opportunities to make good friends during athletic participation.

The benefits and goals of youth sport are more likely to be realized when coaches emphasize positive feedback, encouragement, and technical information, and de-emphasize negative feedback. With this emphasis, the general and athletic self-esteem of young sportspersons is enhanced. Coach Effectiveness Training (CET) is a systematic program developed to teach coaches to emphasize positive feedback, encouragement, and technical information in their interactions with members of their teams. Coaches are even encouraged to wrap corrective feedback in a "positive sandwich." In CET coaches learn to emphasize the goal of giving maximum effort. Youthful athletes enjoy playing for coaches who emphasize positive control, play with less anxiety, and are less likely to drop out of athletics. Effective coaching in youth sport also involves meetings with parents to clarify the roles of coaches, parents, and athletes.

With effective and sensitive coaching, the goals of youth sport are more likely to be realized. Nevertheless, athletic participation is sometimes stressful. Youthful sportspersons are more successful in coping with stress when they practice skills such as the Spaghetti Toes procedure for relaxation. As is true for physical practice, adult supervision of the practice of mental skills is necessary to insure that they are practiced regularly and appropriately.

The benefits of sport accrue for the participants, and therefore the reasons that youngsters drop out or fail to participate are of interest. Youth, who do not experience fun, camaraderie, excitement, challenge, and skill enhancement are more likely to withdraw from or to never initiate athletic participation.

Burnout develops when the costs of sport participation appear to outweigh the benefits. Alternatives to sport may then be pursued if they appear to offer more benefit at less cost. However, even burnt out youngsters may not drop out of sport if more attractive alternative pursuits are not available or if they feel "entrapped" or obliged to participate. Interventions from coaches and parents that encourage intrinsic motivation, self-referenced goals, and self-efficacy help athletes to cope with staleness and temporary loss of interest in sport.

Key Terms

Education experience   493

Public health goal   495

Elite-development goal   495

Sport practices   495

The goal of professional sport   496

Popularity   496

Deliberate play   500

Spaghetti toes   501

Burnout   503

Perfectionism   504

Avoidance coping   506

Interpersonal support   506

Positive feedback   507

Encouragement   507

Technical information   507

Negative feedback   507

Self-esteem   508

Coach Effectiveness Training   509

Positive sandwich   510

5Cs Coaching Efficacy Program   511

Disinterested parents   512

Reversed-dependency trap   512

Preseason meetings   514

Discussion Questions

Q1.   Review the fundamental goal of youth sports.

Q2.   Describe the public health, elite-development, and sports practice goals of youth sports.

Q3.   Differentiate youth and professional sport.

Q4.   Consider the influence of sport on the development of friendships.

Q5.   Review the role of parents in encouraging children to participate in sport.

Q6.   Explain the pros and cons of early specialization in sport.

Q7.   What is deliberate play?

Q8.   Describe mental training practices with children.

Q9.   Review the reasons that children and adolescents discontinue athletic participation.

Q10.   Consider the sources of stress in youth sports.

Q11.   Describe positive forms of coaching in youth sports.

Q12.   Consider coaching interventions that contribute to fears of failure in young sportspersons.

Q13.   How does the self-esteem of young sportspersons influence their responses to coaches?

Q14.   Describe the components of Coach Effectiveness Training (CET).

Q15.   What are the benefits of Coach Effectiveness Training (CET)?

Q16.   Describe the 5Cs.

Suggested Readings

Carr, S. (2009). Adolescent-parent attachment characteristics and quality of youth sport friendship. *Psychology of Sport and Exercise, 10*, 653–661. doi: 10.1016/j.psychsport.2009.04.001

Conroy, D. E., & Coatsworth, J. D. (2007). Coaching behaviors associated with changes in fear of failure: Changes in self-talk and need for satisfaction as potential mechanisms. *Journal of Personality, 75*, 383–419.

Cote, J. (1999). The influence of family in the development of talent. *The Sport Psychologist, 13*, 395–417.

Gaudreau, P., Amiot, C. E., & Vallerand, R. J. (2009). Trajectories of affective states in adolescent hockey players: Turning point and motivational antecedents. *Developmental Psychology, 45*, 307–319. doi: 10.1037/a0014134

Jones, M. I., & Lavallee, D. (2009). Exploring the life skills needs of British adolescent athletes. *Psychology of Sport and Exercise, 10*, 159–167. doi: 10.1016/j.psychsport.2008.06.005

Smith, R. E. (2006). Positive reinforcement, performance feedback, and performance enhancement. In J. M. Williams (Ed.), *Applied sport psychology: Personal growth to peak performance* (5th ed., pp. 40–56). New York, NY: McGraw-Hill.

Smith, R. E., & Smoll, F. L. (2002a). *Way to go, coach! A scientifically-proven approach to coaching effectiveness.* Portola Valley, CA: Warde.

Smith, R. E., & Smoll, F. L. (2002b). Youth sports as a behavior setting for psychosocial interventions. In J. L. Van Raalte & B. W. Brewer (Eds.), *Exploring sport and exercise psychology* (2nd ed., pp. 341–372). Washington, DC: American Psychological Association.

Smoll, F. L., & Cumming, S. P. (2006). Enhancing coach-parent relationships in youth sports: Increasing harmony and minimizing hassle. In J. M. Williams (Ed.), *Applied sport psychology: Personal growth to peak performance* (5th ed., pp. 192–204). Mountain View, CA: Mayfield.

Ullrich-French, S., & Smith, A. L. (2009). Social and motivational predictors of continued youth sport participation. *Psychology of Sport and Exercise, 10*, 87–95. doi: 10.1016/j.psychsport.2008.06.007

Zarrett, N., Fay, K., Li, Y., Carrano, J. Phelps, E., & Lerner, R. M. (2009). More than child's play: Variable- and pattern-centered approaches for examining effects of sports participation on youth development. *Developmental Psychology, 45*, 368–382. doi: 10.1037/a0014577

Chapter 22

LEADERSHIP AND COACHING

Coaches lead athletes (photo by Visions of America/UIG via Getty Images)

Joe Torre, manager of four World Series championship New York Yankee teams, compared teams to families. "I often make the analogy between teams and families. It's been said before, and it may seem old-fashioned. But no matter how often the analogy is applied, I still see teams in sports and business where upper and middle managers don't pay attention to the needs of their team players and don't treat people with fairness. That tells me that they don't understand the ways in which teams are like families.

"Teams are not really families but there are many crucial similarities. Families thrive when members grant one another time; follow agreed-upon rules; treat one another with fairness, respect, and trust; and make togetherness a top priority.

"I'm particularly proud of how my Yankee teams—all of them, but especially the '98 group—have been a collection of diverse personalities from totally different ethnic and religious backgrounds, who've managed to get along and respect one another. With regard to the 1998 Yankees, I've never seen a team develop such strong bonds of love and cooperation, and I'm certain it helped them to achieve their goals" (Torre & Dreher, 1999, pp. 52–53).

LEADERSHIP AND COACHING

The topic of coaching, leadership, and youth sports was reviewed in Chapter 21. In this chapter, the influence of coaches and leaders on adult athletes will be considered.

Simply put, leadership consists of influencing others to strive to reach individual and common goals and to contribute to the good of the group (Kaiser, Hogan, & Craig, 2008). It concerns building and maintaining effective teams (Hogan & Kaiser, 2005). The early study of leadership focused on the personality characteristics or traits common to successful leaders. This line of research was subsequently criticized as successful in describing the personality characteristics of successful leaders in sport in only the most general terms (Murray, Mann, & Mead, 2010). However, personality has proven to be highly important in identifying effective leaders in business, and effective leadership results in gains in productivity and employee satisfaction (Hogan & Kaiser, 2005). **Effective leaders** have **integrity, decisiveness, competence,** and **vision.** Integrity involves keeping one's word and fulfilling promises, not taking advantage of one's position, and not playing favorites. Decisiveness consists of making good decisions quickly, especially under pressure. Competence refers to knowledge and skill at a particular enterprise, and it affords legitimacy to leaders. Finally, a leader with vision is skilled at identifying goals and clarifying the roles of team members. Vision may involve a team's ultimate aspiration, but will also be underpinned by more proximate goals. Individuals may be motivated to look beyond their individual goals and adopt the team vision (Fletcher & Arnold, 2011).

Leaders of winning teams do not focus on "standing out" or drawing attention to themselves. In fact, they are more likely to be modest and humble. They are, however, extraordinarily persistent in pushing teams to reach their goals (Kaiser et al., 2008).

As noted in Chapters 9 and 11, UCLA won ten national championships in basketball with John Wooden as head coach. He was also elected to the NCAA Basketball Hall of Fame as a player and coach. His definition of good leadership requires humility:

> Don't draw attention to yourself; don't be like the fellow in church who coughs loudly just before he puts a coin in the collection plate. A selfless leader puts his team first. I have made a point of refraining from referring to the UCLA Bruins as "my team" or the players as "my players." A team is owned by its members. It was our team (Wooden & Jamison, 2007, p. 143).

To Wooden, selflessness was a powerful leadership asset. He considered the first tool in a leader's tool kit to be consideration and courtesy for those to be led.

The typical interventions of successful coaches are more reliably identified. Effective coaches convince athletes that team and individual goals will be achieved by accepting their leadership. Athletes value the interventions of coaches who know what they are talking about, as well as how to communicate this information. These coaches understand the fundamental components of the skills in their sport. They select and demonstrate specific skills in need of improvement, and do not overload athletes with instruction in single practices. Successful coaches often do not treat each athlete in the same way (Gould & Maynard, 2009). They attempt to understand what interventions best serve to teach and motivate individual athletes. These coaches are sensitive to the relationships between team members and resolve tensions and animosities.

The success of coaching interventions is also determined by the age and maturity of athletes. More-mature athletes are more capable of taking responsibility for and directing their actions. Less-mature athletes are in need of more guidance, direction, and emotional support.

Effective coaches build team morale. Positive moral is evidenced by the confidence and willingness of individual team members to perform assigned tasks and by team dedication to common goals. Positive morale exists when players understand that they will be supported but also held to high standards of effort and performance by coaches. Morale is boosted when athletes believe they are part of something larger than themselves that is good.

RELATIONSHIP AND TASK ORIENTATIONS AND LEADERSHIP

Leaders have different styles or characteristic ways of relating to those under their supervision (Murray et al., 2010). Leaders with a **relationship orientation** focus on giving positive feedback after good performances and encouragement following mistakes. Leaders with **task orientations** focus on providing technical instruction and instruction about how to correct errors after mistakes. Task-oriented leadership is effective when leaders have a great deal of control over subordinates, whereas leaders that are relationship- or people-oriented are more effective when their control is limited (Kaiser et al., 2008).

Successful coaches are likely to manifest both relationship and task orientations. National Collegiate Athletic Association (NCAA) Division I football, basketball, and volleyball coaches who "turned around" failing programs made deliberate efforts to define and reinforce core values with their teams. They attempted to communicate caring about the well-being of the individuals on their teams, as opposed to just whether the athletes could contribute in the athletic arena. Some coaches allowed team members to have input in the recruiting process and to determine if potential recruits would "fit in" with team culture. The coaches considered it essential that they demonstrate core values in their own behavior and that they also model or demonstrate technical skills (Schroeder, 2009).

TRANSFORMATIONAL LEADERSHIP

Superior leaders have been described as charismatic or **transformational** in that they inspire others to adopt their vision and goals for teams. These transformational leaders broaden and elevate the goals and interests of others; team members adopt not only individual goals, but also shared group goals (Bass, 1985; Bass & Avolio, 2005). They establish high performance expectations and lead by example. For example, German karate coaches (*sensei*) who were rated as transformational leaders inspired greater effort from their students (*karatenka*; Rowold, 2006).

Transformational coaches praise team members for good work and instill confidence. They treat team members as individuals and help them to find solutions to problems. Their leadership promotes team cohesion (Callow, Smith, Hardy, Arthur, & Hardy, 2009). Transformational hockey coaches modeled prosocial behavior, and their adolescent teams fouled less and recorded fewer penalty minutes (Tucker, Turner, Barling, & McEvoy, 2010).

Charismatic and transformational leadership qualities are acquired throughout development. For example, Canadian female and male high school athletes who considered their fathers to be transformational leaders and who were rated by coaches as having high levels of athletic skills were more likely to show transformational leadership qualities (Zacharatos, Barling, & Kelloway, 2000).

TRUST AND LEADERSHIP AND COACHING

Trust is an essential component of effective leadership in business and athletic settings. **Trust** has generally been defined as a belief or expectation that one can rely on another person to fulfill expectations and promises and that the other person has good intentions toward other people. Trust is especially important when one is vulnerable in relation to another person. Athletes are in vulnerable positions in relation to coaches because coaches make important decisions about the roles of athletes on teams. For example, coaches make decisions about starting lineups and playing time. Trust is also very important when people are uncertain if their leader is making the right decisions. For example, athletes are asked to accept or "buy into" the goals and tactics of coaches without knowing in advance if these goals and tactics will lead to team and individual success.

Athletes are less likely to accept coaching decisions, especially if they are asked to sacrifice individual goals for team goals, if they do not trust coaches. Sportspersons that trust coaches are more willing to accept their individual roles on the team and to work hard to realize the goals and decisions of coaches (Vallee & Bloom, 2005).

Trust also predicts team success. For example, among 30 NCAA Division I and II male basketball teams, coaches who earned the trust of the teams had the highest winning percentages (Dirks, 2000). The two teams with the highest levels of trust in coaches were very successful. One was ranked number one in the nation before being upset in the NCAA tournament, and the other was defeated in the national championship game. The team with the lowest level of trust in its coach won approximately 10% of its conference games, and the coach was fired after the season. In Spanish professional roller hockey, indoor football (soccer), handball, and basketball teams, trust in coaches fostered team cohesion, trust in teammates, and ultimately better winning percentages (Mach, Dolan, & Tzafrir, 2010). U.S. Olympic athletes at the winter games in Nagano, Japan, in 1998 said their performance improved when they trusted their coaches and believed that coaches were totally committed to their success (Gould, 1999).

Tarnished Credibility

As head basketball coach, Ben Howland led UCLA (University of California, Los Angeles) to three consecutive Final Four appearances, from 2006 through 2008, in the NCAA tournament, and four conference titles. In 2013, he was fired and UCLA paid him "a reported $3.5 million just to go away" (Dohrmann, 2013).

Perhaps the turning point came in 2009 when he reneged on his promise to award Kendall Williams an athletic scholarship. Williams committed to UCLA as a sophomore in high school, and Howland waited to drop him until the last minute, insuring that Williams would not be signed by other teams in UCLA's Pac-12 conference. This soured Howland's relationships with AAU (Amateur Athletic Union) coaches in Los Angeles. Concluding that Williams could not be trusted, several AAU coaches steered their elite players away from UCLA. Thus, Howland's ability to recruit elite players in Los Angeles—one of the most talent-rich areas for basketball players in the country—was irreparably compromised. An opposing coach in the Pac-12 commented: "A lot of coaches on the West Coast will be sad to see Ben go" (Dohrmann, 2013).

Leaders and coaches are judged on the basis of the results of their organizations and teams. Coaches of successful teams are often considered good leaders. Coaches with good track records or histories of prior coaching success are expected to be successful in the future. Athletes are more willing to trust and "put themselves in the hands" of coaches who they expect will make them winners. It is more difficult for coaches with poor records of accomplishment to inspire the trust of teams, and without this trust, these coaches are less likely to be successful in the future.

When athletes trust, like, and respect their coaches, and believe that coaches are committed to them, they are more likely to be satisfied with the coach-athlete relationship (Lorimer & Jowett, 2009). They get more out of training and practice when they understand the motives and reasoning for their coaches' instructions, and when a positive and constructive interpersonal environment is in place.

COMMUNICATION AND COACHING

Trust is the foundation for effective **communication** between coaches and their teams (Yukelson, 2010). Coaches judged to be honest, fair, and consistent are seen as good communicators by their teams. Clearly, effective communication involves more than just what is said and how it is said, as athletes take coaches' "body of work" or record as a coach and a person in evaluating their credibility.

As will be described at later points in this chapter, athletes generally respond more favorably to positive reinforcement, support, and technical instruction from coaches. Criticism often undermines morale. Coaches who emphasize positive control and de-emphasize negative control (Smith & Smoll, 2002b) encourage open communication on teams. Positive control includes reinforcement for good performance, encouragement after mistakes, providing correction in a supportive manner, and technical instruction in the mechanics and strategies of sport. Negative control includes nonreinforcement or failure to respond to good performance or effort, verbal or nonverbal punishment, and providing instruction in a sarcastic and punitive manner. The motivating factor for negative control is fear. Coaches are also more likely to develop skill at communication and maintain team harmony when they are committed to the objectives of positive control (Orlick, 1986).

Athletes also respond favorably to coaches who interact with their athletes at a more personal level. These coaches may refer to personal experience when coaching and instructing, and are available to individual athletes before or after practices and games. These **immediacy behaviors** promote athlete satisfaction and team cohesiveness (Turman, 2008).

COACHING EFFICACY

Coaches who believe they can affect the learning and performance of their teams have coaching efficacy. **Coaching efficacy** consists of four components: **motivation efficacy, technique efficacy, game strategy efficacy,** and **character building efficacy** (Feltz, Chase, Moritz, & Sullivan, 1999; Vealey, 2009). Coaching efficacy in these areas is developed with successful experience in coaching and with coaching preparation and education (Feltz, Short, & Sullivan, 2008). The sources of coaching success are not limited to wins and losses, as coaches focus on improvements in their athletes and in their coaching skills in judging their efficacy (Barber, 1998; Feltz, Hepler, Roman, & Paiement, 2009; Vealey, 2009). Coaching efficacy is enhanced when teams have high ability and when coaches receive social support from school administrators, parents, and the community. Community support is particularly influential in enhancing character building efficacy among female collegiate coaches (Myers, Vargas-Tonsing, and Feltz, 2005). Coaching efficacy is also affected by the feedback from players (Malete & Feltz, 2002).

Prior playing experience contributes to coaching efficacy. Indeed, it was shown to be even more influential than coaching experience in enhancing efficacy for game strategy, or the application of practical game skills and knowledge (Sullivan, Gee, & Feltz, 2006). With more extensive coaching experience, coaches are more confident in their capacity to develop the technical skills of their athletes (Kavussanu, Boardley, Jutkiewicz, Vincent, & Ring, 2008). Soccer coaches who played at the university level or higher may adopt a professional, or "win at all costs," attitude, and their high school players endorsed the use of more aggression in competition (Chow, Murray, & Feltz, 2009).

ethic. Players are likely to recognize coaches who work tirelessly for their development and well-being. Coaches who are most influential convince players to subjugate self-interests to the interests of the team. For example, a great deal of trust in a coach is likely necessary to forego the notoriety of a scorer and move to a defensive position for the good of the team.

Efficacious coaches are also likely to use imagery. Game strategy, technique, motivational, and character building efficacy were all higher among coaches who regularly used imagery in preparation for practice and competition (Short, Smiley, & Ross-Stewart, 2005).

Efficacious coaches excel at developing the talent of their players, and motivating players to believe in themselves and to perform at their highest levels. For example, when rugby union players recognized motivational efficacy in their coaches, they responded with increased effort and commitment and also enjoyed their sport to a greater degree. These players also developed confidence in rugby skills, such as tackling, making accurate passes, and catching balls, when coaches manifested technique efficacy. Players were more likely to show good sportsmanship when coaches exuded character building efficacy (Boardley, Kavussanu, & Ring, 2008). Surprisingly, higher levels of game strategy efficacy among coaches were associated with the endorsement of more aggressive play in competition by high school soccer players (Chow et al., 2009). Efficacious coaches adjust strategies to the talents of their players and the demands of practice and competition (Bandura, 1997; Boardley et al., 2008).

Coaches have been shown to form expectancies for their team's performance (Chase, Lirgg, & Feltz, 1997). The expectations are based on past performances in games, practices, the injury status of players, the strength of opponents, and the coaches' beliefs about the confidence and efficacy of their players. These coaches' expectations in turn influence team efficacy so that teams with higher efficacy perform more successfully (Vargas-Tonsing, Myers, & Feltz, 2004). The performance of teams then ultimately reinforces or supports the original efficacy expectations of coaches.

With higher efficacy, coaches are more likely to be effective, to produce winning teams, and to have players who are confident and satisfied with their coach (Myers et al., 2005). Coaches who had higher efficacy beliefs for their teams believed they had more control over the performance of their teams. Not surprisingly, coaches are more likely to discontinue coaching if they do not perceive themselves to be competent, especially female coaches.

COACHES BUILD THE EFFICACY OF TEAMS

The strategies of efficacious coaches build the individual and group efficacy of their teams (Bandura, 1997). As described in Chapter 10, enactive attainments are the most convincing sources of self-efficacy, and skilled coaches provide teams with goals in practice and competition that are attainable. With the attainment of progressively more difficult goals, individual and team efficacy increases. These coaches avoid placing athletes in situations where they are likely to fail, such as in pressure situations where they are overmatched.

Despite the best efforts and intentions of coaches, athletes still experience failure. Skilled coaches allow athletes opportunities to get themselves out of trouble in matches and games and avoid pulling players at the first sign of trouble. Successful and efficacious coaches blunt discouragement after losses by directing the attention of athletes to aspects of performance that are under the control of athletes. They help athletes to focus on personal and team improvement regardless of wins and losses, and they provide encouragement, corrective instruction, and feedback to teach athletes the skills necessary for more skillful performance. Coaches also support the efficacy of players when they communicate that they have not lost faith in players after failures and that improvement will occur with technical refinements and training. Players are less likely to lose confidence even in prolonged slumps when coaches communicate that they have every confidence that they will return to form. Repeated failure may result in relegation of players to minor leagues or the bench or a reserve role. Relegation is less likely to impact the efficacy of players if it is interpreted as evidence of the need for skill improvement rather than of evidence of a lack of talent.

Effective coaches support beliefs that necessary athletic skills are acquirable. They also adopt styles of play that capitalize on the strengths and hide the weaknesses of their players.

Coaches of Olympic and national level athletes use many of these techniques to build and sustain high efficacy with athletes. They also emphasize conditioning, set specific performance goals, and encourage positive self-talk (Gould, Hodge, Peterson, & Giannini, 1989).

Effective coaches recognize that the time for teams to doubt their likelihood for success is not immediately prior to and during competition. Doubts about efficacy erode performance during competition. However, skillful coaches deliberately **instill doubts** in their team at times distal to competition so as to motivate teams to train and prepare optimally (Bandura, 1997). These coaches also guard against complacency after successful and triumphant seasons by helping athletes understand that without additional improvement, they are unlikely to be equally successful in the future. Continuous improvement is necessary as prior success may well be due to optimal circumstances for the triumphant team, optimal scheduling, luck, and bad breaks or luck and injuries for opponents. Prior success may have also been partially due to optimal team cohesion that was present at a particular period in time.

Efficacious coaches help athletes to not give up in competition, even when teams are clearly beaten. At these times, athletes are instructed to change the focus of their goals so that they still work on aspects of their games in the losing contests. This refocusing provides opportunities for skill development that are not available in practice against lesser competition.

IMPROVING THE INFLUENCE OF COACHES

Coaches and other leaders interested in enhancing their influence have been encouraged to improve their appearance. By tidying up their attire, eliminating obesity and pudginess, and stopping smoking, coaches may present an image of confidence and control, and inspire these reactions in team members (Murray et al., 2010). Coaches are encouraged to acquire necessary expertise in the technical aspects of their sport as well as an understanding of how to motivate individual players (Laios, Theodorakis, & Gargalianos, 2003). Coaches should develop control of their emotions, as athletes often imitate coaches in handling emotions. Coaches use the psychological skills of self-talk, imagery, relaxation, and goal setting to enhance their performance (Thelwell, Weston, Greenlees, & Hutchings, 2008).

EFFECTIVE COACHES RESPOND CONTINGENTLY

Perhaps is goes without saying that effective coaching interventions are given contingently. Comments are **contingent** when they are in response to specific actions or clusters of actions by athletes. Contingent coaching responses are also tailored to fit the level of skill and characteristics of the athlete. Even positive reinforcement that is not contingent on performance does little to enhance feelings of competence (Horn, 1985). In other words, random compliments from coaches have little effect.

MULTIDIMENSIONAL MODEL OF LEADERSHIP

With experience, it was recognized that a single set of characteristics was not associated with successful leadership in all situations. Settings such as sport venues differ in terms of the age of sportspersons, goals for participation, and type of sport. The **Multidimensional Model of Leadership** (Chelladurai, 1980; 2007) was developed specifically for application in sport settings and to account for the interaction of traits and situational factors in explaining effective leadership in sport teams.

The Multidimensional Model of Leadership considers the actual behavior of leaders such as coaches, the style of leadership preferred by subordinates such as team members, and the restrictions placed on leaders by their organizations (Chelladurai, 1980, 1984, 1993, 2012). The accompanying diagram (Figure 22.1) was developed to illustrate this model. Boxes 1, 2, and 3 describe Antecedents of actual leadership behavior, and consist of the characteristics of leaders, team members, and situations. The arrows depict the influences of these Antecedents of Actual Behaviors demonstrated by coaches, favored by team members, and required by sport settings, or on boxes 5, 6, 4, respectively. Situational Characteristics, such as team composition, age, and skill level, influence Required Behavior, such

FIGURE 22.1 Multidimensional Model of Leadership (Chelladurai, 1993)

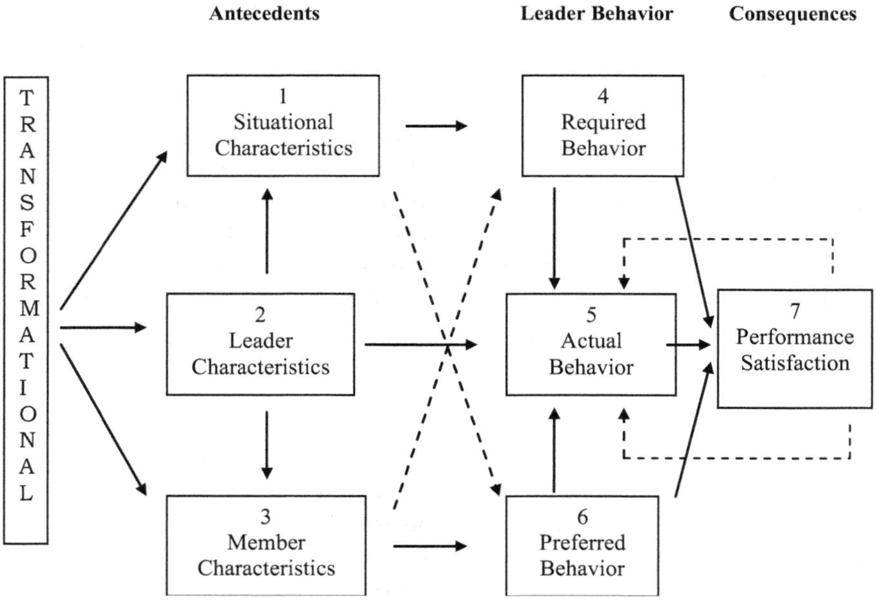

as learning plays during a sport season. Member Characteristics, such as their focus on winning versus having fun, determine Preferred Coaching Behaviors, including the provision of instruction and support. The Actual Behavior of leaders is influenced by Leader Characteristics, such as personality and experience, Required Behavior, and Preferred Behavior or the type of leadership favored by team members. The degree of congruence among the Required, Actual, and Preferred Behavior of coaches is considered to determine the Consequences of leadership or the Performance of teams and Satisfaction of team members with the leadership or coaching (Box 7). Transformational leadership broadens and elevates the Antecedents of leadership (Chelladurai, 2012).

The Leadership Scale for Sport

The **Leadership Scale for Sports** (LSS) was developed to measure the actual leadership behavior of coaches (Chelladurai & Saleh, 1978, 1980). The LSS has five scales. The first scale concerns the degree to which coaches emphasize **training** and **instruction.** This includes strenuous training, providing instruction in the technical aspects of performance in the particular sport, structuring practices, and clarifying roles of team members. A second scale measures the degree to which coaches consider input from team members or allow for **democratic decision making.** The third and fourth scales measure the interpersonal qualities of **social support** and

positive feedback. A fifth scale assesses the degree to which coaches make decisions **autocratically** or without input from team members.

Certain styles of decision making are more appropriate for different situations and different teams (Horn, 1992). There are seven attributes to be considered in mating decision styles to athletic situations (Chelladurai & Doherty, 1998; Chelladurai & Turner, 2006). *First,* when time is limited, coaches are required to be decisive. *Second,* some decisions are more important than others. For example, it is more important to select the most skilled person to be center forward on a soccer team than to select the most skilled player as team captain. Less important decisions can be determined by democratic vote. *Third,* at times coaches have more information about a question, such as the rules of their sport, and in other instances, athletes possess better information. Examples of the latter are questions about athletes' fatigue and injury status. *Fourth,* it is difficult to make complex decisions by committee. The coach or one player is in the best position to make complex decisions such as the sequence of plays in football. *Fifth,* it is more important for teams to accept or "buy into" some decisions than others. Basketball teams are more likely to be successful in applying full-court pressure defense when they agree with coaches that it is an optimal strategy. Group acceptance of the need for sprints to condition them for playing this defense is less important. *Sixth,* teams that are not cohesive have a difficult time with a democratic process of decision making, as they might have a difficult time agreeing on anything. A democratic process of decision-making might result in a weakening of already fragile team spirit.

Seventh, coaches can impose decisions on teams only when they have power over the group. Many coaches have control of important rewards and punishments such as scholarships, playing time, and practice schedules. This form of power is accorded to coaches as a result of their positions. Coaches earn power in relationship to players when players respect and admire their personal qualities and expertise (Janssen & Dale, 2002). On some teams, such as in the National Basketball Association (NBA), players have more status and power than do coaches, and perhaps NBA players respond poorly to autocratic styles (Bandura, 1997).

A Volatile Mix

Coach P. J. Carlissimo was a highly successful collegiate basketball coach. His collegiate career culminated in 1989 when he brought his Seton Hall Pirates to the championship game of Division I American college basketball. His Pirates lost the championship game by a single point. His skills at recruiting, teaching, and motivating athletes were recognized as responsible for returning the Seton Hall men's basketball program to national prominence, and he was twice recognized as the Coach of the Year in the Big East Conference. In 2002, Carlissimo was inducted in the Seton Hall Athletic Hall of Fame.

Carlissimo left Seton Hall in 1994 to assume the head coaching job of the Portland Trailblazers, a professional basketball team in the National Basketball Association (NBA). Carlissimo was fired in Portland in 1997, despite three straight winning seasons. Subsequently, he was hired as the head coach of the Golden State Warriors of the NBA, but was fired from that job in 1999.

Carlissimo's style of coaching was seen as confrontational, aggressive, and "incessantly grating" (Rhoden, 1999, p. D1). The mix of these coaching characteristics with the behavior of an aggressive basketball player proved to be combustible. In 1997, Latrell Sprewell responded to Carlissimo's "ranting and raving" (Rhoden, 1999, p. D1) with violence. He choked Carlissimo and attempted several punches. Sprewell was suspended for 68 games and lost $6.4 million in salary plus his endorsement deal with Converse shoes.

This violent episode notwithstanding, Carlissimo experienced far less success as a professional coach than as a collegiate coach. Assuming that his style of relating to players did not change, differences in the players and in the power associated with collegiate versus professional coaching may explain the difference in success. Collegiate coaches are in a position of power in relation to athletes as they allocate team roles, playing time, and scholarships that are renewable on a yearly basis.

Professional coaches have far less power over athletes who have typically signed long-term contracts for far more money than the contract of the coach. Professional coaches are accorded power when they earn the trust and respect of players and convince athletes that individual and team goals are achievable if they follow his or her direction.

Autocratic Coaching

Autocratic coaches make decisions unilaterally or without input from team members. The response of athletes to **autocratic coaching** styles is not clear-cut. Some members of team sports such as soccer and basketball appear to prefer decisions rendered autocratically. Canadian female and male basketball players (Chelladurai & Arnott, 1985) and Canadian male soccer players (Gordon, 1988) were not adverse to autocratic decision making by coaches. In fact, the soccer players viewed group decision making as appropriate for less than 20% of coaching decisions. Canadian male and female collegiate and high school basketball players preferred autocratic decisions and were also receptive to processes in which coaches consulted with team members and then made decisions (Chelladurai, Haggerty, & Baxter, 1989; Chelladurai & Quek, 1995). Mentally tough English athletes expressed little interest in coaching that emphasized democratic decisions and social support. These efficacious athletes were more interested in training and instruction (Crust & Azadi, 2009). Elite Norwegian soccer players responded favorably to instruction, but also to democratic coaching and positive feedback (Hoigaard, Jones, & Peters, 2008).

Rick Pitino

Athletes in individual sports may be more receptive to cooperative decision making with coaches (Chelladurai & Reimer, 1998). Male and female Canadian tennis players of international, national, or provincial caliber and between the ages of 12 and 25 rated coaches as more autocratic than was to their liking (Prapavessis & Gordon, 1991). This discrepancy between autocratic styles they perceived in their coaches and what they preferred was unique in relation to corresponding perceived coaching behaviors and preferences on the other four scales of the LSS. That is, they perceived that coaches provided preferred supplies of training and instruction, democratic decision making, social support, and positive feedback.

There has been some evidence to indicate that males are more receptive to autocratic styles than are female athletes (Chelladurai, 1993; Holmes, McNeil, Adorna, & Procaccino, 2008; Martin, Jackson, Richardson, & Weiller, 1999). However, this evidence is inconsistent, and males and females appear to be more alike than different in terms of the coaching behaviors they prefer (Horn, 1992). In addition, the actual leadership characteristics of female and male coaches appear to be more alike than different (Jambor & Zhang, 1997).

Culture does appear to influence the coaching preferences of athletes. For example, Japanese collegiate athletes preferred a more autocratic coaching style and social support than did their Canadian counterparts. The Canadians recorded preferences for more democratic training and instruction (Chelladurai, Imamura, Yamaguchi, Oinuma, & Miyauchi,

1988). Chinese high school athletes also expected autocratic behavior from coaches and were less likely to challenge the authority of coaches. Croatian athletes may also expect autocratic behavior from coaches (Baric & Bucik, 2009).

Mothers prefer more democratic coaching styles for their adolescent sportspersons (Martin et al., 1999). Parents and adolescent sportspersons both opt for positive feedback and technical instruction for skill improvement.

Concordance of Actual and Preferred Leadership Styles

Despite differences in the preferred leadership styles among athletes, it is generally true that satisfaction with coaching leadership is greater when the preferences of athletes and the perceived leadership of coaches are in accord. Athletes are generally less satisfied with coaching leadership if there are discrepancies between the levels of training and instruction, social support, and positive feedback that they perceive coaches to supply and the amounts of these resources that they want (Chelladurai, 1990). In addition, satisfaction with leadership is generally higher when the training and instruction of coaches is effective in improving the individual abilities of team members and the performance of the team as a whole, and when coaches provide positive feedback that is contingent on actual good performance (Chelladurai, 1993). Athletes are more satisfied with coaches who foster task-oriented team environments. On these teams, progress is self- as opposed to other-referenced, and coercion is minimized. This coaching style encourages intrinsic interest in sport (Baric & Bucik, 2009).

A **servant leadership** coaching style also contributes to intrinsic interest in sport and satisfaction with team membership. Coaches manifest this style when they manifest sensitivity and humility, and encourage trust and inclusion (Rieke, Hammermeister, & Chase, 2008; Vidic & Burton, 2011). The servant leadership coaching style also encourages intrinsic motivation or enjoyment, interest, and effort from athletes. Rather than encouraging "softness" and a lack of discipline, this style is associated with self-confidence, goal setting, and mental toughness.

Leadership and Performance

In the Multidimensional Model of Leadership (Chelladurai, 1993), the consequences of leadership are defined as both the satisfaction of subordinates or players and the performance of team members. The relationship between coaching and the satisfaction of players is better understood than is the relationship between coaching and performance in the Multidimensional Model of Leadership (Chelladurai & Reimer, 1998). However, athletes hold coaches responsible for the performance of their teams and were less satisfied with coaches when teams fell short of goals and expectations (Chelladurai, 1984).

Athletes also consider performance in identifying peer leaders. For example, female collegiate soccer players were more likely to be identified as leaders if they were highly skilled (Glenn & Horn, 1993). Coaches selected the most skilled players as leaders, and these players were more likely to play in the center of the field, either on the forward, halfback, of fullback line, or as goalie.

ACTUAL BEHAVIOR OF ELITE COACHES

Perhaps it goes without saying that elite coaches have a great deal of knowledge about evaluating athletic talent, training individual athletes and teams, team organization and administration, and strategies and tactics for competition (Vallee & Bloom, 2005). Expert Canadian gymnastics coaches were shown to develop mental models or plans for developing the potential of elite gymnasts (Cote, Salmela, Trudel, Baria, & Russell, 1995). With these mental models, coaches determined what interventions during practice and competition were necessary for the development of young gymnasts. Coaches also considered whether young gymnasts were appropriate candidates for competition at elite levels and whether they had the coaching skills necessary to help the gymnasts reach their potential. Expert coaches altered their mental models or plans for developing elite gymnasts when environmental situations changed or when their coaching was proven to be inadequate to fully develop their gymnasts.

Specific aspects of effective coaching differ depending on the sport. In team sports such as ice hockey, basketball, and soccer, coaches are active in providing instruction and motivating athletes immediately prior to and during competition. Expert male and female gymnastics coaches in Canada tend to not "overcoach" prior to and during competitions. Instead, they monitor the degree of anxiety and mental preparation of their elite gymnasts, and intervene when it appears that athletes are overly anxious or not sufficiently focused and motivated for optimal performance (Cote, Samela, & Russell, 1995). They avoid trying to provide coaching about the technical aspects of routines immediately prior to competition, reasoning that time limitations and stress make it unlikely to be helpful (Cote, Salmela, Trudel, Baria, & Russell, 1995). Only about one-fourth of the coaches attempted to systematically monitor and control aspects of preperformance preparation from the time athletes arrived at competition venues. Coaches exerted control on preperformance preparation when they planned meals, monitored the psychological states of athletes, checked equipment, and anticipated distracting influences prior to and during competition.

During routine practice, gymnastic coaches said that they were supportive, and provided instruction and positive feedback. Coaches of males also acknowledged being dictatorial, demanding respect, and encouraging peer pressure. Coaches of females were more likely to keep an emotional distance and empathize quality training. During practice and training, coaches routinely used simulation training (see Chapter 5) to provide an analogue situation to actual competition.

Elite coaches of adolescent athletes recognize the need to work with parents. For example, Canadian coaches of elite male and female adolescent gymnasts met regularly with parents to explain the roles and expectations for athletes and parents (Cote & Salmela, 1996). These coaches were capable of delegating duty to assistants.

Elite Coaches and Sport Traditions

To this point, the benefits of providing positive feedback, encouragement following mistakes, and technical instruction has been emphasized. Similarly, the liabilities of punitive and negative comments, as well as providing instruction and correction in a hostile and sarcastic manner have been presented. Regardless of the benefits of these coaching characteristics, especially with young sportspersons, it would be inaccurate to assume that elite coaches uniformly emphasize these characteristics. In addition, routine coaching interventions may differ due to the influences of culture and **traditions** for particular sports (Ryska, Yin, Cooley, & Ginn, 1999). For example, the three male coaches responsible for the preparation of the six-member female 1996 French Olympic judo team were authoritarian, made unilateral decisions, and made frequent use of negative feedback (d'Arripe-Longueville, Fournier, & Dubois, 1998). This authoritarian style is traditional for French Olympic judo coaches, and perhaps for judo coaches and instructors in general (Chelladurai, Malloy, Imamura, & Yamaguchi, 1987). Of the six categories of coaching interaction strategies utilized by these judo coaches, five were confrontational or hostile in tone. These consisted of: stimulating rivalries among the six female athletes, provoking athletes with aggressive and ironic comments and negative feedback, displaying indifference and providing no communication and feedback, engaging in direct conflict and threatening athletes with exclusion from the team, and exhibiting favoritism. The sixth coaching strategy involved developing team cohesion.

The coaches believed that these provocative strategies fostered efforts for continuous improvement and helped athletes to develop mental skills and mental toughness. The coaches did not treat all athletes in the same way. They made observations about the personalities of athletes and tailored strategies, such as provocations with hostile comments, to fit the personalities of athletes. Strategies such as ignoring athletes after injuries or when athletes did not follow instructions in matches were seen to not only be effective, but to also comport with judo traditions. The coaches did not believe that selection to an elite athletic team was sufficient to foster team cohesion, and attempted to build cohesion by having the team engage in dangerous tasks. These tasks were intended to promote fearlessness and included driving go-carts, canyoning, and rock climbing.

With power to select athletes for the French Olympic team, these coaches had a great deal of power in relation to the athletes. The responses of athletes to coaches appear to be at least partly determined by their understanding of the power differential between athletes and coaches. Judo athletes were diplomatic and made concessions to the coaches. Athletes gained power in relation to coaches by attempting and accomplishing superiority in their weight class. In this way, they felt less vulnerable to being cut from the team. Athletes solicited feedback and council from coaches after poor performances. By initiating this contact, athletes avoided being ignored by coaches, and coaches also hoped that athletes would initiate this movement. Athletes "shopped" for the best coaching and technical information from the three coaches, perhaps demonstrating that just as coaches could make judgments about them, they could also make decisions about coaches. Another effort at self-determination consisted of soliciting training information from sources outside of the coaching ranks, such as athletic trainers or sport psychologists.

SUMMARY AND APPLICATION

Successful leaders such as coaches know what they are talking about and communicate this understanding to their teams. They appreciate differences among teammates and devise strategies for instructing and motivating them. Effective coaches invest a great deal in teaching and motivating teams and they also hold teams to high standards of effort and performance. Transformational leaders inspire teams to not only improve effort and performance, but to also set higher goals and ask more of themselves.

It is difficult to lead without the trust of team members. Athletes are often asked to put their faith in the decisions of coaches about roles on teams and strategies and tactics for competitions. Sportspersons are less likely to accept coaching decisions that run counter to their individual goals if they do not trust that team goals will be accomplished by cooperating with coaches. It is easier for coaches with histories of success to inspire trust, as athletes expect that they will also become winners if they follow the direction of the successful coaches.

Coaches develop beliefs about the efficacy of their teams and their coaching efficacy. These coaches expect more from their teams, and their teams are more likely to fulfill their expectations. Coaches build the efficacy of teams by setting challenging but attainable goals. With the accomplishment of goals, teams are provided with enactive attainments, the most convincing source of efficacy. Coaches support the efficacy of teams when they monitor the reactions of members to losses and help them to identify unstable factors, such as insufficient practice and skill development that contributed to failures. Coaches intervene when capable athletes become demoralized due to attributing their failures and setbacks to stable, internal factors, such as a lack of talent.

Efficacious coaches dispel doubts about the likelihood for success at times proximal to competition. At times distal, they are vigilant for signs of complacency, and motivate teams to train and practice with a sense of purpose by prompting teams to question their readiness for optimal performance.

Coaches often have distinctive styles of relating to players. Coaches with task orientations focus on providing accurate technical information about how to improve athletic skill and performance. With relationship orientations, coaches emphasize positive feedback and encouragement. Coaches are also distinguished on the basis on the degree to which they emphasize positive control or negative control. With positive control, positive reinforcement, encouragement, and technical instruction are predominant. Negative control encourages fear among team members and emphasizes verbal punishment, sarcasm, and efforts to ignore successful performance. Coaches who emphasize positive control support the self-esteem of their players, build team cohesion, and encourage athletes to stick with their sport.

In the Multidimensional Model of Leadership, the characteristics of leaders and subordinates, such as team members, and leadership requirements demanded by particular environments are represented. Styles of leadership have varying degrees of effectiveness in different environments and with different categories of sportspersons. For example, autocratic coaching styles are more likely to be effective when coaches have a considerable amount of power over athletes. Athletes are generally more satisfied with the leadership of coaches when the levels of instruction, social support, and positive feedback that they perceive coaches to supply are approximately equal to the amounts of these emotional resources that they want.

Key Terms

Discussion Questions

Q1. Define leadership.

Q2. Do leaders share personality traits?

Q3. Consider typical interventions of effective leaders.

Q4. Distinguish leaders with relationship versus task orientations.

Q5. Describe transformational leadership.

Q6. Review the importance of trust in leadership.

Q7. Consider the components of effective communication by leaders.

Q8. Review the four components of coaching efficacy.

Q9. What contributes to the development of coaching efficacy?

Q10. Consider coaching strategies for building team efficacy.

Q11. Provide suggestions for improving the influence of coaches.

Q12. Consider the meaning of contingent coaching interventions.

Q13. Review the seven components of the Multidimensional Model of Leadership.

Q14. Describe the scales of the Leadership Scale for Sport.

Q15. Differentiate autocratic and democratic coaching.

Q16. Are some athletes receptive to autocratic coaching?

Q17. Are leadership styles related to the performance of teams?

Q18. Consider actual coaching behaviors and traditions in sports.

Suggested Readings

Boardley, I. D., Kavussanu, M., & Ring, C. (2008). Athletes' perceptions of coaching effectiveness and athlete-related outcomes in rugby union: An investigation based on the coaching efficacy model. *The Sport Psychologist, 22,* 269–287.

Chelladurai, P. (2007). Leadership in sports. In G. Tenenbaum & R. C. Eklund (Eds.), *Handbook of sport psychology* (3rd ed., pp. 113–135). New York, NY: Wiley.

Cote, J., Salmela, J., Grudel, P., Baria, A., & Storm, R. (1995). The coaching model: A grounded assessment of expert gymnastic coaches' knowledge. *Journal of Sport & Exercise Psychology, 17,* 1–17.

Feltz, D. L., Chase, M. A., Moritz, Se. E., & Sullivan, P. J. (1999). Development of the multidimensional coaching effectiveness scale. *Journal of Educational Psychology, 91,* 765–776.

Feltz, D. L., Short, S. E., & Sullivan, P. J. (2008). *Self-efficacy in sport.* Champaign, IL: Human Kinetics.

Kaiser, R. B., Hogan, R., & Craig, S. B. (2008). Leadership and the fate of organizations. *American Psychologist, 63,* 96–110.

Murray, M. C., Mann, B. L., & Mead, J. K. (2010). Leadership effectiveness. In J. M. Williams (Ed.), *Applied sport psychology: Personal growth to peak performance* (6th ed., pp. 106–131). New York, NY: McGraw-Hill.

Vealey, R. S. (2009). Confidence in sport. (2009). Management of competitive stress in elite sport. In B. W. Brewer (Ed.), *Handbook of sports medicine and science, sport psychology* (pp. 43–52). Chichester, England: Wiley-Blackwell.

Yukelson, D. (2010). Communicating effectively. In J. M. Williams (Ed.), *Applied sport psychology: Personal growth to peak performance* (6th ed., pp. 149–165). New York, NY: McGraw-Hill.

Chapter 23

TEAM COHESION, EFFICACY, AND GOALS

Geno Auriemma, the women's basketball coach at the University of Connecticut, lead his team to eight national championships, four perfect seasons, and winning streaks of 90 and 70 games. He reflected on teamwork:

  "I say to my players, the minute you start thinking you play for Connecticut, or you play for Coach Auriemma, or you play for the fans in the building, you could not be further from the truth. I say that the reason you're going to rotate over and take that charge is because your teammate just got beat on a drive and you just bailed them out. The reason you want to block out and get the rebound that saves the game is that when you get in that locker room, your teammates will let you know how they feel about you. You're playing for each other, so forget all the other stuff" (Cyr, 2004, p. 36).

Cohesion and performance (photo courtesy of Western Connecticut State University)

Individuals become members of teams in order to reach certain goals and to affiliate and socialize with others. For example, individuals interested in a *task*, such as improving individual skills and winning championships in basketball, must become a part of a team. Athletes may also affiliate with teams for *social* reasons, such as the enjoyment of the company of teammates. A form of cohesiveness occurs when individuals perceive teams as meeting their interests in achieving task and social goals. This form of cohesiveness is **Individual Attractions to the Group,** and it includes **Individual Attractions to the Group-Task (ATG-T)**, and **Individual Attractions to the Group-Social (ATG-S)**. Basketball players who join a team that appears most likely to win a championship demonstrate ATG-T, and those that join the same teams as friends demonstrate ATG-S.

Athletes also develop conclusions about the degree to which teammates are united or cohesive in their pursuit of these task and social goals (Carron, Brawley, & Widmeyer, 1998). This form of cohesion is referred to as **Group Integration (GI)**, and Group Integration pertains for task **(GI-T)** and social **(GI-S)** goals. Sportspersons who believe that teammates are united in the pursuit of common tasks experience GI-T, and athletes who find that teammates share their interest in friendship realize GI-S (Carron, Widmeyer, & Brawley, 1985). All four of these forms of cohesiveness (ATG-T, ATG-S, GI-T, GI-S) potentially influence whether sportspersons remain as members of teams. However, the forms of group cohesion may differ in various situations and age groups (Schultz, Eom, Smoll, & Smith, 1994). For example, adolescents between the ages of 13 and 17 identified only task (e.g., "We all share the same commitment to our team's goals") and social (e.g., "Some of my best friends are on this team") forms of group cohesion (Eys, Loughead, Bray, & Carron, 2009a, p. 407; Eys, Loughead, Bray, & Carron, 2009b).

Teams are **cohesive** to the degree that they stick together in pursuit of common goals or for the satisfaction of the emotional needs of the members. Cohesive teams share aspirations, beliefs (Carron, Bray, & Eys, 2002; Carron, Martin, & Loughead, 2012), and a collective identity (Partington & Shangi, 1992). Shared aspirations, goals, and team efficacy influence team performance to a greater degree than friendships among teammates. Cohesive teams resist disruptive influences (Brawley, Carron, & Widmeyer, 1988) such as competing privileges and opportunities (Prapavessis & Carron, 1997), and work harder (Bray & Whaley, 2001). Cohesiveness is enhanced when members demonstrate unselfish play and sacrifice for the good of the team (Holt & Sparkes, 2001), and cohesive teams show good sportspersonship more frequently (Aoyagi, Cox, & McGuire, 2008). Sportspersons approach competition with more facilitative anxiety as members of cohesive teams (Eys, Hardy, Carron, & Beauchamp, 2003).

Athletes are less likely to quit teams when they experience a sense of closeness and belonging to the team. For example, recreational and elite Canadian female ringette players (Spink, 1995) and elite junior male hockey players (Spink, Wilson, & Odnokon, 2010) were more likely to return to play the next season for cohesive teams. (Ringette is a sport that is similar to ice hockey, with modified sticks and a ring rather than a puck.) Various combinations of the forms of cohesiveness also influence attendance at group exercise programs (Paskevich, Estabrooks, Brawley, & Carron, 2001). In cohesive exercise groups, members are more likely to not miss classes, arrive on time, resist disruptions to holding exercise classes, and not drop out.

The beneficial effects of team cohesiveness were traditionally considered to be greater for **interacting** than for **coaching sports** (Carron & Chelladurai, 1981). In coaching sports, such as gymnastics and swimming, athletes compete individually, whereas in interactive sports, such as lacrosse and basketball, teams compete as a unit and individual success is dependent on team function. However, a meta-analysis, or statistical integration of extant research, demonstrated that the beneficial effects of cohesiveness were not mitigated by sport type (Carron, Colman, Wheeler, & Stevens, 2002). Furthermore, even though members of coaching teams do not coordinate their athletic performances, their interactions during competition and practices serve to motivate teammates and foster cohesion (Widmeyer & Williams, 1991).

Cohesiveness is experienced not only in the external interactions between teammates, but also in the individual psychology of team members. Sportspersons incorporate status on cohesive teams and relationships with teammates into their personal identities. That is, they come to define themselves partially as a member of a team. If cohesion has been fostered by effective leadership, relationships with coaches are also integrated into the self-definition of athletes (Blanchard, Perreault, & Vallerand, 1998).

Cohesiveness is more likely when members are satisfied with how they are treated, their training and instruction, and when their individuals goals and goals for the team are met (Aoyagi et al., 2008). Group cohesion does not last forever. It is dynamic, or the result of the confluence of the motives, talents, and efforts of team members that exist in certain periods in time or sport seasons (Carron & Dennis, 1998; Carron & Dennis, 2001).

FOUR FACTORS AFFECTING TEAM COHESION

At least four factors influence team cohesion (Carron, Burke, & Shapcott, 2009; Carron & Dennis, 1998). *First,* **situational factors** influence group cohesion. People who spend time in physical proximity have the opportunity for interaction and communication. Sportspersons have opportunities for spending a considerable amount of time together as they share locker rooms, travel together, and may live in common dormitories and eat at training tables. Individuals that share distinctive characteristics are more likely to feel a sense of oneness and unity. Sportspersons develop this distinctiveness when they earn positions on teams, compete or practice in uniform, or wear clothing such as letter sweaters or jackets that identify them as team members. Coaches and athletic and sport institutions that emphasize the history and tradition of their institution encourage feelings of membership in distinctive sororities and fraternities. Coaches also encourage pride in team membership when they work with athletes to establish team goals and instill a sense of responsibility in team members for the overall team success.

Vince Lombardi and Team Cohesion

In 1958, the Green Bay Packers of the National Football League (NFL) "underwhelmed ten opponents, overwhelmed one, and whelmed one" (Maraniss, 1999, p. 191), or achieved a record of ten losses, one win, and one tie. In 1959, Vince Lombardi was hired as head coach to turn around this professional team. Among his many interventions were efforts to build team cohesion or a sense of family and community. For example, during the final week of training camp, he moved his entire team, including wives and children, to the campus of a suburban Milwaukee boarding school. He instituted a dress code of team blazers and ties for wear on the road, and insisted that team members represent the team in the most dignified manner possible. In a time of segregation in America, he insisted that racial prejudice would not disrupt the cohesion of his team. In a team lecture on racism he stated: "If I ever hear nigger or dago or kike or anything like that around here, regardless of who you are, you're through with me. You can't play for me if you have any kind of prejudice" (Maraniss, 1999, p. 241). Lombardi spread the word in Green Bay that any bar or restaurant that would not serve African American players would also be off limits to his entire team. On road trips, he would not allow his team to stay at segregated hotels, and lodged his team at an army post in Fort Benning, GA, so that they could stay together prior to an exhibition game.

Lombardi succeeded in turning the Packers around. In 1959, the Packers achieved a record of seven wins and five losses. In 1960, they were runners up to the Philadelphia Eagles, losing 17 to 13 in the championship game. They were champions of the NFL in 1961, 1962, 1965, 1966, and 1967. They won the first two Super Bowls that were contested in January of 1967 and 1968. He retired from coaching the Packers in 1968, having won the NFL championship in five of nine years. He was recognized as a transcendent figure and a symbol of modern football during the time that football became the leading American spectator sport. With no political experience, he was considered as a vice presidential candidate by both the Democratic and Republican parties. Reflecting Lombardi's place in its history, the NFL named its championship trophy the Lombardi Trophy.

A number of studies have demonstrated that cohesiveness is greater in smaller groups (Carron & Spink, 1995; Mullen & Cooper, 1994; Widmeyer, Brawley, & Carron, 1990). Membership on elite teams is very limited in relation to the numbers of outsiders, and the distinctiveness bestowed by membership on elite teams creates a sense of unity (Carron & Dennis, 1998). Further, members of a starting team or a travel squad (Widmeyer & Williams, 1991) might experience a greater sense of cohesiveness with fellow first team members than with the larger body or reserves and junior varsity players. For example, starting units on collegiate and high school football teams were more cohesive than nonstarters

(Granito & Rainey, 1988). Regardless of size, cohesiveness is promoted when teammates understand that they must depend on one another for team success (Yukelson, 1997).

A *second* factor demonstrated to influence team cohesion is the **personal characteristics** of the members of teams. Team members may be quite different in terms of socioeconomic background, ethnicity, and athletic experience. These differences need not be divisive, and similarities can be identified. For example, team members may be similar in that they share satisfaction about being a member of a team. Sportspersons are more likely to be satisfied with team membership when relationships with parents, coaches, and other students are positive, and when teammates are showing improvement and commitment to common goals.

No-Swear Zone

In American football, cursing or profanity is a part of the culture, except at Vanderbilt and other universities such as Notre Dame, Stanford, Rice, and Furman. At Vanderbilt, Coach Bobby Johnson instituted a no-profanity rule that extends to players, coaches, and team managers, games and practice, and all athletic facilities. The penalties for inadvertent swearing are "up-and-down" drills—running in place, dropping to the ground, and jumping up—or pushups.

Vanderbilt was considered first in its conference (Southeastern) in decorum (Yantz, 2002).

Third, **effective leadership** fosters team cohesion (Eys, Burke, Carron, & Dennis, 2010; Mach, Dolan, & Tzafrir, 2010). Cohesiveness increases when coaches and athletes pursue common goals and objectives. For example, there was greater cohesiveness on high school basketball and wrestling teams when coaches and athletes were pursuing either team or individual goals, or when both athletes and coaches were focused on maintaining harmonious relationships with teammates (Carron & Chelladurai, 1981). Coaches who are active in providing instruction and training, positive feedback, social support, and who allow athletes to participate in decision making foster team cohesion (Westre & Weiss, 1991). Task cohesion is encouraged when athletes participate in setting team goals. Teams may also be cohesive and not accept the leadership of coaches. This sometimes occurs when a popular coach is replaced and team members compare the replacement with the predecessor.

Leadership is also provided by team members, such as team captains. Effective athlete leaders support teammates and are good communicators (Dupuis, Bloom, & Loughead, 2006; Gould, 1999; Loughead & Hardy, 2005). Not everyone on a team can be a leader, and teams with limited numbers of leaders tend to be more cohesive (Hardy, Eys, & Loughead, 2009). Both junior soccer players who represented England in international tournaments and their coaches considered strong athlete leadership and team cohesion to have the most positive influence on team success (Pain & Harwood, 2008).

Riley's Rules

Pat Riley coached the Los Angeles Lakers to four National Basketball Association (NBA) championships in nine years. A former player, he has also been the head coach of the New York Knicks and the Miami Heat, and the Heat won the 2006 NBA championship. He asked the Lakers to enter into a Core Covenant or commitment to the welfare of the team with him (Riley, 1993). He collaborated with players in making decisions, even about personnel. He asked team members to set standards for practice and games and to monitor these standards. Riley enforced the standards by benching players who did not fulfill the Covenant. However, peer pressure was the primary resource for enforcing the Core Covenant, and he maintained that this replaced blaming and finger-pointing. In this process, members of the Lakers came to trust that Riley's agenda represented their individual and group interests.

Fourth, as teams take shape, members assume roles, acquire status, and develop **norms,** or formal and informal rules or standards, for behavior. On cohesive teams, members understand and accept their roles (George & Feltz, 1995). They attempt to perform their roles to the best of their ability. Role acceptance is increased when coaches make roles explicit and when coaches determine if athletes accept their roles. Role acceptance is enhanced when coaches emphasize that team success is dependent on the successful role performance of all team members, and when differences in status between roles is minimized. Coaches may also assign team and individual goals to increase role clarity and acceptance.

COHESIVENESS AND PERFORMANCE

Better team and individual athletic performances are associated with team cohesiveness (Mach et al., 2010). For example, U.S. Olympic athletes at the winter games in Nagano, Japan, in 1998 rated strong team chemistry and chemistry between teams and coaches as critical determinants of performance (Gould, 1999). Junior soccer players who represented England in international tournaments and their coaches identified strong cohesion on the pitch and positive leadership as the most important factors influencing performance (Pain & Haywood, 2008). Canadian female and male high school athletes were more likely to recognize social and task cohesiveness on successful teams (Partington & Shangi, 1992). Elite Canadian female and male basketball and soccer players from winning collegiate and club teams reported higher levels of GI-T (Group Integration-Task) and ATG-T (Individual Attractions to the Group-Task; Carron et al., 2002).

Cohesiveness was associated with goal celebrations involving physical contact with teammates at the center of pitch among English soccer teams. Teams that celebrated goals in this manner had better records than did teams on which goals were celebrated by running to the edge of the pitch to solicit accolades from the audience (Bornstein & Goldschmidt, 2008).

Team cohesion is also associated with improvement. Collegiate male ice hockey teams in Canada that were cohesive at midseason were more likely to have successful postseasons (Ball & Carron, 1976). The individual performances of female and male high school basketball players improved with the development of team cohesiveness (Bray & Whaley, 2001). High school basketball players demonstrated improvement in terms of field goal and foul shot percentages, points per game, rebounds, and assists per game. As they accepted or bought into the goals and objectives of their teams and developed social relations with teammates, their effort, intensity, and productivity increased.

Application

The need for sport psychologists to develop expertise in team building has been recognized. Despite the importance of this expertise, there is a dearth of scientific literature that details the specific processes for optimizing team cultures (Cruickshank & Collins, 2012). These limitations notwithstanding, an outline for team building may be developed on the bases of the information in this chapter and the suggested readings.

COHESIVENESS LEADS TO SUCCESS, AND VICE VERSA

Cohesion and success

There is general agreement that team cohesiveness and performance improvements are positively correlated. Disagreement exists concerning whether cohesiveness causes performance improvements or successful performance results in cohesiveness. For example, among women's field hockey teams, midseason team records predicted postseason cohesiveness (Williams & Hacker, 1982). More successful teams at midseason were more likely to report interpersonal closeness and teamwork postseason. Success and cohesiveness also predicted greater satisfaction with team participation. Among female athletes in a range of sports, the increase in team cohesiveness after successful performance was greater than the improvement in performance with increasing cohesiveness. Losing appeared to decrease the cohesiveness of teams in interactive sports to a greater degree than the cohesiveness of teams in coacting sports, at least for female athletes (Matheson & Mathes, 1997).

These results were contradicted in a carefully designed study with male and female collegiate field hockey players in England (Slater & Sewell, 1994). These contradictory results demonstrated that team cohesiveness midway through seasons predicted team performance after an additional four weeks. More cohesive teams at midseason were more successful, as determined by wins, ties, and losses, four weeks later. Team performance at the midway point did not predict cohesiveness after the four weeks.

Cohesion Leads to Success

In the previous chapter, the deep bond between University of Louisville Hall of Fame basketball coach Rick Pitino and point guard Russ Smith was recognized. Pitino shared this bond with the entire team, and despite the absence of NBA-caliber players, they won the NCAA basketball championship in 2013.

Pitino beamed about the development of his players: "If I can keep recruiting guys like this, I want to coach until 70 and beyond because I've had such a blast and to see guys work that hard inside just fills you up, really does" (Berman, 2013).

Ultimately, the most comprehensive current research demonstrates that team cohesiveness promotes better performance and that successful performance enhances team cohesiveness (Carron, Colman et al., 2002). Furthermore, teams that are cohesive in their pursuit of task and social goals are likely to be more successful.

Lacking Cohesiveness

The French nation soccer (football) team ("Les Bleus") won the World Cup in 1998, the European championship in 2000, and reached the World Cup final in 2006. Les Bleus exited the 2010 World Cup in the first round without a victory. In their final match against South Africa, they played one man short after a player was given a red card (ejected) for elbowing an opponent in the head. Their coach, Raymond Domenech, refused to shake the hand of his South African counterpart after the watch.

Les Bleus also played the final match without star striker Nicholas Anelka. He was sent home after he profanely insulted Domenech during halftime in their preceding game against Mexico. In protest, the team refused to practice on the day after the loss to Mexico.

Les Bleus were described in the French press as "pitiful, ridiculous, and shameful" (Longman, 2010; "World Cup", 2010). Sports minister Roselyne Bachelot condemned the players as "immature bullies" or "frightened kids" in the national assembly. Anelka characterized this criticism as thinly veiled racism: "When things go wrong, then people come back to talking about the black immigrants. Arabs, housing-project Muslims, even if we aren't" (Peterson, 2010).

Laurent Blanc, a member of the 1998 World Cup champion Les Bleus, replaced Domenech as the national coach in 2010. Blanc established discipline and asserted his authority. One of his first decisions was to exclude all 22 of the players that traveled to South Africa from an exhibition match with Norway. He also hired a psychologist to improve team cohesion.

COHESIVENESS AND SOCIAL LOAFING

Team membership does not also result in improved performance. When group cohesion is low, team members sometimes **loaf** or goof off when they think other group members can make up for their reduction in effort. When cohesion is low, there is less concern for the success of the group (Everett, Smith, & Williams, 1992). In these groups that lack cohesion, there is a diffusion of responsibility, as individuals do not take personal responsibility and reason that jobs are the responsibility of other group members. Loafing is more likely to occur when individual contributions are not critical to the success of the group, when it appears that others are loafing, when it is difficult to identify the contributions of individuals, and in larger groups (Carron et al., 2009). Effort is increased in groups that lack cohesion when the performances of individual members are announced publicly (Paskevich et al., 2001).

Social loafing is less likely to occur in cohesive groups. Responsibility for failure is also shared among the members of cohesive groups (Carron et al., 1998). Failure prompts **scapegoating** in groups that lack cohesion, as members blame teammates for failure. In scapegoating, team members attempt to enhance their image at the expense of teammates.

As has been emphasized at various points in this text, psychological variables, such as team cohesiveness, do not function in isolation from athletic skill, practice, and training. As will be described in the next sections, cohesiveness and team efficacy are positively correlated, and both are associated with better team performance.

TEAM EFFICACY

As explained in Chapter 10, the belief that one has the capacity to organize and execute the actions necessary to realize goals in particular areas or domains of functioning is referred to as self-efficacy. Team members often share efficacy beliefs not only about their potential for reaching athletic goals, but also about the efficacy of the team as a whole to act effectively and reach performance standards (Chow & Feltz, 2008; Magyar, Feltz, & Simpson, 2004). Athletes who consider their teams to be cohesive are more likely to be seen as being efficacious at sports such as soccer and basketball. When cohesion is lacking, athletes are less likely to share team efficacy (Marcos, Miguel, Oliva, & Calvo, 2010).

Collective **team efficacy** is more closely tied to team performance than are the individual efficacy beliefs of team members, especially in interactive sports such as collegiate hockey. It is also a correlate of team cohesion in interactive sports such as basketball and handball (Heuze et al., 2006). Collective efficacy is not only the stronger predictor of hockey team performance, but it is also more directly affected by the performance of hockey teams (Feltz & Lirgg, 2001). Team efficacy has been shown to increase and decrease, respectively, following wins and losses, and individual efficacy did not rise and fall after wins and losses. With high collective team efficacy, team members exert more effort to reach goals, persevere when faced with difficulties and setbacks, and recover confidence more quickly after disappointing defeats.

Past achievements or enactive attainments are important sources of team efficacy. For example, the coach of the Norwegian women's handball team participating in the World Championships and Olympics regularly reminded the team of past successes (Ronglan, 2007). The quality of preparation and training, injury status, and perceptions of the confidence of teammates were also sources of team efficacy. Team members attempted to manifest confidence in their body language and verbal behavior to both boost the confidence of teammates and demoralize and instill doubt in opponents. Coaches emphasized internal, controllable factors in diagnosing problems and explaining successes.

Team efficacy decreases when members are lost to injuries. For example, semiprofessional soccer players were less confident in their team's ability to persevere in response to failure, rebound from losses, and maintain physical endurance following injuries to players (Damato, Grove, Eklund, & Cresswell, 2008).

Sources of Collective Efficacy

As was the case with individual self-efficacy, the most convincing source of collective or team efficacy is **enactive attainments** or actual team accomplishment. Not surprisingly, the efficacy of teams with winning records is likely to increase across the course of athletic seasons (Feltz & Lirgg, 1998; Myers, Payment, & Feltz, 2004). Once established, team efficacy is somewhat resilient (Feltz et al., 2008; Myers, Paiement, & Feltz, 2007), and efficacious teams perform better (Myers, Feltz, & Short, 2004). Successful performance is especially likely to influence team efficacy in sports that require team coordination, cooperation, communication (Gully, Incalcaterra, Joshi, & Beaubien, 2002). Team efficacy is also influenced by the play or enactive attainments of individual players.

As was the case with individual efficacy, observational learning, feedback, and physiological reactions also provide information about the efficacy of teams. Observational learning and feedback are provided as teams estimate their competence in comparison to other teams. Teams are influenced by coaches, and effective coaches model confidence and provide persuasion to enhance team efficacy. Spectators provide feedback, and efficacy is affected by the reactions of the audience. Booing home crowds and hostile media can undermine team efficacy. Team members also monitor their physiological reactions in estimating efficacy (Bandura, 1997). For example, signs of physiological anxiety, physical dysfunction, fatigue, and emotional dysphoria erode efficacy.

Team cohesion also contributes to team efficacy or confidence that team goals will be accomplished, and with heightened team efficacy, team performance improves (Kozub & McDonnell, 2000; Paskevich, Brawley, Dorsch, & Widmeyer, 1995). For example, intercollegiate and recreational collegiate volleyball teams with higher task cohesiveness, both Group Integration-Task (GI-T) and Individual Attractions to Group-Task (ATG-T), also demonstrated higher team efficacy (Paskevich, Brawley, Dorsch, & Widmeyer, 1999). The cohesive teams had confidence in their collective ability to overcome obstacles, sustain motivation and communicate effectively, and in their team's skills. Similar results were also reported for elite Canadian male and female volleyball teams (Spink, 1990). However, in the Canadian study, the ATG-T and Group Integration-Social (GI-S) factors differentiated teams with high and low efficacy. Teams high in the ATG-T and GI-S factors also had higher efficacy. Teams with higher efficacy were more successful in a volleyball tournament. The experience of success enhances both team efficacy and cohesion.

Application

When a team is a decided underdog, collective efficacy may be illusive. It is, therefore, all the more important to focus on the execution of skills, plays, and defensive maneuvers that are under the team's control, rather than the game's outcome. Teams may be reminded that they have "less to lose" than the favorite, and that pressure on the favorite will mount as long as the outcome hangs in the balance.

SETTING TEAM GOALS

Simply put, a group goal is what sufficient numbers of a group, such as a team, attempt to accomplish. Cooperation and collaboration among teammates is necessary for the accomplishment of group goals. Goal setting for teams is complicated by the need to integrate team goals with the individual goals of team members.

Athletes generally endorse team goals, although team goals may not be specific and well defined. Team goals for practice are more likely to be process goals, and team goals for competition are likely to be process and outcome goals (Brawley, Carron, & Widmeyer, 1992). In Chapter 8, process goals were said to relate to objectives for specific skill enhancement and refinement, and outcome goals to results of competition that are defined in relation to competitors. An example of an outcome goal would be to win a particular game.

Group goals that are difficult and specific enhance performance (Widmeyer & Ducharme, 1997). In fact, group goals may increase performance more than individual goals, because the criteria for group goals are more difficult (Burton, Naylor, & Holliday, 2001). Difficult goals motivate greater effort, and effort is also increased when team goals and individual responsibilities for reaching team goals are publicly disclosed. Social loafing is also minimized when individual responsibilities for reaching team goals are defined. However, as was the case with individual goals, sportspersons must accept or buy into the team goals.

When athletes accept team goals, teams develop a shared focus and team cohesion improves. Indeed, athletes rated the acceptance of team goals as the most important source of task cohesion and the second most influential source of social cohesion. Team goals that lead to better team performance are also likely to promote cohesion. Team cohesion is enhanced when team members participate in the goal setting process. This process of setting goals has been identified as a major component of team building or systematically enhancing team cohesion (Rovivo, Arvinen-Barrow, Weigand, Eskola, & Lintunen, 2012). Indeed goal setting is the most influential intervention for enhancing team cohesion (Martin, Carron, & Burke, 2009).

When team members participate in setting goals, they have opportunities to understand the responsibilities of individuals to the team and the degree of cooperation necessary to reach team goals (Eys, Patterson, Loughead, & Carron, 2006). This collaboration is important if athletes are to prioritize team goals over individual goals. Cohesion is also enhanced when team members have opportunities to openly discuss the functioning of teams (Pain & Harwood, 2009). When teammates and coaches collaborate in setting team goals, teams are more likely to resist divisive influences and remain cohesive throughout athletic seasons (Senecal, Loughead, & Bloom, 2008).

Coaches and athletes have been encouraged to collaborate in setting long-term team goals or goals for entire athletic seasons. These goals should be specific and difficult, and team short-term goals should then determine the steps necessary to realize the long-term goals (Widmeyer & Ducharme, 1997). Continuing with this advice, short-term goals should involve outcome, performance, and process aspects. Outcome and process aspects were defined above, and athletic performance goals focus on results measured against individual or team baselines. An example of a performance goal for a basketball team would be to make 80% of free throws during practice and games by the end of a season. Finally, it is important for coaches to provide feedback about progress in meeting short- and long-term goals. This is easily accomplished by posting results and monitoring results in team meetings.

Application

Team members may not be entirely straightforward when their individual goals run counter to team goals. For example, a player may superficially endorse team goals of unselfishness, but covertly prioritize his or her offensive statistics.

The process of openly discussing team goals provides opportunities for coaches and teammates to assess whether team members accept team goals. Covert individual goals may be sussed in these forums. Once identified, the influence of teammates and coaches may come to bear on divisive and ambivalent team members. The influence of the group is considerable.

SUMMARY AND APPLICATION

Team cohesion is associated with team success and successful teams are often more cohesive. Team cohesion does not last forever. It is a dynamic psychological quality that exists in relation to teammates and coaches. Its more indelible representation exists in the identities of athletes as they take aspects of their identities from participation on teams.

Teams that stick together in pursuit of common goals experience a form of task or social cohesiveness. When individual members believe that teams provide opportunities for meeting task goals, they experience Individual Attractions to the Group-Task (ATG-T), and when teams are understood to provide social opportunities, individuals acknowledge Individual Attractions to the Group-Social (ATG-S). Sportspersons also form opinions about the degree to which teammates are united in pursuit of task or social goals, and these opinions are represented on measures of Group Integration for task (GI-T) and social (GI-S) goals.

Opportunities for the development of cohesion occur when teammates spend time in the same sport venues and when they keep to similar schedules. Cohesion is enhanced when sportspersons take pride in team membership and are publicly recognized as a member of an elite corps. Regardless of sociological differences, athletes experience team cohesion when they recognize that team members share a unity of purpose. Coaches have a major role in determining team unity. People are more likely to loaf or avoid work on teams and in groups that lack cohesion.

Teams that are united in the pursuit of goals are more likely to be cohesive. Athletes are more likely to personally endorse goals when they take part in establishing goals and when they understand that teammates share the team goals.

Key Terms

Individual Attractions to the
Group   540

Individual Attractions to the Group-
Task   540

Individual Attractions to the Group-
Social   540

Group integration   540

Group Integration-Task   540

Group Integration-Social   540

Interacting and coaching
sports   541

Team Cohesion: situational factors,
personal characteristics, effective
leadership, norms   541

Social loafing   547

Scapegoating   547

Team efficacy   548

Enactive attainments   548

Discussion Questions

Q1. Review these forms of cohesiveness: Individual Attractions to
     the Group-Task, Individual Attractions to the Group-Social,
     Group Integration-Task, Group Integration-Social.
Q2. Explain the benefits of group cohesion.
Q3. Is group cohesion more important for interacting or coaching
     sports?
Q4. How is team cohesion experienced?
Q5. Review the four factors that influence group cohesion.
Q6. Does team cohesion lead to success or does success lead to
     team cohesion?
Q7. How is team cohesion related to social loafing and scapegoat-
     ing?
Q8. Explain team efficacy.
Q9. What are the sources of collective efficacy?
Q10. How are productive team goals established?

Suggested Readings

Abboud, L., & Colchester, M. (2008, June 6). The flubbing Dutchmen:
    To cure soccer penalty-kick phobias, hugs and psychologists. *The Wall
    Street Journal.* Retrieved from http://www.djreprints.com

Eys, M. A., Burke, S. M., Carron, A. V., & Dennis, P. W. (2010). The sport
    team as an effective group. In J. M. Williams (Ed.), *Applied sport psychol-
    ogy: Personal growth to peak performance* (6th ed., pp. 132–148). New
    York, NY: McGraw-Hill.

Eys, M., Loughead, T., Bray, S. R., & Carron, A. V. (2009a). Development
    of a cohesion questionnaire for youth: The Youth Sport Environment
    Questionnaire. *Journal of Sport and Exercise Psychology, 31*, 390–408.

Eys, M., Loughead, T., Bray, S. R., & Carron, A. V. (2009b). Perceptions of cohesion by youth sport participants. *The Sport Psychologist, 23,* 330–345.

Pain, M., & Harwood, C. (2009). Team building through mutual sharing and open discussion of team functioning. *The Sport Psychologist, 23,* 523–542.

Paskevich, D. M., Brawley, L. R., Dorsch, K. D., & Widmeyer, W. N. (1999). Relationship between collective efficacy and team cohesion: Conceptual and measurement issues. *Group Dynamics: Theory, Research, and Practice, 3,* 210–222.

Widmeyer, W. N., & Ducharme, K. (1997). Team building through team goal setting. *Journal of Applied Sport Psychology, 9,* 97–113.

Appendix

TEST ANXIETY

Like choking, test anxiety is paradoxical because it impairs performance when people are highly motivated to perform optimally. The literature about test anxiety is largely consistent with that of choking and, in addition, there is information about how to ameliorate test anxiety that may have applications in sport settings.

Returning to the model of stress discussed at the beginning of this chapter (Lazarus & Folkman, 1984), test anxiety occurs in the interaction of the test and that test taker. The test would represent the stressor, and tests are interpreted as **threatening** if they are of importance and test takers do not believe that they can "make the grade" or perform adequately (Spielberger & Vagg, 1995). The degree of threat posed by a test is determined by the nature of the test questions, the student's ability in the subject area of the test, the level of the student's preparation for the test, and by their trait anxiety. Students who have not prepared adequately and who lack sophisticated test-taking skills may become increasingly anxious during the course of an examination. This occurs when students cannot answer individual questions and prematurely conclude that they will fail. This definition of threat is similar to the definition of pressure that was discussed in the earlier section on choking.

Tests that are interpreted to be more threatening cause more state anxiety with physiological anxiety and cognitive interference. The cognitive interference includes self-centered and self-critical thoughts, worry about falling behind others, recall of previous test situations that resulted in disaster, anticipated poor grades, and concern about how instructors will view one's performance. Cognitive interference has been more detrimental to test performance than physiological anxiety. As is often the case with cognitive anxiety, the cognitive interference that occurs in test situations has been described as peremptory and automatic. It occurs without conscious volition and preempts concentration on the test itself.

Cognitive interference in the form of self-deprecatory thoughts and test-related worries interferes with concentration, retrieval of information from memory, and decision making, and are especially disruptive on mathematics tasks (Sarason, Sarason, & Pierce, 1995). Approximately one-third of students who sought therapy for test anxiety were most anxious about mathematics tests (Richardson & Suinn, 1972).

Self-Focused Attention and Test Anxiety

The combination of self-focused attention and high levels of test anxiety produces performance deficits, off-task thinking, and a wish to quit (Carver & Scheier, 1992; Kurosawa and Harackiewicz, 1995). This combination is associated with a lack of persistence in solving difficult problems. The single most common thought among anxious students who focus on themselves during examinations was the wish to be somewhere else (Galassi, Frierson, & Sharer, 1981). The experience of test anxiety is unpleasant, and some people avoid situations in which they are evaluated so as to avoid the experience of this anxiety. This avoidance spares people the discomfort of anxiety at the cost of missing opportunities for accomplishments and for the mastery of test anxiety by performing successfully in these evaluations (Sarason, Sarason, & Pierce, 1995).

Social Comparisons and Performance Anxiety

Children as young as 10 to 13 years of age have identified social comparisons as the primary source of information about their competence in sports and academics. This process of comparing oneself to others, and finding oneself less capable is an important source of the anxiety that children in this age range have about evaluations (Weiss, Ebbeck, & Horn, 1997). When forces from the outside issue goals and challenges, people are more likely to have concerns about whether they will be successful. Of course students are routinely faced with the imposition of challenges from the outside in the form of tests and examinations.

Trait Test Anxiety

Some people experience test anxiety during almost all of their examinations and therefore show a trait of test anxiety. This trait test anxiety is similar to the **fear of failure** motive that was described in Chapter 2. Trait test anxiety may lead to the adoption of **performance-avoidance goals** and with these goals performers focus on avoiding failure and the demonstration of incompetence (Elliot & McGregor, 1999). With fear of failure and performance-avoidance goals, people may withdraw from situations involving threat and pressure and conclude that they "don't test well" or are "choke artists." With performance-avoidance goals, standards for successful performance are considered beyond one's reach. Recall that efficacy or confidence that one is capable of realizing performance standards contains cognitive interference, decreases the experience of stress, and limits choking under pressure.

TEST ANXIETY AND DEFENSIVE PESSIMISM

Optimists have been shown to have higher expectations and better performances than do pessimists and people who do not identify any expectations for their performances. Optimists are not particularly fearful of failure. If an optimist fails, they protect their self-esteem by attributing the causes of failure to external, temporary factors that are outside of their control rather than to their talent (Norem & Cantor, 1986a, 1986b). However, some people marshal their resources to prepare for evaluations by considering the consequences of a poor performance. This occurs when people set their expectations at a level lower than would be expected on the basis of their prior performance. With the prospect of performing at a level beneath their usual standards, they experience facilitative anxiety that motivates appropriate preparation for the evaluation. They prepare for examinations to avoid the pain of failure. This pessimism does not lead to lower performance on cognitive tasks, and shields performers from some of the sting of failure. Failure that is anticipated is less aversive than unanticipated failure, and unexpected success is more satisfying than expected success (Feather, 1969).

Although this strategy has been referred to as **defensive pessimism**, it is not the same as the personality trait of pessimism, which inhibits effort and performance. Defensive pessimism is not a global trait, but consists of pessimism in specific domains such as in academic and social functioning. These pessimists acknowledged that their performances generally exceed their gloomy predictions. They therefore appear to be somewhat aware that their expectations for poor performances are cognitive tricks to motive them to work hard to avoid failure. Defensive pessimists are deliberate in approaching problems and think through possible solutions and outcomes to problems as well as worst-case scenarios. Optimists tend to consider fewer outcomes and to look on the bright side (Norem & Illingworth, 1993).

Defensive Pessimism and Reactions of Others

Performance suffers if defensive pessimists experience positive moods and if optimists realize negative moods prior to evaluations. The performance of defensive pessimists also suffers if others make efforts to convince them that their performance will be good (Sanna, 1998). The negative focus of defensive pessimists apparently mobilizes or "psyches them up" to meet a stressor.

How Adaptive is Defensive Pessimism?

The effects of defensive pessimism on sport performance have not been determined. However, as emphasized in this chapter, efficacy that one will meet and surpass standards necessary for success limits choking under pressure. As emphasized in Chapter 11, the time for doubt about one's readiness to perform successfully is at times distal to performances when there is ample time to train and hone skills. Self-doubts during preparatory stages may function similarly to defensive pessimism and motivate more thorough preparation for competition.

However, in the long run defensive pessimism may be a less effective strategy than optimism for students. Over time, defensive pessimists experience more burnout, loss of intrinsic motivation in academics, and, ultimately, diminished achievement (Cantor & Harlow, 1994).

HELP FOR TEST ANXIETY

A simple and straightforward way of limiting test anxiety is to give instructions to concentrate and avoid distractions (Norem & Cantor, 1986b). Apparently, people with both high and low test anxiety follow these instructions, as college students reported less cognitive interference when coached in this manner. The benefits of the instructions to concentrate and avoid distractions may reflect the students' lack of skill in identifying cognitive interference and redirecting attention when interference is detected. Instructions to increase attention to cognitive tasks and decrease negative emotions such as worry or upset following errors have been show to increase the speed of performance and decrease the number of errors on a variety of cognitive tests (Kanfer & Akerman, 1996). These instructions were most influential with those that were least skilled and most likely to make errors.

Social support appears to be an important source of protection from cognitive interference and test anxiety (Yee & Vaughan, 1996). College students who experienced little social support in their personal lives profited from interventions in which authoritative adults demonstrated an interest in their well-being and offered assistance on tests. Apparently there is a threshold of social support below which test anxiety and cognitive interference disrupts test performance and above which additional support is less influential. For example, the performance of students who reported higher levels of social support in their personal lives did not show additional improvement as a result of the expressions of interest and assistance by authoritative adults (Sarason & Sarason, 1986) or apparent college students (Sarason, 1981).

Unfortunately, people with low social support are often inhibited and less able to ask for the support of others. Those with low social support rate themselves as less interesting and worthy of helpful interventions from others, and they are also more likely to have social anxiety and lower self-esteem.

Students with high levels of test anxiety also profit from watching authoritative adults solve problems and **enunciate principles** for solving problems. Whether this intervention provided information about how to solve test problems or again provided social support was not clear, but it did promote attention to the test items and contained cognitive interference (Sarason, 1973). Conversely, the performance of students with high test anxiety deteriorates when they observe other students fail on the same test (Sarason, 1972).

As discussed in Chapter 5, it is unrealistic to expect excellent performance without thorough preparation. Test anxiety is also more likely when students have an inadequate knowledge of the subject matter. Interventions to decrease cognitive interference will be ineffective in improving the performance of people who are not adequately prepared for evaluations (Naveh-Benjamin, 1991).

Self-Efficacy Contains Cognitive Interference and Anxiety

At this point in this book, the construct of self-efficacy is quite familiar. At this point in this chapter, it should be clear that self-efficacy contains cognitive interference and performance anxiety. A leitmotiv in the choking and test anxiety literature has been that anxiety and performance deficits result from a lack of efficacy or belief that one can meet and exceed the standards necessary for successful performances (Jones, 1995; Williams, 1996; Zohar, 1998). A lack of efficacy contributes to attention to the costs of defeat, the formidableness of competitors, and the difficulty of tasks. Attention may also be given to signs of physiological anxiety. The inability to control physiological anxiety may further erode self-efficacy, and performance deteriorates as this spiral continues. Cognitive interference is more likely to occur if a person believes that all of their self-esteem will be lost if they fail an examination or have a poor performance. Less threat will be experienced if success or failure is understood to extend simply to the task at hand and not to the validation of the entire self or person.

People who believe they can handle threats demonstrate less of the cognitive and physiological signs of anxiety. At both the cognitive and physiological level, they act as if they have nothing to be afraid of. They also take action to alleviate the stress related to their performance. For example, by carefully preparing for evaluations, following preperformance routines, developing game plans, engaging in visualization and self-talk, becoming practiced in reducing physiological arousal, predicting contents of evaluations and strategies of opponents, and by having a Plan B, performers enhance their personal control and limit their anxiety.

Preparation and belief in one's capacity to execute components of a performance make worry unnecessary. It is unrealistic and probably unproductive to expect to experience little cognitive and physiological anxiety and cognitive interference during examinations and performances when one has not prepared sufficiently to realize success. Focusing on aspects in a performance over which one has control supports efficacy beliefs. Focusing on aspects that are not under the performer's control, such as the strength of an opponent, diminishes efficacy.

Although self-efficacy is a stable characteristic, **focusing on the positive** prior to evaluations and competitions enhances it. For example, students "primed" to recall accomplishments experienced less cognitive interference when working on insolvable mazes (Sarason, Potter, & Sarason, 1986). U. S. Coast Guard Academy cadets who kept diaries of stressful experiences during an intense six-week summer training period found their training to be more difficult and stressful than a comparable group of cadets who kept a diary of the "good things" that happened to them during the same period. The cadets with the positive focus reported less stress and feelings of defeat. It appears that negative or positive experiences are not recalled in isolation. Their retrieval initiates the recall of thoughts that are related both in content and mood. Focusing on inadequacies prior to evaluations can therefore erode confidence and efficacy. As explained in Chapter 10 and earlier in this chapter, the time to recognize weaknesses is prior to evaluations while there is still time to ameliorate them. Self-talk and mental imagery prior to performances should focus on mastery so that feelings of efficacy can dominate thoughts and moods.

Key Terms

References

Abernethy, B. (2001). Attention. In R. N. Singer, H. A. Hausenblas, & C. M. Janelle (Eds.), *Handbook of sport psychology* (2nd ed., pp. 53–85). New York, NY: Wiley.

Abernethy, B., Maxwell, J. P., Masters, R.S.W., Van Der Kamp, J., & Jackson, R. C. (2007). Attentional processes in skill learning and expert performance. In G. Tennenbaum & R. C. Eklund (Eds.), *Handbook of sport psychology* (3nd ed., pp. 245–263). New York, NY: Wiley.

Abrahamsen, F. E., Roberts, G. C., & Pensgaard, A. M. (2008). Achievement goals and gender effects on multidimensional anxiety in national elite sport. *Psychology of Sport and Exercise, 9,* 449–464. doi: 10.1016/j.psychsport.2007.06.005

Abramson, L. Y., Metalsky, G. I., & Alloy, L. B. (1989). Hopelessness depression: A theory-based subtype of depression. *Psychological Review, 96,* 358–372.

Abramson, L. Y., Seligman, M. E. P., & Teasdale, J. D. (1978). Learned helplessness in humans: Critique and reformulation. *Journal of Abnormal Psychology, 87,* 49–74.

Abuhamdeh, S., & Csikszentmihalyi, M. (2009). Intrinsic and extrinsic motivational orientations in the competitive context: An examination of person-situation interactions. *Journal of Personality, 77,* 1615–1635.

Acosta, R. V., & Carpenter, L. J. (1985). Status of women in athletics: Causes and changes. *Journal of Physical Education, Recreation & Dance, 56,* 35–37.

Adams, J., & White, M. (2003). Are activity promotion interventions based on the transtheoretical model effective? A critical review. *British Journal of Sport Medicine, 37,* 106–114. doi: 10.1136/bjsm.37.2.106

Adie, J. W., Duda, J. L., & Ntoumanis, K. (2008). Achievement goals, competition appraisals, and the psychological and emotional welfare of sport participants. *Journal of Sport & Exercise Psychology, 30,* 302–322.

Adie, J. W., Duda, J. L., & Ntoumanis, K. (2010). Achievement goals, competition appraisals, and well- and ill-being of elite youth soccer players over two competitive seasons. *Journal of Sport & Exercise Psychology, 32,* 555–579.

Adler, A. (1964). *Superiority and social interest: A collection of later writings.* H. L. Ansbacher & R. R. Ansbacher (Eds.), New York, NY: Norton.

Agassi, A. (2009). *Open: An autobiography.* New York, NY: Vintage Books.

Agnew, G. A., & Carron, A. V. (1994). Crowd effects and the home advantage. *International Journal of Sport Psychology, 25,* 53–62.

Agyemang, K., Singer, J. N., DeLorme, J. (2010). An exploratory study of black male college athletes' perceptions on race and athlete activism. *International Review for the Sociology of Sport, 45,* 419–435. doi: 10.1177/1012690210374691

Aherne, C., Moran, A. M., & Lonsdale, C. (2011). The effect of mindfulness training on athletes' flow: An initial investigation. *The Sport Psychologist, 25,* 177–189.

Ahmadiasl, N., Alaei, H., & Hanninen, O. (2003). Effect of exercise on learning, memory, and levels of epinephrine in rat's hippocampus. *Journal of Sports Science and Medicine, 2,* 106–109.

Ainsworth, M. D. S. (1989). Attachments beyond infancy. *American Psychologist, 44,* 709–716.

Ainsworth, M. D. S., Blehar, M. C., Waters, E., & Wall, S. (1978). *Patterns of attachment: A psychological study of the strange situation.* Hillsdale, NJ: Erlbaum.

Ajzens, I. (1985). From intentions to actions: A theory of planned behavior. In J. Huhl & J. Beckmann (Eds.), *Action-control: From cognition to behavior* (pp. 11–39). Heidelberg, Germany: Springer-Verlag.

Albergotti, R. (2009, May 12). Steep hills, skinny tires and guts. *The Wall Street Journal.* Retrieved from http://www.wsj.com

Alfermann, D., & Stambulova, N. (2007). Career transitions and career termination. In G. Tenenbaum & R. C. Eklund (Eds.), *Handbook of sport psychology* (3rd ed., pp. 712–733). New York, NY: Wiley.

Allen, J. B., & Howe, B. L. (1998). Player ability, coach feedback, and female adolescent athletes' perceived competence and satisfaction. *Journal of Sport & Exercise Psychology, 20,* 280–299.

Allen, M. S., Greenlees, I., & Jones, M. (2011). An investigation of the five-factor model of personality and coping behaviour in sport. *Journal of Sports Sciences, 29,* 841–850. doi: 10.1080/02640414.2011.565064

Allen, M. S., Jones, M. V., & Sheffield, D. (2010). The influence of positive reflection on attributions, emotions, and self-efficacy. *The Sport Psychologist, 24,* 211–226.

Allison, M. T., & Meyer, C. (1988). Career problems and retirement among elite athletes: The female tennis professional. *Sociology of Sport Journal, 5, 212–222.*

Allsopp, J., Eysenck, H. J., & Eysenck, S. B. G. (1991). Machiavellianism as a component in psychoticism and extraversion. *Personality and Individual Differences, 12,* 29–41.

American College of Sports Medicine. (1982). Position stand: The use of alcohol in sports. *Medicine Science Sports Exercise, 14,* 9–11.

American Psychiatric Association. (2000). *Diagnostic and statistical manual of mental disorders, fourth edition, text revision.* Washington, DC: American Psychiatric Association.

American Psychological Association. (2002). Ethical principles of psychologists and code of conduct. *American Psychologist, 57,* 1597–1611.

American Psychological Association. (2003). Guidelines on multicultural education, training, research, practice and organizational change for psychologists. *American Psychologist, 58,* 377–402.

American Psychological Association. (2007). Guidelines for psychological practice with girls and women. *American Psychologist, 62,* 949–979.

American Psychological Association. (2012). Guidelines for psychological practice with lesbian, gay, and bisexual clients. *American Psychologist, 67,* 10–42. doi: 10.1037/a0024659

Amorose, A. J., & Horn, T. S. (2000). Intrinsic motivation: Relationships with collegiate athletes' gender, scholarship status, and perceptions of their coaches' behavior. *Journal of Sport and Exercise Psychology, 22,* 63–84.

Andersen, M. B. (1993). Questionable sensitivity: A comment on Lee and Rotella. *The Sport Psychologist, 7,* 1–3.

Anderson, W. A., Albrecht, R. R., McKeag, D. B., Hough, D. O., & McGrew, C. A. (1991). A national survey of alcohol and drug use by college athletes. *The Physician and Sportsmedicine, 19,* 91–104.

Andre, J. D., & Means, J. R. (1986). Rate of imagery in mental practice: An experimental investigation. *Journal of Sport Psychology, 8,* 124–128.

Andre, N., & Metzler, J. N. (2011). Gender differences in fear of success: A preliminary validation of the Performance Success Threat Appraisal Inventory. *Psychology of Sport and Exercise, 12,* 415–422. doi: 10.1016/j.psychsport.2011.02.006

Andre, T., & Holland, A. (1995). Relationship of sport participation to sex role orientation and attitudes toward women among high school athletes. *Journal of Sport Behavior, 18,* 241–253.

Annesi, J. J. (1998). Applications of the Individual Zones of Optimal Functioning model for the multimodal treatment of precompetitive anxiety. *The Sport Psychologist, 12,* 300–316.

Annesi, J. J. (2005). Changes in depressed mood associated with 10 weeks of moderate cardiovascular exercise in formerly sedentary adults. *Psychological Reports, 96,* 855–862.

Anshel, M. H. (1990). Perceptions of black intercollegiate football players: Implications for the sport psychology consultant. *The Sport Psychologist, 4,* 235–248.

Anshel, M. H. (1995). An examination of self-regulatory cognitive-behavioral strategies of Australian elite and non-elite competitive male swimmers. *Australian Psychologist, 30,* 78–83.

Anshel, M. H., & Delany, J. (2001). Sources of acute stress, cognitive appraisals, and coping strategies of male and female child athletes. *Journal of Sport Behavior, 24,* 329–354.

Anshel, M. H., & Kaissidis, A. N. (1997). Coping style and situational appraisals as predictors of coping strategies following stressful events in sport as a function of gender and skill level. *The British Journal of Psychology, 88,* 263–276.

Anshel, M. H., Kim, K-W., Kim, B-H., Chang, K-J., & Eom, H-J. (2001). A model for coping with stressful events in sport: Theory, application, and future directions. *International Journal of Sport Psychology, 32,* 43–75.

Anshel, M. H., & Mansouri, H. (2005). Influences of perfectionism on motor performance, affect, and causal attributions in response to critical information feedback. *Journal of Sport Behavior, 28,* 99–124.

Anshel, M. H., Porter, A., & Quek, J-J. (1998). Coping with acute stress in sport as a function of gender: An exploratory study. *Journal of Sport Behavior, 21,* 363–376.

Anshel. M. H., & Sailes, G. (1990). Discrepant attitudes of intercollegiate team athletes as a function of race. *Journal of Sport Behavior, 13,* 68–77.

Aoyagi, M. W., Cox, R. H., & McGuire, R. T. (2008). Organizational citizenship behavior in sport: Relationships with leadership, team cohesion, and athlete satisfaction. *Journal of Applied Sport Psychology, 20,* 25–41.

Appaneal, R. N., Levine, B. R., Perna, F. M., & Roh, J. L. (2009). Measuring postinjury depression among male and female competitive athletes. *Journal of Sport & Exercise Psychology, 31,* 60–76.

Appleton, P. R., Hall, H. K., & Hill, A. P. (2009). Relations between multidimensional perfectionism and burnout in junior-elite male athletes. *Psychology of Sport and Exercise, 10,* 457–465. doi: 10.1016/j.psychsport.2008.12.006

Appleton, P. R., Hall, H. K., & Hill, A. P. (2010). Family patterns of perfectionism: An examination of elite junior athletes and their parents. *Psychology of Sport and Exercise, 11,* 363–371. doi: 10.1016/j.psychsport.2010.04.005

Arbour, K. P., & Martin Ginis, K. A. (2008). Improving body image one step at a time: Greater pedometer step counts produce greater body image improvements. *Body Image, 5,* 331–336. doi: 10.1016/j.bodyim.2008.05.003

Arbour, K. P., & Martin Ginis, K. A. (2009). A randomized controlled trial of the effects of implementation intentions on women's walking behaviour. *Psychology and Health, 24,* 49–65. doi: 10.1080/08870440801930312

Arent, S. M., Alderman, B. L., Short, E. J., & Landers, D. M. (2007). The impact of the testing environment of affect changes following acute resistance exercise. *Journal of Applied Sport Psychology, 19,* 364–378.

Arent, S. M., & Landers, D. M. (2003). Arousal, anxiety, and performance. A reexamination of the inverted-U hypothesis. *Research Quarterly for Exercise and Sport, 74,* 436–444.

Argus, G., & Thompson, M. (2008). Perceived social problem solving, perfectionism, and mindful awareness in clinical depression: An exploratory study. *Cognitive Therapy and Research, 32,* 745–757.

Arkin, R. M., & Oleson, K. C. (1998). Self-Handicapping. In J. M. Darley, & J. Cooper (Eds.), *Attribution and social interaction* (pp. 313–347). Washington, DC: American Psychological Association.

Armstrong, L., & Jenkins, S. (2003). *Every second counts.* New York, NY: Broadway Books.

Armstrong, L. E., & VanHeest, J. L. (2002). The unknown mechanism of overtraining syndrome. *Sports Medicine, 32,* 185–209.

Arthur, C. A., Woodman, T., Ong, C. W., Hardy, L., & Ntoumanis, N. (2011). The role of athlete narcissism in moderating the relationship between coaches' transformational leader behaviors and athlete motivation. *Journal of Sport & Exercise Psychology, 33,* 3–19.

Arvinen-Barrow, M., Weigand, D. A., Thomas, S., Hemmings, B., & Walley, M. (2007). Elite and novice athletes' imagery use in open and closed sports. *Journal of Applied Sport Psychology, 19,* 93–104. doi: 10.1016/psychsport.2009.05.004

Arvinen-Barrow, M., Penny, G., Hemmings, B., & Corr, S. (2010). UK chartered physiotherapists' personal experiences in using psychological interventions with injured athletes: An interpretative phenomenological analysis. *Psychology of Sport and Exercise, 11,* 58–66. doi: 10.1016/j.psychsport.2009.05.004

Ashe, A. (1993). *A hard road to glory: A history of the African American athlete.* New York, NY: Amistad Press.

Associated Press. (2005, January 16). Kwan wins ninth title. Ties Vinson's U.S. record. *Hartford Courant,* E12.

Associated Press. (2005, March 23). Jury finds for Williams. Romanowski ordered to pay $340,000 in damages. *Hartford Courant,* C7.

Associated Press. (2005, May 18). Romanowski stayed step ahead. *Hartford Courant,* C2.

Associated Press. (2005, June 2). Racy 49ers video is a PR nightmare. *Hartford Courant,* C7.

Association for the Advancement of Applied Sport Psychology. (1994). *Ethical principles of the Association for the Advancement of Applied Sport Psychology.* [Brochure]. Boise, ID: Author.

Astrand, P. O., Rodahl, K., Dahl, H. A., & Stromme, S. B. (2003). *Textbook of work physiology: Physiological bases of exercise.* (4th ed.) Champaign, IL: Human Kinetics.

Atkins, R. (1990, Sunday, June 24). Boris banks on bouncing back. *Observer,* 3–5.

Atkinson, J. W. (1957). Motivational determinants of risk-taking behavior. *Psychological Review, 64,* 359–372.

Atkinson, J. W. (1964). *An introduction to motivation*. Princeton, NJ: Van Nostrand.

Atkinson, J. W. (1978). The mainsprings of achievement-oriented activity. In J. W. Atkinson & J. O. Raynor (Eds.), *Personality, motivation, and achievement* (pp. 11–39). Washington, DC: Halsted Press.

Au, R. C. P., Watkins, D. A., & Hattie, J.A.C. (2010). Academic risk factors and deficits of learned hopelessness: A longitudinal study of Hong Kong secondary school students. *Educational Psychology, 30*, 125–138. doi: 10.1080/01443410903476400

Authur-Banning, S., Wells, M. S., Baker, B. L., & Hegreness, R. (2009). Parents behaving badly? The relationship between the sportsmanship behaviors of adults and athletes in youth basketball games. *Journal of Sport Behavior, 32*, 3–18.

Baar, P., & Wubbels, T. (2011). Machiavellianism in children in Dutch elementary schools and sports clubs: Prevalence and stability according to context, sport type, and gender. *The Sport Psychologist, 25*, 444–464.

Baddeley, A. D. (2001). Is working memory still working? *American Psychologist, 56*, 851–864.

Baer, R. A., & Krietemeyer, J. (2006). Overview of mindfulness- and acceptance-based treatment approaches. In R. A. Baer (Ed.), *Mindfulness-based treatment approaches* (pp. 3–27). Burlington, MA: Academic Press.

Bagby, R. M., Costa, P. T. Jr., Widiger, T. A., Ryder, A. G., & Marshall, M. (2005). DSM-IV personality disorders and the five-factor model of personality: A multi-method examination of domain- and facet-level predictions. *European Journal of Psychology, 19*, 307–324.

Bahrke, M. S., Yesalis, C. E., Brower, K. J. (1998). Anabolic-androgenic steroid abuse and performance-enhancing drugs among adolescents. *Child and Adolescent Psychiatric Clinics of North America, 7*, 821–838.

Bahrke, M. S., Yesalis, C. E., & Wright, J. E. (1996). Psychological and behavioral effects of endogenous testosterone and anabolic-androgenic steroids. An update. *Sports Medicine, 22*, 367–390.

Bailey, R., Armour, K., Kirk, D., Jess, M., Pickup, I., Sandford, R., & the BERA Physical Education and Sport Pedagogy Special Interest Group. (2009). The educational benefits claimed for physical education and school sport: An academic review. *Research Papers in Education, 24*, 1–27. doi: 10.1080/02671520701809817

Bailis, D. S. (2001). Benefits of self-handicapping in sport: A field study of university athletes. *Canadian Journal of Behavioural Science, 33*, 213–223.

Baker, J., Cobley, S., & Fraser-Thomas, J. (2009). What do we know about early sport specialization? Not much! *High Ability Studies, 20*, 77–89. doi: 10.1080/13598130902860507

Baker, J., Cote, J., & Abernethy, B. (2003). Sport specific training, deliberate practice and the development of expertise in team ball sports. *Journal of Applied Sport Psychology, 15*, 12–25.

Bakker, F. C., Oudejans, R. R. D., Binsch, O., & Van der Kamp, J. (2006). Penalty shooting and gaze behavior: Unwanted effects of the wish not to miss. *International Journal of Sport Psychology, 37*, 265–280.

Balaguer, I., Duda, J. L., Atienza, F. L., & Mayo, C. (2002). Situational and dispositional goals as predictors of perceptions of individual and team improvement, satisfaction, and coach ratings among elite female handball teams. *Psychology of Sport and Exercise, 3*, 293–308.

Balaguer, I., Duda, J. L., & Crespo, M. (1999). Motivational climate and goal orientations as predictors of perceptions of improvement, satisfaction and coach ratings among tennis players. *Scandinavian Journal of Medicine and Science in Sports, 9*, 1–8.

Ball, J. R., & Carron, A. V. (1976). The influence of team cohesion and participation motivation upon performance success in intercollegiate ice hockey. *Canadian Journal of Applied Sport Sciences, 1*, 271–275.

Bamberger, M. (2002, February 24). Annika Sorenstam. A woman among men. *Sports Illustrated, 98*, 62–67.

Bandura, A. (1986). *Social foundations of thought and action: A social cognitive theory*. Englewood Cliffs, NJ: Prentice-Hall.

Bandura, A. (1989a). Human agency in social cognitive theory. *American Psychologist, 44*, 1175–1184.

Bandura, A. (1989b). Self-regulation of motivation and action through internal standards and goal systems. In L. A. Pervin (Ed.), *Goal concepts on personality and social psychology* (pp. 19–85). Hillsdale, NJ: Lawrence Erlbaum.

Bandura, A. (1997). *Self-efficacy. The exercise of control*. New York, NY: Freeman.

Bandura, A., Caprara, G. V., Barbaranelli, C., Gerbino, M., & Pastorelli, C. (2003). Role of affective self-regulatory efficacy in diverse spheres of psychosocial functioning. *Child Development, 74*, 769–783. doi: 10.1111/1467-8623.00567

Bandura, A., & Cervone, D. (1983). Self-evaluative and self-efficacy mechanisms governing the motivational effects of goal systems. *Journal of Personality and Social Psychology, 45,* 1017–1028.

Bandura, A., & Cervone, D. (1986). Differential engagement of self-reactive influences in cognitive motivation. *Organizational Behavior and Human Decision Processes, 38,* 92–113.

Bandura, A., Jeffery, R. W., & Gajdos, E. (1975). Generalizing change through participant modeling with self-directed mastery. *Behaviour Research and Therapy, 13,* 141–152.

Bandura, A., & Locke, E. A. (2003). Negative self-efficacy and goal effects revisited. *Journal of Applied Psychology, 88,* 87–99.

Bandura, A., & Simon, K. M. (1977). The role of proximal intentions in self-regulation of refractory behavior. *Cognitive Therapy and Research, 1,* 177–193.

Barber, H. (1998). Examining gender differences in sources and levels of perceived competence in interscholastic coaches. *The Sport Psychologist, 12,* 237–252.

Baric, R., & Bucik, V. (2009). Motivational differences in athletes trained by coaches of different motivational and leadership profiles. *Kinesiology, 41,* 181–194.

Barnett, N. P., Smoll, F. L., & Smith, R. E. (1992). Effects of enhancing coach-athlete relationships on youth sport attrition. *The Sport Psychologist, 6,* 111–127.

Barron, K. E., & Harackiewicz, J. M. (2001). Achievement goals and optimal motivation: Testing multiple goal models. *Journal of Personality and Social Psychology, 80,* 706–722.

Bartholomew, J., Holroyd, S., & Heffernan, T. M. (2010). Does cannabis use affect prospective memory in young adults? *Journal of Psychopharmacology, 24,* 241–246. doi: 10.1177/0269881109106909

Bartholomew, L. K., Parcel, G. S., Kok, G., & Gottlieb, N. H. (2006). *Planned health promotion programs: An intervention mapping approach* (2nd ed.). San Francisco, CA: John Wiley.

Bartlewski, P., Van Raalte, J. L., & Brewer, B. W. (1996). Effects of aerobic exercise on the social physique anxiety and body esteem of female college students. *Women in Sport and Physical Activity Journal, 5,* 49–62.

Bass, B. M. (1985). *Leadership and performance beyond expectations.* New York, NY: Free Press.

Bass. B. M. & Avolio, J. J. (2005). *MLQ: Multifactor Leadership Questionnaire* (2nd ed.). Redwood City, CA: Mind Garden.

Bauer, P. J., Schwade, J. A., Wewerka, S. S., & Delaney, K. (1999). Planning ahead: Goal-directed problem solving by 2–7-year-olds. *Developmental Psychology, 35,* 1321–1337.

Bauman, A., Bull, F., Chey, T., Craig, C. L., Ainsworth, B. E., Sallis, J. F., . . .The ISP Group. (2009). The international Prevalence Study on Physical Activity: Results from 20 countries. *International Journal of Behavioral Nutrition and Physical Activity, 6,* 1–11. doi: 10.1186/1479-5868-6-21

Baumeister, R. F. (1984). Choking under pressure: Self-consciousness and paradoxical effects of incentives on skillful performance. *Journal of Personality and Social Psychology, 46,* 610–620.

Baumeister, R. F. (1995). Disputing the effects of championship pressures and home audiences. *Journal of Personality and Social Psychology, 68,* 644–648.

Baumeister, R. F., Hamilton, J. C., & Tice, D. M. (1985). Public versus private expectancy of success: Confidence booster or performance pressure. *Journal of Personality and Social Psychology, 48,* 1447–1457.

Baumeister, R. F., & Showers, C. J. (1986). A review of paradoxical performance effects: Choking under pressure in sports and mental tests. *European Journal of Social Psychology, 16,* 361–383.

Baumeister, R. F., & Steinhilber, A. (1984). Paradoxical effects of supportive audiences on performance under pressure: The home field disadvantage in sports championships. *Journal of Personality and Social Psychology, 47,* 85–93.

Baumeister, R. F., Tice, D. M., & Hutton, D. G. (1989). Self-presentation motivations and personality differences in self-esteem. *Journal of Personality, 57,* 547–579.

Baumeister, R. F., Twenge, J. M., & Nuss, C. K. (2002). Effects of social exclusion on cognitive processes: Anticipated aloneness reduces intelligent thought. *Journal of Personality and Social Psychology, 83,* 817–827.

Baumgardner, A. H. (1991). Claiming depressive symptoms as a self-handicap: A protective self-presentation strategy. *Basic and Applied Social Psychology 12,* 97–113.

Bawden, M., & Maynard, I. (2001). Towards an understanding of the personal experience of the "yips" in cricketers. *Journal of Sports Sciences, 19,* 937–953.

Beamon, K. K. (2010). Are sport overemphasized in the socialization process of African American males? A qualitative analysis of former collegiate athletes' perception of sport socialization. *Journal of Black Studies, 4,* 281–300. doi: 10.1177/0021934709340873

Beattie, S., Hardy, L., Savage, J., Woodman, T., & Callow, N. (2011). Development and validation of a trait measure of robustness of self-confidence. *Psychology of Sport and Exercise, 12,* 184–191. Doi: 10.1016/j.psychsport.2010.09.008

Beauchamp, P. H., Halliwell, W. R., Fournier, J. F., & Koestner, R. (1996). Effects of cognitive-behavioral psychological skill training on motivation, preparation, and putting performance of novice golfers. *The Sport Psychologist, 10,* 157–170.

Beedie, C. J., Terry, P. C., & Lane, A. M. (2000). The profile of mood states and athletic performance: Two meta-analyses. *Journal of Applied Sport Psychology, 12,* 49–68.

Beilock, S. L., Afremow, J. A., Rabe, A. L., & Carr, T. H. (2001). "Don't miss!" The debilitating effects of suppressive imagery on golf putting performance. *Journal of Sport & Exercise Psychology, 23,* 200–221.

Beilock, S. L., Bertenthal, B. I., McCoy, A. M., & Carr, T. H. (2004). Haste does not always make waste: Expertise, direction of attention, and speed versus accuracy in performing sensorimotor skills. *Psychonomic Bulletin and Review, 11,* 373–379.

Beilock, S. L., & Carr, T. H. (2001). On the fragility of skilled performance: What governs choking under pressure? *Journal of Experimental Psychology: General, 40,* 701–725.

Beilock, S. L., & Carr, T. H. (2005). When high-powered people fail. Working Memory and "choking under pressure" in math. *Psychological Science, 16,* 101–105.

Beilock, S. L., Carr, T. H., MacMahon, C., & Starkes, J. L. (2002). When paying attention becomes counterproductive: Impact of divided versus skill-focused attention on novice and experienced performance of sensorimotor skills. *Journal of Experimental Psychology: Applied, 8,* 6–16.

Beilock, S. L., & Gonzo, S. (2008). Putting in mind versus putting on the green: Expertise, performance time, and the linking of imagery and action. *The Quarterly Journal of Experimental Psychology, 61,* 920–932. doi: 10.1080/17470210701625626

Beilock, S. L., & Gray, R. (2007). Why do athletes choke under pressure? In G. Tenenbaum & R. C. Eklund (Eds.), *Handbook of sport psychology* (3rd ed., pp. 425–444). New York, NY: Wiley.

Beilock, S. L., Jellison, W. A., Rydell, R. J., McConnell, A. R., & Carr, T. H. (2006). On the causal mechanisms of stereotype threat: Can skills that don't rely heavily on working memory still be threatened? *Personality and Social Psychology Bulletin, 32,* 1059–1071.

Beilock, S. L., Kulp, C. A., Holt, L. E., & Carr, T. H. (2004). More on the fragility of performance: Choking under pressure in mathematical problem solving. *Journal of Experimental Psychology: General, 133,* 584–600. doi: 10.1037/0096-3445.133.4.584

Beilock, S. L., & McConnell, A. R. (2004). Stereotype treat and sport: Can athletic performance be threatened? *Journal of Sport and Exercise Psychology, 26,* 597–609.

Beilock, S. L., Rydell, R. J., & McConnell, A. R. (2007). Stereotype threat and working memory: Mechanisms, alleviation, and spillover. *Journal of Experimental Psychology: General, 136,* 256–276.

Belanger-Gravel, A., Godin, G., & Amireault, S. (2011). A meta-analytic review of the effect of implementation intentions on physical activity. *Health Psychology Review, 5,* 1–32. doi: 101080/17437199.2011.560095

Bell, J. L., & Hardy, J. (2009). Effects of attentional focus on skilled performance in golf. *Journal of Applied Sport Psychology, 21,* 163–177.

Bell, R. L., Skinner, C. H., & Fisher, L. A. (2009). Decreasing putting yips in accomplished golfers via solution-focused guided imagery: A single-subject research design. *Journal of Applied Sport Psychology, 21,* 1–14.

Belson, K. (2012, November 8). Joy that lasts, on the poorest of playgrounds. *The New York Times.* Retrieved from http://www.nytimes.com

Bem, S. L. (1974). The measurement of psychological androgyny. *Journal of Consulting and Clinical Psychology, 42,* 155–162.

Bem, S. L. (1978). Beyond androgyny: Some presumptuous prescriptions for a liberated sexual identity. In J. Sherman & F. Denmark (Eds.), *Psychology of women: Future directions for research* (pp. 1–23). New York, NY: Psychological Dimensions.

Bernier, M., Codron, R., Thienot, E., & Fournier, J. F. (2011). The attentional focus of expert golfers in training and competition: A naturalistic investigation. *Journal of Applied Sport Psychology, 23,* 1153–1571. doi: 10.1080/10413200.2011.561518

Benoit, J., & Baker, S. (1987). *Running tide.* New York, NY: Alfred A. Knopf.

Benson, H. (1983). The relaxation response: Its subjective and objective historical precedents and physiology. *Trends in Neurosciences, 6,* 281–284.

Benson, H., Greenwood, M. M., & Klemchuk, H. (1975). The relaxation response: Psychophysiologic aspects and clinical applications. *International Journal of Psychiatry in Medicine, 6,* 87–98.

Benson, P. L. (2002). Adolescent development in social and community context: A program of research. *New Directions for Youth Development, 95,* 123–147.

Ben-Zeev, T., Fein, S., & Inzlicht, M. (2005). Arousal and stereotype threat. *Journal of Experimental Social Psychology, 41,* 174–181.

Berglas, S., & Jones, E. E. (1978). Drug choice as a self-handicapping strategy in response to noncontingent success. *Journal of Personality and Social Psychology, 36,* 405–417.

Berlet, B. (2001, June 18). Gag order. Misses force playoff. *Hartford Courant,* C1, C6.

Berlet, B. (2005, June 2). Not all endorse Wie's career approach. *Hartford Courant,* C3.

Berman, D. K. (2013, March 25). Kentucky basketball's new death star. *The Wall Street Journal.* Retrieved from http://www.wsj.com

Bernier, M., & Fournier, J. F. (2010). Functions of mental imagery in expert golfers. *Psychology of Sport and Exercise, 11,* 444–452. doi: 10.1016/j.psychsport.2010.05.006

Bernier, M., Thienot, E., Codron, R., & Fournier, J. F. (2009). Mindfulness and acceptance approaches in sport performance. *Journal of Clinical Sports Psychology, 4,* 320–333.

Bernstein, N. A. (1967). *The coordination and regulation of movement.* Oxford, England: Pergamon Press.

Berry, D. C., & Dienes, Z. (1993). *Implicit learning: Theoretical and empirical issues.* Hove, England: Lawrence Erlbaum.

Berry, J., & Abernethy, B. (2003, June). *Expert game-based decision-making in Australian football: How it is developed and how can it be trained?* Brisbane, Australia: University of Queensland, School of Human Movement Studies.

Bertollo, M., Robazza, C., Falasca, W. N., Stocchi, M., Babiloni, C., Del Percio, C., Marzano, N., Iacoboni, M., . . .Comani, S. (2012). Temporal pattern of pre-shooting psycho-physiological states in elite athletes: A probabilistic approach. *Psychology of Sport and Exercise, 13,* 91–98. doi: 10.1016/j.psychsport.2011.09.005

Bertollo, M., Saltarelli, B., & Robazza, C. (2009). Mental preparation strategies of elite modern pentathletes. *Psychology of Sport and Exercise, 10,* 244–254. doi: 10.1016/j.psychsport.2008.09.003

Best: Decline of the golden boy.(2005, June 4). *BBC News.* Retrieved from http://news.bbc.co.uk

Bianco, T. (2001). Social support and recovery from sport injury: Elite skiers share their experiences. *Research Quarterly for Exercise and Sport, 72,* 376–388.

Bianco, T., & Eklund, R. C. (2001). Conceptual considerations for social support research in sport and exercise settings: The case of sport injury. *Journal of Sport & Exercise Psychology, 23,* 85–107.

Biddle, S. (1989). Applied sport psychology: A view from Britain. *Applied Sport Psychology, 1,* 23–34.

Biddle, S.J.H., & Hanrahan, S. J. (1998). Attributions and attributional style. In J. L. Duda (Ed.), *Advances in sport and exercise psychology measurement* (pp. 3–19). Morgantown, WV: Fitness Information Technology.

Biddle, S.J.H., Hanrahan, S. J., & Sellars, C. N. (2001). Attributions. Past, present, and future. In N. Singer, H. A. Hausenblas, & C. M. Janelle (Eds.), *Handbook of sport psychology* (2nd ed., pp. 444–471). New York, NY: Wiley.

Biddle, S.J.H., & Nigg, C. R. (2000). Theories of exercise behavior [Special issue: Exercise psychology]. *International Journal of Sport Psychology, 21,* 290-304.

Billing, J. (1980). An overview of task complexity. *Motor Skills: Theory Into Practice, 4,* 18–23.

Birkland, M. S., Torsheim, T., & Wold, B. (2009). A longitudinal study of the relationship between leisure-time physical activity and depressed mood among adolescents. *Psychology of Sport & Exercise, 10,* 25–34. doi: 10.1016/j.psychsport.2008.01.005

Birrer, D., & Morgan, G. (2010). Psychological skills training as a way to enhance an athlete's performance in high-intensity sports. *Scandinavian Journal of Medicine & Science in Sports, 20 (Supplement 2),* 78–87. doi: 10.1111/j.1600-0838.2010.01188.x

Bishop, D. T., Karageorghis, C. I., & Loizou, G. (2007). A grounded theory of young tennis players' use of music to manipulate emotional states. *Journal of Sport & Exercise Psychology, 29,* 584–607.

Bishop, S. R., Lau, M., Shapiro, S., Carlson, L. E., Anderson, N., Carmody, J., . . . Devins, G. (2004). Mindfulness: A proposed operational definition. *Clinical Psychology: Science and Practice, 11,* 230–241.

Black, C. B., & Wright, D. L. (2000). Can observational practice facilitate error recognition and movement production? *Research Quarterly for Exercise and Sport, 71,* 331–339.

Black, S. J., & Weiss, M. R. (1992). The relationship among perceived coaching behaviors, perceptions of ability, and motivation in competitive age-group swimmers. *Journal of Sport & Exercise Psychology, 29,* 289–302.

Blanchard, C. Perreault, S., & Vallerand, R. J. (1998). Participation in team sport: A self-expansion perspective. *International Journal of Sport Psychology, 29,* 289–302.

Blandin, Y., & Proteau, L. (2000). On the cognitive basis of observational learning: Development of mechanisms for the detection and correction of errors. *The Quarterly Journal of Experimental Psychology, 53A,* 846–867.

Blatt, S. J. (1995). The destructiveness of perfectionism. *American Psychologist, 50,* 1003–1020.

Blatt, S. J., & Quinlan, P. (1967). Punctual and procrastinating students: A study of temporal parameters. *Journal of Consulting Psychology, 31,* 169–174.

Bluestein, G. (2004, September 20). Controlling their future. Athletes among those helping steer minority students toward automotive careers. *Hartford Courant,* C13.

Blumenstein, B., Breslav, I., Bar-Eli, M., Tennenbaum, G., & Weinstein, Y. (1995). Regulation of mental states and biofeedback techniques: Effects on breathing patterns. *Biofeedback and Self-Regulation, 20,* 169–182.

Blumenstein, B., & Lidor, R. (2008). Psychological preparation in the Olympic village: A four phase approach. *Athletic Insight, 9,* 15–28.

Blunt, A. K., & Psychl, T. A. (2000). Task aversiveness and procrastination: A multipdimensional approach to task aversiveness across stages of personal projects. *Personality and Individual Differences, 28,* 153–167.

Boardley, I. D., Kavussanu, M., & Ring, C. (2008). Athletes' perceptions of coaching effectiveness and athlete-related outcomes in rugby union: An investigation based on the coaching efficacy model. *The Sport Psychologist, 22,* 269–287.

Boggiano, A. K. (1998). Maladaptive achievement patterns: A test of a diathesis-stress analysis of helplessness. *Journal of Personality and Social Psychology, 74,* 1681–1695.

Boggiano, A. K., & Barrett, M. (1991). Strategies to motivate helpless and mastery-oriented children: The effects of gender based expectancies. *Sex Roles, 25,* 487–510.

Boggiano, A. K., Barrett, M., & Kellam, T. (1993). Competing theoretical analyses of helplessness: A social-developmental analysis. *Journal of Experimental Child Psychology, 55,* 194–207.

Boggiano, A. K., Shields, A., Barrett, M., Kellam, T., Thompson, E., Simons, J., & Katz, P. (1992). Helpless deficits in students: The role of motivational orientation. *Motivation and Emotion, 16,* 271–296.

Bois, J. E., Sarrazin, P. G., Brustad, R. J., Chanal, J. P., & Trouilloud, D. O. (2005). Parents' appraisals, reflected appraisals, and children's self-appraisals of sport competence: A yearlong study. *Journal of Applied Sport Psychology, 17,* 273–289.

Bois, J. E., Sarrazin, P. G., Southon, J., & Boiche, J.C.S. (2009). Psychological characteristics and their relation to performance in professional golfers. *The Sport Psychologist, 23,* 252–270.

Boixados, M., Cruz, J., Torregrosa, M., & Valiente, L. (2004). Relationships among motivational climate, satisfaction, perceived ability, and fair play attitudes in young soccer players. *Journal of Applied Sport Psychology, 16,* 301–317.

Boldizar, J. P. (1991). Assessing sex typing and androgyny in children: The Children's Sex Role Inventory. *Developmental Psychology, 27,* 505–515.

Bond, G. G., Aiken, L. S., & Somerville, S. C. (1992). The health belief model and adolescents with insulin-dependent diabetes mellitus. *Health Psychology, 11,* 190–198.

Bond, K. A., Biddle, S. J. H., & Ntoumanis, N. (2001). Self-efficacy and causal attribution in female golfers. *International Journal of Sport Psychology, 31,* 243–256.

Bonk, T. (2005, October 6). New pro Wie a $20 million teen. *Hartford Courant,* C5.

Borges, G., Walters, E. E., & Kessler, R. C. (2000). Associations of substance use, abuse, and dependence with subsequent suicidal behavior. *American Journal of Epidemiology, 151,* 781–789.

Borkovec, T. D., & Sides, J. K. (1979). Critical procedural variables related to the physiological effects of progressive relaxation: A review. *Behavior Research and Therapy, 17,* 119–125.

Bornstein, G., & Goldschmidt, C. (2008). Post-scoring behaviour and team success in football. In P. Andersson, P. Ayton, & C. Schmidt (Eds.), *Myths and facts about football: The economics and psychology of the world's greatest sport* (pp. 113–123). Newcastle upon Tyne, England: Cambridge Scholars Publishing.

Bortoli, L., Bertollo, M., Comani, S., & Robazza, C. (2011). Competence, achievement goals, motivational climate, and pleasant psychobiosocial states in youth sport. *Journal of Sports Sciences, 29,* 171–180.

Bortoli, L., Bertollo, M., Hanin, Y., & Robazza, C. (2012). Striving for excellence: A multi-action plan intervention model for shooters. *Psychology of Sport and Exercise, 13,* 693–701. doi: 10.1016/j.psychsport.2012.04.006

Bortoli, L., Bertollo, M., & Robazza, C. (2009). Dispositional goal orientations, motivational climate, and psychobiosocial states in youth sport. *Personality and Individual Differences, 47,* 18–24. doi: 10.1016/j.paid.2009.01.042

Boschker, M. S. J., & Bakker, F. C. (2002). Inexperienced sport climbers might perceive and utilize new opportunities for action by merely observing a model. *Perceptual and Motor Skills, 95,* 3–9.

Bosman, J. (2012, May 13). Tiny hand over hand. *The New York Times*, N1, N6, N7.

Botterill, C. (1990). Sport psychology and professional hockey. *The Sport Psychologist, 4*, 358–368.

Bouchard, C., Blair, S. N., & Haskell, W. L. (2007). *Physical activity and health.* Champaign, IL: Human Kinetics.

Bourgeois, A., LeUnes, A., & Meyers, M. (2010). Full-scale and short-form of the Profile of Mood States: A factor analytic comparison. *Journal of Sport Behavior, 33*, 355–376.

Boutcher, S. H. (1992). Attentional and athletic performance: An integrated approach. In T. S. Horn (Ed.), *Advances in sport psychology* (pp. 251–266). Champaign, IL: Human Kinetics.

Boutcher, S. H., & Crews, D. J. (1987). The effect of a preshot attentional routine on a well-learned skill. *International Journal of Sports Psychology, 18*, 30–39.

Bower, B. L., & Martin, M. (1999). African American female basketball players: An examination of alcohol and drug behaviors. *College Health, 48*, 129–133.

Boyce, B. A., Gano-Overway, L. A., & Campbell, A. L. (2009). Perceived motivational climate's influence on goal orientations, perceived competence, and practice strategies across the athletic season. *Journal of Applied Sport Psychology, 21*, 381–394.

Boyce, B. A., Wayda, V. K., Johnston, T., Bunker, L. K., & Eliot, J. (2001). The effects of three types of goal setting conditions on tennis performance: A field-based study. *Journal of Teaching in Physical Education, 20*, 188–200.

Boyce, W. T., & Sobolewski, S. (1989). Recurrent injuries in school children. *American Journal of the Disabled Child, 143*, 338–342.

Bracken, N. M. (2012). Substance use: National study of substance use trends among NCAA college student-athletes. Indianapolis, IN: NCAA.

Brackenridge, C. (2000). Sexual harassment and abuse. In B. L. Drinkwater (Ed.), *Women in sport* (pp. 342–350). Oxford, England: Blackwell Science.

Bratland-Sanda, S., Martinsen, E. W., & Rosenvinge, J. H., Ro, O., Hoffart, A., & Sundgot-Borgen, J. (2011). Exercise dependence score in patients with longstanding eating disorders and controls: The importance of affect regulation and physical activity intensity. *European Eating Disorders Review, 19*, 249–255. doi: 10.1002/erv.971

Brawley, L. R., Carron, A. V., & Widmeyer, W. N. (1988). Exploring the relationship between cohesion and group resistance to disruption. *Journal of Sport & Exercise Psychology, 10*, 199–213.

Brawley, L. R., Carron, A. V., & Widmeyer, W. N. (1992). The nature of group goals in sport teams: A phenomenological analysis. *The Sport Psychologist, 6*, 323–333.

Bray, C. D., & Whaley, D. E. (2001). Team cohesion, effort, and objective individual performance of high school basketball players. *The Sport Psychologist, 15*, 260–275.

Brefczynski-Lewis, J. A., Lutz, A., Schaefer, H. S., Levinson, D. B. & Davidson, R. J. (2007). Neural correlates of attentional expertise in long-term meditation practitioners. *Proceedings of the National Academy of Sciences of the United States of America, 104*, 11483–11488.

Brett, J. F., & VandeWalle, D. (1999). Goal orientation and goal content as predictors of performance in a training program. *Journal of Applied Psychology, 84*, 863–873.

Breuning, J. E., & Dixon, M. A. (2008). Situating work-family negotiations within a life course perspective: Insights on the gendered experiences of NCAA Division I head coaching mothers. *Sex Roles, 58*, 10–23.

Brewer, B. (1993). Self-identity and specific vulnerability to depressed mood. *Journal of Personality, 61*, 343–364.

Brewer, B. W. (2001). Psychology of sport rehabilitation. In R. N. Singer, H. A. Hausenblas, & C. M. Janelle (Eds.), *Handbook of sport psychology* (2nd ed., pp. 787–809). New York, NY: Wiley.

Brewer, B. W. (2007). Psychology of sport injury rehabilitation. In G. Tenenbaum & R. C. Eklund (Eds.), *Handbook of sport psychology* (3rd ed., pp. 404–424). New York, NY: Wiley.

Brewer, B. W. (2009). Injury prevention and rehabilitation. In B. W. Brewer (Ed.), *Handbook of sports medicine and science, sport psychology* (pp. 75–86). Chichester, England: Wiley-Blackwell.

Brewer, B. W., Cornelius, A. E., Van Raalte, J. L., Petitpas, A. J., Sklar, J. H., Pohlman, M. H., Krushell, R. J., & Ditmar, T. D. (2000). Attributions for recovery and adherence to rehabilitation following anterior cruciate ligament reconstruction: A prospective analysis. *Psychology and Health, 15*, 283–291.

Brewer, B. W., Cornelius, A. E., Van Raalte, J. L., Petitpas, A. J., Sklar, J. H., Pohlman, M. H., Krushell, R. J., & Ditmar, T. D. (2003). Protection motivation theory and adherence to sport injury rehabilitation revisited. *The Sport Psychologist, 17*, 95–103.

Brewer, B. W., Van Raalte, J. L., & Petitpas, A. J. (2000). Self-identity issues in sport career transitions. In D. Lavallee & P. Wylleman (Eds.), *Career transitions in sport: International perspectives* (pp. 29–43). Morgantown, WV: Fitness Information Technology.

Bricker, C. (2001, July 7). Rafter never backs down. *Hartford Courant*, C1–C2.

Bridle, C., Riemsma, R. P., Pattenden, J., Sowden, A. J., Mather, L., Watt, I. S., & Walker, A. (2005). Systematic review of the effectiveness of the health behavior interventions based on the transtheoretical model. *Psychology and Health, 20*, 283–301. doi: 10.1080/08870440512331333997

Brink, M. S. (2010). Monitoring stress and recovery: New insights for the prevention of injuries and illnesses in elite youth soccer players. *British Journal of Sports Medicine, 44*, 809–815.

Brink, M. S., Visscher, C., Arends, S., Zwerver, J., Post, W. J., Limmink, K. A. P. M. (2010). Monitoring stress and recovery: New insights for the prevention of injuries and illnesses in elite youth soccer players. *British Journal of Sports Medicine, 44*, 809–815. doi: 10.1136/bjsm.2009.069476

Broman-Fulks, J. J., & Storey, K. M. (2008). Evaluation of a brief exercise intervention for high anxiety sensitivity. *Anxiety, Stress, and Coping, 21*, 117–128.

Brook, J. S., Kessler, R. C., & Cohen, P. (1999). The onset of marijuana use from preadolescence and early adolescence to young adulthood. *Development and Psychopathology, 11*, 901–914.

Brooks, G., & Fahey, T. (1984). *Exercise physiology*. New York, NY: Wiley.

Brown, E. J., Heimberg, R. C., Frost, R. O., Makris, G. S., Juster, H. R., & Leung, A. W. (1999). Relationship of perfectionism to affect, expectations, attributions and performance in the classroom. *Journal of Social and Clinical Psychology, 18*, 98–120.

Brown, G., & Potrac, P. (2009). "You've not made the grade son": De-selection and identity disruption in elite level youth football. *Soccer & Society, 10*, 143–159.

Brown, H., Pearson, N., Braithwaite, R., Brown, W., & Biddle, S. (2013). Physical activity interventions and depression in children and adolescents. *Sports Medicine, 43*, 195–206. doi: 10.1007/s40279-012-0015-8

Brown, J., & Delsohn, S. (1989). *Out of bounds*. New York, NY: Zebra.

Brown, L. J., Malouff, M. J., & Schutte, N. S. (2005). The effectiveness of a self-efficacy intervention for helping adolescents cope with sport-competition loss. *Journal of Sport Behavior, 28*, 136–151.

Brown, P., & Gaines, S. S. (1983). *The love you make. An insider's story of the Beatles*. New York, NY: McGraw-Hill.

Brown, R. W., & Jewell, R. T. (1994). Is there consumer discrimination in college basketball? The premium fans pay for white players. *Social Science Quarterly, 75*, 401–413.

Brown, T. D. Jr., VanRaalte, J. L., Brewer, B. W., Winter, C. R., Cornelius, A. E., & Andersen, M. B. (2002). World Cup soccer home advantage. *Journal of Sport Behavior, 25*, 134–144.

Bruhmann, B., & Schneider, S. (2011). Risk groups for sports injuries among adolescents—representative German national data. *Child: Care, Health and Development, 37*, 597–605. Doi: 10.1111/j.1365-2214.2011.01209.x

Bruner, M. W., & Spink, K. S. (2011). Effects of team building on exercise adherence and group task satisfaction in a youth activity setting. *Group Dynamics: Theory, Research, and Practice, 15*, 161–172. doi: 10.1037/a0021257

Bruni, F. (2012, July 21). Women's time to shine. *The New York Times*. Retrieved from http://www.nytimes.com

Brustad, R. J. (1993). Who will go out and play? Parental and psychological influences on children's attraction to physical activity. *Pediatric Exercise Science, 5*, 210–223.

Buchanan, H. T., Blankenbaker, J., & Cotton, D. (1976) Academic and athletic ability as popularity factors in elementary school children. *Research Quarterly, 47*, 320–325.

Buckolz, E., Prapavesis, H., & Fairs, J. (1988). Advance cues and their use in predicting tennis passing shots. *Canadian Journal of Sport Sciences, 13*, 20–30.

Buckworth, J., & Dishman, R. K. (2007). Exercise adherence. In G. Tenenbaum, & R. C. Eklund (Eds.), *Handbook of sport psychology* (3rd ed., pp. 509–536). New York, NY: Wiley.

Bueno, J., Weinberg, R. S., Fernandez-Castro, J., & Capdevila, L. (2008). Emotional and motivational mechanisms mediating the influence of goal setting on endurance athletes' performance. *Psychology of Sport and Exercise, 9*, 786–799. doi: 10.1016/j.psychsport.2007.11.003

Bull, S. J. (1991). Personal and situational influences on adherence to mental skills training. *Journal of Sport and Exercise Psychology, 13*, 121–132.

Bull, S. J., Shambrook, C. J., James, W., & Brooks, J. E. (2005). Towards an understanding of mental toughness in elite English cricketers. *Journal of Applied Sport Psychology, 17*, 209–227.

Burke, K. L. (1986). Comparison of psychological androgyny within a sample of female college athletes who participate in sports traditionally appropriate and traditionally inappropriate for competition by females. *Perceptual and Motor Skills, 63*, 779–782.

Burke, L. M., & Read, R. S. (1988). A study of dietary patterns of elite Australian football players. *Canadian Journal of Sports Science, 13*, 15–19.

Burton, D., Gillham, A., & Glenn, S. (2011). Motivational styles: Examining the impact of personality on the self-talk patterns of adolescent female soccer players. *Journal of Applied Sport Psychology, 23,* 413–428. doi: 10.1080/10413200.2001.568469

Burton, D., & Naylor, S. (1997). Is anxiety really facilitative? Reaction to the myth that cognitive anxiety always impairs sport performance. *Journal of Applied and Sport Psychology, 9,* 295–302.

Burton, D., Naylor, S., & Holliday, B. (2001). Goal setting in sport. Investigating the goal effectiveness paradox. In R. N. Singer, H. A. Hausenblas, & C. M. Janelle (Eds.), *Handbook of sport psychology* (2nd ed., pp. 497–528). New York, NY: Wiley.

Burton, D., Pickering, M., Weinberg, R., Yukelson, D., & Weigand, D. (2010). The competitive goal effectiveness paradox revisited: Examining the goal practices of prospective Olympic athletes. *Journal of Applied Sport Psychology, 22,* 72–86.

Burton, D., & Weiss, C. L. (2008). The fundamental goal concept: The path to process and performance success. In T. Horn (Ed.), *Advances in sport psychology* (3rd ed., pp. 339–375). Champaign, IL: Human Kinetics.

Butcher, J., Lindner, K. J., & Johns, D. P. (2002). Withdrawal from competitive youth sport: A retrospective ten-year study. *Journal of Sport Behavior, 25,* 145–153.

Butler, J. L., & Baumeister, R. F. (1998). The trouble with friendly faces: Skilled performance with a supportive audience. *Journal of Personality and Social Psychology, 75,* 1213–1230.

Butryn, T. M. (2002). Critically examining white racial identity and privilege in sport psychology consulting. *The Sport Psychologist, 16,* 316–336.

Butt Why? Despite his actions, Zidane wins Golden Ball. (2006, July 11). *Hartford Courant,* C2.

Cacciola, S. (2011, August 30). My last day without a jog: 1971. *Wall Street Journal.* Retrieved from http://www.wsj.com

Caesar, D. (2004, June 10). A (Jim) Gray spot for Bird. *Hartford Courant,* C7.

Caliari, P. (2008). Enhancing forehand acquisition in table tennis: The role of mental practice. *Journal of Applied Sport Psychology, 20,* 88–96.

Callow, N., & Hardy, L. (2001). Types of imagery associated with sport confidence in netball players of varying skill levels. *Journal of Applied Sport Psychology, 13,* 1–17.

Callow, N., Hardy, L., & Hall, C. (2001). The effects of a motivational general-mastery imagery intervention on the sport confidence of high-level badminton players. *Research Quarterly in Exercise and Sport, 72,* 389–400.

Callow, N., & Roberts, R. (2010). Imagery research: An investigation of three issues. *Psychology of Sport and Exercise, 11,* 325–329.

Callow, N., Roberts, R., Bringer, J. D., & Langan, E. (2010). Coach education related to the delivery of imagery: Two interventions. *The Sport Psychologist, 18,* 277–299.

Callow, N., Roberts, R., & Fawkes, J. Z. (2006). Effects of dynamic and static imagery on vividness of imagery skiing performance, and confidence. *Journal of Imagery Research in Sport and Physical Activity, 1,* 1–15.

Callow, N., Smith, M. J., Hardy, L., Arthur, C. A., & Hardy, J. (2009). Measurement of transformational leadership and its relationship with team cohesion and performance level. *Journal of Applied Sport Psychology, 21,* 395–412.

Calmels, C., Berthoumieux, C., & d'Arripe-Longueville, F. (2004). Effects of an imagery training program on selective attention of national softball players. *The Sport Psychologist, 18,* 272–296.

Calmels, C., d'Arripe-Longueville, F., Fournier, J. F., & Soulard, A. (2003). Competitive strategies among elite female gymnasts: An exploration of the relative influences of psychological skills training and natural learning experiences. *International Journal of Sport & Exercise Psychology, 1,* 327–352.

Calmels, C., Holmes, P., Lopez, E., & Naman, V. (2006). Chronometric comparison of actual and imaged complex movement patterns. *Journal of Motor Behavior, 38,* 339–348.

Campbell, A., & Hausenblas, H. A. (2009). Effects of exercise interventions on body image: A meta-analysis. *Journal of Health Psychology, 14,* 780–793. doi: 10.1177/1359105309338977

Campo-Flores, A., & Kirsch, R. (2002, January 21). Sent to the penalty box. *Newsweek, 139,* 38.

Cantor, N., & Harlow, R. E. (1994). Personality, strategic behaviour and daily-life problem solving. *Current Directions in Psychological Science, 3,* 169–172.

Capa, R., Audiffren, M., Andre, N., & Hansenne, M. (2011). Further evidence of the independence between the motive to achieve success and the motive to avoid failure: A confirmatory factor analysis. *Psychologica Belgica, 51,* 93–106.

Capa, R., Audiffren, M., & Ragot, S. (2008). The interactive effect of achievement motivation and task difficulty on mental effort. *International Journal of Psychophysiology, 70,* 114–150.

Cardinal, B. J. (1999). Extended stage model for physical activity behavior. *Journal of Human Movement Sciences, 37,* 37–54.

Carlson, C. R., & Bernstein, D. A. (1995). Relaxation skills training: Abbreviated Progressive Relaxation. In W. O'Donohue, & L. Krasner (Eds.), *Handbook of psychological skills training: Clinical applications and techniques* (pp. 20–35). Boston, MA: Allyn & Bacon.

Carlson, L. E., Speca, M., Patel, K. D., & Faris, P. (2007). One year pre-post intervention follow-up of psychological, immune, endocrine and blood pressure outcomes of mindfulness-based stress reduction (MBSR) in breast and prostate cancer outpatients. *Brain, Behavior, and Immunity, 21,* 1038–1049.

Carlson, L. E., Speca, M., Patel, K. D., & Goodey, E. (2004). Mindfulness-based stress reduction in relation to quality of life, mood, symptoms of stress and levels of cortisol, dehydroepiandrosterone-sulfate (DHEAS) and melatonin in breast and prostate cancer outpatients. *Psychoneuroendocrinology, 29,* 448–474.

Carlson, R. C. (1988). The socialization of elite tennis players in Sweden: An analysis of the players' backgrounds and development. *Sociology of Sport Journal, 5,* 241–256.

Carlson, R. C. (1997). In search of the expert sport performer. *Science in the Olympic Sport, 1,* 1–13.

Carpenter, L. J., & Acosta, R. V. (2008). *Women in intercollegiate sport: A longitudinal, national study thirty-one year update 1977–2008.* Retrieved from http://www.acosta-carpenter.org

Carr, S. (2009). Adolescent-parent attachment characteristics and quality of youth sport friendship. *Psychology of Sport and Exercise, 10,* 653–661. doi: 10.1016/j.psychsport.2009.04.001

Carr, S., & Weigand, D. A. (2002). The influence of significant others on the goal orientations of youngsters in physical education. *Journal of Sport Behavior, 25,* 19–40.

Carron, A. V., Brawley, L. R., & Widmeyer, W. N. (1998). The measurement of cohesiveness in sport groups. In J. L. Duda (Ed.), *Advances in sport and exercise psychology* (pp. 213–226). Morgantown, WV: Fitness Information Technology.

Carron, A. V., Bray, S. R., & Eys, M. A. (2002). Team cohesion and team success in sport. *Journal of Sport Sciences, 20,* 119–126.

Carron, A. V., Burke, S. M., & Shapcott, K. M. (2009). Enhancing team effectiveness. In B. W. Brewer (Ed.), *Handbook of sports medicine and science, sport psychology* (pp. 64–74). Chichester, England: Wiley-Blackwell.

Carron, A. V., & Chelladurai, P. (1981). The dynamics of group cohesion in sport. *Journal of Sport Psychology, 3,* 123–139.

Carron, A. V., Colman, M. M., Wheeler, J., & Stevens, D. (2002). Cohesion and performance in sport: A meta analysis. *Journal of Sport and Exercise Psychology, 24,* 168–188.

Carron, A. V., & Dennis, P. W. (1998). The sport team as an effective group. In J. M. Williams (Ed.), *Applied sport psychology: Personal growth to peak performance* (3rd ed., pp. 127–141). Mountain View, CA: Mayfield.

Carron, A. V., & Dennis, P. W. (2001). The sport team as an effective group. In J. M. Williams (Ed.), *Applied sport psychology: Personal growth to peak performance* (4th ed., pp. 120–134). Mountain View, CA: Mayfield.

Carron, A. V., Martin, L. J., & Loughead, T. M. (2012). Teamwork and performance. In S. M. Murphy (Ed.), *The Oxford handbook of sport and performance psychology* (pp. 309–327). New York, NY: Oxford University Press.

Carron, A. V., Prapavessis, H., & Grove, J. R. (1994). Group effects and self-handicapping. *Journal of Sport and Exercise Psychology, 16,* 246–257.

Carron, A. V., & Spink, K. S. (1995). The group size-cohesion relationship in minimal groups. *Small Group Research, 26,* 86–105.

Carron, A. V., Widmeyer, W. N., & Brawley, L. R. (1985). The development of an instrument to assess cohesion in sport teams: The Group Environment Questionnaire. *Journal of Sport Psychology, 7,* 244–266.

Carson, F., & Polman, R. C. J. (2010). The facilitative nature of avoidance coping within sports injury rehabilitation. *Scandinavian Journal of Medicine & Science in Sports, 20,* 235–240. doi: 10.1111/j.1600–0838.2009.00890.x

Cartwright, W. S. (2008). Economic costs of drug abuse: Financial, cost of illness and services. *Journal of Substance Abuse Treatment, 34,* 224–233. doi: 10.1016/jsat.2007.04.003

Carver, C. S. (1996). Cognitive interference and the structure of behavior. In I. G. Sarason, G. R. Pierce, & B. R. Sarason (Eds.), *Cognitive interference theories, methods, and findings* (pp. 25–45). Mahwah, NJ: Lawrence Erlbaum Associates.

Carver, C. S., & Baird, E. (1998). The American dream revisited: Is it what you want or why you want it that matters? *Psychological Science, 9,* 289–292.

Carver, C. S., Lawrence, J. W., & Scheier, M. F. (1996). A control-process perspective on the origins of affect. In L. M. Martin, & A. Tesser (Eds.), *Striving and feeling.*

Interactions among goals, affect, and self-regulation (pp. 11–52). Mahwah, NJ: Lawrence Erlbaum.

Carver, C. S., & Scheier, M. F. (1992). Confidence, doubt and coping with anxiety. In D. G. Forgays, T. Sosnowski, & K Wresiewski (Eds.), *Anxiety: Recent developments in cognitive, psychophysiological and health research* (pp. 13–22). London, England: Hemisphere.

Carver, C. S., & Scheier, M. F. (1998). A control-process perspective on anxiety. *Anxiety Research, 1,* 17–22.

Carver, C. S., & Scheier, M. F. (1998). *On the self-regulation of behavior.* Cambridge, England: Cambridge University Press.

Carver, C. S., & Scheier, M. F. (2011). Self-regulation of action and affect. In K. K. Vohs & R. F. Baumeister (Eds.), *Handbook of self-regulation research, theory, and applications* (2nd ed., pp. 3–21). New York, NY: Guilford.

Caserta, R., & Singer, R. N. (2007). The effectiveness of situational awareness learning to response to video tennis match situations. *Journal of Applied Sport Psychology, 19,* 125–141.

Caserta, R. J., Young, J., & Janelle, C. M. (2007). Old dogs, new tricks: Training the perceptual skills of senior tennis players. *Journal of Sport & Exercise Psychology, 29,* 479–497.

Cash, T. F. (2004). Body image: Past, present, and future. *Body Image, 1,* 1–5.

Cash, T. F., Melnyk, S. E., & Hrabosky, J. I. (2004). The assessment of body image investment: An extensive revision of the Appearance Schemas Inventory. *International Journal of Eating Disorders, 35,* 305–316. doi: 10.1002/eat.10264

Caspersen, C. J., Powell, K. E., & Christenson, G. M. (1985). Physical activity, exercise, and physical fitness: Definitions and distinctions for health-related research. *Public Health Reports, 100,* 126–131.

Castaneda, B., & Gray, R. (2007). Effects of focus of attention on baseball batting performance in players of differing skill levels. *Journal of Sport & Exercise Psychology, 29,* 60–77.

Castaneda, R., Sussman, N., Levy, R., O'Malley, M., & Westreich, L. (1998). A review of the effects of moderate alcohol intake on psychiatric and sleep disorders. In M. Galanter (Ed.), *Recent developments in alcoholism* (Vol. 14, pp. 197–251). NY: Springer

Castanier, C., Le Scanff, C., & Woodman, T. (2010). Who takes risks in high-risk sports? A typological personality approach. *Research Quarterly for Exercise & Sport, 81,* 478–484.

Castro, J. R., & Rice, K. G. (August, 2003). *Attentional distraction and perfectionism: A test of competing models of moderation and mediation in the cognitive anxiety-performance relationship.* Poster presented at the Annual Convention of the American Psychological Association, Toronto.

Catlin, D. H., Fitch, K. D., & Ljungqvist, A. (2008). Medicine and science in the fight against doping in sport. *Journal of Internal Medicine, 264,* 99–114. doi: 10.1111/j.1365-2796.2008.01993.x

Causer, J., Holmes, P. S., Smith, N. C., & Williams, A. M. (2011). Anxiety, movement kinematics, and visual attention in elite-level performers. *Emotion, 11,* 595–602. doi: 10.1037/a0023225

Cavalli-Sforza, L. L., & Cavalli-Sforza, F. (1995). *The great human diasporas: The history of diversity and evolution.* Reading, MA: Perseus Books.

Cazenvae, N., Le Scanff, C., & Woodman, T. (2007). Psychological profiles and emotional regulation characteristics of women engaged in risk-taking sports. *Anxiety, Stress, & Coping, 20,* 421–435. doi: 10.1080/10615800701330176

Centers for Disease Control and Prevention. (1998). *CDC surveillance summaries,* MMWR; (No. SS-5).

Centers for Disease Control and Prevention. (2006). Sports-related injuries among high school athletes: United States, 2005–06 school year. *MMWR Morbidity and Mortality Weekly Report, 55,* 1037–1040.

Centers for Disease Control and Prevention. (2008). Prevalence of self-reported physically active adults—United States, 2007. *MMWR, 57,* 1297–1300. Retrieved from http://www.cdc.gov/mmwr/preview/mmwrhtml/mm5748a1.htm

Centers for Disease Control and Prevention. (2009, June). Youth Risk Behavior Surveillance. *Surveillance Summaries. MMWR 2010; 59 SS-5.*

Centers for Disease Control and Prevention. (2011). Physical activity and health. Retrieved from http://cdc.gov/physical activity/everyone/health/index.html

Centers for Disease Control and Prevention. (2012). Chronic diseases and health promotion. Retrieved from http://www.cdc.gov/chronicdisease/overview/index.htm

Cerin, E. (2004). Predictors of competitive anxiety direction in male Tae Kwon Do practitioners: A multilevel mixed idiographic/nomothetic interactional approach. *Psychology of Sport and Exercise, 5,* 497–516.

Cervone, D. (2000). Thinking about self-efficacy. *Behavior Modification, 24,* 30–57.

Cervone, D., Kopp, D. A., Schaumann, L., & Scott, W. D. (1994). Mood, self-efficacy, and performance standards: Lower moods induce higher standards for performance. *Journal of Personality and Social Psychology, 67,* 499–512.

Cervone, D., & Wood, R. (1995). Goals, feedback, and the differential influence of self-regulatory processes on cognitively complex performance. *Cognitive Therapy and Research, 19,* 519–545.

Cetinkalp, Z. K., & Turksoy, A. (2011). Goal orientation and self-efficacy as predictors of male adolescent soccer players' motivation to participate. *Social Behavior and Personality, 39,* 925–934. doi: 10.2224/sbp.2011.39.7.925

Chait, L. D. (1990). Subjective and behavioral effects of marijuana the morning after smoking. *Psychopharmacology, 100,* 328–333.

Chalabaev, A., Serrazin, P., Stone, J., & Cury, F. (2008). Do achievement goals mediate stereotype threat? An investigation on females' soccer performance. *Journal of Sport & Exercise Psychology, 30,* 143–158.

Chamberlain, S. T., & Hale, B. D. (2007). Competitive state anxiety and self-confidence: Intensity and direction as relative predictors of performance on a golf putting task. *Anxiety, Stress, and Coping, 20,* 197–207. doi: 10.1080/10615800701288572

Chan, D. K-C., Hagger, M. S., & Spray, C. M. (2011). Treatment motivation for rehabilitation after a sport injury: Application of the trans-contextual model. *Psychology of Sport and Exercise, 12,* 83–92. doi: 10.1016/j.psychsport.2010.08.005

Chantal, Y., Robin, P., Vernat, J-P., & Bernache-Assollant, I. (2005). Motivation, sportspersonship, and athletic aggression: A meditational analysis. *Psychology of Sport and Exercise, 6,* 233–249.

Chase, M. A., & Dummer, G. M. (1992). The role of sports as a social status determinant for children. *Research Quarterly for Exercise and Sport, 63,* 418–424.

Chase, M. A., Feltz, D. L., & Lirgg, C. D. (2003). Sources of collective and individual efficacy of collegiate athletes. *International Journal of Exercise & Sport Psychology, 1,* 180–191.

Chase, M. A., Lirgg, C. D., & Feltz, D. F. (1997). Do coaches' efficacy expectations for their teams predict team performance? *The Sport Psychologist, 11,* 8–23.

Chatzisarantis, N.L.D., Hagger, M. S., Biddle, S.J.H., & Karageorghis, C. (2002). The cognitive processes by which perceived locus of causality predicts participation in physical activity. *Journal of Health Psychology, 7,* 685–699.

Chatzisarantis, N.L.D., Hagger, M. S., & Thogersen-Ntoumani, C. (2008). Effects of implementation intentions and self-concordance on health behavior. *Journal of Applied Biobehavioral Research, 13,* 198–214.

Chavez, E. J. (2008–2009). Flow in sport: A study of college athletes. *Imagination, Cognition, and Personality, 28,* 69–91.

Chelladurai, P. (1980). Leadership in sports organizations. *Canadian Journal of Applied Sport Sciences, 5,* 226–231.

Chelladurai, P. (1984). Discrepancy between preferences and perceptions of leadership behavior and satisfaction of athletes in varying sports. *Journal of Sport Psychology, 6,* 27–41.

Chelladurai, P. (1990). Leadership in sports: A review. *International Journal of Sport Psychology, 21,* 328–354.

Chelladurai, P. (1993). Leadership. In R. N. Singer, M. Murphey, & L. K. Tennant (Eds.), *Handbook of research on sport psychology* (pp. 647–671). New York, NY: Macmillan.

Chelladurai, P. (2007). Leadership in sports. In G. Tenenbaum & R. C. Eklund (Eds.), *Handbook of sport psychology* (3rd ed., pp. 113–135). New York, NY: Wiley.

Chelladurai, P. (2012). Leadership and manifestations of sport. In S. M. Murphy (Ed.), *The Oxford handbook of sport and performance psychology* (pp. 328–341). New York, NY: Oxford University Press.

Chelladurai, P., & Arnott, M. (1985). Decision styles in coaching: Preferences of basketball players. *Research Quarterly for Exercise and Sport, 56,* 15–24.

Chelladurai, P., & Doherty, A. J. (1998). Styles of decision making in coaching. In J. M. Williams (Ed.), *Applied sport psychology: Personal growth to peak performance* (3rd ed., pp. 115–126). Mountain View, CA: Mayfield.

Chelladurai, P., Haggerty, T. R., & Baxter, P. R. (1989). Decision styles choices of university basketball coaches and players. *Journal of Sport and Exercise Psychology, 11,* 201–215.

Chelladurai, P., Imamura, H., Yamaguchi, Y., Oinuma, Y., & Miyauchi, T. (1988). Sport leadership in a cross-national setting: The case of Japanese and Canadian university athletes. *Journal of Sport & Exercise Psychology, 10,* 374–389.

Chelladurai, P., Malloy, D., Imamura, H., & Yamaguchi, Y. (1987). A cross-cultural study of preferred leadership in sports. *Canadian Journal of Sport Sciences, 12,* 106–110.

Chelladurai, P., & Quek, C. B. (1995). Decision style choices of high school coaches: The effects of situational and coach characteristics. *Journal of Sport Behavior, 18,* 91–108.

Chelladurai, P., & Reimer, H. A. (1998). Measurement of leadership in sport. In J. L. Duda (Ed.), *Advances in sport and exercise psychology* (pp. 227–253). Morgantown, WV: Fitness Information Technology.

Chelladurai, P., & Saleh, S. (1978). Preferred leadership in sports. *Canadian Journal of Applied Sport Sciences, 3,* 85–92

Chelladurai, P., & Saleh, S. (1980). Dimensions of leader behavior in sports. *Journal of Sport Psychology, 2,* 34–45.

Chelladurai, P., & Turner, B. A. (2006). Styles of decision making in coaching. In J. M. Williams (Ed.), *Applied sport psychology: Personal growth to peak performance* (5th ed., pp. 140–154), New York, NY: McGraw-Hill.

Chen L. H., Wu, C-H., Kee, Y. H., Lin, M-S., & Shui, S-H. (2009). Fear of failure, 2 × 2 achievement goal and self-handicapping: An examination of the hierarchical model of achievement motivation in physical education. *Contemporary Educational Psychology, 34,* 298–305.

Cheng, W-N. K., Hardy, L., & Markland, D. (2009). Toward a three-dimensional conceptualization of performance anxiety: Rationale and initial measurement development. *Psychology of Sport and Exercise, 10,* 271–278. doi: 10.1016/j.psychsport.2008.08.001

Cheryan, S., & Bodenhausen, G. V. (2000). When positive stereotypes threaten intellectual performance: The psychological hazards of "model minority" status. *Psychological Science, 11,* 399–402.

Chesney, M. A., Neilands, T. B., Chambers, D. B., Taylor, J. M., & Folkman, S. (2006). A validity and reliability study of the coping self-efficacy scale. *British Journal of Health Psychology, 11,* 421–437. doi: 10.1348/135910705X53155

Chi, L., & Duda, J. L. (1995). Multi-sample confirmatory factor analysis of the task and ego orientation in sport questionnaire. *Research Quarterly for Exercise and Sport, 66,* 91–98.

Chief Medical Officers of England, Scotland, Wales, and Northern Ireland. (2011). Start active, stay active: A report on physical activity from the four home countries' Chief Medical Officers. London: Department of Health. Retrieved from http://www.dh.gov.uk/en/Publicationsandstatistics/Publications/PublicationsPolicyAnd Guidance/DH

Chow, G. M., & Feltz, D. L. (2008). Exploring the relationships between collective efficacy, perceptions of success, and team attributions. *Journal of Sports Sciences, 26,* 1179–1189. doi: 10.1080/02640410802101827

Chow, G. M., Murray, K. E., & Feltz, D. L. (2009). Individual, team, and coach predictors of players' likelihood to aggress in youth soccer, *Journal of Sport & Exercise Psychology, 31,* 425–443.

Chu, D. (1982). *Dimensions of sport studies.* New York, NY: Wiley.

Ciani, K. D., & Sheldon, K. M. (2010). Evaluating the mastery-avoidance goal construct: A study of elite college basketball players. *Psychology of Sport and Exercise, 11,* 127–132. doi: 10.1016/j.psychsport.2009.04.005

Clark, R. D. (2002). Do professional golfers "choke"? *Perceptual and Motor Skills, 94,* 1124–1130.

Clark, S. E., & Ste-Marie, D. M. (2002). Peer mastery versus peer coping models: Model type has differential effects on psychological and performance measures. *Journal of Human Movement Studies, 43,* 179–196.

Clegg, J., & Orwall, B. (2010, February 4). Last taboo in English football: Playing footsie with mates' mate. *The Wall Street Journal.* Retrieved from http://online.wsj.com

Clement, D., & Shannon, V. R. (2011). Injured athletes' perceptions about social support. *Journal of Sport Rehabilitation, 20,* 457–470.

Clement, D., Shannon, V. R., & Cannole, I. J. (2011). Performance enhancement groups for injured athletes. *International Journal of Athletic Therapy & Training, 16,* 34–36.

Cloninger, C. R. (1987). Neurogenetic adaptive mechanisms in alcoholism. *Science, 236,* 410–416.

Coakley, J. (1992). Burnout among adolescent athletes: A personal failure or social problem? *Sociology of Sport Journal, 9,* 271–285.

Coakley, J. (2001). *Sport in society. Issues & Controversies.* Boston, MA: McGraw Hill.

Coakley, J. (2006). The good father: Parental expectations and youth sports. *Leisure Studies, 25,* 153–163.

Coates, B. (1997, January 1). Workaholic Vermeil once considered "poster boy of coaching burnout." *St Louis Post-Dispatch,* C3.

Cochran, W., & Tesser, A. (1996). The "What the Hell" effect: Some effects of goal proximity and goal framing on performance. In L. M. Martin, & A. Tesser (Eds.), *Striving and feeling. Interactions among goals, affect, and self-regulation* (pp. 99–120). Mahwah, NJ: Lawrence Erlbaum.

Coen, S. P., & Ogles, B. M. (1993). Psychological characteristics of the obligatory runner: A critical examination of the anorexia analogue hypothesis. *Journal of Sport and Exercise Psychology, 15,* 338–354.

Coffee, P., & Rees, T. (2011). When the chips are down: Effects of attributional feedback on self-efficacy and task performance following initial and repeated failure. *Journal of Sports Sciences, 29,* 235–245. doi: 10.1080/02640414.2010.531752

Coffee, P., Rees, T., & Haslam, A. (2009). Bouncing back from failure: The interactive impact of perceived controllability and stability on self-efficacy beliefs and future task performance. *Journal of Sports Sciences, 27,* 1117–1124. doi: 10.1080/02640410903030297

Cogan, K. D., & Petrie, T. A. (1996). Diversity in sport. In J. L. Van Raalte & B. W. Brewer (Eds.), *Exploring exercise and sport psychology* (pp. 355–373). Washington, DC: American Psychological Association.

Cogan, K. D., & Petrie, T. A. (2002). Diversity in sport. In J. L. Van Raalte & B. W. Brewer (Eds.), *Exploring exercise and sport psychology* (2nd ed., pp. 417–436). Washington, DC: American Psychological Association.

Cohen, B. (2012, December 28). Louisville's strategy: Hug it out. *Wall Street Journal.* Retrieved from htt://www.wsj.com

Cohn, P. J. (1990a). An exploratory study on sources of stress and athlete burnout in youth golf. *The Sport Psychologist, 4,* 95–106.

Cohn, P. J. (1990b). Preperformance routines in sport: Theoretical support and practical applications. *The Sport Psychologist, 4,* 301–312.

Cokley, K., McClain, S., Jones, M., & Johnson, S. (2011). A preliminary investigation of academic disidentification, racial identity, and academic achievement among African American adolescents. *High School Journal, 95,* 54–68.

Colcombe, S. J., & Kramer, A. F. (2003). Fitness effects on the cognitive function of older adults: A meta-analytic study. *Psychological Science, 14,* 125–130.

Collins, D. V., Jones, B., Fairweather, M., Doolan, S., & Priestley, N. (2001). Examining anxiety associated changes in movement patterns. *International Journal of Sport Psychology, 32,* 223–242.

Conn, V. S., Hafdahl, A. R., & Mehr, D. R. (2011). Interventions to increase physical activity among healthy adults: Meta-analysis of outcomes. *American Journal of Public Health, 101,* 751–758. doi: 10.2105/AJPH.2010.194381

Conrad, A., & Roth, W. T. (2007). Muscle relaxation therapy for anxiety disorders: It works but how? *Journal of Anxiety Disorders, 21,* 243–264.

Conroy, D. E. (2003). Representational models associated with fear of failure in adolescents and young adults. *Journal of Personality, 71,* 557–583.

Conroy, D. E. (2004). The unique psychological meanings of multidimensional fears of failing. *Journal of Sport & Exercise Psychology, 26,* 484–491.

Conroy, D E. (2008). Fear of failure in the context of competitive sport: A commentary. *Psychology of Sport and Exercise, 11,* 423–432. doi: 10.1016/j.psychsport.2010.04.013

Conroy, D. E., & Coatsworth, J. D. (2007). Coaching behaviors associated with changes in fear of failure: Changes in self-talk and need for satisfaction as potential mechanisms. *Journal of Personality, 75,* 383–419.

Conroy, D. E., & Elliot, A. J. (2004). Fear of failure and achievement goals in sport: Addressing the issue of the chicken and the egg. *Anxiety, Stress, and Coping, 17,* 271–285.

Conroy, D. E., Elliot, A. J., & Hofer, S. M. (2003). Achievement goals questionnaire for sport: Evidence for factorial invariance, temporal stability, and external validity. *Journal of Sport & Exercise Psychology, 25,* 456–476.

Conroy, D. E., Kaye, M. P., & Coatsworth, J. D. (2006). Coaching climates and the destructive effects of mastery-avoidance achievement goals on situational motivation. *Journal of Exercise & Sport Psychology, 28,* 69–92.

Conroy, D. E., & Metzler, J. N. (2004). Patterns of self-talk associated with different forms of competitive anxiety. *Journal of Sport & Exercise Psychology, 26,* 69–89.

Conroy, D. E., Poczwardowski, A., & Henschen, K. P. (2001). Evaluative criteria and consequences associated with failure and success for elite athletes and performing artists. *Journal of Applied Sport Psychology, 13,* 300–322.

Conroy, D. E., Willow, J. P., & Metzler, J. N. (2002). Multidimensional fear of failure measurement: The Performance Failure Appraisal Inventory. *Journal of Applied Sport Psychology, 14,* 76–90.

Cook, B., Hausenblas, H., Tuccitto, D., & Giacobbi, P. R. Jr. (2011). Eating disorders and exercise: A structural equation modeling analysis of a conceptual model. Special issue article. *European Eating Disorders Review, 19,* 216–225. doi: 10.l002/erv.1111

Cook, T. D., & Campbell, D. T. (1979). *Quasi-experimentation. Design & analysis issues for field settings.* Chicago, IL: Rand McNally.

Cooper, M. L. (1994). Motivations for alcohol use among adolescents: Development and validation of a four-factor model. *Psychological Assessment, 6,* 117–128.

Cooper, M. L., Russell, M., Skinner, J. B., & Windle, M. (1992). Development and validation of a three-dimensional measure of drinking motives. *Psychological Assessment, 4,* 123–132.

Copeland, B., Bonnell, R. J., Reider, L, & Burton, D. (2009). Spawning sliding success: Evaluating a stress management and cohesion development program for young lugers. *Journal of Sport Behavior, 32,* 438–459.

Copeland, J., Peters, R., & Dillon, P. (2000). Anabolic-androgenic steroid use disorders among a sample of Australian competitive and recreational users. *Drug and Alcohol Dependence, 60,* 91–96.

Costa, P. T., Jr., & McCrae, R. R. (1992). *Revised NEO personality inventory and NEO five-factor inventory: Professional manual.* Odessa, FL: Psychological Assessment Resources.

Costa, P. T., Jr., & McCrae, R. R. (1995). Primary traits of Eysenck's P-E-N system: three- and five-factor solutions. *Journal of Personality and Social Psychology, 69,* 308–317.

Costanzo, P. R., Woody, E., & Slater, P. (1992). On being psyched up but not psyched out: An optimal pressure model of achievement motivation. In A. K. Boggiano, & T. S. Pittman (Eds.), *Achievement and motivation. A social developmental perspective* (pp. 215–243). New York, NY: Cambridge University Press.

Cote, J. (1999). The influence of family in the development of talent. *The Sport Psychologist, 13,* 395–417.

Cote, J., Baker, J., & Abernethy, B. (2007). Practice and play in the development of sport expertise. In G. Tenenbaum & R. C. Eklund (Eds.), *Handbook of sport psychology* (3rd ed., pp. 184–202). New York, NY: Wiley.

Cote, J., & Salmela, J. H. (1996). The organizational tasks of high performance gymnastic coaches. *The Sport Psychologist, 10,* 347–260.

Cote, J., Salmela, J. H., Russell, S. (1995). The knowledge of high-performance gymnastic coaches: Competition and training considerations. *The Sport Psychologist, 9,* 76–95.

Cote, J., Salmela, J., Trudel, P., Baria, A., & Russell, S. (1995). The coaching model: A grounded assessment of expert gymnastic coaches' knowledge. *Journal of Sport & Exercise Psychology, 17,* 1–17.

Cotterill, S. T., Sanders, R., & Collins, D. (2010). Developing effective pre-performance routines in golf: Why don't we ask the golfer? *Journal of Applied Sport Psychology, 22,* 51–64.

Cottyn, J., De Clercq, D., Pannier, J-L., Crombez, G., & Lenoir, M. (2006). The measurement of competitive anxiety during balance beam performance in gymnasts. *Journal of Sports Sciences, 24,* 157–164. doi: 10.1080/02640410500131571

Coudevylle, G. R., Gernigon, C., & Ginis, K.A.M. (2011). Self-esteem, self-confidence, anxiety and claimed self-handicapping: A meditational analysis. *Psychology of Sport and Exercise, 12,* 670–675. doi: 10.1016/j.psychsport.2001.05.008

Coudevylle, G. R., Ginis, K.A.M., & Famose, J-P. (2008). Determinants of self-handicapping strategies in sport and their effects on athletic performance. *Social Behavior and Personality, 36,* 391–398.

Coudevylle, G. R., Ginis, K.A.M., Famose, J-P, & Gernigon, C. (2008). Effects of self-handicapping strategies on anxiety before athletic performance. *The Sport Psychologist, 22,* 304–315.

Coudevylle, G. R., Ginis, K.A.M., Famose, J-P, & Gernigon, C. (2009). An experimental investigation of the determinants and consequences of self-handicapping strategies across motivational climates. *European Journal of Sport Science, 9,* 219–227.

Courneya, K. S., & Carron, A. V. (1992). The home advantage in sport competitions: A literature review. *Journal of Sport & Exercise Psychology, 14,* 13–27.

Coutts, A. J., Wallace, L. K., & Slattery, K. M. (2007). Monitoring changes in performance, physiology, biochemistry and psychology during overreaching and recovery in triathletes. *International Journal of Sports Medicine, 28,* 125–134.

Covassin, T., & Pero, S. (2004). The relationship between self-confidence, mood state, and anxiety among collegiate tennis players. *Journal of Sport Behavior, 27,* 230–241.

Covington, M. V. (1992). *Making the grade: A self-worth perspective on motivation and school reform.* New York, NY: Cambridge University Press.

Cox, R. H. (2011). *Sport psychology: Concepts and applications* (7th ed.). New York, NY: McGraw-Hill.

Cox, T., & Ferguson, E. (1991). Individual differences, stress, and coping. In C. L. Cooper & R. Payne (Eds.), *Personality and stress: Individual differences in the stress process* (pp. 7–30). Chichester, England: Wiley.

Cox, T., & Kerr, J. H. (1990). Self-reported mood in competitive squash. *Personality and Individual Differences, 11,* 199–203.

Craft, L. L., & Landers, D. M. (1998). The effects of exercise on clinical depression and depression resulting from mental illness: A meta-analysis. *Journal of Sort & Exercise Psychology, 20,* 339–357.

Craft, L. L., Magyar, T. M., Becker, B. J., & Feltz, D. L. (2003). The relationship between the Competitive State Anxiety Inventory-2 and sport performance: A meta-analysis. *Journal of Sport & Exercise Psychology, 25,* 45–65.

Crant, J. M. (1996). Doing more harm than good: When is impression management likely to evoke a negative response. *Journal of Applied Social Psychology, 16,* 1454–1471.

Cresswell, S. L., & Eklund, R. C. (2005a). Changes in athlete burnout and motivation over a 12-week league tournament. *Medicine and Science in Sports and Exercise, 37,* 1957–1966.

Cresswell, S. L., & Eklund, R. C. (2005b). Motivation and burnout among top amateur rugby players. *Medicine and Science in Sports and Exercise, 37,* 469–477.

Cresswell, S. L., & Eklund, R. C. (2006a). Athlete burnout: Conceptual confusion, current research and future research directions. In S. Hanton & S. D. Mellalieu (Eds.), *Literature reviews in sport psychology* (pp. 91–126), New York, NY: Nova Science Publishers.

Cresswell, S. L., & Eklund, R. C. (2006b). The convergent and discriminant validity of burnout measures in sport: A multi-trait/multi-method analysis. *Journal of Sport Sciences, 24,* 209–220.

Cresswell, S. L., & Eklund, R. C. (2006c). The nature of player burnout in rugby: Key characteristics and attributions. *Journal of Applied Sport Psychology, 18,* 219–239.

Cresswell, S., & Hodge, K. (2004). Coping skills: Role of trait sport confidence and trait anxiety. *Perceptual and Motor Skills, 98,* 433–438.

Crocker, P. R. E., & Graham, T. R. (1995). Coping by competitive athletes with performance stress: Gender differences and relationships with affect. *Sport Psychologist, 9,* 325–338.

Croft, R. J., Mackay, A. J., Mills, A. T., & Gruzelier, J. G. (2001). The relative contributions of ecstasy and cannabis to cognitive impairment. *Psychopharmacology, 153,* 373–379.

Crognier, L., & Fery, Y-A. (2005). Effect of tactical initiative on predicting passing shots in tennis. *Applied Cognitive Psychology, 19,* 647–649. doi: 10.1002/acp.1100

Crossman, J., Vincent, J., & Speed, H. (2007). The times they are a-changin'. *International Review for the Sociology of Sport, 42,* 27–41. doi: 10.1177/1012690207081828

Cruickshank, A., & Collins, D. (2012). Culture change in elite sport performance teams: Examining and advancing effectiveness in the new era. *Journal of Applied Sport Psychology, 24,* 338–355. doi: 10.1080/10413200.2011.650819

Crust, L. (2009). The relationship between mental toughness and affect intensity. *Personality and Individual Differences, 47,* 959–963. doi: 10.1016.j.paid.2009.07.023

Crust, L., & Azadi, K. (2009). Leadership preferences of mentally tough athletes. *Personality and Individual Differences, 47,* 326–330.

Csikszentmihalyi, M. (1990). *Flow: The psychology of optimal experience.* New York, NY: Harper & Row.

Cumming, J., Clark, S. E., Ste-Marie, D. M., McCullagh, P., & Hall, C. (2005). The functions of observational learning questionnaire (FOLQ). *Psychology of Sport and Exercise, 6,* 517–537.

Cumming, J., & Hall, C. (2002). Athletes' use of imagery in the off-season. *The Sport Psychologist, 16,* 160–172.

Cumming, J., Hall, C., Harwood, C., & Gammage, K. (2002). Motivational orientations and imagery use: A goal profiling analysis. *Journal of Sports Sciences, 20,* 127–136.

Cumming, J., Nordin, S. M., Horton, R., & Reynolds, S. (2006). Examining the direction of imagery and self-talk on dart-throwing performance and self-efficacy. *The Sport Psychologist, 20,* 257–274.

Cumming, J. L., & Ste-Marie, D. M. (2001). The cognitive and motivational effects of imagery training: A matter of perspective. *Sport Psychologist, 15,* 276–288.

Cumming, S. P., Smith, R. E., Smoll, F. L., Standage, M., & Grossbard, J. R. (2008). Development and validation of the Achievement Goal Scale for Sports. *Psychology of Sport and Exercise, 9,* 686–703. doi: 10.1016/j.psychsport.2007.09.003

Cumming, S. P., Smoll, F. L., Smith, R. E., & Grossbard, J. R. (2007). Is winning everything? The relative contributions of motivational climate and won-lost percentage in youth sports. *Journal of Applied Sport Psychology, 19,* 322–336.

Cupal, D. D. (1998). Psychological interventions in sport injury prevention and rehabilitation. *Journal of Applied Sport Psychology, 10,* 103–123.

Cupal, D. D., & Brewer, B. W. (2001). Effects of relaxation and guided imagery on knee strength, reinjured anxiety, and pain following anterior cruciate ligament reconstruction. *Rehabilitation Psychology, 46,* 28–43.

Curran, T., Appleton, P. R., Hill, A. P., & Hall, H. K. (2011). Passion and burnout in elite junior soccer players: The mediating role of self-determined motivation. *Psychology of Sport and Exercise, 12,* 655–661. doi: 10.1016/j.psychsport.2011.06.004

Cury, F., Da Fonseca, D., Rufo, M., Peres, C., & Sarrazin, P. (2003). The trichotomous model and investment in learning to prepare a sport test: A mediational analysis. *British Journal of Educational Psychology, 73,* 529–543.

Cury, F., Elliot, A., Sarrazin, P., Da Fonseca, D., & Rufo, M. (2002). The trichotomous achievement goal model and intrinsic motivation: A sequential mediational analysis. *Journal of Experimental Social Psychology, 38,* 473–481.

Cutton, D. M., & Landin, D. (2007). The effects of self-talk and augmented feedback on learning the tennis forehand. *Journal of Applied Sport Psychology, 19*, 288–303. doi: 10.1080/10413200791328664

Cyr, D. (2004, November). King of the court. *U.S. Airways Attaché*, 32–36.

Daino, A. (1985). Personality traits of adolescent tennis players. *International Journal of Sport Psychology, 16*, 120–125.

Dale, G. A. (2000). Distractions and coping strategies of elite decathletes during their most memorable performances. *The Sport Psychologist, 14*, 17–41.

Daly, J. M., Brewer, B. W., Van-Raalte, J. L., Petitpas, A. J., & Sklar, J. H. (1995). Cognitive appraisals, emotional adjustment, and adherence to rehabilitation following knee surgery. *Journal of Sport Rehabilitation, 3*, 23–30.

Damato, G. C., Grove, J. R., Eklund, R. C., & Cresswell, S. (2008). An exploratory examination into the effect of absence due to hypothetical injury on collective efficacy. *The Sport Psychologist, 22*, 253–268.

Danaei, G., Ding, E. L., Mozaffarian, D., Taylor, B., Rehm, J., Murray, C. J. L., & Ezzati, M. (2009). The preventable causes of death in the United States: Comparative risk assessment of dietary, lifestyle, and metabolic risk factors. *PLoS Medicine 6*, e1000058. doi: 10.1371/journal.pmed.1000058

Darling, N., Caldwell, L. L., & Smith, R. (2005). Participation in school-based extracurricular activities and adolescent adjustment. *Journal of Leisure Research, 37*, 51–76.

D'Arripe-Longueville, F., Fournier, J. F., & Dubois, A. (1998). The perceived effectiveness of interactions between expert French judo coaches and elite female athletes. *The Sport Psychologist, 12*, 317–332.

Darrow, C. J., Collins, C. L., Yard, E. E., Comstock, R. D. (2009). Epidemiology of severe injuries among United States high school athletes. *The American Journal of Sports Medicine, 37*, 1798–1805. doi: 10.1177/0363546509333015

Davidson, R., Goleman, D., & Schwartz, G. (1976). Attentional and affective concomitants of meditation: A cross-sectional study. *Journal of Abnormal Psychology, 85*, 235–238.

Davidson, R. J., Kabat-Zinn, J., Schumacher, J., Rosenkranz, M., Muller, D., Santorelli, S., . . . Sheridan, J. F. (2003). Alterations in brain and immune function produced by mindfulness meditation. *Psychosomatic Medicine, 65*, 564–570.

Davies, C. (2009, April 19). George Best and his mother destroyed by the bottle. *The Guardian.* Retrieved from http://www.guardian.co.uk

Davies, C., & Davies, L. (2012, February 13). John Terry cleared of racially abusing Anton Ferdinand. *The Guardian.* Retrieved from http://www.guardian.co.uk

Davis, C., Elliott, S., Dionne, M., & Mitchell, I. (1991). The relationship of personality factors and physical activity to body satisfaction in men. *Personality and Individual Differences, 12*, 689–694.

Davis, C., & Mogk, J. P. (1994). Some personality correlates of interest and excellence in sport. *International Journal of Sport Psychology, 25*, 131–143.

Davis, C. L., Tomporowski, P. D., Boyle, C. A., Waller, J. L., Miller, P. H., Naglieri, J. A., & Gregoski, M. (2007). Effects of aerobic exercise on overweight children's cognitive functioning: A randomized controlled trial. *Research Quarterly for Exercise & Sport, 78*, 510–519.

Davis, J. O. (1991). Sports injuries and stress management: An opportunity for research. *The Sport Psychologist, 5*, 175–182.

Davis, K. (2005, August 6). NCAA rejects "hostile" images. *Hartford Courant*, A1 A4.

Davis, S. F., Huss, M. T., & Becker, A. H. (1995). Norman Triplett and the dawning of sport psychology. *The Sport Psychologist, 9*, 366–375.

Deakin, J. M., & Cobley, S. (2003). An examination of the practice environments in figure skating and volleyball: A search for deliberate practice. In J. Starkes & K. A. Ericsson (Eds.), *Expert performance in sports: Advances in research on sport expertise* (pp. 90–113). Champaign, IL: Human Kinetics.

de Bruijn, G-J., de Groot, R., van den Putte, B., & Rhodes, R. (2009). Conscientiousness, extroversion, and action control: Comparing moderate and vigorous physical activity. *Journal of Sport & Exercise Psychology, 31*, 724–742.

de Bruin, M., Sheeran, P., Kok, G., Hiemstra, A., Prins, J. M., Hosers, H. J., & van Breukelen, G. J. P. (2012). Self-regulatory processes mediate the intention-behavior relation for adherence and exercise behaviors. *Health Psychology, 9*, 1–9. doi: 10.1037/a0027425

Deci, E. L., & Ryan, R. M. (1985). *Intrinsic motivation and self-determination in human behavior.* New York, NY: Plenum Press.

Deci, E. L. & Ryan, R. M. (1987). The support of autonomy and the control of behavior. *Journal of Personality and Social Psychology, 53*, 1024–1037.

Deci, E. L., & Ryan, R. M. (2002). *Handbook of self-determination research.* Rochester, NY: University of Rochester Press.

DeFrancesco, C., & Burke, K. L. (1997). Performance enhancement strategies used in a professional tennis tournament. *International Journal of Sport Psychology, 28*, 185–195.

De La Pena, D., Murray, N. P., & Janelle, C. M. (2008). Implicit overcompensation: The influence of negative self-instructions on performance of a self-paced motor task. *Journal of Sport Sciences, 26*, 1323–1331. doi: 10.1080/02640410802155138

De Moor, M.H.M., Beem, A. L., Stubbe, J. H., Boomsma, D. I., & De Geus, E.J.C. (2006). Regular exercise, anxiety, depression and personality: a population-based study. *Preventive Medicine, 42*, 273-279. doi:10.1016/j.ypmed.2005.12.002

Denmark, F. L., & Fernandez, L. C. (1993). Historical development of the psychology of women. In F. L. Denmark & M. A. Paludi (Eds.), *Psychology of women: A handbook of issues and theories* (pp. 3–22). Westport, CT: Greenwood Press.

De Onis, M., Blossner, M., & Borghi, E. (2010). Global prevalence and trends of over-weight and obesity among preschool children. *American Journal of Clinical Nutrition, 92*, 1257–1264. doi: 10.3945/ajcn.2010.29786

Deppe, R. K., & Harackiewicz, J. M. (1996). Self-handicapping and intrinsic motivation: Buffering intrinsic motivation from threat of failure. *Journal of Personality and Social Psychology, 70*, 868–875.

De Petrillo, L. A., Kaufman, K. A., Glass, C. R., & Arnkoff, D. B. (2009). Mindfulness for long-distance runners: An open trial using Mindful Sport Performance Enhancement (MSPE). *Journal of Clinical Sport Psychology, 4*, 357–376.

Deroche, T., Stepahn, Y., Brewer B. W., & Scanff, C. L. (2007). Predictors of perceived susceptibility to sport-related injury. *Personality & Individual Differences, 43*, 2218–2228. doi: 10.1016/j.paid.2007.06.031

DeSimone, P. (1993). Linguistic assumptions in scientific language. *Contemporary Psychodynamics: Theory, Research & Application, 1*, 8–17.

Developing your mental pacemaker. (1989). *Sport Psychology Training Bulletin, September/October, 1*–8.

Devonport, T. J., Biscomb, K., Lane, A. M., Mahoney, C. M., & Cassidy, T. (2005). Stress and coping in elite junior netball. *Journal of Sports Sciences, 22*, 162–163.

DiBartolo, P. M., Frost, R. O., Chang, P., LaSota, M., & Grills, A. E. (2004). Shedding light on the relationship between personal standards and psychopathology: The case for contingent self-worth. *Journal of Rational-Emotive & Cognitive-Behavior Therapy, 22*, 241–254.

DiBartolo, P. M., Lin, L., Montoya, S., Neal, & Shaffer, C. (2007). Are there 'healthy' and 'unhealthy' reasons for exercise? Examining individual differences in exercise motivations using the Function of Exercise Scale. *Journal of Clinical Sport Psychology, 1*, 93–120.

DiClemente, C. C. (2006). *Addiction and change: How addictions develop and addicted people recover.* New York, NY: Guilford.

Diehl, N., & Petrie, T. (1995). A longitudinal investigation of the effects of different exercise modalities on social physique anxiety. *Journal of Applied Sport Psychology, 7*, S55.

Diener, C. I., & Dweck, C. S. (1978). An analysis of learned helplessness: Continuous changes in performance, strategy, and achievement cognitions following failure. *Journal of Personality and Social Psychology, 36*, 451–462.

Dillbeck, M. C., & Orme-Johnson, D. W. (1987). Physiological differences between transcendental meditation and rest. *American Psychologist, 42*, 879–881.

Dillman, L. (2004, August 22). Phelps: A gold watch. *Hartford Courant*, E13, E14.

Dinges, M. M., & Oettsing, E. R. (1993). Similarity in drug use patterns between adoles-cents and their friends. *Adolescence, 28*, 253–266.

Dirks, K. T. (2000). Trust in leadership and team performance: Evidence from NCAA basketball. *Journal of Applied Psychology, 85*, 1004–1012.

Dishman, R. K. (2001). The problem of exercise adherence: Fighting sloth in nations with market economies. *Quest, 53*, 279–294. doi: 10.1080/003336297.2001.10491745

Dishman, R. K., & Buckworth, J. (1996). Increasing physical activity: A quantitative synthesis. *Medicine and Science in Sports and Exercise, 28*, 706–719.

Dishman, R. K., & Chambliss, H. O. (2010). Exercise psychology. In J. M. Williams (Ed.), *Applied sport psychology: Personal growth to peak performance* (6th ed., pp. 563–595). New York, NY: McGraw-Hill.

Dishman, R. K., Ickes, W., Morgan, W. P., Lavallee, D., Williams, J. M., & Jones, M. V. (2008). Self-motivation and adherence to habitual physical activity. In D. Lavallee, J. M. Williams, & M. V. Jones (Eds.), *Key studies in sport and exercise psychology* (pp. 74–92). Maidenhead, England: Open University Press.

Dishman, R. K., Vandenberg, R. J., Motl, R. W., & Nigg, C. R. (2010). Using constructs of the transtheoretical model to predict classes of change in regular physical activity: A multi-ethnic longitudinal cohort study. *Annuals of Behavioral Medicine, 40*, 150–163. doi: 10.1007/s12160-010-9196-2

Dohrmann, G. (2013, March 25). The moment things started to unravel for Ben Howland at UCLA. *Sports Illustrated.* Retrieved from http://www.si.com

Donahue, E. G., Miguelon, P., Valois, P., Goulet, C., Buist, A., & Vallerand, R. J. (2006). A motivational model of performance-enhancing substance use in elite athletes. *Journal of Sport & Exercise Psychology, 28*, 511–520.

Donovan, J. S., & Williams, K. J. (2003). Minding the mark: Effects of time and causal attributions on goal revision in response to goal performance descriptions. *Journal of Applied Psychology, 88,* 379–390.

Dorsch, T. E., Smith, A. L., & McDonough, M. H. (2009). Parents' perceptions of child-to-parent socialization in organized youth sport. *Journal of Sport & Exercise Psychology, 31,* 444–468.

Douglas, K., & Carless, D. (2009). Abandoning the performance narrative: Two women's stories of transition from professional sport. *Journal of Applied Sport Psychology, 21,* 213–230.

Doyle, P. (2005, January 5). Wade, Ryno get call. *Hartford Courant,* C1, C5.

Draycott, S. G., & Kline, P. (1995). The big three of the five-factor-the EPQ-R vs the NEO-PI: A research note, replication and elaboration. *Personality & Individual Differences, 18,* 801–804.

Drexler, L. P., Ahrens, A. H., & Haaga, D. A. F. (1995). The affective consequences of self-handicapping. *Journal of Social Behavior and Personality, 10,* 861–870.

Driskell, J. E., Copper, C., & Moran, A. (1994). Does mental practice enhance performance? *Journal of Applied Psychology, 79,* 481–492.

Druss, B. G., & Rosenheck, R. A. (1999). Patterns of health care costs associated with depression and substance abuse in a national sample. *Psychiatric Services, 50,* 214–218.

Dubuc, N. G., Schinke, R. J., Eys, M. A., Battochio, R., & Zaichkowsky, L. (2010). Experiences of burnout among adolescent female gymnasts: Three case studies. *Journal of Clinical Sport Psychology, 4,* 1–18.

Duda, J. L. (1985). Goals and achievement orientations of Anglo and Mexican-American adolescents in sport and the classroom. *International Journal of Intercultural Relations, 9,* 131–155.

Duda, J. L. (1986). A cross-cultural analysis of achievement motivation in sport and the classroom. In L. VanderVelden & J. Humphrey (Eds.), *Current selected research in the psychology and sociology of sport* (pp. 115–132). New York, NY: AMS Press.

Duda, J. L. (1989). The relationship between task and ego orientation and the perceived purpose of sport among male and female high school athletes. *Journal of Sport & Exercise Psychology, 11,* 318–335.

Duda, J. L. (1997). Perpetuating myths: A response to Hardy's 1996 Coleman Griffith address. *Journal of Applied Sport Psychology, 9,* 303–309.

Duda, J. L. (2001). Achievement goals research in sport: Pushing the boundaries and clarifying some misunderstandings. In G. C. Roberts (Ed.), *Advances in motivation in sport and exercise* (pp. 129–182). Champaign, IL: Human Kinetics.

Duda, J. L. (2005). Motivation in sport: The relevance of competence and achievement goals. In A. J. Elliot & C. S. Dweck (Eds.), *Handbook of competence and motivation* (pp. 318–335). New York, NY: Guilford.

Duda, J. L., & Allison, M. T. (1982). The nature of sociocultural influences on achievement motivation: The case of the Navajo Indian. In J. W. Loy (Ed.), *Paradoxes of play* (pp. 188–197). West Point, NY: Leisure Press.

Duda, J., & Allison, M. (1990). Cross-cultural analysis in exercise and sport psychology: A void in the field. *Journal of Sport & Exercise Psychology, 12,* 114–131.

Duda, J. L., & Hall, H. (2001). Achievement goal theory in sport. Recent extensions and future directions. In R. N. Singer, H. A. Hausenblas, & C. M. Janelle (Eds.), *Handbook of sport psychology* (2nd ed., pp. 417–443). New York, NY: Wiley.

Duda, J. L., & Kim, M. (1997). Parental and gym motivational climates and the development of eating disorders among young elite gymnasts. *Journal of Sport & Exercise Psychology, 19* (Suppl.), S48.

Duda, J. L., & Nicholls, J. G. (1992). Dimensions of achievement motivation in schoolwork and sport. *Journal of Educational Psychology 84,* 290–299.

Duda, J. L., Olson, L. K., & Templin, T. J. (1991). The relationship of task and ego orientation to sportsmanship attitudes and perceived legitimacy of injurious acts. *Research Quarterly for Exercise and Sport, 62,* 334–343.

Duda, J. L., & Roberts, G. C. (1980). Sex biases in general and causal attributions of outcome in co-ed sport competition. In C. H. Nadeau, W. R. Halliwel, K. M. Newell, & G. C. Roberts (Eds.), *Psychology of motor behavior and sport—1979* (pp. 27–36). Champaign, IL: Human Kinetics.

Duff, C., & Munro, G. (2007). Preventing alcohol-related problems in community sports clubs: The good sports program. *Substance Use & Misuse, 42,* 1991–2001. doi: 10.1080/10826080701533054

Dugdale, J. R., & Eklund, R. C. (2002). Do *not* pay attention to the empires: Thought suppression and task-relevant focusing strategies. *Journal of Sport & Exercise Psychology, 24,* 306–319.

Dunkley, D. M., Blankstein, K. R., Halsall, J., Williams, M., & Winkworth, G. (2000). The relationship between perfectionism and distress: Hassles, coping, and perceived social support as mediators and moderators. *Journal of Counseling Psychology, 47,* 437–453.

Dunkley, D. M., Zuroff, D. C., & Blankstein, K. R. (2006). Specific perfectionism components versus self-criticism in predicting maladjustment. *Personality and Individual Differences, 40,* 665–676.

Dunn, D. L., Madhukar, H., Trivedi, M. D., Kampert, J. B., Clark, C. G., & Chambliss, H. O. (2005). Exercise treatment for depression—efficacy and dose response. *American Journal of Preventive Medicine, 28,* 1–8.

Dunn, J.G.H. (1999). A theoretical framework for structuring the content of competitive worry in ice hockey. *Journal of Sport & Exercise Psychology, 21,* 259–279.

Dunn, J.G.H., & Causgrove Dunn, J. (1999). Goal orientations, perceptions, or aggression, and sportspersonship in elite male youth ice hockey players. *The Sport Psychologist, 13,* 183–200.

Dunn, J.G.H., Causgrove Dunn, J., Gotwals, J. K., Vallance, J.K.H., Craft, J. M., & Syrotuik, D. G. (2006). Establishing construct validity evidence for the Sport Multidimensional Perfectionism Scale. *Psychology of Sport and Exercise, 7,* 57–79.

Dunn, J.G.H., Causgrove Dunn, J., & Syrotuik, D. G. (2002). Relationship between multidimensional perfectionism and goal orientations in sport. *Journal of Sport & Exercise Psychology, 24,* 376–395.

Dunn, J.G.H., Craft, J. M., Dunn, J. C., & Gotwals, J. K. (2011). Comparing a domain-specific and global measure of perfectionism in competitive female figure skaters. *Journal of Sport Behavior, 34,* 25–46.

Dunn, J.G.H., Gotwals, J. K., & Causgrove Dunn, J. (2005). An examination of the domain specificity of perfectionism among intercollegiate student-athletes. *Personality and Individual Differences, 38,* 1439–1448.

Dunn, J.G.H., Gotwals, J. K., Causgrove Dunn, J., & Syrotuik, D. G. (2006). Examining the relationship between perfectionism and trait anger in competitive sport. *International Journal of Sport and Exercise Psychology, 4,* 7–24.

Dupuis, M., Bloom, G. A., & Loughead, T. M. (2006). Team captains' perceptions of athlete leadership. *Journal of Sport Behavior, 29,* 60–78.

Durand, M., Hall, C., & Haslam, I. R. (1997). The effects of combining mental and physical practice on motor skill acquisition: A review of the literature and some practical implications. *The Hong Kong Journal of Sports Medicine and Sports Science, 4,* 36–41.

Durtschi, S., & Weiss, M. (1986). Psychological characteristics of elite and nonelite marathon runners. In D. Landers (Ed.), *Sport and elite performers* (pp. 73–80). Champaign, IL: Human Kinetics.

Dweck, C. S. (1980). Learned helplessness in sport. In C. H. Nadeau, W. R. Halliwell, K. M. Newell, & G. C. Roberts (Eds.), *Psychology of motor behavior and sport—1979* (pp. 1–11). Champaign, IL: Human Kinetics Press.

Dweck, C. S. (1986). Motivational processes affecting learning. *American Psychologist, 41,* 1040–1048.

Dweck, C. S., & Bush, E. S. (1976). Sex differences in learned helplessness: I. Differential debilitation with peer and adult evaluators. *Developmental Psychology, 12,* 147–156.

Dweck, C., & Leggett, E. (1988). A social cognitive approach to motivation and personality. *Psychological Review, 95,* 256–273.

Eagan, M. & Gonzalez, R. (2005, May 19) Attack on coach resonates. *Hartford Courant,* A1, A9.

Eagleton, J. R., McMelvie, & deMan, A. (2007). Extraversion and neuroticism in team sport participants, individual sport participants, and nonparticipants. *Perceptual and Motor Skills, 105,* 265–275.

Eccles, D. W., Ward, P., Janelle, C. M., Le Scanff, C., Ehrlinger, J., Castanier, C., & Coombes, S. A. (2011). Where's the emotion? How sport psychology can inform research on emotion in human factors. *Human Factor, 53,* 180–202. doi: 10.1177/0018720811403731

Eccles, J., Adler, T., & Meece, J. L. (1984). Sex differences in achievement: A test of alternate theories. *Journal of Personality and Social Psychology, 46,* 26–43.

Eccles, J. S. & Barber, B. L. (1999). Student council, volunteering, basketball, or marching band: What kind of extracurricular involvement matters? *Journal of Adolescent Research, 14,* 10–45.

Eccles, J., & Harold, R. (1991). Gender differences in sport involvement: Applying the Eccles expectancy value model. *Journal of Applied Sport Psychology, 3,* 7–35.

Echikson, W. (2008, April 7). The Scandinavian secret. *The Wall Street Journal,* R8.

Edmunds, J., Ntoumanis, N., & Duda, J. L. (2006). A test of self-determination theory in exercise domain. *Journal of Applied Social Psychology, 36,* 2240–2265.

Edmunds, J., Ntoumanis, N., & Duda, J. L. (2007). Understanding exercise adherence and psychological well-being from a self-determination theory perspective among a cohort of obese patients referred to an exercise on prescription scheme. *Psychology of Sport & Exercise, 8,* 722–740.

Edmunds, J., Ntoumanis, N., & Duda, J. L. (2008). Testing a self-determination theory-based teaching style intervention in the exercise domain. *European Journal of Social Psychology, 38,* 375–388.

Edwards, A. (2012). Eyes on the road! Ogling drivers cause nearly one million crashes each year. Retrieved from http://www.dailymail.co.uk

Edwards, H. (1973). *Sociology of sport.* Homewood, IL: Dorsey Press.

Edwards, S. W., Gordin, R. D., Jr., & Henschen, K. P. (1984). Sex-role orientations of female NCAA championship gymnasts. *Perceptual and Motor Skills, 58,* 625–626.

Edwards, T., Kingston, K., Hardy, L., & Gould, D. (2002). A qualitative analysis of catastrophic performances and the associated thoughts, feelings and emotions. *The Sport Psychologist, 16,* 1–19.

Egan, S., & Stelmack, R. M. (2003). A personality profile of Mount Everest climbers. *Personality and Individual Differences, 34,* 1491–1494.

Egli, T., Bland, H. W., Melton, B. F., & Czech, D. R. (2011). Influence of age, sex, and race on college students' exercise motivation of physical activity. *Journal of American College Health, 59,* 399–406.

Egloff, B., & Gruhn, A. J. (1996). Personality and endurance sports. *Personality and Individual Differences, 21,* 223–229.

Eisenberg, M. E., Wall, M., Neumark-Sztainer, D. (2012). Muscle-enhancing behaviors among adolescent girls and boys. *Pediatrics, 130,* 1019–1026. doi: 10.1542/Deds.2012-0095

Eitle, D., Turner, R. J., & Eitle, T. M. (2003). The deterrence hypothesis reexamined: Sports participation and substance use among young adults. *Journal of Drug Issues, 33,* 193–221.

Eklund, R. C. (1994). A season long investigation of competitive cognition in collegiate wrestlers. *Research Quarterly for Exercise and Sport, 65,* 169–183.

Eklund, R. C. (1996). Preparing to compete: A season-long investigation with collegiate wrestlers. *The Sport Psychologist, 10,* 111–131.

Eklund, R. C., & Cresswell, S. L. (2007). Athlete burnout. In G. Tenenbaum & R. C. Eklund (Eds.), *Handbook of Sport Psychology* (3rd ed., pp. 621–641). New York, NY: Wiley.

Elliot, A., J. (1999). Approach and avoidance motivation and achievement goals. *Educational Psychologist, 34,* 169–189.

Elliot, A. J. (2005). A conceptual history of the achievement goal construct. In A. J. Elliot & C. S. Dweck (Eds.), *Handbook of competence and motivation* (pp. 52–72). New York, NY: Guilford.

Elliot, A. J., & Church, M. A. (1997). A hierarchical model of approach achievement motivation. *Journal of Personality and Social Psychology, 72,* 218–232.

Elliot, A. J., Cury, F., Fryer, J. W., & Huguet, P. (2006). Achievement goals, self-handicapping, and performance attainment: A mediational analysis. *Journal of Sport & Exercise Psychology, 28,* 344–361.

Elliot, A. J., & Harackiewicz, J. M. (1994). Goal setting, achievement orientation, and intrinsic motivation: A mediational analysis. *Journal of Personality and Social Psychology 66,* 968–980.

Elliot, A. J., & Harackiewicz, J. M. (1996). Approach and avoidance achievement goals and intrinsic motivation: A mediational analysis. *Journal of Personality and Social Psychology, 70,* 461–475.

Elliot, A. J., & McGregor, H. A. (1999). Test anxiety and the hierarchical model of approach and avoidance achievement motivation. *Journal of Personality and Social Psychology, 76,* 628–644.

Elliot, A. J., & McGregor, H. A. (2001). A 2 × 2 achievement goal framework. *Journal of Personality and Social Psychology, 80,* 501–519.

Elliot, A. J., & Sheldon, K. M. (1997). Avoidance achievement motivation: A personal goals analysis. *Journal of Personality and Social Psychology, 73,* 171–185.

Emmons, R. A., & Kaiser, H. A. (1996). Goal orientation and emotional wellbeing: Linking goals and affect through the self. In L. L. Martin & A. Tesser (Eds.), *Striving and feeling: Interactions among goals, affect, and self-regulation* (pp. 79–98). Hillsdale, NJ: Lawrence Erlbaum Associates.

Engle, R. W. (2002). Working memory capacity as executive attention. *Current Directions in Psychological Science, 11,* 19–23.

Ericsson, K. A. (2003). Development of elite performance and deliberate practice: An update from the perspective of the expert performance approach. In J. Starkes & K. A. Ericsson (Eds.), *Expert performance in sports: Advances in research on sports expertise* (pp. 49–84). Champaign, IL: Human Kinetics.

Ericsson, K. A., Krampe, R. T., & Tesch-Romer, C. (1993). The role of deliberate practice in the acquisition of expert performance. *Psychological Review, 100,* 363–406.

Eriksson, S., & Gard, G. (2011). Physical exercise and depression. *Physical Therapy Reviews, 16,* 261–268. doi: 10.1179/1743288X117.0000000026

Escarti, A., & Guzman, J. F. (1999). Effects of feedback on self-efficacy, performance, and choice in an athletic task. *Journal of Applied Sport Psychology, 11,* 83–96.

Escarti, A., Roberts, G. C., Cervello, E. M., & Guzman, J. F. (1999). Adolescent goal orientations and the perception of criteria of success used by significant others. *International Journal of Sport Psychology, 30,* 309–324.

Eubank, M., Collins, D., Lovell, G., Dorling, D., & Talbot, S. (1997). Individual temporal differences in pre-competition anxiety and hormonal concentration. *Personality and Individual Differences, 23,* 1031–1039.

Evans, L., & Hardy, L. (1995). Sport injury and grief responses: A review. *Journal of Sport & Exercise Psychology, 17,* 227–245.

Evans, L., & Hardy, L. (2002a). Injury rehabilitation: A goal-setting intervention study. *Research Quarterly for Exercise and Sport, 73,* 310–319.

Evans, L., & Hardy, L. (2002b). Injury rehabilitation: A qualitative follow-up study. *Research Quarterly for Exercise and Sport, 73,* 320–329.

Evans, L., Hardy, L, & Fleming, S. (2000). Intervention strategies with injured athletes: An action research study. *The Sport Psychologist, 14,* 188–206.

Evans, L., Jones, L., & Mullen, R. (2004). An imagery intervention during the competitive season with an elite rugby union player. *The Sport Psychologist, 18,* 252–271.

Evans, M., Weinberg, R., & Jackson, A. (1992). Psychological factors related to drug use in college athletes. *The Sport Psychologist, 6,* 24–41.

Evardsson, A., Ivarsson, A., & Johnson, U. (2011). Is a cognitive-behavioural biofeedback intervention useful to reduce injury risk in junior football players? *Journal of Sports Science and Medicine, 11,* 331–338.

Everett, J. L., Smith, R. E., & Williams, K. D. (1992). Effects of team cohesion and identifiability on social loafing in relay swimming performance. *International Journal of Sport Psychology, 23,* 311–324.

Everly, G. S., & Benson, H. (1989). Disorders of arousal and the relaxation response: Speculations on the nature and treatment of stress-related diseases. *International Journal of Psychosomatics, 36,* 15–21.

Ewing, M. E., Seefeldt, V. D., & Brown, T. P. (1996). *Role of organized sport in the education and health of American children and youth. Background Report on the Role of Sports in Youth Development.* New York, NY: Carnegie Corporation of New York.

Eys, M. A., Burke, S. M., Carron, A. V., & Dennis, P. W. (2010). The sport team as an effective group. In J. M. Williams (Ed.), *Applied sport psychology: Personal growth to peak performance* (6th ed., pp. 132–148). New York, NY: McGraw-Hill.

Eys, M. A., Hardy, J., Carron, A. V., & Beauchamp, M. R. (2003). The relationship between task cohesion and competitive state anxiety. *Journal of Sport and Exercise Psychology, 25,* 66–76.

Eys, M., Loughead, T., Bray, S. R., & Carron, A. V. (2009a). Development of a cohesion questionnaire for youth: The Youth Sport Environment Questionnaire. *Journal of Sport and Exercise Psychology, 31,* 390–408.

Eys, M., Loughead, T., Bray, S. R., & Carron, A. V. (2009b). Perceptions of cohesion by youth sport participants. *The Sport Psychologist, 23,* 330–345.

Eys, M. A., Patterson, M. M., Loughead, T. M., & Carron, A. V. (2006). Team building in sport. In J. Duda, D. Hackfort, & R. Lidor (Eds.), *Handbook of research in applied sport psychology: International perspectives* (pp. 219–231). Morgantown, WV: Fitness Information Technology.

Eysenck, H. J. (1952). *The scientific study of personality.* New York, NY: MacMillian.

Eysenck, H. J. (1992). The definition and measurement of psychoticism. *Personality and Individual Differences, 13,* 757–785.

Eysenck, H. J. (1994). Personality. Biological foundations. In P. A. Vernon (Ed.), *The neuropsychology of individual differences* (pp. 151–207). San Diego, CA: Academic Press. Eysenck, H. J., & Eysenck, M. W. (1985). *Personality and individual differences.* New York, NY: Plenum.

Eysenck, H. J., & Eysenck, S. B. G. (1994). *Manual of the Eysenck Personality Questionnaire* (2nd ed.). London, England: Hodder and Stoughton.

Eysenck, H. J., Nias, D.K.B., & Cox, D. N. (1982). Sport and personality. *Advances in Behavior Research & Therapy, 4,* 1–56.

Eysenck, H. J., & Wilson, G. (1976). *Know your own personality.* New York, NY: Barnes & Noble.

Eysenck, M. W., & Calvo, M. G. (1992). Anxiety and performance: The processing efficiency theory. *Cognition and Emotion, 6,* 409–434.

Eysenck, M. W., & Derakshan, N. (1997). Cognitive biases for future negative events as a function of trait anxiety and social desirability. *Personality and Individual Differences, 22,* 597–605.

Eysenck, M. W., Derakshan, N., Santos, R., & Calvo, M. G. (2007). Anxiety and cognitive performance: Attentional control theory. *Emotion, 7,* 336–353.

Fallon, E. A., & Hausenblas, H. A. (2001). Transtheoretical model of behavior change: Does the termination stage really exist? *Journal of Human Movement Studies, 40,* 465–479.

Fallon, E. A., & Hausenblas, H. A. (2004). Transtheoretical model: Is termination applicable to exercise? *American Journal of Health Studies, 19,* 35–44.

Farber, B. A. (1983). *Stress and burnout in the human service professions.* New York, NY: Pergamon Press.

Farber, M. (2004, March 22). Code red. *Sports Illustrated, 100,* 56–59.

Farmer, H. S., & Vispoel, W. P. (1990). Attributions of female and male adolescents for real-life failure experiences. *Journal of Experimental Education, 58,* 127–140.

Farrell, A. (2002, Nov. 17). Golf: Sorenstam driven by perfection; the world's best golfer just gets better and better—and she keeps setting the goals higher. *Independent on Sunday,* p. 23.

Fasting, K. (2000). Women's role in national and international sports governing bodies. In B. L. Drinkwater (Ed.), *Women in sport* (pp. 441–450). Oxford, England: Blackwell Science.

Fasting, K., Brackenridge, C., & Walseth, K. (2007). Women athletes' personal responses to sexual harassment in sport. *Journal of Applied Sport Psychology, 19,* 419–433.

Fasting, K., & Pfister, G. (2000). Female and male coaches in the eyes of female elite soccer players. *European Physical Education Review, 6,* 91–110.

Fatsis, S. (1998, March 6). At last! Here's a way to measure just how pathetic your team is. *Wall Street Journal,* B1.

Faude, O., Kerper, O., Multhaupt, M., Winter, C., Beziel, K., Junge, A., & Meyer, T. (2010). Football to tackle overweight in children. *Scandinavian Journal of Medicine & Science in Sports, 20,* 103–110.

Fauth, R. C., Roth, J. L., & Brooks-Gunn, J. (2007). Does the neighborhood context alter the link between youth's after-school time activities and developmental outcomes? A multilevel analysis. *Developmental Psychology, 43,* 760–777. doi: 10.1037/0012-1649.43.3.760

Fawkner, H. J., McMurray, N. E., & Summers, J. J. (1999). Athletic injury and minor life events: A prospective study. *Journal of Science and Medicine in Sport, 2,* 117–124.

Feather, N. T. (1969). Attribution of responsibility and valence of success and failure in relation to initial confidence and task performance. *Journal of Personality and Social Psychology, 13,* 179–244.

Feick, D. L., & Rhodewalt, F. (1997). The double-edged sword of self-handicapping: discounting, augmentation, and the protection and enhancement of self-esteem. *Motivation and Emotion, 21,* 147–163.

Feltz, D. L. (1982). Path analysis of the causal elements in Bandura's theory of self-efficacy and anxiety-based model of avoidance behavior. *Journal of Personality and Social Psychology, 42,* 764–781.

Feltz, D. L., Chase, M. A., Moritz, Se. E., & Sullivan, P. J. (1999). Development of the multidimensional coaching effectiveness scale. *Journal of Educational Psychology, 91,* 765–776.

Feltz, D. L., Chow, G., & Hepler, T. J. (2006). Path analysis of self-efficacy and diving performance revisited. *Journal of Sport & Exercise Psychology, 28,* 401–411.

Feltz, D. L., Hepler, T. J., Roman, N., & Paiement, C. (2009). Coaching efficacy and volunteer youth sport coaches. *The Sport Psychologist, 23,* 24–41.

Feltz, D. L., & Lirgg, C. D. (1998). Perceived team and player efficacy in hockey. *Journal of Applied Psychology, 83,* 557–564.

Feltz, D. L., & Lirgg, C. D. (2001). Self-efficacy beliefs of athletes, teams, and coaches. In R. N. Singer, H. A. Hausenblas, & C. M. Janelle (Eds.), *Handbook of Sport Psychology* (2nd ed., pp. 340–361). New York, NY: Wiley.

Feltz, D. L., & Magyar, T. M. (2006) Self-efficacy and adolescents in sport and physical activity. In F. Pajares & T. Urdan (Eds.), *Self-efficacy beliefs of adolescents* (pp. 161–179). Greenwich, CT: Information Age.

Feltz, D. L., & Mugno, D. A. (1983). A replication of the causal elements in Bandura's theory of self-efficacy and the influence of autonomic perception. *Journal of Sport Psychology, 5,* 263–277.

Feltz, D. L., Short, S. E., & Sullivan, P. J. (2008). *Self-efficacy in sport.* Champaign, IL: Human Kinetics.

Ferrand, C., Tetard, S., & Fontayne, P. (2006). Self-handicapping in rock climbing: A qualitative approach. *Journal of Applied Sport Psychology, 18,* 271–280.

Ferrari, J. R., Harriott, J. S., & Zimmerman, M. (1999). The social support networks of procrastinators: Friends or family in times of trouble? *Personality and Individual Differences, 26,* 321–331.

Ferrari, J. R., Johnson, J. L., & McCown, W. G. (1995). *Procrastination and task avoidance. Theory, research and treatment.* New York, NY: Plenum.

Ferrari, J. R., & Tice, D. M. (2000). Procrastination as a self-handicap for men and women: A task-avoidance strategy in a laboratory setting. *Journal of Research in Personality, 34,* 73–83.

Fetherman, D. L., Hakim, R. M., & Sanko, J. P. (2011). A pilot study of the application of the transtheoretical model during strength training in older women. *Journal of Women & Aging, 23,* 58–76. doi: 10.1080/08952841.2011.540487

Field, T. (2009). Progressive muscle relaxation. In T. Field (Ed.), *Complementary and alternative therapies research* (pp. 97–101). Washington, DC: American Psychological Association.

Figueiredo, A. J., Goncalves, C. E., Coelho E., Silva, M. J., & Malina, R. M. (2009). Characteristics of youth soccer players who drop out, persist or move up. *Journal of Sports Sciences, 27,* 883–891. doi: 10.1080/02640410902946469

Fincham, F. D., Hokoda, A., Sanders, R. Jr. (1989). Learned helplessness, test anxiety, and academic achievement: A longitudinal analysis. *Child Development, 60,* 138–145.

Finez, L., Berjot, S., Rosnet, E., & Cleveland, C. (2011). Do athletes claim handicaps in low ego-threatening conditions? Re-examining the effect of ego-threat on claimed self-handicapping. *The Sport Psychologist, 25,* 288–304.

Finn, R. (1994, September 26). The second time around for Jennifer Capriati. *The New York Times, 144,* C1, C2.

Firmin, M., Hwang, C-E., Copella, M., & Clark, S. (2004). Learned helplessness: The effect of failure on test-taking. *Education, 124,* 688–693.

Fishbein, M., & Ajzens, I. (2009). *Predicting and changing behavior.* New York, NY: Psychology Press.

Fisher, A., Mancini, V., Hirsch, R., Proulx, T., & Staurowsky, E. (1982). Coach-athlete interactions and team climate. *Journal of Sport Psychology, 4,* 388–404.

Fitts, P. M., & Posner, M. I. (1967). *Human performance.* Belmont, CA: Brooks/Cole.

Fitzsimmons, P. A., Landers, D. M., Thomas, R. J., & Van der Mars, H. (1991). Does self-efficacy predict performance in experienced weightlifters? *Research Quarterly for Exercise and Sport, 62,* 424, 431.

Flegal, K. M., Carroll, M. D., Kit, B. K., & Ogden, C. L. (2012). Prevalence of obesity and trends in the distribution of body mass index among US adults, 1999–2010. *JAMA: Journal of the American Medical Association, 307,* 491–497. doi: 10.1001/jama.2012.39

Fleming, J., & Horner, M. S. (1992). The motive to avoid success. In C. P. Smith (Ed.), *Motivation and personality: Handbook of thematic content analysis* (pp. 278–310). New York, NY: Cambridge University Press.

Fletcher, D., & Arnold, R. (2011). A qualitative study of performance leadership and management in elite sport. *Journal of Applied Sport Psychology, 23,* 223–242. doi: 10.1080/10413200.2011.559184

Fletcher, K. L., Shim, S. S., & Wang, C. (2012). Perfectionistic concerns mediate the relationship between psychologically controlling parenting and achievement goal orientations. *Personality and Individual Differences, 52,* 876–881. doi: 10.1016/j.paid.2012.02.001

Flett, G., & Hewitt, P. (2005). The perils of perfectionism in sports and exercise. *Current Directions in Psychological Science. 14,* 14–18.

Flett, G. L., Blankstein, K. R., Hewitt, P. L., & Koledin, S. (1992). Components of perfectionism and procrastination in college students. *Social Behavior and Personality, 20,* 85–94.

Flett, G. L., Blankstein, K. R., & Martin, T. R. (1995). Procrastination, negative self-evaluation, and stress in depression and anxiety. In J. R. Ferrari, J. L. Johnson, & W. G. McCown (Eds.), *Procrastination and task avoidance. Theory, research and treatment* (pp. 137–167). New York, NY: Plenum.

Flett, G. L., & Hewitt, P. L. (1994). Perfectionism and components of state and trait anxiety. *Current Psychology, 13,* 326–349.

Flett, G. L., & Hewitt, P. L. (1995). Perfectionism, life events, and depressive symptoms: A test of a diathesis-stress mode. *Current Psychology, 14,* 112–138.

Flett, G. L., & Hewitt, P. L. (1998). Perfectionism in relation to attributions for success or failure. *Current Psychology, 17,* 249–263.

Flett, G. L., Hewitt, P. L., Blankstein, K. R., & Gray, L. (1998). Psychological distress and the frequency of perfectionistic thinking. *Journal of Personality and Social Psychology, 75,* 1363–1381.

Flett, G. L., Hewitt, P. L., & De Rosa, T. (1996). Dimensions of perfectionism, psychosocial adjustment, and social skills. *Personality and Individual Differences, 20,* 143–150.

Flett, G. L., Hewitt, P. L., & Martin, T. R. (1995). Dimensions of perfectionism and procrastination. In J. R. Ferrari, J. L. Johnson, & W. G. McCown (Eds.), *Procrastination and task avoidance. Theory, research and treatment* (pp. 113–136). New York, NY: Plenum.

Flett, G. L., Sawatzky, D. L., & Hewitt, P. L. (1995). Dimensions of perfectionism and goal commitment: A further comparison of two perfectionism measures. *Journal of Psychopathology and Behavioral Assessment, 17,* 111–124.

Folkman, S., Chesney, M., McKusick, L., Ironson, G., Johnson, D. S., & Coates, T. J. (1991). Translating coping theory into an intervention. In J. Eckenrode (Ed.), *The social context of coping* (pp. 239–260). New York, NY: Plenum.

Ford, J. A. (2008). Nonmedical prescription drug use among college students: A comparison between athletes and nonathletes. *Journal of American College Health, 57,* 211–219.

Ford, P., Hodges, N. J., & Williams, A. M. (2005). Online attentional focus manipulations in a soccer-dribbling task: Implications for the proceduralization of motor skills. *Journal of Motor Behavior, 37,* 386–394.

Ford, P. R., Ward, P., Hodges, N. J., & Williams, A. M. (2009). The role of deliberate practice and play in career progression in sport: the early engagement hypothesis. *High Ability Studies, 20,* 65–75. doi: 10.1080/13598130902860721

Ford, P. R., Yates, I., & Williams, A. M. (2010). An analysis of practice activities and instructional behaviours used by youth soccer coaches during practice: Exploring the link between science and application. *Journal of Sports Sciences, 28,* 483–495. doi: 10.1080/02640410903582750

Forgeard, M. C., Haigh, E. A. P., Beck, A. T., Davidson, R. J., Henn, F. A., Maier, S. F. . . . Seligman, M. E., P. (2011). Beyond depression: Toward a process-based approach to research, diagnosis, and treatment. *Clinical Psychology: Science and Practice, 18,* 275–299. doi: 10.1111/j.1468-2850.2011.01259.x

Fotheringham, W. (2011, May 9). Belgian cyclist Wouter Weylandt killed in Giro d'Italia crash. *The Guardian.* Retrieved from http://www.guardian.co.uk

Foster, J. J., Weigand, D. A., & Baines, D. (2006). The effect of removing superstitious behavior and introducing a pre-performance routine on basketball free-throw performance. *Journal of Applied Sport Psychology, 18,* 167–172.

Fourkas, A. D., Bonavolonta, V., Avenanti, A., & Agiloti, S. M. (2008). Kinesthetic imagery and tool-specific modulation of corticospinal representations in expert tennis players. *Cerebral Cortex. 18,* 2382–2390. doi: 10.1093/cercor/bhn005

Fournier, J. F., Calmels, C., Durand-Bush, N., & Samela, J. H. (2005). Effects of a season-long PST program on gymnastics performance and on psychological skill development. *International Journal of Sport and Exercise Psychology, 3,* 59–77.

Fournier, J. F., Deremaux, S., & Bernier, M. (2008). Content, characteristics and function of mental images. *Psychology of Sport and Exercise, 9,* 734–748. doi: 10.1016/j.psychsport.2007.12.003

Fowler, G. A. (2012, July 30). Vaulting through the pain. *Wall Street Journal.* Retrieved from http://online.wsj.com

Francis, L. J., Kelly, P., & Jones, S. H. (1998). The personality profile of female students who play hockey. *Irish Journal of Psychology, 19,* 394–399.

Franklin, K. (1989, September). Field of dreams: Little League's not so little anymore. *Sport,* 64–67.

Fredericks, J. A., & Eccles, J. S. (2004). Parental influences on youth involvement in sports. In M. R. Weiss (Ed.), *Developmental sport and exercise psychology: A lifespan perspective* (pp. 145–164). Morgantown, WV: Fitness Information Technology.

Fredericks, J. A., & Eccles, J. S. (2005). Family socialization, gender and sport motivation and involvement. *Journal of Sport & Exercise Psychology, 27,* 3–31.

Freeman, P., Coffee, P., & Rees, T. (2011). The PASS-Q: The Perceived Available Support in Sport Questionnaire. *Journal of Sport & Exercise Psychology, 33,* 54–74.

Freeman, P., & Rees, T. (2009). How does perceived support lead to better performance? An examination of potential mechanisms. *Journal of Applied Sport Psychology, 21,* 429–441.

Freeman, P., & Rees, T. (2010). Perceived social support from team-mates: Direct and stress-buffering effects on self-confidence. *European Journal of Sport Science, 10,* 56–67. doi: 10.1080/17461390903049998

Freixanet, M. G. (1991). Personality profile of subjects engaged in high physical risk sports. *Personality and Individual Differences, 12,* 1087–1093.

French, S. A., Story, M., Downes, B., Resnick, M. D., & Blum, R. W. (1995). Frequent dieting among adolescents: Psychosocial and health behavior correlates. *American Journal of Public Health, 85,* 695–701.

Freud, S. (1917). Mourning and melancholia. In J. Strachey (Ed. & Trans.), *The standard edition of the complete psychological works of Sigmund Freud* (Vol. 14, pp. 243–258). London, England: Hogarth Press.

Freud, S. (1923). The ego and the id. In J. Strachey (Ed. & Trans.), *The standard edition of the complete psychological works of Sigmund Freud* (Vol. 19, pp. 3–69). London, England: Hogarth Press.

Freud. S. (1927). The future of an illusion. In J. Strachey (Ed. & Trans.), *The standard edition of the complete psychological works of Sigmund Freud* (Vol. 21, pp. 5–56). London, England: Hogarth Press.

Freudenberger, H. J. (1974). Staff burnout. *Journal of Social Issues, 30,* 159–165.

Freudenberger, H. J. (1975). The staff burnout syndrome in alternative institutions. *Psychotherapy: Theory, Research, & Practice, 12,* 72–83.

Freudenberger, L. F., & Bergandi, T. A. (1994). Sport psychology research in American football: A review of the literature. *International Journal of Sport Psychology, 25,* 425–434.

Frey, M., Laguna, P. L., & Ravizza, K. (2003). Collegiate athletes' mental skill use and perceptions of success: An exploration of the practice and competition settings. *Journal of Applied Sport Psychology, 15,* 115–128.

Friedman, E., & Berger, B. G. (1991). Influence of gender, masculinity, and femininity on the effectiveness of three stress reduction techniques: Jogging, relaxation response, and group interaction. *Journal of Applied Sport Psychology, 3,* 61–86.

Friedman, N. P., & Miyake, A. (2004). The relations among inhibition and interference control functions: A latent-variable analysis. *Journal of Experimental Psychology: General, 133,* 101–135.

Frisch, A., Seil, R., Urhausen, A., Croisier, J. L., Lair, M. L., & Theisen, D. (2009). Analysis of sex-specific injury patterns and risk factors in young high-level athletes. *Scandinavian Journal of Medicine & Science in Sports, 19,* 834–841. doi: 10.1111/j.1600–0838.2008.00860.x

Frost, R. O., Heimberg, R. G., Holt, C. S., Mattia, J. I., & Neubauer, A. L. (1993). A comparison of two measures of perfectionism. *Personality and Individual Differences, 14,* 119–126.

Frost, R. O., & Henderson, K. J. (1991). Perfectionism and reactions to athletic competition. *Journal of Sport and Exercise Psychology, 13,* 323–335.

Frost, R. O., Lahart, C. M., & Rosenblate, R. (1991). The development of perfectionism: A study of daughters and their parents. *Cognitive Therapy and Research, 15,* 469–489.

Frost, R. O., Marten, P., Lahart, C., & Rosenblate, R. (1990). The dimensions of perfectionism. *Cognitive Therapy and Research, 14,* 449–468.

Frost, R. O., & Marten, P. A. (1990). Perfectionism and evaluative threat. *Cognitive Therapy and Research, 14,* 559–572.

Frost, R. O., Turcotte, T. A., Heimberg, R. G., Mattia, J. I., Holt, C. S., Hope, D. A. (1995). Reactions to mistakes among subjects high and low in perfectionistic concern over mistakes. *Cognitive Therapy and Research, 19,* 195–205.

Fry, M. D., Guivernau, M., Kim, M-s, Newton, M., Gano-Overway, L. A., & Magyar, T. M. (2012). Youth perceptions of a caring climate, emotional regulation, and psychological well-being. *Sport, Exercise, and Performance Psychology, 1,* 44–57. doi: 10.1037/a0025454

Fry, M. D., & Newton, M. (2003). Application of achievement goal theory in an urban youth setting. *Journal of Applied Sport Psychology, 15,* 50–66. doi: 10.1080/10413200390180062

Furley, P., Dicks, M., Stendtke, F., & Memmert, D. (2012). "Get it out the way. The wait's killing me." Hastening and hiding during soccer penalty kicks. *Psychology of Sport and Exercise, 13,* 454–465. doi: 10.1016/j.psychsport.2012.01.009

Futterman, M. (2011, August 1). Klinsmann and the meaning of soccer. *The Wall Street Journal.* Retrieved from http://www.wsj.com

Futterman, M. (2013, January 22). Jurgen Klinsmann sounds off. *The Wall Street Journal.* Retrieved from http://www.wsj.com

Galambos, S. A., Terry, P. C., Moyle, G. M., & Locke, S. A. (2005). Psychological predictors of injury among elite athletes. *British Journal of Sports Medicine, 39,* 351–354. doi: 10.1136/bjsm.2005.018440

Galassi, J. P., Frierson, H. T., Jr., & Sharer, R. (1981). Behavior of high, moderate, and low test-anxious students during an actual test situation. *Journal of Consulting and Clinical Psychology, 49,* 51–62.

Galli, N., & Vealey, R. S. (2008). "Bouncing back" from adversity: Athletes' experiences of resilience. *The Sport Psychologist, 22,* 316–335.

Gallucci, N. T. (1997). On the identification of patterns of substance abuse with the MMPI-A. *Psychological Assessment, 9,* 224–232.

Galper, D. I., Trivedi, M. H., Barlow, C. E., Dunn, A. L., & Kampert, J. B. (2006). Inverse association between physical inactivity and mental health in men and women. *Medicine & Science in Sports & Exercise, 38,* 173–178. doi: 10.1249/01. mss.0000180883.32116.28

Gammons, P. (1988, July 4). Inside baseball: Fatal distraction. *Sports Illustrated,* [Online]. Available: www.elibrary.com

Gano-Overway, L. A. (2008). The effect of goal involvement on self-regulatory processes. *International Journal of Sport and Exercise Psychology, 6,* 132–156.

Gano-Overway, L. A., & Duda, J. L. (1999). Interrelationships between expressive individualism and other achievement goal orientations among African and European American athletes. *Journal of Black Psychology, 25,* 544–563.

Gano-Overway, L. A., Newton, M., Magyar, T. M., Fry, M. D., Kim, M., & Guivernau, M. R. (2009). Influence of caring youth sport contexts on efficacy-related beliefs and social behaviors. *Developmental Psychology, 45,* 329–340. doi: 10.1037/a0014067

Gao, Z., Xiang, P., Harrison, L. Jr., Guan, J., & Rao, Y. (2008). A cross-cultural analysis of achievement goals and self-efficacy between American and Chinese college students in physical education. *International Journal of Sport Psychology, 39,* 312–328.

Garber, G., & Berlet, B. (1996, June 23). Major pressure. Norman regroups after collapse at Masters. *Hartford Courant,* K1, K12.

Gardner, F. L., & Moore, Z. E. (2004). A Mindfulness-Acceptance-Commitment (MAC) based approach to athletic performance enhancement: Theoretical considerations. *Behavior Therapy, 35,* 707–723.

Gardner, F. L., & Moore, Z. E. (2006). *Clinical sport psychology.* Champaign, IL: Human Kinetics.

Gardner, F. L., & Moore, Z. E. (2007). *The psychology of enhancing human performance: The Mindfulness-Acceptance-Commitment (MAC) approach.* New York, NY: Springer Publishing.

Garner, D. M. (1997). The 1997 body image survey results. *Psychology Today, 30,* 30–44, 75–80, 84.

Garza, D. L., & Feltz, D. L. (1998). Effects of selected mental practice on performance, self-efficacy, and competition confidence of figure skaters. *The Sport Psychologist, 12,* 1–15.

Gatewood, J. G., Litchfield, R. E., Ryan, S. J., Geadelmann, J. D. M., Pendergast, J. F., & Ullom, K. K. (2008). Perceived barriers to community-based health promotion program participation. *American Journal of Health Behavior, 32,* 260–271.

Gaudreau, P., Amiot, C. E., & Vallerand, R. J. (2009). Trajectories of affective states in adolescent hockey players: Turning point and motivational antecedents. *Developmental Psychology, 45,* 307–319. doi: 10.1037/a0014134

Gaudreau, P., & Antl, S. (2008). Athletes' broad dimensions of dispositional perfectionism: Examining changes in life satisfaction and the mediating role of sport-related motivation and coping. *Journal of Sport & Exercise Psychology, 30,* 356–382.

Gaudreau, P., & Blondin, J. P. (2002). Development of a questionnaire for the assessment of coping strategies employed by athletes in competitive sport settings. *Psychology of Sport and Exercise, 3,* 1–34.

Gaudreau, P., Nicholls, A., & Levy A. R. (2010). The ups and downs of coping and sport achievement: An episodic process analysis of within-person associations. *Journal of Sport & Exercise Psychology, 32,* 298–311.

Gaudreau, P., & Thompson, A. (2010). Testing a 2 × 2 model of dispositional perfectionism. *Personality and Individual Differences, 48,* 532–537.

Gaudreau, P., & Verner-Filion, J. (2012). Dispositional perfectionism and well-being: A test of the 2 × 2 model of perfectionism in the sport domain. *Sport, Exercise, and Performance Psychology, 1,* 29–43. doi: 10.1037/a0025747

Gay, J. L., Saunders, R. P., & Dowda, M. (2011). The relationship of physical activity and the built environment within the context of self-determination theory. *Annuals of Behavioral Medicine, 42,* 188–196. doi: 10.1007/s12160-011.9292-y

Gay, P. (1999, March 29). Sigmund Freud. *Time, 153,* 66–69.

Gayton, W. F., Matthews, G. R., & Nickless, C. J. (1987). The home field disadvantage in sports championships: Does it exist in hockey? *Journal of Sport Psychology, 9,* 183–185.

Gelantzer-Levy, R., & Cohler, B. (1993). *The essential other.* New York, NY: Basic Books.

Gender-Equity Report, 2001–2002. (2002). Retrieved from http://www.NCAA.org

George Best, a 'genius' on the soccer field dies. (2005, November 25). *The New York Times.* Retrieved from http://www.nytimes.com

George, T. R., & Feltz, D. L. (1995). Motivation in sport from a collective efficacy perspective. *International Journal of Sport Psychology, 26,* 98–116.

George, T. R., Feltz, D. L., & Chase, M. A. (1992). Effects of model similarity on self-efficacy and muscular endurance: A second look. *Journal of Sport and Exercise Psychology 14,* 237–248.

Gernigon, C., Fleurance, P., & Reine, B. (2000). Effects of uncontrollability and failure on the development of learned helplessness in perceptual-motor tasks. *Research Quarterly for Exercise and Sport, 71,* 44–54.

Gernigon, C., Thill, E., & Fleurance, P. (1999). Learned helplessness: A survey of cognitive, motivational and perceptual-motor consequences in motor tasks. *Journal of Sports Sciences, 17,* 403–412.

Gershgoren, L., Tenenbaum, G., Gershgoren, A., & Eklund, R. C. (2011). The effect of parental feedback on young athletes' perceived motivational climate, goal involvement, goal orientation, and performance. *Psychology of Sport and Exercise, 12,* 481–489. doi: 10.1016/j.psychsport.2011.05.003

Ghaye, A., & Ghaye, K. (1998). *Teaching and learning through critical reflective practice.* London, England: David Fulton.

Ghosh, P. R. (2012, August 12). David Rudisha, latest in a long line of superb Kenyan runners. *International Business Times.* Retrieved from http://ibtimes.com

Giacobbi, P. R., Foore, B., & Weinberg, R. S. (2004). Broken clubs and expletives: The sources of stress and coping responses of skilled and moderately skilled golfers. *Journal of Applied Sport Psychology, 16,* 166–182.

Giacobbi, P. R., Jr., & Weinberg, R. S. (2000). An examination of coping in sport: Individual trait anxiety differences and situational consistency. *Sport Psychologist, 14,* 42–62.

Gibson, B., Sachau, D., Doll, B., & Shumate, R. (2002). Sandbagging in competition: Responding to the pressure of being the favorite. *Personality and Social Psychology Bulletin, 28,* 1119–1130.

Gieremek, K., Osialdlo, G., Rudzinska, A., & Nowotny, J. (1994). Physiological responses to selected relaxation techniques. *Biology of Sport, 11,* 109–114.

Gilbert, J. N., Gilbert, W. D., Loney, B., Wahl, M., & Michel, E. (2006). Sport psychology in an urban high school: Overview of a two-year collaboration. *Journal of Education, 187,* 67–95.

Gilbourne, D., & Taylor, A. H. (1998). From theory to practice: The integration of goal perspective theory and life development approaches within an injury-specific goal-setting program. *Journal of Applied Sport Psychology, 10,* 124–139.

Gill, D., & Williams, L. (2008). *Psychological dynamics of sport and exercise.* Champaign, IL: Human Kinetics.

Gill, D. L. (1993). Competitiveness and competitive orientation in sport. In R. N. Singer, M. Murphey, & L. K. Tennant (Eds.), *Handbook of research on sport psychology* (pp. 314–327). New York, NY: Macmillan.

Gill, D. L. (1995). Gender issues: A social-educational perspective. In S. M. Murphey (Ed.), *Sport psychology interventions* (pp. 205–234). Champaign, IL: Human Kinetics.

Gill, D. L. (1998). Gender and competitive motivation: From recreation center to the Olympic arena. In D. Bernstein (Ed.), *Nebraska symposium on motivation* (Vol 45, pp 173–207). Lincoln, NE: University of Nebraska Press.

Gill, D. L. (2002). Gender and sport behavior. In T. S. Horn (Ed.), *Advances in sport psychology* (2nd ed., pp. 355–375). Champaign, IL: Human Kinetics.

Gill, D. L. (2007). Gender and cultural diversity. In G. Tenenbaum & R. C. Eklund (Eds.), *Handbook of sport psychology* (3rd ed., pp. 823–844). New York, NY: Wiley.

Gill, D. L., & Deeter, T. E. (1998). Development of the Sport Orientation Questionnaire. *Research Quarterly for Exercise and Sport, 59,* 191–202.

Gill, D. L., Gross, J. B., & Huddleston, S. (1983). Participation motivation in youth sports. *International Journal of Sport Psychology, 14,* 1–14.

Gill, D. L., & Kamphoff, C. S. (2009). Cultural diversity in applied sport psychology. In R. Schinke & S. J. Hanrahan (Eds.), *Cultural sport psychology* (pp. 45–56). Champaign, IL: Human Kinetics.

Gill, D. L., & Kamphoff, C. S. (2010). Gender and cultural considerations. In J. M. Williams (Ed.), *Applied sport psychology: Personal growth to peak performance* (6th ed., pp. 417–439). New York, NY: McGraw-Hill.

Gillet, N., Berjot, S., & Rosnet, E. (2009). An analysis of the impact of environmental conditions on the relationships between need satisfaction and intrinsic motivation in sport. *International Journal of Sport Psychology, 40,* 249–269.

Gillet, N., Vallerand, R. J., Amoura, S., & Baldes, B. (2010). Influence of coaches' autonomy support on athletes' motivation and sport performance: A test of the hierarchical model of intrinsic and extrinsic motivation. *Psychology of Sport and Exercise, 11,* 155–161. doi: 10.1016/j.psychsport.2009.10.004

Gilovich, T., Medvec, V. H. (1995). Some counterfactual determinants of satisfaction and regret. In N. J. Roese & J. M. Olson (Eds.), *What might have been: The social psychology of counterfactual thinking* (pp. 259- 282). Mahwah, NJ: Lawrence Erlbaum Associates.

Gimmig, D., Huguet, P., Caverni, J-P, & Cury, F. (2006). Choking under pressure and working memory capacity: When performance pressure reduces fluid intelligence. *Psychonomic Bulletin & Review, 13,* 1005–1010.

Glenn, S. D., & Horn, T. S. (1993). Psychological and personal predictors of leadership behavior in female soccer athletes. *Journal of Applied Sport Psychology, 5,* 17–34.

Goldman, T. (2011, January 11). Jack LaLanne: Founding father of fitness. Retrieved from http://www.npr.com

Gollwitzer, P. M., & Sheeran, P. (2006). Implementation intentions and goal achievement: A meta-analysis of effects and processes. *Advances in Experimental Social Psychology, 38,* 69–119.

Gonzalez, R. (2005, May 27). Not injured, but insulted. Volleyball coach describes run-in with Picard. *Hartford Courant, C1, C8.*

Gonzalez, R., & Courchesne, S. (2005, June 1). Batter up in court. Picard arraigned for assault. *Hartford Courant,* C1, C6.

Gonzalez-Cutre, D., Sicilia, A., & Aguila, C. (2011). Interplay of different contextual motivations and their implications for exercise motivation. *Journal of Sports Science and Medicine, 10,* 274–282.

Goodgame, D. (2000, August 14). The game of risk. How the best golfer in the world got even better. *Time, 156,* 56–66.

Goodger, K., Lavallee, D., Gorely, T., & Harwood, C. (2010). Burnout in sport: Understanding the process. In J. M. Williams (Ed.), *Applied sport psychology: Personal growth to peak performance* (6th ed., pp. 492–511). New York, NY: McGraw-Hill.

Goodger, K., Wolfenden, L., & Lavallee, D. (2007). Symptoms and consequences associated with three dimensions of burnout in junior tennis players. *International Journal of Sport Psychology, 38,* 342–364.

Gooding, A., & Gardner, F. L. (2009). An investigation of the relationship between mindfulness, preshot routine, and basketball free throw percentage. *Journal of Clinical Sport Psychology, 4,* 303–319.

Goodwin, R. C. (2003). Association between physical activity and mental disorders among adults in the United States. *Preventive Medicine, 36,* 698–703. doi: 10.1016/S0091-7435

Gordon, R. A. (2008). Attributional style and athletic performance: Strategic optimism and defensive pessimism. *Psychology of Sport and Exercise, 9,* 336–350. doi: 10.1016/j.psychsport.2007.04.007

Gordon, S. (1988). Decision styles and coaching effectiveness in university soccer. *Canadian Journal of Sport Sciences, 13,* 56–65.

Gorely, T., & Bruce, D. (2000). A 6-month investigation of exercise adoption from the contemplation stage of the transtheoretical model. *Psychology of Sport and Exercise, 1,* 89–101. Doi: 10.1016/S1469–0292(00)00012–1

Gotwals, J. K., & Dunn, J.G.H. (2009). A multi-method multi-analytic approach to establishing construct validity evidence: The Sport Multidimensional Perfectionism Scale 2. *Measurement in Physical Education and Exercise Science, 13,* 71–92.

Gotwals, J. K., Dunn, J.G.H., Dunn, J. C., Gamache, V. (2010). Establishing validity evidence for the Sport Multidimensional Perfectionism Scale-2 in intercollegiate sport. *Psychology of Sport and Exercise, 11,* 423–432. doi: 10.1016/j.psychsport.2010.04.013

Gotwals, J. K., Dunn, J.G.H., & Wayment, H. A. (2003). An examination of perfectionism and self-esteem in intercollegiate athletes. *Journal of Sport Behavior, 26,* 17–38.

Gould, D. (1999). Lessons from Nagano. *Olympic Coach, 9*(3), 2–5.

Gould, D. (2010). Goal setting for peak performance. In J. M. Williams (Ed.), *Applied sport psychology: Personal growth to peak performance* (6th ed., pp. 201–220), New York, NY: McGraw-Hill.

Gould, D, & Damarjian, N. (1996). Imagery training for peak performance. In J. L. Van Raalte & B. W. Brewer (Eds.), *Exploring sport and exercise psychology* (pp. 25–50). Washington, DC: American Psychological Association.

Gould, D., Dieffenbach, K., & Moffett, A. (2002). Psychological characteristics and their development in Olympic champions. *Journal of Applied Sport Psychology, 14,* 172–204.

Gould, D., Eklund, R. C., & Jackson, S. A. (1992a). 1988 U.S. Olympic wrestling excellence: I. Mental preparation, competitive cognition, and affect. *The Sport Psychologist, 6,* 358–382.

Gould, D., Eklund, R. C., & Jackson, S. A. (1992b). 1988 U.S. Olympic wrestling excellence: II. Thoughts and affect occurring during competition. *The Sport Psychologist, 6,* 383–402.

Gould, D., Eklund, R. C., & Jackson, S. A. (1993). Coping strategies used by U.S. Olympic wrestlers. *Research Quarterly for Exercise and Sport, 64,* 83–93.

Gould, D., Eklund, R. C., Petlichkoff, L., Peterson, K., & Bump, L. (1991). Psychological predictors of state anxiety and performance in age-group wrestlers. *Pediatric Exercise Science, 3,* 198–206.

Gould, D., Feltz, D., & Weiss, M. R. (1985). Motives for participating in competitive youth swimming. *International Journal of Sport Psychology, 6,* 126–140.

Gould, D., Finch, L. M., & Jackson, S. A. (1993). Coping strategies used national champion figure skaters. *Research Quarterly for Exercise and Sport, 64,* 453–468.

Gould, D., Flett, M. R., & Bean, E. (2009). Management of competitive stress in elite sport. In B. W. Brewer (Ed.), *Handbook of sports medicine and science, sport psychology* (pp. 53–63). Chichester, England: Wiley-Blackwell.

Gould, D., Flett, R., & Lauer, L. (2012). The relationship between psychosocial developmental and the sports climate experienced by underserved youth. *Psychology of Sport and Exercise, 13,* 80–87. doi: 10.1016/j.psychsport.2001.07.005

Gould, D., Greenleaf, C., Guinan, D., & Chung, Y. C. (2002). A survey of U.S. Olympic coaches: Variables perceived to have influenced athlete performances and coach effectiveness. *The Sport Psychologist, 16,* 229–250.

Gould, D., Hodge, K., Peterson, K., & Giannini, J. (1989). An exploratory examination of strategies used by elite coaches to enhance self-efficacy in athletes. *Journal of Sport & Exercise Psychology, 11,* 128–140.

Gould, D., Horn, T., & Spreemann, J. (1983). Sources of stress in junior elite wrestlers. *Journal of Sport Psychology, 5,* 159–171.

Gould, D., Lauer, L., Jannes, C., & Pennisi, N. (2006). Understanding the role parents play in tennis success: A national study of junior tennis players. *British Journal of Sports Medicine, 40,* 632–636. doi: 10.1136/bjsm.2005.024927

Gould, D., Lauer, L., Rolo, C., Jannes, C., & Pennisi, N. (2008). The role of parents in tennis success: Focus group interviews with junior coaches. *The Sport Psychologist, 22,* 18–37.

Gould D., & Maynard, I. (2009). Psychological preparation for the Olympic Games. *Journal of Sports Sciences, 27,* 1393–1408. doi:10.1080/02640410903081845

Gould, D., & Petlichkoff, L. (1988). Participation motivation and attrition in young athletes. In F. Smoll, R. Magill, & M. Ash (Eds.), *Children in sport* (3rd ed., pp. 161–178). Champaign, IL: Human Kinetics.

Gould, D., Petlichkoff, L., Simons, J., & Vevera, M. (1987). Relationship between Competitive State Anxiety Inventory-2 subscale scores and pistol shooting performance. *Journal of Sport Psychology, 6,* 289–304.

Gould, D., & Pick, S. (1995). Sport psychology: The Griffith Era, 1920–1940. *The Sport Psychologist, 9,* 391–405.

Gould, D., Tammen, V., Murphy, S., & May, J. (1989). An examination of U.S. Olympic sport psychology consultants and the services they provide. *The Sport Psychologist, 3,* 300–312.

Gould, D., Tuffey, S., Udry, E., & Loehr, J. (1996). Burnout in competitive junior tennis players: II. Qualitative analysis. *The Sport Psychologist, 10,* 341–366.

Gould, D., Tuffey, S., Udry, E., & Loehr, J. (1997). Burnout in competitive junior tennis players: III. Individual differences in the burnout experience. *The Sport Psychologist, 11,* 257–276.

Gould, D., & Udry, E. (1994). Psychological skills for enhancing performance: arousal regulation strategies. *Medicine and Science in Sports and Exercise, 26,* 478–485.

Gould, D., Udry, E., Bridges, D., & Beck, L. (1997). Coping with season-ending injuries. *The Sport Psychologist, 11,* 379–399.

Gould, D., Udry, E., Tuffey, S., & Loehr, J. (1996). Burnout in competitive junior tennis players: I. A quantitative psychological assessment. *The Sport Psychologist, 10,* 322–340.

Gow, A. J., Bastin, M. E., Maniega, S. M., Hernandez, M. C. V., Morris, Z., Murray, C., . . . Wardlaw, J. M. (2012). Neuroprotective lifestyles and the aging brain. Activity, atrophy, and white matter integrity. *Neurology, 79,* 1802–1808. doi: 10.1212/WNL.0b013e3182703fd2

Graham, S., & Weiner, B. (1996). Theories and principles of motivation. In D. C. Berliner & R. C. Calfee (Eds.), *Handbook of educational psychology* (pp. 63–84). New York, NY: Macmillan.

Graham, T. R., Kowalski, K. C., & Crocker, P. R. E. (2002). The contributions of goal characteristics and causal attributions to emotional experience in youth sport participants. *Psychology of Sport and Exercise, 3,* 273–291.

Granito, Jr., V. J. (2002). Psychological response to athletic injury: Gender differences. *Journal of Sport Behavior, 25,* 243–260.

Granito, V. J., & Rainey, D. W. (1988). Differences in cohesion between high school and college football teams and starters and nonstarters. *Perceptual and Motor Skills, 66,* 471–477.

Grant, B. F., DeBakey, S., & Zobeck, T. S. (1991). *Liver cirrhosis mortality in the United States, 1973–1988* (Surveillance Report No. 18). Rockville, MD: National Institute on Alcohol Abuse & Alcoholism.

Gray, J. (1992). *Men are from Mars, women are from Venus: A practical guide for improving communication and getting what you want in your relationships.* New York, NY: Harper Collins.

Gray, R. (2004). Attending to the execution of a complex sensorimotor skill: Differences, choking, and slumps. *Journal of Experimental Psychology: Applied, 10,* 42–54.

Gray, S. (1990). Effect of visuo-motor rehearsal with videotaped modeling on racquet ball performance of beginning players. *Perceptual and Motor Skills, 70,* 379–385.

Gray, S. W., & Fernandez, S. J. (1989). Effects of Visuo-Motor Behavior Rehearsal with videotaped modeling on basketball shooting performance. *Psychology: A Journal of Human Behavior. 26,* 41–46.

Graydon, J., & Murphy, T. (1995). The effect of personality on social facilitation whilst performing a sports related task. *Personality and Individual Differences, 19,* 265–267.

Graziano, W. G., Feldesman, A. B., & Rahe, D. F. (1985). Extraversion, social cognition, and the salience of aversiveness in social encounters. *Journal of Personality and Social Psychology, 49,* 971–980.

Graziano, W. G., Hair, E. C., & Finch, J. F. (1997). Competitiveness mediates the link between personality and group performance. *Journal of Personality and Social Psychology, 73,* 1394–1408.

Green, C. D. (2003). Psychology strikes out: Coleman R. Griffith and the Chicago Cubs. *History of Psychology, 6,* 267–283. doi: 10.1037/1093-4510.6.3.267

Green, C. D. (2006). Coleman Roberts Griffith: "Adopted" father of sport psychology. In D. A. Dewsbury, L. T. Benjamin Jr., & M. Wertheimer (Eds.), *Portraits of pioneers in psychology* (Vol. 6, pp. 151–166). Mahwah, NJ: Lawrence Erlbaum.

Green, S. L., & Weinberg, R. S. (2001). Relationships among athletic identity, coping skills, social support, and the psychological impact of injury in recreational participants. *Journal of Applied Sport Psychology, 13*, 40–59.

Greenberg, A. (2001, June 18). Into the real world. Former Giant helps players make transition. *The Hartford Courant,* C9.

Greenleaf, C., Petrie, T. A., Carter, J., & Reel, J. J. (2009). Female collegiate athletes: Prevalence of eating disorders and disordered eating behaviors. *Journal of American College Health, 57*, 489–495.

Greenlees, I., Buscombe, R., Thelwell, R., Holder, T., & Rimmer, M. (2005). Impact of opponents' clothing and body language on impression formation and outcome expectations. *Journal of Sport & Exercise Psychology 27*, 39–52.

Greenlees, I., Jones, S., Holder, T., & Thelwell, R. (2006). The effects of self-handicapping on attributions and perceived judo competence. *Journal of Sports Sciences, 24*, 273–280.

Greenlees, I., Leyland, A., Thelwell, R., & Filby, W. (2008). Soccer penalty takers' uniform color and pre-penalty kick gaze affect the impressions formed of them by opposing goalkeepers. *Journal of Sports Sciences, 26*, 569–576. doi: 10.1080/02640410701744446

Greenlees, I., Thelwell, R., & Holder, T. (2006). Examining the efficacy of the concentration grid exercise as a concentration enhancement exercise. *Psychology of Sport and Exercise, 7*, 29–39.

Greenlees, I., Thelwell, R., & Holder, T. (2006). Examining the efficacy of the concentration grid exercise as a concentration enhancement exercise. *Psychology of Sport and Exercise, 7*, 29–39. doi: 10.1016/j.psychsport.2005.02.001

Greenspan, M. J., & Feltz, D. L. (1989). Psychological interventions with athletes in competitive situations: A review. *The Sport Psychologist, 3*, 219–236.

Gregg, M., & Hall, C. (2006). The relationship of skill level and age to the use of imagery of golfers. *Journal of Applied Sport Psychology, 18*, 363–375.

Gregg, M., Hall, C., McGowan, E., & Hall, N. (2011). The relationship between imagery ability and imagery use among athletes. *Journal of Applied Sport Psychology, 23*, 129–141. doi: 10.1080/10413200.10413200.2010.544279

Griffin, J., & Harris, M. B. (1996). Coaches' attitudes, knowledge, experiences, and recommendations regarding weight control. *The Sport Psychologist, 10*, 180–194.

Griffith, C. R. (1939). *General report: Experimental laboratories. Chicago National League Ball Club. Jan 1, 1938-Jan 1, 1939.* Unpublished manuscript, Coleman Griffith Papers, Box 13, Archives of the University of Illinois at Urbana-Champaign.

Grolnick, W. S. (2003). *The psychology of parental control.* Mahwah, NJ: LEA.

Groslambert, A., Candau, R., Grappe, F., Dogue, B., & Rouillon, J. D. (2003). Effects of autogenic and imagery training on the shooting performance in biathlon. *Research Quarterly for Exercise and Sport, 74*, 337–341.

Grossbard, J. R., Cumming, S. P., Standage, M., Smith, R. F., & Smoll, F. L. (2007). Social desirability and relations between goal orientations and competitive trait anxiety in young athletes. *Psychology of Sport and Exercise, 8*, 491–505.

Grossbard, J., Geisner, I. M., Neighbors, C., Kilmer, J. R., & Larimer, M. E. (2007). Are drinking games sports? College athlete participation in drinking games and alcohol-related problems. *Journal of Studies on Alcohol and Drugs, 68*, 97–105.

Grossbard, J., Hummer, J., LaBrie, J., Pederson, E., & Neighbors, C. (2009). Is substance use a team sport? Attraction to team, perceived norms, and alcohol and marijuana use among male and female intercollegiate athletes. *Journal of Applied Sport Psychology, 21*, 247–261.

Grossbard, J. R., Smith, R. E., Smoll, F. L., & Cumming, S. P. (2009). Competitive anxiety in young athletes: Differentiating somatic anxiety, worry, and concentration disruption. *Anxiety, Stress, & Coping, 22*, 153–166. doi: 10.1080/10615800802020643

Grove, J. R., & Heard, N. P. (1997). Optimism and sport confidence as correlates of slump-related coping among athletes. *The Sport Psychologist, 11*, 400–410.

Grove, J. R., Lavallee, D., Gordon, S., & Harvey, J. H. (1998). Account-making: A model of understanding and resolving distressful reactions to retirement from sport. *The Sport Psychologist, 12*, 52–67.

Gucciardi, D. F., & Dimmock, J. A. (2008). Choking under pressure in sensorimotor skills: Conscious processing or depleted attentional resources? *Psychology of Sport & Exercise, 9*, 45–59. doi: 10.1016/j.psychsport.2006.10.007

Gucciardi, D. F., Gordon, S., & Dimmock, J. A. (2008). Towards an understanding of mental toughness in Australian football. *Journal of Applied Sport Psychology, 20*, 261–281.

Gucciardi, D. F., Gordon, S., & Dimmock, J. A. (2009a). Evaluation of a mental tough-ness training program for youth-aged Australian footballers: A quantitative analysis. *Journal of Applied Sport Psychology, 21*, 307–327.

Gucciardi, D. F., Gordon, S., & Dimmock, J. A. (2009b). Evaluation of a mental tough-ness training program for youth-aged Australian footballers: A qualitative analysis. *Journal of Applied Sport Psychology, 21*, 324–339.

Gucciardi, D. F., & Jones, M. I. (2012). Beyond optimal performance: Mental tough-ness profiles and developmental success in adolescent cricketers. *Journal of Sport & Exercise Psychology, 34*, 16–36.

Gucciardi, D. F., Longbottom, J-L., Jackson, B., & Dimmock, J. A. (2010). Experienced golfers' perspectives on choking under pressure. *Journal of Sport & Exercise Psychology, 32*, 61–83.

Gucciardi, D. F., Mahoney, J., Jalleh, G., Donovan, R. J., & Parkes, J. (2012). Perfectionistic profiles among elite athletes and differences in their motivational orientations. *Journal of Sport & Exercise Psychology, 34*, 159–183.

Guevremont, A., Findlay, L., & Kohen, D. (2008). Organized extracurricular activities of Canadian children and youth. *Health Reports, 19*, Statistics Canada, Catalogue no. 82–003-XPE.

Guillot, A., & Collet, C. (2008). Construction of the motor imagery integrative model in sport: A review and theoretical investigation of motor imagery use. *International Review of Sport and Exercise Psychology, 1*, 31–44.

Gully, S. M., Incalcaterra, K. A., Joshi, A., & Beaubien, (2002). A meta-analysis of team-efficacy, potency, and performance: Interdependence and level of analysis as mod-erators of observed relationships. *Journal of Applied Psychology, 87*, 819–832.

Gustafsson, H., Hassmen, P., Kentta, G., & Johansson, M. (2008). A qualitative analysis of burnout in elite Swedish athletes. *Psychology of Sport & Exercise, 9*, 800–816. doi: 10.1016/j.psychsport.2007.11.004

Gutgesell, M., & Canterbury, R. (1999). Alcohol usage in sport and exercise. *Addiction Biology, 4*, 373–383.

Haase, A. M., & Prapavessis, H. (2004). Assessing the factor structure and composition of the Positive and Negative Perfectionism Scale in sport. *Personality and Individual Differences, 36*, 1725–1740.

Haase, A. M., Prapavessis, H., & Owens, R. G. (2002). Perfectionism, social physique anxiety and disordered eating: a comparison of male and female elite athletes. *Psychology of Sport and Exercise, 3*, 209–222.

Haberl, P., & Zaichkowsky, L. (2003). The U.S. Women's Olympic gold medal ice hockey team: Optimal use of sport psychology for developing confidence. In R. Lidor & K. P. Henschen (Eds.), *The psychology of team sports* (pp. 217–233). Morgantown, WV: Fitness Information Technology.

Hadala, M., Cebolla, A., Banos, R., & Barrios, C. (2010). Mood profile of an America's Cup team: Relationship with muscle damage and injuries. *Medicine & Science in Sports & Exercise, 42*, 1403–1408. doi: 10.1249/MSS.0b013e318cd5cb9

Hagan, A. L., & Hausenblas, H. A. (2003). The relationship between exercise depend-ence symptoms and perfectionism. *American Journal of Health Studies, 18*(2/3), 133–137.

Hagger, M. S. (2012). Advances in motivation in exercise and physical activity. In E. O. Acevedo (Ed.), *The Oxford handbook of exercise psychology* (pp. 479–504). New York, NY: Oxford University Press.

Hagger, M. S., & Chatzisarantis, N. L. D. (2005). First- and higher-order models of attitudes, normative influence, and perceived behavioural control in the theory of planned behaviour. *British Journal of Social Psychology, 44*, 513–535. doi: 10.1348/014466604X16219

Hagger, M. S., & Chatzisarantis, N. L. D., & Biddle, S. J. H. (2002). A meta-analytic review of the theories of reasoned action and planned behavior in physical activity: Predictive validity and the contribution of additional variables. *Journal of Sport & Exercise Psychology, 24*, 3–32.

Hale, B. D. (1993). Explanatory style as a predictor of academic and athletic achieve-ment in college athletes. *Journal of Sport Behavior, 16*, 63–75.

Hale, B. D., & Whitehouse, A. (1998). The effects of imagery-manipulated appraisal on intensity and direction of competitive anxiety. *The Sport Psychologist, 12*, 40–51.

Hall, A. E., & Hardy, C. J. (1991). Ready, aim, fire. . . relaxation strategies for enhancing pistol marksmanship. *Perceptual and Motor Skills, 72*, 775–786.

Hall, C., Stevens, D., & Pavio, A. (2005). *The sport imagery questionnaire: Test manual.* West Virginia: Fitness Information Technology.

Hall, C. R. (1985). Individual differences in the mental practice and imagery of motor skill performance. *Canadian Journal of Applied Sport Sciences, 10*, 17S-21S.

Hall, C. R. (2001). Imagery in sport and exercise. In R. N. Singer, H. A. Hausenblas, & C. M. Janelle (Eds.), *Handbook of sport psychology* (2nd ed., pp. 529–549). New York, NY: Wiley.

Hall, C. R., Munroe-Chandler, K. J., Cumming, J., Law, B., Ramsey, R., & Murphy, L. (2009). Imagery and observational learning use and their relationship to sport confidence. *Journal of Sports Sciences, 27,* 327–337. doi: 10.1080/02640410802549769

Hall, C. R., Munroe-Chandler, K. J., Fishburne, G. J., & Hall, N. D. (2009). The Sport Imagery Questionnaire for Children (SIQ-C). *Measurement in Physical Education and Exercise Science, 13,* 93–107. doi: 10.1080/10913670902812713

Hall, E. G., & Erffmeyer, E. S. (1983). The effect of Visuo-Motor Behavior Rehearsal with videotaped modeling on free throw accuracy of intercollegiate female basketball players. *Journal of Sport Psychology, 5,* 343–346.

Hall, H. K., Hill, A. P., Appleton, P. R., & Kozub, S. A. (2009). The mediating influence of unconditional self-acceptance and labile self-esteem on the relationship between multidimensional perfectionism and exercise dependence. *Psychology of Sport & Exercise, 10,* 35–44. doi: 10.1016/j.psychsport.2008.05.003

Hall, H. K., & Kerr, A. W. (1997). Motivational antecedents of precompetitive anxiety in youth sport. *The Sport Psychologist, 11,* 24–42.

Hall, H. K., Kerr, A. W., Kozub, S. A., & Finnie, S. B. (2007). Motivational antecedents of obligatory exercise: The influence of achievement goals and multidimensional perfectionism. *Psychology of Sport and Exercise, 8,* 297–316. doi: 10.1016/j.psychsport.2006.04.007

Hall, H. K., Kerr, A. W., & Matthews, J. (1998). Precompetitive anxiety in sport: The contribution of achievement goals and perfectionism. *Journal of Sport and Exercise Psychology, 20,* 194–217.

Hallagan, J. B., Hallagan, L. F., & Snyder, M. B. (1989). Anabolic-androgenic steroid use by athletes. *The New England Journal of Medicine, 321,* 1042–1045l.

Halliwell, W. (1990). Providing sport psychology consulting services in professional hockey. *The Sport Psychologist, 4,* 369–377.

Halvari, H., & Kjormo, O. (1999). A structural model of achievement motives, performance approach and avoidance goals and performance among Norwegian Olympic athletes. *Perceptual and Motor Skills, 89,* 997–1022.

Hamachek, D. E. (1978). Psychodynamics of normal and neurotic perfectionism. *Psychology, 15,* 27–33.

Hamann, D. L. (1985). The other side of stage fright. *Music Educators Journal, 71,* 26–27.

Hanegby, R., & Tenenbaum, G. (2001). Blame it on the racket: norm-breaking behaviours among junior tennis players. *Psychology of Sport and Exercise, 2,* 117–134.

Haney, C. J., & Long, B. C. (1995). Coping effectiveness: A path analysis of self-efficacy, control, coping, and performance in sport competitions. *Journal of Applied Social Psychology, 25,* 1726–1746.

Haney, M., Ward, A. S., Comer, S. D., Foltin, R. W., Fischman, M. W. (1999). Abstinence symptoms following smoked marijuana in humans. *Psychopharmacology, 141,* 395–404.

Hanin, Y. L. (1980). A study of anxiety in sports. In W. F. Straub (Ed.), *Sport psychology: An analysis of athlete behavior* (pp. 236–249). Ithaca, NY: Mouvement.

Hanin, Y. L. (1986). State-trait research in sports in the USSR. In C. D. Spielberger & R. Diaz-Guerrero (Eds.), *Cross-cultural anxiety* (Vol. 3, pp. 45–64). Washington, DC: Hemisphere.

Hanin, Y. L. (2000a). *Emotions in sport.* Champaign, IL: Human Kinetics.

Hanin, Y. L. (2000b) Individual zones of optimal functioning (IZOF) model: Emotions-performance relationships in sport. In Y. L. Hanin (Ed.), *Emotions in sport* (pp. 65–89). Champaign, IL: Human Kinetics.

Hanin, Y. L. (2000c). Successful and poor performance and emotions. In Y. L. Hanin (Ed.), *Emotions in sport* (pp. 157–187). Champaign, IL: Human Kinetics.

Hanin, Y. L. (2004). Emotion in sports. In C. D. Spielberger (Ed.). *Encyclopedia of applied psychology* (Vol. 1, pp. 739–750). Oxford, England: Elsevier Academic Press.

Hanin, Y. L. (2007). Emotions in sport: Current issues and perspectives. In G. Tenenbaum & R. C. Eklund (Eds.), *Handbook of sport psychology* (3rd ed., pp. 31–58), New York, NY: Wiley.

Hanin, Y. L., & Stambulova, N. B. (2002). Metaphoric description of performance states: An application of the IZOF model. *The Sport Psychologist, 16,* 396–415.

Hanin, Y., & Syrja, P. (1995). Performance affect in junior ice hockey players: An application of the individual zones of optimal functioning model. *The Sport Psychologist, 9,* 169–187.

Hanin, Y., & Syrja, P. (1996). Predicted, actual, and recalled affect in Olympic-level soccer players: Idiographic assessments on individualized scales. *Journal of Sport & Exercise Psychology, 18,* 325–335.

Hanlon, T. (1994). *Sport Parent.* Champaign, IL: Human Kinetics.

Hanton, S., & Connaughton, D. (2002). Perceived control of anxiety and its relationship to self-confidence and performance: A qualitative inquiry. *Research Quarterly for Exercise and Sport, 73,* 87–97.

Hanton, S., Cropley, B., & Lee, S. (2009). Reflective practice, experience, and the interpretation of anxiety symptoms. *Journal of Sports Sciences, 27*, 517–533. doi: 10.1080/02640410802668668

Hanton, S., & Jones, G. (1999a). The acquisition and development of cognitive skills and strategies: I. Making the butterflies fly in formation. *The Sport Psychologist, 13*, 1–21.

Hanton, S., & Jones, G. (1999b). The effects of a multimodal intervention program on performers: II. Training the butterflies to fly in formation. *The Sport Psychologist, 13*, 22–41.

Hanton, S., Jones, G., & Mullen, R. (2000). Intensity and direction of competitive state anxiety as interpreted by rugby players and rifle shooters. *Perceptual and Motor Skills, 90*, 513–521.

Hanton, S., Mellalieu, S. D., & Hall, R. (2002). Re-examining the competitive anxiety trait-state relationship. *Personality and Individual Differences, 33*, 1125–1136.

Hanton, S., Mellalieu, S. D., & Hall, R. (2004). Self-confidence and anxiety interpretation: A qualitative investigation. *Psychology of Sport and Exercise, 5*, 477–495.

Hanton, S., Neil, R., & Mellalieu, S. D. (2008). Recent developments in competitive anxiety direction and competition stress research. *International Review of Sport and Exercise Psychology, 1*, 45–57. doi: 10.1080/17509840701827445

Hanton, S., Thomas, O., & Maynard, I. W. (2004). Competitive anxiety response in the week leading up to competition: The role of intensity, direction and frequency dimensions. *Psychology of Sport and Exercise, 5*, 169–181.

Hanton, S., Thomas, O., & Mellalieu, S. D. (2009). Management of competitive stress in elite sport. In B. W. Brewer (Ed.), *Handbook of sports medicine and science, sport psychology* (pp. 30–42). Chichester, England: Wiley-Blackwell.

Hardy, J. (2006). Speaking clearly: A critical review of the self-talk literature. *Psychology of Sport and Exercise, 7*, 81–97. doi: 10.1016/j.psychsport.2005.04.002

Hardy, J., Eys, M. A., & Loughead, T. M. (2008). Does communication mediate the athlete leadership to cohesion relationship?. *International Journal of Sport Psychology, 39*, 329–345.

Hardy, J., Gammage, K., & Hall, C. (2001). A descriptive study of athlete self-talk. *The Sport Psychologist, 15*, 306–318.

Hardy, J., Roberts, R., & Hardy, L. (2009). Awareness and motivation to change negative self-talk. *The Sport Psychologist, 23*, 435–450.

Hardy, L. (1990). A catastrophe model of anxiety and performance. In J. G. Jones & L. Hardy (Eds.), *Stress and performance in sport* (pp. 81–106). Chichester, England: Wiley.

Hardy, L. (1996). Testing the predictions of the cusp catastrophe model of anxiety and performance. *The Sport Psychologist, 10*, 140–156.

Hardy, L. (1997). The Coleman Roberts Griffith Address: Three myths about applied consultancy work. *Journal of Applied Sport Psychology, 9*, 277–294.

Hardy, L., Beattie, S., & Woodman, T. (2007). Anxiety-induced performance catastrophes: Investigating effort required as an asymmetry factor. *British Journal of Psychology, 98*, 15–31. doi: 10.1348/00712606X103428

Hardy, L., & Callow, N. (1999). Efficacy of external and internal visual imagery perspectives for the enhancement of performance on tasks in which form is important. *Journal of Sport & Exercise Psychology, 21*, 95–112.

Hardy, L., & Hutchinson, A. (2007). Effects of performance anxiety on effort and performance in rock climbing: A test of processing efficiency theory. *Anxiety, Stress, and Coping, 20*, 147–161.

Hardy, L., Jones, G., & Gould, D. (1996). *Understanding psychological preparation for sport.* Chichester, England: Wiley.

Hardy, L., Mullen, R., & Martin, N. (2001). Effect of task-relevant cues and state anxiety on motor performance. *Perceptual and Motor Skills, 92*, 943–946.

Hardy, L., Roberts, R., Thomas, P. R., & Murphy, S. M. (2010). Test of performance strategies: Instrument refinement using confirmatory factor analysis. *Psychology of Sport and Exercise, 11*, 27–35.

Harris, D. V., & Harris, B. L. (1984) *The athlete's guide to sport psychology: Mental skills for physical people.* New York, NY: Leisure Press.

Hars, M., & Calmels, C. (2007). Observation of elite gymnastic performance: Processes and perceived functions of observation. *Psychology of Sport and Exercise, 8*, 337–354. doi: 10.1016/j.psychsport.2006.06.004

Hart, C., Ksir, C., & Ray, O. (2012). *Drugs, society, and human behavior* (14th ed.). Boston, MA: McGraw-Hill.

Hart, C. L., van Gorp, W., Haney, M., Foltin, R. W., Fischman, M. W. (2001). Effects of acute smoked marijuana on complex cognitive performance. *Neuropsychopharmacology, 25*, 757–765.

Hartwig, T. B., Naughton, G., Sear, J. (2011). Motion analyses of adolescent rugby union players: A comparison of training and game demands. *Journal of Strength and Conditioning Research, 25,* 966–972.

Harwitt, S. (1992, January 22). Capriati is feeling the strain. *The New York Times, 141,* B7, B11.

Harwood, C. (2002). Assessing achievement goals in sport: Caveats for consultants and a case for contextualization. *Journal of Applied Sport Psychology, 14,* 106–119.

Harwood, C. (2008). Developmental consulting in a professional football academy: The 5Cs Coaching Efficacy Program. *The Sport Psychologist, 22,* 109–133.

Harwood, C., Cumming, J., Fletcher, D. (2004). Motivational profiles and psychological skills use within elite youth sport. *Journal of Applied Sport Psychology, 16,* 317–332.

Harwood, C. G., Cumming, J., & Hall, C. (2003). Imagery use in elite youth sport participants: Reinforcing the applied significance of achievement goal theory. *Research Quarterly for Exercise and Sport, 3,* 292–300.

Harwood, C., Hardy, L, & Swain, A. (2000). Achievement goals in sport: A critique of conceptual and measurement issues. *Journal of Sport & Exercise Psychology 22,* 235–255.

Harwood, C., & Knight, C. (2009). Stress in youth sport: A developmental investigation of tennis parents. *Journal of Sport and Exercise, 10,* 447–456. doi: 10.1016/j.psychsport.2009.01.005

Harwood, C., & Swain, A. (2002). The development and activation of achievement goals within tennis: II. A player, parent, and coach intervention. *The Sport Psychologist, 16,* 111–137.

Hasbrook, C. A., Hart, B. A., Mathes, S. A., & True, S. (1990). Sex bias and the validity of believed differences between male and female interscholastic athletic coaches. *Research Quarterly for Exercise and Sport, 61,* 259–267.

Hatfield, B. D., Landers, D. L., & Ray, W. J. (1984). Cognitive processes during self-paced motor performance: An electroencephalographic profile of skilled marksmen. *Journal of Sport Psychology, 6,* 42–59.

Hatzigeorgiadis, A., & Biddle, S. (1999). The effects of goal orientation and perceived competence on cognitive interference during tennis and snooker performance. *Journal of Sport Behavior, 22,* 479–401.

Hatzigeorgiadis, A., & Biddle, S. J. H. (2008). Negative self-talk during sport performance: Relationships with pre-competitive anxiety and goal-performance discrepancies. *Journal of Sport Behavior, 31,* 237–253.

Hatzigeorgiadis, A., Theodorakis, Y., & Zourbanos, N. (2004). Self-talk in the swimming pool: The effects of self-talk on thought content and performance on water-polo tasks. *Journal of Applied Sport Psychology, 16,* 138–150. doi: 10.1080/10413200490437886

Hatzigeorgiadis, A., Zourbanos, N., Galanis, E., & Theodorakis, Y. (2012). Self-talk and sports performance: A meta-analysis. *Perspectives on Psychological Science, 6,* 348–356. doi: 10.1177/1745691611413136

Hatzigeorgiadis, A., Zourbanos, N., Goltsios, C., & Theodorakis, Y. (2008). Investigating the functions of self-talk: The effects of motivational self-talk on self-efficacy and performance in young tennis players. *The Sport Psychologist, 22,* 458–471.

Hatzigeorgiadis, A., Zourbanos, N., Mpoumpaki, S., & Theodorakis, Y. (2009). Mechanisms underlying the self-talk-performance relationship: The effects of motivational self-talk on self-confidence and anxiety. *Psychology of Sport and Exercise, 10,* 186–192.

Hatzigeorgiadis, A., Zourbanos, N., & Theodorakis, Y. (2009). The moderating effects of self-talk content on self-talk functions. *Journal of Applied Sport Psychology, 19,* 240–251.

Hausenblas, H. A., & Carron, A. V. (1996). Group cohesion and self-handicapping in female and male athletes. *Journal of Sport and Exercise Psychology, 18,* 132–143.

Hausenblas, H. A., & Giacobbi, P. R. Jr. (2004). Relationship between exercise dependence symptoms and personality. *Personality & Individual Differences, 36,* 1265–1273. doi: 10.1016/S0191–8869(03)00214-9

Hausenblas, H. A., Nigg, C. R., Dannecker, E. A., Downs, D. S., Gardner, R. E., Fallow, E. A., ... & Loving, M. G. (2001). A missing piece of the transtheoretical model applied to exercise: Development and validation of the temptation to not exercise scale. *Psychology and Health, 16,* 381–390. doi: 10.1080/088704401084055514

Hausenblas, H. A., & Symons Downs, D. (2002). How much is too much? The development and validation of the Exercise Dependence Scale. *Psychology and Health, 17,* 387–404.

Hayashi, C. T. (1996). Achievement motivation among Anglo-American and Hawaiian male physical activities participants: Individual differences and social contextual factors. *Journal of Sport & Exercise Psychology, 18,* 194–215.

Hayes, S. C., Strosahl, K., & Wilson, K. G. (1999). *Acceptance and commitment therapy.* New York, NY: Guilford Press.

Hays, K., Thomas, O., Maynard, I., & Bawden, M. (2009). The role of confidence in world-class performance. *Journal of Sports Sciences, 27,* 1185–1199. doi: 10.1080/02640410903089798

Hays, K., Maynard, I., Thomas, O., & Bawden, M. (2007). Sources and types of confidence identified by world class sport performers. *Journal of Applied Sport Psychology, 19,* 434–457.

Hayslip, B. Jr., Petrie, T. A., MacIntire, M. M., & Jones, G. M. (2010). The influences of skill level, anxiety, and psychological skills use on amateur golfers' performances. *Journal of Applied Sport Psychology, 22,* 123–133.

Heath, C., Larrick, R. P., & Wu, G. (1999). Goals as reference points. *Cognitive Psychology, 38,* 79–109.

Heath, T. (2004, July 17). Post-game planning. *Hartford Courant, E1, E8.*

Heaton, A. W., & Sigall, H. (1991). Self-consciousness, self-presentation, and performance under pressure: Who chokes, and when? *Journal of Applied Social Psychology, 21,* 175–188.

Heide, F. J., & Borkovec, T. D. (1983). Relaxation-induced anxiety: Paradoxical anxiety enhancement due to relaxation training. *Journal of Consulting and Clinical Psychology, 51,* 171–182.

Heide, F. J., & Borkovec, T. D. (1984). Relaxation-induced anxiety: Mechanisms and theoretical implications. *Behavioral Research and Therapy, 22,* 1–12.

Heider, F. (1958). *The psychology of interpersonal relations.* New York, NY: Wiley.

Heil, J. (2000). The injured athlete. In Y. L. Hannin (Ed.), *Emotions in sport* (pp. 245–265). Champaign, IL: Human Kinetics.

Heiman, G. W. (2003). *Applied statistics for the behavioral sciences, 5th ed.* Boston, MA: Houghton-Mifflin.

Hellstrom, J. (2009). Psychological hallmarks of skilled golfers. *Sports Medicine, 39,* 845–855.

Helmreich, R. L., & Spence, J. T. (1977). Sex roles and achievement. In R. W. Christiana & D. M. Landers (Eds.), *Psychology of motor behavior and sport-1976* (Vol. 2, pp. 33–46). Champaign, IL: Human Kinetics.

Helms, J. E., Jernigan, M., & Maschler, J. (2005). The meaning of race in psychology and how to change it: A methodological perspective. *American Psychologist, 60,* 16–26.

Helsen, W. F., Starkes, J. L., & Hodges, N. J. (1998). Team sports and the theory of deliberate practice. *Journal of Sport & Exercise Psychology, 20.* 12–34.

Helton, W. S., Dember, W. N., Warm, J. S., & Matthews, G. (1999). Optimism, pessimism, and false failure feedback: Effects on vigilance performance. *Current Psychology: Developmental, Learning, Personality, Social, 18,* 311–325.

Hendrix, A. E., Acevedo, E. O., & Hebert, E. (2000). An examination of stress and burnout in certified athletic trainers at division 1-a universities. *Journal of Athletic Training, 35,* 139–144.

Henschen, K. P. (1998). Athletic staleness and burnout: Diagnosis, prevention, and treatment. In J. M. Williams (Ed.), *Applied sport psychology: Personal growth to peak performance* (3rd ed., pp. 398–408). Mountain View, CA: Mayfield.

Hermann, E. (1921). The psychophysical significance of physical education. *American Physical Education Review, 26,* 282–289.

Hersh, P. (2000, July 10). Just call him Slam-pras. *Hartford Courant, C1, C2.*

Heuschkel, D. (2002, November 8). Pedro: No Cy, just why. *The Hartford Courant, C1, C4.*

Heuze, J-P, Sarrazin, P., Masiero, M., Raimbault, N., & Thomas, J-P. (2006). The relationships of perceived motivational climate to cohesion and collective efficacy in elite female teams. *Journal of Applied Sport Psychology, 18,* 201–218.

Hewitt, P. L., Flett, G. L., & Ediger, E. (1995). Perfectionism traits and perfectionistic self-presentation in eating disorder attitudes, characteristics, and symptoms. *International Journal of Eating Disorders, 18,* 317–326.

Hewitt, P. L., Flett, G. L., & Ediger, E. (1996). Perfectionism and depression: Longitudinal assessment of a specific vulnerability hypothesis. *Journal of Abnormal Psychology, 105,* 276–280.

Hewitt, P. L., Flett, G. L., Ediger, E., Norton, G. R., & Flynn, C. A. (1998). Perfectionism in chronic and state symptoms of depression. *Canadian Journal of Behavioral Science, 30,* 234–242.

Heyman, G. D., Dweck, C. S., & Cain, K. M. (1992). Young children's vulnerability to self-blame and state symptoms of depression. *Canadian Journal of Behavioural Science, 30,* 234–242.

Heyman, J. (1993, March 23). Very superstitious. Boggs unashamed of his mind-boggling habits. *Newsday* [On-line]. Retrieved from http://www.elibrary.com

Heyman, S. R. (1982). Comparisons of successful and unsuccessful competitors: A reconsideration of methodological questions and data. *Journal of Sport Psychology, 4,* 295–300.

Higgins, E. T. (1997). Beyond pleasure and pain. *American Psychologist, 52,* 1280–1300.

Higgins, E. T. (2012). Regulatory focus theory. In P.A.M. Van Lange, A. W. Kruglanski, & E. T. Higgins (Eds.), *Handbook of theories of social psychology* (Vol 1; pp. 483–504). Thousand Oaks, CA: Sage.

Highlen, P. S., & Bennett, B. B. (1983). Elite divers and wrestlers: A comparison between open- and closed-skill athletes. *Journal of Sport Psychology, 5,* 871–890.

Higuchi, T., Imanaka, K., & Hatayama, T. (2002). Freezing degrees of freedom under stress: Kinematic evidence of constrained movement strategies. *Human Movement Science, 21,* 831–846. doi: 10.1016/S0167-9457(02)00174-4

Hildebrand, K. M., Johnson, D. J., & Bogle, K. (2001). Comparison of patterns of alcohol use between high school and college athletes and non-athletes. *College Student Journal, 35,* 358–365.

Hill, A. P., Hall, H. K., & Appleton, P. R. (2010). Perfectionism and athlete burnout in junior elite athletes: The mediating role of coping tendencies. *Anxiety, Stress, & Coping, 23,* 415–430. doi: 10.1080/10615800903330966

Hill, A. P., Hall, H. K., Appleton, P. R., & Kozub, S. A. (2008). Perfectionism and burnout in junior elite soccer players: The mediating influence of unconditional self-acceptance. *Psychology of Sport and Exercise, 9,* 630–644. doi: 10.1016/j.psychsport.2007.09.004

Hill, A. P., Hall, H. K., Appleton, P. R., & Murray, J. J. (2010). Perfectionism and burnout in canoe, polo and kayak slalom athletes: The mediating influence of validation and growth-seeking. *The Sport Psychologist, 24,* 16–34.

Hill, C. E. (2009). *Helping skills. Facilitation, exploration, insight, and action* (3rd ed.). Washington, DC: American Psychological Association.

Hill, D. M., Hanton, S., Fleming, S., & Matthews, N. (2009). A re-examination of choking in sport. *European Journal of Sport Science, 9,* 203–212.

Hill, D. M., Hanton, S., Matthews, N., & Fleming, S. (2010). A qualitative exploration of choking in elite golf. *Journal of Clinical Sport Psychology, 4,* 221–240.

Hill, D. M., Hanton, S., Matthews, N., & Fleming, S. (2011). Alleviation of choking under pressure in elite golf: An action research study. *The Sport Psychologist, 25,* 465–488.

Hill, G. H. (2011, March 17). Grant Hill's response to Jalen Rose. *The New York Times.* Retrieved from http://thequad.blogs.nytimes.com/2011/03/16/grant-hills-response-to-jalen-rose/

Hill, R. A., & Barton, R. A. (2005, May 19). Red enhances human performance in contests. Signals biologically attributed to red coloration in males may operate in the area of combat sports. *Nature, 435,* 293.

Hilton, C. (2006). *Michael Schumacher – the whole story.* England: Haynes Publishing.

Hine, T. (2003a, January 18). Kwan shows others a fine old time. *Hartford Courant,* C1.

Hine, T. (2003b, January 19). National treasure. Kwan wins 7th title; Cohen 3rd behind Hughes. *Hartford Courant,* E2.

Hine, T. (2003c, March 30). As usual, count on Kwan. *Hartford Courant,* E3.

Hine, T. (2004a, August 8). Swimming in hype. *Hartford Courant,* E1, E10.

Hine, T. (2005, December, 16). Great goalie still learning. *Hartford Courant,* C1, C2.

Hirt, E. R., Deppe, R. K., & Gordon, L. J. (1991). Self-reported versus behavioral self-handicapping: Empirical evidence for a theoretical distinction. *Journal of Personality and Social Psychology, 61,* 981–991.

Hjalm, S., Kentta, G., Hassmenan, P., & Gustafsson, H. (2007). Burnout among elite soccer coaches. *Journal of Sport Behavior, 30,* 415–427.

Hoar, S. D., Crocker, P.R.E., Holt, N. L., & Tamminen, K. A. (2010). Gender differences in adolescent athletes' coping and interpersonal stressors in sport: More similarities than differences? *Journal of Applied Sport Psychology, 22,* 134–149.

Hobden, K., & Pliner, P. (1995). Self-handicapping and dimensions of perfectionism: Self-presentation vs self-protection. *Journal of Research in Personality, 29,* 461–474.

Hodge, K., Lonsdale, C., & Jackson, S. A. (2009). Athlete engagement in elite sport: An exploratory investigation of antecedents and consequences. *The Sport Psychologist, 23,* 186–202.

Hodge, K., & Petlichkoff, L. (2000). Goal profiles in sport motivation: A cluster analysis. *Journal of Sport & Exercise Psychology, 22,* 256–272.

Hodges, N. J., Chua, R., & Franks, I. M. (2003). The role of video in facilitating perception and action of a novel coordination movement. *Journal of Motor Behavior, 35,* 247–260.

Hogan, R., & Kaiser, R. B. (2005). What we know about leadership. *Review of General Psychology, 9,* 169–180.

Hoigaard, R., Jones, G. W., & Peters, D. M. (2008). Preferred coach leadership behavior in elite soccer in relation to success and failure. *International Journal of Sports Science & Coaching, 3,* 241–250.

Hokoda, A., & Fincham, F. D. (1995). Origins of children's helpless and mastery achievement patterns in the family. *Journal of Educational Psychology, 87,* 375–385.

Holland, M. J. G., Woodcock, C., Cumming, H., & Duda, J. L. (2010). Mental qualities and employed mental techniques of young elite team sport athletes. *Journal of Clinical Sport Psychology, 4,* 19–38.

Hollander, D., B., & Meyers, M. C. (1995). Psychological factors associated with overtraining: Implications for youth sport coaches. *Journal of Sport Behavior, 18,* 3–20.

Hollembeak, J., & Amorose, A. J. (2005). Perceived coaching behaviors and college athletes' intrinsic motivation: A test of self-determination theory. *Journal of Applied Sport Psychology, 17,* 20–36. doi: 10.1080/10413200590907540

Holmes, D. S. (1984). Meditation and somatic arousal reduction. A review of the experimental evidence. *American Psychologist, 39,* 1–10.

Holmes, P. M., McNeil, M., Adorna, P., & Procaccino, J. K. (2008). Collegiate student athletes' preferences and perceptions regarding peer relationships. *Journal of Sport Behavior, 31,* 338–351.

Holmes, P. S., & Collins, D. J. (2001). THE PETTLEP approach to motor imagery: A functional equivalence model for sport psychologists. *Journal of Applied Sport Psychology, 13,* 60–83.

Holt, N. L., & Dunn, J. G. H. (2004). Toward a grounded theory of the psychosocial competencies and environmental conditions associated with soccer success. *Journal of Applied Sport Psychology, 16,* 199–219.

Holt, N. L., & Sparkes, A. C. (2001). An ethnographic study of cohesiveness in a college soccer team over a season. *The Sport Psychologist, 15,* 237–259.

Holt, N. L., Tamminen, K. A., Black, D. E., Mandigo, J. L., & Fox, K. R. (2009). Youth sport parenting styles and practices. *Journal of Sport & Exercise Psychology, 31,* 37–59.

Holt, R. I. G., & Sonksen, P. H. (2008). Growth hormone, IGF-I and insulin and their abuse in sport. *British Journal of Pharmacology, 154,* 542–556.

Homme, L. E. (1970). *How to use contingency contracting in the classroom.* Champaign, IL: Research Press.

Hootman, J. M., Dick, R., Agel, J. (2007). Epidemiology of collegiate injuries for 15 sports: Summary and recommendations for injury prevention. *Journal of Athletic Training, 42,* 311–319.

Horn, C. M., Gilbert, J. N., Gilbert, W., & Lewis, D. K. (2011). Psychological skills training with community college athletes: The UNIFORM approach. *The Sport Psychologist, 25,* 321–340.

Horn, H. L., Duda, J. L., & Miller, A. (1993). Correlates of goal orientations among young athletes. *Pediatric Exercise Science, 5,* 168–176.

Horn, T. S. (1985). Coaches' feedback and changes in children's perception of their physical competence. *Journal of Educational Psychology, 77,* 174–186.

Horn, T. S. (1992). Leadership effectiveness in the sport domain. In T. S. Horn (Ed.), *Advances in Sport Psychology* (pp. 181–200). Champaign, IL: Human Kinetics.

Hornby, N. (1994). *Fever Pitch.* New York, NY: Penguin Books.

Horner, M. S. (1973). A psychological barrier to achievement in women: The motive to avoid success. In D. C. McClelland, & R. S. Steele (Eds.), *Human motivation. A book of readings* (pp. 222–230). Morristown, NJ: General Learning Press.

Horner, M. S. (1978). The measurement and behavioral implications of fear of success in women. In J. W. Atkinson & J. O. Raynor (Eds.), *Personality, motivation, and achievement* (pp. 41–70). Washington, DC: Halsted Press.

Howard, J. (2002a, February 21). Michelle is experienced in knowing the pitfalls. *Newsday.* Retrieved from http://www.Newsday.com

Howard, J. (2002b, February 22). Sarah tweaks, squeaks by foes. Hughes coach inject big finish into long routine. *Newsday.* Retrieved from http://www.Newsday.com

Howard-Hamilton, M. (1993). African-American female athletes: Issues, implications, and imperatives for educators. *NASPA Journal, 30,* 153–195.

TM-Sidhi Program. (n.d.) Retrieved from http://www.maharishi.org/sidhi

Transcendental Meditation (n.d.). Retrieved from http://www.tm.org

(http://www.wada-ama.org) World Anti-Doping Agency. (2009). *World anti-doping code.* Retrieved from http://www.wada-ama.org

Hudson, J. (1978). Physical parameters used for female exclusion from law enforcement and athletics. In C. Oglesby (Ed.), *Women and sport: From myth to reality.* Philadelphia, PA: Lea & Febiger.

Hughes, R. (2012, September 27). Chelsea's Terry suspended for racial abuse. *The New York Times.* Retrieved from http://www.nytimes.com

Hughes, S. L., Case, H. S., Stuemple, K. J., & Evans, D. S. (2003). Personality profiles of iditasport ultra-marathon participants. *Journal of Applied Sport Psychology, 15,* 256–261.

Humphreys, M. S., & Revelle, W. (1984). Personality, motivation, and performance: A theory of the relationship between individual differences and information processing. *Psychological Review, 91,* 153–184.

Hung, T.-M., Lin, T.-C., Lee, C.-L., & Chen, L.-C. (2008). Provision of sport psychology services to Taiwan archery team for the 2004 Athens Olympic Games. *International Journal of Sport and Exercise Psychology, 6*, 308–318.

Hung, T.-M, Spalding, T. W., Santa Maria, D. L., & Hatfield, B. D. (2004). Assessment of reactive motor performance with event-related brain potentials: Attention processes in elite table tennis players. *Journal of Sport & Exercise Psychology, 26*, 317–337.

Hutchinson, A., Breckon, J. D., & Johnston, L. H. (2008). Physical activity behaviour change interventions based on the transtheoretical model: A systematic review. *Health Behaviour Research, 36*, 829–845. doi: 10.1177/1090198108318491

Hutchinson, J. C., Sherman, T., Martinovic, N., & Tenenbaum, G. (2008). The effect of manipulated self-efficacy on perceived and sustained effort. *Journal of Applied Sport Psychology, 20*, 457–472.

Hyde, J. S. (2005). The gender similarities hypothesis. *The American Psychologist, 60*, 581–592.

International Olympic Committee. (2011). Anti-doping rules. Retrieved from http://www.olympic.org

Irving, P. G., & Goldstein, I. P. (1990). Effect of home-field advantage on peak performance of baseball pitchers. *Journal of Sport Behavior, 13*, 23–27.

Isberg, L. (2000). Anger, aggressive behavior, and athletic performance. In Y. L. Hanin (Ed.), *Emotions in sport*. Champaign, IL: Human Kinetics.

Isoard-Gautheur, S., Guillet-Descas, E., & Lemyre, P-N. (2012). A prospective study of the influence of perceived coaching style on burnout propensity in high level young athletes: Using a self-determination theory perspective. *The Sport Psychologist, 26*, 282–298.

Italian Admits to Insult. (2006, July 12). *Hartford Courant*, C3.

Italian Player Ends Mystery. (2006, September 6) *Hartford Courant*, C7.

Ivarsson, A., & Johnson, U. (2010). Psychological factors as predictors of injuries among senior soccer players. A prospective study. *Journal of Sports Science and Medicine, 9*, 347–352.

Jack, S. J., & Ronan, K. R. (1998). Sensation seeking among high- and low-risk sports participants. *Personality and Individual Differences, 25*, 1063–1083.

Jackson, B., & Beauchamp, M. R. (2010). Efficacy beliefs in coach-athlete dyads: Prospective relationships using actor-partner interdependence models. *Applied Psychology: An International Review, 59*, 220–242. doi: 10.1111/j.1464-0597.009.00388.x

Jackson, B., Beauchamp, M. R., & Knapp, P. (2007). Relational efficacy beliefs in athlete dyads: An investigation using actor-partner interdependence models. *Journal of Sport & Exercise Psychology, 29*, 170–189.

Jackson, B., Dimmock, J. A., Gucciardi, D. F., & Grove, J. R. (2010). Relationship commitment in athletic dyads: Actor and partner effects for Big Five self- and other-ratings. *Journal of Research in Personality, 44*, 641–648. doi: 10.1016/j.jrp.2010.08.004

Jackson, B., Dimmock, J. A., Gucciardi, D. F., & Grove, J. R. (2011). Personality traits and relationship perceptions in coach-athlete dyads: Do opposites really attract? *Psychology of Sport and Exercise, 12*, 222–230. doi: 10.1016/j.psychsport.2010.11.005

Jackson, B., Gucciardi, D. F., & Dimmock, J. A. (2011). Tripartite efficacy profiles: A cluster analytic investigation of athletes' perceptions of their relationship with their coach. *Journal of Sport & Exercise Psychology, 33*, 394–415.

Jackson, B., Harwood, C. G., & Grove, J. R. (2010). On the same page in sporting dyads: Does dissimilarity on 2 × 2 achievement goal constructs impair relationship functioning? *Journal of Sport & Exercise Psychology, 32*, 805–827.

Jackson, B., Knapp, P., & Beauchamp, M. R. (2008). Origins and consequences of tripartite efficacy beliefs within elite athlete dyads. *Journal of Sport and Exercise Psychology, 30*, 512–540.

Jackson, P., & Delehanty, H. (1995). *Sacred hoops: The spiritual lessons of a hardwood warrior*. New York, NY: Hyperion.

Jackson, R. C. (2003). Pre-performance routine consistency: Temporal analysis of goal kicking in the Rugby Union World Cup. *Journal of Sports Sciences, 21*, 803–814.

Jackson, R. C., Ashford, K. J., & Norsworthy, G. (2006). Attentional focus, dispositional reinvestment and skilled motor performance under pressure. *Journal of Sport and Exercise Psychology, 28*, 49–68.

Jackson, R. C., & Baker, J. S. (2001). Routines, rituals, and rugby: Case study of a world class goal kicker. *The Sport Psychologist, 15*, 48–65.

Jackson, R. C., & Mogan, P. (2007). Advance visual information, awareness, and anticipation skill. *Journal of Motor Behavior, 39*, 341–351.

Jackson, R. C., & Wilson, R. J. (1999). Using "swing thoughts" to prevent paradoxical performance effects in golf putting. In M. R. Farrally & A. J. Cochran (Eds.), *Science and golf III: Proceedings of the 1998 world scientific congress of golf* (pp. 166–173). Leeds, England: Human Kinetics.

Jackson, S. A. (1995). Factors influencing the occurrence of flow state in elite athletes. *Journal of Applied Sport Psychology, 7,* 138–166.

Jackson, S. A., & Csikszentmihalyi, M. (1999). *Flow in sports.* Champaign, IL: Human Kinetics.

Jackson, S. A., Kimiecik, J. C., Ford, S. K., & Marsh, H. W. (1998). Psychological correlates of flow in sport. *Journal of Sport & Exercise Psychology, 20,* 358–378.

Jackson, S. A., & Roberts, G. C. (1992) Positive performance states of athletes: Toward a conceptual understanding of peak performance. *The Sport Psychologist, 6,* 156–171.

Jackson, S. A., Thomas, P. R., Marsh, H. W., & Smethurst, C. J. (2001). Relationships between flow, self-concept, psychological skills, and performance. *Journal of Applied Sport Psychology, 13,* 129–153.

Jacobi, M. (1877). *The question of rest for women during menstruation.* New York, NY: G. P. Putnam & Sons.

Jacobs, G. D., Benson, H., & Friedman, R. (1996). Topographic EEG mapping of the relaxation response. *Biofeedback and Self-Regulation, 21,* 121–129.

Jacobs, J. (1999, September 11). It's now shaping up as the right move. *Hartford Courant,* C1, C2.

Jacobson, E. (1938). *Progressive relaxation.* Chicago, IL: University of Chicago Press.

Jambor, E. A., & Zhang, J. J. (1997). Investigating leadership, gender, and coaching level using the revised leadership for sport scale. *Journal of Sport Behavior, 20,* 313–322.

Jamieson, J. P., & Harkins, S. G. (2007). Mere effort and stereotype threat performance effects. *Journal of Personality and Social Psychology, 93,* 544–564.

Janelle, C. M. (2002). Anxiety, arousal and visual attention: A mechanistic account of performance variability. *Journal of Sports Sciences, 20,* 237–251.

Janelle, C. M., Hillman, C. H., Apparies, R., Murray, N. P., Meili, L., & Hatfield, B. D. (2000). Expertise differences in cortical activity and gaze behavior during rifle shooting. *Journal of Sport & Exercise Psychology, 22,* 167–182.

Janelle, C. M., Singer, R. N., & Williams, A. M. (1999). External distraction and attentional narrowing: Visual search evidence. *Journal of Sport & Exercise Psychology, 21,* 70–91.

Janssen, J., & Dale, G. (2002). *The seven secrets of successful coaches.* Cary, NC: Winning the Mental Game.

Jay Williams: Bulls layers got high before 2002–03 games. (2013, February 10). *The Chicago Tribune.* Retrieved from http://chicagotribune.com

Jenkins, S. (1992, March 30). Teenage confidential. *Sports Illustrated, 76,* 26–29.

Jevning, R. Wallace, R. K., & Beidebach, M. (1992). The physiology of meditation: A review. A wakeful hypometabolic integrated response. *Neuroscience and Biobehavioral Reviews, 16,* 415–424.

Jha, A. P., Krompinger, J., & Baime, M. J. (2007). Mindfulness training modifies subsystems of attention. *Cognitive, Affective, & Behavioral Neuroscience, 7,* 107–119.

Joesaar, H., Hein, V., & Hagger, M. S. (2011). Peer influence on young athletes' need satisfaction, intrinsic motivation and persistence in sport: A 12-month prospective study. *Psychology of Sport and Exercise, 12,* 500–508. doi: 10.1016/j.psychsport.2011.04.005

Joesaar, H., Hein, V., & Hagger, M. S. (2012). Youth athletes' perception of autonomy support from the coach, peer motivational climate and intrinsic motivation in sport setting: One-year effects. *Psychology of Sport and Exercise, 13,* 257–262. doi: 10.1016/j.psychsport.2011.12.001

Johnson, E. O., Roehrs, T., Roth, T., & Breslau, N. (1998). Epidemiology of alcohol and medication as aids to sleep in early adulthood. *Sleep, 21,* 178–186.

Johnson, J. J. M., Hrycaiko, D. W., Johnson, G. V., & Halas, J. M. (2004). Self-talk and female soccer performance. *The Sport Psychologist, 18,* 44–56.

Johnson, L., & Biddle, S. J. H. (1989). Persistence after failure: An exploratory look at "learned helplessness" in motor performance. *British Journal of Physical Education Research Supplement, 5,* 7–10.

Johnson, M. B., Tenenbaum, G., Edmonds, W. A., & Castillo, Y. (2008). A comparison of the developmental experiences of elite and sub-elite swimmers: Similar developmental histories can lead to differences in performance level. *Sport, Education and Society, 13,* 453–475.

Johnson, U. (2007). Psychosocial antecedents of sport injury, prevention, and intervention: An overview of theoretical approaches and empirical findings. *International Journal of Sport and Exercise Psychology, 5,* 352–369. doi: 10.1080/1612197X.2007.9671841

Johnson, U., Ekengren, J., & Andersen, M. B. (2005). Injury prevention in Sweden: Helping soccer players at risk. *Journal of Sport & Exercise Psychology, 27,* 32–38.

Johnson, U., & Ivarsson, A. (2011). Psychological predictors of sport injuries among junior soccer players. *Scandinavian Journal of Medicine & Science in Sports, 21,* 129–136. doi: 10.1111/j.1600.0838.2009.01057.x

Johnston, L. H., & Carroll, D. (1998). The context of emotional responses to athletic injury: A qualitative analysis. *Journal of Sport Rehabilitation, 7*, 206–220.

Johnston-O'Connor, E. J., & Kirschenbaum, D. S. (1986). Something success like success: Positive self-monitoring for unskilled golfers. *Cognitive Therapy and Research, 10*, 123–136.

Jones, E. E., & Berglas, S. (1978). Control of attributions about the self through self-handicapping strategies: The appeal of alcohol and the role of underachievement. *Personality and Social Psychology Bulletin, 4*, 200–206.

Jones, E. E., & Davis, K. E. (1965). From acts to dispositions: The attribution process in person perception. In L. Berkowitz (Ed.), *Advances in experimental social psychology* (Vol. 2, pp. 219–266). London, England: Academic Press.

Jones, G. (1995). More than just a game: Research developments and issues in competitive anxiety in sport. *British Journal of Psychology, 86*, 449–478.

Jones, G., & Cale, A. (1989). Relationships between multidimensional competitive state anxiety and cognitive and motor subcomponents of performance. *Journal of Sports Sciences, 7*, 129–140.

Jones, G., & Hanton, S. (1996). Interpretation of competitive anxiety symptoms and goal attainment expectancies. *Journal of Sport and Exercise Psychology, 18*, 144–157.

Jones, G., & Hanton, S. (2001). Pre-competitive feeling states and directional anxiety interpretations. *Journal of Sports Sciences, 19*, 385–395.

Jones, G., Hanton, S., & Connaughton, D. (2002). What is this thing called mental toughness: An investigation of elite sport performers. *Journal of Applied Sport Psychology, 14*, 205–218. doi: 10.1080/10413200290103509

Jones, G., Hanton, S., & Connaughton, D. (2007). A framework for mental toughness in the world's best performers. *The Sport Psychologist, 21*, 243–264.

Jones, G., & Hanton, S., & Swain, A. B. J. (1994). Intensity and interpretation of anxiety symptoms in elite and non-elite sports performers. *Personality & Individual Differences, 17*, 657–663.

Jones, G., & Swain, A. (1995). Predispositions to experience debilitative and facilitative anxiety in elite and nonelite performers. *The Sport Psychologist, 9*, 201–211.

Jones, G., Swain, A., & Cale, A. (1991). Gender differences in precompetition temporal patterning and antecedents of anxiety and self-confidence. *Journal of Sport and Exercise Psychology, 13*, 1–15.

Jones, G., Swain, A. B. J., & Hardy, L. (1993). Intensity and direction dimensions of competitive state anxiety and relationships with performance. *Journal of Sport Sciences, 11*, 525–532.

Jones, K. A., Smith, N. C., & Holmes, P. S. (2004). Anxiety symptom interpretation and performance predictions in high-anxious, low-anxious and repressor sport performers. *Anxiety, Stress and Coping, 17*, 187–199.

Jones, M. I., & Harwood, C. (2008). Psychological momentum within competitive soccer: Players' perspectives. *Journal of Applied Sport Psychology, 20*, 57–72. doi: 10.1080/10413200701784841

Jones, M. I., & Lavallee, D. (2009). Exploring the life skills needs of British adolescent athletes. *Psychology of Sport and Exercise, 10*, 159–167. doi: 10.1016/j.psychsport.2008.06.005

Jonker, L., Elferink-Gemser, M. T., Toering, T. T., Lyons, J., & Visscher, C. (2010). Academic performance and self-regulatory skills in elite youth soccer players. *Journal of Sports Sciences, 28*, 1605–1614. doi: 10.1080/02640414.2010.516270

Jordan, M., & Bestrom, C. (2009, November 9). 10 rules for maximizing your competitiveness. *Golf Digest, 60*, 84–87.

Jordan, W. J. (1999). Black high school students' participation in school-sponsored sports activities: Effects of school engagement and achievement. *Journal of Negro Education, 68*, 54–71.

Jordet, G. (2005). Perceptual training in soccer: An imagery intervention study with elite players. *Journal of Applied Sport Psychology, 17*, 140–156.

Jordet, G. (2009a). When superstars flop: Public status and choking under pressure in international soccer penalty shootouts. *Journal of Applied Sport Psychology, 21*, 125–130.

Jordet, G. (2009b). Why do English players fail in soccer penalty shootouts? A study of team status, self-regulation, and choking under pressure. *Journal of Sports Sciences, 27*, 97–106.

Jordet, G., Elferink-Gemser, M. T., Lemmink, K.A.P.M., & Visscher, C. (2006). The "Russian roulette" of soccer? Perceived control and anxiety in a major tournament penalty shootout. *International Journal of Sport Psychology, 37*, 281–298.

Jordet, G. & Hartman, E. (2008). Avoidance motivation and choking under pressure in soccer penalty shootouts. *Journal of Sport & Exercise Psychology, 30*, 450–457.

Jordet, G., Hartman, E., Visscher, C., & Lemmink, K.A.P.M. (2007). Kicks from the penalty mark in soccer: The roles of stress, skill, and fatigue for kick outcomes. *Journal of Sports Sciences, 25,* 121–129. doi: 10.1080/02640410600624020

Kabat-Zinn, J. (1982). An outpatient program in behavioral medicine for chronic pain patients based on the practice of mindfulness meditation: Theoretical considerations and preliminary results. *General Hospital Psychiatry, 4,* 33–47.

Kabat-Zinn, J. (1990). *Full catastrophe living: Using the wisdom of your body and mind to face stress, pain, and illness.* New York, NY: Delacorte.

Kabat-Zinn, J. (2003). Mindfulness-based interventions in context: Past, present, and future. *Clinical Psychology: Science and Practice, 10,* 144–156.

Kagan, J. (1994). *Galen's prophecy. Temperament in human nature.* New York, NY: Basic Books.

Kagan, J., Snidman, N., McManis, M., & Woodward, S. (2001). Temperamental contributions to the affect family of anxiety. *The Psychiatric Clinics of North America, 24,* 677–688.

Kahn, G. (2006, February 14). Climate of suspicion: High-tech forecasts are a turnoff in Turin. *Wall Street Journal,* A1.

Kahn, R. (1971). *The boys of summer.* New York, NY: Harper & Row.

Kaiseler, M., Polman, R., & Nicholls, A. (2009). Mental toughness, stress, stress appraisal, coping and coping effectiveness in sport. *Personality and Individual Differences, 47,* 728–733. doi: 10.1016/j.paid.2009.06.012

Kaiser, R. B., Hogan, R., & Craig, S. B. (2008). Leadership and the fate of organizations. *American Psychologist, 63,* 96–110.

Kamen, L. P., & Seligman, M. E. P. (1986). *Explanatory style predicts college grade point average.* Unpublished manuscript, University of Pennsylvania.

Kamphoff, C. S., Gill, D. L., Araki, K., & Hammond, C. C. (2010). Content analysis of cultural diversity in the Association for Applied Sport Psychology's conference programs. *Journal of Applied Sport Psychology, 22,* 231–245.

Kanayama, G., Hudson, J. I., & Pope Jr., H. G. (2009). Features of men with anabolic-androgenic steroid dependence: A comparison with nondependent AAS users and with AAS nonusers. *Drug and Alcohol Dependence, 102,* 130–137.

Kanayama, G., Hudson, J. I., & Pope Jr., H. G. (2010). Illicit anabolic-androgenic steroid use. *Hormones and Behavior, 58,* 111–121. doi: 10.1016/j.yhbeh.2009.09.006

Kane, M. (1971, January 18). An assessment of 'Black is best.' *Sports Illustrated.* Retrieved from www.http://si.com

Kane, M. J., Conway, A.R.A., Hambrick, D. Z., & Engle, R. W. (2007). Variation in working memory as variation in executive attention and control. In A.R.A. Conway, C. Jarrold, M. J. Kane, A. Miyake, & J. N. Towse (Eds.), *Variation in working memory* (pp. 21–48). Oxford, England: Oxford University Press.

Kane, M. J., & Engle, R. W. (2000). Working-memory capacity, proactive interference, and divided attention: Limits on long-term memory retrieval. *Journal of Experimental Psychology: Learning, Memory, and Cognition, 26,* 336–358.

Kane, M. J., & Engle, R. W. (2003). Working-memory capacity and the control of attention: The contributions of goal neglect, response competition, and task set to Stroop interference. *Journal of Experimental Psychology: General, 132,* 47–70.

Kane, T. D., Baltes, T. R., & Moss, M. C. (2001). Causes and consequences of free-set goals: An investigation of athletic self-regulation. *Journal of Sport & Exercise Psychology, 23,* 55–75.

Kane, T. D., Marks, M. A., Zaccaro, S. J., & Blair, V. (1996). Self-efficacy, personal goals, and wrestlers' self-regulation. *Journal of Sport and Exercise Psychology, 18,* 36–48.

Kanfer, R., & Ackerman, P. L. (1989). Motivation and cognitive abilities: An integrative/aptitude-treatment interaction approach to skill acquisition. *Journal of Applied Psychology, 74,* 657–690.

Kanfer, R., & Ackerman, P. L. (1996). A self-regulatory skills perspective to reducing cognitive interference. In I. G. Sarason, G. R. Pierce, & B. R. Sarason (Eds.), *Cognitive interference theories, methods, and findings* (pp. 153–171). Mahwah, NJ: Lawrence Erlbaum Associates.

Karageorghis, C. I. (2008). The scientific application of music in sport and exercise. In A. M. Lane (Ed.), *Sport and exercise psychology: Topics in applied psychology* (pp. 109–137). London, England: Hodder Education.

Kareev, Y. (2000). Seven (indeed, plus or minus two) and the detection of correlations. *Psychological Review, 107,* 397–403.

Karp, H. (2011, August 29). Novak Djokovic's secret: Sitting in a pressurized egg. *The Wall Street Journal.* Retrieved from http://online.wsj.com

Kasser, T., & Ryan, R. M. (1993). A dark side of the American dream: Correlates of financial success as a central life aspiration. *Journal of Personality and Social Psychology, 65,* 410–422.

Kasser, T., & Ryan, R. M. (1996). Further examining the American dream: Differential correlates of intrinsic and extrinsic goals. *Personality and Social Psychology Bulletin, 22*, 280–287.

Kaufman, K. A., Glass, C. R., & Arnkoff, D. B. (2009). Evaluation of Mindful Sport Performance Enhancement (MSPE): A new approach to promote flow in athletes. *Journal of Clinical Sport Psychology, 4*, 334–356.

Kavussanu, M., & Boardley, I. D. (2009). The Prosocial and Antisocial Behavior in Sport Scale. *Journal of Sport & Exercise Psychology, 31*, 97–117.

Kavussanu, M., Boardley, I. D., Jutkiewicz, N., Vincent, S., & Ring, C. (2008). Coaching efficacy and coaching effectiveness: Examining their predictors and comparing coaches' and athletes' reports. *The Sport Psychologist, 22*, 383–404.

Kavussanu, M., & Roberts, G. C. (1996). Motivation in physical activity contexts: The relationship of perceived motivational climate to intrinsic motivation and self-efficacy. *Journal of Sport and Exercise Psychology, 18*, 264–280.

Kavussanu, M., Seal, A. R., & Phillips, D. R. (2006). Observed prosocial and antisocial behaviors in male soccer teams: Age differences across adolescence and the role of motivational variables. *Journal of Applied Sport Psychology, 18*, 326–344.

Kawamura, K., Frost, R. O., & Harmatz, M. G. (2002). The relationship of perceived parenting styles to perfectionism. *Personality and Individual Differences, 32*, 317–327.

Kaye, M. P., Conroy, D. E., & Fifer, A. M. (2008). Individual differences in incompetence avoidance. *Journal of Sport & Exercise Psychology, 30*, 110–132.

Kee, Y. H., & Wang, C. K. J. (2008). Relationships between mindfulness, flow dispositions and mental skills adoption: A cluster analytic approach. *Psychology of Sport and Exercise, 9*, 393–411. doi: 10.1016/j.psychsport.2007.07.0010.

Keegan, R. J., Harwood, C. G., Spray, C. M., & Lavallee, D. E. (2009). A qualitative investigation exploring the motivational climate in early career sports participants: Coach, parent and peer influences on sport motivation. *Psychology of Sport and Exercise, 10*, 361–372.

Keegan, R., Spray, C., Harwood, C., & Lavallee, D. (2010). The motivational atmosphere in youth sport: Coach, parent, and peer influences on motivation in specializing sport participants. *Journal of Applied Sport Psychology, 22*, 87–105.

Keele, S. W. (1968). Movement control in skilled motor performance. *Psychological Bulletin, 70*, 387–403.

Keh, A. (2013, January 24). Klinsmann explains, and keeps explaining, his use of "24/7." *The New York Times*. Retrieved from http://www.nyt.com

Kelley, B. C., Eklund, R. C., & Ritter-Taylor, M. (1999). Stress and burnout among collegiate tennis coaches. *Journal of Sport & Exercise Psychology, 21*, 113–130.

Kelley, H. H. (1967). Attribution theory in social psychology. In D. Levine (Ed.), *Nebraska symposium on motivation* (Vol. 15, pp. 192–240). Lincoln, NE: University of Nebraska Press.

Kelley, H. H. (1972). Causal schemata and the attribution process. In E. E. Jones, D. E. Kanouse, H. H. Kelley, R. E. Nisbett, S. Valins, & B. Weiner (Eds.), *Attribution: Perceiving the causes of behaviour* (pp. 1–26). Morristown, NJ: General Learning Press.

Kellmann, M. (2010). Preventing overtraining in athletes in high-intensity sorts and stress/recovery monitoring. *Scandinavian Journal of Medicine & Science in Sports, [Supplement 2], 20*, 95–102. doi: 10.1111/j.1600-0838.2010.01192.x

Kellmann, M., & Kallus, K. W. (2001). *Recovery-stress questionnaire for athletes: User manual*. Champaign, IL: Human Kinetics.

Kentta, G., Hassmen, P., & Raglin, J. S. (2006). Mood state monitoring of training and recovery in elite kayakers, *European Journal of Sport Science, 6*, 245–253. doi: 10.1080/17461390601012652

Kerr, G., & Dacyshyn, A. (2000). The retirement experiences of elite, female gymnasts. *Journal of Applied Sport Psychology, 12*, 115–133.

Kerr, G., & Goss, J. (1996). The effects of a stress management program on injuries and stress levels. *Journal of Applied Sport Psychology, 8*, 109–117.

Kerr, G. A., & Stirling, A. E. (2012). Parents' reflections on their child's experiences of emotionally abusive coaching practices. *Journal of Applied Sport Psychology, 24*, 191–206. doi: 10.1080/10413200.2011.608413

Kerr, J. H. (1997). *Motivation and emotion in sport. Reversal theory*. East Sussex, England: Psychology Press.

Kerr, J. H., & Cox, T. (1991). Arousal and individual differences in sport. *Personality and Individual Differences, 12*, 1075–1085.

Kessler, R. C., Aguilar-Gaxiola, S., Berglund, P. A., Caraveo-Anduaga, J. J., DeWit, D. J., Greenfield, S. F., Kolody, B., Olfson, M., & Vega, W. A. (2001). Patterns and predictors of treatment seeking after onset of a substance use disorder. *Archives of General Psychiatry, 58*, 1065–1071.

Kessler, R. C., Crum, R. M., Warner, L. A., Nelson, C. B., Schulenberg, J., & Anthony, J. C. (1997). Lifetime co-occurrence of DSM-III-R alcohol abuse and dependence with other psychiatric disorders in the National Comorbidity Survey. *Archives of General Psychiatry, 54,* 313–321.

Kessler, R. C., & Frank, R. G. (1997). The impact of psychiatric disorders on work loss days. *Psychological Medicine, 27,* 861–873.

Kessler, R. C., Foster, C. L., Saunders, W. B., & Stang, P. E. (1995). Social consequences of psychiatric disorders, I: Educational attainment. *American Journal of Psychiatry, 152,* 1026–1032.

Kessler, R. C., McGonagle, K. A., Zhao, S., Nelson, C. B., Hughes, M., Eshleman, S., Wittchen, H-U, & Kendler, K. S. (1994). Lifetime and 12-month prevalence of DSM-III-R psychiatric disorders in the United States. Results from the national comorbidity survey. *Archives of General Psychiatry, 51,* 8–19.

Keteyian, A. (1999, October 31). The N.B.A.'s drug program is nothing more than a masquerade. *The New York Times,* Section 8, 17.

Kilpatrick, M., Bartholomew, J., & Riemer, H. (2003). The measurement of goal orientations in exercise. *Journal of Sport Behavior, 26,* 121–136.

Kim, B. J., Williams, L., & Gill, D. L. (2003). A cross-cultural study of achievement orientation and intrinsic motivation in young USA and Korean athletes. *International Journal of Sport Psychology, 34,* 168–184.

King, D., Clark, T., & Kellmann, M. (2010). Changes in stress and recovery as a result of participating in a premier rugby league representative competition. *International Journal of Sports Science & Coaching, 5,* 223–237.

King, P. (2000, February 9). Dick Vermeil: Back to the beginning. *Sports Illustrated.* Retrieved from http://www.si.com

Kingston, K. M., & Hardy, L. (1997). Effects of different types of goals on processes that support performance. *The Sport Psychologist, 11,* 277–293.

Kingston, K. M., Horrocks, C., & Hanton, S. (2006). Do multidimensional intrinsic and extrinsic motivational profiles discriminate between athlete scholarship status? *European Journal of Sport Sciences, 6,* 53–63.

Kingston, K., Lane, A., & Thomas, O. (2010). A temporal examination of elite performers sources of sport confidence. *The Sport Psychologist, 18,* 313–332.

Kirkaldy, B. D. (1980). An analysis of the relationship between psychophysiological variables connected to human performance and the personality variables extraversion and neuroticism. *International Journal of Sport Psychology, 11,* 276–289.

Kirkaldy, B. D. (1984). Clinical psychology in sport. *International Journal of Sport Psychology, 15,* 127–136.

Kirsch, I., & Henry, D. (1979). Self-desensitization and public speaking in the reduction of public speaking anxiety. *Journal of Consulting and Clinical Psychology, 47,* 536–541.

Kirschenbaum, D. S. (1984). Self-regulation and sport psychology: Nurturing and emerging symbiosis. *Journal of Sport Psychology, 6,* 159–183.

Kirschenbaum, D. S., Ordman, A. M., Tomarken, A. J., & Holtzbauer, R. (1982). Effects of differential self-monitoring and level of mastery on sports performance. *Cognitive Therapy and Research, 6,* 335–342.

Kitsantas, A., & Zimmerman, B. J. (1998). Self-regulation of motoric learning: A strategic cycle view. *Journal of Applied Sport Psychology, 10,* 220–239.

Kitsantas, A., & Zimmerman, B. J. (2002). Comparing self-regulatory processes among novice, non-expert, and expert volleyball players: A microanalytic study. *Journal of Applied Sport Psychology, 14,* 91–105.

Kitsantas, A., Zimmerman, B. J., & Cleary, T. (2000). The role of observation and emulation in the development of athletic self-regulation. *Journal of Educational Psychology, 92,* 811–817.

Kiviniemi, M. T., Bennett, A., Zaiter, M., & Marshall, J. R. (2011). Individual-level factors in colorectal cancer screening: A review of the literature on the relation of individual-level health behavior constructs and screening behavior. *Psycho-Oncology, 20,* 1023–1033. doi: 10.1002/pon.1865

Kiviniemi, M. T., Voss-Humke, A. M., & Seifert, A. L. (2007). How do I feel about the behavior? The interplay of affective associations with behaviors and cognitive beliefs as influences on physical activity behavior. *Health Psychology, 26,* 152–158. doi: 10.1037/0278-6133.25.2.152

Kleiber, D. A., & Brock, S. C. (1992). The effects of career-ending injuries on the subsequent well-being of elite college athletes. *Sociology of Sport Journal, 9,* 70–75.

Klein, H. J., Wesson, M. J., Hollenbeck, J. R., & Alge, B. J. (1999). Goal commitment and the goal-setting process: Conceptual clarification and empirical synthesis. *Journal of Applied Psychology, 84,* 885–896.

Klinger, E. (1996). The content of thoughts: Interference as the downside of adaptive normal mechanisms in thought flow. In I. G. Sarason, G. R. Pierce, & B. R. Sarason (Eds.), *Cognitive interference theories, methods, and findings* (pp. 3–23). Mahwah, NJ: Lawrence Erlbaum Associates.

Knowles, Z., Gilbourne, D., Tomlinson, V., & Anderson, A. G. (2007). Reflections on the application of reflective practice for supervision in applied sport psychology. *The Sport Psychologist, 21,* 109–122.

Knubben, K., Reischies, F. M., Adli, M., Schlattmann, P., Bauer, M., & Dimeo, F. A. (2007). A randomized, controlled study on the effects of a short-term endurance training programme in patients with major depression. *British Journal of Sports Medicine, 41,* 29–33. doi: 10.1136/bjsm.2006.030130

Koca, C., Asci, F. H., & Kirazci, S. (2005). Gender role orientation of athletes and non-athletes in a patriarchal society: A study in Turkey. *Sex Roles, 52,* 217–225.

Kochman, T. (1981). *Black and white: Styles in conflict.* Chicago, IL: University of Chicago Press.

Koedijker, J. M., Oudejans, R.R.D., & Beek, P. J. (2008). Table tennis performance following explicit and analogy learning over 10,000 repetitions. *International Journal of Sport Psychology, 39,* 237–256.

Koivula, N. (1999). Sport participation: Differences in motivation and actual participation due to gender typing. *Journal of Sport Behavior, 22,* 360–371.

Koivula, N. (2001). Perceived characteristics of sports categorized as gender-neutral, feminine and masculine. *Journal of Sport Behavior, 24,* 377–393.

Koivula, N., Hassmen, P., & Falby, J. (2002). Self-esteem and perfectionism in elite athletes: effects on competitive anxiety and self-confidence. *Personality and Individual Differences, 32,* 865–875.

Kokkevi, A., Fotiou, A., Chileva, A., Nociar, A., & Miller, P. (2008). Daily exercise and anabolic steroids use in adolescents: A cross-national European study. *Substance Use & Misuse, 43,* 2053–2065. doi: 10.1080/10826080802279342

Kontos, A. P. (2012). Culture/ethnicity and performance. In S. M. Murphy (Ed.), *The Oxford handbook of sport and performance psychology* (pp. 418–432). New York, NY: Oxford University Press.

Kontos, A. P., & Breland-Noble, A. M. (2002). Racial/ethnic diversity in applied sport psychology: A multicultural introduction to working with athletes of color. *The Sport Psychologist, 16,* 296–315

Kornspan, A. S. (2012). History of sport and performance psychology. In S. M. Murphy (Ed.), *The Oxford handbook of sport and performance psychology* (pp. 3–23). New York, NY: Oxford University Press.

Kornspan, A. S., Overby, L. Y., & Lerner, B. S. (2004). Analysis and performance of preperformance imagery and other strategies on a golf putting task. *Journal of Mental Imagery, 28,* 59–74.

Kouli, O., & Papaioannou, A. G. (2009). Ethnic/cultural identity salience, achievement goals and motivational climate in multicultural physical education classes. *Psychology of Sport and Exercise, 10,* 45–51. doi: 10.1016/j.psychsport.2008.06.001

Kowal, J., & Fortier, M. S. (1999). Turning play into work: Effects of adult surveillance and extrinsic rewards on children's intrinsic motivation. *Journal of Personality and Social Psychology, 31,* 479–486.

Kowalski, K. C., & Crocker, P.R.E. (2001). Development and validation of the Coping Function Questionnaire for adolescents in sport. *Journal of Sport and Exercise Psychology, 23,* 136–155.

Kowalski, K. C., Crocker, P.R.E., Hoar, S. D., & Niefer, C. B. (2005). Adolescents' control beliefs and coping with stress in sport. *International Journal of Sport Psychology, 36,* 257–272.

Kozar, B., Whitfield, K. E., Lord, R. H., & Mechikoff, R. A. (1993). Timeouts before free throws: Do the statistics support the strategy? *Perceptual and Motor Skills, 76,* 47–50.

Kozub, S. A., & McDonnell, J. F. (2000). Exploring the relationship between cohesion and collective efficacy in rugby teams. *Journal of Sport Behavior, 23,* 120–129.

Krane, V., & Baird, S. M. (2005). Using ethnography in applied sport psychology. *Journal of Applied Sport Psychology, 17,* 87–107.

Krane, V., Choi, P., Baird, S., Aimar, C., & Kauer, K. (2004). Living the paradox: Female athletes negotiate femininity and muscularity. *Sex Roles, 50,* 315–329.

Krane, V., & Williams, J. M. (2010). Psychological characteristics of peak performance. In J. M. Williams (Ed.), *Applied sport psychology: Personal growth to peak performance* (6th ed., pp. 169–188). New York, NY: McGraw-Hill.

Kraus, H., & Hirschland, P. (1954). Minimum muscular fitness tests in young children. *Research Quarterly, 25,* 178–188.

Kristiansen, E., Halvari, H., & Roberts, G. C. (2011). Organizational and media stress among professional football players: Testing an achievement goal theory model. *Scandinavian Journal of Medicine & Science in Sports.* doi: 10.1111/j.1600-0838.2010.01259.x

Kristiansen, E., Hanstad, D. V., & Roberts, G. C. (2011). Coping with the media at the Vancouver Winter Olympics: "We all make a living out of this." *Journal of Applied Sport Psychology, 23,* 443–458. doi: 10.1080/10413200.2011.598139

Kristiansen, E., Murphy, D., & Roberts, G. C. (2012). Organizational stress and coping in U.S. professional soccer. *Journal of Applied Sport Psychology, 23,* 207–233. doi: 10.1080/10413200.2011.614319

Krohne, H. W. (1993). Vigilance and cognitive avoidance as concepts in coping research. In H. W. Krohne (Ed.), *Attention and avoidance: Strategies in coping with aversiveness* (pp. 19–50). Seattle, WA: Hogrefe & Huber.

Kubler-Ross, E. (1969). *On death and dying.* London, England: Tavistock.

Kuczka, K. K., & Treasure, D. C. (2005). Self-handicapping in competitive sport: Influence of the motivational climate, self-efficacy, and perceived importance. *Psychology of Sport and Exercise, 6,* 539–550.

Kuhn, T. S. (1970). *The structure of scientific revolutions* (2nd ed.). Chicago, IL: University of Chicago Press.

Kumar, S. (2010). Ascending the spiral staircase of grief. In M. Kerman (Ed.); *Clinical pearls of wisdom: Twenty-one leading therapists offer their key insights* (pp. 118–129). New York, NY: Norton.

Kurosawa, K., & Harackiewicz, J. M. (1995). Test anxiety, self-awareness, and cognitive interference: A process analysis. *Journal of Personality, 63,* 931–951.

Kyllo, L. B., & Landers, D. M. (1995). Goal setting in sport and exercise: A research synthesis to resolve the controversy. *Journal of Sport & Exercise Psychology, 17,* 117–137.

LaBrie, J. W., Grossbard, J. R., & Hummer, J. F. (2009). Normative misperceptions and marijuana use among male and female college athletes. *Journal of Applied Sport Psychology, 21 (Supp. 1),* S77-S85.

Laios, A., Theodorakis, N. & Gargalianos, D. (2003). Leadership and power: Two important factors for effective coaching. *International Sports Journal, Winter,* 150–154.

Lally, P., & Kerr, G. (2008). The effects of athlete retirement on parents. *Journal of Applied Sport Psychology, 20,* 42–56.

Lam, W. K., Maxwell, J. P., & Masters, R. (2009). Analogy learning and performance of motor skills under pressure. *Journal of Sport and Exercise Psychology, 31,* 337–357.

Lamarche, L., & Gammage, K. L. (2012). Predicting exercise and eating behaviors from appearance evaluation and two types of investment. *Sport, Exercise, and Performance Psychology, 1,* 145–157. doi: 10.1037/a0026892

Lamb, M. (1986). Self-concept and injury frequency among female college field hockey players. *Athletic Training, 21,* 220–224.

Lambourne, K., & Tomporowski, P. (2010). The effect of exercise-induced arousal on cognitive task performance: A meta-regression analysis. *Brain Research, 1341,* 12–24. doi: 10.1016/j.brainres.2010.03.091

Land, M. F. (2009). Vision, eye movements, and natural behavior. *Visual Neuroscience, 26,* 51–62.

Landers, D. M. (1995). Sport psychology: The formative years, 1950–1980. *The Sport Psychologist, 9,* 406–417.

Landers, D. M., & Arent, S. M. (2010). Arousal-performance relationships. In J. M. Williams (Ed.), *Applied sport psychology: Personal growth to peak performance* (6th ed., pp. 221–246). New York, NY: McGraw-Hill.

Landers, L. M., & Petruzzello, S. J. (1994). Physical activity, fitness, and anxiety. In C. Bouchard, R. J. Shepard, & T. Stevens (Eds.), *Physical activity, fitness, and health* (pp. 868–882). Champaign, IL: Human Kinetics.

Landin, D., & Hebert, E. (1999). The influence of self-talk on the performance of skilled female tennis players. *Journal of Applied Sport Psychology, 111,* 263–282.

Lane, A. M. (2007). The rise and fall of the iceberg: Development of a conceptual model of mood-performance relationships. In A. M. Lane (Ed.), *Mood and human performance: conceptual, measurement, and applied issues* (pp. 1–34). Hauppauge, NY: Nova Science.

Lane, A. M. (2008). Mood and sport performance. In A. M. Lane (Ed.), *Sport and exercise psychology: Topics in applied psychology* (pp. 19–34). London, England: Hodder Education.

Lane, A. M., Beedie, C. J., Devonport, T. J., & Stanley, D. M. (2011). Instrumental emotional regulation in sport: Relationships between beliefs about emotion and emotion regulation strategies used by athletes. *Scandinavian Journal of Medicine & Science in Sports, 2011,* e445-e451. doi: 10.1111/j.1600-0838.3011.01364.x

Lane, A. M., Jones, L., & Stevens, M. J. (2002). Coping with failure: The effects of self-esteem and coping on changes in self-efficacy. *Journal of Sport Behavior, 25,* 331–345.

Lane, A. M., & Terry, P. C. (2000). The nature of mood: Development of a conceptual model with a focus on depression. *Journal of Applied Sport Psychology, 12,* 16–33.

Lane, A. M., Thelwell, R. C., Lowther, J., & Devonport, T. J. (2009). Emotional intelligence and psychological skills use among athletes. *Social Behavior and Personality, 37,* 195–202.

Lanning, W., & Hisanaga, B. (1983). A study of the relation between the reduction of competition anxiety and an increase in athletic performance. *International Journal of Sport Psychology, 14,* 219–227.

LaRocca, T. J., Seals, D. R., & Pierce, G. L. (2010). Leukicyte telomere length is preserved with aging in endurance exercise-trained adults and related to maximal aerobic capacity. *Mechanisms of Aging and Development, 131*, 165–167. doi: 10.1016/j.mad.2009.12.009

Latham, G. P., & Locke, E. A. (2007). New developments in and directions for goal-setting research. *European Psychologist, 12*, 290–300.

Latham, G. P., & Seijts, G. H. (1999). The effects of proximal and distal goals on performance on a moderately complex task. *Journal of Organizational Behavior, 20*, 421–429.

Latinjak, A. J., Terregrosa, M., & Renom, J. (2011). Combining self talk and performance feedback: Their effectiveness with adult tennis players. *The Sport Psychologist, 25*, 18–31.

Lauer, L., Gould, D., Roman, N., & Pierce, M. (2010). How parents influence junior tennis players' development: Qualitative narratives. *Journal of Clinical Sport Psychology, 4*, 69–92.

Lauer, L., & Paiement, C. (2004). The Playing Tough and Clean Hockey Program. *The Sport Psychologist, 23*, 543–561.

Law, B., & Hall, C. (2009). Observational learning use and self-efficacy beliefs in adult sport novices. *Psychology of Sport and Exercise, 10*, 263–270. doi: 10.1016/j.psychsport.2008.08.003

Law, W. P., Cote, J., & Ericsson, K. A. (2007). Characteristics of expert development in rhythmic gymnastics: A retrospective study. *International Journal of Sport and Exercise Psychology, 5*, 82–103.

Lawton, M. (2012, February 4). We don't want you! England team-mates turn on Terry as the FA ditch race case captain. *Mail Online*. Retrieved from http://www.dailymail.co.uk

Lay, C., Kovacs, A., & Danto, D. (1998). The relation of trait procrastination to the big-five factor conscientiousness: An assessment with primary-junior school children based on self-report measures. *Personality and Individual Differences, 25*, 187–193.

Lay, C. H. (1986). At last, my research article on procrastination. *Journal of Research in Personality, 20*, 474–495.

Lay, C. H. (1995). Trait procrastination, agitation, dejection, and self-discrepancy. In J. R. Ferrari, J. L. Johnson, & W. G. McCown (Eds.), *Procrastination and task avoidance. Theory, research and treatment* (pp. 97–112). New York, NY: Plenum.

Lazarus, R. S. (1999). *Stress and emotion: A new synthesis.* New York, NY: Springer.

Lazarus, R. S., & Folkman, S. (1984). *Stress, appraisal, and coping.* New York, NY: Springer.

Leach, J., & Griffith, R. (2008). Restrictions in working memory capacity during parachuting: A possible cause of "no pull" fatalities. *Applied Cognitive Psychology, 22*, 147–157.

Lecoultre, V., & Schutz, Y. (2009). Effects of a small dose of alcohol on the endurance performance of trained cyclists. *Alcohol & Alcoholism, 44*, 278–283.

Leddy, M. H., Lambert, M. J., Ogles, B. M. (1994). *Research Quarterly for Exercise and Sport, 65*, 347–354.

Lederman, D. (2005, October 21). Bradley's "Braves" stays on NCAA "hostile" list. Retrieved from http://www.Insidehighered.com.

Lee, C. C., & Rotella, R. J. (1991). Special concerns and considerations for sport psychology consulting with black student athletes. *The Sport Psychologist, 5*, 365–369.

Lee, D. J. (2010). Adrenal fatigue syndrome, Part 2: Adrenal function and overtraining. *Athletic Therapy Today, 15*, 28–31.

Leerhsen, C. & Barrett, T. (1990, May 14). Teen queen of tennis. *Newsweek, 115*(20), 58–63.

Lefebvre, L. M., & Cunningham, J. D. (1977). The successful football team: Effects of coaching and team cohesiveness. *International Journal of Sport Psychology, 8*, 29–41.

Legrain, P., d'Arripe-Longueville, F., & Gernigon, C. (2003a). The influence of trained peer tutoring on tutors' motivation and performance in a French boxing setting. *Journal of Sports Sciences, 21*, 539–550.

Legrain, P., d'Arripe-Longueville, F., & Gernigon, C. (2003b). Peer tutoring in a sport setting: Are there any benefits for tutors? *The Sport Psychologist, 17*, 77–94.

Legrand, F., & Heuze, J. P. (2007). Antidepressant effects associated with different exercise conditions in participants with depression: A pilot study. *Journal of Sport & Exercise Psychology, 29*, 348–364.

Lehrer, P. M. (1982). How to relax and how not to relax: A re-evaluation of the work of Edmund Jacobson. *Behaviour Research and Therapy, 20*, 417–428.

Lehrer, P. M. (1987). A review of the approaches to the management of tension and stage fright in musical performance. *Journal of Research in Music Education, 35*, 143–152.

Lehrer, P., & Carr, R. (1997). Progressive relaxation. In W. T. Roth (Ed.), *Treating anxiety disorders* (pp. 83–116). San Francisco, CA: Jossey-Bass.

Lehrer, P. M., Carr, R., Sargunaraj, D., Woolfolk, R. L. (1994). Stress management techniques: Are they all equivalent, or do they have specific effects? *Biofeedback and Self-Regulation, 19,* 353–401.

Lehrer, P. M., Woolfolk, R. L., Rooney, A. J., McCann, B., & Carrington, P. (1983). Progressive relaxation and meditation. A study of psychophysiological and thera-peutic differences between two techniques. *Behavior Research and Therapy, 21,* 651–662.

Leichliter, J., Meilman, P., Presley, C., & Cashin, J. (1998). Alcohol use and related consequences among college students with varying levels of involvement in college athletics. *Journal of College Health, 46,* 257–262.

Leith, K. P., & Baumeister, R. F. (1996). Why do bad moods increase self-defeating behavior? Emotion, risk taking, and self-regulation. *Journal of Personality and Social Psychology, 71,* 1250–1267.

Lemyre, P-N, Hall, H. K., & Roberts, G. C. (2008). A social cognitive approach to burnout in elite athletes. *Scandinavian Journal of Medicine & Science in Sports, 18,* 221–234. doi: 10.1111/j.1600–0838.2006.00671.x

Lemyre, P-N., Roberts, G. C., & Ommundsen, Y. (2002). Achievement goal orienta-tions, perceived ability, and sportspersonship in youth soccer. *Journal of Applied Sport Psychology, 14,* 120–136.

Lemyre, P-N, Treasure, D. C., & Roberts, G. C. (2006). Influence of variability in mo-tivation and affect on elite athlete burnout susceptibility. *Journal of Sport & Exercise Psychology, 28,* 32–48.

Lent, R. W., & Lopez, F. G. (2002). Cognitive ties that bind: A tripartite view of efficacy beliefs in growth-promoting relationships. *Journal of Social and Clinical Psychology, 21,* 256–286.

Leonard, W. M. (1989). The "home advantage": The case of the modern Olympiads. *Journal of Sport Behavior, 12,* 227–241.

Lerner, B. S., & Locke, E. A. (1995). The effects of goal setting, self-efficacy, competition, and personal traits on performance of an endurance task. *Journal of Sport & Exercise Psychology, 17,* 138–152.

LeUnes, A., & Burger, J. (2000). Profile of mood states research in sport and exercise psychology: Past, present, and future. *Journal of Applied Sport Psychology, 12,* 5–15.

Levitt, S., & Gutin, B. (1971). Multiple choice reaction time and movement time during physical exertion. *Research Quarterly, 42,* 405–410, 423–433.

Levy, A. R., Polman, R. C. J., Clough, P. J. (2008). Adherence to sport injury rehabilitation programs: an integrated psycho-social approach. *Scandinavian Journal of Medicine & Science in Sports, 18,* 798–809. doi: 10.1111/j.1600–0838.2007.00704.x

Lewis, B. P., & Linder, D. E. (1997). Thinking about choking? Attentional processes and paradoxical performance. *Personality and Social Psychology Bulletin, 23,* 937–944.

Lewis, T. F. (2008). An explanatory model of student-athlete drinking: The role of team leadership, social norms, perceptions of risk, and coaches' attitudes toward alcohol consumption. *College Student Journal, 42,* 818–831.

Li, F. (1999). The exercise motivation scale: Its multifaceted structure and construct validity. *Journal of Applied Sport Psychology, 11,* 97–115.

Li, K-K., & Chan, D. K.-S. (2008). Goal conflict and the moderating effects of inten-tion stability in intention-behavior relations: Physical activity among Hong Kong Chinese. *Journal of Sport & Exercise Psychology, 30,* 39–55.

Liao, C-M, & Masters, R. S. W. (2002). Self-focused attention and performance failure under psychological stress. *Journal of Sport & Exercise Psychology, 24,* 289–305.

Lidor, R. (2007). Preparatory routines in self-paced events. In G. Tenenbaum & R. C. Eklund (Eds.), *Handbook of sport psychology* (3rd ed., pp. 445–465). New York, NY: Wiley.

Lidor, R., & Mayan, Z. (2005). Can beginning learners benefit from preperformance routines when serving in volleyball? *Sport Psychologist, 19,* 343–363.

Lidz, F. (1996, December 23). Different strokes. *Sports Illustrated, 85,* 122–123.

Lincoln, Y. S., & Guba, E. G. (1985) *Naturalistic inquiry.* Newbury Park, CA: Sage Publications.

Linden, W. (1990). *Autogenic training. A clinical guide.* New York, NY: Guilford.

Linden, W. (1994). Autogenic training: A narrative and quantitative review of clinical outcome. *Biofeedback and self-regulation, 19,* 227–264.

Linder, D. E., Brewer, B. W., Van Raalte, J. L., & De Lange, N. (1991). A negative halo for athletes who consult sport psychologists: Replication and extension. *Journal of Sport and Exercise Psychology, 13,* 133–148.

Lindman, H. R. (1974). *Analysis of variance in complex experimental designs.* San Francisco, CA: W. H. Freeman.

Lindsley, D. H., Brass, D. J., & Thomas, J. B. (1995). Efficacy-performance spirals: A multilevel perspective. *Academy of Management Review, 20,* 645–678.

Linver, M. R., Roth, J. L., & Brooks-Gunn, J. (2009). Patterns of adolescents' participation in organized activities: Are sports best when combined with other activities? *Developmental Psychology, 45,* 354–367. doi: 10.1037/a0014133

Litsky, F. (2005, December 14). Steroids, expulsions & suspensions, track & field, drugs & sports. *The New York Times.* D3.

Lobo, R. (2012, June 16). Rebecca Lobo: Empowered by Title IX. *The Hartford Courant.* Retrieved from http://www.courant.com

Locke, E. A. (1996). Motivation through conscious goal setting. *Applied and Preventive Psychology, 5,* 117–124.

Locke, E. A., & Latham, G. P. (2002). Building a practically useful theory of goal setting and task motivation: A 35-year odyssey. *American Psychologist, 57,* 705–717.

Locke, E. A., Latham, G. P., & Erez, M. (1988). The determinants of goal commitment. *Academy of Management Review, 13,* 22–39.

Logan, G. D. (1988). Towards an instance theory of automatization. *Psychological Review, 95,* 492–527.

Lohasz, P. G., & Leith, L. M. (1997). The effect of three mental preparation strategies on the performance of a complex response time task. *International Journal of Sport Psychology, 28,* 25–34.

Lohr, B. A., & Scogin, F. (1998). Effects of self-administered visuo-motor behavior rehearsal on sport performance of collegiate athletes. *Journal of Sport Behavior, 21,* 206–218.

Long, B. C., & Haney, C. J. (1988). Long-term follow-up of stressed working women: A comparison of aerobic exercise and progressive relaxation. *Journal of Sport & Exercise Psychology, 10,* 461–470.

Longman, J. (2010, June 22). Loss completes France's dishonor. *The New York Times.* Retrieved from http://www.nytimes.com

Longman, J. (2012, July 29). A giant leap for women, but hurdles remain. *The New York Times.* Retrieved from http://www.nytimes.com

Lonsdale, C., Hodge, K., & Rose, E. (2009). Athlete burnout in elite sport: A self-determination perspective. *Journal of Sports Sciences, 27,* 875–795.

Lopez-Frias, M., De La Fe Fernandez, M., Planells, E., Miranda, M. T., Mataix, J., & Llopis, J. (2001). Alcohol consumption and academic performance I a population of Spanish high school students. *Journal of Studies on Alcohol, 62,* 741–744.

Lorimer, R. (2006). The relationship between self-presentational concerns and competitive anxiety: The influence of gender. *International Journal of Sport Psychology, 37,* 317–329.

Lorimer, R., & Jowett, S. (2009). Empathic accuracy, meta-perspective, and satisfaction in the coach-athlete relationship. *Journal of Applied Sport Psychology, 21,* 201–212.

Loughead, T. M., Hardy, J., & Eys, M. A. (2006). The nature of athlete leadership. *Journal of Sport Behavior, 29,* 142–158.

Louis, M., Collet, C., & Guillot, A. (2011). Differences in motor imagery times during aroused and relaxed conditions. *Journal of Cognitive Psychology, 23,* 374–382.

Lubker, J. R., Visek, A. J., Geer, J. R., & Watson, J. C. II. (2008). Characteristics of an effective sport psychology consultant: Perspectives from athletes and consultants. *Journal of Sport Behavior, 31,* 147–165.

Lundgren, T., Dahl, J., Melin, L., & Kies, B. (2006). Evaluation of acceptance and commitment therapy for drug refractory epilepsy: A randomized controlled trial in South Africa—a pilot study. *Epilepsia, 47,* 2173–2179.

Lundgren, T., Dahl, J, Yardi, N., & Melin, L. (2008). Acceptance and commitment therapy and yoga for drug-refractory epilepsy: A randomized controlled trial. *Epilepsy & Behavior, 13,* 102–108. doi: 10.1016/j.yebeh.2008.02.009

Lundh, L. G. (2004). Perfectionism and acceptance. *Journal of Rational-Emotive and Cognitive-Behavioral Therapy, 22,* 255–269.

Lundqvist, C., Kentta, G., & Raglin, J. S. (2011). Directional anxiety responses in elite and sub-elite young athletes: Intensity of anxiety symptoms matter. *Scandinavian Journal of Medicine & Science in Sports, 21,* 853–862. doi: 10.1111/j.1600–0838.2010.01102.x

Luszczynska, A., Schwarzer, R., Lippke, S., & Mazurkiewicz, M. (2011). Self-efficacy as a moderator of the planning-behaviour relationship in interventions designed to promote physical activity. *Psychology and Health, 26,* 151–166. doi: 10.1080/08870446.2001.531571

Luthe, W. (1970). *Autogenic therapy, Vol. IV: research and theory.* New York, NY: Grune & Stratton.

Lynskey, M., & Hall, W. (2000). The effects of adolescent cannabis use on educational attainment. *Addiction, 95,* 1621–1630.

MacAndrew, C. (1980). Male alcoholics, secondary psychopathy, and Eysenck's theory of personality. *Personality and Individual Differences, 1,* 151–160.

MacAndrew, C. (1981). What the MAC scale tells us about alcoholics: An interpretive review. *Journal of Studies on Alcohol, 42,* 604–625.

MacDonald, D. J., Cote, J., Eys, M., & Deakin, J. (2011). The role of enjoyment and motivational climate in relation to the personal development of team sport athletes. *The Sport Psychologist, 25,* 32–46.

MacIntyre, T., & Moran, A. (2007a). A qualitative investigation of imagery use and meta-imagery processes among elite canoe-slalom competitors. *Journal of Imagery Research in Sport and Physical Activity, 2,* article 3, 1–23.

MacIntyre, T., & Moran, A. (2007b). A qualitative investigation of meta-imagery processes and imagery direction among elite athletes. *Journal of Imagery Research in Sport and Physical Activity, 2,* article 4, 1–20.

MacIntyre, T., & Moran, A. (2010). Meta-imagery processes among elite sports performers. In A. Guillot & C. Collet (Eds.), *The neuropsychological foundations of mental and motor imagery* (pp. 227–244). Oxford, England: Oxford University Press.

Mach, M., Dolan, S., & Tzafrir, S. (2010). The differential effect of team members' trust on team performance: The mediation role of team cohesion. *Journal of Occupational and Organizational Psychology, 83,* 771–794. doi: 10.1348/096317909X473903

MacLean, C.R.K., Walton, K. G., Wenneberg, S. R., Levitsky, D. K., Mandarino, J. P., Waziri, R., Hillis, S. L., & Schneider, R. H. (1997). Effects of the Transcendental Meditation program on adaptive mechanisms: Changes in hormone levels and responses to stress after 4 months of practice. *Psychoneuroendocrinology, 22,* 277–295.

MacLeod, C. (1996). Anxiety and cognitive processes. In I. G. Sarason, G. R. Pierce, & B. R. Sarason (Eds.), *Cognitive interference theories, methods, and findings* (pp. 47–76). Mahwah, NJ: Lawrence Erlbaum Associates.

Macquet, A. C. (2009). Recognition within the decision-making process: A case study of expert volleyball players. *Journal of Applied Sport Psychology, 21,* 64–79.

Macur, J. (2012, July 26). Once told he'd never walk again, Irish gymnast is not Olympian. Retrieved from http://www.nytimes.com

Madden, C. C., Kirby, R. J., & McDonald, D. (1989). Coping styles of competitive middle distance runners. *International Journal of Sport Psychology, 20,* 287–296.

Maddison, R., & Prapavessis, H. (2005). A Psychological Approach to the Prediction and Prevention of Athletic Injury. *Journal of Sport & Exercise Psychology, 27,* 289–300.

Maddison, R., & Prapavessis, H. (2007). Self-handicapping in sport: A self-presentation strategy. In S. Jowett & D. Lavallee (Eds.), *Social psychology in sport* (pp. 209–220). Champaign, IL: Human Kinetics.

Magyar, T. M., & Duda, J. L. (2000). Confidence restoration following athletic injury. *The Sport Psychologist, 14,* 372–390.

Magyar, T. M., Feltz, D. L., & Simpson, I. P. (2004). Individual and crew level determinants of collective efficacy in rowing. *Journal of Sport & Exercise Psychology, 26,* 136–153.

Mahalik, J. R., & Burns, S. M. (2011). Predicting health behaviors in young men that put them at risk for heart disease. *Psychology of Men and Masculinity, 12,* 1–12. doi: 10.1037/a00021416

Mahoney, J. L., Larson, R. W., Eccles, J. S., & Lord, H. (2005). Organized activities as developmental contexts for children and adolescents. In J. L. Mahoney, R. W. Larson, & J. S. Eccles (Eds.), *Organized activities as contexts of development* (pp. 3–22). Mahwah, NJ: Lawrence Erlbaum Associates.

Mahoney, M. J. (1989). Psychological predictors of elite and non-elite performance in Olympic weightlifting. *International Journal of Sport Psychology, 20,* 1–12.

Mahoney, M. J., & Avener, M. (1977). Psychology of the elite athlete: An exploratory study. *Cognitive Therapy and Research, 1,* 135–141.

Mahoney, M. J., Gabriel, T. J., & Perkins, T. S. (1987). Psychological skills and exceptional athletic performance. *The Sport Psychologist, 1,* 181–199.

Mahoney, P. J. (1997). Freud: Man at work. In C. W. Socarides and S. Kramer (Eds.), *Work and its inhibitions: Psychoanalytic essays* (pp. 79–98). Madison, CT: International Universities Press.

Maior, A. S., Simao, R., de Salles, B. F., Alexander, J. L., Rhea, M., & Nascimento, J.H.M. (2010). Acute cardiovascular response in anabolic androgenic steroid users performing maximal treadmill exercise testing. *Journal of Strength and Conditioning Research, 24,* 1688–1695.

Majors, R. (1998). Cool pose: Black masculinity and sports. In G. Sailes (Ed.), *African Americans in sport* (pp. 15–22). New Brunswick, NJ: Transaction.

Malete, L., & Feltz, D. L. (2000). The effect of a coaching education program on coaching efficacy. *The Sport Psychologist, 14,* 410–417.

Malinauskas, M. (2010). The association among social support, stress, and life satisfaction as perceived by injured college athletes. *Social Behavior and Personality, 38,* 741–752. doi: 10.2224/sbp.2010.38.6.741

Mallett, C. J., & Hanrahan, S. J. (2004). Elite athletes: why does the "fire" burn so brightly? *Psychology of Sport and Exercise, 5,* 183–200.

Malone, D. A., Dimeff, R. J., Lombardo, J. A., & Sample, R.H.B. (1995). Psychiatric effects and psychoactive substance use in anabolic-androgenic steroid users. *Clinical Journal of Sport Medicine, 5*, 25–31.

Malouff, J. M., McGee, J. A., Halford, H. T., & Rooke, S. E. (2008). Effects of pre-competition positive imagery and self-instructions on accuracy of serving in tennis. *Journal of Sport Behavior, 31*, 264–275.

Mamassis, G., & Doganis, G. (2004). The effects of a mental training program on junior's pre-competitive anxiety, self-confidence, and tennis performance. *Journal of Applied Sport Psychology, 16*, 118–137. doi: 10.1080/10413200490437903

Mandel, S. (2011, November 28). Meyer's latest change of heart will wake Ohio State from nightmare. *Sports Illustrated.* Retrieved from http://www.si.com

Mandela, N. (1994). *Long walk to freedom. The autobiography of Nelson Mandela.* Boston, MA: Little, Brown, and Company.

Maniar, S. D., Curry, L. A., Sommers-Flanagan, J., & Walsh, J. A. (2001). Student-athlete preferences in seeking help when confronted with sport performance problems. *The Sport Psychologist, 15*, 205–233.

Maraniss, D. (1999). *When pride still mattered. A life of Vince Lombardi.* New York, NY: Simon & Schuster.

Marcos, F.M.L., Miguel, P.A.S., Olivia, D. S., & Calvo, T. G. (2010). Interactive effects of team cohesion on perceived efficacy in semi-professional sport. *Journal of Sports Science and Medicine, 9*, 320–325.

Marin, G. (1993). Influence of acculturation on familialism and self-identification among Hispanics. In M. E. Bernal & G. P. Knight (Eds.), *Ethnic identity: Formation and transmission among Hispanics and other minorities* (pp. 181–196). Albany, NY: State University of New York Press.

Markman, A. B., Maddox, W. T., & Worthy, D. A. (2006). Choking and excelling under pressure. *Psychological Science, 17*, 944–948.

Marks, D. R. (2008). The Buddha's extra scoop: Neural correlates of mindfulness practice and their relevance for clinical sport psychology. *Journal of Clinical Sports Psychology, 2*, 216–241.

Markus, H. R., & Kitayama, S. (1991). Culture and the self: Implications for cognition, emotion, and motivation. *Psychological Review, 98*, 224–253.

Marquez, D. X., Neighbors, C. J., & Bustamante, E. E. (2010). Leisure time and occupational physical activity among racial or ethnic minorities. *Medicine & Science in Sports & Exercise, 42*, 1086–1093. doi: 10.1249/MSS. 0b013e3181c5ec05

Martens, M. P., Mobley, M., Zizzi, S. J. (2000). Multicultural training in applied sport psychology. *The Sport Psychologist, 14*, 81–97.

Martens, M. P., Watson, J. C. II, & Beck, N. C. (2006). Sport-type differences in alcohol use among intercollegiate athletes. *Journal of Applied Sport Psychology, 18*, 136–150.

Martens, M. P., Watson, J. C., Royland, E. M., & Beck, N. C. (2005). Development of the athlete drinking scale. *Psychology of Addictive Behaviors, 19*, 158–164.

Martens, R. (1977). *Sport Competition Anxiety Test.* Champaign, IL: Human Kinetics.

Martens, R. (1979). About smocks and jocks. *Journal of Sport Psychology, 1*, 94–99.

Martens, R. (1987). *Coaches guide to sport psychology.* Champaign, IL: Human Kinetics.

Martens, R., Burton, D., Vealey, R, Bump, L., & Smith, D. (1990). The development of the Competitive State Anxiety Inventory-2. In R. Martens, R. S. Vealey, & D. Burton (Eds.), *Competitive anxiety in sport* (pp. 117–190). Champaign, IL: Human Kinetics.

Martin, L. J., Carron, A. V., & Burke, S. M. (2009). Team building interventions in sport: A meta-analysis. *Sport & Exercise Psychology Review, 5*, 3–18.

Martha, C., Sanchez, X., & Goma-i-Freixanet, M. (2009). Risk perception as a function of risk exposure amongst rock climbers. *Psychology of Sport and Exercise, 10*, 193–200. doi: 10.1016/j.psychsport.2009.07.004

Martin, A. J., Marsh, H. W., & Debus, R. L. (2001). Self-handicapping and defensive pessimism: Exploring a model of predictors and outcomes from a self-protection perspective. *Journal of Educational Psychology, 93*, 87–102.

Martin, B. A., & Martin, J. H. (1995). Comparing perceived sex role orientations of the ideal male and female athlete to the ideal male and female. *Journal of Sport Behavior, 18*, 286–301.

Martin, B. A., & Murberger, M. A. (1994). Effects of self-esteem and assigned goals on actual and perceived performance. *Journal of Social Behavior and Personality, 9*, 81–87.

Martin, J. J., Kelley, B., & Eklund, R. C. (1999). A model of stress and burnout in male high school athletic directors. *Journal of Sport and Exercise Psychology, 21*, 280–294.

Martin, K. A., & Brawley, L. R. (2002). Self-handicapping in physical achievement settings: The contributions of self-esteem and self-efficacy. *Self and Identity, 1*, 337–351.

Martin, K. A., & Hall, C. R. (1995). Using mental imagery to enhance intrinsic motivation. *Journal of Sport & Exercise Psychology, 17*, 54–69.

Martin, K. A., Moritz, S. E., & Hall, C. R. (1999). Imagery use in sport: A literature review and applied model. *The Sport Psychologist, 13*, 245–268.

Martin, L. J., & Carron, A. V. (2012). Team attributions in sport: A meta-analysis. *Journal of Applied Sport Psychology, 23,* 157–174. doi: 10.1080/10413200.2011.607486

Martin, S. B. (2005). High school and college athletes' attitudes toward sport psychology consulting. *Journal of Applied Sport Psychology, 17,* 127–139.

Martin, S. B., Akers, A., Jackson, A. W., Wrisberg, C. A., Nelson, L., Leslie, P. J., & Leidig, L. (2001). Male and female athletes' and nonathletes' expectations about sport psychology consulting. *Journal of Applied Sport Psychology, 13,* 19–40.

Martin, S. B., Jackson, A. W., Richardson, P. A., & Weiller, K. H. (1999). Coaching preferences of adolescent youths and their parents. *Journal of Applied Sport Psychology, 11,* 247–262.

Martin, S. B., Wrisberg, C. A., Beitel, P. A., & Lounsbury, J. (1997). NCAA Division I athletes' attitudes toward seeking sport psychology consultation: The development of an objective instrument. *The Sport Psychologist, 11,* 201–218.

Martin Ginis, K. A., Eng, J. J., Arbour, K. P., Hartman, J. W., & Phillips, S. M. (2005). Mind over muscle? Sex differences in the relationship between body image change and subjective and objective physical changes following a 12-week strength-training program. *Body Image, 2,* 363–372. doi: 10.1016/j.bodyim.2005.08.003

Martin-Krumm, C. P., Sarrazin, P. G., Peterson, C., & Famose, J-P. (2003). Explanatory style and resilience after sports failure. *Personality and Individual Differences, 35,* 1685–1695.

Martinek, T. J. (1996). Fostering hope in youth: A model for explaining learned helplessness in physical activity. *Quest, 48,* 409–421.

Martinent, G., & Ferrand, C. (2007). A cluster analysis of precompetitive anxiety: Relationship with perfectionism and trait anxiety. *Personality and Individual Differences, 43,* 1676–1686. doi: 10.1016/j.paid.2007.05.005

Martinent, G., & Ferrand, C. (2009). A naturalistic study of the directional interpretation process of discrete emotions during high-stakes table tennis matches. *Journal of Sport and Exercise Psychology, 31,* 318–336.

Martinsen, E., & Raglin, J. (2007). Themed review: Anxiety/depression. *American Journal of Lifestyle Medicine, 1,* 159–166.

Maslach, C., & Jackson, S. E. (1981). The measurement of experienced burnout. *Journal of Occupational Psychology, 2,* 99–113.

Maslach, C., & Jackson, S. E. (1986). *Maslach burnout inventory manual* (2nd ed.). Palo Alto, CA: Consulting Psychologists Press.

Maslach, C., & Schaufeli, W. B. (1993). Historical and conceptual development of burnout. In W. B. Schaufeli, C. Maslach, & T. Marek (Eds.), *Professional burnout: Recent developments in theory and research* (pp. 1–16). Philadelphia, PA: Taylor & Francis.

Maslow, A. (1973). Deficiency motivation and growth motivation. In D. C. McClelland & R. S. Steele (Eds.), *Human motivation. A book of readings* (pp. 233–251). Morristown, NJ: General Learning Press.

Maso, F., Lac, G., Filaire, E., Michaux, O., & Robert, A. (2004). Salivary testosterone and cortisol in rugby layers: Correlation with psychological overtraining items. *British Journal of Sports Medicine, 38,* 260–263. doi: 10.1136/bjsm.2003.000254

Masson, J. F. (1985). *The complete letters of Sigmund Freud to Wilhelm Fliess.* Cambridge, MA: Harvard University Press. (Original work published 1887–1904).

Masters, R.S.W. (1992). Knowledge, nerves, and know-how: The role of explicit versus implicit knowledge in the breakdown of a complex motor skill under pressure. *British Journal of Psychology, 83,* 343–358.

Masters, R.S.W. (2000). Theoretical aspects of implicit learning in sport. *International Journal of Sports Psychology, 31,* 530–541.

Masters, R.S.W., & Maxwell, J. P. (2004). Implicit motor learning, reinvestment and movement disruption: What you don't know won't hurt you. In A. M. Williams & N. J. Hodges (Eds.), *Skill acquisition in sport: Research, theory, and practice* (pp. 207–228). London, England: Routledge.

Masters, R.S.W., Polman, R.C.J., & Hammond, N. V. (1993). "Reinvestment": A dimension of personality implicated in skill breakdown under pressure. *Personality and Individual Differences, 14,* 655–666.

Mata, J., Hogan, C. L., Joormann, J., Waugh, C. E., & Gotlib, I. H. (2012, Sept. 17). Acute exercise attenuates negative affect following repeated sad mood inductions in persons who have recovered from depression. *Journal of Abnormal Psychology,* 1–6. doi: 10.1037/a0029881

Mata, J., Silva, M. N., Vieiera, P. N., Carraca, E. V., Andrade, A. M., Coutinho, S. R.,. . . Teixeira, P. J. (2011). Motivational "spill-over" during weight control: Increased self-determination and exercise intrinsic motivation predict eating self-regulation. *Sport, Exercise, and Performance Psychology, 1,* 49–59. doi: 10.1037/2157-3905.1.S.49

Matheson, H., & Mathes, S. (1997). The effect of winning and losing on female interactive and coactive team cohesion. *Journal of Sport Behavior, 20,* 284–298.

Mattie, P., & Munroe-Chandler, K. (2012). Examining the relationship between mental toughness and imagery use. *Journal of Applied Sport Psychology, 24,* 144–156. doi: 10.1080/10413200.2001.605422

Maughan, R. J. (2006). Alcohol and football. *Journal of Sports Sciences, 24,* 741–748.

May, J. R., & Brown, L. (1989). Delivery of psychological services to the U.S. Alpine ski team prior to and during the Olympics in Calgary. *The Sport Psychologist, 3,* 320–329.

Maynard, I. W., Hemmings, B., Warwick-Evans, L. (1995). The effects of a somatic intervention strategy on competitive state anxiety and performance in semiprofessional soccer players. *The Sport Psychologist, 9,* 51–64.

Maynard, I. W., Warwick-Evans, L., & Smith, M. J. (1995). The effects of a cognitive intervention strategy on competitive state anxiety and performance in semiprofessional soccer players. *Journal of Sport and Exercise Psychology, 17,* 428–446.

McArdle, S., & Duda, J. L. (2008). Exploring the etiology of perfectionism and perceptions of self-worth in young adults. *Social Development, 17,* 980–997.

McArdle, S. (2010). Exploring domain-specific perfectionism. *Journal of Personality, 78,* 493–508. doi: 10.1111/j.1467-6494.2010.00624.x

McAuley, E. (1994). Enhancing psychological health through physical activity. In H. A. Quinney, L. Gauvin, & A.E.T. Wall (Eds.), *Toward active living: proceedings of the International Conference on Physical Activity, Fitness, and Health* (pp. 83–90). Champaign, IL: Human Kinetics.

McAuley, E., Blissmer, B., Katula, J., Duncan, T. E., & Mihalko, S. L. (2000). Physical activity, self-esteem, and self-efficacy relationships in older adults: A randomized controlled trial. *Annals of Behavioral Medicine, 22,* 131–139.

McAuley, E., Duncan, T. E., Wraith, S. C., & Lettunich, M. (1991). Self-efficacy, perceptions of success, and intrinsic motivation. *Journal of Applied Social Psychology, 21,* 139–155.

McAuley, E., Marquez, D. X., Jerome, G. J., Blissmer, B., & Katula, J. (2002). Physical activity and physique anxiety in older adults: Fitness and efficacy influences. *Aging and Mental Health, 6,* 222–230.

McAuley, E., & Mihalko, S. L. (1998). Measuring exercise-related self-efficacy. In J. L. Duda (Ed.), *Advances in sort and exercise psychology measurement* (pp. 371–390). Morgantown, WV: Fitness Information Technology.

McAuley, E., Mullen, S. P., Szabo, A. N., White, S. M., Wojcicki, T. R., Mailey, E. L., . . . Kramer, A. F. (2011). Self-regulatory processes and exercise adherence in older adults: Executive function and self-efficacy effects. *American Journal of Preventive Medicine, 41,* 284–290. doi: 10.1016/j.amere.2011.04.014

McCabe, S. E., Brower, K. J., West, B. T., Nelson, T. F., & Wechsler, H. (2007). Trends in non-medical use of anabolic steroids by U.S. college students: Results from four national surveys. *Drug and Alcohol Dependence, 2-3,* 243–251.

McCarthy, P. J., & Jones, M. V. (2007). A qualitative study of sport enjoyment in the sampling years. *The Sport Psychologist, 21,* 400–416.

McCarthy, P. J., Jones, M. V., & Clark-Carter, D. (2008). Understanding enjoyment in youth sport: A developmental perspective. *Psychology of Sport and Exercise, 9,* 142–156.

McCarthy, P. J., Jones, M. V., Harwood, C. G., & Davenport, L. (2010). Using goal setting to enhance positive affect among junior multievent athletes. *Journal of Clinical Sport Psychology, 4,* 53–68. doi: 10.1016/j.psychsport.2007.01.005

McCarthy, P. J., Jones, M. V., Harwood, C. G., & Olivier, S. (2010). What do young athletes implicitly understand about psychological skills? *Journal of Clinical Sport Psychology, 4,* 158–172.

McCormick, R. E., & Tollison, R. D. (2001). Why do black basketball players work more for less money? *Journal of Economic Behavior & Organization, 44,* 201–219.

McCown, M., & Johnson, J. (1989, May). *Differential arousal gradients in chronic procrastination.* Paper presented at the convention of the American Psychological Society, Alexandria, Vancouver.

McCullagh, P. & Noble, J. M. (2002). Education for becoming a sport psychologist. In J. L. Van Raalte & B. W. Brewer (Eds.), *Exploring sport and exercise psychology* (2nd ed., pp. 439–458). Washington, DC: American Psychological Association.

McCullagh, P. & Weiss, M. R. (2001). Modeling. Considerations for motor skill performance and psychological responses. In R. N. Singer, H. A. Hausenblas, & C. M. Janelle (Eds.), *Handbook of sport psychology* (2nd ed., pp. 205–238). New York, NY: Wiley.

McDaniel, K. D., Cummings, J. L., & Shain, S. (1989). The "yips": A focal dystonia in golfers. *Neurology, 39,* 192–195.

McDermott, B. (1986, August 25). Stormin' Norman. *Sports Illustrated, 65,* 72–76, 78–82, 84.

McDonald, S. A., & Hardy, C. J. (1990). Affective response patterns of the injured athlete: An exploratory analysis. *The Sport Psychologist, 4,* 261–274.

McElroy, M. A., & Willis, J. D. (1979). Women and the achievement conflict: A preliminary study. *Journal of Sport Psychology, 1,* 241–247.

McEnroe, J., & Kaplan, J. (2002). *You cannot be serious.* New York, NY: G. P. Putnam's Sons.

McGinnis, J. M., & Foege, W. H. (1993). Actual causes of death in the United States. *Journal of the American Medical Association, 270,* 2207–2212.

McGlone, S., & Shrier, I. (2000). Does sex the night before competition decrease performance? *Clinical Journal of Sport Medicine, 10,* 233–234.

McGuire, E. J., Courneya, K. S., Widmeyer, W. N., & Carron, A. V. (1992). Aggression as a potential mediator of the home advantage in professional ice hockey. *Journal of Sport and Exercise Psychology, 14,* 148–158.

McGrath, J. E. (1970). Major methodological issues. In J. E. McGrath (Ed.), *Social and psychological factors in stress* (pp. 19–49). New York, NY: Holt, Rinehart, & Winston.

McIntosh, F. (2010, January 31). Dad of the year? Or just bad of the year. *Mirror Online.* Retrieved from http://mirror.co.uk

McIntosh, W. D. (1996). When does goal nonattainment lead to negative emotional reactions, and when doesn't it? The role of linking and rumination. In L. M. Martin, & A. Tesser (Eds.), *Striving and feeling. Interactions among goals, affect, and self-regulation* (pp. 53–77). Mahwah, NJ: Lawrence Erlbaum.

McKay, J. M., Selig, S. E., Carlson, J. S., & Morris, T. (1997). Psychophysiological stress in elite golfers during practice and competition. *The Australian Journal of Science and Medicine in Sport, 29,* 55–61.

McKenzie, A. D., & Howe, B. L. (1997). The effect of imagery on self-efficacy for a motor skill. *International Journal of Sport Psychology, 28,* 196–210.

McKenzie, D. C. (1999). Markers of excessive exercise. *Canadian Journal of Applied Physiology, 24,* 66–73.

McLeod, T.C.V., Decoster, L. C., Loud, K. J., Micheli, L. J., Parker, J. T., Sandrey, M. A., & White, C. (2011). National athletic trainers' association position statement: Prevention of pediatric overuse injuries. *Journal of Athletic Training, 46,* 206–220.

McNair, D. M., Lorr, M., & Droppleman, L. F. (1971). *Profile of mood states manual.* San Diego, CA: Educational and Industrial Testing Service.

McNally, J., & Orlick, T. (1975) Cooperative sport structures: A preliminary analysis. *Movement, 7,* 267–271.

McNamara, J., & McCabe, M. P. (2012). Striving for success or addiction? Exercise dependence among elite Australian athletes. *Journal of Sports Sciences, 30,* 755–766.

Meaney, K. S., Dornier, L. A., & Owens, M. S. (2002). Sex-role stereotyping for selected sport and physical activities across age groups. *Perceptual and Motor Skills, 94,* 743–749.

Mednick, M. T., & Thomas, V. G. (1993). Women and the psychology of achievement: A view from the eighties. In F. L. Denmark, M. A. Paludi (Eds.), *Psychology of women: A handbook of issues and theories* (pp. 585–625). Westport, CT: Greenwood Press.

Medwechuk, N., & Crossman, J. (1994). Effects of gender bias on the evaluation of male and female swim coaches. *Perceptual and Motor Skills, 78,* 163–196.

Meilman, P. W., Leichliter, J. S., & Presley, C. A. (1999). Greeks and athletes: Who drinks more? *College Health, 47,* 187–190.

Mellalieu, S. D., Hanton, S., & Fletcher, D. (2006). A competitive anxiety review: Recent directions in sport psychology research. In S. Hanton & S. D. Mellalieu (Eds.), *Literature reviews in sport psychology.* Hauppauge, NY: Nova Science.

Mellalieu, S. D., Hanton, S., & Jones, G. (2003). Emotional labeling and competitive anxiety in preparation and competition. *The Sport Psychologist, 17,* 157–174.

Mellalieu, S. D., Hanton, S., & O'Brien, M. (2004). Intensity and direction of competitive anxiety as a function of sport type and experience. *Scandinavian Journal of Science & Medicine in Sport, 14,* 326–334.

Mellalieu, S. D., Hanton, S., & Thomas, O. (2009). The effects of a motivational general-arousal imagery intervention upon preperformance symptoms in male rugby union players. *Psychology of Sport and Exercise, 10,* 175–185. doi: 10.1016/j.psychsport.2008.07.003

Mellalieu, S. D., Neil, R., Hanton, S., & Fletcher, D. (2009). Competition stress in sport performers: Stressors experienced in the competition environment. *Journal of Sports Sciences, 27,* 729–744. doi: 10.1080/02640410902889834

Memmert, D., & Furley, P. (2007). "I spy with my little eye!" Breadth of attention, inattentional blindness, and tactical decision making in team sports. *Journal of Sport & Exercise Psychology, 29,* 365–381.

Mend, H., & Federn, E. (1963). *Psychoanalysis and faith: The letters of Sigmund Freud and Oskar Pfister.* London, England: Hogarth Press.

Menzel, K. E., & Carrell, L. J. (1994). The relationship between preparation and performance in public speaking. *Communication Education, 43,* 17–26.

Merikangas, K. R., Mehta, R. L., Molnar, B. E., Walters, E. E., Swendsen, J. D., Aguilar-Gaziola, S., . . . & Kessler, R. C. (1998). Comorbidity of substance use disorders with mood and anxiety disorders: Results of the international consortium in psychiatric epidemiology. *Addictive Behaviors, 23,* 893–907.

Merom, D., Phongsaven, P., Wagner, R., Chey, T., Marnane, C., Steel, Z., Silove, D., & Bauman, A. (2008). Promoting walking as an adjunct intervention to group cognitive behavioral therapy for anxiety disorders—a pilot group randomized trial. *Journal of Anxiety Disorders, 22,* 959–968.

Mesagno, C., Marchant, D., & Morris, T. (2008). A pre-performance routine to alleviate choking in "choking-susceptible" athletes. *The Sport Psychologist, 22,* 439–457.

Metcalf, B., Henley, W., & Wilkin, T. (2012). Effectiveness of intervention on physical activity of children: Systematic review and meta-analysis of controlled trials with objectively measured outcomes (EarlyBird 54). *BMJ: British Medical Journal, 345,* 1–11.

Metheny, E. (1965). Symbolic forms of movement: The feminine image in sports. In E. Metheny (Ed.), *Connotations of movement in sport and dance* (pp. 43–56). Dubuque, IA: Brown.

Metzler, J. N., & Conroy, D. E. (2004). Structural validity of fear of success scale. *Measurement in Physical Education and Exercise Science, 8,* 89–108.

Meyer, C., & Taranis, L. (2011). Exercise in the eating disorders: Terms and definitions. *European Eating Disorders Review, 19,* 169–173. doi: 10.1002/erv.1121

Meyer, C., Taranis, L., Goodwin, H., & Haycraft, E. (2011). Compulsive exercise and eating disorders. *European Eating Disorders Review, 19,* 174–189. doi: 10.1002/erv.1122

Meyers, A. W., Whelan, J. P., & Murphy, S. M. (1996). Cognitive behavioral strategies in athletic performance enhancement. In M. Hersen, R. M. Eisler, & P. M. Miller (Eds.), *Progress in behavioral modification* (Vol. 30, pp. 137–164). Pacific Grove, CA: Brooks/Cole.

Meyers, M. C., & LeUnes, A. (1996). Psychological skills assessment and athletic performance in collegiate rodeo athletes. *Journal of Sport Behavior, 19,* 132–147.

Meyers, M. C., & Sterling, J. C. (1990). Precompetitive mood state changes in collegiate rodeo athletes. *Journal of Sport Behavior, 13,* 114–122.

Meyers, M. C., Stewart, C. C., Laurent, C. M., LeUnes, A. D., & Bourgeois, A. E. (2008). Coping skills of Olympic developmental soccer athletes. *International Journal of Sports Medicine, 29,* 987–993. doi: 10.1055/s-2008-1038679

Mezzich, A., Tarter, R., Kirisci, L., Clark, D., Buckstein, O., & Martin, C. (1993). Subtypes of early age onset alcoholism. *Alcoholism: Clinical and Experimental Research, 17,* 767–770.

Michie, S., Abraham, C., Whittington, C., McAteer, J., & Gupta, S. (2009). Effective techniques in healthy eating and physical activity interventions: A meta-analysis. *Health Psychology, 28,* 590–701. doi: 10.1037/a0016136

Midgley, C., Arunkumar, R., & Urdan, T. C. (1996). "If I don't do well tomorrow, there's a reason": Predictors of adolescents' use of academic self-handicapping strategies. *Journal of Educational Psychology, 88,* 423–434.

Midgley, C., & Urdan, T. (2001). Academic self-handicapping and achievement goals: A further examination. *Contemporary Educational Psychology, 26,* 61–75.

Mikulincer, M. (1986). Attributional processes in the learned helplessness paradigm: Behavioral effects of global attributions. *Journal of Personality and Social Psychology, 51,* 1248–1256.

Mikulincer, M. (1996). Mental rumination and learned helplessness: Cognitive shifts during helplessness training and their behavioral consequences. In I. G. Sarason, G. R. Pierce, & B. R. Sarason (Eds.), *Cognitive Interference. Theories, methods, and findings* (pp. 191–209). Mahwah, NJ: Lawrence Erlbaum Associates.

Millard, L. (1996). Differences in coaching behaviors of male and female high school soccer coaches. *Journal of Sport Behavior, 19,* 19–31.

Miller, B. P., & Miller, A. J. (1985). Psychological correlates of success in elite sportswomen. *International Journal of Sport Psychology, 16,* 289–295.

Miller, G. A. (1956). The magic number seven plus or minus two: Some limits on our capacity for processing information. *Psychological Review, 63,* 81–97.

Miller, W. R., & Rollnick, S. (2013). *Motivational interviewing: Helping people change (applications of motivational interviewing)* (3rd. ed.). New York, NY: Guilford.

Mills, K. D., Munroe, K. J., & Hall, C. R. (2001). The relationship between imagery and self-efficacy in competitive athletes. *Imagery, Cognition, and Personality, 20,* 33–39.

Milmo, C. (2003, July 14). Wife distraught after George Best's alcoholic relapse. *The Independent.* Retrieved from http://www.independent.co.uk

Milner, A. D., & Goodale, M. A. (1995). *The visual brain in action.* Oxford, England: Oxford University Press.

Mio, J. S., Barker-Hackett, L., & Tamambing, J. (2006). *Multicultural psychology: Understanding our diverse communities.* Boston, MA: McGraw-Hill.

Mischel, W., & Shoda, Y. (1995). A cognitive-affective system theory of personality: Reconceptualizing situations, dispositions, dynamics, and invariance in personality structure. *Psychological Review, 102,* 246–268.

Miyake, A., Friedman, N. P., Emerson, M. J., Witzki, A. H., Howerter, A., & Wager, T. D. (2000). The unity and diversity of executive functions and their contributions to complex "frontal lobe" tasks: A latent variable analysis. *Cognitive Psychology, 41,* 49–100.

Mokdad, A. J., Marks, J. S., Stroup, D. F., & Gerberding, J. L. (2004). Actual causes of death in the United States, 2000. *JAMA: Journal of the American Medical Association, 291,* 1238–1245.

Moll, J., Jordet, G., Pepping, G-J. (2010). Emotional contagion in soccer penalty shootouts: Celebration of individual success is associated with ultimate team success. *Journal of Sports Sciences, 28,* 983–992. doi: 10.1080/02640414.2010.484068

Mone, M. A., Baker, D. D., & Jeffries, F. (1995). Predictive validity and time dependency on self-efficacy, self-esteem, personal goals, and academic performance. *Educational and Psychological Measurement, 55,* 716–727.

Montgomery, C., & Fisk, J. E. (2007). Everyday memory deficits in ecstasy-polydrug users. *Journal of Psychopharmacology, 21,* 709–717.

Moore, M. J., & Werch, C. E. (2005). Sport and physical activity participation and substance use among adolescents. *Journal of Adolescent Health, 36,* 486–493. doi: 10.1016/j.adohealth.2004.02.031

Moore, Z. E. (2009). Theoretical and empirical developments of the mindfulness-acceptance-commitment (MAC) approach to performance enhancement. *Journal of Clinical Sports Psychology, 4,* 291–302.

Mor, S., Day, H. I., Flett, G. L., & Hewitt, P. L. (1995). Perfectionism, control, and components of performance anxiety in professional artists. *Cognitive Therapy and Research, 19,* 207–225.

Moran, A. (1996). *The psychology of concentration in sport performers.* East Sussex, England: Psychology Press.

Moran, A. P. (2009). Attention, concentration and thought management. In B. W. Brewer (Ed.), *Handbook of sports medicine and science, sport psychology* (pp. 18–29). Chichester, England: Wiley-Blackwell.

Moran, A. P. (2012). *Sport & exercise psychology* (2nd ed.). East Sussex, England: Routledge.

Moran, M. M., & Weiss, M. R. (2006). Peer leadership in sport: Links with friendship, peer acceptance, psychological characteristics, and athletic ability. *Journal of Applied Sport Psychology, 18,* 97–113.

Moran-Miller, K., & Flores, L. Y. (2011). Where are the women in women's sports? Predictors of female athletes' interest in a coaching career. *Research Quarterly for Exercise and Sport, 82,* 109–117. doi: 10/1080/02701367.2011.10599727

Morgan, L. K., Griffin, J., & Heyward, V. H. (1996). Ethnicity, gender, and experience effects on attributional dimensions. *The Sport Psychologist, 10,* 4–16.

Morgan, W. P. (1980, July). Test of champions: The iceberg profile. *Psychology Today, 14,* 92–99, 101, 108.

Morgan, W. P., Brown, D. R., Raglin, J. S., O'Connor, P. J., & Ellickson, K. A. (1987). Psychological monitoring of overtraining and staleness. *British Journal of Sports Medicine, 21,* 107

Morgan, W. P., & Johnson, R. W. (1978). Personality characteristics of successful and unsuccessful oarsmen. *International Journal of Sport Psychology, 9,* 119–133.

Moritz, S. E., Feltz, D. L., Fahrbach, K. R., & Mack, D. E. (2000). The relation of self-efficacy measures to sport performance: A meta-analytic review. *Research Quarterly for Exercise and Sport, 71,* 280–294.

Moritz, S. E., Martin, K. A., Hall, C. R., & Vadocz, E. (1996). What are confident athletes imaging? An examination of image content. *The Sport Psychologist, 10,* 171–197.

Morrell, E. M. (1986). Meditation and somatic arousal. *American Psychologist, 41,* 712–713.

Morris, J. N. (1994). Exercise in the prevention of coronary heart disease: Today's best buy in public health. *Medicine and Science in Sports and Exercise, 16,* 807–814.

Morris, R. L., & Kavussanu, M. (2008). Antecedents of approach-avoidance goals in sport. *Journal of Sports Sciences, 26,* 465–476. doi: 10.1080/02640410701579388

Morrow, J. R. Jr., Zhu, W., Franks, B. D., Meredith, M. D., & Spain, C. (2009). 1958–2008: 50 years of youth fitness tests in the United States. *Research Quarterly for Exercise and Sport, 80,* 1–11.

Motl, R. W., Dishman, R. K., Saunders, R., Dowda, M., Felton, G., & Pate, R. R. (2001). Measuring enjoyment of physical activity in adolescent girls. *American Journal of Preventive Medicine, 21,* 110–117.

Motl, R. W., Gliottoni, R. C., & Scott, J. A. (2007). Self-efficacy correlates with leg muscle pain during maximal and submaximal cycling exercise. *Journal of Pain, 8,* 583–587.

Motl, R. W., O'Connor, P. J., & Dishman, R. K. (2004). Effects of cycling exercise on state anxiety and the soleur H-reflex among males with low or high trait anxiety. *Psychophysiology, 41,* 96–105.

Mouratidis, A., & Michou, A. (2011). Perfectionism, self-determined motivation, and coping among adolescent athletes. *Psychology of Sport and Exercise, 12,* 355–367. doi: 10.1016/j.psychspor.2011.03.006

Mullen, B., & Cooper, C. (1994). The relation between group cohesiveness and performance: An integration. *Psychological Bulletin, 115,* 210–227.

Mullen, R., & Hardy, L. (2000). State anxiety and motor performance: Testing the conscious processing hypothesis. *Journal of Sports Sciences, 18,* 785–799.

Mullen, R., Hardy, L., & Tattersall, A. (2005). The effects of anxiety on motor performance: A test of the conscious processing hypothesis. *Journal of Sport and Exercise Psychology, 27,* 212–225.

Mullen, R., Lane, A., & Hanton, S. (2009). Anxiety symptom interpretation in high-anxious, defensive high-anxious, low-anxious and repressor sport performers. *Anxiety, Stress & Coping, 22,* 91–100. doi: 10.1080/10615800802203769

Müller-Riemenschneider, F., Reinhold, T., Nocon, M., & Willich, S. N. (2008). Long-term effectiveness of interventions promoting physical activity: A systematic review. *Preventive Medicine, 47,* 354–368. doi: 10.1016/j.ypmed.2008.07.006

Mumenthaler, M. S., & Taylor, J. L. (1999). Gender differences in moderate drinking effects. *Alcohol Health & Research World, 23,* 55–74.

Mummery, W. K., Schofield, G., & Perry, C. (2004). Bouncing back: The role of coping style, social support and self-concept in resilience of sport performance. *Athletic Insight: The Online Journal of Sport Psychology, 6.* Retrieved from http://www.athleticinsight.com

Munroe-Chandler, K., Hall, C., & Fishburne, G. (2008). Playing with confidence: The relationship between imagery use and self-confidence and self-efficacy in youth soccer players. *Journal of Sports Sciences, 26,* 1539–1546. doi: 10.1080/02640410802315419

Munroe-Chandler, K. J., Hall, C. R., Fishburne, G. J., Murphy, L., & Hall, N. D. (2012). Effects of a cognitive imagery intervention on the soccer skill performance of young athletes: Age and group comparisons. *Psychology of Sport and Exercise, 13,* 324–331. doi: 10.1016/j.psychsport.2011.12.006

Munroe-Chandler, K., Hall, C., Fishburne, G., & Strachan, L. (2007). Where, when and why young athletes use imagery: An examination of developmental differences. *Research Quarterly for Exercise and Sport, 78,* 103–116.

Muraven, M., & Baumeister, R. F. (2000). Self-regulation and depletion of limited resources: Does self-control resemble a muscle? *Psychological Bulletin, 126,* 247–259.

Murphy, A. (1998, May 25). Pro football: Taking his medicine Broncos loopy linebacker Bill Romanowski pops a plethora of pills and powders to keep his minerals in balance. To bad they don't do the same for his temper. *Sports Illustrated, 88,* 56–58, 61–63.

Murphy A. J. (2005). Life stories of Black male and female professionals: An inquiry into the salience of race and sports. *The Journal of Men's Studies, 13,* 313–325.

Murphy, J. (2007, September 18). Jack LaLanne on exercise: It's a "pain in the gluties." *Wall Street Journal.* Retrieved from http://www.wsj.com

Murphy, J. B. (1993). *The moral economy of labor: Aristotelian themes in economic theory.* New Haven, CT: Yale Press.

Murphy, S. M. (1994). Imagery interventions in sport. *Medicine and Science in Sports and Exercise, 26,* 486–494.

Murphy, S. M., & Martin, K. A. (2002). The use of imagery in sport. In T. S. Horn (Ed.), *Advances in sport psychology.* Champaign, IL: Human Kinetics.

Murphy, S. M., Nordin, S. M., & Cumming, J. (2008). Imagery in sport, exercise and dance. In T. S. Horn (Ed.), *Advances in sport and exercise psychology* (3rd ed.; pp. 297–324). Champaign, IL: Human Kinetics.

Murray, A. (2010). *The Wall Street Journal essential guide to management.* New York, NY: Harper.

Murray, N. P., & Janelle, C. M. (2003). Anxiety and performance: A visual search examination of the processing efficiency theory. *Journal of Sport and Exercise Psychology, 25,* 171–187.

Murray, M. C., Mann, B. L., & Mead, J. K. (2010). Leadership effectiveness. In J. M. Williams (Ed.), *Applied sport psychology: Personal growth to peak performance* (6th ed., pp. 106–131), New York, NY: McGraw-Hill.

Myers, D. G., & Diener, E. (1995). Who is happy? *Psychological Science, 6,* 10–19.

Myers, N. D., Feltz, D. L., & Short, S. E. (2004). Collective efficacy and team performance: A longitudinal study of collegiate football teams. *Group Dynamics, Theory, Research, and Practice, 8,* 126–138.

Myers, N. D., Paiement, C. A., & Feltz, D. L. (2007). Regressing team performance on collective efficacy: Considerations of temporal proximity and concordance. *Measurement in Physical Education and Exercise Science, 11,* 1–24.

Myers, N. D., Payment, C. A., & Feltz, D. L. (2004). Reciprocal relationships between collective efficacy and team performance in woman's ice hockey. *Group Dynamics: Theory, Research, and Practice, 8,* 182–195.

Myers, N. D., Vargas-Tonsing, T. M., & Feltz, D. L. (2005). Coaching efficacy in intercollegiate coaches: Sources, coaching behavior, and team variables. *Psychology of Sport and Exercise, 6,* 129–143.

Nation, J. R., & LeUnes, A. (1983). A personality profile of the black athlete in college football. *Psychology, 20,* 1–3.

NCAA Research Staff. (2001, June). *NCAA study of substance use habits of college student-athletes.* Indianapolis, IN: Author.

NCAA Research Staff. (2004). *1999–00 – 2003–04 NCAA student-athlete ethnicity report.* Indianapolis, IN: Author.

NCAA Research Staff. (2006). *2006 NCAA Report on the Federal Graduation-Rates Data.* Indianapolis, IN: Author.

Navarro, M., Miyamoto, N., van der Kamp, J., Morya, E., Ranvaud, R., & Savelsbergh, G. J. P. (2012). The effects of high pressure on the point of no return in simulated penalty kicks. *Journal of Sport & Exercise Psychology, 34,* 83–101.

Naveh-Benjamin, M. (1991). A comparison of training programs intended for different types of test-anxious students: Further support for an information-processing mode. *Journal of Educational Psychology, 83,* 134–139.

Navratilova, M. (2006). *Shape your self. My 6-step diet and fitness plan to achieve the best shape of your life.* New York, NY: Rodale.

Neil, R., Fletcher, D., Hanton, S., & Mellalieu, S. D. (2007). (Re)conceptualizing competition stress in sport performers. *Sport and Exercise Psychology Review, 3,* 23–29.

Neil, R., Mellalieu, S. D., & Hanton, S. (2006). Psychological skills usage and the competitive anxiety response as a function of skill level in rugby union. *Journal of Sports Science and Medicine, 5,* 415–423.

Neumeister, K. S. (2004). Perfectionism in gifted students: An overview of current research. *Gifted Education International, 23,* 254–263.

Nevill, A. M., & Holder, R. L. (1999). Home advantage in sport: An overview of studies on the advantage of playing at home. *Sports Medicine, 28,* 221–236.

Nevill, A. M., Balmer, N. J., & Williams, A. M. (2002). The influence of crowd noise and experience upon refereeing decisions in football. *Psychology of Sport and Exercise, 3,* 261–272.

Newcombe, P. A., & Boyle, G. J. (1995). High school students' sports personalities: Variations across participation level, gender, type of sport, and success. *International Journal of Sport Psychology, 26,* 277–294.

Newman, L. S., & Wadas, R. F. (1997). When the stakes are higher: Self-esteem instability and self-handicapping. *Journal of Social Behavior and Personality, 12,* 217–233.

Newmark, T. S., & Bogacki, D. F. (2005). The impact of injury on the adolescent athlete and the family. *Directions in Psychiatry, 25,* 91–99.

Newton, M., Duda, J. L., & Yin, Z. (2000). Examination of the psychometric properties of the Perceived Motivational Climate in Sport Qestionnaire-2 in a sample of female athletes. *Journal of Sport Sciences, 18,* 1–16.

Newton, M., Watson, D. L., Gano-Overway, L., Fry, M. D., Kim, M., & Magyar, M. (2007). The role of a caring-based intervention in a physical domain. *The Urban Review, 39,* 281–299. doi: 10.1007/s11256-007-0065-7

Newton up to 388 lbs.—of pot. (2001, December 13). *Hartford Courant,* C2.

Nicholls, A. R., Holt, N. L., Polman, R.C.J., & Bloomfield, J. (2006). Stressors, coping and coping effectiveness among professional rugby union players. *The Sport Psychologist, 20,* 314–329.

Nicholls, A. R., Holt, N. L., & Polman, R.C.J. (2005). A phenomenological analysis of coping effectiveness in golf. *The Sport Psychologist, 19,* 111–130.

Nicholls, A. R., Holt, N. L., Polman, R.C.J. & James, D.W.G. (2005). Stress and coping among international adolescent golfers. *Journal of Applied Sport Psychology, 17,* 333–340.

Nicholls, A. R., Levy, A. R., Polman, R.C.J., & Crust, L. (2011). Mental toughness, coping self-efficacy, and coping effectiveness among athletes. *International Journal of Sport Psychology, 42,* 513–524.

Nicholls, A. R., & Polman, R.C.J. (2007). Coping in sport: A systematic review. *Journal of Sports Sciences, 25,* 11–31.

Nicholls, A. R., Polman, R., & Levy, A. R. (2010). Coping self-efficacy, pre-competitive anxiety, and subjective performance among athletes. *European Journal of Sport Science, 10,* 97–102. doi: 10.1080/17461390903271592

Nicholls, A. R., Polman, R.C.J., Levy, A. R., & Backhouse, S. H. (2008). Mental toughness, optimism, pessimism, and coping among athletes. *Personality and Individual Differences, 44,* 1182–1192. doi: 10.1016/p.paid.2007.11.011

Nicholls, A. R., Polman, R.C.J., Levy, A. R., & Backhouse, S. H. (2009). Mental toughness in sport: Achievement level, gender, age, experience, and sport type differences. *Personality and Individual Differences, 47*, 73–75. doi: 10.1016/j.paid.2009.02.006

Nicholls, A. R., Polman, R.C.J., Levy, A. R., & Borkoles, E. (2010). The mediating role of coping: A cross-sectional analysis of the relationship between coping self-efficacy and coping effectiveness among athletes. *International Journal of Stress Management, 17*, 181–192. doi: 10.1037/a0020064

Nicholls, A., Poleman, R., Morley, D., & Taylor, N. J. (2009). Coping and coping effectiveness in relation to a competitive sport event: Pubertal status, chronological age, and gender among adolescent athletes. *Journal of Sport and Exercise Psychology, 31*, 299–317.

Nicholls, J. G. (1989). *The competitive ethos and democratic education.* Cambridge, MA: Harvard University Press.

Nicklaus, J. (1976). *Play better golf.* New York, NY: King Features.

Nicolas, M., Gaudreau, P., & Franche, V. (2011). Perception of coaching behaviors, coping, and achievement in a sport competition. *Journal of Sport & Exercise Psychology, 33*, 460–468.

Nideffer, R. M. (1985). *Athletes guide to mental training.* Champaign, IL: Human Kinetics.

Nideffer, R. M. (1993). Attention control training. In R. N. Singer, M. Murphy, & L. K. Tennant (Eds.), *Handbook of research on sport psychology* (pp. 542–556). New York, NY: Macmillan.

Nideffer, R. M., & Sagal, M. (2006). Concentration and attention control training. In J. M. Williams (Ed.), *Applied sport psychology: Personal growth to peak performance* (5th ed., pp. 382–403). Boston, MA: McGraw-Hill.

Nideffer, R. M., Sagal, M-S., Lowry, M., & Bond, J. (2001). Identifying and developing world class performers. In G. Tenenbaum (Ed.), *Reflections and experiences in sport and exercise psychology* (pp. 129–144). Morgantown, WV: Fitness Information Technology.

Niemeier, B. S., Hektner, J. M., & Enger, K. B., (2012). Parent participation in weight-related health interventions for children and adolescents: A systematic review and meta-analysis. *Preventive Medicine, 55*, 3–13. doi:10.1016/j.ypmed.2012.04.021

Nien, C-L., & Duda, J. L. (2008). Antecedents and consequences of approach and avoidance achievement goals: A test of gender invariance. *Psychology of Sport and Exercise, 9*, 352–372. doi: 10.1016/j.psychsport.2007.05.002

Nieuwenhuys, A., Pijpers, J. R., Oudejans, R.R.D., & Bakker, F. C. (2008). The influence of anxiety on visual attention in climbing. *Journal of Sport & Exercise Psychology, 30*, 171–185.

Nieuwenhuys, A., Vos, L., Pijpstra, S., & Bakker, F. C. (2011). Meta experiences and coping effectiveness in sport. *Psychology of Sport and Exercise, 12*, 135–143. doi: 10.1016/j.psychsport.2010.07.008

Nixon, S. J. (1999). Neurocognitive performance in alcoholics: Is polysubstance abuse important? *Psychological Science, 10*, 181–185.

Noel, R. C. (1980). The effects of Visuo-motor Behavior Rehearsal on tennis performance. *Journal of Sport Psychology, 2*, 224–236.

Noh, Y-E., Morris, T., & Andersen, M. B. (2005). Psychosocial factors and ballet injuries. *International Journal of Sport and Exercise Psychology, 3*, 79–90.

Nolen-Hoeksema, S. (1990). *Sex differences in depression.* Stanford, CA: Stanford University Press.

Nolen-Hoeksema, S., Girgus, J. S., & Seligman, M. E. P. (1986). Learned helplessness in children: A longitudinal study of depression, achievement, and explanatory style. *Journal of Personality and Social Psychology, 51*, 435–442.

Nolen-Hoeksema, S., Girgus, J. S., & Seligman, M. E. P. (1992). Predictors and consequences of childhood depressive symptoms: A 5-year longitudinal study. *Journal of Abnormal Psychology, 101*, 405–422.

Nolen-Hoeksema, S., Parker, L. E., & Larson, J. (1994). Ruminative coping with depressed mood following loss. *Journal of Personality and Social Psychology, 67*, 92–104.

Norem, J. K., & Cantor, N. (1986a). Anticipatory and post hoc cushioning strategies: Optimism and defensive pessimism in "risky" situations. *Cognitive Therapy and Research, 10*, 347–362.

Norem, J. K., & Cantor, N. (1986b). Defensive pessimism: Harnessing anxiety as motivation. *Journal of Personality and Social Psychology, 51*, 1208–1217.

Norem, J. K., & Illingworth, K. S. S. (1993). Strategy-dependent effects of reflecting on self and tasks: Some implications of optimism and defensive pessimism. *Journal of Personality and Social Psychology, 65*, 822–835.

Norlander, T., & Archer, T. (2002). Predicting performance in ski and swim championships: Effectiveness of mood, perceived exertion, and dispositional optimism. *Perceptual and Motor Skills, 94*, 153–164.

North, T. C., McCullagh, P., & Tran, Z. V. (1990). Effect of exercise on depression. *Exercise and Sport Science Reviews, 18*, 379–415.

Norton, G. R., & Johnson, W. E. (1983). A comparison of two relaxation procedures for reducing cognitive and somatic anxiety. *Journal of Behavior Therapy and Experimental Psychiatry, 14,* 209–214.

Norton, G. R., Rhodes, L., & Hauch, J. (1985). Characteristics of subjects experiencing relaxation and relaxation-induced anxiety. *Journal of Behavior Therapy and Experimental Psychiatry, 16,* 211–216.

Ntoumanis, N., & Jones, G. (1998). Interpretation of competitive trait anxiety symptoms as a function o locus of control beliefs. *International Journal of Sport Psychology, 29,* 99–114.

Ntoumanis, N., & Standage M. (2009). Morality in sport: A self-determination theory perspective. *Journal of Applied Sport Psychology, 21,* 365–380.

Ntoumanis, N., Taylor, I. M., & Thogersen-Ntoumani, C. (2012). A longitudinal examination of coach and peer motivational climates in youth sport: Implications for moral attitudes, well-being, and behavioral investment. *Developmental Psychology, 48,* 213–223. doi: 10.1037/a0024934

O, J., & Hall, C. (2009). A quantitative analysis of athletes voluntary use of slow motion, real time, and fast motion images. *Journal of Applied Sport Psychology, 21,* 15–30. doi: 10.1080/10413200802541892

Oberhofer, H., Philippovich, T., & Winner, H. (2010). Distance matters in away games: Evidence from the German football league. *Journal of Economic Psychology, 31,* 200–211. doi: 10.1016/j.joep.2009.11.003

O'Brien, M., Mellalieu, S., & Hanton, S. (2009). Goal-setting effects in elite and nonelite boxers. *Journal of Applied Sport Psychology, 21,* 293–306.

O'Connell, J. (1994, October 28). Bagwell can't ask for more. First from state to win award. *Hartford Courant.* C1.

O'Connor, P. J. (2007). Monitoring and titrating symptoms. A science-based approach to using your brain to optimize marathon running performance. *Sports Medicine, 37,* 408–411. doi: 0112–1642/07/0004–44.95/0

Ogbu, J., & Simons, H. (1998). Voluntary and involuntary minorities: A cultural-ecological theory of school performance with some implications for education. *Anthropology & Education Quarterly, 29,* 155–188.

Ogden, C. L., Carroll, M. D., Curtin, L. R., Lamb, M. M., & Flegal, K. M. (2010). Prevalence of high body mass index in US children and adolescents, 2007–2008. *JAMA, 303,* 242–249. doi: 10.1001/jama.2009.2012

Ogden, J., Veale, D., & Summers, Z. (1997). The development and validation of the Exercise Dependence Questionnaire. *Addiction Research, 5,* 343–353.

Ogilvie, B. C., Haase, H., Jokl, E., Kranidiotis, D. T., Mahoney, M., & Nideffer, R. (1979). Critical issues in the application of clinical psychology in the sport setting. *International Journal of Sport Psychology, 10,* 178–183.

Ogilvie, B. C., & Tutko, T. A. (1966). *Problem athletes and how to handle them.* London, England: Pelham Books.

Oglesby, C. A., & Hill, K. L. (1993). Gender and sport. In R. N. Singer, M. Murphey, & L. K. Tennant (Eds.), *Handbook of research on sport psychology* (pp. 718–728). New York, NY: MacMillan.

O'Malley, P. M., & Johnston, L. D. (2007). Drugs and driving by American high school seniors, 2001–2006. *Journal of Studies on Alcohol and Drugs, 68,* 834–842.

Ommundsen, Y. (2001). Self-handicapping strategies in physical education classes: the influence of implicit theories of the nature of ability and achievement goal orientations. *Psychology of Sport and Exercise, 2,* 139–156.

Ommundsen, Y. (2004). Self-handicapping related to task and performance-approach and avoidance goals in physical education. *Journal of Applied Sport Psychology, 16,* 183–197.

Ommundsen, Y. (2006). Pupils' self-regulation in physical education: The role of motivational climates and differential achievement goals. *European Physical Education Review, 10,* 289–315.

Ommundsen, Y., Haugen, R., & Lund, T. (2005). Academic self-concept, implicit theories of ability, and self-regulation strategies. *Scandinavian Journal of Educational Research, 49,* 461–474. doi: 10.1080/00313830500267838

Ommundsen, Y., & Roberts, G. C. (1999). Effect of motivational climate profiles on motivational indices in team sport. *Scandinavian Journal of Medicine and Science in Sports, 9,* 389–397.

Ommundsen, Y., Roberts, G. C., Lemyre, P-N., & Miller, B. W. (2005). Peer relationships in adolescent competitive soccer: Associations to perceived motivational climate, achievement goals and perfectionism. *Journal of Sports Sciences, 23,* 977–989.

Ommundsen, Y., Roberts, G. C., Lemyre, P-N, & Miller, B. W. (2006). Parental and coach support or pressure on psychosocial outcomes of pediatric athletes in soccer. *Clinical Journal of Sport Medicine: Official Journal of the Canadian Academy of Sport Medicine, 6,* 522–526.

Ommundsen, Y., Roberts, G. C., Lemyre, P. N., & Treasure, D. (2003). Perceived motivational climate in male youth soccer: relations to social—moral functioning, sportspersonship, and team norm perceptions. *Psychology of Sport and Exercise, 4,* 397–413.

Onestak, D. M. (1991). The effects of progressive relaxation, mental practice, and hypnosis on athletic performance: A review. *Journal of Sport Behavior, 14,* 247–282.

Onestak, D. (1997). The effects of Visuo-Motor Behavior Rehearsal. *Journal of Sport Behavior, 20,* 185–198.

Orlick, T. (1992). *Freeing children from stress: Focusing and stress control activities for children.* Willits, CA: ITA Publications.

Orlick, T., & McCaffrey, N. (1991). Mental training with children for sport and life. *The Sport Psychologist, 5,* 322–334.

Orlick, T., & Partington, J. (1988). Mental links to excellence. *The Sport Psychologist, 2,* 105–130.

Orlick, T. D. (1986). *Psyching for sport.* Champaign, IL: Human Kinetics.

Orlick, T. D., & Mosher, R. (1978). Extrinsic awards and participant motivation in a sport related task. *International Journal of Sport Psychology, 9,* 27–39.

Orme-Johnson, D. W., Zimmerman, E., & Hawkins, M. (1997). Maharishi's vedic psychology. In H.R.R. Kao & D. Sinha (Eds.), *Asian perspectives on psychology* (pp. 282–308). New Delhi, India: Sage.

O'Rourke, D. J., Smith, R. E., Smoll, F. L., & Cumming, S. P. (2011). Trait anxiety in young athletes as a function of parental pressure and motivational climate: Is parental pressure always harmful? *Journal of Applied Sport Psychology, 23,* 398–412. doi: 10–1080/10413200.2001.552089

Orth, U., Robins, R. W., & Widaman, K. F. (2012). Life-span development of self-esteem and its effects on important life outcomes. *Personality and Individual Differences, 102,* 1271–1288. doi: 10.1037/10025558

Osborn, Z. H., Blanton, P. D., & Schwebel, D. C. (2009). Personality and injury risk among professional hockey players. *Journal of Injury and Violence Research, 1,* 15–19. doi: 10.5249/jivr.v1i1.8

Otten, M. (2009). Choking vs. clutch performance: A study of sport performance under pressure. *Journal of Sport and Exercise Psychology, 31,* 583–601.

Oudejans, R.R.D., & Pijpers, J. R. (2009). Training with anxiety has a positive effect on expert perceptual-motor performance under pressure. *The Quarterly Journal of Experimental Psychology, 62,* 1631–1647. doi: 10.1080/17470210802555702

Oxendine, J. B. (1970). Emotional arousal and motor performance. *Quest, 13,* 23–32.

Oxendine, J. B. (1984). *Psychology of Motor Learning.* Englewood Cliffs, NJ: Prentice-Hall.

Pacht, A. R. (1984). Reflections on perfection. *American Psychologist, 39,* 386–390.

Page, S. J., Sime, W., & Nordell, K. (1999). The effects of imagery on female college swimmers' perceptions of anxiety. *The Sport Psychologist, 13,* 458–469.

Pain, M. A., & Harwood, C. G. (2004). Knowledge and perceptions of sport psychology within English soccer. *Journal of Sports Sciences, 22,* 813–826.

Pain, M. A., & Harwood, C. G. (2008). The performance environment of the England youth soccer teams: A quantitative investigation. *Journal of Sports Sciences, 26,* 1157–1169. doi: 10.1080/02640410802101835

Pain, M., & Harwood, C. (2009). Team building through mutual sharing and open discussion of team functioning. *The Sport Psychologist, 23,* 523–542.

Painter, J. (2010). Lakers standout Metta World Peace awarded for bringing awareness to importance of mental health. Retrieved from http://www.DailyNews.com

Painter, J. E., Borba, C. P., Hynes, M., Mays, D., & Glanz, K. (2008). The use of theory in health behavior research from 2000 to 2005: A systematic review. *Annals of Behavioral Medicine, 35,* 358–362. doi: 10.007/x12160-008-9042-y

Paivio, A. (1985). Cognitive and motivational functions of imagery in human performance. *Canadian Journal of Applied Sport Sciences, 10,* 22–28.

Pajares, F. (1996). Self-efficacy beliefs in academic settings. *Review of Educational Research, 66,* 543–578.

Papaioannou, A., March, H. W., & Theodorakis, Y. (2004). A multilevel approach to motivational climate in physical education and sport settings: An individual or group level construct. *Journal of Sport & Exercise Psychology, 26,* 90–118.

Pargman, D. (1998). *Understanding sport behavior.* Upper Saddle River, NJ: Prentice Hall.

Parham, W. D. (2005). Raising the bar: Developing an understanding of athletes from racially, culturally, and ethnically diverse backgrounds. In M. B. Anderson (Ed.), *Sport psychology in practice* (pp. 201–215). Champaign, IL: Human Kinetics.

Park, C. L., & Gaffey, A. E. (2007). Relationships between psychosocial factors and health behavior change in cancer survivors: An integrative review. *Annals of Behavioral Medicine, 34,* 115–134. doi: 10.1007/BF02872667

Park, J-K. (2000). Coping strategies used by Korean national athletes. *The Sport Psychologist, 14,* 63–80.

Park, S., Tod, D., & Lavallee, D. (2012). Exploring the retirement from sport decision-making process based on the transtheoretical model. *Psychology of Sport and Exercise, 13,* 444–453. doi: 10.1016/j.psychsport.2012.02.003

Parkhouse, B. L., & Williams, J. M. (1986). Differential effects of sex and status on evaluation of coaching ability. *Research Quarterly for Exercise and Sport, 57,* 53–59.

Parsons, C. A., & Soucie, D. (1988). Perceptions of the causes of procrastination by sport administrators. *Journal of Sport Management, 2,* 129–139.

Participation Survey 1999–2000. (1999–2000). National Federation of State High School Associations. Retrieved from http://www.nfhs.org/part_survey99-00.html.

Partington, J. T., & Shangi, G. M. (1992). Developing and understanding of team psychology. *International Journal of Sport Psychology, 23,* 28–47.

Partington, S., Partington, E., & Olivier, S. (2009). The dark side of flow: A qualitative study of dependence in big wave surfing. *The Sport Psychologist, 23,* 170–185.

Paskevich, D. M., Brawley, L. R., Dorsch, K. D., & Widmeyer, W. N. (1995). Implications of individual and group level analyses applied to the study of collective efficacy and cohesion. *Journal of Applied Sport Psychology, 7,* S95.

Paskevich, D. M., Brawley, L. R., Dorsch, K. D., & Widmeyer, W. N. (1999). Relationship between collective efficacy and team cohesion: Conceptual and measurement issues. *Group Dynamics: Theory, Research, and Practice, 3,* 210–222.

Paskevich, D. M., Estabrooks, P. A., Brawley, L. R., & Carron, A. V. (2001). Group cohesion in sport and exercise. In R. N. Singer, H. A. Hausenblas, & C. M. Janelle (Eds.), *Handbook of sport psychology* (2nd ed., pp. 766–786). New York, NY: Wiley.

Patrick, T., D., & Hrycaiko, D. W. (1998). Effects of a mental training package on an endurance performance. *The Sport Psychologist, 12,* 283–299.

Patterson, E. L., & Smith, R. E. (1998). Psychosocial factors as predictors of ballet injuries: Interactive effects of live stress and. *Journal of Sport Behavior, 21,* 101–113.

Patton, M. Q. (1990). *Qualitative evaluation and research methods.* Newbury Park, CA: Sage Publications.

Pearson, R. E., & Petitpas, A. J. (1990). Transitions of athletes: Developmental and preventive perspectives. *Journal of Counseling & Development, 69,* 7–10.

Peddle, C. J., Plotnikoff, R. C., Wild, T. C., Au, H. J., & Courneya, K. S. (2008). Medical, demographic, and psychosocial correlates of exercise in colorectal cancer survivors: An application of self-determination theory. *Support Care in Cancer, 16,* 1–19. doi: 10.1007/s00520-007-0272-5

Pekrun, R., Elliot, A. J., Maier, M. A. (2006). Achievement goals and discrete achievement emotions: A theoretical model and prospective test. *Journal of Educational Psychology, 98,* 583–597. doi: 10.1037/0022-0663.98.3.583

Pellizzari, M., Bertollo, M., & Robazza, C. (2011). Pre- and post-performance emotions in gymnastics competitions. *International Journal of Sport Psychology, 42,* 278–302.

Pelz, D., & Frank, J. A. (1999). *Dave Pelz's short game bible: Master the finesse swing and lower your score.* New York, NY: Doubleday.

Pereira, A., Huddleston, D., Brickman, A., Sosunov, A., Hen, R., McKann, G.,. . . Small, S. (2007). An in vivo correlate of exercise-induced neurogenesis in the adult dentate gyrus. *Proceedings of the National Academy of Science. U.S.A., 104,* 5638–5643.

Peretti-Watel, P., Beck, F., & Legleye, S. (2002). Beyond the U-curve: the relationship between sport and alcohol, cigarette and cannabis use in adolescents. *Addiction, 97,* 707–716.

Perkins-Ceccato, N., Passmore, S. R., & Lee, T. D. (2003). Effects of focus of attention depend on golfers' skill. *Journal of Sports Sciences, 21,* 593–600. doi:10.1080/0264041031000101980

Perna, F. M., Ahlgren, R. L., & Zaichkowsky, L. (1999). The influence of career planning, race, and athletic injury on life satisfaction among recently retired collegiate male athletes. *The Sport Psychologist, 13,* 144–156.

Perna, F. M., Antoni, M. H., Baum, A., Gordon, P., & Schneiderman, N. (2003). Cognitive behavioral stress management effects on injury and illness among competitive athletes: A randomized clinical trial. *Annals of Behavioral Medicine, 25,* 66–73.

Perry, J. D., & Williams, J. M. (1998). Relationship of intensity and direction of competitive trait anxiety to skill level and gender in tennis. *The Sport Psychologist, 12,* 169–179.

Peters, H. J., & Williams, J. M. (2006). Moving cultural background to the foreground: An investigation of self-talk, performance, and persistence following feedback. *Journal of Applied Sport Psychology, 18,* 240–251.

Peters, H. J., & Williams, J. M. (2009). Rationale for developing a cultural sport psychology. In R. Schinke & S. J. Hanrahan (Eds.), *Cultural sport psychology* (pp. 13–21). Champaign, IL: Human Kinetics.

Peters, M. F. (1981). Parenting in black families with young children: A historical perspective. In H. P. McAdoo (Ed.), *Black families* (pp. 211–244). Beverly Hills, CA: Sage.

Peterson, C., & Barrett, L. C. (1987). Explanatory style and academic performance among university freshmen. *Journal of Personality and Social Psychology, 53,* 603–607.

Peterson, C., Maier, S. F., & Seligman, M.E.P. (1993). *Learned helplessness. A theory for the age of personal control.* New York, NY: Oxford.

Peterson, K. (2010, August 10). Blanc aims to revive France. *Wall Street Journal.* Retrieved from http://www.wsj.com

Petherick, C. M., & Weigand, D. A. (2002). The relationship of dispositional goal orientations and perceived motivational climates on indices of motivation in male and female swimmers. *International Journal of Sport Psychology, 33,* 218–237.

Petitpas, A. J. (2009). Sport career termination. In B. W. Brewer (Ed.), *Handbook of sports medicine and science, sport psychology* (pp. 113–120), Chichester, England: Wiley-Blackwell.

Petitpas, A. J., Brewer, B. W., Rivera, P. M., & Van Raalte, J. L. (1994). Ethical beliefs and behaviors in applied sport psychology: The AAASP ethics survey. *Journal of Applied Sport Psychology, 6,* 135–151.

Petri, H. L., & Govern, J. (2004). *Motivation: Theory, research, and applications* (5th ed.). Belmont, CA: Wadsworth/Thomson Learning.

Petrie, T. A. (1993). Coping skills, competitive trait anxiety, and playing status: Moderating effects on the life stress-injury relationship. *Journal of Sport & Exercise Psychology, 15,* 261–274.

Petrie, T. A. (1998). Anxiety management and the elite athlete: A case study. In K. F. Hayes (Ed.), *Integrating exercise, sports, movement, and mind: Therapeutic unity* (pp. 161–173). New York, NY: Haworth Press.

Petrie, T. A., & Falkstein, D. L. (1998). Methodological, measurement, and statistical issues in research on sport injury prediction. *Journal of Applied Sport Psychology, 10,* 26–45.

Pfeffer, I., & Alfermann, D. (2008). Initiation of physical exercise: An intervention study based on the transtheoretical model. *International Journal of Sport Psychology, 39,* 41–58.

Pfister, G. (2000). Women and the Olympic Games: 1900–97. In B. L. Drinkwater (Ed.), *Women in sport* (pp. 3–19). Oxford, England: Blackwell Science.

Phelps, M., & Abrahamson, A. (2008). *No limits. The will to succeed.* New York, NY: Free Press.

Phillips, J. M., & Gully, S. M. (1997). Role of goal orientation, ability, need for achievement, and locus of control in the self-efficacy and goal-setting process. *Journal of Applied Psychology, 82,* 792–802.

Physical Activity Guidelines Advisory Committee. (2008). *Physical Activity Guidelines Advisory Committee Report.* Washington, DC: U.S. Department of Health and Human Services.

Piedmont, R. L. (1988). An interactional model of achievement motivation and fear of success. *Sex Roles, 10,* 89–100.

Piedment, R. L., Hill, D.C., & Blanco, S. (1999). Predicting athletic performance using the five-factor model of personality. *Personality and Individual Differences, 27,* 769–777.

Pikoff, H. (1985). A critical review of autogenic training in America. *Clinical Psychology Review, 4,* 619–639.

Pierce, G. R., Henderson, C. A., Yost, J. H., & Loffredo, C. M. (1996). Cognitive interference and personality: theoretical and methodological issues. In I. G. Sarason, G. R. Pierce, & B. R. Sarason (Eds.), *Cognitive interference theories, methods, and findings* (pp. 285–296). Mahwah, NJ: Lawrence Erlbaum Associates.

Pijpers, J. R., Oudejans, R.R.D., & Bakker, F. C. (2005). Anxiety-induced changes in movement behavior during the execution of a complex whole-body task. *Quarterly Journal of Experimental Psychology, 58A,* 421–445.

Pijpers, J. R., Oudejans, R.R.D., Bakker, F. C., & Beek, P. J. (2006). The role of anxiety in perceiving and realizing affordances. *Ecological Psychology, 18,* 131–161.

Pilon, M. (2012a, April 21). The footprints on a path to gold. *The New York Times.* Retrieved from http://www.nytimes.com

Pilon, M. (2012b, June 2). How do Kenyan 10K runners get to London? Through raindrops in Oregon. *The New York Times.* Retrieved from http://www.nytimes.com

Pleis, J. R., & Lucas, J. W. (2009). Summary health statistics for U.S. adults: National health interview survey, 2007. *Vital and Health Statistics Series, 10*(240), 1–159.

Poczwardowski, A., & Conroy, D. E. (2002). Coping responses to failure and success among elite athletes and performing artists. *Journal of Applied Sport Psychology, 14,* 313–329.

Podlog, L., & Dionigi, R. (2010). Coach strategies for addressing psychosocial challenges during the return to sport from injury. *Journal of Sports Sciences, 28,* 1197–1208. doi: 10.1080/02640414.2010.487873

Podlog, L., & Eklund, R. C. (2007). Professional coaches' perspectives on the return to sport following serious injury. *Journal of Applied Sport Psychology, 19,* 207–225.

Podlog, L., Kleinert, J., Dimmock, J., Miller, J., & Shipherd, A. M. (2012). A parental perspective on adolescent injury rehabilitation and return to sport experiences. *Journal of Applied Sport Psychology, 24,* 175–190. doi: 10.1080/10413200.2011.608102

Podlog, L., Lochbaum, M., & Stevens, T. (2010). Need satisfaction, well-being, and perceived return-to-sport outcomes among injured athletes. *Journal of Applied Sport Psychology, 22,* 167–182.

Poliseo, J. M., & McDonough, M. H. (2012). Coping effectiveness in competitive sport: Linking goodness of fit and coping outcomes, *Sport, Exercise, and Performance Psychology, 1,* 106–119. doi: 10.1037/a0026382

Polivy, J., & Herman, C. P. (2002). Causes of eating disorders. *Annual Review of Psychology, 53,* 187–213.

Pollard, R. (2006). Worldwide regional variations in home advantage in association football. *Journal of Sports Sciences, 24,* 231–240.

Pom, S., Fleig, L., Schwarzer, R., & Lippke, S. (2012). Depressive symptoms interfere with post-rehabilitation exercise: outcome expectancies and experience as mediators. *Psychology, Health & Medicine, 17,* 698–708. doi: 10.1080/13548506.2012.661864

Poolton, J. M., Masters, R.S.W., & Maxwell, J. P. (2007). The development of a culturally appropriate analogy for implicit motor learning in a Chinese population. *The Sport Psychologist, 21,* 375–382.

Pope, H. G., & Katz, D. L. (1994). Psychiatric and medical effects of anabolic-androgenic steroid use. *Archives of General Psychiatry, 51,* 375–382.

Postrel, V. (2011, March 26). "Mommy Track" without shame. *Wall Street Journal.* Retrieved from http://www.wsj.com

Potter, S. (1947). *The theory and practice of gamesmanship.* Harmondsworth, England: Penguin.

Poulter, D. R. (2009). Home advantage and player nationality in international club football. *Journal of Sports Sciences, 27,* 797–805. doi: 10.1080/02640410902893364

Poulton, R. G., Brooke, M., Moffitt, T. E., Stanton, W. R., & Silva, P. A. (1997). Prevalence and correlates of cannabis use and dependence in young New Zealanders. *New Zealand Medical Journal, 110,* 68–70.

Powell, S. (2008). *Souled out?* Champaign, IL: Human Kinetics.

Prapavessis, H. (2000). The POMS and sports performance: A review. *Journal of Applied Sport Psychology, 12,* 34–48.

Prapavessis, H., & Carron, A. V. (1988). Learned helplessness in sport. *The Sport Psychologist, 2,* 189–201.

Prapavessis, H., & Carron, A. V. (1997). Sacrifice, cohesion, and conformity to norms in sport teams. *Group Dynamics: Theory, Research, and Practice, 1,* 231–240.

Prapavessis, H., & Gordon, S. (1991). Coach/player relationships in tennis. *Canadian Journal of Sport Science, 16,* 229–233.

Prapavessis, H., & Grove, J. R. (1991). Precompetitive emotions and shooting performance: The mental health and zone of optimal function models. *The Sport Psychologist, 5,* 223–234.

Prapavessis, H. & Grove, R. (1994). Personality variables as antecedents of precompetitive mood state temporal patterning. *International Journal of Sport Psychology, 22,* 347–365.

Prapavessis, H., & Grove, J. R. (1998). Self-handicapping and self-esteem. *Journal of Applied Sport Psychology, 10,* 175–184.

Prapavessis, H., Grove, J. R., & Eklund, R. C. (2004). Self-presentational issues in competition and sport. *Journal of Applied Sport Psychology, 16,* 19–40.

Prapavessis, H., Grove, J. R., Maddison, R., & Zillmann, N. (2003). Self-handicapping tendencies, coping, and anxiety responses among athletes. *Psychology of Sport and Exercise, 4,* 357–375.

Price, M. S., & Weiss, M. R. (2000). Relationships among coach burnout, coach behaviors, and athletes' psychological responses. *The Sport Psychologist, 14,* 391–409.

Price, S. L. (2001, May 28). Broken promise. *Sports Illustrated, 94,* 82–90.

Price, S. L. (2009, December 7). Urban Meyer. *Sports Illustrated, 111,* 134–147.

Prochaska, J. O. (1979). *Systems of psychotherapy: A transtheoretical analysis.* Homewood, IL: Dorsey Press.

Prochaska, J. O., Wright, J. A., & Velicer, W. F. (2008). Evaluating theories of health behavior change: A hierarchy of criteria applied to the transtheoretical model. *Applied Psychology: An International Review, 57,* 561–588. doi: 10.1111/j.1464-0597.2008.00345.x

Proctor, R. W., & Dutta, A. (1995). *Skill acquisition and human performance.* Thousand Oaks, CA: Sage.

Pryce, C. R., Azzinnari, D., Sigrist, H., Gschwind, T., Lesch, K. P., & Seifritz, E. (2011). Establishing a learned-helplessness effect paradigm in C57BL/6 mice: Behavioral evidence for emotional, motivational and cognitive effects of aversive uncontrollability per se. *Neuropharmacology, 62,* 358–72. doi: 10.1016/j.neuropharm.2011.08.012

Puente, R., & Anshel, M. H. (2010). Exercisers' perceptions of their fitness instructor's interacting style, perceived competence, and autonomy as a function of self-determined regulation to exercise, enjoyment, affect, and exercise frequency. *Scandinavian Journal of Psychology, 51,* 38–45. doi: 10.1111/j.1467–9450.2009.00723.x

Puente-Diaz, R., & Anshel, M. H. (2005). Sources of acute stress, cognitive appraisal, and coping strategies among highly skilled Mexican and U.S. competitive tennis players. *The Journal of Social Psychology, 45,* 429–446.

Pugh, N. E., & Hadjistavropoulos, H. D. (2011). Anxiety about health associated with desire to exercise, physical activity, and exercise dependence. *Personality and Individual Differences, 51,* 1059–1062. doi: 10.1016/j.paid.2011.08.025

Quested, E., & Duda, J. L. (2010). Exploring the social-environmental determinants of well- and ill-being in dancers: A test of basic needs theory. *Journal of Sport & Exercise Psychology, 32,* 39–60.

Quinn, A. M., & Fallon, B. J. (1999). The changes in psychological characteristics and reactions of elite athletes from injury onset until full recovery. *Journal of Applied Sport Psychology, 11,* 210–229.

Radel, R., Sarrazin, P., & Pelletier, L. (2009). Evidence of subliminally primed motivational orientations: The focus of unconscious motivational processes on the performance of a new motor task. *Journal of Sport & Exercise Psychology, 31,* 657–674.

Raedeke, T. D. (1997). Is athlete burnout more than just stress? A sport commitment perspective. *Journal of Sport & Exercise Psychology, 19,* 396–417.

Raedeke, T. D. (2004). Coach commitment and burnout: A one-year follow-up. *Journal of Applied Sport Psychology, 16,* 333–349.

Raedeke, T. D., Granzyk, T. L., & Warren, A. (2000). Why coaches experience burnout: A commitment perspective. *Journal of Sport & Exercise Psychology, 22,* 85–105.

Raedeke, T. D., Lunney, K., & Venables, K. (2002). Understanding athlete burnout: Coach perspectives. *Journal of Sport Behavior, 25,* 181–206.

Raedeke, T. D., & Smith, A. L. (2001). Development and preliminary validation of an athlete burnout measure. *Journal of Sport & Exercise Psychology, 23,* 281–306.

Raffety, B. D., Smith, R. E., & Ptacek, J. T. (1997). Facilitating and debilitating trait anxiety, situational anxiety, and coping with an anticipated stressor: A process analysis. *Journal of Personality and Social Psychology, 72,* 892–906.

Raglin, J. S., & Turner, P. E. (1996). Variability in precompetition anxiety and performance in college track and field athletes. *Medicine & Science in Sports & Exercise, 28,* 378–385.

Raglin, J. S., & Wilson, G. S. (2000). Overtraining in athletes. In Y. L. Hanin (Ed.). *Emotions in sport* (pp. 191–207). Champaign, IL: Human Kinetics.

Raimy, V. C. (1950). *Training in clinical psychology.* New York, NY: Prentice-Hall.

Rain, J. S., Lane, I. M., & Steiner, D. D. (1991). A current look at the job satisfaction/life satisfaction relationship: Review and future considerations. *Human Relations, 44,* 287–307.

Ram, N., Starek, J., & Johnson, J. (2004). Race, ethnicity, and sexual orientation: Still a void in sport and exercise psychology? *Journal of Sport & Exercise Psychology, 26,* 250–268.

Rammsayer, T. H. (2004). Extraversion and the dopamine hypothesis. In R. M. Stelmack (Ed.), *Essays in honor of Marvin Zuckerman* (pp. 409–427). New York, NY: Elsevier Science.

Ramsey, R., Cumming, J., Edwards, M. G., Williams, S., & Brunning, C. (2010). Examining the emotion aspect of PETTLEP-based imagery with penalty taking in soccer. *Journal of Sport Behavior, 33,* 295–314.

Randle, S., & Weinberg, R. (1997). Multidimensional anxiety and performance: An exploratory examination of the Zone of Optimal functioning hypothesis. *The Sport Psychologist, 11,* 160–174.

Randolph, P. D., Caldera, Y. M., Tacone, A. M., & Greak, M. L. (1999). The long-term combined effects of medical treatment and a mindfulness-based behavioral program for the multidisciplinary management of chronic pain in West Texas. *Pain Digest, 9,* 103–112.

Ranking the Dirtiest Teams (2006, July 8). *Hartford Courant,* C3.

Raskin, R., & Hall, C. S. (1981). The Narcissistic Personality Inventory: Alternate form reliability and further evidence of construct validity. *Journal of Personality Assessment, 45,* 159–162.

Raudsepp, L, & Liblik, R. (2002). Relationship of perceived and actual motor competence in children. *Perceptual and Motor Skills, 94,* 1059–1070.

Ravizza, K. (1988). Gaining entry with athletic personnel for season-long consulting. *The Sport Psychologist, 2,* 243–254.

Ravizza, K. (2010). Increasing awareness for sport performance. In J. M. Williams (Ed.), *Applied sport psychology: Personal growth to peak performance* (6th ed., pp. 189–200). M=New York, NY: McGraw-Hill.

Raznahan, A., Lee, Y., Stidd, R., Long, R., Greenstein, D., Clasen, L., . . . & Giedd, J. N. (2010). Longitudinally mapping the influence of sex and androgen signaling on the dynamics of human cortical maturation in adolescence. *Proceedings of the National Academy of Sciences, 107,* 16988–16993. Retrieved from http://www.pnas.org/lookup/suppl/doi:10.1073/pnas.1006025107/-/DCSSupplemental

Reed, C. L. (2002). Chronometric comparisons of imagery to action: Visualizing versus physically performing springboard dives. *Memory and Cognition, 30,* 1169–1178.

Rees, T., & Hardy, L. (2000). An investigation of the social support experiences of high-level sports performers. *The Sport Psychologist, 14,* 327–347.

Rees, T., & Hardy, L. (2004). Matching social support with stressors: Effects on factors underlying performance in tennis. *Psychology of Sport and Exercise, 5,* 319–337. doi: 10.1016/S1469-0292(03)00018-9

Rees, T., Mitchell, I., Evans, L., & Hardy, L. (2010). Stressors, social support and psychological responses to sport injury in high- and low-performance standard participants. *Psychology of Sport and Exercise, 11,* 505–512. doi: 10.1016/j.psychsport.2010.07.002

Reeve, J., & Deci, E. L. (1996). Elements within the competitive situation that affect intrinsic motivation. *Personality and Social Psychology Bulletin, 22,* 24–33.

Reeves, C. W., Nicholls, A. R., & McKenna, J. (2011). Longitudinal analyses of stressors, perceived control, coping, and coping effectiveness among early and middle adolescent soccer players. *International Journal of Sport Psychology, 42,* 186–203.

Reeves, J. L., Tenenbaum, G., & Lidor, R. (2007). Choking in front of the goal: The effects of self-consciousness. *International Journal of Sport and Exercise Psychology, 5,* 240–254.

Rehm, L. P. (1982). Self-management in depression. In P. Karoly & F. H. Kanfer (Eds.), *Self-management and behavior change: From theory to practice* (pp. 522–567). New York, NY: Pergamon.

Reilly, R. (1996, April 22). Master strokes. *Sports Illustrated, 84,* 24–29, 31.

Report finds economic cost of substance abuse exceeds $143 billion. (2002, January 28). *Alcoholism & Drug Abuse Weekly, 14,* 1, 4.

Report on the Committee on Training in Clinical Psychology of the American Psychological Association submitted at the Detroit meeting of the American Psychological Association, September 9–13, 1947. (1947). Recommended training program in clinical psychology. *American Psychologist, 2,* 539–558.

Rethorst, C. D., Wipfli, B. M., & Landers, D. M. (2009). The antidepressive effects of exercise. A meta-analysis of randomized trials. *Sports Medicine, 39,* 491–511. doi: 0112-1642/09/0006-0491/$49.95/0

Rettew, D., & Reivich, K. (1995). Sports and explanatory style. In G. M. Buchanan & M. E. P. Seligman (Eds.), *Explanatory style* (pp. 173–185). Hillsdale, NJ: Lawrence Erlbaum.

Rhea, D. J., & Martin, S. (2010). Personality trait differences of traditional sport athletes, bullriders, and other alternative sport athletes. *International Journal of Sports Science & Coaching, 5,* 75–85.

Rheaume, J., Freeston, M. H., Ladouceur, R., Bouchard, C., Gallant, L., Talbot, F., & Vallieres, A. (2000). Functional and dysfunctional perfectionists: Are they different on compulsive-like behaviors? *Behaviour Research and Therapy, 38,* 119–128.

Rhoden, W. C. (1999, Dec. 30). Just ranting and raving doesn't win. *The New York Times, D1.*

Rhodewalt, F. (1994). Conceptions of ability, achievement goals, and individual differences in self-handicapping behavior: On the application of implicit theories. *Journal of Personality, 62,* 67–85.

Rhodewalt, F., Morf, C., Hazlett, S., & Fairfield, M. (1991). Self-handicapping: The role of discounting and augmentation in the preservation of self-esteem. *Journal of Personality and Social Psychology, 61,* 122–131.

Rhodewalt, F., Sanbonmatsu, D. M., Tschanz, B., Feick, D. L., & Waller, A. (1995). Self-handicapping and interpersonal trade-offs: The effects of claimed self-handicaps on observers' performance evaluations and feedback. *Personality and Social Psychology Bulletin, 21,* 1042–1050.

Rhodewalt, F., Saltzman, A. T., & Wittmer, J. (1984). Self-handicapping among competitive athletes: The role of practice in self-esteem protection. *Basic and Applied Social Psychology, 5,* 197–209.

Richer, I., & Bergeron, J. (2009). Driving under the influence of cannabis: Links with dangerous driving, psychological predictors, and accident involvement. *Accident Analysis and Prevention, 41,* 299–307.

Richardson, F. C., & Suinn, R. M. (1972). The Mathematics Anxiety Rating Scale: Psychometric data and interpersonal trade-offs: The effects of claimed self-handicaps on observers' performance evaluations and feedback. *Personality and Social Psychology Bulletin, 10,* 1042–1050.

Rieke, M., Hammermeister, J., & Chase, M. (2008). Servant leadership in sport: A new paradigm for effective coach behavior. *International Journal of Sports Science and Coaching, 3,* 227–239.

Riggs, J. M. (1992). Self-handicapping and achievement. In A. K. Boggiano & T. S. Pittman (Eds.), *Achievement and motivation. A social-developmental perspective* (pp. 244–267). New York, NY: Cambridge University Press.

Riley, L. (2005, February 1). Working on a comeback. But Hunter may never play again. *Hartford Courant,* C1, C3.

Riley, P. (1993). *The winner within. A life plan for team players.* New York, NY: G. P. Putnam's Sons.

Rink, J. E. (1988). *Teaching physical education for learning* (3rd ed.). Boston, MA: McGraw-Hill.

Rip, B., Fortin, S., & Vallerand, R. J. (2006). The relationship between passion and injury in dance students. *Journal of Dance, Medicine, & Science, 10,* 14–20.

Robazza, C. (2006). Emotion in sport: An IZOF perspective. In S. Hanton & S. D. Mellalieu (Eds.), *Literature reviews in sport psychology* (pp. 127–158). New York, NY: Nova Science Publishers.

Robazza, C., & Bortoli, L. (1998). Mental preparation strategies of Olympic archers during competition: an exploratory investigation. *High Ability Studies, 9,* 219–235.

Robazza, C., & Bortoli, L. (2003). Intensity, idiosyncratic content and functional impact of performance-related emotions in athletes. *Journal of Sport Sciences, 21,* 171–189.

Robazza, C., Bortoli, L., & Hanin, Y. (2004). Precompetition emotions, bodily symptoms, and task-specific qualities as predictors of performance in high-level karate athletes. *Journal of Applied Sport Psychology, 16,* 151–165.

Robazza, C., Pellizzari, M., Bertollo, M., & Hanin, Y. L. (2008). Functional impact of emotions on athletic performance: Comparing the IZOF model and the directional perception approach. *Journal of Sports Sciences, 26,* 1033–1047. doi: 10.1080/02640410802027352

Robazza, C., Pellizzari, M., & Hanin, Y. (2004). Emotion self-regulation and athletic performance: An application of the IZOF model. *Psychology of Sport and Exercise, 5,* 379–404.

Roberts, G. C. (2001). Understanding the dynamics of motivation in physical activity: The influence of achievement goals on motivational processes. In G. C. Roberts (Ed.), *Advances in motivation in sport and exercise* (2nd ed., pp. 1–50). Champaign, IL: Human Kinetics.

Roberts, G. C., Spink, K. S., & Pemberton, C. L. (1999). *Learning experiences in sport psychology* (2nd ed.). Champaign, IL: Human Kinetics Press.

Roberts, G. C., & Treasure, D. C. (1999). Applied sport psychology. In A. M. Stec & D. A. Bernstein (Eds.), *Psychology: Fields of application* (pp. 116–126). Boston, MA: Houghton Mifflin.

Roberts, G. C., Treasure, D. C., & Balague, G. (1998). Achievement goals in sport: The development and validation of the Perceptions of Success Questionnaire. *Journal of Sport Sciences, 16,* 337–347.

Roberts, G. C., Treasure, D. C., & Conroy, D. E. (2007). Understanding the dynamics of motivation in sport and physical activity. Anticipation and decision making. In G. Tenenbaum & R. C. Eklund (Eds.), *Handbook of sport psychology* (3rd ed., pp. 3–30). New York, NY: Wiley.

Roberts, R., Callow, N., Hardy, L., Markland, D., & Bringer, J. (2008). Movement imagery ability: Development and assessment of a revised version of the Vividness of Movement Imagery Questionnaire. *Journal of Sport & Exercise Psychology, 30,* 200–221.

Roberts, R., Callow, N., Hardy, L., Woodman, T., & Thomas, L. (2010). Interactive effects of different visual imagery perspectives and narcissism on motor performance. *Journal of Sport & Exercise Psychology, 32,* 499–517.

Roberts, S. (1997, October 26). N.B.A.'s uncontrolled substance. *The New York Times, Section 8,* 1, 7.

Robson-Ansley, P. J., Gleeson, M., & Ansley, L. (2009). Fatigue management in the preparation of Olympic athletes. *Journal of Sports Sciences, 27,* 1409–1420. doi: 10.1080/02640410802702186

Rogers, C. (1954). *Becoming a person.* Oberlin, OH: Oberlin College.

Rogers, T. J., & Landers, D. M. (2005). Mediating effects of peripheral vision in the life event stress/athletic injury relationship. *Journal of Sport & Exercise Psychology, 27,* 271–288.

Rogerson, L. J., & Hrycaiko, D. W. (2002). Enhancing competitive performance of ice hockey goaltenders using centering and self-talk. *Journal of Applied Sport Psychology, 14,* 14–26.

Rohman, L. (2009). The relationship between anabolic androgenic steroids and muscle dysmorphia: A review. *Eating Disorders, 17,* 187–199. doi: 10.1080/10640260902848477

Romei, V. (2012, November 14). Countries' average body mass: A weighty subject. *Financial Times.* Retrieved from http://blogs.ft.com/ftdata/2012/11/14/countries-average-body-mass-a-weighty-subject/

Ronglan, L. T. (2007). Building and communicating collective efficacy: A season-long in-depth study of an elite sport team. *The Sport Psychologist, 21,* 78–93.

Roper, E. A. (2002). Women working in the applied domain: Examining the gender bias in applied sport psychology. *Journal of Applied Sport Psychology, 14,* 53–66.

Roper, E. A. (2012). Gender, identity, and sport. In S. M. Murphy (Ed.), *The Oxford handbook of sport and performance psychology* (pp. 384–399). New York, NY: Oxford University Press.

Rose, J., & Jevne, R. F. J. (1993). Psychosocial processes associated with athletic injuries. *The Sport Psychologist, 7,* 309–328.

Ross, M. J., & Berger, R. S. (1996). Effects of stress inoculation training on athletes' postsurgical pain and rehabilitation after orthopedic injury. *Journal of Consulting and Clinical Psychology, 64,* 406–410.

Ross-Stewart, L., & Short, S. A. (2009). The frequency and perceived effectiveness of images used to build, maintain, and regain confidence. *Journal of Applied Sport Psychology, 21 (Supp. 1),* S34-S47.

Roth, S., & Cohen, L. J. (1986). Approach, avoidance, and coping with stress. *American Psychologist, 41,* 813–819.

Rovivo, E., Arvinen-Barrow, M., Weigand, D. A., Eskola, J., & Lintunen, T. (2012). Using team building methods with an ice hockey team: An action research case study. *Sport Psychologist, 26,* 584–603.

Rowley, A. J., Landers, D. M., Kyllo, L. B., & Etnier, J. L. (1995). Does the iceberg profile discriminate between successful and less successful athletes? A meta-analysis. *Journal of Sport & Exercise Psychology, 17,* 185–199.

Rowold, J. (2006). Transformational and transactional leadership in martial arts. *Journal of Applied Sport Psychology, 18,* 312–325.

Rozell, E. J., Gundersen, D. E., & Terpstra, D. E. (1997). Gender differences in the factors affecting helplessness behavior and performance. *Journal of Social Behavior and Personality, 13,* 265–280.

Ruch, F. (1937). *Psychology and life.* New York, NY: Scott, Foresman.

Ruddock-Hudson, M., O'Halloran, P., & Murphy, G. (2012) Exploring psychological reactions to injury in the Australian Football League (AFL). *Journal of Applied Sport Psychology, 24,* 375–390. doi: 10.1080/10413200.2011.654172

Rudolph, D. L., & McAuley, E. (1995). Self-efficacy and salivary cortical responses to acute exercise in physically active and less active adults. *Journal of Sport & Exercise Psychology, 17,* 206–213.

Ruiz, M. C., & Hanin, Y. L. (2004). Metaphoric description and individualized emotion profiling of performance related states in high-level karate athletes. *Journal of Applied Sport Psychology, 16,* 258–273.

Ruiz, M. C., & Hanin, Y. L. (2011). Perceived impact of anger on performance of skilled karate athletes. *Psychology of Sport and Exercise, 12,* 242–249. doi: 10.1016/j.psychsport.2011.01.005

Rumbold, J. L., Fletcher, D., & Daniels, K. (2012). A systematic review of stress management interventions with sport performers. *Sport, Exercise, and Performance Psychology, 1,* 173–193. doi: 10.1037/a0026628

Rushall, B., Hall, M., Roux, L., Sasseville, J., & Rushall, A. C. (1988). Effects of three types of thought content instructions on skiing performance. *The Sport Psychologist, 2,* 283–297.

Russell, K. L., & Bray, S. R. (2009). Self-determined motivation predicts independent, home-based exercise following cardiac rehabilitation. *Rehabilitation Psychology, 54,* 150–156. doi: 10.1037/a0015595

Russell, P. (1976). *The TM technique.* London, England: Routledge & Kegan Paul.

Ryan, M. K., Williams, J. M., & Wimer, B. (1990). Athletic aggression: Perceived legitimacy and behavioral intentions in girls' high school basketball. *Journal of Sport & Exercise Psychology, 12,* 48–55.

Ryan, R. M. (1982). Control and information in the interpersonal sphere: An extension of cognitive evaluation theory. *Journal of Personality and Social Psychology, 43,* 450–461.

Ryan, R. M., & Deci, E. L. (2000). Self-determination theory and the facilitation of intrinsic motivation, social development, and well-being. *American Psychologist, 55,* 68–78.

Ryan, R. M., & Deci, E. L. (2007). Active human nature: Self-determination theory and the promotion and maintenance of sport, exercise, and health. In M. S. Hagger, &

N.L.D. Chatzisarantis, (Eds.), *Intrinsic motivation and self-determination in exercise and sport* (pp. 1–19). Champaign, IL: Human Kinetics.

Ryba, T. V., Stambulova, N. B., Wrisberg, C. A. (2005). The Russian origins of sport psychology: A translation of an early work of A. Z. Puni. *Journal of Applied Sport Psychology, 17,* 157–169.

Rymal, A. M., Martini, R., & Ste-Marie, D. M. (2010). Self-regulatory processes employed during self-modeling: A qualitative analysis. *The Sport Psychologist, 24,* 1–15.

Ryska, T. A. (2001). The impact of acculturation on sport motivation among Mexican-American adolescent athletes. *The Psychological Record, 51,* 533–547.

Ryska, T. A. (2009). Multivariate analysis of program goals, leadership style, and occupational burnout among intercollegiate sport coaches. *Journal of Sport Behavior, 32,* 476–488.

Ryska, R. A., & Yin, Z. (1999). The role of dispositional goal orientation and team climate on situational self-handicapping among young athletes. *Journal of Sport Behavior, 22,* 410–425.

Ryska, R. A., Yin, Z., Cooley, D., & Ginn, R. (1999). Developing team cohesion: A comparison of cognitive-behavioral strategies of U.S. and Australian sport coaches. *Journal of Psychology, 133,* 523–539.

Sagar, S. S., Busch, B. K., & Jowett, S. (2010). Success and failure, fear of failure, and coping responses of adolescent academy football players. *Journal of Applied Sport Psychology, 22,* 213–230.

Sagar, S. S., & Lavallee, D. (2010). The developmental origins of fear of failure in adolescent athletes: Examining parental practices. *Psychology of Sport and Exercise, 11,* 177–187. doi: 10.1016.j.psychsport.2010.01.004

Sagar, S. S., & Stoeber, J. (2009). Perfectionism, fear of failure, and affective responses to success and failure: The central role of fear of experiencing shame and embarrassment. *Journal of Sport & Exercise Psychology, 31,* 602–627.

Sage, G. H., & Loudermilk, S. (1979). The female athlete and role conflict. *Research Quarterly, 50,* 88–96.

Sage, L. D., & Kavussanu, M. (2007). Multiple goal orientations as predictors of moral behavior for youth soccer. *The Sport Psychologist, 21,* 417–437.

Sage, L. D., & Kavussanu, M. (2008). Goal orientations, motivational climate, and prosocial and antisocial behavior in youth football: Exploring their temporal stability and reciprocal relationships. *Journal of Sports Sciences, 26,* 717–732. doi: 10.1080/02640410701769716

Sage, L., & Kavussanu, M. (2007). The effects of goal involvement on moral behavior in an experimentally manipulated competitive setting. *Journal of Sport & Exercise Psychology, 29,* 190–207.

Sailes, G. A. (1993). An investigation of campus stereotypes: The myth of black athletic superiority and the dumb jock stereotype. *Sociology of Sport Journal, 10,* 88–97.

Salazar, W., Landers, D. M., Petruzello, S. J., Han, M., Crews, D. J., & Kubitz, K. A. (1990). Hemispheric asymmetry, cardiac response, and performance in elite archers. *Research Quarterly for Exercise and Sport, 61*(4), 351–359.

Salminen, S. (1990). Sex role and participation in traditionally inappropriate sports. *Perceptual & Motor Skills, 71,* 1216–1218.

Salmon, P., Hanneman, S., & Harwood, B. (2010). Associative/dissociative cognitive strategies in sustained physical activity: Literature review and proposal for a mindfulness-based conceptual model. *The Sport Psychologist, 23,* 127–156.

Sanchez, X., Boschker, M.S.J., & Llewellyn, D. J. (2010). Pre-performance psychological states and performance in an elite climbing competition. *Scandinavian Journal of Medicine & Science in Sports, 20,* 356–363. doi: 10.1111/j.1600-0838.2009.00403.x

Sanders, G. S., Baron, R. S., & Moore, D. L. (1978). Distraction and social comparison as mediators of social facilitation effects. *Journal of Experimental Social Psychology, 14,* 291–303.

Sanna, L. J. (1998). Defensive pessimism and optimism: The bitter-sweet influence of mood on performance and prefactual and counterfactual thinking. *Cognition and Emotion, 12,* 635–665.

Sapieja. K. M., Dunn, J. G. H., & Holt, N. L. (2011). Perfectionism and perceptions of parenting styles in male youth soccer. *Journal of Sport & Exercise Psychology, 33,* 20–39.

Sarason, I. G. (1972). Test anxiety and the model who fails. *Journal of Personality and Social Psychology, 22,* 410–413.

Sarason, I. G. (1973). Test anxiety and cognitive modeling. *Journal of Personality and Social Psychology, 28,* 58–61.

Sarason, I. G. (1981). Test anxiety, stress, and social support. *Journal of Personality, 49,* 101–114.

Sarason, I. G., Pierce, G. R., & Sarason, B. R. (1996). Domains of cognitive interference. In I. G. Sarason, G. R. Pierce, & B. R. Sarason (Eds.), *Cognitive interference theories, methods, and findings* (pp. 139–152). Mahwah, NJ: Lawrence Erlbaum Associates.

Sarason, I. G., Potter, E. H., & Sarason, B. R. (1986). Recording and recall of personal events: Effects on cognitions and behavior. *Journal of Personality and Social Psychology, 51*, 347–356.

Sarason, I. G., & Sarason, B. R. (1986). Experimentally provided social support. *Journal of Personality and Social Psychology, 50*, 1222–1225.

Sarason, I. G., Sarason, B. R., & Pierce, G. R. (1995). Cognitive interference. At the intelligence-personality crossroads. In D. H. Saklofske & M. Zeidner (Eds.), *International handbook of personality and intelligence* (pp. 285–296). New York, NY: Plenum Press.

Sarrazin, P., Vallerand, R. J., Guillet, E., Pelletier, L. G., & Cury, F. (2002). Motivation and dropout in female handballers: A 21-month prospective study. *European Journal of Social Psychology, 32*, 395–418.

Sarrazin, P., Biddle, S., Famose, J. P., Cury, F., Fox, K., & Durand, M. (1996). Goal orientations and conceptions of the nature of sport ability in children: A social cognitive approach. *British Journal of Social Psychology, 35*, 399–414.

Sas-Nowosielski, K., & Swiatkowska, L. (2008). Goal orientations and attitudes toward doping. *International Journal of Sports Medicine, 29*, 607–612.

Safdar, A., Bourgeois, J. M., Ogborn, D. I., Little, J. P., Hettinga, B. P., Akhtar, M., . . . Tarnopolsky, M. A. (2011, February 22). Endurance exercise rescues progeroid aging and induces systemic mitochondrial rejuvenation in mtDNA mutator mice. *Proceedings of the National Academy of Sciences of the United States of America, 108*, 4135–4140. doi: 10.1073/pnas.1019581108

Saulny, S. (2011, January 29). Black? White? Asian? More young Americans choose all of the above. *The New York Times*. Retrieved from http://www.nyt.com

Savis, J. C. (1994). Sleep and athletic performance: Overview and implications for sport psychology. *The Sport Psychologist, 8*, 111–125.

Scanlan, T. K., & Lewthwaite, R. (1984). Social psychological aspects of competition for male youth sport participants: I. Predictors of competitive stress. *Journal of Sport Psychology, 6*, 208–226.

Scanlan, T. K., Lewthwaite, R., & Jackson, B. L. (1984). Social psychological aspects of competition for male youth sport participants: II. Predictors of performance outcomes. *Journal of Sport Psychology, 6*, 422–429.

Scanlan, T. K., Russell, D. G., Magyar, T. M., & Scanlan, L. A. (2009). Project on elite athlete commitment (PEAK): III. An examination of the external validity across gender and the expansion and clarification of the Sport Commitment Model. *Journal of Sport & Exercise Psychology, 31*, 685–705.

Scheiber, D. (1990). Tennis' new legend in the making. *Saturday Evening Post, 262, Issue 5*, 68–71.

Scherzer, C. B., Brewer, B. W., Cornelius, A. E., Van Raalte, J. L., Petitpas, A. J., Sklar, J. H., Pohlman, M. H., Krushell, R. J., & Ditmar, T. D. (2001). Psychological skills and adherence to rehabilitation after reconstruction of the anterior cruciate ligament. *Journal of Sport Rehabilitation, 10*, 165–172.

Schlenker, B. R., Phillips, S. T., Boniecki, K. A., & Schlenker, D. R. (1995). Championship pressures: Choking or triumphing in one's own territory. *Journal of Personality and Social Psychology, 68*, 632–643.

Schmader, T., Johns, M., & Forbes, C. (2008). An integrated process model of stereotype threat effects on performance. *Psychological Review, 115*, 336–356.

Schmid, A., & Peper, E. (1993). Training strategies for concentration. In J. M. Williams (Ed.), *Applied sport psychology. Personal growth to peak performance* (2nd ed., pp. 262–273). Mountain View, CA: Mayfield.

Schmidt, G. W., & Stein, G. L. (1991). Sport commitment: A model integrating enjoyment, dropout, and burnout. *Journal of Sport & Exercise Psychology, 8*, 254–265.

Schmidt, R. A. (1975). A schema theory of discrete motor learning. *Psychological Review, 82*, 225–260.

Schmidt, R. A. (1982). More on motor programs. In J. A. S. Kelso (Ed.), *Human motor behavior: An introduction* (pp. 219–235). Hillsdale, NJ: Erlbaum.

Schneider, R. H., Alexander, C. N., & Wallace, R. K. (1992). In search of an optimal behavioral treatment for hypertension: A review and focus on Transcendental Meditation. In E. H. Johnson, W. D. Gentry, & S. Julius (Eds.), *Personality, elevated blood pressure, & essential hypertension* (pp. 291–316). Washington, DC: Hemisphere.

Schommer, N. C., Hellhammer, D. H., & Kirschbaum, C. (2003). Dissociation between reactivity of the hypothalamus-pituitary-adrenal axis and the sympathetic-adrenal-medullary system to repeated psychosocial stress. *Psychosomatic Medicine, 65*, 450–460.

Schouwenburg, H. C. (1995). Academic procrastination. Theoretical notions, measurement, and research. In J. R. Ferrari, J. L. Johnson, & W. G. McCown (Eds.), *Procrastination and task avoidance. Theory, research and treatment* (pp. 71–96). New York, NY: Plenum.

Schroeder, P. J. (2009). Changing team culture: The perspectives of ten successful head coaches. *Journal of Sport Behavior, 32,* 63–88.

Schuckit, M. A. (1994). Low level of response to alcohol as a predictor of future alcoholism. *American Journal of Psychiatry, 151,* 184–189.

Schuler, J., & Brunner, S. (2009). The rewarding effect of flow experience on performance in a marathon race. *Psychology of Sport and Exercise, 10,* 168–174. doi: 10.1016.j.psychsport.2008.07.001

Schuler, J., & Langens, T. A. (2007). Psychological crisis in a marathon and the buffering effects of self-verbalizations. *Journal of Applied Social Psychology, 37,* 2319–2344.

Schultz, J. (1932). Das Autogene Training (Konzentrative Selbstentspannung). Leipzig, Germany: Thieme.

Schultz, R. W., Eom, H. J., Smoll, F. L., & Smith, R. E. (1994). Examination of the factorial validity of the Group Environment Questionnaire. *Research Quarterly for Exercise and Sport, 65,* 226–236.

Schunk, D. H. (1989). Self-efficacy and achievement behaviors. *Educational Psychology Review, 1,* 173–208.

Schurr, K. T., Ashley, M. A., & Joy, K. L. (1977). A multivariate analysis of male athlete personality characteristics: Sport type and success. *Multivariate Experimental Clinical Research, 3,* 53–68.

Schwanhausser, L. (2009). Application of the Mindfulness-Acceptance-Commitment (MAC) protocol with an adolescent springboard diver. *Journal of Clinical Sports Psychology, 4,* 377–395.

Schwartz, G. E., Davidson, R. J., & Goleman, D. J. (1978). Patterning of cognitive and somatic processes in the self-regulation of anxiety: Effects of meditation versus exercise. *Psychosomatic Medicine, 40,* 321–328.

Schwarzer, R. (1996). Thought control of action: Interfering self-doubts. In I. G. Sarason, G. R. Pierce, & B. R. Sarason (Eds.), *Cognitive interference theories, methods, and findings* (pp. 99–115). Mahwah, NJ: Lawrence Erlbaum Associates.

Scott, J. P. R., McNaughton, L. R., & Polman, R. C. J. (2006). Effects of sleep deprivation and exercise on cognitive, motor performance and mood. *Physiology & Behavior, 87,* 396–408. doi: 10.1016/j.physbeh.2005.11.009

Scripture, E. W. (1900). Cross-education. *Popular Science, 56,* 589–596.

Seabourne, T. G., Weinberg, R. S., Jackson, A., & Suinn, R. M. (1985). Effect of individualized, nonindividualized and package intervention strategies on karate performance. *Journal of Sport Psychology, 7,* 40–50.

Sedek, G., & Kofta, M. (1990). When cognitive exertion does not yield cognitive gain: Toward an informational explanation of learned helplessness. *Journal of Personality and Social Psychology, 58,* 729–743.

Segal, B. (1986). Confirmatory analyses of reasons for experiencing psychoactive drugs during adolescence. *International Journal of the Addictions, 20,* 1649–1662.

Segal, Z. V., Williams, J. M., & Teasdale, J. D. (2002). *Mindfulness-based cognitive therapy for depression: A new approach to preventing relapse.* New York, NY: Guilford Press.

Seibt, B., & Förster, J. (2004). Stereotype threat and performance: How self-stereotypes influence processing by inducing regulatory foci. *Journal of Personality and Social Psychology, 87,* 38–56.

Seligman, M. (1975). *Helplessness: On depression, development, and death.* San Francisco, CA: Freeman.

Seligman, M. E. P. (1990). *Learned optimism.* New York, NY: Pocket Books.

Seligman, M. E. P., Abramson, L. Y., Semmel, A., & von Baeyer, C. (1979). Depressive attributional style. *Journal of Abnormal Psychology, 88,* 242–247.

Seligman, M. E., & Maier, S. F. (1967). Failure to escape traumatic shock. *Journal of Experimental Psychology, 74,* 1–9.

Seligman, M. E., Maier, S. F., & Geer, J. H. (1968). Alleviation of learned helplessness in the dog. *Journal of Abnormal Psychology, 73,* 256–262.

Seligman, M. E. P., Nolen-Hoeksema, S., Thornton, N., & Thornton, K. M. (1990). Explanatory style as a mechanism of disappointing athletic performance. *Psychological Science, 1,* 143–146.

Senecal, J., Loughead, T. M., & Bloom, G. A. (2008). A season-long team-building intervention: Examining the effect of team goal setting on cohesion. *Journal of Sport & Exercise Psychology, 30,* 186–199.

Serrao, H. F., Martens, M. P., Martin, J. L., & Rocha, T. L. (2008). Competitiveness and alcohol use among recreational and elite collegiate athletes. *Journal of Clinical Sport Psychology, 2,* 205–215.

Seve, C., Saury, J., Leblanc, S., & Durand, M. (2005). Course of action theory in table tennis: a qualitative analysis of the knowledge used by three elite players during matches. *Revue Europeene de Psychologie Appliquee, 55,* 145–155. doi: 10.1016/j.erap.2005.04.001

Seve, C., Saury, J., Theureau, J., & Durand, M. (2002). Activity organization and knowledge construction during competitive table tennis. *Cognitive Systems Research, 3,* 501–522.

Shadish, W. R., Cook, T. D., & Campbell, D. T. (2002). *Experimental and quasi-experimental designs for generalized causal inference.* Boston, MA: Houghton-Mifflin.

Shain, J. (2001, July 23). Du-validation. Leaves field behind for 1st major title. *Hartford Courant,* C1, C7.

Shambrook, C. J., & Bull, S. J. (1999). Adherence to psychological preparation in sport. In S. J. Bull (Ed.), *Adherence issues in sport and exercise* (pp. 169–196). Chichester, England: Wiley.

Shapiro, S. L., & Carlson, L. E. (2009). *The art and science of mindfulness. Integrating mindfulness into psychology and the helping professions.* Washington, DC: American Psychological Association.

Shapiro, S. L., Carlson, L. E., Astin, J. A., & Freedman, B. (2006). Mechanisms of mindfulness. *Journal of Clinical Psychology, 62,* 373–386.

Sharp, L-A., & Hodge, K. (2011). Sport psychology consulting effectiveness: The sport psychology consultant's perspective. *Journal of Applied Sport Psychology, 23,* 360–376. doi: 10.1080/10413200.2011.583619

Shaw, L., & Sichel, H. (1971). *Accident proneness.* London, England: Penguin.

Shea, J. (2002). Buzz on. Caffeine spreads from coffee to soft drinks, candy, even soap. *Hartford Courant,* D1.

Sheard, M., & Golby, J. (2006). Effect of a psychological skills training program on swimming performance and positive psychological development. *International Journal of Sport and Exercise Psychology, 4,* 149–169.

Sheldon, J. P., & Eccles, J. S. (2005). Physical and psychological predictors of perceived ability in adult male and female tennis players. *Journal of Applied Sport Psychology, 17,* 48–63.

Sheldon, K. M., Elliot, A. J. (1999). Goal striving, need satisfaction, and longitudinal well-being: The self-concordance model. *Journal of Personality and Social Psychology, 76,* 482–497.

Sheldon, W. H. (1940). *The varieties of human physique.* New York, NY: Harper.

Sheldon, W. H. (1942). *The varieties of human temperament.* New York, NY: Harper.

Sherman, C. A., Fuller, R., & Speed, H. D. (2000). Gender comparisons of preferred coaching behaviors in Australian sports. *Journal of Sport Behavior, 23,* 389–406.

Sherman, E. (2001, July 23). Those extra drivers. Extra club costs Woosnam. *Hartford Courant,* C7.

Shields, C. A., Paskevich, D. M., & Brawley, L. R. (2003). Self-handicapping in structured and unstructured exercise: Toward a measurable construct. *Journal of Sport & Exercise Psychology, 25,* 267–283.

Short, S. E., Bruggeman, J. M., Engel, S. G., Marback, T. L., Wang, L. J., Willandsen, A., & Short, M. W. (2002). The effect of imagery function and imagery direction on self-efficacy and performance on a golf-putting task. *The Sport Psychologist, 16,* 48–67.

Short, S. E., Monsma, E. A., & Short, M. W. (2004). Is what you see really what you get? Athletes' perceptions of imagery's functions. *The Sport Psychologist, 10,* 341–349.

Short, S. E., Smiley, M., & Ross-Stewart, L. (2005). The relationships among imagery use and efficacy beliefs in coaches. *The Sport Psychologist, 19,* 380–394.

Siedentop, D. (2002). Junior sport and the evolution of sport cultures. *Journal of Teaching in Physical Education, 21,* 392–401.

Siegel, D. J. (2007). *The mindful brain: Reflection and attunement in the cultivation of well-being.* New York, NY: W.W. Norton & Company.

Silva, J. M., III. (1982). An evaluation of fear of success in female and male athletes and nonathletes. *Journal of Sport Psychology, 4,* 92–96.

Silva, J. M., III. (1989).The evolution of the association for the advancement of applied sport psychology and the Journal of Applied Sport Psychology. *Applied Sport Psychology, 2,* 5–20.

Silva, J. M., III. (1990). An analysis of the training stress syndrome in competitive athletics. *Applied Sport Psychology, 2,* 5–20.

Silva, J. M. III, & Andrew, J. A. (1987). An analysis of game location and basketball performance in the Atlantic Coast Conference. *International Journal of Sport Psychology, 18,* 188–204.

Silva, J. M., III, & Conroy, D. E. (1995). Understanding aggressive behavior and its effects upon athletic performance. In K. P. Henschen & W. F. Straub (Eds.), *Sport psychology an analysis of athlete behavior* (3rd ed., pp. 149–159). Longmeadow, MA: Mouvement.

Silva, J. M., III, Conroy, D. E., & Zizzi, S. J. (1999). Critical issues confronting the advancement of applied sport psychology. *Journal of Applied Sport Psychology, 11,* 298–320.

Singer, J. N. (2009). African American football athletes' perspectives on institutional integrity in college sport. *Research Quarterly for Exercise and Sport, 80,* 102–116.

Singer, R. N. (1989). Applied sport psychology in the United States. *Applied Sport Psychology, 1,* 61–80.

Singer, R. N. (2002). Preperformance state, routines, and automaticity: What does it take to realize expertise in self-paced events? *Journal of Sport & Exercise Psychology, 24,* 359–375.

Singer, R. N., Cauraugh, J. H., Chen, D., Steinberg, G. M., & Frehlich, S. G. (1996). Visual search, anticipation, and reactive comparisons between highly-skilled and beginning tennis players. *Journal of Applied Sport Psychology, 8,* 9–26.

Singh, G. K., Kogan, M. D., & van Dyck, P. C. (2010). Changes in state-specific childhood obesity and overweight prevalence in the United States from 2003 to 2007. *Archives of Pediatrics & Adolescent Medicine, 164,* 598–607.

Singh, N. A., Clements, K. M., Fiatarone Singh, M. A. (2001). The efficacy of exercise as a long-term antidepressant in elderly subjects: A randomized, controlled trial. *Journal of Gerontology: Medical Sciences, 56,* M497-M504. doi: 10.1093/Gerona/56.8.M497

Singh, N. A., Stavrinos, T. M., Scarbek, Y, Galambos, G., Liber, C., & Singh, M. A. F. (2005). A randomized controlled trial of high versus low intensity weight training versus general practitioner care for clinical depression in older adults. *Journal of Gerontology: Medical Sciences, 60,* 768–776. doi: 10.1093/Gerona/60.9.768

Sisley, B. L., Weiss, M. R., Barber, H., & Ebbeck, V. (1990). Developing competence and confidence in novice women coaches-A study of attitudes, motives, and perceptions of ability. *Journal of Physical Education, Recreation & Dance, 61,* 60–64.

Slade, P. D., Coppel, D. B., & Townes, B. D. (2009). Neurocognitive correlates of positive and negative perfectionism. *International Journal of Neuroscience, 119,* 1741–1754. doi: 10.1080/00207450902915212

Slanger, E., & Rudestam, K. E. (1997). Motivation and disinhibition in high risk sports: Sensation seeking and self-efficacy. *Journal of Research in Personality, 31,* 355–373.

Slater, A., & Tiggemann, M. (2010). "Uncool to do sport": A focus group study of adolescent girls' reasons for withdrawing from physical activity. *Psychology of Sport and Exercise, 11,* 619–626.

Slater, M. R., & Sewell, D. F. (1994). An examination of the cohesion-performance relationship in university hockey teams. *Journal of Sports Sciences, 12,* 423–431.

Slobounov, S., Yukelson, D., & O'Brien, R. (1997). Self-efficacy and movement variability of Olympic-level springboard divers. *Journal of Applied Sport Psychology, 9,* 171–190.

Smedley, A., & Smedley, B. D. (2005). Race as biology is fiction, racism as a social problem is real: Anthropological and historical perspectives on the social construction of race. *American Psychologist, 60,* 16–26.

Smeeton, N. J., Williams, A. M., Hodges, N. J., & Ward, P. (2005). The relative effectiveness of various instructional approaches in developing anticipation skills. *Journal of Experimental Psychology: Applied, 11,* 98–110.

Smith, A., Adler, C., Crews, D., Wharen, R., Laskowski, E., Barnes, K., . . . Kaufman, K. R. (2003). The "yips" in golf: A continuum between a focal dystonia and choking. *Sports Medicine, 33,* 13–31.

Smith, A., Ntoumanis, N., & Duda, J. (2010). An investigation of coach behaviors, goal motives, and implementation intentions as predictors of well-being in sport. *Journal of Applied Sport Psychology, 22,* 17–33.

Smith, A.C.T., & Stewart, B. (2008). Drug policy in sport: Hidden assumptions and inherent contradictions. *Drug and Alcohol Review, 27,* 123–129. doi: 10.1080/09595230701829355

Smith, D., Wright, C., Allsopp, A., & Westhead, H. (2007). It's all in the mind: PETTLEP-Based imagery and sports performance. *Journal of Applied Sport Psychology, 19,* 80–92.

Smith, D., Wright, C., & Winrow, D. (2010). Exercise dependence and social physique anxiety in competitive and non-competitive runners. *International Journal of Sport and Exercise Psychology, 8,* 61–69. doi: 10.1080/1612197X.2010.9671934

Smith, H. W. (1994). *The 10 natural laws of successful time and life management: Proven strategies for increased productivity and inner peace.* New York, NY: Warner.

Smith, J. C. (1990). *Cognitive-behavioral relaxation training: A new system of strategies for treatment and assessment.* New York, NY: Springer.

Smith, J. C., Amutio, A., Anderson, J. P., & Aria, L. A. (1996). Relaxation: Mapping an uncharted world. *Biofeedback and Self-Regulation, 21,* 63–90.

Smith, M., & Lee, C. (1992). Goal setting and performance in a novel coordination task: Mediating mechanisms. *Journal of Sport & Exercise Psychology, 14,* 169–176.

Smith, N. C., Bellamy, M., Collins, D. J., & Newell, D. (2001). A test of processing efficiency theory in a team sport context. *Journal of Sport Sciences, 19,* 321–332.

Smith, P. J., Humiston, S. G., Marcuse, E. K., Zhao, Z., Dorell, C. g., Howes, C., & Hibbs, B. (2011). Parental delay or refusal of vaccine doses, childhood vaccination coverage at 24 months of age, and the health belief model [Supplement 2]. *Public Health Reports, 126,* 135–146.

Smith, R. E. (1986). Toward a cognitive-affective model of athletic burnout. *Journal of Sport Psychology, 8,* 36–50.

Smith, R. E. (1996). Performance anxiety, cognitive interference, and concentration enhancement strategies in sports. In I. G. Sarason, G. R. Pierce, & B. R. Sarason (Eds.), *Cognitive interference theories, methods, and findings* (pp. 261–283). Mahwah, NJ: Lawrence Erlbaum Associates.

Smith, R. E. (1999). Generalization effects in coping skills training. *Journal of Sport and Exercise Psychology, 21,* 189–204.

Smith, R. E. (2006). Understanding sport behavior: A cognitive-affective processing systems approach. *Journal of Applied Sport Psychology, 18,* 1–27.

Smith, R. E. (2010). A positive approach to coaching effectiveness and performance enhancement. In J. M. Williams (Ed.), *Applied sport psychology: Personal growth to peak performance* (6th ed., pp. 42–58). New York, NY: McGraw-Hill.

Smith, R. E., Cumming, S. P., & Smoll, F. L. (2008). Development and validation of the Motivational Climate Scale for Youth Sports. *Journal of Applied Sport Psychology, 20,* 116–136.

Smith, R. E., & Christensen, D. S. (1995). Psychological skills as predictors of performance and survival in professional baseball. *Journal of Sport & Exercise Psychology, 17,* 399–415.

Smith, R. E., Schutz, R. W., Smoll, F. L., & Ptacek, J. T. (1995). Development and validation of a multidimensional measure of sport-specific psychological skills: The Athletic Coping Skills Inventory-28. *Journal of Sport & Exercise Psychology, 17,* 379–398.

Smith, R. E., & Smoll F. L. (1990). Self-esteem and children's reactions to youth sport coaching behaviors: A field study of self-enhancement processes. *Developmental Psychology, 26,* 987–993.

Smith, R. E., & Smoll, F. L. (1997). Coach-mediated team building in youth sports. *Journal of Applied Sport Psychology, 9,* 114–132.

Smith, R. E., & Smoll, F. L. (2002a). *Way to go, coach! A scientifically-proven approach to coaching effectiveness* (2nd ed.). Portola Valley, CA: Warde.

Smith, R. E., & Smoll, F. L. (2002b). Youth sports as a behavior setting for psychosocial interventions. In J. L. Van Raalte & B. W. Brewer (Eds.), *Exploring sport and exercise psychology* (2nd ed., pp. 341–372). Washington, DC: American Psychological Association.

Smith, R. E., & Smoll, F. L. (2005). Assessing psychosocial outcomes in coach training programs. In D. Hackfort, J. Duda, & R. Lidor (Eds.), *Handbook of applied sport and exercise psychology* (pp. 293–316). Morgantown, WV: Fitness Technology.

Smith, R. E., Smoll, F. L., & Barnett, N. P. (1995). Reduction of children's sport performance anxiety through social support and stress-reduction training for coaches. *Journal of Applied Developmental Psychology, 16,* 125–142.

Smith, R. E., Smoll, F. L., & Cumming, S. P. (2007). Effects of a motivational climate intervention for coaches on young athletes' sport performance anxiety. *Journal of Sport & Exercise Psychology, 29,* 39–59.

Smith, R. E., Smoll, F. L., & Cumming, S. P. (2009). Motivational climate and changes in young athletes' achievement goal orientations. *Motivation and Emotion, 33,* 173–183.

Smith, R. E., Smoll, F. L., Cumming, S. P., & Grossbard, J. R. (2006). Measurement of multidimensional sport performance anxiety in children and adults: The Sport Anxiety Scale-2. *Journal of Sport & Exercise Psychology, 28,* 479–501.

Smith, R. E., Smoll, R. L., & Curtis, B. (1979). Coach effectiveness training: A cognitive-behavioral approach to enhancing relationship skills in youth sport coaches. *Journal of Sport Psychology, 1,* 59–75.

Smith, R. E., Smoll, F. L., & Passer, M. W. (2002). Sport performance anxiety in young athletes. In F. L. Smoll & R. E. Smith (Eds.), *Children and youth in sport: A biosocial perspective* (2nd ed.). Dubuque, IA: Kendall/Hunt.

Smith, R. E., Smoll, E. L., & Ptacek, J. T. (1990). Conjunctive moderator variables in vulnerability and resiliency research: Life stress, social support, coping skills, and adolescent sport injuries. *Journal of Personality and Social Psychology, 58,* 360–370.

Smith, R. E., Smoll, F. L., & Schultz, R. W. (1990). Measurement and correlates of sport-specific cognitive and somatic trait anxiety: The Sport Anxiety Scale. *Anxiety Research, 2,* 263–280.

Smith, R. E., Smoll, F., & Smith, N. J. (1989). *Parents complete guide to youth sports.* Costa Mesa, CA: HDL.

Smith, R. E., Zane, N. W. S., Smoll, F. L., & Coppel, D. B. (1983). Behavioral assessment in youth sports: Coaching behaviors and children's attitudes. *Medicine and Science in Sports and Exercise, 15,* 208–214.

Smith, S. (2010, October 17, 19). Ron Artest: An unlikely advocate. Retrieved from http://www.ESPN.com

Smith, T. W., Snyder, C. R., & Handelsman, M. M. (1982). On the self-serving function of an academic wooden leg: Test anxiety as a self-handicapping strategy. *Journal of Personality and Social Psychology, 42,* 314–321.

Smits, A. J., Berry, A. C., Rosenfield, D., Powers, M. B., Behar, E., & Otto, M. W. (2008). Reducing anxiety sensitivity with exercise, *Anxiety and Depression, 25,* 689–699. doi: 10.1002/da.20411

Smoll, F. L. (1998). Improving the quality of coach-parent relationships in youth sports. In J. M. Williams (Ed.), *Applied sport psychology: Personal growth to peak performance* (3rd ed., pp. 63–73). Mountain View, CA: Mayfield.

Smoll, F. L., & Cumming, S. (2006). Enhancing coach-parent relationships in youth sports: Increasing harmony and minimizing hassle. In J. M. Williams (Ed.), *Applied sport psychology: Personal growth to peak performance* (5th ed., pp. 192–204). New York, NY: McGraw-Hill.

Smoll, F. L., & Smith, R. E. (1988). Reducing stress in youth sport: Theory and application. In F. L. Smoll, R. A. Magill, & M. J. Ash (Eds.), *Children in sport* (3rd. ed., pp. 229–249). Champaign, IL: Human Kinetics.

Smoll, F. L., & Smith, R. E. (1989). Leadership behaviors in sport: A theoretical model and research paradigm. *Journal of Applied Social Psychology, 19,* 1522–1551.

Smoll, F. L., & Smith, R. E. (2002). Coaching behavior research and intervention in youth sports. In F. L. Smoll & R. E. Smith (Eds.), *Children and youth in sport: A biopsychosocial perspective* (pp. 211–231). Dubuque, IA: Kendall/Hunt.

Smoll, F. L., & Smith, R. E. (2010). Development and implementation of coach-training programs. In J. M. Williams (Ed.), *Applied sport psychology: Personal growth to peak performance* (6th ed., pp. 458–482). New York, NY: McGraw-Hill.

Solomon, G. B., Wiegardt, P. A., Wayda, V. K., Yusuf, F. R., Kosmitzki, C., Williams, J., & Stevens, C. E. (1996). Expectancies and ethnicity: The self-fulfilling prophecy in college basketball. *Journal of Sport & Exercise Psychology, 18,* 83–88.

Solowij, N., Stephens, R. S., Roffman, R. A., Babor, T., Kadden, R., Miller, M., Christiansen, K., McRee, B., & Vendetti, J. (2002). Cognitive functioning of long-term heavy cannabis users seeking treatment. *Journal of the American Medical Association, 287,* 1123–1131.

Sordoni, C., Hall, C., & Forwell, L. (2000). The use of imagery by athletes during injury rehabilitation. *Journal of Sport Rehabilitation, 9,* 329–338.

Spencer, J. (February, 8). For some athletes, the road to victory starts with restraint. *Wall Street Journal,* A1.

Spencer, S. J., Steele, C. M., & Quinn, D. M. (1999). Stereotype threat and women's math performance. *Journal of Experimental Social Psychology, 35,* 4–28.

Spielberger, C. D., Gorsuch, R. L., & Lushene, R. E. (1970). *Manual for the State-Trait Anxiety Inventory (STAI).* Palo Alto, CA: Consulting Psychologists Press.

Spielberger, C. D., & Vagg, P. R. (1995). Test anxiety: A transactional process model. In C. D. Spielberger & P. R. Vagg (Eds.), *Test anxiety: Theory, assessment, and treatment* (pp. 3–13). Washington, DC: Taylor & Francis.

Spieler, M., Czech, D. R., Joyner, A. B., Munkasy, B., Gentner, N., & Long, J. (2007). Predicting athletic success: Factors contributing to the success of NCAA Division I AA collegiate football players. *Athletic Insight: The Online Journal of Sport Psychology, 9,* 22–33. Retrieved from http://www.athleticinsight.com

Spink, K. S. (1990). Group cohesion and collective efficacy of volleyball teams. *Journal of Sport & Exercise Psychology, 12,* 301–311.

Spink, K. S. (1995). Cohesion and intention to participate of female sport team athletes. *Journal of Sport & Exercise Psychology, 17,* 416–427.

Spink, K. S., Wilson, K. S., & Odnokon, P. (2010). Examining the relationship between cohesion and return to team in elite athletes. *Psychology of Sport and Exercise, 11,* 6–11. doi: 10.1016/j.psychsport.2009.06.002

Spink, K. S., Wilson, K. S., & Priebe, C. S. (2010). Groupness and adherence in structured exercise settings. *Group Dynamics: Theory, Research, and Practice, 14,* 163–173. doi: 10.1037/a0017596

Stafstrom, M., Ostergren, P-O, & Larsson, S. (2005). Risk factors for frequent high alcohol consumption among Swedish secondary-school students. *Journal of Studies on Alcohol, 66,* 776–783.

Stainback, R. D. (1997). *Alcohol and sport.* Champaign, IL: Human Kinetics.

Stambulova, N., Stambulov, A., & Johnson, U. (2012). 'Believe in yourself, channel energy, and play your trumps': Olympic preparation in complex coordination sports. *Psychology of Sport and Exercise, 13,* 679–686. doi: 10.1016/j.psychsport.2012.04.009

Stambulova, N. B., Wrisberg, C. A., & Ryba, T. V. (2006). A tale of two traditions in applied sport psychology: The heyday of Soviet sport and wake-up calls for North America. *Journal of Applied Sport Psychology, 18,* 173–184.

Standage, M., Gillison, F. B., Ntoumanis, N., & Treasure, D. C. (2012). A prospective cross-domain investigation of motivation across school physical education and exercise settings. *Journal of Sport & Exercise Psychology, 34,* 36–60.

Standage, M., Treasure, D. C., Hooper, K., & Kuczka, K. (2007). Self-handicapping in school physical education: The influence of the motivational climate. *British Journal of Educational Psychology, 77,* 81–99.

Starr, M. (2002a, February 23). Kwan Song. *Newsweek,* 50–55.

Starr, M. (2002b, March 4). Sarah-dipity! *Newsweek, 39,* 34–37.

Starr, M., & Reiss, S. (1994, September 30). Fault, Miss Capriati. *Newsweek, 123,* 70–72.

Stavrou, N. A., Jackson, S. A., Zervas, Y., & Karteroliotis, K. (2007). Flow experience and athletes' performance with reference to the orthogonal model of flow. *The Sport Psychologist, 21,* 438–457.

Stavrou, N. A., & Zervas, Y. (2004). The confirmatory factor analysis of the slow state scale in sports. *International Journal of Sport and Exercise Psychology, 2,* 161–181.

Steel, P., Brothen, T., & Wambach, C. (2001). Procrastination and personality, performance, and mood. *Personality and Individual Differences, 30,* 95–106.

Steele, C. M. (1997). A threat in the air: How stereotypes shape intellectual ability and performance. *American Psychologist, 52,* 613–629.

Steenland, K., & Deddens, J. A. (1997). Effect of travel and rest on performance of professional basketball players. *Sleep, 20,* 366–369.

Steffen, K., Pensgaard, A. M., & Bahr, R. (2008). Self-reported psychological characteristics as risk factors for injuries in female youth football. *Scandinavian Journal of Medicine & Science in Sports, 18,* 1–10. doi: 10.1111/j.1600–0838.2008.00797.x

Stein, J., Bloom, G. A., & Sabiston, C. M. (2012). Influence of perceived and preferred coach feedback on youth athletes' perceptions of team motivational climate. *Psychology of Sport and Exercise, 13,* 484–490. doi: 10.1016/j.psychsport.2012.02.004

Steinfeldt, M., & Steinfeldt, J. A. (2012). Athletic identity and conformity to masculine norms among college football players. *Journal of Applied Sport Psychology, 24,* 115–128. doi: 10.1808/10413200.2011.603405

Stephan, Y., Deroche, T., Brewer, B. W., Caudroit, J., & Le Scanff, C. (2009). Predictors of perceived susceptibility to sport-related injury among competitive runners: The role of previous experience, neuroticism, and passion for running. *Applied Psychology: An International Review, 58,* 672–687. doi: 10.1111/j.464–0597.2008.00373.x

Stice, E. Y., & Whitenton, K. (2002). Risk factors for body dissatisfaction in adolescent girls: A longitudinal investigation. *Developmental Psychology, 38,* 669–678.

Stinear, C. M., Coxon, J. P., Fleming, M. K., Lim, V. K., Prapavessis, H., Byblow, W. D. (2006). The yips in golf: Multimodal evidence for two subtypes. *Medicine & Science in Sports & Exercise, 38,* 1980–1989. doi: 10.1249/01.mss0000233792.93540.10

Stirling, A. E., Cruz, L. C., & Kerr, G. A. (2012). Influence of retirement on body satisfaction and weight control behaviors: Perceptions of elite rhythmic gymnasts. *Journal of Applied Sport Psychology, 24,* 129–143. doi: 10.1080/10413200.2011.603718

Stoeber, J., & Crombie, R. (2010). Achievement goals and championship performance: Predicting absolute performance and qualification success. *Psychology of Sport and Exercise, 11,* 513–521. doi: 10.1016/j.psychsport.2010.07.007

Stoeber, J., & Otto, K. (2006). Positive conceptions of perfectionism: Approaches, evidence, challenges. *Personality and Social Psychology Review, 10,* 295–319.

Stoeber, J., Otto, K., Pescheck, E., Becker, C., & Stoll, O. (2007). Perfectionism and competitive anxiety in athletes: Differentiating striving for perfection and negative reactions to imperfection. *Personality and Individual Differences, 42,* 959–969.

Stoeber, J., & Rambow, A. (2007). Perfectionism in adolescent school students: Relations to motivation, achievement, and well-being. *Personality and Individual Differences, 42,* 1379–1389.

Stoeber, J., Stoll, O., Pescheck, E., & Otto, K. (2008). Perfectionism and achievement goals in athletes: Relations with approach and avoidance orientations in mastery and performance goals. *Psychology of Sport and Exercise, 9,* 102–121. doi: 10.1016/j.psychsport.2007.02.002

Stoeber, J., Stoll, O., Salmi, O., & Tiikkaja, J. (2009). Perfectionism and achievement goals in young Finnish ice-hockey players aspiring to make the Under-16 national team. *Journal of Sports Sciences, 27,* 85–94.

Stoeber, M., Uphill, M. A., & Hotham, S. (2009). Predicting race performance in triathlon: The role of perfectionism, achievement goals, and personal goal setting: Erratum. *Journal of Sport & Exercise Psychology, 31,* 575.

Stone, J., Lynch, C. I., Sjomeling, M., & Darley, J. M. (1999). Stereotype threat effects on Black and White athletic performance. *Journal of Personality and Social Psychology, 77,* 1213–1227.

Stone, J., Perry, Z. W., & Darley, J. M. (1997). "White men can't jump": Evidence for the perceptual confirmation of racial stereotypes following a basketball game. *Basic and Applied Social Psychology, 19,* 291–306.

Strachan, L., Cote, J., & Deakin, J. (2009). An evaluation of personal and contextual factors in competitive youth sport. *Journal of Applied Sport Psychology, 21,* 340–355.

Strean, W. B. (1995). Youth sport contexts: Coaches' perceptions and implications for intervention. *Journal of Applied Sport Psychology, 7*, 23–37.

Students' Vote on the Graduate Training Accreditation Issue. (1997, September 25). The Annual Conference of the Association for the Advancement of Applied Sport Psychology.

Substance Abuse and Mental Health Services Administration (2011). *Results from the 2010 national survey on drug use and health: Summary of national findings.* NSDUH Series H-41, HHS Publication No. (SMA) 11–4658. Rockville, MD: Substance Abuse and Mental Health Services Administration.

Sue, D. W., & Sue, D. (1999). *Counseling the culturally different: Theory and practice* (3rd ed.). New York, NY: Wiley.

Sue, S. (2006). Cultural competency: From philosophy to research and practice. *Journal of Community Psychology, 34*, 237–245.

Suinn, R. M. (1980). *Psychology in sport. Methods and applications.* Minneapolis, MN: Burgess.

Suinn, R. M. (1985). The 1984 Olympics and sport psychology. *Journal of Sport Psychology, 7*, 321–329.

Suinn, R. M. (1986). *Seven steps to peak performance: The mental training manual for athletes.* Toronto, Ontario: H. Huber.

Suinn, R. M. (1987). Behavioral approaches to stress management in sport. In J. R. May & M. J. Asken (Eds.), *Sport psychology* (pp. 59–75). New York, NY: PMA.

Sullivan, K. A., White, K. M., Young, R. McD., Chang, A., Roos, C., & Scott, C. (2008). Predictors of intention to reduce stroke risk among people at risk of stroke: An application of an extended health belief model. *Rehabilitation Psychology, 53*, 505–512.

Sullivan, P. J., Gee, C. J., & Feltz, D. L. (2006). Playing experience: The content knowledge source of coaching efficacy beliefs. In A. V. Mitel (Ed.), *Trends in educational psychology.* New York, NY: Nova Publishers.

Swenson, D. M., Yard, E. E., Fields, S. K., & Comstock, R. D. (2009). Patterns of recurrent injuries among US high school athletes, 2005–2008. *The American Journal of Sports Medicine, 37*, 1586–1593. doi: 10.1177/0363546509332500

Swift, E. M. (1989, March 6). Facing the music. Wade Boggs stayed cool despite his ex-lover's steamy revelations. *Sports Illustrated, 70*, 38–40, 45.

Symons Downs, D., & Hausenblas, H. A. (2005). Exercise behavior and the theories of reasoned action and planned behavior: A meta-analytic update. *Journal of Physical Activity and Health, 2*, 76–97.

Symons Downs, D., Hausenblas, H. A., & Nigg, C. R. (2005). Factor validity and psychometric examination of the Exercise Dependence Scale-Revised. *Measurement in Physical Education and Exercise Science, 8*, 183–201.

Tainsky, S., & Winfree, J. A. (2010). Discrimination and demand: The effect of international players on attendance in Major League Baseball. *Social Science Quarterly, 91*, 117–128.

Taktek, K. (2004). The effects of mental imagery on the acquisition of motor skills and performance: A literature review with theoretical implications. *Journal of Mental Imagery, 28*, 79–114.

Taliaferro, L. A., Rienzo, B. A., & Donovan, K. A. (2010). Relationships between youth sport participation and selected health risk behaviors from 1999 to 2007. *Journal of School Health, 80*, 399–410.

Tallis, F., & Eysenck, M. W. (1994). Worry: Mechanisms and modulating influences. *Behavioural and Cognitive Psychotherapy, 22*, 37–56.

Tanaka, S. (2012, July 17). How shark-attack survivor got fitter. *Wall Street Journal.* Retrieved from http://online.wsj.com

Tang, T. L., & Reynolds, D. B. (1993). Effects of self-esteem and perceived goal difficulty on goal setting, certainty, task performance, and attributions. *Human Resource Development Quarterly, 4*, 153–170.

Tanner, M. A., Travis, F., Gaylord-King, C., Haaga, D.A.F., Grosswald, S., & Schneider, R. H. (2009). The effects of the Transcendental Meditation program on mindfulness. *Journal of Clinical Psychology, 65*, 574–589. doi: 10.1002/jclp.20544

Tashman, L., S., Tenenbaum, G., & Eklund, R. (2010). The effect of perceived stress on the relationship between perfectionism and burnout in coaches. *Anxiety, Stress, & Coping, 23*, 195–212. doi: 10.1080/10615800802629922

Tauer, J. M., Guenther, C. L., & Rozek, C. (2009). Is there a home choke in decisive playoff basketball games? *Journal of Applied Sport Psychology, 21*, 148–162.

Tauer, J. M., & Harackiewicz, J. M. (2004). The effects of cooperation and competition on intrinsic motivation and performance. *Journal of Personality and Social Psychology. 86*, 849–861. doi: 10.1037/0022-3514.86.6.849

Taylor, D. R., Poulton, R., Moffitt, T. E., Ramankutty, P., & Sears, M. R. (2000). The respiratory effects of cannabis dependence in young adults. *Addiction, 95*, 1669–1677.

Taylor, J. (1988). Slumpbusting: A systematic analysis of slumps in sports. *The Sport Psychologist, 2,* 39–48.

Taylor, J. (1996). Intensity regulation and athletic performance. In J. L. Van Raalte & B. W. Brewer (Eds.), *Exploring sport and exercise psychology* (pp. 75–106). Washington, DC: APA.

Taylor, J. & Lavallee, D. (2010). Career transition among athletes: Is there life after sports? In J. M. Williams (Ed.), *Applied sport psychology: Personal growth to peak performance* (6th ed., pp. 542–562). New York, NY: McGraw-Hill.

Taylor, J. & Ogilvie, B. C. (2001). Career termination among athletes. In R. N. Singer, H. A. Hausenblas, & C. M. Janelle (Eds.), *Handbook of sport psychology* (2nd ed., pp. 787–809). New York, NY: Wiley.

Taylor, J., & Wilson, G. S. (2002). Intensity regulation and sport performance. In J. L. Van Raalte & B. W. Brewer (Eds.), *Exploring sport and exercise psychology* (2nd ed., pp. 99–130). Washington, DC: APA.

Taylor, S. E., Pham, L. B., Rivkin, I. D., & Armor, D. A. (1998). Harnessing the imagination. Mental simulation, self-regulation, and coping. *American Psychologist, 53,* 429–439.

Teasdale, J. D., Segal, Z. V., Williams, J. M. G., Ridgeway, V. A., Soulsby, J. M., & Lau, M. A. (2000). Prevention of relapse/recurrence in major depression by mindfulness-based cognitive therapy. *Journal of Consulting and Clinical Psychology, 68,* 615–623.

Tellegen, A. (1981). Practicing the two disciplines for relaxation and enlightenment: Comment on "Role of the feedback signal in electromyograph biofeedback: The relevance of attention" by Qualls and Sheehan. *Journal of Experimental Psychology: General, 110,* 217–226.

Tenenbaum, G., Stewart, E., Singer, R. N., & Duda, J. (1996). Aggression and violence in sport: An ISSP position stand. *International Journal of Sport Psychology, 27,* 229–236.

Tenga, A. P. C., Holme, I., Ronglan, L. T., & Rahr, R. (2010) Effects of match location on playing tactics for goal scoring in Norwegian professional soccer. *Journal of Sport Behavior, 33,* 89–109.

Terry to fight Anton racism charge as FA grant Chelsea star personal hearing. (2012, August 3). *Mail Online.* Retrieved from http://daily mail.co.uk

Tests show impairment at low BACs (2000, August, 21). *Alcoholism and Drug Abuse Week, 33,* 8.

Terry, P. C. (1993). Mood state profiles as indicators of performance among Olympic and World Championship athletes. In S. Serpa, J. Alves, V. Ferreira, & A. Paulo-Brito (Eds.), *Proceedings of the VIIIth ISSP World Congress of Sport Psychology* (pp. 963–967). Lisbon, Portugal: International Society of Sport Psychology.

Terry, P. (1995). The efficacy of mood state profiling with elite performers: A review and synthesis. *The Sport Psychologist, 9,* 309–324.

Terry-Short, L. A., Owens, R. G., Slade, P. D., & Dewey, M. E. (1995). Positive and Negative Perfectionism, *Personality and Individual Differences, 18,* 663–668.

Thamel, P. (2009, December 28). Florida's Meyer will take leave, not resign. *The New York Times,* Retrieved from http://www.nyt.com

The Queen (2002, December/January). *Sports Illustrated,* 63.

Thelwell, R. (2008). Applied sport psychology: Enhancing performance using psychological skills. In A. M. Lane (Ed.), *Sport and exercise psychology: Topics in applied psychology* (pp. 1–15). London, England: Hodder Education.

Thelwell, R. C., & Greenlees, I. A. (2003). Developing competitive endurance performance using mental skills training. *The Sport Psychologist, 17,* 318–337.

Thelwell, R. C., Greenlees, I. A., & Weston, N.J.V. (2006). Using psychological skills training to develop soccer performance. *Journal of Applied Sport Psychology, 18,* 254–270.

Thelwell, R. C., Greenlees, I. A., & Weston, N.J.V. (2009). The influence of game location and level of experience on psychological skill usage. *International Journal of Sport and Exercise Psychology, 7,* 203–211.

Thelwell, R. C., Greenlees, I. A., & Weston, N.J.V. (2010). Examining the use of psychological skills throughout soccer performance. *Journal of Sport Behavior, 33,* 109–127.

Thelwell, R. C., & Maynard, I. W. (1998). Anxiety-performance relationships in cricketers: Testing the zone of optimal functioning hypothesis. *Perceptual and Motor Skills, 87,* 675–698.

Thelwell, R. C., & Maynard, I. W. (2002). A triangulation of findings of three studies investigating repeatable good performance in professional cricketers. *International Journal of Sport Psychology, 33,* 247–268.

Thelwell, R. C., Weston, N. .V., & Greenlees, I. A. (2005). Defining and understanding mental toughness within soccer. *Journal of Applied Sport Psychology, 17,* 326 -332.

Thelwell, R. C., Weston, N.J.V., Greenlees, I. A., & Hutchings, N. V. (2008). A qualitative exploration of psychological-skills use in coaches. *The Sport Psychologist, 22,* 38–53.

Theodorakis, Y. (1995). Effects of self-efficacy, satisfaction, and personal goals on swimming performance. *The Sport Psychologist, 9*, 245–253.

Theodorakis, Y. (1996). The influence of goals, commitment, self-efficacy and self-satisfaction on motor performance. *Journal of Applied Sport Psychology, 8*, 171–182.

Theodorakis, Y., Hatzigeorgiadis, A., & Chroni, S. (2008). Self-talk: it works, but How? Development and preliminary validation of the functions of self-talk questionnaire. *Measurement in Physical Education and Exercise Science, 12*, 10–30.

Theodosiou, A., & Papaioannou, A. (2006). Motivational climate, achievement goals and metacognitive activity in physical education and exercise involvement in out-of-school settings. *Psychology of Sport and Exercise, 7*, 361–379.

Thibault, V., Guillaume, M., Berthelot, G., El Helou, N., Schaal, K., Quinquis, L., . . .Toussaint, J-F. (2010). Women and men in sport performance: The gender gap has not evolved since 1983. *Journal of Sports Science and Medicine, 9*, 214–223.

Thiese, K. E., & Huddleston, S. (1999). The use of psychological skills by female collegiate swimmers. *Journal of Sport Behavior, 22*, 602–610.

Thill, E. E., & Cury, F. (2000). Learning to play golf under different goal conditions: their effects on irrelevant thoughts and subsequent control strategies. *European Journal of Social Psychology, 30*, 101–122.

Thomas, A. G., Dennis, A., Bandettini, P. A., & Johansen-Berg, H. (2012). The effects of aerobic activity on brain structure. *Frontiers in Psychology, 3*, 1–9. doi: 10.3389/fpsyg.2012.00086

Thomas, O., Hanton, S., & Maynard, I. (2007). Anxiety responses and psychological skill use during the time leading up to competition: Theory to practice I. *Journal of Applied Sport Psychology, 19*, 379–397.

Thomas, O., Maynard, I., & Hanton, S. (2007). Intervening with athletes during the time leading up to competition: Theory to practice II. *Journal of Applied Sport Psychology, 19*, 398–418. doi: 10.1080/10413200701599140

Thomas, P. R., & Fogarty, G. J. (1997). Psychological skills training in golf: The role of individual differences in cognitive preferences. *The Sport Psychologist, 11*, 86–106.

Thomas, P. R., & Over, R. (1994). Psychological and psychomotor skills associated with performance in golf. *The Sport Psychologist, 8*, 73–86.

Thomassen, R. O., & Hallgeir, H. (2007). A hierarchical model of approach achievement motivation and effort regulation during a 90-min. soccer match. *Perceptual and Motor Skills, 105*, 609–635.

Thome, P., Wahrborg, P., Borjesson, M., Thome, R., Eriksson, B. I., & Karlsson, J. (2007). Self-efficacy, symptoms and physical activity in patients with an anterior cruciate ligament injury: A prospective study. *Scandinavian Journal of Medicine & Science in Sports, 17*, 238–245. doi: 10.1111/j.1600-0838.2006.00557.x

Thompson, T. (2004). Re-examining the effects of noncontingent success on self-handicapping behaviour. *British Journal of Educational Psychology, 74*, 239–260.

Thompson, T., Davidson, J. A., & Barber, J. G. (1995). Self-worth protection in achievement motivation: Performance effects and attributional behavior. *Journal of Educational Psychology, 87*, 598–610.

Thompson, T., & Dinnell, D. L. (2007). Is self-worth protection best regarded as intentional self-handicapping behavior or an outcome of choking under pressure. *Educational Psychology, 27*, 509–531. doi: 1080/01443410601159910

Thompson, T., & Richardson, A. (2001). Self-handicapping status, claimed self-handicaps and reduced practice effort following success and failure feedback. *British Journal of Educational Psychology, 71*, 151–170.

Throll, D. A. (1982). Transcendental Meditation and progressive relaxation: Their physiological effects. *Journal of Clinical Psychology, 38*, 522–530.

Tice, D. M. (1991). Esteem protection or enhancement? Self-handicapping motives and attributions differ by trait self-esteem. *Journal of Personality and Social Psychology, 60*, 711–725.

Tice, D. M., & Baumeister, R. F. (1990). Self-esteem, self-handicapping, and self-presentation: The strategy of inadequate practice. *Journal of Personality, 58*, 443–464.

Tice, D. M., & Baumeister, R. F. (1997). Longitudinal study of procrastination, performance, stress, and health: The costs and benefits of dawdling. *Psychological Science, 8*, 454–458.

TM-Sidhi Program. (n.d.) Retrieved from http://www.maharishi.org/sidhi

Tobar, D. A. (2005). Overtraining and staleness: The importance of psychological monitoring. *International Journal of Sport and Exercise Psychology, 3*, 455–468.

Tod, D., Hardy, J., & Oliver, E. (2011). Effects of self-talk: A systematic review. *Journal of Sport & Exercise Psychology, 33*, 666–687.

Tod, D. A., Thatcher, R., McGuigan, M., & Thatcher, J. (2009). Effects of instructional and motivational self-talk on the vertical jump. *The Journal of Strength and Conditioning Research, 23*, 196–202.

Todd, P. M., & Gigerenzer, G. (2000). Precis of simple heuristics that make us smart. *Behavioral and Brain Sciences, 23,* 727–741.

Toering, T. T., Elferink-Gemser, M. T., Jordet, G., & Visscher, C. (2009). Self-regulation and performance level of elite and non-elite youth soccer players. *Journal of Sports Sciences, 27,* 1509–1517. doi: 10.1080/02640410903369919

Toftegaard-Stoeckel, J., Groenfeldt, V., & Andersen, L. B. (2010). Children's self-perceived bodily competencies and associations with motor skills, body mass index, teachers' evaluations, and parents' concerns. *Journal of Sports Sciences, 28,* 1369–1375. doi: 10.1080/02640414.2010.510845

Tofler, I. R., Knapp, P. K., & Drell, M. J. (1998). The achievement by proxy spectrum in youth sports: Historical perspective and clinical approach to pressured and high-achieving children and adolescents. *Sport Psychiatry, 7,* 803–820.

Tok, S. (2011). The big five personality traits and risky sport participation. *Social Behavior and Personality, 39,* 1105–1112. doi: 10.2224/sbp.2011.39.8.1105

Top 10 Chokes in Majors (2002, December). *Golf Magazine, 44,* 117.

Top of the world. Italy wins shootout with France for fourth Cup title. (2006, July 9). Retrieved from http://www.SI.com.

Torre, J., & Dreher, H. (1999). *Joe Torre's ground rules for winners.* New York, NY: Hyperion.

Tracey, J. (2011). Benefits and usefulness of a personal motivational video: A case study of a professional mountain bike racer. *Journal of Applied Sport Psychology, 23,* 308–325. doi: 10.1080/10413200.2011.558364

Transcendental Meditation (n.d.). Retrieved from http://www.tm.org

Travis, R. (1994). The junction point model: A field model of waking, sleeping, and dreaming, relating dream witnessing, the waking/sleeping transition, and transcendental meditation in terms of a common psychophysiologic state. *Dreaming, 4,* 91–104.

Treasure, D. C., Duda, J. L., Hall, H. K., Roberts, G. C., Ames, C., & Maehr, M. L. (2001). Clarifying misconceptions and misrepresentations in achievement goal research in sport: A response to Harwood, Hardy, and Swain. *Journal of Sport & Exercise Psychology, 23,* 317–329.

Treasure, D. C., Monson, J., & Lox, C. L. (1996). Relationship between self-efficacy, wrestling performance, and affect prior to competition. *The Sport Psychologist, 10,* 73–83.

Treasure, D. C., & Roberts, G. C. (1998). Relationship between female adolescents' achievement goal orientations, perceptions of the motivational climate, belief about success and sources of satisfaction in basketball. *International Journal of Sport Psychology, 29,* 211–230.

Trezza, V., Campolong, P., Cassano, T., Macheda, T., Dipasquale, P., Carratu, M. R., . . . Cuomo, V. (2008). Effects of perinatal exposure to delta-9-tetrahydrocannabinol on the emotional reactivity of the offspring: A longitudinal behavioral study in Wistar rats. *Psychopharmacology (Berl), 198,* 529–537.

Triplett, N. L. (1898). Dynamogenic factors in pacemaking and competition. *The American Journal of Psychology, 9,* 507–533.

Trivedi, M. H., Greer, T. L., Church, T. S., Carmody, T. J., Grannemann, B. D., Galper, D. I., . . . Blair, S. N. (2011). Exercise as an augmentation treatment for nonremitted major depressive disorder: A randomized, parallel dose comparison. *Journal of Clinical Psychiatry, 72,* 677–684. doi: 10.4088/JCP.10m06743

Troiano, R. P., Berrigan, D., Dodd, K. W., Masse, L. C., Tilert, T., & McDowell, M. (2008). Physical activity in the United States measured by accelerometer. *Medicine & Science in Sport & Exercise, 34,* 350–355.

Trost, S. G., Owen, N., Bauman, A. E., Sallis, J. F., & Brown, W. (2002). Correlates of adults participation in physical activity: Review and update. *Medicine and Science in Sports and Exercise, 34,* 196–201.

Tucker, S., Turner, N., Barling, J., & McEvoy, M. (2010). Transformational leadership and children's' aggression in team settings: A short-term longitudinal study. *The Leadership Quarterly, 21,* 389–399.

Turman, P. D. (2008). Coaches' immediacy behaviors as predictors of athletes' perceptions of satisfaction and team cohesion. *Western Journal of Communication, 72,* 162–179.

Turman, P. D., Zimmerman, A., & Dobesh, B. (2009). Parent-talk and sport participation: Interaction between parents, children, and coaches regarding level of play in sports. In T. J. Socha, J. Thomas, & G. H. Stamp (Eds.), *Parents and children communicating with society: Managing relationships outside of home* (pp. 171–188). New York, NY: Routledge.

Turrisi, R., Mastroleo, N. R., Mallett, K. A., & Larimer, M. E. (2007). Examination of the meditational influences of peer norms, environmental influences, and parent communications on heavy drinking in athletes and nonathletes. *Psychology of Addictive Behaviors, 21,* 453–461. doi: 10.1037/0893-164X.21.4.453

Udry, E. (1996). Social support: Exploring its role in the context of athletic injuries. *Journal of Sport Rehabilitation, 5,* 151–163.

Udry, E. (1997). Coping and social support among injured athletes following surgery. *Journal of Sport & Exercise Psychology, 19*, 71–90.

Udry, E. (1999). The paradox of injuries: Unexpected positive consequences. In D. Pargman (Ed.), *Psychological bases of sport injuries* (pp. 79–88). Morgantown, WV: Fitness Information Technology.

Udry, E., Gould, D., Bridges, D., & Beck, L. (1997). Down but not out: Athlete responses to season-ending injuries. *Journal of Sport & Exercise Psychology, 19*, 229–248.

Udry, E., Gould, D., Bridges, D., & Tuffey, S. (1997). People helping people? Examining the social ties of athletes coping with burnout and injury stress. *Journal of Sport & Exercise Psychology, 19*, 368–395.

Ullrich-French, S., Cox, A. E., & Bumppus, M. F. (2012). Physical activity motivation and behavior across the transition to university. *Sport, Exercise, and Performance Psychology, 1*, 1–12. doi: 10.1037/a0030632

Ullrich-French, S., & Smith, A. L. (2009). Social and motivational predictors of continued youth sport participation. *Psychology of Sport and Exercise, 10*, 87–95. doi: 10.1016/j.psychsport.2008.06.007

Ungerleider, S. (2001). *Faust's gold. Inside the East German doping machine.* New York, NY: Thomas Dunne.

U.S. Department of Education. (1972). *Nondiscrimination on the basis of sex ineducation programs or activities receiving federal financial assistance.* Retrieved from http://www.ed.gov/legislation/FedRegister.

U.S. Department of Education. (2002). *Postsecondary institutions in the United States: Fall 2000 and degrees and other awards conferred: 1999–2000.* National Center for Education Statistics, Integrated post secondary data system (IPEDS). Retrieved from http://nces.ed.gov/pubsearch/pubinfo.asp?pubid = 2002156

U.S. Department of Health and Human Services. (2008). *2008 physical activity guidelines for Americans.* Washington, DC: U.S. Department of Health and Human Services. Retrieved from http://www.health.gov/paguidelines/pdf/paguide.pdf.

U.S. Department of Health and Human Services, National Institute on Drug Abuse. (2010). *Marijuana abuse* (NIH Publication No. 10–3859). Retrieved from http://www.drugabuse.gov/publications/research-reports/marijuana-abuse

U.S. Olympic Committee. (1983). U.S. Olympic Committee establishes guidelines for sport psychology services. *Journal of Sport Psychology, 5*, 4–7.

Universal language of sport (2005). Retrieved from http://www.un.org/News/Press/docs/2004/sgsm9579.doc.htm

Uphill, M. (2008). Anxiety in sport: Should we be worried or excited? In A. M. Lane (Ed.), *Sport and exercise psychology: Topics in applied psychology* (pp. 35–51). London, England: Hodder Education.

Upthegrove, T. R., Roscigno, V. J., & Charles, C. Z. (1999). Big money collegiate sports: Racial concentration, contradictory pressures, and academic performance. *Social Science Quarterly, 80*, 718–737.

Urdan, T., Midgley, C., & Anderman, E. (1998). The role of classroom goal structure in students' use of self-handicapping strategies. *American Educational Research Journal, 35*, 101–122.

Vadocz, E. A., Hall, C., & Moritz, S. E. (1997). The relationship between competitive anxiety and imagery use. *Journal of Applied Sport Psychology, 9*, 241–252.

Vallance, J. K. H., Dunn, H.G.H., & Dunn, J. L. C. (2006). Perfectionism, anger, and situation criticality in competitive youth hockey. *Journal of Sport & Exercise Psychology, 28*, 383–406.

Vallee, C. N., & Bloom, G. A. (2005). Building a successful university program: Key and common elements of expert coaches. *Journal of Applied Sport Psychology, 17*, 179–196.

Vallerand, R. J. (2001). A hierarchical model of intrinsic and extrinsic motivation in sport and exercise. In G. C. Roberts (Ed.), *Advances in motivation in sport and exercise* (2nd ed., pp. 263–319). Champaign, IL: Human Kinetics.

Vallerand, R. J. (2007). Intrinsic and extrinsic motivation in sport and physical activity. In G. Tenenbaum & R. C. Eklund (Eds.), *Handbook of sport psychology* (3rd ed., pp. 59–83). New York, NY: Wiley.

Vallerand, R. J., Blanchard, C., Mageau, G. A., Koestner, R., Ratelle, C., Léonard, M., Gagné, M., & Marsolais, J. (2003). *Journal of Personality and Social Psychology, 85*, 756–767.

Vallerand, R. J., Deci, E. L., & Ryan, R. M. (1987). Intrinsic motivation in sport. *Exercise and Sport Sciences Reviews, 15*, 389–425.

Vallerand, R. J., & Losier, G. F. (1994). Self-determined motivation and sportsmanship orientations: An assessment of their temporal relationship. *Journal of Sport & Exercise Psychology, 16*, 229–245.

Vallerand, R. J., & Losier, G. F. (1999). An integrative analysis of intrinsic and extrinsic motivation in sport. *Journal of Applied Sport Psychology, 11*, 142–169.

Vallerand, R. J. & Rousseau, F. L. (2001). Intrinsic and extrinsic motivation in sport and exercise. A review using the hierarchical model of intrinsic and extrinsic motivation.

In R. N. Singer, H. A. Hausenblas, & C. M. Janelle (Eds.), *Handbook of sport psychology* (2nd ed., pp. 389–416). New York, NY: Wiley.

Vallerand, R. J., Rousseau, F. L., Grouzet, F.M.E., Dumais, A., Grenier, S., & Blanchard, C. M. (2006). Passion in sport: A look at determinants and affective experiences. *Journal of Sport & Exercise Psychology, 28*, 454–478.

van de Pol, P.K.C., Kavussanu, M., & Ring, C. (2012). Goal orientations, perceived motivational climate, and motivational outcomes in football: A comparison between training and competition contexts. *Psychology of Sport and Exercise, 13*, 491–499. doi: 10.1016/j.psychsport.2011.12.002

van de Pol, P.K.C., & Kavussanu, M. (2011). Achievement goals and motivational responses in tennis: Does the context matter? *Psychology of Sport and Exercise, 12*, 176–183. doi: 10.1016/j.psychsport.2010.09.005

van der Kamp, J., & Masters, R. S. W. (2008). The human Muller-Lyer illusion in goal-keeping. *Perception, 37*, 951–954. doi: 10.1068/p6010

Van Eerde, W. (2000). Procrastination: Self-regulation in initiating aversive goals. *Applied Psychology: An International Review, 49*, 372–389.

Van Raalte, J. L., Brewer, D. D., Brewer, B. W., & Linder, D. E. (1992). NCAA division II college football players' perceptions of an athlete who consults a sport psychologist. *Journal of Sport & Exercise Psychology, 14*, 273–282.

Van Raalte, J. L., Brewer, B. W., Linder, D. E., & DeLange, N. (1990). Perceptions of sport-oriented professionals: A multidimensional scaling analysis. *The Sport Psychologist, 4*, 228–234.

Van Raalte, J. L., Brewer, D. D., Matheson, H., & Brewer, B. W. (1996). British athletes' perceptions of sport and mental health practitioners. *Journal of Applied Sport Psychology, 8*, 102–108.

Van Raalte, J. L., Brewer, B. W., Rivera, P. M., & Petitpas, A. J. (1994). The relationship between self-talk and performance of competitive junior tennis players. *NASPSPA Conference Abstracts, 16 Supplement*, S118 (abstract).

Van Raalte, J. L., Cornelius, A. E., Hatten, S. J., & Brewer, B. W. (2000). The antecedents and consequences of self-talk in competitive tennis. *Journal of Sport and Exercise Psychology, 22*, 345–356.

Vansteenkiste, M., & Deci, E. L. (2003). Competitively contingent rewards and intrinsic motivation: Can losers remain motivated. *Motivation and Emotion, 27*, 273–299.

Vansteenkiste, M., Simons, J., Soenens, B., & Lens, W. (2004). How to become a persevering exerciser? Providing a clear, future intrinsic goal in an autonomy supportive way. *Journal of Sport & Exercise Psychology, 26*, 232–249.

Van Vianen, A.E.M., & De Dreu, C.K.W. (2001). Personality in teams: Its relationship to social cohesion, task cohesion, and term performance. *European Journal of Work and Organizational Psychology, 10*, 97–120.

Van Wilgen, C. P., Kaptein, AD. A., & Brink, M. S. (2010). Illness perceptions and mood states are associated with injury-related outcomes in athletes. *Disability and Rehabilitation, 32*, 1576–1585. doi: 10.3109/09638281003596857

VanYperen, N. W. (1995). Interpersonal stress, performance level, and parental support: A longitudinal study among highly skilled young soccer players. *The Sport Psychologist, 9*, 225–241.

Vargas-Tonsing, T. M., Myers, N. D., & Feltz, D. L. (2004). Coaches' and athletes' perceptions of efficacy enhancing techniques. *The Sport Psychologist, 18*, 397–414.

Vast, R. L., Young, R. L., & Thomas, P. R. (2010). Emotions in sport: Perceived effects on attention, concentration, and performance. *Australian Psychologist, 45*, 132–140. doi: 10.1080/000500060903261538

Vazou, S. (2010). Variations in the perceptions of peer and coach motivational climate. *Research Quarterly for Exercise and Sport, 81*, 199–211.

Vazou, S., Ntoumanis, N., & Duda, J. L. (2006). Predicting young athletes' motivational indices as a function of the perceptions of coach- and peer-created climate. *Psychology of Sport and Exercise, 7*, 215–233. doi: 10.1016/j.psychsport.2005.08.007

Vealey, R. S. (2001). Understanding and enhancing self-confidence in athletes. In R. N. Singer, H. A. Hausenblas, & C. M. Janelle (Eds.), *Handbook of sport psychology* (2nd ed., pp. 550–565). New York, NY: Wiley.

Vealey, R. S. (2007). Mental skills training in sport. In G. Tenenbaum & R. C. Eklund (Eds.), *Handbook of sport psychology* (3rd ed., pp. 287–309). New York, NY: Wiley.

Vealey, R. S. (2009). Confidence in sport. (2009). Management of competitive stress in elite sport. In B. W. Brewer (Ed.), *Handbook of sports medicine and science, sport psychology* (pp. 43–52). Chichester, England: Wiley-Blackwell.

Vealey, R. S., Armstrong, L., Comar, W, & Greenleaf, C. A. (1998). Influence of perceived coaching behaviors on burnout and competitive anxiety in female college athletes. *Journal of Applied Sport Psychology, 10*, 297–318.

Vealey, R. S., & Greenleaf, C. A. (2010). Seeing is believing: Understanding and using imagery in sport. In J. M. Williams (Ed.), *Applied sport psychology: Personal growth to peak performance* (6th ed., pp. 267–299). New York, NY: McGraw-Hill.

Vealey, R. S., Hayashi, S. W., Garner-Holman, G., & Giacobbi, P. (1998). Sources of sport-confidence: Conceptualization and instrument development. *Journal of Sport & Exercise Psychology, 20*, 54–80.

Vealey, R. S., Udry, E. M., Zimmerman, V., & Soliday, J. (1992). Intrapersonal and situational predictors of coaching burnout. *Journal of Sport & Exercise Psychology, 14*, 40–58.

Velentzas, K., Heinen, T., & Schack, T. (2011). Routine integration strategies and their effects on volleyball serve performance and players' movement mental representation. *Journal of Applied Sport Psychology, 23*, 209–222. doi: 10.1080/10413200.2010.546826

Vereijken, B., van Emmerik, R.E.A., Whiting, H.T.A., & Newell, K. M. (1992). Free(z) ing degrees of freedom in skill acquisition. *Journal of Motor Behavior, 23*, 133–142.

Veroff, J. (1992). Power motivation. In C. P. Smith (Ed.), *Motivation and personality: Handbook of thematic content analysis* (pp. 278–310). New York, NY: Cambridge University Press.

Vickers, J. N. (1992). Gaze control in putting. *Perception, 21*, 117–132.

Vickers, J. N. (1996). Visual control when aiming at a far target. *Journal of Experimental Psychology: Human Perception and Performance, 22*, 342–354.

Vickers, J. N., Rodrigues, S. T., & Edworthy, G. (2000). Quiet eye and accuracy in the dart throw. *International Journal of Sports Vision, 6*, 30–36.

Vickers, J. N., & Williams, A. M. (2007). Performing under pressure: The effects of physiological arousal, cognitive anxiety, and gaze control in biathlon. *Journal of Motor Behavior, 39*, 381–394.

Vidic, Z., & Burton, D. (2011). Developing effective leaders: Motivational correlates of leadership styles. *Journal of Applied Sport Psychology, 23*, 1533–1571. doi: 10.1080/10413200.3010.546827

Vine, S. J., & Wilson, M. R. (2010). Quiet eye training: Effects on learning and performance under pressure. *Journal of Applied Sport Psychology, 22*, 361–376. doi: 10.1080/10413200.2010.495106

Visek, A. J., Harris, B. S., & Blom, L. C. (2009). Doing sport psychology: A youth sport consulting model for practitioners. *The Sport Psychologist, 23*, 271–291.

Vlachopoulos, S. P., & Michailidou, S. (2006). Development and initial validation of a measure of autonomy, competence, and relatedness in exercise: The Basic Psychological Needs in Exercise Scale. *Measurement in Physical Education and Exercise Science, 10*, 179–201.

Vorauer, J. D., & Turpie, C. A. (2004). Disruptive effects of vigilance on dominant group members' treatment of outgroup members: Choking versus singing under pressure. *Journal of Personality and Social Psychology, 87*, 384–399. doi: 10.1037/0022-3514.87.3.384

Voss, M. W., Erickson, K. I., Prakash, R. S., Chaddock, L., Malkowski, E., Alves, H., . . . Kramer, A. F. (2010). Functional connectivity: A source of variance in the association between cardiorespiratory fitness and cognition? *Neuropsychologia, 48*, 1394–1406. doi: 10.1016/j.neuropsychologia.2010.01.005

Wadden, T. A., Brownell, K. D., & Foster, G. D. (2002). Obesity: Responding to the global epidemic. *Journal of Consulting and Clinical Psychology, 70*, 510–525.

Wadey, R., Evans, L., Evans, K., & Mitchell, I. (2011). Perceived benefits following sport injury: A qualitative examination of their antecedents and underlying mechanisms. *Journal of Applied Sport Psychology, 23*, 142–158. doi: 10.1080/10413200.2010.543119

Wahl, G. (2009). Political futbol. *Sports Illustrated, 111*, 16–17.

Wahl, G., Wertheim, L. J., & Dohrmann, G. (2001, September 10). Special report. Passion play. *Sports Illustrated, 95*, 58–70.

Wakefield, C. J., & Smith, D. (2009). Impact of differing frequencies of PETTLEP imagery on netball shooting performance. *Journal of Imagery Research in Sport and Physical Activity, 4*: Article 7, 1–12.

Wallace, H. M., & Baumeister, R. F. (2002). The performance of narcissists rises and falls with perceived opportunity for glory. *Journal of Personality and Social Psychology, 82*, 819–834.

Wallace, H. M., Baumeister, R. F., & Vohs, K. D. (2005). Audience support and choking under pressure: A home disadvantage? *Journal of Sports Sciences, 23*, 429–438.

Wallace, R. K., & Benson, H. (1972). The physiology of meditation. *Scientific American, 226*, 84–90.

Walling, M. D., Duda, J. L., Chi, L. (1993). The Perceived Motivational Climate in Sport Questionnaire: Construct and predictive validity. *Journal of Sport and Exercise Psychology, 15*, 172–183.

Walling, M., & Martinek, T. (1995). Learned helplessness: A case study of a middle school student. *Journal of Teaching in Physical Education, 14*, 454–456.

Walsh, A. E. (2011). The Relaxation Response: A strategy to address stress. *International Journal of Athletic Therapy & Training, 16*, 20–23.

Wang, C.K.J., Sproule, J., McNeill, M., Martindale, R.J.J., & Lee, K. S. (2011). Impact of the talent development environment on achievement goals and life aspirations in Singapore. *Journal of Applied Sport Psychology, 23,* 263–276. doi: 10.1080/10413200.2010.543120

Wang, J., Marchant, D., & Morris, T. (2004). Coping style and susceptibility to choking. *Journal of Sport Behavior, 27,* 75–92.

Wang, J., Marchant, D., Morris, T., & Gibbs, P. (2004). Self-consciousness and trait anxiety as predictors of choking in sport. *Journal of Science in Medicine and Sport, 7,* 174–185.

Wanjek, B., Rosendahl, J., Strauss, B., & Gabriel, H. H. (2007). Doping, drugs and drug abuse among adolescents in the state of Thuringia (Germany): Prevalence, knowledge and attitudes. *International Journal of Sports Medicine, 28,* 346–353. doi: 10.1055/s-2006-924353

Ward, P. (2011). Goal setting and performance feedback. In J. K. Luiselli & D. D. Reed (Eds.), *Behavioral sport psychology* (pp. 99–112). New York, NY: Springer. doi: 10.1007/978-1-4614-0070-7_6

Ward, P., & Williams, A. M. (2003). Perceptual and cognitive skill development in soccer: The multidimensional nature of expert performance. *Journal of Sport & Exercise Psychology 25,* 93–111.

Warner, L. M., & Lippke, S. (2008). Psychological stage models of physical exercise—Research advances. In M. P. Simmons & L. A. Foster (Eds.), *Sport and exercise psychology research advances* (pp. 19–51). Hauppauge, NY: Nova Biomedical Books.

Warriner, K., & Lavallee, D. (2008). The retirement experiences of elite female gymnasts: Self identity on the physical self. *Journal of Applied Sport Psychology, 20,* 301–317.

Watkins, C. E., Jr., Terrell, F., Miller, F. S., & Terrell, S. L. (1989). Cultural mistrust and its effects on expectational variables in Black client-White counselor relationships. *Journal of Counseling Psychology, 36,* 447–450.

Watson, A. E., & Pulford, B. D. (2004). Personality differences in high risk sports amateurs and instructors. *Perceptual and Motor Skills, 99,* 83–94.

Watson, G. G. (1986). Approach-avoidance behaviour in team sports: An application to leading Australian national hockey players. *International Journal of Sport Psychology, 17,* 136–155.

Watson, J. C., Clement, D., Blom, L. C., & Grindley, E. (2009). Mentoring: Processes and perceptions of sport and exercise psychology graduate students. *Journal of Applied Sport Psychology, 21,* 231–246.

Webb, T. L., & Sheeran, P. (2006). Does changing behavior intentions engender behavior change? A meta-analysis of the experimental evidence. *Psychological Bulletin, 132,* 249–268. doi: 10.1037/0033-2909.132.2.249

Webbe, R. M., & Ochs, S. R. (2007). Personality traits relate to heading frequency in male soccer players. *Journal of Clinical Sport Psychology, 1,* 379–389.

Weber, M. (1930). *The Protestant work ethic and the spirit of capitalism* (T. Parsons,Trans.). New York, NY: Scribner. (Original work published 1904).

Wechsler, H., Davenport, A. E., Dowdall, G. W., Grossman, S. J., & Zanakos, S. I. (1997). Binge drinking, tobacco, and illicit drug use and involvement in college athletics. A survey of students at 140 American colleges. *College Health, 45,* 195–200.

Weierich, M. R., Treat, T. A., & Hollingworth, A. (2008). Theories and measurement of visual attentional processing in anxiety. *Cognition and Emotion, 22,* 985–1018. doi: 10.1080/02699930701597601

Wegner, D. M. (1994). Ironic processes of mental control. *Psychological Review, 101,* 34–52.

Wegner, D. M. (1997a). When the antidote is the poison: Ironic mental control processes. *Psychological Science, 8,* 148–150.

Wegner, D. M. (1997b). Why the mind wanders. In J. D. Cohen & J. W. Schooler (Eds.), *Scientific approaches to consciousness* (pp. 295–315). Hillsdale, NJ: Erlbaum.

Wegner, D. M. (2011). Setting free the bears: Escape from thought suppression. *American Psychologist, 66,* 671–680.

Wegner, D. M., Broome, A., & Blumberg, S. J. (1997). Ironic effects of trying to relax under stress. *Behavioral Research and Therapy, 35,* 11–21.

Weik, M. (2009). Contrasting gender differences on two measures of exercise dependence. *British Journal of Sports Medicine, 43,* 204–207. doi: 10.1136/bjsm.2007.045138

Weinberg, R. S. (1977). Anxiety and motor behavior: A new direction. In R. W. Christina & D. M. Landers (Eds.), *Psychology of motor behavior and sport-1976* (Vol. 2, pp. 132–139). Champaign, IL: Human Kinetics.

Weinberg, R. S. (1985). Relationship between self-efficacy and cognitive strategies in enhancing endurance performance. *International Journal of Sport Psychology, 17,* 280–292.

Weinberg, R., Bruya, L., Jackson, A., & Garland, H. (1987). Goal difficulty and endurance performance: A challenge to the goal attainability assumption. *Journal of Sport Psychology, 10,* 82–92.

Weinberg, R., Bruya, L., & Jackson, A. (1985). The effects of goal proximity and goal specificity on endurance performance. *Journal of Sport & Exercise Psychology, 7,* 296–305.

Weinberg, R. S., Burke, K. L., & Jackson, A. W. (1997). Coaches' and players' perceptions of goal setting in junior tennis: An exploratory investigation. *The Sport Psychologist, 11,* 426–439.

Weinberg, R. S., Burton, D., Yukelson, D., & Weigand, D. (1993). Goal setting in competitive sport: An exploratory investigation of practices of collegiate athletes. *The Sport Psychologist, 7,* 275–289.

Weinberg, R. S., Burton, D., Yukelson, D., & Weigand, D. (2000). Perceived goal setting practices of Olympic athletes: An exploratory investigation. *The Sport Psychologist, 14,* 279–295.

Weinberg, R., Butt, J., & Knight, B. (2001). High school coaches' perceptions of the process of goal setting. *The Sport Psychologist, 15,* 20–47.

Weinberg, R., Butt, J., Knight, B., Burke, K. L., & Jackson, A. (2003). The relationship between the use and effectiveness of imagery: An exploratory investigation. *Journal of Applied Sport Psychology, 15,* 26–40.

Weinberg, R. S., & Gould, D. (2010). *Foundations of sport and exercise psychology* (5th ed.). Champaign, IL: Human Kinetics Press.

Weinberg, R. S., Gould, D., & Jackson, A. (1979). Expectations and performance: An empirical test of Bandura's self-efficacy theory. *Journal of Sport Psychology, 1,* 320–331.

Weinberg, R. S., Gould, D., Yukelson, D., & Jackson, A. (1981). The effects of pre-existing and manipulated self-efficacy on a competitive muscular endurance task. *Journal of Sport Psychology, 3,* 345–354.

Weinberg, R. S., Seabourne, T. G., & Jackson, A. (1981). Effects of visuomotor behavior rehearsal, relaxation, and imagery on karate performance. *Journal of Sport Psychology, 3,* 228–238.

Weinberg, R., Tenenbaum, G., McKenzie, A., Jackson, S., Anshel, M., Grove, R., & Fogerty, G. (2000). Motivation for youth participation in sport and physical activity: Relationships to culture, self-reported activity levels, and gender. *International Journal of Sport Psychology, 31,* 321–346.

Weinberg, R. S., & Williams, J. M. (2010). Integrating and implementing a psychological skills training program. In J. M. Williams (Ed.), *Applied sport psychology: Personal growth to peak performance* (6th ed., pp. 361–391). New York, NY: McGraw-Hill.

Weinstein, M., & Smith, J. C. (1992). Isometric squeeze relaxation (Progressive Relaxation) vs meditation: Absorption and focusing as predictors of state effects. *Perceptual and Motor Skills, 75,* 1263–1271.

Weinstein, A. A., Deuster, P. A., Francis, J. L., Beadling, C., & Kop, W. J. (2010). The role of depression in short-term mood and fatigue response to acute exercise. *International Journal of Behavioral Medicine, 17,* 51–57. doi: 10.1007/s12529-009-9046-4

Weisenberg, M., Gerby, Y., & Mikulincer, M. (1993). Aerobic exercise and chocolate as means for reducing learned helplessness. *Cognitive Therapy and Research, 17,* 579–592.

Weiss, M. R. (1991). Psychological skill development in children and adolescents. *The Sport Psychologist, 5,* 335–354.

Weiss, M. R., Amorose, A. J., & Allen, J. B. (2000). The young elite athlete: The good, the bad, and the ugly. In B. L. Drinkwater (Ed.), *Women in sport* (pp. 409–429). Oxford, England: Blackwell Science.

Weiss, M. R., & Barber, H. (1995). Socialization influences of collegiate female athletes: A tale of two decades. *Sex Roles, 33,* 129–140.

Weiss, M. R., Barber, H., Ebbeck, V., & Sisley, B. L. (1991). Developing competence and confidence in novice female coaches: II. Perceptions of ability and affective experiences following a season-long coaching internship. *Journal of Sport & Exercise Psychology, 13,* 336–363.

Weiss, M. R., & Chaumeton, N. (2002). Motivational orientations in sport. In T. S. Horn (Ed.), *Advances in sport psychology* (2nd ed., pp. 61–99). Champaign, IL: Human Kinetics.

Weiss, M. R., Ebbeck, V., & Horn, T. S. (1997). Children's self-perceptions and sources of physical competence information: A cluster analysis. *Journal of Sport and Exercise Psychology 19,* 52–70.

Weiss, M. R., & Gill, D. L. (2005). What goes around comes around: Re-emerging themes in sport and exercise psychology. *Research Quarterly for Exercise and Sport, 76,* S71-S87.

Weiss, M. R., McCullagh, P., Smith, A. L., & Berlant, A. R. (1998). Observational learning and the fearful child: Influence of peer models on swimming skill performance and psychological responses. *Research Quarterly for Exercise and Sport, 69,* 380–394.

Weiss, M. R., Smith, A. L., & Theeboom, M. (1996). "That's what friends are for": Children's and teenagers' perceptions of peer relationships in the sport domain. *Journal of Sport & Exercise Psychology, 18,* 347–379.

Weiss, M. R., & Stevens, C. (1993). Motivation and attrition of female coaches: An application of social exchange theory. *The Sport Psychologist, 7,* 244–261.

Weissensteiner, J., Abernethy, B., & Farrow, D. (2009). Towards the development of a conceptual model of expertise in cricket batting: A grounded theory approach. *Journal of Applied Sport Psychology, 21,* 276–292.

Weitlauf, J. C., Cervone, Smith, R. E., & Wright, P. M. (2001). Assessing generalization in perceived self-efficacy: Multidomain and global assessments of the effects of self-defense training for women. *Personality and Social Psychology Bulletin, 27,* 1683–1691.

Weitlauf, J. C., Smith, R. E., & Cervone, D. (2000). Generalization effects of coping skills training: Influence of self-defense training on women's efficacy beliefs, assertiveness, and aggression. *Journal of Applied Psychology, 85,* 625–633.

Wenzlaff, R. M., & Wegner, D. M. (2000). Thought suppression. *Annual Review of Psychology, 51,* 59–91.

Wertheim, J. (2013, January 27). Serenity now: Djokovic calmly bags third straight Australian Open. *Sports Illustrated.* Retrieved from http://www.si.com

Wesch, N. N., Law, B., & Hall, C. R. (2007). The use of observational learning by athletes. *Journal of Sport Behavior, 30,* 219–231.

Weston, N. J. V., Thelwell, R. C., Bond, D., & Hutchings, N. V. (2009). Stress and coping in single-handed round-the-world ocean sailing. *Journal of Applied Sport Psychology, 21,* 460–470.

Westre, K., & Weiss, M. (1991). The relationship between perceived coaching behaviors and group cohesion in high school football teams. *The Sport Psychologist, 5,* 41–54.

Wethe, D. (2004, March 11). Suddenly on sidelines. *Hartford Courant,* E1, E6.

Whaley, D. E., & Krane, V. (2012). Resilient excellence: Challenges faced by trailblazing women in U.S. sport psychology. *Research Quarterly for Exercise and Sport, 83,* 65–76.

Whelan, J. P., Epkins, C. C., & Meyers, A. W. (1990). Arousal interventions for athletic performance: Influence of mental preparation and competitive experience. *Anxiety Research, 2,* 293–307.

Whelan, J. P., Meyers, A. W., & Elkins, T. D. (2002). Ethics in sport and exercise psychology. In J. L. Van Raalte & B. W. Brewer (Eds.), *Exploring sport and exercise psychology* (2nd ed., pp. 503–524). Washington, DC: American Psychological Association.

Whisenant, W., Miller, J., & Pedersen, P. (2005). Systemic barriers in athletic administration: An analysis of job descriptions for interscholastic athletic directors'. *Sex Roles, 53,* 911–918.

Whisenant, W. A., Pedersen, P. M., & Clavio, G. (2010). Analyzing ethics in the administration of interscholastic sports. *Educational Management Administration & Leadership, 38,* 107–118.

White, S. A., Duda, J. L., & Keller, M. R. (1998). The relationship between goal orientation and perceived purposes of sport among youth sport participants. *Journal of Sport Behavior, 21,* 474–483.

White, A., & Hardy, L. (1995). Use of different imagery perspectives on the learning and performance of different motor skills. *British Journal of Psychology, 86,* 169–180.

White, S. A., & Zellner, S. R. (1996). The relationship between goal orientation, beliefs about the causes of sport success, and trait anxiety among high school, intercollegiate, and recreational sport participants. *The Sport Psychologist, 10,* 58–72.

Wichstrøm, T., & Wichstrøm, L. (2009). Does sports participation during adolescence prevent later alcohol, tobacco and cannabis use? *Addiction, 104,* 138–149.

Widmeyer, W. N., & Birch, J. S. (1979). The relationship between aggression and performance outcome in ice hockey. *Canadian Journal of Applied Sport Science, 4,* 91–94.

Widmeyer, W. N., Brawley, L. R., & Carron, A. V. (1990). The effects of group size in sport. *Journal of Sport & Exercise Psychology, 12,* 177–190.

Widmeyer, W. N., Brawley, L. R., & Carron, A. V. (2002). Group dynamics in sport. In T. S. Horn (Ed.), *Advances in Sport Psychology* (2nd ed., pp. 163–180). Champaign, IL: Human Kinetics.

Widmeyer, W. N., & Ducharme, K. (1997). Team building through team goal setting. *Journal of Applied Sport Psychology, 9,* 97–113.

Widmeyer, W. N., & Williams, J. M. (1991). Predicting cohesion in a coaching sport. *Small Group Research, 22,* 548–570.

Wiese, B. S., & Freund, A. M. (2005). Goal progress makes one happy, or does it? Longitudinal findings from the work domain. *Journal of Occupational and Organizational Psychology, 78,* 287–304.

Wiese, J. G., Shilpak, M. G., & Browner, W. S. (2000). The alcohol hangover. *Annals of Internal Medicine, 132,* 897–902.

Wiese-Bjornstal, D. M., LaVoi, N. M., & Omli, J. (2009). Child and adolescent development and sport participation. In B. W. Brewer (Ed.), *Handbook of sports medicine and science, sport psychology* (pp. 97–112), Chichester, England: Wiley-Blackwell.

Wiese-Bjornstal, D. M., Smith, A. S., Shaffer, S. M., & Morrey, M. A. (1998). An integrated model of response to sport injury: Psychological and sociological dynamics. *Journal of Applied Sport Psychology, 10*, 46–69.

Wiggins, D. K. (1984). The history of sport psychology in North America. In J. M. Silva & R. S. Weinberg (Eds.), *Psychological foundations of sport* (pp. 9–22). Champaign, IL: Human Kinetics.

Wiggins, D. K. (1997). "Great speed but little stamina": The historical debate over Black athletic superiority. In S. W. Pope (Ed.), *The new American sport history: Recent approaches and perspectives* (pp. 312–338). Urbana, IL: University of Illinois Press.

Wiggins, M. S. (1998). Anxiety intensity and direction: Preperformance temporal patterns and expectations in athletes. *Journal of Applied Sport Psychology, 10*, 201–211.

Wilkes, S., MacDonald, D. J., Horton, S., & Cote, J. (2009). The benefits of sampling sports during childhood. *The Physical and Health Education Journal, 74*, 6–11.

Williams, A. M., & Elliott, D. (1999). Anxiety, expertise, and visual search strategy in karate. *Journal of Sport & Exercise Psychology, 21*, 362–375.

Williams, A. M., Janelle, C. M., & Davids, K. (2004). Constraints on the search for visual information in sport. *International Journal of Sport and Exercise Psychology, 2*, 301–318.

Williams, A. M., Singer, R. N., & Frehlich, S. G. (2002). Quiet eye duration, expertise, and task complexity in near and far aiming tasks. *Journal of Motor Behavior, 34*, 197–207.

Williams, A. M., Vickers, J., & Rodrigues, S. (2002). The effects of anxiety on visual search, movement kinematics, and performance in table tennis: A test of Eysenck and Calvo's Processing Efficiency Theory. *Journal of Sport & Exercise Psychology, 24*, 438–455.

Williams, A. M., & Ward, P. (2007). Anticipation and decision making. In G. Tenenbaum & R. C. Eklund (Eds.), *Handbook of sport psychology* (3rd ed., pp. 203–223). New York, NY: Wiley.

Williams, A. M., Ward, P., Knowles, J. M., & Smeeton, N. J. (2002). Anticipation skill in a real-world task: Measurement, training, and transfer in tennis. *Journal of Experimental Psychology: Applied, 8*, 259–270.

Williams, A. M., Ward, P., Smeeton, N. J., & Allen, D. (2004). Developing anticipation skills in tennis using on-court instruction: Perception versus perception and action. *Journal of Applied Sport Psychology, 16*, 350–360.

Williams, J. E. (1996). The relation between efficacy for self-regulated learning and domain-specific academic performance, controlling for test anxiety. *Journal of Research and Development in Education, 29*, 77–80.

Williams, J. M. (2001). Psychology of injury risk and prevention. In R. N. Singer, H. A. Hausenblas, & C. M. Janelle (Eds.), *Handbook of sport psychology* (2nd ed., pp. 766–786). New York, NY: Wiley.

Williams, J. M. (2010). Relaxation and energizing techniques for regulation of arousal. In J. M. Williams (Ed.), *Applied sport psychology: Personal growth to peak performance* (6th ed., pp. 247–266). New York, NY: McGraw-Hill.

Williams, J. M., & Anderson, M. B. (2007). Psychosocial antecedents of sport injury and interventions for risk reduction. In G. Tenenbaum & R. C. Eklund (Eds.), *Handbook of sport psychology* (3rd ed., pp. 379–403). New York, NY: Wiley.

Williams, J. M., & Hacker, C. M. (1982). Causal relationships among cohesion, satisfaction, and performance in women's intercollegiate field hockey teams. *Journal of Sport Psychology, 4*, 324–337.

Williams, J. M., Hogan, T. D., & Andersen, M. B. (1993). Positive states of mind and athletic injury risk. *Psychosomatic Medicine 55*, 468–472.

Williams, J. M., & Leffingwell, T. R. (1996). Cognitive strategies in sport and exercise psychology. In J. L. Van Raalte & B. W. Brewer (Eds), *Exploring sport and exercise psychology (pp.* 25–50). Washington, DC: American Psychological Association.

Williams, J. M., Nideffer, R. M., Wilson, V. E., Sagal, M-S., & Peper, E. (2010). Concentration and strategies for controlling it. In J. M. Williams (Ed.), *Applied sport psychology: Personal growth to peak performance* (6th ed., pp. 336–358), New York, NY: McGraw-Hill.

Williams, J. M., & Parkhouse, B. L. (1988). Social learning theory as a foundation for examining sex bias in evaluation of coaches. *Journal of Sport & Exercise Psychology, 10*, 322–333.

Williams, J. M., & Scherzer, C. B. (2003). Tracking the training and careers of graduates of advanced degree programs in sport psychology, 1994 to 1999. *Journal of Applied Sport Psychology, 15*, 335–353.

Williams, J. M., & Scherzer, C. B. (2010). Injury risk and rehabilitation: Psychological considerations. In J. M. Williams (Ed.), *Applied sport psychology: Personal growth to peak performance* (6th ed., pp. 512–541). New York, NY: McGraw-Hill.

Williams, J. M., & Straub, W. F. (2010). Sport psychology: Past, present, future. In J. M. Williams (Ed.), *Applied sport psychology: Personal growth to peak performance* (6th ed., pp. 1–17). New York, NY: McGraw-Hill.

Williams, J. M., Tonymon, P., & Andersen, M. B. (1991). The effects of stressors and coping resources on anxiety and peripheral narrowing. *Journal of Applied Sport Psychology, 3,* 126–141

Williams, K. J., Donovan, J. J., & Dodge, T. L. (2000). Self-regulation of performance: Goal establishment and goal revision processes in athletes. *Human Performance, 13,* 159–180.

Williams, L. (1994). Goal orientations and athletes' preferences for competence information sources (1994). *Journal of Sport & Exercise Psychology, 16,* 416–430.

Williams, R., & Youssef, Z. (1975). Division of labor in college football along racial lines. *International Journal of Sport Psychology, 3,* 3–11.

Williams, S. E., & Cumming, J. (2011). Measuring athlete imagery ability: The Sport Imagery Ability Questionnaire. *Journal of Sport & Exercise Psychology, 33,* 416–440.

Williams, S. E., Cumming, J., & Balanos, G. M. (2010). The use of imagery to manipulate challenge and threat appraisal states in athletes. *Journal of Sport & Exercise Psychology, 32,* 339–358.

Williams, T., & Underwood, J. (1970). *The science of hitting.* New York, NY: Simon & Schuster.

Williamson, S. Y. (2010). Within-group ethnic differences of black male STEM majors and factors affecting their persistence in college. *Journal of International & Global Studies, 1,* 45–73.

Wilson, K. M., Hardy, L., & Harwood, C. G. (2006). Investigating the relationship between achievement goals and process goals in rugby union players. *Journal of Applied Sport Psychology, 18,* 297–311.

Wilson, M. (2008). From processing efficiency to attentional control: A mechanistic account of the anxiety-performance relationship. *International Review of Sport and Exercise Psychology, 1,* 184–201. doi: 10.1080/17509840802400787

Wilson, M., & Smith, N. C. (2007). A test of the predictions of processing efficiency theory during elite team competition using the Thought Occurrence Questionnaire for Sport. *International Journal of Sport Psychology, 38,* 245–262.

Wilson, M., Smith, N., Chattington, M., Ford, M., & Marple-Horvat, D. E. (2006). The role of effort in moderating the anxiety-performance relationship: Testing the prediction of processing efficiency theory in simulated rally driving. *Journal of Sports Sciences, 24,* 1223–1233. doi: 10.1080/02640410500497667

Wilson, M., Smith, N. C., & Holmes, P. S. (2007). The role of effort in influencing the effect of anxiety on performance: Testing the conflicting predictions of processing efficiency theory and the conscious processing hypothesis. *British Journal of Psychology, 98,* 411–428. doi: 10.1348/000712606X133047

Wilson, M. R., Wood, G., & Vine, S. J. (2009). Anxiety, attentional control, and performance impairment in penalty kicks. *Journal of Sport & Exercise Psychology, 31,* 761–775.

Wilson, P. M., Mack, D. E., & Grattan, K. P. (2008). Understanding motivation for exercise: A self-determination theory perspective. *Canadian Psychology, 49,* 250–256. doi: 10.1037/a0012762

Wilson, P. M., & Rodgers, W. M. (2004). The relationship between perceived autonomy support, exercise regulations and behavioural intentions in women. *Psychology of Sport & Exercise, 5,* 229–242.

Wilson, R. C., Sullivan, P. J., Myers, N. D., & Feltz, D. L. (2004). Sources of sport confidence of master athletes. *Journal of Sport & Exercise Psychology, 26,* 369–384.

Wilson, V. E., Peper, E., & Schmid, A. (2006). Strategies for training concentration. In J. M. Williams (Ed.), *Applied sport psychology: Personal growth to peak performance* (5th ed., pp. 404–422). New York, NY: McGraw-Hill.

Wilson, M., Chattington, M. Marple-Horvat, D. E., & Smith, N. C. (2007). A comparison of self-focused versus attentional explanations of choking. *Journal of Sport & Exercise Psychology, 29,* 439–456.

Wilson, M., & Smith, N. C. (2007). A test of the predictions of processing efficiency theory during elite team competition using the Thought Occurrence Questionnaire in Sport. *International Journal of Sport Psychology, 38,* 245–165.

Wilson, M., Smith, N. C., Ford, M., & Chattington, M., Marple-Horvat, D. E. (2006). The role of effort in moderating the anxiety-performance relationship: Testing the prediction of processing efficiency theory in simulated rally driving. *Journal of Sports Sciences, 23,* 1223–1233.

Wilson, M., Smith, N. C., & Holmes, P. S. (2007). The role of effort in influencing the effect of anxiety on performance: Testing the conflicting predictions of processing efficiency theory and the conscious processing hypothesis. *British Journal of Psychology, 98,* 411–428.

Wilson, M. R., Vine, S. J., & Wood, G. (2009). The influence of anxiety on visual attentional control in basketball free throw shooting. *Journal of Sport & Exercise Psychology, 31,* 152–168.

Wilson, M. R., Wood, G., & Vine, S. J. (2009). Anxiety, attentional control, and performance impairment in penalty kicks. *Journal of Sport & Exercise Psychology, 31,* 761–775.

Wine, J. (1971). Test anxiety and direction of attention. *Psychological Bulletin, 76*, 92–104.Winter, B., Breitenstein, C., Mooren, F. C., Voelker, K., Fobker, M., Lechtermann, A.,. . . & Knecht, S. (2007). High impact running improves learning. *Neurobiology of Learning and Memory, 87*, 597–609. doi: 10.1016/j.nlm.2006.11.003

Winter, D. G. (1992). Power motivation revisited. In C. P. Smith (Ed.), *Motivation and personality: Handbook of thematic content analysis* (pp. 301–310). New York, NY: Cambridge University Press.

Wise, M. (2000, February, 2). N.B.A. finds minimal use of marijuana in first tests. *The New York Times*, D1.

Woitalla, M. (2010, July 6). Diego Forlán keeps his promises. *Soccer America Daily*, Retrieved from http://www.socceramerica.com

Wolf, E. S. (1997). A self psychological perspective of work and its inhibitions. . In C. W. Socarides and S. Kramer (Eds.), *Work and its inhibitions. Psychoanalytic essays.* (pp. 99–114). Madison, CT: International Universities Press.

Wolfe, R. N., & Kasmer, J. A. (1988). Type versus trait: Extraversion, impulsivity, sociability, and preferences for cooperative and competitive activities. *Journal of Personality and Social psychology, 54*, 864–871.

Wolfenden, L. E., & Holt, N. L. (2005). Talent development in elite junior tennis: Perceptions of players, parents, and coaches. *Journal of Applied Sport Psychology, 17*, 1–19.

Wood, R., & Bandura, A. (1989). Impact of conceptions of ability on self-regulatory mechanisms and complex decision-making. *Journal of Personality and Social Psychology, 56*, 407–415.

Wood, G., & Wilson, M. R. (2008). Gaze behavior and shooting strategies in football penalty kicks: Implications of a "keeper-dependent" approach. *International Journal of Sport Psychology, 39*, 1–18.

Woodgate, J., & Brawley, L. R. (2008). Self-efficacy for exercise in cardiac rehabilitation—review and recommendations. *Journal of Health Psychology, 13*, 366–387. doi: 10.1177/1359105307088141

Woods, T. (2008, June). My new stinger: It's my knockout punch for pressure situations. *Golf Digest*, 55.

Woodcock, C., Cumming, J., Duda, J. L., & Sharp, L-A. (2012). Working within an Individual Zone of Optimal Functioning (IZOF) framework: Consultant practice and athlete reflections on refining emotion regulation skills. *Psychology of Sport and Exercise, 13*, 291–302. doi: 10.1016/j.psychsport.2011.11.011

Wooden, J., & Jamison, S. (2007). *The essential Wooden. A lifetime of lessons on leaders and leadership.* New York, NY: McGraw-Hill.

Woodman, T., Akehurst, S., Hardy, L., & Beattie, S. (2010). Self-confidence and performance: A little self-doubt helps. *Psychology of Sport and Exercise, 11*, 467–470. doi: 10.1016/j.psychsport.2010.05.009

Woodman, T., Albinson, J. G., & Hardy, L. (1997). An investigation of the zones of optimal functioning hypothesis within a multidimensional framework. *Journal of Sport and Exercise Psychology, 19*, 131–141.

Woodman, T., Davis, P. A., Hardy, L., Callow, N., Glasscock, I., & Yuill-Proctor, J. (2009). Emotions and sport performance: An exploration of happiness, hope, and anger. *Journal of Sport & Exercise Psychology, 31*, 169–188.

Woodman, T., & Hardy, L. (2001). Stress and anxiety. In R. N. Singer, H. A. Hausenblas, & C. M. Janelle (Eds.), *Handbook of sport psychology* (2nd ed., pp. 290–318). New York, NY: Wiley.

Woodman, T., Roberts, R., Hardy, L., Callow, N., & Rogers, C. H. (2011). There is an "I" in TEAM: Narcissism and social loafing. *Research Quarterly for Exercise and Sport, 82*, 285–290.

Woodman, T., Zourbanos, N., Hardy, L., Beattie, S., & McQuillan, A. (2010). Do performance strategies moderate the relationship between personality and training behaviors? An exploratory study. *Journal of Applied Sport Psychology, 22*, 183–197.

Woolsey, C., Waigandt, A., & Beck, N. C. (2010). Athletes and energy drinks: Reported risk-taking and consequences from the combined use of alcohol and energy drinks. *Journal of Applied Sport Psychology, 22*, 65–71.

World Anti-Doping Agency. (2009). *World anti-doping code.* Retrieved from http://www. wada-ama.org

World Cup 2010: French press rages after first round exit. *The Guardian.* Retrieved from http://www.guardian.co.uk

World Health Organization (2011). *Global status report on alcohol and health.* Retrieved from http://www.who.int/substance_abuse/publications/global_alcohol_report/msbgsruprofiles.pdf

Wright, A., & Cote, J. (2003). A retrospective analysis of leadership development through sport. *The Sport Psychologist, 17*, 268–291.

Wright, E. F., & Jackson, W. (1991) The home-course disadvantage in golf championships: Further evidence for the undermining effect of supportive audiences on performance under pressure. *Journal of Sport Behavior, 14*, 51–60.

Wright, E. F., & Voyer, D. (1995). Supporting audiences and performance under pressure: The home-ice disadvantage in hockey championships. *Journal of Sport Behavior, 18*, 21–28.

Wrisberg, C. A., & Pein, R. L. (1992). The pre-shot interval and free throw shooting accuracy: An exploratory investigation. *Sport Psychologist, 6*, 14–23.

Wroblewski, A. P., Amati, F., Smiley, M. A., Goodpaster, B., & Wright, V. (2011). *The Physician and Sportsmedicine, 39*, 172–178. doi: 10.3810/psm.2011.09.1933

Wulf, G. (2007). *Attention and motor skill learning.* Champaign, IL: Human Kinetics.

Wulf, G., & Prinz, W. (2001). Direction attention to movement effects enhances learning: A review. *Psychonomic Bulletin & Review, 8*, 648–660.

Wulf, G., & Su, J. (2007). An external focus of attention enhances golf shot accuracy in beginners and experts. *Research Quarterly for Exercise and Sport, 78*, 384–389.

Wurtele, S. K. (1986). Self-efficacy and athletic performance: A review. *Journal of Social and Clinical Psychology, 4*, 290–301.

Wylleman, P., Alfermann, D., & Lavallee, D. (2004). Career transitions in sport: European perspectives. *Psychology of Sport and Exercise, 5*, 7–20. doi: 10.1016/S1469-0292(02)00049-3

Wylleman, P., & Lavallee, D. (2004). A developmental perspective on transitions faced by athletes. In M. Weiss (Ed.), *Developmental sport psychology* (pp. 507–527). Morgantown, WV: Fitness Information Technology.

Yaeger, D. (2000, August, 21). Rx for trouble. Did Romo's fondness for pharmaceuticals go too far? *Sports Illustrated, 93*, 27–28.

Yan, J. H., & McCullagh, P. (2004). Cultural influence on youth's motivation of participation in physical activity. *Journal of Sport Behavior, 27*, 378–390.

Yang, J., Peek-Asa, C., Lowe, J. B., Heiden, E., & Foster, D. T. (2010). Social support patterns of collegiate athletes before and after injury. *Journal of Athletic Training, 45*, 372–379.

Yantz, T. (2002, October 25). Coach's four-letter word: Stop. *Hartford Courant*, C6.

Yasunaga, M., & Inomata, K. (2004). Factors associated with helplessness among Japanese collegiate swimmers. *Perceptual and Motor Skills, 99*, 581–590.

Yee, P. L., & Vaughan, J. (1996). Integrating cognitive, personality, and social approaches to cognitive interference and distractibility. In I. G. Sarason, G. R. Pierce, & B. R. Sarason (Eds.), *Cognitive interference theories, methods, and findings* (pp. 77–97). Mahwah, NJ: Lawrence Erlbaum Associates.

Yeh, S. S. (2010). Understanding and addressing the achievement gap through individualized instruction and formative assessment. *Assessment in Education: Principles, Policy, and Practice, 17*, 169–182.A

Yerkes, R. M., & Dodson, J. D. (1908). The relation of strength of stimulus to rapidity of habit formation. *Journal of Comparative Neurology of Psychology, 18*, 459–482.

Yocom, G., Woods, T., Williams, T., Cooke, A., Venturi, K., Bush, G., Runyan, P., Mandela, N., Rawls, B., Tatum, F. D., Snead, S., Aaron, H., Alliss, P., Seitz, N., Miller, J., Thompson, P., Richards, A., Andrew, P., Anderson, D. . . . et al. (2000, July). 50 greatest golfers of all time and what they taught us. *Golf Digest, 51*, 87–109, 113–114, 116, 118, 120, 124, 126, 130, 132, 134, 136, 138, 142, 144, 146, 148, 150, 152, 154, 156, 158, 160, 164, 166, 169, 171–174.

Yoo, J. (2000). Factorial validity of the coping scale for Korean athletes. *International Journal of Sport Psychology, 31*, 391–404.

Yoo, J. (2001). Coping profile of Korean competitive athletes. *International Journal of Sport Psychology, 32*, 290–303.

Yoo, J, & Park, S. J. (1998a). Development of a sport coping scale. *Korean Journal of Physical Education, 37*, 151–168.

Yoo, J, & Park, S. J. (1998b). A test of the causal-structural model on coping effectiveness in sport. *Korean Journal of Physical Education, 37*, 141–152.

York, J. L., Hirsch, J. A., Pendergast, D. R., & Glavy, J. S. (1999). Muscle performance in detoxified alcoholics. *Journal of Studies on Alcohol, 60*, 413–421.

Young, B. W., Medic, N., & Starkes, J. L. (2009). Effects of self-monitoring training logs on behaviors and beliefs of swimmers. *Journal of Applied Sport Psychology, 21*, 313–428.

Yukelson, D. (1997). Principles of effective team building interventions in sport: A direct services approach at Penn State University. *Journal of Applied Sport Psychology, 9*, 73–96.

Yukelson, D. (2010). Communicating effectively. In J. M. Williams (Ed.), *Applied sport psychology: Personal growth to peak performance* (6th ed., pp. 149–165). New York, NY: McGraw-Hill.

Yusko, D. A., Buckman, J. F., White, H. R., & Pandina, R. J. (2008a). Alcohol, tobacco, illicit drugs, and performance enhancers: A comparison of use by college student athletes and nonathletes. *Journal of American College Health, 57*, 281–289.

Yusko, D. A., Buckman, J. F., White, H. R., & Pandina, R. J. (2008b). Risk for excessive alcohol use and drinking-related problems in college student athletes. *Addictive Behaviors, 33*, 1546–1556.

Zacharatos, A., Barling, J., & Kelloway, E. K. (2000). Development and effects of transformational leadership in adolescents. *Leadership Quarterly, 11*, 211–226.

Zador, P. L. (1991). Alcohol-related relative risk of fatal driver injuries in relation to driver age and sex. *Journal of Studies on Alcohol, 52*, 302–310.

Zaichkowsky, L. D., & Baltzell, A. (2001). Arousal and performance. In R. N. Singer, H. A. Hausenblas, & C. M. Janelle (Eds.), *Handbook of Sport Psychology* (2nd ed., pp. 319–339). New York, NY: Wiley.

Zajonc, R. B. (1965). Social facilitation. *Science, 149*, 269–274.

Zamboanga, B. L., Rodriguez, L., & Horton, N. J. (2008). Athletic involvement and its relevance to hazardous alcohol use and drinking game participation in female college athletes: A preliminary investigation. *Journal of American College Health, 56*, 651–656.

Zanich, M. L., & Grover, D. E. (1989). Introductory psychology from the standpoint of the consumer. *Teaching of Psychology, 16*, 72–74.

Zarrett, N., Fay, K., Li, Y., Carrano, J. Phelps, E., & Lerner, R. M. (2009). More than child's play: Variable- and pattern-centered approaches for examining effects of sports participation on youth development. *Developmental Psychology, 45*, 368–382. doi: 10.1037/a0014577

Zeidner, M. (1994). Personal and contextual determinants of coping and anxiety in an evaluative situation: A prospective study. *Personality and Individual Differences, 16*, 899–918.

Zehsaz, F., Azarbaijani, M. A., Farhangimaleki, N., & Tiidus, P. (2011). Effect of tapering period on plasma hormone concentrations, mood state, and performance of elite male cyclists. *European Journal of Sport Science, 11*, 183–190. doi: 10.1080/17461391.2010.499976

Zelli, A., Lucidi, F., & Mallia, L. (2010). The relationships among adolescents' drive for muscularity, drive for thinness, doping attitudes, and doping intentions. *Journal of Clinical Sport Psychology, 4*, 39–52.

Zervas, Y., Stavrou, N. A., & Psychountaki, M. (2007). Development and validation of the self-talk questionnaire (S-TK) for Sports. *Journal of Applied Sport Psychology, 19*, 142–159.

Zidane: "I don't regret anything that happened." (2006, July 13). *Hartford Courant*, C5.

Zimmerman, B. J. (2000). Attaining self-regulation: A social cognitive perspective. In M. Boekaerts, P. Pintich, & M. Seidner (Eds.), *Self-regulation: Theory, research and application* (pp. 13–39). Orlando, FL: Academic Press.

Zimmerman, B. J. & Kitsantas, A. (1997). Developmental phases in self-regulation. Shifting from process goals to outcome goals. *Journal of Educational Psychology, 89*, 29–36.

Zinsser, N., Bunker, L., & Williams, J. M. (1998). Cognitive techniques for building confidence and enhancing performance. In J. M. Williams (Ed.), *Applied sport psychology: Personal growth to peak performance* (3rd ed., pp. 270–295). Mountain View, CA: Mayfield.

Zinsser, N., Bunker, L., & Williams, J. M. (2006). Cognitive techniques for building confidence and enhancing performance. In J. M. Williams (Ed.), *Applied sport psychology: Personal growth to peak performance* (5th ed., pp. 349–381). New York, NY: McGraw-Hill.

Zizzi, S. Zaichkowsky, L., & Perna, F. M. (2002). Certification in sport and exercise psychology. In J. L. Van Raalte & B. W. Brewer (Eds.), *Exploring exercise and sport psychology* (2nd ed., pp. 417–436). Washington, DC: American Psychological Association.

Zohar, D. (1998). An additive model of test anxiety: Role of exam-specific expectations. *Journal of Educational Psychology, 90*, 330–340.

Zouhal, H., Jacob, C., Delamarche, P., & Gratas-Delamarche, A. (2008). Catecholamines and the effects of exercise, training and gender. *Sports Medicine, 38*, 401–42.

Zourbanos, N., Hatzigeorgiadis, A., Chroni, S., Theodorakis, Y., & Papaioannou, A. (2009). The Automatic Self-Talk Questionnaire for Sports (ASTQS): Development and preliminary validation. *The Sport Psychologist, 23*, 233–251.

Zuckerman, M. (1994). *Behavioral expressions and biosocial bases of sensation seeking*. Cambridge, England: Cambridge University Press.

Zuckerman, M., Kieffer, S. C., & Knee, C. R. (1998). Consequences of self-handicapping: Effects on coping, academic performance, and adjustment. *Journal of Personality and Social Psychology, 74*, 1619–1628.

Zuckerman, M., & Wheeler, L. (1975). To dispel fantasies about the fantasy-based measure of fear of success. *Psychological Bulletin, 82*, 932–946.

Zuroff, D. C., & Schwarz, J. C. (1978). Effects of Transcendental Meditation and muscle relaxation on trait anxiety, maladjustment, locus of control, and drug use. *Journal of Consulting and Clinical Psychology, 46*, 264–271.

INDEX

Page numbers in italics refer to figures and photographs.